DIGITAL SAT® TOTAL PREP 2025

T0345899

Editor-in-Chief
Heather Waite

Contributing Editors
J. Scott Mullison, Ethan Weber, and Melissa McLaughlin

Special thanks to our faculty authors and reviewers:
Michael Collins, Bonnie Wang, Jo L'Abbate, Aisa Diaz, Mark Feery, Boris Dvorkin, Karen McCulloch, Michelle Hunt, Steve Cisar, Gordon Spector, and David Staples

Additional special thanks to the following:
Nancy Greenspan; Isaac Botier; Laurel Hanson; Brian Carlidge; Jessica Gleicher; Amy Zarkos; Alexandra Strelka, MA; Heather Wilcox; Megan Buckman; Denise Pangia; and the countless others who made this project possible

TABLE OF CONTENTS

K   v

How to Use This Book

As of the spring of 2024, the SAT fully retired its traditional pencil-and-paper test and transitioned to an adaptive, digital exam. This book is designed to help you achieve your highest score on this updated version of the SAT.

We at Kaplan understand that your time is limited and that this book is hefty, but nobody expects you to read every word. Nor do we expect you to go through the chapters in order. If you need more work on the Reading and Writing section than on the Math section, for example, then feel free to skip over the math chapters. The most efficient way to use this book is to spend the most time on those areas that give you trouble, starting with those that are tested most often. If you're not sure, use the "How Much Do You Know?" pretests provided to figure out how much time to spend on that material. See the Table of Contents to quickly find them.

Chapter Organization

After reading the introductory material, we recommend completing one of the previously mentioned "How Much Do You Know?" pretests that roughly fall into the domains of the material tested by the College Board™ on the digital SAT: Algebra, Problem-Solving and Data Analysis, Advanced Math, Geometry and Trigonometry, Reading and Writing: Reading Skills, or Reading and Writing: Writing Skills.

After you've completed a "How Much Do You Know?" pretest, you should have a sense of how comfortable you already are with the material in that section. Answers and explanations follow immediately in the "Check Your Work" section. For areas where you are comfortable, you may consider moving on to another pretest, but for other areas where there are opportunities to score more points on test day, work through the chapters of that section. Chapter lessons start with a question typical of the way the SAT tests a given topic and end with a set of practice questions called "Try on Your Own." Answers are provided at the end of the chapter. To reinforce what you have learned, you'll find "How Much Have You Learned?" post-tests for each section as well. They will be similar to the pretests, so that you have a good means of measuring your progress. Answers will be provided after those as well.

Practice Tests

While the SAT is digital, we are including two paper tests at the end of this book to help you learn about the test and be able to practice even when you are not online. The Practice Tests have full answers and explanations and demonstrate the adaptive structure of the digital test.

You're Already on Your Way

You already have many of the skills you'll need to excel on the SAT, but you'll need to adapt those skills to the structure of the exam. This book will teach you to adapt your math, reading, and writing skills to solve questions more efficiently and to confidently tackle even the toughest SAT questions.

Extra Practice

This book will help you answer the most common questions on test day, but there is even more practice for you online. We highly recommend that you make use of both your book and digital resources.

K

Online Resources

To access the online resources that accompany this book, follow these steps:

www.kaptest.com/moreonline

1.   Go to **www.kaptest.com/moreonline.**

2.   Have this book available as you complete the on-screen instructions. Then, whenever you want to use your online resources, go to **www.kaptest.com/login** and sign in using the email address and password you used to register your book.

Are You Registered for the SAT?

Kaplan cannot register you for the official SAT. If you have not already registered for the upcoming SAT, talk to your high school guidance counselor or visit the College Board's website at www.collegeboard.org to register online and for information on registration deadlines, test sites, accommodations for students with disabilities, and fees.

Don't Forget Your Strengths

As your test date approaches, shift your practice to your strengths. Let's say you're good at geometry. You might not need the instructional text covering geometry in this book, but in the final week before your test date, you should still do a few geometry practice questions. Think about it: your strengths are your most reliable source of points on test day. Build that confidence in the final stretch. And just as if the SAT were an athletic event, get plenty of sleep in the days leading up to it.

Let's Get Started

Want to get a feel for the SAT before you start studying? Take the Practice Tests at the back of this book. Otherwise, start by identifying the sections of the test you think will give you the most trouble. On test day, you'll be glad you did!

PART 1

THE SAT AND YOU

[CHAPTER 1]

INSIDE THE SAT

> **LEARNING OBJECTIVES**
>
> After completing this chapter, you will be able to:
> - Recall the timing and scope of each section in anticipation of section management
> - State what the SAT scoring system means for you, the test taker

THE DIGITAL SAT

With the exception of certain students with accommodations, all students take the digital SAT on a computer. The digital SAT format includes helpful features—such as a built-in graphing calculator, text annotation tools, a timer, a zooming tool, and the ability to "cross out" answer choices you want to eliminate—that will make it easy for you to navigate the test and manage the questions. To best use the digital format to your advantage, it will be important to familiarize yourself with the online practice tests.

Compared to the old pencil-and-paper SAT, the digital SAT is shorter in length (by about 45 minutes) and has fewer, more concise questions. This also means that you'll have more time to spend per question. All of these changes are good news for test takers like you!

This book will explain every digital SAT question type in detail and teach you simple methods and strategies to help you tackle every question efficiently. Even if this is your first time taking a standardized admissions test, this book will help give you the confidence you need for SAT success.

SAT STRUCTURE

The SAT, like any standardized test, is **predictable**. The more comfortable you are with the test structure, the more confidently you will approach each question type, thus maximizing your score.

The digital SAT is **2 hours and 14 minutes** long. The SAT is made up of mostly multiple-choice questions in two main sections: the Math section and the Reading and Writing section. Each section is divided into **two modules**.

SECTION	MODULE	ALLOTTED TIME (MINUTES)	TOTAL TIME (MINUTES)	QUESTION COUNT	TOTAL QUESTION COUNT
Reading and Writing	Module 1	32	64	27	54
	Module 2	32		27	
Math	Module 1	35	70	22	44
	Module 2	35		22	
Total			134		98

K   3

The two-module format divides each section into two parts, each timed separately (see table shown). Once you submit your answers for the first module of either the Reading and Writing or the Math section, you won't be able to return to that module. This is because the digital SAT is an **adaptive test**. In other words, your performance on the first module of each section will determine the difficulty level of the second module you'll take.

SAT Scoring

As you just learned, the SAT is adaptive. How well you do on your first module determines the questions you see in the second. This is often called a multi-staged test. Doing well on the first module, also known as the routing module, will send you to a higher difficulty second module. This will give you a chance to earn the very top scores for a section (either Reading and Writing or Math). Bear in mind that even if you are routed to an easier second module, you can still earn a competitive score on the SAT. Don't spend time trying to figure out which difficulty level you were routed to; this will only waste your brainpower and time. Your focus should be to do your best on every question, regardless of which module it is in. While their exact formula is proprietary, your total score is based on how you do on both modules of Reading and Writing and both modules of Math. There is very likely an overlapping range of scores possible for students routed to the easier or harder second module.

You will receive one score ranging from 200–800 for Reading and Writing and another for Math. Your overall SAT score will range from 400–1600 and is calculated by adding these two scores together.

The SAT also gives you a percentile ranking, which allows you to compare your scores with those of other test takers. For example, a student who scored in the 63rd percentile did better than 63 percent of all others who took that test.

The scores that you need depend primarily on which colleges you are planning to apply to. For example, if you want to attend an engineering school, you'll typically need a higher math score than if you want to attend a liberal arts college. Research the colleges you are interested in, find out what scores they require, and structure your SAT studying accordingly.

How to Maximize Your Score

You'll find advice on test-taking strategies in this chapter and in the section management chapters at the end of the Math and the Reading and Writing sections of this book. In addition, make sure to read the instructional text in the lessons throughout this book for those topics you feel less confident about, and then work your way through the lesson's practice questions. There are hundreds of practice questions in this book, and they are very similar to those that you will see on test day. Practice will not only improve your skills; it will also raise your confidence, and that's very important for test-day success. Remember, you can go through the chapters in this book in any order you like, and you don't need to review the whole book. Prioritize additional review on those topics from which you'd benefit the most.

Where and When to Take the SAT

The SAT is offered every year on multiple Saturday test dates. Typically, exams are offered in August, October, November, December, March, May, and June. You can take the SAT multiple times. Some states offer special administrations of the SAT on different dates. Sunday tests are available by request for students requiring religious or other exemptions. The SAT is administered at high schools around the country that serve as testing centers. Your high school may or may not be a testing center. Check www.collegeboard.org for a list of testing centers near you. Note that you must register for the SAT approximately one month in advance to avoid paying a late fee.

The SAT Math Section

The SAT Math section consists of two modules of 22 questions each. Of these 22 questions, there will be two pretest questions that the College Board will use for research purposes, while the other 20 will count toward your score. These pretest questions are not marked in any way that is visible to you, so it is in your best interest to try your best on every question you see. You may use the provided built-in graphing calculator or your own approved calculator on every question. Questions across the section will consist of both **multiple-choice** and **student-produced response** questions. About 25%, or 11 of the questions, will be student-produced responses, for which you will type your answers, and the rest will be four-option multiple-choice questions. With 44 questions to answer in 70 minutes, this gives you about a **minute and a half per question**.

	ALLOTTED TIME (MINUTES)	QUESTION COUNT
Module 1	35	22
Module 2	35	22
Total	70	44

QUESTION TYPE	QUESTION COUNT
Multiple-Choice Questions	~33
Student-Produced Responses	~11
Total	44

About a third of the questions in the SAT Math section will be **word problems** that are situated in a real-world context; the rest will be straightforward math questions. The SAT Math section includes questions in **four major content areas**: Algebra, Advanced Math, Problem-Solving and Data Analysis, and Geometry and Trigonometry.

SAT MATH SECTION CONTENT AREA DISTRIBUTION	

Algebra (13–15 questions)	• Solving, creating, and using:
	  • Linear equations
	  • Linear functions
	  • Linear inequalities
	  • Systems of linear equations
	• Making connections between different representations of linear relationships

Advanced Math (13–15 questions)	• Interpreting, solving, creating, and using:
	  • Equations with absolute value
	  • Equations with radicals
	  • Quadratic equations
	  • Exponential equations
	  • Polynomial equations
	  • Rational equations
	  • Other nonlinear equations
	• Making connections between different representations of nonlinear relationships between two variables

SAT MATH SECTION CONTENT AREA DISTRIBUTION	

Problem-Solving and Data Analysis (5–7 questions)	• Solving questions involving:
	   • Ratios
	   • Rates
	   • Proportions
	   • Units
	   • Percentages
	 • Analyzing and interpreting data, including distributions and scatterplots
	 • Calculating and interpreting:
	   • Probability and conditional probability
	   • Mean, median, range, standard deviation, and margin of error
	 • Evaluating statistical claims

Geometry and Trigonometry (5–7 questions)	• Solving questions involving:
	   • Area and volume
	   • Lines, angles, and triangles
	   • Right triangles and trigonometry
	   • Circles

The SAT Reading and Writing Section

The SAT Reading and Writing section will focus on your comprehension, reasoning, and editing skills with questions based on short academic passages taken from a variety of content areas.

The SAT Reading and Writing section consists of two modules of 27 questions each. Of these 27 questions, there will be two pretest questions that the College Board will use for research purposes, while the other 25 will count toward your score. These pretest questions are not marked in any way that is visible to you, so it is in your best interest to try your best on every question you see. All the questions in this section are four-option multiple-choice questions. With 54 questions to answer in 64 minutes, this gives you about a **minute and 10 seconds per question**.

	ALLOTTED TIME (MINUTES)	QUESTION COUNT
Module 1	32	27
Module 2	32	27
Total	64	54

Each question on the SAT Reading and Writing section is accompanied by a **short passage**, usually a paragraph in length. Some questions may have two short passages about the same topic, and a few questions will have a bullet point list of notes about a topic. Passages will draw from literature, history/social studies, the humanities (topics such as the arts), and science. Some questions will also be accompanied by a graphical representation of data, such as a graph or table.

The SAT Reading and Writing section includes questions in **four major content areas**: Information and Ideas, Craft and Structure, Expression of Ideas, and Standard English Conventions.

SAT READING AND WRITING SECTION CONTENT AREA DISTRIBUTION	
Information and Ideas (12–14 questions)	• Using reading comprehension, analysis, and reasoning skills to answer questions about: • Main ideas • Details • Command of evidence (text and graphs/tables) • Inferences • Interpreting, evaluating, and integrating ideas
Craft and Structure (13–15 questions)	• Using reading comprehension, analysis, and reading skills to answer questions about: • The meaning of words in context • The purpose of texts • Connections between related texts
Expression of Ideas (8–12 questions)	• Using revision skills to answer questions about: • Synthesizing ideas to achieve rhetorical goals • Making effective transitions
Standard English Conventions (11–15 questions)	• Using editing skills to follow Standard English conventions, including: • Sentence structure • Punctuation • Verb agreement • Pronoun agreement • Modifier agreement

Test-Taking Strategies

The SAT is different from the tests you are used to taking in school. The good news is that you can use the SAT's particular structure to your advantage.

For example, on a test given in school, you probably go through the questions in order. You spend more time on the harder questions than on the easier ones because harder questions are usually worth significantly more points. You also probably show your work because your teacher tells you that how you approach a question is as important as getting the correct answer.

This approach is not optimal for the SAT. On the SAT, you benefit from moving around within a section. If you come across tough questions, it's most efficient to save those until the end. This allows you to answer the easiest questions for *you* before attempting *your* most challenging ones. Similarly, showing your work on the SAT is unimportant. It doesn't matter how you arrive at the correct answer—only that you select the correct answer choice.

The following strategies can be used in both the Reading and Writing section and the Math section of the digital SAT.

Strategy #1: Triaging the Test

You do not need to complete questions on the SAT in order. Every student has different strengths and should attack the test with those strengths in mind. Your main objective on the SAT should be to score as many points as you can. While approaching questions out of order may seem counterintuitive, it is a surefire way to achieve your best score.

Just remember, you can skip around within each module, but you cannot return to work on a module once you've submitted your answers for that module.

To triage a section effectively, do the following:

- First, work through all the easy questions that you can do quickly. Skip questions that are hard or time-consuming. Use the digital test's tool to **flag** any questions you are initially skipping. Before you leave the question, you might want to mark a guess, just in case you don't have time to return to it.
- Second, use the **module review screen** to return to any questions you skipped. Work through the questions that are doable but time-consuming.
- Third, work through the hard questions.

Strategy #2: Elimination

If you can determine that one or more answer choices are definitely incorrect, you can increase your chances of getting the correct answer by paring the selection down.

To eliminate answer choices, do the following:

- Read each answer choice.
- Use the digital test's **elimination tool** to cross out any answer choices that you determine are incorrect.
- If only one answer choice is left, select it and move on.
- If more than one answer choice remains, remember that there is no wrong-answer penalty, so take your best guess.

The specific lessons in this book will teach you about the different incorrect answer types that commonly appear on the SAT. When you see one of these incorrect answer types, you can quickly eliminate it.

Strategy #3: Strategic Guessing

Each multiple-choice question on the SAT has four answer choices and no wrong-answer penalty. That means if you have no idea how to approach a question, you have a 25 percent chance of randomly choosing the correct answer. Even though there's a 75 percent chance of selecting the incorrect answer, you won't lose any points for doing so. And often, you'll be able to eliminate one or more choices as incorrect (see Strategy #2), improving your chances of getting the correct answer even more. The worst that can happen on the SAT is that you'll earn zero points on a question, which means you should *always* **at least take a guess**, even when you have no idea what to do.

When guessing on a question, do the following:

- Try to strategically eliminate answer choices before guessing.
- If you are almost out of time or have no idea what a question is asking, pick a **Letter of the Day**. A Letter of the Day is an answer choice letter (A, B, C, or D) that you choose before test day to select for questions you guess on.
- If a question is taking too long, skip it and guess. Spend your time on those questions that you know how to do; don't allow yourself to get bogged down in fighting it out with a question that is too time-consuming.
- Leave yourself a few minutes before you run out of time on each module to check the **module review screen**. Make sure you have an answer selected for every question.

Strategy #4: Living in the Question

As discussed previously, the digital SAT is an adaptive test. This means that your performance on the first module of the Math section or the Reading and Writing section will determine the difficulty of the second module you see in that section. On any adaptive test, it can be tempting to try to guess how you performed on the first module based on the questions you are seeing on the second module. However, it is important to **keep all your focus on answering the current question**.

People are typically not great at assessing their own test performance in the moment. We tend to focus on the questions that we found difficult rather than on the questions we answered easily. Thinking too much about your overall performance during the test will draw your attention away from where it needs to be: **answering as many questions correctly as you can *on your current module***. Don't attempt to make guesses about how you're doing during the exam. Don't attempt to try to identify which questions are operational questions that count and which are the two-per-module pretest questions that are used for research. Don't attempt to determine whether the test has adapted to harder difficulty questions or think about what that means for your overall score during the test. Instead, take action that will help you continue to improve your score: focus on the question you're on. Take confidence in your preparation and in the methods and strategies you'll learn throughout this book, and apply your skills to each individual question as you encounter it.

PART 2

SAT MATH

[CHAPTER 2]

PREREQUISITE SKILLS AND CALCULATOR USE

LEARNING OBJECTIVES

After completing this chapter, you will be able to:

- Identify skills necessary to obtain the full benefits of the Math sections of this book
- Use efficiency tips to boost your test-day speed
- Distinguish between questions that need a calculator and questions for which manual calculations are more efficient

---

MATH FUNDAMENTALS

LEARNING OBJECTIVES

After this lesson, you will be able to:

- Identify skills necessary to obtain the full benefits of the Math sections of this book
- Use efficiency tips to boost your test-day speed

Prerequisites

This book focuses on the skills that are tested on the SAT. It assumes a working knowledge of arithmetic, algebra, and geometry. Before you dive into the subsequent chapters where you'll try testlike questions, there are a number of concepts—ranging from basic arithmetic to geometry—that you should master. The following sections contain a brief review of these concepts.

Algebra and Arithmetic

Order of operations is one of the most fundamental of all arithmetic rules. A well-known mnemonic device for remembering this order is PEMDAS: Please Excuse My Dear Aunt Sally. This translates to Parentheses, Exponents, Multiplication/Division, Addition/Subtraction. Perform multiplication and division from left to right (even if it means division before multiplication) and treat addition and subtraction the same way:

$$(14 - 4 \div 2)^2 - 3 + (2 - 1)$$
$$= (14 - 2)^2 - 3 + (1)$$
$$= 12^2 - 3 + 1$$
$$= 144 - 3 + 1$$
$$= 141 + 1$$
$$= 142$$

Three basic properties of number (and variable) manipulation—commutative, associative, and distributive—will assist you with algebra on test day:

- **Commutative:** Numbers can swap places and still provide the same mathematical result. This is valid only for addition and multiplication:

$$a + b = b + a \rightarrow 3 + 4 = 4 + 3$$
$$a \times b = b \times a \rightarrow 3 \times 4 = 4 \times 3$$

BUT: $3 - 4 \neq 4 - 3$ and $3 \div 4 \neq 4 \div 3$

- **Associative:** Different number groupings will provide the same mathematical result. This is valid only for addition and multiplication:

$$(a + b) + c = a + (b + c) \rightarrow (4 + 5) + 6 = 4 + (5 + 6)$$
$$(a \times b) \times c = a \times (b \times c) \rightarrow (4 \times 5) \times 6 = 4 \times (5 \times 6)$$

BUT: $(4 - 5) - 6 \neq 4 - (5 - 6)$ and $(4 \div 5) \div 6 \neq 4 \div (5 \div 6)$

- **Distributive:** A number that is multiplied by the sum or difference of two other numbers can be rewritten as the first number multiplied by the two others individually. This does *not* work with division:

$$a(b + c) = ab + ac \rightarrow 6(x + 3) = 6x + 6(3)$$
$$a(b - c) = ab - ac \rightarrow 3(y - 2) = 3y + 3(-2)$$

BUT: $12 \div (6 + 2) \neq 12 \div 6 + 12 \div 2$

Note: When subtracting an expression in parentheses, such as in $4 - (x + 3)$, distribute the negative sign outside the parentheses first: $4 + (-x - 3) \rightarrow 1 - x$.

Subtracting a positive number is the same as adding its negative. Likewise, subtracting a negative number is the same as adding its positive:

$$r - s = r + (-s) \rightarrow 22 - 15 = 7 \text{ and } 22 + (-15) = 7$$
$$r - (-s) = r + s \rightarrow 22 - (-15) = 37 \text{ and } 22 + 15 = 37$$

You should be comfortable manipulating both proper and improper fractions:

- To add and subtract fractions, first find a common denominator, then add the numerators together:

$$\frac{2}{3} + \frac{5}{4} \rightarrow \left(\frac{2}{3} \times \frac{4}{4}\right) + \left(\frac{5}{4} \times \frac{3}{3}\right) = \frac{8}{12} + \frac{15}{12} = \frac{23}{12}$$

- Multiplying fractions is straightforward: multiply the numerators together, then repeat for the denominators. Cancel when possible to simplify the answer:

$$\frac{5}{8} \times \frac{8}{3} = \frac{5}{\overset{}{\underset{1}{8}}} \times \frac{\overset{1}{8}}{3} = \frac{5 \times 1}{1 \times 3} = \frac{5}{3}$$

- Dividing by a fraction is the same as multiplying by its reciprocal. Once you've rewritten a division problem as multiplication, follow the rules for fraction multiplication to simplify:

$$\frac{3}{4} \div \frac{3}{2} = \frac{\overset{1}{3}}{\underset{2}{4}} \times \frac{\overset{1}{2}}{\underset{1}{3}} = \frac{1 \times 1}{2 \times 1} = \frac{1}{2}$$

Whatever you do to one side of an equation, you must do to the other. For instance, if you multiply one side by 3, you must multiply the other side by 3 as well.

The ability to solve straightforward one-variable equations is critical on the SAT. For example:

$$\frac{4x}{5} - 2 = 10$$

$$\frac{4x}{5} = 12$$

$$\frac{5}{4} \times \frac{4x}{5} = 12 \times \frac{5}{4}$$

$$x = 15$$

Note: $\frac{4x}{5}$ is the same as $\frac{4}{5}x$. You could see either form on the SAT.

You will encounter **irrational numbers**, such as common radicals and π, on test day. These are numbers that cannot be expressed as the ratio of two integers (i.e., they have no equivalent fraction). You can carry an irrational number through your calculations as you would a variable (e.g., $4 \times \sqrt{2} = 4\sqrt{2}$). Only convert to a decimal when you have finished any intermediate steps.

Mental Math

Even if you're a math whiz, you need to adjust your thought process in terms of the SAT to give yourself the biggest advantage you can. Knowing a few extra things will boost your speed on test day:

- Don't abuse your calculator by using it to determine something as simple as $15 \div 3$ (we've seen it many times). Save time on test day by reviewing multiplication tables. At a bare minimum, work up through the 10s. If you know them through 12 or 15, that's even better!

- You can save a few seconds of number crunching by memorizing **perfect squares**. Knowing perfect squares through 10 is a good start; go for 15 or even 20 if you can.

- **Percent** means "out of a hundred." For example, $27\% = \frac{27}{100}$. You can write percents as decimals; for example, $27\% = 0.27$.

- The ability to recognize a few simple fractions masquerading in decimal or percent form will save you time on test day, as you won't have to turn to your calculator to convert them. Memorize the content of the following table.

FRACTION	DECIMAL	PERCENT
$\frac{1}{10}$	0.1	10%
$\frac{1}{5}$	0.2	20%
$\frac{1}{4}$	0.25	25%
$\frac{1}{3}$	$0.333\overline{3}$	$33.3\overline{3}\%$
$\frac{1}{2}$	0.5	50%
$\frac{3}{4}$	0.75	75%

Tip: If you don't have the decimal (or percent) form of a multiple of one of the fractions shown in the table memorized, such as $\frac{2}{5}$, just take the fraction with the corresponding denominator ($\frac{1}{5}$ in this case), convert to a decimal (0.2), and multiply by the numerator of the desired fraction to get its decimal equivalent:

$$\frac{2}{5} = \frac{1}{5} \times 2 = 0.2 \times 2 = 0.4 = 40\%$$

Math

Graphing

- Basic two-dimensional graphing is performed on a **coordinate plane**. There are two **axes**, *x* and *y*, that meet at a central point called the **origin**. Each axis has both positive and negative values that extend outward from the origin at evenly spaced intervals. The axes divide the space into four sections called **quadrants**, which are labeled I, II, III, and IV. Quadrant I is always the upper-right section and the rest follow counterclockwise, as shown:

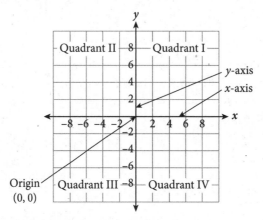

- To plot points on the coordinate plane, you need their coordinates. The **x-coordinate** is where the point falls along the *x*-axis, and the **y-coordinate** is where the point falls along the *y*-axis. The two coordinates together make an **ordered pair** written as (*x*, *y*). When writing ordered pairs, the *x*-coordinate is always listed first (think alphabetical order). Four points are plotted in the figure as examples:

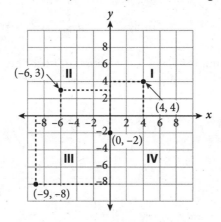

- When two points are vertically or horizontally aligned, calculating the distance between them is easy. For a horizontal distance, only the *x*-value changes; for a vertical distance, only the *y*-value changes. Take the positive difference of the *x*-coordinates (or *y*-coordinates) to determine the distance—that is, subtract the smaller number from the larger number so that the difference is positive. Two examples are presented here:

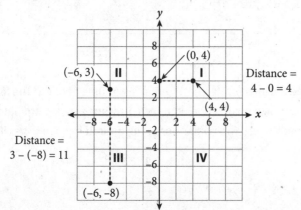

- Two-variable equations have an **independent variable** (input) and a **dependent variable** (output). The dependent variable (often y), depends on the independent variable (often x). For example, in the equation $y = 3x + 4$, x is the independent variable; any y-value depends on what you plug in for x. You can construct a table of values for the equation, or you can graph the equation on your calculator.

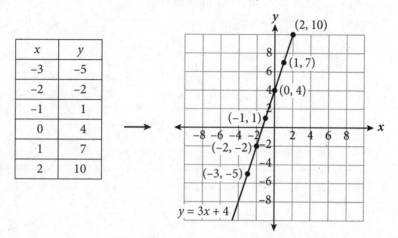

- You may be asked to infer relationships from graphs. In the first of the following graphs, the two variables are year and population. Clearly, the year does not depend on how many people live in the town; rather, the population increases over time and thus depends on the year. In the second graph, you can infer that plant height depends on the amount of rain; thus, rainfall is the independent variable. Note that the independent variable for the second graph is the vertical axis; this can happen with certain nonstandard graphs. On the standard coordinate plane, however, the independent variable is always plotted on the horizontal axis as shown:

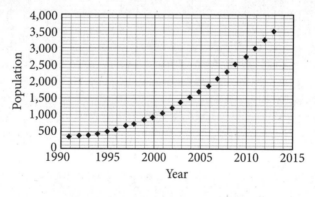

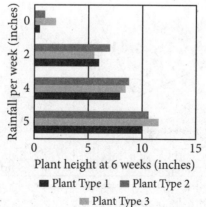

- When two straight lines are graphed simultaneously, one of three possible scenarios will occur:
  - The lines will not intersect at all (no solution).
  - The lines will intersect at one point (one solution).
  - The lines will lie on top of each other (infinitely many solutions).

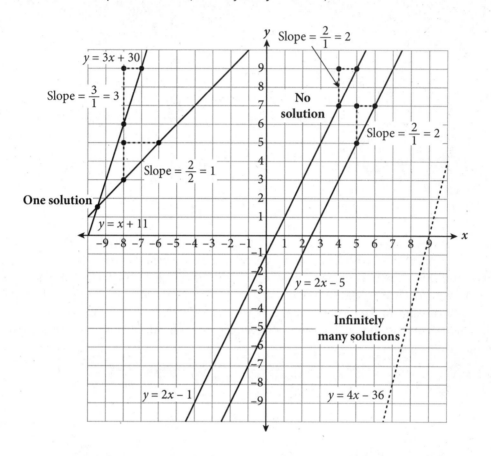

Geometry

- **Adjacent angles** can be added to find the measure of a larger angle. The following diagram demonstrates this:

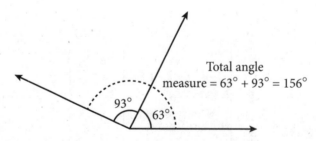

- Two angles that sum to 90° are called **complementary angles**. Two angles that sum to 180° are called **supplementary angles**.
- Two distinct lines in a plane will either intersect at one point or extend indefinitely without intersecting. If two lines intersect at a right angle (90°), they are **perpendicular** and are denoted with ⊥. If the lines never intersect, they are **parallel** and are denoted with ‖:

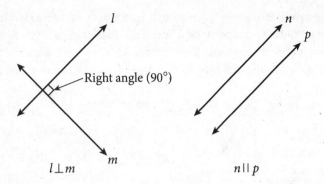

$l \perp m$ $n \parallel p$

- **Perimeter** and **area** are basic properties that all two-dimensional shapes have. The perimeter of a polygon can easily be calculated by adding the lengths of all its sides. Area is the amount of two-dimensional space a shape occupies. The most common shapes for which you'll need these two properties on test day are triangles, parallelograms, and circles.

- The **area (A) of a triangle** is given by $A = \frac{1}{2}bh$, where b is the base of the triangle and h is its height. The base and height are always perpendicular. Any side of a triangle can be used as the base; just make sure you use its corresponding height (a line segment perpendicular to the base, terminating in the opposite vertex). You can use a right triangle's two legs as the base and height, but in non-right triangles, if the height is not given, you'll need to draw it in (from the vertex of the angle opposite the base down to the base itself at a right angle) and compute it.

- The **interior angles** of a triangle sum to 180°. If you know any two interior angles, you can calculate the third.

- **Parallelograms** are quadrilaterals with two pairs of parallel sides. Rectangles and squares are subsets of parallelograms. You can find the **area of a parallelogram** using $A = bh$. As with triangles, you can use any side of a parallelogram as the base, and again, the height is perpendicular to the base. For a rectangle or square, use the side perpendicular to the base as the height. For any other parallelogram, the height (or enough information to find it) will be given.

- A circle's perimeter is known as its **circumference (C)** and is found using $C = 2\pi r$, where r is the **radius** (distance from the center of the circle to its edge). The **area of a circle** is given by $A = \pi r^2$. The strange symbol is the lowercase Greek letter pi (π, pronounced "pie"), which is approximately 3.14. As mentioned in the algebra section, you should carry π throughout your calculations without rounding unless instructed otherwise.

- A **chord** is any line segment connecting two points located on the circumference of the circle. The **diameter** of a circle is a chord that passes through the center; its length is equal to twice that of the radius.

- A **tangent line**, shown in the figure that follows, touches a circle at exactly one point and is perpendicular to a circle's radius at the point of contact:

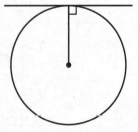

The presence of a right angle opens up the opportunity to draw otherwise hidden shapes, so pay special attention to tangents when they're mentioned.

- A shape is said to have **symmetry** when it can be split by a line (called an **axis of symmetry**) into two identical parts. Consider folding a shape along a line: if all sides and vertices align once the shape is folded in half, the shape is symmetrical about that line. Some shapes have no axis of symmetry, some have one, some have multiple axes, and still others can have infinite axes of symmetry (e.g., a circle):

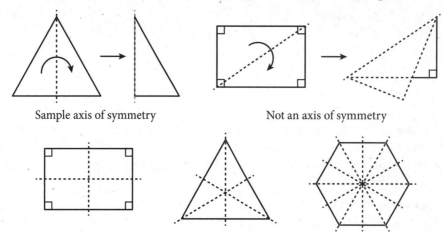

Sample axis of symmetry   Not an axis of symmetry

Sample shapes with corresponding axes of symmetry

- **Congruence** is simply a geometry term that means identical. Angles, lines, and shapes can be congruent. Congruence is indicated by using hash marks. Everything with the same number of hash marks is congruent:

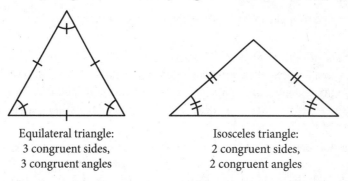

Equilateral triangle: Isosceles triangle:
3 congruent sides,   2 congruent sides,
3 congruent angles   2 congruent angles

- **Similarity** between shapes indicates that they have identical angles and proportional sides. Think of taking a shape and stretching or shrinking each side by the same ratio. The resulting shape will have the same angles as the original. While the sides will not be identical, they will be proportional:

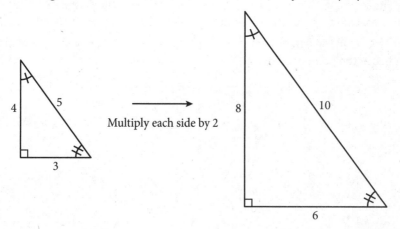

Multiply each side by 2

If you're comfortable with these concepts, read on for tips on calculator use. If not, review this lesson and remember to refer to it for help if you get stuck in a later chapter.

CALCULATOR USE

LEARNING OBJECTIVE

After this lesson, you will be able to:

- Distinguish between questions that need a calculator and questions for which manual calculations are more efficient

Calculators and the SAT

Many students never stop to ask whether using a calculator is the most efficient way to answer a math question. This chapter will show you how the strongest test takers use their calculators strategically; that is, they carefully evaluate when to use the calculator and when to skip it in favor of a more streamlined approach. As you will see, even though you can use a calculator, sometimes it's more beneficial to save your energy by approaching a question more strategically. Work smarter, not harder.

Which Calculator Should You Use?

The SAT allows four-function, scientific, and graphing calculators; additionally, it features a built-in graphing calculator. No matter which calculator you choose, start practicing with it now. You don't want to waste valuable time on test day looking for the exponent button or figuring out how to correctly graph equations. Due to the wide range of math topics you'll encounter on test day, **we recommend using the graphing calculator**.

A graphing calculator's capabilities extend well beyond what you'll need for the test, so don't worry about memorizing every function. The next section will cover which calculator functions you'll want to know how to use for the SAT. If you'd prefer to use your own graphing calculator, you'll want to get the user manual; you can find this on the Internet by searching for your calculator's model number. Identify the calculator functions necessary to answer various SAT Math questions, then write down the directions for each to make a handy study sheet.

When Should You Use a Calculator?

Some SAT question types are designed based on the idea that students will do some or all of the work using a calculator. As a master test taker, you want to know what to look for so you can identify when calculator use is advantageous. Questions involving statistics, determining roots of complicated quadratic equations, and other topics are generally designed with calculator use in mind.

Other questions aren't intentionally designed to involve calculator use. Solving some with a calculator can save you time and energy, but you'll waste both if you go for the calculator on others. You will have to decide which method is best when you encounter the following topics:

- Long division and other extensive calculations
- Graphing quadratics
- Simplifying radicals and calculating roots
- Plane and coordinate geometry

Practicing **long computations** by hand and with the calculator will not only boost your focus and mental math prowess but will also help you determine whether it's faster to do the work for a given question by hand or by reaching for the calculator on test day.

Graphing quadratic equations is a big reason why many students get a fancy calculator in the first place; it makes answering these questions a snap! This is definitely an area where you need to have an in-depth knowledge of the function of the calculator you'll be using on test day. The key to making these questions easy with the calculator is being meticulous when entering the equation.

Another stressful area for many students is **radicals**, especially when the answer choices are written as decimals. Those two elements are big red flags that trigger a reach for the calculator. Beware: not all graphing calculators have a built-in radical simplification function, so consider familiarizing yourself with this process.

Geometry can be a gray area for students when it comes to calculator use. Consider working by hand when dealing with angles and lines, specifically when filling in information on complementary, supplementary, and congruent angles. You should be able to work fluidly through most of those questions without using your calculator.

If you choose to use **trigonometric functions** to get to the answer on triangle questions, make sure you have your calculator set to degrees or radians as required by the question.

In short, be sure to understand how the calculator that you will be using on test day works, whether that's your own approved for use on the test or the one included with the College Board's testing application. You can get more practice with the College Board's included calculator by taking a practice test on College Board's website.

To Use or Not to Use?

A calculator is a double-edged sword on the SAT: using one can be an asset for verifying work if you struggle when doing math by hand, but turning to it for the simplest computations will cost you time that you could devote to more complex questions. Practice solving questions with and without a calculator to get a sense of your personal style as well as your strengths and weaknesses. Think critically about when a calculator saves you time and when mental math is faster. Use the exercises in this book to practice your calculations so that by the time test day arrives, you'll be in the habit of using your calculator as effectively as possible.

[CHAPTER 3]

THE METHOD FOR SAT MATH QUESTIONS

HOW TO DO SAT MATH

SAT Math questions can seem more difficult than they actually are, especially when you are working under time pressure. The method we are about to describe will help you answer SAT questions, whether you are comfortable with the math content or not. This method is designed to give you the confidence you need to get the right answers on the SAT by helping you think through a question logically, one piece at a time.

Take a look at this question and think about how you would attack it if you saw it on test day:

Of the 150 apartments in building M, 24% have at least 3 bedrooms. If building M is representative of the 1,350 apartment buildings in city Z, then approximately how many apartments in city Z have fewer than 3 bedrooms?

A) 49,000

B) 114,000

C) 154,000

D) 203,000

Many test takers will see a question like this and panic. Others will waste a great deal of time reading and rereading without a clear goal. You want to avoid both of those outcomes.

First, ask yourself, **What is the question asking?** In other words, what do the answer choices represent? In this question, they represent *the number of apartments in city Z with fewer than 3 bedrooms.*

Second, ask yourself, **What does the question tell me?** In other words, what information did the test makers give you? Here, you know that 24% of the 150 apartments in building M have 3 or more bedrooms, that building M is one of 1,350 apartment buildings in city Z, and that all 1,350 apartment buildings are similar.

Third, ask yourself, **What strategy is best for me?** The answer to this question is personal. What works best for you might not work best for other test takers, and vice versa. The answer choices to this question are far apart, so you might consider rounding 24% to $\frac{1}{4}$ and estimating. Alternatively, you could use your calculator to make precise calculations easily. If you decide to use your calculator, start by finding the percentage of apartments with fewer than 3 bedrooms: 100% − 24% = 76%. Next, calculate the number of apartments in building M with fewer than 3 bedrooms:

Fewer than 3 bedrooms total in building M: $0.76 \times 150 = 114$

Finally, ask yourself, **Am I done?** This step is an important step. Does your answer make sense? Did you answer what the question asked? Panicked students who skip this step might see the number 114 in choice (B) and be tempted to choose it. The percentage you are looking for is sizeable, and 114 should strike you as too low for 1,350 apartment building with 150 apartments each. The number calculated so far (114), is off by orders of magnitudes from the answers given and probably not what you would have expected, so instead of just assuming that you made a slight math mistake and missed multiplying by 1,000 somewhere, take a moment to stop and review those first questions you asked yourself when answering this question.

A quick review will let you know that you're not done yet! You calculated the number of fewer-than-3-bedroom apartments in *building M*, but the question asks for the total in *the entire city*. There are 1,350 apartment buildings in the city—all of which are similar to building M—so you need to multiply your answer by 1,350:

$$114 \times 1,350 = 153,900$$

Again, ask yourself, **Am I done?** This time, you are! You want the number of apartments in the city that have fewer than 3 bedrooms, and that's what you calculated. The correct answer is **(C)**.

Here are the steps of the method we just used:

THE METHOD FOR SAT MATH QUESTIONS

STEP 1 What is the question asking?

STEP 2 What does the question tell me?

STEP 3 What strategy is best for me?

STEP 4 Am I done?

The amount of time you spend on each step may vary from question to question. This question, because it is an in-context word problem, required a fair amount of analysis in steps 1 and 2, but choosing an approach (step 3) was straightforward; the calculations were quick to do on a calculator, so there was no need to estimate. Other questions will require less thought in steps 1 and 2 but will benefit from a careful strategy decision in step 3. Step 4 is quick, but you should always do it: just stop for a moment to make sure you answered the question that was actually asked and that the answer makes sense to you before selecting or entering your response. Doing so will save you from making mistakes on questions that you know how to do and should be getting credit for.

There are several approaches you can choose from in step 3: doing the traditional math, as we did in the previous question; picking numbers; backsolving; estimating; or taking a strategic guess. In the next two examples, you'll see Picking Numbers and Backsolving in action.

Here's another example. This one is not an in-context word problem, so steps 1 and 2 require less mental energy, but pay attention when you get to step 3.

Which of the following is equivalent to the expression $\frac{8x-2}{x+1}$?

A) $8 - \frac{10}{x+1}$

B) $8 - \frac{2}{x+1}$

C) $8 + \frac{2}{x+1}$

D) $\frac{8-2}{1}$

Step 1: What is the question asking? An answer choice that is equal to $\frac{8x-2}{x+1}$.

Step 2: What does the question tell me? Only the expression $\frac{8x-2}{x+1}$.

Step 3: What strategy is best for me?

Here's where it gets interesting. The creator of this question may be expecting you to use polynomial long division to solve. But if you don't know how to do polynomial long division (or find it very time-consuming), there's no need to panic. You could use an alternate approach called **Picking Numbers** that will work just as well: choose a number to substitute for x in the question, then substitute the same number for x in the choices and see which one matches. Like this:

Pick a small number for x, say 2. When $x = 2$, the original expression becomes:

$$\frac{8x-2}{x+1} = \frac{8(2)-2}{2+1} = \frac{14}{3}$$

Now, plug $x = 2$ into the choices:

(A) $8 - \frac{10}{x+1} = 8 - \frac{10}{3} = \frac{24}{3} - \frac{10}{3} = \frac{14}{3}$

This is a match. It is always possible that another answer choice can produce the same result, so check the rest to be sure there isn't another match when $x = 2$. (If there is, go back and pick another number to distinguish between the choices that match.)

(B) $8 - \frac{2}{x+1} = 8 - \frac{2}{3} = \frac{24}{3} - \frac{2}{3} = \frac{22}{3}$

Eliminate (B).

(C) $8 + \frac{2}{x+1} = 8 + \frac{2}{3} = \frac{24}{3} + \frac{2}{3} = \frac{26}{3}$

Eliminate (C).

(D) $\frac{8-2}{1} = 6$

Eliminate (D).

Step 4: Am I done? You eliminated (B), (C), and (D), so only **(A)** is a match. Select it and move on.

When picking numbers, use numbers that are **permissible** and **manageable**. That is, use numbers that follow the rules of the question and are easy to work with. In this question, you could have picked any real number because x was not defined as positive, negative, odd, even, a fraction, etc. A small positive integer is usually the best choice in this situation. In other questions, other kinds of numbers may be more manageable. For example, in percent questions, 100 is typically a good number to pick.

Try one more:

> Mr. Dvorkin distributes colored markers to a group of children. If he gives each child 4 markers, he will have 3 markers left over. In order to give each child 5 markers, with no markers left over, he will need 17 additional markers. How many markers does Mr. Dvorkin have?
>
> A) 55
> B) 68
> C) 83
> D) 100

Step 1: What is the question asking? The number of markers Mr. Dvorkin has.

Step 2: What does the question tell me? Two unknowns (the number of children and the number of markers) and sufficient information to set up a system of equations.

Step 3: What strategy is best for me? You could set up the system of equations, but it might be faster to use a technique called **Backsolving**: plug the choices in for the unknown and see which one works. Here, you need an answer choice that will leave a remainder of 3 when divided by 4. Choices (B) and (D) don't meet this condition, so the answer must be (A) or (C). (Both 68 and 100 are evenly divisible by 4, so if they were divided by 4, there would be 0 markers left over, not 3.)

(A) If Mr. Dvorkin has 55 markers, and gives each child 4 markers, he will indeed have 3 markers left over, since $55 \div 4 = 13$ R3. Now, what happens in the other situation? With an extra 17 markers, Mr. Dvorkin should be able to give each child exactly 5 markers. But $55 + 17 = 72$, which is not evenly divisible by 5. Eliminate (A).

Step 4: Am I done? You've now eliminated every choice but **(C)**, so it must be correct—you don't even need to test it! For the record:

(C) If Mr. Dvorkin has 83 markers and gives each child 4 markers, he will indeed have 3 left over, since $83 \div 4 = 20$ R3. With an extra 17 markers, Mr. Dvorkin should be able to give each child exactly 5 markers, and this is in fact what happens: $83 + 17 = 100$, which is evenly divisible by 5.

Although it wasn't the case in this question, when backsolving, it often makes sense to start with (B) or (C) in case you can tell from the context whether you'll need a larger or smaller answer choice if the one you're testing fails. For example, if you test (B) and it's too big, then the answer must be (A).

Now, it's your turn. Be deliberate with these questions. If there is analysis to do up front, do it. If there is more than one way to do a question, consider carefully before choosing your approach. And be sure to check whether you answered the right question. Forming good habits now, in slow and careful practice, will build your confidence for test day.

Try on Your Own

Directions

Take as much time as you need on these questions. Work carefully and methodically. There will be an opportunity for timed practice later in the book.

1

A cargo airplane has a maximum takeoff weight of 19,000 kilograms. The airplane, crew, and fuel have a combined weight of 14,750 kilograms. The airplane will be loaded with n 125-kilogram cargo containers. What is the greatest value of n such that the airplane doesn't exceed its maximum takeoff weight?

- (A) 28
- (B) 34
- (C) 118
- (D) 152

2

A laptop costs $550 at an electronics store. An online retailer sells the laptop for $\frac{9}{10}$ of the price. A luxury department store sells the laptop for $\frac{7}{5}$ of the price. How much more does the laptop cost at the luxury department store than at the online retailer?

- (A) $198
- (B) $220
- (C) $275
- (D) $495

3

A stack of 75 identical plastic plates forms a column approximately $9\frac{7}{8}$ inches tall. At this rate, which of the following is closest to the number of plates that would be needed to form a column 20 inches tall?

- (A) 125
- (B) 150
- (C) 185
- (D) 220

4

Last month, Kiera ran 22 more miles than Bianca did. If they ran a combined total of 86 miles, how many miles did Bianca run?

- (A) 27
- (B) 32
- (C) 43
- (D) 54

5

If $\frac{4x}{2y} = 4$, what is the value of $\frac{3y}{x}$?

- (A) $\frac{3}{4}$
- (B) $\frac{4}{3}$
- (C) $\frac{3}{2}$
- (D) 2

6

x	2	4	6	8	10
y	$\frac{7}{5}$	$\frac{11}{5}$	$\frac{15}{5}$	$\frac{19}{5}$	$\frac{23}{5}$

Which of the following equations relates y to x according to the values shown in the table?

(A) $y = \left(\frac{2}{5}\right)^x - \frac{7}{5}$

(B) $y = \left(\frac{3x}{5}\right)^2 - 2$

(C) $y = \frac{5}{2}x - \frac{3}{5}$

(D) $y = \frac{2}{5}x + \frac{3}{5}$

7

$$n - \sqrt{c + 5} = 1$$

In the given equation, c is a constant. If $n = 5$, what is the value of c?

(A) -1

(B) 0

(C) 3

(D) 11

8

At a child's lemonade stand, p pitchers of lemonade are made by adding m packets of lemonade mix to cold water. If $m = 2p + 4$, how many more packets of lemonade mix are needed to make each additional pitcher of lemonade?

(A) 1

(B) 2

(C) 4

(D) 6

9

A health club charges a one-time membership fee of $125 plus n dollars for each month. If a member pays $515 dollars for the first six months, including the membership fee, what is the value of n?

(A) 55

(B) 65

(C) 75

(D) 85

10

If $x > 0$, which of the following is equivalent to $\dfrac{2}{\dfrac{1}{x + 6} + \dfrac{1}{x + 2}}$?

(A) $x^2 + 8x + 12$

(B) $\dfrac{x + 4}{x^2 + 8x + 12}$

(C) $2x + 8$

(D) $\dfrac{x^2 + 8x + 12}{x + 4}$

A NOTE ABOUT STUDENT-PRODUCED RESPONSES

You will see questions without answer choices throughout the Math chapters of this book, starting in the next chapter, and on the SAT itself. Instead of selecting an answer choice, you'll enter your responses to these questions into a box that looks like this:

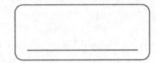

It is possible that such a question may have more than one possible answer, such as the two roots of a quadratic equation. In that case, only enter one of the answers; either one will receive credit. For a positive answer, you can enter up to five characters; for a negative answer, you can enter six characters (which includes the negative sign). Do not enter symbols like dollar signs, percent signs, or commas. You can enter answers as either a fraction or a decimal (with or without the leading zero); the decimal point will count against the five- or six-character limit. If the answer is $\frac{1}{2}$, you can enter 1/2, 0.5, or .5.

Some types of answers require a bit more care. If your answer is a decimal longer than the allotted space, you can either round it or truncate it at the final digit. A mixed number must be entered as either an improper fraction or a decimal; anything to the left of the fraction bar will be read as the numerator of a fraction. The table shows some examples of acceptable and unacceptable answers.

ANSWER	ACCEPTABLE	UNACCEPTABLE
$\frac{5}{9}$	5/9 0.555 0.556 .5555 .5556	0.55 0.56 .555 .556
$-4\frac{1}{4}$	−17/4 −4.25 −4.250	−4 1/4 −41/4

If you arrive at a fraction for an answer that will not fit into the space provided in the student-produced response box, such as the seven characters needed for $\frac{901}{990}$, enter the decimal equivalent of the fraction into the box using the rules shown in the table.

REFLECT

Directions: Take a few minutes to recall what you've learned and what you've been practicing in this chapter. Consider the following questions, jot down your answer for each one, and then compare your reflections to the expert responses that follow. Use your level of confidence to determine what to do next.

Think about your current habits when attacking SAT questions. Are you a strategic test taker? Do you take the time to think through what would be the fastest way to the answer?

_____

_____

_____

Do word problems give you trouble?

_____

_____

_____

What are the steps of the Method for SAT Math and why is each step important?

_____

_____

_____

Expert Responses

Think about your current habits when attacking SAT questions. Are you a strategic test taker? Do you take the time to think through what would be the fastest way to the answer?

If yes, good for you! If not, we recommend doing questions more than one way whenever possible as part of your SAT prep. If you can discover now, while you're still practicing, that Picking Numbers is faster for you on certain types of questions but not on others, you'll be that much more efficient on test day.

Do word problems give you trouble?

If word problems are difficult for you, get into the habit of taking an inventory, before you do any math, of what the question is asking for and what information you have.

What are the steps of the Method for SAT Math, and why is each step important?

Here are the steps:

Step 1. *What is the question asking?*

Step 2. *What does the question tell me?*

(Taking an inventory is especially important in word problems.)

Step 3. *What strategy is best for me?*

(Taking a moment to decide which approach will be the fastest way for you to get to the correct answer will ultimately save you time.)

Step 4. *Am I done?*

(Making sure that you solved for the right thing will save you from missing out on points on questions that you know how to do and should be getting credit for.)

Next Steps

If your approach to most questions in the "Try on Your Own" section generally resembled that of the experts using Kaplan methods and strategies and if your responses to the Reflect questions were similar to those of the SAT expert, then consider the Method for SAT Math an area of strength and move on to the next chapter. Do keep using the Method as you work on the questions in future chapters.

If you don't yet feel confident, review those parts of this chapter that you have not yet mastered and try the questions that you missed again. As always, be sure to review the explanations closely.

Check Your Work – Chapter 3

1. B
Difficulty: Medium
Category: Algebra
Getting to the Answer: You need to find the maximum number of cargo containers that can fit on this plane. You're given the weight of everything on the airplane except the combined weight of the cargo containers (which weigh 125 kilograms each), and you're given the maximum takeoff weight of the plane. Therefore, the difference between the maximum takeoff weight and the weight of the plane, crew, and fuel must be the maximum combined weight of the cargo containers.

The maximum takeoff weight of the plane is 19,000 kilograms, and the weight of the plane, crew, and fuel is 14,750 kilograms. Hence, the maximum number of cargo containers can have a combined weight no greater than $19,000 - 14,750 = 4,250$ kilograms. That means that the maximum number of containers, n, must be 4,250 kilograms ÷ 125 kilograms = 34 containers. Thus, **(B)** is correct.

2. C
Difficulty: Medium
Category: Algebra
Getting to the Answer: You need to find the difference between the price of a particular laptop at a luxury department store and at an online retailer. The price of the laptop at the electronics store is $550. You also know that the price at the online retailer is $\frac{9}{10}$ of this, and the price at the luxury store is $\frac{7}{5}$ of the price at the electronics store. Determine those two prices: $\frac{9}{10} \times \$550 = \$495$ and $\frac{7}{5} \times \$550 = \$770$. You're not done yet, though; the answer is the difference in prices between the places of purchase, not either of the individual prices. The difference between the price at the luxury department store and the price at the online retailer is $\$770 - \$495 = \$275$. Choice **(C)** is correct.

3. B
Difficulty: Easy
Category: Problem-Solving and Data Analysis
Getting to the Answer: You need to determine how many plates would be in a stack 20 inches tall, given that 75 plates make a stack $9\frac{7}{8}$ inches tall. You could use the given information to determine the height of

each plate, and then divide 20 by that height to see how many plates are needed. However, this is a good opportunity for estimating. Notice the relationship between the height of the stack of 75 plates and the height of the unknown number of plates: $9\frac{7}{8}$ inches is *about half* of 20 inches. So, a 20-inch stack of plates will be about twice as tall as a stack of 75 plates. Therefore, approximately twice as many plates, or about $2 \times 75 = 150$, will be needed to form a stack 20 inches tall. Hence, **(B)** is correct.

4. B
Difficulty: Medium
Category: Algebra
Getting to the Answer: You're asked to determine how many miles Bianca ran. The question gives two unknowns (the distances Kiera and Bianca each ran) and enough information (the total distance run and the difference between their individual distances) to create a system of equations; therefore, it could be solved with a traditional algebraic approach.

There is, however, a more efficient way: assess the answer choices to see which makes sense for Bianca's distance. Since Kiera ran 22 miles farther than Bianca, and the combined distance they ran is 86 miles, Bianca must have run less than half of the 86 miles. Since one-half of 86 is 43, you can quickly eliminate (C) and (D), which are both too big.

Now check (B) against the known information. If Bianca ran 32 miles, then Kiera ran $32 + 22 = 54$ miles. Check if Bianca's distance and Kiera's distance add up to 86: $32 + 54 = 86$; thus, **(B)** is correct.

If you're curious about the algebraic approach, here it is: let b represent the number of miles Bianca ran and k represent the number of miles Kiera ran. Then $b + k = 86$, and $k = b + 22$. Now, substitute the value of k in terms of b into the first equation:

$$b + (b + 22) = 86$$
$$2b + 22 = 86$$
$$2b = 64$$
$$b = 32$$

Again, Bianca ran 32 miles, and **(B)** is correct.

5.   C
Difficulty: Medium
Category: Algebra
Getting to the Answer: Instead of solving for the value of a variable, you're solving for the value of an expression, $\frac{3y}{x}$, given that $\frac{4x}{2y} = 4$. You can approach this by picking numbers. Pick a simple number for y, solve for x, and if x is also easy to work with, plug them into the expression you're trying to find. Say $y = 1$; then you have $\frac{4x}{2(1)} = 4$, which simplifies to $2x = 4$, so $x = 2$, another manageable number.

Now, plug these same values of x and y into $\frac{3y}{x}$ to get $\frac{3(1)}{(2)} = \frac{3}{2}$. Thus, **(C)** is correct.

6.   D
Difficulty: Medium
Category: Algebra
Getting to the Answer: The correct answer will be an equation that represents the relationship between x and y. You're given a table with a series of x- and y-values. Notice that, for every increase of 2 in the x-value, the y-value increases by $\frac{4}{5}$. Therefore, they have a linear relationship, so you can eliminate (A) and (B), which are both exponential functions.

Now, plug values from the table into the remaining answers to see whether the math works out. Try the first column in the table and plug in 2 for x and $\frac{7}{5}$ for y:

(C): $\frac{7}{5} = \frac{5}{2} \times 2 - \frac{3}{5} = 5 - \frac{3}{5} = \frac{25}{5} - \frac{3}{5} = \frac{22}{5}$. This doesn't work out, so **(D)** must be correct. No need to check it. For the record:

(D): $\frac{7}{5} = \frac{2}{5} \times 2 + \frac{3}{5} = \frac{4}{5} + \frac{3}{5} = \frac{7}{5}$.

7.   D
Difficulty: Medium
Category: Advanced Math
Getting to the Answer: You're asked to find the value of c. The question provides an equation in terms of n and c and the value of n.

Since you're told that $n = 5$, fill this value into the equation, and then simplify to find the root:

$$5 - \sqrt{c + 5} = 1$$
$$-\sqrt{c + 5} = -4$$
$$\sqrt{c + 5} = 4$$
$$c + 5 = 4^2$$
$$c + 5 = 16$$
$$c = 11$$

(D) is correct.

8.   B
Difficulty: Medium
Category: Algebra
Getting to the Answer: You need to determine how many extra packets of lemonade mix would be needed to make one more pitcher of lemonade. You're given a linear equation in terms of m and p. Try picking numbers. If $p = 2$, then $m = 2(2) + 4 = 8$, so there are 8 packets of mix needed to make 2 pitchers of lemonade. Now try $p = 3$: $m = 2(3) + 4 = 10$. For one additional pitcher, the packets needed increased from 8 to 10, which is a change of 2. Therefore, **(B)** is correct.

9.   B
Difficulty: Medium
Category: Algebra
Getting to the Answer: The question asks for the value of n, which is the monthly fee at a health club; you're given the cost of a six-month membership, which includes a one-time membership fee. Try backsolving, starting with (B) or (C). If the answer you choose is too large or too small, you'll know which direction to go when testing the next choice. Multiply the value in the answer choice by the six months and then add the $125 membership fee.

(B): $65 \times 6 = 390$. $390 + 125 = 515$. This is a match, so **(B)** is correct. Since there can be only one correct answer, you're finished.

Alternatively, you can solve algebraically:

$$\$125 + 6n = \$515$$
$$6n = \$390$$
$$\frac{6n}{6} = \frac{\$390}{6}$$
$$n = \$65$$

Again, **(B)** is correct.

Math

10. D
Difficulty: Medium
Category: Advanced Math
Getting to the Answer: The correct answer will be an expression equal to the one given in the question, which also specifies that x must be positive. Try using the Picking Numbers strategy. To make calculations easy, say $x = 1$; then the given expression becomes $\dfrac{2}{\dfrac{1}{1+6} + \dfrac{1}{1+2}}$. Now, simplify this expression:

$$\dfrac{2}{\dfrac{1}{7} + \dfrac{1}{3}}$$

$$= \dfrac{2}{\dfrac{3}{21} + \dfrac{7}{21}}$$

$$= \dfrac{2}{\left(\dfrac{10}{21}\right)}$$

$$= 2 \times \dfrac{21}{10}$$

$$= \dfrac{21}{5}$$

Next, plug 1 in for x in the answer choices to see which yields the same value:

(A): $1^2 + 8 \times 1 + 12 = 21$. Eliminate.

(B): $\dfrac{1+4}{1^2 + 8 \times 1 + 12} = \dfrac{5}{21}$. Eliminate.

(C): $2 \times 1 + 8 = 10$. Eliminate. You have eliminated three answer choices, so the one left is correct; **(D)** is correct. For the record: (D): $\dfrac{1^2 + 8 \times 1 + 12}{1 + 4} = \dfrac{21}{5}$. This is a match, which confirms that **(D)** is correct.

You might also have noticed that (B) gave you the reciprocal of the value you were looking for; therefore, the reciprocal of the expression in (B) must give you the correct answer, and that is **(D)**.

ALGEBRA

HOW MUCH DO YOU KNOW: ALGEBRA

Directions

Try the questions that follow, using the Method for SAT Math Questions. When you're done, check your answers and read through the explanations in the "Check Your Work" section.

There will be an opportunity for timed practice at the end of the Algebra unit.

1

The farmers market usually sells potatoes for $0.90 per pound. On Fridays, it sells potatoes at a 30 percent discount. The market also sells cantaloupes for $3.50 each. Which of the following represents the total cost, c, if a customer buys 2 cantaloupes and p pounds of potatoes on a Friday?

Ⓐ $c = 0.63p + 7$

Ⓑ $c = 0.9p + 7$

Ⓒ $c = 0.3p + 3.5$

Ⓓ $c = 0.9p + 3.5$

2

$$\frac{x}{5} + \frac{y}{3} = \frac{21}{15}$$

$$\frac{3}{7}x + 4y = 3$$

What is the value of y?

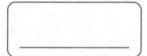

3

x	$f(x)$
-2	-2.5
0	-3
2	-3.5

The table shows some values of the linear function f. What is the value of $f(5)$?

4

Which value of x makes the equation $\frac{3}{2}(x + 7) = 6$ true?

Ⓐ -5

Ⓑ -3

Ⓒ 9

Ⓓ 11

5

x	-9	0	3	9
y	11	8	7	$?$

If the values in the table represent a linear relationship, what is the missing value?

Ⓐ 5

Ⓑ 6

Ⓒ 11

Ⓓ 13

6

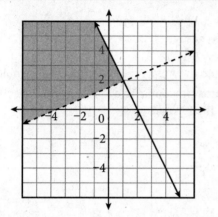

The shaded region on the graph shows the solution for a system of inequalities. Which of the following is the system of inequalities depicted on the graph?

- Ⓐ $x + 2y \leq 4$ and $5y - 2x > 8$

- Ⓑ $y + 2x \leq 4$ and $5x - 2y > 8$

- Ⓒ $2x + y \leq 4$ and $5y - 2x > 8$

- Ⓓ $2x + y < 4$ and $5y - 2x \geq 8$

7

$$4x > y + 8$$
$$8y > 20 + 3y$$

Which of the following describes the values of x that satisfy the system of inequalities?

- Ⓐ $x > 3$

- Ⓑ $x > 4$

- Ⓒ $3 < x < 12$

- Ⓓ $x > 12$

8

$$ax + 9y = 1$$
$$2x + 6y = 5$$

If the given system of equations has no solution, what is the value of a?

- Ⓐ 0

- Ⓑ 1

- Ⓒ 2

- Ⓓ 3

9

$$2x = 3y - 10$$
$$7y + 5 = 4x$$

What is the value of $6x - 10y$?

- Ⓐ -10

- Ⓑ -5

- Ⓒ 5

- Ⓓ 10

10

$$f(x) = 2x - 1$$
$$g(x) = 3 - f(x)$$

What is the value of $g(4)$?

_____

Math

Check Your Work – How Much Do You Know: Algebra

1.   A
Difficulty: Easy
Category: Algebra
Getting to the Answer: To find the cost of potatoes on Friday, multiply their weight p by the sale price. If there is a 30% discount, then the customer actually pays $100\% - 30\% = 70\%$. Therefore, p pounds of potatoes costs $0.90 \times 70\% \times p = 0.90 \times 0.70 \times p = 0.63p$. Now, add the cost of two cantaloupes, $3.50 \times 2 = 7$, to get the total cost: $c = 0.63p + 7$. Choice **(A)** is correct.

2.   0
Difficulty: Medium
Category: Algebra
Getting to the Answer: The first equation contains fractions, which are difficult to work with. Clear the fractions by multiplying both sides of the equation by 15:

$$15\left(\frac{x}{5} + \frac{y}{3} = \frac{21}{15}\right) \rightarrow 3x + 5y = 21$$

Using similar logic, multiply both sides of the second equation by 7:

$$7\left(\frac{3}{7}x + 4y = 3\right) \rightarrow 3x + 28y = 21$$

The question asks for the value of y. You can eliminate the x terms by subtracting the second equation from the first:

$$\begin{aligned} 3x + 5y &= 21 \\ -(3x + 28y &= 21) \\ \hline -23y &= 0 \\ y &= 0 \end{aligned}$$

Enter **0**.

3.   −4.25 or −17/4
Difficulty: Hard
Category: Algebra
Getting to the Answer: Linear functions have a constant rate of change, or slope. Examining the table, you see that every time x is increased by 2 units, $f(x)$ decreases by 0.5 units. This means that the slope is $\frac{-0.5}{2} = -0.25$. The point $(0, -3)$ in the table indicates that the y-intercept is -3. Plugging these values into $y = mx + b$ yields $f(x) = -0.25x - 3$. The question asks for $f(5)$, so plug in 5 for x and simplify: $f(5) = -0.25(5) - 3 = -1.25 - 3 = -4.25$. Enter **−4.25 or −17/4**.

4.   B
Difficulty: Easy
Category: Algebra
Getting to the Answer: Distributing the $\frac{3}{2}$ would create more messy fractions. To avoid this, multiply both sides of the equation by 2:

$$2\left[\frac{3}{2}(x + 7) = 6\right]$$
$$3(x + 7) = 12$$
$$3x + 21 = 12$$
$$3x = -9$$
$$x = -3$$

Choice **(B)** is correct. Backsolving is another viable approach. When backsolving, start with either (B) or (C). Try plugging in $x = -3$:

$$\frac{3}{2}(x + 7) = 6$$
$$\frac{3}{2}(-3 + 7) = 6$$
$$\frac{3}{2}(4) = 6$$
$$6 = 6$$

Since this results in a true statement, **(B)** is correct.

5.   A
Difficulty: Medium
Category: Algebra
Getting to the Answer: The rate of change (or slope) of a linear relationship is constant, so find the slope and use it to determine the missing value. Examine the points $(-9, 11)$ and $(0, 8)$. When x increased by 9, y decreased by 3. Therefore, if x increases by 9 again, y should decrease by 3 again. This means that the y-value when $x = 9$ is $8 - 3 = 5$. Choice **(A)** is correct.

6.   C
Difficulty: Hard
Category: Algebra
Getting to the Answer: Use known points from the graph to determine the equations for the two lines. Then convert them into inequalities.

The solid line passes through the points $(0, 4)$ and $(1, 2)$. Its slope is therefore $\frac{y_2 - y_1}{x_2 - x_1} = \frac{2 - 4}{1 - 0} = \frac{-2}{1} = -2$. The graph shows that the y-intercept is 4, so the equation for the solid line is $y = -2x + 4$. This can be restated as $y + 2x = 4$. Because the shaded region is below this line and the line is solid, the inequality defined by the line is $y + 2x \leq 4$. Eliminate (A) and (D).

The dotted line passes through the points $(-4, 0)$ and $(1, 2)$. Thus, the slope of this line is $\frac{2 - 0}{1 - (-4)} = \frac{2}{5}$. The y-intercept is unclear from the graph, so plug the x-intercept $(-4, 0)$ into $y = \frac{2}{5}x + b$ to get $0 = \frac{2}{5}(-4) + b$. Thus, $b = \frac{8}{5}$. The equation for this line is therefore $y = \frac{2}{5}x + \frac{8}{5}$. Since the line is dotted and the values of the solution are above the line, the inequality is $y > \frac{2}{5}x + \frac{8}{5}$. Simplify this by multiplying all the terms by 5 to get $5y > 2x + 8$, which converts to $5y - 2x > 8$. These two inequalities match the ones in **(C)**.

7.   A
Difficulty: Medium
Category: Algebra
Getting to the Answer: Solve the second inequality for y and substitute this result into the first inequality. If $8y > 20 + 3y$, then $5y > 20$ and $y > 4$. Plugging into the second inequality gives $4x > 4 + 8$, or $4x > 12$. This means that $x > 3$. Choice **(A)** is correct.

8.   D
Difficulty: Hard
Category: Algebra
Getting to the Answer: Graphically, a "solution" to a system of equations is where the two lines touch each other. For a system of equations to have no solution, they must never touch each other. This means that they are parallel. Parallel lines have the same slope but different y-intercepts. Although you could rearrange each equation to get it into $y = mx + b$ form, it is easier to recognize that the slope of each line is determined by the x- and y-coefficients. If the two lines have the same x- and y-coefficients, then they have the same slope.

Examining the equations, you see that the first one has a $9y$ and the second has a $6y$. If you multiply the second equation by $\frac{3}{2}$, you can make the coefficient of the y term 9:

$$\frac{3}{2}(2x + 6y = 5) \rightarrow 3x + 9y = \frac{15}{2}$$

Since the y-coordinates are now the same, you can simply match up the x-coordinates in both equations. This means that $a = 3$. Choice **(D)** is correct.

9.   B
Difficulty: Medium
Category: Algebra
Getting to the Answer: Rather than solving for each variable individually, see if you can solve for the desired expression all at once. Begin by getting the x and y variables together on the left-hand side of the equation and the constants on the right:

$$2x - 3y = -10$$
$$-4x + 7y = -5$$

Look carefully at what the question is asking you to find. You can obtain this expression simply by subtracting the two equations:

$$\begin{array}{r} 2x - 3y = -10 \\ -(-4x + 7y = -5) \\ \hline 6x - 10y = -5 \end{array}$$

Choice **(B)** is correct.

10.   −4
Difficulty: Medium
Category: Algebra
Getting to the Answer: To evaluate $g(4)$, replace x with 4 in the g function: $g(4) = 3 - f(4)$. Next, find $f(4)$ by replacing x with 4 in the f function: $f(4) = 2(4) - 1 = 8 - 1 = 7$. Finally, plug this value of $f(4)$ back into the g function: $g(4) = 3 - 7 = -4$. Enter **−4**.

[CHAPTER 4]

LINEAR EQUATIONS AND GRAPHS

LEARNING OBJECTIVES

After completing this chapter, you will be able to:

- Isolate a variable
- Translate word problems into equations
- Match an expression or equation to a real-life context, table, or graph
- Calculate the slope of a line given two points
- Write the equation of a line in slope-intercept form
- Discern whether the slope of a line is positive, negative, zero, or undefined based on its graph
- Describe the slopes of parallel and perpendicular lines

HOW MUCH DO YOU KNOW?

Directions

Try the questions that follow. Show your work so that you can compare your solutions to the ones found in the "Check Your Work" section immediately after this question set. If you answered the question(s) on a specific topic correctly, and if your scratchwork looks like ours, you may be able to move quickly through the lesson covering that topic. If you answered incorrectly or used a different approach, you may want to take your time on that lesson.

1

The tangential velocity, v, of an object traveling at constant speed around a circle is calculated using the formula $v = \frac{2\pi r}{T}$, where r is the radius of the circle and T is the time it takes for the object to make one complete circle, called a period. Which of the following formulas expresses T in terms of v and r?

(A) $T = \frac{v}{2\pi r}$

(B) $T = \frac{2\pi r}{v}$

(C) $T = 2\pi rv$

(D) $T = \frac{1}{2\pi rv}$

2

If $x = z\left(\frac{ab}{y}\right)$, where z, a, and b are constants and x and y are not equal to zero, then which of the following gives y in terms of a, b, x, and z?

(A) $y = \frac{ab}{xz}$

(B) $y = \frac{bx}{az}$

(C) $y = \frac{az}{bx}$

(D) $y = \frac{abz}{x}$

3

Andrew, a travel agent, gets paid $120 for a day's work, plus a bonus of $25 for each cruise he books. Which of the following represents the total that Andrew earns in a day, d, based on the number of cruises he books, c?

(A) $c = 25d + 120$

(B) $c = 120d + 25$

(C) $d = 25c + 120$

(D) $d = 120c + 25$

4

In a practice long-jump competition, Vera gets 5 points for landing over the nearer line and 10 points for landing over the more distant line. Out of 7 jumps, x jumps are over the more distant line and the rest are over the nearer line. Which of the following equations represents the relationship between Vera's total score, y, and x?

(A) $y = 10x$

(B) $y = 5x + 35$

(C) $y = 10x + 5$

(D) $y = 70 - 5x$

5

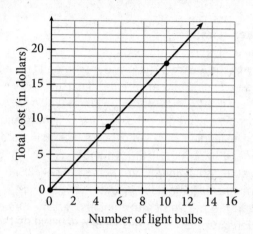

The graph shows the cost of various quantities of light bulbs sold at a store. According to the graph, what is the cost of a single light bulb?

Ⓐ $0.56

Ⓑ $1.80

Ⓒ $2.50

Ⓓ $3.60

6

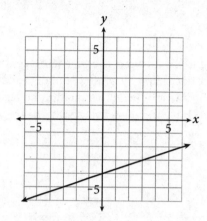

The graph shown represents which of the following equations?

Ⓐ $y = -3x + 4$

Ⓑ $y = -\dfrac{1}{3}x + 4$

Ⓒ $y = \dfrac{1}{3}x - 4$

Ⓓ $y = 3x - 4$

Check Your Work

1.   B
Difficulty: Easy
Category: Algebra
Getting to the Answer: The goal here is to solve the equation for T. Start by getting T out of the denominator of the fraction. To do this, multiply both sides of the equation by T, and then divide both sides by v:

$$v = \frac{2\pi r}{T}$$
$$T \times v = \left(\frac{2\pi r}{T}\right) \times T$$
$$Tv = 2\pi r$$
$$T = \frac{2\pi r}{v}$$

Choice **(B)** is the correct answer.

2.   D
Difficulty: Easy
Category: Algebra
Strategic Advice: Even when the equation is entirely made up of variables, the process for isolating one variable is still the same.
Getting to the Answer: The given equation needs to be rearranged to solve for y, so start by multiplying both sides by y to get that expression out of the denominator:

$$yx = abz$$

Next, divide both sides by x:

$$y = \frac{abz}{x}$$

(D) is correct.

3.   C
Difficulty: Easy
Category: Algebra
Getting to the Answer: When writing a linear equation to represent a real-world scenario, a flat rate is a constant, while a unit rate is always multiplied by the independent variable. You can identify the unit rate by looking for words like *per* or *for each*.

Because the amount Andrew gets paid daily, $120, is a flat rate that doesn't depend on the number of cruises he books, 120 should be the constant in the equation. This means you can eliminate (B) and (D). You can infer from the question that you need to multiply $25 by the number of cruises he books, c, so the equation is *total pay* $= 25 \times$ *number of cruises* $+ 120$, or $d = 25c + 120$, making **(C)** correct.

4.   B
Difficulty: Hard
Category: Algebra
Getting to the Answer: The key to answering this question is determining how many jumps land across each line. If Vera gets 7 jumps total and x jumps land over the more distant line, then the rest, or $7 - x$, must land over the nearer line. Now, write the expression in words: points per distant line (10) times number of jumps landing over the distant line (x), plus points per near line (5) times number of jumps landing over the near line ($7 - x$). Next, translate the words into numbers, variables, and operations: $10x + 5(7 - x)$. This is not one of the answer choices, so simplify the expression by distributing the 5 and combining like terms: $10x + 5(7 - x) = 10x + 35 - 5x = 5x + 35$, so the equation is $y = 5x + 35$. **(B)** is correct.

5.   B
Difficulty: Easy
Category: Algebra
Getting to the Answer: The x-axis represents the number of light bulbs, so find 1 on the x-axis and follow it up to where it meets the graph of the line. The y-value is somewhere between $1 and $2, so the only possible correct answer choice is $1.80. **(B)** is correct.

You could also find the unit rate by calculating the slope of the line using two of the points shown on the graph: the graph rises 9 units and runs 5 units from one point to the next, so the slope is $\frac{9}{5}$, or 1.8, which confirms that **(B)** is correct.

6.   C
Difficulty: Medium
Category: Algebra
Getting to the Answer: Use the graph to identify the y-intercept and the slope of the line, and then write an equation in slope-intercept form, $y = mx + b$. Once you have your equation, look for the answer choice that matches. The line crosses the y-axis at $(0, -4)$, so the y-intercept, b, is -4. The line rises 1 unit for every 3 units that it runs to the right, so the slope, m, is $\frac{1}{3}$. The equation of the line is $y = \frac{1}{3}x - 4$, which matches **(C)**.

You could also graph each of the answer choices in your calculator to see which one matches the given graph, but this is not the most time-efficient strategy. You also have to be very careful when entering fractions into the calculator. **(C)** is correct.

SOLVING EQUATIONS

LEARNING OBJECTIVE

After this lesson, you will be able to:

- Isolate a variable

To answer a question like this:

$$\frac{1}{2}(3x + 14) = \frac{1}{6}(7x - 10)$$

Which value of x satisfies the given equation?

A) -26

B) 2

C) 8

D) 16

You need to know this:

Isolating a variable means getting that variable by itself on one side of the equation. To do this, use inverse operations to manipulate the equation, remembering that whatever you do to one side of the equation, you must do to *both* sides.

You need to do this:

It usually makes sense to proceed in this order:

1. Eliminate any fractions.

2. Collect and combine like terms.

3. Divide to leave the desired variable by itself.

Explanation:

Eliminate the fractions by multiplying both sides of the equation by 6:

$$\left(\frac{6}{1}\right)\frac{1}{2}(3x + 14) = \left(\frac{6}{1}\right)\frac{1}{6}(7x - 10)$$

$$3(3x + 14) = (7x - 10)$$

In order to collect all the x terms on one side, you'll first need to distribute the 3 on the left side of the equation:

$$9x + 42 = 7x - 10$$

Next, subtract $7x$ from both sides:

$$2x + 42 = -10$$

Now, subtract 42 from both sides:

$$2x = -52$$

Finally, divide both sides by 2 to leave x by itself:

$$x = -26$$

Choice **(A)** is correct.

If you find isolating a variable to be challenging, try these Drill questions before proceeding to the "Try on Your Own" set. Isolate the variable in each equation. Drill answers can be found in the Check Your Work section at the end of the chapter.

Drill

a. $3(x + 2) = 14 - 2(3 - 2x)$

b. $5(6 - 3b) = 3b + 3$

c. $\dfrac{r}{6} - \dfrac{3r}{5} = \dfrac{1}{2}$

d. Isolate F: $C = \dfrac{5}{9}(F - 32)$

e. Isolate b: $A = \dfrac{1}{2}(a + b)h$

Try on Your Own

Directions

Take as much time as you need on these questions. Work carefully and methodically. There will be an opportunity for timed practice later in the book.

1

HINT: For Q1, what do you need to do before you can collect all the y terms on one side?

$$3y + 2(y - 2) = \frac{3y}{2} + 1$$

What value of y satisfies the given equation?

Ⓐ $-\dfrac{10}{7}$

Ⓑ $-\dfrac{6}{13}$

Ⓒ $\dfrac{7}{9}$

Ⓓ $\dfrac{10}{7}$

2

$$S = \frac{C - \frac{1}{4}I}{C + I}$$

A student's score, S, is determined by the given formula, where C represents the number of correct answers and I represents the number of incorrect answers. Which of the following expresses I in terms of C and S?

Ⓐ $\dfrac{C(1 - 4S)}{4S + 1}$

Ⓑ $\dfrac{C(1 + 4S)}{4S - 1}$

Ⓒ $\dfrac{4C(1 - S)}{4S + 1}$

Ⓓ $\dfrac{4C(1 + S)}{4S - 1}$

3

What value of n satisfies the equation

$$\frac{7}{8}(n - 6) = \frac{21}{2}?$$

4

HINT: For Q4, use $\frac{a}{b}$ as your target and solve for that expression rather than trying to solve for a and b separately.

If $b \neq 0$ and $\frac{3a + b}{b} = \frac{11}{2}$, which of the following could be the value of $\frac{a}{b}$?

Ⓐ $\frac{3}{2}$

Ⓑ $\frac{7}{2}$

Ⓒ $\frac{9}{2}$

Ⓓ It is not possible to determine a value of $\frac{a}{b}$.

5

HINT: For Q5, simplify the numerators before clearing the equation of fractions.

$$\frac{4 + z - (3 + 2z)}{6} = \frac{-z - 3(5 - 2)}{7}$$

What is the value of z?

Ⓐ -61

Ⓑ $-\frac{61}{27}$

Ⓒ $\frac{61}{27}$

Ⓓ 61

WORD PROBLEMS

LEARNING OBJECTIVES

After this lesson, you will be able to:

- Translate word problems into expressions and equations
- Match an expression or equation to a real-life context, table, or graph

To answer a question like this:

A laser tag arena sells two types of one-year memberships. Package A costs $325 and includes an unlimited number of visits. Package B has a $125 enrollment fee, includes five free visits, and costs an additional $8 per visit after the first five. How many visits would a person need to use for Package B to cost the same amount as Package A?

A) 20

B) 25

C) 30

D) 40

You need to know this:

SAT word problems test your understanding of how to describe real-world situations using math equations. For some questions, it will be up to you to extract and solve an equation; for others, you'll have to interpret an equation in a real-life context. The following table shows some of the most common phrases and mathematical equivalents you're likely to see on the SAT.

WORD PROBLEMS TRANSLATION TABLE	
English	**Math**
equals, is, equivalent to, was, will be, has, costs, adds up to, the same as, as much as	$=$
times, of, multiplied by, product of, twice, double	$\times$
divided by, out of, ratio	$\div$
plus, added to, sum, combined, increased by	$+$
minus, subtracted from, smaller than, less than, fewer, decreased by, difference between	$-$
a number, how much, how many, what	x, n, etc.

You need to do this:

When translating from English to math, *start by defining the variables*, choosing letters that make sense. Then, *break down the question into small pieces*, writing down the translation for one phrase at a time.

Explanation:

The phrase "how many visits" indicates an unknown, so you need a variable. Use an intuitive letter to represent the number of visits; call it v. The question asks when the two memberships will cost the "same amount," so write an equation that sets the total membership costs equal to each other.

Package A costs $325 for unlimited visits, so write 325 on one side of the equal sign. Package B costs $8 per visit (not including, or *except*, the first 5 visits), or $8(v - 5)$, plus a flat $125 enrollment fee, so write $8(v - 5) + 125$ on the other side of the equal sign. That's it! Now solve for v:

$$325 = 8\,(v - 5) + 125$$
$$200 = 8v - 40$$
$$240 = 8v$$
$$30 = v$$

The answer is **(C)**.

Try on Your Own

Directions

Take as much time as you need on these questions. Work carefully and methodically. There will be an opportunity for timed practice later in the book.

6

After a couple dances for three hours in a charity dance-a-thon, they earn $50 per half-hour of additional dancing. Assuming they dance for at least three hours, which expression represents the total number of dollars earned by a couple who dances continuously for h hours?

(A) $25h$

(B) $100h$

(C) $50(h - 3)$

(D) $100h - 300$

7

HINT: For Q7, start with the most concrete information: 1 is the second value.

The final value, v, in a four-digit lock code is determined by multiplying the second value by 2, subtracting that expression from the first value, and dividing the resulting expression by half of the third value. If the second value is 1, what is v in terms of the first value, f, and the third value, t?

(A) $\dfrac{f - 2}{t}$

(B) $\dfrac{2f - 4}{t}$

(C) $\dfrac{t}{2f - 4}$

(D) $\dfrac{2t - 4}{f}$

8

HINT: For Q8, profit = sales — expenses

A pizzeria charges $17 for Pizza A and $13 for Pizza B. Ingredient costs are $450 per week for Pizza A and $310 per week for Pizza B. Last week, the pizzeria sold an equal number of both pizza types, and the weekly profit from the sale of each pizza type was the same. If x represents the number of Pizza B sold, what is the value of x?

Ⓐ 30

Ⓑ 35

Ⓒ 140

Ⓓ 145

9

If an employee works n hours a week for w weeks, she will earn $10nw + 50$ dollars. Which of the terms in the expression most logically will change if the employee gets a raise?

Ⓐ 10

Ⓑ n

Ⓒ w

Ⓓ The expression will not change if the employee gets a raise.

10

Malik's salary is $25,500 per year, which he expects will increase by a constant dollar amount annually. In 12 years, his salary will have doubled. Assuming salary increases take place only at the end of a full year, how many years must Malik wait until his salary is at least $40,000 annually?

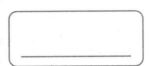

LINEAR GRAPHS

LEARNING OBJECTIVES

After this lesson, you will be able to:

- Calculate the slope of a line given two points
- Write the equation of a line in slope-intercept form
- Discern whether the slope of a line is positive, negative, zero, or undefined based on its graph
- Describe the slopes of parallel and perpendicular lines

To answer a question like this:

What is the equation of the line that passes through the points $(-3, -1)$ and $(1, 3)$?

A) $y = -x + 2$

B) $y = -x - 2$

C) $y = x - 2$

D) $y = x + 2$

You need to know this:

The answer choices in this question are written in slope-intercept form: $y = mx + b$. In this form of a linear equation, m represents the **slope** of the line and b represents the **y-intercept**. You can think of the slope of a line as how steep it is. The y-intercept is the y-coordinate of the point where the line crosses the y-axis. If the point where the line crosses the y-axis is $(0, b)$, the y-intercept is b.

You can calculate the slope of a line if you know any two points on the line. The formula is $m = \dfrac{y_2 - y_1}{x_2 - x_1}$, where (x_1, y_1) and (x_2, y_2) are the coordinates of the two points on the line.

A line that moves from the bottom left to the top right has a positive slope. A line that moves from the top left to the bottom right has a negative slope. A horizontal line has a slope of 0, and a vertical line has an undefined slope.

Some SAT questions ask about parallel or perpendicular lines. Parallel lines have the same slope, while perpendicular lines that are not parallel to the axes have slopes that are negative reciprocals.

You need to do this:

- Find the slope of the line.
- Write the equation in slope-intercept form, substituting the value of the slope you found and one of the known points for x and y.
- Solve for the y-intercept.

Explanation:

In this question, $m = \dfrac{3 - (-1)}{1 - (-3)} = \dfrac{4}{4} = 1$. Of the answer choices, only (C) and (D) have a slope of 1, so rule out (A) and (B), which both have a slope of -1.

To find the y-intercept of the line, write the equation for the line in slope-intercept form and plug in one of the known points for x and y:

$$y = 1x + b$$
$$3 = 1(1) + b$$
$$2 = b$$

The correct answer is **(D)**. For the record, here is the graph of the line. Note that as you would expect from the fact that m is positive, the line moves from the lower left to upper right, and it crosses the y-axis at the y-intercept of $b = 2$.

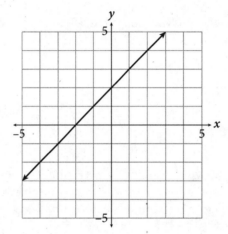

Try on Your Own

Directions

Take as much time as you need on these questions. Work carefully and methodically. There will be an opportunity for timed practice later in the book.

11

HINT: For Q11, what do you know about lines that never intersect?

Line A passes through the coordinate points $\left(-\frac{2}{5}, 0\right)$ and $(0, 1)$. Which of the following lines will line A never intersect?

Ⓒ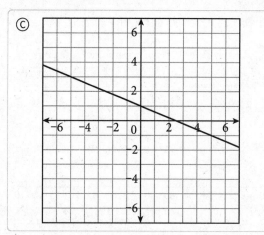

Ⓐ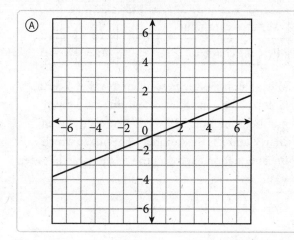

Ⓑ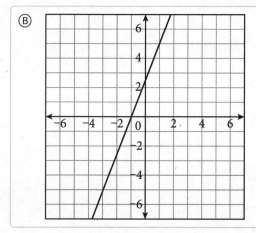

Ⓓ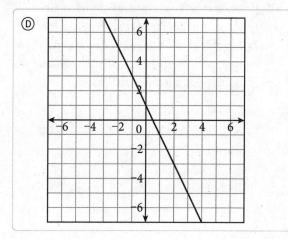

12

In the xy-plane, the point $(4, 7)$ lies on line t, which is perpendicular to the line $y = -\frac{4}{3}x + 6$. What is the equation of line t?

Ⓐ $y = \frac{3}{4}x + 4$

Ⓑ $y = -\frac{4}{3}x + 4$

Ⓒ $y = \frac{3}{4}x + 7$

Ⓓ $y = -\frac{3}{4}x + 4$

13

HINT: For Q13, remember that at the *y*-intercept, $x = 0$.

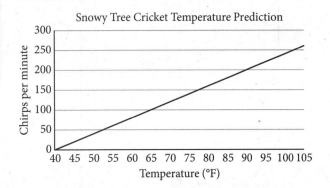

Snowy Tree Cricket Temperature Prediction

The graph shows the correlation between air temperature, *t*, in degrees Fahrenheit and the number of chirps per minute, *c*, that a snowy tree cricket makes. Which of the following equations represents the line shown in the graph?

(A) $c = 4t - 160$

(B) $c = \frac{1}{4}t - 160$

(C) $c = \frac{1}{2}t - 40$

(D) $c = 4t + 160$

14

HINT: For Q14, the starting point (flat fee) is the *y*-intercept. The rate of change (price per pound) is the slope.

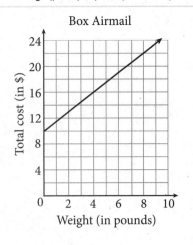

Box Airmail

To ship a box, one company charges a flat fee, plus an additional charge for each pound the box weighs. The graph shows the relationship between the box's weight and the total cost to ship it. Based on the graph, how much would it cost in dollars to ship a 40-pound box?

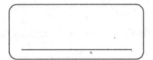

15

Minutes charging	10	15	30
Percent charged	34	41.5	64

The table shows the percent charge that a certain laptop battery has after recharging for a given number of minutes. If *y* is the battery's percent charge and *x* is the number of minutes, which linear equation expresses the relationship between *y* and *x*?

(A) $y = 1.5x + 19$

(B) $y = 2x + 14$

(C) $y = 2.5x + 9$

(D) $y = 10x + 34$

ON TEST DAY

Remember that the SAT doesn't ask you to show your work. If you find the algebra in a question challenging, there is often another way to get to the answer.

Try this question first using algebra and then using the Picking Numbers strategy you learned in chapter 3. Time yourself. Which approach did you find easier? Which one was faster? Did you get the correct answer both times? Remember your preferred approach and try it first if you see a question like this on test day.

$$\frac{2(a - 3)}{b} = \frac{4}{7}$$

16.   If the given equation is true, which of the following must be true?

A) $\dfrac{b}{a - 3} = \dfrac{7}{2}$

B) $\dfrac{2a}{b} = -\dfrac{10}{7}$

C) $7a - 21 = b$

D) $\dfrac{14a - 21}{b} = 4$

The correct answer and both ways of solving can be found at the end of this chapter.

HOW MUCH HAVE YOU LEARNED?

Directions

For testlike practice, give yourself 14 minutes to complete this question set. Be sure to study the explanations, even for questions you answered correctly. They can be found at the end of this chapter.

17

Which value of x makes the equation $\frac{8}{5}\left(x + \frac{33}{12}\right) = 16$ true?

(A) 7.25

(B) 8.75

(C) 12.75

(D) 13.25

18

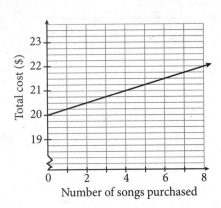

The graph shows the cost of joining and buying music from a music subscription service. What does the y-intercept of the line most likely represent?

(A) The cost per song

(B) The cost to join the service

(C) The cost of buying 20 songs

(D) The cost of 20 subscriptions to the service

19

If $\frac{3}{4}y = 6 - \frac{1}{3}c$, then what is the value of $2c + \frac{9}{2}y$?

20

Each year, a high school increases the cost, c, of a ticket to a basketball game by a constant amount. This year, a ticket costs \$2. In three years, after three annual cost increases, the cost will be \$2.50. Which of the following equations shows how much a ticket will cost in y years?

(A) $c = 6y + 2$

(B) $c = \frac{y}{6} + 2.5$

(C) $c = \frac{y}{6} + 2$

(D) $c = \frac{y}{2} + 2$

21

Price of one pound	Projected number of pounds sold
$1.20	15,000
$1.40	12,500
$1.60	10,000
$1.80	7,500
$2.00	5,000
$2.20	2,500

Which of the following equations best describes the linear relationship shown in the table, where g represents the number of pounds of grain sold and d represents the price in dollars of one pound of grain?

Ⓐ $g = 1.2d + 12,500$

Ⓑ $g = 12,500d + 15,000$

Ⓒ $g = -12,500d + 17,500$

Ⓓ $g = -12,500d + 30,000$

22

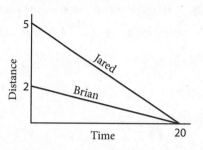

The graph shows a typical commute home by bicycle for Brian and Jared. Based on the graph, which of the following statements is true?

Ⓐ   It takes Brian longer to bike home because his work is farther away.

Ⓑ   It takes Jared longer to bike home because his work is farther away.

Ⓒ   Jared and Brian arrive home at the same time, so they must bike at about the same rate.

Ⓓ   Jared bikes a longer distance than Brian in the same amount of time, so Jared must bike at a faster rate.

23

If $b > 0$ in the equation of a line written in the form $y = mx + b$, which of the following best describes how reversing the sign of b will affect the graph?

Ⓐ   The new line will be shifted down b units.

Ⓑ   The new line will be shifted down $2b$ units.

Ⓒ   The new line will be a perfect reflection across the x-axis.

Ⓓ   The new line will be a perfect reflection across the y-axis.

24

The graph of a line in the xy-plane passes through the points $(5, 4)$ and $\left(3, \frac{1}{2}\right)$. Which of the following equations describes the line?

Ⓐ $y = \frac{7}{4}x + \frac{19}{4}$

Ⓑ $y = -\frac{7}{4}x - \frac{19}{4}$

Ⓒ $y = \frac{7}{4}x - \frac{19}{4}$

Ⓓ $y = \frac{4}{7}x + \frac{8}{7}$

25

Line f in the xy-plane passes through the origin and has a slope of $-\frac{2}{5}$. Line z is perpendicular to line f and line z passes through the point $(6, 2)$. Which of the following is the equation of line z?

Ⓐ $y = -\frac{2}{5}x$

Ⓑ $y = -\frac{2}{5}x - 13$

Ⓒ $y = \frac{5}{2}x$

Ⓓ $y = \frac{5}{2}x - 13$

REFLECT

Directions: Take a few minutes to recall what you've learned and what you've been practicing in this chapter. Consider the following questions, jot down your best answer for each one, and then compare your reflections to the expert responses that follow. Use your level of confidence to determine what to do next.

What should you do to isolate a particular variable in an equation?

_____

_____

_____

What types of keywords should you look for when translating English into math?

_____

_____

_____

What is the most useful equation for a line in the coordinate plane? Why?

_____

_____

_____

When the SAT gives you two points on a line, what can you figure out?

_____

_____

_____

What are the properties of parallel and perpendicular lines?

_____

_____

_____

Expert Responses

What should you do to isolate a particular variable in an equation?

Perform inverse operations until the variable is by itself on one side of the equal sign. If the equation has fractions, make them disappear by multiplying both sides of the equation by the denominator(s). If like terms appear on different sides of the equation, collect them on the same side so that you can combine them.

What types of keywords should you look for when translating English into math?

Look for keywords that signal equality ("is," "has," "was"), variable names ("Marina's age," "the cost of one bathtub"), or one of the four arithmetic operations (addition, subtraction, multiplication, and division).

Math

What is the most useful equation for a line in the coordinate plane? Why?

The best equation is slope-intercept form, $y = mx + b$, *because it tells you the slope (m) and the y-intercept (b). Conversely, if you need to derive an equation yourself, you can plug the slope and y-intercept into slope-intercept form, and you're done.*

When the SAT gives you two points on a line, what can you figure out?

If you know two points, you can figure out the slope of the line with the equation $m = \dfrac{y_2 - y_1}{x_2 - x_1}$. *From there, you can plug one of the points and the slope into slope-intercept form and find the y-intercept.*

What are the properties of parallel and perpendicular lines?

Parallel lines never intersect, and they have equal slopes. Perpendicular lines intersect at a 90° angle, and they have negative reciprocal slopes.

Next Steps

If you answered most questions correctly in the "How Much Have You Learned?" section, and if your responses to the Reflect questions were similar to those of the SAT expert, then consider linear equations and graphs an area of strength and move on to the next chapter. Come back to this topic periodically to prevent yourself from getting rusty.

If you don't yet feel confident, review those parts of this chapter that you have not yet mastered. In particular, review the variable isolation drills in the Solving Equations lesson and the definition of slope-intercept form in the Linear Graphs lesson. Then try the questions you missed again. As always, be sure to review the explanations closely. Finally, **go online** (www.kaptest.com/moreonline) for additional practice.

Check Your Work – Chapter 4

Drill Answers for Solving Equations

a. $3x + 6 = 14 - 6 + 4x$

$$3x = 2 + 4x$$
$$x = -2$$

b. $30 - 15b = 3b + 3$

$$-18b = -27$$
$$\frac{-18b}{-18} = \frac{-27}{-18}$$
$$b = \frac{3}{2}$$

c. $30 \times \left(\frac{r}{6} - \frac{3r}{5}\right) = \left(\frac{1}{2}\right) \times 30$

$$5r - 6(3r) = 15$$
$$-13r = 15$$
$$r = -\frac{15}{13}$$

d. $\frac{9}{5} \times C = \frac{9}{5} \times \frac{5}{9}(F - 32)$

$$\frac{9}{5}C = F - 32$$
$$\frac{9}{5}C + 32 = F$$

e. $A = \frac{1}{2}(a + b)h$

$$2A = (a + b)h$$
$$\frac{2A}{h} = a + b$$
$$\frac{2A}{h} - a = b$$

Try on Your Own Answers

1. D

Difficulty: Easy

Category: Algebra

Getting to the Answer: Distribute the factor of 2, combine like terms, multiply both sides of the equation by 2 to clear the fraction, and then solve for y:

$$3y + 2y - 4 = \frac{3y}{2} + 1$$
$$5y - 4 = \frac{3y}{2} + 1$$
$$10y - 8 = 3y + 2$$
$$7y = 10$$
$$y = \frac{10}{7}$$

Choice **(D)** is correct.

2. C

Difficulty: Hard

Category: Algebra

Strategic Advice: Complicated-looking equations may appear difficult, but they always succumb to the steps of solving an equation. First, clear the equation of fractions, then collect like terms, and solve for the desired variable.

Getting to the Answer: Clear the equation of the fraction in the numerator by multiplying both sides by 4 to yield:

$$4S = \frac{4C - I}{C + I}$$

Now, multiply both sides by the denominator $C + I$ to clear the equation of fractions:

$$4S(C + I) = 4C - I$$

Distribute the $4S$:

$$4SC + 4SI = 4C - I$$

To solve for I, collect all the terms that include I on one side of the equation:

$$4SI + I = 4C - 4SC$$

Factor out the I:

$$I(4S + 1) = 4C - 4SC$$

Divide to isolate I, and factor out $4C$ from the numerator:

$$I = \frac{4C - 4SC}{4S + 1} = \frac{4C(1 - S)}{4S + 1}$$

(C) is correct.

3. 18

Difficulty: Easy

Category: Algebra

Getting to the Answer: First, clear the fractions by multiplying both sides of the equation by 8. Then, solve for n using inverse operations:

$$\frac{7}{8}(n - 6) = \frac{21}{2}$$
$$8\left[\frac{7}{8}(n - 6)\right] = 8\left[\frac{21}{2}\right]$$
$$7(n - 6) = 4(21)$$
$$7n - 42 = 84$$
$$7n = 126$$
$$n = 18$$

Enter **18**.

4.   A
Difficulty: Medium
Category: Algebra
Strategic Advice: Noticing key information about the answer choices and using that information to pick numbers saves time by eliminating algebra.
Getting to the Answer: Rearranging the terms of the equation such that $\frac{a}{b}$ is on one side and the constants are all on the other will work for this question. First, cross-multiply to get rid of the fractions. Then, use inverse operations to isolate $\frac{a}{b}$:

$$\frac{\boxed{3a+b}}{\boxed{b}} \times \frac{\boxed{11}}{\boxed{2}}$$

$$2(3a+b) = 11b$$
$$6a + 2b = 11b$$
$$6a = 9b$$
$$a = \frac{9}{6}b$$
$$\frac{a}{b} = \frac{3}{2}$$

The answer is **(A)**.

There is a faster approach. Notice that 2 shows up in the denominator in most of the choices, indicating that it is likely that b equals 2. If $b = 2$, then a must be 3 for the numerator to equal 11. Test this by plugging the numbers into the equation:

$$\frac{3(3)+2}{2} = \frac{11}{2}$$

Thus, $\frac{a}{b} = \frac{3}{2}$, confirming **(A)** as the answer. You can avoid a lot of work by using key information in the answer choices to pick numbers.

5.   D
Difficulty: Medium
Category: Algebra
Getting to the Answer: Simplify the numerators as much as possible, then isolate the variable. Begin by combining like terms on both sides of the equation. Then cross-multiply and solve for z:

$$\frac{4+z-(3+2z)}{6} = \frac{-z-3(5-2)}{7}$$
$$\frac{1-z}{6} = \frac{-z-9}{7}$$
$$7 - 7z = -6z - 54$$
$$-z = -61$$
$$z = 61$$

Choice **(D)** is correct.

6.   D
Difficulty: Medium
Category: Algebra
Getting to the Answer: Use the information in the question to write your own expression, then look for the answer choice that matches. Simplify your expression only if you don't find a match. If a couple earns $50 *per half-hour* that they dance, then they earn $50 \times 2 = \$100$ *per hour*. Multiply this amount by the number of hours (not including the first 3 hours). This can be expressed as $100(h - 3)$. This is not one of the answer choices, so simplify by distributing the 100 to get $100h - 300$, which is **(D)**.

If you're struggling with the algebra, try picking numbers. Pick a number of hours a couple might dance, such as 5. They don't earn anything for the first 3 hours, but they earn $50 per half-hour for the last 2 hours, which is 50 times 4 half-hours, or $200. Now, find the expression that gives you an answer of $200 when $h = 5$ hours: $100(5) - 300 = 500 - 300 = 200$. If you use Picking Numbers, remember that it is possible that the number you choose satisfies more than one answer choice, so plug it into the other three choices. In this case, $h = 5$ does not give a value of 200 in any other expression, which confirms that **(D)** is correct.

7.   B
Difficulty: Medium
Category: Algebra
Getting to the Answer: Translate piece by piece to get a final expression for the final value, v. Multiply the second value by 2 to get $2(1) = 2$. Subtract that from the first value to get $f - 2$. Divide this expression by half of the third value to get $\frac{f-2}{\frac{t}{2}}$, which you can simplify by multiplying by the reciprocal of the denominator: $\left(\frac{f-2}{1}\right)\left(\frac{2}{t}\right) = \left(\frac{2f-4}{t}\right)$. Choice **(B)** matches the final expression. Watch out for (D), the trap answer choice that switches the variables.

8.   B
Difficulty: Medium
Category: Algebra
Getting to the Answer: Write expressions to represent the profit generated by selling each type of pizza. You're told Pizza A sells for $17 each and that its ingredients cost the pizzeria $450 per week. This means the weekly profit generated by this pizza's sales can be represented by the expression $17x - 450$. Do the same for Pizza B:

each one sells for $13, but the pizzeria loses $310 to pay for ingredients each week. Therefore, the weekly profit from this pizza can be represented by $13x - 310$. To determine the value of x at which the profit from the sale of each type of pizza is the same, set the two profit expressions equal to each other and solve:

$$17x - 450 = 13x - 310$$
$$4x = 140$$
$$x = 35$$

Thus, **(B)** is correct.

9. A
Difficulty: Easy
Category: Algebra
Getting to the Answer: When faced with a question that includes abstract expressions, it is often helpful to pick concrete numbers to work with. These numbers don't have to be realistic; just choose numbers that are easy to work with. Suppose the student works 3 hours a week for 2 weeks. She would have worked a total of 6 hours, which would have to be multiplied by the amount she is paid per hour to get her total pay. In the expression, plugging in $w = 2$ and $n = 3$ demonstrates that the number 10 in the expression must be the amount that she is paid per hour, and thus is the term that would change if the employee got a raise. **(A)** is correct.

10. 7
Difficulty: Medium
Category: Algebra
Getting to the Answer: First, notice that the actual dollar amount of the increase each year is unknown, so assign a variable like d. After 12 increases, his salary will rise by $25,500, so write a formula: $12d = 25,500$. Solve for d to find that Malik will receive an increase of $2,125 per year.

The question asks how many years must go by until Malik's salary is at least $40,000; the number of years is another unknown, so assign it a variable like n. Multiplying n by the amount of each increase will give you the total increase of dollars over n years, but don't forget to add in the current salary to reflect his total salary amount:

$$25,500 + 2,125n = 40,000$$
$$2,125n = 14,500$$
$$n \approx 6.8$$

The question asks you to assume that salary increases only take place at the end of a full year. If you are unsure and want to prove that the answer is not 6, check by using $n = 6$ to calculate the total dollar amount: $25,500 + 2,125(6) = 38,250$. Six years is not long enough; enter **7**.

11. B
Difficulty: Easy
Category: Algebra
Getting to the Answer: You're asked to identify the line that the one described in the question stem will never intersect. Lines that never intersect are parallel and therefore have identical slopes, so start by finding the slope of the line whose two coordinate pairs are given. You'll find:

$$m = \frac{1 - 0}{0 - \left(-\frac{2}{5}\right)} = \frac{1}{\frac{2}{5}} = \frac{5}{2}$$

Choices (C) and (D) have negative slopes, so eliminate them. Next, find the slopes of (A) and (B). No need to use the slope formula; counting units on the graphs will be faster. The slope of (A) is $\frac{2}{5}$ because for every 2 units the line rises, it runs 5 units to the right. The slope of (B) is $\frac{5}{2}$ because when the line goes up 5 units, it goes 2 units to the right. Therefore, **(B)** is correct.

12. A
Difficulty: Medium
Category: Algebra
Strategic Advice: Remember that parallel lines have the same slope and perpendicular lines have opposite sign reciprocal slopes.
Getting to the Answer: The first useful piece of information is that the slope of the line perpendicular to line t is $-\frac{4}{3}$. Perpendicular lines have negative reciprocal slopes, so the slope of line t is $\frac{3}{4}$. Eliminate (B) and (D) because they have incorrect slopes.

Plug the values for the slope and the coordinates of the point (4, 7) into the slope-intercept equation to solve for b:

$$7 = \frac{3}{4}(4) + b$$
$$7 = 3 + b$$
$$7 - 3 = b$$
$$b = 4$$

Eliminate (C) because it does not have the correct y-intercept. Choice **(A)** is correct.

13. A
Difficulty: Medium
Category: Algebra
Getting to the Answer: Start by finding the slope of the line by picking a pair of points, such as (40, 0) and (65, 100): $m = \dfrac{100 - 0}{65 - 40} = \dfrac{100}{25} = 4$. Choices (B) and (C) have slopes other than 4, so eliminate them. Choices (A) and (D) have y-intercepts of -160 and 40, respectively. Now, read the axis labels carefully: the horizontal axis begins at 40 (not 0). The line is trending downward as x-values get smaller, so the y-intercept (when $x = 0$) must be well below 0 on the vertical axis. Therefore, the answer must be **(A)**.

14. 70
Difficulty: Hard
Category: Algebra
Getting to the Answer: Because 40 pounds is not shown on the graph, you need more information. In a real-world scenario, the y-intercept of a graph usually represents a flat fee or a starting amount. The slope of the line represents a unit rate, such as the cost per pound to ship the box.

The y-intercept of the graph is 10, so the flat fee is $10. To find the cost per pound (the unit rate), substitute two points from the graph into the slope formula. Using the points (0, 10) and (4, 16), the cost per pound is $\dfrac{16 - 10}{4 - 0} = \dfrac{6}{4} = 1.5$, which means it costs $1.50 per pound to ship a box. The total cost to ship a 40-pound box is $\$10 + 1.50(40) = \$10 + \$60 = \$70$. Enter **70**.

15. A
Difficulty: Hard
Category: Algebra
Getting to the Answer: The question tells you that the relationship is linear, so start by finding the rate of change (the slope, m) using any two pairs of values from the table and the slope formula.

$$m = \frac{y_2 - y_1}{x_2 - x_1} = \frac{64 - 34}{30 - 10} = \frac{30}{20} = 1.5$$

You can stop right there! The next step would be to use the slope and a pair of values from the table to determine b; however, only **(A)** has a slope of 1.5, so it must be the correct answer. For the record:

$$34 = 1.5(10) + b$$
$$34 = 15 + b$$
$$19 = b$$

16. A
Difficulty: Hard
Category: Algebra
Strategic Advice: Picking numbers based on clues in the equation may be faster than doing the algebra.
Getting to the Answer: To find the answer using Picking Numbers, take advantage of the fact that the equation is a proportion (that is, two fractions equal to each other). If $b = 7$ and $2(a - 3) = 4$, then both fractions will be the same and the numbers you've picked will be valid. Solve for a: $a - 3 = 2$, and $a = 5$. Now plug $b = 7$ and $a = 5$ into the choices, looking for one that is true.

(A) $\dfrac{b}{a - 3} = \dfrac{7}{5 - 3} = \dfrac{7}{2}$, so keep this one for now. If another answer choice also works, pick another set of valid numbers.

(B) $\dfrac{2a}{b} = \dfrac{2(5)}{7} = \dfrac{10}{7} \neq -\dfrac{10}{7}$. Eliminate.

(C) $7a - 21 = 7(5) - 21 = 35 - 21 = 14$. This is not equal to b, so it can be eliminated.

(D) $\dfrac{14a - 21}{b} = \dfrac{14(5) - 21}{7} = 2(5) - 3 = 7$. This is not equal to 4, so it can be eliminated.

(A) is the only choice that works, so it's correct.

To solve this question using algebra, first cross-multiply and simplify the original equation:

$$\frac{2(a - 3)}{b} = \frac{4}{7}$$
$$14(a - 3) = 4b$$
$$7(a - 3) = 2b$$
$$7a - 21 = 2b$$
$$7a - 2b = 21$$

Then, repeat this entire process for each answer choice, looking for the one that yields the same equation:

(A) $\dfrac{b}{a - 3} = \dfrac{7}{2}$, $2b = 7a - 21$, $21 = 7a - 2b$. This matches the given equation, so **(A)** is correct.

17. A
Difficulty: Medium
Category: Algebra
Getting to the Answer: This question has multiple fractions, so clear the $\dfrac{8}{5}$ by multiplying both sides of the equation by its reciprocal, $\dfrac{5}{8}$. Then, because the answers are given in decimal form, change the other

fraction to a decimal by dividing the numerator by the denominator:

$$\frac{8}{5}\left(x + \frac{33}{12}\right) = 16$$

$$\frac{5}{8} \times \left[\frac{8}{5}\left(x + \frac{33}{12}\right)\right] = \frac{5}{8} \times 16$$

$$x + 2.75 = 10$$

$$x = 7.25$$

(A) is correct.

18. B
Difficulty: Easy
Category: Algebra
Getting to the Answer: Read the axis labels carefully. The y-intercept is the point at which $x = 0$, which means the number of songs purchased is 0. The y-intercept is (0, 20), so the cost is $20 before buying any songs and therefore most likely represents a flat membership fee for joining the service. **(B)** is correct.

19. 36
Difficulty: Medium
Category: Algebra
Getting to the Answer: When you're asked to find an expression rather than a variable value, it means there's likely a shortcut: try to make the expression you have look like the expression you want. Start by eliminating the fractions. A common multiple of 4 and 3 is 12, so multiply both sides of the equation by that. Once the fractions are gone, move both variable terms to the same side. Finally, divide each side by 2:

$$12\left(\frac{3}{4}y = 6 - \frac{1}{3}c\right)$$

$$9y = 72 - 4c$$

$$4c + 9y = 72$$

$$2c + \frac{9}{2}y = 36$$

The expression on the left side is precisely what you're looking for, so enter **36**.

20. C
Difficulty: Medium
Category: Algebra
Getting to the Answer: The stimulus describes a linear relationship between cost and time. Use the given information in the stimulus to find two sets of coordinates to determine the equation of the line. Admission is $2 now and will increase to $2.50 after 3 years, making the

coordinates (0, 2) and (3, 2.5). The slope of the line passing through these is $m = \frac{2.5 - 2}{3 - 0} = \frac{0.5}{3} = \frac{1}{6}$. Eliminate (A) and (D). Because the admission fee is $2 this year, the y-intercept is 2, so the full equation is $c = \frac{y}{6} + 2$. **(C)** is correct.

21. D
Difficulty: Medium
Category: Algebra
Getting to the Answer: Take a quick peek at the answer choices. The equations are given in slope-intercept form, so start by finding the slope. Substitute two pairs of values from the table (try to pick easy ones, if possible) into the slope formula, $m = \frac{y_2 - y_1}{x_2 - x_1}$. Keep in mind that the projected number of pounds sold *depends* on the price, so the price is the independent variable (x) and the projected number is the dependent variable (y). Using the points (1.2, 15,000) and (2.2, 2,500), you can find the slope:

$$m = \frac{2,500 - 15,000}{2.2 - 1.2}$$

$$m = \frac{-12,500}{1}$$

$$m = -12,500$$

This means you can eliminate (A) and (B) because the slope is not correct. Don't let (B) fool you—the projected number of pounds sold goes *down* as the price goes *up*, so there is an inverse relationship, which means the slope must be negative. To choose between (C) and (D), you could find the y-intercept of the line. Pick a point with easy values, such as (2, 5,000), and plug in 5,000 for y and 2 for x:

$$y = mx + b$$

$$5,000 = -12,500(2) + b$$

$$5,000 = -25,000 + b$$

$$30,000 = b$$

(D) is correct. Another option is to substitute (2, 5,000) into (C) and (D) only. Again, **(D)** is correct because $5,000 = -12,500(2) + 30,000$ is a true statement.

22. D
Difficulty: Medium
Category: Algebra
Getting to the Answer: Consider each choice systematically, using the numbers on the figure to help you evaluate each statement.

It takes Brian and Jared each 20 minutes to bike home, so (A) and (B) are false. Jared bikes 5 miles in 20 minutes, while Brian only bikes 2 miles in 20 minutes; their rates are not the same, so (C) is false. This means **(D)** must be true. Jared starts out farther away than Brian, so Jared must bike at a faster rate to arrive home in the same amount of time.

23. B
Difficulty: Hard
Category: Algebra
Getting to the Answer: You aren't given any numbers in this question, so make some up. On the on-screen calculator or scratch paper, plot a quick graph of any simple linear equation that has a positive y-intercept (because it is given that $b > 0$). Then, change the sign of the y-intercept and plot the new graph on the same coordinate plane. Pick a simple equation that you can plot quickly, such as $y = x + 3$, and then change the sign of b. The new equation is $y = x - 3$. Plot both graphs. The second line is shifted down 6 units, and because $b = 3$, 6 is $2b$ units. **(B)** is correct. The graph that follows illustrates this. If you're still unsure, try another pair of equations.

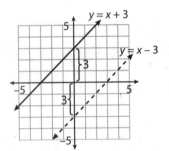

24. C
Difficulty: Medium
Category: Algebra
Strategic Advice: Be careful when the answer choices look very similar to each other. Eliminating incorrect answers during intermediate steps lowers your odds of making a careless mistake.
Getting to the Answer: The question provides two coordinate points, which means that the best approach is to find the slope using the formula $m = \dfrac{y_2 - y_1}{x_2 - x_1}$, then use the slope-intercept equation for a line to find b, the y-intercept. Plugging the points into the slope formula results in:

$$\frac{\frac{1}{2} - 4}{3 - 5} = \frac{\frac{1}{2} - \frac{8}{2}}{-2} = \frac{-\frac{7}{2}}{-2} = -\frac{7}{2} \times \left(-\frac{1}{2}\right) = \frac{7}{4}$$

Eliminate (B) and (D) because they do not have the slope $\dfrac{7}{4}$. Plug the slope and one of the given points, (5, 4), into the slope-intercept equation to solve for b:

$$4 = \frac{7}{4}(5) + b$$

$$4 = \frac{35}{4} + b$$

$$\frac{16}{4} - \frac{35}{4} = b$$

$$b = -\frac{19}{4}$$

Eliminate (A) because it does not have the correct y-intercept; therefore, only **(C)** is left and is correct. Plugging the calculated values for the slope and the y-intercept into the slope-intercept equation indeed gives you choice **(C)**: $y = \dfrac{7}{4}x - \dfrac{19}{4}$.

After eliminating (B) and (D), you can save time by noticing that the two possible y-intercepts are $\dfrac{19}{4}$ and $-\dfrac{19}{4}$. You really only need to determine whether b is positive or negative.

25. D
Difficulty: Easy
Category: Algebra
Getting to the Answer: This question provides an equation for a line perpendicular to line z and a coordinate point for line z, (6, 2). The negative reciprocal of the slope of the perpendicular line, $\dfrac{5}{2}$, is the slope of line z. Eliminate (A) and (B) because they have the incorrect slope.

Plug the values for the slope and the coordinate point (6, 2) into the slope-intercept equation to solve for b:

$$2 = \frac{5}{2}(6) + b$$

$$2 = 15 + b$$

$$2 - 15 = b$$

$$b = -13$$

Plug the values for the slope and the y-intercept into the slope-intercept equation to get $y = \dfrac{5}{2}x - 13$. **(D)** is correct.

You can save a little time if you eliminate (C) when you notice that $b \neq 0$, which you should be able to tell as soon as you see that $2 = 15 + b$.

CHAPTER 5

SYSTEMS OF LINEAR EQUATIONS

Math

LEARNING OBJECTIVES

After completing this chapter, you will be able to:

- Solve systems of linear equations by substitution
- Solve systems of linear equations by combination
- Determine the number of possible solutions for a system of linear equations, if any

HOW MUCH DO YOU KNOW?

Directions

Try the questions that follow. Show your work so that you can compare your solutions to the ones found in the "Check Your Work" section immediately after this question set. If you answered the question(s) on a specific topic correctly, and if your scratchwork looks like ours, you may be able to move quickly through the lesson covering that topic. If you answered incorrectly or used a different approach, you may want to take your time on that lesson.

1

$$-7x + 2y = 18$$
$$x + y = 0$$

In the system of equations shown, what is the value of x?

(A) -2

(B) 0

(C) 2

(D) 4

2

At a certain movie theater, there are 16 rows and each row has either 20 or 24 seats. If the total number of seats in all 16 rows is 348, how many rows have 24 seats?

(A) 7

(B) 9

(C) 11

(D) 13

3

If $17x - 5y = 8$ and $14x - 7y = -7$, what is the value of $3x + 2y$?

(A) -15

(B) -5

(C) 5

(D) 15

4

If $0.2x = 10 - 0.5y$, what is $10y + 4x$?

5

$$\frac{1}{2}x - \frac{2}{3}y = 7$$
$$ax - 8y = -1$$

If this system of linear equations has no solution, and a is a constant, then what is the value of a?

(A) -2

(B) $-\frac{1}{2}$

(C) 2

(D) 6

This page is intentionally blank.

Check Your Work

1.   A

Difficulty: Easy

Category: Algebra

Getting to the Answer: Solve the second equation for y in terms of x, then substitute into the first equation and solve:

$$y = -x$$
$$-7x - 2x = 18$$
$$-9x = 18$$
$$x = -2$$

(A) is correct.

2.   A

Difficulty: Hard

Category: Algebra

Getting to the Answer: Create a system of equations in which x represents the number of rows with 20 seats and y represents the number of rows with 24 seats. The first equation should represent the total *number of rows*, each with 20 or 24 seats, or $x + y = 16$. The second equation should represent the total *number of seats*. Because x represents rows with 20 seats and y represents rows with 24 seats, the second equation should be $20x + 24y = 348$. Now solve the system using substitution. Since the question asks for the number of rows with 24 seats, y, solve the first equation for x and substitute the result into the second equation:

$$x + y = 16$$
$$x = 16 - y$$
$$20(16 - y) + 24y = 348$$
$$320 - 20y + 24y = 348$$
$$320 + 4y = 348$$
$$4y = 28$$
$$y = 7$$

So 7 rows have 24 seats, which means **(A)** is correct. This is all the question asks for, so you don't need to find the value of x.

3.   D

Difficulty: Medium

Category: Algebra

Getting to the Answer: Since the question asks for the value of an expression, rather than just the value of a variable, look for a shortcut. Subtract the second equation from the first to find that $3x + 2y = 15$, making **(D)** the correct answer.

4.   200

Difficulty: Medium

Category: Algebra

Getting to the Answer: Rearrange the equation so that the y and x terms appear, in that order, on the left side: $0.5y + 0.2x = 10$. What number do you need to multiply $0.5y$ by to get $10y$? Twenty. Notice that $10y + 4x$ is 20 times $0.5y + 0.2x$. Multiply both sides of the equation by 20 to find that $10y + 4x = \mathbf{200}$. Note that both of these equations describe the same line.

5.   D

Difficulty: Hard

Category: Algebra

Getting to the Answer: Graphically, a system of linear equations that has no solution indicates two parallel lines—that is, two lines that have the same slope but different y-intercepts. To have the same slope, the x- and y-coefficients must be the same. To get from $-\frac{2}{3}y$ to $-8y$, you multiply by 12, so multiply $\frac{1}{2}x$ by 12 as well to yield $6x$. Because the other x-coefficient is a, it must be that $a = 6$, and **(D)** is correct. Note that, even though it is more work, you could also write each equation in slope-intercept form and set the slopes equal to each other to solve for a.

SUBSTITUTION

LEARNING OBJECTIVE

After this lesson, you will be able to:

- Solve systems of linear equations by substitution

To answer a question like this:

If $3x + 2y = 15$ and $x + y = 10$, what is the value of y?

A) -15

B) -5

C) 5

D) 15

You need to know this:

A **system** of two linear equations simply refers to the equations of two lines. "Solving" a system of two linear equations usually means finding the point where the two lines intersect. (However, see the lesson titled "Number of Possible Solutions" later in this chapter for exceptions.)

There are multiple ways to solve a system of linear equations. For some SAT questions, substitution is fastest; for others, combination is fastest. There is also the possibility of using the test's built-in graphing calculator, although this can sometimes be more time-consuming. The next lesson will cover combination.

You need to do this:

To solve a system of two linear equations by substitution:

- Isolate a variable (ideally, one whose coefficient is 1) in one of the equations.
- Substitute the result into the other equation.

Explanation:

Isolate x in the second equation, then substitute the result into the first equation:

$$x = 10 - y$$
$$3(10 - y) + 2y = 15$$
$$30 - 3y + 2y = 15$$
$$-y = -15$$
$$y = 15$$

If you needed to know the value of x as well, you could now substitute 15 for y into either equation to find that $x = -5$. The correct answer is **(D)**.

Try on Your Own

Directions

Solve these questions by substitution. Take as much time as you need on these questions. Work carefully and methodically. There will be an opportunity for timed practice later in the book.

1

HINT: For Q1, which equation is the easier one to solve for one variable in terms of the other?

If $7c + 8b = 15$ and $3b - c = 2$, what is the value of b?

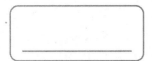

2

HINT: For Q2, the second equation is in a convenient form for substitution. But look at the first equation: what can you learn quickly about x and y?

$$3x - 3y = 0$$
$$y = 2x + 5$$

Given this system of equations, what is the sum of x and y?

Ⓐ -10

Ⓑ -5

Ⓒ 0

Ⓓ 5

3

$$4x + 3y = 14 - y$$
$$x - 5y = 2$$

If (x, y) is a solution to the given system of equations, then what is the value of $x - y$?

Ⓐ $\dfrac{1}{4}$

Ⓑ 1

Ⓒ 3

Ⓓ 18

4

If $5a = 6b + 7$ and $a - b = 3$, what is the value of $\dfrac{b}{2}$?

Ⓐ 2

Ⓑ 4

Ⓒ 5.5

Ⓓ 11

5

The owner of a snack stand purchases nuts in cases of 24 bags and granola bars in cases of 20 bars. She sells nuts for \$1.25 a bag and granola bars for \$1.75 each. If the snack stand sold 112 items for a total of \$160, how many cases of granola bars did the owner purchase?

Ⓐ 2

Ⓑ 3

Ⓒ 40

Ⓓ 72

Math

COMBINATION

LEARNING OBJECTIVE

After this lesson, you will be able to:

- Solve systems of linear equations by combination

To answer a question like this:

$$4x - 5y = 10$$
$$2x + 3y = -6$$

If the solution to the given system of equations is (x, y), what is the value of y?

A) -2

B) -1

C) 1

D) 2

You need to know this:

Combining two equations means adding or subtracting them. Most often the goal is to eliminate one of the variables; hence, this is also known as elimination, but combining equations can also be used to solve for a combination of variables (e.g., $5m + 7n$).

You need to do this:

To solve a system of two linear equations by combination:

- Make sure that the coefficients for one variable have the same absolute value. (If they don't, multiply one equation by an appropriate constant. Sometimes, you'll want to multiply both equations by constants.)
- Either add or subtract the equations to eliminate one variable.
- Solve for the remaining variable, then substitute its value into either equation to solve for the variable you eliminated in the preceding step.

Explanation:

Both variables have different coefficients in the two equations, but you can convert the $2x$ in the second equation to $4x$ by multiplying the entire second equation by 2:

$$2(2x + 3y = -6)$$
$$4x + 6y = -12$$

Now that the coefficients for one variable are the same, subtract the second equation from the first to eliminate the x variable. (Note that if the x-coefficients were 4 and -4, you would add the equations instead of subtracting.)

$$\begin{array}{r} 4x - 5y = 10 \\ -(4x + 6y = -12) \\ \hline 0x - 11y = 22 \end{array}$$

Solve this equation for y:

$$-11y = 22$$
$$y = -2$$

(A) is the correct answer. If the question asked for x as well, you would now substitute -2 for y in either of the original equations and solve for x. (For the record, $x = 0$.)

Try on Your Own

Directions

Answer these questions using combination. Take as much time as you need on these questions. Work carefully and methodically. There will be an opportunity for timed practice later in the book.

6

HINT: For Q6, should you add or subtract these equations to eliminate a variable?

If $2x - 3y = 14$ and $5x + 3y = 21$, what is the value of x?

Ⓐ -1

Ⓑ 0

Ⓒ $\dfrac{7}{3}$

Ⓓ 5

7

If $7c - 2b = 15$ and $3b - 6c = 2$, what is the value of $b + c$?

Ⓐ -27

Ⓑ -3

Ⓒ 8

Ⓓ 17

8

HINT: For Q8, there's no need to solve for x and y separately.

If $y = -x - 15$ and $\dfrac{5y}{2} - 37 = -\dfrac{x}{2}$, what is the value of $2x + 6y$?

9

If $5x + 3y = 13$ and $8x + 5y = 21$, what is the value of $\dfrac{y}{x}$?

10

Restaurant A sells tacos for $2.20 and bags of chips for $1.95. Restaurant B sells tacos for $3.00 and bags of chips for $1.50. A certain purchase of tacos and chips would cost $18.55 at restaurant A or $19.50 at restaurant B. How many bags of chips are in this purchase?

NUMBER OF POSSIBLE SOLUTIONS

LEARNING OBJECTIVE

After this lesson, you will be able to:

• Determine the number of possible solutions for a system of linear equations, if any

To answer a question like this:

$$5x - 3y = 10$$
$$6y = kx - 42$$

In the given system of linear equations, k represents a constant. If the system of equations has no solution, what is the value of $2k$?

A) $\dfrac{5}{2}$

B) 5

C) 10

D) 20

You need to know this:

The solution to a system of linear equations consists of the values of the variables that make both equations true.

A system of linear equations may have one solution, infinitely many solutions, or no solution.

If a system of equations represents two lines that intersect, then the system will have exactly **one solution** (in which the x- and y-values correspond to the point of intersection).

If a system of equations has **infinitely many solutions**, the two equations actually represent the same line. For example, $2x + y = 15$ and $4x + 2y = 30$ represent the same line. If you divide the second equation by 2, you arrive at the first equation. Every point along this line is a solution.

If a system of equations has **no solution**, as in the question above, the lines are parallel: there is no point of intersection.

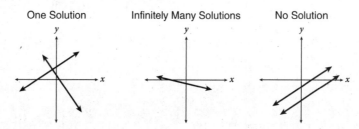

One Solution   Infinitely Many Solutions   No Solution

You need to do this:

• If the question states that the system has one solution and provides the point of intersection, substitute the values at that point of intersection for x and y in the equations.

• If the question states that the system has infinitely many solutions, make the x-coefficients equal to each other, the y-coefficients equal to each other, and the y-intercepts (or constant terms) equal to each other. This will result in two equations that represent the same line.

- If the question states that the system has no solution, manipulate the equations to make the x-coefficients equal to each other and the y-coefficients equal to each other, but be sure that the y-intercepts (or constant terms, if the equations are in $ax + by + c$ form) are different. This will result in two equations with the same slope but different y-intercepts, or, in other words, parallel lines.

Explanation:

Start by recognizing that for two lines to be parallel, the coefficients for x must be identical in the two equations; ditto for the coefficients for y. Manipulate the second equation so that it is in the same format as the first one:

$$kx - 6y = 42$$

The y-coefficient in the first equation, $5x - 3y = 10$, is 3. Divide the second equation by 2 in order to make the y-coefficients in both equations equal:

$$\frac{k}{2}x - 3y = 21$$

Now set the x-coefficient equal to the x-coefficient in the first equation:

$$\frac{k}{2} = 5$$
$$k = 10$$

Note that the question asks for the value of $2k$, so the correct answer is **(D)**, 20.

Try on Your Own

Directions

Take as much time as you need on these questions. Work carefully and methodically. There will be an opportunity for timed practice later in the book.

11

$$21x - 6y = 54$$
$$9 + y = 3.5x$$

The system of equations shown has how many solutions?

- (A) Zero

- (B) One

- (C) Two

- (D) Infinitely many

12

HINT: For Q12, if a system of equations has infinitely many solutions, what do you know about the two equations?

$$6x + 3y = 18$$
$$qx - \frac{y}{3} = -2$$

In the given system of linear equations, q is a constant. If the system has infinitely many solutions, what is the value of q?

- (A) -9

- (B) $-\frac{2}{3}$

- (C) $\frac{2}{3}$

- (D) 9

13

HINT: For Q13, the point of intersection is the solution to the system of equations. Use those concrete x- and y-values.

$$hx - 4y = -10$$
$$kx + 3y = -15$$

If the graphs of the lines in this system of equations intersect at $(-3, 1)$, what is the value of $\frac{k}{h}$?

Ⓐ $\frac{1}{3}$

Ⓑ 2

Ⓒ 3

Ⓓ 6

14

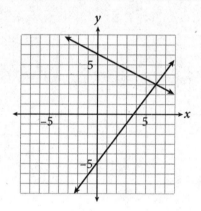

What is the y-coordinate of the solution to the system of equations shown in the graph?

Ⓐ −5

Ⓑ 3

Ⓒ 5

Ⓓ 6

15

$$3x - 9y = -6$$
$$\frac{1}{2}x - \frac{3}{2}y = c$$

If the system of linear equations shown has infinitely many solutions, and c is a constant, what is the value of c?

Ⓐ −6

Ⓑ −3

Ⓒ −2

Ⓓ −1

ON TEST DAY

Many SAT Math questions can be solved in more than one way. A little efficiency goes a long way in helping you get through the Math modules on time, so it's useful to try solving problems more than one way to learn which way is fastest.

Try this question using two approaches: both substitution and combination. Time yourself on each attempt. Which approach allowed you to get to the answer faster?

16.   If $28x - 5y = 36$ and $15x + 5y + 18 = 68$, what is the value of x?

A)   1

B)   2

C)   3

D)   4

The answer and both ways of solving can be found at the end of this chapter.

HOW MUCH HAVE YOU LEARNED?

Directions

For testlike practice, give yourself 16 minutes to complete this question set. Be sure to study the explanations, even for questions you answered correctly. They can be found at the end of this chapter.

17

If $8x - 2y = 10$ and $3y - 9x = 12$, then what is the value of $y - x$?

Ⓐ -8

Ⓑ 2

Ⓒ 12

Ⓓ 22

18

At a particular college, fees are $421 per semester for resident students and $879 for nonresident students. This semester, the sophomore class of 1,980 students had total fees of $1,170,210. Which of the following systems of equations represents the number of resident (r) and nonresident (n) students and the fees the two groups paid?

Ⓐ $r + n = 1{,}170{,}210$
$421r + 879n = 1{,}980$

Ⓑ $r + n = 1{,}980$
$879r + 421n = 1{,}170{,}210$

Ⓒ $r + n = 1{,}980$
$421r + 879n = 1{,}170{,}210$

Ⓓ $r + n = 1{,}170{,}210$
$879r + 421n = 1{,}980$

19

A sofa costs $50 less than three times the cost of a chair. If the sofa and chair together cost $650, how much more does the sofa cost than the chair?

Ⓐ $175

Ⓑ $225

Ⓒ $300

Ⓓ $475

20

Equation 1		Equation 2	
x	y	x	y
-2	6	-8	-8
0	4	-4	-7
2	2	0	-6
4	0	4	-5
		8	-4
		12	-3

The tables represent data points for two linear equations. If the two equations form a system, what is the x-coordinate of the solution to that system?

21

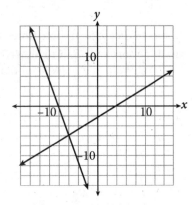

If (A, B) is the solution to the system of equations shown in the graph, and A and B are integers, then what is the value of $A + B$?

- (A) -12
- (B) -6
- (C) 0
- (D) 6

22

$$-16 = 7y + 4x$$

$$k = \frac{7}{8}y + \frac{1}{2}x$$

If this system of linear equations has infinitely many solutions, and k is a constant, what is the value of k?

- (A) -8
- (B) -4
- (C) -2
- (D) -1

23

$$-\frac{3}{2} = ay + 3x$$

$$9 + 24x = 6y$$

If the system of equations shown has no solution, and a is a constant, then what is the value of a?

- (A) -6
- (B) $-\frac{3}{4}$
- (C) $\frac{3}{4}$
- (D) 6

24

If $\frac{1}{4}x + 2y = \frac{11}{4}$ and $-6y - x = 7$, what is half of y?

$$\boxed{\underline{\qquad\qquad}}$$

25

At a certain toy store, tiny stuffed pandas cost $3.50 and giant stuffed pandas cost $14. If the store sold 29 panda toys and made $217 in revenue in one week, how many tiny stuffed pandas and giant stuffed pandas were sold?

Ⓐ 18 tiny stuffed pandas, 11 giant stuffed pandas

Ⓑ 11 tiny stuffed pandas, 18 giant stuffed pandas

Ⓒ 12 tiny stuffed pandas, 17 giant stuffed pandas

Ⓓ 18 tiny stuffed pandas, 13 giant stuffed pandas

26

A bead shop sells wooden beads for $0.20 each and crystal beads for $0.50 each. If a jewelry artist buys 127 beads total and pays $41 for them, how much more did she spend on crystal beads than wooden beads?

Ⓐ $11

Ⓑ $15

Ⓒ $23

Ⓓ $26

REFLECT

Directions: Take a few minutes to recall what you've learned and what you've been practicing in this chapter. Consider the following questions, jot down your best answer for each one, and then compare your reflections to the expert responses that follow. Use your level of confidence to determine what to do next.

When is substitution a good choice for solving a system of equations?

_____

_____

_____

When is combination a good choice for solving a system of equations?

_____

_____

_____

What does it mean if a system of linear equations has no solution? Infinitely many solutions?

_____

_____

_____

Expert Responses

When is substitution a good choice for solving a system of equations?

Substitution works best when at least one of the variables has a coefficient of 1, making the variable easy to isolate. This system, for example, is well suited for substitution:

$$a + 3b = 5$$
$$4a - 6b = 21$$

That's because in the first equation, you can easily isolate a as $a = 5 - 3b$ *and plug that in for* a *in the other equation. By contrast, substitution would not be a great choice for solving this system:*

$$2a + 3b = 5$$
$$4a - 6b = 21$$

If you used substitution now, you'd have to work with fractions, which is messy.

When is combination a good choice for solving a system of equations?

Combination is always a good choice. It is at its worst in systems such as this one:

$$2a + 3b = 5$$
$$3a + 5b = 7$$

Neither of the a-coefficients *is a multiple of the other, and neither of the* b-coefficients *is a multiple of the other, so to solve this system with combination you'd want to multiply both equations by a constant (e.g., multiply the first equation by 3 and the second equation by 2 to create a* 6a *term in both equations). But substitution wouldn't be stellar in this situation, either.*

Note that combination may be particularly effective when the SAT asks for a variable expression. For example, if a question based on the previous system of equations asked for the value of 5a + 8b, then you could find the answer instantly by adding the equations together.

What does it mean if a system of linear equations has no solution? Infinitely many solutions?

A system of linear equations with no solution represents two parallel lines, which never cross. The coefficient of a variable in one equation will match the coefficient of the same variable in the other equation, but the constants will be different. For example, this system has no solution:

$$2x + 3y = 4$$
$$2x + 3y = 5$$

Subtracting one equation from the other yields the equation $0 = -1$, which makes no sense.

If a system of linear equations has infinitely many solutions, then the two equations represent the same line. For example, this system has infinitely many solutions:

$$2x + 3y = 4$$
$$4x + 6y = 8$$

Dividing the second equation by 2 yields $2x + 3y = 4$, so although the two equations look different, they are actually the same.

Next Steps

If you answered most questions correctly in the "How Much Have You Learned?" section, and if your responses to the Reflect questions were similar to those of the SAT expert, then consider Systems of Linear Equations an area of strength and move on to the next chapter. Come back to this topic periodically to prevent yourself from getting rusty.

If you don't yet feel confident, review those parts of this chapter that you have not yet mastered. In particular, review the mechanics for solving a system of equations by substitution and by combination. Then try the questions you missed again. As always, be sure to review the explanations closely. Finally, **go online** (www.kaptest.com/moreonline) for additional practice.

Check Your Work – Chapter 5

1.   1
Difficulty: Medium
Category: Algebra
Getting to the Answer: Start by isolating c in the second equation: $c = 3b - 2$. Then substitute c into the first equation and solve:

$$7(3b - 2) + 8b = 15$$
$$21b - 14 + 8b = 15$$
$$29b - 14 = 15$$
$$29b = 29$$
$$b = 1$$

Enter **1**.

2.   A
Difficulty: Easy
Category: Algebra
Getting to the Answer: The quickest way to solve this question is to realize that you can rearrange the first equation to find that $x = y$. Then substitute y in for x in the second equation: $y = 2y + 5$. Solve to find that $y = -5$. Because $x = y$, x also equals -5, and $x + y = -10$. **(A)** is correct.

3.   C
Difficulty: Medium
Category: Algebra
Getting to the Answer: Because x has a coefficient of 1 in the second equation, solve the system using substitution. Before you select your answer, make sure you found the right quantity (the difference between x and y).

First, solve the second equation for x and substitute:

$$x - 5y = 2$$
$$x = 2 + 5y$$
$$4(2 + 5y) + 3y = 14 - y$$
$$8 + 20y + 3y = 14 - y$$
$$8 + 23y = 14 - y$$
$$24y = 6$$
$$y = \frac{6}{24} = \frac{1}{4}$$

Next, substitute this value back into $x = 2 + 5y$ and simplify:

$$x = 2 + 5\left(\frac{1}{4}\right)$$
$$x = \frac{8}{4} + \frac{5}{4}$$
$$x = \frac{13}{4}$$

Finally, evaluate $x - y$ to find the difference:

$$\frac{13}{4} - \frac{1}{4} = \frac{12}{4} = 3$$

(C) is correct.

4.   B
Difficulty: Medium
Category: Algebra
Getting to the Answer: Since the second equation is easier to solve for one variable and the question asks for $\frac{b}{2}$, solve the second equation for a. Then substitute the result into the first equation to create an equation in only one variable:

$$a = b + 3$$
$$5(b + 3) = 6b + 7$$
$$5b + 15 = 6b + 7$$
$$8 = b$$

So $\frac{b}{2} = 4$, and **(B)** is correct.

5.   A
Difficulty: Medium
Category: Algebra
Getting to the Answer: Set up two equations: one for the number of items sold and one for the money collected. Let $N =$ the number of bags of nuts sold and $G =$ the number of granola bars sold.

The equation for the total items is $N + G = 112$.

The equation for the money collected is $1.25N + 1.75G = 160$.

At this point, you could solve by either combination or substitution. If you use substitution, solve the first equation for N, the number of bags of nuts, because the question asks for G, the number of granola bars. Solving the first equation for N yields $N = 112 - G$. Substituting that equation into the second equation gives:

$$1.25(112 - G) + 1.75G = 160$$
$$140 - 1.25G + 1.75G = 160$$
$$0.5G = 20$$
$$G = 40$$

Remember that the question asks for the number of cases of granola bars the owner purchased, so divide 40 by 20, the number of granola bars per case. **(A)** is correct.

As an alternative approach, if you read the question carefully and recognize that you're solving for the number of cases, not the number of granola bars, the correct answer would have to be either (A) or (B), since (C) and (D) are way too big. You could then test one of those choices, for example, (A) 2, by multiplying by 20 granola bars per case: $2 \times 20 = 40$. Subtract that number from 112 to get the number of bags of nuts: $112 - 40 = 72$. Multiply each quantity by the price per package: $72 \times 1.25 = 90$ and $40 \times 1.75 = 70$. Then add the sales of the two items together: $90 + 70 = 160$. You've now confirmed the correct answer because $160 is the total sale amount. If you had tested (B) instead, then you could have eliminated it and still arrived at the correct answer with no more work because you eliminated all choices except **(A)**.

If you chose any of the other options, you likely answered the wrong question. (B) is the number of cases of nuts purchased, (C) is the number of granola bars sold, and (D) is the number of bags of nuts sold.

6.   D
Difficulty: Easy
Category: Algebra
Getting to the Answer: This system is already set up perfectly to solve using combination because the y terms ($-3y$ and $3y$) are opposites. Add the two equations to cancel $-3y$ and $3y$. Then solve the resulting equation for x:

$$\begin{array}{r} 2x - 3y = 14 \\ +(5x + 3y = 21) \\ \hline 7x \quad\;\; = 35 \\ x \quad\;\; = 5 \end{array}$$

Choice **(D)** is correct. The question asks only for the value of x, so you don't need to substitute x back into either equation to find the value of y.

7.   D
Difficulty: Easy
Category: Algebra
Getting to the Answer: If you're not asked to find the value of an individual variable, the question may lend itself to combination. This question asks for $b + c$, so don't waste your time finding the variables individually if you can avoid it. After rearranging the equations so

that variables and constants are aligned, you can add the equations together:

$$\begin{array}{r} -2b + 7c = 15 \\ +(3b - 6c = 2) \\ \hline b + c = 17 \end{array}$$

This matches **(D)**.

8.   59
Difficulty: Hard
Category: Algebra
Getting to the Answer: You're asked for the value of an expression rather than the value of one of the variables, so try combination. Start by rearranging the two equations so that variables and constants are aligned:

$$x + y = -15$$
$$\frac{x}{2} + \frac{5y}{2} = 37$$

Clear the fractions in the second equation and then add the equations:

$$2\left(\frac{x}{2} + \frac{5y}{2} = 37\right) \rightarrow x + 5y = 74$$
$$\begin{array}{r} x + y = -15 \\ + (x + 5y = 74) \\ \hline 2x + 6y = 59 \end{array}$$

This is precisely what the question asks for, so you're done. Enter **59**.

9.   1/2, .5, or 0.5
Difficulty: Medium
Category: Algebra
Getting to the Answer: None of the coefficients in either equation is 1, so using combination is a better strategy than substitution here. Examine the coefficients, looking for whether the x or the y terms will be easier to cancel. The y terms are both factors of 15, so multiply each equation to give y a coefficient of 15.

$$5(5x + 3y = 13) \rightarrow 25x + 15y = 65$$
$$3(8x + 5y = 21) \rightarrow 24x + 15y = 63$$

Subtract the second equation from the first:

$$\begin{array}{r} 25x + 15y = 65 \\ -(24x + 15y = 63) \\ \hline x \quad\quad\;\; = 2 \end{array}$$

Next, you need y so you can determine the value of $\frac{y}{x}$. Substitute 2 for x in one of the original equations:

$$5(2) + 3y = 13$$
$$10 + 3y = 13$$
$$3y = 3$$
$$y = 1$$

Plug your x- and y-values into $\frac{y}{x}$ to get $\frac{1}{2}$. Enter **1/2, .5,** or **0.5.**

10. 5
Difficulty: Hard
Category: Algebra
Getting to the Answer: Begin by choosing variables to represent tacos, t, and bags of chips, c. Then set up equations to represent the total purchase price at both restaurants. Restaurant A's total is $2.2t + 1.95c = 18.55$. Restaurant B's total is $3t + 1.5c = 19.5$. You're asked to find the number of bags of chips, so rewrite the equations to eliminate the t variable with combination. Multiply each equation by the t-coefficient of the other equation:

$$3(2.2t + 1.95c = 18.55) \rightarrow 6.6t + 5.85c = 55.65$$
$$2.2(3t + 1.5c = 19.5) \rightarrow 6.6t + 3.3c = 42.9$$

Subtract the second equation from the first to cancel the t terms:

$$\begin{array}{r} 6.6t + 5.85c = 55.65 \\ -(6.6t + 3.3c = 42.9) \\ \hline 2.55c = 12.75 \\ c = 5 \end{array}$$

You only need the number of bags of chips, so enter **5.**

An alternate strategy, which eliminates many of the calculations above, is to make use of the built-in graphing calculator. Again, determine the two costs equations, $2.2t + 1.95c = 18.55$ and $3t + 1.5c = 19.5$. Enter these into the graphing calculator using x for t and y for c, and note the point of intersection, $(4, 5)$. Since the y variable represents the number of bags of chips, **5** is your final answer.

11. D
Difficulty: Medium
Category: Algebra
Strategic Advice: Note that (C) is impossible. There are only three possibilities: the lines intersect, in which case there is one solution; the lines are parallel, in which case there is no solution; or the equations

describe the same line, in which case there are infinitely many solutions.
Getting to the Answer: Get the two equations into the same format so that you can distinguish among these possibilities:

$$21x - 6y = 54$$
$$3.5x - y = 9$$

Now it's easier to see that the first equation is equivalent to multiplying every term in the second equation by 6. Both equations describe the same line, so there are infinitely many solutions; **(D)** is correct.

12. B
Difficulty: Hard
Category: Algebra
Getting to the Answer: A system of equations that has infinitely many solutions describes a single line. Therefore, manipulation of one equation will yield the other. Look at the constant terms: to turn the 18 into a -2, divide the first equation by -9:

$$\frac{(6x + 3y = 18)}{-9} \rightarrow -\frac{6}{9}x - \frac{3}{9}y = -2$$
$$\rightarrow -\frac{2}{3}x - \frac{1}{3}y = -2$$

The y terms and constants in the second equation now match those in the first; all that's left is to set the coefficients of x equal to each other: $q = -\frac{2}{3}$. Choice **(B)** is correct.

Note that you could also write each equation in slope-intercept form and set the slopes equal to each other to solve for q.

13. C
Difficulty: Medium
Category: Algebra
Getting to the Answer: If the graphs intersect at $(-3, 1)$, then the solution to the system is $x = -3$ and $y = 1$. Substitute these values into both equations and go from there:

$$\begin{array}{ll} hx - 4y = -10 & kx + 3y = -15 \\ h(-3) - 4(1) = -10 & k(-3) + 3(1) = -15 \\ -3h - 4 = -10 & -3k + 3 = -15 \\ -3h = -6 & -3k = -18 \\ h = 2 & k = 6 \end{array}$$

So, $\frac{k}{h} = \frac{6}{2} = 3$, making **(C)** correct.

14. B
Difficulty: Easy
Category: Algebra
Getting to the Answer: The solution to a system of linear equations represented graphically is the point of intersection. If the lines do not intersect, the system has no solution.

According to the graph, the lines intersect, or cross each other, at (6, 3). The question asks for the y-coordinate of the solution, which is 3, so **(B)** is correct.

15. D
Difficulty: Hard
Category: Algebra
Getting to the Answer: A system of linear equations has infinitely many solutions if both lines in the system have the same slope and the same y-intercept (in other words, they are the same line).

To have the same slope, the x- and y-coefficients of the two equations must be the same. Use the x-coefficients here: to turn $\frac{1}{2}$ into 3, multiply by 6. So c becomes $6c$, and $6c = -6$, or $c = -1$, which is **(D)**.

Note that you could also write each equation in slope-intercept form and set the y-intercepts equal to each other to solve for c.

16. B
Difficulty: Medium
Category: Algebra
Strategic Advice: The numbers here are fairly large, so substitution is not likely to be convenient. Moreover, the y-coefficients have the same absolute value, so combination will probably be the faster way to solve for most students.
Getting to the Answer: Start by writing the second equation in the same form as the first, then use combination to solve for x:

$$\begin{array}{r} 28x - 5y = 36 \\ +15x + 5y = 50 \\ \hline 43x \quad\quad = 86 \\ x \quad\quad = 2 \end{array}$$

Choice **(B)** is correct.

If you feel more comfortable using substitution, you can maximize efficiency by solving one equation for $5y$ and substituting that value into the other equation:

$$\begin{aligned} 15x + 5y &= 50 \\ 5y &= 50 - 15x \\ 28x - (50 - 15x) &= 36 \\ 43x - 50 &= 36 \\ 43x &= 86 \\ x &= 2 \end{aligned}$$

Note that the arithmetic is fundamentally the same, but the setup using combination is quicker and visually easier to follow.

17. D
Difficulty: Medium
Category: Algebra
Strategic Advice: When a question asks for a sum or difference of variables, consider solving by combination.
Getting to the Answer: Rearrange the equations to be in the same form, with the y terms before the x terms, and then add:

$$\begin{array}{r} -2y + 8x = 10 \\ +(3y - 9x = 12) \\ \hline y - x = 22 \end{array}$$

The correct answer is **(D)**.

18. C
Difficulty: Medium
Category: Algebra
Getting to the Answer: Because you're given the variables (r for resident and n for nonresident), the only thing left for you to do is to break the wording apart into phrases and translate into math. Add together both student types to get the first equation: $r + n = 1,980$. This eliminates (A) and (D). Residents pay \$421 in fees ($421r$), which eliminates (B). Only **(C)** is left, so it has to be the answer.

19. C
Difficulty: Medium
Category: Algebra
Getting to the Answer: Write a system of equations, where $c =$ the cost of the chair in dollars and $s =$ the cost of the sofa in dollars. A sofa costs \$50 less than three times the cost of the chair, or $s = 3c - 50$; together, a sofa and a chair cost \$650, so $s + c = 650$.

The system is:

$$s = 3c - 50$$
$$s + c = 650$$

The top equation is already solved for s, so substitute $3c - 50$ into the bottom equation for s and solve for c:

$$3c - 50 + c = 650$$
$$4c - 50 = 650$$
$$4c = 700$$
$$c = 175$$

Remember to check if you solved for the right thing! The chair costs $175, so the sofa costs $3(175) - 50 = 525 - 50 = \$475$. This means the sofa costs $\$475 - \$175 = \$300$ more than the chair. Therefore, **(C)** is correct.

20. 8
Difficulty: Medium
Category: Algebra
Strategic Advice: The solution to the system is the point that both tables will have in common, but the tables, as given, do not share any points. You could use the data to write the equation of each line and then solve the system, but this will use up valuable time on test day. Instead, look for patterns that can be extended.
Getting to the Answer: In the table for Equation 1, the x-values increase by 2 each time the y-values decrease by 2. In the table for Equation 2, the x-values increase by 4 each time and the y-values increase by 1. Use these patterns to continue the tables.

Equation 1	
x	y
−2	6
0	4
2	2
4	0
6	−2
8	−4

Equation 2	
x	y
−8	−8
−4	−7
0	−6
4	−5
8	−4
12	−3

The point $(8, -4)$ satisfies both equations, so the x-coordinate of the solution to the system is **8**.

21. A
Difficulty: Easy
Category: Algebra
Getting to the Answer: The solution to a system of equations shown graphically is the point of intersection. Read the axis labels carefully. Each grid line represents 2 units. The two lines intersect at the point $(-6, -6)$, so $A + B = -6 + (-6) = -12$, which means **(A)** is correct.

22. C
Difficulty: Hard
Category: Algebra
Getting to the Answer: The system has infinitely many solutions, so both equations must describe the same line. Notice that if you multiply the x- and y-coefficients in the second equation by 8, you arrive at the x- and y-coefficients in the first equation. The constant k times 8 must then equal the constant in the first equation, or -16:

$$8k = -16$$
$$k = -2$$

The correct answer is **(C)**.

23. B
Difficulty: Hard
Category: Algebra
Getting to the Answer: First, rearrange the equations and write them on top of each other so that the x and y variables line up vertically:

$$3x + ay = -\frac{3}{2}$$
$$24x - 6y = -9$$

In a system of equations that has no solution, the x-coefficients must equal each other and the y-coefficients must equal each other. So, multiply the first equation by 8 to make the x-coefficients equal.

$$24x + 8ay = 8\left(-\frac{3}{2}\right)$$
$$24x - 6y = -9$$

The x-coefficients are now equal at 24. For the y-coefficients to be equal, $8a = -6$, which means that $a = -\frac{6}{8} = -\frac{3}{4}$. For a system with no solution, the difference in the constant (-12 vs. -9) is expected. **(B)** is correct.

24. 9/2 or 4.5

Difficulty: Medium

Category: Algebra

Getting to the Answer: Start by clearing the fractions from the first equation (by multiplying by 4) to make the numbers easier to work with. Then use combination to solve for y:

$$
\begin{aligned}
x + 8y &= 11 \\
+ (-x - 6y) &= 7 \\
\hline
2y &= 18 \\
y &= 9
\end{aligned}
$$

Take half of 9 to get $\frac{9}{2}$, then enter **9/2** or **4.5**.

25. A

Difficulty: Medium

Category: Algebra

Getting to the Answer: Choose intuitive letters for the variables: t for tiny pandas, g for giant pandas. You're given the cost of each as well as the number of each sold and the total revenue generated. Then write the system of equations that represents the information given:

$$
\begin{aligned}
t + g &= 29 \\
3.5t + 14g &= 217
\end{aligned}
$$

Multiplying the top equation by -14 allows you to solve for t using combination:

$$
\begin{aligned}
-14t - 14g &= -406 \\
+ (3.5t + 14g &= 217) \\
\hline
-10.5t &= -189 \\
t &= 18
\end{aligned}
$$

Solving for t gives 18, which eliminates (B) and (C). Plugging 18 into t in the first equation allows you to find g, which is 11. Choice **(A)** is correct.

You can also use the on-screen graphing calculator. After setting up the two equations, $t + g = 29$ and $3.5t + 14g = 217$, enter them into the graphing calculator using x for t and y for g. The point of intersection is (18, 11). The x-coordinate represents tiny pandas and the y-coordinate represents giant pandas; thus, **(A)** is correct.

26. A

Difficulty: Hard

Category: Algebra

Getting to the Answer: Choose letters that make sense for the variables: w for wooden and c for crystal. You know the jewelry artist bought 127 beads total. You're also told each wooden bead costs $0.20 ($0.2w$) and each crystal bead costs $0.50 ($0.5c$), as well as the fact that she spent $41 total. You'll have two equations: one relating the number of wooden beads and crystal beads and a second relating the costs associated with each:

$$
\begin{aligned}
w + c &= 127 \\
0.2w + 0.5c &= 41
\end{aligned}
$$

Either combination or substitution is a good choice for solving this system. Both are shown here:

Combination:

$$
2(0.2w + 0.5c = 41) \rightarrow 0.4w + c = 82
$$

$$
\begin{aligned}
w + c &= 127 \\
- (0.4w + c) &= 82 \\
\hline
0.6w &= 45 \\
w &= 75
\end{aligned}
$$

Substitution:

$$
w + c = 127 \rightarrow c = 127 - w
$$

$$
\begin{aligned}
0.2w + 0.5(127 - w) &= 41 \\
0.2w + 63.5 - 0.5w &= 41 \\
-0.3w &= -22.5 \\
w &= 75
\end{aligned}
$$

$$
75 + c = 127 \rightarrow c = 52
$$

You can also use the on-screen graphing calculator to determine how many wooden and crystal beads there are. Set up the equations $w + c = 127$ and $0.2w + 0.5c = 41$ and graph them, with x representing w and y representing c. The point of intersection is (75, 52), meaning that there are 75 wooden beads and 52 crystal beads.

The question asks for the difference in the amount spent on each type of bead, not the difference in the quantity of each type. Multiply the bead counts by the correct pricing to get $75 \times \$0.2 = \$15$ for the wooden beads and $52 \times \$0.5 = \$26$ for the crystal beads. Take the difference to get $\$26 - \$15 = \$11$, which is **(A)**.

[CHAPTER 6]

INEQUALITIES

HOW MUCH DO YOU KNOW?

Directions

Try the questions that follow. Show your work so that you can compare your solutions to the ones found in the "Check Your Work" section immediately after this question set. If you answered the question(s) on a specific topic correctly, and if your scratchwork looks like ours, you may be able to move quickly through the lesson covering that topic. If you answered incorrectly or used a different approach, you may want to take your time on that lesson.

1

If $\frac{3}{5}p - 2 \geq 5$, what is the least possible value of $\frac{6}{5}p + 2$?

- Ⓐ   7
- Ⓑ   10
- Ⓒ   16
- Ⓓ   18

2

If $-1 < \frac{4}{3}h + \frac{1}{6} < \frac{1}{2}$, and $12h + 2$ is an integer greater than 0, then what is one possible value of $12h + 2$?

3

$$y > 2x - 3$$
$$5y \leq 3x$$

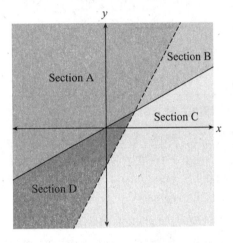

The graph depicts the given system of inequalities. Which of the labeled section or sections of the graph could represent all of the solutions of the system?

- Ⓐ   Sections A and D
- Ⓑ   Section B
- Ⓒ   Sections C and D
- Ⓓ   Section D

4

A bowling alley charges a flat $6.50 fee for shoe rental, plus $3.75 per game and 6.325 percent sales tax. If each person in a group of seven has $20 to spend and at least some of them must rent shoes, which inequality best describes this situation, given r is the number of shoe rentals and g is the number of games purchased?

(A) $1.06325(6.5r + 3.75g) \leq 140$

(B) $1.06325(6.5r + 3.75g) \leq 20$

(C) $1.06325\left(\dfrac{6.5}{r} + \dfrac{3.75}{g}\right) \leq 140$

(D) $0.06325(6.5r + 3.75g) \leq 20$

5

Marco is paid $80 per day, plus $15 per hour for overtime. If he works five days per week and wants to make a minimum of $520 this week, what is the fewest number of hours of overtime he must work?

$$\boxed{\underline{}}$$

6

The initial installation of arid-zone landscaping would cost a business $15,900 but would lower its electricity bill from $1,640 to $770 a month. Which of the following inequalities can be used to find m, the number of months after installation that the savings in water costs will be at least as much as the cost of the installation?

(A) $15,900 \geq (1,640 - 770)m$

(B) $15,900 > 770m$

(C) $15,900 \leq (1,640 - 770)m$

(D) $15,900 \leq 770m$

Check Your Work

1.   C
Difficulty: Medium
Category: Algebra
Getting to the Answer: You might be tempted to solve for p, but some critical thinking and algebra make that unnecessary. First, get $\frac{3}{5}p$ by itself by adding 2 to both sides: $\frac{3}{5}p \geq 7$. Next, multiply both sides by 2 to get the value range of $\frac{6}{5}p \geq 14$. Finally, add 2 to both sides to get $\frac{6}{5}p + 2 \geq 14 + 2$. Thus, $\frac{6}{5}p + 2 \geq 16$, so **(C)** is correct.

2.   1, 2, 3, or 4
Difficulty: Hard
Category: Algebra
Getting to the Answer: Don't automatically start solving the two inequalities separately. Instead, look for a series of quick manipulations to convert $\frac{4}{3}h + \frac{1}{6}$ to $12h + 2$. Start by multiplying the entire inequality by 9 to yield $-9 < 12h + \frac{3}{2} < \frac{9}{2}$. Next, add $\frac{1}{2}$ (to get the desired $+2$) to all parts of the inequality (converting the fraction component to a decimal will make this step easier), which will become $-8.5 < 12h + 2 < 5$. You now know that the value $12h + 2$ is greater than -8.5 and less than 5. Since the question stem states that $12h + 2$ is an integer greater than 0, enter **1, 2, 3,** or **4**.

3.   D
Difficulty: Medium
Category: Algebra
Getting to the Answer: Sections A and D are all the y-values greater than $2x - 3$, so those sections are the solution set for the inequality $y > 2x - 3$. Similarly, Sections C and D are the solution set for $5y \leq 3x$. The solutions for a system of inequalities are all the points that satisfy all (both, in this case) of the inequalities. The points in Section D are in the solution set for both inequalities, so **(D)** is correct.

4.   A
Difficulty: Medium
Category: Algebra
Getting to the Answer: The question has defined the variables for you (r and g). The bowling alley charges $6.50 for shoe rental and $3.75 per game. Sales tax is 6.325% (0.06325 in decimal form). Rental and game costs are given by $6.5r$ and $3.75g$, respectively. To incorporate sales tax into the total cost, multiply the sum of $6.5r$ and $3.75g$ by 1.06325 (not 0.06325, which gives the cost of sales tax only). The question asks for an inequality that represents the amount that the group can spend, which can be no more than $7 \times 20 = 140$; therefore, the correct inequality is $1.06325(6.5r + 3.75g) \leq 140$. This matches **(A)**.

5.   8
Difficulty: Medium
Category: Algebra
Getting to the Answer: Translate from English into math to create an inequality in which h represents the number of hours of overtime Marco must work. Marco gets paid a daily wage plus an hourly rate for overtime, so his weekly pay is his daily rate ($80) times 5 days, plus the number of hours of overtime he works (h) times his overtime rate ($15). If he wants to make *at least* $520, which means that much or more, the inequality is $(80 \times 5) + 15h \geq 520$. Solve for h:

$$400 + 15h \geq 520$$
$$15h \geq 120$$
$$h \geq 8$$

Marco must work at least 8 hours of overtime to make $520 or more this week. Enter **8**.

6.   C
Difficulty: Medium
Category: Algebra
Getting to the Answer: The question asks for the point at which the savings will be *at least as much* as the cost of installing the landscaping, so the value range could include a value equal to the exact cost of installation; eliminate (B). Because you need a value range that is at least as much as the cost of landscaping, you need the cost of landscaping, $15,900, to be *less than* or equal to the value range. Eliminate (A).

The value range will be the value of the monthly savings times the number of months, which will be m times the difference between the old monthly water cost and the new monthly water cost: $(1,640 - 770)m$. Therefore, the entire inequality expression is $15,900 \leq (1,640 - 770)m$, so **(C)** is correct.

LINEAR INEQUALITIES

LEARNING OBJECTIVES

After this lesson, you will be able to:

- Solve an inequality for a range of values
- Identify the graph of an inequality

To answer a question like this:

Which of the graphs represents the solution set for $5x - 10y > 6$?

A)

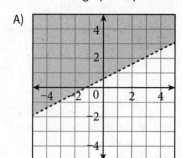

B)

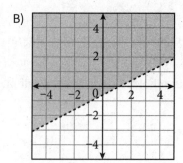

C)

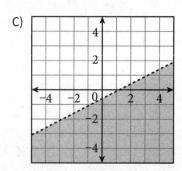

D)

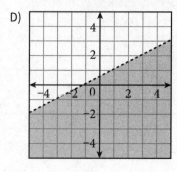

You need to know this:

Linear inequalities are similar to linear equations but have two differences:

- You are solving for a **range of values** rather than a single value.
- If you multiply or divide both sides of the inequality by a negative, you must **reverse the inequality sign**.

While linear equations graph as simple lines, inequalities graph as shaded regions. Use solid lines for inequalities with $\leq$ or $\geq$ signs because the line itself is included in the solution set. Use dashed lines for inequalities with $<$ or $>$ signs because, in these cases, the line itself is not included in the solution set. The shaded region represents all points that make up the solution set for the inequality.

You need to do this:

To graph an inequality, start by writing the inequality in slope-intercept form, then graph the solid or dashed line. Finally, add shading:

- For $y > mx + b$ and $y \geq mx + b$, shade the region *above* the line.
- For $y < mx + b$ and $y \leq mx + b$, shade the region *below* the line.

If it's hard to tell which region is above/below the line (which can happen when the line is steep), compare the y-values on both sides of the line.

Explanation:

Rewrite the inequality in slope-intercept form and then identify which half-plane should be shaded. Subtract $5x$ from both sides of the inequality, divide both sides by -10, and flip the inequality symbol to yield $y < \frac{1}{2}x - \frac{3}{5}$.

Eliminate (A) and (D) because they have positive y-intercepts. The less-than symbol indicates that the half-plane below the line should be shaded, making **(C)** the correct answer.

Try on Your Own

Directions

Take as much time as you need on these questions. Work carefully and methodically. There will be an opportunity for timed practice later in the book.

1

$$-\frac{a}{6} - a > -\frac{4}{3}$$

Which of the following is equivalent to the given inequality?

Ⓐ $a < \frac{7}{8}$

Ⓑ $a > \frac{7}{8}$

Ⓒ $a < \frac{8}{7}$

Ⓓ $a > \frac{8}{7}$

2

HINT: For Q2, save time by solving for the entire expression, not c.

If $-5c - 7 \le 8$, what is the least possible value of $15c + 7$?

Ⓐ -38

Ⓑ -4

Ⓒ 15

Ⓓ 22

3

HINT: For Q3, be careful not to "lose" a negative sign.

$$-\frac{1}{8}(8 - 10x) > 3x - 2$$

Which of the following describes all possible values of x?

Ⓐ $x < -\frac{12}{7}$

Ⓑ $x > -\frac{4}{7}$

Ⓒ $x < \frac{4}{7}$

Ⓓ $x > \frac{4}{7}$

4

$$\frac{1}{4}a - \frac{1}{16}b + 3 < 5$$

Which of the following is equivalent to the inequality shown?

Ⓐ $4a - b < 8$

Ⓑ $4a - b < 32$

Ⓒ $a - 4b < 32$

Ⓓ $4b - a < 4$

5

If $4c + 20 \ge 31$, what is the least possible value of $12c + 7$?

Ⓐ 18

Ⓑ 40

Ⓒ 51

Ⓓ 58

SYSTEMS OF INEQUALITIES

LEARNING OBJECTIVES

After this lesson, you will be able to:

- Identify the graph of a system of inequalities
- Solve for the point of intersection of the boundary lines of a system of inequalities
- Solve algebraically a system of one inequality with two variables and another inequality with one variable

To answer a question like this:

If $12x - 4y > 8$ and $\frac{2}{3}x + 6y \geq 14$ form a system of inequalities, which of the graphs shows the solution set for the system?

A)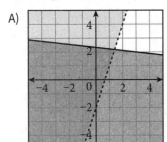

B)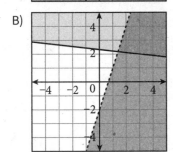

C)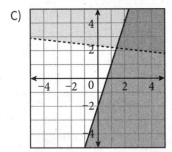

D)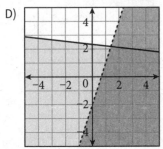

You need to know this:

The solution set for a system of inequalities is not a single point (a single *x*-value and *y*-value) but a region of overlap between the two inequalities: that is, a range of *x*-values and *y*-values. It is easiest to see this graphically.

Systems of inequalities can be presented graphically with multiple boundary lines and multiple shaded regions. Follow the same rules as for graphing single inequalities, but keep in mind that **the solution set is the region where the shading overlaps**.

Note that you generally cannot use substitution or combination to solve a system of two inequalities in which both have two variables. You won't be able to come up with a single statement that describes all possible solutions to the system. That said, the SAT may ask for the maximum or minimum *x*- or *y*-value of a system of inequalities. These questions are actually asking about the intersection of the **boundary lines** of the system. If you see one of these questions, use substitution or combination to solve for the point of intersection, as you learned to do in chapter 5. For an example of this type of question, see question number 8 in the "Try on Your Own" set for this lesson.

You may also see a question without a graph asking you to solve a system of one inequality in two variables and another inequality in one variable. As long as both inequalities have the same symbol (for instance, both have the greater-than sign), you can do this by substitution. Question number 6 in this lesson's "Try on Your Own" set is an example of this question type.

You need to do this:

- To identify the graph of a system of inequalities, follow the same rules as for single inequalities. The solution set is the region where the shading overlaps.
- For a question asking for a maximum or minimum, solve for the intersection point of the boundary lines.
- For a question asking for the range of values that satisfies a system of one inequality in two variables and one inequality in one variable (both with the same sign), solve by substitution.

Explanation:

Rewrite the inequalities in slope-intercept form. Once complete, determine whether each line should be solid or dashed and which half of the plane (above or below the line) should be shaded for each. The correct graph should have a dashed line with a positive slope ($y < 3x - 2$) and a solid line with a negative slope $\left(y \geq -\frac{1}{9}x + \frac{7}{3}\right)$; eliminate (C) because the dashed and solid lines are incorrect. According to the inequality symbols, the half-plane above the solid line and the half-plane below the dashed line should be shaded; the only match is **(B)**.

Try on Your Own

Directions

Take as much time as you need on these questions. Work carefully and methodically. There will be an opportunity for timed practice later in the book.

6

$$a < 6b + 4$$
$$3b < 8$$

Which of the following consists of all the a-values that satisfy the given system of inequalities?

Ⓐ $a < 20$

Ⓑ $a < 16$

Ⓒ $a < 12$

Ⓓ $a < \dfrac{8}{3}$

7

HINT: For Q7, remember that the solution set is the overlap between both inequalities. Make a sketch or use a graphing calculator.

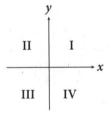

If the system of inequalities $y \le -x + 1$ and $y < \dfrac{1}{2}x$ is graphed on the coordinate plane, which of the quadrants contain(s) no solution to the system?

Ⓐ Quadrant I

Ⓑ Quadrant II

Ⓒ Quadrant III

Ⓓ Quadrants I and II

8

$$-y \le 6x - 2{,}200$$
$$3y \ge 9x - 1{,}500$$

Given this system of inequalities, if point (a, b) lies within the solution set, what is the minimum possible value of b?

9

$$x < 4 - 2y$$
$$y \le -2x + 1$$

Which of the following ordered pairs satisfies both of the given inequalities?

Ⓐ $(-1, 3)$

Ⓑ $(1, 1)$

Ⓒ $(2, -3)$

Ⓓ $(4, 4)$

10

HINT: For Q10, remember that "solution" means an (x, y) pair that is true for both inequalities.

$$y > x + r$$
$$y < s - x$$

If $x = y = 1$ is a solution to the system of inequalities shown, which of the following ordered pairs could correspond to (r, s)?

Ⓐ $(-1, 1)$

Ⓑ $\left(-\dfrac{1}{2}, 2\right)$

Ⓒ $\left(-\dfrac{1}{10}, 3\right)$

Ⓓ $(3, -1)$

MODELING REAL-LIFE SITUATIONS WITH INEQUALITIES

LEARNING OBJECTIVE

After this lesson, you will be able to:

- Identify one or more inequalities that match a real-life situation

To answer a question like this:

A toy company sells toy hoops for $8 and basketballs for $25. The company hopes to sell more than three times as many basketballs as toy hoops to meet its sales goal of at least $10,400. If h represents the number of toy hoops and b represents the number of basketballs, which of the following systems of inequalities describes this situation?

A) $8h + 25b \geq 10{,}400$
   $b > 3h$

B) $8h + 25b \geq 10{,}400$
   $h > 3b$

C) $25h + 8b \geq 10{,}400$
   $b > 3h$

D) $25h + 8b \geq 10{,}400$
   $h > 3b$

You need to know this:

Word problems involving inequalities require you to do the same sort of translation that you learned in chapter 4. They also require you to get the direction of the inequality sign right. The following table shows which symbols correspond to which words.

ENGLISH	SYMBOL
more, greater, longer, heavier	$>$
less, fewer, shorter, lighter	$<$
no less than, no fewer than, at least	$\geq$
no more than, no greater than, at most	$\leq$

You need to do this:

Break down the word problem one inequality at a time. For each one:

- Identify the correct symbol based on the preceding table.
- Use logic to determine the relationship between the values given in the word problem.

Explanation:

"At least $10,400" means $\geq 10{,}400$. It's the money from the sales of toy hoops and basketballs that has to be greater than or equal to $10,400, so that's what needs to go on the left of the $\geq$ sign. Each toy hoop costs $8, so the money generated by sales of toy hoops will be $8h$. Each basketball costs $25, so basketballs will generate $25b$. Add them: $8h + 25b \geq 10{,}400$. Eliminate (C) and (D).

The company wants to sell "*more than* three times as many basketballs as toy hoops," so write down $>$ and work out what needs to go on each side. The company wants to sell more basketballs than toy hoops, so b should go on the left. Specifically, they want basketball sales to be more than 3 times toy hoop sales, so the final statement is $b > 3h$. **(A)** is correct.

Try on Your Own

Directions

Take as much time as you need on these questions. Work carefully and methodically. There will be an opportunity for timed practice later in the book.

11

HINT: For Q11, set up one inequality for the number of ads and a second inequality for the money the ads bring in.

To qualify for a prize, a student has to sell at least $1,500 worth of yearbook advertisements consisting of no fewer than 15 individual ads. If x is the number of full-page ads sold for $110 each, y is the number of half-page ads sold for $70 each, and z is the number of quarter-page ads sold for $50 each, which of the following systems of inequalities represents this situation?

Ⓐ $110x + 70y + 50z \geq 1{,}500$
$x + y + z \leq 15$

Ⓑ $110x + 70y + 50z \leq 1{,}500$
$x + y + z \leq 15$

Ⓒ $110x + 70y + 50z \geq 1{,}500$
$x + y + z \geq 15$

Ⓓ $110x + 70y + 50z \leq 1{,}500$
$x + y + z \geq 15$

12

A farmer needs to sell at least $200 of produce each day. The cart she uses for transport can hold no more than 250 pounds. Which inequality represents this scenario, if w is the number of pounds of watermelons sold at $0.50 per pound, c is the number of pounds of cantaloupes sold at $1 per pound, and t is the number of pounds of tomatoes sold at $2.50 per pound?

Ⓐ $0.5w + 1c + 2.5t \geq 200$
$w + c + t \leq 250$

Ⓑ $0.5w + 1c + 2.5t \leq 200$
$w + c + t \leq 250$

Ⓒ $0.5w + 1c + 2.5t \geq 200$
$w + c + t \geq 250$

Ⓓ $0.5w + 1c + 2.5t \leq 200$
$w + c + t \geq 250$

13

A garden will be planted with at least 15 trees. There will be x apple trees, which cost $120 each, and y pear trees, which cost $145 each. The budget for purchasing the trees is no more than $2,050. There must be at least 5 apple trees and at least 3 pear trees. Which of the following systems of inequalities represents the situation?

Ⓐ $120x + 145y \geq 2,050$
$x + y \leq 15$
$x \geq 5$
$y \geq 3$

Ⓑ $120x + 145y \geq 2,050$
$x + y \geq 15$
$x \leq 5$
$y \leq 3$

Ⓒ $120x + 145y \leq 2,050$
$x + y \geq 15$
$x \leq 5$
$y \leq 3$

Ⓓ $120x + 145y \leq 2,050$
$x + y \geq 15$
$x \geq 5$
$y \geq 3$

14

A utility shelf is used to store x containers of paint, which weigh 50 pounds each, and y containers of varnish, which weigh 35 pounds each. The shelf can hold up to 32 containers, the combined weight of which must not exceed 1,450 pounds. Which of the following systems of inequalities represents this relationship?

Ⓐ $50x + 35y \leq 32$
$x + y \leq 1,450$

Ⓑ $50x + 35y \leq 1,450$
$x + y \leq 32$

Ⓒ $85x + y \leq 1,450$
$x + y \leq 32$

Ⓓ $50x + 35y \leq 1,450$
$x + y \leq 85$

15

HINT: For Q15, read carefully. *At least* is a minimum, so which way should the inequality sign point?

A bakery is buying f 50-pound bags of flour and s 20-pound bags of sugar. The supplier will deliver no more than 750 pounds in a shipment. The bakery wants to buy at least three times as many bags of sugar as bags of flour. Which of the following systems of inequalities represents this situation?

Ⓐ $50f + 60s \leq 750$
$f \leq 3s$

Ⓑ $50f + 20s \leq 750$
$f \leq 3s$

Ⓒ $50f + 20s \leq 750$
$3f \leq s$

Ⓓ $150f + 20s \leq 750$
$3f \leq s$

ON TEST DAY

Modeling real-life situations with inequalities can be tricky, especially when there are multiple inequalities involved or when a question doesn't state the information in the most straightforward way. The good news is that you can often make use of the answer choices to get to the answer quickly.

Try the question below. If you use the choices, you shouldn't have to do any calculations. Just pay close attention to the direction of the inequality signs.

16. At a flower sale, a florist sold x carnations at a price of \$4 for 10 and y daisies at a price of \$7 for 5. The florist had 500 flowers in stock for the sale and the revenue from the sale was least \$400. Which system of inequalities best describes this situation?

A) $0.4x + 1.4y \geq 400$
   $x + y \leq 500$

B) $0.4x + 1.4y \leq 400$
   $x + y \leq 500$

C) $0.4x + 1.4y \geq 400$
   $x + y \geq 500$

D) $0.4x + 1.4y \leq 400$
   $x + y \geq 500$

The answer and explanation can be found at the end of this chapter.

HOW MUCH HAVE YOU LEARNED?

Directions

For testlike practice, give yourself 14 minutes to complete this question set. Be sure to study the explanations, even for questions you answered correctly. They can be found at the end of this chapter.

17

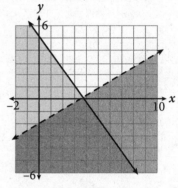

The graph shows the solution set for this system of inequalities:

$$y < \frac{3}{5}x - 2$$

$$y \leq -\frac{4}{3}x + 5$$

Which of the following is a solution to this system?

Ⓐ $(6, -1)$

Ⓑ $(1, -1)$

Ⓒ $(6, -3)$

Ⓓ $(0, -2)$

18

Ezekiel has $5.00 to spend on snacks. Candy bars cost $0.60 each, gum costs $0.50 per pack, and nuts are priced at $1.29 per small bag. If Ezekiel buys c candy bars, g packs of gum, and n bags of nuts, which of the following inequalities correctly describes Ezekiel's choices?

Ⓐ $\dfrac{c}{0.60} + \dfrac{g}{0.50} + \dfrac{n}{1.29} \leq \dfrac{1}{5}$

Ⓑ $c + g + n \leq 5$

Ⓒ $0.60c + 0.50g + 1.29n \leq 5.00$

Ⓓ $0.60c + 0.50g + 1.29n \geq 5.00$

19

A cargo container, which can hold a maximum of 300 cubic feet, can fit a maximum of 50 microwaves or a maximum of 15 refrigerators. Each microwave takes up 6 cubic feet of space, and each refrigerator takes up 20 cubic feet. Which of the following systems of inequalities describes how many of each item (microwaves, m, and refrigerators, r) can fit into one cargo container?

Ⓐ $m \leq 6$
$r \leq 20$
$50m + 15r \leq 300$

Ⓑ $m \leq 50$
$r \leq 15$
$m + r \leq 300$

Ⓒ $m \leq 50$
$r \leq 15$
$6m + 20r \leq 300$

Ⓓ $m \leq 50$
$r \leq 15$
$50m + 15r \leq 300$

20

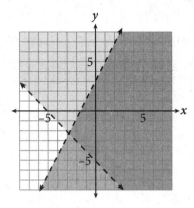

$$y > -x - 5$$
$$y < 2x + 3$$

The figure shows the solution for the system of inequalities shown. Suppose (a, b) is a solution to the system. If $a = 0$, what is the greatest possible integer value of b?

21

$$3x + 2 > 5$$
$$-2x + 8 > -10$$

Which of the following describes the range of x based on the given inequalities?

(A) $x > 1$

(B) $x > 9$

(C) $-1 < x < 9$

(D) $9 > x > 1$

22

$$y \geq -3x + 18$$
$$y \geq 9x$$

In the xy plane, the point (a, b) lies in the solution set of the system of inequalities shown. What is the minimum possible value of b?

(A) $1\frac{1}{2}$

(B) 3

(C) $7\frac{1}{2}$

(D) $13\frac{1}{2}$

23

Francine is able to make up to 15 sales calls per week. Of these calls, p successfully sell advertisers a prime package for $12,000, b successfully sell a basic package for $8,000, and u calls are unsuccessful. Her weekly sales goal is to sell more than $20,000 worth of advertising. Which of the following systems of inequalities represents this situation?

(A) $p + b + u \leq 15$
  $12,000p + 8,000b > 20,000$

(B) $p + b + u \geq 15$
  $12,000p + 8,000b > 20,000$

(C) $p + b + u \leq 15$
  $12,000p + 8,000(b + u) > 20,000$

(D) $p + b + u \leq 15$
  $12,000p + 8,000b < 20,000$

24

Luis has $25 to spend on school supplies. Pencils (p) cost $1.25 per package, notebooks (n) are priced at $2.50 each, and markers ($m$) sell for $4 per pack. He must buy exactly one calendar for $5.75. Which of the following describes how many markers Luis can buy?

Ⓐ $m \leq \dfrac{1.25p + 2.5n + 5.75}{25}$

Ⓑ $m \leq \dfrac{19.25 - 1.25p - 2.5n}{4}$

Ⓒ $m \leq \dfrac{25 - 1.25p - 2.5n}{4} - 5.75$

Ⓓ $m \leq 19.25 - 1.25p - 2.5n$

25

The variable x is a positive integer.
If $3(x - 1) + 5 > 11$ and $-5x + 18 \geq -12$, how many possible values are there for x?

REFLECT

Directions: Take a few minutes to recall what you've learned and what you've been practicing in this chapter. Consider the following questions, jot down your best answer for each one, and then compare your reflections to the expert responses that follow. Use your level of confidence to determine what to do next.

What is the difference between a linear inequality and a linear equation?

_____

_____

_____

The rules for manipulating an inequality are very similar to those for manipulating an equation. What is the major difference?

_____

_____

_____

When two lines representing a system of inequalities intersect in the coordinate plane, they create four regions. What does each of these regions represent?

_____

_____

_____

Expert Responses

What is the difference between a linear inequality and a linear equation?

A linear equation is solved for a single value. A linear inequality is solved for a range of values.

The rules for manipulating an inequality are very similar to those for manipulating an equation. What is the major difference?

When solving an inequality, you can do the same thing to both sides, just as you could for an equation. The big difference is that if you divide or multiply both sides of an inequality by a negative number, you have to flip the inequality sign.

When two lines representing a system of inequalities intersect in the coordinate plane, they create four regions. What does each of these regions represent?

Of the four regions, one represents values that satisfy neither inequality. One represents values that satisfy both inequalities. The other two regions represent values that satisfy one inequality but not the other.

Next Steps

If you answered most questions correctly in the "How Much Have You Learned?" section, and if your responses to the Reflect questions were similar to those of the SAT expert, then consider inequalities an area of strength and move on to the next chapter. Come back to this topic periodically to prevent yourself from getting rusty.

If you don't yet feel confident, review those parts of this chapter that you have not yet mastered and try the questions you missed again. As always, be sure to review the explanations closely. Finally, **go online** (www. kaptest.com/moreonline) for additional practice.

Check Your Work – Chapter 6

1. C
Difficulty: Easy
Category: Algebra
Getting to the Answer: Begin by multiplying all parts of the inequality by 6 to clear the fractions: $-a - 6a > -\frac{24}{3}$, which, when simplified, is $-7a > -8$. Divide both sides by -7, remembering to switch the direction of the sign: $a < \frac{8}{7}$. Therefore, **(C)** is correct.

2. A
Difficulty: Medium
Category: Algebra
Getting to the Answer: Don't solve for c on autopilot. Instead, solve for $15c$, then add 7 to both sides. To do this, first multiply both sides of the inequality by -1 to get $5c + 7 \geq -8$. (Notice that the inequality sign had to be flipped due to multiplication by a negative number.) Then subtract 7 from both sides to yield $5c \geq -15$. Multiply both sides by 3: $15c \geq -45$. Finally, add 7 to both sides: $15c + 7 \geq -38$. Choice **(A)** is correct.

3. C
Difficulty: Medium
Category: Algebra
Getting to the Answer: First, to clear the fraction, multiply both sides of the inequality by -8, remembering to flip the direction of the inequality sign: $8 - 10x < -24x + 16$.

Next, subtract 8 from both sides, and then add $24x$ to both sides. Divide both sides by 14, and then simplify the fraction:

$$-10x < -24x + 8$$
$$14x < 8$$
$$x < \frac{8}{14}$$
$$x < \frac{4}{7}$$

Thus, **(C)** is correct.

4. B
Difficulty: Medium
Category: Algebra
Getting to the Answer: Begin by subtracting 3 from both sides of the inequality to get $\frac{1}{4}a - \frac{1}{16}b < 2$. Next, clear the fractions in that inequality by multiplying all terms by 16: $16 \times \left(\frac{1}{4}a - \frac{1}{16}b < 2\right) \rightarrow 4a - b < 32$. **(B)** is correct.

5. B
Difficulty: Medium
Category: Algebra
Strategic Advice: Because the given inequality contains $4c$ and the value you're solving for has $12c$ (a multiple of $4c$), solve for $4c$ and then multiply by 3 to find $12c$.
Getting to the Answer: Subtract 20 from both sides of the inequality to find that $4c \geq 11$. Multiply by 3: $12c \geq 33$. Finally, add 7 to both sides: $12c + 7 \geq 40$. So the least permissible value for $12c + 7$ is 40. **(B)** is correct.

6. A
Difficulty: Easy
Category: Algebra
Getting to the Answer: The question offers a value range of a in terms of $6b$ and a value range for $3b$. Therefore, use the known value range of $3b$ to find the value range of $6b$.

Since $6b$ is two times $3b$, multiply both sides of the second inequality by 2 to find the value range of $6b$: $2 \times 3b < 2 \times 8$, so $6b < 16$.

Because the signs are the same in the two inequalities (both are less-than signs), you can plug 16 in for $6b$ in the first inequality: $a < 16 + 4$, or $a < 20$. Hence, **(A)** is correct.

7. B
Difficulty: Medium
Category: Algebra
Getting to the Answer: Draw a sketch of the two lines (or use the graphing calculator) to visualize the system of inequalities.

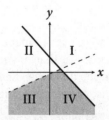

Quadrants III and IV contain solutions to the system. Eliminate (C). Quadrant II contains no solutions, so you can also eliminate (A). Look closely at quadrant I. The line for $y \leq -x + 1$ intersects both the x and y axes at $+1$. The line for $y < \frac{1}{2}x$ passes through the origin and upward into quadrant I. Thus, there is a very small triangle of solutions to both inequalities that lies in quadrant I. Therefore, **(B)** is correct.

8. 400
Difficulty: Medium
Category: Algebra
Getting to the Answer: The first task is to express both inequalities in terms of y. Multiply $-y \leq 6x - 2,200$ by -1 to get $y \geq -6x + 2,200$; don't forget to flip the sign since you are multiplying by a negative number. Divide $3y \geq 9x - 1,500$ by 3 to get $y \geq 3x - 500$.

The solution set for these inequalities is the area of the coordinate plane on or above both lines. Thus, the minimum y-value will occur at the intersection of the two lines, whose equations are $y = -6x + 2,200$ and $y = 3x - 500$. To find the point of intersection, set the equations equal to each other: $-6x + 2,200 = 3x - 500$. Isolate the x-values on one side to yield $-9x = -2,700$ and $x = 300$. Plug this value into one of the equations (it doesn't matter which one because $x = 300$ is where they intersect) to obtain the y-coordinate at the point of intersection: $3(300) - 500 = 400$. The y-coordinate at the point of intersection is the minimum possible value of b that the question is asking for, so enter **400**.

Alternatively, you could graph each inequality in the graphing calculator. Again, since the solution set will be above the lines, the minimum y-value will be at the intersection of the lines. Inspect the intersection to find that its y-value is **400**.

9. C
Difficulty: Medium
Category: Algebra
Getting to the Answer: You could plot the two lines on the graphing calculator and identify the solution set on a graph, checking to see if each ordered pair falls within it. However, testing the choices to see if they satisfy both inequalities may be a more efficient approach, particularly since one inequality is "less than" and the other is "less than or equal to." If you take this approach, you don't even need to rearrange the inequalities to isolate y on one side.

(A): Substituting these values for x and y in $x < 4 - 2y$ gives you $(-1) < 4 - 2(3)$, which is $-1 < -2$ (not a true statement). You don't need to evaluate the other inequality since this ordered pair is not in the solution set for $x < 4 - 2y$. Eliminate (A).

(B): Substituting these values for x and y in $x < 4 - 2y$ gives you $(1) < 4 - 2(1)$, or $1 < 2$. The ordered pair is in the solution set for this inequality, so plug the values into $y \leq -2x + 1$ to get $(1) \leq -2(1) + 1$, which

simplifies to $1 \leq -1$. Thus, this ordered pair is not in the solution set for the second inequality. Eliminate (B).

(C): Substituting these values for x and y in $x < 4 - 2y$ gives you $(2) < 4 - 2(-3)$, or $2 < 10$. The ordered pair is in the solution set for this inequality, so plug the values into $y \leq -2x + 1$ to get $(-3) \leq -2(2) + 1$, which simplifies to $-3 \leq -3$. Since the sign for this inequality is "less than or equal to," this ordered pair is in the solution set. **(C)** is correct.

(D): Since you already identified the correct choice, you do not need to check this pair, but, for the record, substituting these values for x and y in $x < 4 - 2y$ gives you $(4) < 4 - 2(4)$, or $4 < -4$. Since this is incorrect, this ordered pair is not in the solution set for the first inequality.

10. C
Difficulty: Hard
Category: Algebra
Getting to the Answer: Since the question states that $x = y = 1$ is a solution to the system, plug those values in to get $1 > 1 + r$ and $1 < s - 1$. These inequalities further simplify to $r < 0$ and $s > 2$. Check each pair of values in the answer choices to see which complies with these limitations. Only **(C)** has both $r < 0$ and $s > 2$, and is correct. (B) is incorrect because s must be greater than 2, and (D) reverses r and s.

11. C
Difficulty: Medium
Category: Algebra
Getting to the Answer: Translate each part of the word problem into its mathematical equivalent. Because x, y, and z represent the numbers of each of the three ad sizes, the total number of ads will be $x + y + z$. "No fewer than 15" ads means $x + y + z \geq 15$, so eliminate (A) and (B).

The total cost of the ads sold will be represented by the number of each size ad sold times the respective cost of each size ad. Thus, $110x + 70y + 50z$ represents the total cost of all of the ads; "at least \$1,500" means that $110x + 70y + 50z \geq 1,500$. Therefore, **(C)** is correct.

12. A
Difficulty: Medium
Category: Algebra
Getting to the Answer: Translate each part of the word problem into its mathematical equivalent. The total weight of produce will be represented by the combined

pounds of watermelons, w, cantaloupes, c, and tomatoes, t. This combined weight cannot exceed 250 pounds, so the inequality is $w + c + t \leq 250$. Eliminate (C) and (D).

The total money for the produce sold is represented by the price per pound of each type of produce times the number of pounds of that type. This must be "at least" (greater than or equal to) $200, so the inequality is $0.5w + 1c + 2.5t \geq 200$. **(A)** is correct.

13. D
Difficulty: Medium
Category: Algebra
Getting to the Answer: Translate each part of the word problem into its mathematical equivalent, beginning with the easiest-to-translate components. There needs to be at least 5 apple trees and at least 3 pear trees, so the correct inequalities are $x \geq 5$ and $y \geq 3$. Eliminate (B) and (C). The total number of apple and pear trees must be at least 15, so the correct inequality is $x + y \geq 15$. Eliminate (A). Only **(D)** is left and is correct.

Note that, by being strategic, you never even have to determine the first, most complicated inequality in each of the answer choices. For the record: apple trees cost $120 and pear trees cost $145, so the total amount spent on trees is $120x + 145y$. This total amount cannot go above $2,050, which means it must be less than or equal to $2,050. Therefore, $120x + 145y \leq 2,050$.

14. B
Difficulty: Medium
Category: Algebra
Getting to the Answer: First, define the relationship between the weight of each kind of container and the weight the shelf can hold. Since x is the number of 50-pound containers of paint and y is the number of 35-pound containers of varnish, the combined weight of the containers will be represented by $50x + 35y$. This needs to be no more than 1,450 pounds, so the inequality that represents this is $50x + 35y \leq 1,450$. Eliminate (A) and (C).

The question also states that the total number of containers the shelf can hold is no more than 32, so the combined number of containers of paint and containers of varnish must be no more than 32. This is represented by the inequality $x + y \leq 32$. Thus, **(B)** is correct.

15. C
Difficulty: Hard
Category: Algebra
Getting to the Answer: Begin by translating the weight of the combined bags of flour and sugar. The weight of each bag of flour times the number of bags of flour—plus the weight of each bag of sugar times the number of bags of sugar—will yield the total. Thus, $50f + 20s$ will describe the weight of all of the bags combined. Since the weight that the supplier can deliver is no more than 750 pounds, the inequality that describes this situation is $50f + 20s \leq 750$. Eliminate (A) and (D).

The question also specifies that the bakery needs to buy at least three times as many bags of sugar as bags of flour. In other words, the number of bags of sugar must be equal to or greater than three times the number of bags of flour. This is represented by $s \geq 3f$, which can be rewritten as $3f \leq s$. **(C)** is correct.

16. A
Difficulty: Hard
Category: Algebra
Strategic Advice: All the numbers in the answer choices are the same, so you don't actually have to calculate the cost of one carnation or one daisy. The answer choices have done that for you.
Getting to the Answer: Focus on the keywords that tell you the direction of the inequality signs. The florist had 500 flowers in stock, so that's ≤ 500. Eliminate (C) and (D). The florist earned "at least" $400, or ≥ 400. The correct answer is **(A)**.

17. C
Difficulty: Medium
Category: Algebra
Getting to the Answer: The intersection (overlap) of the two shaded regions under both lines is the solution to the system of inequalities. Check each point to see whether it lies in the region where the shading overlaps. (A), $(6, -1)$, is under the dashed line but not the solid line, so it is incorrect. (B), $(1, -1)$, is under the solid line but not the dashed line, so it is incorrect. (C), $(6, -3)$, is under the dashed line and lies on the solid line. Because the line is solid, the point *is* included in the solution region. Thus, **(C)** is correct. For the record, (D) is incorrect because $(0, -2)$ lies on the dashed line, which means it is not included in the solution set.

18. C

Difficulty: Easy
Category: Algebra
Getting to the Answer: The fact that Ezekiel has exactly $5.00 means that he can spend up to and including $5.00, so use the less than or equal symbol ($\leq$) for the limit on how much he can spend. Because (D) has an inequality with something greater than or equal to 5, it can be eliminated. The amount of money Ezekiel spends on each type of snack is the number of units of that snack times its price. So, $0.60c + 0.50g + 1.29n \leq 5.00$. **(C)** is correct.

19. C

Difficulty: Medium
Category: Algebra
Getting to the Answer: The clue "maximum" means the container can hold exactly that much or less, so use the less than or equal to symbol ($\leq$) throughout. The cargo container can hold a maximum of 50 microwaves, so the first inequality is $m \leq 50$. Eliminate (A). The container can hold a maximum of 15 refrigerators, so the second inequality is $r \leq 15$. The third inequality deals with the size of each appliance. The cargo container can hold m microwaves multiplied by the size of the microwave, which is 6 cubic feet; it can hold r refrigerators multiplied by the size of the refrigerator, which is 20 cubic feet; and it can hold a maximum of 300 cubic feet total. Put these together to write the final inequality: $6m + 20r \leq 300$, which is **(C)**.

20. 2

Difficulty: Hard
Category: Algebra
Getting to the Answer: If (a, b) is a solution to the system, then a is the x-coordinate of any point in the region where the shading overlaps, and b is the corresponding y-coordinate. When $a = 0$ (or $x = 0$), the maximum possible value for b lies just under the upper boundary line, $y < 2x + 3$. It looks like the y-coordinate is 3, but to be sure, substitute $x = 0$ into the equation and simplify. You can replace the inequality symbol with an equal sign to make it an equation because you are finding a point on the boundary line, not a range:

$$y = 2(0) + 3$$
$$y = 3$$

The point on the boundary line is $(0, 3)$. The boundary line is dashed (because the inequality is strictly less than), so $(0, 3)$ is *not* a solution to the system. This

means 2 is the greatest possible *integer* value for b when $a = 0$. Enter **2**.

21. D

Difficulty: Medium
Category: Algebra
Getting to the Answer: Isolate x in each of the given inequalities, then consider the results in combination. For $3x + 2 > 5$, subtract 2 from each side to get $3x > 3$, which means that $x > 1$. For $-2x + 8 > -10$, subtract 8 from each side to get $-2x > -18$. Divide each side by -2 (which means that you have to flip the inequality sign) to get $x < 9$. Taking the two inequalities together, x must be greater than 1 but less than 9. This can be expressed as $1 < x < 9$ or, alternatively, $9 > x > 1$. **(D)** is correct.

22. D

Difficulty: Medium
Category: Algebra
Strategic Advice: If the given inequalities are graphed in the xy-plane, the solution set is the portion of the plane on or above both lines. Thus, the minimum value of y will occur at the intersection of these lines, which is the point (a, b).
Getting to the Answer: The boundary lines of this system of inequalities are $y = -3x + 18$ and $y = 9x$. To find their intersection point, set them equal to each other to get $9x = -3x + 18$. So, $12x = 18$ and $x = 1\frac{1}{2}$. That represents a, but the question asks for the value of b. Substitute $1\frac{1}{2}$ for x in either equation, preferably the simpler one: use $y = 9x$ to get $y = 9\left(1\frac{1}{2}\right) = 13\frac{1}{2}$. Therefore, **(D)** is correct.

Alternatively, you could use the test's on-screen graphing calculator and graph both inequalities. You'll see the intersection point at (1.5, 13.5), which also leads to **(D)**.

23. A

Difficulty: Medium
Category: Algebra
Strategic Advice: Translating English into math, set up one inequality for Francine's number of sales calls and another for the dollar amount of sales in terms of her goal.
Getting to the Answer: Since Francine can make "up to" 15 sales calls per week and there are three categories of the results of her efforts, you can write the inequality $p + b + u \leq 15$. Eliminate (B). For the monetary goal, that is "more than" $20,000, so this inequality is $12,000p + 8,000b > 20,000$. Note that

the unsuccessful sales calls are not included in this inequality since they do not generate any revenue. **(A)** is correct.

24. B
Difficulty: Medium
Category: Algebra
Getting to the Answer: The amount Luis spends on each item is that item's price times the quantity he buys. The total amount must be less than or equal to $25. Thus, you can write the inequality $1.25p + 2.50n + 4.00m + 1(5.75) \leq 25.00$. Since the question asks for the number of markers, isolate m on one side of the inequality: $4m \leq 25 - 1.25p - 2.5n - 5.75$. Therefore, $m \leq \dfrac{19.25 - 1.25p - 2.5n}{4}$. **(B)** is correct.

25. 3
Difficulty: Hard
Category: Algebra
Strategic Advice: Isolate x in each of the two inequalities to determine a range for x.
Getting to the Answer: Expand the first inequality to get $3x - 3 + 5 > 11$, so $3x > 9$ and $x > 3$. Multiply the second inequality by -1 (remembering to flip the inequality sign), so that $5x - 18 \leq 12$. This simplifies to $x \leq 6$. Combine the two results: $3 < x \leq 6$. There are three allowable integer values for x: 4, 5, and 6. Enter **3**.

[CHAPTER 7]

LINEAR FUNCTIONS

LEARNING OBJECTIVES

After completing this chapter, you will be able to:

- Apply function notation
- Define the domain and range of a linear function
- Evaluate the output of a linear function for a given input
- Interpret the graph of a linear function
- Write a linear function to describe a rule or data set

HOW MUCH DO YOU KNOW?

Directions

Try the questions that follow. Show your work so that you can compare your solutions to the ones found in the "Check Your Work" section immediately after this question set. If you answered the question(s) on a specific topic correctly, and if your scratchwork looks like ours, you may be able to move quickly through the lesson covering that topic. If you answered incorrectly or used a different approach, you may want to take your time on that lesson.

1

$$p(x) = 7x + 4$$
$$s(x) = 7 - p(x)$$

What is the value of $s(-1)$?

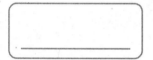

2

$$f(x) = 8x - 5$$
$$f(x + a) = 8x + 19$$

What is the value of a?

- (A) 1.75
- (B) 3
- (C) 14
- (D) 24

3

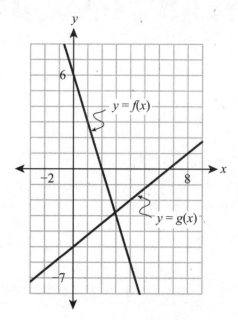

The figure shows the graphs of the linear functions f and g. What is the value of $2g(0) - f(4)$?

- (A) -16
- (B) -4
- (C) 10
- (D) 14

4

x	2	3	4	5
$f(x)$	7	13	19	25

Some values of the function f are shown in the table. Which of the following defines f?

(A) $f(x) = 7x - 1$

(B) $f(x) = 6x - 5$

(C) $f(x) = 5x + 1$

(D) $f(x) = 4x + 5$

5

Brianna is typing a 500-word essay and averages 45 words per minute. Which of the following correctly estimates the number of words, w, Brianna has left to type after typing for t minutes?

(A) $w(t) = -\dfrac{45}{t} + 500$

(B) $w(t) = \dfrac{45}{t} + 500$

(C) $w(t) = -45t + 500$

(D) $w(t) = 45t + 500$

Check Your Work

1.   10
Difficulty: Medium
Category: Algebra
Getting to the Answer: To evaluate a function at any value, substitute that value for the variable in the function definition. The question asks for the value of $s(-1)$, so replace the x in the s function with -1: $s(-1) = 7 - p(-1)$. To find the value of $p(-1)$, replace the x in the p function with -1: $p(-1) = 7(-1) + 4 = -3$. Replace $p(-1)$ with its value, -3, in the s function: $s(-1) = 7 - (-3) = 10$. Enter **10**.

2.   B
Difficulty: Hard
Category: Algebra
Getting to the Answer: Evaluate $f(x)$ when x is $x + a$ by replacing x with $x + a$: $f(x + a) = 8(x + a) - 5$. Then set this expression equal to $8x + 19$ and solve for a.

$$8(x + a) - 5 = 8x + 19$$
$$8x + 8a - 5 = 8x + 19$$
$$8a = 24$$
$$a = 3$$

(B) is correct.

3.   B
Difficulty: Medium
Category: Algebra
Getting to the Answer: To find the value of $2g(0)$, first, use the graph of g to find $g(0)$. The graph of g crosses the y-axis at -5, so $g(0) = -5$ and $2g(0) = -10$. Similarly, use the graph of f to find the value of $f(4)$. At $x = 4$, the graph of f has a y-value of -6, so $f(4) = -6$. Thus, the value of $2g(0) - f(4)$ is $-10 - (-6) = -10 + 6 = -4$.
(B) is correct.

4.   B
Difficulty: Easy
Category: Algebra
Getting to the Answer: Pick one of the given points to test the functions. Choose the point that is easiest for you to test. When $x = 2$, $y = 7$, so plug $x = 2$ into the choices and find the one that yields $y = 7$.

Test (A): $f(2) = 7(2) - 1 = 13$. Eliminate (A).

Test (B): $f(2) = 6(2) - 5 = 7$. Keep (B).

Test (C): $f(2) = 5(2) + 1 = 11$. Eliminate (C).

Test (D): $f(2) = 4(2) + 5 = 13$. Eliminate (D).

Only **(B)** remains, and it is correct.

Since all the choices have different slopes, an alternative approach would be to find the slope of the line by using two points.

Use the formula slope $= \frac{\text{rise}}{\text{run}}$ to get $\frac{13 - 7}{3 - 2} = 6$.
(B) is correct.

5.   C
Difficulty: Hard
Category: Algebra
Getting to the Answer: Note that the answer choices are in slope-intercept form. The y-intercept is 500 for each answer choice and represents the starting number of words Brianna has left to type. The slope is the rate at which Brianna types, which is 45 words per minute. Multiplying Brianna's rate by t gets you the number of words typed after t minutes, which can then be subtracted from the starting word count, 500, to get the number of words Brianna has left to type. The function should read $w(t) = -45t + 500$, which matches **(C)**.

FUNCTION NOTATION

LEARNING OBJECTIVES

After this lesson, you will be able to:

- Apply function notation
- Define the domain and range of a linear function
- Evaluate the output of a linear function for a given input

To answer a question like this:

$h(x) = 2x + 7$

Which of the following must be true about $h(x)$?

A) $h(3) = 15$

B) $h(14) = 35$

C) The domain of $h(x)$ consists only of integers.

D) $h(x)$ may only be positive.

You need to know this:

A **function** is a rule that generates one unique output for a given input. In function notation, the x-value is the input and the y-value, designated by $f(x)$, is the output. (Note that other letters besides x and f may be used.)

A linear function is a function that describes a line; as such, it is generally expressed in slope-intercept form with $f(x)$ equivalent to y:

$$f(x) = mx + b$$

In questions that describe real-life situations, the y-intercept will often be the starting point for the function. You can think of it as $f(0)$, or the value of the function where $x = 0$.

The set of all possible x-values is called the **domain** of the function, while the set of all possible y-values is called the **range**. For most linear functions, the range and domain consist of all real numbers, since lines are infinitely long. However, a constant function, such as $f(x) = 4$, produces a horizontal line, since every x-value produces the same y-value, and thus has a range consisting of just that one number.

You need to do this:

- To find $f(x)$ for some value of x, substitute the concrete value in for the variable and do the arithmetic.
- For questions that ask about a function of a function, for example, $g(f(x))$, start on the inside and work your way out.

Explanation:

Check each answer choice, plug in 3 for x:

$$h(3) = 2(3) + 7 = 6 + 7 = 13$$

This doesn't match. Eliminate choice (A).

Check answer choice (B), plug in 14 for x:

$$h(14) = 2(14) + 7 = 28 + 7 = 35$$

That is true, so choice **(B)** is correct.

On test day, you would select **(B)** and move on to the next question, but for the record: Since $h(x)$ is a linear function, any possible x-values, not just integers, will correspond with points along the line. Choice (C) is incorrect.

Choice (D) is also incorrect. Any non-horizontal line will cross the x-axis at some point, which means that it has both positive and negative y-values. The given equation for $h(x)$ is already in $y = mx + b$ form, so you can see that it has a positive slope. So, $h(x)$ can be either positive or negative.

Try on Your Own

Directions

Take as much time as you need on these questions. Work carefully and methodically. There will be an opportunity for timed practice later in the book.

1

HINT: For Q1, replace x in the function definition with $(x - 2)$.

If $g(x) = 7x - 3$, what is $g(x - 2)$?

Ⓐ $7x - 17$

Ⓑ $7x - 11$

Ⓒ $7x - 5$

Ⓓ $7x - 1$

2

If $k(x) = 5x + 2$, what is the value of $k(4) - k(1)$?

3

HINT: For Q3, work from the inside parentheses out.

x	$g(x)$
-6	-3
-3	-2
0	-1
3	0
6	1

x	$h(x)$
0	6
1	4
2	2
3	0
4	-2

Several values for the functions $g(x)$ and $h(x)$ are shown in the tables. What is the value of $g(h(3))$?

Ⓐ -1

Ⓑ 0

Ⓒ 3

Ⓓ 6

LINEAR FUNCTIONS

Math

4

If $p(x) = 2x + 8$ and $q(x) = x - 3$, what is the value of $\dfrac{q(p(5))}{p(q(5))}$?

Ⓐ 0

Ⓑ 0.8

Ⓒ 1

Ⓓ 1.25

5

n	$f(n)$	$g(n)$
2	11.6	1.5
3	13.9	1
4	16.2	0.5

The table shows some values of the linear functions f and g. If $h(n) = 2 \times f(n) - g(n)$, what is the value of $h(6)$?

Ⓐ 21.3

Ⓑ 35.0

Ⓒ 41.1

Ⓓ 42.1

GRAPHS OF LINEAR FUNCTIONS

LEARNING OBJECTIVE

After this lesson, you will be able to:

- Interpret the graph of a linear function

To answer a question like this:

x	$h(x)$
-2	-5
-1	-4
0	-3
1	-2
2	-1

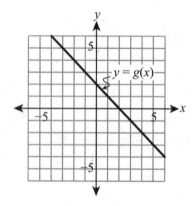

The graph shows $g(x) = mx + b$, where m and b are constants. Values for the function h are shown in the table. What is the value of $h(m)$?

A) -4

B) -2

C) 1

D) 2

You need to know this:

Interpreting graphs of linear functions uses the same skills as interpreting graphs of linear equations. For example:

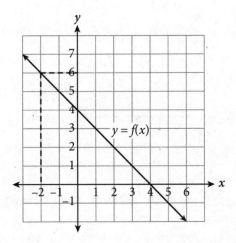

Say the graph above represents the function $f(x)$ and you're asked to find the value of x for which $f(x) = 6$. Because $f(x)$ represents the output value, or range, you can translate this to, "When does the y-value equal 6?" To answer the question, find 6 on the y-axis, then trace over to the function (the line). Read the corresponding x-value: it's -2, so when $f(x) = 6$, x must be -2.

You need to do this:

- Use the skills you learned for dealing with graphs of linear equations.
- Treat $f(x)$ as the y-coordinate on a graph.

Explanation:

The linear function $g(x)$ is given in slope-intercept form, so m represents the function's slope. You can determine the slope by visually inspecting the graph: for every unit the line moves to the right, it also goes down one, so $m = -1$. You could also plug two points from the graph of $g(x)$, such as $(1, 1)$ and $(0, 2)$ into the slope formula: $m = \dfrac{y_2 - y_1}{x_2 - x_1} = \dfrac{2 - 1}{0 - 1} = \dfrac{1}{-1} = -1$. Next, use the table to find $h(-1)$, which is the y-value of function h when $x = -1$. According to the table, when $x = -1$, $h(x) = -4$. **(A)** is correct.

Try on Your Own

Directions

Take as much time as you need on these questions. Work carefully and methodically. There will be an opportunity for timed practice later in the book.

6

HINT: For Q6, at the point where the graphs of *f* and *g* intersect, both graphs have exactly the same *x*- and *y*-values.

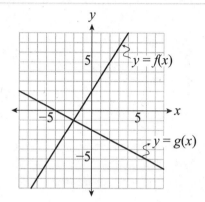

The graphs of functions *f* and *g* are shown in the figure. At what value of *x* does $f(x) - g(x) = 0$?

Ⓐ   −2

Ⓑ   −1

Ⓒ   0

Ⓓ   2

7

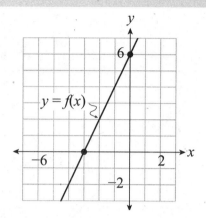

The graphs of linear functions *f* (shown) and *g* (not shown) are parallel. The graph of *g* passes through the point (1, 1). What is the value of *g*(0)?

Ⓐ   −3

Ⓑ   −1

Ⓒ   3

Ⓓ   6

8

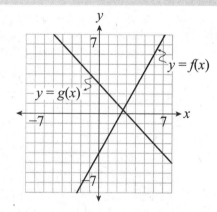

The graphs of the linear functions *f* and *g* are shown in the *xy*-plane. What is $f(6) - g(-3)$?

9

The graph of the linear function f has intercepts at $(c, 0)$ and $(0, d)$ in the xy-plane. If $2c = d$ and $d \neq 0$, which of the following is true about the slope of the graph of f?

(A) It is positive.

(B) It is negative.

(C) It equals zero.

(D) It is undefined.

10

HINT: For Q10, first determine $f(0)$.

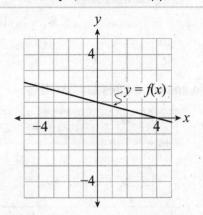

The graph of function f is shown in the xy-plane. The equation for function g (not shown) is $g(x) = 2f(x) - 9$. What is the value of $g(0)$?

(A) -9

(B) -7

(C) -1

(D) 1

DESCRIBING REAL-LIFE SITUATIONS WITH LINEAR FUNCTIONS

LEARNING OBJECTIVE

After this lesson, you will be able to:

- Write a linear function to describe a rule or data set

To answer a question like this:

COOKIE VARIETY	NUMBER OF COOKIES PER BOX	PRICE PER BOX (DOLLARS)
Walnut	22	1.26
Pecan	20	1.10
Butterscotch	24	1.42
Mint	18	0.94
Macadamia	12	0.46
Hazelnut	16	0.78

The number of cookies per box and the price per box for the different varieties of cookies sold by a cookie company are shown in the table. The relationship between the number of cookies per box and the price, in dollars, per box can be represented by which of the following linear functions?

A) $p(n) = 0.11n - 0.25$

B) $p(n) = 0.1n - 0.35$

C) $p(n) = 0.09n - 0.45$

D) $p(n) = 0.08n - 0.5$

You need to know this:

Modeling real-life situations using functions is the same as modeling them using equations; the only difference is the function notation and a function's rule that each input has only one output.

For example, suppose a homeowner wants to determine the cost of installing a certain amount of carpet in her living room. Say that the carpet costs $0.86 per square foot, the installer charges a $29 installation fee, and sales tax on the total cost is 7%. Using your algebra and function knowledge, you can describe this situation in which the cost, c, is a function of square footage, f. The equation would be $c = 1.07(0.86f + 29)$. In function notation, this becomes $c(f) = 1.07(0.86f + 29)$, where $c(f)$ is shorthand for "cost as a function of square footage." The following table summarizes what each piece of the function represents in the scenario.

ENGLISH	Overall cost	Square footage	Material cost	Installation fee	Sales tax
MATH	c	f	$0.86f$	29	1.07

You need to do this:

For word problems involving function notation, translate the math equations exactly as you learned in the Word Problems lesson in the Linear Equations and Graphs chapter, but substitute $f(x)$ for y.

Explanation:

Note that the question asks for the relationship between the number of cookies per box and the price per box and that the answer choices all start with $p(n)$. Given the context, this translates to the relationship "price as a function of the number of cookies." All the choices express a linear relationship, so you can't rule out any of them on that basis.

There are several approaches you could take to find the correct answer. One would be to recognize that all the choices are in the form $p(n) = mn + b$ (a variation of the slope-intercept form $y = mx + b$) and that you can set up a system of linear equations using the data from any two rows, such as "walnut" ($p(n) = 1.26$ and $n = 22$) and "pecan" ($p(n) = 1.10$ and $n = 20$), to solve for m and b. That approach would look like this:

$$1.26 = 22m + b$$
$$\underline{- (1.10 = 20m + b)}$$
$$0.16 = 2m$$
$$0.08 = m$$

$$1.10 = 20(0.08) + b$$
$$1.10 = 1.60 + b$$
$$b = -0.5$$

Because $m = 0.08$ and $b = -0.5$, the correct function is $p(n) = 0.08n - 0.5$, so **(D)** is correct.

Another approach would be to use two of the pairs of data points from the table to calculate a slope; for example, using the "walnut" and "pecan" rows would yield $\frac{1.26 - 1.10}{22 - 20} = \frac{0.16}{2} = 0.08$. Because only one answer has a slope of 0.08, you can pick **(D)**.

Finally, you could pick numbers from the table. Plug any one of the rows of data, such as "pecan," from the table into all four answer choices to check which equation will produce a price of $1.10 per box given 20 cookies per box:

A) $0.11(20) - 0.25 = 1.95 \neq 1.10$

B) $0.1(20) - 0.35 = 1.65 \neq 1.10$

C) $0.09(20) - 0.45 = 1.35 \neq 1.10$

D) $0.08(20) - 0.5 = 1.10$

Choice **(D)** is confirmed as the only one that works. It is correct.

Try on Your Own

Directions

Take as much time as you need on these questions. Work carefully and methodically. There will be an opportunity for timed practice later in the book.

11

HINT: For Q11, pick the easiest number of days from the chart, plug that into the choices, and eliminate any that don't give you the correct vote count. Repeat if necessary until only one choice is left.

Day	Vote count
3	21
4	28
5	35
6	42
7	49

Paulo is running for class president. He recorded his vote count for each day. Data for five days are shown in the table. Which of the following represents Paulo's vote count, v, as a function of time, t, in days?

Ⓐ $v(t) = \dfrac{t}{7}$

Ⓑ $v(t) = \dfrac{t}{7} + 21$

Ⓒ $v(t) = 7t$

Ⓓ $v(t) = 7t + 21$

12

HINT: For Q12, the faster the rate of change, the steeper the slope.

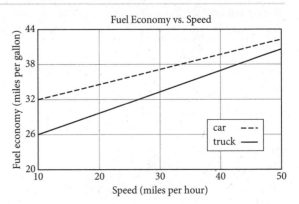

The graph shows a car's and a truck's fuel economy as a function of speed. Which of the following is true?

Ⓐ The rate of increase in fuel economy of the car is greater than the rate of increase in fuel economy of the truck.

Ⓑ The rate of increase in fuel economy of the car is equal to the rate of increase in fuel economy of the truck.

Ⓒ The rate of increase in fuel economy of the car is less than the rate of increase in fuel economy of the truck.

Ⓓ Nothing can be said about the rates of change in fuel economy.

13

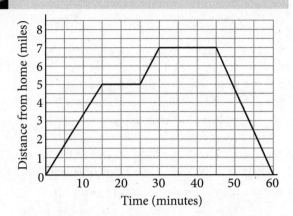

The graph shows Carmel's distance from home over a one-hour period, during which time she first went to the library, then went to the grocery store, and then returned home. Which of the following statements must be true?

Ⓐ   The grocery store is 5 miles from Carmel's house.

Ⓑ   Carmel traveled a total of 7 miles from the time she left home until she returned.

Ⓒ   The grocery store is 7 miles farther from Carmel's house than the library is.

Ⓓ   Carmel spent 10 minutes at the library and 15 minutes at the grocery store.

14

HINT: For Q14, which two readings will be easiest to use to find the number of visitors admitted every 15 minutes?

Time	Total number of visitors for the day
10:10 a.m.	140
12:30 p.m.	420
2:00 p.m.	600
2:50 p.m.	700

The gates at a museum allow a constant number of visitors to enter every 15 minutes. The cumulative number of visitors at various times are shown in the table. The museum does not admit any visitors after 4:45 p.m. What is the projected total number of visitors for the day, assuming that the same number of visitors are granted entrance each 15-minute period throughout the day?

ON TEST DAY

The SAT tests the modeling of real-life situations. Get comfortable with function notation in these questions. Remember that you can write the equation of a line as $y = mx + b$ or as $f(x) = mx + b$, where m is the slope and b is the y-intercept. Recall that the slope indicates the rate of change. Often, in questions asking about real-life situations, the x variable indicates time. In that case, the y-intercept (that is, the value of the function at $x = 0$, or $f(0)$) indicates the starting point.

15. An environmental agency plans to increase its recycling capacity at a constant rate to eliminate 6.2 million pounds of plastic waste by the end of eight years. Which of the following linear functions, f, models the amount of remaining plastic waste (in millions of pounds) t years into the program?

    A) $f(t) = -\dfrac{62}{40}t + 6.2$

    B) $f(t) = -\dfrac{31}{40}t + 6.2$

    C) $f(t) = \dfrac{31}{40}t + 6.2$

    D) $f(t) = \dfrac{62}{40}t + 6.2$

The correct answer and explanation can be found at the end of the chapter.

HOW MUCH HAVE YOU LEARNED?

Directions

For testlike practice, give yourself 13 minutes to complete this question set. Be sure to study the explanations, even for questions you answered correctly. They can be found at the end of this chapter.

16

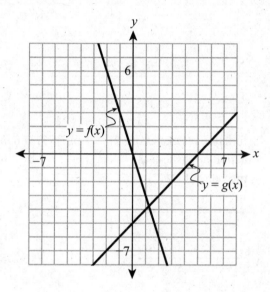

Based on the figure, what is the value of $f(-2) + g(2)$?

Ⓐ -3

Ⓑ 0

Ⓒ 3

Ⓓ 6

17

A company uses the function $P(x) = 150x - x^2$ to determine how much profit the company will make when it sells 150 units of a certain product that sells for x dollars per unit. How much more profit per unit, in dollars, will the company make if it charges \$25 for the product than if it charges \$20?

18

The function $C(t) = 12t + 5$ approximates the number of calls received by a call center after t hours. Based on this function, how many calls can be expected by the end of one 10-hour day?

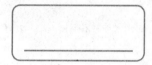

19

A biologist uses the function $n(p)$ to represent the number of seeds that germinate, where p represents the number of seeds planted. Which of the following lists could represent a portion of the domain for the biologist's function?

Ⓐ $\{ \ldots -150, -100, -50, 0, 50, 100, 150 \ldots \}$

Ⓑ $\{ -150, -100, -50, 0, 50, 100, 150 \}$

Ⓒ $\{ 0, 0.25, 0.5, 0.75, 1, 1.25, 1.5 \ldots \}$

Ⓓ $\{ 0, 20, 40, 60, 80 \ldots \}$

20

$$g(x) = -3x - 5$$

What is the value of $g(-4x)$?

Ⓐ 7

Ⓑ $-12x - 5$

Ⓒ $12x - 5$

Ⓓ $12x^2 - 20x$

21

$$r(x) = 3x - 7$$
$$t(x) = 3x + r(x)$$

What is the value of $t(2)$?

Ⓐ -3

Ⓑ -1

Ⓒ 0

Ⓓ 5

22

$$f(x) = ax + 5$$

If a is a constant and $f(3) = -4$, what is the value of $f(2)$?

Ⓐ -3

Ⓑ -1

Ⓒ 1

Ⓓ 3

23

A function a satisfies $a(-2) = 3$ and $a(3) = 8$. A function b satisfies $b(3) = 4$ and $b(7) = -2$. What is the value of $a(b(7))$?

REFLECT

Directions: Take a few minutes to recall what you've learned and what you've been practicing in this chapter. Consider the following questions, jot down your best answer for each one, and then compare your reflections to the expert responses that follow. Use your level of confidence to determine what to do next.

What are the domain and range of a function?

_____

_____

_____

What is another way to write the function $f(x) = x + 4$?

_____

_____

_____

In a function, what does x represent? What does $f(x)$ represent?

_____

_____

_____

What will the function $f(x) = x + 4$ look like when graphed?

_____

_____

_____

In a function whose x-value represents time, what does the y-intercept represent?

_____

_____

_____

Expert Responses

What are the domain and range of a function?

The domain of a function indicates the possible x-values and the range of a function indicates the possible y-values. In a linear function, the domain is all real numbers, and, for non-horizontal lines, the range is all real numbers.

What is another way to write the function $f(x) = x + 4$?

When you graph the function on the xy-coordinate plane, you can replace f(x) with y. This function is equivalent to y = x + 4.

In a function, what does x represent? What does $f(x)$ represent?

In a function, x is the input and f(x) is the output.

What will the function $f(x) = x + 4$ look like when graphed?

The slope of the line is 1 and its y-intercept is 4, so it will move from the lower left to the upper right and cross the y-axis at y = 4.

In a function whose *x*-value represents time, what does the *y*-intercept represent?

The y*-intercept represents the initial quantity when* t = 0. *Say a function represents the progress of a machine manufacturing widgets at a rate of 6 widgets per hour. The machine adds the widgets it makes to a growing pile that consisted of 12 widgets when the machine started working. If this function were graphed as a function of time, the y-intercept would be 12—the pile of 12 widgets that were there when the machine started its task.*

Next Steps

If you answered most questions correctly in the "How Much Have You Learned?" section, and if your responses to the Reflect questions were similar to those of the SAT expert, then consider functions an area of strength and move on to the next chapter. Come back to this topic periodically to prevent yourself from getting rusty.

If you don't yet feel confident, review those parts of this chapter that you have not yet mastered. Then try the questions you missed again. As always, be sure to review the explanations closely. Finally, **go online** (www.kaptest.com/moreonline) for additional practice.

Check Your Work – Chapter 7

1.   A
Difficulty: Medium
Category: Algebra
Getting to the Answer: The notation $g(x-2)$ asks for the value of $g(x)$ when x is $x-2$, so substitute $x-2$ for x and simplify. Don't forget to use the correct order of operations as you work.

$$\begin{aligned} g(x-2) &= 7(x-2) - 3 \\ &= 7x - 14 - 3 \\ &= 7x - 17 \end{aligned}$$

Choice **(A)** is correct.

2.   15
Difficulty: Easy
Category: Algebra
Getting to the Answer: The notation $k(4)$ is the output value of the function k when 4 is substituted for the input x. Similarly, $k(1)$ is the output value of the function k when 1 is substituted for the input x. Substitute 4 and 1 into the function, one at a time, and then subtract the results.

$$\begin{aligned} k(4) &= 5(4) + 2 = 20 + 2 = 22 \\ k(1) &= 5(1) + 2 = 5 + 2 = 7 \\ k(4) - k(1) &= 22 - 7 = 15 \end{aligned}$$

Enter **15**.

3.   A
Difficulty: Medium
Category: Algebra
Getting to the Answer: The notation $g(h(x))$ is read "g of h of x." It means that the output of $h(x)$ becomes the input of $g(x)$. First, use the table on the right to find the value of $h(x)$ when x is 3. At $x = 3$, $h(3) = 0$. This is your new input. Now, use the table on the left to find $g(0)$, which is -1, making **(A)** the correct answer.

4.   D
Difficulty: Medium
Category: Algebra
Getting to the Answer: Evaluate the numerator and denominator separately. Start with the innermost parentheses and work your way out.

$$\begin{aligned} p(5) &= 2(5) + 8 = 18 \\ q(p(5)) &= q(18) = 18 - 3 = 15 \\ q(5) &= 5 - 3 = 2 \\ p(q(5)) &= p(2) = 2(2) + 8 = 12 \end{aligned}$$

Combine to get $\dfrac{q(p(5))}{p(q(5))} = \dfrac{15}{12} = \dfrac{5}{4} = 1.25$. The correct answer is **(D)**.

5.   D
Difficulty: Hard
Category: Algebra
Getting to the Answer: Determine the linear change of the functions relative to the change in n, and then extrapolate to get the values of $f(6)$ and $g(6)$. You don't need to determine the algebraic expressions for the functions. As a shortcut, find the changes per a 2-unit increase of n and apply that to the values of the functions when $n = 4$. For $f(n)$, the increase from $n = 2$ to $n = 4$ is $16.2 - 11.6 = 4.6$. Thus, the value of $f(6)$ is $f(4) + 4.6 = 16.2 + 4.6 = 20.8$. The change in $g(n)$ from $n = 2$ to $n = 4$ is $0.5 - 1.5 = -1$. So the value of $g(6)$ is $g(4) + (-1) = 0.5 - 1 = -0.5$. Now, calculate $h(6)$: $h(6) = 2 \times f(6) - g(6) = 2(20.8) - (-0.5) = 41.6 + 0.5 = 42.1$. Choice **(D)** is correct.

6.   A
Difficulty: Easy
Category: Algebra
Getting to the Answer: Rewrite $f(x) - g(x) = 0$ as $f(x) = g(x)$. You're looking for the x-value that gives the same y-value in each function; that is, the point where the functions f and g intersect. According to the graph, the functions intersect at $(-2, -1)$, so the value of x for which $f(x) - g(x) = 0$ is -2. **(A)** is correct.

7.   B
Difficulty: Hard
Category: Algebra
Getting to the Answer: Parallel lines have the same slope. First, determine the slope of linear function f from the graph. Function f passes through the points $(-3, 0)$ and $(0, 6)$. Thus, the slope is $\dfrac{y_2 - y_1}{x_2 - x_1} = \dfrac{6 - 0}{0 - (-3)} = \dfrac{6}{3} = 2$. Now use the slope-intercept form, $y = mx + b$, to determine b, the y-intercept, which is the y-value when x is 0 or $g(0)$. Plugging in $(1, 1)$ for (x, y) and 2 for m gives $1 = 2(1) + b$, and $b = -1$. **(B)** is correct.

8.   0
Difficulty: Medium
Category: Algebra
Getting to the Answer: According to the graph, when $x = 6$, the y-value of the graph of f is 6, so $f(6) = 6$. When

$x = -3$, the y-value of the graph of g is 6, so $g(-3) = 6$. Thus, $f(6) - g(-3) = 6 - 6 = 0$. Enter **0**.

9. B
Difficulty: Medium
Category: Algebra
Strategic Advice: Quickly sketching the different possibilities can be helpful.
Getting to the Answer: Because $2c = d$, both the x-intercept, c, and the y-intercept, d, must have the same sign. If both are positive, then d would be greater than c, and the graph of f would look something like this:

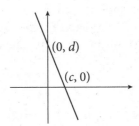

This is all you need to answer the question. According to the choices, the slope is always the same regardless of the sign of c and d. In other words, if the slope is negative at one point, then it must be negative all the time. Therefore, **(B)** is correct. On test day, you would move on to the next question without needing to check what the line looks like when c and d are negative. For the record, if c and d are negative, then d will be less than c, and the graph would look like this:

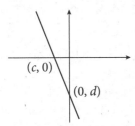

If you're curious to see the algebra, plug $(0, d)$ and $(c, 0)$ into the slope formula:

$$m = \frac{y_2 - y_1}{x_2 - x_1} = \frac{d - 0}{0 - c} = -\frac{d}{c}$$

The question states that $d = 2c$, so sub in $2c$ for d:

$$-\frac{d}{c} = -\frac{(2c)}{c} = -2$$

Therefore, the slope is -2, and the answer is indeed **(B)**.

10. B
Difficulty: Medium
Category: Algebra
Getting to the Answer: Since $g(x) = 2f(x) - 9$, when $x = 0$, $g(0) = 2f(0) - 9$. Begin by using the graph of f to find $f(0)$. At $x = 0$, $f(x) = 1$. Then substitute 1 for $f(0)$ into $g(0) = 2f(0) - 9$ to solve for $g(0)$. This gives $g(0) = 2(1) - 9 = -7$. **(B)** is correct.

11. C
Difficulty: Medium
Category: Algebra
Getting to the Answer: Thinking about the y-intercept (the starting amount) for the function will reduce the amount of work you need to do. The table indicates that Paulo had 21 votes on day 3, when $t = 3$, not at the start, when $t = 0$. This means that (B) and (D) are incorrect. To evaluate the remaining answer choices, pick a point and try it in a function. If it works, then you've found the correct answer. If it doesn't work, then you can confidently select the other answer choice. The result of checking the point $(4, 28)$ is as shown.

$$(A): 28 \neq \frac{4}{7}$$

Choice (A) is incorrect, so **(C)** must be correct. On test day, you would stop here. For the record, here is the reason why **(C)** is correct.

$$(C): 28 = 7(4)$$

12. C
Difficulty: Medium
Category: Algebra
Getting to the Answer: The words "rate of increase" (more generally, "rate of change") mean slope. Examine the graph and look for trends in the slope of the two lines. The line representing the truck has a significantly steeper slope than the line representing the car. Choice **(C)** is correct.

13. D
Difficulty: Medium
Category: Algebra
Getting to the Answer: Compare each answer choice to the graph, eliminating false statements as you go.

(A): Carmel went to the library first, so the library (not the grocery store) is 5 miles from her home. Eliminate (A).

(B): Carmel traveled 7 miles away from her home (between $t = 0$ minutes and $t = 30$ minutes), but then also traveled 7 miles back (between $t = 45$ minutes and $t = 60$ minutes), so she traveled a total of 14 miles. Eliminate (B).

(C): When Carmel reached the library, she was 5 miles from home; when she reached the grocery store, she was 7 miles from home. This means the grocery store must be $7 - 5 = 2$ miles farther away. Eliminate (C).

(D) must be correct. Carmel is the same distance from home (5 miles) between $t = 15$ minutes and $t = 25$ minutes, so she spent 10 minutes at the library. She is stopped once again (at the grocery store) between $t = 30$ minutes and $t = 45$ minutes, so she spent 15 minutes at the grocery store.

14. 930
Difficulty: Hard
Category: Algebra
Strategic Advice: The fact that the number of visitors each 15 minutes is constant means that the cumulative number of visitors is a linear function.
Getting to the Answer: Because the time between the numbers of cumulative visitors in the table varies, pick an interval that is easy to work with to determine the number of visitors who enter every 15 minutes. Next, use that value to find how many entered by 4:45 p.m. There are six 15-minute periods between 12:30 p.m. and 2:00 p.m. The number of visitors admitted during that time was $600 - 420 = 180$. So, $\frac{180}{6} = 30$ visitors enter every 15 minutes.

In order to project the cumulative, or total, number of visitors for a specific time, set up a function, $f(v)$. Pick a time that is convenient, such as 2:00 p.m. Since you know that there were 600 visitors by 2:00 p.m. you can write $f(v) = 600 + 30v$, where v is the number of 15-minute periods after 2:00 p.m. The question asks for the cumulative visitors admitted by 4:45 p.m. Thus, v is the number of 15-minute periods between 2:00 and 4:45, which is 11. So, $f(11) = 600 + 30(11) = 930$. Enter **930**.

15. B
Difficulty: Medium
Category: Algebra
Strategic Advice: When modeling a real-life situation with a linear function, the starting point in the description is the y-intercept of the equation and the rate of change is the slope. Eliminate choices as you go; you may find that you are able to answer the question after only one or two steps. Never do more math than necessary to answer the question.
Getting to the Answer: In this question, the agency is reducing the amount of plastic waste, so the slope must be negative. Eliminate (C) and (D) because their positive slopes indicate an *increasing* function.

The starting point, or y-intercept, is the amount of plastic waste the agency plans to eliminate, or 6.2 million pounds. Unfortunately, this value is the same in (A) and (B), so you will need to determine the slope: the amount of plastic waste eliminated per year. Since the agency wants to eliminate 6.2 million pounds of plastic waste in 8 years, the amount of plastic eliminated per year is 6.2 divided by 8.

Although $-\frac{6.2}{8}$ does not appear in the choices, the value is between 0 and -1, so **(B)** is correct. You can confirm $-\frac{6.2}{8} = -\frac{31}{40}$ by using your calculator to convert the fractions to decimals: $-\frac{6.2}{8} = -0.775$ and $-\frac{31}{40} = -0.775$.

Alternatively, since the amount of plastic waste at the end of 8 years is 0, that is, $f(8) = 0$, you could plug $(8, 0)$ into (A) and (B) to determine which equation is correct.

(A) $f(8) = -\frac{62}{40}(8) + 6.2 \neq 0$, eliminate.

Thus, **(B)** is correct.

16. C
Difficulty: Medium
Category: Algebra
Getting to the Answer: Graphically, the notation $f(-2)$ means the y-value when x is -2. Pay careful attention to which graph is which. Find $x = -2$ along the horizontal axis and trace up to the graph of $f(x)$. Then trace down the graph to find $g(2)$.

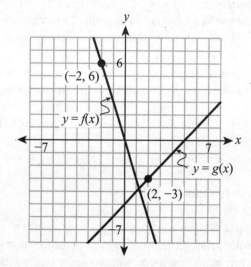

Now, read the y-coordinates from the graph and add them together: $f(-2)$ is 6 and $g(2)$ is -3, so $f(-2) + g(2) = 6 + (-3) = 3$, which is **(C)**.

17. 3.5 or 3.50
Difficulty: Hard
Category: Algebra
Getting to the Answer: Start by evaluating the function at $x = 25$ and at $x = 20$. Make sure you follow the correct order of operations as you simplify:

$$P(25) = 150(25) - (25)^2$$
$$= 3{,}750 - 625$$
$$= 3{,}125$$
$$P(20) = 150(20) - (20)^2$$
$$= 3{,}000 - 400$$
$$= 2{,}600$$

The question asks how much more profit *per unit* the company makes, so find the difference in the amounts of profit and divide by the number of units (150) to get $\frac{3{,}125 - 2{,}600}{150} = \frac{525}{150} = 3.50$. Enter **3.5**.

18. 125
Difficulty: Easy
Category: Algebra
Getting to the Answer: Evaluate the function at $t = 10$.

$$C(10) = 12(10) + 5$$
$$= 120 + 5$$
$$= 125$$

Enter **125**.

19. D
Difficulty: Easy
Category: Algebra
Getting to the Answer: The domain of a function includes every possible input value, which is usually represented by x. In this function, instead of x, the input is represented by p, which is the number of seeds planted. Because there cannot be a negative number of seeds planted or a fraction of a seed planted, the list in **(D)** is the only one that could represent a portion of the function's domain.

20. C
Difficulty: Medium
Category: Algebra
Getting to the Answer: To evaluate a function at a particular value, replace the variable in the function with the value. In this question, replace x in the function definition with $-4x$ to get $g(-4x) = -3(-4x) - 5 = 12x - 5$. **(C)** is correct.

Note that you can replace one variable with another. In this question, $-4x$ replaces x. If you chose (A), you likely replaced x in the function definition with -4. If you chose (B), you may have "lost" a negative sign. Finally, (D) results if you multiply each term in the definition by $-4x$ instead of replacing x with $-4x$.

21. D
Difficulty: Medium
Category: Algebra
Getting to the Answer: To evaluate the value of a function, replace the variable in the definition with the given value. Since the question asks for $t(2)$, and the definition of the t function includes the r function, evaluate $r(2)$ first, then use that result to evaluate $t(2)$:

$$r(2) = 3(2) - 7 = 6 - 7 = -1$$

Because $t(2) = 3(2) + r(2) = 6 - 1 = 5$, **(D)** is correct.

22. B
Difficulty: Medium
Category: Algebra
Getting to the Answer: Use the given statement $f(3) = -4$ to solve for a in $f(x)$. Then use this value of a to find $f(2)$.

To evaluate a function for a particular value, substitute the value for the variable in the function. In this case, substitute 3 for x and then use the given value for $f(3)$ to solve for the value of a.

$$f(3) = 3a + 5$$
$$-4 = 3a + 5$$
$$-9 = 3a$$
$$-3 = a$$

Since $a = -3$, the function becomes $f(x) = -3x + 5$. Now find $f(2)$:

$$f(2) = -3(2) + 5$$
$$= -6 + 5$$
$$= -1$$

(B) is correct.

23. 3
Difficulty: Medium
Category: Algebra
Getting to the Answer: To evaluate a composite function (a set of nested functions), start with the innermost function and work outward. For this question, begin by evaluating $b(7)$. Because $b(7) = -2$, you know that $a(b(7)) = a(-2)$, so next, evaluate $a(-2)$. The question states that $a(-2) = 3$. Enter **3**.

HOW MUCH HAVE YOU LEARNED: ALGEBRA

Directions

This "How Much Have You Learned" section will allow you to measure your growth and confidence in Algebra skills.

For testlike practice, give yourself 15 minutes for this question set. Be sure to use the Method for SAT Math Questions. When you're done, check your answers and read through the explanations, even for the questions you got correct. Don't forget to celebrate your progress!

1

A warehouse club usually sells carrots for $0.50 per pound. On Saturdays, it sells carrots at a 10 percent discount. The club also sells bags of oranges for $7.25 each. Which of the following represents the total cost, c, if a customer buys 3 bags of oranges and a pounds of carrots on a Saturday?

- (A) $c = 0.45a + 7.25$
- (B) $c = 0.45a + 21.75$
- (C) $c = 0.50a + 7.25$
- (D) $c = 0.50a + 21.75$

2

$$\frac{x}{4} + \frac{y}{3} = 5$$

$$2x + \frac{4}{5}y = 5$$

What is the value of x?

3

x	$f(x)$
-4	5
0	13
2	17

The table shows some values of the linear function f. What is the value of $f(9.5)$?

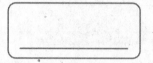

4

Which value of x makes the equation $\frac{4}{9}(x - 8) = 2$ true?

- (A) 9
- (B) 11.5
- (C) 12.5
- (D) 18

5

x	y
-6	-5
0	7
2	?
6	19

If the values in the table represent a linear relationship, what is the missing value?

- (A) 2
- (B) 7
- (C) 9
- (D) 11

PART 2A
ALGEBRA

Math

6

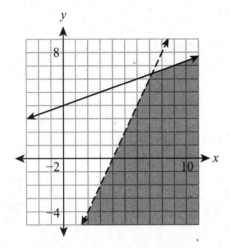

The shaded region on the graph shows the solution for a system of inequalities. Which of the following is the system of inequalities depicted on the graph?

(A) $2x - y < -12$ and $3y - x > 8$

(B) $2x - y > 8$ and $3y - x \leq 12$

(C) $2x + y < 12$ and $3y - x > 8$

(D) $2x + y > -8$ and $3y - x \leq 12$

7

$$5y < 2x - 22$$
$$x > 2x + 4$$

Which of the following describes the values of y that satisfy the system of inequalities?

(A) $y < -6$

(B) $y < -4$

(C) $-6 < y < -4$

(D) $y > 6$

8

$$\frac{2}{7}x - 6 = 3ay$$
$$2x - 14y = 42$$

If the system of equations shown has infinitely many solutions, what is the value of a?

(A) $-\frac{3}{2}$

(B) $-\frac{2}{3}$

(C) $\frac{2}{3}$

(D) $\frac{3}{2}$

9

$$-2y = 3x + 1$$
$$4x = -3y + 8$$

What is the value of $8x + 8y$?

(A) 9

(B) 17

(C) 72

(D) 80

10

$$f(x) = \frac{x}{3} - 1$$
$$g(x) = 2x + 5$$

What is the value of $f(g(8))$?

Check Your Work – How Much Have You Learned: Algebra

1. B
Difficulty: Easy
Category: Algebra
Getting to the Answer: To find the cost of carrots on Saturday, multiply their weight a by the sale price. If there is a 10% discount, then the customer actually pays $100\% - 10\% = 90\%$. Therefore, a pounds of carrots cost $0.50 \times 90\% \times a = 0.50 \times 0.90 \times a = 0.45a$. Now, add the cost of three bags of oranges, $7.25 \times 3 = 21.75$, to get the total cost: $c = 0.45a + 21.75$. Choice **(B)** is correct.

2. −5
Difficulty: Medium
Category: Algebra
Getting to the Answer: The first equation contains fractions, which are difficult to work with. Clear the fractions by multiplying both sides of the equation by 12, the least common denominator:

$$12\left(\frac{x}{4} + \frac{y}{3} = 5\right) \rightarrow 3x + 4y = 60$$

Using similar logic, multiply both sides of the second equation by 5:

$$5\left(2x + \frac{4}{5}y = 5\right) \rightarrow 10x + 4y = 25$$

The question asks for the value of x. You can eliminate the y terms by subtracting the second equation from the first:

$$
\begin{array}{r}
3x + 4y = 60 \\
-(10x + 4y = 25) \\
\hline
-7x = 35 \\
x = -5
\end{array}
$$

Enter **−5**.

3. 32
Difficulty: Hard
Category: Algebra
Getting to the Answer: Linear functions have a constant rate of change, or slope. Examining the bottom two rows of the table, you see that as x is increased by 2 units, $f(x)$ is increased by 4 units. Therefore, the slope is $\frac{4}{2} = 2$. The table also supplies the point $(0, 13)$, which means that the y-intercept is 13. Therefore, the equation of this linear function is $f(x) = 2x + 13$. The question asks for $f(9.5)$, so plug in 9.5 for x and simplify: $f(9.5) = 2(9.5) + 13 = 19 + 13 = 32$. Enter **32**.

4. C
Difficulty: Easy
Category: Algebra
Getting to the Answer: Distributing the $\frac{4}{9}$ would create more messy fractions. To avoid this, multiply both sides of the equation by 9:

$$9\left[\frac{4}{9}(x - 8) = 2\right]$$
$$4(x - 8) = 18$$
$$4x - 32 = 18$$
$$4x = 50$$
$$x = 12.5$$

Choice **(C)** is correct. Backsolving is another viable approach. When backsolving, start with either (B) or (C). Try plugging in $x = 11.5$:

$$\frac{4}{9}(x - 8) = 2$$
$$\frac{4}{9}(11.5 - 8) = 2$$
$$\frac{4}{9}(3.5) = 2$$
$$\frac{14}{9} = 2$$

This does not result in a true statement, so (B) is incorrect. Since the left-hand side is smaller than the right-hand side, move up to (C):

$$\frac{4}{9}(x - 8) = 2$$
$$\frac{4}{9}(12.5 - 8) = 2$$
$$\frac{4}{9}(4.5) = 2$$
$$2 = 2$$

This is a true statement, so **(C)** is correct.

5. D
Difficulty: Medium
Category: Algebra
Getting to the Answer: A linear relationship can be modeled by $y = mx + b$. Begin by choosing any two points from the table and substituting them into the slope formula. Using the points $(0, 7)$ and $(-6, -5)$, the slope is $\frac{y_2 - y_1}{x_2 - x_1} = \frac{-5 - 7}{-6 - 0} = \frac{-12}{-6} = 2$. The point $(0, 7)$ indicates that 7 is the y-intercept. Plugging these values in for m and b in the $y = mx + b$ equation yields $y = 2x + 7$. Finally, substitute in $x = 2$ to find the missing value of y. This yields $y = 2(2) + 7 = 4 + 7 = 11$. Choice **(D)** is correct.

6. B
Difficulty: Hard
Category: Algebra
Getting to the Answer: Use known points from the graph to determine the equations for the two lines. Then convert them into inequalities.

The solid line passes through the points (9, 7) and (0, 4). Its slope is therefore $\frac{y_2 - y_1}{x_2 - x_1} = \frac{4 - 7}{0 - 9} = \frac{-3}{-9} = \frac{1}{3}$. The graph shows that the y-intercept is 4, so the equation for the solid line is $y = \frac{1}{3}x + 4$. Multiply both sides by 3 to clear the fraction: $3y = x + 12$. This can be restated as $3y - x = 12$. Because the shaded region is below this line and the line is solid, the inequality defined by the line is $3y - x \leq 12$. Eliminate (A) and (C).

The dotted line passes through the points (4, 0) and (7, 6). Thus, the slope of this line is $\frac{6 - 0}{7 - 4} = \frac{6}{3} = 2$. The y-intercept is unclear from the graph, so plug the x-intercept (4, 0) into $y = 2x + b$ to get $0 = 2(4) + b$. Thus, $b = -8$. The equation for this line is therefore $y = 2x - 8$. Since the line is dotted and the values of the solution are below the line, the inequality is $y < 2x - 8$. This converts to $2x - y > 8$. These two inequalities match the ones in **(B)**.

7. A
Difficulty: Medium
Category: Algebra
Getting to the Answer: Solve the second inequality for x and substitute this result into the first inequality. If $x > 2x + 4$, then $-x > 4$. This simplifies to $x < -4$ (remember that you must flip the inequality if you multiply or divide by a negative number). Plugging into the first inequality gives $5y < 2(-4) - 22$, or $5y < -30$. This means that $y < -6$. Choice **(A)** is correct.

8. C
Difficulty: Hard
Category: Algebra
Getting to the Answer: Graphically, a "solution" to a system of equations is where the two lines touch each other. For a system of equations to have infinitely many solutions, they must touch each other in an infinite number of places. This means that the two lines must be on top of each other. In other words, the two lines are identical and have the same slope and y-intercept. Although you could rearrange each equation into $y = mx + b$ form, it is easier to get both equations into the same format and simply compare each part of the equations piece by piece.

Since the first equation contains fractions and the second does not, multiply the first equation by 7 to clear the fractions:

$$7\left(\frac{2}{7}x - 6 = 3ay\right) \rightarrow 2x - 42 = 21ay$$

Next, rearrange the equation so that the x and y variables are on the left and the constant is on the right. This will make it match the format of the second equation.

$$2x - 21ay = 42$$

Now compare this to the second equation. Both contain a $2x$ and a 42. For the first equation to match the second, $-21ay$ must equal $-14y$. This means that $a = \frac{-14y}{-21y} = \frac{2}{3}$. Choice **(C)** is correct.

9. C
Difficulty: Medium
Category: Algebra
Getting to the Answer: Rather than solving for each variable individually, see if you can solve for the desired expression all at once. Begin by getting the x and y variables together on the left-hand side of the equation and the constants on the right:

$$-3x - 2y = 1$$
$$4x + 3y = 8$$

There isn't a quick way to simply add or subtract these equations to get to $8x + 8y$, but since $8x + 8y = 8(x + y)$, finding $x + y$ and multiplying the results by 8 will be an efficient route to get to the answer. You can obtain $x + y$ by adding the two equations:

$$-3x - 2y = 1$$
$$\underline{+(4x + 3y = 8)}$$
$$x + y = 9$$

Since $x + y = 9$, $8(x + y) = 8(9) = 72$. Choice **(C)** is correct.

10. 6
Difficulty: Medium
Category: Algebra
Getting to the Answer: To evaluate $f(g(8))$, start with the innermost function. Plug 8 into g to obtain $g(8) = 2(8) + 5 = 16 + 5 = 21$. Now take this value and plug it into the f function: $f(21) = \frac{21}{3} - 1 = 7 - 1 = 6$. Enter **6**.

[PART 2B]

PROBLEM-SOLVING AND DATA ANALYSIS

HOW MUCH DO YOU KNOW: PROBLEM-SOLVING AND DATA ANALYSIS

Directions

Try the questions that follow, using the Method for SAT Math Questions. When you're done, check your answers and read through the explanations in the "Check Your Work" section.

There will be an opportunity for timed practice at the end of the "Problem-Solving and Data Analysis" unit.

1

A contractor quotes $5,200 as the cost of materials for an addition to a house. If he budgets 20 percent for materials, 55 percent for labor, 10 percent for equipment rental, and the remainder is his fee, then how much is his fee?

(A) $2,600

(B) $3,900

(C) $5,200

(D) $6,500

2

An online movie subscription service charges a dollars for the first month of membership and b dollars per month after that. If a customer has paid $108.60 so far for the service, which of the following expressions represents the number of months this customer has subscribed to the service?

(A) $\dfrac{108.60}{a + b}$

(B) $\dfrac{108.60 - a}{b}$

(C) $\dfrac{108.60 - a - b}{b}$

(D) $\dfrac{108.60 - a + b}{b}$

3

The ratio of angelfish to rainbow fish in Mikal's fish tank at home is 5 to 2. Mikal wants to put a tank in his office with 21 fish total, using the same ratio he has at home. How many rainbow fish does he need for the tank in his office?

(A) 2

(B) 5

(C) 6

(D) 15

4

If Jordan ran 11.5 miles, and 1 kilometer equals around 0.62 miles, approximately how many kilometers did Jordan run?

Math

5

Approximately 40 percent of 3,000 local high school athletes surveyed said they would purchase the latest athletic shoe design over the old design. Based on the study, the company concludes that 40 percent of shoe customers would purchase the new design. Which of the following is true about the study?

Ⓐ The data from the survey represents the whole population because a large sample was surveyed.

Ⓑ The data from the survey does not represent the whole population because it was not conducted across the whole country.

Ⓒ The data from the survey likely underestimates the number of people interested in the new product because it compared the new product only to athletic shoes, not to all types of shoes.

Ⓓ The data from the survey likely overestimates the number of people interested in the new product because the survey targeted respondents already interested in athletics.

6

On a used vehicle lot, 50 percent of the vehicles are cars, $\frac{3}{4}$ of which have automatic transmissions. Of the cars with automatic transmissions, $\frac{1}{3}$ have leather interiors. If a vehicle is chosen from the lot at random, what is the probability that it will be a car with an automatic transmission and a leather interior?

Ⓐ $\frac{1}{8}$

Ⓑ $\frac{1}{6}$

Ⓒ $\frac{1}{4}$

Ⓓ $\frac{1}{3}$

7

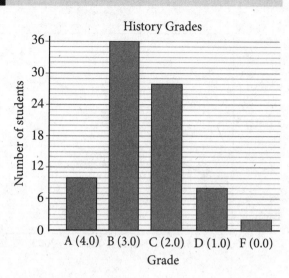

History Grades

The figure shows the distribution of grades and corresponding GPA scores among 84 students in a history class. What is the approximate mean history GPA for this class of students?

Ⓐ 2.0

Ⓑ 2.5

Ⓒ 2.7

Ⓓ 3.0

8

If a basketball team wants to report that in at least half of the games in the season the team scored more than 50 points, which measure of center should the team use to describe the results?

Ⓐ Mean

Ⓑ Range

Ⓒ Median

Ⓓ Standard deviation

PROBLEM-SOLVING AND DATA ANALYSIS

Math

9

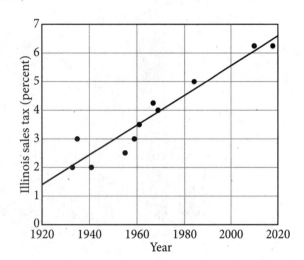

The scatterplot shows the change in Illinois sales tax over the years. According to the line of best fit, which of the following is closest to the estimated yearly percent increase in sales tax?

Ⓐ 0.05

Ⓑ 0.5

Ⓒ 5

Ⓓ 50

10

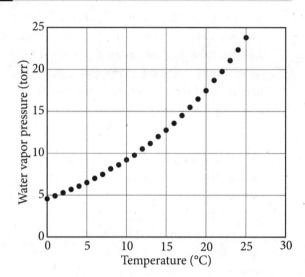

The scatterplot shows the water vapor pressure in torr as a function of temperature in degrees Celsius. Which of the following statements is true about the relationship between water vapor pressure and temperature?

Ⓐ The water vapor pressure doubles when the temperature is halved.

Ⓑ The water vapor pressure doubles when the temperature is doubled.

Ⓒ The rate of increase of water vapor pressure every 5°C is greater at lower temperatures than at higher temperatures.

Ⓓ The rate of increase of water vapor pressure every 5°C is greater at higher temperatures than at lower temperatures.

Check Your Work – How Much Do You Know: Problem-Solving and Data Analysis

1. B
Difficulty: Medium
Category: Problem-Solving and Data Analysis
Getting to the Answer: The percent of the contractor's fee on the quoted budget is $100\% - 20\% - 55\% - 10\% = 15\%$. You're told that the estimate for materials is $5,200, which represents 20% of the total budget. Let x be the total amount of the budget in dollars. Then 20% of x is $5,200, or $0.2x = 5,200$. Solve this equation for x:

$$0.2x = 5,200$$
$$x = 26,000$$

The total budget is $26,000. The contractor's fee represents 15% of this amount, or $0.15 \times \$26,000 = \$3,900$, which means **(B)** is correct. You could also set up the proportion $\frac{15\%}{20\%} = \frac{x}{5,200}$ and solve for x.

2. D
Difficulty: Hard
Category: Problem-Solving and Data Analysis
Getting to the Answer: The key to answering this question is an accurate translation from English into math. Start by assigning a variable to what you're looking for. Let m be the number of months the customer has subscribed to the service. The first month costs a dollars and the remaining months ($m - 1$) are charged at a rate of b dollars per month. So, the total charge for the subscription so far is $a + b(m - 1)$. Set this equal to the amount the customer has paid and solve for m. Note that you're not going to get a nice numerical answer because the question doesn't give you the actual rates:

$$a + b(m - 1) = 108.60$$
$$a + bm - b = 108.60$$
$$bm = 108.60 - a + b$$
$$m = \frac{108.60 - a + b}{b}$$

The expression for m matches the one in **(D)**.

3. C
Difficulty: Easy
Category: Problem-Solving and Data Analysis
Getting to the Answer: You need to find the number of rainbow fish out of a total of 21 that will yield a 5:2 ratio of angelfish to rainbow fish.

Add the parts of the given ratio together to get the total number of parts: $2 + 5 = 7$, so the total number of fish will always be a multiple of 7. Divide the total number of fish Mikal wants by 7 to find the multiple that he'll use for his office tank: $\frac{21}{7} = 3$. Multiply the original ratio by 3 to get the actual numbers of fish. The question asks for rainbow fish, so $2(3) = 6$. **(C)** is correct.

4. 18.54 or 18.55
Difficulty: Easy
Category: Problem-Solving and Data Analysis
Getting to the Answer: Use unit conversion to convert from miles to kilometers, which is the unit you need the answer in:

$$11.5 \text{ miles} \times \frac{1 \text{ kilometer}}{0.62 \text{ miles}} \approx 18.548 \text{ kilometers}$$

You may either truncate or round. Enter **18.54** or **18.55**.

5. D
Difficulty: Easy
Category: Problem-Solving and Data Analysis
Getting to the Answer: When considering the validity of a study, always look for possible sources of bias. In other words, look for things that might skew the results in either direction. Only surveying high school athletes is likely to skew the results. The respondents are already interested in athletics and so are likely to respond more positively than the average shoe customer. Therefore, the data from the survey likely overestimates the number of people interested in the new product, making **(D)** the correct answer.

6. A
Difficulty: Medium
Category: Problem-Solving and Data Analysis
Getting to the Answer: Convert 50% to a fraction $\left(\frac{1}{2}\right)$ and then approach logically—the final probability is $\frac{1}{3}$ of $\frac{3}{4}$ of $\frac{1}{2}$. When dealing with fractions, "of" means multiply. So the probability of randomly choosing a vehicle that is a car with an automatic transmission and a leather interior is $\frac{1}{3} \times \frac{3}{4} \times \frac{1}{2} = \frac{1}{8}$. **(A)** is correct.

7.   B

Difficulty: Easy

Category: Problem-Solving and Data Analysis

Getting to the Answer: The mean of a set of numbers is the same as the average, which is the sum of the values divided by the number of values: $\text{Average} = \frac{\text{sum of values}}{\text{number of values}}$. Use the graph to find the sum of the GPA values, and then calculate the mean. Read the graph carefully—each grid line represents one student. There are 10 students who received a 4.0, 36 who received a 3.0, 28 with a 2.0, 8 with a 1.0, and 2 with a 0.0. You can save time by multiplying the frequency in each category by the GPA value. This calculation is called a weighted average. For example, instead of adding ten 4.0s together, just multiply 10 by 4. The sum of all the values, then, is $(10 \times 4) + (36 \times 3) + (28 \times 2) + (8 \times 1) + (2 \times 0) = 212$. Now, divide by the number of values, which is 84 students: $\frac{212}{84} \approx 2.523$, or about 2.5, which is **(B)**.

8.   C

Difficulty: Easy

Category: Problem-Solving and Data Analysis

Getting to the Answer: Eliminate (B) and (D) right away because range and standard deviation are measures of spread, not of center. The median is the middle number of a set, so if you want to describe half of the games as above a certain score, the median is perfect since it divides the data into two parts. **(C)** is correct.

9.   A

Difficulty: Medium

Category: Problem-Solving and Data Analysis

Getting to the Answer: The estimated increase in sales tax every year is represented by the slope of the line of best fit. Recall that slope is equal to $\frac{y_2 - y_1}{x_2 - x_1}$. Estimate any two points on the line, for instance (1920, 1.5) and (1960, 3.5), to approximate the slope. The slope is about $\frac{3.5 - 1.5}{1960 - 1920} = \frac{2}{40} = 0.05$. The unit of the sales tax in the graph is percent, so no conversion is needed. **(A)** is correct.

10.   D

Difficulty: Medium

Category: Problem-Solving and Data Analysis

Getting to the Answer: The data in the scatterplot can be modeled with a concave up curve (such as quadratic or exponential) that has an increasing positive slope. To visualize this, for every 5°C interval, draw a line of best fit through the data. The slopes of the lines of best fit are steeper at higher temperatures. Thus, at higher temperatures, the rate of increase of water vapor pressure every 5°C is greater than at lower temperatures. **(D)** is correct.

CHAPTER 8

RATES, RATIOS, PROPORTIONS, PERCENTS, AND UNITS

LEARNING OBJECTIVES

After completing this chapter, you will be able to:

- Given any two values in a three-part rate equation, solve for the third
- Set up and solve a proportion for a missing value
- Use ratios to perform unit conversions
- Calculate percents
- Calculate percent change

HOW MUCH DO YOU KNOW?

Directions

Try the questions that follow. Show your work so that you can compare your solutions to the ones found in the "Check Your Work" section immediately after this question set. If you answered the question(s) on a specific topic correctly, and if your scratchwork looks like ours, you may be able to move quickly through the lesson covering that topic. If you answered incorrectly or used a different approach, you may want to take your time on that lesson.

1

A theory states that a person's height is proportional to the length of the person's palm. Don's palm is 5 centimeters in length and he is 120 centimeters tall. Mateo's palm is 7.5 centimeters in length. Assuming the theory is correct, how tall, in centimeters, is Mateo?

(A) 60

(B) 80

(C) 160

(D) 180

2

As of 2009, there were about 225 quarters for every 2 half-dollar coins in circulation. If there were 380 million quarters in circulation that year, approximately how many total quarters and half-dollar coins, in millions, were there in circulation?

(A) 383

(B) 415

(C) 493

(D) 605

3

If $\dfrac{5}{7a} = \dfrac{1}{b-a}$, which of the following proportions is equivalent?

(A) $\dfrac{a}{b} = \dfrac{5}{12}$

(B) $\dfrac{a}{b} = \dfrac{5}{2}$

(C) $\dfrac{b-a}{a} = \dfrac{5}{7}$

(D) $\dfrac{b-a}{a} = -\dfrac{7}{5}$

4

British Thermal Units (BTUs) and calories are two measures of heat energy. If there are 2,016 calories in 8 BTUs, how many calories are in 3 BTUs?

5

A car's engine is leaking oil at a rate of 2.5 milliliters per hour. If the engine contains 6 liters of oil, what will be the amount of oil, in milliliters, remaining in the engine after 24 hours? (Note: There are 1,000 milliliters in 1 liter.)

6

Category	Percentage
Completely satisfied	
Somewhat satisfied	
Somewhat dissatisfied	15%
Completely dissatisfied	25%

A company conducts a customer satisfaction survey. The results are partly summarized in the table. If 240 customers responded to the survey, how many customers were either completely or somewhat satisfied?

Ⓐ 60

Ⓑ 96

Ⓒ 144

Ⓓ 204

7

In a week, a light bulb factory produces 12,500 light bulbs. The ratio of light-emitting diodes (LED bulbs) to compact fluorescent lamps (CFL bulbs) is 2:3. Of the LED bulbs produced, 3 percent were defective. If only LED and CFL bulbs were produced, how many LED bulbs were NOT defective?

Ⓐ 2,425

Ⓑ 4,850

Ⓒ 7,275

Ⓓ 8,083

8

In 1950, scientists estimated a certain animal population in a particular geographical area to be 6,400. In 2000, the population had risen to 7,200. If this animal population experiences the same percent increase over the next 50 years, what will the approximate population be?

Ⓐ 8,000

Ⓑ 8,100

Ⓒ 8,400

Ⓓ 8,600

Check Your Work

1. D
Difficulty: Easy
Category: Problem-Solving and Data Analysis
Getting to the Answer: Since you are given the palm-to-height ratio for Don's as well as Mateo's palm length, set up a proportion using M to represent Mateo's height:

$$\frac{5 \text{ cm}}{120 \text{ cm}} = \frac{7.5 \text{ cm}}{M}$$

Cross-multiply to solve for M:

$$5M = 7.5(120)$$
$$5M = 900$$
$$M = 180$$

The correct answer is **(D)**.

2. A
Difficulty: Medium
Category: Problem-Solving and Data Analysis
Getting to the Answer: Notice that the question asks you for the total number of coins in millions, but the ratio given specifies the parts only. Set up a proportion using the given ratio:

$$\frac{2 \text{ half-dollar coins}}{225 \text{ million quarters}} = \frac{x \text{ half-dollar coins}}{380 \text{ million quarters}}$$

Cross-multiply to obtain $225x = 760$. Solve for x to find that $x = 3.3\overline{7}$ million half-dollar coins in circulation. To calculate the total number of half-dollar coins and quarters in circulation in millions in 2009, add the number of half-dollar coins to the number of quarters: $3.3\overline{7}$ million $+$ 380 million $\approx$ 383 million. Choice **(A)** is correct.

3. A
Difficulty: Medium
Category: Problem-Solving and Data Analysis
Getting to the Answer: Since the answer choices are expressed as $\frac{a}{b} =$ and $\frac{b-a}{a} =$, cross-multiply the proportion and rewrite it to get an expression that matches one of the answer choices. Solving for $\frac{b-a}{a}$, you get the following:

$$\frac{5}{7a} = \frac{1}{b-a}$$
$$5(b-a) = 7a$$
$$\frac{b-a}{a} = \frac{7}{5}$$

This does not match (C) or (D), so eliminate them. Now cross-multiply and solve for $\frac{a}{b}$:

$$5(b-a) = 7a$$
$$5b - 5a = 7a$$
$$5b = 12a$$
$$\frac{5}{12} = \frac{a}{b}$$

This matches **(A)**.

4. 756
Difficulty: Easy
Category: Problem-Solving and Data Analysis
Getting to the Answer: Let x represent the number of calories in 3 BTUs, and then set up a proportion equating the ratio of 8 BTUs to 2,016 calories to the ratio of 3 BTUs to x calories: $\frac{8 \text{ BTU}}{2,016 \text{ cal}} = \frac{3 \text{ BTU}}{x \text{ cal}}$. Solving for x gives 756 calories. Enter **756**.

5. 5940
Difficulty: Medium
Category: Problem-Solving and Data Analysis
Getting to the Answer: First, determine the amount of oil that will leak out of the engine after 24 hours: $\frac{2.5 \text{ mL}}{1 \text{ hr}} \times 24 \text{ hr} = 60$ mL. Then, use the conversion to determine the amount of oil, in milliliters, initially in the engine: $6 \text{ L} \times \frac{1,000 \text{ mL}}{1 \text{ L}} = 6,000$ mL. Calculate the difference between the two to find the amount of oil remaining in the engine after 24 hours: 6,000 mL $-$ 60 mL $=$ 5,940 mL. Enter **5940**.

6. C
Difficulty: Easy
Category: Problem-Solving and Data Analysis
Getting to the Answer: According to the table, 25% of the customers are completely dissatisfied and 15% are somewhat dissatisfied. So, 100% $-$ 25% $-$ 15% $=$ 60% of the customers are completely or somewhat satisfied. Thus, the number of customers who are completely or somewhat satisfied is 60% of 240, or $0.6 \times 240 = 144$ customers, making **(C)** correct.

7. B
Difficulty: Hard
Category: Problem-Solving and Data Analysis
Getting to the Answer: Approach the question as a series of steps. Before you select your answer, check that you answered the right question (the number of LED bulbs that were *not* defective).

First, find the total number of LED bulbs produced. Since the ratio of LED to CFL is 2:3 and a total of 12,500 of both kinds of bulbs were produced, two parts LED plus three parts CFL equals 12,500. Let x be the number of LED bulbs produced and use the part-to-whole ratio to set up a proportion:

$$\frac{2}{5} = \frac{x}{12,500}$$

Solve for x by cross-multiplying:

$$2(12,500) = 5x$$
$$25,000 = 5x$$
$$5,000 = x$$

Now find the number of LED bulbs that were not defective: $5,000 \times 97\% = 5,000 \times 0.97 = 4,850$. Choice **(B)** is correct.

8. B
Difficulty: Medium
Category: Problem-Solving and Data Analysis
Getting to the Answer: Find the percent increase in the population from 1950 to 2000 using this formula: percent increase $= \frac{\text{amount of increase}}{\text{original amount}} \times 100\%$. Then apply the same percent increase to the animal population in 2000.

The amount of increase is $7,200 - 6,400 = 800$, so the percent increase is $\frac{800}{6,400} \times 100\% = 0.125 \times 100\% = 12.5\%$ between 1950 and 2000. If the total percent increase over the next 50 years is the same, the animal population should be about $7,200 \times (100\% + 12.5\%) = 7,200 \times (112.5\%) = 7,200 \times 1.125 = 8,100$.

(B) is correct.

RATES

> **LEARNING OBJECTIVE**
>
> After this lesson, you will be able to:
>
> - Given any two values in a three-part rate equation, solve for the third

To answer a question like this:

Tanks A and B are both used to store the same chemical. Tank A, which holds 108 gallons when full, takes 18 minutes to empty when the valve is opened. Tank B, which holds 196 gallons when full, takes 28 minutes to empty when the valve is opened. What is the positive difference, in gallons per minute, between the rates at which tanks A and B empty?

A) 1

B) 6

C) 7

D) 9

You need to know this:

A **rate** is an expression of the amount of something done per unit of time. Speed, for example, represents the distance something travels in a particular amount of time. The general three-part rate formula is **Rate** $= \dfrac{\textbf{amount}}{\textbf{time}}$, although you may see this in a number of different ways. With a little math, the equation becomes **Amount = rate × time**, or you might find it helpful to use **Distance = rate × time** or even **Work = rate × time**. We'll use several ways in this chapter. For example, say a cyclist rides 30 miles in 2 hours. To determine her speed(rate), plug in 30 miles for the amount and 2 hours for the time to get Speed $= \dfrac{30 \text{ miles}}{2 \text{ hours}} =$ 15 miles per hour. Since a rate also represents the work done in one unit of time, its reciprocal represents the amount of time taken to do one unit of work. The bike being ridden at 15 miles per hour takes $\dfrac{1}{15}$ of an hour to ride one mile.

Like other three-part formulas, you may need to rearrange the rate formula to solve for the other two parts: the previously mentioned **Amount = rate × time** as well as **Time** $= \dfrac{\textbf{amount}}{\textbf{rate}}$.

Sometimes, you'll be given the rates of two separate workers attempting to complete a task, and you'll need to combine their rates to figure out how long they'd take to complete the task together. Suppose that it takes Dorian 3 hours to paint a room and Clarice 2 hours to paint a room of the same size. So, Dorian's rate is $\dfrac{1 \text{ room}}{3 \text{ hours}} = \dfrac{1}{3}$ room per hour and Clarice's rate is $\dfrac{1 \text{ room}}{2 \text{ hours}} = \dfrac{1}{2}$ room per hour. If they work together, their combined progress is the sum of their individual rates: $\dfrac{1}{3} + \dfrac{1}{2} = \dfrac{2}{6} + \dfrac{3}{6} = \dfrac{5}{6}$ room per hour. You could then take the reciprocal to find that it would take them $\dfrac{6}{5}$ of an hour to paint one room.

There is also a simplified formula for two workers. If a and b represent the time each worker takes to complete the task and T is their combined time, then $T = \dfrac{ab}{a+b}$.

You need to do this:

- Determine which two parts of the rate formula are given and use them to solve for the third.
- If there are multiple workers collaborating on a task, use their individual rates to determine their combined rate.

Explanation:

First, find the rates at which each individual tank drains using the rate formula, **Rate** $= \dfrac{\textbf{amount}}{\textbf{time}}$. For tank A, the amount is 108 gallons and the time is 18 minutes, so Rate $= \dfrac{108 \text{ gallons}}{18 \text{ minutes}} = 6$ gallons per minute. For tank B, the amount is 196 gallons and the time is 28 minutes, so Rate $= \dfrac{196 \text{ gallons}}{28 \text{ minutes}} = 7$ gallons per minute. Remember, though, that the question asks for the positive difference between these rates, not either of the rates themselves. Since $7 - 6 = 1$, **(A)** is correct.

Try on Your Own

Directions

Take as much time as you need on these questions. Work carefully and methodically. There will be an opportunity for timed practice later in the book.

1

A sprinter can run 29 feet in 1 second. How many seconds will it take the sprinter to run 300 feet?

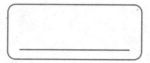

2

Pump A can transfer 3 gallons of water per minute, and pump B can work twice as fast as pump A. How many minutes will it take pump A and pump B, working together, to transfer 279 gallons of water?

- Ⓐ 30
- Ⓑ 31
- Ⓒ 46.5
- Ⓓ 93

3

An airplane travels 900 miles at 300 miles per hour and then an additional 500 miles at 250 miles per hour. What is the airplane's average speed, in miles per hour, over the entire trip?

- Ⓐ 260
- Ⓑ 275
- Ⓒ 280
- Ⓓ 290

4

An asteroid travels 30,000 kilometers per hour. It rotates on its axis one time for every 600,000 kilometers it travels. How many hours will it take for the asteroid to rotate on its axis 12 times?

- Ⓐ 20
- Ⓑ 24
- Ⓒ 120
- Ⓓ 240

5

HINT: For Q5, calculate the distance left to travel
in the time remaining.

At noon, a car departs on a 270-mile trip. It travels for the first 1.5 hours at 40 miles per hour. It completes the trip at 5:00 p.m. on the same day. What was the car's average speed, in miles per hour, from 1:30 to 5:00 p.m.?

(A) 35

(B) 40

(C) 60

(D) 70

6

Tavish can clean his room in 2 hours. His brother can clean the same room in 4 hours. If they work together, how many hours will it take them to clean their room?

(A) 1

(B) $\frac{4}{3}$

(C) $\frac{3}{2}$

(D) 6

7

HINT: For Q7, determine the net rate at which the pond
is being filled.

A 2,100-gallon fish pond has a circulation drain at the bottom that drains at a rate of 20 gallons per hour. A pump adds water to the pond at a rate of 55 gallons per hour. If the pond starts out empty, how many hours will it take the pump to completely fill it?

8

If cyclist A travels at 6 miles per hour and cyclist B travels at 8 miles per hour, how much longer, in hours, will it take cyclist A than cyclist B to travel 24 miles?

(A) $\frac{3}{8}$

(B) $\frac{3}{4}$

(C) 1

(D) 2

RATIOS AND PROPORTIONS

LEARNING OBJECTIVE

After this lesson, you will be able to:

- Set up and solve a proportion for a missing value

To answer a question like this:

The aircraft carrier *Essex* was 872 feet long with a beam (width) of 147 feet. A museum wishes to build an exact replica scale model of the *Essex* that is 8 feet long. Approximately how many feet wide will the scale model's beam be?

A) 1.35

B) 2.14

C) 2.68

D) 5.93

You need to know this:

A **ratio** is a comparison of one quantity to another. When writing ratios, you can compare one part of a group to another part of that group, or you can compare a part of the group to the whole group. Suppose you have a bowl of apples and oranges: you can write ratios that compare apples to oranges (part to part), apples to total fruit (part to whole), and oranges to total fruit (part to whole).

Keep in mind that ratios convey *relative* amounts, not necessarily actual amounts, and that they are typically expressed in lowest terms. For example, if there are 10 apples and 6 oranges in a bowl, the ratio of apples to oranges would likely be expressed as $\frac{5}{3}$ on the SAT, rather than as $\frac{10}{6}$. However, if you know the ratio of apples to oranges and either the actual number of apples or the total number of pieces of fruit, you can find the actual number of oranges by setting up a proportion.

Note that the SAT may occasionally use the word "proportion" to mean "ratio."

A **proportion** is simply two ratios set equal to each other, such as $\frac{a}{b} = \frac{c}{d}$. Proportions are an efficient way to solve certain problems, but you must exercise caution when setting them up. Noting the units of each piece of the proportion will help you put each piece of the proportion in the right place.

Sometimes the SAT may ask you to determine whether certain proportions are equivalent—check this by cross-multiplying. You'll get results that are much easier to compare.

$$\text{If } \frac{a}{b} = \frac{c}{d}, \text{ then: } ad = bc, \frac{a}{c} = \frac{b}{d}, \frac{d}{b} = \frac{c}{a}, \frac{b}{a} = \frac{d}{c}, \text{ BUT } \frac{a}{d} \ne \frac{c}{b}$$

Each derived ratio shown except the last one is simply a manipulation of the first, so all except the last are correct. You can verify this via cross-multiplication ($ad = bc$ in each case except the last).

Alternatively, you can pick equivalent fractions $\frac{2}{3}$ and $\frac{6}{9}$ ($a = 2$, $b = 3$, $c = 6$, $d = 9$). Cross-multiplication gives $2 \times 9 = 3 \times 6$, which is a true statement. Dividing 2 and 3 by 6 and 9 gives $\frac{2}{6} = \frac{3}{9}$, which is also true, and so on. However, attempting to equate $\frac{2}{9}$ and $\frac{3}{6}$ will not work.

If you know any three numerical values in a proportion, you can solve for the fourth. For example, say a fruit stand sells 3 peaches for every 5 apricots, and you are supposed to calculate the number of peaches sold on a day when 20 apricots were sold. You would use the given information to set up a proportion and solve for the unknown:

$$\frac{3}{5} = \frac{p}{20}$$

You can now solve for the number of peaches sold, p, by cross-multiplying:

$$60 = 5p$$
$$p = 12$$

Alternatively, you could use the common multiplier to solve for p: the numerator and denominator in the original ratio must be multiplied by the same value to arrive at their respective terms in the new ratio. To get from 5 to 20 in the denominator, you multiply by 4, so you also have to multiply the 3 in the numerator by 4 to arrive at the actual number of peaches sold: $4(3) = 12$.

You need to do this:

Set up a proportion and solve for the unknown, either by cross-multiplying or by using the common multiplier.

Explanation:

The ratio of the length of the real *Essex* to that of the scale model is $\frac{872 \text{ ft}}{8 \text{ ft}}$. You know the actual beam width (147 feet), so set up a proportion and solve for the scale model's beam width:

$$\frac{872 \text{ ft}}{8 \text{ ft}} = \frac{147 \text{ ft}}{x \text{ ft}}$$
$$872x = 1{,}176 \text{ ft}$$
$$x \approx 1.349 \text{ ft}$$

The correct answer is **(A)**.

Try on Your Own

Directions

Take as much time as you need on these questions. Work carefully and methodically. There will be an opportunity for timed practice later in the book.

9

The number of topics teachers at a certain school can cover is directly proportional to the length of time they have to review. If teachers can cover 9 topics in a single 45-minute period, how many topics can they cover in a 60-minute period?

10

One pound on Earth is equal to approximately 0.166 pounds on the Moon. If a person weighs 29 pounds on the Moon, approximately how much, in pounds, does the person weigh on Earth?

(A) 21

(B) 48

(C) 175

(D) 196

11

A machine produces 6 defective parts out of every 3,500 it makes. How many total parts were made during the time the machine produced 27 defective parts?

Ⓐ 14,000

Ⓑ 15,750

Ⓒ 17,500

Ⓓ 21,000

12

HINT: For Q12, designate the unknown starting number of first-year students and second-year students with the ratio $\frac{f}{s} = \frac{3}{10}$.

The ratio of first-year students to second-year students in an auditorium was 3 to 10. After an additional 270 first-year students and 120 second-year students entered the auditorium, the ratio of first-year students to second-year students was 6 to 5. No other students entered or left the auditorium. How many first-year students were in the auditorium before the additional students entered?

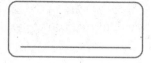

13

Riding her bicycle, Reyna can travel 1 mile in 5.5 minutes. If she rides at a constant rate, which of the following is closest to the distance she will travel in 90 minutes?

Ⓐ 9 miles

Ⓑ 11 miles

Ⓒ 13 miles

Ⓓ 16 miles

14

If $\frac{x + y}{x} = \frac{4}{9}$, which of the following proportions is equivalent?

Ⓐ $\frac{y}{x} = -\frac{5}{9}$

Ⓑ $\frac{y}{x} = \frac{13}{9}$

Ⓒ $\frac{y - x}{x} = -\frac{4}{9}$

Ⓓ $\frac{y - x}{x} = -\frac{9}{4}$

15

HINT: For Q15, start with the proportion $\frac{physicists}{total} = \frac{2}{5}$, then think about what to substitute for "physicists" and "total."

All of the attendees at a symposium are either physicists or biologists. If there are 123 physicists and 270 biologists, then how many additional physicists must arrive at the symposium in order for the ratio of physicists to total attendees to become 2 to 5?

Ⓐ 25

Ⓑ 50

Ⓒ 57

Ⓓ 114

Math

UNIT CONVERSION

LEARNING OBJECTIVE

After this lesson, you will be able to:

- Use ratios to perform unit conversions

To answer a question like this:

Proxima Centauri is approximately 4.3 light-years away from the Sun. Another star, Sirius A, is twice that distance from the Sun. If 1 light-year equals 63,000 astronomical units (AU), and 1 AU equals 150 million kilometers, approximately how far is Sirius A from the Sun in trillions of kilometers? (1 trillion = 1,000,000,000,000)

A) 2.2

B) 20

C) 41

D) 81

You need to know this:

You can use ratios to perform unit conversions. This is especially useful when there are multiple conversions or when the units are unfamiliar.

For example, though these units of measurement are no longer commonly used, there are 8 furlongs in a mile and 3 miles in a league. Say you're asked to convert 4 leagues to furlongs. A convenient way to do this is to set up the conversion ratios so that equivalent units cancel:

$$4 \text{ leagues} \times \frac{3 \text{ miles}}{1 \text{ league}} \times \frac{8 \text{ furlongs}}{1 \text{ mile}} = 4 \times 3 \times 8 = 96 \text{ furlongs}$$

Notice that all the units cancel out except the furlongs, which is the one you want.

You need to do this:

Set up a series of ratios to make equivalent units cancel. (Keep track of the units by writing them down next to the numbers in the ratios.) You should be left with the units you're converting into.

Explanation:

Sirius A is twice as far from the Sun as Proxima Centauri, so it is $2(4.3) = 8.6$ light-years away from the Sun. Set up a series of ratios to convert to trillion kilometers:

$$8.6 \text{ light-years} \times \frac{63,000 \text{ AU}}{1 \text{ light-year}} \times \frac{150 \text{ million km}}{1 \text{ AU}} = 8.6 \times 63,000 \times 150 \text{ million km}$$

$$= 81,270,000 \text{ million km}$$

$$= 81.27 \text{ trillion km}$$

Because there are 6 zeros in a million, 81,270,000 million is 81,270,000,000,000. There are 12 zeros in a trillion, so this number equals 81.27 trillion. The correct answer is **(D)**.

Try on Your Own

Directions

Take as much time as you need on these questions. Work carefully and methodically. There will be an opportunity for timed practice later in the book.

16

HINT: For Q16, *cubic feet* means ft³, or ft × ft × ft.

Quinn estimates that she will need 700 cubic feet of storage space, but the dimensions of the storage units are in cubic meters. If 1 meter is approximately 3.28 feet, approximately how many cubic meters of space will Quinn need?

Ⓐ 19.84

Ⓑ 25.93

Ⓒ 65.07

Ⓓ 213.41

17

A court reporter types 3.75 words per second. If a trial transcript contains 25 pages with an average of 675 words per page, how much time did the court reporter spend typing?

Ⓐ 1 hour, 15 minutes

Ⓑ 1 hour, 45 minutes

Ⓒ 2 hours, 30 minutes

Ⓓ 3 hours

18

HINT: For Q18, "how many more" means you're solving for a difference. Subtract, then convert pounds per hour to ounces per minute.

At 350°F, an oven can cook approximately 3 pounds of turkey per hour. At 450°F, it can cook approximately 4.5 pounds per hour. How many more ounces of turkey can the oven cook at 450°F than at 350°F in 10 minutes? (1 pound = 16 ounces)

Ⓐ 4

Ⓑ 6

Ⓒ 8

Ⓓ 12

19

A doctor prescribes 800 milliliters of a medication to be delivered via IV fluid over the course of 8 hours. The IV delivers 1 milliliter of medication over the course of 30 drips. How many drips per minute are needed to deliver the prescribed dosage?

20

A tree grew 46 meters in the first 50 years of its life. On average, how many centimeters per day did it grow during this period? Assume that there are 365 days in a year. (1 meter = 100 centimeters)

PERCENTS

> **LEARNING OBJECTIVE**
>
> After this lesson, you will be able to:
>
> • Calculate percents

To answer a question like this:

Political canvassers polled 125 voters in District 18 and of those, 22.4 percent responded favorably. In District 19, 37.5 percent of 272 people responded favorably. Approximately what percent of all the people surveyed responded favorably?

A) 25.7%

B) 30.0%

C) 31.5%

D) 32.7%

You need to know this:

Percent means "per one hundred." Knowing this definition helps you understand that 25% means 25 out of every hundred. For instance, 25% of 500 students can be found by setting up a proportion: $\frac{25}{100} = \frac{x}{500}$, where x represents 25% of 500 students and equals 125.

To calculate percent, you can use this basic equation:

$$\text{Percent} = \frac{\text{part}}{\text{whole}} \times 100\%$$

In the example, the whole is 500 students and the part is 125 students. Plugging the values into the equation gives $\frac{125}{500} \times 100\% = 25\%$.

Alternatively, use this statement: _____ percent of _____ is _____. Translating from English into math, you get _____% × _____ = _____. For example, "25 percent of 500 is 125" translated is "25% × 500 = 125."

In some calculations, you may find it convenient to express percentages as decimals: 25% as a decimal is 25 divided by 100 or 0.25. Thus, 25% × 500 can be written as 0.25 × 500.

You need to do this:

• Translate from English into math.
• Plug in the values for any two parts of the formula and solve for the third.

Explanation:

First, find the number of people in each district who responded favorably. Start with District 18: 22.4% of 125 is $0.224 \times 125 = 28$. Move on to District 19: $0.375 \times 272 = 102$. Next, find the total number of people who were surveyed at both locations, which is $125 + 272 = 397$, and the total number who responded favorably, $28 + 102 = 130$. Finally, find the percent of people who responded favorably by using the formula:

$$\text{percent} = \frac{130}{397} \times 100\%$$
$$\approx 0.327 \times 100\%$$
$$= 32.7\%$$

Of all the people surveyed, about 32.7% responded favorably, making **(D)** the correct answer.

Try on Your Own

Directions

Take as much time as you need on these questions. Work carefully and methodically. There will be an opportunity for timed practice later in the book.

21

A college athletics program found that 3 percent of 300 runners were injured during workouts, while 6 percent of 250 weight lifters were injured during workouts. Which of the following is the total number of runners and weight lifters who were injured?

(A) 24

(B) 50

(C) 142

(D) 240

22

HINT: For Q22, what percent of the attendees are teachers?

At a high school event, 15 percent of the attendees are sophomores, 30 percent are juniors, 25 percent are seniors, and the remaining 18 attendees are teachers. How many more juniors are there than seniors at the event?

23

HINT: For Q23, how many gallons of *pigment* is the painter starting with? How many gallons of *pigment* are needed for the final mix? How many gallons of the final paint will it take to provide the needed pigment?

A painter has 20 gallons of a paint mixture that is 15 percent blue pigment. How many gallons of a mixture that is 40 percent blue pigment would the painter need to add to achieve a mixture that is 20 percent blue pigment?

(A) 4

(B) 5

(C) 8

(D) 12

24

The price of one share of a company's stock on August 1 was $75. On September 1, the price of one share was $10 more than it was on August 1 and 80 percent of the price of one share on October 1. To the nearest dollar, what was the price of one share on October 1?

(A) $68

(B) $99

(C) $102

(D) $106

25

The sum of x, y, and z is 63. If x is 60% less than the sum of y and z, what is the value of x?

_____

PERCENT CHANGE

LEARNING OBJECTIVE

After this lesson, you will be able to:

- Calculate percent change

To answer a question like this:

A power company increases the power allocated to a neighborhood by 20 percent in the morning and then decreases the power by 12 percent in the afternoon. What is the net percent increase in this neighborhood's power allocation from the morning to the afternoon?

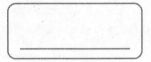

You need to know this:

You can determine the **percent change** in a given situation by applying this formula:

$$\text{Percent increase or decrease} = \frac{\text{amount of increase or decrease}}{\text{original amount}} \times 100\%$$

Sometimes, more than one change will occur. Be careful here, as it can be tempting to take a shortcut by just combining percent changes together (which will almost always lead to an incorrect answer). Instead, you'll need to find the total amount of increase or decrease and then apply the formula.

In some instances, a question will ask you for the final amount as a percent of the original amount. In those cases, use this formula: $\text{Percent} = \frac{\text{final amount}}{\text{original amount}} \times 100\%$. Pay attention to the distinction between these two question types.

You need to do this:

- Calculate the actual change (increase or decrease).
- Divide by the *original* amount (not the new amount!).
- Multiply by 100%.

Explanation:

The question does not give an initial value for power allocation, so pick 100 (often the best number to use when picking numbers for questions involving percents) and then calculate the actual change. A 20% increase from 100 is $100 + (0.2 \times 100)$ and brings the power allocation to $100 + 20 = 120$. A 12% decrease from 120 is $120 - (0.12 \times 120)$ and brings the power allocation to $120 - 14.4 = 105.6$. The actual increase, then, is $105.6 - 100 = 5.6$. (Again, note that simply combining the percents would get you the incorrect answer: $20\% - 12\% = 8\%$.)

Plugging this increase into the percent change formula yields the following (remember to divide by the *original* amount, 100, rather than by the new amount, 105.6):

$$\text{Percent change} = \frac{5.6}{100} \times 100\% = 5.6\%$$

Enter **5.6**.

Try on Your Own

Directions

Take as much time as you need on these questions. Work carefully and methodically. There will be an opportunity for timed practice later in the book.

26

The price of a single ticket for admission to an amusement park rose from $35 to $49. To the nearest percent, what was the percent increase in the price per ticket?

Ⓐ 14%

Ⓑ 29%

Ⓒ 40%

Ⓓ 48%

27

HINT: For Q27, remember to divide by the *original* value.

A homeowner's annual property tax payment was $1,494. Due to a property value reassessment, the tax payment was increased to $1,572. To the nearest tenth of a percent, by what percent was the homeowner's property tax payment increased?

Ⓐ 0.1%

Ⓑ 5.0%

Ⓒ 5.2%

Ⓓ 7.9%

28

HINT: For Q28, how does the wording of the question help you determine which container of coins is the original amount?

The number of coins in jar X is 75. The number of coins in jar Y is 54. By what percent is the number of coins in jar Y less than the number of coins in jar X?

Ⓐ 21%

Ⓑ 28%

Ⓒ 39%

Ⓓ 72%

29

HINT: For Q29, if you have 75% more seniors than juniors, you have all the juniors (100%) plus 75%, or 175%. Adding the percentages at the start saves a calculation step.

At a school rally, there are 50 sophomores, 80 juniors, and 75 percent more seniors than juniors. By what percent is the number of seniors greater than the number of sophomores?

Ⓐ 80%

Ⓑ 140%

Ⓒ 150%

Ⓓ 180%

30

HINT: For Q30, the final 25% discount is applied to an already reduced price. You *cannot* add the percent discounts together.

A smartphone originally priced at y dollars loses 36 percent of its original value after a year. If the phone is sold at a price that is 25 percent less than the depreciated cost, by what percent is the discounted price less than y?

(A) 27%

(B) 48%

(C) 52%

(D) 61%

31

Season 2 of a TV show opened with 1.8 million total viewers, which was down from its Season 1 average of 2.4 million. The number of viewers for Season 2, Episode 2, is 15 percent lower than that for Episode 1. What percent of the average number of Season 1 viewers is the number of viewers of Season 2, Episode 2?

(A) 15%

(B) 36.25%

(C) 63.75%

(D) 75%

ON TEST DAY

When a question features multiple percentages, you have to make a key strategic decision: can I do the arithmetic on the percentages themselves and get the answer right away, or do I have to calculate each percentage individually and do the arithmetic on the actual values?

For example, suppose a car traveling 50 miles per hour increases its speed by 20 percent and then decreases its speed by 20 percent. If you were to calculate $+20\% - 20\% = 0$, you might conclude that the speed of the car did not change and that the final speed is 50 miles per hour. However, this answer would be incorrect; you must calculate each percentage individually. After a 20% increase, the car's speed becomes 120% of the original: $1.2(50) = 60$ miles per hour. Then when the car "decreases its speed by 20 percent," that 20% is calculated based on the *new* speed, 60 miles per hour, not the original speed: $60 - 0.2(60) = 60 - 12 = 48$. Since 20% of 60 is greater than 20% of 50, the car's final speed is *lower* than its starting speed.

On the other hand, suppose you have to find how many more car owners than motorcycle owners live in a certain region where there are 13,450 residents, given that 60 percent of the residents own cars and 10 percent own motorcycles. It may be tempting to find 60 percent of 13,450 ($0.60 \times 13,450 = 8,070$), then find 10 percent of 13,450 ($0.10 \times 13,450 = 1,345$), and finally subtract those two numbers to get the answer ($8,070 - 1,345 = 6,725$). However, you can more quickly find the correct answer by calculating the difference between the two percentages ($60\% - 10\% = 50\%$) and then take 50 percent of the total to get the answer: $13,450 \times 0.50 = 6,725$. Since you are working with percentages of the same total, you can do arithmetic on the percentages first.

The fundamental principles are:

- If the percentages are out of the same total, then you can do arithmetic on the percentages.
- If the totals are different, then you must convert the percentages into actual values.

Practice applying these principles on the following question.

32. A company has 250 full-time and 250 part-time employees. If 92 percent of the full-time employees qualify for benefits, and 74 percent of the part-time employees do not qualify for benefits, then how many more full-time than part-time employees qualify for benefits?

    A) 45
    B) 90
    C) 165
    D) 330

The answer and explanation can be found at the end of this chapter.

HOW MUCH HAVE YOU LEARNED?

Directions

For testlike practice, give yourself 14 minutes to complete this question set. Be sure to study the explanations, even for questions you answered correctly. They can be found at the end of this chapter.

33

Undergraduate Costs at a State University

2014–15	2015–16	2016–17	2017–18	2018–19	2019–20
$12,192	$12,804	$13,446	$14,118	$14,820	$15,564

The table summarizes the total cost per undergraduate student per year for each academic year from 2014–15 to 2019–20. If fees account for 8.75 percent of one year's total costs, what is the average fee increase per academic year? Round your answer to the nearest dollar.

34

A gardener planted a 20-inch-tall sapling in his yard. Four months later, the sapling was 27 inches tall. By what percent did the height of the sapling increase over the four months?

(A) 7%

(B) 26%

(C) 35%

(D) 74%

35

From 1997 to 1998, company T's profits increased by 25 percent. From 1998 to 1999, company T's profits rose from $375 million to $483 million. By what percent did company T's profits increase from 1997 to 1999?

(A) 38%

(B) 49%

(C) 54%

(D) 61%

36

The price of a calculator is $150, the price of a radio is $75, and the price of a printer is 16 percent less than the price of a radio. By what percent is the price of a printer less than the price of a calculator?

(A) 42%

(B) 58%

(C) 63%

(D) 87%

37

A car that is traveling at a constant speed of 9 miles per hour is traveling at a constant speed of how many feet per second? (1 mile = 5,280 feet)

(A) 1.5

(B) 6.1

(C) 13.2

(D) 79.2

38

A bag contains only red and blue marbles. The ratio of red to blue marbles in the bag is 4 to 15, and there is a total of 114 marbles in the bag. How many marbles in the bag are red?

Ⓐ 24

Ⓑ 29

Ⓒ 34

Ⓓ 46

39

The population of a town was 84,600. One year later, it was 74,025. By what percent did the population of the town decrease?

Ⓐ 10.5%

Ⓑ 12.5%

Ⓒ 14.5%

Ⓓ 17%

40

A jar contains only red, white, and yellow candies in the ratio of 9:5:4, respectively. When 7 red candies and 5 white candies are removed from the jar, and 3 yellow candies are added, the ratio of red to white to yellow becomes 4:2:3. How many candies were originally in the jar?

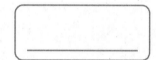

41

An air mattress deflates at a constant rate of 100 milliliters per minute. If the air mattress contains 300 liters of air, how many hours will it take to completely deflate? (Note: There are 1,000 milliliters in 1 liter.)

REFLECT

Directions: Take a few minutes to recall what you've learned and what you've been practicing in this chapter. Consider the following questions, jot down your best answer for each one, and then compare your reflections to the expert responses that follow. Use your level of confidence to determine what to do next.

What is a ratio and how is it different from a proportion?

_____

_____

_____

If you're given a ratio of one quantity to another, what can you say about the total number of quantities?

_____

_____

_____

When doing unit conversions, how can you make sure you're setting them up correctly?

_____

_____

_____

Suppose the value of something increases by 20 percent. How can you calculate the final value in the fewest number of steps? What if the value decreases by 20 percent?

_____

_____

_____

What is the percent change formula, and what is the biggest pitfall to avoid when using it?

_____

_____

_____

Expert Responses

What is a ratio and how is it different from a proportion?

A ratio is the relative comparison of one quantity to another. For example, if the ratio of dogs to cats in an animal shelter is 3 to 5, then there are 3 dogs for every 5 cats. A proportion is two ratios set equal to each other.

If you're given a ratio of one quantity to another, what can you say about the total number of quantities?

Given a ratio, you know that the total must be a multiple of the sum of the ratio's parts. For example, if the ratio of dogs to cats is 3 to 5, then the total number of dogs and cats must be a multiple of 3 + 5, or 8. This means that when the SAT gives you one ratio, it's actually giving you several. If you're told that dogs:cats = 3:5, then you also know that dogs:total = 3:8 and cats:total = 5:8. You can use this "hidden" knowledge to your advantage.

When doing unit conversions, how can you make sure you're setting them up correctly?

To do unit conversions correctly, set up the conversion in whichever way makes the unwanted units cancel each other out. For example, to convert 3 feet into inches, you multiply 3 feet by 12 inches per foot because it cancels out the feet unit. If instead you multiplied 3 feet by 1 foot per 12 inches, then the resulting units would be "feet squared per inch," which makes no sense.

Suppose the value of something increases by 20 percent. How can you calculate the final value in the fewest number of steps? What if the value decreases by 20 percent?

The fastest way to increase a value by 20 percent is to multiply it by 1.2, which is 100% + 20% = 120%. Similarly, to decrease something by 20 percent, you multiply it by 0.8, which is 100% − 20% = 80%.

What is the percent change formula, and what is the biggest pitfall to avoid when using it?

The percent change formula is as follows:

$$\text{Percent change} = \frac{\text{amount of increase or decrease}}{\text{original amount}} \times 100\%$$

A common mistake is to put the new amount on the bottom of the fraction rather than the original amount. Be sure to avoid that pitfall on test day.

Next Steps

If you answered most questions correctly in the "How Much Have You Learned?" section, and if your responses to the Reflect questions were similar to those of the SAT expert, then consider Rates, Ratios, Proportions, Percents, and Units an area of strength and move on to the next chapter. Come back to this topic periodically to ensure your skills stay sharp.

If you don't yet feel confident, review those parts of this chapter that you have not yet mastered and try the questions you missed again. As always, be sure to review the explanations closely. Finally, **go online** (www.kaptest.com/moreonline) for additional practice on the highest yield topics in this chapter.

Check Your Work – Chapter 8

1. 10.34
Difficulty: Easy
Category: Problem-Solving and Data Analysis
Getting to the Answer: To answer a question involving time and distance, use the rate (speed) formula Distance = rate × time.

In this case, you have a rate, 29 feet per second, and a distance, 300 feet. Plug these into the formula to solve for time:

300 feet = 29 feet per second × time. Now divide both sides by 29 to solve for time:

$$\frac{300 \text{ feet}}{29 \text{ feet per second}} \cong 10.34 \text{ seconds}$$

Since you can enter up to five characters for a positive student-produced response answer, enter **10.34**.

2. B
Difficulty: Medium
Category: Problem-Solving and Data Analysis
Getting to the Answer: To answer a question that relates work to time, use the work rate formula Work = rate × time. In this case, the total amount of work to be performed is the total gallons of water to be transferred, 279 gallons.

A complication in this question is the presence of two pumps. Since they're working together, it's necessary to combine their rates. The question specifies that pump A's rate is 3 gallons per minute, and pump B's rate is twice that, or 6 gallons per minute. Therefore, their combined rate is 3 gpm + 6 gpm = 9 gpm. Plug in the total work and the rate to the $W = RT$ formula and then solve for time:

279 gallons = 9 gallons per minute × time. Divide both sides by 9 gpm to solve for time:

$$\frac{279 \text{ gallons}}{9 \text{ gpm}} = \text{time}$$
$$31 \text{ minutes} = \text{time}$$

Choice **(B)** is correct.

3. C
Difficulty: Hard
Category: Problem-Solving and Data Analysis
Getting to the Answer: When a trip has multiple legs at different speeds, you'll need to use the average speed formula:

$$\text{Average Speed} = \frac{\text{total distance}}{\text{total time}}$$

The question presents the two legs of the trip by providing distances and speeds for each leg, so you'll need to use the rate formula to calculate the time of each leg. For the first leg:

$$900 \text{ miles} = 300 \text{ mph} \times t_1$$
$$\frac{900 \text{ miles}}{300 \text{ mph}} = t_1$$
$$3 \text{ hours} = t_1$$

For the second leg:

$$500 \text{ miles} = 250 \text{ mph} \times t_2$$
$$\frac{500 \text{ miles}}{250 \text{ mph}} = t_2$$
$$2 \text{ hours} = t_2$$

Now plug in the times and distances into the average speed formula:

$$\frac{\text{total distance}}{\text{total time}} = \frac{900 \text{ mi} + 500 \text{ mi}}{3 \text{ hrs} + 2 \text{ hrs}} = \frac{1,400 \text{ mi}}{5 \text{ hrs}} = 280 \text{ mph}$$

Thus, the average speed is 280 miles per hour, so **(C)** is correct.

4. D
Difficulty: Medium
Category: Problem-Solving and Data Analysis
Getting to the Answer: This question involves two separate rates: the number of kilometers the asteroid travels per hour and the number of kilometers traveled per rotation.

First, find the distance that the asteroid travels while it rotates 12 times. If it travels 600,000 km during one rotation, it must travel the following distance for 12 rotations: 600,000 km × 12 = 7,200,000 km.

To find how many hours it took to travel this distance (and rotate 12 times), use Distance = rate × time, with 30,000 kph (kilometers per hour) as the rate.

$$7,200,000 \text{ km} = 30,000 \text{ kph} \times \text{time}$$
$$\frac{7,200,000 \text{ km}}{30,000 \text{ kph}} = \text{time}$$
$$240 \text{ hours} = \text{time}$$

This means **(D)** is correct.

5. C
Difficulty: Hard
Category: Problem-Solving and Data Analysis
Getting to the Answer: You're given the total distance of a trip as well as the start and end times of the trip. You're

also given the speed of a car for the first 1.5 hours of the trip. You need to find the average speed of the car for the remaining trip time.

First, determine how far the car travels during the initial 1.5 hours using the formula $D = RT$: $D = 40$ mph × 1.5 hours = 60 miles.

From this, you can determine the remaining distance of the trip: 270 miles − 60 miles = 210 miles. Since the entire trip lasts from noon to 5:00 p.m., you know the entire trip time is 5 hours. You've accounted for the first 1.5 hours, so the rest of the trip lasts 5 hours − 1.5 hours = 3.5 hours.

Therefore, you know the car takes 3.5 hours to cover the remaining 210 miles of the trip. Use the $D = RT$ formula to find the speed over this part of the trip: 210 miles = R × 3.5 hours, so $R = 60$ miles per hour. Thus, **(C)** is correct.

6.   B
Difficulty: Hard
Category: Problem-Solving and Data Analysis
Getting to the Answer: First, use Work = rate × time to determine the rate that each of the brothers can clean the room.

Tavish: 1 room = rate × 2 hours
$$rate = \frac{1 \text{ room}}{2 \text{ hours}}$$

Tavish's brother: 1 room = rate × 4 hours
$$rate = \frac{1 \text{ room}}{4 \text{ hours}}$$

Rates simply add, so to clean 1 room together use their combined rate in Work = rate × time.

$$1 = \left(\frac{1}{2} + \frac{1}{4}\right) \times time$$
$$1 = \left(\frac{3}{4}\right) \times time$$
$$\frac{4}{3} = time$$

Therefore, **(B)** is correct.

7.   60
Difficulty: Medium
Category: Problem-Solving and Data Analysis
Getting to the Answer: The questions asks for the time needed to do a certain amount of work. You can use the $W = RT$ formula here, where W is the work to be done. In this case, that's to fill a 2,100-gallon pond, so $W = 2,100$ gallons.

To solve for T, time, you'll also need to fill the rate into the formula. The complication here is that the pond is

both draining and being filled at the same time, so you need to determine the net rate at which the pond is being filled. It's being filled at a rate of 55 gallons per hour while simultaneously being drained at a rate of 20 gallons per hour, so the net fill rate is 55 gallons per hour − 20 gallons per hour = 35 gallons per hour. Thus, R is 35 gph.

Filling in $W = RT$, you get 2,100 gallons = 35 gph × number of hours. Now solve for time:

$$\frac{2,100 \text{ gallons}}{35 \text{ gallons per hour}} = 60 \text{ hours}$$

Enter **60**.

8.   C
Difficulty: Medium
Category: Problem-Solving and Data Analysis
Getting to the Answer: Since you need to determine the difference in the time it takes the two cyclists to travel 24 miles, figure out the time it takes for each and then calculate the difference.

Cyclist A: 24 miles = 6 mph × time, so
$$\frac{24 \text{ miles}}{6 \text{ mph}} = 4 \text{ hours}$$
Cyclist B: 24 miles = 8 mph × time, so
$$\frac{24 \text{ miles}}{8 \text{ mph}} = 3 \text{ hours}$$

4 hours − 3 hours = 1 hour. Therefore, **(C)** is correct.

9.   12
Difficulty: Easy
Category: Problem-Solving and Data Analysis
Getting to the Answer: To answer a question that says "directly proportional," set two ratios equal to each other and solve for the missing amount. Be sure to match the units in the numerators and in the denominators on both sides of the proportion.

Let t equal the number of topics the teachers can cover in a 60-minute period. Set up a proportion and solve for t:

$$\frac{9 \text{ topics}}{45 \text{ minutes}} = \frac{t \text{ topics}}{60 \text{ minutes}}$$
$$9(60) = 45(t)$$
$$540 = 45t$$
$$12 = t$$

Enter **12**.

10. C

Difficulty: Easy

Category: Problem-Solving and Data Analysis

Getting to the Answer: Think about how your answer should look. A person weighs *less* on the Moon, so that person should weigh *more* on Earth. This means your answer must be greater than 29, so you can eliminate (A) right away.

Now, set up a proportion:

$$\frac{0.166 \text{ lb on Moon}}{1 \text{ lb on Earth}} = \frac{29 \text{ lb on Moon}}{p \text{ lb on Earth}}$$
$$0.166p = 29(1)$$
$$p \approx 174.7$$

The person weighs about 175 pounds on Earth. Choice **(C)** is correct.

11. B

Difficulty: Easy

Category: Problem-Solving and Data Analysis

Getting to the Answer: This is a typical proportion question. Let *n* equal the total number of parts made. Set up a proportion and solve for *n*. Be sure to match the number of defective parts in the numerators and the total manufactured parts in the denominators on both sides of the proportion:

$$\frac{6}{3,500} = \frac{27}{n}$$
$$6n = 27(3,500)$$
$$6n = 94,500$$
$$n = 15,750$$

This means **(B)** is correct.

12. 42

Difficulty: Hard

Category: Problem-Solving and Data Analysis

Getting to the Answer: This question has two unknowns: you don't know the starting number of either first-year students or second-year students. To solve for two unknowns, you need two equations. Let *f* represent the original number of first-year students in the auditorium and *s* represent the original number of second-year students. The starting ratio is $\frac{f}{s} = \frac{3}{10}$. Cross-multiplying yields $10f = 3s$. This is your first equation.

Set up a second equation to represent the adjusted number of first-year students and second-year students:

$$\frac{f + 270}{s + 120} = \frac{6}{5}$$
$$5(f + 270) = 6(s + 120)$$
$$5f + 1,350 = 6s + 720$$

You've determined from the first ratio that $10f = 3s$, and if you multiply this equation by 2, you get $20f = 6s$. Now substitute $20f$ for $6s$ in the above equation:

$$5f + 1,350 = 20f + 720$$
$$630 = 15f$$
$$42 = f$$

There were 42 first-year students in the auditorium to start, so enter **42**.

13. D

Difficulty: Medium

Category: Problem-Solving and Data Analysis

Getting to the Answer: Use the known time of 5.5 minutes it takes Reyna to travel 1 mile to calculate the distance she can cover in 90 minutes. Let *d* be the unknown distance and then set up a proportion to solve for *d*:

$$\frac{1}{5.5} = \frac{d}{90}$$
$$90 = 5.5d$$
$$\frac{90}{5.5} = d$$
$$d \approx 16$$

Therefore, **(D)** is correct.

14. A

Difficulty: Medium

Category: Problem-Solving and Data Analysis

Getting to the Answer: Since the answer choices are expressed as $\frac{y}{x} =$ and $\frac{y-x}{x} =$, cross-multiply the proportion and rewrite it to get an expression that matches the form of one of the answer choices. Solve for $\frac{y}{x}$:

$$\frac{x+y}{x} = \frac{4}{9}$$
$$9(x+y) = 4x$$
$$9x + 9y = 4x$$
$$9y = -5x$$
$$\frac{y}{x} = -\frac{5}{9}$$

This matches **(A)**.

15. C

Difficulty: Hard

Category: Problem-Solving and Data Analysis

Getting to the Answer: The ratio of physicists to total attendees is the number of physicists divided by the number of all attendees. Suppose *x* new physicists arrive at the symposium. The new number of physicists will be $123 + x$, and the new number of all attendees will be the original physicists (123) + biologists (270) + the newcomer physicists (x). The ratio of the first number over the second equals 2 to 5, so set up a proportion and solve for x:

$$\frac{123 + x}{123 + 270 + x} = \frac{2}{5}$$
$$\frac{123 + x}{393 + x} = \frac{2}{5}$$
$$5(123 + x) = 2(393 + x)$$
$$615 + 5x = 786 + 2x$$
$$3x = 171$$
$$x = 57$$

Therefore, **(C)** is correct.

16. A

Difficulty: Medium
Category: Problem-Solving and Data Analysis
Getting to the Answer: Map out your route from starting units to ending units, being mindful of the fact that the question deals with units of volume (cubic units). The starting quantity is in ft^3, and the desired quantity is in m^3. The only conversion factor you need is $1 \text{ m} \approx 3.28 \text{ ft}$, but you'll need to use it three times because ft^3 is really ft × ft × ft. Setting up your equation to get to m^3, you get:

$$700 \text{ ft}^3 \times \frac{1 \text{ m}}{3.28 \text{ ft}} \times \frac{1 \text{ m}}{3.28 \text{ ft}} \times \frac{1 \text{ m}}{3.28 \text{ ft}} = \frac{700}{(3.28)^3} \text{m}^3 \approx 19.84 \text{ m}^3$$

This matches **(A)**.

17. A

Difficulty: Hard
Category: Problem-Solving and Data Analysis
Getting to the Answer: Whenever multiple rates are given, pay very careful attention to the units. Starting with the number of pages the reporter typed, set up your conversion ratios so that equivalent units cancel. Be sure that your final units match those in the answer choices:

$$25 \text{ pages} \times \frac{675 \text{ words}}{1 \text{ page}} \times \frac{1 \text{ second}}{3.75 \text{ words}} \times \frac{1 \text{ minute}}{60 \text{ seconds}}$$
$$\times \frac{1 \text{ hour}}{60 \text{ minutes}} = 1.25 \text{ hours}$$

Because 1.25 hours is not an answer choice, convert 0.25 to minutes: 0.25 hours × 60 minutes per hour = 15 minutes. Therefore, **(A)** is the correct answer.

18. A

Difficulty: Medium
Category: Problem-Solving and Data Analysis
Getting to the Answer: The 450°F oven cooks $4.5 - 3 = 1.5$ more pounds per hour than the 350°F oven. The question asks for the difference in ounces after 10 minutes, so start there when setting up the conversion ratios:

$$10 \text{ min} \times \frac{1 \text{ hr}}{60 \text{ min}} \times \frac{1.5 \text{ lb}}{1 \text{ hr}} \times \frac{16 \text{ oz}}{1 \text{ lb}} = 4 \text{ oz}$$

Choice **(A)** is correct.

19. 50

Difficulty: Medium
Category: Problem-Solving and Data Analysis
Getting to the Answer: Starting with the prescribed dosage, set up your conversion ratios so that you get drips per minute:

$$\frac{800 \text{ mL}}{8 \text{ hours}} \times \frac{30 \text{ drips}}{1 \text{ mL}} \times \frac{1 \text{ hour}}{60 \text{ minutes}} = 50 \frac{\text{drips}}{\text{minute}}$$

Enter **50**.

20. 0.252, .2520, or .2521

Difficulty: Easy
Category: Problem-Solving and Data Analysis
Getting to the Answer: The question provides the growth rate, in meters, over a 50-year period. You need to convert this to a rate of centimeters per day. Set up your conversion ratios to make the unwanted units cancel:

$$\frac{46 \text{ meters}}{50 \text{ years}} \times \frac{100 \text{ centimeters}}{1 \text{ meter}} \times \frac{1 \text{ year}}{365 \text{ days}}$$
$$\approx 0.25205 \frac{\text{centimeters}}{\text{day}}$$

You may enter up to five characters for positive numbers, and since both truncating and rounding are acceptable, **0.252, .2520,** and **.2521** are all acceptable numbers to enter.

21. A

Difficulty: Easy
Category: Problem-Solving and Data Analysis
Getting to the Answer: The question asks for the combined number of runners and weight lifters who were injured. Calculate the number from each group who were injured and then add the numbers together:

$$3\% \times 300 = 0.03 \times 300 = 9$$
$$6\% \times 250 = 0.06 \times 250 = 15$$
$$9 + 15 = 24$$

Therefore, **(A)** is correct.

22. 3
Difficulty: Medium
Category: Problem-Solving and Data Analysis
Strategic Advice: First find the total number of attendees. Then calculate the difference in the actual number of juniors and seniors.
Getting to the Answer: The question gives you the percentage of sophomores, juniors, and seniors attending the event, as well as the actual number of teachers. Add up all of the percentages to find the total percent of the attendees who are *not* teachers: 15% + 30% + 25% = 70%. Therefore, the 18 teachers account for 100% − 70% = 30% of the attendees.

You can solve for the total number of attendees (the whole) by creating an equation relating the percent (30%) and the part (18). Say the total number of attendees is t:

$$0.30t = 18$$
$$t = \frac{18}{0.30}$$
$$t = 60$$

Thus, the total number of attendees is 60. Juniors are 30% of this number and seniors are 25%, so the difference between juniors and seniors is 30% − 25% = 5%. Now calculate 5% of the total: $0.05 \times 60 = 3$. Thus, there are 3 more juniors than seniors at the event. Alternatively, the number of juniors is $60 \times 0.30 = 18$ and the number of seniors is $60 \times 0.25 = 15$. Subtract the number of seniors from the number of juniors: 18 − 15 = 3. Either way you choose, enter **3**.

23. B
Difficulty: Hard
Category: Problem-Solving and Data Analysis
Getting to the Answer: The question gives you the amount of 15% mixture and the desired concentration (20%) that the painter wants to achieve by adding an unknown quantity of 40% mixture.

Let x represent the unknown number of gallons of the 40% mixture that the painter needs to add. Then use the formula Part = $\frac{\text{percent}}{100\%} \times$ whole to determine the part of each mixture that is blue pigment. The amount of blue pigment in the 15% mixture is 0.15×20 and the amount of blue pigment in the 40% mixture is $0.40x$. Set the sum of these two amounts equal to the amount of

blue pigment in the 20% mixture, which is $0.2 \times (20 + x)$, and solve for x.

$$0.15(20) + 0.40x = 0.20(20 + x)$$
$$3 + 0.40x = 4 + 0.20x$$
$$0.20x = 1$$
$$x = 5$$

Thus, the painter needs to add 5 gallons of the 40% mixture to achieve the desired 20% concentration of blue pigment. **(B)** is correct.

24. D
Difficulty: Medium
Category: Problem-Solving and Data Analysis
Getting to the Answer: You need to find the price of a share of the stock on October 1. You know that the price of a share was $75 on August 1 and that on September 1 the price was $10 higher than it was on August 1. Thus, on September 1, it was $75 + $10 = $85.

The question also states that the September 1 price is 80% of the October 1 price. Set up an equation where p represents the October 1 price:

$$0.8p = \$85$$
$$p = \frac{\$85}{0.8}$$
$$p = \$106.25$$

The question asks for the price to the nearest dollar, so **(D)** is correct.

25. 18
Difficulty: Hard
Category: Problem-Solving and Data Analysis
Getting to the Answer: Be sure to read the question carefully. The question tells you that x is 60% *less* than the sum of y and z, not 60% of the sum. Translate English to math and write a system of equations:

$$x + y + z = 63$$
$$x = (y + z) - 0.6(y + z)$$

Solve the second equation for $y + z$ in terms of x.

$$x = 0.4(y + z)$$
$$\frac{1}{0.4}x = y + z$$
$$2.5x = y + z$$

Then substitute $2.5x$ for $y + z$ in the first equation.

$$x + 2.5x = 63$$
$$3.5x = 63$$
$$x = 18$$

Enter **18**.

26. C
Difficulty: Easy
Category: Problem-Solving and Data Analysis
Getting to the Answer: The formula for percent increase or decrease is $\frac{actual\ change}{original\ amount} \times 100\%$. Since the price per ticket started at \$35 and ended up at \$49, that's $\frac{49 - 35}{35} \times 100\% = 40\%$.
Therefore, **(C)** is correct.

27. C
Difficulty: Easy
Category: Problem-Solving and Data Analysis
Getting to the Answer: The formula for percent increase or decrease is $\frac{actual\ change}{original\ amount} \times 100\%$. In this case, that's $\frac{1,572 - 1,494}{1,494} \times 100\% \approx 5.2\%$. Therefore, **(C)** is correct.

If you chose (B), you likely divided by the new amount, \$1,572, instead of the original amount, \$1,494.

28. B
Difficulty: Medium
Category: Problem-Solving and Data Analysis
Getting to the Answer: The question asks for a percent decrease in the number of coins from the larger jar to the smaller one. The formula for percent decrease is $\frac{actual\ change}{original\ amount} \times 100\%$. Jar X has 75 coins and jar Y has 54 coins. The phrase "less than" means that you're calculating percent decrease from a starting value of 75 coins. In other words, 75 is the "original amount." The calculation is $\frac{75 - 54}{75} \times 100\% = \frac{21}{75} \times 100\% = 28\%$.
Therefore, **(B)** is correct.

29. D
Difficulty: Medium
Category: Problem-Solving and Data Analysis
Strategic Advice: Begin by calculating the number of seniors. Then figure out what percent greater this number is than the number of sophomores.
Getting to the Answer: The number of seniors is 75% greater than the number of juniors, so there are $80 + (0.75 \times 80)$, or $1.75 \times 80 = 140$ seniors.

The formula for percent increase is $\frac{actual\ change}{original\ amount} \times$ 100%. In this case, the actual change is the number

of seniors minus the number of sophomores, $140 - 50$. The question asks for a percent greater than the number of sophomores, so the original amount is the number of sophomores, or 50: $\frac{140 - 50}{50} \times 100\% = \frac{90}{50} \times 100\% = 180\%$.

Thus, **(D)** is correct.

30. C
Difficulty: Hard
Category: Problem-Solving and Data Analysis
Strategic Advice: When presented with a two-part percent change scenario, you cannot simply add the two percents. Instead, you have to calculate the second percent change based on the adjusted value that results from the first percent change.
Getting to the Answer: The price of the phone goes through two different changes: an initial decrease of 36% and a second reduction of 25% from that depreciated cost. Because you don't know y, the original price of the phone, you can pick a number to make calculations easier.

Usually, the best number to pick when calculating the percent change of an unknown value is 100, so assume that the initial price of the phone was \$100 (the numbers don't have to be realistic, just easy to work with). Now, calculate the resulting value after the first decrease: 36% of \$100 is $0.36 \times \$100 = \$36$, so the new value of the phone will be $\$100 - \$36 = \$64$.

Next, calculate the change in price after an additional 25% is taken off of the current value of \$64: 25% of \$64 is $0.25 \times \$64 = \$16$, so the final price will be $\$64 - \$16 = \$48$. (Note that you could have also calculated the new price by subtracting the percent discount from 100 percent: $100\% - 25\% = 75\%$, so $0.75 \times \$64 = \$48$.)

The formula for percent change is $\frac{actual\ change}{original\ amount} \times 100\%$. Use the starting price of \$100 and the final price of \$48: $\frac{100 - 48}{100} \times 100\% = \frac{52}{100} \times 100\% = 52\%$.
Thus, **(C)** is correct.

31. C
Difficulty: Hard
Category: Problem-Solving and Data Analysis
Getting to the Answer: First, find the number of viewers for Season 2, Episode 2. The number of viewers for this episode is 15% lower than the number for Episode 1

(1.8 million), which is $1.8 - 0.15(1.8) = 1.53$ million. Divide this number by the average number of Season 1 viewers (2.4 million) to get the percentage. The number of viewers of Season 2, Episode 2, is $\frac{1.53}{2.4} \times 100\% = 63.75\%$ of the average number of Season 1 viewers. **(C)** is correct.

32. C
Difficulty: Hard
Category: Problem-Solving and Data Analysis
Getting to the Answer: Although the full-time and part-time employees are separate groups, the total number of employees in each group is the same. Thus, you don't need to calculate the individual number of full- and part-time employees who have benefits. Instead, find the difference of the percents. Then find that percent of 250 to get the answer in one step.

Remember the second step of the method "What does the question tell me?" and be careful: 74 percent of part-time employees *don't* qualify for benefits. This means that $100\% - 74\% = 26\%$ of them *do* qualify. Since 92% of full-time employees qualify for benefits, the percent difference is $92\% - 26\% = 66\%$. Find 66% of 250: $250 \times 0.66 = 165$. Choice **(C)** is correct.

33. 59
Difficulty: Hard
Category: Problem-Solving and Data Analysis
Getting to the Answer: Don't switch on autopilot and do five separate cost increase calculations! You can do just one and save time. First, determine the total increase from 2014–15 through 2019–20: $\$15,564 - \$12,192 = \$3,372$. Dividing $\$3,372$ by 5 (the number of increases) gives $\$674.40$, the average increase per year. To determine what portion of this amount is fees, find 8.75% of $\$674.40$: $0.0875 \times \$674.40 = \$59.01$. The question asks you to round to the nearest dollar, so enter **59**.

34. C
Difficulty: Easy
Category: Problem-Solving and Data Analysis
Getting to the Answer: The formula for percent increase or decrease is $\frac{\text{actual change}}{\text{original amount}} \times 100\%$. In this case, that works out to
$$\frac{27 - 20}{20} \times 100\% = \frac{7}{20} \times 100\% = 0.35 \times 100\% = 35\%.$$
Hence, **(C)** is correct.

35. D
Difficulty: Hard
Category: Problem-Solving and Data Analysis
Strategic Advice: Begin by determining how much profit company T made in 1997 so that you can calculate the percent increase in profit from 1997 to 1999.
Getting to the Answer: The question indicates that the 1998 profit of $375 million was 25% greater than the 1997 profit. Therefore, you can set up this equation: $125\% \times 1997$ profit $= \$375$ million. This can be written as $1.25p = \$375$ million, where p represents the 1997 profit. Divide both sides by 1.25 to find that $p = \$300$ million. The formula for percent increase or decrease is $\frac{\text{actual change}}{\text{original amount}} \times 100\%$. The actual change in profit from 1997 to 1999 was $\$483$ million $- \$300$ million $= \$183$ million. Therefore, the percent change is $\frac{183}{300} \times 100\% = 61\%$. **(D)** is correct.

36. B
Difficulty: Medium
Category: Problem-Solving and Data Analysis
Strategic Advice: Before you can calculate the percent difference between the price of the printer and the price of the calculator, you need to determine the price of the printer.
Getting to the Answer: The question indicates that the price of the printer is 16% less than the price of the radio, or 16% less than $75. Therefore, the price of the printer is $(100 - 16)\% \times \$75 = 0.84 \times \$75 = \$63$.

The formula for percent increase or decrease is $\frac{\text{actual change}}{\text{original amount}} \times 100\%$. The difference in price between the calculator and the printer is $\$150 - \$63 = \$87$. Here, the price of the calculator is functioning as the original amount. Hence, the price of the printer is $\frac{87}{150} \times 100\% = 58\%$ less than the price of the calculator. Choice **(B)** is correct.

37. C
Difficulty: Easy
Category: Problem-Solving and Data Analysis
Getting to the Answer: The question provides the speed of a car in miles per hour and asks for the speed

in feet per second. Set up your conversion ratios so that the unwanted units cancel:

$$\frac{9 \text{ miles}}{1 \text{ hour}} \times \frac{5{,}280 \text{ feet}}{1 \text{ mile}} \times \frac{1 \text{ hour}}{60 \text{ minutes}} \times \frac{1 \text{ minute}}{60 \text{ seconds}}$$

$$= 13.2 \frac{\text{feet}}{\text{second}}$$

Hence, **(C)** is correct.

38. A
Difficulty: Medium
Category: Problem-Solving and Data Analysis
Getting to the Answer: This is a proportions question that requires you to relate the total known number of marbles to the given ratio in order to find the unknown number of red marbles. First, define the relationship in the proportion with words. Then, translate from English into math. Let r equal the unknown number of red marbles. Set up a proportion and cross-multiply to solve for r:

$$\frac{\text{number of red marbles in the ratio}}{\text{total number of marbles in the ratio}}$$

$$= \frac{\text{actual number of red marbles}}{\text{actual total number of marbles}}$$

$$\frac{4}{4+15} = \frac{r}{114}$$

$$4 \times 114 = (4+15)r$$

$$456 = 19r$$

$$24 = r$$

Thus, **(A)** is correct.

Here's another way to approach this question. The total of the two values in the ratio 4:15 is 19. The total number of marbles is 114, which is 6×19. Thus, the number of red marbles is $6 \times 4 = 24$.

39. B
Difficulty: Easy
Category: Problem-Solving and Data Analysis
Getting to the Answer: The formula for percent decrease is $\frac{\text{amount of decrease}}{\text{original amount}} \times 100\%$. In this case, that works out to $\frac{84{,}600 - 74{,}025}{84{,}600} \times 100\% = \frac{10{,}575}{84{,}600} \times 100\% = 12.5\%$. Choice **(B)** is correct.

40. 54
Difficulty: Hard
Category: Problem-Solving and Data Analysis
Getting to the Answer: Since you are given both the initial values of the different-colored candies and their values after additions and removals in terms of ratios, you can express these as amounts relative to each other. There are the least number of yellow candies, so you can write that the initial number of yellow candies

is y. Because the ratio of white to yellow candles is 5:4, the number of white candies is $\frac{5}{4}y$, and, because the ratio of red to yellow candles is 9:4, the number of red candies is $\frac{9}{4}y$.

Now you can compare the "before and after" quantities of the red or white candies in terms of y. If you choose to look at the red candies, after the removals and additions, the number of red candies is $\frac{4}{3}(y+3)$ because 3 yellow candies were added. But 7 reds were removed, so the equation is $\frac{9}{4}y - 7 = \frac{4}{3}(y+3)$. Multiply both sides by 12 to clear the fractions: $27y - 84 = 16y + 48$. So, $11y = 132$, and $y = 12$.

The original number of white candies is $\frac{5}{4}(12) = 15$, and the original number of red is $\frac{9}{4}(12) = 27$. So, the total number of all three colors before the changes is $12 + 15 + 27 = 54$. Enter **54**.

Another way to solve this question is by picking numbers, making sure that they obey the rules of the ratios. You know that the ratio of red to white is 9 to 5, and that after 7 red and 5 white are removed, the ratio will be 4 to 2—in other words, there will be twice as many red as white. Start with 9 red and 5 white candies and work up from there until you find a multiple that works in this scenario:

9 red, 5 white
2 red, 0 white: doesn't work

18 red, 10 white
11 red, 5 white: doesn't work

27 red, 15 white
20 red, 10 white: this works!

Also, the common multiplier is 3, so there are $4 \times 3 = 12$ yellow candies. Therefore, the total is $27 + 15 + 12 = 54$ candies. Enter **54**.

41. 50
Difficulty: Medium
Category: Problem-Solving and Data Analysis
Getting to the Answer: Since the rate of deflation is $100 \frac{\text{mL}}{\text{min}}$, convert the air mattress's initial volume of 300 liters into milliliters: $300 \text{ L} \times \frac{1{,}000 \text{ mL}}{1 \text{ L}} = 300{,}000 \text{ mL}$. Then, to determine the number of hours it will take for the mattress to completely deflate, set up conversion factors so that unwanted units cancel out:

$$300{,}000 \text{ mL} \times \frac{1 \text{ min}}{100 \text{ mL}} \times \frac{1 \text{ hr}}{60 \text{ min}} = 50 \text{ hr}$$

Enter **50**.

CHAPTER 9

TABLES, STATISTICS, AND PROBABILITY

LEARNING OBJECTIVES

After completing this chapter, you will be able to:

- Draw inferences about data presented in a variety of graphical formats
- Find an unknown value given the average
- Calculate mean, median, mode, and range
- Describe standard deviation and margin of error
- Determine whether a survey is valid or biased
- Draw inferences about surveys and data samples
- Calculate probabilities based on data sets

HOW MUCH DO YOU KNOW?

Directions

Try the questions that follow. Show your work so that you can compare your solutions to the ones found in the "Check Your Work" section immediately after this question set. If you answered the question(s) on a specific topic correctly, and if your scratchwork looks like ours, you may be able to move quickly through the lesson covering that topic. If you answered incorrectly or used a different approach, you may want to take your time on that lesson.

1

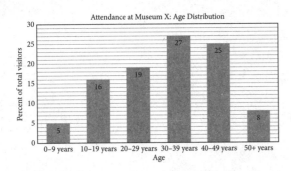

The graph shows the percent distribution of visitors to museum X by age. If 553 people aged 20 years and older visited museum X, then how many total people visited museum X?

- (A) 116
- (B) 437
- (C) 700
- (D) 2633

2

Age group	Healthy	At risk	Diabetic	Total
18–25	9	22	17	48
26–35	16	48	34	98
36–45	19	35	40	94
Older than 45	12	27	21	60
Total	56	132	112	300

Based on the table, if a single participant is selected at random from all the participants, what is the probability that he or she will be at risk for diabetes and be at least 36 years old?

- (A) $\frac{7}{60}$
- (B) $\frac{31}{150}$
- (C) $\frac{31}{77}$
- (D) $\frac{11}{25}$

3

History Majors Declared at College X

Year	Number of history majors
2010	225
2011	287
2012	162
2013	240
2014	s

The table shows the number of history majors declared each year at a certain college from 2010 to 2014. If the median number of history majors declared for the five years was 225, what is the greatest possible value of s?

Ⓐ 161

Ⓑ 225

Ⓒ 239

Ⓓ 288

4

A certain convention is attended by 1,650 people. Before the convention, 150 of the people who are planning to attend were surveyed about their lunch preferences. Of these, 38 preferred salads, 23 preferred pizza, 59 preferred sandwiches, and 30 preferred chicken. Based on the results of this survey, how many of the people attending the convention can be expected to want sandwiches for lunch?

5

A researcher conducted a poll to determine how many people in a city of 100,000 residents drink nondairy milks. The researcher polled 800 city residents who are sensitive to dairy. Of those polled, 72 percent responded that they drink nondairy milks.

Which of the following indicates why the survey results would not allow for a reliable conclusion about the preferences of the city's residents?

Ⓐ The researcher did not ask people if they prefer the taste of dairy milk to nondairy milks.

Ⓑ The survey sample is not representative of the city's residents.

Ⓒ The population of the city is too large to get a reliable survey sample.

Ⓓ The survey sample likely consisted of only adults and did not consider the opinion of children.

6

Cookies Baked

	Chocolate chip	Oatmeal raisin	Total
With nuts		40	
Without nuts			104
Total			186

A baker makes 186 cookies: $\frac{2}{3}$ are chocolate chip and $\frac{1}{3}$ are oatmeal raisin. Both kinds are made with and without nuts, as shown in the table. If a chocolate chip cookie is chosen at random, what is the probability that it will have nuts?

Ⓐ $\frac{21}{93}$

Ⓑ $\frac{21}{62}$

Ⓒ $\frac{41}{93}$

Ⓓ $\frac{21}{41}$

Check Your Work

1. C
Difficulty: Medium
Category: Problem-Solving and Data Analysis
Getting to the Answer: Although you could use the bar graph to find the percentage of people aged 20 or older, it is tedious to add up all of these individual values. It is faster to find the percentage of people who are *not* aged 20 or older and subtract this value from 100%. You know from the bar graph that 21% (5% + 16%) of the visitors were *not* aged 20 or older. This means that 100% − 21% = 79% *were* aged 20 or older. Let the total number of visitors in the museum be *x*. Since the number of visitors aged 20 or older is 553, you can conclude that $0.79x = 553$. This gives $x = 700$. Choice **(C)** is correct.

2. B
Difficulty: Medium
Category: Problem-Solving and Data Analysis
Getting to the Answer: This question requires careful reading of the table. The first criterion is fairly straightforward—you're looking for a participant who is at risk, so focus on that column in the table. The second criterion is a bit trickier—"at least 36 years old" means you'll need to use the values in both the row for 36–45 and the row for older than 45. Within the at risk column, there are 35 in the 36–45 age group and 27 in the older than 45 age group, resulting in a total of 35 + 27 = 62 out of 300 total participants overall. The probability of randomly selecting one participant who fits the criteria is therefore $\frac{62}{300}$, which reduces to $\frac{31}{150}$. Choice **(B)** is correct.

3. B
Difficulty: Hard
Category: Problem-Solving and Data Analysis
Getting to the Answer: The median of a list of numbers is the middle number when the list is written in ascending order. Begin by arranging the number of history majors from least to greatest, making sure that 225 is in the middle. Use *s* to balance out the number of history majors on either side of 225. Because there are already two numbers above the median (240 and 287), there must be two numbers below the median. There are two ways that this could happen:

s, 162, 225, 240, 287

or

162, *s*, 225, 240, 287

The number could be anything less than or equal to 225. Its greatest possible value is therefore 225, which is **(B)**.

4. 649
Difficulty: Easy
Category: Problem-Solving and Data Analysis
Getting to the Answer: The question indicates that of the 150 survey respondents, 59 wanted sandwiches. To find the number of the people attending the convention who can be expected to want sandwiches for lunch, set up a proportion using the number of survey respondents who want sandwiches, the total number of survey respondents, and the total number of people attending the convention: $\frac{59}{150} = \frac{x}{1,650}$. Cross-multiply to find that $97,350 = 150x$. Therefore, $x = 649$. Enter **649**.

5. B
Difficulty: Easy
Category: Problem-Solving and Data Analysis
Getting to the Answer: Determine who is being surveyed and what results are intended. In this question, the goal is to determine whether people in a large city drink nondairy milks. To obtain a representative sample of the population, the survey should randomly select individuals from the population. However, the researcher polled only people who have a dairy sensitivity. Since these people are a special subset of the general population, they do not represent the population of the city as a whole. Therefore, **(B)** is the correct answer.

6. B

Difficulty: Hard

Category: Problem-Solving and Data Analysis

Getting to the Answer: The table is not complete, so your first step is to transfer the table quickly to scratch paper and fill in the missing values. Start with what you know and work from there. There are 186 cookies total, and 104 are without nuts. This means that $186 - 104 = 82$ have nuts. Because the table already indicates that 40 of those cookies are oatmeal raisin, $82 - 40 = 42$ are chocolate chip. The table you drew on the scratch paper might now looks like this:

	C C	O R	Total
W/ nuts	42	40	82
W/O nuts			104
Total			186

Recall that $\frac{2}{3}$ of the total number of cookies are chocolate chip. This means that there are $\frac{2}{3} \times 186 = 124$ chocolate chip cookies.

	C C	O R	Total
W/ nuts	42	40	82
W/O nuts			104
Total	124		186

You do not need to fill in any more values because the question asks only about chocolate chip cookies with nuts. There are 124 chocolate chip cookies total and 42 of them have nuts, so the probability of randomly choosing one with nuts is $\frac{42}{124}$, or $\frac{21}{62}$. This matches **(B)**.

Math

TABLES AND GRAPHS

LEARNING OBJECTIVES

After this lesson, you will be able to:

- Draw inferences about data presented in a variety of graphical formats
- Find an unknown value given the average

To solve a question like this:

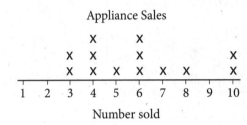

Appliance Sales

An appliance salesperson sets a goal to sell an average of 6 appliances per day for the first two weeks of his new job. The dot plot shows the number he sold each day during the first 13 days. What is the minimum number of appliances he must sell on the 14th day in order to reach his goal?

A) 5

B) 6

C) 7

D) 8

You need to know this:

The SAT uses some straightforward methods of representing data sets that you are likely already familiar with. For example, you may have to look up information in a table or read a bar chart. There are, however, some less common types of plots that show up from time to time that can be confusing at first glance. Graphics you may see on test day include the following:

- **Tables, bar charts, and line graphs** show up all the time in the Math section (and in the Reading and Writing section, too). They shouldn't be difficult to interpret, but it's helpful to keep in mind that the test maker often includes more information than you actually need. It's important to consider what the question asks for so that you find only the information that you need.

- **Frequency tables and dot plots** are ways of representing how many times a data point appears within a data set. The sample question presents its data as a dot plot:

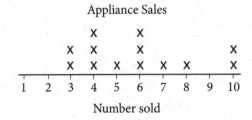

Appliance Sales

Each "X" represents one instance in the data set of each "number sold." So, for example, there were two different days on which this person sold 3 appliances, three different days on which this person sold 4 appliances, and so on. The data could just as easily be written as a data set: {3, 3, 4, 4, 4, 5, 6, 6, 6, 7, 8, 10, 10}. Or it could be placed in a frequency table:

NUMBER SOLD	FREQUENCY
1	0
2	0
3	2
4	3
5	1
6	3
7	1
8	1
9	0
10	2

- **Histograms** look a lot like bar charts and can be read in the same way, but they are similar to frequency tables and dot plots in that they show how many times a certain value shows up in a data set for a variable. The histogram for the appliances data set would look like this:

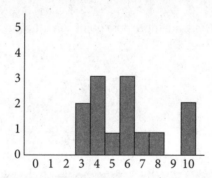

Notice that the histogram is basically the same as the dot plot for this data set. Histograms are better for representing larger data sets for which individual dots would be difficult to count.

- **Skew** is a measure of the symmetry of the data in a chart or graph.

An unskewed graph is perfectly symmetrical. Its mean, median, and mode are equal. (Don't worry if you're not familiar with these statistics terms yet; they'll be covered in the next lesson.) An unskewed graph looks like this:

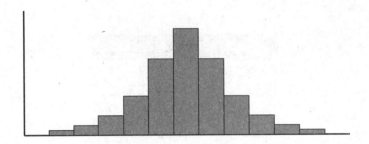

In a right-skewed graph, there are more data points on the left. The distribution is often said to have a "tail" on the right. The statistics are: Mode < Median < Mean

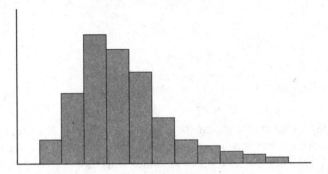

A left-skewed graph is the opposite. There are more data points on the right, and the "tail" is said to be on the left. Mean < Median < Mode

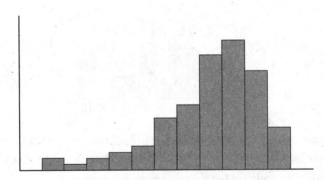

You need to do this:

- When presented with a question that uses a graph or table to present information, first inspect the format of the graph or table. What kind of graph or table is it? What information is presented on each axis? What information do you need to find in order to answer the question?

- Find the information you need from the table or graph and then use the information for any calculation the question might require, such as taking the average, finding the median, or thinking about standard deviation.

- Use the average formula, $\text{Average} = \dfrac{\text{sum}}{\text{number of items}}$, to find unknowns. For example, if you know that the average of 5 terms is 7, and you know that 4 of the terms are 3, 6, 8, and 9, you can call the last term x and plug it into the equation, then solve for x:

$$7 = \frac{3 + 6 + 8 + 9 + x}{5}$$

$$35 = 26 + x$$

$$x = 9$$

- If the data is skewed, determine the effect on the mean, median, and mode.

Explanation:

This question gives you an average and asks for a missing value. First, set up a general equation for the average:

$$\text{Average} = \frac{\text{sum}}{\text{number of items}}$$

The scenario takes place over 14 days, and the average is given as 6 items per day. Let a represent the unknown number of appliances sold on the 14th day and then fill in the number of appliances sold the previous days from the dot plot:

$$6 = \frac{3 + 3 + 4 + 4 + 4 + 5 + 6 + 6 + 6 + 7 + 8 + 10 + 10 + a}{14}$$

Multiply both sides by 14 to get rid of the fraction and simplify the addition on the right before isolating a:

$$84 = 3 + 3 + 4 + 4 + 4 + 5 + 6 + 6 + 6 + 7 + 8 + 10 + 10 + a$$

$$84 = 76 + a$$

$$a = 8$$

Choice **(D)** is correct.

Try on Your Own

Directions

Take as much time as you need on these questions. Work carefully and methodically. There will be an opportunity for timed practice later in the book.

1

HINT: For Q1, fraction $= \dfrac{\text{part}}{\text{whole}}$. Which *part* is the question asking for? Out of which *whole*?

	Bob's bookshop	Clara's bookshop	Derek's bookshop	Evelyn's bookshop	Total
Monday	14	7	15	12	48
Tuesday	8	13	15	13	49
Wednesday	10	13	12	14	49
Thursday	8	15	14	10	47
Friday	13	7	10	9	39
Total	53	55	66	58	232

Which of the four bookshops made the greatest fraction of its total sales on Tuesday?

(A) Bob's Bookshop

(B) Clara's Bookshop

(C) Derek's Bookshop

(D) Evelyn's Bookshop

2

Group	Proportion
A: inert, mild or no side effects	34.5%
B: inert, moderate side effects	9.2%
C: inert, severe side effects	6.2%
D: drug, mild or no side effects	9.5%
E: drug, moderate side effects	12.8%
F: drug, severe side effects	27.8%

Dr. Hunter is overseeing a treatment-resistant influenza Phase I trial with 400 healthy participants: half are given the drug and half are given an inert pill. Dr. Hunter records the severity of gastrointestinal side effects.

Of the participants who had severe side effects, approximately what percent were administered the drug?

(A) 28%

(B) 34%

(C) 82%

(D) 95%

3

HINT: For Q3, which group in the study is of interest?

Numerous health studies have found that people who eat breakfast are generally healthier and weigh less than people who skip this meal.

Breakfast Study Results

	Breakfast ≤1 time per week	Breakfast 2–4 times per week	Breakfast 5–7 times per week	Total
Within healthy weight range	6	15	36	57
Outside healthy weight range	38	27	9	74
Total	44	42	45	131

Approximately what percent of the participants who were outside a healthy weight range ate breakfast one or fewer times per week?

Ⓐ 29%

Ⓑ 51%

Ⓒ 56%

Ⓓ 86%

4

Scientists have classified a sleeping person's brain activity into four sleep stages: 1 (light sleep), 2 (medium sleep), 3 (deep sleep), and 4 (REM). A technician monitored a person's brainwaves in 15-minute intervals for 8 continuous hours, and categorized them into one of the four stages, as shown in the bar graph.

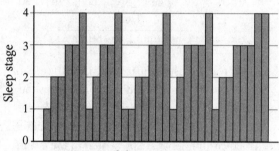

8-Hour Sleep Study Results

Each bar = 15 minutes

Based on the graph, how many minutes did the patient spend in non-deep sleep over the course of the entire night?

5

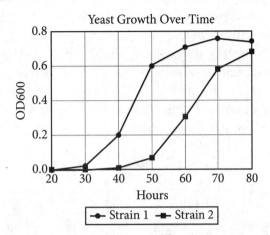

A microbiologist compares the growth rates of two yeast strains. She indirectly measures the number of yeast cells by recording the optical density (OD600) of each strain every 10 hours. The measurements are presented in the graph shown. Based on the data, which of the following statements is false?

(A) Between hours 30 and 80, Strain 1 had a higher OD600 reading than Strain 2.

(B) The growth rate of Strain 2 was less than the growth rate of Strain 1 until hour 50, at which point Strain 1's growth rate became the lesser one.

(C) Between hours 50 and 70, Strain 2's OD600 reading increased by approximately 0.03 every hour.

(D) The growth rate of Strain 1 was greater than the growth rate of Strain 2 throughout the monitored period.

STATISTICS

LEARNING OBJECTIVES

After this lesson, you will be able to:

• Calculate mean, median, mode, and range

• Describe standard deviation and margin of error

To answer a question like this:

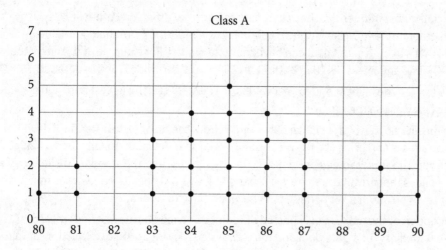

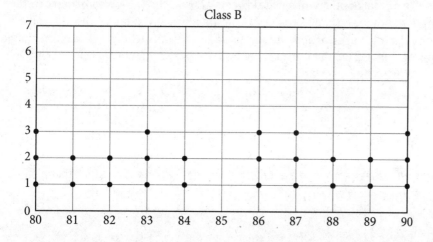

Two classes of 25 students each took an identical exam. Their percent correct scores are shown in the dot plots. If M_A and S_A are the median and standard deviation, respectively, of class A, and M_B and S_B are the median and standard deviation, respectively, of class B, then which of the following statements is true?

A) $M_A < M_B$ and $S_A < S_B$

B) $M_A > M_B$ and $S_A < S_B$

C) $M_A > M_B$ and $S_A > S_B$

D) $M_A < M_B$ and $S_A > S_B$

You need to know this:

The following are six fundamental statistical measures you can determine for a data set. For example, suppose a nurse took a patient's pulse at different times of day and found it to be 75, 78, 71, 71, and 68.

- **Mean (also called arithmetic mean or average):** The sum of the values divided by the number of values. For this data set, the mean pulse is $\frac{75 + 78 + 71 + 71 + 68}{5} = \frac{363}{5} = 72.6$.

- **Median:** The value that is in the middle of the set *when the values are arranged in ascending order*. The pulse values in ascending order are 68, 71, 71, 75, and 78. The middle term is the third term, making the median 71. (If the list consists of an even number of values, the median is the average of the middle two values.)

- **Mode:** The value that occurs most frequently. The value that appears more than any other is 71, which appears twice (while all other numbers appear only once), so it is the mode. If more than one value appears the most often, that's okay; a set of data can have multiple modes. For example, if the nurse took the patient's pulse a sixth time and it was 68, then both 71 and 68 would be modes for this data set.

- **Range:** The difference between the highest and lowest values. In this data set, the lowest and highest values are 68 and 78, respectively, so the range is $78 - 68 = 10$.

- **Standard deviation:** A measure of how far a typical data point is from the mean. A low standard deviation means most values in the set are fairly close to the mean; a high standard deviation means there is much more spread in the data set. The standard deviation of this data set is 3.91, and the standard deviation of a data set containing five values that are all the same is 0. On the SAT, you will need to know what standard deviation is and what it tells you about a set of data, but you won't have to calculate it.

- **Margin of error:** A description of the maximum expected difference between a true statistics measure (for example, the mean or median) for a data pool and that same statistics measure for a random sample from the data pool. If 72.6% of a random sample reported yes, and there is a 10% margin of error, then the percentage of the data pool (e.g., real population) who said yes is 72.6% ± 10%. A lower margin of error is achieved by increasing the size of the random sample. As with standard deviation, on the SAT, you will need to know how to interpret margin of error and perform some simple calculations with a given margin of error and statistics measure, but you won't be asked to determine what a margin of error is for a given sample.

You need to do this:

- To compare two standard deviations, look at how spread out the data set is. The more clustered the data, the lower the standard deviation.

- To find the median, arrange *all* values in order. In a dot plot or frequency distribution table, that means finding the group with the middle value.

Explanation:

Start with the standard deviation. The scores in class A are more clustered around the mean, so the standard deviation for class A will be smaller than that for class B, where the scores are more spread out. Eliminate (C) and (D).

To calculate the medians of the two classes, you need to find the middle value in each data set. Each class has 25 students, so the middle score will be the 13th term. Count from the left of each dot plot to find that the 13th score for class A is 85 and for class B is 86. So the median for class B is greater. **(A)** is correct.

Try on Your Own

Directions

Take as much time as you need on these questions. Work carefully and methodically. There will be an opportunity for timed practice later in the book.

6

Number of Languages	Country A	Country B
1	55	70
2	80	50
3	50	50
4	40	45
5	25	35

An anthropologist chose 250 citizens at random from each of two European countries and separated them into groups based on how many languages they spoke. The results are shown in the table. What is the median number of languages spoken by the sample of citizens from country B?

Ⓐ 1

Ⓑ 2

Ⓒ 3

Ⓓ 4

7

The average of x and 5 is c, and the average of $3x$ and 3 is d. What is the average of c and d in terms of x?

Ⓐ $\frac{1}{2}x + 1$

Ⓑ $x + 2$

Ⓒ $2x - 1$

Ⓓ $2x + 4$

8

HINT: For Q8, when you see the word "consistent," think "standard deviation."

	Charles	Gautam	Brin
Run 1	8.3	8.5	8.4
Run 2	7.7	8.0	8.0
Run 3	7.1	8.5	7.5
Run 4	6.6	7.8	9.0
Run 5	8.0	8.1	7.5
Run 6	6.6	7.5	7.2
Mean score	7.38	8.07	7.93
Standard deviation	0.73	0.39	0.67

Charles, Gautam, and Brin participated in a snowboarding competition. The scores for each of their six qualifying runs are shown in the table. According to the data, which of the following is a valid conclusion?

Ⓐ Charles had the smallest mean score, so his performance was the least consistent.

Ⓑ Gautam had the smallest standard deviation, so his performance was the most consistent.

Ⓒ Charles had the largest standard deviation, so his performance was the most consistent.

Ⓓ Brin had the highest score on any one run, so her performance was the most consistent.

9

Ages of Used Cars in Dealer Inventory

Age (model years)	Number of cars
1	3
2	5
3	18
4	17
5	11
6	6
7	2

The table shows the distribution of the ages (in model years) of the cars in a certain dealer's inventory. Which of the following correctly lists the mean, median, and mode of the ages of the cars in ascending order?

Ⓐ Mean, Median, Mode

Ⓑ Median, Mode, Mean

Ⓒ Mode, Mean, Median

Ⓓ Mode, Median, Mean

10

HINT: For Q10, start with the most definite information. What do you know about the past 11 days?

Credit Card Applicants

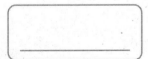

The dot plot shows the number of credit card applicants Amara obtained in the past 11 days. How many applicants must Amara obtain on the 12th day to reach an average of 4 applicants a day?

11

Number of Persons in 65 Households

y-axis: Number of households (0, 2, 4, 6, 8, 10, 12, 14, 16, 18, 20)
x-axis: Number of persons in household (1, 2, 3, 4, 5, 6)

Based on the graph, how many households have a number of persons greater than the median number of persons?

Ⓐ 2

Ⓑ 10

Ⓒ 22

Ⓓ 37

12

A random sample of college students was asked how often they eat out. Based on the sample data, a marketing team estimated that 87% of the college students on campus ate out at least once a week. If the margin of error is 5%, which of the following is a valid conclusion?

Ⓐ The marketing team has 95% confidence that most college students eat out at least once a week.

Ⓑ No more than 89.5% of college students eat out at least once a week.

Ⓒ The percentage of college students who eat out at least once a week is between 82% and 92%.

Ⓓ Less than 87% of college students eat out 5% of the time.

SURVEYS AND DATA SAMPLES

LEARNING OBJECTIVES

After this lesson, you will be able to:

- Determine whether a survey is valid or biased
- Draw inferences about surveys and data samples

To answer a question like this:

A book club wanted to determine the average number of books read each year by residents of a certain town, so it conducted a survey of 100 patrons of the town's public library. The average number of books read per year by these 100 patrons was 51.5. Which of the following statements must be true based on this information?

A) The survey is biased due to a poor choice of sampling method.

B) The survey is not biased and will likely produce a correct estimate of the number of books read annually by the town's residents.

C) The average number of books read annually by all the town's residents is 51.5.

D) The average number of books read per town resident per year cannot be determined from such a small sample.

You need to know this:

You will see occasional questions on the SAT Math section that do not test any calculation or even your ability to interpret numerical data. Instead, these questions test your ability to draw logical conclusions about surveys and data sampling methods.

Answering these questions correctly hinges on your ability to tell whether a data sample is **representative** of the larger population. A **representative sample** is a small group that shares key characteristics with the larger group you are trying to draw conclusions about.

A sample that is selected truly at random is generally representative of the larger group. For example, a scientist who wants to learn the average height of penguins in a colony of 200 might measure the heights of a random sample of only 20 penguins. As long as the 20 penguins are selected at random, their average height will approximate the average height of the birds in the entire colony.

On the other hand, a sample that is not selected at random may not be representative and may lead to a biased conclusion. For instance, imagine that a small town uses volunteer firefighters and that a stipulation for becoming a volunteer firefighter is living within a mile of the fire station. If you wanted to know what percent of households in the town include at least one volunteer firefighter, you would need to survey a random sample of households from the entire town, not just a sample of households within a mile of the fire station. A sample of households within a mile of the fire station would be a biased sample and would lead to an erroneous conclusion (namely, that the percent of households in the town that include at least one volunteer firefighter is higher than it actually is).

You need to do this:

- Check whether the data sample represents the larger population of interest. If it doesn't, the survey is biased.
- In questions that ask you to draw a conclusion from a random (unbiased) sample, look for the answer choice for which the representative sample accurately reflects the larger population. For example, in a question asking for a conclusion based on a sample of librarians, the correct answer will match the sample to a larger population of librarians, not to a population of, say, accountants.

Explanation:

The sample in this question includes 100 public library patrons. This is not a randomly selected sample. It's a good bet that frequent readers of books will be overrepresented at a public library. Thus, the survey is biased, so **(A)** is correct. (B) and (C) are incorrect because they both imply the survey is accurate. (D) misstates the reason the survey is inaccurate; the problem is not that the sample is too small, it's that it's biased.

Try on Your Own

Directions

Take as much time as you need on these questions. Work carefully and methodically. There will be an opportunity for timed practice later in the book.

13

HINT: For Q13, who is in the survey group? Who is in the larger population? Are these groups different? If so, the survey is likely biased.

A railroad company is planning to build a new station in a town's downtown area where many commuters work. To assess public opinion, the company surveys a sample of 200 residents who commute to the downtown area for work. Over 80 percent of those surveyed are in favor of building the new station.

Which of the following is true about the survey's reliability?

- Ⓐ It is unreliable because the survey sample is not representative of the entire town.

- Ⓑ It is unreliable because the survey sample is too small.

- Ⓒ It is reliable because nobody in the survey sample works for the railroad company.

- Ⓓ It is reliable because the survey sample excludes people who do not ride the train.

14

A bottled water company conducts a survey to find out how many bottles of water people consume per day. If a representative and random sample of 500 people is chosen from a population estimated to be 50,000, which of the following accurately describes how the mean of the sample data relates to the estimated mean of the entire population?

- Ⓐ The mean of the sample data is equal to the estimated mean of the population.

- Ⓑ The mean of the sample data cannot be used to estimate the mean of the much larger population.

- Ⓒ The mean of the sample data should be multiplied by 100 to get the estimated mean of the population.

- Ⓓ The mean of the sample data should be multiplied by 1,000 to get the estimated mean of the population.

15

A store manager surveyed randomly selected customers to determine why they were returning their products. This sample included 70 customers who were returning dinnerware, of whom 80 percent indicated that at least one piece of dinnerware was chipped or broken.

Which of the following conclusions is best supported by the sample data?

Ⓐ Most of the products returned to the store contain chipped or broken pieces.

Ⓑ Dinnerware products are more likely to contain chipped or broken pieces than other products.

Ⓒ Most customers returning dinnerware returned products containing chipped or broken pieces.

Ⓓ At least 80 percent of the products sold at the store contain chipped or broken pieces.

16

The owner of a miniature golf course asked 150 randomly surveyed children at the course what color golf ball they prefer. Approximately 60 percent of them said they prefer red, while approximately 30 percent of them said blue.

This data best supports which of the following conclusions?

Ⓐ Most people prefer a red golf ball when playing miniature golf.

Ⓑ Red golf balls are used twice as often for miniature golf as blue golf balls.

Ⓒ Most children at the miniature golf course preferred a red golf ball.

Ⓓ Approximately 10 percent of miniature golf players prefer a white golf ball.

17

HINT: For Q17, remember that a valid sample must be unbiased and representative of the larger population.

A state politician appears on a local television show to discuss his response to Issue X. He asks people to text "1" if they support his response and "2" if they do not. 75% of the texts are 1s. He concludes that the majority of the state's residents support his response to Issue X.

Which of the following indicates why the survey results would not allow for a reliable conclusion about the preferences of the entire state?

Ⓐ The politician did not ask people's opinions about Issue Y.

Ⓑ The survey sample is not representative of the state's residents.

Ⓒ The television show is streamed online for free.

Ⓓ The survey sample was only 75% likely to be accurate.

PROBABILITY

LEARNING OBJECTIVE

After this lesson, you will be able to:

- Calculate probabilities based on data sets

To answer a question like this:

Number of Cyclists in Regional Race, by Age and Town

TOWN	AGE (YEARS)					TOTAL
	15 TO 18	19 TO 25	26 TO 34	35 TO 46	47 AND OLDER	
Pine Falls	9	52	31	26	29	147
Greenville	14	38	42	53	30	177
Salem	5	17	18	13	10	63
Fairview	19	41	32	34	27	153
Total	47	148	123	126	96	540

The table shows the number of participants in a regional bicycle race, categorized by town and age group. Based on the table, if a cyclist from Fairview is chosen at random, which of the following is closest to the probability that the cyclist was 35 or older at the time of the race?

A) 0.40

B) 0.18

C) 0.11

D) 0.05

You need to know this:

Probability is a fraction or decimal between 0 and 1 comparing the number of desired outcomes to the number of total possible outcomes. A probability of 0 means that an event will not occur; a probability of 1 means that it definitely will occur. The formula is as follows:

$$\text{Probability} = \frac{\text{number of desired outcomes}}{\text{number of total possible outcomes}}$$

For instance, if you roll a six-sided die, each side showing a different number from 1 to 6, the probability of rolling a number higher than 4 is $\frac{2}{6} = \frac{1}{3}$, because there are two numbers higher than 4 (5 and 6) and six numbers total (1, 2, 3, 4, 5, and 6).

To find the probability that an event will **not** happen, subtract the probability that the event will happen from 1. Continuing the previous example, the probability of **not** rolling a number higher than 4 would be:

$$1 - \frac{1}{3} = \frac{2}{3}$$

You might also be tested on the probability of two independent events both happening. **Independent events** are those in which the probability of one has no influence on the probability of the other. To find the probability of both events happening, multiply the probability of the first event times the probability of the second. For example, the probability of getting "heads" on a single coin toss is $\frac{1}{2}$. The probability of rolling a number greater than 4 on a six-sided die is $\frac{1}{3}$. Thus, the probability of getting "heads" on a coin toss *and* rolling a number greater than 4 on a die is $\frac{1}{2} \times \frac{1}{3} = \frac{1}{6}$.

Note that a probability can be expressed as a fraction, a decimal, or a percent; for example, a probability of $\frac{1}{2}$ can also be expressed as 0.5 or 50%.

The SAT may test probability in the context of data tables. Using a table, you can find the probability that a randomly selected data value (be it a person, object, etc.) will fit a certain profile. For example, the following table summarizing a survey on water preference might be followed by a question asking for the probability that a person randomly selected for a follow-up survey falls into a given category.

	TAP	CARBONATED	BOTTLED	TOTAL
Female	325	267	295	887
Male	304	210	289	803
Total	629	477	584	1,690

If the question asked for the probability of randomly selecting a female who prefers tap water from all the participants of the original survey, you would calculate it using the same general formula as before:

$$\frac{\text{\# female, tap}}{\text{\# total}} = \frac{325}{1{,}690} = \frac{5}{26} \approx 0.192$$

If the question asked for the probability of randomly selecting a female for the follow-up survey, given that the chosen participant prefers tap water, the setup is a little different. This time, the number of possible outcomes is the total number of participants **who prefer tap water**, which is 629, not the grand total of 1,690. The calculation is now $\frac{\text{\# female, tap}}{\text{\# total, tap}} = \frac{325}{629} \approx 0.517$.

Conversely, if you needed to find the probability of selecting someone who prefers tap water for the follow-up survey, given that the chosen participant is female, the new number of possible outcomes would be the female participant total (887). The calculation becomes $\frac{\text{\# female, tap}}{\text{\# total, females}} = \frac{325}{887} \approx 0.366$.

You need to do this:

- Determine the number of desired and total possible outcomes by looking at the table.
- Read the question carefully when determining the number of possible outcomes: do you need the entire set or a subset?

Explanation:

The number of desired outcomes is the number of cyclists from Fairview who are 35 or older. That means you need to add the "35 to 46" and "47 and Older" categories: $34 + 27 = 61$. The number of possible outcomes is the total number of cyclists from Fairview. The number is given in the totals column: 153. Plug these numbers into the probability formula and divide:

$$\text{Probability} = \frac{\text{\# Fairview, 35 and Older}}{\text{\# Fairview, Total}} = \frac{61}{153} \approx 0.40$$

The correct answer is **(A)**.

Try on Your Own

Directions

Take as much time as you need on these questions. Work carefully and methodically. There will be an opportunity for timed practice later in the book.

18

	Marked defective	Not marked defective	Total
Defective bearing	392	57	449
Non-defective bearing	168	49,383	49,551
Total	560	49,440	50,000

A factory produces 50,000 bearings per week. A device is installed that is designed to detect defective bearings and mark them. According to the results shown in the table, what is the approximate probability that a part that is marked defective will actually be defective?

(A) 30%

(B) 43%

(C) 70%

(D) 87%

19

HINT: For Q19, what percentage of the fish at the hatchery are salmon? How many salmon are there? How many of those were tested?

The table shows the distribution of four species of fish at a hatchery that has approximately 6,000 fish.

Species	Percent of total
Carp	50
Salmon	25
Tilapia	15
Tuna	10

A biologist randomly tests 5 percent of each species of fish for mercury content. Her findings are shown in the following table.

Mercury Content Test Results

Species	Number of fish with dangerous mercury levels
Carp	11
Salmon	6
Tilapia	5
Tuna	8

Based on the biologist's findings, if a single salmon is randomly selected from those that were tested, what is the probability that this particular fish would have a dangerous mercury level?

(A) 0.001

(B) 0.004

(C) 0.02

(D) 0.08

20

Type of engineer	Preference		Total
	Robotics	AV	
Mechanical	198	245	443
Electrical	149	176	325
Total	347	421	768

In a survey, a group of mechanical and electrical engineers marked their preference between robotics and autonomous vehicles (AV). The results are shown in the table. What is the probability that a randomly selected engineer will be a mechanical engineer who prefers autonomous vehicles?

Ⓐ 0.229

Ⓑ 0.319

Ⓒ 0.553

Ⓓ 0.582

21

HINT: For Q21, how many groups have *at least* 8 days vacation?

	0–7	8–14	15–30	Total
Hourly	79	183	38	300
Salaried	8	27	65	100
Total	87	210	103	400

A company collected data on the paid vacation days accrued by hourly and salaried employees. The table shows the results of the data collection. If an employee has at least 8 paid vacation days, what is the probability that the person is a salaried employee?

Ⓐ $\dfrac{92}{313}$

Ⓑ $\dfrac{221}{300}$

Ⓒ $\dfrac{313}{400}$

Ⓓ $\dfrac{92}{100}$

22

Egg Production by Size and Color		
Egg type	Brown	White
Large		
Jumbo		
Total	750	3,880

A farm's daily egg production is shown in the table. The farm produces six times as many large white eggs as large brown eggs and five times as many jumbo white eggs as jumbo brown eggs. What is the approximate probability that a brown egg selected at random will be large?

Ⓐ 0.173

Ⓑ 0.307

Ⓒ 0.440

Ⓓ 0.827

ON TEST DAY

The average formula will serve you well on questions that ask about a sum of values or the average of a set of values. However, for questions that give you the average and ask for a missing value in the data set, there is a potentially faster alternative: the balance approach.

The balance approach conceptualizes the average as the "center" of the data set. You can find the totals on both "sides" of the average and then add the missing value that makes both sides balance out. This approach is especially helpful if the values are large and closely spaced. Imagine that a question gives you the set {976, 980, 964, 987, x} and tells you that the average is 970. You would reason as follows: 976 is 6 over the average, 980 is 10 over, 964 is 6 under, and 987 is 17 over. That's a total of $6 + 10 - 6 + 17 = 27$ over. Therefore, x needs to be 27 under the average, or $970 - 27 = 943$, to make everything balance out.

Try solving the question that follows both ways, using first the average formula and then the balance approach. If you find the latter to be fast and intuitive, add it to your test day arsenal.

	Height Change (inches)						
Plant type	Week 3	Week 4	Week 5	Week 6	Week 7	Week 8	Week 9
Zinnia	3	2	1	4	2	1	1
Sunflower	3		8	6	7	2	5
Marigold	1	1	3	2	4	4	3

23. The table summarizes the height change (in inches) over a seven-week period of three different plants grown in a biology class. If the mean height change for the sunflower plant over the seven-week period is 5 inches, what was the height change in week 4?

The correct answer and both ways of solving can be found at the end of the chapter.

HOW MUCH HAVE YOU LEARNED?

Directions

For testlike practice, give yourself 10 minutes to complete this question set. Be sure to study the explanations, even for questions you answered correctly. They can be found at the end of this chapter.

24

	Freshmen	Sophomores	Juniors	Seniors	Total
Sports	144	122	134	115	515
Video games	126	140	152	148	566
Music	120	117	153	148	538
Reading	110	114	63	98	385
Total	500	493	502	509	2,004

The table summarizes the results of a survey about favorite leisure activities for a group of high school students. Assume that every student has a favorite leisure activity and that each student could select only one favorite.

What is the probability that a sophomore will prefer a type of leisure activity other than video games?

(A) $\dfrac{140}{2,004}$

(B) $\dfrac{353}{2,004}$

(C) $\dfrac{140}{493}$

(D) $\dfrac{353}{493}$

25

A gym is opening a new branch in a town of 12,600 people. The gym surveys 300 randomly selected residents. Of these 300, 40 claim that they would join the gym. However, only 30 percent of these 40 will actually join. About how many people in town will join the gym?

(A) 134

(B) 504

(C) 1,680

(D) 3,780

26

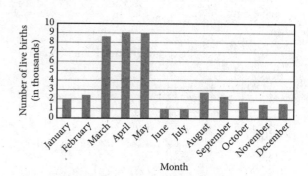

The bar graph shows the number of live births of the black-tailed jackrabbit in California over the course of a year. Based on the data, which of the following would be an appropriate conclusion?

(A) In general, rabbits give birth during March, April, and May.

(B) In general, rabbits give birth during June and July.

(C) In general, black-tailed jackrabbits in California give birth during March, April, and May.

(D) In general, black-tailed jackrabbits in the United States give birth during March, April, and May.

27

The average (arithmetic mean) of $p + 12t - 5$, $q + 16t + 4$, and $r - 7t + 25$ is $10t + 34$. In terms of t, what is the average of p, q, and r?

(A) $3t + 26$

(B) $4t + 16$

(C) $6t + 16$

(D) $8t - 37$

28

A company sent out a survey to see how much consumers would be willing to pay for a certain product. A summary of the results is shown in the bar graph.

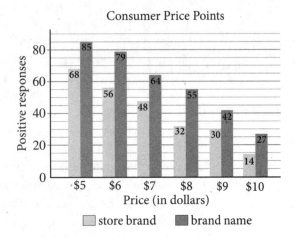

Consumer Price Points

If a consumer is chosen at random from the 600 respondents, what is the probability that the consumer is willing to pay at least $8 for the product?

29

A company produces an equal number of a certain product each working day in the month. The daily reject rates for the first 12 days of this month ranged from 0 percent to 1.5 percent with an average of 0.4 percent. If there are 22 working days this month and the company's monthly reject goal is 0.5 percent or less, what is the maximum reject rate, as a percent, for the 13th day that would still enable the company to attain its goal for the month?

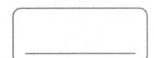

REFLECT

Directions: Take a few minutes to recall what you've learned and what you've been practicing in this chapter. Consider the following questions, jot down your best answer for each one, and then compare your reflections to the expert responses that follow. Use your level of confidence to determine what to do next.

What are some common ways that the SAT may present data?

_____

_____

_____

What is the difference between median, mode, and range?

_____

_____

_____

What does the standard deviation of a data set tell you?

_____

_____

_____

When can you generalize the results of a survey of a small group to a larger group?

_____

_____

_____

What are two ways to calculate the probability of a single event?

_____

_____

_____

Expert Responses

What are some common ways that the SAT may present data?

The SAT may present data in tables, bar charts, line graphs, dot plots, and histograms.

What is the difference between median, mode, and range?

The median of a set with an odd number of values is the middle value, and the median of a set with an even number of values is the average of the two values that share the middle. Regardless of the number of values in the set, the mode is the most common value (or values if two or more numbers are equally common), while the range is the largest value minus the smallest one.

What does the standard deviation of a data set tell you?

A data set's standard deviation reflects how far apart the numbers are from each other. The standard deviation of a set whose numbers are all the same—for example, {5, 5, 5, 5}—is 0. The greater the distance between the numbers, the greater the standard deviation.

When can you generalize the results of a survey of a small group to a larger group?

A survey can be generalized to a larger population if the data sample is representative. To be representative, the data sample needs to be drawn at random from the larger population.

What are two ways to calculate the probability of a single event?

One way is to use the basic probability formula:

$$\text{Probability} = \frac{\text{number of desired outcomes}}{\text{number of total outcomes}}$$

Alternatively, the probability that an event happens is 1 minus the probability that it doesn't happen.

Next Steps

If you answered most questions correctly in the "How Much Have You Learned?" section and if your responses to the Reflect questions were similar to those of the SAT expert, then consider Tables, Statistics, and Probability an area of strength and move on to the next chapter. Come back to this topic periodically to ensure your skills stay sharp.

If you don't yet feel confident, review those parts of this chapter that you have not yet mastered, then try the questions you missed again. In particular, make sure that you understand the terms explained in the Statistics lesson and the probability formulas explained in the Probability lesson. As always, be sure to review the explanations closely. Finally, **go online** (www.kaptest.com/moreonline) for additional practice on the highest yield topics in this chapter.

Check Your Work – Chapter 9

1.   B
Difficulty: Easy
Category: Problem-Solving and Data Analysis
Getting to the Answer: The trickiest part of this question is understanding what is being asked. You need to find the shop that had the most Tuesday sales as a fraction of its own total sales, so the only rows that matter are "Tuesday" and "Total." For each shop, divide the number of books it sold on Tuesday by the total number of books it sold all week. Use your calculator to speed up this step.

Bob's Bookshop: $\dfrac{\text{Tuesday total}}{\text{weekly total}} = \dfrac{8}{53} \approx 0.1509$

Clara's Bookshop: $\dfrac{\text{Tuesday total}}{\text{weekly total}} = \dfrac{13}{55} \approx 0.2364$

Derek's Bookshop: $\dfrac{\text{Tuesday total}}{\text{weekly total}} = \dfrac{15}{66} \approx 0.2273$

Evelyn's Bookshop: $\dfrac{\text{Tuesday total}}{\text{weekly total}} = \dfrac{13}{58} \approx 0.2241$

The greatest fraction belongs to Clara's Bookshop, so **(B)** is correct.

2.   C
Difficulty: Medium
Category: Problem-Solving and Data Analysis
Getting to the Answer: The table indicates that 27.8% of participants who got the drug experienced severe side effects, as did 6.2% of participants who got the placebo. Add these percentages together: $27.8\% + 6.2\% = 34\%$ of participants had severe side effects. Therefore, 34% of $400 = 0.34 \times 400 = 136$ participants who had severe side effects. The table indicates that 27.8% of the 400 participants were given the drug and sustained severe side effects, which equates to $0.278 \times 400 \approx 111$ participants. So, 111 out of the 136 participants who had severe side effects were given the drug:

$$\frac{111}{136} \times 100\% = 81.6\%$$

This is approximately 82%. Choice **(C)** is correct.

3.   B
Difficulty: Easy
Category: Problem-Solving and Data Analysis
Getting to the Answer: The question asks only about participants who were outside a healthy weight range,

so focus on this row: 38 out of the 74 participants who were outside a healthy weight range ate breakfast one or fewer times per week. This expressed as a percent is $\dfrac{38}{74} \times 100\% \approx 0.5135 \times 100\% = 51.35\%$, which is closest to **(B)**.

4.   300
Difficulty: Medium
Category: Problem-Solving and Data Analysis
Getting to the Answer: Read the graph carefully, including the key at the bottom indicating that each bar represents 15 minutes. The paragraph identifies stage 3 as deep sleep, and the question asks how much time was spent in *non*-deep sleep. There are 12 bars that represent stage 3, which means the person spent $12 \times 15 = 180$ minutes in deep sleep. The study was for 8 hours, or 480 minutes, so the person spent $480 - 180 = 300$ minutes in non-deep sleep. Enter **300**.

5.   D
Difficulty: Medium
Category: Problem-Solving and Data Analysis
Getting to the Answer: Compare each statement to the line graph one at a time, eliminating true statements as you work. Start with (A): at every reading after 20 hours, Strain 1 has a higher OD600 level than Strain 2, so this statement is true. Eliminate (A). Choice (B) states that Strain 2's growth rate (slope) overtook Strain 1's at hour 50, which is consistent with the line graph; eliminate it. It looks as though (C) requires time-consuming calculations, so skip it for now. Choice (D) states that Strain 1's growth rate was greater than Strain 2's over the entire period. This statement contradicts what you already confirmed in (B), which makes **(D)** false and, therefore, correct. There's no need to check (C).

6.   C
Difficulty: Medium
Category: Problem-Solving and Data Analysis
Strategic Advice: The median is the middle value when all of the values are in numerical order, so find the total number of values in the set and determine which one is the middle value.
Getting to the Answer: The total number of people who were surveyed in country B is 250. Since it is an even set of values, the median will be the average of the 125th and 126th values. To get to those values, add the

number of citizens who speak one or two languages: $70 + 50 = 120$. Keep going because this group does not include the 125th and 126th values. Add the citizens who speak three languages: $120 + 50 = 170$. This means that the 125th and 126th values are both 3, so the median is 3. **(C)** is correct.

7. B
Difficulty: Hard
Category: Problem-Solving and Data Analysis
Getting to the Answer: Since the average of x and 5 is c, $c = \dfrac{x+5}{2}$. Similarly, $d = \dfrac{3x+3}{2}$. To find the average of c and d in terms of x, substitute $\dfrac{x+5}{2}$ for c and $\dfrac{3x+3}{2}$ for d into $\dfrac{c+d}{2}$. This gives $\dfrac{\dfrac{x+5}{2} + \dfrac{3x+3}{2}}{2}$, which simplifies to $\dfrac{\dfrac{4x+8}{2}}{2} = \dfrac{4x+8}{4} = x+2$. Choice **(B)** is correct.

8. B
Difficulty: Easy
Category: Problem-Solving and Data Analysis
Getting to the Answer: Consider the definitions of mean and standard deviation: mean is a measure of center, while standard deviation is a measure of spread. The closer the data points for a given snowboarder are to the mean, the more consistent that snowboarder's performance. Since consistency is measured by standard deviation, you can eliminate (A) and (D). Greater consistency means lower standard deviation (and vice versa); the only choice that reflects this—and correctly represents the data in the table—is **(B)**.

9. C
Difficulty: Hard
Category: Problem-Solving and Data Analysis
Getting to the Answer: You'll have to determine the values of all three measurements before you can place them in ascending order. The *mode* is 3 because there are 18 cars of that age, which is the most of any age. The total number of cars is $3 + 5 + 18 + 17 + 11 + 6 + 2 = 62$. Since this is an even number, the *median* age will be the average of the 31st and 32nd values. There are $3 + 5 + 18 = 26$ cars that are 1, 2, and 3 years old and 17 that are 4 years old. Thus, the 27th through 43rd ($26 + 17 = 43$) values are 4, and that is the median.

To find the *mean*, multiply each value by its frequency, add up those values, and divide by 62. So, $1 \times 3 = 3$, $2 \times 5 = 10$, $3 \times 18 = 54$, $4 \times 17 = 68$, $5 \times 11 = 55$, $6 \times 6 = 36$, $7 \times 2 = 14$, and $3 + 10 + 54 + 68 + 55 + 36 + 14 = 240$. Divide 240 by 62 to get approximately 3.87. The ascending order of the three values is mode (3), mean (3.87), and median (4), so **(C)** is correct.

10. 7
Difficulty: Medium
Category: Problem-Solving and Data Analysis
Getting to the Answer: Understanding how averages and sums are connected is the key to answering a question like this. Recall the formula, $\text{average} = \dfrac{\text{sum of terms}}{\text{number of terms}}$. If the average of 12 numbers is 4, then the sum of the 12 numbers must be $4 \times 12 = 48$. Use the dot plot to find the total number of credit card applicants Amara obtained. Then, subtract this number from 48. Each X on the dot plot represents one day, and it is placed in the column that shows the number of applicants for that day. Amara has already obtained $1 + 3(2) + 2(3) + 4 + 5 + 2(6) + 7 = 41$ applicants, so she needs to obtain $48 - 41 = 7$ applicants on the 12th day. Enter **7**.

11. C
Difficulty: Medium
Category: Problem-Solving and Data Analysis
Getting to the Answer: There are 65 data points, so the median will be the middle data point, or the 33rd data point once the data are listed in order. Count the number of data points from the end. There are 10 households with 1 person and 18 households with 2 persons, which adds up to 28 households. Since there are 15 households with 3 persons, the 33rd household will fall in that group. Therefore, the median household size is 3 persons. Finally, add up the number of households with more than 3 persons: $12 + 8 + 2 = 22$. **(C)** is correct.

12. C
Difficulty: Medium
Category: Problem-Solving and Data Analysis
Getting to the Answer: The margin of error corresponds to the amount of random sampling error and is the interval in which a population likely falls. Thus, the smaller the margin of error, the more confidence the results of the sample population reflect the larger population. If the sample data estimates 87% with a margin of error of 5%, the percentage of college

students who eat out at least once a week will fall in the interval 87% ± 5%; that is, between 82% and 92%. **(C)** is correct.

13. A
Difficulty: Easy
Category: Problem-Solving and Data Analysis
Getting to the Answer: Any sample used to determine a general opinion needs to be representative and unbiased. The railroad company fails to meet that requirement by surveying only people who commute to work and who would probably benefit from the station. This leaves out a large portion of the population who may not share the commuters' opinion. The use of a biased sample group makes the survey unreliable and not representative. Choice **(A)** is correct.

14. A
Difficulty: Medium
Category: Problem-Solving and Data Analysis
Getting to the Answer: As long as a sample is representative (without bias and relatively large), the mean and median of the sample data will be the same as the expected mean and median of the population from which the sample was taken. Since the question tells you that the sample is random and representative, the mean of the sample equals the estimated mean of the general population. Choice **(A)** is the correct answer.

15. C
Difficulty: Medium
Category: Problem-Solving and Data Analysis
Getting to the Answer: As the customers were selected at random, it is reasonable to assume that the survey results will be representative of what is true for customers in general. However, the data provided refers only to people who bought dinnerware. Thus, an inference can be drawn only about dinnerware returns and nothing else. Since 80% of surveyed customers returned dinnerware items because of damage, it is reasonable to infer that this statistic will be similar for all customers who return dinnerware. Choice **(C)** is correct.

Choices (A) and (D) incorrectly generalize from dinnerware to all the products in the store. You have no information about any other products, so you cannot draw conclusions about all the products in the store. Choice (B) also goes outside the scope of the question. While the 80% indicated in the question may seem like a high percentage, other products may be even more likely to be damaged. There is no way to know.

16. C
Difficulty: Medium
Category: Problem-Solving and Data Analysis
Getting to the Answer: To make a reliable inference from a survey, the survey sample needs to be unbiased and relatively large. In this case, the miniature golf course owner surveyed only children who played at that course. Thus, any inference drawn from the data must be about children at this golf course only and cannot be generalized to the entire population. Since 60% of the surveyed children prefer a red golf ball, it is reasonable to infer that a similar percentage of total children at that golf course would prefer red golf balls. Thus, **(C)** is correct.

17. B
Difficulty: Medium
Category: Problem-Solving and Data Analysis
Getting to the Answer: To make a reliable inference from a survey, the survey sample needs to be unbiased and relatively large. Here, the survey responses are drawn only from people who happen to be watching this particular television show and those who have the ability to send text messages. Therefore, it may not represent the preferences of the entire state's population. **(B)** is correct.

Choice (A) is incorrect because Issue Y is never mentioned in the question. Choice (C) is irrelevant. Choice (D) misinterprets the percent by mistakenly applying it to accuracy rather than the raw number of votes.

18. C
Difficulty: Medium
Category: Problem-Solving and Data Analysis
Getting to the Answer: The number of desired outcomes is 392 (bearings marked defective that are actually defective). The number of total possible outcomes is 560 (all the bearings that are marked defective). Thus, the probability that a bearing marked defective is in fact defective is $\frac{392}{560} \times 100\% = 0.70 \times 100\% = 70\%$. **(C)** is correct.

19. D
Difficulty: Hard
Category: Problem-Solving and Data Analysis
Getting to the Answer: The probability that one randomly selected salmon from those that were tested would have a dangerous level of mercury is equal to

the number of salmon that had dangerous mercury levels divided by the total number of salmon that were tested.

$$\frac{\text{\# salmon with dangerous mercury levels}}{\text{\# of salmon tested}}$$

This means you need only two numbers to answer this question. One of those numbers is in the second table—6 salmon had dangerous mercury levels. Finding the other number is the tricky part. Use information from the question stem and the first table. The biologist tested 5% of the total number of each species of fish, and 25% of the 6,000 fish are salmon. So, the biologist tested 5% of 25% of 6,000 fish. Multiply to find that $0.05 \times 0.25 \times 6{,}000 = 75$ salmon were tested. This means the probability is $\frac{6}{75} = 0.08$, which matches **(D)**.

20. B
Difficulty: Medium
Category: Problem-Solving and Data Analysis
Strategic Advice: Recognizing which value goes in the denominator, whether it is the grand total or the total of a subgroup, is essential for probability questions that are based on data in a table.
Getting to the Answer: The question indicates that the random selection is from all the engineers, or the grand total of 768. The specific engineer to be selected is a mechanical engineer who prefers autonomous vehicles, and the table indicates that there are 245 such engineers. Therefore, the probability of selecting a mechanical engineer who prefers autonomous vehicles from all the engineers is $\frac{245}{768}$, which is approximately 0.319. **(B)** is correct.

Note that the incorrect answer choices often reflect common misunderstandings and simple table-reading errors. For example, (C) and (D) both use the wrong total, and (A) is the probability of choosing an electrical engineer who prefers autonomous vehicles.

21. A
Difficulty: Medium
Category: Problem-Solving and Data Analysis
Strategic Advice: Be on the lookout for "at least" language. It will usually require adding data from multiple rows or columns.
Getting to the Answer: The probability of choosing an employee with "at least" 8 paid vacation days who is

salaried is the number of salaried employees with 8 or more paid vacation days divided by the total number of employees with 8 or more paid vacation days.

$$\frac{\text{\# salaried employees with 8 or more paid vacation days}}{\text{total \# employees with 8 or more paid vacation days}}$$

Find the number of salaried employees with 8 or more paid vacation days by adding the salaried employees with 8–14 paid vacation days, 27, and the salaried employees with 15–30 paid vacation days, 65. That means there are $27 + 65$, or 92, salaried employees with 8 or more paid vacation days. The total number of employees with 8 or more paid vacation days is 210 (the total number of employees with 8–14 paid vacation days) plus 103 (the total number of employees with 15–30 paid vacation days), or 313. The probability is $\frac{92}{313}$. **(A)** is correct.

22. A
Difficulty: Hard
Category: Problem-Solving and Data Analysis
Strategic Advice: If totals and the relationships between the data are the only information provided, write out a system of equations.
Getting to the Answer: The question gives the relationships between unknown values in the table, so you may want to draw this table out on your scratch paper and fill it in accordingly. For large eggs, let l be the number that is brown. There are 6 times as many large eggs that are white, so that is $6l$. Similarly, for jumbo eggs, let j be the number of jumbo brown eggs. Because the farm produces five times as many jumbo eggs that are white, fill in that blank with $5j$:

Egg Production by Size and Color		
Egg type	Brown	White
Large	l	$6l$
Jumbo	j	$5j$
Total	750	3,880

Write a system of equations based on the brown and white columns:

$$l + j = 750$$
$$6l + 5j = 3{,}880$$

Solve the first equation for j and substitute the result into the second equation to solve for l:

$$j = 750 - l$$
$$6l + 5(750 - l) = 3,880$$
$$6l + 3,750 - 5l = 3,880$$
$$l = 130$$

Therefore, there are 130 large brown eggs. The total number of brown eggs is 750. Thus, the probability of a brown egg selected at random being large is $\frac{130}{750}$, or approximately 0.173. **(A)** is correct. Notice that there is no need to actually calculate j or the other values in the table to answer this question.

23. 4
Difficulty: Medium
Category: Problem-Solving and Data Analysis
Getting to the Answer: The question asks about the sunflower plant, so ignore the data for the other plants. The given height changes for the other six weeks are 3, 8, 6, 7, 2, and 5. The average change in height for the sunflower plant is given as 5. Call the missing value x. Plugging the known values into the average formula yields the following:

$$\text{average} = \frac{\text{sum of terms}}{\text{\# of terms}}$$
$$5 = \frac{3 + 8 + 6 + 7 + 2 + 5 + x}{7}$$
$$5 = \frac{31 + x}{7}$$
$$35 = 31 + x$$
$$4 = x$$

Enter **4**.

To use the balance approach, write down how much each value is above or below the average of 5. For example, the Week 3 value of 3 is 2 below the average of 5.

Week 3	Week 5	Week 6	Week 7	Week 8	Week 9
−2	+3	+1	+2	−3	+0

Excluding Week 4, the values are $-2 + 3 + 1 + 2 - 3 = 1$. In other words, the total is 1 more than what you'd expect based on the average. For the values to balance out, the Week 4 value must be 1 less than the average of 5, or $5 - 1 = 4$. Enter **4**.

24. D
Difficulty: Easy
Category: Problem-Solving and Data Analysis
Getting to the Answer: Recall that Probability $= \frac{\text{desired}}{\text{total}}$. The research firm is choosing one student from among the sophomores, so the total is 493. There are $493 - 140 = 353$ sophomores who prefer activities other than video games, so the probability of choosing a sophomore who does not prefer video games is $\frac{353}{493}$. Choice **(D)** is correct.

25. B
Difficulty: Medium
Category: Problem-Solving and Data Analysis
Getting to the Answer: According to the survey, $\frac{40}{300}$ say that they would join the gym. But the gym estimates that only 30% of these respondents would actually join, so multiply $\frac{40}{300}$ by 30% to find that the gym can expect $\frac{40(0.30)}{300} = \frac{12}{300} = 0.04$ of the respondents to join. Therefore, $12,600 \times 0.04 = 504$ residents can be expected to join. Choice **(B)** is correct.

26. C
Difficulty: Easy
Category: Problem-Solving and Data Analysis
Getting to the Answer: The question states that the data collected was from black-tailed jackrabbits in California, so any conclusion can be applied only to that particular species of rabbit in California, not to all rabbits in general. According to the data, the California black-tailed jackrabbit gives birth mostly during March, April, and May, so **(C)** is correct.

27. A
Difficulty: Hard
Category: Problem-Solving and Data Analysis
Getting to the Answer: Use the average formula to set up an equation using the information in the question. Even though you are given expressions with variables, the average formula is still the sum of the terms divided by the number of terms:

$$\frac{(p + 12t - 5) + (q + 16t + 4) + (r - 7t + 25)}{3} = 10t + 34$$

Because the question asks for the average of p, q, and r in terms of t, solve the equation for $\frac{p + q + r}{3}$:

$$\frac{p + 12t - 5 + q + 16t + 4 + r - 7t + 25}{3} = 10t + 34$$
$$\frac{p + q + r + 21t + 24}{3} = 10t + 34$$
$$\frac{p + q + r}{3} + \frac{21t}{3} + \frac{24}{3} = 10t + 34$$
$$\frac{p + q + r}{3} + 7t + 8 = 10t + 34$$
$$\frac{p + q + r}{3} = 3t + 26$$

Choice (**A**) is correct.

28. 1/3, 0.333, or .3333
Difficulty: Medium
Category: Problem-Solving and Data Analysis
Getting to the Answer: Recall that Probability = $\frac{\text{desired}}{\text{total}}$. Begin by finding the number of respondents willing to pay at least $8 (which means $8 or more). The question doesn't specify store brand or brand name, so use both versions: $32 + 55 + 30 + 42 + 14 + 27 = 200$.

Now find the total number of people in the survey. Again, the question doesn't specify store brand or brand name. The question stem states that there is a total of 600 respondents. This means that the probability that a randomly chosen respondent is willing to pay at least $8 is $\frac{200}{600}$, or $\frac{1}{3}$. Enter **1/3, 0.333, or .3333**.

29. 6.2
Difficulty: Hard
Getting to the Answer: The company's goal is a 0.5% average reject rate for the month. Express this using the average formula:

$$0.5\% = \frac{\text{sum of daily reject rates}}{22}$$

This tells you that the sum of the daily reject rates is $22 \times 0.5\% = 11\%$. Since 12 days have already passed with an average reject rate of 0.4%, the sum of the daily rates so far is $12 \times 0.4\% = 4.8\%$. Thus, the sum of the daily rates over the next 10 days cannot exceed $11\% - 4.8\% = 6.2\%$.

The question asks for the *maximum* reject rate on the next single day that would still allow the company to meet its monthly goal. Call this day x. To *maximize* day x, the remaining 9 days must be *minimized*. The question states that the minimum possible rejection rate is 0%, so set up an equation and solve for x:

$$6.2\% = 9(0\%) + x$$
$$6.2\% = x$$

Enter **6.2**.

[CHAPTER 10]

SCATTERPLOTS

LEARNING OBJECTIVES

After completing this chapter, you will be able to:

- Determine the average rate of change
- Write an equation for a line of best fit
- Extrapolate values from the line of best fit
- Determine whether a linear, a quadratic, or an exponential model describes the data presented in a scatterplot

Math

HOW MUCH DO YOU KNOW?

Directions

Try the questions that follow. Show your work so that you can compare your solutions to the ones found in the "Check Your Work" section immediately after this question set. If you answered the question(s) on a specific topic correctly, and if your scratchwork looks like ours, you may be able to move quickly through the lesson covering that topic. If you answered incorrectly or used a different approach, you may want to take your time on that lesson.

1

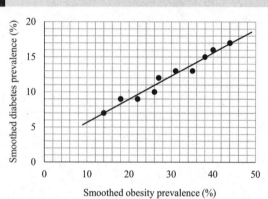

Source: CDC

The scatterplot shows the prevalence of obesity plotted against the prevalence of diabetes in various areas of the United States. Which of the following best estimates the average rate of change in the prevalence of diabetes as compared to the prevalence of obesity?

Ⓐ 0.3

Ⓑ 0.9

Ⓒ 1.1

Ⓓ 3

2

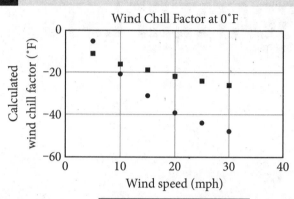

- ● 1939 wind chill formula
- ■ 2001 wind chill formula

Wind chill, a measurement that reflects perceived temperature based on the actual temperature and the wind speed, was first introduced in 1939, and the formula was revised in 2001. If the outside temperature is 0°F, what is the approximate wind chill at 40 miles per hour, based on the 2001 formula?

Ⓐ −20°F

Ⓑ −30°F

Ⓒ −40°F

Ⓓ −50°F

3

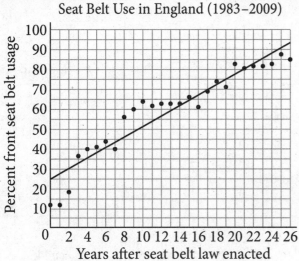

Seat Belt Use in England (1983–2009)

The scatterplot shows data collected each year after the British Parliament enacted a mandatory seat belt law and the line of best fit for the data. Which of the following equations best represents the trend of the data shown in the figure?

- Ⓐ $y = 0.4x + 25$
- Ⓑ $y = 1.8x + 15$
- Ⓒ $y = 2.1x + 35$
- Ⓓ $y = 2.6x + 25$

4

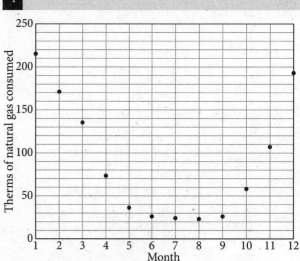

The scatterplot shows the average therms of natural gas used by residential customers over a 12-month period. Of the following equations, which best models the data in the scatterplot?

- Ⓐ $y = 1.061x + 312.9$
- Ⓑ $y = -1.061x - 312.9$
- Ⓒ $y = 6.1x^2 - 85.1x + 312.9$
- Ⓓ $y = -6.1x^2 + 85.1x - 312.9$

5

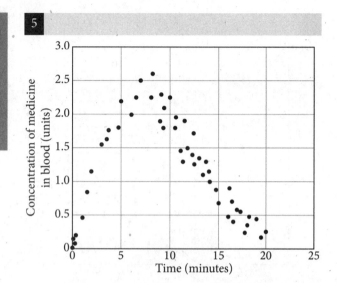

Scientists measured the concentration of an experimental medication in blood samples over time. If a quadratic function is used to model the data, which of the following best explains the meaning of the vertex?

Ⓐ The average maximum medicine concentration in the blood sample is 7.5 units.

Ⓑ The average maximum medicine concentration is more than 20 units.

Ⓒ The average maximum medicine concentration in the blood samples occurs around 2.5 minutes.

Ⓓ The average maximum medicine concentration in the blood sample occurs between 5 and 10 minutes.

6

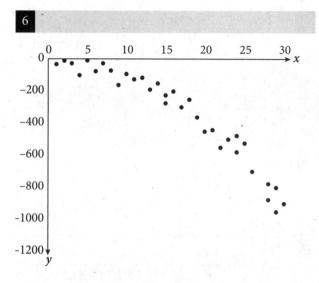

For which of the following values of a and b could the equation $y = ax^b$ model the data in the scatterplot shown?

Ⓐ $a < 0, b < 0$

Ⓑ $a < 0, b > 0$

Ⓒ $a > 0, b < 0$

Ⓓ $a > 0, b > 0$

Check Your Work

1.   A
Difficulty: Easy
Category: Problem-Solving and Data Analysis
Getting to the Answer: The scatterplot shows obesity prevalence plotted against diabetes prevalence, and because the line goes up as it moves to the right, there is a positive linear correlation between the two. The phrase "rate of change" is the same as the slope of the line of best fit, so pick two points to plug into the slope formula. Estimating, the endpoints appear to be (14, 7) and (44, 17). (If your estimate is different, that's okay—whenever the SAT requires you to make an estimate, the answer choices will be spread far enough apart that you'll get the correct answer as long as you're looking in the right place and thinking the right way.) Calculate the slope, m:

$$m = \frac{y_2 - y_1}{x_2 - x_1} = \frac{17 - 7}{44 - 14} = \frac{10}{30} = \frac{1}{3} \approx 0.3$$

This matches **(A)**.

2.   B
Difficulty: Medium
Category: Problem-Solving and Data Analysis
Getting to the Answer: The 2001 formula plot has a slight curve that becomes nearly linear as wind speed increases above 10 miles per hour. Imagine this nearly linear relationship extending to the 40 mph on the x-axis. On test day, you may be able to place your finger on the screen and follow the square dots to the 40 mph line to help you visualize. You'll see the imagined line crossing nearly halfway between the −20 and −40 lines. Therefore, the correct answer must be about halfway between −20°F and −40°F. Choice **(B)**, −30°F, is correct.

3.   D
Difficulty: Medium
Category: Problem-Solving and Data Analysis
Getting to the Answer: A line that "represents the trend of the data" is another way of referring to the line of best fit, which is linear in this diagram. Use the y-intercept and slope of the line of best fit to eliminate the choices.

Start by finding the y-intercept. For this graph, it's about 25, so eliminate (B) and (C). To choose between (A) and (D), find the approximate slope using two points that lie on (or very close to) the line of best fit. Use the y-intercept (0, 25) as one of the points to save time (it's

easy to subtract 0) and estimate the second, such as (21, 80). Then, use the slope formula to find the slope:

$$m = \frac{y_2 - y_1}{x_2 - x_1} = \frac{80 - 25}{21 - 0} = \frac{55}{21} \approx 2.6$$

The result is approximately the slope in **(D)**, making it the correct answer.

4.   C
Difficulty: Medium
Category: Problem-Solving and Data Analysis
Getting to the Answer: The data in the scatterplot can be modeled by a parabola opening upward. (A) is an exponential growth equation, and (B) is an exponential decay equation. Neither will graph as a parabola, so eliminate both. A parabola is the graph of a quadratic. For a quadratic equation in the form $ax^2 + bx + c$, a determines whether the parabola opens upward or downward and c is the y-intercept. The y-intercept is positive, so (D) can be eliminated. Choice **(C)** is correct. Also note that when, $a > 0$, the parabola opens upward, which also leads to **(C)** as the correct answer. Additional practice with quadratics can be found in the Advanced Math section of this book.

5.   D
Difficulty: Medium
Category: Problem-Solving and Data Analysis
Getting to the Answer: For this scatterplot, the medicine concentration is measured on the y-axis, and the maximum value (the vertex) is about 2.6 units, so the average maximum medicine concentration cannot be above 2.6 units. Eliminate (A) and (B). The x-value of the maximum occurs between 5 and 10 minutes; therefore, **(D)** is correct.

6.   B
Difficulty: Hard
Category: Problem-Solving and Data Analysis
Getting to the Answer: The shape of the data is concave down with an increasingly negative slope as x increases. The y-values of the data are negative, which indicates $a < 0$. Eliminate (C) and (D). As x increases, the magnitude of the y-values increases. This indicates $b > 0$. Note that if $b < 0$, the y-values would approach 0 as x increases. Thus, **(B)** is correct.

If you were uncertain how different values of a and b affect the shape of the curve, you could experiment by picking numbers in various combinations of positive and negative values as allowed by the answer choices and then graphing them to see how the results appear.

LINE OF BEST FIT

To answer a question like this:

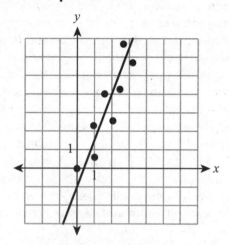

Which of the following equations corresponds to the line of best fit for the data set shown in the scatterplot?

A) $y = 0.4x - 1$

B) $y = 0.4x + 1$

C) $y = 2.5x + 1$

D) $y = 2.5x - 1$

You need to know this:

A **scatterplot** is a visual representation of a set of data points. The data points are plotted on the x- and y-axes such that each axis represents a different characteristic of the data set. For example, in the scatterplot that follows, each data point represents a dachshund. The x-axis represents the dog's height and the y-axis represents its length.

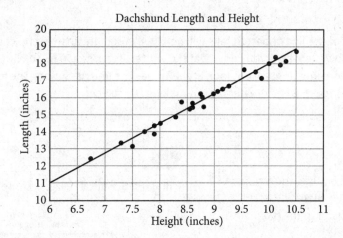

The **line of best fit**, or trend line, is drawn through the **data points** to describe the relationship between the two variables as an equation. This line does not necessarily go through any single data point, but it does accurately reflect the trend shown by the data with about half the points above the line and half below.

The **equation of the line of best fit** is the equation that describes the line of best fit algebraically. On test day, you'll most likely encounter this equation as linear, quadratic, or exponential, though it can also be other types of equations. The next lesson will cover these various forms.

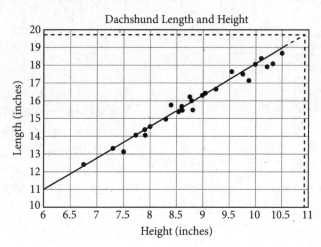

Some SAT questions will require you to extrapolate from the line of best fit. For example, you might be asked to predict the length of a dachshund that is 10.9 inches in height. Find where on the line of best fit it is from the given x-value and observe the corresponding y-value, in this case about 19.7 inches.

You need to do this:

To determine the equation of the line of best fit for a linear equation, like the one in the dachshund scatterplot, start by finding the slope, also called the **average rate of change**. Watch out for the units when you do this. In the dachshund example, using the points (6, 11) and (10, 18), the slope is $\frac{y_2 - y_1}{x_2 - x_1} = \frac{18 - 11}{10 - 6} = \frac{7}{4} = 1.75$.

Next, find the y-intercept. Using the point (10, 18) and plugging those values into slope-intercept form yields $18 = 1.75(10) + b$.

Thus, $b = 0.5$ in the dachshund example. So the equation in slope-intercept form is length $= 1.75x + 0.5$.

You can also extrapolate using the equation for the line of best fit. For a dachshund that is 11 inches tall, the calculation would be length $= 1.75(11) + 0.5 = 19.75$.

Explanation:

Knowing where the y-intercept of the line of best fit falls will help you eliminate answer choices. Because the line of best fit intersects the y-axis below the x-axis, you know that the y-intercept is negative, so eliminate (B) and (C) (the y-intercept is +1 for each of those equations). Now, look at the slope. The line rises along the y-axis much faster than it runs along the x-axis, so the slope must be greater than 1, making **(D)** correct.

Try on Your Own

Directions

Take as much time as you need on these questions. Work carefully and methodically. There will be an opportunity for timed practice later in the book.

1

HINT: For Q1, look at the slope. Which two choices can you eliminate immediately?

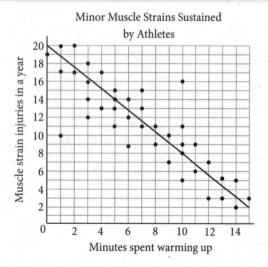

The scatterplot shows the number of minor muscle strain injuries sustained in a year by athletes plotted against the amount of time warming up before engaging in rigorous physical activity. Which of the following best estimates the average rate of change in the number of injuries compared with the number of minutes spent warming up?

(A) −1.2

(B) −0.8

(C) 2

(D) 20

2

HINT: For Q2, rate of change, increase or decrease, means slope.

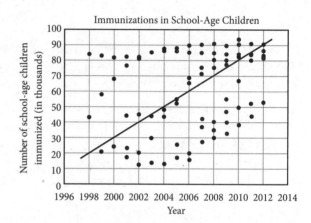

The scatterplot shows the number of school-age children in a particular state who received immunizations for various illnesses between 1996 and 2012. What was the average rate of increase in the number of children immunized, in thousands, per year over the given time period?

(A) 5

(B) 10

(C) 25

(D) 70

3

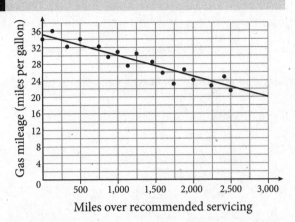

The scatterplot shows the gas mileage as a function of the number of miles driven over recommended servicing. The equation for the line of best fit shown is $y = -\frac{1}{200}x + 35$. How many miles per gallon could be expected if a car is driven 3,400 miles over the recommended miles between servicing?

4

HINT: For Q4, how many tick marks on the *y*-axis represent 5 eggs?

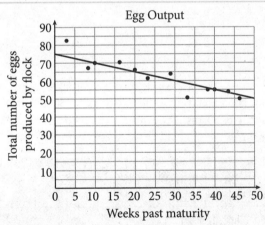

The scatterplot shows the daily egg output for 100 chickens at random intervals. The line of best fit for the data has been drawn. How many times did the farmer's data differ by more than 5 eggs from the number of eggs predicted by the line of best fit?

5

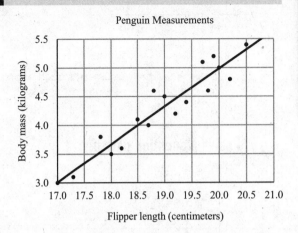

The scatterplot shows the body mass of penguins against penguin flipper length and a line of best fit for the data. Which of the following might be the equation of the line of best fit?

Ⓐ $y = \frac{2}{3}x - \frac{25}{3}$

Ⓑ $y = \frac{2}{3}x + 3$

Ⓒ $y = \frac{3}{2}x - 25$

Ⓓ $y = \frac{3}{2}x + 3$

SCATTERPLOT MODELING

LEARNING OBJECTIVE

After this lesson, you will be able to:

• Determine whether a linear, a quadratic, or an exponential model describes the data presented in a scatterplot

To solve a question like this:

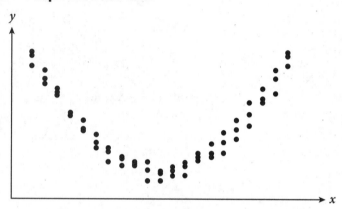

Given that a, b, and c are constants and that $a > 0$, which of the following is the equation for the line or curve of best fit for the scatterplot?

A) $y = ax + b$

B) $y = a^{bx}$

C) $y = -ax^2 + bx + c$

D) $y = ax^2 + bx + c$

You need to know this:

Scatterplots are typically constructed so that the variable on the x-axis is the independent variable (input) and the variable on the y-axis is the dependent variable (output). The equation for the line or curve of best fit quantifies the relationship between the variables represented by the two axes. The patterns that you are most likely to encounter on the SAT are shown in the table that follows.

BEST FIT DESCRIPTION	RELATIONSHIP BETWEEN VARIABLES
Upward-sloping straight line	Linear and positive
Downward-sloping straight line	Linear and negative
Upward-opening parabola	Quadratic with a positive coefficient in front of the squared term
Downward-opening parabola	Quadratic with a negative coefficient in front of the squared term
Upward-sloping curve with an increasing slope	Exponential and positive (e.g., compound interest)
Downward-sloping curve with a flattening slope	Exponential and negative (e.g., radioactive decay)

Here are visual representations of linear, quadratic, and exponential models:

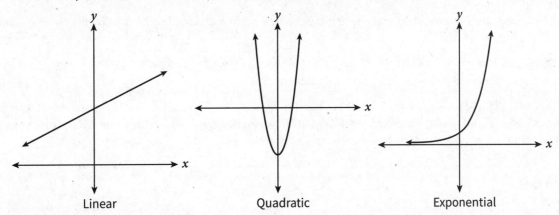

Linear   Quadratic   Exponential

Correlation measures the strength of the relationship between the two variables. A strong correlation means there is a close connection between the independent and dependent variables; this means the data points will be clustered around the line or curve of best fit. Conversely, a weak correlation means the data points will be spread farther from the line or curve of best fit.

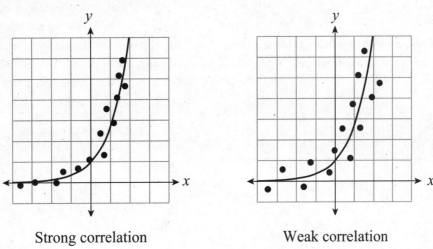

Strong correlation   Weak correlation

You need to do this:

- First, examine the line or curve of best fit and determine its curvature.
- If it is a straight line of best fit, the scatterplot represents a linear relationship and the equation will not contain any exponents. It will likely be in slope-intercept form, $y = mx + b$.
- If the curve of best fit is a parabola, the equation will be quadratic, generally in the form $y = ax^2 + bx + c$. If the parabola opens downward, a will be negative; if upward, a will be positive. (The quadratics chapter presents more detailed information about parabolas, but this will suffice for now.)
- If the curve of best fit is represented by an exponential relationship, the equation will generally be in the form $y = a(1 + r)^x$, where a is the initial amount and r is the rate of change. If r is positive, the graph will increase, slowly at first and then more rapidly as x increases. If r is negative, it will decrease, rapidly at first and then more gradually as x increases.

Explanation:

The best fit for this scatterplot would be a curve, so it is not a straight line as would be created by the linear equation $y = ax + b$. Eliminate (A).

The exponential equation $y = a^{bx}$ would result in a curve that opens upward in one direction. The curve of best fit of the scatterplot opens upward in two directions, so (B) is incorrect.

Quadratic equations create parabolas when graphed, but the negative coefficient of the x^2 term means that (C) would be a downward-opening parabola, whereas the scatterplot shows an upward-opening parabola. Thus, **(D)** is correct since that equation would be graphed as an upward-opening parabola.

Try on Your Own

Directions

Take as much time as you need on these questions. Work carefully and methodically. There will be an opportunity for timed practice later in the book.

6

Which of the following is best modeled using a linear equation, $y = ax + b$, where $a < 0$?

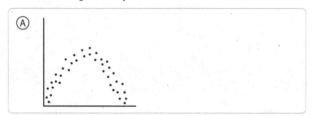

(A)

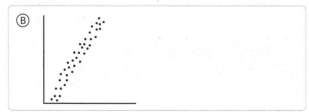

(B)

(C)

(D)

7

HINT: For Q7, in an exponential equation, you're taking a starting value and multiplying repeatedly by some other value.

In a scatterplot of population data over time, an exponential growth equation of the form $y = x_0(1 + r)^x$ models the relationship between the population in the area where Adriana lives and the number of years, x, after she was born. Which of the following does x_0 most likely represent in the equation?

(A) The population in the year that she was born

(B) The rate of change of the population over time

(C) The maximum population reached during her lifetime

(D) The number of years after her birth when the population reached its maximum

8

Suppose a scatterplot shows a weak negative linear correlation. Which of the following statements must be true?

(A) The slope of the line of best fit will be a number less than −1.

(B) The slope of the line of best fit will be a number between −1 and 0.

(C) The data points will follow, but not closely, the line of best fit.

(D) The data points will be closely gathered around the line of best fit.

9

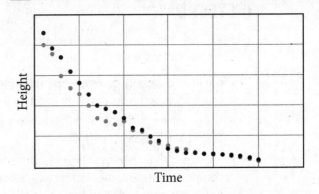

Time

A drain at the bottom of a cylindrical water tank is opened and the height of the water is measured at regular time intervals. The tank is refilled and the process is then repeated. The scatterplot shows the measured height on the y-axis and time on the x-axis for the two trials. Which of the following conclusions can be drawn from the observations in the scatterplot?

(A) Water flows out of the drain at a constant rate.

(B) The flow rate from the tank decreases as the height of the water in the tank decreases.

(C) The data in the scatterplot can be represented with a quadratic model.

(D) The is no relationship between the height of the water in the tank and time.

ON TEST DAY

The SAT often tests your understanding of the real-world meaning of the *y*-intercept of the line of best fit. Scatterplots will test your ability to recognize the meaning of the *y*-intercept in various ways:

- For lines of best fit, common examples include the flat fee for renting an item before the hourly rate begins or the down payment on an item before the monthly payments begin.
- For quadratic curves of best fit modeling the path of a projectile, the *y*-intercept is the starting height of the projectile.
- For exponential curves of best fit, common examples include the principal when calculating compound interest, the starting amount of an isotope with a specific half-life (radioactive decay), or the initial population when calculating population growth over time.

In short, the *y*-intercept models the initial amount of what is measured on the *y*-axis. Try the following question to see if you can recognize the real-world meaning of the *y*-intercept of the line or curve of best fit.

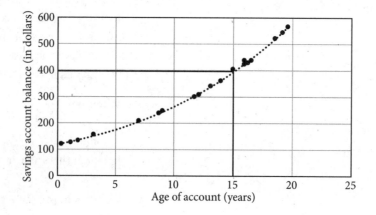

10. The scatterplot shows data collected from "Stock Market Special" account holders at a certain bank. The bank promises a 10% annual interest rate for this account. However, independent analysts found that the equation of the curve of best fit was actually $y = 120\left(1 + \dfrac{0.08}{12}\right)^{12x}$. Which of the following best explains how the number 120 in the equation relates to the scatterplot?

A) A "Stock Market Special" account with $120 initially will likely have less than $350 after 15 years.

B) A "Stock Market Special" account will earn $120 per year.

C) The difference between the promised 10 percent annual interest rate and the actual 8 percent rate is $120 a year.

D) A "Stock Market Special" account with $120 initially will likely have more than $350 after 15 years.

HOW MUCH HAVE YOU LEARNED?

Directions

For testlike practice, give yourself 9.5 minutes to complete this question set. Be sure to study the explanations, even for questions you answered correctly. They can be found at the end of this chapter.

11

Employee Sick Day Usage

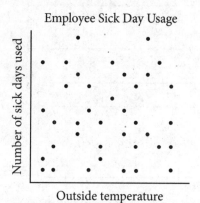

A certain company tracks employee sick day usage against outside temperature. The information is compiled in the scatterplot. Which of the following conclusions can be drawn based on this data?

(A) There is no relationship between the number of sick days used by employees in general and outside temperature.

(B) There is no relationship between the number of sick days used by this company's employees and outside temperature.

(C) No conclusions can be drawn about the number of sick days used by this company's employees and outside temperature.

(D) There is a relationship, but not a causal link, between the number of sick days used by this company's employees and outside temperature.

12

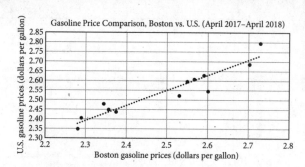

The scatterplot compares the average gasoline prices per gallon in Boston to the average gasoline prices per gallon across the United States during a one-year period from 2017 to 2018. Of the following equations, which best models the data in the scatterplot?

(A) $y = -1.7848x + 0.5842$

(B) $y = 1.7848x + 1.5842$

(C) $y = 0.7848x + 0.5842$

(D) $y = -0.7848x + 0.5842$

13

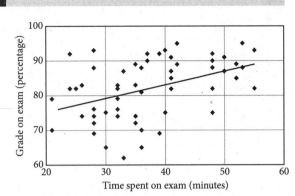

A physics professor presented the scatterplot shown to her students. What is the significance of the slope of the line of best fit?

(A) The slope represents the estimated rate at which time spent on an exam increases based on a student's exam performance.

(B) The slope represents the average grade on the exam.

(C) The slope represents the estimated rate at which a student's exam grade increases based on time spent on the exam.

(D) The slope has no significance.

14

Which of the following scatterplots shows a relationship that is appropriately modeled by the equation $y = -ax^2 + bx - c$, where a and c are negative and b is positive?

(A)
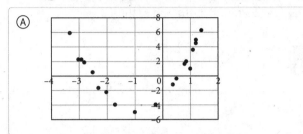

(B)
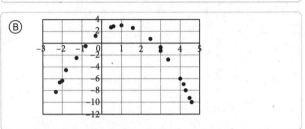

(C)
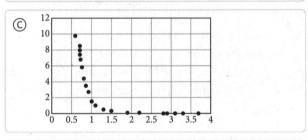

(D)
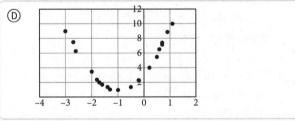

15

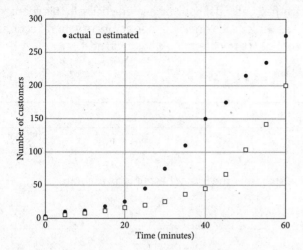

The scatterplot shows the actual and estimated number of customers visiting a new shopping plaza within the first hour of opening. Which of the following statements correctly compares the rates of increase for the actual and estimated numbers of customers?

(A) The rate of increase for the actual number of customers is greater than that of the estimated number in every 20-minute interval.

(B) The rate of increase for the actual number of customers is less than that of the estimated number in every 20-minute interval.

(C) The rate of increase for the actual number of customers is greater than that of the estimated number in the interval from 20 to 40 minutes and less in the interval 40 to 60 minutes.

(D) The rate of increase for the actual number of customers is less than that of the estimated number in the interval from 20 to 40 minutes and greater in the interval 40 to 60 minutes.

16

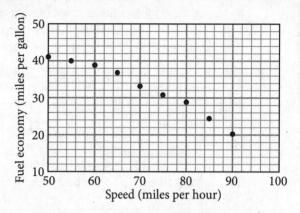

A certain car's fuel economy is depicted in the graph. What is the best estimate of this car's fuel economy, in miles per gallon, at 100 miles per hour?

(A) 0

(B) 10

(C) 17

(D) 41

REFLECT

Directions: Take a few minutes to recall what you've learned and what you've been practicing in this chapter. Consider the following questions, jot down your best answer for each one, and then compare your reflections to the expert responses that follow. Use your level of confidence to determine what to do next.

What is the significance of a scatterplot's line of best fit?

_____

_____

_____

Given a scatterplot and a line of best fit, how can you tell whether the line of best fit is an accurate representation?

_____

_____

_____

What are the three most common patterns for modeling scatterplots that you'll see on test day?

_____

_____

_____

Expert Responses

What is the significance of a scatterplot's line of best fit?

The line of best fit describes the relationship between the two variables of the scatterplot. For example, if the line of best fit is linear and has a positive slope, then the two variables have a linear and positive relationship: as one variable increases, the other one also increases at a constant rate.

Given a scatterplot and a line of best fit, how can you tell whether the line of best fit is an accurate representation?

A line of best fit should be drawn such that approximately half the points are above it and half are below it.

What are the three most common patterns for modeling scatterplots that you'll see on test day?

Most test day scatterplots can be modeled by a linear ($y = mx + b$), quadratic ($y = ax^2 + bx + c$), or exponential ($y = ab^x + c$) relationship.

Next Steps

If you answered most questions correctly in the "How Much Have You Learned?" section and if your responses to the Reflect questions were similar to those of the SAT expert, then consider Scatterplots an area of strength and move on to the next chapter. Come back to this topic periodically to ensure your skills stay sharp.

If you don't yet feel confident, review those parts of this chapter that you have not yet mastered and try the questions you missed again. In particular, make sure that you feel comfortable gathering data from a line of best fit. As always, be sure to review the explanations closely.

Check Your Work – Chapter 10

1.   A
Difficulty: Medium
Category: Problem-Solving and Data Analysis
Getting to the Answer: Examine the graph, paying careful attention to units and labels. The average rate of change is the same as the slope of the line of best fit. The data is decreasing (going down from left to right), so eliminate (C) and (D). To choose between (A) and (B), find the slope of the line of best fit using the slope formula, $m = \dfrac{y_2 - y_1}{x_2 - x_1}$, and any two points that lie on (or very close to) the line. Using the two points (5, 14) and (10, 8), the average rate of change is about $\dfrac{8 - 14}{10 - 5} = \dfrac{-6}{5} = -1.2$, which matches **(A)**.

2.   A
Difficulty: Easy
Category: Problem-Solving and Data Analysis
Getting to the Answer: The question asks for a rate of change, which means you'll need the slope of the line of best fit. Pick a pair of points to use in the slope formula, such as (1998, 20) and (2012, 90):

$$m = \frac{y_2 - y_1}{x_2 - x_1} = \frac{90 - 20}{2012 - 1998} = \frac{70}{14} = 5$$

Choice **(A)** is correct.

3.   18
Difficulty: Medium
Category: Problem-Solving and Data Analysis
Getting to the Answer: Because the y-value of the graph when $x = 3,400$ is not shown, this question requires a mathematical solution; extending the line of best fit will not provide an accurate enough answer. The equation of the model is given as $y = -\dfrac{1}{200}x + 35$. Miles over recommended servicing are graphed along the x-axis, so substitute 3,400 for x to find the answer:

$$y = -\frac{1}{200}(3,400) + 35 = -17 + 35 = 18$$

Enter **18**.

4.   2
Difficulty: Easy
Category: Problem-Solving and Data Analysis
Getting to the Answer: Examine the graph, including the axis labels and numbering. Each vertical grid line represents 5 eggs, so look to see how many data points are more than a complete grid space away from the

line of best fit. Only 2 data points meet this requirement—the first data point at about 3 weeks and the one between 30 and 35 weeks, making **2** the correct answer. Enter **2**.

5.   A
Difficulty: Medium
Category: Problem-Solving and Data Analysis.
Getting to the Answer: First, find the slope of the line of best fit using the slope formula, $m = \dfrac{y_2 - y_1}{x_2 - x_1}$, and any two points that lie on the line. Using the two points (17.0, 3.0) and (20.0, 5.0), the slope is $\dfrac{5.0 - 3.0}{20.0 - 17.0} = \dfrac{2}{3}$. Eliminate (C) and (D). The y-intercept occurs when x is 0. According to the scatterplot, y is 3 when x is 17, not when x is 0, so eliminate (B). **(A)** is correct.

You can determine the exact y-intercept by plugging one of the points into the slope-intercept form:

$$5 = \frac{2}{3}(20) + b$$
$$\frac{15}{3} = \frac{40}{3} + b$$
$$-\frac{25}{3} = b$$

6.   C
Difficulty: Easy
Category: Problem-Solving and Data Analysis
Getting to the Answer: The equation given is that of a line in slope-intercept form, so a represents the slope. Since a is negative, you are looking for data that is linear and decreasing or falling from left to right. You can eliminate (A), which is a parabola, and (D), an exponential curve. You can also eliminate (B) because it is increasing (rising from left to right) instead of decreasing (falling from left to right). **(C)** is correct.

7.   A
Difficulty: Easy
Getting to the Answer: When an exponential equation is written in the form $y = x_0(1 + r)^x$, the value of x_0 gives the y-intercept of the equation's graph. To answer this question, you need to think about what the y-intercept would represent in the context described.

Whenever time is involved in a relationship that is modeled by an equation or a graph, it is almost always the independent variable and therefore graphed on the *x*-axis. Therefore, for this question, population would be graphed on the *y*-axis, so x_0 most likely represents the population when the time elapsed was zero, or in other words, in the year that Adriana was born, making **(A)** correct.

8. C
Difficulty: Medium
Getting to the Answer: "Correlation" simply means relationship. The word "weak" refers to the strength of the relationship (how close the data lies to the line of best fit), which has no effect on slope. Be careful not to confuse slope and strength. The fact that a data set shows a weak correlation does not give you any information about the magnitude of the slope. This means you can eliminate (A) and (B). In a weak correlation, the data points will loosely follow the line of best fit, which makes **(C)** the correct answer. (D) describes a strong correlation.

9. B
Difficulty: Easy
Getting to the Answer: A curve of best fit for the scatterplot would show that the measured height of the water decreases over time, but the curve becomes less steep over time, too. Since the flow changes as the height of the water changes, (A) is incorrect. Because the curve of best fit becomes less steep as the height of the water decreases, it follows that the flow rate decreases as the height of the water decreases. **(B)** is correct. (D) is incorrect because the height of the water decreases (though at an ever slower rate) as time progresses, so there is a relationship between the height of the water and time. (C) is incorrect because a downward-sloping curve with a flattening slope is represented by an exponential model, not a quadratic model.

10. D
Difficulty: Medium
Category: Problem-Solving and Data Analysis
Getting to the Answer: In the curve of best fit equation, the initial principal is $120. However, this does not mean that the account will earn $120 per year. Eliminate (B).

To test (A) and (D), examine the curve of best fit:

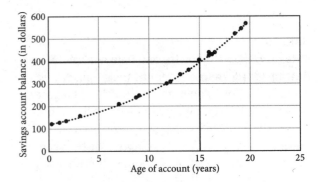

Notice that the curve of best fit is definitely above $350 at the 15-year mark, so **(D)** is correct.

On test day, you would stop here. But for the record, since the curve of best fit is exponential, not linear, there will not be a constant difference between the 10% annual rate and 8% annual rate. This makes (C) incorrect.

11. B
Difficulty: Medium
Category: Problem-Solving and Data Analysis
Getting to the Answer: Work through each answer choice systematically. The population in the study is only the employees at this particular company, not all employees in general, so eliminate (A). The data points are scattered and do not form any discernible pattern. This means there is no correlation, which is another way of saying that the two variables aren't related. Eliminate (D). You can also eliminate (C) because it *is* possible to draw a conclusion—that there is no relationship between sick days and temperature. Therefore, **(B)** is correct.

12. C
Difficulty: Medium
Category: Problem-Solving and Data Analysis
Getting to the Answer: The slope of the line of best fit is positive. Eliminate (A) and (D) because they have negative slopes. Determining the *y*-intercept is a little trickier, since the *x*-axis begins at 2.2, not 0. Since only two choices are left, you could plug in a point from the line of best fit to test it. If the equation you test works, then it is correct. If the equation you test does not work, the other is correct.

Choose a point that is easy to approximate, like (2.7, 2.7). Plugging 2.7 in for x should give approximately $y = 2.7$. Try plugging this into (B):

$$y = 1.7848(2.7) + 1.5842$$
$$y = 4.81896 + 1.5842$$
$$y = 6.40316$$

This does not match, so **(C)** is correct.

13. C
Difficulty: Easy
Category: Problem-Solving and Data Analysis
Getting to the Answer: Recall that slope is change in y over change in x. The slope of a line is a rate of change, so you can eliminate (B) and (D). The graph indicates that exam performance is the dependent variable, y, and that time spent on the exam is the independent variable, x. Choice **(C)** correctly describes this relationship.

14. D
Difficulty: Hard
Category: Problem-Solving and Data Analysis
Getting to the Answer: Examine the curves of best fit in the answer choices. (A) and (D) are parabolas that open up, (B) is a parabola that opens down, and (C) is an exponential curve. The equation that needs to be modeled is $y = -ax^2 + bx - c$. This is a quadratic and thus graphs as a parabola. Eliminate (C).

The question says that a and c are negative and b is positive. The coefficient in front of the x^2 term determines whether the parabola opens up or down. The negative sign in front of a multiplied by the negative value of a creates a positive coefficient in front of the x^2 term. This means that the parabola opens up. Eliminate (B).

Finally, the c coefficient in the equation determines the y-intercept of the graph. Again, the negative sign in front of c multiplied by the negative value of c creates a positive y-intercept. Eliminate (A) because the parabola has a negative y-intercept. Choice **(D)** is correct.

15. C
Difficulty: Hard
Category: Problem-Solving and Data Analysis
Getting to the Answer: The words "rate of increase" mean slope. For every 20-minute interval, either quickly sketch a line of best fit through estimations of data for the actual number of customers and for the

estimated number of customers on your scratch paper or, better yet, simply mentally visualize it on the graph given to you (as shown). Compare the steepness of the slopes of the lines of best fit for actual and estimated for each 20-minute interval.

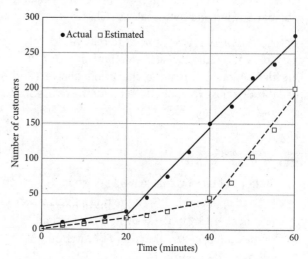

In the interval from 0 to 20 minutes, the slope of the line of best fit for the actual number of customers is slightly greater (steeper) than that of the estimated model. In the interval from 20 to 40 minutes, the slope of the line of best fit for the actual data is greater than that of the estimated data. In the interval from 40 to 60 minutes, the slope of the line of best fit for the actual data is less than that of the estimated data. Thus, **(C)** is correct.

16. B
Difficulty: Easy
Category: Problem-Solving and Data Analysis
Getting to the Answer: Mentally visualize a curve of best fit on the graph. Extending the regression curve to the x-axis allows you to estimate what the fuel economy at 100 miles per hour (mph) will be. Notice that the miles per gallon (mpg) drop from 80 mph to 90 mph is slightly less than 10, so it is reasonable to expect a drop of another full 10 mpg as the curve steepens from 90 mph to 100 mph. Therefore, the mpg at 100 mph would be about 10. Choice **(B)** is correct.

HOW MUCH HAVE YOU LEARNED: PROBLEM-SOLVING AND DATA ANALYSIS

Directions

This "How Much Have You Learned" section will allow you to measure your growth and confidence in Problem-Solving and Data Analysis skills.

For testlike practice, give yourself 15 minutes for this question set. Be sure to use the Method for SAT Math Questions. When you're done, check your answers and read through the explanations, even for the questions you got correct. Don't forget to celebrate your progress!

1

Stafford books a venue for $5,950, which is 35% of his budget. Food is 40% of the budget and entertainment is 15% of the budget. If the remainder of the budget covers the cost of decorations, how much are decorations?

(A) $1,700

(B) $2,550

(C) $5,100

(D) $6,800

2

Ayesha signs up for an e-book subscription service for which the monthly fee is e dollars. She budgets to spend $100 for the service. If the first two months are half-off, then which of the following expressions represents the number of months Ayesha will subscribe to the service?

(A) $\dfrac{100 - \frac{1}{2}e}{e}$

(B) $\dfrac{100 - e}{e}$

(C) $\dfrac{100 + e}{e}$

(D) $\dfrac{100 + \frac{3}{2}e}{e}$

3

The ratio of washing machines to dryers at a laundromat is 4 to 3. The laundromat opens a second location with a total of 42 washing machines and dryers, using the same ratio as the first location. How many washing machines are at the second location?

(A) 18

(B) 24

(C) 32

(D) 56

4

If Simritha consumes 8 cups of water a day, and 1 cup equals approximately 0.24 liters, how many liters did Simritha consume?

5

A marketing team was provided data from a survey of 1,000 pet owners with cars. The data indicated that approximately 35% of respondents planned to purchase car seat covers within the next six months. Which of the following conclusions is best supported by the sample data?

(A) The number of car owners who will purchase seat covers is less than 35%.

(B) The number of car owners who will purchase seat covers is 35%.

(C) The number of car owners who will purchase seat covers is greater than 35%.

(D) The number of car owners who will not purchase seat covers is 65%.

6

At an ice skating rink, $\frac{3}{5}$ of the skaters were teenagers, $\frac{2}{3}$ of whom were wearing gloves. Of the teenagers wearing gloves, 10 percent also wore hats. If a skater is chosen at random, what is the probability that the skater is a teenager wearing both a hat and gloves?

(A) $\frac{1}{25}$

(B) $\frac{1}{15}$

(C) $\frac{1}{10}$

(D) $\frac{2}{5}$

7

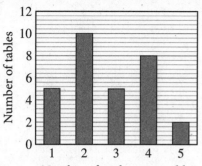

The number of students at tables in a library is shown in the figure. What is the median number of students at a table in the library?

(A) 2

(B) 2.5

(C) 2.73

(D) 3

8

The skill level of a dart player corresponds to the distribution of the player's darts around the bullseye. Which measure should be used to determine a player's skill?

(A) Mean

(B) Range

(C) Median

(D) Standard deviation

9

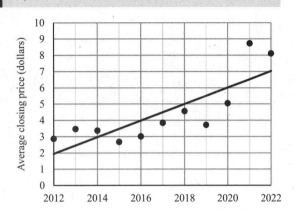

The scatterplot shows the average closing price of lumber over time and the line of best fit. Which of the following is closest to the estimated yearly increase in the average closing price of lumber, in dollars?

Ⓐ 0.50

Ⓑ 1

Ⓒ 2

Ⓓ 5

10

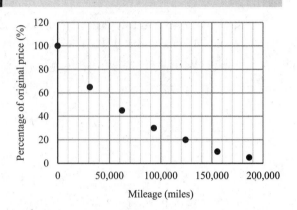

The scatterplot shows the resale value of a car as a function of miles driven. Which of the following statements is true about the relationship between the resale value of a car and its mileage?

Ⓐ The resale value of a car increases every 50,000 miles.

Ⓑ The rate of decrease in the resale value per mile is constant.

Ⓒ The rate of decrease in the resale value of a car every 50,000 miles is greater at lower mileage than at higher mileage.

Ⓓ The rate of decrease in the resale value of a car every 50,000 miles is greater at higher mileage than at lower mileage.

Check Your Work – How Much Have You Learned: Problem-Solving and Data Analysis

1. A
Difficulty: Medium
Category: Problem-Solving and Data Analysis
Getting to the Answer: The percent of the budget spent on the decorations is $100\% - 35\% - 40\% - 15\% = 10\%$. You're told that the cost of the venue is $5,950, which represents 35% of the total budget. Let x be the total amount of the budget in dollars. Then 35% of x is $5,950, or $0.35x = 5,950$. Solve this equation for x:

$$0.35x = 5,950$$
$$x = 17,000$$

The total budget is $17,000. Decorations represent 10% of this amount, or $0.10 \times \$17,000 = \$1,700$, which means **(A)** is correct. You could also set up the proportion $\frac{10\%}{35\%} = \frac{x}{5,950}$ and solve for x.

2. C
Difficulty: Hard
Category: Problem-Solving and Data Analysis
Getting to the Answer: Let m be the number of months Ayesha will subscribe to the service. Since the first two months are half-off, the first two months cost $2 \times 0.5e$ dollars. The remaining months $(m - 2)$ are charged at a rate of e dollars per month. So, the total charge for the subscription so far is $e + e(m - 2)$. Set this equal to $100 and solve for m:

$$e + e(m - 2) = 100$$
$$e + em - 2e = 100$$
$$em - e = 100$$
$$m = \frac{100 + e}{e}$$

The expression for m matches the one in **(C)**.

3. B
Difficulty: Easy
Category: Problem-Solving and Data Analysis
Getting to the Answer: You need to find the number of washing machines out of a total of 42 washers and dryers that will yield a 4:3 ratio of washers to dryers.

Add the parts of the given ratio together to get the total number of parts: $4 + 3 = 7$, so the total number of washers and dryers will always be a multiple of 7. Divide the total number of washers and dryers at the second location by 7 to find the multiple that the laundromat has at the second location: $\frac{42}{7} = 6$. Multiply the

original ratio by 6 to get the actual number of washers: $4(6) = 24$. **(B)** is correct.

4. 1.92
Difficulty: Easy
Category: Problem-Solving and Data Analysis
Getting to the Answer: Use unit conversion to convert from cups to liters, which is the unit you want the answer in:

$$8 \text{ cups} \times \frac{0.24 \text{ liter}}{1 \text{ cup}} = 1.92 \text{ liters}$$

Enter **1.92**.

5. A
Difficulty: Easy
Category: Problem-Solving and Data Analysis
Getting to the Answer: When considering the validity of a study, always look for possible sources of bias. In other words, look for things that might skew the results in either direction. Because the survey only sampled car owners who had pets, the results of the survey are likely skewed. The respondents of pet owners with cars are likely to respond more positively than the average car owner to seat covers. Therefore, the data from the survey likely overestimates the number of car owners interested in seat covers, making **(A)** the correct answer.

6. A
Difficulty: Medium
Category: Problem-Solving and Data Analysis
Getting to the Answer: Convert 10% to a fraction $\left(\frac{1}{10}\right)$ and then approach logically—the final probability is $\frac{1}{10}$ of $\frac{2}{3}$ of $\frac{3}{5}$. When dealing with fractions, "of" means multiply. So, the probability of randomly choosing a skater who is a teenager wearing a hat and gloves is $\frac{1}{\overset{1}{5}\cancel{10}} \times \frac{2}{3} \times \frac{\cancel{3}}{5} = \frac{1}{25}$. **(A)** is correct.

7. B
Difficulty: Easy
Category: Problem-Solving and Data Analysis
Getting to the Answer: There are $5 + 10 + 5 + 8 + 2 = 30$ tables with students, so the median will be the average of the 15th and 16th groups. The 15th table falls under 2 students per table since $5 + 10 = 15$, and the 16th table falls under 3 students per table. Thus, the median, which is the average of the 15th and 16th groups, is $\frac{2 + 3}{2} = \frac{5}{2} = 2.5$. Choice **(B)** is correct.

8. D
Difficulty: Easy
Category: Problem-Solving and Data Analysis
Getting to the Answer: Both range and standard deviation are measures of spread, while mean and median are a measure of center. Eliminate (A) and (C). The range tells you the maximum value minus the minimum value but not the distribution. Thus, standard deviation should be used to determine a player's skill. **(D)** is correct. The distribution over a broader region indicates a low-skilled darts player (high standard deviation), while a good darts player will have shots closely clustered around the bullseye (low standard deviation).

9. A
Difficulty: Medium
Category: Problem-Solving and Data Analysis
Getting to the Answer: The estimated yearly increase in the average closing price of lumber is represented by the slope of the line of best fit. Recall that the slope is equal to $\frac{y_2 - y_1}{x_2 - x_1}$. Estimate any two points on the line, for instance (2012, 2) and (2022, 7), to approximate the slope. The slope is about $\frac{7 - 2}{2022 - 2012} = \frac{5}{10} = 0.5$. The estimated yearly increase in the average closing price of lumber is $0.50. **(A)** is correct.

10. C
Difficulty: Medium
Category: Problem-Solving and Data Analysis
Getting to the Answer: The data in the scatterplot can be modeled with a concave up curve (such as quadratic or exponential) that has a decreasing negative slope. The rate of decrease is not constant. Eliminate (A) and (B). To visualize this, for every 50,000 miles, draw a line of best fit through the data. The slopes of the lines of best fit are steeper at lower mileage. Thus, at lower mileage, the rate of decrease in the resale value of a car every 50,000 is greater than at higher mileage. **(C)** is correct.

ADVANCED MATH

HOW MUCH DO YOU KNOW: ADVANCED MATH

Directions

Try the questions that follow, using the Method for SAT Math Questions. When you're done, check your answers and read through the explanations in the "Check Your Work" section.

There will be an opportunity for timed practice at the end of the Advanced Math unit.

1

If $|3x - 14| = x + 4$, which of the following gives all possible values of x?

(A) $-5, 9$

(B) 9

(C) $-2.5, 18$

(D) $2.5, 9$

2

If the quadratic equation $y = 3(x + 5)^2 + 12$ is rewritten in standard form, $y = ax^2 + bx + c$, what is the value of c?

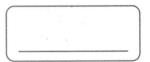

3

Which of the following is equivalent to the expression $4\sqrt[3]{ab^9}$?

(A) $4a^{\frac{1}{3}}b^3$

(B) $4a^3b^{\frac{1}{3}}$

(C) $4a^3b^{27}$

(D) $\dfrac{4}{a^{\frac{1}{3}}b^3}$

4

$$\sqrt{0.75} \times \sqrt{0.8}$$

Which of the following has the same value as the expression above?

(A) $\dfrac{3}{5}$

(B) $\dfrac{\sqrt{15}}{5}$

(C) $\sqrt[4]{0.6}$

(D) $\sqrt{1.55}$

5

If the equation of the axis of symmetry of the parabola given by $y = 3x^2 + 12x - 8$ is $x = m$, then what is the value of m?

K

6

If $f(x) = \sqrt[3]{x} + 3$ and $f(x) \leq 0$, what is the maximum value of x?

7

Which of the following best describes the solutions to the rational equation $\dfrac{3}{x-2} - \dfrac{12}{x^2-4} = 1$?

Ⓐ No solution

Ⓑ Two valid solutions

Ⓒ Two extraneous solutions

Ⓓ One valid solution and one extraneous solution

8

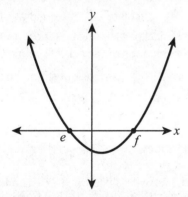

If e is half as far from the origin as f in the figure shown, which of the following could be the factored form of the graph's equation?

Ⓐ $y = \left(x - \dfrac{1}{2}\right)(x + 1)$

Ⓑ $y = (x - 1)(x + 2)$

Ⓒ $y = (x - 1)(2x + 1)$

Ⓓ $y = \left(x + \dfrac{1}{2}\right)(2x + 1)$

9

If $f(x) = \dfrac{x^2 - x - 12}{3x - 4}$ and $g(x) = x^2 - 7x + 8$, what is $f(2g(2))$?

Ⓐ -2

Ⓑ $-\dfrac{1}{2}$

Ⓒ 2

Ⓓ $\dfrac{7}{2}$

10

If $j(x) = 3x^2 + 6x - 24$, $k(x) = x + 4$, and $x = z - 5$, what is the value of $\dfrac{j(x)}{k(x)}$ when $z = 8$?

Ⓐ -3

Ⓑ 1

Ⓒ 3

Ⓓ 7

Check Your Work – How Much Do You Know: Advanced Math

1. D

Difficulty: Medium

Category: Advanced Math

Getting to the Answer: With absolute value equations, you must solve twice: once for the positive version of the given value and once for the negative version of that value. Start by solving for the positive version:

$$3x - 14 = x + 4$$
$$3x = x + 18$$
$$2x = 18$$
$$x = 9$$

Next, solve for the negative version:

$$3x - 14 = -(x + 4)$$
$$3x - 14 = -x - 4$$
$$3x = -x + 10$$
$$4x = 10$$
$$x = 2.5$$

So both 2.5 and 9 are the values of x. **(D)** is correct.

2. 87

Difficulty: Easy

Category: Advanced Math

Getting to the Answer: Use FOIL to expand the factored form of the quadratic into standard form:

$$y = 3(x + 5)^2 + 12$$
$$= 3(x + 5)(x + 5) + 12$$
$$= 3(x^2 + 5x + 5x + 25) + 12$$
$$= 3(x^2 + 10x + 25) + 12$$
$$= 3x^2 + 30x + 75 + 12$$
$$= 3x^2 + 30x + 87$$

The question asks for the value of c, so enter **87**.

3. A

Difficulty: Medium

Category: Advanced Math

Getting to the Answer: Write each factor in the expression in exponential form and use exponent rules to simplify the expression. The number 4 is being multiplied by the variables, which will not go into the denominator. Eliminate (D). The power of a under the radical is 1 and the root is 3, so a is raised to the power of $\frac{1}{3}$. Eliminate (B) and (C). Only **(A)** is left and is correct. On test day, you would move on, but for the record: the power of b is 9 and the root is 3, so the exponent on b is $\frac{9}{3} = 3$. Therefore, $4\sqrt[3]{ab^9} = 4a^{\frac{1}{3}}b^3$. **(A)** is indeed correct.

4. B

Difficulty: Medium

Category: Advanced Math

Getting to the Answer: When you see decimals that do not simplify, change them to an equivalent form, such as fractions. Then simplify:

$$\sqrt{0.75} \times \sqrt{0.8} = \sqrt{\frac{3}{4}} \times \sqrt{\frac{4}{5}} = \sqrt{\frac{3}{\cancel{4}} \times \frac{\cancel{4}}{5}} = \sqrt{\frac{3}{5}} = \frac{\sqrt{3}}{\sqrt{5}}$$

A radical is not allowed in the denominator of a fraction, so rationalize it by multiplying the numerator and the denominator by the same radical that you are trying to rationalize: $\frac{\sqrt{3}}{\sqrt{5}} \times \frac{\sqrt{5}}{\sqrt{5}} = \frac{\sqrt{15}}{5}$. Alternatively, you can evaluate the expression in the question on your calculator, 0.77459..., and then evaluate the expressions in the answer choices until you find a match. This might, however, consume time that could be better spent on other questions. Either way, **(B)** is correct.

5. −2

Difficulty: Medium

Category: Advanced Math

Getting to the Answer: The axis of symmetry of a parabola always passes through the x-coordinate of the parabola's vertex. The trick for finding the x-coordinate of the vertex is to calculate $\frac{-b}{2a}$ (the quadratic formula without the radical part). In the equation, $a = 3$ and $b = 12$, so the equation of the axis of symmetry is $x = \frac{-(12)}{2(3)} = \frac{-12}{6} = -2$. In the question, the equation is $x = m$, so m must be −2. Enter **−2**.

6. −27

Difficulty: Medium

Category: Advanced Math

Getting to the Answer: Since $f(x) = \sqrt[3]{x} + 3$, and the question states that this value can be no greater than 0, set up an inequality to solve for the maximum value of x:

$$\sqrt[3]{x} + 3 \leq 0$$
$$\sqrt[3]{x} \leq -3$$
$$(\sqrt[3]{x})^3 \leq (-3)^3$$
$$x \leq -27$$

Enter **−27**.

7. D

Difficulty: Hard

Category: Rational Expressions and Equations

Getting to the Answer: Factor the denominator in the second term to find that the common denominator for all three terms is $(x-2)(x+2)$. Multiply each term in the equation by the common denominator (in factored form or the original form, whichever is more convenient) to clear the fractions. Then solve the resulting equation for x:

$$(x+2)(x^2-4)\left(\frac{3}{x-2}\right)-(x^2-4)\left(\frac{12}{x^2-4}\right)=1(x^2-4)$$

$$3(x+2)-12=x^2-4$$

$$3x+6-12=x^2-4$$

$$3x-6=x^2-4$$

$$0=x^2-3x+2$$

$$0=(x-1)(x-2)$$

Set each factor equal to 0 to find that the potential solutions are $x=1$ and $x=2$. Note that these are only *potential* solutions because the original equation was a rational equation. When $x=2$, the denominators in both terms on the left side are equal to 0, so 2 is an extraneous solution, which means **(D)** is correct.

8. C

Difficulty: Medium

Category: Advanced Math

Getting to the Answer: According to the graph, one x-intercept is to the left of the y-axis and the other is to the right. Therefore, one value of x is positive, while the other is negative. Eliminate (D) because both factors have the same sign. To evaluate the remaining equations, find the x-intercepts by setting each factor equal to 0 and solving for x. In (A), the x-intercepts are $\frac{1}{2}$ and -1, but that would mean that e (the negative intercept) is twice as far from the origin as f, not half as far, so eliminate (A). In (B), the x-intercepts are 1 and -2. Again, e is twice as far from the origin as f, not half, so eliminate (B). Only **(C)** is left and must be correct. The x-intercepts are 1 and $-\frac{1}{2}$, which fits the criterion that e is half as far from the origin as f.

9. B

Difficulty: Medium

Category: Advanced Math

Getting to the Answer: Work from the inside out. Find $g(2)$, multiply it by 2 to find $2g(2)$ and then use the result as the input for $f(x)$: $g(2)=2^2-7(2)+8=4-14+8=-2$. Next, $2g(2)=2(-2)=-4$. Now, find $f(-4)$:

$$\frac{(-4)^2-(-4)-12}{3(-4)-4}=\frac{16+4-12}{-12-4}=\frac{8}{-16}=-\frac{1}{2}$$

(B) is correct.

10. C

Difficulty: Medium

Category: Advanced Math

Getting to the Answer: There are two ways to approach this question. After determining the value of x when $z=8$, you can either plug that value into both functions, or you can write out the equations for $j(x)$ and $k(x)$ and see if there are any common factors that can be canceled out. Both methods begin the same way: $x=8-5=3$.

The function $j(x)$ is $3(3)^2+6(3)-24=27+18-24=21$ when $x=3$. Similarly, $k(x)=3+4=7$. So, $\frac{j(x)}{k(x)}=\frac{21}{7}=3$. **(C)** is correct.

Alternatively, factoring an $(x+4)$ out of $j(x)$ and canceling with $k(x)$ in the denominator will leave you with just $3(x-2)$. At $x=3$, this also evaluates to 3.

CHAPTER 11

ABSOLUTE VALUE AND NONLINEAR FUNCTIONS

LEARNING OBJECTIVES

After completing this chapter, you will be able to:

- Solve an equation containing an absolute value expression
- Interpret the graph of an equation containing an absolute value expression
- Interpret the domain, range, and properties of nonlinear functions and their graphs
- Evaluate the output of a given nonlinear function

HOW MUCH DO YOU KNOW?

Directions

Try the questions that follow. Show your work so that you can compare your solutions to the ones found in the "Check Your Work" section immediately after this question set. If you answered the question(s) on a specific topic correctly, and if your scratchwork looks like ours, you may be able to move quickly through the lesson covering that topic. If you answered incorrectly or used a different approach, you may want to take your time on that lesson.

1

$$|-2x + 2| - 1 = 5$$

Based on the equation shown, which of the following shows all values of x?

Ⓐ -2 and 3

Ⓑ 2 and 3

Ⓒ -2 and 4

Ⓓ 2 and 4

2

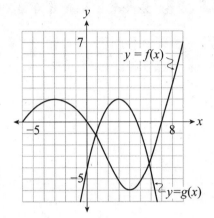

In the figure shown, what is the value of $g(0)$ divided by $f(-3)$?

3

A function is defined by the equation $f(x) = x^3 + 3x + 11$. What is the value of $f(2) - f(5)$?

Ⓐ -151

Ⓑ -126

Ⓒ 151

Ⓓ 176

4

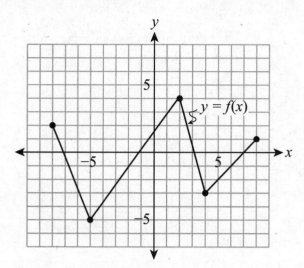

The graph of the function $y = f(x)$ is shown. The coordinates of the maximum of f are (a, b) and the coordinates of the minimum of f are (c, d). What is the value of $(a + b) - (c + d)$?

Ⓐ   −10

Ⓑ   −4

Ⓒ   6

Ⓓ   16

5

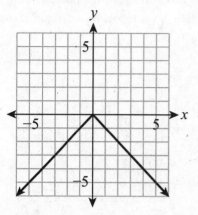

The figure shows the function $f(x) = -|x|$. Which statement about the function is true?

Ⓐ   The domain of $f(x)$ is all negative numbers and zero.

Ⓑ   The range of $f(x)$ is all negative numbers and zero.

Ⓒ   The range of $f(x)$ is all real numbers.

Ⓓ   The range of $f(x)$ is zero.

6

The function h is defined by $h(x) = 2x^2 - 11$. Which of the following is a value of x when $h(x)$ equals 39?

- (A) 5
- (B) 11
- (C) 25
- (D) 50

7

$$6x = |12 - 3x|$$

Which of the following lists all of the solutions to the given equation?

- (A) -4
- (B) -4 and $\frac{4}{3}$
- (C) $-\frac{4}{3}$ and 4
- (D) $\frac{4}{3}$

Check Your Work

1.   C
Difficulty: Medium
Category: Advanced Math
Getting to the Answer: To solve an absolute value equation, you need to solve twice: for both the positive and the negative version of the expression inside the absolute value symbols. First, the positive version:

$$|-2x + 2| - 1 = 5$$
$$|-2x + 2| = 6$$
$$-2x + 2 = 6$$
$$-2x = 4$$
$$x = -2$$

So one of the values of x is -2; eliminate (B) and (D). Now solve for the negative version of the expression:

$$|-2x + 2| - 1 = 5$$
$$|-2x + 2| = 6$$
$$-2x + 2 = -6$$
$$-2x = -8$$
$$x = 4$$

Choice **(C)** is correct.

2.   −2
Difficulty: Medium
Category: Advanced Math
Getting to the Answer: Use the graph to find the y-value of each function at the specified x-value; $g(0)$ occurs on the g-function where $x = 0$, and that's a y-value of -4; $f(-3)$ occurs at a y-value of 2. Thus, $\dfrac{g(0)}{f(-3)} = -\dfrac{4}{2} = -2$.

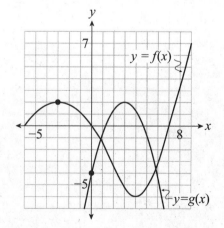

Enter **−2**.

3.   B
Difficulty: Medium
Category: Advanced Math
Getting to the Answer: Calculate the value of $f(2)$ by plugging 2 in for x in the function, and then calculate the value of $f(5)$ by plugging 5 in for x in the function. Then subtract the second value from the first.

$$f(2) = 2^3 + 3(2) + 11 = 8 + 6 + 11 = 25$$
$$f(5) = 5^3 + 3(5) + 11 = 125 + 15 + 11 = 151$$

Thus, the value of $f(2) - f(5)$ is $25 - 151 = -126$.

(B) is correct.

4.   D
Difficulty: Medium
Category: Advanced Math
Getting to the Answer: The maximum of f occurs at the point where the y-value is the greatest, which in this case is $(2, 4)$. Thus, $a = 2$ and $b = 4$. The point with the smallest y-value is $(-5, -5)$. So $c = -5$ and $d = -5$. Thus, the value of $(a + b) - (c + d)$ is $(2 + 4) - (-5 + -5) = 6 + 10 = 16$. Choice **(D)** is correct.

5.   B
Difficulty: Easy
Category: Advanced Math
Getting to the Answer: The function graphed is a negative of an absolute value function. The range (the output, or the y-values) of this function shows all negative numbers and zero. Therefore, choice **(B)** is correct.

6.   A
Difficulty: Medium
Category: Advanced Math
Getting to the Answer: The function is defined by the equation $h(x) = 2x^2 - 11$. You need to find the value of x when $2x^2 - 11$ equals 39, so substitute 39 for $h(x)$ and solve for x:

$$39 = 2x^2 - 11$$
$$50 = 2x^2$$
$$25 = x^2$$
$$5 \text{ or } -5 = x$$

Only 5 is among the answer choices, so **(A)** is correct.

7. D

Difficulty: Medium

Category: Advanced Math

Getting to the Answer: This question can be solved very quickly by noting that an absolute value can never be negative, so the $6x$ term of the equation must also never be negative. Choices (A), (B), and (C) all have negative answers and may be eliminated, leaving only choice **(D)** as correct.

For the record, to solve an absolute value question in a more traditional manner, you need to solve for both the positive and the negative version of the expression inside the absolute value symbols. Set up two equations, one for each version:

$$6x = |12 - 3x|$$
$$6x = 12 - 3x$$
$$9x = 12$$
$$x = \frac{12}{9}$$
$$x = \frac{4}{3}$$

Since one of the values of x is $\frac{4}{3}$, eliminate answer choices that don't include it; that's (A) and (C).

$$6x = |12 - 3x|$$
$$-6x = 12 - 3x$$
$$-3x = 12$$
$$x = \frac{12}{-3}$$
$$x = -4$$

Note that when you plug -4 back into the original equation, you get $-24 = |12 - 3(-4)|$. Again, since an absolute value can never be negative, this is not a valid solution, so the value of x cannot be -4. Therefore, **(D)** is correct.

ABSOLUTE VALUE

LEARNING OBJECTIVES

After this lesson, you will be able to:

- Solve an equation containing an absolute value expression
- Interpret the graph of an equation containing an absolute value expression

To answer a question like this:

If $|2x - 14| = 4$ and $x^2 + 11 = 36$, what is the value of x?

A) -5

B) 5

C) 6

D) 9

You need to know this:

The **absolute value** of a number represents its distance from zero on a number line. It is represented by a set of vertical lines around a number, variable, or expression. For example, $|x| = 4$ means that x is four units away from zero on the number line, which means that x itself could be either 4 or -4.

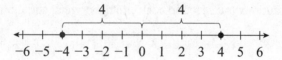

Thus, the effect of putting something inside a set of absolute value bars is to take any nonzero number and make it positive (if it wasn't already). The absolute value of 0 is simply 0.

When you see an equation involving absolute value, you'll need to consider both possible values of the expression inside the absolute value bars. Say that $|x + 8| = 11$. Then, you know that either $x + 8 = 11$ or $x + 8 = -11$, and you could solve each equation to find that $x = 3$ or $x = -19$. Both of these possible values for x satisfy the original equation; if a question asks you to narrow it down to a single value for x, you'd need more information—such as another equation.

You may see a question involving an absolute value function, where the entire function is in absolute value bars. The domain of such a function is the same as it would be if there were no absolute value bars. For instance, $f(x) = |x^2 - 3|$ has a domain of all real numbers, since any real number can be squared, while $f(x) = \left|\dfrac{1}{x+1}\right|$ has a domain of all real numbers other than -1, since $\dfrac{1}{x+1}$ is undefined when the denominator is 0. The range of an absolute value function will consist only of non-negative numbers because the absolute value bars turn any otherwise negative output positive.

The graph of an absolute value function will look similar to what it would look like without the absolute value bars; the only difference is that any point on the graph that would have appeared below the y-axis will instead appear an equal distance above the x-axis. For instance, consider the graphs of $f(x) = x^2 - 3x + 1$ and $f(x) = |x^2 - 3x + 1|$:

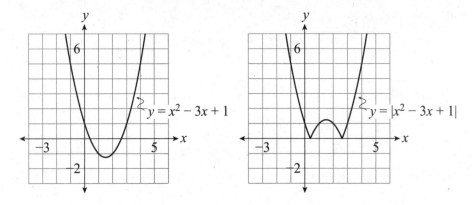

You need to do this:

- Set up equations with both the positive and negative values of the expression inside the absolute value bars.
- If needed, use any other given information to narrow down the possible values of x.
- In some more complicated absolute value equations, you may need to check for extraneous solutions by plugging the potential solutions you've found back into the original equation to see if they work.

Explanation:

You need a value of x that satisfies both of these equations. Start by considering the absolute value equation. If $|2x - 14| = 4$, then $2x - 14 = 4$ or $2x - 14 = -4$. Solve each of these equations: $2x = 18$ and $x = 9$, or $2x = 10$ and $x = 5$. Now, solve the other equation. If $x^2 + 11 = 36$, then $x^2 = 25$, and $x = \pm 5$. Thus, $x = 5$ is the only solution that satisfies both equations, and **(B)** is correct.

Try on Your Own

Directions

Take as much time as you need on these questions. Work carefully and methodically. There will be an opportunity for timed practice later in the book.

1

HINT: For Q1, $p(x)$ means the y-value of the function at x.

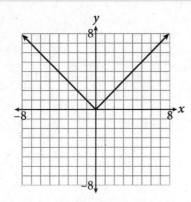

The figure shows the absolute value function $p(x) = |x|$. Which statement about the function is true?

Ⓐ The range of $p(x)$ is zero.

Ⓑ The domain of $p(x)$ is all positive numbers and zero.

Ⓒ The range of $p(x)$ is all real numbers.

Ⓓ The domain of $p(x)$ is all real numbers.

2

For what values of x is $|2x - 8| + 1$ equal to 3?

Ⓐ -3 and -5

Ⓑ -2 and -5

Ⓒ 2 and 5

Ⓓ 3 and 5

3

$$4x = |9 - 2x|$$

What is the solution to the equation shown?

4

HINT: For Q4, the absolute value of a number is its distance from zero on a number line.

Points c and d on a number line are both 4 units from point a. Which of the following gives the coordinates of c and d?

Ⓐ $|x + a| = 4$

Ⓑ $|x - a| = 4$

Ⓒ $|x + 4| = a$

Ⓓ $|x - 4| = a$

5

Which of the following equations is true for some value of x?

Ⓐ $|-x + 3| + 3 = 0$

Ⓑ $|x - 3| + 3 = 0$

Ⓒ $|x + 3| - 3 = 0$

Ⓓ $|x + 3| + 3 = 0$

NONLINEAR FUNCTIONS

> **LEARNING OBJECTIVES**
>
> After this lesson, you will be able to:
>
> * Interpret the domain, range, and properties of nonlinear functions and their graphs
> * Evaluate the output of a given nonlinear function

To answer a question like this:

$$f(x) = \begin{cases} 2x + 4, & x \le -2 \\ -x^2 + 4, & -2 < x < 3 \\ -x - 2, & x \ge 3 \end{cases}$$

What is the maximum value of $f(x)$?

A) 0

B) 2

C) 4

D) $f(x)$ does not have a maximum.

You need to know this:

You learned about linear functions earlier in the book. Like a linear function, a nonlinear function takes a number as an input and generates a unique output. Unlike a linear function, however, a nonlinear function's graph will be something other than a line. Here are some examples of nonlinear functions you may encounter on the SAT:

* Parabola: A curve generated by a function in the form $f(x) = ax^2 + bx + c$. You'll learn more about parabolas in the chapter on quadratics.

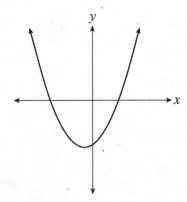

- Cubic function: A curve generated by a function with an x^3 term. The function's graph can cross the x-axis either one, two, or three times.

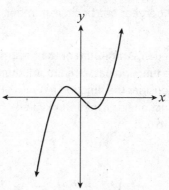

- Square root function: A curve generated by a function with a $\sqrt{x}$ term.

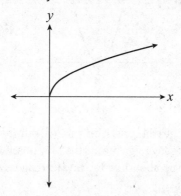

- Piecewise function: A function may have different equations for different x-values. For instance, a function may be defined as $f(x) = \begin{cases} (x-2)^2, & x \le 4 \\ x, & x > 4 \end{cases}$

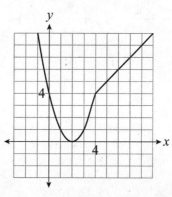

The **domain** is the set of all possible inputs to a function, and the **range** is the set of all possible outputs of a function. In a linear function, other than one representing a horizontal line, the domain and range both consist of all real numbers; a line is infinitely long, and every possible x-value has a different associated y-value. In a nonlinear function, you'll have to consider the domain and range more carefully.

The domain of a function includes every value of x that would result in a real number when plugged into the function. Consider the function $f(x) = \sqrt{x}$. A non-negative number would result in a real number: the positive square root. A negative number would not, since the square root of a negative number is imaginary. Thus, the domain of $f(x) = \sqrt{x}$ is all non-negative numbers. Another common issue to look out for with the domain was division by zero; the domain of $f(x) = \frac{1}{x}$ is all real numbers except 0, as that would make the function undefined:

Math

To determine the range of a function, think about what kind of numbers can be output by the function. Consider again $f(x) = \sqrt{x}$. Since the radical sign by convention refers to the positive square root, the output of this function must be non-negative: either zero or a positive number. So, the range of $f(x) = \sqrt{x}$ is all real numbers greater than or equal to 0.

The SAT may sometimes ask about a function's **minimum** or **maximum**. These terms mean the least and greatest value of the function, respectively. If a function has a minimum, then its range will consist only of numbers greater than or equal to the minimum. Consider the function $f(x) = x^2$. Because squaring any real number results in a non-negative number, this function has a minimum value of 0 at the parabola's vertex, and its range is all real numbers greater than or equal to 0.

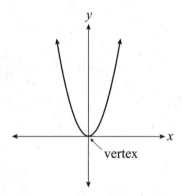

If a function has a maximum, then its range will consist only of real numbers less than or equal to the maximum. Consider the function $f(x) = -x^2$. The negative sign means that any possible output can't be positive; thus, this function has a maximum value of 0 at the parabola's vertex, and its range is all real numbers less than or equal to 0.

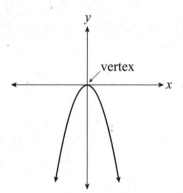

Not all functions have a maximum or minimum (for instance, $f(x) = x^3$ has a range of all real numbers). Some may have both a maximum and a minimum; $f(x) = \sin x$ has a maximum of 1 and a minimum of -1.

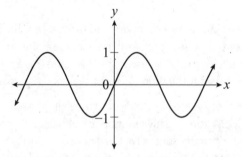

In many other ways, working with nonlinear functions is no different from what was done with linear functions earlier in the book. For example, evaluating a nonlinear function is just like evaluating a linear one. Take $f(x) = \sqrt{x} + 5$. To evaluate at $x = 4$, it's just a matter of substituting 4 for every x in the equation: $f(4) = \sqrt{4} + 5 = 2 + 5 = 7$.

You need to do this:

If you're given the graph of a function, use it to find out what you need to know about the function, such as its domain, range, minimum, maximum, x- or y-intercepts, or the equation that matches the graph. If you're not given a graph, use the equation to find out the same information.

Explanation:

Check for a maximum in each part of this piecewise function. The first part of the function, $2x + 4$, is a line segment with a positive slope. Since the line increases as the x-values increase, this portion of the function will have its maximum value at its rightmost point, which, according to the function's definition, is at $x = -2$. Plug this into the line's equation to get $f(-2) = 2(-2) + 4 = 0$. Now, consider the maximum of the middle piece of the function, which is defined by $-x^2 + 4$. The first term in the expression, $-x^2$, will be negative unless $x = 0$. So, the maximum value this piece of the function can have is $f(0) = -(0)^2 + 4 = 4$. Since the maximum can't be less than 4, eliminate (A) and (B).

Finally, check the third segment, $-x - 2$. Since this line segment has a negative slope, its greatest value will be at the leftmost point of the segment, which, according to the given information, is at $x = 3$. Plug this in to get $f(3) = -3 - 2 = -5$. So, the function's maximum is 4, and **(C)** is correct.

Alternatively, you could graph the three sections on the calculator and look for the value of the maximum point, making sure to pay attention to only the correct intervals of each section.

Try on Your Own

Directions

Take as much time as you need on these questions. Work carefully and methodically. There will be an opportunity for timed practice later in the book.

6

HINT: For Q6, remember that $f(x)$ and $g(x)$ are found on the y-axis on the graphs.

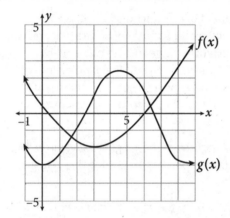

In the figure shown, what is the value of $f(3) - g(3)$?

Ⓐ -3

Ⓑ 0

Ⓒ 3

Ⓓ 6

7

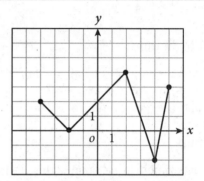

Based on the graph, if the coordinates of the maximum of $f(x)$ are (a, b) and the coordinates of the minimum of $f(x)$ are (c, d), what is the value of $a + b + c + d$?

8

HINT: For Q8, the *x*-values determine the domain, while the *y*-values determine the range.

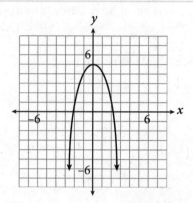

The graph of $f(x)$ is shown. Which of the following represents the domain and range of the function?

Ⓐ   Domain: $f(x) \geq 5$
    Range: all real numbers

Ⓑ   Domain: $f(x) \leq 5$
    Range: all real numbers

Ⓒ   Domain: all real numbers
    Range: $f(x) \geq 5$

Ⓓ   Domain: all real numbers
    Range: $f(x) \leq 5$

9

$$f(y) = y^3 - 7y + 5$$

What is $f(5) - f(1)$?

Ⓐ -96

Ⓑ -95

Ⓒ 95

Ⓓ 96

10

x	$f(x)$
-4	4
-1	0
0	-3
3	-9
7	1

The table shows some values for a polynomial defined by the function f. Which of the following is a factor of $f(x)$?

Ⓐ $x - 1$

Ⓑ $x - 3$

Ⓒ $x + 1$

Ⓓ $x + 3$

ON TEST DAY

The SAT likes to test nonlinear functions abstractly and with the modeling of real-life situations. Get comfortable with function notation in these questions. When solving absolute values, you must solve for both the negative and positive version of the value shown.

11. Given the equation $|8x + 4| = 108$, what is the minimum possible value of $2x + 1$?

   A) -27
   B) -13
   C) 13
   D) 27

The correct answer and explanation can be found at the end of the chapter.

HOW MUCH HAVE YOU LEARNED?

Directions

For testlike practice, give yourself 13 minutes to complete this question set. Be sure to study the explanations, even for questions you got right. They can be found at the end of this chapter.

12

The function a is defined by $a(x) = 5x^4$. In the xy-plane, the graph of $b(x)$ results from shifting the graph of $a(x)$ up 9 units. Which equation defines function b?

(A) $b(x) = x + 9$

(B) $b(x) = 5x^4 + 9$

(C) $b(x) = 5x^4 - 9$

(D) $b(x) = (5x^4)^9$

13

If $\left|\frac{1}{2}x - 8\right| = 14$, what is the least possible value of $x - 8$?

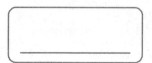

14

The function f is defined by $f(x) = 160(0.5)^x$. What is the value of $f(4)$?

(A) 10

(B) 20

(C) 80

(D) 320

15

An internet provider has found that on weekdays, the function $v(h) = 0.85h^4 + h^3 + 12h$ approximates the total number of visitors to a website, where h represents the number of hours that have passed since 12:00 midnight. Based on this function, how many visitors can be expected by 10:00 a.m. on a weekday?

16

$$|3x - 3| = x + 15$$

What is the minimum value of x that solves the equation shown?

(A) -12

(B) -3

(C) 9

(D) 18

17

x	$g(x)$
-3	4
0	2
1	0
3	-2
7	-5

The table shows some values for a nonlinear polynomial defined by the function g. Which of the following is a factor of $g(x)$?

Ⓐ $(x + 1)$

Ⓑ $(x + 2)$

Ⓒ $(x - 1)$

Ⓓ $(x - 4)$

18

$$f(x) = ax^3 + 2x^2 + 2$$

In the function f, a is a constant. If $f(3) = 101$, what is the value of $f(1)$?

Ⓐ 1

Ⓑ 3

Ⓒ 7

Ⓓ 27

19

The function f is defined by the equation $f(x) = (x - 3)(x - 5)(x + 7)$. The function $g(x)$ is equal to $f(x) + 4$. Which of the following is a possible value of x when $g(x) = 4$?

Ⓐ -7

Ⓑ -4

Ⓒ 1

Ⓓ 105

REFLECT

Directions: Take a few minutes to recall what you've learned and what you've been practicing in this chapter. Consider the following questions, jot down your best answer for each one, and then compare your reflections to the expert responses that follow. Use your level of confidence to determine what to do next.

What are the domain and range of a function?

_____

_____

_____

Where do the factors of a polynomial function occur?

_____

_____

_____

On the graph of a function, what does $f(x)$ represent?

_____

_____

_____

Why do absolute value equations need to be solved twice?

_____

_____

_____

Does every absolute value equation have two valid solutions?

_____

_____

_____

Expert Responses

What are the domain and range of a function?

The domain of a function indicates the possible x-values and the range of a function indicates the possible y-values. For example, in the function f(x) = x², the domain is all real numbers because any number can be squared, and the range is any number greater than or equal to 0, because x² can't be negative.

Where do the factors of a polynomial function occur?

The factors of a polynomial function occur when the value of the function   the output   is equal to 0.

On the graph of a function, what does $f(x)$ represent?

In functions, f(x) is the output value, which is the y-value on a graph.

Why do absolute value equations need to be solved twice?

Because absolute value expressions represent the positive value of the expression inside the absolute value symbols, the actual value of that expression might be either positive or negative. Therefore, it's necessary to solve for both the positive and the negative version of the expression.

Does every absolute value equation have two valid solutions?

Not necessarily. While it's necessary to solve an absolute value equation twice, which will usually yield two distinct values for the variable within the equation, it's possible that one of those values will not work when plugged back into the original absolute value. That's called an extraneous solution, and it's not a valid one.

Next Steps

If you answered most questions correctly in the "How Much Have You Learned?" section, and if your responses to the Reflect questions were similar to those of the SAT expert, then consider Functions an area of strength and move on to the next chapter. Come back to this topic periodically to prevent yourself from getting rusty.

If you don't yet feel confident, review those parts of this chapter that you have not yet mastered. Both of the lessons in this chapter cover question types that are fairly common on the SAT, and it is to your advantage to have a firm grasp on this material, so go back over it until you feel more confident. Then try the questions you missed again. As always, be sure to review the explanations closely. Finally, **go online** (www.kaptest.com/moreonline) for additional practice on the highest yield topics in this chapter.

Check Your Work – Chapter 11

1. D
Difficulty: Easy
Category: Advanced Math
Getting to the Answer: The function graphed is the absolute value function. The range (*y*-values) of this function is all positive numbers and zero. Eliminate (A) and (C). Also eliminate (B); it is the range, not the domain, that fits this; all real numbers can be inputted as the *x*-values (domain) for this function. Choice **(D)** is correct.

2. D
Difficulty: Easy
Category: Advanced Math
Getting to the Answer: First set $|2x - 8| + 1$ equal to 3 and then subtract 1 from both sides.

$$|2x - 8| + 1 = 3$$
$$|2x - 8| = 2$$

Since absolute value gives a non-negative value, the expression inside the absolute value may be equal to 2 or −2. Solving for each case gives the values of *x*.

$$2x - 8 = 2 \qquad 2x - 8 = -2$$
$$2x = 10 \qquad 2x = 6$$
$$x = 5 \qquad x = 3$$

(D) is correct.

3. 3/2 or 1.5
Difficulty: Hard
Category: Advanced Math
Getting to the Answer: Since absolute value gives a non-negative value, the expression inside the absolute value may be equal to $4x$ or $-4x$. Solving for each case gives the solutions to the equation.

$$4x = 9 - 2x \qquad -4x = 9 - 2x$$
$$6x = 9 \qquad -2x = 9$$
$$x = \frac{9}{6} \qquad x = -\frac{9}{2}$$
$$x = \frac{3}{2}$$

Check to see if these are valid solutions. Substituting $x = \frac{3}{2}$ back into the equation gives us $6 = |9 - 3|$. That works. However, substituting $x = -\frac{9}{2}$ back into the equation gives $-18 = |9 + 9|$. It is impossible for an absolute value to be negative, so this is not a solution. The only solution is $x = \frac{3}{2}$. Enter **3/2** or **1.5**.

4. B
Difficulty: Hard
Category: Advanced Math
Getting to the Answer: By definition, $|x|$ indicates the distance of *x* from 0. Thus, $|x| = 4$ says that *x* is 4 units from 0. That is, $x = 4$ or $x = -4$. Since *c* and *d* are 4 units from *a*, then the coordinates of *c* and *d* are $x = a + 4$ and $x = a - 4$. Subtracting *a* from both sides gives $x - a = 4$ and $x - a = -4$, which can be written more concisely as $|x - a| = 4$. **(B)** is correct.

5. C
Difficulty: Easy
Category: Advanced Math
Getting to the Answer: The absolute value of a number is always non-negative. Thus, for the expression to equal 0, the result of the absolute value must be combined with a negative number. Only (C) subtracts 3 from the absolute value. Thus, **(C)** is correct. If you isolated the absolute value term in (A), (B), and (D), you would find that the absolute value term equals −3, which can never be true.

6. A
Difficulty: Medium
Category: Advanced Math
Getting to the Answer: Graphically, the notation $f(3)$ means the *y*-value when $x = 3$. Find $x = 3$ on the *x*-axis. Then, read the *y*-coordinates from the graph, paying close attention to which function is which:

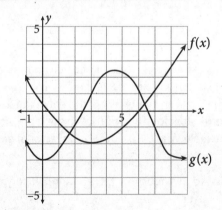

$f(3) = -2$ and $g(3) = 1$, so $f(3) - g(3) = -2 - 1 = -3$. **(A)** is correct.

7. 8
Difficulty: Medium
Category: Advanced Math
Getting to the Answer: The maximum of $f(x)$ occurs at the point where the y-value is the greatest, which in this case is (2, 4). So, $a = 2$ and $b = 4$. The point with the smallest y-value is (4, −2). Thus, $c = 4$ and $d = −2$. The total of the four values is $2 + 4 + 4 + (−2) = 8$. Enter **8**.

8. D
Difficulty: Easy
Category: Advanced Math
Getting to the Answer: To determine the domain, look at the x-values. Since the domain is the set of inputs, not outputs, it will not include $f(x)$. This means you can eliminate (A) and (B). Note that the graph is continuous and has arrows on both sides, so the domain is all real numbers.

To determine the range, look at the y-values. For the range, the function's maximum is located at (0, 5), which means the highest possible value of $f(x)$ is 5. The graph is continuous and opens downward, so the range of the function is $f(x) \leq 5$, making **(D)** correct.

9. D
Difficulty: Easy
Category: Advanced Math
Getting to the Answer: Evaluate this function at $y = 5$ and $y = 1$. At $y = 5$, $f(5) = (5)^3 − 7(5) + 5 = 125 − 35 + 5 = 95$. At $y = 1$, $f(1) = (1)^3 − 7(1) + 5 = 1 − 7 + 5 = −1$. Your final answer is $95 − (−1) = 96$. Choice **(D)** is correct.

10. C
Difficulty: Medium
Category: Advanced Math
Getting to the Answer: A factor of a polynomial is equal to 0. So if $x − a$ is a factor of $f(x)$, then $x − a = 0$ and $x = a$, where a is an x-intercept of the polynomial. In other words, look for when $f(a) = 0$ in the table. According to the table, $f(−1) = 0$, so $x + 1$ is a factor of $f(x)$. **(C)** is correct.

If you missed this question, there's more on polynomials in the next chapter.

11. A
Difficulty: Medium
Category: Advanced Math
Getting to the Answer: While answering absolute value questions usually involves isolating the variable, in this instance, doing so is unnecessary. Note that the value the question asks for is simply one-fourth of the value inside the absolute value expression. That is, $2x + 1 = \frac{1}{4}(8x + 4)$. Therefore, finding one-fourth of the possible values of $8x + 4$ will lead to the answer:

$$|8x + 4| = 108$$
$$8x + 4 = 108 \text{ or } −108$$
$$\frac{8x + 4}{4} = \frac{108}{4} \text{ or } \frac{−108}{4}$$
$$2x + 1 = 27 \text{ or } −27$$

The question asks for the *minimum* possible value of $2x + 1$, so that's −27. Thus, **(A)** is correct.

12. B
Difficulty: Easy
Category: Advanced Math
Getting to the Answer: When the graph of a function shifts up or down, the change occurs only in the y-values. In this case, the question specifies that the graph shifts up 9. Therefore, adding 9 to the original function expresses this shift. That's choice **(B)**.

13. −20
Difficulty: Medium
Category: Advanced Math
Getting to the Answer: Since the question asks for the least possible value of $x − 8$, start by solving for the negative version of the original absolute value equation:

$$\frac{1}{2}x − 8 = −14$$
$$\frac{1}{2}x = −6$$
$$x = −12$$

Therefore, $x − 8 = −12 − 8 = −20$. (For the record, solving for the positive version of the equation would have resulted in 36.) Enter −**20**.

14. A
Difficulty: Easy
Category: Advanced Math
Getting to the Answer: In this question, the expression $f(4)$ indicates that $x = 4$ in the given function. Plug 4 in for x and calculate with your calculator:

$f(4) = 160(0.5)^4 = 160(0.0625) = 10$. Choice **(A)** is correct.

15. 9620
Difficulty: Easy
Category: Advanced Math
Getting to the Answer: While the function may look complicated, the question simply requires you to plug in 10 for h and calculate the value that results. In this case, that's $0.85(10)^4 + 10^3 + 12(10) = 8,500 + 1,000 + 120 = 9,620$. Enter **9620**.

16. B
Difficulty: Medium
Category: Advanced Math
Getting to the Answer: Solving absolute value equations means solving twice, for both the positive and negative version of the value given. Start with the positive version:

$$|3x - 3| = x + 15$$
$$3x - 3 = x + 15$$
$$2x - 3 = 15$$
$$2x = 18$$
$$x = 9$$

Next, solve for the negative version:

$$|3x - 3| = x + 15$$
$$3x - 3 = -x - 15$$
$$4x - 3 = -15$$
$$4x = -12$$
$$x = -3$$

This is the type of question where you should check for extraneous solutions before finishing. An absolute value operator makes everything inside of it positive, so if the $x + 15$ side of the equation results in a negative value when plugging your answers back in, it'll be an extraneous solution that isn't valid. In this case, $9 + 15$ and $-3 + 15$ are both positive, so both solutions are valid.

The question asked for the minimum value of x that solves the equation, so that's -3. **(B)** is correct.

17. C
Difficulty: Medium
Category: Advanced Math
Getting to the Answer: A factor of a polynomial is equal to 0 when $y = 0$ on the graph of the polynomial. In other words, you want to find the x-value where $g(x) = 0$ in the table. According to the table, $g(x) = 0$ where $x = 1$, meaning $(x - 1) = 0$. That makes it a factor of $f(x)$. Hence, **(C)** is correct.

18. C
Difficulty: Medium
Category: Advanced Math
Getting to the Answer: To evaluate a function for a particular value, substitute the value for the variable in the function. In this case, substitute 3 for x and then use the given value for $f(3)$ to solve for the value of a:

$$f(3) = a(3)^3 + 2(3)^2 + 2$$
$$101 = 27a + 18 + 2$$
$$81 = 27a$$
$$\frac{81}{27} = a$$
$$3 = a$$

Next, use the known value of a to find $f(1)$:

$$f(1) = 3(1)^3 + 2(1)^2 + 2$$
$$f(1) = 3 + 2 + 2$$
$$f(1) = 7$$

(C) is correct.

19. A
Difficulty: Medium
Category: Advanced Math
Getting to the Answer: The question asks for a possible value of x when $g(x) = 4$. The question also specifies that $g(x)$ is equal to $f(x) + 4$. You can restate this as $f(x) = g(x) - 4$. Thus, you can say that when $g(x) = 4$, $f(x) = 4 - 4 = 0$.

Therefore, you're really being asked to find a value of x that would make $f(x)$ equal to 0. $f(x)$ is defined as $(x - 3)(x - 5)(x + 7)$; that's the product of three binomial factors. The only way for the product of multiplication to equal 0 is for at least one of the factors to equal 0. Don't try to multiply the factors together; instead, determine which value of x will make one of the binomials equal to 0: $(x - 3)$ is equal to 0 when $x = 3$, $(x - 5)$ is equal to 0 when $x = 5$, and $(x + 7)$ is equal to 0 when $x = -7$. Of these values, only -7 is an answer choice. Therefore, **(A)** is correct.

[CHAPTER 12]

EXPONENTS, RADICALS, POLYNOMIALS, AND RATIONAL EXPRESSIONS

LEARNING OBJECTIVES

After completing this chapter, you will be able to:

- Apply exponent rules
- Apply radical rules
- Add, subtract, multiply, and factor polynomials
- Divide polynomials
- Define root, solution, zero, and *x*-intercept and identify them on the graph of a nonlinear function
- Determine whether the growth or decay described in a question is linear or exponential
- Apply the linear and exponential equations to answer growth and decay questions
- Simplify rational expressions
- Isolate a variable in a rational equation

HOW MUCH DO YOU KNOW?

Directions

Try the questions that follow. Show your work so that you can compare your solutions to the ones found in the "Check Your Work" section immediately after this question set. If you answered the question(s) on a specific topic correctly, and if your scratchwork looks like ours, you may be able to move quickly through the lesson covering that topic. If you answered incorrectly or used a different approach, you may want to take your time on that lesson.

1

Which expression is equivalent to $2(-4j^3k^{-4})^{-3}$?

(A) $-\dfrac{k^{12}}{512j^9}$

(B) $-\dfrac{k^{12}}{32j^9}$

(C) $-\dfrac{j^9}{32k^{12}}$

(D) $-\dfrac{k^{12}}{128j^9}$

2

The formula $T = 2\pi\sqrt{\dfrac{L}{g}}$ describes the time it takes for a pendulum to complete a swing—called its period, T—in terms of the length of the pendulum, L, and the force of gravity, g. Based on the equation above, which of the following equations could be used to find the length of the pendulum given its period?

(A) $L = \dfrac{gT}{2\pi}$

(B) $L = \dfrac{gT^2}{4\pi^2}$

(C) $L = \dfrac{T^2}{4\pi^2 g}$

(D) $L = \dfrac{g}{4\pi^2 T^2}$

3

Which of the following represents $\dfrac{\sqrt[6]{x^{10}y^{12}}}{\sqrt[3]{x^5 y^6}}$ written in simplest form, given that $x > 0$ and $y > 0$?

(A) 1

(B) 2

(C) $x^2 y^3 \sqrt{x}$

(D) $xy^2\sqrt[3]{x^2}$

4

What is the result when $4x^3 - 5x^2 + x - 3$ is divided by $x - 2$?

(A) $4x + 3 + \dfrac{11}{x-2}$

(B) $4x^2 + 3x - 6$

(C) $4x^2 + 3x + 18$

(D) $4x^2 + 3x + 7 + \dfrac{11}{x-2}$

5

The function f is a parabolic function that intersects the x-axis. Which of the following statements must be true?

(A) The function has at least one real root.

(B) The function has no real roots.

(C) The function intersects the positive y-axis.

(D) The function has two zeros.

6

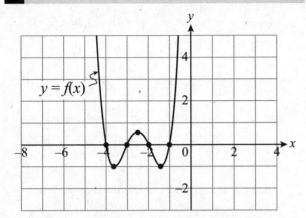

$y = f(x)$

The graph shows the function defined by $f(x) = (x + 1)(x + 2)(x + 3)(x + 4)$. If k is a constant such that $g(x) = k$ and the system of functions f and g have exactly two real solutions, which of the following could be a value of k?

Ⓐ -2

Ⓑ 0

Ⓒ 0.5

Ⓓ 1

7

In the equation $ax^4 + bx^3 + cx^2 - dx = 0$, a, b, c, and d are constants. If the equation crosses the x-axis at 0, -2, 3, and 5, which of the following is a factor of $ax^4 + bx^3 + cx^2 - dx$?

Ⓐ $x - 2$

Ⓑ $x + 3$

Ⓒ $x - 5$

Ⓓ $x + 5$

8

Age (months)	Height (centimeters)
15	80
18	82.5
21	85
24	87.5
27	90

The growth of a young child is given in the chart. If t represents the number of months after 15 months and $f(t)$ represents the child's height, which of the following equations is the best model for the data in the age range shown?

Ⓐ $f(t) = 80t + 3$

Ⓑ $f(t) = \frac{5}{6}t + 80$

Ⓒ $f(t) = 80 \left(\frac{5}{6}\right)^t$

Ⓓ $f(t) = \frac{5}{6}(80)^t$

9

$$\frac{8x}{3(x-5)} + \frac{2x}{3x-15} = \frac{50}{3(x-5)}$$

What value(s) of x satisfy the equation above?

Ⓐ 0

Ⓑ 5

Ⓒ No solution

Ⓓ Any value such that $x \neq 5$

10

If $\dfrac{6}{2x-3} + 6a = \dfrac{10}{2x-3} + 4b$ and $3a - 2b = 2$, what is the value of x?

Ⓐ $\dfrac{1}{2}$

Ⓑ 2

Ⓒ No solution

Ⓓ The value cannot be determined from the information given.

Check Your Work

1. B
Difficulty: Easy
Category: Advanced Math
Getting to the Answer: Move the expression in parentheses to the denominator to make the sign of the exponent outside positive; do not change the signs of the exponents inside the parentheses. Next, distribute the exponent as usual. Divide the 2 into -64, and move k^{-12} back to the numerator and change the sign of its exponent. Work for these steps is shown below:

$$2\left(-4j^3k^{-4}\right)^{-3} = \frac{2}{\left(-4j^3k^{-4}\right)^3}$$

$$= \frac{2}{(-4)^3(j^3)^3(k^{-4})^3}$$

$$= \frac{\cancel{2}}{\cancel{-64}j^9k^{-12}}$$

$$= -\frac{k^{12}}{32j^9}$$

Choice **(B)** is the correct answer.

2. B
Difficulty: Medium
Category: Advanced Math
Getting to the Answer: The question asks you to solve the equation for L. Use inverse operations to accomplish the task. Divide both sides of the equation by 2π and then square both sides. You'll need to apply the exponent to all the terms on the left side of the equation, including the π:

$$T = 2\pi\sqrt{\frac{L}{g}}$$

$$\frac{T}{2\pi} = \sqrt{\frac{L}{g}}$$

$$\left(\frac{T}{2\pi}\right)^2 = \left(\sqrt{\frac{L}{g}}\right)^2$$

$$\frac{T^2}{4\pi^2} = \frac{L}{g}$$

Finally, multiply both sides by g to remove g from the denominator and isolate L:

$$L = \frac{gT^2}{4\pi^2}$$

The correct answer is **(B)**.

3. A
Difficulty: Hard
Category: Advanced Math
Getting to the Answer: Because the expression has different roots, sixth and third, rewrite the expression with fractional exponents first, and then use exponent rules to simplify it. The rule for fraction exponents is "power over root"; use this to rewrite the expression:

$$\frac{\sqrt[6]{x^{10}y^{12}}}{\sqrt[3]{x^5y^6}} = \frac{x^{\frac{10}{6}}y^{\frac{12}{6}}}{x^{\frac{5}{3}}y^{\frac{6}{3}}} = \frac{x^{\frac{10}{6}}y^2}{x^{\frac{5}{3}}y^2}$$

When dividing like bases, subtract the exponents. Find common denominators as needed:

$$x^{\frac{10}{6}-\frac{5}{3}}y^{2-2} = x^{\frac{10}{6}-\frac{10}{6}}y^0 = x^0y^0$$

Any nonzero number raised to the power of zero becomes 1, and the question specifies that x and y are both greater than zero, so the expression becomes $1 \times 1 = 1$. Choice **(A)** is correct.

4. D
Difficulty: Medium
Category: Advanced Math
Getting to the Answer: Since factoring the numerator does not appear to be practical, use polynomial division to find the result:

$$x-2\overline{)4x^3-5x^2+x-3}$$

The first number in this process will be $4x^2$ since $4x^2 \cdot x = 4x^3$:

$$
\begin{array}{r}
4x^2 \\
x-2\overline{)4x^3-5x^2+x-3} \\
-(4x^3-8x^2) \\
\hline
3x^2
\end{array}
$$

Next, complete the rest of the polynomial division process:

$$\begin{array}{r}
4x^2 + 3x + 7 \\
x-2\overline{)4x^3 - 5x^2 + x - 3} \\
\underline{-(4x^3 - 8x^2)} \\
3x^2 + x \\
\underline{-(3x^2 - 6x)} \\
7x - 3 \\
\underline{-(7x - 14)} \\
11
\end{array}$$

Remember that you are dividing by $x - 2$, so put the remainder over the divisor to get $\frac{11}{x-2}$. **(D)** is correct.

5. A
Difficulty: Easy
Category: Advanced Math
Getting to the Answer: The key to this question is knowing that an x-intercept is another word for root or zero; those three terms are synonyms. Even though the question stem does not say how many roots f has, you know it must have at least one if it intersects the x-axis. **(A)** is correct. Watch out for trap answer (D), which does not consider the case when a parabola touches the x-axis at one point but does not cross it.

6. D
Difficulty: Medium
Category: Advanced Math
Strategic Advice: Working backward from the answer choices saves time.
Getting to the Answer: The solution or solutions of a system of functions, like a system of equations, can be found at the points of intersection. Because the function $g(x)$ is equal to a constant, all x-values produce the same output—it must represent a horizontal line. A horizontal line and a 4th-degree function could intersect 0, 1, 2, 3, or 4 times. Visually inspect the graph to determine how many times the function $f(x)$ intersects with each answer choice's given y-value/constant function $g(x)$. You'll see that only $g(x) = 1$ intersects f exactly twice, so **(D)** is correct.

7. C
Difficulty: Medium
Category: Advanced Math
Getting to the Answer: The question is asking for a factor of the function and tells you where the function crosses the x-axis. The roots are the x-values where the graph crosses the x-axis. To find the factors from the roots, consider what expressions would produce a value of zero. Thus, if the roots are at 0, -2, 3, and 5, then the factored form of this equation must be $x(x + 2)(x - 3)(x - 5)$ because plugging in any one of the four roots will equal zero. The only factor that appears in the answer choices is $x - 5$, so **(C)** is correct.

8. B
Difficulty: Easy
Category: Advanced Math
Strategic Advice: Determining the type of growth represented by the data will help to eliminate half of the choices immediately. Look at what happens to the height from each measurement to the next. From 15 to 18 months, the child's height increases by 2.5 centimeters. The same is true for 18 to 21 months, and for 21 to 24 months, and so on. Since 2.5 centimeters are added each equal time interval, the best model for this data would be linear.
Getting to the Answer: Because this growth is linear, eliminate choices (C) and (D), which represent exponential growth. The remaining two choices differ in both the coefficient of t and the value being added. When linear growth is modeled with the equation $y = mx + b$, m represents the rate of growth and b represents the starting amount. In this case, the starting height is 80 centimeters; thus, **(B)** is correct, as (A) has a different value for b. For the record, the growth rate is 2.5 centimeters every 3 months, or $\frac{5}{6}$ centimeter per month.

9. C
Difficulty: Hard
Category: Advanced Math
Getting to the Answer: Because the denominators are the same (just written in different forms), multiplying both sides of the equation by $3x - 15$ will immediately clear all the fractions, the result of which is a much easier equation to solve:

$$8x + 2x = 50$$
$$10x = 50$$
$$x = 5$$

Because there are variables in the denominator, you must check the solution to make sure it is not extraneous. When $x = 5$, each of the denominators is equal to 0, and division by 0 is not possible. Therefore, there is no solution to the equation, making **(C)** the correct answer.

10. B
Difficulty: Hard
Category: Advanced Math
Getting to the Answer: Begin by putting the x terms on one side and the a and b terms on the other for the first equation:

$$6a - 4b = \frac{10}{2x - 3} - \frac{6}{2x - 3} = \frac{10 - 6}{2x - 3} = \frac{4}{2x - 3}$$

Now note that the left side of the equation is $6a - 4b$, which is equivalent to $2(3a - 2b)$. The question states that $3a - 2b = 2$. So $6a - 4b = 2(3a - 2b) = 2(2) = 4$. Substitute 4 for $6a - 4b$, multiply both sides by $2x - 3$ to clear the fractions, and solve for x:

$$4 = \frac{4}{2x - 3}$$
$$4(2x - 3) = 4$$
$$2x - 3 = 1$$
$$2x = 4$$
$$x = 2$$

Because "No solution" is an answer choice, make sure that $x = 2$ is not an extraneous solution before selecting choice (B). When $x = 2$, the denominator $2x - 3 \neq 0$. Thus, $x = 2$ is a valid solution, and the answer is **(B)**.

EXPONENTS

LEARNING OBJECTIVE

After this lesson, you will be able to:

- Apply exponent rules

To answer a question like this:

The expression $x(x^3y^2)^{-4}$ is equivalent to which of the following?

A) $\dfrac{1}{y^2}$

B) $\dfrac{1}{x^4}$

C) $\dfrac{1}{x^{11}y^8}$

D) $\dfrac{1}{x^{16}y^8}$

You need to know this:

RULE	EXAMPLE
When multiplying two terms with the same base, add the exponents.	$a^b \cdot a^c = a^{(b+c)} \rightarrow 4^2 \cdot 4^3 = 4^{2+3} = 4^5$
When dividing two terms with the same base, subtract the exponents.	$\dfrac{a^b}{a^c} = a^{(b-c)} \rightarrow \dfrac{4^3}{4^2} = 4^{3-2} = 4^1$
When raising a power to another power, multiply the exponents.	$(a^b)^c = a^{(bc)} \rightarrow (4^3)^2 = 4^{3 \cdot 2} = 4^6;$ $(2x^2)^3 = 2^3x^{2 \cdot 3} = 8x^6$
When raising a product to a power, apply the power to all factors in the product.	$(ab)^c = a^c \cdot b^c \rightarrow (2m)^3 = 2^3 \cdot m^3 = 8m^3$
Any nonzero term raised to the zero power equals 1.	$a^0 = 1 \rightarrow 4^0 = 1$
A base raised to a negative exponent can be rewritten as the reciprocal raised to the positive of the original exponent.	$a^{-b} = \dfrac{1}{a^b}, \dfrac{1}{a^{-b}} = a^b \rightarrow 4^{-2} = \dfrac{1}{4^2}, \dfrac{1}{4^{-2}} = 4^2$
A negative number raised to an even exponent will produce a positive result; a negative number raised to an odd exponent will produce a negative result.	$(-2)^4 = 16$, but $(-2)^3 = -8$

You need to do this:

- Identify the appropriate rule by looking at the operation.
- Apply the rule.
- Repeat as necessary.

SAT exponent questions can often result in quick points. Make sure you memorize the rules in the preceding table before test day.

Explanation:

You'll need several exponent rules to answer the question at the beginning of this lesson. The order of operations dictates that you start with the negative exponent. When one power is raised to another, multiply the exponents:

$$x\left(x^3y^2\right)^{-4} = x\left(x^{3(-4)}y^{2(-4)}\right) = x\left(x^{-12}y^{-8}\right)$$

The x out front has no exponent, which means it is raised to the power of 1. To do the multiplication, add the exponents:

$$x^1\left(x^{-12}y^{-8}\right) = x^{-11}y^{-8}$$

Finally, because this expression is not among the choices, you'll need the rule for negative exponents: you can write them as the reciprocal of the positive exponent. Like this:

$$x^{-11}y^{-8} = \frac{1}{x^{11}y^8}$$

The correct answer is **(C)**.

If exponents give you trouble, study the rules in the preceding table and try these Drill questions before completing the "Try on Your Own" questions that follow. Simplify each expression (without using a calculator). Drill answers can be found in the Check Your Work section at the end of the chapter.

Drill

a. 3^4

b. $(-5)^3$

c. $4^2 \times 2^{-4}$

d. $\dfrac{2^4}{2^3}$

e. $\left(\dfrac{1}{3}\right)^{-2}$

f. $\left(2^2\right)^3$

g. $(7x)^2$

h. $\left(-\dfrac{1}{2}\right)^{-2}$

i. $\left(a^2\right)^5$

j. $\left(b^3\right)^{-6}$

Try on Your Own

Directions

Take as much time as you need on these questions. Work carefully and methodically. There will be an opportunity for timed practice later in the book.

1

HINT: For Q1, think about the exponent rules that you will need to apply.

If $\dfrac{x^c(3x)^2}{9x^3} = x^6$ and $x \neq 0$, what is the value of c?

2

HINT: For Q2, look for common factors in the numerator and denominator.

$$\frac{18x^4 + 27x^3 - 36x^2}{9x^2}$$

If $x \neq 0$, which of the following is equivalent to the given expression?

Ⓐ $2x^2 + 3x - 4$

Ⓑ $2x^2 + 3x - 6$

Ⓒ $2x^4 + 3x^3 - 4x^2$

Ⓓ $2x^6 + 3x^5 - 4x^4$

3

If a and b are positive integer constants and $x^a y^b = -128$, where $x < 0$ and $y < 0$, which of the following must be true?

Ⓐ a is even

Ⓑ a is odd

Ⓒ ab is odd

Ⓓ ab is even

4

If $n^3 = -8$, what is the value of $\dfrac{\left(n^2\right)^3}{\frac{1}{n^2}}$?

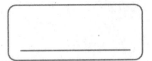

5

HINT: For Q5, how can you get rid of the fraction on the left side?

$$\frac{x^{5r}}{x^{3r-2s}} = x^t$$

If $r + s = 6$ and $x \neq 0$, what is the value of t in the equation shown?

Ⓐ   6

Ⓑ   12

Ⓒ   18

Ⓓ   30

RADICALS

LEARNING OBJECTIVE

After this lesson, you will be able to:

- Apply radical rules

To answer a question like this:

$$\frac{\sqrt[3]{x} \cdot x^{\frac{5}{2}} \cdot x}{\sqrt{x}}$$

If x^n is the simplified form of the given expression, what is the value of n?

You need to know this:

RULE	EXAMPLE
When a fraction is under a radical, you can rewrite it using two radicals: one containing the numerator and the other containing the denominator.	$\sqrt{\frac{a}{b}} = \frac{\sqrt{a}}{\sqrt{b}} \rightarrow \sqrt{\frac{4}{9}} = \frac{\sqrt{4}}{\sqrt{9}} = \frac{2}{3}$
Two factors under a single radical can be rewritten as separate radicals multiplied together.	$\sqrt{ab} = \sqrt{a} \times \sqrt{b} \rightarrow \sqrt{75} = \sqrt{25} \times \sqrt{3} = 5\sqrt{3}$
A radical can be written using a fractional exponent.	$\sqrt{a} = a^{\frac{1}{2}} \rightarrow \sqrt{289} = 289^{\frac{1}{2}}$ $\sqrt[3]{a} = a^{\frac{1}{3}} \rightarrow \sqrt[3]{729} = 729^{\frac{1}{3}}$
When you have a fractional exponent, the numerator is the power to which the base is raised, and the denominator is the root to be taken.	$a^{\frac{b}{c}} = \sqrt[c]{a^b} \rightarrow 5^{\frac{2}{3}} = \sqrt[3]{5^2}$
When a number is squared, the original number can be positive or negative, but the radical sign implies the positive square root.	$\sqrt{x^2} = |x|$ If $a^2 = 81$, then $a = \pm 9$, BUT $\sqrt{81} = 9$ only.
Cube roots of negative numbers are negative.	$\sqrt[3]{-27} = -3$

You need to do this:

- Identify the appropriate rule by looking at the answer choices. What form do you need to get the expression into? What rule do you need to apply to get there?
- Apply the rule.
- Repeat as necessary.

SAT Radicals questions are often quick points. Make sure you memorize the rules in the preceding table before test day.

Explanation:

Write each factor in the expression in exponential form (using fractional exponents for the radicals). Next, use exponent rules to simplify the expression:

$$\frac{\sqrt[3]{x} \cdot x^{\frac{5}{2}} \cdot x}{\sqrt{x}} = \frac{x^{\frac{1}{3}} \cdot x^{\frac{5}{2}} \cdot x^1}{x^{\frac{1}{2}}}$$

Now add the exponents of the factors that are being multiplied and subtract the exponent of the factor that is being divided, find common denominators, and simplify:

$$= x^{\frac{1}{3} + \frac{5}{2} + \frac{1}{1} - \frac{1}{2}} = x^{\frac{2}{6} + \frac{15}{6} + \frac{6}{6} - \frac{3}{6}}$$

$$= x^{\frac{20}{6}} = x^{\frac{10}{3}}$$

The question states that n is the power of x, so the value of n is $\frac{10}{3}$.

If radicals give you trouble, study the rules in the table and try these Drill questions before completing the following "Try on Your Own" questions. Simplify each expression (without using a calculator). Drill answers can be found in the Check Your Work section at the end of the chapter.

Drill

a. $\sqrt{\frac{121}{9}}$

b. $\sqrt{225}$

c. $\sqrt{\frac{16 \times 125}{5}}$

d. $\sqrt{\frac{50}{288}}$

e. $\sqrt[3]{-64}$

f. $\frac{\sqrt{5}\,\sqrt{60}}{\sqrt{3}}$

g. $\frac{4\sqrt{21} \times 5\sqrt{2}}{10\sqrt{7}}$

h. $9^{\frac{1}{2}} \times \sqrt{4} \times 81^{\frac{1}{4}}$

i. $\frac{\sqrt{81x^2}}{\sqrt{64y^4}}$

j. $\sqrt{\frac{x^8}{y^{12}}}$

Try on Your Own

Directions

Take as much time as you need on these questions. Work carefully and methodically. There will be an opportunity for timed practice later in the book.

6

HINT: For Q6, what do you need to do before squaring both sides?

$$8 + \frac{\sqrt{2x + 29}}{3} = 9$$

For what value of x is this equation true?

Ⓐ -10

Ⓑ -2

Ⓒ 19

Ⓓ No solution

7

$$3x = x + 14$$

$$\sqrt{3z^2 - 11} + 2x = 22$$

If $z > 0$, what is the value of z?

Ⓐ 1

Ⓑ 3

Ⓒ 5

Ⓓ 8

8

Which of the following expressions is equivalent to $-x^{\frac{1}{4}}$?

Ⓐ $-\dfrac{1}{4x}$

Ⓑ $-\dfrac{1}{x^4}$

Ⓒ $-\sqrt[4]{x}$

Ⓓ $\dfrac{1}{\sqrt[4]{-x}}$

9

HINT: For Q9, remember that the denominator of the exponent becomes the root, and the numerator remains the exponent.

When simplified, $8^{\frac{4}{3}}$ is what number?

$$\boxed{ \\ \underline{}}$$

10

HINT: For Q10, which approach is faster for you: Algebra or Backsolving?

$$\sqrt{3a + 16} - 3 = a - 1$$

In the equation above, if $a \geq 0$, which of the following is a possible value of a?

Ⓐ 3

Ⓑ 2

Ⓒ 1

Ⓓ 0

POLYNOMIALS

LEARNING OBJECTIVE

After this lesson, you will be able to:

* Add, subtract, multiply, and factor polynomials

To answer a question like this:

If $-2x^2 + 5x - 8$ is multiplied by $4x - 9$, what is the coefficient of x in the resulting polynomial?

A) -77

B) -45

C) -32

D) -13

You need to know this:

A **polynomial** is an expression composed of variables, exponents, and coefficients. By definition, a polynomial cannot have a variable in a denominator, and all exponents must be integers. Here are some examples of polynomial and non-polynomial expressions:

POLYNOMIAL	$23x^2$	$\dfrac{x}{5} - 6$	$y^{11} - 2y^6 + \dfrac{2}{3}xy^3 - 4x^2$	$z + 6$
NOT A POLYNOMIAL	$\dfrac{10}{z} + 13$	$x^3 y^{-6}$	$x^{\frac{1}{2}}$	$\dfrac{4}{y - 3}$

You need to do this:

To add and subtract polynomials, start by identifying **like terms**—that is, terms in which the types of variables and their exponents match. For example, x^2 and $3x^2$ are like terms; adding them would give $4x^2$ and subtracting them would give $x^2 - 3x^2 = -2x^2$. Note that you cannot add or subtract unlike terms. For example, there is no way to simplify $x^2 + y$. You can, however, multiply unlike terms: $x^2 \cdot y = x^2 y$.

To multiply two polynomials, multiply each term in the first factor by each term in the second factor, then combine like terms.

To factor a polynomial, find a value or variable that divides evenly into each term, for example: $2x^3 + 2x^2 + 2x = 2x(x^2 + x + 1)$. (Factoring quadratics into binomials is discussed in the Quadratics chapter.)

Explanation:

Multiply each term in the first factor by each term in the second factor, then combine like terms:

$$(-2x^2 + 5x - 8)(4x - 9)$$
$$= -2x^2(4x - 9) + 5x(4x - 9) - 8(4x - 9)$$
$$= -8x^3 + 18x^2 + 20x^2 - 45x - 32x + 72$$
$$= -8x^3 + 38x^2 - 77x + 72$$

The coefficient of x is -77, so **(A)** is correct.

If you are confident with polynomials, you may be able to save time by noting that when multiplying these expressions, only the $5x \times (-9)$ and $(-8) \times 4x$ operations will result in x terms: $-45x - 32x = -77x$, which brings you to the same answer. The coefficient of x is -77, so **(A)** is correct.

Try on Your Own

Directions

Take as much time as you need on these questions. Work carefully and methodically. There will be an opportunity for timed practice later in the book.

11

What is the sum of the polynomials $6a^2 - 17a - 9$ and $-5a^2 + 8a - 2$?

(A) $a^2 - 9a - 11$

(B) $a^2 - 25a - 7$

(C) $11a^2 - 9a - 11$

(D) $11a^2 - 25a - 7$

12

What is the difference when $3x^3 + 7x - 5$ is subtracted from $8x^2 + 4x + 10$?

(A) $5x^2 - 3x + 15$

(B) $-3x^3 - 3x + 5$

(C) $3x^3 - 8x^2 + 3x - 15$

(D) $-3x^3 + 8x^2 - 3x + 15$

13

HINT: For Q13, as you calculate each term, eliminate choices. Stop when there's only one choice left.

If $A = 4x^2 + 7x - 1$ and $B = -x^2 - 5x + 3$, then what is $\frac{3}{2}A - 2B$?

(A) $4x^2 + \frac{31}{2}x - \frac{9}{2}$

(B) $4x^2 + \frac{41}{2}x - \frac{15}{2}$

(C) $8x^2 + \frac{31}{2}x - \frac{9}{2}$

(D) $8x^2 + \frac{41}{2}x - \frac{15}{2}$

14

HINT: For Q14, which is more efficient for you: Algebra or backsolving the choices?

If $x^3 - 9x = 9 - x^2$, which of the following CANNOT be the value of x?

(A) -3

(B) -1

(C) 1

(D) 3

15

$(2x^2 + 3x - 4)(3x + 2) = 6x^3 + ax^2 - 6x - 8$

In the given equation, a is a constant. If the equation is true for all values of x, what is the value of a?

(A) 4

(B) 9

(C) 13

(D) 16

POLYNOMIAL DIVISION

LEARNING OBJECTIVE

After this lesson, you will be able to:

• Divide polynomials

To answer a question like this:

Which of the following is equivalent to $\dfrac{x^2 + 3x + 7}{x + 4}$?

A) $\dfrac{3 + 7}{4}$

B) $x + \dfrac{3}{4}$

C) $3 + \dfrac{7}{x + 4}$

D) $x - 1 + \dfrac{11}{x + 4}$

You need to know this:

To divide polynomials, you can use an approach called **polynomial long division**. This process is similar to ordinary long division, except that you use polynomials instead of numbers. In the process described in this lesson, the *dividend* is the polynomial to be divided, the *divisor* is the polynomial you are dividing the dividend by, and the *quotient* is the result of the division.

You need to do this:

• Start with the dividend arranged so that the powers are in descending order, for example: $x^4 + x^3 + x + 1$. If any terms are missing, put in zeros, like this: $x^4 + x^3 + 0x^2 + x + 1$. Write the expression using a long division sign.

• Divide the first term of the dividend by the first term of the divisor to yield the first term of the quotient.

• Multiply the divisor by the first term of the quotient.

• Subtract the product you got in the last step from the dividend, then bring down the next term, just as you would in ordinary long division. Use the result as the new dividend.

• Repeat the process until you arrive at the remainder.

Explanation:

To divide $x^2 + 3x + 7$ by $x + 4$, set up a long division problem:

$$x + 4 \overline{) x^2 + 3x + 7}$$

Start by dividing the first term of the dividend, x^2, by the first term of the divisor, x. Multiply the entire divisor by x and subtract this product from the dividend:

$$
\begin{array}{r}
x \\
x + 4 \overline{) x^2 + 3x + 7} \\
\underline{-(x^2 + 4x)} \\
-x + 7
\end{array}
$$

Next, divide the first term of the result of this subtraction, $-x$, by the first term of the divisor, x, to get -1. Repeat the process of multiplying and subtracting:

$$\require{enclose}\begin{array}{r}x-1\\x+4\enclose{longdiv}{x^2+3x+7}\\-(x^2+4x)\\\hline-x+7\\-(-x-4)\\\hline+11\end{array}$$

You're left with a remainder of 11. Put this over the divisor, $x + 4$, and you're done. The result of the division is $x - 1 + \dfrac{11}{x+4}$, which is choice **(D)**.

Try on Your Own

Directions

Take as much time as you need on these questions. Work carefully and methodically. There will be an opportunity for timed practice later in the book.

16

HINT: For Q16, because $a - 3$ is not a factor of the numerator, you'll have to use polynomial long division.

Which of the following is equivalent to $\dfrac{2a^2 - 5a - 1}{a - 3}$?

(A) $2a - 2$

(B) $2a + 1 - \dfrac{2}{a-3}$

(C) $2a + \dfrac{2}{a-3}$

(D) $2a + 1 + \dfrac{2}{a-3}$

17

HINT: For Q17, if the fraction simplifies to $ax + b$, the denominator divides evenly into the numerator. Does that suggest another approach?

$$\dfrac{6x^2 + 19x + 10}{2x + 5}$$

If $ax + b$ represents the simplified form of the expression shown, then what is the value of $a + b$?

(A) 2

(B) 3

(C) 5

(D) 6

18

Which of the following is equivalent to $\dfrac{4x^2 - 6x}{2x + 2}$?

(A) $2x - \dfrac{10}{2x+2}$

(B) $2x - 5 + \dfrac{10}{2x+2}$

(C) $2x - 3$

(D) $2x + 5 - \dfrac{10}{2x+2}$

19

HINT: For Q19, the quotient (result of division) times the divisor (the denominator) equals the dividend (the numerator). Stop as soon as you have the value of t.

The equation $\dfrac{36x^2 + 16x - 21}{tx - 4} = -9x + 5 - \dfrac{1}{tx - 4}$ is true for all values of x for which $x \neq \dfrac{4}{t}$, where t is a constant. What is the value of t?

Ⓐ -20

Ⓑ -4

Ⓒ 4

Ⓓ 12

20

If the polynomial $f(x)$ is evenly divisible by $x - 5$ and the polynomial $g(x) = f(x) + 4$, what is the value of $g(5)$?

Ⓐ -4

Ⓑ 0

Ⓒ 4

Ⓓ 9

GRAPHS OF POLYNOMIAL FUNCTIONS

LEARNING OBJECTIVE

After this lesson, you will be able to:

- Define root, solution, zero, and *x*-intercept and identify them on the graph of a nonlinear function

To answer a question like this:

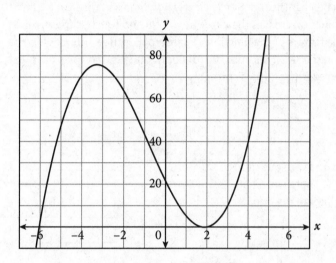

Which of the following could be the function shown on the graph?

A) $f(x) = (x - 6)(x + 2)^2$

B) $f(x) = (x + 6)(x - 2)^2$

C) $f(x) = 3x + 23$

D) $f(x) = 6x + 23$

You need to know this:

When applied to polynomial functions, the words **root**, **solution**, **zero**, and **x-intercept** all mean the same thing: the *x*-values on the function's graph where the function touches or crosses the *x*-axis. You can find the roots of a polynomial function by setting each factor of the polynomial equal to zero. For example, the polynomial function $f(x) = x^2 + x$ factors into $f(x) = x(x + 1)$. Set each factor equal to zero to find that $x = 0$ and $x = -1$. These are the function's solutions, also known as zeros. A solution can be represented using the coordinate pair $(x, 0)$.

Note that if a function crosses the *x*-axis, the factor associated with that *x*-intercept will have an odd exponent. If the function touches but does not cross the *x*-axis, the factor associated with that *x*-intercept will have an even exponent. For example, the function $f(x) = x(x + 1)$ will cross the *x*-axis at $x = 0$ and $x = -1$, while the function $f(x) = x^2(x + 1)$ will cross the *x*-axis at $x = -1$ but only touch the *x*-axis at $x = 0$.

You need to do this:

- Identify the *x*-values where the function crosses or touches the *x*-axis.
- For each *x*-intercept, change the sign of the *x*-value and add it to the variable *x* to find the associated factor. For example, if the function crosses the *x*-axis at $x = -1$, then the factor associated with that root must be $x + 1$ (since $x + 1 = 0$ will produce the solution $x = -1$).
- Recognize that if the function only touches the *x*-axis without crossing it, the factor must have an even exponent.

Explanation:

Start by looking at the answer choices. The function is clearly not linear, so rule out (C) and (D). Next, look at the *x*-intercepts on the graph: the function crosses the *x*-axis at $x = -6$ and touches the *x*-axis at $x = 2$. Remember that the *x*-intercepts occur where the factors of the function equal zero. For the *x*-intercepts to be -6 and 2, the factors of the function must be $(x + 6)$ and $(x - 2)$. Because the function touches, but does not cross, the *x*-axis at $x = 2$, the $(x - 2)$ factor must have an even exponent. **(B)** is correct.

Try on Your Own

Directions

Take as much time as you need on these questions. Work carefully and methodically. There will be an opportunity for timed practice later in the book.

21

HINT: For Q21, set each factor equal to 0 and solve for x to find the *x*-intercepts.

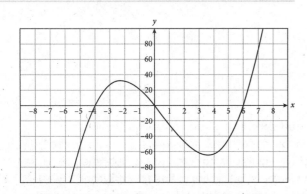

Which of the following could be the equation of the function in the graph?

Ⓐ $f(x) = x^2(x + 4)(x - 6)$

Ⓑ $f(x) = x(x + 4)(x - 6)$

Ⓒ $f(x) = x^2(x - 4)(x + 6)$

Ⓓ $f(x) = x(x - 4)(x + 6)$

22

x	*h(x)*
-3	6
-1	0
0	-5
2	-8

The function *h* is defined by a polynomial. The table shown gives some of the values of *x* and *h(x)*. Which of the following must be a factor of *h(x)*?

Ⓐ $x - 8$

Ⓑ $x - 1$

Ⓒ $x + 1$

Ⓓ $x + 5$

23

HINT: In Q23, the definition of the *b* function has a variable in the denominator. What does this tell you about the value of *x*?

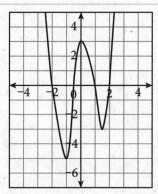

The graph of the function $a(x)$ is shown. If $b(x) = \frac{1}{x}$, which of the following is a true statement about $b(a(x))$?

Ⓐ $b(a(x))$ is defined for all real numbers.

Ⓑ $b(a(x))$ is undefined for exactly one real value of x.

Ⓒ $b(a(x))$ is undefined for at least four real values of x.

Ⓓ $b(a(x))$ is undefined for all real numbers.

24

If function f has exactly two distinct real zeros, which of the following graphs could be the complete graph of $f(x)$?

Ⓐ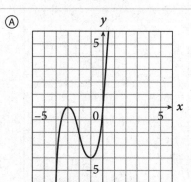

Ⓑ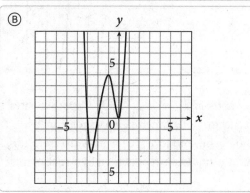

Ⓒ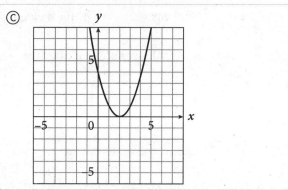

Ⓓ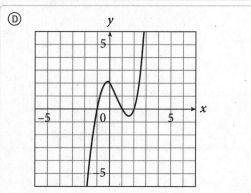

25

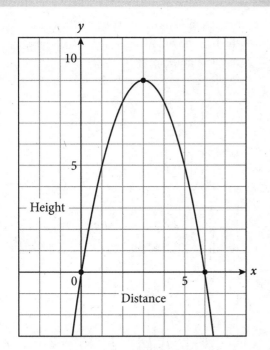

The graph of $f(x) = -(x - 3)^2 + 9$ approximates the trajectory of a water balloon shot from a cannon at ground level. In terms of the trajectory, what information is represented by a root of this function?

Ⓐ   The maximum height achieved by the balloon

Ⓑ   The total horizontal distance traveled by the balloon

Ⓒ   The maximum speed of the balloon

Ⓓ   The initial acceleration of the balloon

MODELING GROWTH AND DECAY

LEARNING OBJECTIVES

After this lesson, you will be able to:

- Determine whether the growth or decay described in a question is linear or exponential
- Apply the linear and exponential equations to answer growth and decay questions

To answer a question like this:

A certain car costs $20,000. If the car loses 15 percent of its value each year, approximately how much will the car be worth after 5 years?

A) $5,000

B) $8,900

C) $11,200

D) $15,000

You need to know this:

The terms **growth** and **decay** refer to situations in which some quantity is increased or decreased over time according to a rule:

- If the rule is to add or subtract the same amount each time, then the growth or decay is **linear**. Because the graph of linear growth and decay is a line, you can describe it using the slope-intercept form of a line, $y = mx + b$, where b is the starting amount and m is the amount added or subtracted each time x increases by 1.

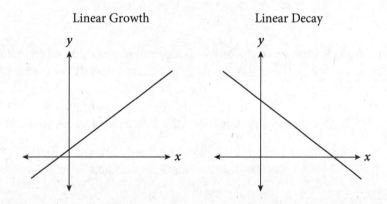

Linear Growth   Linear Decay

- If the rule is to multiply or divide by the same amount each time, then the growth or decay is **exponential**. The general form of an exponential function is $y = ab^x$, where a is the y-intercept and b is the amount multiplied or divided each time x increases by 1. Given that $a > 0$ and $b > 1$, when x is positive, the equation describes exponential growth, and when x is negative, the equation describes exponential decay.

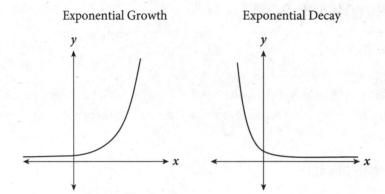

- When an exponential growth or decay question gives you a growth rate over time, you can use a modified version of the exponential function, $f(t) = f(0)(1 + r)^t$, where $f(0)$ is the amount at time $t = 0$ and r is the growth rate (or decay rate, if negative) expressed as a decimal.

You need to do this:

- First, determine whether the situation described is linear or exponential. If an amount is added or subtracted each time, then the growth is linear; if the quantity is multiplied or divided by some amount each time, then the growth is exponential.
- Plug the values from the question into an appropriate linear or exponential growth equation and solve for the missing quantity.
- When the numbers are manageable, you might be able to avoid using the equations by simply carrying out the operations described. For example, if the question says that an amount doubles each day and asks for the amount after three days, then doubling the initial quantity three times will likely be more efficient than plugging the numbers into the exponential growth equation.

Explanation:

The question says that the car loses value at a certain percentage rate per year, which means the question involves exponential decay. The question asks for the approximate value of the car after 5 years, which is $f(5)$. The rate must be expressed as a decimal, and since the value of the car is decreasing, the rate is also negative. The question gives three pieces of important information: the initial value $f(0) = \$20,000$, the rate $r = -0.15$, and the time $t = 5$. Plug these values into the equation $f(t) = f(0)(1 + r)^t$ and use your calculator to solve:

$$f(5) = 20,000(1 - 0.15)^5$$
$$= 20,000(0.85)^5 \approx \$8,900$$

Choice **(B)** is correct.

Try on Your Own

Directions

Take as much time as you need on these questions. Work carefully and methodically. There will be an opportunity for timed practice later in the book.

26

HINT: For Q26, keep track of your calculations by making a chart with the number of applicants at the start of the day and the number of applicants eliminated.

In determining the winner of a speech-writing competition, a panel of judges eliminates one-quarter of the remaining applicants per day of deliberations. If 128 students entered the competition, how many applicants have been eliminated by the end of the third day of deliberations?

27

A health club's membership has increased at a rate of 16 percent per year for the past four years. The club currently has 42 members. If this trend continues, how many years will it take for the club's membership to exceed 100 members?

- (A) 4 years
- (B) 5 years
- (C) 6 years
- (D) 7 years

28

HINT: For Q28, no original amount is given. What would be a good number to pick for that amount?

^{14}C (an isotope of carbon) has a half-life of 5,600 years, which means half of the ^{14}C in the remains of an organism will decay in that time period. If a sample of a petrified tree contains 6.25 percent of its original ^{14}C, how long ago did the tree die?

- (A) 22,400 years
- (B) 28,000 years
- (C) 35,000 years
- (D) 89,600 years

29

HINT: For Q29, is she saving more, the same, or less each month? What does that tell you about the function?

Penelope receives the same amount of money each month for her allowance. Each month she spends half of her allowance and puts the rest in a piggy bank. On her 8th birthday, the piggy bank contains $40. If the piggy bank contains $244 after 2 years, what is her monthly allowance in dollars?

30

Account X earns a monthly interest equal to 2 percent of the original investment, while account Y earns a monthly interest equal to 2 percent of the current value of the account. If $500 is invested into each account, what is the positive difference between the value of account X and account Y after three years? (Round your answer to the nearest dollar.)

RATIONAL EXPRESSIONS AND EQUATIONS

> **LEARNING OBJECTIVES**
>
> After this lesson, you will be able to:
>
> - Simplify rational expressions
> - Isolate a variable in a rational equation

To answer a question like this:

$$\frac{5y+7}{(y+4)^2} - \frac{5}{(y+4)}$$

If the expression shown is equal to $\dfrac{-b}{(y+4)^2}$, where b is a positive constant and $y \neq -4$, what is the value of b?

A) 4

B) 7

C) 13

D) 27

You need to know this:

A **rational expression** is a ratio expressed as a fraction with a polynomial in the denominator. A **rational equation** is an equation that includes at least one rational expression.

- Factors in a rational expression can be canceled when simplifying, but under no circumstances can you do the same with individual terms. Consider, for instance, the expression $\dfrac{x^2 - x - 6}{x^2 + 5x + 6}$. Some test takers will attempt to cancel the x^2, x, and 6 terms to give $\dfrac{1-1-1}{1+5+1} = \dfrac{-1}{7}$, which is *never* correct. Instead, factor the numerator and denominator: $\dfrac{(x+2)(x-3)}{(x+2)(x+3)}$. Cancel the $x+2$ factors to get $\dfrac{x-3}{x+3}$.

- If a rational expression has a higher-degree numerator than denominator $\left(\text{e.g., } \dfrac{x^2+3}{1-x}\right)$, it can be simplified using polynomial long division. If a rational expression has a lower-degree numerator than denominator $\left(\text{e.g., } \dfrac{1-x}{x^2+3}\right)$, it cannot.

- Because rational expressions have polynomial denominators, they will often be undefined for certain values. For example, the expression $\dfrac{x-4}{x+2}$ is defined for all values of x except -2. This is because when $x = -2$, the denominator of the expression is 0, which would make the expression undefined.

- When solving rational equations, beware of undefined expressions. Take the equation $\dfrac{1}{x+4} + \dfrac{1}{x-4} = \dfrac{8}{(x+4)(x-4)}$, for instance. After multiplying both sides by the common denominator $(x+4)(x-4)$, you have $(x-4) + (x+4) = 8$. Solving for x yields $2x = 8$, which simplifies to $x = 4$. When 4 is substituted for x, however, you get 0 in the denominator of both the second and third terms of the original equation. Therefore, this equation is said to have no solution. (A value that causes a denominator to equal 0 is called an **extraneous solution**.)

You need to do this:

- Find a common denominator.
- Multiply each term by the common denominator and simplify.
- Make sure you haven't found an extraneous solution.

Explanation:

Start by setting the two expressions equal:

$$\frac{5y + 7}{(y + 4)^2} - \frac{5}{y + 4} = \frac{-b}{(y + 4)^2}$$

Next, get rid of the fractions. To do this, multiply both sides of the equation by the common denominator, $(y + 4)^2$:

$$\left(\frac{5y + 7}{(y + 4)^2} - \frac{5}{y + 4} = \frac{-b}{(y + 4)^2}\right)(y + 4)^2$$

$$5y + 7 - 5(y + 4) = -b$$

Now all that remains is to solve for b:

$$5y + 7 - 5y - 20 = -b$$
$$-13 = -b$$
$$b = 13$$

The correct answer is **(C)**.

Try on Your Own

Directions

Take as much time as you need on these questions. Work carefully and methodically. There will be an opportunity for timed practice later in the book.

31

HINT: For Q31, multiply both sides by a common denominator or cross-multiply. (They are the same thing.)

Given the equation $\frac{6}{x} = \frac{3}{k + 2}$ and the constraints $x \neq 0$ and $k \neq -2$, what is x in terms of k?

- Ⓐ $x = 2k + 4$
- Ⓑ $x = 2k + 12$
- Ⓒ $x = 2k - \frac{1}{4}$
- Ⓓ $x = \frac{1}{4}k + 12$

32

HINT: For Q32, how do you add fractions with different denominators?

$$\frac{3a + 9}{(a - 3)^2} + \frac{-9}{3a - 9}$$

In the given expression, $(a - 3)^2 = 6$. What is the value of the expression?

33

If $a > 6$, which of the following is equivalent to

$$\dfrac{\dfrac{2}{a}}{\dfrac{1}{a-2}+\dfrac{1}{a-6}}?$$

Ⓐ $2a^2 - 16a + 24$

Ⓑ $a(2a - 8)$

Ⓒ $\dfrac{a^2 - 8a + 12}{a^2 - 4a}$

Ⓓ $\dfrac{2a - 8}{a^2 - 8a + 12}$

34

If $\dfrac{x^3 - 3x^2}{x - 3} = 9$, what is the value of x?

Ⓐ -3

Ⓑ 0

Ⓒ 3

Ⓓ 9

35

If $\dfrac{16}{7x + 4} + A$ is equivalent to $\dfrac{49x^2}{7x + 4}$, what is A in terms of x?

Ⓐ $7x + 4$

Ⓑ $7x - 4$

Ⓒ $49x^2$

Ⓓ $49x^2 + 4$

36

HINT: For Q36, make sure you pay attention to all of the information given to you.

If $\dfrac{1 - 2c}{3c} - \dfrac{c - 8}{12} = 0$ and $c < 0$, what is the value of c?

Ⓐ -4

Ⓑ -2

Ⓒ 1

Ⓓ 2

ON TEST DAY

Remember that the SAT doesn't ask you to show your work. If you find the algebra in a question challenging, there is often another way to get to the answer.

Try this question first using algebra and then using the Picking Numbers strategy. Which approach do you find easier? There's no right or wrong answer—just remember your preferred approach and try it first if you see a question like this on test day.

37. The expression $\dfrac{3x - 1}{x - 4}$ is equivalent to which of the following?

A) $3x + \dfrac{1}{x - 4}$

B) $3x - \dfrac{1}{x - 4}$

C) $3 - \dfrac{11}{x - 4}$

D) $3 + \dfrac{11}{x - 4}$

The correct answer and both ways of solving can be found at the end of this chapter.

HOW MUCH HAVE YOU LEARNED?

Directions

For testlike practice, give yourself 19 minutes to complete this question set. Be sure to study the explanations, even for questions you got right. They can be found at the end of this chapter.

38

The height, h, of a projectile at time t is given by the equation $h = \frac{1}{2}at^2 + v_v t + h_0$, where a is the acceleration due to gravity, v_v is the vertical component of the velocity, and h_0 is the initial height. Which of the following equations correctly represents the object's acceleration due to gravity in terms of the other variables?

(A) $a = \dfrac{h - v_v t - h_0}{t}$

(B) $a = \dfrac{h - v_v t - h_0}{2t^2}$

(C) $a = \dfrac{2(h - v_v t - h_0)}{t^2}$

(D) $a = t\sqrt{2(h - v_v t - h_0)}$

39

If $(16^{3x})(32^x)(8^{3x}) = \dfrac{(4^{6x})(32^{3x})}{4}$, what is the value of x?

(A) -2

(B) -1

(C) 1

(D) 2

40

Given that $\dfrac{y}{\sqrt{x} - 3} = \dfrac{\sqrt{x} + 3}{3}$ and $2x + 42 = 9x - 63$, what is the value of y?

41

$$y = \frac{3x^2 + 7}{x - 3}$$

Which of the following expressions is equivalent to y?

(A) $3x + 9 - \dfrac{20}{x - 3}$

(B) $3x + 9 + \dfrac{34}{x - 3}$

(C) $3x + 43$

(D) $3x^2 + \dfrac{9}{x - 3}$

42

$$z = 15x^2 + 10xy - 6x - 4y$$

For which of the following ordered pairs, (x, y), is $z \neq 0$?

(A) $(-3, 2)$

(B) $(-2, 3)$

(C) $\left(\dfrac{2}{5}, 0\right)$

(D) $\left(\dfrac{2}{5}, 10\right)$

43

$$\sqrt{27^{\frac{2}{3}} + 128^{\frac{4}{7}}} =$$

44

Which of these expressions is equivalent to $\dfrac{4x^2 - 8}{2x + 3}$?

Ⓐ $2x - 3 + \dfrac{1}{2x + 3}$

Ⓑ $2x - 2$

Ⓒ $2x + 3 - \dfrac{1}{2x + 3}$

Ⓓ $2x + 4$

45

$$g(x) = \frac{2}{2x^3 - 12x^2 - 14x}$$

For which of the following values of x is the function $g(x)$ defined?

Ⓐ -1

Ⓑ 0

Ⓒ 1

Ⓓ 7

46

$$x^3 + 4 = 3x^2 - 7x + 25$$

For what real value of x is the given equation valid?

Ⓐ 0

Ⓑ 3

Ⓒ 4

Ⓓ 7

47

Which of the following equations has a graph for which all roots are greater than 0?

Ⓐ $y = 4|x|$

Ⓑ $y = x^2 - 4$

Ⓒ $y = (x - 2)^2$

Ⓓ $y = x(x - 2)^2$

48

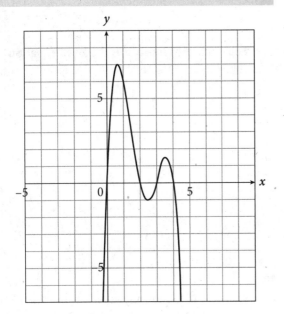

The graph of the function
$f(x) = -x(x - 4)(x - 3)(x - 2)$ is shown.
If $f(x) = 0$, how many real solutions exist?

Ⓐ 0

Ⓑ 2

Ⓒ 3

Ⓓ 4

49

In a certain city, there were 1.6 million smart-phone users at the end of 2021. It is expected that the number of smartphone users will increase by 35 percent each year beginning in 2022. If y represents the number of smartphone users in this metropolitan area x years after 2021, then which of the following equations best models the number of smartphone users in this city over time?

Ⓐ $y = 1,600,000(1.35)^x$

Ⓑ $y = 1,600,000(35)^x$

Ⓒ $y = 35x + 1,600,000$

Ⓓ $y = 1.35x + 1,600,000$

REFLECT

Directions: Take a few minutes to recall what you've learned and what you've been practicing in this chapter. Consider the following questions, jot down your best answer for each one, and then compare your reflections to the expert responses that follow. Use your level of confidence to determine what to do next.

How do you multiply two polynomials?

_____

_____

_____

What are the zeros of a polynomial function?

_____

_____

_____

Describe the difference between linear and exponential growth.

_____

_____

_____

Describe two ways to simplify rational expressions.

_____

_____

_____

Expert Responses

How do you multiply two polynomials?

Distribute each term in the first set of parentheses to each term in the second set, then combine like terms.

What are the zeros of a polynomial function?

The zeros are the points at which the value of the function (i.e., the y-value) is zero. Think of the zeros as the x-intercepts of the function. The words "roots" and "solutions" mean the same thing.

Describe the difference between linear and exponential growth.

Linear growth is modeled by a linear function, with the equation $y = mx + b$, such that the slope of the line is positive. You're essentially adding the same amount over and over again. (In linear decay, the slope of the line is negative, and you're subtracting the same amount over and over again.)

Exponential growth is modeled by an exponential function in the form $y = ab^x$, where a is the y-intercept and b is the amount multiplied each time, over and over. The slope of an exponential growth function steepens with increasing x-values. (In exponential decay, b is the amount divided by each time, and the slope starts out steeply negative and flattens with increasing x-values.)

Describe two ways to simplify rational expressions.

One way is to use polynomial long division, though this will work only if the higher-order polynomial is in the numerator. Another way is to cancel factors that appear in both the numerator and denominator.

Next Steps

If you answered most questions correctly in the "How Much Have You Learned?" section, and if your responses to the Reflect questions were similar to those of the SAT expert, then consider Exponents, Radicals, Polynomials, and Rational Expressions an area of strength and move on to the next chapter. Come back to this topic periodically to ensure your skills stay sharp.

If you don't yet feel confident, review those parts of this chapter that you have not yet mastered; then, try the questions you missed again. As always, be sure to review the explanations closely.

Check Your Work – Chapter 12

Drill Answers for Exponents

a. $3^4 = 3 \times 3 \times 3 \times 3 = 81$

b. $(-5)^3 = (-5) \times (-5) \times (-5) = -125$

c. $4^2 \times 2^{-4} = \dfrac{16}{16} = 1$

d. $\dfrac{2^4}{2^3} = 2^{4-3} = 2^1 = 2$

e. $\left(\dfrac{1}{3}\right)^{-2} = \left(\dfrac{3}{1}\right)^2 = 9$

f. $(2^2)^3 = 2^{2 \times 3} = 2^6 = 64$

g. $(7x)^2 = 49x^2$

h. $\left(-\dfrac{1}{2}\right)^{-2} = (-2)^2 = 4$

i. $(a^2)^5 = a^{10}$

j. $(b^3)^{-6} = b^{-18} = \dfrac{1}{b^{18}}$

Drill Answers for Radicals

a. $\dfrac{\sqrt{121}}{\sqrt{9}} = \dfrac{11}{3}$

b. $\sqrt{25} \times \sqrt{9} = 5 \times 3 = 15$

c. $\dfrac{4 \times 5\sqrt{5}}{\sqrt{5}} = 20$

d. $\dfrac{5\sqrt{2}}{12\sqrt{2}} = \dfrac{5}{12}$

e. -4

f. $\dfrac{\sqrt{5} \times 2\sqrt{3}\,\sqrt{5}}{\sqrt{3}} = 2 \times 5 = 10$

g. $\dfrac{4\sqrt{3}\sqrt{7} \times 5\sqrt{2}}{10\sqrt{7}} = \dfrac{20\sqrt{6}}{10} = 2\sqrt{6}$

h. $3 \times 2 \times 3 = 18$

i. $\dfrac{9|x|}{8y^2}$

j. $\dfrac{x^4}{y^6}$

Try on Your Own Answers

1. 7

Difficulty: Easy

Category: Advanced Math

Getting to the Answer: Simplify the fraction on the left side of the equation using exponent rules. Start by distributing the power of 2 outside the parentheses to both the 3 and the x inside:

$$\frac{x^c(3x)^2}{9x^3} = x^6$$

$$\frac{x^c(3)^2(x^2)}{9x^3} = x^6$$

$$\frac{9(x^c)(x^2)}{9x^3} = x^6$$

Now, cancel the 9s in the numerator and denominator, and add the exponents of the two x terms, since it's multiplication of the same base to different exponents:

$$\frac{\cancel{9}(x^{c+2})}{\cancel{9}x^3} = x^6$$

There's now an x in both the numerator and the denominator raised to different exponents, so subtract them:

$$x^{(c+2)-3} = x^6$$

$$x^{c-1} = x^6$$

Since, according to the question, $x \neq 0$, this means that $c - 1 = 6$, or $c = 7$. Enter **7**.

2. A

Difficulty: Easy

Category: Advanced Math

Getting to the Answer: Find the greatest common factor (GCF) of both the numerator and the denominator, which in this question happens to be the denominator. Factor out the GCF, $9x^2$, from the numerator and denominator and then cancel what you can:

$$\frac{18x^4 + 27x^3 - 36x^2}{9x^2} = \frac{\cancel{9x^2}(2x^2 + 3x - 4)}{\cancel{9x^2}}$$

$$= 2x^2 + 3x - 4$$

This matches **(A)**. As an alternate method, you could split the expression up and reduce each term, one at a time:

$$\frac{18x^4 + 27x^3 - 36x^2}{9x^2} = \frac{18x^4}{9x^2} + \frac{27x^3}{9x^2} - \frac{36x^2}{9x^2}$$

$$= 2x^2 + 3x - 4$$

3.   D

Difficulty: Hard

Category: Advanced Math

Getting to the Answer: If the product of x^a and y^b is negative, then either x^a is positive and y^b is negative, or vice versa. A negative number raised to an even exponent is positive, and a negative number raised to an odd exponent is negative. Since x and y are both negative, then either a is even and b odd, or vice versa.

Now, evaluate the choices to see what must be true. (A) says that a is even; this is possibly true, but it's also possible that b is even and a is odd. Thus, (A) can be eliminated. (B) can be eliminated for the same reason. (C) says that ab is odd. The only way for the product of two integers to be odd is if both of the integers are odd; since one of either a or b must be even, ab must be even. Eliminate (C); **(D)** is correct.

If you are ever unsure of even and odd rules, you can pick numbers to test them out: Odd × Even = Even; $3 \times 4 = 12$.

4.   256

Difficulty: Medium

Category: Advanced Math

Getting to the Answer: If $n^3 = -8$, then $n = -2$. Plug -2 in for n and simplify the given expression via exponent rules:

$$\frac{((-2)^2)^3}{\frac{1}{(-2)^2}} = \frac{4^3}{\frac{1}{4}} = 4^3 \times 4 = 4^4 = 256$$

Enter **256**.

5.   B

Difficulty: Hard

Category: Advanced Math

Getting to the Answer: Because the bases are the same, to simplify the fraction on the left side of the equation just subtract the powers and combine:

$$\frac{x^{5r}}{x^{3r-2s}} = x^{5r-(3r-2s)}$$
$$= x^{5r-3r+2s}$$
$$= x^{2r+2s}$$

Note that in the expression $2r + 2s$, it is possible to factor out a 2. Thus, $x^{2r+2s} = x^{2(r+s)}$. The question indicates that $r + s = 6$, so $x^{2(r+s)} = x^{2(6)} = x^{12}$. This is equal to x^t, so $t = 12$. The answer is **(B)**.

6.   A

Difficulty: Medium

Category: Advanced Math

Getting to the Answer: Solve equations containing radical expressions the same way you solve any other equation: isolate the variable using inverse operations. Start by subtracting 8 from both sides of the equation and then multiply by 3. Then, square both sides to remove the radical:

$$8 + \frac{\sqrt{2x+29}}{3} = 9$$
$$\frac{\sqrt{2x+29}}{3} = 1$$
$$\sqrt{2x+29} = 3$$
$$2x + 29 = 9$$

Now you have a simple linear equation that you can solve using more inverse operations: subtract 29 and divide by 2 to find that $x = -10$. Be careful—just because the equation started with a radical and the answer is negative, it does not follow that *No solution* is the correct answer. If you plug -10 into the expression under the radical, the result is a positive number, which means -10 is a perfectly valid solution. Therefore, **(A)** is correct.

7.   C

Difficulty: Medium

Category: Advanced Math

Getting to the Answer: Subtract x from both sides of the first equation to get $2x = 14$. You could solve for x, but since $2x$ appears in the second equation, plug it in to get $\sqrt{3z^2 - 11} + 14 = 22$. Thus, $\sqrt{3z^2 - 11} = 8$. Square both sides of this equation and solve for z:

$$3z^2 - 11 = 64$$
$$3z^2 = 75$$
$$z^2 = 25$$
$$z = \pm 5$$

Since the question specifies that $z > 0$, **(C)** is correct.

8.   C

Difficulty: Easy

Category: Advanced Math

Getting to the Answer: Follow the standard order of operations—deal with the exponent first and then attach the negative sign (because a negative in front of an expression means multiplication by -1). The variable x is being raised to the $\frac{1}{4}$ power, so rewrite the term as a radical expression with 4 as the degree of the root and 1 as the power to which the radicand, x, is being raised:

$$x^{\frac{1}{4}} = \sqrt[4]{x^1} = \sqrt[4]{x}$$

Now attach the negative to arrive at the correct answer, $-\sqrt[4]{x}$, which is **(C)**.

9. 16
Difficulty: Medium
Category: Advanced Math
Getting to the Answer: While this could be solved for with a calculator, learning exponent rules may save you time in the long run. The following calculation could also be done quickly with mental math after some practice. Rewrite the exponent in a way that makes it easier to evaluate: use exponent rules to rewrite $\frac{4}{3}$ as a unit fraction raised to a power. Then write the expression in radical form and simplify:

$$8^{\frac{4}{3}} = \left(8^{\frac{1}{3}}\right)^4$$
$$= (\sqrt[3]{8})^4$$
$$= 2^4$$
$$= 2 \times 2 \times 2 \times 2$$
$$= 16$$

Enter **16**.

10. A
Difficulty: Medium
Category: Advanced Math
Getting to the Answer: This is a question that lends itself to backsolving. Each answer is easily plugged into the equation and checked:

Choice (A):

$$\sqrt{3a + 16} - 3 = a - 1$$
$$\sqrt{3(3) + 16} - 3 = 3 - 1$$
$$\sqrt{25} - 3 = 2$$
$$5 - 3 = 2$$

Choice **(A)** is correct. For the record:

Choice (B) would yield the false statement $\sqrt{22} - 3 = 1$ and would be eliminated.

Choice (C) would yield the false statement $\sqrt{19} - 3 = 0$ and would be eliminated.

Choice (D) would yield the false statement $4 - 3 = -1$ and would be eliminated.

You could also solve this with quadratics (which is covered in a later chapter). Start by isolating the radical on the left side of the equation by adding 3 to both sides to get $\sqrt{3a + 16} = a + 2$. Now you can square both sides to get rid of the radical: $3a + 16 = (a + 2)^2 = a^2 + 4a + 4$. Since the right side of this equation is a quadratic, set it equal to 0 in order to determine the solutions: $0 = a^2 + 4a + 4 - (3a + 16) = a^2 + a - 12$. Next, factor the quadratic using reverse FOIL. The two factors of -12 that add up to 1 are -3 and 4, so $(a - 3)(a + 4) = 0$. Thus, a can be either 3 or -4, but the question says $a \geq 0$, so the only permissible value is 3. **(A)** is correct.

11. A
Difficulty: Easy
Category: Advanced Math
Getting to the Answer: Add polynomial expressions by combining like terms. Be careful of the signs of each term. It may help to write the sum vertically, lining up the like terms:

$$\begin{array}{r} 6a^2 - 17a - 9 \\ +(-5a^2 + 8a - 2) \\ \hline a^2 - 9a - 11 \end{array}$$

The correct choice is **(A)**.

12. D
Difficulty: Medium
Category: Advanced Math
Getting to the Answer: First, write the question as a subtraction problem. Pay careful attention to which expression is being subtracted so that you distribute the negative sign correctly, and make sure you only subtract terms with the same base and exponent.

$$8x^2 + 4x + 10 - (3x^3 + 7x - 5) = -3x^3 + 8x^2 - 3x + 15$$

This expression matches **(D)**.

13. D
Difficulty: Medium
Category: Advanced Math
Getting to the Answer: Multiply each term in the first expression by $\frac{3}{2}$ and each term in the second expression by 2. Then, subtract the two polynomials by writing them vertically and combining like terms. You'll have to find a common denominator to combine the x-coefficients and to combine the constant terms:

$$\frac{3}{2}A = \frac{3}{2}\left(4x^2 + 7x - 1\right) = 6x^2 + \frac{21}{2}x - \frac{3}{2}$$
$$2B = 2\left(-x^2 - 5x + 3\right) = -2x^2 - 10x + 6$$

$$\begin{array}{r} 6x^2 + \frac{21}{2}x - \frac{3}{2} \\ -\left(-2x^2 - \frac{20}{2}x + \frac{12}{2}\right) \\ \hline 8x^2 + \frac{41}{2}x - \frac{15}{2} \end{array}$$

This means **(D)** is correct. Notice that if you are simplifying the expression from left to right, after you find the x^2-coefficient, you can eliminate (A) and (B). After you find the x-coefficient, you can eliminate (C) and stop your work.

14. C
Difficulty: Hard
Category: Advanced Math
Getting to the Answer: In order to solve the equation, move all the terms to one side of the equation to set them equal to 0, then factor the expression. Thus, the given equation becomes $x^3 + x^2 - 9x - 9 = 0$. Think of this as two pairs of terms, $(x^3 + x^2)$ and $(-9x - 9)$. The first pair of terms share a common factor of x^2, so they can be written as $x^2(x + 1)$. The second pair share the common factor of -9, so they are equivalent to $-9(x + 1)$. So, the equation becomes $x^2(x + 1) - 9(x + 1) = 0$. Now, factor out the $(x + 1)$ term: $(x^2 - 9)(x + 1) = 0$.

In order for the product of two terms to be 0, either one or both must be 0. If $x^2 - 9 = 0$, then $x^2 = 9$ and $x = \pm 3$. Eliminate (A) and (D). If $x + 1 = 0$, then $x = -1$. Eliminate (B), so **(C)** is correct. You could also answer the question using Backsolving by plugging in each answer choice until you find the value for x that does *not* satisfy the equation.

15. C
Difficulty: Medium
Category: Advanced Math
Strategic Advice: To multiply two polynomials, multiply each term in the first factor by each term in the second factor, then combine like terms.

Getting to the Answer: Multiply each part of the trinomial expression by each part of the binomial one piece at a time and then combine like terms:

$$(2x^2 + 3x - 4)(3x + 2)$$
$$= 2x^2(3x + 2) + 3x(3x + 2) - 4(3x + 2)$$
$$= 6x^3 + 4x^2 + 9x^2 + 6x - 12x - 8$$
$$= 6x^3 + 13x^2 - 6x - 8$$

Because a represents the coefficient of x^2, $a = 13$. Hence, **(C)** is correct.

16. D
Difficulty: Medium
Category: Advanced Math
Getting to the Answer: Use polynomial long division to simplify the expression:

$$\begin{array}{r} 2a + 1 \phantom{{}-1} \\ a - 3 \overline{)\, 2a^2 - 5a - 1} \\ \underline{-(2a^2 - 6a)} \\ a - 1 \\ \underline{-(a - 3)} \\ 2 \end{array}$$

The quotient is $2a + 1$ and the remainder is 2, which will be divided by the divisor in the final answer: $2a + 1 + \frac{2}{a - 3}$. Thus, **(D)** is correct.

17. C
Difficulty: Hard
Category: Advanced Math
Getting to the Answer: A fraction is the same as division, so you can use polynomial long division to simplify the expression:

$$\begin{array}{r} 3x + 2 \phantom{{}+10} \\ 2x + 5 \overline{)\, 6x^2 + 19x + 10} \\ \underline{-(6x^2 + 15x)} \\ 4x + 10 \\ \underline{-(4x + 10)} \\ 0 \end{array}$$

The simplified expression is $3x + 2$, so $a = 3$ and $b = 2$, and $a + b = 3 + 2 = 5$, which is **(C)**. As an alternate approach, you could factor the numerator of the expression and cancel common factors:

$$\frac{6x^2 + 19x + 10}{2x + 5} = \frac{(2x + 5)(3x + 2)}{(2x + 5)} = 3x + 2$$

18. B
Difficulty: Medium
Category: Advanced Math
Getting to the Answer: Use polynomial long division to simplify the expression:

$$
\begin{array}{r}
2x - 5 \\
2x+2\overline{)4x^2 - 6x} \\
\underline{-(4x^2 + 4x)} \\
-10x \\
\underline{-(-10x - 10)} \\
+10
\end{array}
$$

The quotient is $2x - 5$ and the remainder is 10. Put the remainder over the divisor and add this to the quotient: $2x - 5 + \dfrac{10}{2x+2}$. **(B)** is correct.

19. B
Difficulty: Hard
Category: Advanced Math
Getting to the Answer: The question provides the quotient of $-9x + 5$ of a division problem and asks you to find the coefficient of the first term of the divisor $tx - 4$. Set this up in polynomial long division form to better understand the relationship between t and the other terms:

$$
\begin{array}{r}
-9x + 5 \\
tx - 4\overline{)36x^2 + 16x - 21}
\end{array}
$$

Viewed this way, it becomes apparent that $36x^2 \div tx = -9x$. Multiplying both sides by tx gives you $tx(-9x) = 36x^2$; therefore, $t(-9) = 36$, so $t = -4$. **(B)** is correct.

20. C
Difficulty: Hard
Category: Advanced Math
Getting to the Answer: Because $f(x)$ is divisible by $x - 5$, the value $x - 5$ must be a factor of $f(x)$. Therefore, you can define $f(x)$ as $(x - 5)(n)$, where n is some unknown polynomial. Since $g(x)$ is $f(x) + 4$, you can say that $g(x)$ must be $(x - 5)(n) + 4$.

Thus, $g(5)$ will be $(5 - 5)(n) + 4 = 0(n) + 4 = 0 + 4 = 4$. Therefore, **(C)** is correct.

21. B
Difficulty: Medium
Category: Advanced Math
Getting to the Answer: The solutions, or x-intercepts, of a polynomial are the factors of that polynomial. This polynomial has x-intercepts of -4, 0, and 6. The factors that

generate those solutions are $(x + 4)$, x, and $(x - 6)$. Eliminate (C) and (D) because they do not include those three factors. Because the graph *crosses* the x-axis at each x-intercept (rather than merely touching the x-axis), none of the factors can be raised to an even exponent. Therefore, eliminate (A) because of the x^2 term. **(B)** is correct.

22. C
Difficulty: Medium
Category: Advanced Math
Getting to the Answer: To find the solutions to a polynomial function, factor the polynomial and set each factor equal to 0. The solutions of a function are the x-intercepts, so $h(x)$ or the y-coordinate of the solution must equal 0. From the chart, the only point with $h(x) = 0$ is at $x = -1$. If $x = -1$, the factor that generates that solution is $x + 1 = 0$ because $(-1) + 1 = 0$. **(C)** is correct.

23. C
Difficulty: Hard
Category: Advanced Math
Getting to the Answer: Translate the notation: $b(a(x))$ means b of $a(x)$. This tells you to use $a(x)$ as the input for $b(x)$. You can rewrite this as $\dfrac{1}{a(x)}$, which is the reciprocal of $a(x)$. This new function will be undefined anywhere that $a(x) = 0$ because a denominator of 0 is not permitted. Looking at the graph, you can see that $a(x)$ crosses the x-axis four times, at which point the value of $a(x)$ is 0. Since division by 0 is undefined, $b(a(x))$ will be undefined for at least these four points, so **(C)** is correct.

24. A
Difficulty: Easy
Category: Advanced Math
Getting to the Answer: The phrase "exactly 2 distinct real zeros" means that the graph must have exactly two different x-intercepts on the graph. An x-intercept is indicated any time that the graph either crosses or touches the x-axis. (B) and (D) have three distinct zeros, and (C) has two zeros, but because the graph only touches the x-axis, they are the same, not distinct. The only graph with exactly two distinct zeros is **(A)**.

25. B
Difficulty: Easy
Category: Advanced Math
Getting to the Answer: The keyword "root" in the question stem means that you should examine the places at which the graph intersects the x-axis. Thus,

this graph has roots at (0, 0) and (6, 0). The x-axis, according to the graph, represents the horizontal distance traveled by the balloon. When $x = 0$, the distance the water balloon has traveled is 0, which is the balloon's starting position. The initial location of the balloon is not an answer choice, so the correct answer must be what the other root represents. When $x = 6$, the balloon's height is 0, which is the end point of the balloon's trajectory. This value, 6, is a root that represents the total horizontal distance traveled. **(B)** is correct.

26. 74
Difficulty: Medium
Category: Advanced Math
Strategic Advice: The goal is to find the number of applicants *eliminated* after three days, not the number remaining.
Getting to the Answer: The question describes the decay as the result of removing a certain fraction of the remaining applicants each day. The situation involves repeated division, so this is an example of exponential decay. You could use the exponential decay formula for a given rate, but it may be more straightforward to determine how many applicants are eliminated each day and tally them up.

After the first day, the judges eliminate one-fourth of 128, or 32, applicants. This leaves $128 - 32 = 96$ applicants. On the second day, one-fourth of 96, or 24, applicants are eliminated, leaving $96 - 24 = 72$. Finally, on the third day, one-fourth are eliminated again; one-fourth of 72 is 18, so there are $72 - 18 = 54$ applicants remaining. If 54 applicants remain, then $128 - 54 = 74$ applicants have been eliminated. Enter **74**.

27. C
Difficulty: Medium
Category: Advanced Math
Strategic Advice: This question gives you a percent increase per year, so use the exponential growth equation to solve for the number of years.
Getting to the Answer: Use the formula for exponential growth and plug in the values from the question. The rate is 16%, which as a decimal is 0.16. The rate will remain positive because the question asks about increase, or growth; therefore, $r = 0.16$. The current number of members is 42, so this will be $f(0)$. The goal is at least

100 members, so that will be the output, or $f(t)$. Put it all together:

$$f(t) = f(0)(1 + r)^t$$
$$100 = 42(1 + 0.16)^t$$
$$100 = 42(1.16)^t$$

At this point, backsolving is the best approach. Plug in the number of years for t. Because the answer choices are in ascending order, try one of the middle options first. You might be able to eliminate more than one choice at a time. Choice (B) is $t = 5$:

$$42(1.16)^5 \approx 88$$

Since (B) is too small, (A) must be as well. Eliminate them both. Unfortunately, 88 is not close enough to 100 to be certain that **(C)** is the correct answer, so test it:

$$42(1.16)^6 \approx 102$$

Six years is enough to put the club over 100 members. **(C)** is correct.

28. A
Difficulty: Hard
Category: Advanced Math
Strategy Advice: The term "half-life" signals exponential decay because it implies repeated division by 2. Using the exponential decay formula here could be complicated. Instead, you can use the percentage given in the question, along with the Picking Numbers strategy, to figure out how many half-lives have elapsed.
Getting to the Answer: Instead of providing an actual amount of ^{14}C, this question tells you what percent is left. For questions involving percentages of unknown values, it is often a good idea to pick 100. So, assume that the amount of ^{14}C in the sample when the tree died is 100. (Fortunately, there is no need to worry about the units here.) After one half-life, the amount of ^{14}C is halved to 50. A second half-life leaves 25, a third leaves 12.5, and a fourth leaves 6.25, which is 6.25% of 100. So four half-lives have elapsed. Since each half-life is 5,600 years, the tree died $4 \times 5,600$ or 22,400 years ago. Choice **(A)** is correct.

29. 17
Difficulty: Medium
Category: Advanced Math
Strategic Advice: The question describes a situation with linear growth since Penelope is adding the same amount of money to her piggy bank each month. Note:

the question is asking for her monthly allowance, but she puts in only half that amount each month. **Getting to the Answer:** Use the linear growth equation $y = mx + b$. The question gives you the starting amount b ($40), the final amount y ($244), and the amount of time x (2 years, which is 24 months). Plug these values into the equation and solve for m, which is the slope, or the rate of change—or in this case, how much Penelope puts in her piggy bank each month:

$$y = mx + b$$
$$244 = m(24) + 40$$
$$24m = 204$$
$$m = 8.5$$

Remember that what she puts in the piggy bank is only half of her allowance, so her total monthly allowance is twice $8.50. Enter **17**.

30. 160
Difficulty: Hard
Category: Advanced Math
Strategic Advice: This question describes both types of growth. Account X adds a percentage of the original amount, which never changes, so the same amount of money is added each month. Account X grows linearly. Account Y, however, adds a percentage of the current balance, which grows monthly, so account Y grows exponentially.
Getting to the Answer: Account X begins with $500 (the y-intercept, or b) and adds 2% of $500, or $500 \times 0.02 = \$10$ (the rate of change, or m), each month for 3 years, which is 36 months (the input, or x). Plug these values into the linear growth equation to solve for the final value of the account:

$$y = mx + b$$
$$y = 10(36) + 500$$
$$y = 360 + 500 = \$860$$

Account Y begins with $500 ($f(0)$) and adds 2%, or 0.02, (r) each month for 36 months (t). Plug these values into the exponential growth equation to solve for the final value of the account:

$$f(t) = f(0)(1 + r)^t$$
$$f(t) = 500(1 + 0.02)^{36}$$
$$f(t) = 500(1.02)^{36} \approx \$1,019.94$$

The positive difference between the two accounts is therefore $1,019.94 − $860 = $159.94. Round up to the nearest dollar, and enter **160**.

31. A
Difficulty: Medium
Category: Advanced Math
Getting to the Answer: There are two variables and only one equation, but because you're asked to solve for one of the variables *in terms of* the other, you solve the same way you would any other equation, by isolating x on one side of the equation. Cross-multiplying is a quick route to the solution:

$$\frac{6}{x} = \frac{3}{k+2}$$
$$6(k + 2) = 3x$$
$$6k + 12 = 3x$$
$$\frac{6k}{3} + \frac{12}{3} = \frac{3x}{3}$$
$$2k + 4 = x$$

Switch x to the left side of the equation and the result matches **(A)**.

32. 3
Difficulty: Hard
Category: Advanced Math
Getting to the Answer: Because the expression is adding fractions with different denominators, you'll need to establish a common denominator. Note that the second fraction is divisible by 3, so you can simplify the expression and then create the common denominator. Since both fractions now have denominators involving $(a − 3)$, wait to substitute 6 for $(a − 3)^2$ until you've added the two fractions.

$$\frac{3a + 9}{(a-3)^2} + \frac{-3}{a-3}$$
$$= \frac{3a + 9}{(a-3)^2} + \frac{-3}{a-3} \times \frac{a-3}{a-3}$$
$$= \frac{3a + 9}{(a-3)^2} + \frac{-3a + 9}{(a-3)^2}$$
$$= \frac{18}{(a-3)^2}$$

The question specifies that $(a − 3)^2 = 6$, so $\frac{18}{(a-3)^2} = \frac{18}{6} = 3$. Therefore, the expression equals 3. Enter **3**.

33. C
Difficulty: Medium
Category: Advanced Math
Getting to the Answer: The denominator of the expression contains the sum of two fractions that

themselves have different denominators, so start by finding a common denominator:

$$\frac{\frac{2}{a}}{\frac{a-6}{(a-2)(a-6)} + \frac{a-2}{(a-2)(a-6)}} = \frac{\frac{2}{a}}{\frac{2a-8}{a^2-8a+12}}$$

Next, multiply the numerator of the expression by the reciprocal of the denominator and simplify:

$$\frac{2}{a} \times \frac{a^2-8a+12}{2a-8}$$
$$= \frac{2(a^2-8a+12)}{2a^2-8a}$$
$$= \frac{a^2-8a+12}{a^2-4a}$$

This expression matches **(C)**.

34. A
Difficulty: Easy
Category: Advanced Math
Getting to the Answer: Both terms in the numerator share a common x^2 term, so factor that out:

$$\frac{x^2(x-3)}{x-3} = 9$$

Now, cancel $(x-3)$ in the numerator and the denominator to get $x^2 = 9$. Normally, this would mean that x could be 3 or -3. However, remember to check for extraneous solutions. If $x = 3$, then the denominator in the original equation would be equal to 0; thus, $x = -3$, and **(A)** is correct.

35. B
Difficulty: Hard
Category: Advanced Math
Getting to the Answer: Because the question states that the expressions are equivalent, set up the equation $\frac{16}{7x+4} + A = \frac{49x^2}{7x+4}$ and solve for A. Start by subtracting the first term from both sides of the equation to isolate A. Then, simplify. The denominators of the rational terms are the same, so they can be combined. Then, cancel common factors.

$$\frac{16}{7x+4} + A = \frac{49x^2}{7x+4}$$
$$A = \frac{49x^2}{7x+4} - \frac{16}{7x+4}$$
$$A = \frac{49x^2-16}{7x+4}$$
$$A = \frac{(7x+4)(7x-4)}{7x+4}$$
$$A = 7x-4$$

The correct choice is **(B)**.

36. B
Difficulty: Medium
Category: Advanced Math
Getting to the Answer: Move the second fraction over to the other side of the equation by subtracting it from both sides, then cross-multiply to simplify:

$$\frac{1-2c}{3c} = \frac{c-8}{12}$$
$$12(1-2c) = 3c(c-8)$$
$$12-24c = 3c^2-24c$$
$$12 = 3c^2$$
$$c^2 = 4$$

Therefore, either $c = -2$ or $c = 2$. The question specifies that $c < 0$, so c must equal -2. **(B)** is correct.

37. D
Difficulty: Medium
Category: Advanced Math
Getting to the Answer: Your first thought at seeing this question may be to try to break the expression into two separate fractions or see if some expression can be factored out. Unfortunately, that does not help with simplifying the expression. You'll need polynomial long division if you're going to use algebra:

$$\begin{array}{r} 3 \\ x-4\overline{)3x-1} \\ -(3x-12) \\ \hline 11 \end{array}$$

That results in the expression $3 + \frac{11}{x-4}$, so the correct answer is **(D)**.

Another effective alternative for solving this question is to use Picking Numbers. Choose a small, permissible value like $x = 2$ to find a value for the original expression:

$$\frac{3(2)-1}{(2)-4} = \frac{6-1}{-2} = -\frac{5}{2}$$

Now check each answer choice to see which one is equal to $-\frac{5}{2}$ when you plug in $x = 2$:

(A): $3(2) + \frac{1}{(2)-4} = 6 + \frac{1}{-2} = 6 + \left(-\frac{1}{2}\right) = 6 - \frac{1}{2} = 5\frac{1}{2} = \frac{11}{2}$, eliminate.

(B): $3(2) - \frac{1}{(2)-4} = 6 - \frac{1}{-2} = 6 - \left(-\frac{1}{2}\right) = 6 + \frac{1}{2} = 6\frac{1}{2} = \frac{13}{2}$, eliminate.

(C): $3 - \dfrac{11}{(2) - 4} = 3 - \dfrac{11}{-2} = 3 - \left(-\dfrac{11}{2}\right) =$

$3 + \dfrac{11}{2} = \dfrac{17}{2}$, eliminate.

(D): $3 + \dfrac{11}{(2) - 4} = 3 + \dfrac{11}{-2} = 3 + \left(-\dfrac{11}{2}\right) = -\dfrac{5}{2}$

38. C

Difficulty: Medium

Category: Advanced Math

Getting to the Answer: When solving polynomial equations for one variable, begin by moving all terms that don't contain that variable (in this case a) to one side of the equation. Once there, multiply both sides by 2 to eliminate the fraction, and then divide by t^2 to isolate a:

$$h = \frac{1}{2}at^2 + v_v t + h_0$$

$$h - v_v t - h_0 = \frac{1}{2}at^2$$

$$2(h - v_v t - h_0) = at^2$$

$$\frac{2(h - v_v t - h_0)}{t^2} = a$$

Choice **(C)** is the correct answer.

39. D

Difficulty: Medium

Category: Advanced Math

Getting to the Answer: In order to combine terms with exponents by multiplication or division, the terms must all have the same base. All the bases in the given equation are powers of 2, so restate the equation with all the terms in base two: $\left(2^4\right)^{3x}\left(2^5\right)^x\left(2^3\right)^{3x} = \dfrac{\left(2^2\right)^{6x}\left(2^5\right)^{3x}}{2^2}$.

When a base with an exponent is raised to a power, multiply the exponents. An exponent in a denominator is equivalent to the same exponent in the numerator with the sign flipped, so $\left(2^{12x}\right)\left(2^{5x}\right)\left(2^{9x}\right) = \left(2^{12x}\right)\left(2^{15x}\right)\left(2^{-2}\right)$.

When the numbers with exponents and the same base are multiplied, add the exponents. Thus, the equation further simplifies to $2^{12x + 5x + 9x} = 2^{12x + 15x - 2}$. Because the base on each side of the equation is the same, the total of the exponents on both sides must be equal. Therefore, $12x + 5x + 9x = 12x + 15x - 2$. This further simplifies to $26x = 27x - 2$, so $x = 2$. **(D)** is correct.

40. 2

Difficulty: Medium

Category: Advanced Math

Getting to the Answer: Conveniently, the conjugate of the denominator, $\sqrt{x} - 3$, is the numerator of the other fraction, $\sqrt{x} + 3$, so cross-multiplying will rationalize the fraction.

Cross-multiplying the first equation yields $(y)(3) = (\sqrt{x} + 3)(\sqrt{x} - 3)$, which simplifies to $3y = x - 9$. (If this is a difficult simplification for you, study FOIL and the classic quadratics in the Quadratics chapter.) In the second equation, you are given that $2x + 42 = 9x - 63$, so $7x = 105$, and $x = 15$. Therefore, $3y = 15 - 9 = 6$, and $y = 2$. Enter **2**.

You could have chosen to solve the second equation for the value of x, then substituted the result into the proportion and solved for y. Either approach would be equally effective.

41. B

Difficulty: Medium

Category: Advanced Math

Getting to the Answer: Since there's no common factor in the numerator and denominator, you'll need to use polynomial long division. Notice that the numerator does not have an x term, so include $0x$ in the long division:

$$
\begin{array}{r}
3x + 9 \\
x - 3 \overline{\smash{\big)}\, 3x^2 + 0x + 7} \\
\underline{-(3x^2 - 9x)} \\
9x + 7 \\
\underline{-(9x - 27)} \\
34
\end{array}
$$

The result of the long division is $3x + 9$ with a remainder of 34. The remainder is the "leftover" part that hasn't yet been divided by $x - 3$, so it can be expressed as $\dfrac{34}{x - 3}$.

Thus, **(B)** is correct.

42. A

Difficulty: Medium

Category: Advanced Math

Strategic Advice: You could plug the x- and y-values from each choice into the given equation to see which does not equal zero. However, if you factor the polynomial, you'll save time by avoiding extra calculations.

Getting to the Answer: Look for common factors in the polynomial by groups. The first two terms, $15x^2$ and $10xy$, share the common factor $5x$. The third and fourth terms share a common factor of -2, so you can write the equation as $z = 5x(3x + 2y) - 2(3x + 2y)$. Next, factor out the $(3x + 2y)$ to regroup this as $z = (5x - 2)(3x + 2y)$. Since z is the product of two factors, if either factor equals 0, then $z = 0$.

If $5x - 2 = 0$, then $x = \frac{2}{5}$. You can immediately eliminate (C) and (D) because, if $x = \frac{2}{5}$, $z = 0$ no matter what the value of y might be. Plug the other two ordered from (A) and (B) into $3x + 2y$ to see which one makes $z = 0$. If $x = -3$ and $y = 2$, then $3x + 2y = 3(-3) + 2(2) = -9 + 4 = -5$. Thus, **(A)** is an ordered pair for which $z \neq 0$, so it is correct. For the record, (B) is incorrect because if $x = -2$ and $y = 3$, then $3x + 2y = 3(-2) + 2(3) = -6 + 6 = 0$, which would result in $z = 0$.

43. 5
Difficulty: Medium
Category: Advanced Math
Getting to the Answer: Remember that the rules for combining terms under a radical are different for addition and multiplication. Although $\sqrt{xy}$ can be written as $\sqrt{x} \times \sqrt{y}$, terms that are added under a radical, such as $\sqrt{x + y}$, must be combined before taking the root. Now, find the value of each term in the radical above, add them, and then take the square root of the sum.

The term, $27^{\frac{2}{3}}$, is the square of the cube root of 27. Since $3 \times 3 \times 3 = 27$, the cube root of 27 is 3, which squared is $3^2 = 9$. The denominator of the exponent in $128^{\frac{4}{7}}$ quite likely means that 128 is some number to the seventh power. A good place to start would be to try 2 because it is small and easy to raise to high powers. Indeed, you'll find that $2 \times 2 \times 2 \times 2 \times 2 \times 2 \times 2 = 128$. So $128^{\frac{4}{7}} = \left(2^7\right)^{\frac{4}{7}} = 2^4 = 16$. Thus, $\sqrt{27^{\frac{2}{3}} + 128^{\frac{4}{7}}} = \sqrt{9 + 16} = \sqrt{25} = 5$. Enter **5**.

44. A
Difficulty: Medium
Category: Advanced Math
Strategic Advice: Since there is no common factor in the numerator and denominator, you might be tempted to dive into polynomial long division. However, if you notice that the numerator, $4x^2 - 8$, is very close to being the difference of two squares, $4x^2 - 9$, there is a more efficient way to unravel this fraction.

Getting to the Answer: Restate the fraction as $\frac{4x^2 - 9}{2x + 3} + \frac{1}{2x + 3}$. Now factor the numerator and cancel like terms: $\frac{\cancel{(2x + 3)}(2x - 3)}{\cancel{2x + 3}} + \frac{1}{2x + 3}$.
(A) is correct.

45. C
Difficulty: Medium
Category: Advanced Math
Strategic Advice: Recall that a denominator equal to zero results in an undefined value for the fraction. To answer this question, determine which of the choices does *not* result in the denominator being equal to zero.
Getting to the Answer: Factor the denominator first to simplify the identification of those values. Start by factoring out $2x$ to show the denominator as $2x(x^2 - 6x - 7)$. The denominator is the product of the two factors, so if either one is 0, the denominator will be 0. If $2x = 0$, $x = 0$, so eliminate (B) because $x = 0$ makes $g(x)$ undefined.

Next, you could either plug the remaining choices into $x^2 - 6x - 7$ to see which choice does not produce a result of zero or you could factor the expression into $(x - 7)(x + 1)$. Thus, either $x = 7$ or $x = -1$ results in the denominator of $g(x)$ being zero. Eliminate (A) and (D); **(C)** is correct. For the record, $g(1) = \frac{2}{-24}$.

You could also graph the function on the calculator. If you did so, you would see that the function is undefined at -1, 0, and 7, leaving **(C)**, 1, as the only answer choice for which the function is defined.

46. B
Difficulty: Medium
Category: Advanced Math
Getting to the Answer: In order to solve for possible values of x, first group all the terms on one side of the equation and set the other side to 0. Thus, $x^3 + 4 = 3x^2 - 7x + 25$ can be written as $x^3 - 3x^2 + 7x - 21 = 0$. Factor this by grouping the terms into two pairs. The first pair, $x^3 - 3x^2$, contains the common factor x^2, so it is equivalent to $x^2(x - 3)$. The second pair, $7x - 21$, factors to $7(x - 3)$. Thus, another form of the entire equation is $x^2(x - 3) + 7(x - 3) = 0$. Factor out $(x - 3)$ to get $(x^2 + 7)(x - 3) = 0$.

If the product of two factors is zero, one or both of the factors must be zero. If $(x^2 + 7) = 0$, then $x^2 = -7$. Since the square root of a negative number is not a real number, move on to $x - 3 = 0$. In this case, $x = 3$, so **(B)** is correct.

47. C

Difficulty: Medium

Category: Advanced Math

Strategic Advice: Equations with roots of 0, as well as roots that are less than 0, will be incorrect and can be eliminated. When using Elimination, start with the easiest-looking choice first, then proceed to the next easiest, and so forth.

Getting to the Answer: Roots on a graph are the points at which $y = 0$. Start by plugging in 0 for y in each choice and solving for x, and then eliminate those choices for which x could be 0 or less. For (A), you would plug in 0 such that $0 = 4|x|$, which is true only for $x = 0$. Eliminate (A). For (B), plug in 0 for y and solve for x:

$$0 = x^2 - 4$$
$$x^2 = 4$$
$$\sqrt{x^2} = \sqrt{4}$$
$$x = \pm 2$$

Since x could equal -2, eliminate (B) as well. Choices (C) and (D) are the products of two factors. If the product of 2 factors is 0, then one of the factors must be 0. In (C), the only value for x that would make the equation equal to 0 is 2, which is greater than 0, so **(C)** is correct. On test day, you would move on, but for the record, in choice (D), $x = 0$ is a root, so (D) is incorrect.

48. D

Difficulty: Easy

Category: Advanced Math

Getting to the Answer: The notation $f(x) = 0$ is another way of describing the x-axis, so this question is asking how many times the graph intersects or touches the x-axis. This graph crosses the x-axis four times, once each at $x = 0$, $x = 4$, $x = 3$, and $x = 2$, so **(D)** is correct.

49. A

Difficulty: Easy

Category: Advanced Math

Getting to the Answer: If the number of smartphone users increases by 35% each year, then the amount of the increase is variable (because it's 35% of a bigger number each time), which means exponential growth. Eliminate (C) and (D). Consider the two remaining equations in terms of the exponential growth function, $f(x) = f(0)(1 + r)^x$. Note that the only difference between the two remaining choices is the r value. Recall that when assembling an exponential growth model, r (the rate) must be in decimal form. Therefore, the number raised to the power of x should be $1 + 0.35$, or 1.35. Choice **(A)** is the only one that fits these criteria.

[CHAPTER 13]

QUADRATICS

LEARNING OBJECTIVES

After completing this chapter, you will be able to:

- Solve a quadratic equation by factoring
- Expand quadratics using FOIL
- Recognize the classic quadratics
- Solve a quadratic equation by completing the square
- Solve a quadratic equation by applying the quadratic formula
- Use the discriminant to determine the number of real solutions to a quadratic equation
- Relate properties of a quadratic function to its graph and vice versa
- Solve a system of one quadratic and one linear equation

HOW MUCH DO YOU KNOW?

Directions

Try the questions that follow. Show your work so that you can compare your solutions to the ones found in the "Check Your Work" section immediately after this question set. If you answered the question(s) on a specific topic correctly, and if your scratchwork looks like ours, you may be able to move quickly through the lesson covering that topic. If you answered incorrectly or used a different approach, you may want to take your time on that lesson.

1

Which of the following expressions is equivalent to $x^2 - 10x - 7$?

(A) $(x - 5)^2 - 32$

(B) $(x - 5)^2 + 32$

(C) $(x + 5)^2 - 32$

(D) $(x + 5)^2 + 32$

2

$$3x^2 - 5x = -k$$

In the given equation, k is a constant. For which of the following values of k does the equation have at least one real solution?

(A)   2

(B)   3

(C)   4

(D)   5

3

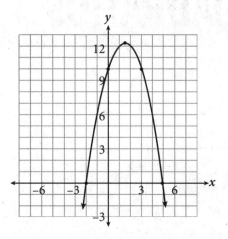

Which of the following could be the equation of the graph shown?

(A) $y = 2x + 10$

(B) $y = x^2 + \frac{3}{2}x + 10$

(C) $y = -(x - 2)(x + 5)$

(D) $y = -(x + 2)(x - 5)$

4

The x-coordinates of the solutions to a system of equations are 3.5 and 6. Which of the following could be the system?

(A) $y = x + 3.5$
$y = x^2 + 6$

(B) $y = 2x - 7$
$y = -(x - 6)^2$

(C) $y = \frac{1}{2}x + 3$
$y = -(x - 5)^2 + 7$

(D) $y = \frac{1}{2}x + 7$
$y = -(x - 6)^2 + 3.5$

5

The graph of the equation $y = -4x^2 - 3x + 49$ intersects the line $x = -4$ at a point whose y-coordinate is g. The same graph intersects the line $x = 1$ at a point whose y-coordinate is h. What is the value of $g + h$?

(A) -6

(B) 27

(C) 39

(D) 46

6

If $x + y > 0$, $x^2 + 3xy = 90$, and $-xy + y^2 = -9$, what is the value of $x + y$?

Check Your Work

1. A
Difficulty: Medium
Category: Advanced Math
Getting to the Answer: There are no integer factors of $x^2 - 10x - 7$, since no two integers whose product is -7 add up to -10. Note that the answer choices are stated in vertex format, the same as you would obtain by completing the square of the given expression. Half of the x-coefficient, -10, is -5, so the constant term needed to complete the square is $(-5)^2 = 25$. Thus, you can rewrite and group the given expression as $(x^2 - 10x + 25) - 25 - 7$. This simplifies to $(x - 5)^2 - 32$, which is **(A)**. Noticing that $x^2 - 10x + 25$ is a classic quadratic makes the process of factoring very quick.

2. A
Difficulty: Medium
Category: Advanced Math
Getting to the Answer: Rearrange the equation into "standard" quadratic form, $3x^2 - 5x + k = 0$. A quadratic equation has two real solutions if the discriminant, $b^2 - 4ac$, is positive. The equation has one real solution if the discriminant is 0. For the given equation, $a = 3$, $b = -5$, and $c = k$, so you can set up the inequality $(-5)^2 - 4(3)k \geq 0$. This simplifies to $25 \geq 12k$. The only choice for which this is true is (A), since plugging in any of the other answers for k yields a value greater than 25. **(A)** is correct.

If you didn't know of the shortcut about the discriminant, consider the quadratic formula, $x = \dfrac{-b \pm \sqrt{b^2 - 4ac}}{2a}$. If the term inside the radical, $b^2 - 4ac$, is negative, then there are no real solutions.

3. D
Difficulty: Easy
Category: Advanced Math
Getting to the Answer: The graph is a parabola, so you can eliminate (A) because its equation is linear. The parabola opens downward, so there should be a negative sign in front of the factors or the a-coefficient; eliminate (B). The x-intercepts of the graph are -2 and 5, so the factors of the quadratic are $(x + 2)$ and $(x - 5)$. These factors make $y = 0$ when $x = -2$ and $x = 5$. Eliminate (C). Only (D) is left, so **(D)** is correct.

4. C
Difficulty: Hard
Category: Advanced Math
Getting to the Answer: You don't actually need to solve each system. Instead, plug 3.5 or 6 into each answer choice and eliminate each one whose y-values don't come out the same. (If the same x-value produces different y-values in two equations, then it is not the x-coordinate of the solution to the system.) Because 3.5 is a decimal, doing arithmetic with it is likely to be messy. So start with 6:

(A): $y = 6 + 3.5 = 9.5$
$\quad\quad y = 6^2 + 6 = 36 + 6 = 42$
Different y-values; eliminate.

(B): $y = 2(6) - 7 = 12 - 7 = 5$
$\quad\quad y = -(6 - 6)^2 = -(0)^2 = 0$
Different y-values; eliminate.

(C): $y = \frac{1}{2}(6) + 3 = 3 + 3 = 6$
$\quad\quad y = -(6 - 5)^2 + 7 = -(1)^2 + 7 = -1 + 7 = 6$
Keep for now. You need to test (D) because it's possible that (D) is the correct answer and (C) just happens to work for $x = 6$ (but not for $x = 3.5$).

(D): $y = \frac{1}{2}(6) + 7 = 3 + 7 = 10$
$\quad\quad y = -(6 - 6)^2 + 3.5 = -(0)^2 + 3.5 = 3.5$
Different y-values; eliminate.

Alternatively, you might graph each of the answer choices to see which one produces intersections at 3.5 and 6.

(C) is correct.

5. C
Difficulty: Medium
Category: Advanced Math
Getting to the Answer: The question is asking for the sum of the y-coordinates of the points where two vertical lines intersect a parabola. You might use a graphing calculator to graph all three equations to determine the intersection points. Otherwise, to find the first intersection point, g, substitute -4 for x into the equation $y = -4x^2 - 3x + 49$: $y = -4(-4)^2 - 3(-4) + 49 = -4(16) + 12 + 49 = -64 + 12 + 49 = -52 + 49 = -3$. Thus, $g = -3$.

To find the second intersection point, h, substitute 1 for x into the same equation: $y = -4(1)^2 - 3(1) + 49 = -4(1) - 3 + 49 = -4 - 3 + 49 = -7 + 49 = 42$. Thus, $h = 42$.

Finally, add g and h: $g + h = -3 + 42 = 39$. **(C)** is correct.

6.   9

Difficulty: Hard

Category: Advanced Math

Getting to the Answer: Add the two equations as shown.

$$(x^2 + 3xy) + (-xy + y^2) = 90 + (-9)$$
$$x^2 + 3xy - xy + y^2 = 81$$
$$x^2 + 2xy + y^2 = 81$$

Recognizing that $x^2 + 2xy + y^2$ is a classic quadratic makes it easy to rewrite $x^2 + 2xy + y^2 = 81$ as $(x + y)^2 = 81$. Take the square root of both sides to find that $x + y = 9$ or $x + y = -9$. The question says that $x + y > 0$, so discard -9 as a possible solution. Enter **9**.

SOLVING QUADRATICS BY FACTORING

LEARNING OBJECTIVES

After this lesson, you will be able to:

- Solve a quadratic equation by factoring
- Expand quadratics using FOIL

To answer a question like this:

If $x^2 - 7x = 30$ and $x > 0$, what is the value of $x - 5$?

A) 5

B) 6

C) 10

D) 25

You need to know this:

A quadratic expression is a second-degree polynomial—that is, a polynomial containing a squared variable. You can write a quadratic expression as $ax^2 + bx + c$.

The **FOIL** acronym (which stands for First, Outer, Inner, Last) will help you remember how to multiply two binomials of the form $(a + b)(c + d)$: multiply the first terms together (ac), then the outer terms (ad), then the inner terms (bc), and finally the last terms (bd):

$$(a + b)(c + d) = ac + ad + bc + bd$$

FOIL can also be done in reverse if you need to go from a quadratic to its factors.

To solve a quadratic equation by factoring, the quadratic must be set equal to 0. For example:

$$x^2 + x - 56 = 0$$
$$(x + 8)(x - 7) = 0$$

From the binomial factors, you can find the **solutions**, also called **roots** or **zeros**, of the equation. For two factors to be multiplied together and produce zero as the result, one or both of those factors must be zero. In the example above, either $x + 8 = 0$ or $x - 7 = 0$, which means that $x = -8$ or $x = 7$.

You need to do this:

Here are the steps for solving a quadratic equation by factoring:

- Set the quadratic equal to zero, so it looks like this: $ax^2 + bx + c = 0$.
- Factor the squared term. (For factoring, it's easiest when a, the coefficient in front of x^2, is equal to 1.)
- Make a list of the factors of c. Remember to include negatives.
- Find the factor pair that, when added, equals b, the coefficient in front of x.
- Write the quadratic as the product of two binomials.
- Set each binomial equal to zero and solve.

Explanation:

Set the equation equal to zero and factor the first term:

$$x^2 - 7x = 30$$
$$x^2 - 7x - 30 = 0$$
$$(x \pm ?)(x \pm ?) = 0$$

Next, consider factors of -30, keeping in mind that they must sum to -7, so the factor with the greater absolute value must be negative. The possibilities are: -30×1, -15×2, -10×3, and -6×5. The factor pair that sums to -7 is -10 and 3. Write that factor pair into your binomials:

$$(x - 10)(x + 3) = 0$$

Set each factor equal to zero and solve:

$$(x - 10) = 0 \quad (x + 3) = 0$$
$$x = 10 \quad\quad x = -3$$

The question says that $x > 0$, so $x = 10$. Now that you solved for x, you can answer the question, which asks for $x - 5$: $10 - 5 = 5$. **(A)** is correct.

If factoring quadratics gives you trouble, study the steps above and try these Drill questions before completing the following "Try on Your Own" questions. Factor each quadratic expression (without using a calculator). Drill answers can be found in the Check Your Work section at the end of the chapter.

Drill

a. $a^2 + 8a + 15$

b. $x^2 + 4x - 21$

c. $b^2 - 7b - 18$

d. $y^2 - 10y + 24$

e. $x^2 + \frac{1}{2}x - \frac{1}{2}$

f. $5x^2 + 10x + 5$

g. $2x^2 + 12x - 54$

h. $3x^2 - 6x + 3$

i. $x^2 + 3xy + 2y^2$

j. $4a^2 + 4ab - 8b^2$

Try on Your Own

Directions

Take as much time as you need on these questions. Work carefully and methodically. There will be an opportunity for timed practice later in the book.

1

Which of the following is an equivalent form of the expression $(6 - 5x)(15x - 11)$?

Ⓐ $\quad -75x^2 + 35x - 66$

Ⓑ $\quad -75x^2 + 145x - 66$

Ⓒ $\quad 90x^2 - 141x + 55$

Ⓓ $\quad 90x^2 + 9x + 55$

2

HINT: For Q2, what is the easiest way to factor the denominator?

Which of the following is equivalent to $\dfrac{x^2 - 10x + 25}{3x^2 - 9x - 30}$?

Ⓐ $\quad \dfrac{3(x - 2)}{(x + 5)}$

Ⓑ $\quad \dfrac{3(x + 2)}{(x - 5)}$

Ⓒ $\quad \dfrac{(x - 5)}{3(x + 2)}$

Ⓓ $\quad \dfrac{(x + 5)}{3(x - 2)}$

3

HINT: For Q3, what value in the denominator would make the fraction undefined?

For what positive value of x is the equation $\dfrac{3}{2x^2 + 4x - 6} = 0$ undefined?

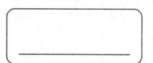

4

What is the sum of the roots of $3x^2 + 9x = 54$?

Ⓐ $\quad -6$

Ⓑ $\quad -3$

Ⓒ $\quad 3$

Ⓓ $\quad 6$

5

$$f(x) = (1.3x - 3.9)^2 - (0.69x^2 - 0.14x - 9.79)$$

Which of the following functions is equivalent to the function given?

Ⓐ $\quad f(x) = (x - 5)^2$

Ⓑ $\quad f(x) = x^2 + 10.28x + 5.42$

Ⓒ $\quad f(x) = 0.61x^2 + 0.14x + 25$

Ⓓ $\quad f(x) = 1.3(x - 3)^2 - 0.69x^2 + 0.14x + 9.79$

CLASSIC QUADRATICS

LEARNING OBJECTIVE

After this lesson, you will be able to:

- Recognize the classic quadratics

To answer a question like this:

Which of the following expressions is equivalent to $25x^2y^4 - 1$?

A) $5(x^2y^4 - 1)$

B) $-5(xy^2 + 1)$

C) $(5xy - 1)(5xy + 1)$

D) $(5xy^2 - 1)(5xy^2 + 1)$

You need to know this:

Quadratic expressions often follow certain patterns that will show up on the SAT. Memorizing the following classic quadratics will save you time on test day:

- $x^2 - y^2 = (x + y)(x - y)$
- $x^2 + 2xy + y^2 = (x + y)^2$
- $x^2 - 2xy + y^2 = (x - y)^2$

You need to do this:

When you see a pattern that matches either the left or the right side of one of the above equations, simplify by substituting its equivalent form. For example, say you need to simplify the following:

$$\frac{a^2 - 2ab + b^2}{a - b}$$

You would substitute $(a - b)(a - b)$ for the numerator and cancel to find that the expression simplifies to $a - b$:

$$\frac{a^2 - 2ab + b^2}{a - b} = \frac{(a - b)(a - b)}{a - b} = \frac{a - b}{1} = a - b$$

Explanation:

The expression $25x^2y^4 - 1$ is a difference of perfect squares. It corresponds to the first of the three classic quadratic patterns. The square root of $25x^2y^4$ is $5xy^2$ and the square root of 1 is 1, so the correct factors are $(5xy^2 - 1)$ $(5xy^2 + 1)$. Choice **(D)** is correct.

Try on Your Own

Directions

Take as much time as you need on these questions. Work carefully and methodically. There will be an opportunity for timed practice later in the book.

6

For all a and b, what is the sum of $(a - b)^2$ and $(a + b)^2$?

Ⓐ $2a^2$

Ⓑ $2a^2 - 2b^2$

Ⓒ $2a^2 + 2b^2$

Ⓓ $2a^2 + 4ab + 2b^2$

7

HINT: For Q7, how can you remove the fraction to make factoring easier?

What is the positive difference between the roots of the equation $y = \frac{1}{3}x^2 - 2x + 3$?

$$\boxed{\\ \rule{3cm}{0.4pt}}$$

8

HINT: For Q8, look for a classic quadratic in the denominator.

$$f(x) = \frac{3}{(x - 7)^2 + 6(x - 7) + 9}$$

For which value of x is the function $f(x)$ undefined?

$$\boxed{\\ \rule{3cm}{0.4pt}}$$

9

HINT: One of the given equations in Q9 is a classic quadratic.

A rectangle has an area of $x^4 - 196$. If the width of the rectangle is $x^2 - 14$, what is the length? (The area of a rectangle is its length times its width.)

Ⓐ $x + 14$

Ⓑ $x^2 + 14$

Ⓒ $x^2 - 14$

Ⓓ $x - 14$

10

In the expression $2x^2 - 28x + 98 = a(x - b)^2$, $a > 1$ and both a and b are constants. Which of the following could be the value of b?

Ⓐ -7

Ⓑ 7

Ⓒ 14

Ⓓ 49

 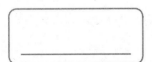

COMPLETING THE SQUARE

LEARNING OBJECTIVE

After this lesson, you will be able to:

- Solve a quadratic equation by completing the square

To answer a question like this:

Which of the following equations has the same solutions as the equation $42 - 6x = x^2 - y$?

A) $y = (x - 6)^2 - 42$

B) $y = (x - 6)^2 + 42$

C) $y = (x + 3)^2 - 51$

D) $y = (x + 3)^2 + 51$

You need to know this:

For quadratics that do not factor easily, you'll need one of two strategies: completing the square or the quadratic formula (taught in the next lesson). To complete the square, you'll create an equation in vertex form $(x - h)^2 = k$, where h and k are constants that represent the vertex of the parabola.

As with factoring, completing the square is most convenient when the coefficient in front of the x^2 term is 1.

You need to do this:

Here are the steps for completing the square, demonstrated with a simple example.

STEP	SCRATCHWORK
Starting point:	$x^2 + 8x - 8 = 0$
1. Move the constant to the opposite side.	$x^2 + 8x = 8$
2. Divide b, the x-coefficient, by 2 and square the quotient.	$b = 8$; $\left(\dfrac{b}{2}\right)^2 = \left(\dfrac{8}{2}\right)^2 = (4)^2 = 16$
3. Add the number from the previous step to both sides of the equation and factor.	$x^2 + 8x + 16 = 8 + 16$ $(x + 4)(x + 4) = 24$ $(x + 4)^2 = 24$
4. Take the square root of both sides.	$x + 4 = \pm\sqrt{24}$ $x + 4 = \pm\sqrt{4}\sqrt{6}$ $x + 4 = \pm 2\sqrt{6}$
5. Split the result into two equations and solve each one.	$x + 4 = 2\sqrt{6} \rightarrow x = 2\sqrt{6} - 4$ $x + 4 = -2\sqrt{6} \rightarrow x = -2\sqrt{6} - 4$

Explanation:

First, write the equation in standard form: $y = x^2 + 6x - 42$. Add 42 to both sides and complete the square on the right-hand side. Find $\left(\dfrac{b}{2}\right)^2 = \left(\dfrac{6}{2}\right)^2 = 3^2 = 9$, and add the result to both sides of the equation:

$$y = x^2 + 6x - 42$$
$$y + 42 = x^2 + 6x$$
$$y + 42 + 9 = x^2 + 6x + 9$$
$$y + 51 = x^2 + 6x + 9$$

Note that all of the answer choices are in factored form. The right side of the equation is a classic quadratic that factors as follows:

$$y + 51 = (x + 3)(x + 3)$$
$$y + 51 = (x + 3)^2$$

Finally, solve for y to get $y = (x + 3)^2 - 51$, which means **(C)** is correct.

If you find completing the square to be challenging, study the steps in the preceding table and try these Drill questions before completing the following "Try on Your Own" questions. Drill answers can be found in the Check Your Work section at the end of the chapter.

Drill

a. $x^2 = 10x + 2$

b. $-9 = 2x^2 + 16x + 3$

c. $x^2 - x - 11 = 0$

d. $x^2 + \dfrac{x}{2} = 4$

e. $-x^2 + 6ax = 2a^2$

Try on Your Own

Directions

Take as much time as you need on these questions. Work carefully and methodically. There will be an opportunity for timed practice later in the book.

11

Which of the following is a value of x that satisfies the equation $x^2 + 2x - 5 = 0$?

Ⓐ -1

Ⓑ $1 - \sqrt{6}$

Ⓒ $1 + \sqrt{6}$

Ⓓ $-1 - \sqrt{6}$

12

$$a^2 - 12a - 72 = 0$$

Which of the following is the greatest possible value of a?

Ⓐ $12\sqrt{3}$

Ⓑ $36\sqrt{3}$

Ⓒ $6 + \sqrt{3}$

Ⓓ $6(1 + \sqrt{3})$

13

HINT: For Q13, treat the square root in the b term just like any other: divide it by 2, then square it.

$$x^2 - (6\sqrt{5})x = -40$$

What is the sum of the possible values of x in the given equation?

Ⓐ 15

Ⓑ $4\sqrt{5}$

Ⓒ $6\sqrt{5}$

Ⓓ 60

14

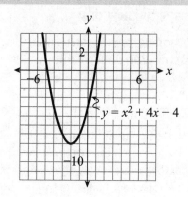

Which of the following is equivalent to the equation of the graph shown?

Ⓐ $(x - 2)^2 - 8$

Ⓑ $(x + 2)^2 - 8$

Ⓒ $(x - 2)^2 + 8$

Ⓓ $(x + 2)^2 + 8$

Math

THE QUADRATIC FORMULA

LEARNING OBJECTIVES

After this lesson, you will be able to:

- Solve a quadratic equation by applying the quadratic formula
- Use the discriminant to determine the number of real solutions to a quadratic equation

To answer a question like this:

Which of the following are the real values of x that satisfy the equation $2x^2 - 5x - 2 = 0$?

A) 1 and 4

B) $-\dfrac{5}{4} + \dfrac{\sqrt{41}}{4}$ and $-\dfrac{5}{4} - \dfrac{\sqrt{41}}{4}$

C) $\dfrac{5}{4} + \dfrac{\sqrt{41}}{4}$ and $\dfrac{5}{4} - \dfrac{\sqrt{41}}{4}$

D) No real solutions

You need to know this:

The quadratic formula can be used to solve any quadratic equation. It yields solutions to a quadratic equation that is written in standard form, $ax^2 + bx + c = 0$:

$$x = \frac{-b \pm \sqrt{b^2 - 4ac}}{2a}$$

The $\pm$ sign that follows $-b$ indicates that you will have two solutions, so remember to find both.

The expression under the radical ($b^2 - 4ac$) is called the **discriminant**, and its value determines the *number* of real solutions. If the discriminant is positive, the equation has two distinct real solutions. If the discriminant is equal to 0, there is only one distinct real solution. If the discriminant is negative, there are no real solutions because you cannot take the square root of a negative number.

The arithmetic can get complicated, so reserve the quadratic formula for equations that cannot be solved by factoring and those in which completing the square is difficult because $a \neq 1$.

You need to do this:

Get the quadratic equation into the form $ax^2 + bx + c = 0$. Then substitute a, b, and c into the quadratic formula and simplify.

Explanation:

In the given equation, $a = 2$, $b = -5$, and $c = -2$. Plug these values into the quadratic formula and simplify:

$$x = \frac{-b \pm \sqrt{b^2 - 4ac}}{2a}$$

$$x = \frac{-(-5) \pm \sqrt{(-5)^2 - 4(2)(-2)}}{2(2)}$$

$$x = \frac{5 \pm \sqrt{25 - (-16)}}{4}$$

$$x = \frac{5 \pm \sqrt{41}}{4}$$

$$x = \frac{5}{4} + \frac{\sqrt{41}}{4} \text{ and } x = \frac{5}{4} - \frac{\sqrt{41}}{4}$$

The correct answer is **(C)**.

If you find the quadratic formula to be challenging, study the formula and try these Drill questions before completing the following "Try on Your Own" questions. Drill answers can be found in the Check Your Work section at the end of the chapter.

Drill

a. $x^2 - 2x - 20 = 0$

b. $3x^2 - 5x - 2 = 0$

c. $-7x^2 + 14x + 24 = -4$

d. $0.3x^2 + 0.7x - 1 = 0$

e. $\frac{x^2}{2} - x\sqrt{2} - 2 = 0$

Try on Your Own

Directions

Take as much time as you need on these questions. Work carefully and methodically. There will be an opportunity for timed practice later in the book.

15

HINT: For Q15, use the discriminant.

Given the equation $2x^2 + 8x + 4 + 2z = 0$, for what value of z is there exactly one solution for x?

_____

16

The product of all the solutions to the equation $3v^2 + 4v - 2 = 0$ is M. What is the value of M?

(A) -3

(B) $-\dfrac{2}{3}$

(C) $-\dfrac{1}{3}$

(D) $\dfrac{4}{3}$

17

What are the solutions to the equation $4x^2 - 24x + 16 = 0$?

(A) $x = 3 \pm \sqrt{5}$

(B) $x = 4 \pm \sqrt{6}$

(C) $x = 5 \pm \sqrt{3}$

(D) $x = 5 \pm 2\sqrt{2}$

18

$$3x^2 = m(5x + v)$$

What are the values of x that satisfy the equation above, where m and v are constants?

(A) $x = -\dfrac{5m}{6} \pm \dfrac{\sqrt{25m^2 + 12mv}}{6}$

(B) $x = \dfrac{5m}{6} \pm \dfrac{\sqrt{25m^2 + 12mv}}{6}$

(C) $x = -\dfrac{5m}{3} \pm \dfrac{\sqrt{12m^2 + 25mv}}{3}$

(D) $x = \dfrac{5m}{3} \pm \dfrac{\sqrt{25m^2 + 12mv}}{3}$

19

HINT: For Q19, start with the standard form of a quadratic equation.

$$x(dx + 10) = -3$$

The equation shown, where d is a constant, has no real solutions. The value of d could be which of the following?

(A) -12

(B) 4

(C) 8

(D) 10

20

Which equation has no real solutions?

(A) $x^2 + 8x - 12 = 0$

(B) $x^2 - 8x + 12 = 0$

(C) $x^2 - 9x + 21 = 0$

(D) $x^2 + 100x - 1 = 0$

GRAPHS OF QUADRATICS

LEARNING OBJECTIVE

After this lesson, you will be able to:

- Relate properties of a quadratic function to its graph and vice versa

To answer a question like this:

Given the equation $y = -(2x - 4)^2 + 7$, which of the following statements is true?

A) The vertex is (4, 7).

B) The y-intercept is $(0, -9)$.

C) The parabola opens upward.

D) The graph does not cross the x-axis.

You need to know this:

A quadratic function is a quadratic equation set equal to y or $f(x)$ instead of 0. Remember that the solutions (also called "roots" or "zeros") of any polynomial function are the same as the x-intercepts. To solve a quadratic function, substitute 0 for y, or $f(x)$, then solve algebraically. Alternatively, you can plug the equation into your graphing calculator and read the x-intercepts from the graph. Take a look at the following examples to see this graphically.

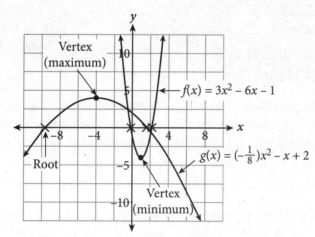

The graph of every quadratic equation (or function) is a **parabola**, which is a symmetric U-shaped graph that opens either upward or downward. To determine which way a parabola will open, examine the value of a in the quadratic equation. If a is positive, the parabola will open upward. If a is negative, it will open downward.

Like quadratic equations, quadratic functions will have zero, one, or two distinct real solutions, corresponding to the number of times the parabola touches or crosses the *x*-axis. Graphing is a powerful way to determine the number of solutions a quadratic function has.

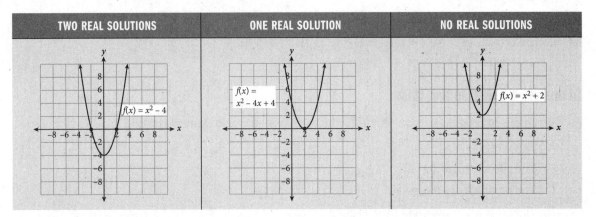

STANDARD	FACTORED	VERTEX
$y = ax^2 + bx + c$	$y = a(x - m)(x - n)$	$y = a(x - h)^2 + k$
The *y*-intercept is *c*.	Solutions are *m* and *n*.	The vertex is (h, k).
In real-world contexts, the starting quantity is *c*.	The *x*-intercepts are *m* and *n*.	The minimum/maximum of the function is *k*.
Can use quadratic formula to solve.	The vertex is halfway between *m* and *n*.	The axis of symmetry is given by $x = h$.

There are three algebraic forms that a quadratic equation can take: standard, factored, and vertex. Each is provided in the following table along with the graphical features that are revealed by writing the equation in that particular form.

You've already seen standard and factored forms earlier in this chapter, but vertex form might be new to you. In vertex form, *a* is the same as the *a* in standard form, and *h* and *k* are the coordinates of the **vertex** (h, k). If a quadratic function is not in vertex form, you can still find the *x*-coordinate of the vertex by plugging the appropriate values into the equation $h = \frac{-b}{2a}$, which is the quadratic formula without the discriminant. Once you determine *h*, plug this value into the quadratic function and solve for *y* to determine *k*, the *y*-coordinate of the vertex.

The equation of the **axis of symmetry** of a parabola is $x = h$, where *h* is the *x*-coordinate of the vertex.

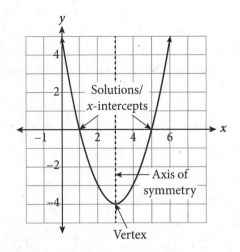

You need to do this:

- To find the vertex of a parabola, get the function into vertex form: $y = a(x - h)^2 + k$ or use the formula $h = \frac{-b}{2a}$.
- To find the y-intercept of a quadratic function, plug in 0 for x.
- To determine whether a parabola opens upward or downward, look at the coefficient of a. If a is positive, the parabola opens upward. If negative, it opens downward.
- To determine the number of x-intercepts, set the quadratic function equal to 0 and solve or examine its graph.
- Graph the function on a graphing calculator and efficiently interpret the results.

Explanation:

Be careful—the equation looks like vertex form, $y = a(x - h)^2 + k$, but it's not quite there because of the 2 inside the parentheses. You could rewrite the equation in vertex form, but this would involve squaring the quantity in parentheses and then completing the square, which would take quite a bit of time. Instead, use the graphing calculator to graph the function.

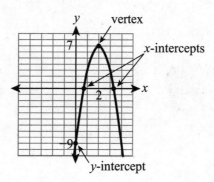

On the graph, you can see that the vertex is at (2, 7), not (4, 7). Eliminate (A). The y-intercept is indeed (0, −9); plugging 0 in for x will result in −9. Select **(B)** and move on. For the record, there is a negative in front of the squared term, so the parabola opens downward, not upward. (C) is incorrect. Because the parabola has a vertex of (2, 7) and opens downward, the parabola must cross the x-axis twice. (D) is incorrect.

Try on Your Own

Directions

Take as much time as you need on these questions. Work carefully and methodically. There will be an opportunity for timed practice later in the book.

21

HINT: For Q21, which form of a quadratic equation tells you the *x*-intercepts?

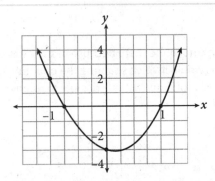

Which of the following equations represents the graph shown? Which equation represents the exact values of the *x*-intercepts of the graph?

Ⓐ $y = (4x - 3)(x + 1)$

Ⓑ $y = (4x + 3)(x - 1)$

Ⓒ $y = (3x - 4)(x + 1)$

Ⓓ $y = (3x + 4)(x - 1)$

22

HINT: For Q22, through which point on a parabola does the axis of symmetry pass?

Which equation represents the axis of symmetry for the graph of the quadratic function $f(x) = -\frac{11}{3}x^2 + 17x - \frac{43}{13}$?

Ⓐ $x = -\frac{102}{11}$

Ⓑ $x = -\frac{51}{22}$

Ⓒ $x = \frac{51}{22}$

Ⓓ $x = \frac{102}{11}$

23

$$f(x) = -(x - p)^2 + q$$

Which of the following represents the graph of $y = f(x)$ if $p < 0$ and $q > 0$?

(A)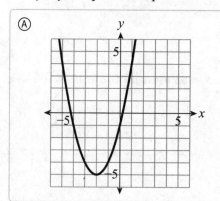

(B)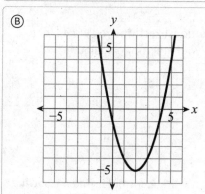

(C)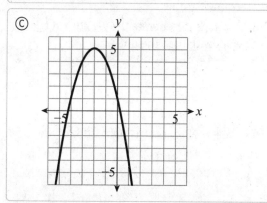

(D)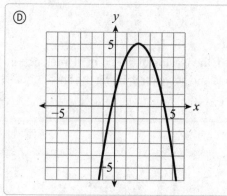

24

The graph of $y = a(x + 1)(x - 6)$ has a vertex at (h, k). What is the value of h?

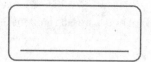

25

HINT: For Q25, what does "maximum height" correspond to on the graph of a quadratic equation?

A toy rocket is fired from ground level. The height of the rocket with respect to time can be represented by a quadratic function. If the toy rocket reaches a maximum height of 34 feet 3 seconds after it was fired, which of the following functions could represent the height, h, of the rocket t seconds after it was fired?

(A) $h(t) = -16(t - 3)^2 + 34$

(B) $h(t) = -16(t + 3)^2 + 34$

(C) $h(t) = 16(t - 3)^2 + 34$

(D) $h(t) = 16(t + 3)^2 + 34$

SYSTEMS OF QUADRATIC AND LINEAR EQUATIONS

LEARNING OBJECTIVE

After this lesson, you will be able to:

- Solve a system of one quadratic and one linear equation

To answer a question like this:

In the *xy*-plane, the graphs of $y + 3x = 5x^2 + 6$ and $y - 6 = 2x$ intersect at points (a, b) and (c, d), where $c > a$. What is the value of d?

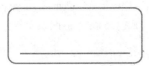

You need to know this:

You can solve a system of one quadratic and one linear equation by substitution, exactly as you would for a system of two linear equations. Alternatively, you can plug the system into your graphing calculator.

You need to do this:

- Isolate y in both equations.
- Set the equations equal to each other.
- Put the resulting equation into the form $ax^2 + bx + c = 0$.
- Solve this quadratic by factoring, completing the square, or using the quadratic formula. (You are solving for the x-values at the points of intersection of the original two equations.)
- Plug the x-values you get as solutions into one of the original equations to generate the y-values at the points of intersection. (Usually, the linear equation is easier to work with than the quadratic.)
- Graph the equations in the graphing calculator.

Explanation:

Start by isolating y in both equations to get $y = 5x^2 - 3x + 6$ and $y = 2x + 6$. Next, set the right sides of the equations equal to each other and solve for x:

$$5x^2 - 3x + 6 = 2x + 6$$
$$5x^2 - 5x = 0$$
$$5x(x - 1) = 0$$
$$x = 0 \text{ or } x = 1$$

The two points of intersection are (a, b) and (c, d) and you need to find d, the y-value of the point of intersection with the higher x-value, so plug $x = 1$ into either of the original equations and solve for y. Using the linear equation will be faster:

$$y = 2(1) + 6$$
$$y = 8$$

Therefore, the point (c, d) is $(1, 8)$. Enter **8**.

Alternatively, you could graph both equations in the graphing calculator and note the two points of intersection. Since it asks about the point of intersection with the higher *x*-value, inspect the point of intersection to the right on the graph to see that its *y*-value is **8**.

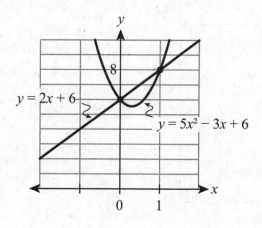

Try on Your Own

Directions

Take as much time as you need on these questions. Work carefully and methodically. There will be an opportunity for timed practice later in the book.

26

HINT: For Q26, note that both equations are equal to *a*.

$$a = b^2 + 4b - 12$$
$$a = -12 + b$$

The ordered pair (a, b) satisfies the system of equations shown. What is one possible value of *b*?

Ⓐ -6

Ⓑ -3

Ⓒ 2

Ⓓ 3

27

In the *xy*-coordinate plane, the graph of $y = 5x^2 - 12x$ intersects the graph of $y = -2x$ at points $(0, 0)$ and (a, b). What is the value of *a*?

28

The graph of $f(x) = x^2 + x$ intersects the graph of $g(x) = d$, where *d* is a constant, at exactly one point. What is the value of *d*?

29

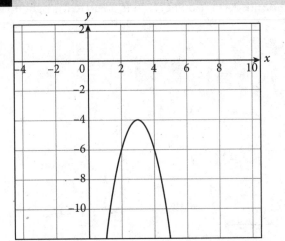

The graph of the function f, defined by $f(x) = -2(x-3)^2 - 4$, is shown in the xy-plane. The function g (not shown) is defined by $g(x) = 2x - 10$. If $f(c) = g(c)$, what is one possible value of c?

(A) -6

(B) -4

(C) 2

(D) 4

30

HINT: For Q30, solve for the points of intersection, then use the formula for distance in the coordinate plane.

On the xy-plane, points P and Q are the two points where the parabola with the equation $y = 3x^2 + \frac{14}{3}x - \frac{73}{3}$ and the line with the equation $y = -\frac{4}{3}x - \frac{1}{3}$ meet. What is the distance between point P and point Q?

(A) 5

(B) 8

(C) 10

(D) 12

ON TEST DAY

On the SAT, there is often more than one strategy that will get you to the answer. When a question involves a graph of two functions of *x* that intersect, you can either set the two functions equal to each other and solve for *x*, or you can use the coordinates of an intersection of the functions and set the values of both functions for that point equal to each other.

Try this question using both approaches. Which approach do you find easier? There's no right or wrong answer—just remember your preferred approach and use it if you see a question like this on test day.

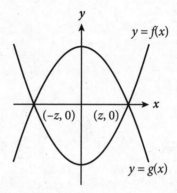

31. The functions $f(x) = 4x^2 - 25$ and $g(x) = -4x^2 + 25$ are graphed in the *xy*-plane. The points where the two functions intersect are $(z, 0)$ and $(-z, 0)$. What is the value of z?

A) 0.5

B) 1.0

C) 2.5

D) 4.0

The correct answer and both ways of solving can be found at the end of the chapter.

HOW MUCH HAVE YOU LEARNED?

Directions

For testlike practice, give yourself 17 minutes to complete this question set. Be sure to study the explanations, even for questions you got right. They can be found at the end of this chapter.

32

The equation $\frac{1}{4}(4x^2 - 8x - k) = 30$ has two solutions: $x = -5$ and $x = 7$. What is the value of k?

33

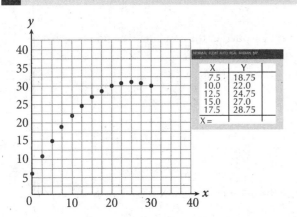

The maximum value of the data shown in the scatterplot occurs at $x = 25$. If the data is modeled using a quadratic regression and the correlation coefficient is 1.0 (the fit is exact), then what is the y-value when $x = 35$?

Ⓐ 10

Ⓑ 15

Ⓒ 22

Ⓓ 27

34

The height of a model rocket can be described as a function of time according to the following quadratic equation: $h(t) = -16t^2 + 224t + 240$. What is the maximum height that the rocket attains?

Ⓐ 240

Ⓑ 784

Ⓒ 1,024

Ⓓ 1,696

35

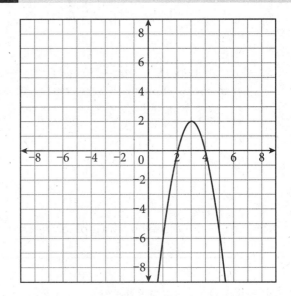

If the function in the graph is represented by $f(x) = a(x - h)^2 + k$, which of the following statements is false?

Ⓐ The value of a is negative.

Ⓑ $f(x)$ is symmetrical across the line $y = 3$.

Ⓒ The function $g(x) = \frac{2x}{3}$ intersects $f(x)$ at its vertex.

Ⓓ The value of h is positive.

36

$$y = -2$$
$$y = x^2 - 6x + 7$$

If point (a, b) is the only solution to the system of equations shown, what is the value of a?

37

What are the x-intercepts of the quadratic function $f(x) = x^2 - 7x + 8\frac{1}{4}$?

Ⓐ $-1\frac{1}{2}$ and $3\frac{1}{2}$

Ⓑ 1 and $8\frac{1}{4}$

Ⓒ $1\frac{1}{4}$ and $5\frac{3}{4}$

Ⓓ $1\frac{1}{2}$ and $5\frac{1}{2}$

38

If $g(x) = (x - 2)^2 - 5$, which of the following statements is true?

Ⓐ The function $g(x)$ is increasing over the entire domain.

Ⓑ The function $g(x)$ is decreasing over the entire domain.

Ⓒ The function $g(x)$ is increasing for $x < 2$ and decreasing for $x > 2$.

Ⓓ The function $g(x)$ is decreasing for $x < 2$ and increasing for $x > 2$.

39

$$4x - 12\sqrt{x} + 9 = 16$$

If the equation shown is true, what is the positive value of the expression $10\sqrt{x} - 15$?

Ⓐ 20

Ⓑ 25

Ⓒ 30

Ⓓ 35

40

Given the equation $5x^2 = 4x - z$, for what value of z is there exactly one solution for x?

41

If $x - 6 = \dfrac{-11}{x + 6}$, and $x < 0$, what is the value of x?

Ⓐ -11

Ⓑ -6

Ⓒ -5

Ⓓ 5

42

If $\dfrac{z^{x^2+y^2}}{z^{-2xy}} = \left(z^3\right)^3$, x and y are positive integers, $z > 3$, and $x > y$, what is the value of $x - y$?

- (A) 1
- (B) 2
- (C) 3
- (D) 8

REFLECT

Directions: Take a few minutes to recall what you've learned and what you've been practicing in this chapter. Consider the following questions, jot down your best answer for each one, and then compare your reflections to the expert responses that follow. Use your level of confidence to determine what to do next.

What features in a quadratic equation should you look for to decide whether to factor, complete the square, or apply the quadratic formula?

_____

_____

_____

Which constant in the vertex form of a quadratic function gives its maximum or minimum?

_____

_____

_____

Which form of a quadratic equation gives its y-intercept?

_____

_____

_____

Which form of a quadratic equation gives its x-intercepts, assuming the equation has two real roots?

_____

_____

_____

How do you solve a system of one linear and one quadratic equation?

_____

_____

_____

Expert Responses

What features in a quadratic equation should you look for to decide whether to factor, complete the square, or apply the quadratic formula?

Get the equation into standard form. If the coefficient in front of the squared term is 1, try factoring, but don't spend longer than about 15 seconds on the attempt. If you can't get the quadratic factored quickly, look at the coefficient on the middle term: if it is even, completing the square will be an efficient approach. Finally, the quadratic formula will work for any quadratic, no matter what the coefficients are.

Which constant in the vertex form of a quadratic function gives its maximum or minimum?

The vertex form is $y = a(x - h)^2 + k$. *The constant* k *is the* y*-value at the vertex, which occurs at the maximum or minimum.*

Which form of a quadratic equation gives its *y*-intercept?

In the standard form, $y = ax^2 + bx + c$, *the* y*-intercept is given by* c.

Which form of a quadratic equation gives its *x*-intercepts, assuming the equation has two real roots?

In the factored form, $y = a(x - m)(x - n)$, *the x-intercepts are at* $x = m$ *and* $x = n$.

How do you solve a system of one linear and one quadratic equation?

Put the linear equation in the form $y = mx + b$ *and the quadratic in the form* $y = ax^2 + bx + c$. *Either graph these and look for the intersection point(s) or set the right sides of the equations equal to each other and solve.*

Next Steps

If you answered most questions correctly in the "How Much Have You Learned?" section, and if your responses to the Reflect questions were similar to those of the SAT expert, then consider Quadratics an area of strength and move on to the next chapter. Come back to this topic periodically to prevent yourself from getting rusty.

If you don't yet feel confident, review those parts of this chapter that you have not yet mastered. In particular, study the table describing the different forms of quadratics in the Graphs of Quadratics lesson. Then try the questions you missed again. As always, be sure to review the explanations closely. Finally, **go online** (www.kaptest.com/moreonline) for additional practice on the highest yield topics in this chapter.

Check Your Work – Chapter 13

Drill Answers for Solving Quadratics by Factoring

a. $a^2 + 8a + 15 = (a + 3)(a + 5)$

b. $x^2 + 4x - 21 = (x - 3)(x + 7)$

c. $b^2 - 7b - 18 = (b + 2)(b - 9)$

d. $y^2 - 10y + 24 = (y - 4)(y - 6)$

e. $x^2 + \frac{1}{2}x - \frac{1}{2} = (x + 1)\left(x - \frac{1}{2}\right)$

f. $5x^2 + 10x + 5 = 5(x + 1)(x + 1)$

g. $2x^2 + 12x - 54 = 2(x - 3)(x + 9)$

h. $3x^2 - 6x + 3 = 3(x - 1)(x - 1)$

i. $x^2 + 3xy + 2y^2 = (x + y)(x + 2y)$

j. $4a^2 + 4ab - 8b^2 = 4(a - b)(a + 2b)$

Drill Answers for Completing the Square

a. $x = 5 \pm 3\sqrt{3}$

b. $x = -4 \pm \sqrt{10}$

c. $x = \dfrac{1 \pm 3\sqrt{5}}{2}$

d. $x = \dfrac{-1 \pm \sqrt{65}}{4}$

e. $x = 3a \pm a\sqrt{7}$

Drill Answers for The Quadratic Formula

a. $x = 1 \pm \sqrt{21}$

b. $x = 2, x = -\dfrac{1}{3}$

c. $x = 1 \pm \sqrt{5}$

d. $x = -\dfrac{10}{3}, x = 1$

e. $x = \sqrt{2} \pm \sqrt{6}$

Try on Your Own Answers

1. B
Difficulty: Easy
Category: Advanced Math
Getting to the Answer: FOIL the binomials $(6 - 5x)$ $(15x - 11)$. First: $(6)(15x) = 90x$. Outer: $(6)(-11) = -66$. Inner: $(-5x)(15x) = -75x^2$. Last: $(-5x)(-11) = 55x$. Combining like terms gives $90x - 66 - 75x^2 + 55x = -75x^2 + 145x - 66$. The correct answer is **(B)**.

2. C
Difficulty: Easy
Category: Advanced Math
Getting to the Answer: First, factor out a 3 in the denominator to make that quadratic a bit simpler. Next, factor the numerator and denominator using reverse-FOIL to reveal an $x - 5$ term that will cancel out.

$$\frac{x^2 - 10x + 25}{3x^2 - 9x - 30} = \frac{x^2 - 10x + 25}{3(x^2 - 3x - 10)}$$

$$= \frac{(x - 5)(x - 5)}{3(x - 5)(x + 2)} = \frac{x - 5}{3(x + 2)}$$

The correct answer is **(C)**.

3. 1
Difficulty: Medium
Category: Advanced Math
Getting to the Answer: An expression is undefined when it involves division by 0, so the key to the question is to recognize that the denominator will be 0 if either of the factors of the quadratic are 0. Factoring 2 out of the denominator leaves a relatively easy-to-factor quadratic:

$$\frac{3}{2x^2 + 4x - 6} = 0$$

$$\frac{3}{2(x^2 + 2x - 3)} = 0$$

$$\frac{3}{2(x + 3)(x - 1)} = 0$$

The denominator will be 0 if the value of x is either 1 or -3. Because the question asks for a positive value of x, enter **1**.

4. B
Difficulty: Medium
Category: Advanced Math
Getting to the Answer: Set the equation equal to zero and then divide by 3 to remove the x^2 coefficient:

$$3x^2 + 9x - 54 = 0$$
$$x^2 + 3x - 18 = 0$$
$$(x - 3)(x + 6) = 0$$
$$x = 3 \text{ or } -6$$

The question asks for the sum of the roots, which is $3 + (-6) = -3$. The correct answer is **(B)**.

5. A
Difficulty: Hard
Category: Advanced Math
Strategic Advice: The question asks for an equivalent expression, so ignore the function notation and focus on simplifying the polynomial so that it looks more like the answer choices.
Getting to the Answer: Expand the polynomial and distribute as necessary so that all of the parentheses are eliminated:

$$(1.3x - 3.9)^2 - (0.69x^2 - 0.14x - 9.79)$$
$$= (1.3x - 3.9)(1.3x - 3.9) - 0.69x^2 + 0.14x + 9.79$$
$$= 1.69x^2 - 10.14x + 15.21 - 0.69x^2 + 0.14x + 9.79$$

Combine like terms:

$$x^2 - 10x + 25$$

Then factor the polynomial by finding two integers that multiply to 25 and add up to -10: $x^2 - 10x + 25 = (x - 5)(x - 5) = (x - 5)^2$. **(A)** is correct.

6. C
Difficulty: Easy
Category: Advanced Math
Getting to the Answer: Expand both classic quadratics and combine like terms to find the sum:

$$(a - b)^2 + (a + b)^2$$
$$= (a^2 - 2ab + b^2) + (a^2 + 2ab + b^2)$$
$$= 2a^2 + 2b^2$$

This matches **(C)**.

7. 0
Difficulty: Medium
Category: Advanced Math
Getting to the Answer: To find the roots, set the equation equal to 0, factor it, and then solve. Clear the fraction the same way you do when solving equations, multiplying both sides of the equation by the denominator of the fraction:

$$0 = \frac{1}{3}x^2 - 2x + 3$$

$$3(0) = 3\left(\frac{1}{3}x^2 - 2x + 3\right)$$

$$0 = x^2 - 6x + 9$$
$$0 = (x - 3)(x - 3)$$

The equation has only one unique solution ($x = 3$), so the positive difference between the roots is $3 - 3 = 0$. Enter **0**.

8. 4
Difficulty: Hard
Category: Advanced Math
Getting to the Answer: A fraction is undefined when the denominator equals 0. To find the value of x where $f(x)$ is undefined, set the denominator equal to 0 and solve for x.

The equation $(x - 7)^2 + 6(x - 7) + 9 = 0$ is the expansion of the classic quadratic $a^2 + 2ab + b^2 = (a + b)^2$, where $a = (x - 7)$ and $b = 3$, so the denominator will factor as $[(x - 7) + 3]^2$. That's equivalent to $(x - 4)^2$. Set this expression equal to 0 to find that the function is undefined when $x - 4 = 0$, or $x = 4$. Enter **4**.

9. B
Difficulty: Medium
Category: Advanced Math
Getting to the Answer: Start by noticing that $x^4 - 196$ is a difference of perfect squares. Use the pattern for difference of squares $a^2 - b^2 = (a + b)(a - b)$ where $x^4 - 196 = (x^2 + 14)(x^2 - 14)$. Because area is length times width ($A = lw$) and the width is $x^2 - 14$, the length must be $x^2 + 14$. Choice **(B)** is correct.

10. B
Difficulty: Medium
Category: Advanced Math
Strategic Advice: Recognizing the classic quadratic $(x - y)^2 = x^2 - 2xy + y^2$ will save you time when factoring.

Getting to the Answer: In this question, the goal is to manipulate the polynomial so that it matches the factored form given. First, recognize that 2 can be factored out. The resulting expression is then $2(x^2 - 14x + 49)$. Notice that $\sqrt{49} = 7$ and factor the quadratic to get $2(x - 7)(x - 7) = 2(x - 7)^2$. Now the expression is in the same form as $a(x - b)^2$. Therefore, $b = 7$, so **(B)** is correct.

11. D

Difficulty: Medium

Category: Advanced Math

Getting to the Answer: Factoring won't work here because no two factors of -5 sum to 2. However, the coefficient of x^2 is 1, so try completing the square:

$$x^2 + 2x - 5 = 0$$
$$x^2 + 2x = 5$$
$$\left(\frac{b}{2}\right)^2 = \left(\frac{2}{2}\right)^2 = 1^2 = 1$$
$$x^2 + 2x + 1 = 5 + 1$$
$$(x + 1)^2 = 6$$
$$x + 1 = \pm\sqrt{6}$$
$$x = -1 \pm \sqrt{6}$$

(D) matches one of the two possible values of x, so it's correct.

12. D

Difficulty: Medium

Category: Advanced Math

Getting to the Answer: To complete the square, restate this as $a^2 - 12a = 72$. One-half of the x-coefficient is -6, which, when squared, becomes 36. So, $a^2 - 12a + 36 = 108$. Factor to find that $(a - 6)^2 = 108$ and then take the square root of both sides to get $a - 6 = \pm\sqrt{108}$. Since $108 = 36 \times 3$, the radical simplifies to $6\sqrt{3}$.

Since the question asks for the root with the greatest value, you can ignore the root with the minus sign, so $a = 6 + 6\sqrt{3} = 6(1 + \sqrt{3})$. **(D)** is correct.

13. C

Difficulty: Hard

Category: Advanced Math

Getting to the Answer: The radical looks as if it will make the calculation difficult, but it will drop out when you complete the square. The coefficient, b, is $6\sqrt{5}$, so $\left(\frac{6\sqrt{5}}{2}\right)^2 = \left(\frac{36 \times 5}{4}\right) = 45$. Adding 45 to both sides of the equation gives you $x^2 - (6\sqrt{5})x + 45 = 5$, so the factored form is $(x - 3\sqrt{5})^2 = 5$. Take the square root of both sides to get $x - 3\sqrt{5} = \pm\sqrt{5}$. The two possible values of x are $3\sqrt{5} + \sqrt{5} = 4\sqrt{5}$ and $3\sqrt{5} - \sqrt{5} = 2\sqrt{5}$. The question asks for the sum of these values, which is $4\sqrt{5} + 2\sqrt{5} = 6\sqrt{5}$. **(C)** is correct.

14. B

Difficulty: Medium

Category: Advanced Math

Getting to the Answer: Rewrite the equation of the graph by completing the square. The coefficient, b, is 4, so $\left(\frac{4}{2}\right)^2 = 2^2 = 4$. Completing the square gives you $y + 4 = x^2 + 4x + 4 - 4$. Isolate y and then factor.

$$y = x^2 + 4x + 4 - 4 - 4$$
$$y = (x + 2)^2 - 8$$

(B) is correct.

In the upcoming lesson, Graphs of Quadratics, you'll see how to solve this question by noting that in this form, the vertex of the parabola can be read: $(-2, -8)$.

15. 2

Difficulty: Hard

Category: Advanced Math

Strategic Advice: Recall that when the value of the discriminant, $b^2 - 4ac$, is 0, there is exactly one solution to the quadratic equation.

Getting to the Answer: The given equation is $2x^2 + 8x + 4 + 2z = 0$, but there is a common factor of 2 in all the terms, so this becomes $x^2 + 4x + 2 + z = 0$. Thus, $a = 1$, $b = 4$, and $c = 2 + z$. Set the discriminant $4^2 - 4(1)(2 + z)$ equal to 0 so that there is only one solution. Expand the equation to $16 - 8 - 4z = 0$. Thus, $8 = 4z$, and $z = 2$. Enter **2**.

16. B

Difficulty: Hard

Category: Advanced Math

Getting to the Answer: The question presents a quadratic equation that cannot be easily factored. Therefore, use the quadratic formula to solve. The quadratic formula states that $x = \dfrac{-b \pm \sqrt{b^2 - 4ac}}{2a}$.

In this case, $a = 3$, $b = 4$, and $c = -2$. Plug in these values to get:

$$x = \frac{-4 \pm \sqrt{4^2 - 4(3)(-2)}}{2(3)}$$
$$= \frac{-4 \pm \sqrt{16 - (-24)}}{6}$$
$$= \frac{-4 \pm \sqrt{40}}{6}$$

Thus, the solutions to the equation are $\dfrac{-4+\sqrt{40}}{6}$ and $\dfrac{-4-\sqrt{40}}{6}$. The question asks for their product, so multiply the solutions:

$$\left(\frac{-4+\sqrt{40}}{6}\right)\left(\frac{-4-\sqrt{40}}{6}\right)$$

$$=\frac{16+4\sqrt{40}-4\sqrt{40}-40}{36}$$

$$=\frac{-24}{36}$$

$$=-\frac{2}{3}$$

(B) is correct.

17. A

Difficulty: Medium
Category: Advanced Math
Strategic Advice: When all of the coefficients in a quadratic equation are divisible by a common factor, simplify the equation by dividing all terms by that factor before solving.
Getting to the Answer: The given equation is $4x^2 - 24x + 16 = 0$, but there is a common factor of 4 in all the terms, so this becomes $x^2 - 6x + 4 = 0$.

The radicals in the answer choices are a strong clue that the quadratic formula is the way to solve this equation. The quadratic formula is $x = \dfrac{-b \pm \sqrt{b^2 - 4ac}}{2a}$, and after you plug in the coefficients, $a = 1$, $b = -6$, and $c = 4$, you get:

$$x = \frac{-(-6) \pm \sqrt{(-6)^2 - 4(1)(4)}}{2(1)}$$

$$= \frac{6 \pm \sqrt{36 - 16}}{2}$$

$$= \frac{6 \pm \sqrt{20}}{2}$$

This doesn't resemble any of the answer choices, so continue simplifying:

$$\frac{6 \pm \sqrt{20}}{2}$$

$$= \frac{6 \pm \sqrt{4}\sqrt{5}}{2}$$

$$= \frac{6 \pm 2\sqrt{5}}{2}$$

$$= \frac{6}{2} \pm \frac{2\sqrt{5}}{2}$$

$$= 3 \pm \sqrt{5}$$

Hence, **(A)** is correct.

18. B

Difficulty: Hard
Category: Advanced Math
Getting to the Answer: A glance at the radicals in the answer choices suggests that using the quadratic formula to solve is appropriate. Because there are so many variables, it might help to write down the quadratic formula on your scratch paper as a guide: $x = \dfrac{-b \pm \sqrt{b^2 - 4ac}}{2a}$.

Begin by reorganizing the quadratic into the standard form $ax^2 + bx + c = 0$:

$$3x^2 = m(5x + v)$$
$$3x^2 = 5mx + mv$$
$$3x^2 - 5mx - mv = 0$$

In this case, $a = 3$, $b = -5m$, and $c = -mv$. Now solve:

$$x = \frac{-(-5m) \pm \sqrt{(-5m)^2 - 4(3)(-mv)}}{2(3)}$$

$$= \frac{5m \pm \sqrt{25m^2 - (-12mv)}}{6}$$

$$= \frac{5m \pm \sqrt{25m^2 + 12mv}}{6}$$

$$= \frac{5m}{6} \pm \frac{\sqrt{25m^2 + 12mv}}{6}$$

Therefore, **(B)** is correct.

19. D

Difficulty: Medium
Category: Advanced Math
Getting to the Answer: Get the equation $x(dx + 10) = -3$ into the form $ax^2 + bx + c = 0$. Multiply out the left side of the equation $x(dx + 10) = -3$ to get $dx^2 + 10x = -3$. Add 3 to both sides to obtain $dx^2 + 10x + 3 = 0$.

The equation $ax^2 + bx + c = 0$ (when $a \neq 0$) does not have real solutions if the discriminant, which is $b^2 - 4ac$, is negative. In the equation $dx^2 + 10x + 3 = 0$, $a = d$, $b = 10$, and $c = 3$. The discriminant in this question is $10^2 - 4(d)(3) = 100 - 12d$.

Since you're looking for a negative discriminant, that is, $b^2 - 4ac < 0$, you need $100 - 12d < 0$. Solve the inequality $100 - 12d < 0$ for d:

$$100 - 12d < 0$$
$$100 < 12d$$
$$\frac{100}{12} < d$$
$$\frac{25}{3} < d$$
$$8\frac{1}{3} < d$$

Among the answer choices, only 10 is greater than $8\frac{1}{3}$, so **(D)** is correct.

20. C
Difficulty: Medium
Category: Advanced Math
Getting to the Answer: Recall that when a quadratic equation has no real solutions, its discriminant, which is $b^2 - 4ac$, will be less than 0. Calculate the discriminant of each answer choice and pick the one that's negative. You don't need to actually solve for x.

(A): $8^2 - 4(1)(-12) = 64 + 48 > 0$. Eliminate.

(B): $(-8)^2 - 4(1)(12) = 64 - 48 > 0$. Eliminate.

(C): $(-9)^2 - 4(1)(21) = 81 - 84 = -3 < 0$. Pick **(C)** and move on. For the record:

(D): $(100)^2 - 4(1)(-1) = 10,000 + 4 > 0$. Eliminate.

21. B
Difficulty: Easy
Category: Advanced Math
Getting to the Answer: The factored form of a quadratic equation makes it easy to find the solutions to the equation, which graphically represent the x-intercepts. The graph shows x-intercepts at $x = -\frac{3}{4}$ and $x = 1$. For each answer choice, set each factor equal to 0 and quickly solve to find the x-intercepts and see which ones agree with the graph.

(A): $x = \frac{3}{4}$ and $x = -1$. This does not match the graph; eliminate.

(B): $x = -\frac{3}{4}$ and $x = 1$. This matches the graph, so **(B)** is correct. You do not need to check the remaining choices.

22. C
Difficulty: Medium
Category: Advanced Math
Getting to the Answer: An axis of symmetry splits a parabola in half and travels through the vertex. Use the formula to find h, plug in the correct values from the equation, and simplify:

$$x = -\frac{b}{2a}$$
$$= -\frac{17}{2\left(\frac{-11}{3}\right)}$$
$$= -\frac{17}{\left(\frac{-22}{3}\right)}$$
$$= -17 \cdot \frac{-3}{22}$$
$$= \frac{51}{22}$$

The correct answer is **(C)**. Note that you could have also graphed the function on your calculator to determine the axis of symmetry. Use the approach that is best for you.

23. C
Difficulty: Medium
Category: Advanced Math
Getting to the Answer: The given function is in vertex form, $y = a(x - h)^2 + k$, where (h, k) is the vertex and the sign of a indicates whether the parabola opens up or down. Since $a = -1$ for $f(x) = -(x - p)^2 + q$, the parabola opens downward. Eliminate (A) and (B). The vertex is (p, q), and the question tells you that p is negative, so **(C)** is correct.

24. 5/2 or 2.5
Difficulty: Easy
Category: Advanced Math
Getting to the Answer: The factored form of the equation $y = a(x + 1)(x - 6)$ tells you that the x-intercepts of the parabola are -1 and 6. The x-coordinate of the vertex (h) is the axis of symmetry, which is halfway between the x-intercepts. Thus, $h = \frac{-1 + 6}{2} = \frac{5}{2}$.

Enter **5/2** or **2.5**.

25. A
Difficulty: Hard
Category: Advanced Math
Getting to the Answer: The answer choices are all similar, so pay careful attention to their differences and see if you can eliminate any choices logically. A rocket goes up and then comes down, which means that the graph will be a parabola opening downward. The equation, therefore, should have a negative sign in front. Eliminate (C) and (D).

To evaluate the two remaining choices, recall the *vertex form* of a quadratic, $y = a(x - h)^2 + k$, and what it tells you: the vertex of the graph is (h, k). The h is the x-coordinate of the maximum (or minimum) and k is the y-coordinate of the maximum (or minimum). In this situation, x has been replaced by t, or time, and y is now $h(t)$, or height. The question says that the maximum height occurs at 3 seconds and is 34 feet, so h is 3 and k is 34. Substitute these values into vertex form to find that the correct equation is $y = -16(x - 3)^2 + 34$. The function that matches is **(A)**.

26. B
Difficulty: Medium
Category: Advanced Math
Strategic Advice: Because each of the two expressions containing b is equal to a, the two expressions must be equal to each other.
Getting to the Answer: Set the two expressions equal to each other and then solve for b:

$$b^2 + 4b - 12 = -12 + b$$
$$b^2 + 4b = b$$
$$b^2 + 3b = 0$$
$$b(b + 3) = 0$$

If $b(b + 3) = 0$, then $b = 0$ or $b = -3$. Of these two values, only -3 is among the answer choices, so **(B)** is correct.

27. 2
Difficulty: Medium
Category: Advanced Math
Getting to the Answer: The points of intersection of the graphs are the points at which the equations are equal. Since (a, b) is the label for an (x, y) point, set the two equations equal to each other and solve for the value of x to find the value of a:

$$-2x = 5x^2 - 12x$$
$$0 = 5x^2 - 10x$$
$$0 = 5x(x - 2)$$

Thus, $x = 0$ or $x = 2$. The question states that the intersection points are $(0, 0)$ and (a, b), so a must equal 2. Enter **2**.

Alternatively, you could graph the two equations on the calculator to determine the point of intersection.

28. −1/4, −0.25, or −.25
Difficulty: Hard
Category: Advanced Math
Getting to the Answer: Since $f(x)$ and $g(x)$ intersect, set the equations equal to each other: $x^2 + x = d$. Then subtract d from both sides to set the quadratic equal to 0: $x^2 + x - d = 0$.

Recall that when there is exactly one solution, the discriminant, $b^2 - 4ac$, equals 0. In the equation $x^2 + x - d = 0$, $a = 1$, $b = 1$, and $c = -d$. Therefore, $1^2 - 4(1)(-d) = 0$. Solving for d gives $d = -\frac{1}{4}$. Enter **−1/4, −0.25, or −.25**

29. C
Difficulty: Hard
Category: Advanced Math
Getting to the Answer: Because the question states that $f(c) = g(c)$, set the two functions equal to each other and solve for x. To make calculations easier, begin by converting $f(x)$ into standard form:

$$f(x) = -2(x - 3)^2 - 4$$
$$= -2(x - 3)(x - 3) - 4$$
$$= -2(x^2 - 6x + 9) - 4$$
$$= -2x^2 + 12x - 18 - 4$$
$$= -2x^2 + 12x - 22$$

Now set the two functions equal to each other:

$$-2x^2 + 12x - 22 = 2x - 10$$

Simplify by dividing all terms by -2:

$$x^2 - 6x + 11 = -x + 5$$

Next, combine like terms and solve for x:

$$x^2 - 6x + 11 = -x + 5$$
$$x^2 - 5x + 6 = 0$$
$$(x - 2)(x - 3) = 0$$

Therefore, $x = 2$ or $x = 3$, which means that c could also be either 2 or 3. Because 3 is not an answer choice, the answer must be 2. **(C)** is correct.

If you find it faster, you could graph the two functions to determine the points of intersection.

30. C
Difficulty: Hard
Category: Advanced Math
Strategic Advice: When you need to find the points of intersection of two equations, set the equations equal to each other.
Getting to the Answer: The question indicates that points P and Q are the points of intersection of the two equations, so set the two equations equal to each other and consolidate terms to get a single quadratic equation equal to 0:

$$3x^2 + \frac{14}{3}x - \frac{73}{3} = -\frac{4}{3}x - \frac{1}{3}$$

$$3x^2 + \frac{18}{3}x - \frac{72}{3} = 0$$

$$3x^2 + 6x - 24 = 0$$

$$x^2 + 2x - 8 = 0$$

Factor the equation to find the values of x:

$$x^2 + 2x - 8 = 0$$

$$(x+4)(x-2) = 0$$

$$x = -4 \text{ or } 2$$

You can plug each value of x into either of the original equations to find the corresponding values of y, but the linear equation is easier to work with. For $x = -4$:

$$y = -\frac{4}{3}(-4) - \frac{1}{3}$$

$$y = \frac{16}{3} - \frac{1}{3}$$

$$y = \frac{15}{3} = 5$$

Therefore, one of the points of intersection is $(-4, 5)$. Find the other point of intersection by plugging $x = 2$ into the linear equation:

$$y = -\frac{4}{3}(2) - \frac{1}{3}$$

$$y = -\frac{8}{3} - \frac{1}{3}$$

$$y = -\frac{9}{3} = -3$$

Thus, the other point of intersection is $(2, -3)$.

Note that you could have also found the points of intersection by graphing the two equations.

The question asks for the distance between these two points. The formula for the distance, d, between the points (x_1, y_1) and (x_2, y_2) is $d = \sqrt{(x_2 - x_1)^2 + (y_2 - y_1)^2}$. Find the distance between points P and Q:

$$d = \sqrt{(-4 - 2)^2 + (5 - (-3))^2}$$

$$= \sqrt{(-6)^2 + 8^2}$$

$$= \sqrt{36 + 64}$$

$$= \sqrt{100}$$

$$= 10$$

Therefore, the distance between points P and Q is 10. **(C)** is correct.

31. C
Difficulty: Medium
Category: Advanced Math
Getting to the Answer: The first approach is to set $f(x)$ equal to $g(x)$: $4x^2 - 25 = -4x^2 + 25$. Isolate the x^2 terms on one side to get $8x^2 = 50$, so $x^2 = \frac{50}{8} = \frac{25}{4}$. Take the square root of both sides to see that $x = \pm\frac{5}{2} = \pm 2.5$, which means that the two intersections of the functions occur where $x = -2.5$ and $x = 2.5$. From the graph, you can see that these are the values of $\pm z$, so $z = 2.5$. **(C)** is correct. (Note that even if you had not been given the y-coordinates of the points of intersection, you could have calculated them from knowing their corresponding x-coordinates.)

The second approach is to plug in the coordinates of one of the intersections into either function. Using $f(x)$, the y-coordinate is 0 and the x-coordinate is z. So, $0 = 4z^2 - 25$. The math works out exactly the same as the first method: $4z^2 = 25$, so $z = \pm 2.5$. Note that you could also graph the functions on the calculator to identify the points of intersection.

32. 20
Difficulty: Medium
Category: Advanced Math
Getting to the Answer: Since the given equation is valid for both $x = -5$ and $x = 7$, you can plug in either of those values and solve for k. Using 7 as the value of x gives you $\frac{1}{4}(4(7)^2 - 8(7) - k) = 30$. Multiply both sides by 4 to get $4(49) - 56 - k = 120$. Thus, $-k = 120 - 196 + 56 = -20$, so $k = 20$. Enter **20**.

33. D
Difficulty: Hard
Category: Advanced Math
Getting to the Answer: Because the quadratic regression is an exact fit of the data, you can treat the data points as a quadratic function.

The graph of a quadratic function (a parabola) is symmetric with respect to its axis of symmetry, which passes through the x-value of the vertex, or the maximum (or minimum) of the function. The question tells you the maximum occurs at $x = 25$, which makes it the line of symmetry. Because 35 is $35 - 25 = 10$ units to the right of the axis of symmetry, you know that the y-value will be the same as the point that is 10 units to the left of the axis of symmetry, which is $x = 25 - 10 = 15$. Find the corresponding y-value in the table: 27. Therefore, **(D)** is correct.

34. C
Difficulty: Hard
Category: Advanced Math
Getting to the Answer: Because the height of the rocket is expressed as a quadratic equation with a negative t^2 coefficient, its path is a downward-facing parabola. Therefore, the maximum height occurs at the vertex of the parabola. The t-coordinate (generally called the x-coordinate) of the vertex of a parabola is given by $t = \frac{-b}{2a} = \frac{-224}{2(-16)} = 7$, where a and b come from the standard form of a quadratic, $h(t) = at^2 + bt + c$. Plug the result into the function to get the h-coordinate (the y-coordinate of the vertex): $h(7) = -16(7)^2 + 224(7) + 240 = 1,024$. **(C)** is correct.

35. B
Difficulty: Medium
Category: Advanced Math
Getting to the Answer: Keep in mind that the question asks for the statement that's false, so eliminate the true choices as you go, from easiest to hardest to check. The parabola opens downward, so the a term must be negative. Eliminate (A). The parabola's vertex is in quadrant I, so h and k are both positive. That makes choice (D) true as well; eliminate it. According to the graph, the vertex is (3, 2). The axis of symmetry is $x = h$, so $x = 3$. Choice (B), however, claims that the axis of symmetry is $y = 3$. Choice **(B)** is false and is therefore the correct answer.

For the record, (C) is a true statement because the line $g(x) = \frac{2x}{3}$ passes through the point (3, 2), which is indeed the vertex of $f(x)$.

36. 3
Difficulty: Medium
Category: Advanced Math
Getting to the Answer: The question is asking for a, which is the x-value of the solution point of the system of equations. It also tells you that $y = -2$, so solving the system using substitution is a good option:

$$-2 = x^2 - 6x + 7$$
$$0 = x^2 - 6x + 9$$
$$0 = (x - 3)(x - 3)$$
$$0 = (x - 3)$$
$$3 = x$$

Thus, $a = 3$. Enter **3**.

37. D
Difficulty: Hard
Category: Advanced Math
Getting to the Answer: The x-intercepts of a function are the values of x that make the function equal to 0. Factoring this function would be cumbersome because you would need to determine two numbers whose product is $8\frac{1}{4}$ and whose sum is -7. You could solve with the quadratic formula or completing the square.

To solve with completing the square: start with $x^2 - 7x + 8\frac{1}{4} = 0$, then subtract $8\frac{1}{4}$ from each side to get $x^2 - 7x = -8\frac{1}{4}$. Half of the b-coefficient, -7, is $-3\frac{1}{2}$, which, when squared, is $12\frac{1}{4}$. Add that to both sides to get $x^2 - 7x + 12\frac{1}{4} = 4$. So $\left(x - 3\frac{1}{2}\right)^2 = 4$.

Take the square root of both sides to get $x - 3\frac{1}{2} = \pm 2$.

Therefore, the x-intercepts are $3\frac{1}{2} \pm 2$, or $1\frac{1}{2}$ and $5\frac{1}{2}$.

(D) is correct.

38. D
Difficulty: Medium
Category: Advanced Math
Getting to the Answer: Either graph this equation on your graphing calculator or draw out a quick sketch on scratch paper:

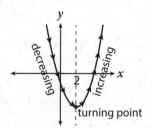

Based on the equation, the graph is a parabola that opens upward with a vertex of $(2, -5)$. A parabola changes direction at the x-coordinate of its vertex. You can immediately eliminate (A) and (B). To the left of 2 on the x-axis (or $x < 2$), the parabola is decreasing, and to the right of 2 on the x-axis (or $x > 2$), it is increasing. **(D)** is correct.

39. A
Difficulty: Hard
Category: Advanced Math
Strategic Advice: Technically, this isn't a quadratic equation because the highest power on the variable isn't 2. However, it is a "quadratic-type" equation because the square of the variable part of the middle term is equal to the variable in the leading term. In other words, squaring $\sqrt{x}$ gives you x. You can use factoring techniques you learned for quadratics to answer the question.
Getting to the Answer: The presence of 4, 9, and 16—all perfect squares—is a big clue. Note that $4x - 12\sqrt{x} + 9$ is an instance of the classic quadratic $(a - b)^2 = a^2 - 2ab + b^2$. Use this shortcut to factor the equation and see where that leads you:

$$4x - 12\sqrt{x} + 9 = 16$$
$$(2\sqrt{x} - 3)^2 = 16$$
$$2\sqrt{x} - 3 = \pm 4$$

The question asks for $10\sqrt{x} - 15$, which happens to be 5 times the quantity on the left side of the last equation above, so multiply the positive result, 4, (-4 is an extraneous solution and can be ignored) by 5 to get 20. The correct answer is **(A)**.

40. 16/20, 4/5, or 0.8
Difficulty: Medium
Category: Advanced Math
Strategic Advice: Recall that when the value of the discriminant, $b^2 - 4ac$, is 0, there is exactly one solution to the quadratic equation.
Getting to the Answer: First set the given equation equal to 0 by rearranging it into the standard quadratic form: $5x^2 - 4x + z = 0$. Now determine the values in the discriminant: $a = 5$, $b = -4$, and $c = z$. So the discriminant is $(-4)^2 - 4(5)(z)$. Simplify this and set

it equal to 0 (meaning there is only one solution) and then solve for z:

$$16 - 20z = 0$$
$$16 = 20z$$
$$\frac{16}{20} = z$$
$$\frac{4}{5} = z$$

Enter **16/20, 4/5,** or **0.8**.

41. C
Difficulty: Medium
Category: Advanced Math
Getting to the Answer: This is a good candidate to solve by backsolving. There's no need to try choice (D) as the question specifies that $x < 0$, and the only negative number from the answer choices that you can plug into the equation to make it work is **(C)**. To solve with straightforward math: get the x-terms to one side of the equation by multiplying both sides by the denominator, $x + 6$. This yields $(x - 6)(x + 6) = -11$. You might recognize that the left side of this equation is the classic quadratic known as the "difference of squares." This simplifies to $x^2 - 6^2 = -11$. Now solve for x:

$$x^2 - 36 = -11$$
$$x^2 = 25$$
$$x = \pm 5$$

The question specifies that $x < 0$, so **(C)** is also correct using this strategy.

42. A
Difficulty: Hard
Category: Advanced Math
Getting to the Answer: Use exponent rules to simplify the fraction. Since the terms in the numerator and denominator have the same base, z, subtract the exponent of the denominator from that of the numerator: $z^{x^2 + y^2 - (-2xy)} = z^{x^2 + 2xy + y^2}$. When a value with an exponent is raised to another exponent, multiply the exponents. So, for the term on the right side, $(z^3)^3 = z^9$. Now the equation is $z^{x^2 + 2xy + y^2} = z^9$. Since both sides have the common base, z, their exponents must be equal and you can write $x^2 + 2xy + y^2 = 9$.

Factor $x^2 + 2xy + y^2$, a classic quadratic, to get $(x + y)^2 = 9$. Thus, $x + y$ must be either 3 or -3. However, the question limits x and y to positive integers, so they must be 1 and 2. Furthermore, since $x > y$, x must be 2 and y must be 1. Consequently, $x - y = 2 - 1 = 1$. **(A)** is correct.

HOW MUCH HAVE YOU LEARNED: ADVANCED MATH

Directions

This "How Much Have You Learned?" section will allow you to measure your growth and confidence in Advanced Math skills.

For test-like practice, give yourself 15 minutes for this question set. Be sure to use the Method for SAT Math Questions. When you're done, check your answers and read through the explanations, even for the questions you answered correctly. Don't forget to celebrate your progress!

1

If $|5a| = 2a - 15$, which of the following gives all possible values of a?

Ⓐ -5

Ⓑ $\dfrac{15}{7}$

Ⓒ $-5, \dfrac{15}{7}$

Ⓓ No solution

2

If the quadratic equation $y = 4(x + 3)^2 + 7$ is rewritten in standard form, $y = ax^2 + bx + c$, what is the value of $b + c$?

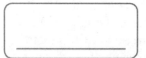

3

Which of the following is equivalent to $\sqrt{0.5} \times \sqrt{0.4}$?

Ⓐ $\dfrac{1}{5}$

Ⓑ $\dfrac{\sqrt{5}}{5}$

Ⓒ $\sqrt[4]{0.2}$

Ⓓ $\sqrt{0.9}$

4

Which of the following is equivalent to the expression $\dfrac{\sqrt[3]{8a^9 b^6}}{a b^2}$?

Ⓐ $2a^2$

Ⓑ $\dfrac{2a^2}{b}$

Ⓒ $8a^2 b$

Ⓓ $\dfrac{8a^2}{b^3}$

5

If $h(x) = x^2 + 14$, what is the minimum value of $h(x)$?

6

The vertex of the parabola given by $y = 2x^2 - 8x - 3$ is at point (h, k). What is the value of k?

7

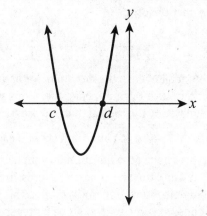

If c is three times farther from the origin than d in the figure shown, which of the following could be the factored form of the graph's equation?

Ⓐ $y = (x + 2)(2x + 12)$

Ⓑ $y = (x - 2)(2x - 12)$

Ⓒ $y = (3x + 3)(x + 4)$

Ⓓ $y = (x + 2)(3x + 12)$

8

If $f(x) = \dfrac{x^2 + 5x + 10}{3x}$ and $g(x) = x + 4$, what is $f(g(1))$?

Ⓐ 1

Ⓑ 4

Ⓒ 15

Ⓓ 60

9

Which of the following best describes the solutions to the rational equation $\dfrac{2}{x+3} - \dfrac{-12}{x^2 - 9} = 1$?

Ⓐ No solution

Ⓑ Two extraneous solutions

Ⓒ Two valid solutions

Ⓓ One valid solution and one extraneous solution

10

If $f(x) = 2x^2 - 14x + 20$, $g(x) = x - 5$, and $x = 10$, what is the value of $\dfrac{f(x)}{g(x)}$?

Ⓐ 5

Ⓑ 16

Ⓒ 80

Ⓓ 160

Check Your Work – How Much Have You Learned: Advanced Math

1.   D
Difficulty: Medium
Category: Advanced Math
Getting to the Answer: With absolute value equations, you must solve twice: once for the positive version of the given value and once for the negative version of that value. Start by solving for the positive version:

$$5a = 2a - 15$$
$$3a = -15$$
$$a = -5$$

However, plugging -5 back into the right side of the original equation yields $2(-5) - 15 = -25$. Since an absolute value can never be negative, -5 is not a solution; therefore, you can eliminate (A) and (C). Next, solve for the negative version:

$$5a = -2a + 15$$
$$7a = 15$$
$$a = \frac{15}{7}$$

Again, when you plug $\frac{15}{7}$ into the right side of the original equation, you get

$$2\left(\frac{15}{7}\right) - 15 = \frac{30}{7} - 15 = \frac{30}{7} - \frac{105}{7} = -\frac{75}{7}.$$

That's a negative value, so $\frac{15}{7}$ is not a solution either.

There is no solution, so **(D)** is correct.

2.   67
Difficulty: Medium
Category: Advanced Math
Getting to the Answer: Use FOIL to expand the vertex form of the quadratic into standard form:

$$y = 4(x + 3)^2 + 7$$
$$= 4(x + 3)(x + 3) + 7$$
$$= 4(x^2 + 3x + 3x + 9) + 7$$
$$= 4(x^2 + 6x + 9) + 7$$
$$= 4x^2 + 24x + 36 + 7$$
$$= 4x^2 + 24x + 43$$

The question asks for the value of $b + c$, which is $24 + 43 = 67$, so enter **67**.

3.   B
Difficulty: Medium
Category: Advanced Math
Getting to the Answer: Start by multiplying and combining the values under each root:

$$\sqrt{0.5} \times \sqrt{0.4} = \sqrt{0.5 \times 0.4} = \sqrt{0.2}$$

When you have a root of a decimal, you can simplify by changing the decimal to a fraction. Then simplify the root of the fraction form:

$$\sqrt{0.2} = \sqrt{\frac{2}{10}} = \sqrt{\frac{1}{5}} = \frac{\sqrt{1}}{\sqrt{5}} = \frac{1}{\sqrt{5}}$$

A radical is not allowed in the denominator of a fraction, so rationalize it by multiplying the numerator and the denominator by the radical that you are trying to rationalize: $\frac{1}{\sqrt{5}} \times \frac{\sqrt{5}}{\sqrt{5}} = \frac{\sqrt{5}}{5}$. Alternatively, you can evaluate the expression in the question on your calculator, 0.44721..., and then evaluate the expressions in the answer choices until you find a match. This might, however, consume time that could be better spent on other questions. Choice **(B)** is correct.

4.   A
Difficulty: Medium
Category: Advanced Math
Getting to the Answer: Cancel the root on top by separating each of the terms underneath it. First, $\sqrt[3]{8} = 2$, so you can pull that to the outside of the expression: $\frac{2\left(\sqrt[3]{a^9 b^6}\right)}{ab^2}$. Next, convert the cube root of the variable terms using fractional exponents and simplify step-by-step:

$$\frac{2a^{\frac{9}{3}}b^{\frac{6}{3}}}{ab^2}$$
$$= \frac{2a^3 b^2}{ab^2}$$
$$= \frac{2a^3 \cancel{b^2}}{ab \cancel{^2}}$$
$$= \frac{2a^3}{a}$$
$$= 2a^2$$

Choice **(A)** is correct.

5.   14
Difficulty: Medium
Category: Advanced Math
Getting to the Answer: You could graph this function on a calculator to see where its minimum value falls. Without graphing, the key to answering this question is to determine the minimum value of x^2 and then add 14 to that value. Numbers that have been squared can never be negative, so the smallest possible value of x^2 is $0^2 = 0$. Therefore, the minimum value of the function is $0 + 14 = 14$. Enter **14**.

6.   −11
Difficulty: Medium
Category: Advanced Math
Getting to the Answer: You could graph this on a calculator to locate the vertex. Otherwise, the first step is to find h, the x-coordinate of the vertex. The formula for finding the x-coordinate of the vertex is $\frac{-b}{2a}$ (the quadratic formula without the radical part). In the equation, $a = 2$ and $b = -8$, so the equation is $h = \frac{-(-8)}{2(2)} = \frac{8}{4} = 2$.

To find the value of k, which is the y-coordinate of the vertex, plug 2 in for x in the original quadratic equation: $k = 2(2)^2 - 8(2) - 3 = 8 - 16 - 3 = -11$. Enter **−11**.

7.   A
Difficulty: Medium
Category: Advanced Math
Getting to the Answer: According to the graph, both x-intercepts are to the left of the y-axis. Therefore, both values of x are negative. Eliminate (B) because both x values are positive when y equals 0. To evaluate the remaining equations, find the x-intercepts by setting each factor equal to 0 and solving for x. In (A), the x-intercepts are -2 and -6, which means that one intercept is 3 times farther from the origin than the other, which matches the description in the question, so this must be the correct answer. For the record, in (C), the x-intercepts are -1 and -4, making one intercept 4 times farther from the origin than the other; in (D), the x-intercepts are -2 and -4, making one intercept 2 times farther from the origin than the other. Thus, **(A)** is correct.

8.   B
Difficulty: Medium
Category: Advanced Math
Getting to the Answer: Work from the inside out. First find $g(1)$ and then plug the result into $f(x)$: $g(1) = 1 + 4 = 5$. Now, find $f(5)$: $\frac{5^2 + 5(5) + 10}{3(5)} = \frac{25 + 25 + 10}{15} = \frac{60}{15} = 4$.
(B) is correct.

9.   D
Difficulty: Hard
Category: Advanced Math
Getting to the Answer: Factor the denominator in the second term to find that the common denominator for all three terms is $(x - 3)(x + 3)$. Multiply each term in the equation by the common denominator (in factored form or the original form, whichever is more convenient) to clear the fractions. Then solve the resulting equation for x:

$$(x-3)(x^2-9)\left(\frac{2}{x+3}\right) - (x^2-9)\left(\frac{-12}{x^2-9}\right) = 1(x^2 - 9)$$

$$2(x - 3) - (-12) = x^2 - 9$$

$$2x - 6 + 12 = x^2 - 9$$

$$2x + 6 = x^2 - 9$$

Subtract the left side of the equation to yield a quadratic equation, set equal to zero, and then factor the equation to find the values of x:

$$0 = x^2 - 2x - 15$$

$$0 = (x + 3)(x - 5)$$

Set each factor equal to 0 to find that the potential solutions are $x = -3$ and $x = 5$. Note that these are only *potential* solutions because the original equation was a rational equation. When $x = -3$, both denominators on the left side of the original equation are equal to 0, so -3 is an extraneous solution, which means **(D)** is correct.

10. B

Difficulty: Medium

Category: Advanced Math

Getting to the Answer: There are two ways to approach this question. One is to plug the value of x, 10, into both functions and then calculate the value of the fraction:

The function $f(x)$ is $2(10)^2 - 14(10) + 20 = 200 - 140 + 20 = 80$ when $x = 10$. The function $g(x) = 10 - 5 = 5$.

So $\dfrac{f(x)}{g(x)} = \dfrac{80}{5} = 16$.

Alternatively, you could factor the $f(x)$ equation to see if there are any common factors with the $g(x)$ equation that can be canceled out:

$2x^2 - 14x + 20 = 2(x^2 - 7x + 10) = 2(x - 2)(x - 5)$.

So the fraction becomes

$\dfrac{2(x - 2)\cancel{(x - 5)}}{\cancel{(x - 5)}} = 2(x - 2) = 2(10 - 2) = 2(8) = 16$.

(B) is correct.

GEOMETRY AND TRIGONOMETRY

Math

HOW MUCH DO YOU KNOW: GEOMETRY AND TRIGONOMETRY

Directions

Try the questions that follow, using the Method for SAT Math Questions. When you're done, check your answers and read through the explanations in the "Check Your Work" section.

There will be an opportunity for timed practice at the end of the Geometry and Trigonometry unit.

1

The longer leg of a right triangle is three times the length of the shorter leg. Given that the length of each leg is a whole number, which of the following could be the length of the hypotenuse?

(A) $\sqrt{40}$

(B) $\sqrt{47}$

(C) $\sqrt{55}$

(D) $\sqrt{63}$

2

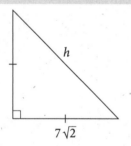

What is the value of h in the figure shown?

(A) 3.5

(B) 7

(C) 12.5

(D) 14

3

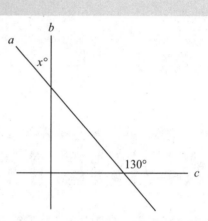

In the figure shown, line b is perpendicular to line c. What is the value of x?

4

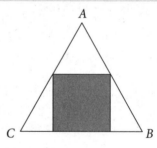

In the figure, the shaded region is a square with an area of 12 square units, inscribed inside equilateral triangle ABC. What is the perimeter of triangle ABC?

(A) $18\sqrt{3}$

(B) $12 + 6\sqrt{3}$

(C) $4 + 6\sqrt{3}$

(D) $4 + \sqrt{3}$

5

Triangle *ABC* has side lengths of 8, 15, and 17. Which of the following could be the side lengths of a triangle that is similar to *ABC*?

Ⓐ 3, 4, 5

Ⓑ 5, 12, 13

Ⓒ 10, 17, 19

Ⓓ 24, 45, 51

6

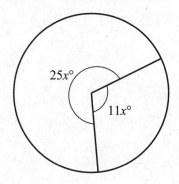

For the circle shown, what is the measure, in degrees, of the smallest angle?

Ⓐ 10

Ⓑ 55

Ⓒ 110

Ⓓ 250

7

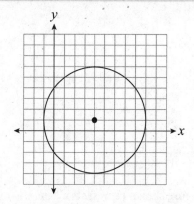

If each grid line of the *xy*-plane shown is 3 units, what is the equation of the circle?

Ⓐ $(x - 4)^2 + (y - 1)^2 = 25$

Ⓑ $(x + 4)^2 + (y + 1)^2 = 25$

Ⓒ $(x - 12)^2 + (y - 3)^2 = 225$

Ⓓ $(x + 12)^2 + (y + 3)^2 = 225$

8

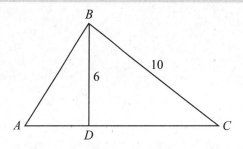

In the figure shown, $\overline{AC} \perp \overline{BD}$ and $\overline{AB} \perp \overline{BC}$. What is the length of *AB*?

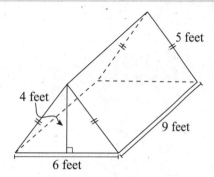

The figure shown represents a camping tent that will be sprayed with a waterproofing agent. If it takes 1 ounce of the agent to cover 3 square feet, how many ounces will it take to spray the entire outside of the tent, excluding the tent bottom?

Ⓐ   38

Ⓑ   72

Ⓒ   114

Ⓓ   216

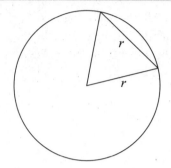

Note: Figure not drawn to scale.

What is the sine of the central angle of the circle shown?

Ⓐ $\dfrac{1}{2}$

Ⓑ $\dfrac{1}{\sqrt{3}}$

Ⓒ $\dfrac{\sqrt{2}}{\sqrt{3}}$

Ⓓ $\dfrac{\sqrt{3}}{2}$

Check Your Work – How Much Do You Know: Geometry and Trigonometry

1.   A

Difficulty: Medium

Category: Geometry and Trigonometry

Getting to the Answer: Start by translating from English into math. Because one leg of the triangle is three times as long as the other, let x and $3x$ represent the lengths. Use the Pythagorean theorem to find the hypotenuse:

$$a^2 + b^2 = c^2$$
$$x^2 + (3x)^2 = c^2$$
$$x^2 + 9x^2 = c^2$$
$$10x^2 = c^2$$
$$\sqrt{10x^2} = c$$

Although you can't find a numerical value for c, $\sqrt{10x^2}$ tells you that the number under the radical is a multiple of 10. The only choice with a multiple of 10 under the radical is (A), so **(A)** is correct.

Note that when $\sqrt{10x^2} = \sqrt{40}$, $x = 2$.

2.   D

Difficulty: Medium

Category: Geometry and Trigonometry

Getting to the Answer: Because one angle of the triangle measures 90° and the two legs are congruent (notice the tick marks), this is a 45-45-90 triangle. The side lengths of a 45-45-90 triangle are in the ratio $x:x:x\sqrt{2}$, where x represents the length of a leg and $x\sqrt{2}$ represents the length of the hypotenuse. Set up an equation using $x\sqrt{2}$ from the ratio and the length of the leg, $7\sqrt{2}$, to find h:

$$\begin{aligned} h &= x\sqrt{2} \\ &= 7\sqrt{2} \times \sqrt{2} \\ &= 7\sqrt{4} \\ &= 7(2) \\ &= 14 \end{aligned}$$

The length of the hypotenuse is 14, so **(D)** is correct.

3.   40

Difficulty: Medium

Category: Geometry and Trigonometry

Getting to the Answer: Since line b is perpendicular to line c, the triangle formed by lines a, b, and c is a right triangle. The angle supplementary to 130° is $180° - 130° = 50°$, so the remaining angle in the triangle is $180° - (90° + 50°) = 40°$. Since $x°$ is vertical to that angle, $x°$ is also 40°.

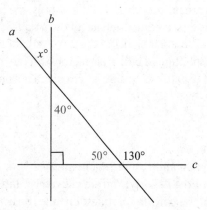

Enter **40**.

4.   B

Difficulty: Hard

Category: Geometry and Trigonometry

Getting to the Answer: Start with what you know about the shaded square. Because its area is 12, each side must be $\sqrt{12} = 2\sqrt{3}$.

Triangle ABC is an equilateral triangle, so each of its interior angles measures 60°. The two vertical sides of the square, therefore, each represent the longer leg of a 30-60-90 triangle (the small white triangles on the sides). The side lengths of a 30-60-90 triangle are in the ratio $x:x\sqrt{3}:2x$, where x represents the length of the short leg. For the small white triangles, the long leg has a length of $2\sqrt{3}$, which means the length of each short leg is 2.

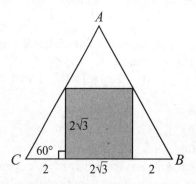

You now have the length of the base of the large equilateral triangle: $2 + 2\sqrt{3} + 2 = 4 + 2\sqrt{3}$. Thus, each side of the large equilateral triangle has length $4 + 2\sqrt{3}$. The perimeter is the sum of all three sides, so multiply by 3 to get $12 + 6\sqrt{3}$, making **(B)** correct.

5. D

Difficulty: Easy

Category: Geometry and Trigonometry

Getting to the Answer: Corresponding sides of similar triangles are proportional. In other words, the larger triangle is a "scaled-up" version of the smaller triangle. Therefore, you're looking for the same ratio of sides (8:15:17), multiplied by a scale factor. This means **(D)** is correct because each side length of *ABC* has been scaled up by a factor of 3.

6. C

Difficulty: Easy

Category: Geometry and Trigonometry

Getting to the Answer: You are given the relative size of each of the parts in this question, and the *whole* is the total number of degrees in a circle, which is 360. Now, set up an equation:

$$25x + 11x = 360$$
$$36x = 360$$
$$x = 10$$

Note that the question asks for the measure of the smallest angle, which is represented by 11*x*. The correct answer is 11(10) = 110, which is **(C)**.

7. C

Difficulty: Hard

Category: Geometry and Trigonometry

Getting to the Answer: To find the equation of a circle, you need the radius and the *x*- and *y*-coordinates of the center point. Then, you can use the standard equation: $(x - h)^2 + (y - k)^2 = r^2$, where (h, k) is the center of the circle and *r* is the length of the radius.

Since each grid line is 3 units, the center of the circle is $(3 \times 4, 3 \times 1)$, or $(12, 3)$, and its radius is $3 \times 5 = 15$. Thus, the equation must be $(x - 12)^2 + (y - 3)^2 = 15^2$, or $(x - 12)^2 + (y - 3)^2 = 225$. **(C)** is the correct answer.

8. 60/8 or 7.5

Difficulty: Hard

Category: Geometry and Trigonometry

Getting to the Answer: Triangles *ABC*, *BDC*, and *ADB* are similar triangles because their corresponding angles are congruent.

A right triangle with side length 6 and hypotenuse 10 means a 3:4:5 triangle, but you could also use the Pythagorean theorem to find that *DC* = 8.

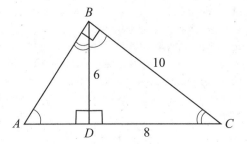

To find the length of *AB*, set up a proportion using the lengths of triangle *ADB* and triangle *BDC* and solve:

$$\frac{AB}{10} = \frac{6}{8}$$
$$8AB = 60$$
$$AB = \frac{60}{8}$$
$$AB = 7.5$$

Enter **60/8 or 7.5**.

Alternatively, you could set up a proportion using the lengths of triangle *ABC* and triangle *BDC*

$$\frac{AB}{6} = \frac{10}{8}$$
$$8AB = 60$$
$$AB = \frac{60}{8}$$
$$AB = 7.5$$

9. A

Difficulty: Medium

Category: Geometry and Trigonometry

Strategic Advice: You're looking for surface area because you need to spray all of the faces of the tent, *excluding* the bottom. Decompose the figure into 2-D shapes, and add their areas together. Lastly, find the number of ounces of waterproofing agent using unit conversion.

Getting to the Answer: The two sides of the tent are rectangles: 2*A* = 2(*lw*) = 2(9)(5) = 90. The front and back of the tent are triangles:

$$2A_{\text{triangle}} = 2\left(\frac{1}{2}bh\right) = bh = (6)(4) = 24$$

Thus, the total surface area of the tent is 90 + 24 = 114 square feet. Use unit conversion to find the number of ounces of waterproofing agent needed:

$$114 \text{ square feet} \times \frac{1 \text{ ounce}}{3 \text{ square feet}} = 38 \text{ ounces}$$

(A) is correct.

10. D

Difficulty: Hard

Category: Geometry and Trigonometry

Getting to the Answer: The chord (the line segment that connects two points on the circle's circumference) forms a triangle with the two radii of the central angle. Since the chord is the same length as the radii, this is an equilateral triangle. Therefore, each angle, including the central angle, is 60°. Although this triangle does not have a right angle, it can be split into two 30-60-90 triangles. So, you can use the side ratios of a 30-60-90 triangle to find sin 60°. That ratio is $1:\sqrt{3}:2$.

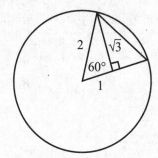

Because $\sin x = \dfrac{\text{opposite}}{\text{hypotenuse}}$, the sine of 60° is $\dfrac{\sqrt{3}}{2}$.
(D) is correct.

CHAPTER 14

GEOMETRY

LEARNING OBJECTIVES

After completing this chapter, you will be able to:

- Apply the properties of lines and angles to solve geometry questions
- Use area calculations to solve questions
- Apply scale factors to solve geometry questions
- Identify similar triangles and apply their properties
- Calculate the length of one side of a right triangle, given the lengths of the other two sides
- Recognize the most common Pythagorean triples
- Calculate the other two sides of a 45-45-90 or 30-60-90 triangle, given one side length
- Interpret and manipulate the equation for a circle
- Calculate the length of an arc or the area of a sector defined by a central angle
- Convert degrees to radians
- Calculate the volume of common solids
- Calculate the surface area of common solids

HOW MUCH DO YOU KNOW?

Directions

Try the questions that follow. Show your work so that you can compare your solutions to the ones found in the "Check Your Work" section immediately after this question set. If you answered the question(s) on a specific topic correctly, and if your scratchwork looks like ours, you may be able to move quickly through the lesson covering that topic. If you answered incorrectly or used a different approach, you may want to take your time on that lesson.

Make use of the formula sheet below as needed; you'll have these same formulas available when you take the real SAT.

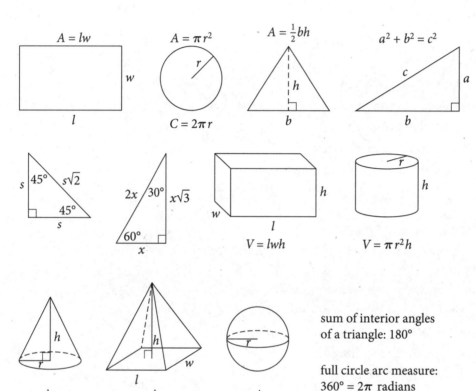

1

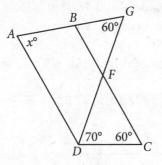

In the figure shown, line segments AD and BC are parallel. What is the value of x?

(A) 60

(B) 70

(C) 80

(D) 110

2

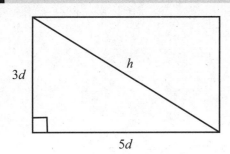

The diagonal of the rectangle shown has length h. What is the value of h in terms of d?

(A) $2\sqrt{2}d$

(B) $4d$

(C) $\sqrt{34d}$

(D) $d\sqrt{34}$

3

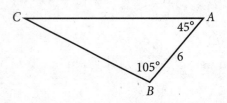

What is the area of the triangle shown in the figure?

(A) $18\sqrt{3}$

(B) $9 + 9\sqrt{3}$

(C) $9 + 18\sqrt{3}$

(D) $18 + 18\sqrt{3}$

4

What is the maximum value of y on the circumference of the circle defined by the equation $x^2 + y^2 + 6x - 10y - 47 = 0$?

(A) 9

(B) 14

(C) 16

(D) 19

Math

5

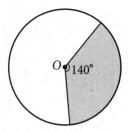

If the area of the shaded sector in circle O is 14π square units, what is the radius of the circle?

Ⓐ 6

Ⓑ 8

Ⓒ 9

Ⓓ 12

6

A cylinder that is 4 inches in diameter and 6 inches tall has a volume of 24π. If a second 6-inch tall cylinder has a volume of 216π, how much wider, in inches, will its diameter be?

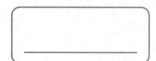

Check Your Work

1.   B

Difficulty: Medium

Category: Geometry and Trigonometry

Getting to the Answer: Notice that $\triangle CDF$ and $\triangle GBF$ are similar: they share a 60° angle, and the vertical angles formed at point F are equal, so their third angles must be equal as well. It follows that $\angle FBG = 70°$. Because line segments AD and BC are parallel, $\angle FBG$ and $\angle DAG$ are corresponding angles (and are therefore equal). You can now conclude that $\angle x = 70°$, so **(B)** is correct.

2.   D

Difficulty: Medium

Category: Geometry and Trigonometry

Getting to the Answer: The sides $3d$, $5d$, and h form a right triangle, so plug these values into the Pythagorean theorem and then solve for h. When you square $3d$ and $5d$, be sure to square both the coefficient and the variable:

$$a^2 + b^2 = c^2$$
$$(3d)^2 + (5d)^2 = h^2$$
$$9d^2 + 25d^2 = h^2$$
$$34d^2 = h^2$$
$$\sqrt{34d^2} = h$$
$$d\sqrt{34} = h$$

Choice **(D)** is correct.

3.   B

Difficulty: Hard

Category: Geometry and Trigonometry

Getting to the Answer: First, find the measure of the missing angle in the triangle: $180° - 105° - 45° = 30°$. Next, draw the height of the triangle up from B to a point, D, on side AC to create two right triangles:

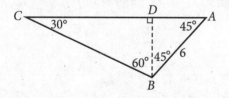

Triangle ABD is a 45-45-90 triangle, so its side lengths are in the ratio $x:x:x\sqrt{2}$. Because side AB is the hypotenuse, set up an equation using the ratio of the sides:

$$6 = x\sqrt{2}$$
$$\frac{6}{\sqrt{2}} = x$$
$$\frac{6}{\sqrt{2}}\left(\frac{\sqrt{2}}{\sqrt{2}}\right) = x$$
$$\frac{6\sqrt{2}}{2} = x$$
$$3\sqrt{2} = x$$

This is the length of both AD and BD. Triangle BDC is a 30-60-90 triangle, so its side lengths are in the ratio of $x:x\sqrt{3}:2x$. You just found that the length of the shorter leg, BD, is $3\sqrt{2}$, so multiply it by $\sqrt{3}$ to find the length of the longer leg ($\sqrt{3} \times 3\sqrt{2} = 3\sqrt{6}$). Now, find the length of AC, which is the base of triangle ABC, by adding length AD to DC. The result is $3\sqrt{2} + 3\sqrt{6}$. Finally, use the area formula, $A = \frac{1}{2}bh$, to find the area of the whole triangle:

$$A = \frac{1}{2}(3\sqrt{2} + 3\sqrt{6})(3\sqrt{2})$$
$$= \frac{1}{2}(18 + 9\sqrt{12})$$
$$= \frac{1}{2}(18 + 9 \cdot 2\sqrt{3})$$
$$= \frac{1}{2}(18 + 18\sqrt{3})$$
$$= 9 + 9\sqrt{3}$$

Choice **(B)** is correct.

4.   B

Difficulty: Medium

Category: Geometry and Trigonometry

Getting to the Answer: You can plot this equation with either the test's or your own graphing calculator and look for the maximum y-value on the circle, or you can solve this algebraically. If you opt for the second way, complete the square of the given equation to arrange it into the standard format for a circle, $(x - h)^2 + (y - k)^2 = r^2$, to determine the center and the radius. The maximum value of y on the circle will be the point where a radius drawn straight up from the center touches the circumference.

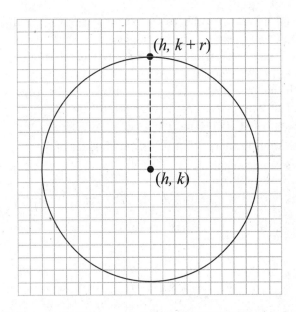

Rearrange the given equation to combine like terms: $(x^2 + 6x) + (y^2 - 10y) - 47 = 0$. Completing the square for the x and y terms yields $(x^2 + 6x + 9) + (y^2 - 10y + 25) - 47 = 0 + 9 + 25$.

Next, simplify the x and y expressions and add 47 to each side to yield $(x + 3)^2 + (y - 5)^2 = 9 + 25 + 47 = 81$. So, the y-coordinate of the center is 5. Since $r^2 = 81$, the radius of the circle is 9. Therefore, the y-coordinate of the point straight above the center is $5 + 9 = 14$. **(B)** is correct.

5.   A

Difficulty: Medium

Category: Geometry and Trigonometry

Getting to the Answer: The question asks for the radius. If you know the area of the circle, you can find the radius. The question gives enough information to find the area of the circle. Use the relationship $\dfrac{\text{area of sector}}{\text{area of circle}} = \dfrac{\text{central angle}}{360°}$:

$$\frac{14\pi}{A} = \frac{140}{360}$$
$$5{,}040\pi = 140A$$
$$36\pi = A$$

Now, solve for r using $A = \pi r^2$:

$$36\pi = \pi r^2$$
$$36 = r^2$$
$$\pm 6 = r$$

The radius can't be negative, so the correct answer is 6, which is **(A)**.

6.   8

Difficulty: Hard

Category: Geometry and Trigonometry

Getting to the Answer: Find the diameter of the second cylinder using the formula for volume of a cylinder, $V = \pi r^2 h$. The question gives you the height of the cylinder, 6 inches, and its volume, 216π, so plug these into the formula to solve for the radius.

$$V = \pi r^2 h$$
$$216\pi = \pi r^2 6$$
$$36\pi = \pi r^2$$
$$36 = r^2$$
$$6 = r$$

The diameter is twice the radius, so the larger cylinder has a diameter of 12. The question asks how much larger this is compared to the diameter of the first cylinder, and that's $12 - 4 = 8$. Enter **8**.

LINES AND ANGLES

LEARNING OBJECTIVE

After this lesson, you will be able to:

- Apply the properties of lines and angles to solve geometry questions

To answer a question like this:

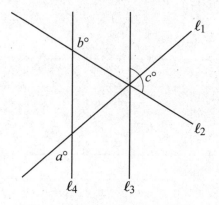

In the figure shown, lines l_3 and l_4 are parallel, and line l_1 bisects angle c. If $95 < b < 100$, which of the following is a possible value of a?

A) 45

B) 47

C) 48

D) 50

You need to know this:

A **line** is a one-dimensional geometrical abstraction—infinitely long with no width. Two points determine a straight line; given any two points, there is exactly one straight line that passes through them both.

A **line segment** is a section of a straight line of finite length with two endpoints.

An **angle** is formed by two lines or line segments intersecting at a point. The point of intersection is called the **vertex** of the angle. Angles can be measured in degrees (°) or radians.

Familiarity with angle types will often unlock information that is not explicitly given in a question. This makes getting to the answer much easier for even the toughest geometry questions. First, take a look at the types of angles you should be able to recognize.

Math

ANGLE TYPE	ANGLE MEASUREMENT	EXAMPLE
Acute	Less than 90°	
Right	90°	
Obtuse	Between 90° and 180°	
Straight	180°	

Two angles are **supplementary** if together they make up a straight angle; that is, if the sum of their measures is 180°. In the following figure, c and d are supplementary.

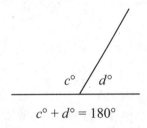

$$c° + d° = 180°$$

Two angles are **complementary** if together they make up a right angle: i.e., if the sum of their measures is 90°. In the following figure, a and b are complementary.

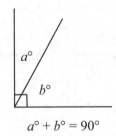

$$a° + b° = 90°$$

Note: Angle pairs do not need to be adjacent (next to each other) to be supplementary or complementary.

Intersecting lines create angles with special relationships. When two lines intersect, adjacent angles are supplementary, and **vertical angles** (two angles opposite a vertex) are equal, or congruent. Take a look at the following figure for an example.

The angles marked $a°$ and $b°$ are supplementary; therefore, $a + b = 180$. The angle marked $a°$ is vertical (and thus equal) to the one marked 60°, so $a = 60$. With this new information, you can find b: $a + b = 60 + b = 180$, so $b = 120$.

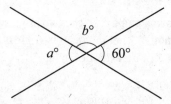

Two lines are **parallel** if they lie in the same plane and never intersect each other regardless of how far they are extended. If line 1 is parallel to line 2, it can be written as 1 ∥ 2.

When two parallel lines are intersected by another line (called a **transversal**), all acute angles are equal, and all obtuse angles are equal. Additionally, **corresponding angles** are angles that are in the same position but on different parallel lines/transversal intersections; they are also equal.

Alternate interior angles and alternate exterior angles are equal. **Alternate interior angles** are angles that are positioned between the two parallel lines on opposite sides of the transversal, while **alternate exterior angles** are positioned on the outside of the parallel lines on opposite sides of the transversal. Consider the following figure:

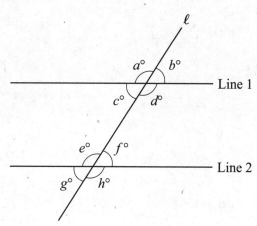

- Line 1 and Line 2 are parallel and cut by transversal ℓ.
- Angles a, d, e, and h are obtuse and equal.
- Angles b, c, f, and g are acute and equal.
- Angle pairs (b and f), (c and g), (a and e), and (d and h) are corresponding angles.
- Angle pairs (a and h) and (b and g) are alternate exterior angles.
- Angle pairs (d and e) and (c and f) are alternate interior angles.

You need to do this:

- Determine which angles in a figure are equal and which are supplementary or complementary.
- Find a missing angle by identifying its relationship to known angles in a figure.

Explanation:

Lines l_3 and l_4 are parallel. Line l_2 is a transversal that crosses l_3 and l_4, so the obtuse angles formed with the parallel lines must be equal. That means angles b and c are equal.

Additionally, the question states that line l_1 bisects angle c, so the two angles formed by the division of angle c are equal. One of those angles is formed by l_1 and l_3. That means this angle is equal to angle a; since l_1 is another transversal that crosses l_3 and l_4, the two are alternate exterior angles.

The question specifies that $95 < b < 100$, so, since c is equal to b, you can say that $95 < c < 100$. You've already established that a is half the value of c, so $47.5 < a < 50$. Among the answer choices, only 48 falls within that range.

Choice **(C)** is correct.

Try on Your Own

Directions

Take as much time as you need on these questions. Work carefully and methodically. There will be an opportunity for timed practice later in the book.

1

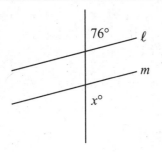

In the figure shown, l and m are parallel. Which of the following is the value of x?

Ⓐ 76

Ⓑ 96

Ⓒ 104

Ⓓ 124

2

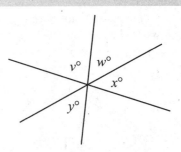

The figure shows three lines that meet at a point. Given that $x = 45$ and $v = 65$, what is the value of y?

3

HINT: In a pair of supplementary angles, 180° minus one angle will always equal the other angle. How can you use this fact in Q3?

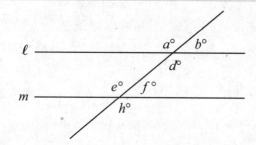

In the figure shown, if line l is parallel to line m, which of the following is NOT necessarily equal to a?

Ⓐ $b + f$

Ⓑ d

Ⓒ $180 - b$

Ⓓ $\dfrac{e + h}{2}$

4

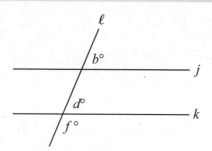

Lines j and k are parallel in the figure shown. If $f = 9b$, what is the value of $2d$?

Ⓐ 18

Ⓑ 36

Ⓒ 162

Ⓓ 324

5

HINT: For Q5, keep in mind that supplementary angles need not be adjacent.

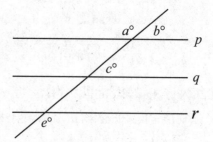

Note: Figure not drawn to scale.

In the figure shown, lines p, q, and r are all parallel. If $b = 30$, what is the value of $a + c + e$?

6

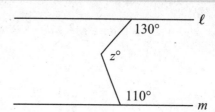

In the figure shown, lines l and m are parallel. What is the value of z?

Ⓐ 50

Ⓑ 70

Ⓒ 110

Ⓓ 120

AREA, PERIMETER, AND SCALE

LEARNING OBJECTIVES

After this lesson, you will be able to:

- Use area calculations to solve questions
- Apply scale factors to solve geometry questions

To answer a question like this:

A square has sides of length $x + 5$. If it had sides $\frac{1}{2}$ that length, its area would be 9. What is the value of x?

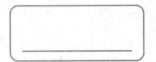

You need to know this:

The **perimeter** of a shape is the length of the shape's border. For any shape, you can find the perimeter by adding up the lengths of all of its sides. However, for some shapes, there are shortcuts. For an equilateral triangle, a square, or another polygon with equal side lengths, you can simply multiply the side length by the number of sides. For a rectangle, the perimeter is $2(l + w)$, where l and w are the rectangle's length and width.

The **area** of a shape is the amount of space it occupies. Different shapes have different formulas for calculating their area:

- The area of a square is s^2, where s is the side length.

- The area of a parallelogram is $b \times h$, where b is one side of the parallelogram and h is a line perpendicular to that side and extending to its opposite side.

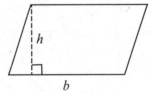

- The area of a rectangle is $l \times w$, where l and w are the rectangle's length and width, respectively.

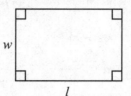

- The area of a triangle is $\frac{1}{2}bh$, where b is the base of the triangle (one of its sides) and h is its height, a line perpendicular to the base extending to the opposite vertex. Note that the height can only be a side of the triangle in a right triangle.

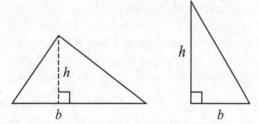

- The area of a trapezoid is $\frac{1}{2}(b_1 + b_2)h$, where b_1 and b_2 are the two parallel sides of the trapezoid and h is the height, a line connecting the two bases and perpendicular to both.

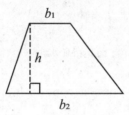

If you're asked to find the area of a polygon other than those shown, it's likely that the most efficient way is to break the polygon into shapes for which you do know the area formula. For instance, you may not know how to calculate the area of a hexagon directly, but you can split a regular hexagon into six equilateral triangles, which you can then use the triangle area formula on.

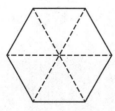

Or, consider this figure:

There's no area formula for this shape, but you may still see a question on the SAT asking you to find the area of such a shape. Notice that it can be split into a rectangle and a triangle:

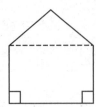

On test day, you'd be given enough information to determine the length and width of the rectangle and the base and height of the triangle, which would give you all you need to determine the area of the whole shape.

Sometimes, a question may ask you to consider what effect scaling up the size of a polygon's sides has on either the perimeter or area. Take a square that has side lengths of 1. The perimeter would be $4(1) = 4$. Then, double the side lengths to 2. The new perimeter would be $4(2) = 8$, which is also twice the original perimeter. This relationship holds for any polygon; if you multiply the side lengths by a certain number, the perimeter of the new shape is equal to the original perimeter multiplied by that same number.

Doubling the side lengths of a polygon, however, does not simply double the area. Consider again a square with side length 1; it has an area of $(1)^2 = 1$. Doubling the length of the sides yields a square with side length 2 and area $(2)^2 = 4$. This new area is 4 (or 2^2) times as big as the original. Similarly, tripling the side length results in a square with an area of $(3)^2 = 9$, which is 9 (or 3^2) times as big as the original. Thus, if you multiply the side lengths of a polygon by a number n, the area of the new polygon will be n^2 times bigger than the original.

You need to do this:

- Determine whether you can use a formula to find the area of the shape or if you have to split up the shape into smaller component shapes.
- Determine the effect of scaling up the sides of a shape on its perimeter and area.

Explanation:

You can use the formula for the area of a square, $A = s^2$, to solve for x. After the change to the side length, the new area is 9 and each side length is then $\frac{x + 5}{2}$.

$$9 = \left(\frac{x + 5}{2}\right)^2$$
$$3 = \frac{x + 5}{2}$$
$$6 = x + 5$$
$$1 = x$$

Enter **1**.

Alternatively, you can use a scale factor to answer this question. When the side lengths of a shape are multiplied by a number, you can find the new area by multiplying the original area by the square of that number. Since the sides of this square are being multiplied by $\frac{1}{2}$, the new area would be $\left(\frac{1}{2}\right)^2 = \frac{1}{4}$ of the original area.

Since the new area is 9, the original area of the square would be 36. Since the area of a square is its side length squared, you can set up the equation $(x + 5)^2 = 36$. Because $x + 5$ represents the side length of a square, it must be positive; therefore, $x + 5 = 6$ and $x = 1$. Enter **1**.

Try on Your Own

Directions

Take as much time as you need on these questions. Work carefully and methodically. There will be an opportunity for timed practice later in the book.

7

What is the positive difference in area between a parallelogram with a height of 9 and a base length of 8 and a triangle with a height of 7 and a base length of 6?

Ⓐ 72

Ⓑ 51

Ⓒ 30

Ⓓ 5

8

The rectangular top of a balance beam is w centimeters wide. If the length of the beam is 50 times its width, what is the perimeter of the top surface of the beam, in centimeters, in terms of w?

Ⓐ 51w

Ⓑ 50w^2

Ⓒ 102w

Ⓓ 102w^2

9

The height of a billboard is 34 feet less than its width. If the area of the billboard is 672 square feet, what is the height of the billboard, in feet?

10

The area of a triangle is x square inches. If both the base and height of the triangle are doubled, what is the area of the new triangle in terms of x?

Ⓐ 2x

Ⓑ 4x

Ⓒ 2x^2

Ⓓ 4x^2

11

HINT: The area of a square is s^2, and the perimeter is 4s. How can you use this fact in Q11?

The area of Square A is 4 times the area of Square B. How many times greater is the perimeter of Square A than the perimeter of Square B?

(A) 2

(B) 4

(C) 8

(D) 16

12

HINT: For Q12, a decrease by x percent can be written as $1 - \dfrac{x}{100}$.

The height of a triangle is increased by 50 percent, and its base is decreased by x percent. If the area of the triangle increased by 20 percent, what is the value of x?

(A) 20

(B) 30

(C) 70

(D) 80

SIMILAR TRIANGLES

To answer a question like this:

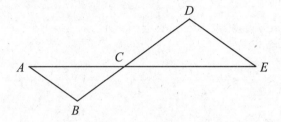

In the figure shown, segments *AE* and *BD* intersect at point *C*, and $\angle ABC \cong \angle CDE$. If $BC = DE = 5$ and $AB = 2$, what is the measure of *CD*?

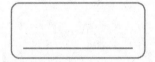

You need to know this:

The corresponding angles and side lengths of **congruent triangles** are equal. **Similar triangles** have the same angle measurements and proportional sides. In the figure that follows, the two triangles have the same angle measurements, so the side lengths can be set up as the following proportion: $\frac{A}{D} = \frac{B}{E} = \frac{C}{F}$.

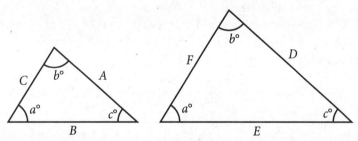

Two triangles are similar if three specific conditions are met:

• Two of their three angles are congruent (**angle-angle**). For example, two triangles that each have one 40° and one 55° angle are similar.

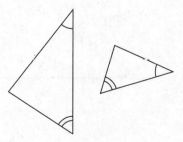

- Two of their three sides are in the same proportion and the intervening angle is congruent (**side-angle-side**). For example, a triangle with sides of 10 and 12 and an intervening angle of 40°, and another triangle with sides of 20 and 24 and an intervening angle of 40°, are similar.

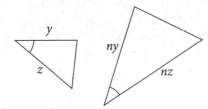

- Their three sides are in the same proportion (**side-side-side**). For example, a triangle with sides of 5, 6, and 8 and a triangle with sides of 15, 18, and 24 are similar.

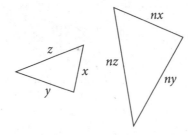

You need to do this:

- Determine whether two triangles are similar by checking for angle-angle, side-angle-side, or side-side-side relationships.
- Find a missing side length by setting up a proportion.

Explanation:

Label the figure with information from the question stem and information you can deduce from geometry principles. These two triangles are similar because they have two sets of congruent angles: one set is the set of vertical angles ($\angle ACB \cong \angle DCE$) and one set is given in the question stem ($\angle ABC \cong \angle CDE$). Corresponding sides in similar triangles are proportional to each other, so set up a proportion to find the missing side length. In this case, CD corresponds to BC and DE corresponds to AB. Solve for CD:

$$\frac{CD}{BC} = \frac{DE}{AB}$$
$$\frac{CD}{5} = \frac{5}{2}$$
$$CD = \frac{25}{2}$$

Enter **25/2** or **12.5**.

Try on Your Own

Directions

Take as much time as you need on these questions. Work carefully and methodically. There will be an opportunity for timed practice later in the book.

13

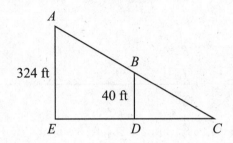

The diagram shows similar triangles *ACE* and *BCD*. If segment *DC* is 50 percent longer than segment *BD*, how long, in feet, is segment *DE*?

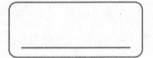

14

HINT: Triangles with a shared angle and parallel sides are similar. How can you use this fact in Q14?

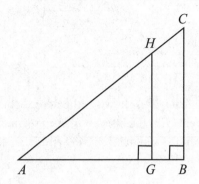

Triangle *ABC* shown has an area of 150 square units. If lengths $AB = AH = 20$, then what is the length of *HG*?

Ⓐ 5

Ⓑ 12

Ⓒ 16

Ⓓ 20

15

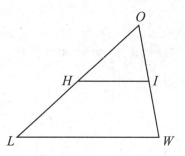

Triangle *LOW* is shown in the figure, where segment *HI* is the bisector of both segments *LO* and *OW*. Given that $LW = 30$ and $HI = 4x - 1$, what is the value of *x*?

Ⓐ 3.5

Ⓑ 4

Ⓒ 7.75

Ⓓ 8

16

Right triangle *DEF* is similar to right triangle *ABC*, and both are plotted on a coordinate plane (not shown). The vertices of triangle *DEF* are $D(3, 2)$, $E(3, -1)$, and $F(-1, -1)$. The vertices that form triangle *ABC*'s longer leg are $(-8, -3)$ and $(8, -3)$. If vertex *A* is in the same quadrant of the coordinate plane as vertex *D*, what is the *y*-coordinate of vertex *A*?

17

HINT: For Q17, translate carefully from English into math and fill in the lengths on the figure.

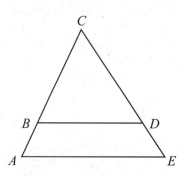

In the figure above, $\overline{BD} \parallel \overline{AE}$ and $AB = 5$. If *BC* is three times *AB*, and if *CD* is 2 more than half *AC*, then what is the length of segment *DE*?

Ⓐ 3

Ⓑ 4

Ⓒ 5

Ⓓ 6

PYTHAGOREAN THEOREM

LEARNING OBJECTIVES

After this lesson, you will be able to:

- Calculate the length of one side of a right triangle given the lengths of the other two sides
- Recognize the most common Pythagorean triples

To answer a question like this:

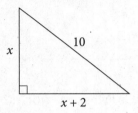

What is the area of the triangle shown?

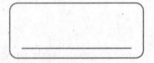

You need to know this:

The **Pythagorean theorem** states that in any right triangle (and *only* in right triangles), the square of the hypotenuse (the longest side) is equal to the sum of the squares of the legs (the shorter sides). If you know the lengths of any two sides of a right triangle, you can use the Pythagorean equation, $a^2 + b^2 = c^2$, to find the length of the third. In this equation, a and b are the legs of the triangle and c is the hypotenuse, the side across from the right angle of the triangle.

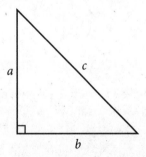

Consider an example: a right triangle has a leg of length 9 and a hypotenuse of length 14. To find the missing leg length, plug the known values into the Pythagorean equation: $9^2 + b^2 = 14^2$. This simplifies to $81 + b^2 = 196$, which becomes $b^2 = 115$. Take the square root of both sides to find that $b = \sqrt{115}$.

Some right triangles have three side lengths that are all integers. These sets of integer side lengths are called **Pythagorean triples**. The two most common Pythagorean triples on the SAT are 3:4:5 and 5:12:13. Look for multiples of these (e.g., 6:8:10 and 10:24:26) as well. Memorizing these triples now can save you valuable calculation time on test day.

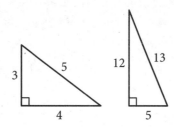

You need to do this:

- Keep in mind that the Pythagorean theorem applies only to right triangles.
- When you need to find a side length of a right triangle, look first for the common Pythagorean triples or their multiples.
- If you cannot identify any Pythagorean triples, substitute any two known side lengths into the equation $a^2 + b^2 = c^2$, where c represents the hypotenuse, to find the third.

Explanation:

You could answer this question by applying the Pythagorean equation, but you would have to do a fair amount of algebra. It's much faster if you recognize that this is a 6:8:10 Pythagorean triple, where $x = 6$ and $x + 2 = 8$. Then it's just a matter of calculating the area, using the legs as the base and height:

$$A = \frac{1}{2}bh = \frac{1}{2}(8)(6) = 24$$

For the record, here's the solution using the Pythagorean equation:

$$x^2 + (x + 2)^2 = 10^2$$
$$x^2 + x^2 + 4x + 4 = 100$$
$$2x^2 + 4x - 96 = 0$$
$$x^2 + 2x - 48 = 0$$
$$(x + 8)(x - 6) = 0$$
$$x = -8 \quad \text{or} \quad x = 6$$

At this point, you would throw out the negative root because length must be positive, so you would use 6 and $6 + 2 = 8$ as the legs and calculate the area as shown above.

Enter **24**.

Try on Your Own

Directions

Take as much time as you need on these questions. Work carefully and methodically. There will be an opportunity for timed practice later in the book.

18

HINT: For Q18, draw the direct path and use it as the hypotenuse of a right triangle.

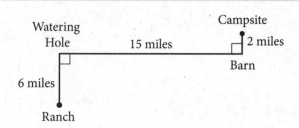

A tourist ranch built the horse-riding trail shown in the figure. The trail takes a rider from the ranch to a watering hole, then to a barn, and finally to a campsite. If a rider took a horse on a direct path from the ranch to the campsite instead, how long, in miles, would the trip be?

(A) 6

(B) 17

(C) 23

(D) 40

19

Ted wants to visit his friend. If he bikes, he can cut through the yards of neighbors to travel in a straight line. If he drives, however, he must follow the streets. He travels 6 miles east, 6 miles south, and 2 more miles east by car. How much shorter, in miles, is Ted's bike route than his car route?

20

Sage takes a trail to a campsite that travels 5 miles south, 6 miles east, 7 miles south, and 2 miles west to a campsite. Annette uses a cross-country route that starts at the same point as Sage's trail but goes in a straight line from there to the campsite. About how many miles total will the two travel?

(A) 32.65

(B) 33.42

(C) 34.00

(D) 34.42

21

The lengths of the legs of a right triangle are $3x$ and $x + 1$. The hypotenuse is $3x + 1$. What is the value of x?

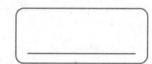

22

HINT: In Q22, an isosceles right triangle has two equal sides.

If an isosceles right triangle has a hypotenuse of 4 inches, what is the perimeter, in inches, of the triangle?

(A) $4\sqrt{2}$

(B) $4 + 4\sqrt{2}$

(C) $4 + 8\sqrt{2}$

(D) 8

SPECIAL RIGHT TRIANGLES

> **LEARNING OBJECTIVE**
>
> After this lesson, you will be able to:
>
> * Calculate the other two sides of a 45-45-90 or 30-60-90 triangle, given one side length

To answer a question like this:

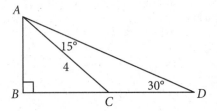

Note: Figure not drawn to scale.

Given triangle *ABC* and triangle *ABD* above, what is the perimeter of triangle *ACD*?

A) $2\sqrt{6} - 2\sqrt{2}$

B) $4\sqrt{3}$

C) $4 + 2\sqrt{6} + 2\sqrt{2}$

D) $2\sqrt{6} + 6\sqrt{2}$

You need to know this:

Special right triangles are defined by their angles. As a result, the ratios of their side lengths are always the same. If you know the length of any one of the three sides of a special right triangle, you can find the lengths of the other two.

The ratio of the sides of a **45-45-90** triangle is $x:x:x\sqrt{2}$, where x is the length of each leg and $x\sqrt{2}$ is the length of the hypotenuse:

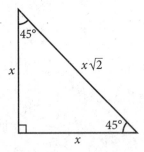

The ratio of the sides of a **30-60-90** triangle is $x:x\sqrt{3}:2x$, where x is the shorter leg, $x\sqrt{3}$ is the longer leg, and $2x$ is the hypotenuse:

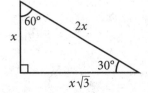

For example, if the shorter leg of a 30-60-90 triangle has a length of 5, then the longer leg has a length of $5\sqrt{3}$, and the hypotenuse has a length of $5 \times 2 = 10$. These side length ratios are given on the SAT reference sheet, but for the sake of efficiency on test day, we recommend that you memorize them.

You need to do this:

- Look for hidden special right triangles within other shapes. For example, an equilateral triangle can be bisected (cut in half) to form two congruent 30-60-90 triangles, and a square can be divided with a diagonal into two congruent 45-45-90 triangles.
- Use one known side length to deduce the other two.

Explanation:

Look for hidden special right triangles and add new information to your diagram as you go. Since $\angle ADB$ is 30° and $\angle ABC$ is 90°, $\angle BAD$ is 60°, so $\triangle ABD$ is a 30-60-90 triangle. Subtracting $\angle CAD$ from $\angle BAD$ leaves $60° - 15° = 45°$, meaning $\angle BAC$ is 45°. Since $\triangle ABC$ is a right triangle, its missing angle ($\angle ACB$) is also 45°, making $\triangle ABC$ a 45-45-90 triangle.

Knowing that you have two special right triangles will allow you to unlock the unknown side lengths. AC is the hypotenuse of the 45-45-90 triangle (side ratio of $x{:}x{:}x\sqrt{2}$), so AB and BC (the two legs) can be found by solving the equation $4 = x\sqrt{2}$:

$$4 = x\sqrt{2}$$
$$\frac{4}{\sqrt{2}} = \frac{x\sqrt{2}}{\sqrt{2}}$$
$$\frac{4}{\sqrt{2}} = x$$
$$\frac{4}{\sqrt{2}} \cdot \frac{\sqrt{2}}{\sqrt{2}} = x \cdot \frac{\sqrt{2}}{\sqrt{2}}$$
$$\frac{4\sqrt{2}}{2} = x \cdot 1$$
$$2\sqrt{2} = x$$

Therefore, both legs of the 45-45-90 triangle are $2\sqrt{2}$. AB is also the shorter leg of the 30-60-90 triangle (side ratio of $x{:}x\sqrt{3}{:}2x$), so BD (the longer leg) is $2\sqrt{2} \times \sqrt{3} = 2\sqrt{6}$ and AD (the hypotenuse) is $2 \times 2\sqrt{2} = 4\sqrt{2}$. To determine CD, take the difference of BD and BC: $2\sqrt{6} - 2\sqrt{2}$. With all sides and angles labeled, the figure looks like this:

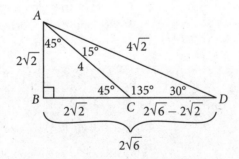

You now have all three sides of triangle ACD, so add them together for the perimeter:

$$4 + (2\sqrt{6} - 2\sqrt{2}) + 4\sqrt{2}$$

This simplifies to $4 + 2\sqrt{6} + 2\sqrt{2}$, so **(C)** is correct.

Try on Your Own

Directions

Take as much time as you need on these questions. Work carefully and methodically. There will be an opportunity for timed practice later in the book.

23

HINT: For Q23, don't rush to use the Pythagorean theorem. What kind of special triangle is triangle *BCD*?

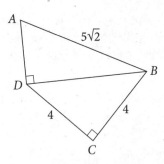

What is the area of triangle *ABD*?

Ⓐ $3\sqrt{2}$

Ⓑ 8

Ⓒ 12

Ⓓ $20\sqrt{2}$

24

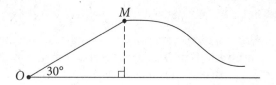

The distance from point *O* to point *M* of an amusement ride course shown in the figure is $200\sqrt{3}$ feet. If the angle of ascent is 30°, what is the height, in feet, of the amusement ride at point *M*?

Ⓐ $\dfrac{20}{3}\sqrt{3}$

Ⓑ $100\sqrt{3}$

Ⓒ 200

Ⓓ 300

25

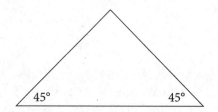

The triangle shown in the figure has a hypotenuse length of 16 inches. What is the area of the triangle, in square inches?

Ⓐ 32

Ⓑ 64

Ⓒ $64\sqrt{2}$

Ⓓ 128

26

HINT: Q26: Whenever a right triangle question involves $\sqrt{3}$, suspect a 30-60-90 special right triangle.

A rectangle has a 12-inch diagonal. If the length of the rectangle is $\sqrt{3}$ times longer than the width, what is the area, in square inches, of the rectangle?

Ⓐ 12

Ⓑ $18\sqrt{3}$

Ⓒ 36

Ⓓ $36\sqrt{3}$

27

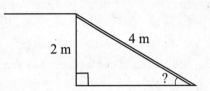

A theater is building a portable ramp to allow equipment and people easy access to the stage, which is 2 meters high. If the ramp is 4 meters long, what is the angle of the incline, in degrees?

CIRCLES

Math

LEARNING OBJECTIVE

After this lesson, you will be able to:

- Interpret and manipulate the equation for a circle

To answer a question like this:

Which of the following points in the xy-plane represents the center of the circle defined by the equation $x^2 + y^2 - 4x - 8y - 16 = 0$?

A) $(-4, -8)$

B) $(-2, -4)$

C) $(2, 4)$

D) $(4, 8)$

You need to know this:

The equation of a circle in the coordinate plane is as follows:

$$(x - h)^2 + (y - k)^2 = r^2$$

In this equation, called the **standard form**, r is the radius of the circle, and h and k are the x- and y-coordinates of the circle's center, respectively: (h, k).

You might also see what is referred to as **general form**:

$$x^2 + y^2 + Cx + Dy + E = 0$$

In the general form, the fact that there are x^2 and y^2 terms with coefficients of 1 is an indicator that the equation does indeed graph as a circle. To convert to standard form, complete the square for the x terms, then repeat for the y terms. Refer to the lessons on quadratics for a review of completing the square if needed.

You need to do this:

- Get the circle into standard form.
- Determine the center and radius using the standard form equation.
- Use the center and/or radius to answer the question.

Explanation:

The equation given is in general form rather than in standard form, so complete the square for both x and y. Start by grouping the x terms together and the y terms together:

$$x^2 - 4x + y^2 - 8y = 16$$
$$(x^2 - 4x + ?) + (y^2 - 8y + ?) = 16$$
$$(x^2 - 4x + 4) + (y^2 - 8y + 16) = 16 + 4 + 16$$
$$(x - 2)^2 + (y - 4)^2 = 36$$

With the equation in standard form, it is now clear that the center is $(2, 4)$. Choice **(C)** is correct.

Try on Your Own

Directions

Take as much time as you need on these questions. Work carefully and methodically. There will be an opportunity for timed practice later in the book.

28

HINT: For Q28, which part of the circle's equation would be the easiest to use to eliminate answer choices? The coordinates of the circle's center? The radius?

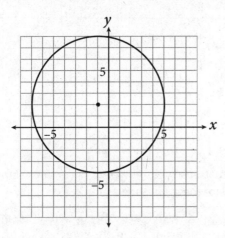

Which of the following represents the equation of the circle shown?

Ⓐ $(x - 1)^2 + (y + 2)^2 = 6$

Ⓑ $(x + 1)^2 + (y - 2)^2 = 6$

Ⓒ $(x - 1)^2 + (y + 2)^2 = 36$

Ⓓ $(x + 1)^2 + (y - 2)^2 = 36$

29

A circle in the standard (x, y) coordinate plane is tangent to the x-axis at 4 and tangent to the y-axis at 4. Which of the following is the equation of the circle?

Ⓐ $x^2 + y^2 = 4$

Ⓑ $x^2 + y^2 = 16$

Ⓒ $(x - 4)^2 + (y - 4)^2 = 4$

Ⓓ $(x - 4)^2 + (y - 4)^2 = 16$

30

HINT: For Q30, complete the square for the x and y terms.

$$x^2 + y^2 + 8x - 20y = 28$$

What is the diameter of the circle given by the equation?

Ⓐ 12

Ⓑ 24

Ⓒ 28

Ⓓ 56

31

A circle in the xy-plane is defined by the equation $(x - 4)^2 + (y + 2)^2 = 100$. Which of the following points is located on the circumference of the circle?

Ⓐ $(-3, 5)$

Ⓑ $(0, 9)$

Ⓒ $(4, -2)$

Ⓓ $(4, 8)$

ARC LENGTH AND SECTORS

LEARNING OBJECTIVES

After this lesson, you will be able to:

- Calculate the length of an arc or the area of a sector defined by a central angle
- Convert degrees to radians

To answer a question like this:

A circle with a diameter of 8 inches is divided into a number of equal sectors such that each sector has an area of $\frac{4\pi}{3}$ square inches. What is the central angle of each sector, in radians?

A) $\frac{\pi}{12}$

B) $\frac{\pi}{6}$

C) $\frac{\pi}{3}$

D) $\frac{2\pi}{3}$

You need to know this:

The SAT may ask you about the following parts of circles: arcs, central angles, inscribed angles, and sectors. The ability to set up ratios and proportions correctly is essential for these questions.

- An **arc** is part of a circle's circumference. If the circumference is divided into exactly two arcs, the smaller one is called the **minor arc** and the larger one is called the **major arc**. If a diameter cuts the circle in half, the two arcs formed are called **semicircles**. An arc length can never be greater than the circle's circumference.

- An angle formed by two radii is called a **central angle**. Because a full circle contains 360°, a central angle measure cannot be greater than this.

- The part of a circle's area defined by a central angle is called a **sector**. The area of a sector cannot be greater than the circle's total area.

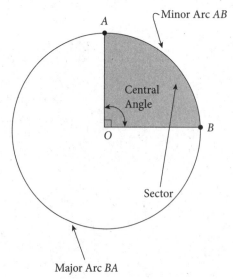

Minor Arc *AB*

Central Angle

Sector

A

O

B

Major Arc *BA*

The ratios formed by these three parts and their whole counterparts are:

$$\frac{\text{central angle}}{360°} = \frac{\text{arc length}}{\text{circumference}} = \frac{\text{sector area}}{\text{circle area}}$$

Notice that all of these ratios are equal. Intuitively, this should make sense: when you slice a pizza into four equal slices, each piece should have $\frac{1}{4}$ of the cheese, crust, and sauce. If you slice a circle into four equal pieces, the same principle applies: each piece should have $\frac{1}{4}$ of the degrees, circumference, and area.

An angle whose vertex is on the edge of the circle is called an **inscribed angle**. As this vertex moves along the edge, the measure of the inscribed angle remains constant as long as the minor arc created does not change. When the line segments that create an inscribed angle define the same minor arc that a pair of radii do, a special relationship appears: the central angle measure is twice that of the inscribed angle.

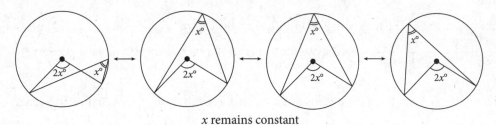

x remains constant

Most geometry questions present angle measures in degrees, but some may present angle measures in radians. To convert between degrees and radians, use this relationship as a conversion factor: $180° = \pi$ radians. For instance, if you're asked to convert 90° into radians: $90° \times \frac{\pi}{180°} = \frac{\pi}{2}$. Note that there isn't a symbol for radians, so $\frac{\pi}{2}$ is read as "$\frac{\pi}{2}$ radians." This conversion works in the opposite direction as well: to convert radians to degrees, multiply by $\frac{180°}{\pi}$.

Most graphing calculators have both degree and radian modes, so make sure you're in the correct mode for the question you're working on.

The following figure shows a detailed unit circle diagram with common degree and radian measures (and the coordinates of the ends of their respective radii):

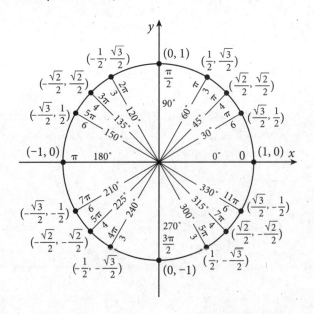

The coordinates at a particular angle measure translate into the leg lengths of the triangle created when a vertical line is drawn from the end of the radius down (or up if you're in quadrant III or IV) to the *x*-axis. For example, at 60°, the horizontal leg has a length of $\frac{1}{2}$ and the vertical leg has a length of $\frac{\sqrt{3}}{2}$.

You need to do this:

- To find the length of an arc or the area of a sector, you need to know the angle that defines the arc or sector as well as the radius of the circle. Questions that are especially tricky might not give you those values directly but will instead give you a way of calculating them.

- When converting between degrees and radians, set up the conversion fraction so that the units cancel.

Explanation:

First, use the radius to find the area of the circle. Then find the central angle by plugging the known values into $\frac{\text{central angle}}{360°} = \frac{\text{sector area}}{\text{circle area}}$. Since the question asks for the central angle in radians, convert 360° to 2π radians.

The question says the diameter of the circle is 8 inches, so the radius is 4 inches. A circle with a radius of 4 inches has an area of $\pi r^2 = 16\pi$. The area of each sector is $\frac{4\pi}{3}$, so $\frac{\text{central angle}}{2\pi} = \frac{\frac{4}{3}\pi}{16\pi}$.

Cross-multiply to solve for the central angle:

$$\text{central angle} \times 16\pi = \frac{4}{3}\pi(2\pi)$$

$$\text{central angle} = \frac{\frac{8}{3}\pi^2}{16\pi}$$

$$\text{central angle} = \frac{\pi}{6}$$

Choice **(B)** is correct.

Try on Your Own

Directions

Take as much time as you need on these questions. Work carefully and methodically. There will be an opportunity for timed practice later in the book.

32

HINT: For Q32, what do you need to calculate before using the circle ratios?

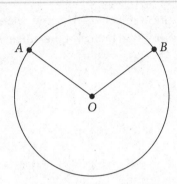

Note: Figure not drawn to scale.

In the figure, circle O has a radius of 120 centimeters. If the length of minor arc AB is 200 centimeters, what is the measure of central angle AOB, to the nearest tenth of a degree?

- (A) 95.5

- (B) 98.2

- (C) 102.1

- (D) 105.4

33

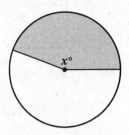

In the figure, the ratio of the shaded area to the non-shaded area is 4 to 5. What is the value of x, in degrees?

- (A) 135

- (B) 145

- (C) 160

- (D) 288

34

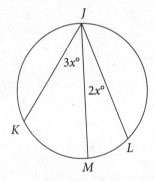

In the figure, points J, K, L, and M lie on the circle. If minor arc KL has a measure of 150°, what is the value of x?

- (A) 12

- (B) 15

- (C) 30

- (D) 60

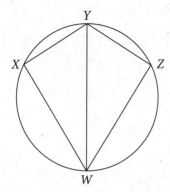

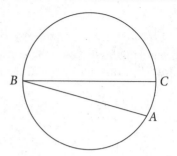

In the figure, points W, X, Y, and Z lie on the circle. Semicircle YW has a measure of 180°, and minor arcs XY and YZ each have a measure of 60°. If the length of chord YZ is 3, then what is the length of chord WX?

Ⓐ $\sqrt{3}$

Ⓑ 3

Ⓒ $3\sqrt{3}$

Ⓓ 6

In the figure, BC is the diameter of the circle. If the measure of minor arc AC is 30°, then what is the measure of minor arc BA, in radians?

Ⓐ $\dfrac{\pi}{2}$

Ⓑ $\dfrac{2\pi}{3}$

Ⓒ $\dfrac{3\pi}{4}$

Ⓓ $\dfrac{5\pi}{6}$

THREE-DIMENSIONAL FIGURES

LEARNING OBJECTIVES

After this lesson, you will be able to:

- Calculate the volume of common solids
- Calculate the surface area of common solids

To answer a question like this:

The side lengths inside a sandbox in the shape of a square prism are 24 feet, and the box is currently one-third full of sand from the bottom up. Marcus adds 480 cubic feet of sand to completely fill the sandbox. How many inches deep is the sandbox? (Note: 1 foot = 12 inches)

A) 10

B) 15

C) 20

D) 25

You need to know this:

Over the last several sections, you learned about two-dimensional (2-D) shapes and how to tackle SAT questions involving them. Now you'll learn how to do the same for questions containing three-dimensional (3-D) shapes, also called solids. There are several different types of solids that might appear on the SAT—rectangular solids, cubes, cylinders, prisms, spheres, cones, pyramids—and knowing their structures will help you on test day.

The following diagram shows the basic anatomy of a 3-D shape:

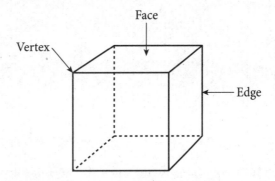

A **face** (or **surface**) is a 2-D shape that acts as one of the sides of the solid. Two faces meet at a line segment called an **edge**, and three faces meet at a single point called a **vertex**.

Volume

Volume is the amount of 3-D space occupied by a solid. You can find the volume of many 3-D shapes by finding the area of the base and multiplying it by the height. In the table of formulas, the pieces that represent the areas of the bases are enclosed in parentheses.

RECTANGULAR SOLID	CUBE	RIGHT CYLINDER
$(l \times w) \times h$	$(s \times s) \times s = s^3$	$(\pi \times r^2) \times h$

The three 3-D shapes shown above are prisms. Almost all prisms on the SAT are right prisms; that is, all faces are perpendicular to those with which they share edges. For any other right prism, use the general volume formula ($V = A_{\text{base}} \times h$).

More complicated 3-D shapes include the right pyramid, right cone, and sphere. The vertex of a right pyramid or right cone will always be centered above the middle of the base. Their volume formulas are similar to those of prisms, albeit with different coefficients.

Some of these formulas might look daunting, but you won't have to memorize them for test day. They'll be provided on the reference sheet at the beginning of each Math module.

RIGHT RECTANGULAR PYRAMID	RIGHT CONE	SPHERE
$\frac{1}{3} \times (l \times w) \times h$	$\frac{1}{3} \times (\pi \times r^2) \times h$	$\frac{4}{3} \times \pi \times r^3$

A right pyramid can have any polygon as its base, but the square variety is the one you're most likely to see on the SAT. Also note that the vertex above the base of a right pyramid or cone is not necessarily formed by an intersection of exactly three faces, as in prisms, but it is still a single point and is still called a vertex.

Surface Area

Surface area is the sum of the areas of all faces of a solid. To calculate the surface area of a solid, simply find the area of each face using your 2-D geometry skills, then add them all together.

You might think that finding the surface area of a solid with many sides, such as a right hexagonal prism, is a tall order. However, you can save time by realizing that this prism has two identical hexagonal faces and six identical rectangular faces. Don't waste time finding the area of each of the eight surfaces. Find the area of one hexagonal face and one rectangular face only. Then multiply the area of the hexagonal face by 2 and the area of the rectangular face by 6, add the products together, and you're done. The same is true for other 3-D shapes such as rectangular solids (including cubes), other right prisms, and certain pyramids.

You need to do this:

- To answer questions that involve regular solids, look for ways to find the area of the base and the height.
- To answer questions that involve solids that are not regular, look up and apply the appropriate formula.
- To answer questions that involve surface area, look for surfaces that are the same. Calculate the area of each kind of surface once, and then multiply by the number of identical surfaces in the solid.

Explanation:

One way to approach this question is to find the total volume of the sandbox first and then use that volume to calculate its depth. If the sandbox is one-third full, it is two-thirds empty, and, according to the question, this empty space is 480 cubic feet. So two-thirds of the total volume is 480:

$$\frac{2}{3} \times V = 480 \text{ ft}^3$$

$$V = 480 \times \frac{3}{2} = 720 \text{ ft}^3$$

The volume of the sandbox is also equal to the product of its length, width, and height. The question states that the length and width are each 24 feet, so plug these values into the formula and solve for height:

$$V = l \times w \times h$$

$$720 = 24 \times 24 \times h$$

$$\frac{720}{24 \times 24} = h$$

$$\frac{720}{576} = h$$

$$1.25 \text{ feet} = h$$

The question asks for inches, so use 12 inches = 1 foot to convert from feet to inches:

$$1.25 \text{ feet} \times \frac{12 \text{ inches}}{1 \text{ foot}} = 15 \text{ inches}$$

Choice (**B**) is correct.

Try on Your Own

Directions

Take as much time as you need on these questions. Work carefully and methodically. There will be an opportunity for timed practice later in the book.

37

HINT: For Q37, refer to the formulas given in the lesson. On test day, they are provided.

Two ornamental glass spheres have diameters of 6 centimeters and 12 centimeters, respectively. What is the positive difference, in cubic centimeters, in their volumes?

Ⓐ 36π

Ⓑ 252π

Ⓒ 288π

Ⓓ $2,016\pi$

38

HINT: For Q38, when the water is poured into a larger glass, what information about the water does not change?

Alma completely fills a small cylindrical glass with a height of 6 inches and a diameter of 3 inches with water. She then pours the water from the small glass into a larger cylindrical glass that is 8 inches tall and 4 inches in diameter. Assuming Alma doesn't spill any water, how many inches high will the water reach in the larger glass?

Ⓐ   1.5

Ⓑ   2.25

Ⓒ   3.375

Ⓓ   6.0

39

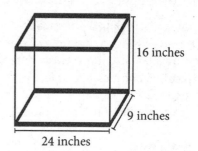

16 inches

9 inches

24 inches

Staff at a pet store want to fill the bottom of 50 fish tanks (one shown) with two inches of sand. Sand comes in full-size 40-pound bags. If 1 cubic inch of sand weighs 0.125 pounds, how many bags of sand does the pet store need to buy?

40

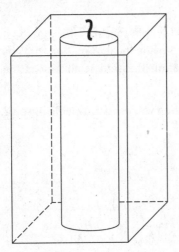

In the figure, a cylindrical candle with a diameter of 2 inches and height of 8 inches sits within a rectangular glass box. The box is the same height as the candle and the area of the base of the box is 15 square inches. If Felipe wants to fill the space between the candle and the box with wax, how many cubic inches of wax does he need?

Ⓐ $120 - 8\pi$

Ⓑ $120 - 32\pi$

Ⓒ $225 - 8\pi$

Ⓓ $225 - 32\pi$

41

The perimeter of one face of a cube is $4x$. What is the surface area of the cube in terms of x?

Ⓐ $6x$

Ⓑ $24x$

Ⓒ $6x^2$

Ⓓ $16x^2$

42

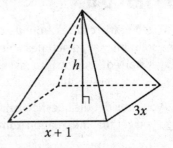

If the volume of the pyramid shown in the figure can be represented by the function $V(x) = x^3 - x$, which of the following expressions represents the pyramid's height?

Ⓐ x

Ⓑ $2x$

Ⓒ $x - 1$

Ⓓ $x - 3$

ON TEST DAY

SAT geometry revolves around a small set of basic formulas and simple concepts. Though the path to the solution may sometimes seem hidden, the test will always provide the information that you need to get started. Your job is to make deductions from that information to assemble all the facts necessary to answer the question.

As you consider the question below, ask yourself what information you need to be able to solve. How can you get that information from what you're given?

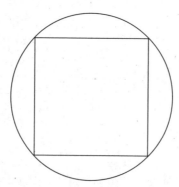

43. In the figure shown, a square is inscribed in a circle, and the area of the square is 400 square units. What is the area of the circle in square units?

A) 50π

B) 100π

C) 200π

D) 400π

The explanation appears at the end of this chapter.

HOW MUCH HAVE YOU LEARNED?

Directions

For testlike practice, give yourself 19 minutes to complete this question set. Be sure to study the explanations, even for questions you got right. They can be found at the end of this chapter. Note that this question set includes foundational topics in Geometry covered in Math Fundamentals in chapter 2.

Make use of the formula sheet below as needed; you'll have these same formulas available in your test booklet when you take the real SAT.

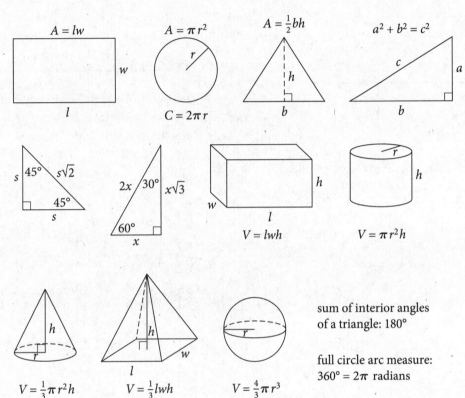

44

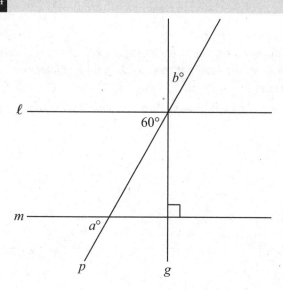

In the figure shown, lines l and m are parallel. What is the value of $a - b$?

(A) 30

(B) 40

(C) 60

(D) 90

45

A full cylindrical container of juice concentrate has a diameter of 6 inches and a height of 12 inches. The concentrate must be diluted with water to make a mix that is 75 percent water and 25 percent concentrate. Approximately, what is the total volume of juice, in cubic inches, after the concentrate is diluted?

(A) 108

(B) 339

(C) 452

(D) 1,357

46

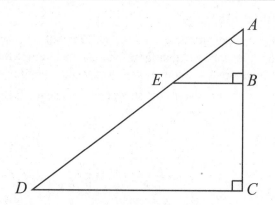

Triangles ABE and ACD are shown above. If AB is 3, DC is 12, and AD is 15, which of the following is equal to the ratio 1:3?

(A) $\dfrac{EB}{AC}$

(B) $\dfrac{AE}{DC}$

(C) $\dfrac{EB}{DC}$

(D) $\dfrac{AE}{AC}$

47

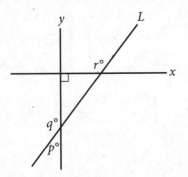

In the figure shown, if $q = 140$, what is the value of $r - p$?

Ⓐ 0

Ⓑ 40

Ⓒ 90

Ⓓ 130

48

The area of a right triangle is 35 square inches. If the longer leg is 3 inches longer than the shorter leg, what is the length of the hypotenuse, in inches?

Ⓐ $\dfrac{\sqrt{35}}{2}$

Ⓑ $\sqrt{10}$

Ⓒ 10

Ⓓ $\sqrt{149}$

49

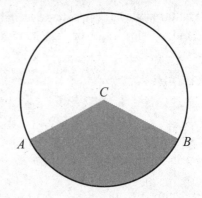

The circle shown has center C and a circumference of 40π. The area of the shaded sector is 140π. What is the degree measure of central angle ACB?

50

A cube with an edge length of x has a volume of a. In terms of a, what is the volume of a cube with an edge length of $2.5x$?

Ⓐ $2.5a$

Ⓑ $6.25a$

Ⓒ $7.5a$

Ⓓ $15.625a$

51

A right triangle has a hypotenuse length of $\sqrt{7}$ and one side length of $\sqrt{2}$. What is the area of the triangle?

(A) $\dfrac{\sqrt{10}}{2}$

(B) $\dfrac{\sqrt{14}}{2}$

(C) $\sqrt{10}$

(D) 5

52

The diameter of circle B is 30 percent larger than the diameter of circle A. What is circle B's area as a percentage of circle A's area?

(A) 49%

(B) 70%

(C) 130%

(D) 169%

53

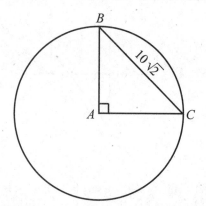

In the circle shown, point A is the center of the circle and points B and C lie on its circumference. The length of BC is $10\sqrt{2}$. What is the circumference of the circle?

(A) 5π

(B) $5\sqrt{2}\,\pi$

(C) 10π

(D) 20π

54

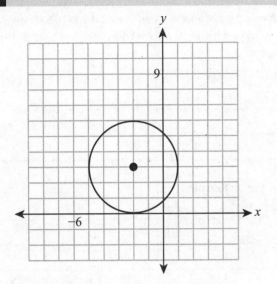

Which of the following is the equation of the circle shown?

- Ⓐ $(x + 2)^2 + (y - 3)^2 = 9$

- Ⓑ $(x + 2)^2 + (y - 3)^2 = 6$

- Ⓒ $(x + 2)^2 + (y - 3)^2 = 3$

- Ⓓ $(x - 2)^2 + (y + 3)^2 = 9$

55

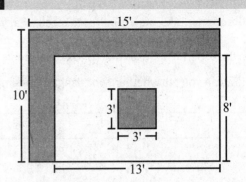

The diagram represents the floor plan of a rectangular kitchen. The shaded regions represent countertop space. All interior angles are 90°, and all dimensions are shown in feet. What is the combined area of the countertop space, in square feet?

REFLECT

Directions: Take a few minutes to recall what you've learned and what you've been practicing in this chapter. Consider the following questions, jot down your best answer for each one, and then compare your reflections to the expert responses that follow. Use your level of confidence to determine what to do next.

How can you tell whether two triangles are similar?

_____

_____

_____

What are the two Pythagorean triples you are most likely to see on test day?

_____

_____

_____

What are the ratios of the side lengths of a 45-45-90 triangle? Of a 30-60-90 triangle?

_____

_____

_____

What is the standard form for the equation of a circle?

_____

_____

_____

What is the relationship of a circle's central angle to the arc and sector the angle defines?

_____

_____

_____

How would you find the surface area of a right triangular prism with equilateral triangles as its bases?

_____

_____

_____

Expert Responses

How can you tell whether two triangles are similar?

There are three ways to tell:

- *Two of their three angles are congruent (angle-angle).*
- *Two of their three sides are in the same proportion and the intervening angle is congruent (side-angle-side).*
- *Their three sides are in the same proportion (side-side-side).*

What are the two Pythagorean triples you are most likely to see on test day?

The two most common Pythagorean triples on the SAT are 3:4:5 and 5:12:13. You may also see multiples of these, e.g., 6:8:10 or 10:24:26.

What are the ratios of the side lengths of a 45-45-90 triangle? Of a 30-60-90 triangle?

The side lengths of a 45-45-90 triangle are always in the ratio of $x:x:x\sqrt{2}$. The side lengths of a 30-60-90 triangle are always in the ratio of $x:x\sqrt{3}:2x$. Remember that the shortest side of any triangle is across from the smallest angle and the longest side is across from the greatest angle.

What is the standard form for the equation of a circle?

The equation of a circle in the coordinate plane is $(x - h)^2 + (y - k)^2 = r^2$, where r is the radius of the circle and (h, k) is the ordered pair representing its center.

What is the relationship of a circle's central angle to the arc and sector the angle defines?

The central angle, the arc, and the sector are all in proportion to the full circle:

$$\frac{\text{central angle}}{360°} = \frac{\text{arc length}}{\text{circumference}} = \frac{\text{sector area}}{\text{circle area}}$$

How would you find the surface area of a right triangular prism with equilateral triangles as its bases?

Calculate the area of one of the equilateral triangles and multiply by 2. Calculate the area of one of the rectangular faces and multiply by 3. Then add the results.

Next Steps

If you answered most questions correctly in the "How Much Have You Learned?" section, and if your responses to the Reflect questions were similar to those of the SAT expert, then consider Geometry an area of strength and move on to the next chapter. Come back to this topic periodically to ensure your skills stay sharp.

If you don't yet feel confident, review those parts of this chapter that you have not yet mastered. In particular, review the lessons on similar triangles, the Pythagorean theorem, and special right triangles, as these are high-yield topics on the SAT. Then try the questions you missed again. As always, be sure to review the explanations closely. Finally, **go online** (www.kaptest.com/moreonline) for additional practice on the highest yield topics in this chapter.

Math

Check Your Work – Chapter 14

1.   C

Difficulty: Easy

Category: Geometry and Trigonometry

Getting to the Answer: When a line intersects two parallel lines, it intersects each of the parallel lines at the same angle. Therefore, the value of x will equal the value of the angle supplementary to 76.

Since $180 - 76 = 104$, $x = 104$, so choice **(C)** is correct.

2.   70

Difficulty: Easy

Category: Geometry and Trigonometry

Getting to the Answer: When two or more angles combine to form a straight line, the sum of the angles is $180°$. Therefore, $v + w + x = 180$.

The question states that $x = 45$ and $v = 65$, so you can say that $65 + w + 45 = 180$. That means $180 - 65 - 45 = w$. Thus, $w = 70$.

Angle w forms a vertical angle with angle y. Therefore, $y = w$, so $y = 70$. Enter **70**.

3.   A

Difficulty: Medium

Category: Geometry and Trigonometry

Getting to the Answer: When a transversal crosses two or more parallel lines, all acute angles formed will be equal and all obtuse angles formed will be equal.

The question asks for the answer choice that does NOT necessarily correspond to the value of angle a, which is an obtuse angle. Check each answer and eliminate any choice that is equal to the value of an obtuse angle in the diagram.

Angles b and f are both acute angles in the diagram; while it's possible that the sum of two acute angles is equal to one obtuse angle, this is not *necessarily* true. Therefore, choice **(A)** is correct.

For the record, d forms a vertical angle with a, so $d = a$. Eliminate (B). Since any obtuse and acute angle pair in the diagram form a straight line (that is, the pair are supplementary angles) $180 - b = a$. Eliminate (C). Finally, e and h are both obtuse angles, so they are each equal to a. So

$$\frac{e + h}{2} = \frac{a + a}{2} = \frac{2a}{2} = a$$

This allows you to eliminate (D). Thus, every other answer choice is a match in value for angle a and can be eliminated. Choose **(A)**.

4.   B

Difficulty: Medium

Category: Geometry and Trigonometry

Getting to the Answer: Since lines j and k are parallel, and line l is a transversal passing through j and k, all obtuse angles formed by the transversal will be identical, and all acute angles formed will also be identical. Therefore, acute angles b and d are equal.

The question specifies that $f = 9b$. Therefore, you can say that the value of each obtuse angle in the diagram is 9 times the value of each acute angle. Since an acute angle and an obtuse angle in the figure are supplementary—they sum to $180°$—you can say that $f + b = 180°$. Substituting $9b$ for f, the equation becomes $9b + b = 180°$, so $10b = 180°$. Now isolate b:

$$10b = 180°$$
$$\frac{10b}{10} = \frac{180°}{10}$$
$$b = 18°$$

The question asks for the value of $2d$. Since $d = b$, $2d = 2b$. That is $2 \times 18 = 36$. Choice **(B)** is correct.

5.   330

Difficulty: Medium

Category: Geometry and Trigonometry

Getting to the Answer: When a transversal crosses parallel lines, all the acute angles are equal, and all the obtuse angles are equal.

Since $b = 30$ and $a + b = 180$, you know that $a = 180 - 30 = 150$. The angles represented by b and c are both acute angles formed by the same transversal, so $b = c$. Since $b = 30$, $c = 30$. Similarly, the angles represented by a and e are both obtuse angles formed by the same transversal, so $a = e$.

Since $a = 150$, you know that $e = 150$. The question asks for the sum of a, c, and e, which is $a + c + e = 150 + 30 + 150 = 330$.

Enter **330**.

6. D

Difficulty: Hard

Category: Geometry and Trigonometry

Getting to the Answer:

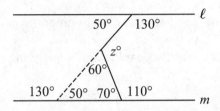

Continue the transversal as shown until it intersects line m to create a triangle. The base interior angles of the triangle are $180° - 130° = 50°$ and $180° - 110° = 70°$ (from alternate interior angles of the transversals). Since the sum of the interior angles in a triangle is always $180°$, the remaining angle in the triangle is $180° - 50° - 70° = 60°$. Therefore, z equals $180° - 60° = 120°$. Choice **(D)** is correct.

7. B

Difficulty: Easy

Category: Geometry and Trigonometry

Getting to the Answer: This is a matter of plugging into the formulas and subtracting the results. The area of a parallelogram is base times height, or $A = 8 \times 9 = 72$. The area of a triangle is $A = \frac{1}{2}bh$, or $A = \frac{1}{2}(6)(7) = 21$. Subtract to find the difference of $72 - 21 = 51$. **(B)** is correct.

8. C

Difficulty: Easy

Category: Geometry and Trigonometry

Getting to the Answer: The perimeter of a rectangle is $2l + 2w$, where l is the length and w is the width. Since the length is 50 times its width, or $l = 50w$, the perimeter of the beam is $2(50w) + 2w = 102w$ centimeters. **(C)** is correct.

9. 14

Difficulty: Medium

Category: Geometry and Trigonometry

Getting to the Answer: Use the formula for the area of a rectangle: $A = l \times w$. In this case, l is height and

equals $w - 34$. Plugging that and the area into the formula and solving for w by factoring gives:

$$672 = (w - 34)(w)$$
$$672 = w^2 - 34w$$
$$0 = w^2 - 34w - 672$$
$$0 = (w - 48)(w + 14)$$
$$w = 48 \text{ and } -14$$

Because the width cannot be negative, the width is 48 ft. The height is $48 - 34 = 14$ ft. Enter **14**.

10. B

Difficulty: Medium

Category: Geometry and Trigonometry

Getting to the Answer: The formula for the area of a triangle is $A = \frac{1}{2}bh$, so $x = \frac{1}{2}bh$. Since both the base and height of the triangle are doubled, the base of the new triangle is $2b$ and the height of the new triangle is $2h$. This gives an area of $\frac{1}{2}(2b)(2h)$ or $\frac{1}{2}bh \times 4$. Given that $x = \frac{1}{2}bh$, the area of the new triangle in terms of x is $4x$. **(B)** is correct.

11. A

Difficulty: Hard

Category: Geometry and Trigonometry

Getting to the Answer: Let x be a side of Square B. The area of a square is equal to its side length squared, so the area of Square B is x^2. Since the area of Square A is 4 times the area of Square B, the area of Square A is $4x^2$. Taking the square root gives $2x$ as the side of Square A. The perimeter of a square is 4 times its side length. Thus, the perimeter of Square A is $4(2x) = 8x$ and the perimeter of Square B is $4x$. The perimeter of Square A is $\frac{8x}{4x} = 2$ times greater than the perimeter of Square B. **(A)** is correct.

12. A

Difficulty: Hard

Category: Geometry and Trigonometry

Getting to the Answer: Let h represent the height of the original triangle and b the base. By definition, x percent is $\frac{x}{100}$. Thus, the new triangle has a height of $1.5h$ and a base of $\left(1 - \frac{x}{100}\right)b$. The new area is $1.2A$. Plugging these into the formula for the area of a triangle, $A = \frac{1}{2}bh$, gives:

$$1.2A = \frac{1}{2}\left(1 - \frac{x}{100}\right)b(1.5h)$$

$$1.2\left(\frac{1}{2}bh\right) = \frac{1}{2}\left(1 - \frac{x}{100}\right)b(1.5h)$$

$$1.2 = \left(1 - \frac{x}{100}\right)(1.5)$$

$$0.8 = 1 - \frac{x}{100}$$

$$-0.2 = -\frac{x}{100}$$

$$20 = x$$

(A) is correct.

13. 426

Difficulty: Medium

Category: Geometry and Trigonometry

Strategic Advice: The figure contains a pair of similar triangles. Use the fact that their sides are proportional to find the required length.

Getting to the Answer: The question asks for the length of *DE*. First, find the length of *EC* by setting up a proportion where *BD* is related to *AE* in the same way that *DC* is related to the unknown *EC*. *AE* is 324 and *DC* is 50% longer than segment *BD*, or $1.5 \times 40 = 60$ feet:

$$\frac{BD}{AE} = \frac{DC}{EC}$$

$$\frac{40}{324} = \frac{60}{EC}$$

$$40(EC) = 19{,}440$$

$$EC = 486$$

Note that $DE + DC = EC$, which means $DE = EC - DC$. Subtract the length of *DC*, 60, from the length of *EC*, 486, to obtain 426, the length of *DE*. Enter **426**.

14. B

Difficulty: Medium

Category: Geometry and Trigonometry

Getting to the Answer: Given the area of $\triangle ABC$ and the length of the base *AB*, you can find *BC*, its height. Use the triangle area formula:

$$\text{Area} = \frac{1}{2}b \times h$$

$$150 = \frac{1}{2}(20)(BC)$$

$$150 = 10(BC)$$

$$15 = BC$$

Because lengths $BC = 15$ and $AB = 20$, $\triangle ABC$ is a 3:4:5 triangle with dimensions scaled up by a factor of 5. The hypotenuse, *AC*, must be $5 \times 5 = 25$. $\triangle ABC$ and $\triangle AGH$ are similar triangles because they share an angle at vertex *A* and they each have a right angle. Therefore, their corresponding sides must be proportional. The question says that the hypotenuse of $\triangle AGH$, *AH*, is 20, so use this information to create a proportion:

$$\frac{AH}{AC} = \frac{HG}{BC}$$

$$\frac{20}{25} = \frac{HG}{15}$$

$$300 = 25(HG)$$

$$HG = 12$$

Choice **(B)** is the correct answer.

15. B

Difficulty: Medium

Category: Geometry and Trigonometry

Getting to the Answer: The question says that segment *HI* is the bisector of segments *LO* and *OW*. This tells you two things: 1) *HI* divides both *LO* and *OW* exactly in half and 2) *HI* is parallel to *LW*.

Because *HI* is parallel to *LW*, angles *L* and *H* must be congruent (they are corresponding angles), and angles *W* and *I* must be congruent (they are also corresponding angles). Angle *O* is shared by both triangles. The triangles, therefore, are similar. Side lengths of similar triangles are in proportion to one another. Because *I* is the midpoint of *OW*, *OI* is half as long as *OW*. The same is true for the other side: *OH* is half as long as *OL*. Thus, the sides are in the ratio 1:2. The question gives the side lengths of *LW* and *HI*. Use this ratio and these side lengths to set up a proportion and solve for *x*:

$$\frac{1}{2} = \frac{HI}{LW}$$

$$\frac{1}{2} = \frac{4x - 1}{30}$$

$$30 = 2(4x - 1)$$

$$30 = 8x - 2$$

$$32 = 8x$$

$$4 = x$$

The correct answer is **(B)**.

16. 9

Difficulty: Hard

Category: Geometry and Trigonometry

Getting to the Answer: Corresponding sides of similar triangles are proportional. Draw a quick sketch to find as many side lengths as you can, determine the ratio of the sides between the two triangles, and use that ratio to obtain the missing vertex.

On either the included graphing calculator or your scratch paper, plot all the points given in the question, labeling them as you go so you don't get confused. You know that D and A are in the same quadrant, which means the triangles are both oriented the same way, so make your sketch accordingly:

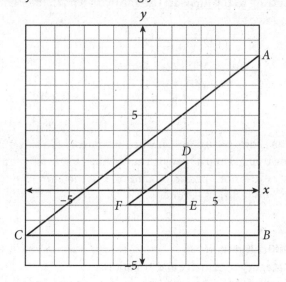

Once you have plotted triangle DEF and the base of triangle ABC, you can determine that the ratio of the triangles is 1:4 (the base of DEF has a length of 4 and the base of ABC has a length of 16). To determine where you should put A, find the length of side DE and then multiply by 4. The length of the vertical side of triangle ABC is $3 \times 4 = 12$. Because one vertex is at $(8, -3)$, vertex A must be 12 vertical units above that point, or $(8, 9)$. The y-coordinate of A is 9. Enter **9**.

17. B

Difficulty: Hard

Category: Geometry and Trigonometry

Getting to the Answer: The figure gives two nested triangles that share angle C. And, because BD is parallel to AE, angles CAE and CBD are congruent—they are corresponding angles. Two pairs of congruent angles means that triangles ACE and BCD are similar. (You could also have analyzed angles CDB and CEA, but you

need only two pairs of congruent angles to conclude that two triangles are similar.)

Set up a proportion using the triangles' side lengths. You'll need to translate from English into math as you go: $AB = 5$ and BC is three times that, or 15. This means $AC = 5 + 15 = 20$. CD is 2 more than half AC, $\frac{20}{2} + 2 = 10 + 2 = 12$. Use the three known side lengths to create a proportion and solve for EC:

$$\frac{BC}{AC} = \frac{CD}{EC}$$
$$\frac{15}{20} = \frac{12}{EC}$$
$$15(EC) = 240$$
$$EC = 16$$

The question asks for the length of segment DE, which is $EC - CD$, or $16 - 12 = 4$. **(B)** is correct.

18. B

Difficulty: Medium

Category: Geometry and Trigonometry

Getting to the Answer: Start by connecting the ranch to the campsite. Then draw in a horizontal line and a vertical line to form a right triangle.

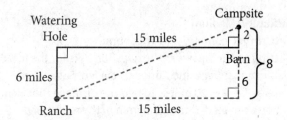

The length of one leg of the triangle is 15 miles, the distance from the watering hole to the barn. The length of the other leg is $6 + 2 = 8$ miles, the distance from the ranch to the watering hole plus the distance from the barn to the campsite. The two legs of the right triangle are 8 and 15. You may recognize the Pythagorean triple 8:15:17, but if you don't, you can always use the Pythagorean theorem:

$$8^2 + 15^2 = c^2$$
$$64 + 225 = c^2$$
$$289 = c^2$$
$$17 = c$$

The direct route is 17 miles, so **(B)** is correct.

19. 4

Difficulty: Medium

Category: Geometry and Trigonometry

Getting to the Answer: Draw Ted's car and bike routes and label your diagram with the distances that you know. To find the distance of Ted's bike route, create a right triangle:

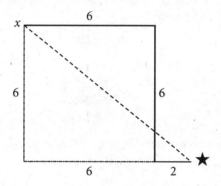

You can use the Pythagorean theorem to find the hypotenuse (bike route), but you can save time if you recognize the 6:8:10 Pythagorean triple. Ted's car route is $6 + 6 + 2 = 14$ miles, and his bike route is 10 miles. The difference between the two is **4**.

20. A

Difficulty: Medium

Category: Geometry and Trigonometry

Getting to the Answer: The question asks for the total distance that Sage and Annette traveled. Sage hiked $5 + 6 + 7 + 2 = 20$ miles. To find the distance that Annette traveled, draw a diagram of the routes and make Annette's direct route the hypotenuse of a right triangle:

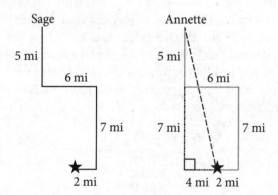

Use the Pythagorean theorem to calculate the distance that Annette traveled:

$$c^2 = (5 + 7)^2 + 4^2$$
$$c^2 = 144 + 16$$
$$c^2 = 160$$
$$c = \sqrt{160}$$
$$c \approx 12.65$$

Add this to Sage's distance to find the total distance: $20 + 12.65 = 32.65$ miles. Choice **(A)** is correct.

21. 4

Difficulty: Medium

Category: Geometry and Trigonometry

Getting to the Answer: Use the Pythagorean theorem to solve for x:

$$(3x)^2 + (x + 1)^2 = (3x + 1)^2$$
$$9x^2 + x^2 + 2x + 1 = 9x^2 + 6x + 1$$
$$x^2 + 2x + 1 = 6x + 1$$
$$x^2 - 4x = 0$$
$$x(x - 4) = 0$$

Therefore, $x = 0$ or $x = 4$. Since $3x$ represents a side of the triangle and a triangle cannot have a side length of 0, $x = 0$ is not a possible solution. This means that $x = 4$ must be correct. Enter **4**.

22. B

Difficulty: Hard

Category: Geometry and Trigonometry

Getting to the Answer: The word "isosceles" means that the triangle has two equal sides, so you can call them both x. The hypotenuse is given as 4. Plug these values into the Pythagorean theorem and solve for x:

$$a^2 + b^2 = c^2$$
$$x^2 + x^2 = 4^2$$
$$2x^2 = 16$$
$$x^2 = 8$$
$$x = \sqrt{8}$$
$$x = \sqrt{4}\,\sqrt{2}$$
$$x = 2\sqrt{2}$$

The question asks for the perimeter, which is the sum of all of the sides. Use this value of x to find the perimeter: $4 + 2\sqrt{2} + 2\sqrt{2} = 4 + 4\sqrt{2}$. Choice **(B)** is correct.

23. C

Difficulty: Medium

Category: Geometry and Trigonometry

Getting to the Answer: Triangle BCD is an isosceles right triangle, which means that it is a 45-45-90 right triangle with side length ratios of $x:x:x\sqrt{2}$. Because the two legs are each 4 units long, the hypotenuse BD is $4\sqrt{2}$. BD also acts as one leg of right triangle ABD. Since this leg is $4\sqrt{2}$ and the hypotenuse is $5\sqrt{2}$, triangle ABD is a 3:4:5 right triangle. Thus, the length of AD is $3\sqrt{2}$. The legs of a right triangle are also its base and height, so plug the lengths of the legs into the formula for the area of a triangle, $\frac{1}{2}bh$, to get $\frac{1}{2} \times 4\sqrt{2} \times 3\sqrt{2} = \frac{1}{2} \times 12 \times \sqrt{2} \times \sqrt{2} = 6 \times 2 = 12$. The correct answer is **(C)**.

24. B

Difficulty: Easy

Category: Geometry and Trigonometry

Getting to the Answer: The height of the amusement ride at point M is perpendicular to the ground, and the ride's angle of ascent is 30°, which creates a 30-60-90 triangle. Use the ratio of the sides, $x:x\sqrt{3}:2x$, to find the height at point M. Because the distance from point O to point M is $200\sqrt{3}$ and corresponds to the hypotenuse of the triangle, you can conclude that $2x = 200\sqrt{3}$. Solving for x by dividing both sides by 2 gives the length of the side opposite the 30° angle. This corresponds to the height of the amusement ride at point M: $x = 100\sqrt{3}$ feet. **(B)** is correct.

25. B

Difficulty: Medium

Category: Geometry and Trigonometry

Getting to the Answer: The two given 45° angles mean that the triangle must be a 45-45-90 triangle. Define the length of each of the legs as x and use the ratio of the sides $x:x:x\sqrt{2}$ to solve for x:

$$x\sqrt{2} = 16$$
$$\frac{x\sqrt{2}}{\sqrt{2}} = \frac{16}{\sqrt{2}}$$
$$x = \frac{16}{\sqrt{2}}$$

Next, determine the triangle's area using $\frac{1}{2}bh$. Note that in a right triangle, the sides that form the 90° angle can form the base and height. Thus, the area is $\frac{1}{2}\left(\frac{16}{\sqrt{2}}\right)\left(\frac{16}{\sqrt{2}}\right) = \frac{1}{2}\left(\frac{256}{2}\right) = \frac{256}{4} = 64$ square inches. Choice **(B)** is correct.

26. D

Difficulty: Hard

Category: Geometry and Trigonometry

Getting to the Answer: To find the area of the rectangle, you need to determine its length and width. On scratch paper, sketch a rectangle with a diagonal of 12. Note that the diagonal splits the rectangle into two right triangles and is the hypotenuse of each. The length and width of the rectangle correspond to the base and height of the right triangles.

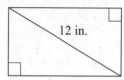

The question says that the length is $\sqrt{3}$ times the width, so the ratio of the triangle's short leg to its long leg is $x:x\sqrt{3}$, where x represents the shorter leg and $x\sqrt{3}$ represents the longer leg. This relationship is part of the ratio of the side lengths of a 30-60-90 triangle: $x:x\sqrt{3}:2x$.

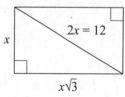

The hypotenuse is 12, which corresponds to $2x$, so $x = 6$. Therefore, the width is 6, and the length is $\sqrt{3} \times 6 = 6\sqrt{3}$. Use $l \times w$ to calculate the area: $6\sqrt{3} \times 6 = 36\sqrt{3}$ square inches. The correct answer is **(D)**.

27. 30

Difficulty: Medium

Category: Geometry and Trigonometry

Getting to the Answer: Note the right triangle with a height of 2 and hypotenuse of 4 formed by the ramp to the stage. The ratio of the short side to the hypotenuse is 2:4, or 1:2. Notice that this matches the ratio of the short side to the hypotenuse for a 30-60-90 triangle: $x:x\sqrt{3}:2x$. The angle of incline is opposite the short side, so that is 30°. Enter **30**.

28. D

Difficulty: Easy
Category: Geometry and Trigonometry
Getting to the Answer: The standard form of the equation of a circle is $(x - h)^2 + (y - k)^2 = r^2$, where (h, k) is the center of the circle and r is the length of the radius.

The answer choices have many similarities, which will make them easy to eliminate piece by piece. Use the graph to find the radius. From the center, you can count horizontally or vertically to the edge of the circle to find that its radius is 6. If $r = 6$, then $r^2 = 36$. Eliminate (A) and (B). Now find the x-coordinate of the center of the circle, -1. This means the $(x - h)^2$ part of the equation is $(x - (-1))^2 = (x + 1)^2$. Eliminate (C). Only **(D)** is left and is correct. Note that you do not even need to find the $(y - k)^2$ part of the equation, but for the record: because the y-coordinate of the center of the circle is 2, then $(y - k)^2$ becomes $(y - 2)^2$, and the full equation is $(x + 1)^2 + (y - 2)^2 = 36$. **(D)** is correct.

29. D

Difficulty: Medium
Category: Geometry and Trigonometry
Getting to the Answer: Draw a quick sketch on your scratch paper to help visualize the circle:

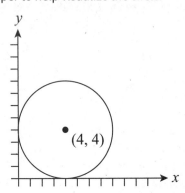

You can see from the diagram that the center of the circle is at (4, 4), and the radius is 4. In the equation of a circle, $(x - h)^2 + (y - k)^2 = r^2$, the center is at (h, k), and the radius is r. Plug in the information you know to get $(x - 4)^2 + (y - 4)^2 = 4^2$, which matches choice **(D)**.

Alternatively, you can input each of the equations in the answer choices into the graphing calculator to see which matches the description of the circle given the question. This will also lead you to the correct answer of **(D)**.

30. B

Difficulty: Hard
Category: Geometry and Trigonometry
Getting to the Answer: The question asks for the diameter, which is twice the radius. When the equation of a circle is in the form $(x - h)^2 + (y - k)^2 = r^2$, the r represents the length of the radius. The question gives the equation in general form, so you need to complete the square to put the equation into standard form.

You already have an x^2 and a y^2 in the given equation and the coefficients of x and y are even, so completing the square is fairly straightforward—there are just a lot of steps. Start by grouping the x's and y's together. Then, take the coefficient of the x term and divide it by 2, square it, and add it to the two terms with x variables.

Do the same with the y term. Remember to add these amounts to the other side of the equation as well. Then factor the perfect squares and simplify:

$$x^2 + y^2 + 8x - 20y = 28$$
$$x^2 + 8x + y^2 - 20y = 28$$
$$(x^2 + 8x + 16) + (y^2 - 20y + 100) = 28 + 16 + 100$$
$$(x + 4)^2 + (y - 10)^2 = 144$$

This equation tells you that r^2 is 144, which means that the radius is 12, and the diameter is twice that, or 24, which is **(B)**.

31. D

Difficulty: Medium
Category: Geometry and Trigonometry
Getting to the Answer: The given equation defines a circle with its center at $(4, -2)$ and a radius of 10. Any point on the circumference of the circle must satisfy that equation. Eliminate (C) because it is the center of the circle. Plug the other choices into the equation to see if they satisfy the given equation:

(A): $(-3 - 4)^2 + (5 + 2)^2 = (-7)^2 + (7)^2 = 49 + 49 = 98$. Since $98 < 100$, this is inside the circle. Eliminate (A).

(B): $(0 - 4)^2 + (9 + 2)^2 = (-4)^2 + (11)^2$. Since the second term alone is greater than 100, this is outside the circle. Eliminate (B).

Only **(D)** is left and is correct. For the record:

(D): $(4 - 4)^2 + (8 + 2)^2 = (0)^2 + (10)^2 = 100$. This point satisfies the equation and is, therefore, on the circumference. **(D)** is indeed correct.

32. A

Difficulty: Medium

Category: Geometry and Trigonometry

Getting to the Answer: To find a central angle based on a known arc length, use the relationship $\frac{\text{arc length}}{\text{circumference}} = \frac{\text{central angle}}{360°}$. The unknown in the relationship is the central angle, so call it a. Before you can fill in the rest of the equation, you need to find the circumference of the circle: $C = 2\pi r = 2\pi(120) = 240\pi$. Now, you're ready to solve for a:

$$\frac{\text{arc length}}{\text{circumference}} = \frac{\text{central angle}}{360°}$$

$$\frac{200}{240\pi} = \frac{a}{360°}$$

$$\frac{200(360)}{240\pi} = a$$

$$95.5° \approx a$$

(A) is correct.

33. C

Difficulty: Medium

Category: Geometry and Trigonometry

Getting to the Answer: Because the ratio of the shaded area to the non-shaded area is 4:5, the ratio of the shaded area to the entire circle is $4:(4 + 5) = 4:9$. This ratio is the same as the ratio of the interior angle of the shaded sector to 360°, or $x:360$. Set up a proportion using these ratios:

$$\frac{4}{9} = \frac{x}{360}$$

$$360(4) = 9x$$

$$1{,}440 = 9x$$

$$160 = x$$

Choice **(C)** is correct.

34. B

Difficulty: Medium

Category: Geometry and Trigonometry

Getting to the Answer: The measure of an arc is directly related to the degree measure of its central angle. The measure of an inscribed angle is half of that of the central angle. Because the measure of arc KL is 150°, the degree measure of the inscribed angle is half

of that. The inscribed angle for arc KL can be written as $3x + 2x$. Set up an equation to solve for x:

$$3x + 2x = \frac{1}{2}(150)$$

$$5x = 75$$

$$x = 15$$

Choice **(B)** is correct.

35. C

Difficulty: Hard

Category: Geometry and Trigonometry

Getting to the Answer: Note that the figure is composed of two triangles inscribed in a circle. If you have enough information about the triangles, you can find the length of WX. Arcs XY and YZ are each 60°. Because an inscribed angle is half of its corresponding arc, the inscribed angles XWY and ZWY are each 30°. Similarly, since arc YXW is 180°, the inscribed angle YZW is 90°. Therefore, both triangles are 30-60-90 special right triangles. Use the ratio of the sides $x:x\sqrt{3}:2x$ to find the length of WX. Given $YZ = 3$, XY also equals 3 and $\frac{3}{WX} = \frac{1}{\sqrt{3}}$, so $WX = 3\sqrt{3}$. Choice **(C)** is correct.

36. D

Difficulty: Medium

Category: Geometry and Trigonometry

Getting to the Answer: Since BC is the diameter, the measure of arc BAC is 180°. Therefore, the measure of arc BA is the measure of arc BAC minus the measure of arc AC: $180° - 30° = 150°$. Use $180° = \pi$ to convert to radians: $150° \times \frac{\pi}{180°} = \frac{5\pi}{6}$. Thus, **(D)** is correct.

37. B

Difficulty: Medium

Category: Geometry and Trigonometry

Getting to the Answer: Begin by finding the volume of each sphere using the volume formula for a sphere, remembering to halve the diameters first:

$$V_1 = \frac{4}{3}\pi r^3 = \frac{4}{3}\pi(3)^3 = \frac{4}{3}\pi(27) = 36\pi \text{ cm}^3$$

$$V_2 = \frac{4}{3}\pi r^3 = \frac{4}{3}\pi(6)^3 = \frac{4}{3}\pi(216) = 288\pi \text{ cm}^3$$

The positive difference is $288\pi \text{ cm}^3 - 36\pi \text{ cm}^3 = 252\pi \text{ cm}^3$, which is **(B)**.

38. C

Difficulty: Medium

Category: Geometry and Trigonometry

Getting to the Answer: After the water is poured into the larger glass, the volume of the water in the glass will be the same as the volume when it was in the smaller glass. Find the volume of the water in the smaller glass, whose height is 6 inches and diameter is 3 inches. Then, substitute this volume into a second equation where the height is unknown and the radius is 2 inches (the radius of the larger glass) and solve for h. The volume of a cylinder equals the area of its base times its height, or $V = \pi r^2 h$:

$$V = \pi r^2 h$$
$$V = \pi (1.5)^2 (6)$$
$$V = \pi (2.25)(6)$$
$$V = 13.5\pi$$

$$13.5\pi = \pi (2)^2 h$$
$$13.5\pi = 4\pi h$$
$$3.375 = h$$

The water will be 3.375 inches high in the larger glass. **(C)** is correct.

39. 68

Difficulty: Hard

Category: Geometry and Trigonometry

Getting to the Answer: When a question involves many steps, as this one does, plan out the order of your calculations and conversions. In this case, you can go from the volume of sand in 1 tank to the volume of sand in 50 tanks, to the weight of sand in pounds, to the number of bags of sand.

The volume of sand in one tank (only 2 inches of the height) will be $V = 24 \times 9 \times 2 = 432$ cubic inches, which means the volume of sand in all 50 tanks will be $50 \times 432 = 21,600$ cubic inches. Each cubic inch of sand weighs 0.125 pounds, so the weight of all the sand will be $0.125 \times 21,600 = 2,700$ pounds. Finally, each bag contains 40 pounds of sand, so the pet store needs to buy $2,700 \text{ pounds} \times \dfrac{1 \text{ bag}}{40 \text{ pounds}} = 67.5$ bags. Because the store cannot buy one-half of one 40-pound bag of sand, it will need to buy 68 bags of sand. Enter **68**.

40. A

Difficulty: Medium

Category: Geometry and Trigonometry

Getting to the Answer: Determine the volumes of the rectangular box and of the cylindrical candle. Then calculate the difference between the two to find the volume of space between them. The volume of the box is the area of the base times its height: $15 \times 8 = 120$ cubic inches. Eliminate (C) and (D). Next, use $\pi r^2 h$ to calculate the volume of the cylinder. The diameter is 2 inches, so the radius is 1 inch: $\pi (1)^2 (8) = 8\pi$. Felipe needs $120 - 8\pi$ cubic inches of wax, so **(A)** is correct

41. C

Difficulty: Medium

Category: Geometry and Trigonometry

Getting to the Answer: A cube consists of 6 square faces. If the perimeter of one square face of the cube is $4x$, the length of one side is $\dfrac{4x}{4} = x$. The surface area of a cube is the sum of the areas of all 6 square faces or $6 \times \text{side}^2$. Thus, the surface area of the cube in terms of x is $6x^2$. **(C)** is correct.

42. C

Difficulty: Hard

Category: Geometry and Trigonometry

Getting to the Answer: The formula for finding the volume of a pyramid with a rectangular base is $V = \dfrac{1}{3}lwh$. Start by substituting what you know into the formula. The volume is represented by $x^3 - x$, the length is $x + 1$, and the width is $3x$:

$$V = \frac{1}{3}lwh$$
$$x^3 - x = \frac{1}{3}(x + 1)(3x)h$$
$$x(x^2 - 1) = (x + 1)xh$$

Notice that if you divide both sides of the equation by x, you'll be left with $x^2 - 1$ on the left side and $(x + 1)$ times h on the right side. Note that this is a classic quadratic: the factors of $x^2 - 1$ are $x + 1$ and $x - 1$. So:

$$(x + 1)(x - 1) = (x + 1)h$$
$$x - 1 = h$$

This means the height of the pyramid must be represented by $x - 1$. Therefore, **(C)** is correct.

43. C

Difficulty: Hard

Category: Geometry and Trigonometry

Strategic Advice: The diagonal of the square divides it into two 45-45-90 triangles. Use this information to find the diagonal of the square, which is also the diameter of the circle. From there, you can calculate the area of the circle.

Getting to the Answer: The area of the square is 400, so each side of the square is $\sqrt{400} = 20$. The sides of a 45-45-90 triangle are in the ratio $x{:}x{:}x\sqrt{2}$, so the diagonal of the square is $20\sqrt{2}$ and the radius of the circle is half of that, or $10\sqrt{2}$. The area formula for a circle is πr^2. Thus, the area of the given circle is:

$$\pi(10\sqrt{2})^2 = \pi(10)^2(\sqrt{2})^2 = \pi(100)(2) = 200\pi$$

Choice **(C)** is correct.

44. A

Difficulty: Medium

Category: Geometry and Trigonometry

Getting to the Answer: Because line p is a transversal intersecting the parallel lines l and m, all acute angles formed by the intersections must be the same. Therefore, since one of these angles is shown to be 60°, angle a must also be 60°. Additionally, the angle directly across from the 60° angle (the angle adjacent to b) must also be 60°. Line g intersects lines l and m at a 90° angle, so that means $b + 60 = 90$. Therefore, $b = 30$. Thus, you can say $a - b = 60 - 30 = 30$. **(A)** is correct.

45. D

Difficulty: Hard

Category: Geometry and Trigonometry

Getting to the Answer: The question asks for the total volume of juice, which is the volume of the cylinder that contains the concentrate plus the amount of water that is added. The height of the container of concentrate is 12 inches, and its diameter is 6 inches, making the radius 3 inches. Plug this information into the formula for the volume of a cylinder, $V = \pi r^2 h$:

$$V_{conc} = \pi \times 3^2 \times 12 = 108\pi \text{ inches}^3$$

The ratio of concentrate to total juice is $V_{conc}{:}(V_{conc} + V_{water})$ or $25{:}(25 + 75)$, which simplifies to 1:4. Set up the following ratio to calculate the total volume:

$$\frac{108\pi}{V_{Total}} = \frac{1}{4}$$

Cross-multiply to find the total volume of juice:

$$V_{Total} = (108\pi)(4)$$
$$V_{Total} = 432\pi \approx 1{,}357$$

This approximation matches **(D)**.

46. C

Difficulty: Medium

Category: Geometry and Trigonometry

Strategic Advice: For questions with right triangles, look for Pythagorean triples and special right triangles.

Getting to the Answer: Begin by making a quick sketch of the figure on scratch paper and transferring all of the information in the question stem to the diagram:

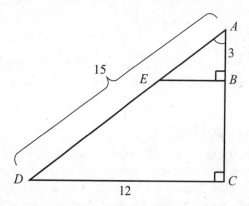

Triangle ACD is a right triangle with side length 12 and a hypotenuse of 15; these side lengths are the 3:4:5 triple multiplied by 3, which means its other side length, AC, is 9. Because they share angle A and both have a right angle, the two triangles are similar by way of angle-angle. Therefore, triangle ABE is also a 3:4:5 triangle, and the side lengths of triangle ACD correspond to the side lengths of triangle ABE. Since AB is 3 and AC is 9, you can find a ratio of 1:3 with each set of corresponding sides. Look for a choice with a side of ABE in the numerator and the corresponding side of ACD in the denominator. Only **(C)** correctly matches up the corresponding sides of ABE and ACD.

Another option to answer this question is to plug in the values for all of the sides based on the Pythagorean triples and plug those lengths into the answer choices. The diagram that follows shows the side lengths of the two triangles:

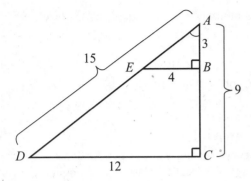

Plugging the lengths into the choices results in:

(A): $\dfrac{EB}{AC} = \dfrac{4}{9}$

(B): $\dfrac{AE}{DC} = \dfrac{5}{12}$

(C): $\dfrac{EB}{DC} = \dfrac{4}{12} = \dfrac{1}{3}$

There is no need to check (D) because there will be only one set of lengths that work. **(C)** is indeed correct.

47. C

Difficulty: Medium
Category: Geometry and Trigonometry
Getting to the Answer: Line L forms a right triangle whose right angle is created by the intersection of the x- and y-axes. The figure shows that q and p are supplementary, as they form a straight line—the y-axis—which means $q + p = 180$. The question says that $q = 140$, so $p = 180 - 140 = 40$. One of the interior angles of the triangle, the one created by the y-axis and line L, is vertical to p, so that angle is also 40. Now, find the last angle measure inside the triangle by subtracting: $180 - 90 - 40 = 50$. This angle is supplementary to r, so $r = 180 - 50 = 130$. This means that $r - p$ is $130 - 40 = 90$. **(C)** is correct.

48. D

Difficulty: Hard
Category: Geometry and Trigonometry
Getting to the Answer: In a right triangle, one leg is the base and the other is the height. Because the question states that one leg is 3 inches longer than the other, you can use x as the length of the shorter leg and $x + 3$

as the length of the longer leg. Use the formula for the area of a triangle, $A = \frac{1}{2}bh$, to solve for x, the shorter leg:

$$35 = \frac{1}{2}(x)(x + 3)$$

$$2(35) = 2\left(\frac{1}{2}(x)(x + 3)\right)$$

$$70 = (x)(x + 3)$$

$$70 = x^2 + 3x$$

Next, subtract 70 to make the equation equal 0. Use reverse-FOIL to find that the factors are $(x + 10)$ and $(x - 7)$, which means $x = -10$ and $x = 7$. Lengths cannot be negative, so the shorter leg has a length of 7, and the longer leg has a length of $7 + 3 = 10$. Now, use the Pythagorean theorem to find the length of the hypotenuse:

$$a^2 + b^2 = c^2$$
$$7^2 + 10^2 = c^2$$
$$49 + 100 = c^2$$
$$149 = c^2$$
$$\sqrt{149} = \sqrt{c^2}$$
$$\sqrt{149} = c$$

Choice **(D)** is correct.

49. 126

Difficulty: Hard
Category: Geometry and Trigonometry
Getting to the Answer: You're given the circle's circumference and the area of the sector. With this information, you can find what fraction of the circle is made up of the sector. From there, you can set up a proportion to determine the sector's central angle.

Start by finding the circle's radius by plugging the known value of the circumference into the circumference formula, $C = 2\pi r$: $40\pi = 2\pi r$, so $r = 20$. Now find the area of the circle: $\pi r^2 = \pi \times 20^2 = 400\pi$.

So the fraction of the circle's area represented by the sector is $\dfrac{140\pi}{400\pi} = 0.35$. Thus, the sector is 35% of the circle. That means its central angle has to be 35% of $360°$, which is $0.35 \times 360 = 126$. Enter **126**.

50. D

Difficulty: Medium

Category: Geometry and Trigonometry

Getting to the Answer: The formula for the volume of a cube is edge³ (edge × edge × edge). So the cube described has a volume of x^3, which is equal to a.

Next, find the volume of a cube with an edge of $2.5x$: $(2.5x)^3 = 15.625x^3$. Since $x^3 = a$, $15.625x^3 = 15.625a$.

Note that you could also pick numbers here; if the original edge length, x, is 2, then the volume of the cube is $2^3 = 8$, meaning $a = 8$. Next, $2.5x = 2.5(2) = 5$. So the volume of this larger cube would be $5^3 = 125$. Since $125 \div 8 = 15.625$, again, the volume of the second cube, in terms of a, is $15.625a$. Thus, **(D)** is correct.

51. A

Difficulty: Medium

Category: Geometry and Trigonometry

Getting to the Answer: The area formula for a triangle is $\frac{1}{2}$ × base × height. In a right triangle, the sides are the base and height. You have one side length already, so you'll need to find the other. Use the Pythagorean theorem, $a^2 + b^2 = c^2$, to find the missing side by plugging in the known hypotenuse and side length:

$$a^2 + b^2 = c^2$$
$$(\sqrt{2})^2 + b^2 = (\sqrt{7})^2$$
$$2 + b^2 = 7$$
$$b^2 = 5$$
$$b = \sqrt{5}$$

Now plug the known side lengths into the area formula: area $= \frac{1}{2} \times \sqrt{2} \times \sqrt{5} = \frac{1}{2} \times \sqrt{10} = \frac{\sqrt{10}}{2}$. Choice **(A)** is correct.

52. D

Difficulty: Hard

Category: Geometry and Trigonometry

Getting to the Answer: The question does not provide the dimensions of either circle, only a percentage relationship of the diameters. This is a great situation to pick numbers. Say the diameter of circle A is 10; that means the diameter of circle B is $10 + 0.30 \times 10 = 10 + 3 = 13$. Since radius is half of diameter, the radius of circle A is 5 and the radius of circle B is 6.5.

Now calculate the area of each circle, using the circle area formula, πr^2:

Circle A: $\pi \times 5^2 = 25\pi$.

Circle B: $\pi \times 6.5^2 = 42.25\pi$.

Now calculate the percentage of circle B's area in relation to circle A's: $\frac{42.25\pi}{25\pi} = 1.69 = 169\%$.

(D) is correct.

53. D

Difficulty: Medium

Category: Geometry and Trigonometry

Getting to the Answer: The triangle shown in the diagram is a right triangle, and both legs form radii of the circle. That means they're both the same length, which means the triangle is an isosceles right triangle. By definition, an isosceles right triangle is a 45-45-90 special right triangle.

The ratio of sides of a 45-45-90 triangle can be expressed as $x{:}x{:}x\sqrt{2}$, where x is the length of each leg and $x\sqrt{2}$ is the length of the hypotenuse. In this case, the hypotenuse is $10\sqrt{2}$, so $x = 10$. That makes the radius of the circle 10. Using this information, solve for the circumference using the circumference formula, $2\pi r$: $2\pi(10) = 20\pi$. Thus, **(D)** is correct.

54. A

Difficulty: Medium

Category: Circles

Getting to the Answer: In the standard form of the equation of a circle, $(x - h)^2 + (y - k)^2 = r^2$, the coordinates of the center of the circle are (h, k) and the radius is r. The center of the circle shown is at $(-2, 3)$. Eliminate (D), since it indicates a center at $(2, -3)$. Examining the diagram shows that the radius of the circle is 3, so $r^2 = 3^2 = 9$. **(A)** is correct.

55. 55

Difficulty: Medium
Category: Geometry and Trigonometry
Getting to the Answer: To calculate the area of the L-shaped shaded region, divide it into two rectangles. It may help to quickly sketch this on scratch paper. The shaded rectangle formed along the entire left side of the figure is 10 feet by 2 feet, so its area is $10 \times 2 = 20$ square feet. The remaining shaded rectangle across the top of the figure is 13 feet by 2 feet, so its area is $13 \times 2 = 26$ square feet. The separate shaded square is 3 by 3 feet, or 9 square feet.

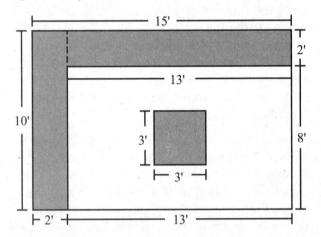

Adding these areas together yields a total of $20 + 26 + 9 = 55$ square feet. Enter **55**.

[CHAPTER 15]

TRIGONOMETRY

LEARNING OBJECTIVES

After completing this chapter, you will be able to:

- Calculate trigonometric ratios from side lengths of right triangles
- Calculate side lengths of right triangles using trigonometric ratios
- Describe the relationship between the sine and cosine of complementary angles

HOW MUCH DO YOU KNOW?

Directions

Try the questions that follow. Show your work so that you can compare your solutions to the ones found in the "Check Your Work" section immediately after this question set. If you answered most of the questions correctly, and if your scratchwork looks like ours, you may be able to move quickly through this chapter. If you answered incorrectly or used a different approach, you may want to take your time on this chapter.

1

If $\tan x = \dfrac{7}{24}$, what is the value of $\sin x$?

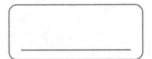

2

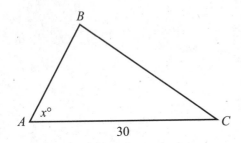

Note: Figure not drawn to scale.

If the area of $\triangle ABC$ is 225 and $AB = 17$, what is the value of $\cos x$?

Ⓐ $\dfrac{8}{17}$

Ⓑ $\dfrac{8}{15}$

Ⓒ $\dfrac{17}{30}$

Ⓓ $\dfrac{15}{17}$

3

In a right triangle, one of the acute angles measures $\dfrac{\pi}{3}$, and $\cos\left(\dfrac{\pi}{3}\right) = \sin x$. What is the measure of x?

Ⓐ $\dfrac{\pi}{12}$

Ⓑ $\dfrac{\pi}{6}$

Ⓒ $\dfrac{\pi}{3}$

Ⓓ $\dfrac{2\pi}{3}$

4

In a right triangle, if $\sin y = 0.8$, what is the value of $\cos y$?

Ⓐ 0.08

Ⓑ 0.4

Ⓒ 0.6

Ⓓ 0.75

This page is intentionally blank.

Check Your Work

1.   7/25, 0.28, or .28

Getting to the Answer: Recall that $\tan x = \dfrac{\text{opp}}{\text{adj}}$. This means you know the lengths of the two legs of the right triangle but not its hypotenuse. Draw a picture with the given lengths:

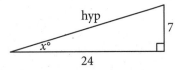

Remember that $\sin x = \dfrac{\text{opp}}{\text{hyp}}$, so use the Pythagorean theorem to calculate the length of the hypotenuse:

$$7^2 + 24^2 = \text{hyp}^2$$
$$49 + 576 = \text{hyp}^2$$
$$\sqrt{625} = \sqrt{\text{hyp}^2}$$
$$25 = \text{hyp}$$

Plug the length of the hypotenuse into the sine ratio: $\sin x = \dfrac{7}{25}$. Enter **7/25**, **0.28**, or **.28**.

2.   A

Difficulty: Hard

Category: Geometry and Trigonometry

Getting to the Answer: Begin by drawing a height from B to AC to create a perpendicular altitude in the triangle:

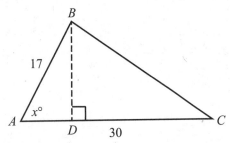

Next, find the length of BD using the triangle area formula:

$$A = \frac{1}{2}bh$$
$$225 = \frac{1}{2} \times 30 \times BD$$
$$\frac{225}{15} = BD$$
$$15 = BD$$

You now have two sides of a right triangle ($\triangle ABD$)—but not necessarily the two sides you need. To find the value of $\cos x$, you need the side adjacent to x and the hypotenuse. Here, you have the opposite side (BD) and the hypotenuse (AB), so you need to find the length of the third side (AD). You might recognize $\triangle ABD$ as an 8-15-17 Pythagorean triple, but if you don't, you can use the Pythagorean theorem:

$$AD^2 + 15^2 = 17^2$$
$$AD^2 = 17^2 - 15^2$$
$$AD^2 = 289 - 225$$
$$AD = \sqrt{64} = 8$$

You can now find $\cos x$: $\dfrac{\text{adj}}{\text{hyp}} = \dfrac{8}{17}$. **(A)** is correct.

3.   B

Difficulty: Medium

Category: Geometry and Trigonometry

Getting to the Answer: The sine and cosine of complementary angles are equal, meaning $\cos(90 - x) = \sin x$ and $\sin(90 - x) = \cos x$. The sum of the two acute angles in a right triangle is always 90°. Convert this to radians to find the measure of the missing angle. The sum of the acute angles in a right triangle, in radians, is $90° \times \dfrac{\pi}{180°} = \dfrac{90\pi}{180} = \dfrac{\pi}{2}$. Subtract the known angle to find the other angle: $\dfrac{\pi}{2} - \dfrac{\pi}{3} = \dfrac{3\pi}{6} - \dfrac{2\pi}{6} = \dfrac{\pi}{6}$. **(B)** is correct.

4.   C

Difficulty: Medium

Category: Geometry and Trigonometry

Getting to the Answer: Don't let the decimal point confuse you. A sine value equal to 0.8 is the same as $\dfrac{4}{5}$. We have a 3:4:5 right triangle with hypotenuse of 5 and the leg opposite y equal to 4. The cosine of y will be the other leg over the same hypotenuse, or $\dfrac{3}{5}$, which is equal to 0.6, or choice **(C)**.

SINE, COSINE, AND TANGENT

LEARNING OBJECTIVES

After this lesson, you will be able to:

- Calculate trigonometric ratios from side lengths of right triangles
- Calculate side lengths of right triangles using trigonometric ratios
- Describe the relationship between the sine and cosine of complementary angles

To answer a question like this:

One angle in a right triangle measures $y°$ such that $\cos y° = \frac{24}{25}$. What is the measure of $\sin(90° - y°)$?

You need to know this:

The SAT tests three trigonometric functions: **sine**, **cosine**, and **tangent**. All three are the ratios of side lengths within a right triangle. The notation for sine, cosine, and tangent functions always includes a reference angle; for example, $\cos x$ or $\cos \theta$. That's because you'll need to refer to the given angle within a right triangle to determine the appropriate side ratios.

There is a common mnemonic device for the sine, cosine, and tangent ratios: SOHCAHTOA (commonly pronounced: so-kuh-TOE-uh). Here's what it represents: **S**ine is **O**pposite over **H**ypotenuse, **C**osine is **A**djacent over **H**ypotenuse, and **T**angent is **O**pposite over **A**djacent. See the following triangle and the table for a summary of the ratios and what each equals for angle A in triangle CAB:

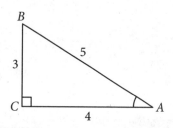

SINE (SIN)	COSINE (COS)	TANGENT (TAN)
$\dfrac{\text{opposite}}{\text{hypotenuse}}$	$\dfrac{\text{adjacent}}{\text{hypotenuse}}$	$\dfrac{\text{opposite}}{\text{adjacent}}$
$\dfrac{3}{5}$	$\dfrac{4}{5}$	$\dfrac{3}{4}$

Complementary angles (angles that sum to 90°) have a special relationship relative to sine and cosine:

- $\sin x° = \cos(90° - x°)$
- $\cos x° = \sin(90° - x°)$

In other words, if two angles add up to 90°, the sine of one equals the cosine of the other (and vice versa). For example, $\cos 30° = \sin 60°$, $\cos 60° = \sin 30°$, $\cos 45° = \sin 45°$, and so on.

You need to do this:

Apply the appropriate trigonometric ratio to a right triangle or use the relationship between the sine and cosine of complementary angles.

Explanation:

There are two ways to approach this question. You might choose to draw the triangle on your scratch paper:

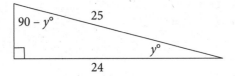

To find $\sin(90° - y°)$, put the side opposite the angle labeled $90° - y°$ over the hypotenuse. You'll get $\frac{24}{25}$, exactly the same as $\cos y°$. (Note that the third angle is $90° - y°$ because the angles of a triangle always add up to 180°, and $90° + y° + (90° - y°) = 180°$.)

Alternatively, you could use the property of complementary angles that says that $\cos x° = \sin(90° - x°)$ to find that $\sin(90° - y°) = \frac{24}{25}$.

Enter your answer: **24/25**, **.96**, and **0.96** are all acceptable.

Try on Your Own

Directions

Take as much time as you need on these questions. Work carefully and methodically. There will be an opportunity for timed practice later in the book.

1

HINT: Pythagorean triples frequently appear in trig questions. What is the triangle's missing side length in Q1?

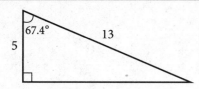

Based on the figure, which of the following is true?

Ⓐ $\sin 22.6° = \dfrac{5}{12}$

Ⓑ $\sin 67.4° = \dfrac{5}{13}$

Ⓒ $\cos 22.6° = \dfrac{12}{13}$

Ⓓ $\cos 67.4° = \dfrac{5}{12}$

2

The triangle shown is a cross-section of a feeding trough. The triangular cross-section is 24 inches deep and 36 inches across the top. If $\cos x = B$, what is the value of B?

3

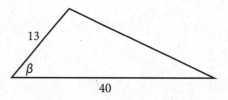

Note: Figure not drawn to scale.

If the area of the triangle shown is 240 square inches, what is $\tan \beta$?

4

HINT: For Q4, what do you know about triangles with a shared angle and parallel sides?

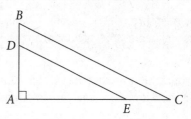

In the figure, DE is parallel to BC and $\sin \angle C = 0.6$. Side $AC = 16$ and side $BD = 3$. What is the length of side AE?

Math

5

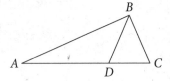

If sin $\angle A = \cos \angle C$, what is sin $\angle ABD - \cos \angle DBC$?

(A)   0

(B) $\dfrac{1}{2}$

(C)   1

(D)   The result of the subtraction cannot be determined without additional information.

ON TEST DAY

As you read through this question, think about what information you really need to arrive at the answer before you begin your calculations so that you don't get sidetracked and spend time doing unnecessary work.

Plan your strategy to get the correct value and identify what information you need to carry out that strategy. Note if there is any unnecessary information that you can ignore.

6.   Triangle PQR is a right triangle with the 90° angle at vertex Q. The length of side PQ is 25 and the length of side QR is 60. Triangle STU is similar to triangle PQR. The vertices S, T, and U correspond to vertices P, Q, and R, respectively. What is the value of $\cos\angle U$?

A) $\dfrac{5}{13}$

B) $\dfrac{5}{12}$

C) $\dfrac{5}{6}$

D) $\dfrac{12}{13}$

The answer and explanation can be found at the end of this chapter.

HOW MUCH HAVE YOU LEARNED?

Directions

For testlike practice, give yourself 8 minutes to complete this question set. Be sure to study the explanations, even for questions you answered correctly. They can be found at the end of this chapter.

7

If $\sin x = \cos\left(\dfrac{13\pi}{6}\right)$, which of the following could be the value of x?

(A) $\dfrac{\pi}{6}$

(B) $\dfrac{\pi}{4}$

(C) $\dfrac{\pi}{3}$

(D) $\dfrac{\pi}{2}$

8

If $\cos z$ in a right triangle is $\dfrac{12}{13}$, what is $\tan z$?

(A) $\dfrac{12}{5}$

(B) $\dfrac{13}{12}$

(C) $\dfrac{5}{12}$

(D) $\dfrac{5}{13}$

9

Angle x is one of the acute angles in a right triangle. If the measure of angle x is 30°, what is the value of $(\sin x)^2 + (\cos x)^2$?

(A) $\dfrac{1}{4}$

(B) $\dfrac{1}{2}$

(C) 1

(D) 2

10

In a certain right triangle, the measures of $\angle A$ and $\angle B$ are $(6k - 8)°$ and $(7k - 45)°$, respectively. If $\dfrac{\sin \angle A}{\cos \angle B} = 1$, what is the value of k?

11

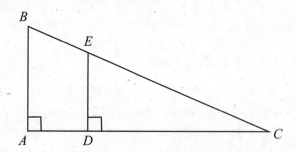

In the triangle shown, if side $AB = 5$, segment $AD = 3$, and $\tan \angle B = 2.4$, what is the length of segment BE?

(A) 3

(B) $3\dfrac{1}{4}$

(C) $3\dfrac{3}{4}$

(D) $4\dfrac{1}{4}$

REFLECT

Directions: Take a few minutes to recall what you've learned and what you've been practicing in this chapter. Consider the following questions, jot down your best answer for each one, and then compare your reflections to the expert responses that follow. Use your level of confidence to determine what to do next.

What are the definitions of sine, cosine, and tangent?

_____

_____

_____

What is the special relationship of sine to cosine in complementary angles?

_____

_____

_____

Expert Responses

What are the definitions of sine, cosine, and tangent?

Sine *is defined as opposite over hypotenuse,* cosine *as adjacent over hypotenuse, and* tangent *as opposite over adjacent. The acronym SOHCAHTOA can help you remember these definitions.*

What is the special relationship of sine to cosine in complementary angles?

For two complementary angles, $\sin x° = \cos(90° - x°)$ and $\cos x° = \sin(90° - x°)$. In other words, if two angles are complementary (add up to 90 degrees), the sine of one equals the cosine of the other.

Next Steps

If you answered most questions correctly in the "How Much Have You Learned?" section, and if your responses to the Reflect questions were similar to those of the SAT expert, then consider Trigonometry an area of strength and move on to the next chapter. Come back to this topic periodically to ensure your skills stay sharp.

If you don't yet feel confident, review those parts of this chapter that you have not yet mastered, then try the questions you missed again. As always, be sure to review the explanations closely. Finally, **go online** (www.kaptest.com/moreonline) for additional practice on the highest yield topics in this chapter.

Check Your Work – Chapter 15

1.   C
Difficulty: Medium
Category: Geometry and Trigonometry
Getting to the Answer: Find the unknown leg length and angle measure. The triangle is a right triangle with one leg length of 5 and a hypotenuse of 13, so the other leg is length 12. (If you didn't see the Pythagorean triple 5:12:13, you could have used the Pythagorean theorem to find the missing leg length.) Use the measures of the internal angles to find the missing angle. It may be helpful to sketch this figure out:

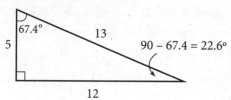

Sine and cosine both involve the hypotenuse, 13, so you can eliminate (A) and (D). Compare the remaining answer choices to the trig ratios given by SOHCAHTOA. Sine is opposite over hypotenuse, but the side opposite the 67.4° angle has length 12 (not 5), so eliminate (B). Only **(C)** is left and must be correct. For the record, the side adjacent to the 22.6° angle has length 12 and the hypotenuse has length 13, so $\cos 22.6° = \frac{5}{13}$.

2.   18/30, 3/5, 0.6, or .6
Difficulty: Hard
Category: Geometry and Trigonometry
Getting to the Answer: Because trig functions typically apply to right triangles, draw in an altitude and label what you know. You know the trough is 24 inches deep and 36 inches across the top. Because the given angles have equal measures, $x°$, the triangle is isosceles and the altitude bisects the top. Draw a figure:

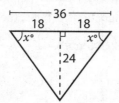

You're given that $R = \cos x$, and the cosine of an angle involves the hypotenuse, so you need to find the length of the hypotenuse. The triangle is a 3:4:5 triple multiplied by 6: $3 \times 6 = 18$ and $4 \times 6 = 24$, so the hypotenuse must

be $5 \times 6 = 30$. If you didn't notice the triple, you could find the hypotenuse using the Pythagorean theorem:

$$18^2 + 24^2 = c^2$$
$$324 + 576 = c^2$$
$$\sqrt{900} = \sqrt{c^2}$$
$$30 = c$$

Thus, $\cos x = \frac{\text{adj}}{\text{hyp}} = \frac{18}{30} = \frac{3}{5}$. Enter **18/30, 3/5, 0.6, or .6**.

3.   12/5 or 2.4
Difficulty: Hard
Category: Geometry and Trigonometry
Getting to the Answer: Find the height of the triangle using the information given about the area and add it to the figure:

$$A = \frac{1}{2}bh$$
$$240 = \frac{1}{2}(40)h$$
$$240 = 20h$$
$$12 = h$$

After you find the height, you might recognize the 5:12:13 Pythagorean triple, which gives you another side of the triangle that contains β:

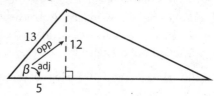

Now use SOHCAHTOA: $\tan \beta = \frac{\text{opp}}{\text{adj}} = \frac{12}{5}$. Enter **12/5 or 2.4**.

4.   12
Difficulty: Hard
Category: Geometry and Trigonometry
Getting to the Answer: The fact that DE is parallel to BC means that triangles ABC and ADE are similar. Convert $\sin C$, 0.6, to a fraction, $\frac{3}{5}$. Because $\sin x$ is $\frac{\text{opposite}}{\text{hypotenuse}}$, both triangles have the side ratio 3:4:5. The question states that $AC = 16$. This is the long leg of a 3:4:5 right triangle multiplied by 4 (4×4), so $AB = 3 \times 4 = 12$ and $BC = 5 \times 4 = 20$.

The other known dimension is $BD = 3$. Since the length of AB is 12, the length of AD is $12 - 3 = 9$. Thus, the ratio of the sides of triangle ADE to those of triangle ABC is $\frac{9}{12} = \frac{3}{4}$. Therefore, AE is $\frac{3}{4}$ of AC, which is $\frac{3}{4} \times 16 = 12$. Enter **12**.

5.   A

Difficulty: Hard
Category: Geometry and Trigonometry
Getting to the Answer: The sine of an angle is equal to the cosine of its complementary angle, so $\angle A + \angle C = 90°$. Since $\angle B$ is the third interior angle of the triangle ABC, $\angle B = 180° - 90° = 90°$. Therefore, the measures of angles ABD and DBC must total 90°, which means they are complementary angles. Thus, $\sin \angle ABD = \cos \angle DBC$, and $\sin \angle ABD - \cos \angle DBC = 0$. **(A)** is correct.

6.   D

Difficulty: Medium
Category: Geometry and Trigonometry
Getting to the Answer: The question tells you that triangles PQR and STU are similar. Therefore, their corresponding angles are equal, and all sides of STU have the same ratio to their corresponding sides in PQR. Since the angles of both triangles are the same, their trig functions are also the same, so there is no need to know the lengths of the sides of triangle STU. Because they are the same ratio, cosine of U will have the same value as the cosine of R, so just calculate the cosine of R value using the side lengths of triangle PQR.

Since $\angle Q = 90°$, sides PQ and QR are legs of the right triangle and PR is the hypotenuse. (If you have trouble visualizing this, you can draw a quick sketch.) Thus, $\cos R = \frac{QR}{PR}$. You can calculate the value of PR using the Pythagorean theorem:

$$25^2 + 60^2 = PR^2$$
$$625 + 3{,}600 = PR^2$$
$$\sqrt{4{,}225} = \sqrt{PR^2}$$
$$PR = 65$$

Note that you can save a lot of calculation time if you recognize that the two legs, 25 and 60, are the legs of a 5:12:13 Pythagorean triple triangle multiplied by 5. You can calculate PR as $5 \times 13 = 65$. Either way, that means $\cos R = \frac{60}{65} = \frac{12}{13}$. Since $\cos U = \cos R$, **(D)** is correct.

7.   C

Difficulty: Hard
Category: Geometry and Trigonometry
Getting to the Answer: Dealing with smaller angles usually makes trig questions easier, so start by subtracting 2π from $\frac{13\pi}{6}$ to get $\frac{13\pi}{6} - 2\pi = \frac{13\pi}{6} - \frac{12\pi}{6} = \frac{\pi}{6}$. (This is permissible because 2π is once around the unit circle; you are not changing the quadrant of the angle.) The equation in the question stem becomes $\sin x = \cos\left(\frac{\pi}{6}\right)$. Complementary angles have a special relationship relative to trig values—the cosine of an acute angle is equal to the sine of the angle's complement and vice versa. The angle measures are given in radians, so you're looking for an angle that, when added to $\frac{\pi}{6}$, gives $\frac{\pi}{2}$ (because $\frac{\pi}{2} = 90°$); $\frac{\pi}{2}$ is the same as $\frac{3\pi}{6}$. Since $\frac{2\pi}{6} + \frac{\pi}{6} = \frac{3\pi}{6}$, the two angles, $\frac{\pi}{6}$ and $\frac{2\pi}{6}$, are complementary angles. Since $\frac{2\pi}{6} = \frac{\pi}{3}$, **(C)** is correct.

8.   C

Difficulty: Easy
Category: Geometry and Trigonometry
Getting to the Answer: It may be useful to quickly sketch a triangle on your scratch paper. Using "the cosine is adjacent over hypotenuse" in SOHCAHTOA, the side of the triangle adjacent to the sketched angle z will be 12 and the hypotenuse will be 13. Now, use the Pythagorean 5:12:13 triple or the Pythagorean theorem to find that the final, opposite, side of the triangle is 5. The tangent (opposite over adjacent) must be $\frac{5}{12}$, or answer choice **(C)**.

9.   C

Difficulty: Medium
Category: Geometry and Trigonometry
Getting to the Answer: Use the definitions of the common trig functions to put some context to this question. Substitute $\left(\frac{\text{opposite}}{\text{hypotenuse}}\right)^2 + \left(\frac{\text{adjacent}}{\text{hypotenuse}}\right)^2$ for $(\sin x)^2 + (\cos x)^2$. This simplifies to $\frac{\text{opposite}^2 + \text{adjacent}^2}{\text{hypotenuse}^2}$. The Pythagorean theorem states $a^2 + b^2 = c^2$, which is equivalent to $\text{opposite}^2 + \text{adjacent}^2 = \text{hypotenuse}^2$, so this fraction is actually $\frac{\text{hypotenuse}^2}{\text{hypotenuse}^2} = 1$. **(C)** is correct.

If you prefer to work with actual values, recall that the side ratio of a 30-60-90 triangle is $1:\sqrt{3}:2$. So, $\sin x = \frac{1}{2}$ and $\cos x = \frac{\sqrt{3}}{2}$. The question asks for the sum of the squares of those values: $\left(\frac{1}{2}\right)^2 + \left(\frac{\sqrt{3}}{2}\right)^2 = \frac{1}{4} + \frac{3}{4} = 1$. **(C)** is indeed correct.

10. 11
Difficulty: Hard
Category: Geometry and Trigonometry

Getting to the Answer: If $\frac{\sin \angle A}{\cos \angle B} = 1$, then $\sin A = \cos B$, so $\angle A$ and $\angle B$ are complementary. Therefore, the sum of the measures of $\angle A$ and $\angle B$ is 90°, and you can write the equation $(6k - 8) + (7k - 45) = 90$. This simplifies to $13k - 53 = 90$ and then to $13k = 143$. Divide both sides by 13 to see that $k = 11$. Enter **11**.

11. B
Difficulty: Hard
Category: Geometry and Trigonometry

Getting to the Answer: Since BA and ED are both perpendicular to AC, they are parallel, and triangles ABC and DEC are similar. If $\tan \angle B = \frac{AC}{AB}$, then $2.4 = \frac{AC}{5}$, and $AC = 12$. Triangle ABC is a 5:12:13 right triangle, and the length of BC is 13. (If you didn't recall the Pythagorean triple, you could have calculated the hypotenuse using the Pythagorean theorem.) Given that $AD = 3$ and $AC = 12$, it follows that $DC = 12 - 3 = 9$, and the ratio of the side lengths of $\triangle DEC$ to $\triangle ABC$ is 9:12, which simplifies to 3:4.

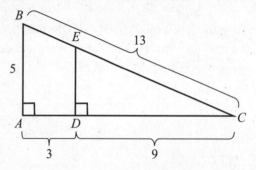

Because this ratio is the same for all sides, BE is $\frac{1}{4}$ the length of BC, or $\frac{1}{4}(13) = 3\frac{1}{4}$. **(B)** is correct.

Math

HOW MUCH HAVE YOU LEARNED: GEOMETRY AND TRIGONOMETRY

Directions

This "How Much Have You Learned?" section will allow you to measure your growth and confidence in Geometry and Trigonometry skills.

For testlike practice, give yourself 15 minutes for this question set. Be sure to use the Method for SAT Math Questions. When you're done, check your answers and read through the explanations, even for the questions you got correct. Don't forget to celebrate your progress!

1

The base, b, of a right triangle is $\frac{2}{3}$ the height, h, of the triangle. Which of the following is the length of the hypotenuse in terms of h?

(A) $\sqrt{\frac{5}{3}}h$

(B) $\frac{\sqrt{13}}{3}h$

(C) $\sqrt{\frac{5}{6}}h$

(D) $\frac{\sqrt{13}}{18}h$

2

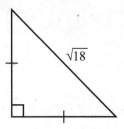

What is the length of each leg in the figure shown?

(A) 3

(B) $3\sqrt{2}$

(C) $3\sqrt{3}$

(D) 9

3

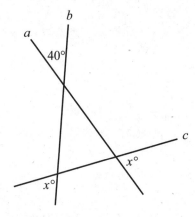

In the figure shown, what is the value of x?

4

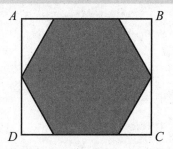

In the figure shown, the shaded region is a regular hexagon inscribed in rectangle *ABCD*. If each side length of the hexagon is 2 units, what is the area of rectangle *ABCD* in square units?

Ⓐ $4 + 4\sqrt{3}$

Ⓑ   12

Ⓒ $8\sqrt{3}$

Ⓓ $8 + 4\sqrt{3}$

5

Triangle *PQR* has angles measuring 23° and 48°. Which of the following could be the measure of an angle in a triangle similar to *PQR*?

Ⓐ   24°

Ⓑ   69°

Ⓒ   96°

Ⓓ   109°

6

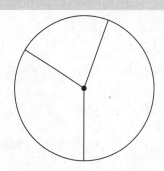

If the central angles in the circle shown are in the ratio 4:3:2, what is the measure, in degrees, of the smallest angle?

Ⓐ   40

Ⓑ   60

Ⓒ   72

Ⓓ   80

7

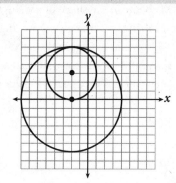

If the area of the smaller circle shown is 144π square units, what is the equation of the larger circle?

Ⓐ $(x + 2)^2 + y^2 = 36$

Ⓑ $(x + 2)^2 + (y - 3)^2 = 9$

Ⓒ $(x + 8)^2 + (y - 12)^2 = 144$

Ⓓ $(x + 8)^2 + y^2 = 576$

8

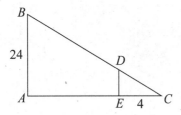

In the figure shown, $\overline{DE} \parallel \overline{AB}$ and $\overline{DE} \perp \overline{AC}$. If $AE = 28$, what is the length of DE?

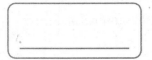

9

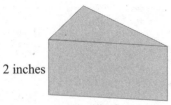

2 inches

4 inches

A piece of cheese in the shape of a triangular prism, consisting of 2 triangles, 2 rectangles and 1 square, as shown in the figure is coated with a layer of wax. If 2 grams of wax covers 1 square inch, how many grams will it take to coat the piece of cheese?

(A) $20 + 2\sqrt{15}$

(B) 28

(C) $40 + 2\sqrt{15}$

(D) $40 + 4\sqrt{15}$

10

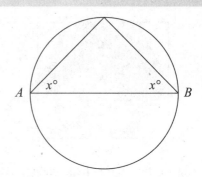

In the figure shown, AB is the diameter of the circle. What is $\cos x$?

(A) $\dfrac{1}{2}$

(B) $\dfrac{1}{\sqrt{2}}$

(C) $\dfrac{\sqrt{3}}{2}$

(D) 1

Check Your Work – How Much Have You Learned: Geometry and Trigonometry

1. B

Difficulty: Medium

Category: Geometry and Trigonometry

Getting to the Answer: Start by translating from English into math. Because the base of the triangle is $\frac{2}{3}$ the height of the triangle, $b = \frac{2}{3}h$. Use the Pythagorean theorem to find the hypotenuse:

$$h^2 + b^2 = c^2$$

$$h^2 + \left(\frac{2}{3}h\right)^2 = c^2$$

$$\frac{9}{9}h^2 + \frac{4}{9}h^2 = c^2$$

$$\frac{13}{9}h^2 = c^2$$

$$\sqrt{\frac{13}{9}h^2} = c$$

$$\frac{\sqrt{13}}{3}h = c$$

(B) is correct.

2. A

Difficulty: Medium

Category: Geometry and Trigonometry

Getting to the Answer: Because one angle of the triangle measures 90° and the two legs are congruent (notice the tick marks), this is a 45-45-90 triangle. The side lengths of a 45-45-90 triangle are in the ratio x:x:$x\sqrt{2}$, where x represents the length of a leg and $x\sqrt{2}$ represents the length of the hypotenuse. Set up an equation using the ratio and the length of the hypotenuse, $\sqrt{18}$, to find the length of each leg:

$$x\sqrt{2} = \sqrt{18}$$

$$x\sqrt{2} = \sqrt{9}\sqrt{2}$$

$$x\sqrt{2} = 3\sqrt{2}$$

$$x = 3$$

The length of each leg is 3, so **(A)** is correct.

3. 70

Difficulty: Medium

Category: Geometry and Trigonometry

Getting to the Answer: The angle in the triangle that is vertical to 40° is also 40°, and the angles in the triangle vertical to x° are also x°. Thus, the triangle formed by lines a, b, and c is an isosceles triangle. Since angles in a triangle sum to 180°, $40° + x° + x° = 180°$, and $x° = 70°$.

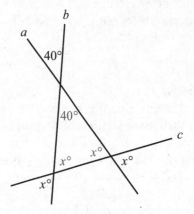

Enter **70**.

4. C

Difficulty: Hard

Category: Geometry and Trigonometry

Getting to the Answer: Start with the shaded hexagon. One way to determine the sum of the interior angles of the hexagon is to use $180°(n-2)$, where n represents the number of sides of the polygon. Since the hexagon has six sides, the sum of the interior angles equals $180°(6-2) = 720°$. Thus, each angle is $720° \div 6 = 120°$. (You could also note that a hexagon can be thought of as made of 6 smaller equilateral triangles whose angles are all 60°. Two of those angles form the same 120°.) The angle in the white right triangle supplementary to 120° is then $180° - 120° = 60°$, indicating the white triangles are 30-60-90 triangles with ratio side lengths of x:$x\sqrt{3}$:$2x$. The question tells you that each side length of the hexagon, which is also the hypotenuse of the triangles, is 2 units. Thus, the leg lengths of the triangle are 1 and $\sqrt{3}$.

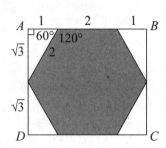

You now have the length of the rectangle, $1 + 2 + 1 = 4$, and the width of the rectangle: $\sqrt{3} + \sqrt{3} = 2\sqrt{3}$. The area of the rectangle is therefore, $l \times w = 4 \times 2\sqrt{3} = 8\sqrt{3}$ square units, making **(C)** correct.

5. D

Difficulty: Easy
Category: Geometry and Trigonometry
Getting to the Answer: Corresponding angles of similar triangles are congruent. Therefore, the similar triangle will also have angles measuring 23° and 48° and $180° - (23° + 48°) = 109°$. **(D)** is correct.

6. D

Difficulty: Easy
Category: Geometry and Trigonometry
Strategic Advice: Whenever you're given a ratio, you can set up an equation. Sometimes the equation takes the form of a proportion and sometimes it takes the form of the sum of the parts equals the whole. In this question, the *whole* is the total number of degrees in a circle, which is 360.

Getting to the Answer: You know the relative size of each of the parts in this question. You don't know the exact size of one part, so call it *x*. Now, set up an equation:

$$4x + 3x + 2x = 360$$
$$9x = 360$$
$$x = 40$$

Note that the question asks for the measure of the smallest angle, which is represented by 2*x*. The correct answer is $2(40) = 80$, which is **(D)**.

7. D

Difficulty: Hard
Category: Geometry and Trigonometry
Strategic Advice: Note that the graph is not labeled with any units, which means that one square does not necessarily equal one unit.

Getting to the Answer: To find the equation of a circle, you need the radius and the *x*- and *y*-coordinates of the center point. Then, you can use the standard equation: $(x - h)^2 + (y - k)^2 = r^2$, where (h, k) is the center of the circle and *r* is the length of the radius.

Be careful—choice (A) is incorrect, but might appear correct if you assume that one square represents one unit. The graph has no number labels on it, so you'll need to use the information given in the question about the smaller circle to determine the value of each grid line:

$$A = \pi r^2$$
$$144\pi = \pi r^2$$
$$144 = r^2$$
$$\pm 12 = r$$

The radius can't be negative, so it must be 12. There are only 3 grid lines between the center of the smaller circle and its edge, so each grid line must be equal to $\frac{12}{3} = 4$ units. The center of the larger circle, therefore, is $(-8, 0)$, and its radius is $6 \times 4 = 24$. Thus, the equation must be $(x - (-8))^2 + (y - 0)^2 = 24^2$, or written in simplified form, $(x + 8)^2 + y^2 = 576$. **(D)** is the correct answer.

8. 3

Difficulty: Medium
Category: Geometry and Trigonometry
Getting to the Answer: Start by determining whether there is a relationship between triangles *ABC* and *EDC*. The two triangles share a common angle, *C*. It is given that $\overline{DE} \perp \overline{AC}$, so angle *DEC* is a right angle. Because $\overline{DE} \parallel \overline{AB}$, *BA* is also perpendicular to $\overline{AC}$, making angle *BAC* another right angle. Triangles that have two congruent interior angles are similar, so triangle *ABC* is similar to triangle *EDC*.

The length of *AE* is 28, which means the length of *AC* is $28 + 4 = 32$. The length of *EC* is 4, which means that the side lengths of triangle *ABC* are 8 times the side lengths of triangle *EDC*. Use this ratio to find *DE* : $\frac{24}{8} = 3$. Enter **3**.

9.   D

Difficulty: Medium

Category: Geometry and Trigonometry

Getting to the Answer: To calculate the amount of wax needed to cover the piece of cheese, first determine the surface area of the cheese by summing the areas of the faces (one square, two rectangles, and two triangles). The square side of the cheese has an area of $s^2 = 2^2 = 4$, and the two rectangular sides of the cheese have an area of $2A = 2(lw) = 2(2)(4) = 16$. The bottom and top of the cheese are triangles; each can be split into two right triangles.

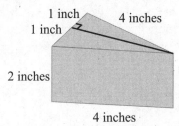

The height of the triangles can be found by splitting the triangle into two right triangles and then using the Pythagorean theorem: $\text{height} = \sqrt{4^2 - 1^2} = \sqrt{15}$. Thus, the area of the top and bottom triangles, which have a base of 2, is $2A_{\text{triangle}} = 2\left(\frac{1}{2}bh\right) = bh = (2)(\sqrt{15}) = 2\sqrt{15}$.

The total surface area of the cheese is $4 + 16 + 2\sqrt{15} = 20 + 2\sqrt{15}$ square inches. Note that the question asks for the amount of wax needed to coat the piece of cheese. Use unit conversion to find the number of grams of wax needed:

$$20 + 2\sqrt{15} \text{ square inches} \times \frac{2 \text{ grams}}{1 \text{ square inches}} =$$
$$40 + 4\sqrt{15} \text{ grams}$$

(D) is correct.

10.   B

Difficulty: Hard

Category: Geometry and Trigonometry

Getting to the Answer: Although the triangle containing $x°$ does not have a right angle, it can be split into two 45-45-90 triangles. So, $x° = 45°$. You can use the side ratios of a 45-45-90 triangle to find cos 45°. That ratio is $r:r:r\sqrt{2}$.

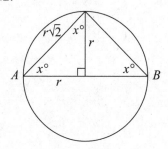

Because $\cos x = \frac{\text{adjacent}}{\text{hypotenuse}}$, the cos x is $\frac{1}{\sqrt{2}}$.

(B) is correct.

CHAPTER 16

SAT MATH: TIMING AND SECTION MANAGEMENT STRATEGIES

LEARNING OBJECTIVE

After completing this chapter, you will be able to:

* Make quick decisions about which questions to do right away and which to save for later

SAT MATH: TIMING AND SECTION MANAGEMENT

Timing

The Math section is made up of two 35-minute modules, for a total of 70 minutes for the section. Each of the two modules has 22 questions, for a total of 44 Math questions. This gives you a little over one and a half minutes for each question.

Section Management

To help you navigate the Math section accurately and efficiently, recall the test-taking strategies discussed in the Inside the SAT chapter. Review chapter 1 for more details about the strategies.

1. **Triaging the Test**—Start with the questions you find easiest and flag more difficult or time-consuming questions to do later. Use the module review screen to help you navigate through each module.

2. **Elimination**—Strategically eliminate answer choices that you know are incorrect by crossing them out with the on-screen elimination tool.

3. **Strategic Guessing**—Be sure to answer every question, since there is no wrong-answer penalty. If you're not sure how to do a question or you're nearly out of time, strategically eliminate answer choices, and then use a Letter of the Day to guess an answer.

4. **Living in the Question**—Focus all your energy on the current question.

Keep reading for specifics on how to apply these strategies to the Math section.

Pacing

SAT Math questions vary both in difficulty and in length, so the time you'll spend on each will vary. Further, some question types will require more time than others. Consider the following questions, which you practiced in the Math lessons of this book, and think about how you might approach a Math module that contains these questions on test day.

1.

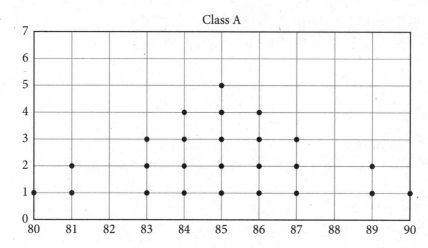

Class A

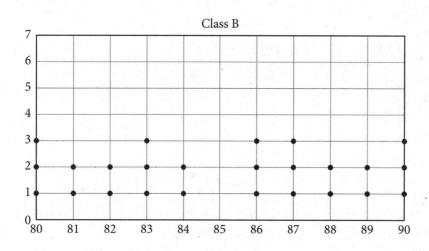

Class B

Two classes of 25 students each took an identical exam. Their percent correct scores are shown in the dot plots. If M_A and S_A are the median and standard deviation, respectively, of class A, and M_B and S_B are the median and standard deviation, respectively, of class B, then which of the following statements is true?

A) $M_A < M_B$ and $S_A < S_B$

B) $M_A > M_B$ and $S_A < S_B$

C) $M_A > M_B$ and $S_A > S_B$

D) $M_A < M_B$ and $S_A > S_B$

2. $\frac{1}{2}(3x + 14) = \frac{1}{6}(7x - 10)$

Which value of x satisfies the equation above?

A) -26

B) 2

C) 8

D) 16

Think about everything the first question requires you to do. You need to interpret *two* dot plots and a lengthy question. Then, you have to determine the relationship between both the standard deviation and the mean in each graph. On the other hand, the second question simply asks you to solve an equation with just one variable. No matter which question you may personally find *easier*, the first question here will likely take you substantially longer to read, analyze, and answer correctly. Adopt the mindset that every question is equally important to your best score. You might decide to flag question 1 and move on to questions like the second one, returning to question 1 from the review screen later as you have time. (See the Statistics lesson in chapter 9 and the Solving Equations lesson in Chapter 4 for the answers and explanations to these questions.)

Because this is a timed exam, be sure to complete the questions you find easiest to answer first. Questions in the Math modules are arranged in approximate order of difficulty, from easiest to most difficult. Use this knowledge to help you navigate each module. If a particular question is challenging or is taking you an especially long time, eliminate any answer choices you can, mark a guess, and flag the question to come back to it if you have time. Once you submit your answers for a module, you will not be able to return to it. So before you exit a module, make sure you have an **answer selected for every question**, since there is no penalty for guessing.

Using the Digital SAT Test Application Tools

The digital test application includes a **countdown timer** that can help you keep track of your remaining time and manage your pace. Every time you complete a practice test, make sure you time yourself so you can practice your pacing.

In addition to the graphing calculator, the digital testing application will also provide you with a reference sheet containing formulas, a way to mark questions for review, and an elimination tool to help you cross out incorrect choices as you go. *Practice with the tools ahead of time so you can determine if you want to use them, and, if so, figure out how you will use them to your advantage on test day.*

Practicing the SAT Math Section

Mastering your section management strategy for SAT Math will require practice. **Every time you complete a practice test, apply the strategies from this chapter:** flag questions you find too time-consuming and return to them if you have time while keeping an eye on the clock. Eliminate incorrect answer choices, strategically guess if you need to, and keep your focus on the current question. Make sure you answer every question before you finish each module. And when taking online practice tests, practice navigating the section and using the available tools so you'll be comfortable with the format on test day.

Now that you've learned about section management for the SAT Math section, your next step is to **take a practice test**. Be sure to apply the section management strategies you've learned and, as always, carefully **review the practice test answers and explanations** to reflect on your performance.

PART 3

SAT READING AND WRITING

HOW MUCH DO YOU KNOW: READING SKILLS

Directions

Try the questions that follow, using the Method for SAT Reading and Writing Questions. When you're done, check your answers and read through the explanations in the "Check Your Work" section.

There will be an opportunity for timed practice at the end of the Reading Skills unit.

1

The following text is from Hilaire Belloc's 1926 comic novel *The Emerald of Catherine the Great*.

It may or may not interest the reader to know that upon his father's death it was discovered that the Emerald of Catherine the Great had been made an heirloom and was devised by an explanatory letter—since the law could not enforce such a succession—for the eldest son, or, failing sons, the eldest daughter of the reigning de Bohun on arriving at his twenty-first, or her eighteenth birthday, his or her parents or trustees being its successive custodians until that date. Failing such a personage, the jewel was to be passed to any cadet branch, the eldest in succession. If the great line of de Bohun should fail—which Heaven forfend!—the sacred object was to be buried with the last of that illustrious lineage. The legal complications to which such a disposition would give rise need not concern us, for in fact they never arose.

As used in the text, what does the word "disposition" most nearly mean?

- (A) Attitude
- (B) Character
- (C) Inclination
- (D) Arrangement

The following text is from John Galsworthy's 1922 novel *The Forsyte Saga*.

Those privileged to be present at a family festival of the Forsytes have seen that charming and instructive sight—an upper middle-class family in full plumage. But whosoever of these favored persons has possessed the gift of psychological analysis . . . has witnessed a spectacle, not only delightful in itself, but illustrative of an obscure human problem. In plainer words, he has gleaned from a gathering of this family—no branch of which had a liking for the other, between no three members of whom existed anything worthy of the name of sympathy—evidence of that mysterious concrete tenacity which renders a family so formidable a unit of society, so clear a reproduction of society in miniature. He has been admitted to a vision of the dim roads of social progress, has understood something of patriarchal life, of the swarmings of savage hordes, of the rise and fall of nations.

Which choice best states the function of the underlined sentence in the text as a whole?

- (A) It sets up the conflict presented in the sentences that follow.

- (B) It establishes a contrast with the description in the previous sentence.

- (C) It elaborates on the previous sentence's description of the family.

- (D) It introduces the setting that is described in the sentences that follow.

3

It is unlikely that pioneers in the field of quantum computing—Stephen Wiesner, Richard Feynman, and Paul Benioff—could have foreseen the rapid progress that has been made. In 1960, when Wiesner first developed conjugate coding with the goal of improving cryptography, his paper on the subject was rejected for publication because it contained logic far ahead of its time. Feynman proposed a basic quantum computing model at the 1981 First Conference on the Physics of Computation. At that same conference, Benioff spoke on the ability of discrete mechanical processes to erase their own history and the application to Turing machines, a natural extension of Wiesner's earlier work. A year later, Benioff more clearly outlined the theoretical framework of a quantum computer. By the early 2000s development accelerated, and in 2018, the first computer chip capable of quantum computing was produced.

According to the text, which of the following factors slowed early developments in the theory of quantum computing?

(A) Feynman and Benioff were discouraged that their computing models were rejected.

(B) At least one academic journal was reluctant to publish papers containing advanced logic.

(C) Quantum computing was too expensive for colleges and universities to support effectively during the 1980s.

(D) A focus on cryptology in the early 1960s drew the most talented researchers away from quantum computing.

4

Hydroponics is a method of growing fruits and vegetables in water-based nutrient solutions rather than in soil. Plants have all needed nutrients directly in contact with their roots, so hydroponic plants grow much faster and much larger since they do not have to send roots through soil in search of nutrients. However, the ingredients for the nutrient solutions are produced in factories and shipped to hydroponic growers. This suggests that hydroponic growers _____

Which choice most logically completes the text?

(A) are able to produce crops more profitably than growers who use soil.

(B) produce crops that are more appealing to consumers.

(C) are able to grow a wider variety of crops than growers who use soil.

(D) are dependent upon the nutrient factories for the success of their crops.

5

Doctors are recognizing the importance of the bacteria found in the human gut, called the microbiome, in malnutrition. Dr. Jeffrey Gordon studied pairs of twins, assuming that, since the twins have identical genes and grew up in the same household, they would have similar nutritional outcomes. However, Dr. Gordon's research found several instances where one twin was healthy and the other twin was malnourished. When he compared the twin's microbiomes, he found substantial differences between the types of bacteria that populated their guts.

Which choice best describes the function of the third sentence in the overall structure of the text?

(A) It presents the central finding of Dr. Gordon's study.

(B) It describes the results of Dr. Gordon's research that contradicted the hypothesis.

(C) It explains how Dr. Gordon's results demonstrate the hypothesis is correct.

(D) It shows that the method Dr. Gordon used is seriously limited.

6

Text 1

Although electric vehicles may seem promising, they present many difficult challenges. For example, residents of apartment buildings, who must park either on the street or in multi-story garages, have no access to electricity to recharge their vehicle's batteries.

Text 2

Japanese light-truck manufacturers have agreed to have a standard battery configuration in their new electric trucks so that the batteries will be interchangeable. The manufacturers are planning to build kiosks throughout Japan where drained batteries can be quickly replaced with fully charged ones.

Based on the texts, what would Japanese light-truck manufacturers (Text 2) most likely say about Text 1's characterization of electric vehicles?

(A) They would argue that residents of apartment buildings would be unlikely to want an electric vehicle.

(B) They would claim that their use of electric trucks will substantially improve inner-city air quality.

(C) They would encourage the author to examine the possibility of a battery exchange.

(D) They would recommend that the author compare the costs of electric vehicles with gasoline vehicles.

7

The following text is from A. E. Housman's 1919 poem, "A Shropshire Lad."

When I was one-and-twenty
I heard a wise man say,
"Give crowns and pounds and guineas
But not your heart away;
Give pearls away and rubies
But keep your fancy free."
But I was one-and-twenty,
No use to talk to me.

What is the main idea of the text?

(A) The narrator did not take the wise man's advice and fell in love.

(B) The narrator carefully followed the wise man's excellent advice.

(C) The narrator followed the wise man's advice but found the advice incorrect.

(D) The wise man encouraged the narrator to give away the narrator's wealth.

8

The Oort cloud is composed of icy and rocky remnants from the formation of the solar system and surrounds its far outer reaches. If one of these remnants collides with another or is pulled out of orbit by an interaction with a passing star, the remnant can fall out of orbit and enter the Earth's atmosphere. Dr. Denis Vida observed a fireball in the atmosphere unusually close to Earth, at about 46 kilometers above the surface. Dr. Vida argues that this fireball was a rocky remnant from the Oort cloud that burned up upon the remnant's entry into Earth's atmosphere.

Which finding, if true, would most directly support Dr. Vida's claim?

(A) Icy remnants from the Oort cloud usually burn up at about 75 kilometers above the Earth's surface.

(B) In any given time period, many more icy, rather than rocky, remnants from the Oort cloud enter the Earth's atmosphere.

(C) Icy remnants from the Oort cloud normally burn up closer to the Earth's surface, at about 40 kilometers above it.

(D) Rocky remnants from the Oort cloud are more difficult to observe and record than are icy remnants.

9

Unlike physical card catalogs, which are no longer maintained, the Dewey decimal system has _____ the transition of libraries to increasingly electronic environments. Although your computer can tell you if your library owns a book, the Dewey decimal number is needed to find the book on the library shelf.

Which choice completes the text with the most logical and precise word or phrase?

(A) hindered

(B) survived

(C) facilitated

(D) encouraged

10

	Capital ships	Ratio
British Empire	525,000 tons	5
United States	525,000 tons	5
Empire of Japan	315,000 tons	3
France	175,000 tons	1.75
Italy	175,000 tons	1.75

Signed in 1922, the Washington Naval Treaty set a ratio of warship tonnage among the world's most powerful navies. This meant that each nation could build only so many capital ships (battleships); the treaty also put limits on smaller ships such as destroyers. However, not all the signatories were allowed the same ratio tonnage. For example, for every 5 tons Britain got, France got 1.75 tons. According to naval historian Dr. A. Suzuki, Japanese public opinion was outraged at the treaty's terms. However, Japanese negotiators agreed to the limits partly due to the urgent need to reduce military spending, which was straining Japan's economy. Suzuki argues that the Japanese negotiators, not wanting to admit the country's economic woes publicly, defended the treaty's terms by claiming that it still established Japan as more prestigious than certain other countries.

Which choice best describes data from the table that support Suzuki's claim?

(A) Although Britain and the United States were allowed more tonnage than Japan, France and Italy were allowed even less tonnage than Japan.

(B) Japan was allowed to build 175,000 tons of capital ships for every 315,000 tons that France built.

(C) Although Britain and the United States were allowed twice as much tonnage as Japan, France and Italy were allowed less than half of Japan's tonnage.

(D) Britain was allowed 525,000 tons under the treaty, while Japan and the United States were each allowed 315,000 tons.

Check Your Work – How Much Do You Know: Reading Skills

1.   D
Difficulty: Hard
Category: Craft and Structure
Getting to the Answer: In the text, the "disposition" mentioned is the transfer of the emerald to the successive heirs, so *settlement* or *plan* are good predictions. **(D)** is correct.

The incorrect choices are all alternative definitions for "disposition" that refer to a person, and so, do not fit this context.

2.   A
Difficulty: Hard
Category: Craft and Structure
Getting to the Answer: The passage introduces the Forsyte family, and the descriptive phrases "charming," "upper middle-class," and "full-plumage" present an image of a wealthy, attractive family. The contrast keyword "but" indicates a change of direction, and the purpose of the underlined portion is introduced by the phrase "in plainer words." In the remainder of the text, conflicts are outlined—the different branches of the family dislike each other and no three members of the family care for each other—the same types of conflicts that are part of wider society. This structure matches **(A)**, the correct answer.

Although the underlined portion opens with the contrast keyword "but," the contrast is not explained until the *following* sentence, so (B) is incorrect. Choices (C) and (D) are incorrect because the underlined portion does not contain any description of the family (C) or the setting (D).

3.   B
Difficulty: Medium
Category: Information and Ideas
Getting to the Answer: Most of the details in the text are positive and speak to a consistent advancement in theorizing and modeling quantum computing. The one setback that is mentioned is the rejection of Wiesner's paper by an academic journal hesitant to publish logic that was "far ahead of its time." That's described in the correct answer, **(B)**.

Choice (A) distorts the text, which does not suggest that Feynman's and Benioff's models were rejected. (C) is not mentioned in the text; the expense of quantum

computing is never discussed. (D) contradicts the passage; Wiesner's interest in cryptology appears to have promoted his work leading to early quantum computing models.

4.   D
Difficulty: Easy
Category: Information and Ideas
Getting to the Answer: The correct answer to a "logically completes the text" inference question will refer to ideas mentioned in the text and will not introduce a new concept. Inventory the ideas in the text, then work through the choices by elimination. Here, the first sentence defines hydroponics, the second explains why hydroponic plants grow faster and larger than plants grown in soil, and the third discusses the source of the ingredients for the nutrient solutions needed for hydroponics. Eliminate (A) because there is no discussion of profit. Eliminate (B) since the text never mentions consumer appeal. Eliminate (C) because the text does not discuss the variety of crops that can be grown. Choice **(D)** must be correct, and on test day, mark it confidently and move on. For practice, though, (D) draws a reasonable inference. If hydroponics requires "nutrient solutions" that are "produced in factories and shipped to hydroponic growers," it is likely that growers "are dependent upon the nutrient factories."

5.   B
Difficulty: Medium
Category: Craft and Structure
Getting to the Answer: The question asks for the "function of the third sentence," so this is a purpose question. As you read, categorize the *type* of information presented, not the details of the content. Here, the first sentence mentions that doctors may have found a new factor contributing to malnutrition. The second sentence provides the reason Dr. Gordon's research studied twins: Dr. Gordon assumed their nutritional outcomes would be similar. The third sentence starts with the contrast keyword "However," so predict that the twins' nutritional outcomes were *not* similar. Indeed, the sentence supports that prediction. Matching this to the choices yields **(B)**, the correct answer.

For the incorrect choices: (A) is the role of the fourth, and final, sentence, not the third sentence. Choice (C) is opposite; Dr. Gordon's hypothesis was that the twins' nutritional outcomes would be similar. Choice (D) is incorrect because Dr. Gordon's method was not flawed.

6.   C

Difficulty: Medium

Category: Craft and Structure

Getting to the Answer: Since the question asks for the response of the Text 2 Japanese light-truck manufacturers, read Text 1 quickly and focus on the ideas presented in Text 2. Text 1 presents a point against electric vehicles: residents in apartment buildings can't recharge a battery. Text 2 describes the Japanese light-truck manufacturer's plan to exchange, rather than recharge, batteries. Identify the choice that uses this concept to respond to the author of Text 1. Choice **(C)** does so and is correct.

The incorrect choices all introduce ideas not mentioned in Text 2. The Japanese light-truck manufacturers never mention the desirability of an electric vehicle (A), air quality (B), or the comparative cost of an electric vehicle (D).

7.   A

Difficulty: Medium

Category: Information and Ideas

Getting to the Answer: In the first four lines of the poem, the narrator hears the wise man's advice to give away money ("crowns and pounds and guineas") but not "your heart." If you weren't sure what "crowns and pounds and guineas" were, the narrator restates the advice in the next two lines: "Give pearls away and rubies," but keep your "fancy," or *affections*, free. The final two lines conclude the poem: the narrator was young and did not listen to the wise man's advice "no use to talk to me." This summary matches **(A)**, the correct answer.

The incorrect choices all misinterpret the poem's meaning. The narrator did not follow the wise man's advice, so (B) and (C) are incorrect. For (D), the wise man encouraged the narrator to give away wealth *instead* of the narrator's heart. The main idea of the poem is not about giving away property.

8.   A

Difficulty: Medium

Category: Information and Ideas

Getting to the Answer: To efficiently "support Dr. Vida's claim," quickly scan the text and identify what the claim is. The last sentence states "Dr. Vida argues,"

so note the key idea in your own words: *this "fireball" was a piece of rock from the Oort cloud*. With this idea in mind (or on your scratch paper) start reading the text from the beginning, focusing on the ideas mentioned in the claim. The first sentence describes the Oort cloud as "composed of icy and rocky remnants" that "can fall out of orbit and enter the Earth's atmosphere." The second sentence describes Dr. Vida's "fireball" and uses the emphasis keyword "unusually" to explain Dr. Vida's interest: the fireball came unusually close to the Earth's surface. Although you may find it challenging to predict the exact words the correct answer will take, the answer must include *only* these ideas, so evaluate the choices using this summary. **(A)** is correct; if icy remnants burn up farther away from the Earth's surface, it is more likely that the fireball that was "unusually" close to that surface was composed of rock, not ice.

Incorrect choices (B) and (D) bring in ideas that were not discussed in the text, and therefore, cannot support the claim. The passage never compares the numbers of the different kinds of remnants (B) or the relative difficulty of observing them (D). Choice (C) is opposite; if the icy remnants normally burn up closer to Earth's surface, then it is more likely Dr. Vida's fireball was ice, not rock.

9.   B

Difficulty: Easy

Category: Craft and Structure

Getting to the Answer: The first sentence uses a contrast keyword "unlike" to draw a comparison between "card catalogs" that are gone to "the Dewey decimal system." The second sentence explains that the "Dewey decimal number is needed." A good prediction for the blank is any word or phrase that indicates the Dewey decimal system *successfully made* the transition to an electronic environment. Choice **(B)**, the correct answer, matches this prediction.

The incorrect choices all change the meaning of the sentence. There is no evidence in the text that the Dewey decimal *held back* (A) or *assisted* the transition to a more electronic environment in libraries as in (C) and (D).

10. A

Difficulty: Medium

Category: Information and Ideas

Getting to the Answer: Suzuki's claim is that, while the country was not allowed the maximum tonnage of some nations, Japan was able to claim that the treaty "still established Japan as more prestigious than certain other countries." According to the data table, Japan was limited to 315,000 tons, while France and Italy were limited to 175,000 tons. Thus, you can predict that the correct answer will favorably contrast Japan with France and/or Italy. **(A)** best matches this prediction and is correct.

Choice (B) misreads the data table; Japan was allowed 315,000 tons, while France was allowed 175,000 tons. (C) is incorrect because Britain and the United States were allowed tonnage on a 5:3 ratio with Japan, not a 2:1 ratio. Furthermore, Japan held a 3:1.75 ratio of tonnage with France and Italy, not a 2:1 ratio. (D) is incorrect because the table lists the United States as being allowed 525,000 tons.

[CHAPTER 17]

THE METHOD FOR SAT READING AND WRITING QUESTIONS

LEARNING OBJECTIVES

After completing this chapter, you will be able to:

- Apply the Method to SAT Reading and Writing questions
- Identify useful keywords and use them to answer questions

HOW TO DO SAT READING AND WRITING

LEARNING OBJECTIVES

After this lesson, you will be able to:

- Apply the Method to SAT Reading and Writing questions
- Identify useful keywords and use them to answer questions

The SAT Reading and Writing section contains 54 questions, divided into two 27-question modules of 32 minutes each. Every question has its own short passage (or sometimes a short pair of passages) that accompanies it. To tackle this section effectively in the 64 minutes allotted, the most successful test takers:

- **Approach the questions with a method that minimizes rereading and leads directly to correct answers.** (See "The Method for SAT Reading and Writing Questions" section of this chapter.)

- **Read the passages strategically to focus in on the text that leads to points.** (See the "Strategic Reading" section of this chapter.)

In this chapter, we'll give you an overview of how to tackle Reading and Writing passages and questions. The following chapters in this unit will teach you the unique strategies that will help you maximize your efficiency and accuracy on each Reading and Writing question type. Chapter 21 will also provide review of the Standard English conventions topics that are tested on the SAT.

To get started, try the questions that follow on your own. Then, keep reading to compare your approach to ours.

The careful design of the rock garden at the Ryōan-ji Zen temple in Kyoto, Japan, is meant to facilitate meditation. Like all karesansui, or dry landscape gardens, the Ryōan-ji garden reflects the principle of minimalism and evokes the quality of stillness. Most of the garden is covered by small white pebbles, which the temple monks rake into linear designs meant to mimic water ripples; both the practice of raking and the appearance of the small rocks encourage calm contemplation. On top of the pebbles, the garden at Ryōan-ji features fifteen larger rocks organized into groups, though only fourteen can be viewed from any one position. The arrangement creates a rhythmic and soothing viewing experience as observers' eyes drift among the groupings.

Which choice best states the main idea of the text?

A) The Ryōan-ji garden is the most well-known karesansui garden in Japan.

B) The Ryōan-ji garden has a purposeful arrangement that is intended to influence viewers' mental state.

C) The organization of the large rocks at the Ryōan-ji garden is different from that of most dry landscape gardens.

D) Raking the small pebbles in the Ryōan-ji garden is a physically challenging, yet mentally rewarding, practice.

In order to assess test subjects' decisions related to risk-taking, psychologists at the University of Iowa developed the so-called Iowa Gambling Task, a computer-based _____ allows participants to wager fake money as they select cards from four decks with differing levels of potential rewards and losses. Risk-tolerant individuals tend to keep selecting cards from decks with the highest probability of both big wins and big losses.

Which choice completes the text so that it conforms to the conventions of Standard English?

A) game

B) game,

C) game that

D) game, that

The Method for SAT Reading and Writing Questions

The digital SAT presents a total of 54 questions. SAT experts use a simple three-step method that takes advantage of this test format to help them tackle each question quickly and confidently.

THE METHOD FOR SAT READING AND WRITING

STEP 1 What is the question asking?

- Standard English Conventions questions ONLY: Look at the answer choices for clues

STEP 2 What do I need to look for in the passage?

STEP 3 What answer strategy is best?

- Predict and Match
- Eliminate

Take another look at the first question from the set, and then read through how and why an expert would apply the steps of the Method.

The careful design of the rock garden at the Ryōan-ji Zen temple in Kyoto, Japan, is meant to facilitate meditation. Like all karesansui, or dry landscape gardens, the Ryōan-ji garden reflects the principle of minimalism and evokes the quality of stillness. Most of the garden is covered by small white pebbles, which the temple monks rake into linear designs meant to mimic water ripples; both the practice of raking and the appearance of the small rocks encourage calm contemplation. On top of the pebbles, the garden at Ryōan-ji features fifteen larger rocks organized into groups, though only fourteen can be viewed from any one position. The arrangement creates a rhythmic and soothing viewing experience as observers' eyes drift among the groupings.

Which choice best states the main idea of the text?

A) The Ryōan-ji garden is the most well-known karesansui garden in Japan.

B) The Ryōan-ji garden has a purposeful arrangement that is intended to influence viewers' mental state.

C) The organization of the large rocks at the Ryōan-ji garden is different from that of most dry landscape gardens.

D) Raking the small pebbles in the Ryōan-ji garden is a physically challenging, yet mentally rewarding, practice.

Step 1. What is the question asking?

The format of the SAT provides you with an excellent time-saving strategy. Because each passage only has one question, *reading the question before you jump into the passage* will allow you to focus in on exactly what you need from the passage.

In the previous question, you're asked to identify the answer choice that gives the "main idea" of the passage.

Step 2. What do I need to look for in the passage?

Next, strategically read the passage based on what the question asks. Some question types, which you'll learn about in the following chapters, can be answered by focusing on just a specific part of the passage. And whether you closely read the entire passage or only part of it, your reading approach will differ depending on the question type.

Note that, on this Main Idea question, an SAT expert would likely read the entire passage, but would especially focus on the first and last sentences of the passage, which are the most likely to summarize the main idea of the passage. Here, the first sentence states that the "careful design" of a certain rock garden "is meant to facilitate meditation."

Since all you need is the main idea, you should avoid getting bogged down in the details of this passage. A quick skim of the details, however, can confirm that they all support the main idea that the design of the rock garden facilitates meditation: the other sentences include details such as the garden's minimalism evoking stillness, the small pebbles encouraging contemplation, and the arrangement of the larger rocks creating a soothing viewing experience.

Step 3. What answer strategy is best?

Finally, consider which strategy will be your best approach for answering the question efficiently and correctly. Once you have identified what the question is asking and tailored your reading approach appropriately, there are two strategies you can use to help you identify the correct answer:

- **Predict and Match**—Based on the question and your reading of the passage, make a prediction of the correct answer in your own words. Then look for an answer choice that matches your prediction.

- **Eliminate**—Analyze the answer choices one by one and rule out any that do not directly answer the question based upon the information in the passage.

On the previous Main Idea question, use the main idea identified in the first sentence of the passage to make a **prediction** of the correct answer in your own words: *the rock garden was designed to encourage meditation.* This prediction matches **(B)**. The other answer choices reflect details that were mentioned in the passage, but they all misrepresent the information presented; further, each incorrect choice focuses on one detail from the passage rather than summarizing the big picture of the passage.

Some question types tend to lend themselves to one strategy or the other. For instance, as in the example question, Main Idea questions allow you to paraphrase the main idea from the passage in your own words, which serves as your **prediction**. When predicting, be sure to make your prediction *before looking at the answer choices*; your prediction will help you quickly identify the correct answer and avoid wasting time considering the incorrect answer choices. Check your prediction against the choices and find the *one* correct answer that **matches**. If you can't find a match, you can check the passage again and try rephrasing your prediction or try the strategy of elimination.

Eliminating entails reading the answer choices one by one and rejecting those that don't answer the question. Although this can be more time-consuming than predicting and matching, some questions are difficult to predict and require using this more thorough approach. Eliminate answer choices that misrepresent the passage, as well as those that fail to address the question asked. See the "Incorrect Answer Types" section in this chapter for information about the incorrect answer types you are most likely to encounter—and be able to quickly eliminate—on test day. Note that the digital format of the SAT provides an option that allows you to eliminate individual answer choices by clicking an icon that appears next to each choice. An icon at the far right of the question number box will enable this option, which can be very helpful for keeping track of the answer choices on test day.

While some question types may typically lend themselves to one answer strategy or the other, keep in mind that you should use whichever strategy is best *for you*. If you struggle to make a prediction on a Main Idea question, for instance, don't sweat it! Move on to the elimination strategy and get rid of those answer choices you recognize as incorrect.

Let's walk through the steps of the Method one more time, this time on a question that highlights the answer strategy of elimination and presents the slight adjustment you should make to the Method when answering a question about Standard English conventions.

> In order to assess test subjects' decisions related to risk-taking, psychologists at the University of Iowa developed the so-called Iowa Gambling Task, a computer-based _____ allows participants to wager fake money as they select cards from four decks with differing levels of potential rewards and losses. Risk-tolerant individuals tend to keep selecting cards from decks with the highest probability of both big wins and big losses.
>
> Which choice completes the text so that it conforms to the conventions of Standard English?
>
> A) game
>
> B) game,
>
> C) game that
>
> D) game, that

Step 1. What is the question asking?

Note that this question stem asks you to choose the answer choice that "conforms to the conventions of Standard English." Since this question concerns English conventions, add an additional part to this step: look at the answer choices for clues before looking at the passage. Doing so will often enable you to identify the English convention that the question is testing, which will help you focus on that issue as you read.

This question, for example, has two answer choices that contain commas, so you can anticipate that the question tests punctuation.

Step 2. What do I need to look for in the passage?

Strategically read the passage based on what the question asks. Since the question and answer choices indicate that the missing portion may contain a comma and/or the word "that," read the passage with the goal of determining the structure of the sentence with the blank. The portion of the sentence beginning with "a computer-based [game] . . ." seems to be a phrase that describes the "Iowa Gambling Task."

Step 3. What answer strategy is best?

Consider which answer strategy—Predict and Match or Eliminate—is your best approach. For questions like these, it may be easier to identify which answer choice correctly completes the descriptive phrase by reading the answer choices back into the blank and eliminating any that result in an illogical or ungrammatical sentence.

First, eliminate (A); inserting the word "game" without any punctuation results in a run-on because two complete sentences are connected with only the comma that follows "Iowa Gambling Task." The comma in (B) sets off the phrase "a computer-based game" as parenthetical. This parenthetical is logical, but reading the sentence without the parenthetical phrase results in a non-grammatical sentence (psychologists . . . developed the so-called Iowa Gambling Task. . . allows participants to wager). Eliminate (B). Next, consider the use of "that" in the remaining choices. Adding "that" results in a logical phrase (a computer-based [game that] allows participants to wager . . .) that describes the "Iowa Gambling Task." No comma is needed before a descriptive phrase beginning with "that," so (D) can be eliminated and **(C)** is correct.

Make the Method Work for You

Overall, remember that the Method for SAT Reading and Writing is *flexible*, allowing you to efficiently answer each question using the strategy that is best for you. Always use the question to help you tailor your reading of the passage, and then determine which answer strategy—Predict and Match or Eliminate—will enable you to confidently answer the question asked. Expert SAT test takers consistently apply the three-step Method, but they vary their specific approach from question to question, depending on what is asked and their own strengths. As you practice SAT questions, follow the Method, but practice both answer strategies so you can learn what works best for you.

Incorrect Answer Types on SAT Reading and Writing

Whether you predict and match or eliminate when answering a question, being aware of the most common types of incorrect answer choices can help you focus on the correct choice and quickly rule out the incorrect choices. Incorrect answer choices on the SAT often fall into one of five categories:

- **Out of Scope**—contains a statement that is too broad, too narrow, or beyond the purview of the passage
- **Extreme**—contains language that is too strong (*all, never, always, every, none*) to be supported by the passage
- **Distortion**—based on details or ideas from the passage but distorts or misstates what the author says or implies
- **Opposite**—directly contradicts what the correct answer must say
- **Misused Detail**—accurately states something from the passage but in a manner that incorrectly answers the question

Strategic Reading

Every question on the SAT Reading and Writing section is accompanied by a short passage, typically about a paragraph in length. The SAT includes passages in the following subject areas: literature, history/social studies, the humanities (topics such as the arts), and science.

The process of reading passages on the SAT is not the same as reading materials for leisure or even for textbooks or other books you read for school. As demonstrated in the Method for SAT Reading and Writing, your reading of each short passage should be tailored exactly to the question that is asked; you are not reading to learn everything about the passage, but only with the goal of answering a specific question. The following chapters will provide tips about how to read the passage for each particular question type. For example, as demonstrated in the Method section, you'll typically focus on sentence structure when answering a Standard English Conventions question that tests punctuation.

Keywords

No matter what type of question you're answering, there are special types of words you should be on the look-out for in every SAT Reading and Writing passage. These words will help you understand the structure and viewpoints in every passage; *the test makers specifically include these words as hints to help you answer the questions asked*. The following table shows types of SAT keywords.

TYPES OF KEYWORDS IN SAT PASSAGES		
Keyword Type	**What the Keywords Indicate**	**Examples**
Opinion	the author's viewpoint	*fortunately, disappointing, I suggest, it seems likely*
Emphasis	what the author finds noteworthy	*especially, crucial, important, above all*
Continuation	a continuation of the same point	*moreover, in addition, also, further*
Contrast	a change in direction or a point of difference	*but, yet, despite, on the other hand, however*
Argument	the use of evidence to support a conclusion	*thus, therefore, because, for example, to illustrate*

Keywords indicate opinions and signal structures that make the difference between correct and incorrect answers on SAT questions. Consider this question:

With which one of the following statements would the author most likely agree?

1. Coffee beans that grow at high altitudes typically produce dark, mellow coffee when brewed.

2. Coffee beans that grow at high altitudes typically produce light, acidic coffee when brewed.

To answer this question, look at this excerpt from its associated passage next. Pay special attention to the keywords in bold.

Type X coffee beans grow at very high altitudes **and so** produce a dark, mellow coffee when brewed.

The continuation keywords "and so" indicate a connection between the ideas in the sentence, so choice (1) would be correct.

However, if the excerpt instead said:

Type X coffee beans grow at very high altitudes **but** produce a **surprisingly** dark, mellow coffee when brewed.

In this case, the contrast keyword "but" and the emphasis keyword "surprisingly" indicate a contrast between Type X coffee beans and their growing at high altitudes, making choice (2) correct. The other words in the excerpts did not change at all, but the correct answer to the SAT question would be different in each case because of the keywords the author chose to include.

Passage Blurbs

Some passages are preceded by a **short blurb** that identifies the author, the year written, and the source of the passage. The blurbs may also provide some additional context to keep in mind that will help you understand the passage. These blurbs most often accompany literature passages. Be sure to read any blurbs to help you understand the context of the passage.

Literature Passages

Many of the passages on the SAT will be literature passages. These will be short excerpts from literary works, such as novels, short stories, and poems. Don't worry if you haven't read the source before; like every SAT

Reading and Writing question, everything you need to answer the question is found on the test. In fact, if you are familiar with the source, be careful to use *only* the excerpt provided on the SAT, not your outside knowledge, to answer the question.

Literature passages are naturally less factual than other SAT passages. When you encounter a literature passage, approach it as you would any SAT Reading and Writing question: first analyze the question stem, then the passage, before you use an answering strategy. When reading the passage, keep in mind that literature passages often emphasize literary elements: characters, settings, themes (the main idea or message of the passage), and figurative language. Questions on literature passages often concern these types of literary elements.

Putting it All Together

By using the Method for SAT Reading and Writing on every question and strategically reading every passage, expert test takers set themselves up for success with an approach that will be efficient and effective on every question they'll encounter. Like learning any new skill, mastering these strategies will take practice. So on every practice question you try, work on getting in the habit of following the steps: read the question, read the passage strategically, and predict and match or eliminate answer choices. Always read the question explanations, and reflect upon how your own approach compares. Keep asking yourself: *What did I do well on this question? How can I improve my strategy on a similar question in the future?* With practice, the method and strategies will become second nature by test day. Give it a try now by applying what you've learned to the questions that follow.

Try on Your Own

Directions

Take as much time as you need on these questions. On each question, use the three-step Method for SAT Reading and Writing. Look for keywords as you strategically read each passage.

1

Psychologist Barry Schwartz describes a phenomenon called the "paradox of choice," which entails the counter-intuitive idea that people are actually less satisfied when presented with a relatively high number of alternatives. For instance, the opportunity to choose among three desserts at a restaurant may be delightful, but a dessert menu with 30 choices might be overwhelming. Schwartz attributes this condition to three main factors. When presented with an overabundance of choice, test subjects tend to have more difficulty making decisions, make generally poorer decisions, and ultimately tend to feel discontented with whatever decisions they make. The paradox of choice therefore implies that

_____

Which choice most logically completes the text?

A) consumers always prefer to have a high number of potential selections for a product than a small number of higher quality potential selections.

B) consumers would likely experience greater satisfaction when presented with fewer, rather than more, potential selections for a product.

C) the perception of choice plays a significant role in many psychological phenomena.

D) the quantity of potential selections is the most important factor for people to consider when they engage in rational decision making.

2

The following text is from Emily Brontë's 1847 novel *Wuthering Heights*.

[Cathy's] spirit was high, though not rough, and qualified by a heart sensitive and lively to excess in its affections. That capacity for intense attachments reminded me of her mother. Still she did not resemble her: for she could be soft and mild as a dove, and she had a gentle voice and pensive expression. Her anger was never furious; her love never fierce: it was deep and tender. However, it must be acknowledged, she had faults to foil her gifts. <u>A propensity to be saucy was one; and a perverse will, that indulged children invariably acquire, whether they be good tempered or cross</u>. If a servant chanced to vex her, it was always—"I shall tell papa!"

Which choice best states the function of the underlined sentence in the text as a whole?

(A) It introduces a significant event in the plot of the narrative.

(B) It provides a contrast with the description in the previous sentence.

(C) It establishes a context that makes the conversation that follows unexpected.

(D) It elaborates on a character description from the previous sentence.

3

Walt Disney's first full-length animated feature, *Snow White and the Seven Dwarfs*, faced skepticism at its 1937 release. Critics questioned whether children would be able to sit still for the full 80 minutes of the film and doubted that a cartoon would be able to earn back its nearly $1.5 million production costs. _____ the movie was a resounding success. *Snow White* earned five times its costs during its initial release, received an honorary Oscar award, and jump-started the animated film industry.

Which choice completes the text with the most logical transition?

(A) However,

(B) For instance,

(C) Likewise,

(D) Hence,

4

Goodnight Moon is a children's book that features engaging illustrations and a soothing rhyming _____ the writing approach of author and educator Margaret Wise Brown, who believed in showing the world through children's eyes. The book presents a bedtime ritual in which a young bunny bids goodnight to the objects in the bedroom. Its sweet simplicity has made it a bedtime classic across generations, selling almost 50 million copies since its publication in 1947.

Which choice completes the text so that it conforms to the conventions of Standard English?

(A) scheme. Reflecting

(B) scheme; reflecting

(C) scheme, reflecting

(D) scheme reflecting

REFLECT

Directions: Take a few minutes to recall what you've learned and what you've been practicing in this chapter. Consider the following questions, jot down your best answer for each one, and then compare your reflections to the expert responses that follow. Use your level of confidence to determine what to do next.

Identify the steps of the Method for SAT Reading and Writing. What additional task should you perform when answering a Standard English Conventions question?

_____

_____

_____

Why do expert SAT test takers look at the question before reading the passage?

_____

_____

_____

What are the two answer strategies you can use when answering a Reading and Writing question? When might one strategy be preferable over the other?

_____

_____

_____

What types of incorrect answer types can you quickly eliminate?

_____

_____

_____

What are some types of keywords that appear in SAT passages? What is the benefit of noting keywords as you read?

_____

_____

_____

What will you do differently on future passages and their questions?

_____

_____

_____

Expert Responses

Identify the steps of the Method for SAT Reading and Writing. What additional task should you perform when answering a Standard English Conventions question?

The steps of the Method are: 1) What is the question asking?, 2) What do I need to look for in the passage?, and 3) What answer strategy is best? When answering a Standard English Conventions question, you should look at the answer choices for clues during Step 1 before reading the passage.

Why do expert SAT test takers look at the question before reading the passage?

Because each passage only has one question, reading the question before you jump into the passage will allow you to focus in on exactly what you need from the passage.

What are the two answer strategies you can use when answering a Reading and Writing question? When might one strategy be preferable over the other?

The two answer strategies are Predict and Match, in which you make a prediction of the correct answer in your own words before looking for a match in the answer choices, and Eliminate, in which you analyze the answer choices one-by-one and rule out any that do not directly answer the question based on the information in the passage. Predicting works well when it is easy to predict the answer to the question. Eliminating works well when it is difficult to make a specific prediction.

What types of incorrect answer types can you quickly eliminate?

Incorrect answer choices include those that are out of scope (state something that goes beyond the passage), extreme (contain language that is too strong to be supported by the passage), distortions (misstate what the author says or implies), opposite (directly contradict what the correct answer must say), and misused details (state something from the passage but don't answer the question). Don't worry if you couldn't remember all these types—you'll learn to recognize them as you practice more Reading and Writing questions.

What are some types of keywords that appear in SAT passages? Provide some examples of each type. What is the benefit of noting keywords as you read?

Keyword types include opinion (such as fortunately *and* disappointing*), emphasis (such as* especially *and* crucial*), continuation (such as* moreover *and* further*), contrast (such as* despite *and* however*), and argument (such as* therefore *and* because*) words. These words will help you understand the structure and viewpoints in every passage; the test makers specifically include these words as hints to help you answer the questions asked.*

What will you do differently on future passages and their questions?

There is no one-size-fits-all answer to this question. Each student has his or her own initial strengths and opportunities in the Reading and Writing section. What's important here is that you're honestly self-reflective. Take what you need from the expert's examples and strive to apply it to your own performance. Many test takers convince themselves that they'll never get faster or more confident in SAT Reading and Writing, but the truth is, many test takers who now routinely ace the Reading and Writing section were much slower and more hesitant before they learned to approach this section systematically and strategically.

Next Steps

If your responses to the Reflect questions were similar to those of the SAT expert, then consider How to Do SAT Reading and Writing an area of strength.

If you don't yet feel confident, review the information in this chapter that you have not yet mastered. Then, try the questions you missed again. As always, be sure to review the explanations closely.

In either case, make sure you apply the strategies from this chapter and the Method for SAT Reading and Writing to every question you practice as you move on to the following chapters, which cover each of the Reading and Writing question types.

Check Your Work – Chapter 17

1. B
Difficulty: Hard
Category: Information and Ideas
Getting to the Answer: The question stem asks which choice logically flows from the ideas in the passage. The sentence with the blank identifies that the correct answer will be something implied by the paradox of choice, so look for a description of the paradox as you read. The first sentence defines the paradox: people are less satisfied when they have more choices. The rest of the passage gives an example of the paradox and three reasons for the paradox.

Many students would find it hard to predict an answer here, so you may want to choose the elimination strategy for questions such as this. Evaluate the answer choices with these ideas just identified in mind; you can always go back to the passage to clarify specific details if needed. Choice (A) can be eliminated because it is the opposite of the paradox of choice; further, the word "always" makes this answer choice extreme. Choice **(B)**, however, is a logical inference based on the paradox of choice: if people are less satisfied with lots of choices, they will likely be more satisfied with fewer choices; **(B)** is correct. Choices (C) and (D) are out of scope. The passage does not discuss "many" psychological phenomena, just the paradox of choice, and factors in rational decision making are never mentioned.

2. D
Difficulty: Medium
Category: Craft and Structure
Getting to the Answer: The question stem asks for the function of an underlined sentence, so think about the structure of the passage as you read. Ask yourself, *Why did the author include this sentence?* The first sentences of the passage describe the character Cathy. Pay attention to the sentence before the underline, since it begins with the contrast transition "However." Here, the narrator states that Cathy "had faults to foil her gifts"; expect that the passage will shift from describing Cathy's positive traits to describing her negative traits. Indeed, the underlined sentence describes negative traits, including her being "saucy" and having "a perverse will." The keywords in this question are enough for many students to make a prediction, but others will still choose elimination. If the latter is the case for you, evaluate the answer choices with this passage structure in mind.

Eliminate (A), since the underlined sentence is a character description, not an event. Be careful with (B). The underlined sentence elaborates on a contrast that was introduced

in the *previous* sentence; the underlined sentence itself does not contrast with the previous sentence. Eliminate (B). Eliminate (C) because the next sentence does not contain a conversation. Rather, it provides a statement Cathy often makes that is an example of her "perverse will"; Cathy's statement is thus not "unexpected," but in keeping with her character description. Choice **(D)** is correct; the underlined sentence gives examples of the character "faults" mentioned in the previous sentence.

3. A
Difficulty: Easy
Category: Expression of Ideas
Getting to the Answer: The question stem asks for the most logical transition, so as you read the passage, identify what ideas are being connected by the transition. The idea before the blank is that *Snow White* faced "skepticism." The idea after the blank is that the movie was a "success." The clear contrast will make prediction the best strategy for most students on this question. Predict that the correct answer will be a contrast transition word: the movie was a success *even though* critics doubted it. This prediction matches **(A)**, which is correct. Choice (B) is incorrect because the movie's success is not *an example* of the doubts about it. Choice (C) is incorrect because it is a continuation transition, while the ideas in the passage contrast. Choice (D) is incorrect because it creates an illogical cause-and-effect relationship; the movie was a success *in spite of*, not *due to*, early skepticism about the film.

4. C
Difficulty: Medium
Category: Standard English Conventions
Getting to the Answer: Since this question asks about Standard English conventions, read the answer choices before looking at the passage. The choices signal that this question deals with punctuation, most likely testing how to connect the parts of a sentence. The portion of the sentence before the blank is a complete thought ("*Goodnight Moon* is a children's book . . ."). The portion after the punctuation is *not* a complete thought ("reflecting the writing approach . . . through children's eyes"). Predict that a comma should be used to join a complete thought to an incomplete thought. **(C)** is correct. If you prefer elimination, you can rule out incorrect answer choices. Choices (A) and (B) are incorrect because they are ways to join two complete thoughts. Choice (D) is incorrect because it omits all punctuation.

[CHAPTER 18]

INFORMATION AND IDEAS

LEARNING OBJECTIVES

After completing this chapter, you will be able to:

- Identify the main idea of a passage
- Identify a detail explicitly stated in the text
- Identify the conclusion and evidence in an argument
- Identify additional relevant information that strengthens or weakens a claim
- Use quantitative information to logically complete, support, or weaken a statement
- Determine what must be true based on given information

HOW MUCH DO YOU KNOW?

Directions

Try the questions that follow. When you're done, check your answers and reasoning against ours in the "Check Your Work" section. If they closely match, you may be able to move quickly through the chapter. If they do not, spend some extra time with the chapter to grow your SAT Reading and Writing skills.

1

Those who experience recurrent nightmares may be diagnosed as having nightmare disorder; fortunately, researchers have developed a new treatment that has shown promising results. Patients in a 2022 study were divided into two groups. Half were treated using only Imagery Rehearsal Therapy (IRT), a commonly used technique for treating nightmare disorder, and half were treated with traditional IRT in combination with a new method, Targeted Memory Reactivation (TMR). TMR involves playing a repeated major piano chord as patients engage in positive thinking while awake. Then, the piano chord is played while the patients sleep. In the study, these patients experienced a greater decrease in the occurrence of nightmares and a greater increase in the occurrence of positive dreams in comparison with the patients who received only IRT. The researchers hope that this combination of IRT and TMR therapy will improve the condition of patients with nightmare disorder.

Which choice best describes the main idea of the text?

(A) Imagery Rehearsal Therapy is the most common and effective method for treating patients who experience nightmare disorder.

(B) A 2022 study about nightmare disorder treated some patients with only a traditional technique and some patients with both the traditional technique and a new technique.

(C) Based on a 2022 study, the use of a new technique along with a traditional technique may be an effective treatment for nightmare disorder.

(D) The Targeted Memory Reactivation method involves teaching patients with nightmare disorder to associate a piano chord with positive thoughts.

2

The following text is adapted from George Eliot's 1871 novel *Middlemarch*.

It was hardly a year since they had come to live at Tipton Grange with their uncle, a man nearly sixty, of acquiescent temper, miscellaneous opinions, and uncertain vote. He had traveled in his younger years, and was held in this part of the county to have contracted a too rambling habit of mind. Mr. Brooke's conclusions were as difficult to predict as the weather: it was only safe to say that he would act with benevolent intentions, and that he would spend as little money as possible in carrying them out.

According to the text, what is true about Mr. Brooke?

(A) Others are unable to anticipate what choices he will make.

(B) He becomes angry and agitated for minor reasons.

(C) Others assume that he will usually act in his own self-interest.

(D) He has only lived at Tipton Grange for about a year.

3

Female mosquitoes bite humans in order to gain nourishment that contributes to the production of the insects' eggs. However, scientists have long been puzzled as to why some people are plagued by mosquitoes while others seem to be practically ignored by the insects. Researchers Leslie Vosshall and Maria Elena De Obaldia predicted that different variations of human body odor are more or less likely to attract mosquitoes. To test their hypothesis, the researchers created an apparatus in which *Aedes Aegypti* mosquitoes could choose one of two nylon stockings that had been worn on the arms of two different participants. Researchers measured the level of carboxylic acids, from which bacteria create each person's individual body odor, produced by each participant's skin.

Which finding, if true, would most strongly support the researchers' prediction?

(A) The mosquitoes' preference for stockings worn by different people was no different than would be expected by random chance.

(B) The stockings worn by the people whose skin produced the highest levels of carboxylic acids attracted the most mosquitoes.

(C) The mosquitoes were significantly less attracted to stockings that were worn by people who wore the stockings on their legs rather than their arms.

(D) All participants, regardless of the level of carboxylic acids produced by their skin, reported that they typically receive about the same quantity of mosquito bites when outdoors.

4

"Birds of Passage" is an 1858 poem by Henry Wadsworth Longfellow. In the poem, Longfellow compares poetry to the flight of birds, writing, _____

Which quotation from "Birds of Passage" most effectively illustrates the claim?

(A) "But the night is fair, / And everywhere / A warm, soft vapor fills the air, / And distant sounds seem near,"

(B) "And above, in the light / Of the star-lit night, / Swift birds of passage wing their flight / Through the dewy atmosphere."

(C) "O, say not so! / Those sounds that flow / In murmurs of delight and woe / Come not from wings of birds."

(D) "They are the throngs / Of the poet's songs, / Murmurs of pleasures, and pains, and wrongs, / The sound of winged words."

5

Congressional Amendment: Time Spans from Congressional Passage to Ratification

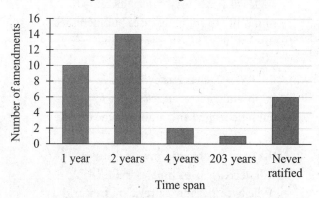

The writers of the U.S. Constitution intended it to be a "living document"; in other words, the government it outlined could be adapted over time as the needs of the country and its people changed. Still, they believed that changes to the Constitution should not be made lightly. As a result, they structured the Constitution so that the process for adding amendments was intentionally deliberate and complex. Of the two possible processes they outlined for amending the Constitution, only one has been utilized: if two-thirds of both houses of Congress pass a proposed amendment, it is then sent to the state legislatures. The amendment is only ratified—or added to the Constitution—if three-fourths of the state legislatures approve it. Given the complexity of this ratification process, political scientists argue that amendments are an ineffective way to address immediate matters of public policy; indeed, _____

Which choice most effectively uses data from the graph to illustrate the claim?

Ⓐ the majority of amendments sent to the states for approval that were eventually ratified took two or more years to complete the process.

Ⓑ only one amendment sent to the states for approval took over 200 years to complete the ratification process and be added to the Constitution.

Ⓒ the majority of amendments sent to the states for approval that were eventually ratified took just one year to complete the process.

Ⓓ a total of 33 amendments have been passed by Congress and sent to the states for possible ratification.

6

In a wide-ranging study, researchers from institutions including McMaster University and the University of Chicago analyzed immunity during the Black Death, the highly fatal bubonic plague that first spread through Africa and Eurasia in the fourteenth century. The study identified that a certain allele of the gene *ERAP2* provided those who had it with a significantly higher survival rate when they contracted the plague. As a result, this version of *ERAP2* was passed on by plague survivors to their descendants, though worldwide cases of bubonic plague are low in modern times. The researchers also found, however, that this *ERAP2* allele today is associated with an increased risk of autoimmune disease. Thus, the researchers suggest that _____

Which choice most logically completes the text?

Ⓐ alleles of genes may confer increased immunity to some diseases but increased susceptibility to others over time.

Ⓑ the *ERAP2* allele has evolved over time to provide increased resistance to both bubonic plague and autoimmune disease.

Ⓒ the severity of autoimmune diseases will decrease over time as the *ERAP2* allele becomes more prevalent in world populations.

Ⓓ the fourteenth-century bubonic plague was more likely to be fatal than the modern day strand of the bubonic plague.

Check Your Work

1.   C

Difficulty: Medium
Category: Information and Ideas
Getting to the Answer: The question asks for the main idea of the passage, so paraphrase the primary point of the passage as you read, keeping in mind that the first and last sentences may address the main idea. Here, the first sentence introduces nightmare disorder and claims that researchers have a promising new treatment. The following sentences describe the study, in which patients were treated with only traditional IRT or with both IRT and the new method, TMR. The next-to-last sentence concludes that the combination therapy was more effective, and the last sentence affirms that researchers hope the combined therapy will help patients. Predict that the main idea is that *the new combination of IRT and TMR might be effective based on the study;* choice **(C)** is correct.

Choice (A) is incorrect because it does not discuss the new TMR method or the study. Choices (B) and (D) are incorrect because although they describe the study, they do not address its results or the researchers' conclusion that the combined therapy might be effective.

2.   A

Difficulty: Easy
Category: Information and Ideas
Getting to the Answer: The question asks for something that is true about Mr. Brooke, so look for qualities of Mr. Brooke as you read the passage. Since the passage contains many details about Mr. Brooke, it might be easiest to check the answer choices against the passage. Choice **(A)** is correct because the passage indicates that Mr. Brooke is "difficult to predict." The phrases "miscellaneous opinions," "uncertain vote," and "rambling habit of mind" suggest that he has a variety of ideas and that people are never sure about how he will vote.

Choice (B) is opposite, as the passage states Mr. Brooke has an "acquiescent," or *accepting,* temper. Choice (C) is also opposite; others think it is "safe to say" that Mr. Brooke will "act with benevolent," or *good,* intentions. Choice (D) is incorrect because those who have lived at Tipton Grange for "hardly a year" are the nieces and/or nephews of their "uncle," Mr. Brooke.

3.   B

Difficulty: Medium
Category: Information and Ideas
Getting to the Answer: To determine which answer choice supports the researchers' prediction, first paraphrase the prediction in your own words. The third sentence states that Vosshall and de Obaldia predicted that differences in body odor influence mosquitoes' level of attraction. Thus, the correct answer should provide a result of the study that shows that *body odor impacted mosquitoes' selection of the stockings.* The description of the experiment indicates that carboxylic acids influence body odor, so the correct choice will likely entail different levels of carboxylic acids causing differing levels of attraction by the mosquitoes: choice **(B)** is correct.

Choices (A) and (D) are incorrect because they describe results that support different body odors not impacting mosquito attraction. Choice (C) is incorrect because the passage does not mention participants wearing stockings on their legs; thus, this choice is unrelated to the researchers' prediction.

4.   D

Difficulty: Medium
Category: Information and Ideas
The correct answer must illustrate how the author compares poetry to the flight of birds, so look for the quote that makes a connection between the two ideas. Choice **(D)** is correct because it describes "poet's songs" as "The sound of winged words"; the poetry is "winged," like the flying birds.

Choice (A) is incorrect because it only describes the night; the "distant sounds" that are mentioned are not implied to be poetry. Choice (B) mentions flying birds, but it is incorrect because it does not compare the flying birds to poetry. Choice (C) is incorrect because it does not specify that the "sounds that flow" are poetry. Further, the quote does not compare the sounds to flying birds; it just states that the sounds are *not* made by birds.

5.   A
Difficulty: Hard
Category: Information and Ideas
Getting to the Answer: Since the question stem asks you to illustrate a claim, identify the specific claim from the passage. The last sentence states that political scientists argue that amendments are "ineffective" for "immediate" public policy, since the ratification process is complex. Thus, you need data from the graph that demonstrates that amendments are not a good way to address "immediate," or short-term, policies. Analyze the graph: it shows how many amendments have taken 1, 2, 4, or 203 years to be ratified, as well as how many were never ratified. The passage may help you better understand the graph. The passage specifies that the amendment process entails a proposed amendment being "pass[ed]" by Congress and then "ratified" if enough states approve it. So according to its title, the graph shows how long it took between the time amendments were passed by Congress until they were added to the Constitution. Choice **(A)** is correct because it accurately reflects the graph and it provides evidence that amendments are not a good way to address short-term policy: most took two or more years to be ratified.

Choice (B) is incorrect because the word "only" portrays the amendment that took 203 years as an outlier rather than as evidence that the amendment process takes a long time. Choice (C) is incorrect because the phrase "just one year" implies that amendments do not take long; further, it is not the case that a majority of amendments took one year. Choice (D) is incorrect because the correct answer must address how long it takes to ratify amendments, not how many have been ratified in total.

6.   A
Difficulty: Hard
Category: Information and Ideas
The question asks for a logical suggestion made by the researchers, based upon their finding that the *ERAP2* allele associated with higher survival rates during the historic Black Death is now associated with a higher risk of autoimmune disease. Evaluate the answer choices to determine which provides a logical suggestion. Choice **(A)** is correct because the findings about the allele indicate an increased immunity to bubonic plague in the fourteenth century but an increased susceptibility to autoimmune disease today.

Choice (B) is incorrect because the researchers found an increased *risk of*, not an increased *resistance to*, autoimmune disease. Choice (C) is incorrect because the passage indicates that the *ERAP2* allele is associated with an increased risk of autoimmune disease, so it is not logical that the severity of the disease would decrease as the allele becomes more prevalent. Further, the passage does not discuss disease severity. Choice (D) is incorrect because the fatality of the modern day bubonic plague is outside the scope of the passage.

MAIN IDEA QUESTIONS

LEARNING OBJECTIVE

After this lesson, you will be able to:

• Identify the main idea of a passage

To answer a question like this:

Although scholars generally agree that the primary focus of the Puranas, a collection of Sanskrit verse writings, is the Hindu gods, the texts also provide insight into daily life in historic India. For example, the *Agni Purana* includes not only accounts of court and tax structures during Gupta-era India but also descriptions of herb usage in medicinal applications. With the Puranas' focus on deities, it is unsurprising that the writings discuss religious practices; the *Skanda Purana*, for instance, provides guidance for travelers to religious pilgrimage sites.

Which choice best states the main idea of the text?

A) The Puranas were widely read Sanskrit texts in historic India.

B) The topic of medicine is not commonly addressed in the Puranas.

C) The Puranas can reveal information about aspects of life in India's past.

D) The *Agni Purana* differs from most of the Puranas in that it does not include religious topics.

You need to know this:

How to Identify Main Idea Questions

Main Idea questions can be identified by the keywords "main idea" in the question stem: *Which choice best states the main idea of the text?*

How to Identify the Main Idea

The main idea is the big picture of the passage. The main idea is not just the *topic* of the passage (for instance, dogs) but the author's *main point* about that topic (perhaps, why dogs are good pets). The main idea can sometimes be found in the first or last sentence of the passage. The other sentences in the passage include details that support the main idea of the passage (perhaps, details that dogs are loyal, protective, and playful—and, thus, are good pets).

More difficult Main Idea questions will not have a clear topic sentence. They will instead require you to pull together the main points from the passage and summarize them in your own words. For instance, if each sentence in a passage identifies a different breed of dog and explains why that breed makes a good pet for kids, the main idea of the paragraph would be *dog breeds that are good pets for kids*.

When you need to identify the main idea, don't get caught up in the details of the passage. In fact, incorrect answers on Main Idea questions often address just a specific detail, rather than the overall main idea, of the passage.

Incorrect answers to a Main Idea question may be:

• **Misused Details**—Incorrect answers to Main Idea questions often address just a specific detail, rather than the overall main idea, of the passage.

• **Distortions**—Incorrect answers to Main Idea questions may be based on ideas from the passage but may distort or misstate what the author says.

• **Out of Scope**—Incorrect answers to Main Idea questions may contain ideas that are simply not covered in the passage. These incorrect answers go beyond what the passage states or logically implies.

The **correct answer** to a Main Idea question will:

- Summarize the author's main point about the topic of the passage, which is sometimes found in the first or last sentence
- Be supported by the details within the passage

You need to do this:

THE METHOD FOR SAT READING AND WRITING

STEP 1   What is the question asking?

STEP 2   What do I need to look for in the passage?

STEP 3   What answer strategy is best?

- Predict and Match
- Eliminate

Step 1. What is the question asking?

If the question stem asks for the "main idea" of the passage, proceed through the rest of the steps of the Method with your focus on finding the main idea.

Step 2. What do I need to look for in the passage?

As discussed in the Method for SAT Reading and Writing Questions chapter, your approach to reading the passage should vary depending on what the question asks for. Since you need to identify the main idea, focus on the first and last sentences of the passage; the main idea will sometimes be stated there. To make sure you've identified the main idea, skim the other sentences in the passage. The other sentences should be details that provide support for the main idea you've identified.

If the main idea is not clear from the first and last sentences, read the passage more closely. Think about how the details relate to each other, and summarize in your own words a main idea that pulls together all the details from the passage.

Step 3. What answer strategy is best?

Main Idea questions lend themselves to the strategy of predicting the correct answer. Take a moment to paraphrase the main idea you identified in Step 2 in your own words. The correct answer will probably not be a word-for-word match of the wording in the passage, so having a prediction in your own words will make it easier to efficiently focus in on the answer choice that reflects the main idea. If needed, eliminate answer choices that address only specific details from the passage, as well as answer choices that are outside the scope of the passage.

Once you find the answer choice that matches your prediction and provides the main idea—not a detail—from the passage, select it and move on.

Explanation:

The question asks for the main idea, so focus on the big picture rather than the details as you read the passage. The first sentence identifies the topic, the Puranas, and states that the Puranas focus on Hindu gods but also "provide insight into daily life in historic India." The remaining sentences provide examples of the Puranas giving details about daily life, as indicated by the keywords "For example" and "for instance." Paraphrase the main idea in your own words: *the Puranas can teach us about daily life in historic India*. Use this paraphrase as your prediction; **(C)** matches this prediction and is correct.

The remaining answer choices are incorrect because they are misused or out of scope details rather than the main idea of the passage. The fact about the Puranas in (A) fails to address the main idea (that the Puranas give insight into daily life); further, the passage never addresses how "widely read" the texts were. Choice (B) is incorrect because the passage does not indicate how often medicine is addressed in the Puranas; further, medicine in the Puranas is too narrow to be the main idea of the passage. Finally, the passage discusses details about the *Agni Purana*, but it does not indicate the specific detail in (D).

Try on Your Own

Directions

Take as much time as you need on these questions. Work carefully and methodically. There will be an opportunity for timed practice later in the book.

1

In 1908, Charles Henry Turner, the first African American to be published in the prestigious journal *Science*, devised a simple, yet intriguing experiment that seemed to indicate that bees have some perception of time. He started by placing plates of strawberry jam on an outdoor table at dawn, noon, and dusk. Bees soon began arriving regularly at those times to feed. Then, Turner stopped the noon and dusk feedings. At first, the bees continued to arrive at all three times, but soon adjusted their feeding times and only came in the mornings. This was one of the first of Turner's seminal insights into insect cognition.

Which choice best states the main idea of the text?

(A) Insects do not have the capacity to perceive time.

(B) Turner's many achievements have not been recognized.

(C) Turner found that bees can adapt their behavior patterns.

(D) Experiments have shown that bees prefer to feed at dawn.

2

Violent video games played for long periods of time inadvertently mimic the same type of repetition used by teachers to reinforce students' ability to retain subject matter. This method makes the content of these games, including overall aggressive themes, easy to absorb, and studies performed in the 1990s connected some violent video games to anger issues, obesity, and addiction.

Which choice best states the main idea of the text?

(A) People who have anger issues, obesity, and addictions should not play video games.

(B) Some learning strategies are used by both video games and educators.

(C) Video games are always harmful, and should be avoided.

(D) Repetition is the most important way students learn.

3

An important piece of modern Cairo history may soon be no more. Cairo's houseboats on the Nile have been docked at the river's shore for generations, and several of the owners were born on the boats. A symbol of Egyptian intellectual life made famous by Nobel laureate Naguib Mahfouz in *The Cairo Trilogy* and *Adrift on the Nile*, houseboats were the locations of restaurants and cafes where authors, poets, and scholars would meet to exchange ideas. Many Cairenes are petitioning the government to retain the houseboats for their cultural and historic importance.

Which choice best states the main idea of the text?

(A) The government of Cairo should preserve the houseboats on the Nile.

(B) The existence of the historic Cairo houseboats is threatened.

(C) Naguib Mahfouz won the Nobel prize for writing about the Cairo houseboats.

(D) Many intellectual and cultural gatherings were held on Cairo houseboats.

4

The following text is from Emily Brontë's 1845 poem "Remembrance."

Cold in the earth—and the deep snow piled above thee.
Far, far removed, cold in the dreary grave!
Have I forgot, my Only Love, to love thee,
Severed at last by Time's all-severing wave?

Now, when alone, do my thoughts no longer hover
Over the mountains, on that northern shore,
Resting their wings where heath and fern-leaves cover
Thy noble heart forever, ever more?

Cold in the earth—and fifteen wild Decembers,
From those brown hills, have melted into spring:
Faithful, indeed, is the spirit that remembers
After such years of change and suffering!

Sweet Love of youth, forgive, if I forget thee,
While the world's tide is bearing me along;
Other desires and other hopes beset me,
Hopes which obscure, but cannot do thee wrong!

Which choice best states the main idea of the text?

(A) Although gone, the author's beloved is not forgotten.

(B) After death, the author's beloved is largely forgotten.

(C) Everyday events have distracted the author from caring for the beloved.

(D) Loyalty to the memory of the beloved is the most important aspect of a relationship.

5

The following text is from the 1867 speech of Satanta, Chief of the Kiowa, at the Medicine Lodge Treaty council.

I have heard that you intend to settle us on a reservation near the mountains. I don't want to settle. I love to roam over the prairies. There I feel free and happy, but when we settle down, we grow pale and die. I have laid aside my lance, bow, and shield, and yet I feel safe in your presence. I have told you the truth. I have no little lies hid about me, but I don't know how it is with the commissioners. Are they as clear as I am? A long time ago this land belonged to our fathers; but when I go up the river, I see camps of soldiers on its banks. These soldiers cut down my timber; they kill my buffalo; and when I see that, my heart feels like bursting. I have spoken.

Which choice best states the main idea of the text?

(A) The speaker embraces the notion of settling on a reservation near the mountains.

(B) The speaker insists on being told the truth and not the usual falsehoods.

(C) The speaker needs to feel safe in the presence of the audience.

(D) The speaker wants to continue a nomadic life on the prairie.

6

Anna Rosa Ziefuss, a German doctoral candidate, may have overcome the greatest hurdle to producing cold-brewed coffee: time. Cold-brewed coffee is usually made by pouring cold water over ground coffee beans and allowing the mixture to stand for at least 12 hours before straining out the bean particles. The flavor of cold-brewed coffee is said to be superior to that of traditionally brewed coffee, which uses hot water to extract the liquid coffee in a much shorter time. Ziefuss' breakthrough uses a three-second laser pulse applied to a suspension of finely ground coffee beans in water and creates coffee chemically identical to cold-brew, as measured by spectrometry and chromatography.

Which choice best states the main idea of the text?

(A) Lasers may make it possible to make cold-brew coffee quickly.

(B) The taste of cold-brew coffee is superior to that of traditionally brewed coffee.

(C) Ziefuss' new process will enable more consumers to purchase cold-brew coffee.

(D) Because lasers are expensive, Ziefuss' new process is not suitable for home use.

7

Petra, an ancient Nabataean city in the mountains of Jordan, is a marvel of ancient engineering. Although primarily known today for its remarkable buildings carved from sandstone, Petra may have been most famous in its own time for its stable water supply. Completely surrounded by desert, Petra was an artificial oasis. Nabataean engineers designed an ingenious system of cisterns, dams, and water conduits to divert and store water from seasonal rainfall and flash flooding. However, in modern times, these ancient systems have been overwhelmed. To safeguard tourists and guides, the Jordanian government now closes the site when flash flooding is predicted.

Which choice best states the main idea of the text?

- (A) Because of its clever engineering, ancient Petra never flooded.

- (B) Frequent flash flooding makes Petra a risky place for tourists.

- (C) Despite its inventive design, Petra is susceptible to flooding.

- (D) As an artificial oasis, Petra was unique among ancient desert cities.

8

For the first time, scientists have demonstrated the possibility of artificial photosynthesis. Researchers at the University of Cambridge have designed artificial leaves, light and thin enough to float on water, that convert sunlight to fuel, just as plants do via photosynthesis. If successful, the scientists hope to deploy the artificial leaves in sufficient numbers to reduce maritime shipping's dependence on fossil fuels.

Which choice best states the main idea of the text?

- (A) Only green plants are able to convert sunlight to usable energy.

- (B) Floating artificial leaves can only be used in maritime applications.

- (C) Innovative technology may become available that will replace some fossil fuels.

- (D) Artificial leaves will soon enable maritime shipping to operate more efficiently.

DETAIL QUESTIONS

LEARNING OBJECTIVE

After this lesson, you will be able to:

- Identify a detail explicitly stated in the text

To answer a question like this:

A research team led by Raz Jelinek at Ben-Gurion University of Negev is developing an "e-nose" that can detect nanoplastic particles in the air. A source of potential health issues if inhaled, microscopic plastic particles can enter the air as discarded plastic erodes. Jelinek's team is working to detect air-borne nanoplastics by utilizing carbon dots—small, carbon-heavy materials—attached to electrodes, which exhibit a measurable change in charge when they interact with nanoplastics. The technology has proven successful at indicating different types and quantities of nanoplastics in the air, and the team hopes that additional developments will make it possible to accurately measure nanoplastics levels in living and working spaces.

According to the text, how does the "e-nose" indicate the presence of nanoplastics in the air?

A) The discarded nanoplastic particles are inhaled by living organisms.

B) The charges of electrodes that are covered in carbon dots change.

C) The carbon dots become saturated with high concentrations of carbon.

D) The eroding carbon dots float into the air along with the nanoplastics.

You need to know this:

How to Identify Detail Questions

Detail questions test your ability to interpret the details that support the main idea of a passage. Key phrases that signal a Detail question include "according to the text," "based on the text," "presented in the text," and "the text most strongly suggests"; for instance: *According to the text, why are beagles considered proficient hunting dogs?*

How to Locate the Relevant Detail

Although the wording of Detail questions can vary, the correct answer will always be explicitly stated in the passage. Clue words in the question stem can help you focus in on the specific detail(s) needed to answer the question. For instance, in the example above (*According to the text, why are beagles considered proficient hunting dogs?*), the words "beagles," "proficient," and "hunting" indicate that you need to locate a detail about the qualities of beagles that make them good at hunting.

Sometimes, a single sentence in the passage may be enough to answer the question—in this case, you can ignore the other details, find the correct answer, and move on. Other times, you may need additional context from the passage in order to understand the detail needed to answer the question. Be flexible in your approach, using only as much of the passage as you need.

Although the correct answer is explicitly stated in the passage, the wording of the correct answer choice will not exactly match the wording in the passage. Rather, it will be a paraphrase of the detail in the passage. For this reason, making your own paraphrased prediction of the correct answer will help you efficiently focus in on the one correct answer choice.

Incorrect answers to a Detail question may be:

- **Misused Details**—Don't select an answer choice just because you recognize it from the passage. The most common type of incorrect answer to Detail questions mentions a detail that appears in the passage but does not answer the question that was asked.

- **Distortions**—Incorrect answers to Detail questions may reflect the relevant detail that answers the question but may misstate the detail in a way that contradicts the information in the passage.

- **Opposite**—Incorrect answers to Detail questions may even state the opposite of the details from the passage.

The **correct answer** to a Detail question will:

- Specifically answer the question, not just provide a detail from the passage
- Paraphrase a detail explicitly stated in the passage

You need to do this:

THE METHOD FOR SAT READING AND WRITING

STEP 1 What is the question asking?

STEP 2 What do I need to look for in the passage?

STEP 3 What answer strategy is best?

- Predict and Match
- Eliminate

Step 1. What is the question asking?

Key phrases such as "according to the text," "based on the text," "presented in the text," and "the text most strongly suggests" signal a Detail question. Use the other clue words in the question stem to state, in your own words, exactly what the question is asking.

Step 2. What do I need to look for in the passage?

Once you've identified what the question is asking, skim the passage for clue words that reflect the detail(s) you need. It's possible that a single sentence may be all that is required to answer the question, though be ready to read more of the passage for additional context if needed.

Step 3. What answer strategy is best?

Making a prediction can make it easier to efficiently answer Detail questions. Using the relevant detail(s) you located in the passage, paraphrase the correct answer in your own words. Then look for a match for your prediction among the answer choices. Remember that the correct answer will not be an *exact* match for the wording in the passage. Rather, one answer choice will match the *idea* you identified in your prediction. If needed, eliminate answer choices that distort or misuse details from the passage—any detail that does not specifically answer the question.

Once you find the answer choice that matches your prediction and provides the specific answer to the question asked, select it and move on.

Explanation:

The key phrase "According to the text" indicate that this is a Detail question. The question is asking how the "e-nose" indicates when nanoplastics are in the air, so search the passage for a detail that explains how the "e-nose" works. The first sentence identifies the topic (the "e-nose" that detects nanoplastics), but it is the third sentence that explains how the "e-nose" operates. Summarize the explanation in your own words: *carbon dots are attached to electrodes, and the electrodes change their charge when nanoplastics are present.* Use this prediction to find a match among the answer choices; **(B)** is correct.

The other answer choices can be eliminated because they either reflect details that do not specifically answer the question or they distort details from the passage. Choice (A) describes the potential health risk of airborne nanoplastics. Choices (C) and (D) are distortions of the description of the "e-nose" provided in the third sentence.

Try on Your Own

Directions

Take as much time as you need on these questions. Work carefully and methodically. There will be an opportunity for timed practice later in the book.

9

One proposal for reducing breakdowns on the New York City subway is to end 24-hour service and to shut down for a few hours nightly. Proponents of this plan argue that this would regularly allow time for preventative maintenance, leading to more consistent service; rather than shutting down for long periods of time, there would be shorter outages at night. This may seem a preferable outcome to the consequences of a shutdown resulting from a breakdown, but it has its liabilities. Most subway trips occur during rush hour, but not everyone works during the day. Doctors, nurses, bartenders, police officers, and firefighters are examples of occupations whose workers travel at all hours. Rather than be subjected to a period of inconvenience, these workers would find their commutes irrevocably altered. Clearly, the city must consider many factors to design a subway maintenance plan.

According to the text, what is true about non-rush-hour commuters?

(A) They would risk losing public transportation options if 24-hour subway service were suspended.

(B) They would face only minor inconveniences if 24-hour subway service were suspended.

(C) They work primarily in health care and its related fields.

(D) They are among the strongest advocates for a change to the current subway maintenance plan.

Reading & Writing

Reading & Writing

10

One persistent, albeit erroneous, view is that real estate is a better investment than a stock market portfolio. While it is true that home equity is the stepping-stone from which most individuals begin to build their personal wealth, statistics make it clear that stock market investments are a more stable and lucrative source of long-term wealth. A London Business School study found that over the same 90-year period, the average rate of return on a real estate investment was 1.3% compared to the 9.8% return for the S&P Stock 500 index. Investing $5,500 in an IRA for 25 years would result in a return of over $600,000 based on this return rate. Investment in stock requires a smaller overhead than that of real estate, and the liquid nature of stocks makes them ideal for retirement: stocks allocated to retirement accounts remain tax-free until they are drawn on.

According to the text, what is true about investing in the stock market?

- Ⓐ It is the stepping stone from which most individuals begin to build personal wealth.
- Ⓑ It remains less stable and lucrative than home ownership as a source of wealth.
- Ⓒ It has tax implications well suited to retirement planning.
- Ⓓ It requires a minimum investment of $5,500 according to IRS rules.

11

As a graduate student, Urmila Mahadev devoted over a decade to creating a verification process for quantum computing. The result is an interactive protocol, based on a type of cryptography called Learning With Errors (LWE), that is similar to "blind computing" used in cloud computing to mask data while still performing calculations. Given current limitations, Mahadev's protocol remains purely theoretical, but rapid progress in quantum computing combined with further refinement of the protocol will likely result in real-world implementation within the next decade or two.

According to the text, what is true about Urmila Mahadev's graduate work?

- Ⓐ It was focused on ways to improve cloud computing.
- Ⓑ Its results cannot be confirmed by classical computing techniques.
- Ⓒ It will make Learning With Errors cryptography obsolete.
- Ⓓ It may lead to verification of quantum computing calculations.

12

The following passage is adapted from Jules Verne's *Around the World in Eighty Days*, first published in 1873.

A package of banknotes, to the value of fifty-five thousand pounds, had been taken from the principal cashier's table, that functionary being at the moment engaged in registering the receipt of three shillings and sixpence. Let it be observed that the Bank of England reposes a touching confidence in the honesty of the public. There are neither guards nor gratings to protect its treasures; gold, silver, banknotes are freely exposed, at the mercy of the first comer. A keen observer of English customs relates that, being in one of the rooms of the Bank one day, he had the curiosity to examine a gold ingot weighing some seven or eight pounds. He took it up, scrutinized it, passed it to his neighbor, he to the next man, and so on until the ingot, going from hand to hand, was transferred to the end of a dark entry; nor did it return to its place for half an hour.

According to the text, what is true about the Bank of England?

(A) The public has faith in the integrity of the bank.

(B) The bank has taken few precautions to guard against theft.

(C) The bank has a history of money being stolen.

(D) The bank has carefully managed public relations.

13

Bioluminescence, the production of light by chemical reactions associated with biological activity, occurs in a variety of life forms and is more common in marine organisms than in terrestrial or freshwater life. There is considerable diversity in how light is produced, but most processes involve the reaction of a light-emitting molecule with oxygen, catalyzed by an enzyme. The light-emitting molecule varies from one organism to another, but all are grouped under the generic name luciferin. The enzymes catalyzing the reaction fall into two groups: photoproteins and luciferases.

According to the text, what is true about the process of bioluminescence?

(A) It requires luciferin.

(B) It requires seawater.

(C) It requires luciferase.

(D) It requires photoproteins.

14

The recent discovery of marine and land bacteria similar to species found on Earth in cosmic dust present on the exterior of the International Space Station (ISS) is not evidence of panspermia, the hypothesis that life on Earth originated in outer space. Even if the discovery is genuine and not the result of cross-contamination of the samples at any stage between their collection and their analysis in a laboratory on Earth, it by no means indicates that the bacteria arrived at the ISS from an extraterrestrial source. It is far more likely that they are ordinary Earth bacteria that were transported to the ISS on the surfaces of supplies or other objects as part of routine restocking, as is known to have occurred in the past. It is also possible, though less likely, that they are ordinary Earth bacteria that were hurled into the outer atmosphere by storm systems.

Based on the text, why is the author skeptical of the idea that discoveries of bacteria on extraterrestrial objects are evidence for panspermia?

(A) Scientists cannot avoid bias when examining evidence for hypotheses they believe to be true.

(B) A large number of highly improbable events would need to have occurred at precisely the same time.

(C) It is very unlikely that such bacteria would have survived the lengthy journey from another planet to Earth.

(D) There is high probability that the bacteria came from some terrestrial source.

15

The following text is adapted from Wilkie Collins' 1859 novel, *The Woman in White*.

I have observed, not only in my sister's case, but in the instances of others, that we of the young generation are nowhere near as hearty and impulsive as some of our elders. I constantly see old people flushed and excited by the prospect of some anticipated pleasure which altogether fails to ruffle the tranquility of their serene grandchildren. Has the great advance in education taken rather too long a stride, and are we in these modern days just the least trifle in the world too well brought up?

Based on the passage, how does the author view young people?

(A) They are more reserved than older people.

(B) They are stronger and more healthy than their parents.

(C) They are too disrespectful of the older generation.

(D) They are too enthusiastic when faced with opportunities.

The following text is from Wells Hastings's 1914 short story "Gideon."

The house . . . roared with laughter, and shook with a storming volley of applause. Gideon bowed . . . Dramatic judgment, as well as dramatic sense of delivery, was native to him, qualities which the shrewd Felix Stuhk, his manager and exultant discoverer, recognized . . .

Stuhk deemed himself one of the cleverest managers in the business. He was rapidly becoming rich, and there were bright prospects of even greater triumphs, with proportionately greater reward. He had made Gideon a national character, a headliner, a star . . . and all in six short months. Or, at any rate, he had helped to make him all this; he had booked him well and given him his opportunity. To be sure, Gideon had done the rest; Stuhk was as ready as anyone to do credit to Gideon's ability. Still, after all, he, Stuhk, was the discoverer, the theatrical Columbus who had had the courage and the vision.

According to the passage, what does Stuhk believe about Gideon's success?

(A) It is the result of a natural talent.

(B) It developed because Stuhk trained him.

(C) It would have been impossible if Stuhk had not been the one to discover him.

(D) It is needed for Stuhk's wealth to continue to increase.

COMMAND OF EVIDENCE QUESTIONS (TEXTUAL)

LEARNING OBJECTIVES

After this lesson, you will be able to:

- Identify the conclusion and evidence in an argument
- Identify additional relevant information that strengthens or weakens a claim

To answer a question like this:

In questionnaire-based studies, students typically self-report that they perceive themselves as having different psychological responses to online learning compared to in-person learning. But a team led by Morris Gellisch and Beate Brand-Saberi hypothesized that students also experience differing physiological stress responses in the two learning environments. To evaluate their hypothesis, the researchers conducted various physiological measures of students in a blended learning anatomy course, in which students alternated between attending class sessions remotely and in-person. One measure conducted, for instance, was the students' concentration of cortisol in saliva; a lower concentration indicates a lower level of physiological stress. The researchers also administered questionnaires for students to complete at the end of the course.

Which finding from the study, if true, would most strongly support Gellisch and colleagues' hypothesis?

A) In the end-of-course survey, a majority of students indicated that they thought anatomy was a subject better taught in-person than online.

B) In the end-of-course survey, students reported feeling less stressed during the online sessions than they did during the in-person sessions.

C) Students in the online sessions had significantly lower measures of cortisol concentration than did students in the in-person sessions.

D) Students in the online sessions and students in the in-person sessions had similar measures of cortisol concentration.

You need to know this:

How to Identify Textual Command of Evidence Questions

Textual Command of Evidence questions require you to select additional information, beyond what is provided in the passage, that would support or weaken a hypothesis or claim from the passage. These questions can be identified by key phrases such as "most strongly supports," "most directly weakens," or "most effectively illustrates." Here are some sample Textual Command of Evidence question stems:

- *Which finding, if true, would most strongly support the hypothesis?*
- *Which quotation from the poem most effectively illustrates the claim?*

How to Identify Evidence that Supports or Weakens

Since Textual Command of Evidence questions typically ask you to support or weaken a hypothesis or claim, the first step is to identify the specific hypothesis or claim. Paraphrase the hypothesis or claim in your own words.

Next, depending on what is asked for in the question stem, think about what type of additional information could potentially strengthen, weaken, or illustrate that claim or hypothesis.

For instance, suppose someone claims that basset hounds bark louder than do German shepherds. What type of additional information would strengthen, weaken, or illustrate that claim? An experiment that records a louder average decibel level for basset hound barks than for German shepherd barks would strengthen the claim, an experiment that records the opposite would weaken the claim, and an anecdote about a basset hound—but not a German shepherd—activating a noise-activated alarm would illustrate the claim.

Incorrect answers to a Textual Command of Evidence question may be:

- **Out of Scope**—Incorrect answers to Textual Command of Evidence questions often include additional information that has no relationship to the claim or hypothesis.

- **Opposite**—Incorrect answers to Textual Command of Evidence questions may include additional information that provides the *opposite* of what is asked for in the question, for instance, information that weakens a claim when the question asks for information that strengthens the claim.

The **correct answer** to a Textual Command of Evidence question will:

- Provide additional information, beyond what is provided in the passage, that strengthens, weakens, or illustrates a claim or hypothesis, as identified in the question

- Have a direct, logical relationship to the claim or hypothesis

Reading & Writing

You need to do this:

THE METHOD FOR SAT READING AND WRITING

STEP 1 What is the question asking?

STEP 2 What do I need to look for in the passage?

STEP 3 What answer strategy is best?

- Predict and Match
- Eliminate

Step 1. What is the question asking?

Textual Command of Evidence questions will ask you to strengthen, weaken, or illustrate a claim or hypothesis using additional information that is not in the passage. These questions can be identified by key phrases such as "most strongly supports," "most directly weakens," or "most effectively illustrates."

Step 2. What do I need to look for in the passage?

The question stem will mention a claim or hypothesis, so focus on identifying this claim or hypothesis as you read the passage. Paraphrase the claim or hypothesis in your own words.

Step 3. What answer strategy is best?

After identifying the claim or hypothesis, decide on your answer strategy. You might be able to quickly make a prediction about what type of additional information would help to answer the question that you have been given. If so, use your prediction to help you focus in on the one answer choice that clearly meets the criteria.

If you *can't* make a prediction or choose not to, eliminate any answer choices one by one that fail to directly support, discredit, or illustrate the hypothesis or claim (depending on what the question asks you to do). Once you find the answer choice that is logically related to the hypothesis or claim and that addresses the task in the question stem, select it and move on.

Note that some Textual Command of Evidence questions may present a claim about a writing sample and answer choices that provide quotes from the writing sample. On these questions, follow the same steps: identify what the question is asking, paraphrase the claim, and eliminate answer choices that do not illustrate that claim.

Explanation:

The key phrase "most strongly support" identifies this as a Textual Command of Evidence question. You need to identify support for a hypothesis, so begin by identifying that hypothesis. The researchers' hypothesis is identified in the second sentence: students have different physiological stress responses in two different learning environments. Read the rest of the passage to put this hypothesis in context. The researchers are comparing online and in-person learning, focusing on physiological rather than psychological responses. They did a study of students in both learning environments, conducting both physiological measures and questionnaires. The first sentence identifies questionnaires with *psychological* responses. So predict that the needed support for the hypothesis about *physiological* responses will likely involve different results on the physiological measures for online versus in-person students.

Since the questionnaires involve psychological responses, eliminate (A) and (B). Choice **(C)** is correct because it supports a *difference* in a physiological stress response, as cortisol concentration is identified in the fourth sentence as an indicator of physiological stress. Choice (D) is incorrect because it supports the *opposite* of the hypothesis—a similar rather than a differing physiological response.

Try on Your Own

Directions

Take as much time as you need on these questions. Work carefully and methodically. There will be an opportunity for timed practice later in the book.

17

Roundabouts are circular intersections that restrict the flow of traffic to a single direction around a center island. The U.S. Department of Transportation (DoT) claims that roundabouts are a "Proven Safety Countermeasure" that decreases the high rates of collisions and injuries that occur at traditional intersections, which employ traffic lights for controlling two-way traffic flow. The DoT explains that demonstrated effectiveness of roundabouts stems from the elimination of left turns and traffic cross-flow.

Which study, if true, would best support the DoT's claim about the safety of roundabouts?

(A) A DoT traffic study reported that roundabouts are only effective at high-traffic intersections.

(B) A DoT traffic study reported that roundabouts reduced the number of head-on collisions, nationwide, by 85%.

(C) A DoT traffic study reported that the construction of roundabouts resulted in a 20% increase in city expenditures.

(D) A DoT traffic study reported that roundabouts increased the rate of the left turns flow by 15%.

18

Originally developed for treating kidney stones, lithotripsy is a non-surgical, painless procedure that uses a series of shock waves to break up calcification within targeted areas of the body. Some doctors are eager to apply this technology to treat coronary artery disease, believing that lithotripsy may improve the treatment process and the long-term recovery of patients. Without this innovative application of lithotripsy, the only option for coronary artery disease treatment is atherectomy, a similar intervention using a drill instead of sound waves. Atherectomy requires more time to complete and may result in damage to the diseased arteries.

Which finding, if true, would most directly weaken the doctors' belief?

- (A) Patients have better recovery outcomes when treated using lithotripsy.

- (B) The process of lithotripsy is simpler to administer than that of atherectomy.

- (C) Lithotripsy may increase patients' susceptibility to future heart attacks.

- (D) Calcified debris created by the drill may create additional stress on the heart.

19

"Somebody's Song" is a 1926 poem by Dorothy Parker. In the poem, Parker describes an experience of love while using contrasting images:

_____

Which quotation from "Somebody's Song" most effectively illustrates the claim?

- (A) Swift the measured sands may run; / Love like this is never done; / He and I are welded one: / This is what I vow.

- (B) This is what I pray: / Keep him by me tenderly; / Keep him sweet in pride of me, / Ever and a day;

- (C) This is what I know: / Lovers' oaths are thin as rain; / Love's a harbinger of pain— / Would it were not so!

- (D) Ever is my heart a-thirst, / Ever is my love accurst; / He is neither last nor first— / This is what I know.

Food historians believe that croissants, the iconic French pastry, were inspired by the Austrian *kipferl*, a crescent-shaped roll that originated in the thirteenth century. Chefs consider the croissant to be the far more complicated and time-consuming pastry to make despite both recipes using a yeasted dough and the finished pastries sharing the familiar shape.

Which quotation from a cookbook best supports the chefs' claim?

(A) "Both recipes can be made by mixing butter or other fat directly into the yeasted dough, but this process yields an inferior croissant."

(B) "The hallmark of the croissant is a number of flakey layers that require laminating a dough with butter, a process that takes many steps, with time to chill the dough between them."

(C) "A finished croissant is lighter and crisper than a *kipferl*, but both pastries can be prepared plain or topped with sugar, chocolate, or almonds."

(D) "Many families prepare various types of *kipferl* at home, but croissants are usually purchased from bakeries, where the pastries are prepared by professional bakers, or groceries, where the pastries are produced in factories."

21

Alzheimer's disease is a progressive brain disorder that causes memory and other cognitive functions to deteriorate. Current medical standards require that a patient have years of observable symptoms and multiple brain scans prior to receiving a formal diagnosis of the disorder. Some researchers now believe they have identified non-invasive methods that will allow doctors to diagnose the occurrence of Alzheimer's disease in a person before the onset of symptoms.

Which finding, if true, would most directly support the researchers' belief?

(A) Alzheimer's disease is caused by the presence of an abnormal build-up of beta amyloid plaques and neurofibrillary tangles of the tau protein.

(B) Specific language characteristics in writing samples are an accurate indicator of Alzheimer's disease seven years before typical symptoms begin occurring.

(C) Some patients have Alzheimer's disease without observable symptoms, indicating that examining the brain after death is the best method of diagnosis.

(D) Staying physically active, adhering to a largely plant-based diet, and building a healthy network of social connections all contributed to a delay in the onset of Alzheimer's disease.

Reading & Writing

John Swierk, a chemist at Binghamton University, leads an inorganic chemistry research group in the study of the molecular composition of commercial tattoo inks to help identify and disclose potential health risks that may be posed by the particles of pigments, carrier solution, and additives. Current scientific literature documents only the instances of undesired reactions, most often a long-term allergy, after receiving a tattoo, while Swierk and his research team hypothesize that there may be long-term health risks posed by chemicals in tattoo inks that are currently unknown to both tattoo artists and consumers.

Which finding from the study, if true, would most strongly support Swierk and his team's hypothesis?

(A) Of the commercial tattoo inks analyzed during this study, over half of them either did not have an ingredient list or did not list all the ingredients on the manufacturers' labels.

(B) All of the pigments used to create color in the tattoo ink that was analyzed were found to be the same pigments that are used in paint and textile manufacturing.

(C) The Food and Drug Administration considers tattoos, along with permanent make-up and henna (mehndi), a cosmetic, and regulates them as such.

(D) The nanometric size of the pigment particles was small enough to raise concerns about their ability to penetrate cell walls and damage the nucleus, possibly causing cancer.

COMMAND OF EVIDENCE QUESTIONS (QUANTITATIVE)

Reading & Writing

LEARNING OBJECTIVE

After this lesson, you will be able to:

- Use quantitative information to logically complete, support, or weaken a statement

To answer a question like this:

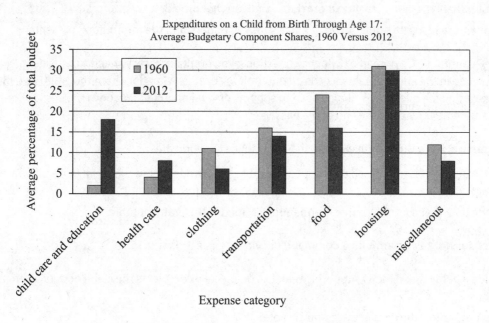

Expenditures on a Child from Birth Through Age 17: Average Budgetary Component Shares, 1960 Versus 2012

The average cost of raising a single child in 2012 approached a quarter million dollars, and with additional children in the family, that financial burden increased accordingly. Adjusting for inflation, however, the real costs of raising a child may not have increased significantly since the mid-1900s, but how parents allocated those costs evolved over time; for example, _____

Which choice most effectively uses data from the graph to complete the example?

A) the percent of the average expenditure budget spent on housing stayed approximately the same, about 30%, from 1960 to 2012.

B) food costs constituted approximately 15% of the average expenditure budget in 2012.

C) parents in 2012 spent a much greater percent of the average expenditure budget on child care and education than did parents in 1960.

D) parents in 1960 spent approximately the same percent of the average expenditure budget on clothing as on miscellaneous costs.

You need to know this:

How to Identify Quantitative Command of Evidence Questions

Quantitative Command of Evidence questions are easy to identify, since they are accompanied by a graph or table. The question stem will refer to the "graph" or "table."

How to Read Tables and Graphs

To answer these Command of Evidence questions, you need to carefully analyze the graph or table to be sure you understand exactly what type of information it provides (and what information it does *not* provide). For instance, a table that displays only the *percentage* of students in a grade that have pet dogs might not provide the *actual number* of students who own dogs.

To effectively analyze the graph or table:

- Examine its titles and labels.
- Identify what type of information it provides (and does *not* provide).
- Optionally, read a data point or two to make sure you understand the information presented.

To answer Quantitative Command of Evidence questions, you don't necessarily need to consider *all* the information provided in the graph or table. Focus on determining exactly what data from the graph or table is relevant for answering the question. You may need to support or weaken a claim made in the passage or logically complete a statement made at the end of the passage.

Incorrect answers to a Quantitative Command of Evidence question may:

- Provide data that is true based on the graph or table but is irrelevant to the claim or detail from the passage
- Provide data that contradicts the information provided in the graph or table

The **correct answer** to a Quantitative Command of Evidence question will:

- Provide a detail that directly supports, weakens, or logically completes the claim or detail from the passage
- Accurately reflect the data in the graph or table

You need to do this:

THE METHOD FOR SAT READING AND WRITING

STEP 1 What is the question asking?

STEP 2 What do I need to look for in the passage?

STEP 3 What answer strategy is best?

- Predict and Match
- Eliminate

Step 1. What is the question asking?

The presence of a graph or table indicates a Quantitative Command of Evidence question. The question stem will ask you for an answer choice that provides specific evidence that supports, weakens, or logically completes a claim or detail from the passage, such as, *Which choice best describes data from the graph that support the researchers' conclusion?*

Step 2. What do I need to look for in the passage?

Next, read the passage. Pay careful attention to locating the claim or detail that you need to support, weaken, or logically complete using the information in the graph or table. You may need to read the entire passage to understand the full context of the provided graph or table.

Now analyze the graph or table itself. Note any titles and labels, and make sure you understand exactly what type of information the graph or table provides. You may want to read a data point or two to confirm that you understand the graph or table.

Step 3. What answer strategy is best?

You may be able to predict what kind of data from the graph or table would provide the evidence needed to answer the question, but often, you will need to evaluate the answer choices one by one. Eliminate answer choices that contradict the data in the graph or table, as well as any that are irrelevant to the claim or detail from the passage. If you find an answer choice that provides the needed evidence *and* is true based on the graph or table, select it and move on.

Explanation:

The presence of the graph signals a Quantitative Command of Evidence question, and the question stem indicates that you need to complete an example with relevant data from the graph. The passage discusses the costs of raising children in 2012 and in the mid-1900s. The sentence with the blank makes the claim that "how parents allocated those costs evolved over time"; the correct answer will thus be an example of how costs were allocated differently over time.

According to its title, the graph displays the average percentage components of expenditures on a child in both 1960 and 2012, and the *x*-axis identifies various budget categories. For instance, clothing made up, on average, 6% of child expenditures in 2012. Based on the passage and graph, you could predict that the correct answer will provide an example of an expenditure category in which the percentage has changed significantly between 1960 and 2012.

Evaluate the answer choices, eliminating any that do not show a significant percent change and any that do not accurately reflect the graph. Eliminate (A), as it reflects a category that stayed about the same. Also eliminate (B), as it only reflects data from 2012, not a change over time. Choice **(C)** is correct because it identifies a category, child care and education, that experienced a significant change (from less than 5% to almost 20%) over time. Choice (D) is also incorrect because it only addresses categories from 1960, not a change over time.

Try on Your Own

Directions

Take as much time as you need on these questions. Work carefully and methodically. There will be an opportunity for timed practice later in the book.

23

Median Home Appreciation & Median Financial Portfolio Return (2010–2018)

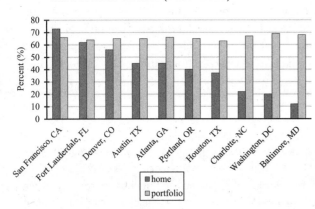

A team of economists and sociologists were interested in the long-term profitability of home appreciation compared to the financial returns of a stock portfolio. They studied several hundred test subjects in various city markets. The team concluded that although the returns on stock portfolios were relatively consistent nationwide, median home appreciation was dependent on the city.

Which choice most effectively uses data from the graph to support the research team's conclusion?

(A) Investment in the stock market generated more wealth than home ownership in every market listed in the graph.

(B) Portland, Oregon, saw a greater home appreciation than did Fort Lauderdale, Florida.

(C) The value of a home appreciated by a greater percentage in Portland, Oregon, than in Charlotte, North Carolina.

(D) Austin, Texas, saw a greater disparity between home appreciation and return on financial portfolios than did Washington, DC.

24

Bridge Name & Location	Date Completed	Length	Largest Single Span
Akashi Kaikyo Bridge, Kobe, Japan	1998	12,828 feet	6,527 feet
Brooklyn Bridge, New York, USA	1883	5,989 feet	1,595 feet
Golden Gate Bridge, San Francisco, USA	1937	8,981 feet	4,200 feet
Tower Bridge, London, UK	1894	880 feet	200 feet

One of New York City's most iconic landmarks, the Brooklyn Bridge spans 5,989 feet across the East River. Connecting the boroughs of Brooklyn (Kings County) and Manhattan, this bridge was a fantastic marvel of engineering _____

Which choice most effectively uses data from the table to complete the statement?

(A) with the largest single span of any bridge in the world until the 1998 completion of the Akashi Kaikyo Bridge in Japan.

(B) when it was completed in 1883, about a decade before the Tower Bridge in London, England, was built.

(C) that boasted the world's longest length for any bridge until the construction of the Tower Bridge in London, UK.

(D) and remains the longest single bridge in the United States even to this day.

Reading & Writing

25

Percentage of U.S. Corn Used to Produce Ethanol and Price per Bushel, 1980–2007

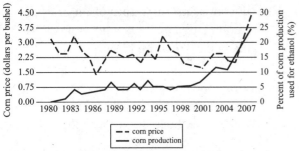

Adapted from United States Department of Agriculture-Economic Research Service and United States Energy Information Administration, 1980–2007.

Ethanol is created from plants such as corn, sugarcane, soybeans, and rice. While ethanol is a viable energy source, very large areas of cropland must be dedicated to growing these plants in order to produce enough ethanol to be designated for commercial use. Ethicists raised questions about such production because it meant farmers were growing food sources earmarked solely for fuel when there were many people around the world in dire need of food. These ethicists claim that the situation has become even more concerning over time, noting that since 1995, _____

Which choice most effectively uses data from the graph to support the ethicists' claim?

(A) the price of corn increased while the percentage of corn produced for ethanol stayed the same.

(B) the price of corn stayed the same while the percentage of corn produced for ethanol decreased.

(C) the price of corn increased and the percentage of corn produced for ethanol increased.

(D) the price of corn decreased while the percentage of corn produced for ethanol increased.

Trade Between Japan and the Netherlands

Year	To Japan (florins)	From Japan (florins)	Net Profit (florins)
1825	373,853	875,405	501,552
1826	23,366	161,615	138,249
1827	409,270	663,405	254,135
1828	313,313	1,067,231	753,918
1829	407,145	692,979	285,834

The Dutch East India Company, Vereenigde Oostindische Compagnie (VOC), maintained a monopoly on trade with Japan during its sakoku period of strict isolationism. A single Dutch ship was allowed to make port in Nagasaki each year, and a variety of goods were exchanged. The most notable export was Japanese copper, which the VOC would then resell on the global market. A historian analyzed data about trade between Japan and the Netherlands from 1825 to 1829 and claimed that these trade practices provided relatively high profits for the VOC in some years.

Which choice best describes data from the table that support the historian's claim?

(A) Net profits never fell below a quarter million florins.

(B) The company saw only 138,249 florins of net profit in 1826.

(C) 1825 and 1828 saw net profits of over half a million florins.

(D) Over one million florins were gained from Japan in 1828 alone.

Reading & Writing

27

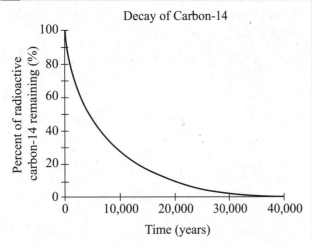

Decay of Carbon-14

Adapted from the *Journal of Research of the National Bureau of Standards*, April 1951.

According to Professor Kim Geon-Woo of Yonsei University, humans have a built-in clock, one that only starts "ticking" at the moment of death. This clock is the "half-life" of their carbon-14. The half-life of a radioactive material is the amount of time it takes for half of a sample of that material to decay. All plants and animals consume carbon-14 while alive. Once they are deceased, however, the carbon-14 in their remains begins to decay into nitrogen-14. By measuring the amount of carbon-14 left in an organic sample, scientists can precisely determine how old that sample is, up to the point all the carbon-14 has totally decayed. For example, paleontologists can use this technique to date ancient human remains up to _____.

Which choice most effectively uses data from the graph to complete the example?

Ⓐ 20,000 years old.

Ⓑ millions of years old.

Ⓒ 5,000 years old.

Ⓓ 40,000 years old.

28

Comparison of First-Class Berth Fares in Sleeping Cars on Trains (1889)		
Train Routes—Europe	Distance in Miles	Berth Fare (in dollars)
Paris, France, to Marseilles, France	536	$11.00
Paris, France, to Rome, Italy	901	$12.75
Train Routes—North America	Distance in Miles	Berth Fare (in dollars)
New York, USA, to Buffalo, USA	440	$2.00
New York, USA, to Chicago, USA	912	$5.00

On trains in the late 19th century, first-class berths were a luxury good. Travelers who purchased them enjoyed heated train cars, good ventilation, ice-water, toilet accommodations, and additional storage for baggage. Today, such amenities are expected on any train trip, but for their era, these conveniences were indulgences only for those travelers who could afford them. Historians at Barnett College wanted to compare European and North American railways to determine which system in the 19th century was more affordable to passengers. The comparison yielded a stark result; for example, _____.

Which choice most effectively uses data from the table to complete the example?

Ⓐ the cost of a first-class berth fare from Paris to Marseilles was over five times that of a comparable first-class berth fare from New York to Buffalo.

Ⓑ despite the distance from New York to Chicago being less than half the distance from Paris to Rome, the first-class berth fare for both trips was roughly the same.

Ⓒ a train route from Paris to Rome covered over two hundred more miles than a train route from Paris to Marseilles, despite the tickets costing roughly the same.

Ⓓ the cost of a first-class berth fare from New York to Chicago was more than twice that of a first-class berth fare from New York to Buffalo.

INFERENCE QUESTIONS

LEARNING OBJECTIVE

After this lesson, you will be able to:

- Determine what must be true based on given information

To answer a question like this:

The Caño Cristales River in Colombia has been called the "Liquid Rainbow" because of its unique quality of appearing in a variety of vibrant colors for several months of the year. Most notably, proliferations of *Macarenia clavigera* riverweed cause the water's distinct red-pink hue. Yet the river, part of Serranía de la Macarena national park, faces challenges today. After officials placed strict limits on tourism for eighteen months, biologists reported a marked increase in local plant life at the end of the restriction period. Further, the river's *Macarenia clavigera* are threatened by a cycle of events in which deforestation leads to decreased rainfall, which causes an increase in debris in the Caño Cristales. Overall, in light of these dangers to the vegetation of the Caño Cristales's ecosystem, biologists and ecologists agree that the key to preserving this natural site is _____.

Which choice most logically completes the text?

A) addressing the potential threats posed by human activity.

B) creating stricter anti-pollution laws in Colombia.

C) understanding why *Macarenia clavigera* make the river water appear red.

D) eliminating all future tourism in the Serranía de la Macarena national park.

You need to know this:

How to Identify Inference Questions

Inference questions can be identified by key phrases such as "logically completes" in the question stem, for instance: *Which choice most logically completes the text?*

What an Inference Is

While the correct answer to a Detail question is something explicitly stated in the passage, the correct answer to an Inference question is *not* stated explicitly in the passage. However, you can still be confident about your answer to an Inference question because the correct answer is something *logically supported by what is stated in the passage.*

Incorrect answers to an Inference question may be:

- **Out of Scope**—Incorrect answers to Inference questions often include a statement that is related to the passage but is too broad to be logically supported by the passage. (For instance, if a passage argues that one dog breed, beagles, makes a good pet, it would be out of scope to infer that the passage argues *all* dog breeds make good pets.)

- **Extreme**—Incorrect answers to Inference questions may include language that is too strong (*all, never, every, none*) to be supported by the passage.

- **Distortions**—Incorrect answers to Inference questions may be based on details from the passage but distort or misstate the author's ideas.

The **correct answer** to an Inference question will:

- Be a conclusion that can be logically supported by what is stated in the passage

You need to do this:

THE METHOD FOR SAT READING AND WRITING

STEP 1   What is the question asking?

STEP 2   What do I need to look for in the passage?

STEP 3   What answer strategy is best?

- Predict and Match
- Eliminate

Step 1. What is the question asking?

Key phrases such as "logically completes" in the question stem signal an Inference question. Keep in mind that the correct answer will be something that is *not* explicitly stated in the passage, but is *logically supported by the passage*.

Step 2. What do I need to look for in the passage?

If the question stem asks you to logically complete a blank, focus on the context near the blank to determine what type of inference is required.

You will usually need to read the entire passage so that you can understand the author's logical flow of ideas. Pay special attention to transition words, such as those that indicate contrast (*but, however, although*) or logical connections (*therefore, because*). These transition words will help you paraphrase the passage in your own words.

Step 3. What answer strategy is best?

In some cases, you may be able to make at least a general prediction about the inference in the correct answer. If so, use your prediction to help you focus in on the correct answer.

Alternatively, you may need to use elimination. Immediately eliminate answer choices that are out of scope—those that make a statement that is too broad to be supported by the passage. Similarly, eliminate answer choices that use language that is too extreme (*all, never, every, none*) to be supported by the passage. Also eliminate answer choices that distort the ideas from the passage.

Remember, the correct answer to an Inference question goes a step beyond what is stated in the passage, but it can always be fully and logically supported by what is stated in the passage.

Explanation:

The phrase "most logically completes the text" signals that this is an Inference question, so the correct answer will be something that is not explicitly stated in the passage but is logically supported by the passage. The last sentence of the passage, which contains the blank, states that you are looking for "the key to preserving" Caño Cristales, specifically "in light of these dangers to the vegetation." As you read the rest of the passage, look for these "dangers" so that you can draw a logical conclusion about how to preserve Caño Cristales.

Read through the passage and paraphrase its flow of ideas. The first sentences identify the topic of the Caño Cristales River and explain why it has unique colorings. The contrast word "Yet" signals a transition to the river's "challenges." Look for these challenges—or "dangers," as mentioned in the last sentence—in the following sentences. First, since decreased tourism improved plant life, it must be the case that tourism was threatening plant life. The transition word "Further" indicates another challenge: deforestation threatens the *Macarenia clavigera* riverweed.

Predict that the inference in the correct answer will be *a way to preserve the river, in light of the dangers of tourism and deforestation*.

Evaluate the answer choices. Choice (**A**) is correct because it is a logical inference based on the passage: the issues of tourism and deforestation are both "human activities" that the author has identified as threats to Caño Cristales. Although tourism could conceivably cause pollution, the passage never identifies pollution as the threat posed by tourists, so (B) is out of scope. Further, anti-pollution laws would not address the problem of deforestation, so eliminate (B). Eliminate (C) because it distorts the author's use of the detail about *Macarenia clavigera*; why the river appears red is unrelated to how to preserve the site. Eliminate (D) because it is too extreme; although the author identifies tourism as a threat, "eliminating all" tourism is too extreme of a conclusion to be supported by the passage.

Try on Your Own

Directions

Take as much time as you need on these questions. Work carefully and methodically. There will be an opportunity for timed practice later in the book.

29

The Great Recession left many investors wary of stock market volatility, and that hesitancy was exacerbated among young people, who saw a considerable portion of their families' wealth erased in short order. One study posited that the average American household lost a third of its wealth during the Great Recession. This was at the exact moment when many millennials were making decisions about attending college, pursuing post-graduate studies, or entering the workforce. Those decisions were all directly correlated to household wealth. The ripple effects of the Great Recession left many millennials ascribing blame directly to the stock market for their missed opportunities. Even with a full awareness that the stock market has rebounded and far exceeded the highs seen prior to the Great Recession, many millennials _____

Which choice most logically completes the text?

(A) continue to believe that the Great Recession could have been avoided by continued funding of Social Security and Medicare.

(B) have continued to wait for indications of an economic recovery rather than risk prematurely investing a percentage of their savings in the stock market.

(C) argue that the Great Recession resulted from misconceptions about the stability of stock market investments, especially as it related to housing.

(D) still feel trepidation about investing in the stock market, preferring to save a larger percentage of their salaries than their parents and grandparents did.

30

The drive to share scary stories is common across human history, with all cultures having their own share of folklore dealing with ghosts, monsters, and fiends. The modern internet is no different. Creepypastas are a type of internet folklore that focuses on horror, with topics ranging from incomprehensible supernatural beings to liminal space. In contrast to the elaborate single-author horror novels of the twentieth century, creepypastas _____

Which choice most logically completes the text?

- (A) focus on scares that appeal to the modern youth, such as liminal space, which is akin to endless hallways stretching out to an uncertain destination.

- (B) more closely resemble internet memes, with multiple creators offering their own spin on a simple core concept.

- (C) have more in common with the scary stories of previous generations, with their focus on ghosts and monsters.

- (D) avoid the use of monsters in favor of topics that focus on real-world horrors.

31

It would not be until 1861 that Louis Pasteur would propose the link between microorganisms and disease, now known as the germ theory. Before Pasteur's breakthrough, the predominant explanation for the cause of most illnesses was the so-called miasma theory, which held that noxious fumes and pollution—quite literally, as the theory's name implies, "bad air"—were responsible for making people sick. Consequently, during the 1854 outbreak of cholera in Westminster, London, doctors and government officials alike _____

Which choice most logically completes the text?

- (A) were skeptical of claims that the disease outbreak was due to microorganisms in the water supply.

- (B) blamed "miasmatic particles" released into the air by decaying organic matter in the soil of the River Thames.

- (C) tackled the disease with newfound efficiency due to understanding the true source of the disease.

- (D) blamed the public's moral shortcomings for causing God to punish the city with such a terrible disease.

Reading & Writing

32

Officials in the movie industry report that over half of the films released in the United States in the 2010s targeted an audience ranging in age from 13–25. Moreover, national sales data indicate that pizza is a favorite food among this age group. Since Filmmax opened a theater in a Chicago area mall in 2022 close to one of their existing MyPie subsidiary stores, pizza sales at that MyPie location have been higher than at any other restaurant in their nationwide chain. Because watching movies seems to stimulate pizza sales, Filmmax has decided that _____

Which choice most logically completes the text?

(A) additional MyPie restaurants should be opened around Chicago to take advantage of pizza's popularity in that city.

(B) the simplest way to increase their profits is to expand by opening new MyPie restaurants near every Filmmax theater nationwide.

(C) it would be more profitable to sell off their Filmmax business and focus on opening new MyPie locations near theaters.

(D) a marketing campaign to boost pizza sales must necessarily involve product placement for MyPie restaurants in major Hollywood movies.

33

One persistent, albeit erroneous, view is that real estate is a better investment instrument than a stock market portfolio. A London Business School study found that over the same 90-year period, the average rate of return on a real estate investment was 1.3% compared to the 9.8% annualized total return for the S&P stock 500 index. Investing the $5,500 IRS-imposed annual limit in an IRA for 25 years would result in a return of over $600,000 based on the annualized return rate. Stock investment requires a smaller overhead than real estate investment, and the liquid nature of stocks makes them ideal for retirement: stocks allocated to retirement accounts remain tax-free until they are drawn on. Despite this tangible evidence, though, the stock market _____

Which choice most logically completes the text?

(A) is the main stepping stone from which most individuals begin to build personal wealth.

(B) remains less stable and lucrative than home ownership as a source of wealth.

(C) retains a stigma in the minds of many.

(D) is limited by IRS rules to a $5,500 annual maximum.

34

Long theoretical, quantum computers have finally seen concrete developments in recent years. Around the turn of the century, the first 5- and 7-qubit nuclear magnetic resonance (NMR) computers were demonstrated in Munich, Germany, and Santa Fe, New Mexico, respectively. In 2006, researchers at Oxford were able to cage a qubit within a "buckyball," a buckminsterfullerene molecule, and maintain its state for a short time using precise, repeated microwave pulses. The first company dedicated to quantum computing software, 1QB Information Technologies, was founded in 2012. In 2018, Google announced the development of the 72-qubit Bristlecone chip designed to prove "quantum supremacy," the ability of quantum computers to solve problems beyond the reach of classical computing. Compared to the theoretical work being slowly sketched out in the 1980s, the early 21st century _____

Which choice most logically completes the text?

(A) will eventually see those theories finally put into practice with the first quantum computer.

(B) lacks the government-backed funding that propelled quantum computing forward during the Cold War.

(C) has seen the general public adopt quantum computers at a terrific rate compared to classical computers.

(D) has brought quantum computing advancements at an impressive pace.

35

Walter Alvarez, a professor at the University of California, Berkeley, is best known for proposing the theory that the dinosaurs were killed off by an asteroid strike 66 million years ago. Beyond the immediate effects of fire, flood, and storm, dust darkened the atmosphere, cutting off plant life. Many animal species disappeared as the food chain was snapped at its base. Alvarez's main evidence is an abundance of iridium in the KT boundary, a thin stratum dividing Cretaceous rocks from rocks of the Tertiary period. Iridium normally accompanies the slow fall of interplanetary debris, but the KT boundary strata implies _____

Which choice most logically completes the text?

(A) a rapid, massive deposition, given its iridium content is 10–100 times more abundant than normal.

(B) whole species of small organisms vanishing from the fossil record.

(C) the formation of basaltic spheres and deformed quartz grains, both of which could have resulted from high-velocity impact.

(D) that iridium in the KT boundary was gradually deposited over a period of 50,000 to 100,000 years.

Solo concert pianists, by convention, are not permitted to use musical scores during their performances. However, most members of chamber groups and orchestras are permitted to use sheet music during performances and perform well as a result. Why is this? Audience expectations are one reason. The piano soloist is expected to know both the piano score and the orchestral score by heart. This allows for a high degree of collaboration during a performance. The orchestra does not move in lockstep behind the piano soloist. Instead, the soloist _____

Which choice most logically completes the text?

(A) is considered more experienced than typical members of the orchestra, who require a musical score.

(B) uses a musical score in the same way as does a member of a chamber group or orchestra.

(C) deals with a less complex instrument as a single performer, while the orchestra must manage mass coordination despite boasting a variety of instruments.

(D) is expected to adjust their performance to best match the orchestra and the acoustics of the hall.

HOW MUCH HAVE YOU LEARNED?

Directions

For testlike practice, give yourself 7 minutes to complete this question set. When you're finished, be sure to study the explanations, even for questions you answered correctly. Full explanations can be found at the end of this chapter.

37

The following text is adapted from Archibald Lampman's 1895 poem "The Poet's Possession." The poem appears in the autumn harvest section of Lampman's poetry collection *Lyrics of Earth*, which includes poems about each season of the calendar year.

Think not, oh [farmer] of the well-tilled field,
This earth is only thine; for after thee,
When all is sown and gathered and put by,
Comes the grave poet with creative eye,
And from these silent acres and clean plots,
Bids with his wand the fancied after-yield,
A second tilth and second harvest, be,
The crop of images and curious thoughts.

Which choice best describes the main idea of the text?

(A) The farmer's land really belongs to the whole community.

(B) It will require multiple harvests to clear the farmer's field.

(C) Poets are the only ones who express their creativity.

(D) The harvested field will provide inspiration for poetry.

38

Since the 1960s, Japanese artist Yayoi Kusama has created performances, sculptures, and installations that captivate viewers and, as described by the artist, foster connections between the natural world and humans. One example of her installation art is *Ascension of Polkadots on the Trees*, which Kusama has created in public parks in Singapore, Helsinki, and New York City. To install *Ascension of Polkadots*, Kusama uses large staples and elastic bungee cords to tightly wrap trees in bright red fabric adorned with large white dots. The resulting groups of decorated trees create whimsical, immersive experiences that bridge nature and the human imagination.

According to the text, how did Kusama make *Ascension of Polkadots on the Trees*?

(A) She incorporated plants and animals in public parks into the designs.

(B) She built structures out of red and white fabric.

(C) She arranged tree branches into unusually shaped bridges.

(D) She affixed fabric around trees using fasteners and cords.

Reading & Writing

Scientists previously assumed that insects, unlike some mammals and birds, do not engage in play—actions that have no known survival purpose but rather seem motivated by pleasure. However, researchers from Queen Mary University of London studied play in bees, hypothesizing that the insects will actively seek out the opportunity to engage in play. In one test, bees could choose to proceed directly to food or to divert to spaces containing miniature wooden balls. The bees rolled the balls repeatedly—one bee doing so over a hundred times. This result caused the researchers to conclude that the bees were indeed playing, as they apparently obtained pleasure from rolling the balls. In a second test, bees were placed in an enclosure with two differently-colored spaces; only one of the spaces had wooden balls. The bees were later given the opportunity to choose to enter one of the two differently-colored spaces.

Which finding from the second test, if true, would most strongly support the researchers' hypothesis?

(A) Bees that initially engaged in high amounts of ball rolling typically decreased their ball-rolling activity over the course of the tests.

(B) The bees showed a preference for the space that was the same color as the one previously containing balls.

(C) The vast majority of bees tended to bypass the opportunity to roll balls in order to access food more quickly.

(D) The bees preferred spaces that were darker colors, regardless of whether darker spaces previously contained balls.

Incidents in the Life of a Slave Girl is an 1861 autobiography by Harriet Jacobs. In the book, Jacobs suggests that although she found her family to be a source of comfort, the stability of her family was insecure: _____

Which quotation from *Incidents in the Life of a Slave Girl* most effectively illustrates the claim?

Ⓐ "When [my brother] put his arms round my neck, and looked into my eyes, as if to read there the troubles I dared not tell, I felt that I still had something to love. But even that pleasant emotion was chilled by the reflection that he might be torn from me at any moment."

Ⓑ "I had one brother, William, who was two years younger than myself—a bright, affectionate child. I had also a great treasure in my maternal grandmother, who was a remarkable woman in many respects."

Ⓒ "The laugh of the . . . children sounded harsh and cruel. It was selfish to feel so about the joy of others. My brother moved about with a very grave face. I tried to comfort him, by saying, 'Take courage, Willie; brighter days will come by and by.'"

Ⓓ "A streak of moonlight was on the floor before me, and in the midst of it appeared the forms of my two children. They vanished; but I had seen them distinctly. Some will call it a dream, others a vision. I know not how to account for it, but it made a strong impression on my mind."

Reading & Writing

Select U.S. Cabinet Departments

Department	Year Created	Year Disbanded	Purpose
State	1789	n/a	coordinate foreign policy
Treasury	1789	n/a	manage government revenue and create currency
War	1789	1947	operate the U.S. Army
Navy	1798	1949	operate the U.S. Navy
Air Force	1947	1949	operate the U.S. Air Force
Army	1947	1949	operate the U.S. Army
Defense	1947	n/a	operate the entire U.S. military

The function of the executive departments of the U.S. federal government, also known as the federal bureaucracy, is to implement federal law. The head, or secretary, of each department is appointed by the president and serves in the president's advisory Cabinet. While there are currently fifteen executive departments, there were originally only three: the Departments of State, Treasury, and War. The organization of the federal bureaucracy has been in continual flux; departments have both dissolved and combined over time. For instance, _____

Which choice most effectively uses data from the table to complete the example?

(A) the State and Treasury Departments were first established in 1789 and still exist under these same department titles today.

(B) although the Department of the Navy dates to 1798, while the Departments of the Army and Air Force began in 1947, all three of them ceased to exist in 1949.

(C) the original War Department was retired in 1947, and the Departments of the Navy, Army, and Air Force came under the Department of Defense in 1949.

(D) the Treasury and War Departments both dissolved in 1947 and were incorporated into the newly formed Department of Defense.

Dogs that assist humans who have post-traumatic stress disorder (PTSD) are currently taught to respond to mostly visual and auditory cues, both those exhibited by the humans they serve and those in the surrounding environment. Researchers in a 2022 study analyzed whether PTSD service dogs also use their acute sense of smell to detect and respond to negative stress in humans. The researchers found that trained dogs were highly accurate—about 94% on average—in detecting the odors of breath and sweat samples that were taken from participants who were experiencing stress. As a result, the researchers suggest that _____

Which choice most logically completes the text?

(A) the current methods of PTSD service dog training are highly effective and should not undergo any revisions.

(B) PTSD service dogs are more accurate at detecting smell-based cues that indicate states of stress than states of calm.

(C) the chemical odors in human sweat are more acute to dogs' sense of smell than are the chemical odors in human breath.

(D) PTSD service dog training could incorporate teaching them to respond to smell-based stress cues.

Reading & Writing

REFLECT

Directions: Take a few minutes to recall what you've learned and what you've been practicing in this chapter. Consider the following questions, jot down your best answer for each one, and then compare your reflections to the expert responses that follow. Use your level of confidence to determine what to do next.

How should you approach reading the passage when the question stem asks you to identify its main idea?

_____

_____

_____

How can you effectively analyze graphs or tables on Quantitative Command of Evidence questions?

_____

_____

_____

How do Detail questions differ from Inference questions?

_____

_____

_____

How can predicting help you correctly answer Information and Ideas questions? What types of answer choices can you eliminate on Information and Ideas questions?

_____

_____

_____

What are the main differences you see between SAT Information and Ideas questions and those you're used to from tests in school?

_____

_____

_____

How will you approach SAT Reading and Writing questions more strategically as you continue to practice and improve on your performance? Are there any specific habits you will practice to make your approach to SAT Reading and Writing more effective and efficient?

_____

_____

_____

K

Expert Responses

How should you approach reading the passage when the question stem asks you to identify its main idea?

On Main Idea questions, don't get caught up in the details of the passage. Instead, locate the author's main point about the topic of the passage, which is sometimes found in the first or last sentence. Otherwise, pull together all the details from the passage into one main idea. Paraphrasing the main idea in your own words can help you predict the correct answer choice.

How can you effectively analyze graphs or tables on Quantitative Command of Evidence questions?

When analyzing a graph or table, you should pay attention to its titles and labels, and you should also identify what type of information it does (and does not) provide. Reading a data point or two might help you make sure you understand the data presented. Just as importantly, make sure you carefully analyze the passage so that you can determine what data from the graph or table is relevant for answering the question.

How do Detail questions differ from Inference questions?

The correct answer to a Detail question is something explicitly stated in the passage. The correct answer to an Inference question is not explicitly stated in the passage, but it is logically supported by what is stated in the passage.

How can predicting help you correctly answer Information and Ideas questions? What types of answer choices can you eliminate on Information and Ideas questions?

When you are able to do so, predicting the correct answer can increase your accuracy and speed by helping you focus in on the one correct answer and avoid spending time comparing the answer choices to one another. Main Idea and Detail questions often lend themselves to predicting. When eliminating answer choices, toss out any that misuse or distort information from the passage, any that use language that is too extreme for the passage, and any that are out of the scope of the passage.

What are the main differences you see between SAT Information and Ideas questions and those you're used to from tests in school?

Depending on the kinds of classes and teachers you've had in high school, the skills rewarded on SAT Information and Ideas questions may be more or less familiar. In general, Information and Ideas questions do not ask you to simply recall facts, but they instead require you to identify main ideas and details from a passage and to logically support ideas or draw inferences from a passage.

How will you approach SAT Reading and Writing questions more strategically as you continue to practice and improve your performance? Are there any specific habits you will practice to make your approach to SAT Reading and Writing more effective and efficient?

There is no one-size-fits-all answer here. Reflect on your own habits in answering SAT Reading and Writing questions and give yourself an honest assessment of your strengths and weaknesses. Consider the strategies you've seen experts use in this chapter, and put them to work in your own practice to increase your accuracy, speed, and confidence.

Next Steps

If you answered most questions correctly in the "How Much Have You Learned?" section, and if your responses to the Reflect questions were similar to those of the SAT expert, then consider Information and Ideas questions an area of strength and move on to the next chapter. Come back to this topic periodically to prevent yourself from getting rusty.

If you don't yet feel confident, review the lessons in this chapter that you have not yet mastered. Then, try the questions you missed again. As always, be sure to review the explanations closely.

Check Your Work – Chapter 18

1.   C
Difficulty: Medium
Category: Information and Ideas
Getting to the Answer: The passage describes an experiment performed by Charles Henry Turner that showed bees changed their feeding patterns when the food sources changed. This matches **(C)**, the correct answer.

The passage says that the bees changed the time they arrived for food, so (A) is incorrect. Choice (B) is incorrect because the text never discusses Taylor's recognition, and says he was published in a "prestigious" journal. The passage never discusses the times that bees prefer to feed, so (D) is incorrect.

2.   B
Difficulty: Medium
Category: Information and Ideas
Getting to the Answer: The passage describes how repetition is used by teachers and video games, so **(B)** is correct.

Although the studies mentioned in the text connect anger, obesity, and addiction to video game use, they do not say that people with these issues should avoid video games. Choice (A) is incorrect. The passage only discusses violent video games, not all video games, so (C) is incorrect. You may believe (D) to be true, but the text never mentions the most important way students learn, making (D) incorrect.

3.   B
Difficulty: Hard
Category: Information and Ideas
Getting to the Answer: The passage opens with the idea that the historic houseboats of Cairo may be lost and closes with the opposition of local citizens to this situation. Choice **(B)** is correct.

Based on the passage, you might believe (A) to be true, but the author never makes this suggestion in the text, so (A) is incorrect. Choice (C) is also not stated in the passage. You know that Naguib Mahfouz won the Nobel prize, and that he wrote about the houseboats, but there is no evidence in the passage that he won the prize *because* he wrote about the houseboats. You will always be able to point to words in the passage that will "prove" the correct answer to a Main Idea question.

Choice (D) is mentioned in the passage, but is a detail supporting the historic importance of the houseboats, not the main idea. This choice is also incorrect.

4.   A
Difficulty: Hard
Category: Information and Ideas
Getting to the Answer: The poem opens with the description of the grave of the poet's beloved, followed by the rhetorical question, "Have I forgotten you?" The answer comes in the final lines of the excerpt: although the events of life have gone on, these have "obscure[d]" but not violated the memory of the beloved. **(A)** is correct.

Choices (B) and (C) are mentioned as possibilities in the poem, but are contradicted by the last lines. The poet still honors the memory of the beloved, even though new events have occurred. These choices are incorrect. Choice (D) is not discussed in the poem; the poet never discusses the most important aspect of relationships.

5.   D
Difficulty: Easy
Category: Information and Ideas
Getting to the Answer: The passage makes clear that Satanta wants to continue life on the prairies, making **(D)** correct.

In the second sentence, the speaker clearly states, "I don't want to settle." Choice (A) is incorrect. Satanta clearly says, "I have told you the truth . . . [but] I don't know how it is with the commissioners," but this is not strong enough to support (B). The speaker neither makes the definite statement "usual falsehoods" nor insists on the honesty of his audience. Although Satanta feels safe in the presence of the audience, this is more a declaration of courage than a need to be protected, so (C) is also incorrect.

6.   A
Difficulty: Easy
Category: Information and Ideas
Getting to the Answer: The main idea of the passage is a description of a new laser technology that can make cold-brew coffee quickly, so **(A)** is correct.

Choice (B) is a statement made in the passage, but is not the main idea. This choice is incorrect. You may have thought (C) or (D) were correct, but they are not mentioned in the text. Even though Ziefuss' process is faster, there may be a reason that consumers may not purchase cold-brew coffee (C) or a way that the process could be used in the home (D). The passage never addresses these topics, so these choices are incorrect.

7.   C
Difficulty: Medium
Category: Information and Ideas
Getting to the Answer: The passage discusses the ancient city of Petra, its design, and one problem in modern times. Choice **(C)** sums these features up nicely, and is correct.

The incorrect choices all go beyond the statements in the passage. The text does not claim that "ancient Petra never flooded " (A), that the floods are "frequent " (B), or that "Petra was unique among ancient desert cities" (D).

8.   C
Difficulty: Easy
Category: Information and Ideas
Getting to the Answer: Use the text to predict that a new technology, floating artificial leaves, may eventually be used in maritime shipping to reduce amount of fossil fuels needed. Choice **(C)** matches this prediction, and is correct.

All the incorrect choices make statements that are not supported by the text. The passage never discusses green plants (A) or the full extent of eventual uses of the artificial leaves (B). (D) is incorrect because the text never mentions the timetable for the use of the artificial leaves.

9.   A
Difficulty: Medium
Category: Information and Ideas
Getting to the Answer: The phrase "According to the text" shows this to be a Detail question. The correct answer will paraphrase a statement made explicitly in the text. The author discusses non–rush hour commuters toward the end of the text, listing some examples of these commuters—"doctors, nurses, bartenders, police officers, and firefighters"—and explaining that a cessation of 24-hour subway service could permanently alter their commutes. That matches choice **(A)**, the correct answer here.

(B) is the opposite of what the passage says. The current system creates inconveniences for these workers when their subway lines are rerouted or closed for

repair, but a suspension of 24-hour service would entail a permanent disruption. (C) distorts the paragraph. Doctors and nurses are *among* the non–rush hour commuters, but that doesn't mean the commuters are *primarily* health care workers. The passage never states that health care workers are the majority of commuters. (D) is incorrect because the author does not discuss which occupations show the strongest support for a change in subway maintenance.

10.   C
Difficulty: Medium
Category: Information and Ideas
Getting to the Answer: The passage compares investment in the stock market favorably to home ownership. The author demonstrates the large return on a modest investment and then points out other reasons why they are well suited to retirement income. One of those reasons is the investments' tax-free status; that matches the correct answer, **(C)**.

(A) is a misused detail; this answer choice virtually quotes the passage, but the piece of text it cites refers to home ownership, not to stock market investments. (B) says the opposite of what's in the passage; the author demonstrates that the stock market is more stable and lucrative than home ownership is. (D) is never mentioned in the text; $5,500 is the investment mentioned in the example, but a minimum amount required is not discussed.

11.   D
Difficulty: Medium
Category: Information and Ideas
Getting to the Answer: From the passage you know Mahadev dedicated her graduate studies to "creating a verification process for quantum computing." Her studies were based on a type of cryptography, and she came up with a theoretical solution that the author concludes will likely have real-world application in the coming years. Matching these details to the choices yields **(D)**, the correct answer.

(A) distorts the passage. Part of Mahadev's protocol is similar to techniques used in cloud computing, but nothing indicates that she was trying to improve cloud computing. (B) and (C) are not mentioned in the text. How Mahadev's results will be confirmed (B) and whether they will replace Learning With Errors (C) are not discussed.

12. B

Difficulty: Medium

Category: Information and Ideas

Getting to the Answer: This passage describes the lack of security measures at the bank: "There are neither guards nor gratings," "banknotes are freely exposed," and a gold bar is passed "from hand to hand." These details match the correct answer **(B)**.

Choice (A) is a distortion of information in the excerpt. The second sentence states that the bank had faith in its customers, not that the customers have faith in the bank. (C) and (D) are not mentioned in the passage at all.

13. A

Difficulty: Hard

Category: Information and Ideas

Getting to the Answer: The description of the process of bioluminescence starts in the last part of the second sentence. There, the passage describes three necessary components: a light-emitting molecule, oxygen, and an enzyme. Since none of these are among the choices, continue researching. The following sentence groups all of the light-emitting molecules under "the generic name luciferin," making **(A)** the correct answer.

Choice (B) is incorrect because although most biolu-minescent organisms are marine life, sea water is not identified as a necessary part of the process of bioluminescence. Incorrect choices (C) and (D) are the two types of enzymes used in bioluminescent processes, so one of them must be present, but neither is required. An organism that requires luciferase for its bioluminescence will not require photoproteins, and the converse is true.

14. D

Difficulty: Medium

Category: Information and Ideas

Getting to the Answer: The passage contains infor-mation about bacteria found on the exterior of the International Space Station. The author then engages in a lengthy discussion describing the likely terrestrial origins of these bacteria. This matches **(D)**, which is correct.

The author never mentions bias among scientists, so (A) is incorrect. While the author might agree with the statements in (B) and (C), neither of these is the reason given for skepticism about the possibility of extraterres-trial origins for the bacteria found on the ISS, so both are incorrect.

15. A

Difficulty: Medium

Category: Information and Ideas

Getting to the Answer: The passage describes the young generation as "serene" and not "as hearty and impulsive" as their elders, matching **(A)**, the correct answer.

Choices (B) and (C) are never mentioned in the passage, and so, are incorrect. (D) states the opposite of the passage. The author describes older people as "flushed and excited by the prospect of some anticipated pleasure."

16. A

Difficulty: Hard

Category: Information and Ideas

Getting to the Answer: The first paragraph tells you that Gideon's talent "is native to him," and the second paragraph says that Stuhk recognizes "Gideon's ability," making **(A)** correct.

Choice (B) is never mentioned in the passage, so this choice is incorrect. Stuhk's contribution is described as booking Gideon and giving "him his opportunity," not training him. Incorrect choices (C) and (D) go beyond the passage. You do know that "Stuhk, was the discover," but not that Gideon would never have been successful if Stuhk had not been the one to discover him (C). Similarly, you know that Stuhk has become rich, but not that Gideon was the only source of that wealth.

17. B

Difficulty: Medium

Category: Information and Ideas

Getting to the Answer: The question is asking for a study that supports the DoT's claim that roundabouts are safer than traditional intersections. Predict that the correct answer will either include evidence that refers to the safety of the roundabout or the dangers of the traditional intersection. Choice **(B)** includes data on the reduction of head-on collisions, supporting the claim of increased safety, and it is correct.

Choice (A) is incorrect because it states that there are limitations to the effectiveness of roundabouts. Elimi-nate (C) because it is out of scope; the passage does not include references to the cost associated with round-abouts. (D) weakens the author's claim that left turns were eliminated.

18. C

Difficulty: Medium

Category: Information and Ideas

Getting to the Answer: This question is asking you to identify the statement that weakens the doctors' belief, so begin by identifying that belief and paraphrasing it in your own words. The keywords in the second sentence, "Some doctors . . . believ[ing]," mark off the claim: lithotripsy may help patients with cardiac artery disease. Predict that the correct answer will provide some reason *lithotripsy may not help these patients* and work through the choices by elimination.

Recovery outcomes are mentioned in the second sentence as an outcome that is *improved* by lithotripsy, so eliminate (A). This choice supports, not weakens, the doctors' belief. Similarly, (B) supports the use of lithotripsy over atherectomy and strengthens the author's belief; eliminate it. Choice **(C)** is the only claim to indicate that lithotripsy may increase the risk to heart health; this matches the prediction and is correct. Atherectomy is the procedure that uses a drill and may cause additional damage, so (D) is incorrect.

19. A

Difficulty: Hard

Category: Information and Ideas

Getting to the Answer: The claim is found in the second sentence. Predict that the correct answer will contain three concepts: an experience of love, and at least two contrasting images. Choice **(A)** contrasts the image of quickly moving time ("Swift . . . sands may run") with the permanence of the lovers' "vow" to describe an experience of love ("Love like this is never done;"). This choice matches the prediction and is correct.

The incorrect choices all portray experiences of love without conflicting images and do not satisfy the claim that Parker "us[ed] contrasting images."

20. B

Difficulty: Medium

Category: Information and Ideas

Getting to the Answer: The chefs' claim is found in the second sentence, identified by the key phrase "Chefs consider." Summarize the claim in your own words; anything like *croissants are harder and take longer to make than kipferl* is a good paraphrase. Predict that the correct answer will mention a difficult and/or time-consuming aspect of croissant production and work through the choices by elimination.

Eliminate (A); this choice describes a process that doesn't produce the best croissant but does not indicate that the croissant process is particularly difficult or time-consuming. Choice **(B)** is correct. The "hallmark," or distinguishing feature of a croissant, takes "many steps" and needs "time to chill" the sheet of dough and butter between the "many steps." The process is both difficult and time-consuming. Choice (C) is out of scope; the production process is never mentioned. Choice (D) is tempting because you may *think* that the reason croissants are not usually made at home is because they are hard to make, but the choice never states this. The locations where the pastries are produced is out of scope.

21. B

Difficulty: Medium

Category: Information and Ideas

Getting to the Answer: Start by identifying the researchers' belief and putting it into your own words. The key phrase "researchers now believe" locates the belief in the third sentence: *a way has been found to diagnose if someone has Alzheimer's disease before symptoms show up*. This is all the expert test-taker needs to evaluate the choices. If you prefer to read the entire text for background, do so, but return to your paraphrase of the claim to focus your search on the precise information needed.

Eliminate (A); this choice describes a characteristic of Alzheimer's disease, not a method of diagnosis. Choice **(B)** cites a specific indicator that can be used seven years before the onset of the disorder's typical symptoms and is correct. Eliminate (C); this choice weakens the researchers' claim by stating that examining the brain after death is the best tool for diagnosis. Eliminate (D); methods of preventing Alzheimer's are out of scope.

22. D

Difficulty: Hard

Category: Information and Ideas

Getting to the Answer: The hypothesis put forth by Swierk and his team is that "there may be long-term health risks posed by chemicals in tattoo inks." Predict that the correct answer will include specific health risks. Eliminate choice (A), because having an accurate label does not change whether or not the ink itself poses a health risk. Choice (B) provides information about the ink's pigments but does *not* make a connection to any health risk. Choice (C) is out of scope; the passage does not mention tattoo ink regulation, and may be eliminated. Choice **(D)** is correct, as it is the only choice that makes the connection between the pigment particles' size and the potential cancer risks.

23. C

Difficulty: Medium
Category: Information and Ideas
Getting to the Answer: On Quantitative Command of Evidence questions, begin by determining what information you are being asked to support (or weaken). Sometimes, you may be required to complete a blank from the passage. On this question, the question stem indicates that you must support the research team's conclusion. The final sentence of the passage states that the team "concluded" that "although . . . stock portfolios" were relatively consistent in profit nationwide, "median home appreciation" was dependent on the city. The correct answer must use data from the graph to support this conclusion.

On the graph, make sure you understand what is being represented and look for trends. Here, the x-axis shows 10 different cities. For each one, the long-term profitability of home appreciation compared to the financial returns of a stock portfolio are given on the y-axis. Note that, along the x-axis, the cities are arranged from greatest increase in home value to least. The increases in stock portfolios, while roughly similar to one another, are not in a particular order.

(C) is correct; its information matches the graph. It provides an example of how median home appreciation varied by city, making it the only answer choice that supports the statement made in the passage. (A) is contradicted by the case of San Francisco, the one market in which home ownership outperformed stock market investments. (B) is the reverse of the graph; Fort Lauderdale, Florida, saw greater home value appreciation than Portland, Oregon, did. (D) is incorrect because it does not address the question; instead, it focuses on the merits of particular cities rather than home ownership versus stock market investments in general.

24. B

Difficulty: Easy
Category: Information and Ideas
Getting to the Answer: The passage discusses specifics about the Brooklyn Bridge, which are further elaborated upon in the table. Since no specific detail or claim is made in the final sentence, an elimination strategy is

the best approach. Go through the answer choices and compare them to the passage and the table, eliminating any option that is contradicted by the existing data there.

The claim in (A) is contradicted by the data table; the Golden Gate Bridge, completed in 1937, had a longer single span than the Brooklyn Bridge. Choice **(B)** accurately reflects the information in the table since the Tower Bridge was built in 1894. Examine the remaining answer choices just to be safe. (C) is incorrect because the Tower Bridge in London, UK, has a shorter length overall and a shorter "largest single span" when compared to the Brooklyn Bridge. (D) is incorrect for the same reason as (A); the Golden Gate Bridge surpassed the Brooklyn Bridge in 1937.

25. C

Difficulty: Medium
Category: Information and Ideas
Getting to the Answer: Since the sentence with the blank concerns the years since 1995, look at the data after 1995 in the graph. Pay attention to the relationship between the two lines: the solid line represents the percentage of corn production used for ethanol, and the dotted line reflects the price of corn. In the most recent year displayed in the graph, 2007, the price of corn and the percentage of corn production used for ethanol have both increased compared to the date listed near the blank, 1995. Choice **(C)** is correct. Choices (A), (B), and (D) do not accurately reflect the graph.

26. C

Difficulty: Medium
Category: Information and Ideas
Getting to the Answer: When analyzing a graph or table for a Quantitative Command of Evidence question, be sure to carefully examine any titles or labels. In the table provided, three categories are listed: the amount (in Dutch florins) for goods sent to Japan, the amount for goods received from Japan, and the net profit for those goods. Also, keep in mind that incorrect answer choices may contain data that is factually true based on the graph or table but does not directly support the claim or detail from the passage.

The question stem asks you to support the historian's claim. The claim is identified in the last sentence of the passage, which states that trade with Japan provided the VOC with "relatively high profits" in "some years."

Choice **(C)** correctly supports this claim, as it identifies years in which the Dutch had the highest net profits according to the table. (A) is incorrect because it is contradicted by the graph; only 138,249 florins in net profit were made in 1826. (B) is factually true based on the table but does not support the claim, as 1826 had the lowest net profit listed rather than "relatively high" profit. (D) does not address the claim. The Dutch gained over a million florins in goods from Japan in 1828, but the claim must address the VOC's *profits*.

27. D

Difficulty: Medium
Category: Information and Ideas
Getting to the Answer: The passage discusses the concept of a radioactive half-life and how the half-life of carbon-14 allows for the dating of "an organic sample" until "all the carbon-14 has totally decayed." The blank refers to an example of how paleontologists can use this technique to date human remains up to a certain age. Pick the answer choice that is true based on the contents of the passage and the graph.

Choice **(D)** is correct because the x-axis on the graph goes to 40,000 years, at which point the carbon-14 reduces to close to 0% and is finally "totally decayed." Choice (A) can be eliminated because, per the graph, at 20,000 years old roughly 10% of the carbon-14 will still remain in a sample. This means the carbon-14 has not "totally decayed" yet. Choice (B) is contradicted by the graph, which only goes up to 40,000 years on the x-axis. Choice (C) can be eliminated because at 5,000 years old only 50% of the carbon-14 will have decayed.

28. A

Difficulty: Hard
Category: Information and Ideas
Getting to the Answer: It can be useful to predict what kind of data from the graph or table would support the passage. Consider the claim made before the blank. The passage discusses first-class berths on trains. It compares the affordability of European to North American railways and then says that comparison "yielded a stark result." The example is blank, so what fills it should support that claim.

The data table contrasts routes of comparable distance (901/912 and 536/440 miles, respectively) with their prices. What can you predict from the data shown? That first-class berth fares in North America were consistently cheaper than comparable fares in Europe, and

by a lot. **(A)** is the answer choice that best fits that prediction.

Choice (B) is incorrect; New York to Chicago and Paris to Rome are roughly the same distance, while the first-class berth fare for the former costs less than half of the latter. (C) is incorrect; it compares two European berth fares, while the point of the passage is to compare the affordability of European and North American railroads. Likewise, (D) is incorrect because it compares two North American berth fares.

29. D

Difficulty: Medium
Category: Information and Ideas
Getting to the Answer: The passage discusses why millennials distrust the stock market. Many of these young people blamed the 2007 stock market crash, which lead to the Great Recession, for the "missed opportunities" within their college and career options. This directly supports **(D)**, which is the correct answer. Choice (A) is outside the scope; the author does not draw a connection between the Great Recession and the two social programs named here. Choice (B) is contradicted by the passage; the author states that the market "has rebounded" and "far exceeded" its levels from prior to the Great Recession, which means indications of economic recovery already exist. Choice (C) is outside the scope; the author does not discuss any cause of the Great Recession.

30. B

Difficulty: Medium
Category: Information and Ideas
Getting to the Answer: The correct answer to an Inference question is logically supported by the passage. The passage's final sentence, which contains the blank, may also contain important context clues. This passage briefly reviews the history of horror stories, then discusses modern internet horror known as creepypasta. The final sentence contrasts creepypasta with "single-author horror novels" of last century. With that context in mind, you can predict that the answer will be something akin to "Creepypasta does not have a singular author." Choice **(B)** best fits that prediction.

Choice (A) is too extreme. There is nothing in the passage to suggest that liminal space was not the subject of pre-internet horror stories, only that it is a popular topic in creepypastas. (C) is contradicted by the passage; ghosts and monsters are said to be popular in horror across "all cultures" throughout history. (D) is likewise contradicted; the passage mentions that creepypasta may focus on "supernatural beings."

31. B
Difficulty: Easy
Category: Information and Ideas
Getting to the Answer: When tackling an Inference question, it can be useful to consider the chain of thought in a passage. Here, Pasteur's germ theory is introduced; then it is contrasted with the explanation for a disease that it replaced—miasma theory. Finally, a specific example is offered of miasma theory in practical use. Choice **(B)** correctly continues that chain of thought, as the London officials blamed the disease on bad air from decaying matter. The other answer choices all incorrectly break that chain of thought. Note the use of the word "Consequently" in the sentence with the blank; it implies that London officials were working off the miasma theory of disease rather than germ theory, making (A) and (C) incorrect. Nothing in the passage hints at a theological or moral explanation for the cholera outbreak; (D) is incorrect because it is out of scope.

32. B
Difficulty: Easy
Category: Information and Ideas
Getting to the Answer: The passage describes a simple binary relationship, in that theaters attract an audience that is already predisposed to pizza as their favorite food. Therefore, the simplest way for the company to increase their profits is to open new MyPie pizzerias near Filmmax theaters nationwide; **(B)** is correct. Note how the passage discusses films and pizza in broad terms. Chicago is used as a model for how theaters and pizzerias could be exploited by the company on a nationwide basis; (A) is incorrect. The passage does not indicate that the Filmmax theaters are unprofitable or that the MyPie pizzerias make for a better investment; (C) is incorrect because it is too extreme. Choice (D) is contradicted by the passage, which indicates that films drive pizza sales even without product placement.

33. C
Difficulty: Hard
Category: Information and Ideas
Getting to the Answer: The passage argues that the idea of real estate being a better investment than the stock market is wrongheaded. Various statistics are offered to support this claim, which the author terms "tangible evidence." The word "despite" in the final sentence means that the blank will be filled by something about the stock market that goes against that "tangible evidence." Choice **(C)** is correct because it states that stock market investment retains a stigma. Choice (A) is incorrect because it does not fit the inference of the final sentence, which sets up a contrast with the "tangible evidence." Choice (B) says the opposite of what is in the passage; the author demonstrates that the stock market is more stable and lucrative than home ownership is. Choice (D) misuses a detail; the $5,500 annual cap applies to IRA contributions, not to stock market investments in general.

34. D
Difficulty: Hard
Category: Information and Ideas
Getting to the Answer: The passage lays out, in chronological order, a series of milestones in the development of quantum computers. It culminates in an overview of quantum computing over the twenty-first century so far, contrasting it with the "slowly sketched out" theoretical work of the 1980s. Choice **(D)** correctly fills in the blank, contrasting the slow-paced 1980s with the rapid advancements of the twenty-first century as outlined in the rest of the passage. Choice (A) contradicts the rest of the passage, as the first quantum computer had already been built "around the turn of the century." Choice (B) is out of scope; there is no mention of government financing or the Cold War elsewhere in the piece. Choice (C) is incorrect because it overstates the development of quantum computers; the milestones listed are for basic concepts related to quantum computing, and the only reference to classical computers is in the context of the type of problems they cannot solve that quantum computers can solve.

35. A
Difficulty: Medium
Category: Information and Ideas
Getting to the Answer: The answer to an Inference question should be logically supported by the passage, so pay special attention to the author's logical flow of ideas. In this passage, the case for Alvarez's theory of dinosaur extinction is laid out. The effects of the asteroid impact are described, and then the "main evidence" is described as the "abundance of iridium in the KT boundary." Finally, the typically "slow" build-up of iridium from space debris is contrasted with something about the KT boundary. Predict an answer that

best fits this inference, such as "Something must have introduced a lot of iridium rapidly." **(A)** best fits this prediction.

Choice (B) is a distortion; although the extinction of animals is mentioned in the passage, the logical flow of the passage would not bring it up while discussing iridium. (C) is out of scope; there is no discussion of basaltic spheres and deformed quartz grains prior to this point. (D) contradicts the flow of the passage, since "but" in the final sentence sets up a contrast with the typically slow build-up of iridium from space debris.

36. D
Difficulty: Medium
Category: Information and Ideas
Getting to the Answer: The passage explores the reasons why solo concert pianists do not use musical scores during their performances. The second-to-last sentence sets up a contrast, where an orchestra is said to not "move in lockstep" with the piano player. The final sentence, with the blank, explains that contrast. If the orchestra does not move in lockstep "behind" the pianist, then what does happen? The correct answer should explain. Eliminate any answer choice that does not fit.

Choices (A) and (C) can be eliminated as they do not explain how the pianist and the orchestra relate during a performance. (B) is contradicted by the passage; the pianist is said to NOT use a musical score. That leaves **(D)**, which correctly addresses how the piano soloist relates to the orchestra during a performance.

37. D
Difficulty: Medium
Category: Information and Ideas
Getting to the Answer: The question asks for the main idea of the passage, so paraphrase the main point of the poem as you read. The first lines admonish the farmer to not think of the field as belonging only to him. Then the speaker claims that after the field is harvested ("gathered and put by") by the farmer, the poet will come and make a "second harvest" of "images and curious thoughts." In other words, the poet, when looking at the harvested field, will think of ideas for poems. This prediction matches **(D)**, which is correct.

Choices (A) and (B) are incorrect because they focus only on the field, not the poetry it inspires. Further, (A) is incorrect because the poem does not imply the field

belongs to *everyone*, and (B) is incorrect because the "second harvest" is one of poetry, not of actual crops. Although the poem states that the poet has a "creative eye," choice (C) is incorrect because the poem does not imply that no one else expresses creativity.

38. D
Difficulty: Easy
Category: Information and Ideas
Getting to the Answer: The question asks how Kusama made *Ascension of Polkadots on the Trees*, so look for this detail as you read the passage. The phrases "To install" and "uses" in the third sentence indicate that this sentence describes her process: she uses staples and bungee cords to wrap trees in red and white-dotted fabric. Use this description as your prediction; **(D)** is correct.

The other answer choices distort details from the passage. Choice (A) is incorrect because the passage does not mention the use of animals, only trees. Choice (B) is incorrect because Kusama does not build fabric structures, but rather wraps fabric around trees. Choice (C) is incorrect because "bridges" are only mentioned figuratively in the passage: her installations "bridge" nature and the imagination.

39. B
Difficulty: Hard
Category: Information and Ideas
Getting to the Answer: To determine which answer choice supports the researchers' hypothesis, first paraphrase the hypothesis in your own words. Since the second sentence states that the researchers hypothesized that bees will seek opportunities to play, the correct answer will provide support for this idea. Look for details about the second test, as referenced in the question stem, as you read the rest of the passage. This test entailed bees choosing between two spaces of different colors, one of which previously had wooden balls. Since the first test associated ball rolling with play, predict that *bees choosing the color of the space that held balls would support the hypothesis* that bees seek out play. Choice **(B)** is correct.

Choice (A) is incorrect because it suggests a decreased interest in playing over time, rather than evidence that bees seek out play. Choice (C) is incorrect because it provides the opposite of the required support, indicating instead that bees skip the opportunity to play if food is involved. Choice (D) is incorrect because it suggests that the room color itself, rather than the presence of balls for play, motivated the bees' preferences.

40. A

Difficulty: Medium
Category: Information and Ideas
Getting to the Answer: The correct answer must reflect the two ideas expressed in the introduction to Harriet Jacobs's autobiography: Jacobs was comforted by her family and her family experienced insecurity. Choice **(A)** is correct because it addresses both of these ideas. Her brother made her feel that she "still had something to love," and the contrast word "But" signals that her "pleasant emotion was chilled" because he could be taken from her.

Choice (B) is incorrect because it only describes Jacobs's family and does not address the sense of insecurity. Choice (C) is incorrect because it does not reflect Jacobs herself being comforted by her family; instead, she attempts to comfort her brother. Choice (D) uses a dream or vision to suggest the instability of the family, but it is incorrect because it does not indicate Jacobs was comforted by the vision; the "strong impression" it created could have been positive or negative.

41. C

Difficulty: Hard
Category: Information and Ideas
Getting to the Answer: Use the passage to determine what "example" you are being asked to complete: the previous sentence claims that departments have both dissolved and combined over time, so the correct answer will contain examples of both from the table. Analyze the table. It shows a selection of Cabinet departments, including when they began, when/if they ended, and their purpose. Since some departments show a year that they "disbanded" and the correct answer must include an example of a department "dissolving," expect one of these instances to appear in the correct answer.

Eliminate any answer choices that fail to address both a dissolution *and* a combination, as well as any that misrepresent information from the table. Choice (A) is incorrect because it is an example of a continuation, rather than a dissolution or combination, of departments. Choice (B) can be eliminated because it does not mention departments combining. Choice **(C)** is correct; it accurately reflects the years in the table and mentions both a dissolution (the War Department in 1947) and a combination (the Navy, Army, and Air Force Departments into the Department of Defense). This combination is supported by the table, as the Defense Department's purpose supplants those of the dissolved War, Navy, Army, and Air Force Departments. Choice (D) is incorrect because it misrepresents the table; the Treasury Department did not disband in 1947.

42. D

Difficulty: Medium
Category: Information and Ideas
Getting to the Answer: The question asks for a logical suggestion made by the researchers, based upon their finding that the dogs tested were highly accurate in detecting odor samples from stressed participants. Evaluate the answer choices to determine which provides a logical suggestion. Choice (A) can be eliminated because the passage does not address how effective current PTSD service dog training programs are. Choice (B) can be eliminated because the passage does not report the results of dogs detecting odor cues from calm people, so a comparison of accuracy between detecting stressed and calm states cannot be made. Choice (C) is also incorrect, as the study did not compare dogs' ability to smell sweat versus breath odors. Choice **(D)** is correct because it is a logical suggestion based on the finding that dogs accurately detected smell-based stress cues. Further, the passage states that current dog training involves visual and auditory cues, so incorporating smell-based training, in light of the study results, would be a logical addition.

CHAPTER 19

CRAFT AND STRUCTURE

LEARNING OBJECTIVES

After completing this chapter, you will be able to:

- Use surrounding context to infer the meaning of a word
- Identify the word that best conveys the intended meaning
- Identify the main purpose of a paragraph
- Identify the purpose of a phrase or sentence within a paragraph
- Identify the structure of a text
- Identify connections between two texts

HOW MUCH DO YOU KNOW?

Directions

Try the questions that follow. When you're done, check your answers and reasoning against ours in the "Check Your Work" section. If they closely match, you may be able to move quickly through the chapter. If they do not, spend some extra time with the chapter to grow your SAT Reading and Writing skills.

1

Composed of enzymes, peptides, and proteins with many toxic properties, snake venom must be _____ , but recent medical research has demonstrated the potential therapeutic effects of snake venom as well, such as treatments for some forms of arthritis and cancer.

Which choice completes the text with the most logical and precise word or phrase?

Ⓐ feared

Ⓑ respected

Ⓒ exalted

Ⓓ disdained

2

The following text is from Emilia Pardo-Bazan's 1898 short story "First Love."

I was very fond—as soon as my aunt had gone to church to perform her evening devotions—of slipping into her bedroom and rummaging her chest of drawers, which she kept in admirable order. Those drawers were to me a museum; in them I always came across something rare or antique, which exhaled an archaic and mysterious scent, the aroma of the sandal-wood fans which perfumed her white linen.

As used in the text, what does the word "exhaled" most nearly mean?

Ⓐ breathed

Ⓑ exuded

Ⓒ inhaled

Ⓓ respired

3

The following text is from Kate Chopin's 1894 short story, "A Respectable Woman."

Mrs. Baroda was a little provoked to learn that her husband expected his friend, Gouvernail, up to spend a week or two on the plantation. ... This was a man she had heard much of but never seen. He had been her husband's college friend; was now a journalist, and in no sense a society man or "a man about town," which were, perhaps, some of the reasons she had never met him. But she had unconsciously formed an image of him in her mind. She pictured him tall, slim, cynical; with eyeglasses, and his hands in his pockets; and she did not like him. Gouvernail was slim enough, but he wasn't very tall nor very cynical; neither did he wear eyeglasses nor carry his hands in his pockets. And she rather liked him when he first presented himself. But why she liked him she could not explain satisfactorily to herself when she partly attempted to do so.

Which choice best states the function of the underlined sentence in the text as a whole?

(A) It establishes an important physical description of a character mentioned earlier.

(B) It sets up the contrast with the character description that follows.

(C) It provides the background explanation for the emotional reaction that introduces the text.

(D) It introduces the situation that leads to the conflict presented in the sentences that follow.

4

Jane Goodall, a British researcher who studies chimpanzees in their native habitats, was sharply criticized in the 1960s for ascribing human personality traits to chimpanzees. At the time, it was believed that only humans developed and employed tools. After recording chimpanzees extracting termites from their underground nests with long thin blades of grass and eating them, Goodall demonstrated that the ability to make tools and utilize them for benefit is not limited to humans. Since then, Goodall has been vindicated as other researchers continue to document many more examples of animals displaying behaviors and personality traits that had previously been believed to be specific to humans.

Which choice best states the function of the underlined sentence in the overall structure of the text?

(A) To identify a claim Goodall refutes

(B) To summarize Goodall's methodology

(C) To justify the criticism of Goodall

(D) To provide support for Goodall's results

Reading & Writing

5

Text 1

Invasive species must be rigorously attacked and eliminated. These plants and animals that humans have relocated to new environments out-compete native species and damage local ecosystems. Zebra mussels attach to hydro-power plants and obstruct the water flow. Feral pigs contaminate and destroy crops. Japanese knotweed and kudzu overwhelm landscapes.

Text 2

Not all invasive species are harmful. Honey-bees were imported into North America and have become invaluable pollinators. Earthworms transported during colonial times have dramatically improved soil fertility. Dov Sax and his colleagues have devised a series of analyses to more accurately assess the impact of invasive species. They suggest the benefit to humans, the benefit to the ecosystem, and the relationship of the new species to humans all be evaluated to more objectively measure the effects of these species.

Based on the texts, how would Sax and colleagues (Text 2) most likely characterize the conclusion presented in Text 1?

- (A) As unexpected, because the instances of humans introducing new species into environments are limited

- (B) As premature, because researchers have only recently begun to catalog damages caused by invasive species

- (C) As questionable, because it ignores the possibility that some invasive species may provide benefits that outweigh their harms

- (D) As puzzling, because it is unusual for invasive species to be the sole cause of the damage to a local ecosystem

Text 1

Earth shares many characteristics with Venus, its closest planetary neighbor. However, Earth enjoys a wet, temperate climate while it appears that all the water once present on Venus has boiled away in its fierce heat. Because the planets are otherwise so similar, experts believe that a catastrophic event caused Venus to lose its water.

Text 2

Michael Way, Richard Ernst, and Jeffery Scargle posit that volcanic activity on Earth could cause the planet to overheat and become uninhabitable. They cite the massive amounts of carbon dioxide released into the atmosphere by volcanic activity that usually cause a period of hotter temperatures followed by a return to Earth's normal, cooler temperature. But, it is possible that several large volcanic events occurring in rapid succession could raise temperatures high enough that Earth would be unable to recover.

Based on the texts, what would the author of Text 2 most likely say about the conclusion drawn in Text 1?

(A) It is questionable, since the similarities between the planets indicate the temperature of Venus should be comparable to that of Earth.

(B) It is unlikely, given the similarities between the planets and the theory of Way, Ernst, and Scargle.

(C) It is valid, despite the differences between the temperature of Venus and that of Earth.

(D) It is reasonable, given the similarities between the planets and the theory of Way, Ernst, and Scargle.

Check Your Work

1.   B
Difficulty: Medium
Category: Craft and Structure
Getting to the Answer: In this Words in Context question, read enough of the text to determine the author's view of "snake venom." The first clause mentions its "many toxic properties" followed by the contrast keyword "but." In spite of its dangers, venom has helpful, or "therapeutic," effects as well. Since both positive and negative effects are mentioned, a good prediction for what the author believes "must be" done with snake venom would be something like "handled carefully" or "used with caution." This prediction matches **(B)**, the correct answer.

Incorrect choices (A) "feared" and (D) "disdained" are too negative and ignore the positive benefits of snake venom. Choice (D) "disdained" means *scorned*. Choice (C) "exalted" means *praised* and doesn't match the neutral tone required by the text.

2.   B
Difficulty: Medium
Category: Craft and Structure
Getting to the Answer: In the passage, the narrator is searching through the aunt's drawers where something "rare and antique," or old, *gave off* or "exhaled" a "scent . . . the aroma of the sandalwood . . . ." Choice **(B)** "exuded" or *spread out* is the best match to the context and is the correct answer.

The incorrect choices are all related to the action of breathing, but in the context of the passage, the *narrator* is breathing in the fragrance. The "rare and antique" item has not "breathed" (A), "inhaled" (C), or "respired" (D).

3.   B
Difficulty: Medium
Category: Craft and Structure
Getting to the Answer: When identifying the author's reason for including a portion of the passage, consider the structure of the entire passage. Here, the text starts with a description of Mrs. Baroda as "provoked," or irritated that her husband's friend is coming to visit. The next sentence states that she has never met the man and is followed by the contrast keyword "But" that starts the next sentence. Even though she never

met Gouvernail, she had a mental picture of him. The underlined sentence is that image, followed by the strong opinion, "she did not like him." The next sentence contains the actual description of Gouvernail, which points out that Mrs. Baroda's mental image was incorrect in many aspects, leading up to her new opinion, "she rather liked him." Predict that the author provided the first description *to highlight the differences between Mrs. Baroda's imagined view of Gouvernail and the way he actually presented himself*. Choice **(B)** is correct.

Choice (A) is incorrect because the underlined sentence is Mrs. Baroda's imagined view of Gouvernail, not his physical description. Choice (C) is incorrect because although Mrs. Baroda is described as "provoked" by Gouvernail's visit, the text never connects her displeasure to the imagined description. Choice (D) is incorrect because the description in the sentence is of a character, not a situation.

4.   A
Difficulty: Medium
Category: Craft and Structure
Getting to the Answer: When identifying the author's reason for including a portion of the passage, consider the structure of the entire passage. Here, the text starts with a discussion of how Jane Goodall was once "sharply criticized." In the underlined portion, the narrator introduces what "was believed" at the time of this criticism: "only humans developed and employed tools." The next sentence describes Goodall's observations, which contradicted the prevailing belief. The final sentence discusses how Goodall's observation was the first of many that proved her to be correct and her critics incorrect. With that in mind, predict what function the underlined portion might serve: *it establishes a belief that Goodall demonstrates to be incorrect*. This best fits **(A)**.

Choice (B) is incorrect because Goodall's methodology is discussed in the sentence following the underlined sentence. Choice (C) is incorrect because the text refutes the criticism of Goodall, not justifies it. Choice (D) is incorrect because the underlined sentence refers to a belief of her critics, not Goodall's results.

5. C

Difficulty: Medium

Category: Craft and Structure

Getting to the Answer: The main idea of Text 1 is that invasive species should be eliminated. The main idea of Text 2 is that the impact of invasive species should be carefully evaluated, because not all invasive species have been harmful. Predict that Sax and colleagues would disagree with the conclusion of Text 1, because some invasive species have been beneficial. This prediction matches **(C)**, the correct answer.

Each of the incorrect choices introduces a reason for disagreement that is not mentioned in the texts. There is no mention of the frequency of introductions of new species (A), the study of the extent of damages caused by invasive species (B), or other causes for habitat damage (D).

6. D

Difficulty: Hard

Category: Craft and Structure

Getting to the Answer: The main idea of Text 1 is that, despite their similarities, the Earth and Venus have very different temperatures and amounts of water. The author concludes that experts believe this difference was caused by a catastrophic event. The main idea of Text 2 is that Way, Ernst, and Scargle believe Earth could become overheated and uninhabitable if several large volcanic events happened close together. Predict that the author of Text 2 would say that several large volcanic events happening at the same time might have been the "catastrophic event" that caused Venus to lose its water. This prediction matches **(D)**, the correct answer.

Incorrect choices (A) and (B) can be eliminated, because Text 2 provides support for the conclusion of Text 1, so the author of Text 2 would not consider that conclusion to be "questionable" or "unlikely." Incorrect choice (C) goes too far. The theory presented in Text 2 is not strong enough evidence to claim the conclusion of Text 1 is "valid."

WORDS IN CONTEXT QUESTIONS

LEARNING OBJECTIVES

After this lesson, you will be able to:

- Use surrounding context to infer the meaning of a word
- Identify the word that best conveys the intended meaning

To answer a question like this:

Hoop trundling, an activity in which a player typically uses a short stick to keep a large hoop rolling upright, was briefly considered _____ pastime in the 19th century: critics cited pedestrian and horse leg injuries as potential issues associated with children trundling down crowded city streets.

Which choice completes the text with the most logical and precise word or phrase?

A) a hazardous

B) a challenging

C) a harmless

D) an inexplicable

You need to know this:

How to Identify Words in Context Questions

Words in Context questions can be identified by the words or short phrases in their answer choices. These questions include the keyword "word," and typically appear in two types:

- *Which choice completes the text with the most logical and precise word or phrase?*
- *As used in the text, what does the word "example" most nearly mean?*

How to Predict a Word in Context

As indicated by the sample question stems above, there are two different forms of Words in Context questions: one kind will ask you to fill in a blank with a missing word or phrase, and the other kind will ask you to choose a word with the same meaning as a word from the passage.

The key to answering both types of Words in Context questions is to use the clues in the passage to make a strong prediction of the correct answer *before looking at the answer choices*. When analyzing the context of a passage:

- Determine which words in the passage indicate the meaning of the needed word.
- Consider both the immediate context around the word and, if needed, the broader context in the passage.
- Pay special attention to keywords and punctuation that indicate transitions.

Consider how to analyze the context in this short excerpt, spoken by Dr. John H. Watson from Arthur Conan Doyle's *The Adventures of Sherlock Holmes*:

> I took a good look at the man and endeavored, after the fashion of my companion, to read the indications which might be presented by his dress or appearance. I did not gain very much, however, by my inspection.

A Words in Context question might ask you: *As used in the text, what does the word "read" most nearly mean?*

To determine the meaning of the word "read," look for clues in the passage. Begin by considering the immediate context: the word "read" appears in the first sentence, and the narrator is "read[ing] the indications" of someone's dress and appearance by taking "a good look" at him. These clues suggest that the narrator is looking closely at someone to try to learn about him. This paraphrase is confirmed by the context in the rest of the passage. The contrast transition word "however" in the next sentence indicates that the narrator was not very successful in his attempt to "read" the man, as the narrator "did not gain very much" by the "inspection."

This analysis of the immediate context, the broader context, and the transition words in the passage enables you to make a prediction about the meaning of the word "read" as used in this passage: if the narrator is making an "inspection," he is trying to *observe* or *figure out* the indications about the man. Suppose the answer choices are A) memorize, B) discern, C) skim, and D) predict. The prediction matches (**B**); to *figure out* is to "discern." The other answer choices are alternate meanings for "read," but none are suggested by the context of the passage.

Incorrect answers to a Words in Context question may be words that are:

- Related to words in the passage but do not logically complete the blank
- Synonyms of the word in the passage but do not match the context of the passage

The **correct answer** to a Words in Context question will:

- Provide a word that matches the context of the passage

You need to do this:

THE METHOD FOR SAT READING AND WRITING

STEP 1 What is the question asking?

STEP 2 What do I need to look for in the passage?

STEP 3 What answer strategy is best?

- Predict and Match
- Eliminate

Step 1. What is the question asking?

Words in Context questions will make reference to "words" in the question stem. Some Words in Context questions will ask you to choose a missing word or phrase that logically completes a blank in the passage; others will ask you to choose a word that is closest in meaning to a word as it is used in the passage.

Step 2. What do I need to look for in the passage?

For both types of Words in Context questions, you need to use the context of the passage to determine the meaning of the word in question. Locate the blank or indicated word in the passage, and first consider the context of the phrase in which the blank or word appears. Most of the time, you will need to read the rest of the passage for additional clues to help you determine the meaning of the word. Pay careful attention to any transition words (such as *however*, *but*, *although*, *and*, *because*—words that signal connections between ideas), transition punctuation (such as a colon or dash—punctuation that signals a continuation between ideas), and other clue words.

Step 3. What answer strategy is best?

Using your analysis of context, make a prediction for the meaning of the word. Occasionally, you may find an exact match for your prediction among the answer choices. Even if there isn't an exact match, your prediction should make it easier to eliminate incorrect answer choices that give a different meaning for the word and identify the correct answer.

Explanation:

The question mentions a "word or phrase" and asks you to logically complete a blank, so this is a Words in Context question. The context immediately around the blank indicates that the missing word describes how a "pastime" was "briefly considered"; since this isn't enough information to make a prediction, examine the context of the entire passage for more hints about the pastime. The pastime is identified as "hoop trundling," and the last part of the sentence provides clues about it. A colon signals a connection between the blank and what "critics" said about trundling: it could cause injuries. Predict that the critics must have thought trundling could be a *dangerous* pastime; this matches **(A)**.

Choice (B) is incorrect because, although the description of hoop trundling in the passage makes it sound like a challenging activity, the blank must logically reflect the criticisms against trundling. Choice (C) is incorrect because it is the opposite of the required meaning, and, for (D), while trundling may seem like an unusual pastime, nothing in the passage indicates it is "inexplicable."

Try on Your Own

Directions

Take as much time as you need on these questions. Work carefully and methodically. There will be an opportunity for timed practice later in the book.

1

In 2014, accusations were made that a global mobile communications carrier had clipped its clients for millions of dollars. The company was adding one-time and recurring service fees to their monthly bills without the clients' knowledge or consent. An investigation by the U.S. Federal Trade Commission resulted in substantial refunds to over 40% of its clients.

As used in the text, what does the word "clipped" most nearly mean?

Ⓐ Cut

Ⓑ Overcharged

Ⓒ Busted

Ⓓ Curtailed

2

The following text is from Jules Verne's 1863 novel *Five Weeks in a Balloon*.

Notwithstanding fatigues of every description, and in all climates, Ferguson's constitution continued marvelously sound. He felt at ease in the midst of the most complete privations; in fine, he was the very type of the thoroughly accomplished explorer whose stomach expands or contracts at will; whose limbs grow longer or shorter according to the resting-place that each stage of a journey may bring; who can fall asleep at any hour of the day or awake at any hour of the night.

As used in the text, what does the word "constitution" most nearly mean?

(A) Statute

(B) Principles

(C) Health

(D) Ordinance

3

In 1990, Carl Woese proposed that bacteria and archaea were disparate domains of prokaryotes based on the analysis of their ribosomal RNA, the genetic material that plays an active role in the formation of proteins. Today, the phylogenetic branches of bacteria, archaea, and eukarya form the basis of the three-domain system of classification that is still in use.

As used in the text, what does the word "branches" most nearly mean?

(A) Boughs

(B) Offices

(C) Chapters

(D) Groupings

4

Paleontologist Jingmai O'Connor is an expert in Mesozoic bird phylogeny and the evolution of birds. By researching the development and diversification of extinct paravian biology, she hopes to discover the link between the dinosaur-bird _____.

Which choice completes the text with the most logical and precise word or phrase?

(A) disconnection

(B) transition

(C) imitation

(D) history

5

In the United States, child welfare congregate care facilities are intended to be a home-like environment that provides food, shelter, and limited mental health services to youth and young adults. Historically, they had _____ oversight, which resulted in poor outcomes for their residents. Recent reforms now require that the facilities complete a rigorous licensing process, implement evidence-based interventions, and participate in collaborative treatment plans that support the residents' transition to family-based care.

Which choice completes the text with the most logical and precise word or phrase?

- (A) insufficient
- (B) valuable
- (C) stringent
- (D) effective

6

The following text is from Leo Tolstoy's 1869 novel *War and Peace.*

Everyone brightened at the sight of this pretty young woman, so soon to become a mother, so full of life and health, and carrying her burden so lightly. Old men and dull dispirited young ones who looked at her, after being in her company and talking to her a little while, felt as if they too were becoming, like her, full of life and health. All who talked to her, and at each word saw her bright smile and the constant gleam of her white teeth, thought that they were in a specially _____ mood that day.

Which choice completes the text with the most logical and precise word or phrase?

- (A) amiable
- (B) miserable
- (C) insufferable
- (D) disagreeable

7

Built in the late 19th century as a place of worship in Shiraz, Iran, the Nasir al-Mulk Mosque is colloquially hailed as the "Pink Mosque." In the morning, the building's facade of _____ stained glass windows dazzles worshippers; the rising sunlight filters through the panes and illuminates the interior's rose-colored tiles with a stunning array of vibrant colors.

Which choice completes the text with the most logical and precise word or phrase?

- (A) translucent
- (B) darkened
- (C) murky
- (D) opaque

8

The following text is from Charlotte Brontë's 1853 novel *Villette*.

The next day, on my return from a long walk, I found, as I entered my bedroom, an unexpected change. In addition to my own French bed in its shady recess, appeared in a corner a small crib, draped with white; and in addition to my mahogany chest of drawers, I saw a tiny rosewood chest. I stood still, gazed, and considered.

As used in the text, what does the word "recess" most nearly mean?

- Ⓐ Break
- Ⓑ Cleft
- Ⓒ Alcove
- Ⓓ Intermission

PURPOSE QUESTIONS

> **LEARNING OBJECTIVES**
>
> After this lesson, you will be able to:
> - Identify the main purpose of a paragraph
> - Identify the purpose of a phrase or sentence within a paragraph
> - Identify the structure of a text

To answer a question like this:

The following excerpt is from Lucy Maud Montgomery's 1908 novel *Anne of Green Gables*.

Mrs. Rachel Lynde lived just where the Avonlea main road dipped down into a little hollow, fringed with alders and ladies' eardrops and traversed by a brook that had its source away back in the woods of the old Cuthbert place; it was reputed to be an intricate, headlong brook in its earlier course through those woods, with dark secrets of pool and cascade; but by the time it reached Lynde's Hollow it was a quiet, well-conducted little stream, <u>for not even a brook could run past Mrs. Rachel Lynde's door without due regard for decency and decorum</u>; it probably was conscious that Mrs. Rachel was sitting at her window, keeping a sharp eye on everything that passed, from brooks and children up, and that if she noticed anything odd or out of place she would never rest until she had ferreted out the whys and wherefores thereof.

Which choice best states the function of the underlined portion in the text as a whole?

A) It elaborates on the character description provided in the previous sentences.

B) It establishes a contrast between two different settings in the story.

C) It interrupts a character description with a surprising fact about an element in the setting.

D) It transitions between a description of the setting and a description of a character.

You need to know this:

How to Identify Purpose Questions

Purpose questions ask you to identify the purpose of a passage or a specified portion of a passage or to describe the overall structure of a passage. You can identify Purpose questions because they contain words such as "purpose," "function," or "structure." Note that in the following sample questions, the first two ask about the entire passage and the third asks about a portion of the passage:

- *Which choice best states the main purpose of the text?*
- *Which choice best describes the overall structure of the text?*
- *Which choice best states the function of the underlined sentence in the text as a whole?*

How to Identify Purpose and Structure

On SAT Reading and Writing, "purpose" and "function" refer to the author's *reason* for writing something, whether an entire passage or a portion of a passage. The "structure" of a passage refers to how the ideas in a passage are organized so that they can effectively achieve the author's purpose.

Identifying the Purpose of a Passage

When identifying the purpose of an entire passage, you can use many of the same strategies you used when identifying the main idea on Main Idea questions. Begin by determining the author's *main point* about the topic of the passage, which will be supported by the details in the rest of the passage. The first and last sentences may identify the author's main idea.

Where Purpose questions differ from Main Idea questions is in the form of the answer choices. Whereas the correct answer to a Main Idea question summarizes the main point of the passage, the correct answer to a Purpose question will contain a verb that describes the author's specific *reason* for writing the passage. For instance, while a passage about dogs might have the main idea of *why dogs make good pets*, its purpose might be <u>*to argue*</u> that *dogs make good pets*. The purpose of a passage should answer the question *Why did the author write this?*

Identifying the Structure of a Passage

Passages on the SAT are carefully crafted; each sentence and phrase intentionally contributes to the passage as a whole. If a question asks about a passage's structure, mentally map out the passage's organization as you read. A few examples of basic passage structures include:

- topics and examples
- hypothesis, experiment, and results
- cause and effect
- claim and support
- counter-claim and support
- descriptive elements

Consider an example literature passage structure: perhaps a passage first introduces a character, then describes that character, then gives an example of the character behaving according to the description.

Identifying the Purpose of a Portion of the Passage

On Purpose questions that ask about the function of a specified portion of a passage, again ask yourself, *Why did the author write this?* or *Why did the author include this?* To identify the purpose of a portion of a passage, first determine its overall structure, as discussed above. The placement of the specified portion will indicate its function within the passage.

For example, again consider the sample literature passage described above: a passage first introduces a character, then describes that character, then gives an example of the character behaving according to the description. If a portion appears in the example section, for instance, its function might be: *it illustrates a character's nature by providing an example*. Once again, the correct answer will include a verb that accurately reflects the function of the specified portion.

Incorrect answers to a Purpose question may:

- Include ideas from the passage but misrepresent the author's reason for writing about them
- Include verbs that misrepresent the author's reason for writing the passage or underlined portion
- Inaccurately reflect the structure of the passage

The **correct answer** to a Purpose question will:

- Correctly identify the author's reason for writing a passage, using an appropriate verb OR
- Correctly describe the structure of a passage in a way that accounts for every part of the passage and reflects the author's overall purpose OR
- Correctly identify the author's reason for including a portion of the passage, in light of the structure of the entire passage, using an appropriate verb

You need to do this:

> **THE METHOD FOR SAT READING AND WRITING**
>
> **STEP 1** What is the question asking?
>
> **STEP 2** What do I need to look for in the passage?
>
> **STEP 3** What answer strategy is best?
>
> - Predict and Match
> - Eliminate

Step 1. What is the question asking?

If the question stem contains the keyword "purpose" or "function," ask yourself, *Why did the author write/ include this?* If the question stem contains the keyword "structure," ask yourself, *How are the ideas in the passage organized?*

Step 2. What do I need to look for in the passage?

If asked about the purpose of the entire passage, identify its *main idea*, which is sometimes reflected in the first or last sentence. Then ask yourself what the author's *reason* is for writing about that main idea. Is the author making an argument? Responding to an objection? Critiquing another idea?

If asked about the structure of the entire passage, mentally map out how the ideas in the passage are organized as you read. See if you can identify one of the commonly used passage structures, such as a topic and examples or a claim and support.

If asked about the function of a portion of the passage, analyze the structure of the passage—what role does the tested portion serve in the overall organization and structure of the passage? Ask yourself, *Why did the author decide to include this portion? What would the passage be lacking if the portion were missing?*

Step 3. What answer strategy is best?

Questions that ask about purpose lend themselves to making a prediction. Paraphrase, in your own words, the author's *reason* for writing the passage or portion. Look for an answer choice that matches your prediction. If needed, eliminate any answer choices that use an inappropriate verb (for instance, one that states the passage "critiques" an idea, when the passage never explicitly analyzes that idea). Also, eliminate any answer choices that mention ideas from the passage but misrepresent the author's purpose for mentioning them.

On questions that ask about the structure of the passage, make a prediction about the passage's overall organization, if you are able. These questions often become easier to answer when you evaluate the answer choices and eliminate any that misrepresent a portion of the structure of the passage. For instance, if a passage begins by describing a character, eliminate an answer choice that begins "It describes the setting of the passage, the…." Remember that the correct answer will accurately reflect the *entire* structure of the passage.

Reading & Writing

Explanation:

This is a Purpose question (indicated by the keyword "function"); the question asks for the reason the author included a phrase. To determine how the phrase functions within the passage, read through the passage to determine its structure. The passage begins by identifying a character (Mrs. Rachel) and describing the surroundings, particularly focusing on a brook. The underlined portion states that even a brook would act with "decency" as it passed by Mrs. Rachel's house. The rest of the passage describes traits of Mrs. Rachel. So before the underlined portion, the passage discusses the setting; after the underlined portion, it discusses a character. Further, the portion ties together the ideas of the brook (the setting) and Mrs. Rachel (the character). Thus, predict that the portion provides a transition between ideas; choice **(D)** is correct.

Choice (A) can be eliminated because it misrepresents the structure of the passage: the character description is after, not before, the underlined portion. Choice (B) is incorrect because it misuses details; the passage mentions the brook in different settings, but the underlined portion does not serve the function of contrasting different settings. Choice (C) is incorrect because it uses an inappropriate verb: the underlined portion does not interrupt the flow of ideas in the passage.

Try on Your Own

Directions

Take as much time as you need on these questions. Work carefully and methodically. There will be an opportunity for timed practice later in the book.

9

The following text is from Jane Austen's 1813 novel *Pride and Prejudice*.

"Well," said Charlotte, "I wish Jane success with all my heart. And if she were married to him tomorrow, I should think she had as good a chance of happiness as if she were to be studying his character for a twelvemonth. Happiness in marriage is entirely a matter of chance. If the dispositions of the parties are ever so well known to each other, or ever so similar beforehand, it does not advance their felicity in the least. They always continue to grow sufficiently unlike afterwards to have their share of vexation; and it is better to know as little as possible of the defects of the person with whom you are to pass your life."

Which choice best states the main purpose of the text?

- (A) It establishes that Charlotte thinks Jane has a good chance at happiness even if Jane rushes into her marriage.

- (B) It lays out how Charlotte believes that being happy in your marriage is not something that can be assured.

- (C) It chronicles the events that caused Charlotte to believe what she does about marriage.

- (D) It shows that Charlotte did nothing to improve her own happiness in marriage by getting to know her partner first.

10

The following text is from H.G. Wells' 1898 novel *The War of the Worlds*.

No one gave a thought to the older worlds of space as sources of human danger, or thought of them only to dismiss the idea of life upon them as impossible or improbable. <u>It is curious to recall some of the mental habits of those departed days.</u> At most terrestrial men fancied there might be other men upon Mars, perhaps inferior to themselves and ready to welcome a missionary enterprise. Yet across the gulf of space, minds that are to our minds as ours are to those of the beasts that perish, intellects vast and cool and unsympathetic, regarded this earth with envious eyes, and slowly and surely drew their plans against us.

Which choice best states the function of the underlined portion in the text as a whole?

Ⓐ It elaborates on the danger posed by the Martians.

Ⓑ It establishes a contrast with the idea introduced in the preceding sentence.

Ⓒ It presents specific examples of what humans once thought about the Martians.

Ⓓ It sets up the specific beliefs presented in the next sentence.

11

The following text is from Etsu Inagaki Sugimoto's 1926 novel *A Daughter of the Samurai*.

Early one morning there passed an old man who had the slight droop of the left shoulder that always marks the man who once wore two swords. He went into the office building, in a moment reappearing in the cap and coat of a uniform, and taking his stand at the door, opened and closed it for the people passing in and out. It was Mr. Toda. A number of young clerks in smart European dress pushed hastily by without even a nod of thanks. It was the new foreign way assumed by so-called progressive youths. It is well for the world to advance, but I could not help thinking how, less than a generation before, the fathers of these same youths would have had to bow with their foreheads to the ground when Mr. Toda, sitting erect on his horse, galloped by. The door swung to and fro, and he stood with his head held high and on his lips the same half-humorous smile. Brave, unconquered Mr. Toda!

Which choice best states the main purpose of the text?

Ⓐ It presents a formerly high-status warrior serving as a doorman and uses it as a reason to condemn the state of the modern world.

Ⓑ It illustrates how Japanese society banned the use of its traditional clothing in favor of European dress.

Ⓒ It chronicles how a man from the former social elite continued to live a proud life in a changing society.

Ⓓ It explains how an old man was able to come to work as a doorman for a building where clerks were employed.

12

The following text is from Homer's eighth-century B.C.E. work *The Odyssey*.

As the two men were talking, a dog that had been lying asleep raised his head and pricked his ears. This was Argos, whom Ulysses had bred before setting out for Troy. In the old days he used to be taken out by the young men when they went hunting wild goats, or deer, or hares, but now that his master was gone he was lying neglected in front of the stable doors till the men should come and draw it away to manure the great close; he was full of fleas. As soon as he saw Ulysses standing there, Argos dropped his ears and wagged his tail, but he could not rise to greet master. When Ulysses saw the dog on the other side of the yard, he dashed a tear from his eyes without Eumaeus seeing it.

Which choice best states the main purpose of the text?

(A) It establishes why a random man has an emotional reaction to the sight of an old, flea-infested dog he has never met before.

(B) It shows how a dog suffering from poor treatment reacts in fear at the mere sight of its owner.

(C) It illustrates a man concealing his emotional reaction to the poor state of a dog and why he would hide a tear.

(D) It explains why a dog and its owner have the emotional responses they do upon finally seeing one another again.

13

The following text is adapted from a 1961 speech by President Dwight D. Eisenhower.

Until the latest of our world conflicts, the United States had no armaments industry. American makers of plowshares could, with time and as required, make swords as well. But we can no longer risk emergency improvisation of national defense. We have been compelled to create a permanent armaments industry of vast proportions. We recognize the imperative need for this development. Yet, we must not fail to comprehend its grave implications. Our toil, resources, and livelihood are all involved. So is the very structure of our society. In the councils of government, we must guard against the acquisition of unwarranted influence, whether sought or unsought, by the military-industrial complex.

Which choice best describes the function of the fifth sentence in the overall structure of the text?

(A) It allows President Eisenhower to present himself as a credible authority on this situation, which then allows him to make the case for disbanding the armaments industry.

(B) It establishes why President Eisenhower tolerates the existence of the military-industrial complex despite going on to describe it as a potential threat to American society.

(C) It illustrates why the creation of the military-industrial complex was an unreasonable act.

(D) It introduces the idea that America can build up its national defense over time, as new threats arise.

Parfleche, the widely adopted French name for rawhide items fashioned by the Native Americans of the Great Plains, has especially come to mean an envelope-shaped container used to store clothes, food, and personal items. These wallets or bags, depending on the size, served not only as a practical and durable storage solution but also as a decorative object of spiritual significance. Among certain tribes, notably the Cheyenne, *parfleches* were decorated by the women's painting society, whose members among the Cheyenne were known as the Selected Ones. Although similar in economic and social importance to craft guilds in medieval and Renaissance Western Europe, the painting society also had a spiritual or religious nature. The shamanistic society required application for admission and held its members to high artistic and moral standards. The society further established its importance by defining aspects of Cheyenne wealth and status.

Which choice best states the main purpose of the text?

(A) It analyzes the social connotations of a particular craft.

(B) It chronicles how a particular craft came into existence.

(C) It explains why a particular craft came to be known as the *parfleche* to the French.

(D) It disputes the spiritual significance associated with the making of the *parfleche*.

15

The following text is from Henry Wadsworth Longfellow's 1869 poem "The Building of the Ship." The poem describes the work of a master shipbuilder.

"Build me straight, O worthy Master!
Staunch and strong, a goodly vessel,
That shall laugh at all disaster,
And with wave and whirlwind wrestle!"

The merchant's word,
Delighted the Master heard;
For his heart was in his work, and the heart
Giveth grace unto every Art.

… And first with nicest skill and art,
Perfect and finished in every part,
A little model the Master wrought,
Which should be to the larger plan,
What the child is to the man,
Its counterpart in miniature;
That with a hand more swift and sure
The greater labor might be brought,
To answer to his inward thought.

Which choice best describes the overall structure of the text?

(A) It establishes the Master's satisfaction at his charge to build a ship, and then explains why he will first construct a model.

(B) It presents the words of the Master's speech about shipbuilding, and then puts forth the claim that the Master is especially skilled at his craft.

(C) It emphasizes the Master's reluctance to agree to a new shipbuilding project, and then explains why he concedes to make a miniature ship.

(D) It details the Master's entire process for shipbuilding, and then describes an alternative method used by shipbuilders in the past.

16

The following text is from P. G. Wodehouse's 1923 novel *The Inimitable Jeeves.*

When I had scrubbed my face and got my eye to stop watering for a moment, I saw that the evening's entertainment had begun to resemble one of Belfast's livelier nights. The air was thick with shrieks and fruit. The kids on the stage, with Bingo buzzing distractedly to and fro in their midst, were having the time of their lives. I suppose they realized that this couldn't go on for ever, and were making the most of their chances. The Tough Eggs had begun to pick up all the oranges that hadn't burst and were shooting them back, so that the audience got it both coming and going. In fact, take it all round, there was a certain amount of confusion; and, just as things had begun really to hot up, out went the lights again.

Which choice best states the function of the underlined sentence in the text as a whole?

(A) It characterizes the fruit-throwing as an exciting opportunity that would not likely happen again.

(B) It establishes that the people on stage are happy with the events going on around them.

(C) It provides specific details about how the people on stage were using the thrown fruit against the audience.

(D) It disputes the excitement the people on stage were feeling at their treatment by the audience.

CONNECTIONS QUESTIONS

LEARNING OBJECTIVE

After this lesson, you will be able to:

- Identify connections between two texts

To answer a question like this:

Text 1

Many neurologists in the past assumed that, since the ability is so fundamental to human social interactions, facial recognition would have been highly selected for from an evolutionary standpoint, so that all modern humans would possess a relatively similar level of facial recognition ability.

Text 2

A team of researchers led by Jeremy Wilmer conducted a facial recognition study by administering the CFMT, an evaluation tool in which participants must study and then select certain faces from a lineup. Subjects included both fraternal twins and identical twins, the latter of which share much more of their genetic material in common. Participants showed a wide variety of accuracy on the CFMT, and identical twins' results were much more strongly correlated than fraternal twins' results, suggesting a significant genetic determinant in facial recognition ability.

Based on the texts, how would Wilmer and colleagues (Text 2) most likely describe the view of the neurologists presented in Text 1?

A) It is plausible and has been further supported by the research team's results.

B) It has been unquestionably confirmed by the research team's study.

C) It probably is inaccurate, regardless of the findings of the research team.

D) It has decreased in credibility in light of their own CFMT research results.

You need to know this:

How to Identify Connections Questions

Connections questions are easy to identify: they present two different texts (labeled "Text 1" and "Text 2") and ask a question related to both texts. A Connections question will likely ask about how a viewpoint in one text would respond to a viewpoint in the other text.

How to Make Connections Between Texts

The key to correctly answering Connections questions is keeping straight all the viewpoints in the passages. Viewpoints could be those of the text authors, as well as those of anyone (such as a researcher) mentioned in the texts. Fortunately, you can use the question stem to identify which viewpoints you need to understand to correctly answer the question.

If the question asks about the view of an author, determine the main idea of the text, just as you would for a Main Idea question. Remember, you need to identify not just the topic of the passage but the author's main point about that topic. Paraphrase the author's view in your own words.

If the question asks about the view of someone mentioned in the passage, also paraphrase this view in your own words. These views might be explicitly stated in the passage (for example, "Some scientists have argued that . . ."), or they might be based upon information given in the passage (for instance, the results of a research study).

In either case, pay attention to any clue words in the passages that provide hints about viewpoints. Emphasis words such as "terrible" or "exciting" signal opinions. There may also be subtle words or phrases, such as "contrary to what she expected," that can provide strong hints about a viewpoint.

Make sure that you carefully distinguish between the view of the text author and the view of someone mentioned in a text—these viewpoints are not necessarily the same!

Incorrect answers to a Connections question may be:

- **Distortions**—Incorrect answers to Connections questions may distort the viewpoints in the passages by making unsupported connections between them.

- **Extreme**—Incorrect answers to Connections questions may make connections that are more extreme than those supported by the viewpoints in the passages. These incorrect answers might include extreme words, such as *always*, *never*, or *regardless*.

- **Opposites**—Incorrect answers to Connections questions may make connections that are opposite of the connection that is supported by the viewpoints in the passages.

The **correct answer** to a Connections question will:

- Provide a relevant and accurate connection
- Correctly reflect the viewpoints from both texts

You need to do this:

> ### THE METHOD FOR SAT READING AND WRITING
>
> **STEP 1** What is the question asking?
>
> **STEP 2** What do I need to look for in the passage?
>
> **STEP 3** What answer strategy is best?
>
> - Predict and Match
> - Eliminate

Step 1. What is the question asking?

When a question includes two texts, look at the question stem to determine which viewpoints are needed to answer the question. In your own words, briefly state what the question asks, for instance, *how the author of Text 2 would respond to the researchers in Text 1*.

Step 2. What do I need to look for in the passage?

Next, read the passages with the goal of identifying the viewpoints needed to answer the question. Use clue words to help you understand the nuances of each viewpoint, and make sure you keep different viewpoints (such as those of an author versus those of someone mentioned in the passage) straight. Paraphrase the two relevant viewpoints in your own words.

Step 3. What answer strategy is best?

Making a prediction about the connection between the viewpoints will make it easier to focus in on the one correct answer. Even if you are unable to make a specific prediction (such as, *the researchers in Text 2 would agree with the hypothesis presented in Text 1*), you may be able to make a general prediction about the connection (such as, *the views agree* or *the views disagree*).

Whether or not you make a prediction, eliminate answer choices that misrepresent the connection between the views. Eliminate any answer choices that distort the logical connection between the views; some answer choices may even provide the opposite of the correct connection. Also eliminate any answer choices that make connections that are too extreme; if the passages themselves lack extreme language, an extreme answer choice will likely be incorrect.

Once you identify the answer choice that presents a logical connection based on an accurate representation of both relevant viewpoints, select it and move on.

Explanation:

The question includes two texts, and the question asks how one group would most likely describe the view of another group, so this is a Connections question. Based on the question, the correct answer will describe how a group from Text 2 would describe the view of neurologists in Text 1; read the passages with these needed viewpoints in mind. The end of Text 1 presents the assumption of the neurologists: all humans have similar facial recognition ability. Text 2 describes a study led by Wilmer. The passage does not explicitly state the Wilmer team's viewpoint, but you can infer their view based on the results of their study. The study showed a "wide variety of accuracy" on a facial recognition test and suggested genetics plays a role in the ability.

Predict the connection. The view in Text 1 is that all humans have a similar facial recognition ability; the view in Text 2 is that a facial recognition study showed different accuracy levels of facial recognition ability. Predict that the researchers of Text 2 would think their study casts doubt on the view in Text 1. This matches **(D)**, which is correct.

Choices (A) and (B) are incorrect because they are opposite of the logical connection; the study in Text 2 casts strong doubt on the view in Text 1. Choice (C) is incorrect because making a conclusion "regardless" of the team's findings is too extreme to be supported by the passage.

Try on Your Own

Directions

Take as much time as you need on these questions. Work carefully and methodically. There will be an opportunity for timed practice later in the book.

 17

Text 1

Dinosaurs came to dominate the Earth by surviving a mass extinction event, which paleontologists believe occurred at a time of intense volcanic activity. Since volcanoes emit carbon dioxide, which traps heat close to the Earth's surface, some paleontologists argue that the planet warmed sufficiently to drive the dinosaurs' competitors to extinction.

Text 2

Paul Olsen, Sha Jingeng, and their research team propose that dinosaurs survived a mass extinction event because they were able to endure colder temperatures than other species could. The researchers note that volcanoes produce sulfur dioxide that forms atmospheric particles that reflect sunlight, thereby cooling the planet. Unlike their competing species, dinosaurs were covered in fine, hair-like filaments that retained their body heat. After their competitors died, dinosaurs were able to move into wider territories and grow to enormous sizes.

Based on the texts, how would Olsen's and Jingeng's team (Text 2) most likely respond to the paleontologists' argument in Text 1?

- (A) By agreeing that the carbon dioxide released by volcanic activity elevated the temperatures on Earth's surface and enabled the dinosaurs to survive

- (B) By declaring that the higher temperatures on Earth's surface encouraged abundant plant life that provided plentiful food for many types of dinosaurs

- (C) By questioning why the paleontologists assume that volcanic activity contributed to the dominance of dinosaurs during their time on Earth

- (D) By asserting that, while volcanic activity contributed to the dominance of dinosaurs, the effect of that activity was the cooling of the Earth's surface

18

Text 1

During the Great Recession (which began in December 2007 and ended in June 2009), the average American household lost a third of its wealth, approximately $28,000. Even though the stock market rebounded and far exceeded the highs seen prior to the Great Recession, many people who lost part of their retirement savings in the Great Recession remain hesitant about investing in the stock market. These retirement savers are investing their savings in real estate, which they believe is safer and will generate more income.

Text 2

Economists believe that stock market investments are a more stable and lucrative source of retirement wealth than real estate. They cite a London Business School study that found that over the same 90-year period, real estate investment earned the equivalent of 1.3% interest annually on the funds invested compared to the 9.8% earned by the most popular stock index.

Based on the texts, how would the economists (Text 2) most likely respond to the belief of the retirement savers (Text 1)?

(A) By arguing that investments in the stock market can be easily sold at any time, while real estate can be difficult and time consuming to sell

(B) By explaining that taxes must be paid on real estate every year, but taxes are only paid on stock when it is sold

(C) By suggesting that, although there are times when the stock market loses money, those losses are generally made up when the stock market is strong

(D) By admitting that most stock market investors are not knowledgeable about real estate and so prefer the ease of purchasing stock

Text 1

Genetic modification of plants involves inserting or deleting the genes for a particular trait. The <u>conventional wisdom</u> has long held that photosynthesis, the crucial mechanism by which plants convert sunlight into food, cannot be made more efficient. So, most crop scientists focus their genetic modifications of food crops on improving crop yields by increasing resistance to disease and pests.

Text 2

Plants must increase photosynthesis during times of shading from the sun and then slow down photosynthesis when full sunlight returns. Stephen Long and colleagues genetically modified soybean plants by inserting extra copies of a gene that is crucial to the process of regulating these changes in photosynthetic rates. Long's research had surprising results: average soybean yield increased 24.5%.

Based on the texts, how would Long and colleagues (Text 2) most likely respond to the "conventional wisdom" discussed in Text 1?

(A) By suggesting that their own findings help clarify how soybean yields can be raised through improving disease resistance

(B) By acknowledging that while it may have been true in the past, their research indicates that increasing the rate of photosynthesis of soybeans may be possible

(C) By asserting that it fails to recognize that genetic manipulation is too expensive a process for most crop producers

(D) By recommending that crop scientists research the disease and pest resistance of a variety of types of soybeans

Text 1

Many teenagers have heard that playing video games can negatively affect their learning and socialization. Studies performed in the 1990s supported this claim. Scientists evaluated the content of popular video games and the amount of time teenagers were allowed to spend playing them, connecting video game use to anger issues, obesity, and addiction. The scientists found that the only positive effect of playing video games was an improvement in manual dexterity and computer literacy.

Text 2

Researchers from the National Academy of Sciences found in a 2013 study that playing fast-paced video games can improve performance in many areas, such as attention span, spatial navigation, cognition, reasoning, and memory. Researchers tested small pools of gamers and found that those who played action-packed video games were better at tasks involving pattern discrimination and conceptualizing 3-D objects.

Based on the texts, how would the researchers from the National Academy of Sciences (Text 2) most likely respond to the scientists' findings presented in Text 1?

- (A) They would argue that the time spent playing video games per day increased dramatically in the years between the studies.

- (B) They would recommend that the scientists compare the effects of playing video games to those of playing contact sports.

- (C) They would encourage the scientists to evaluate the effects of video games on a wide variety of learning and performance skills.

- (D) They would claim that video games have different effects on people in different age groups.

Text 1

Why is difficult mental work so fatiguing? The <u>conventional wisdom</u> is that, like physical work, mental work is fueled by glucose, a simple sugar. As mental effort continues, the brain consumes available glucose, and glucose levels decline. Mental fatigue is the result of a lack of glucose to fuel cognitive processes.

Text 2

Antonius Wiehler and a team of scientists divided subjects into two groups: one was assigned difficult mental tasks and the other easier ones. While the subjects performed the tasks, the scientists examined the subjects' brains with magnetic-resonance spectroscopy to identify any biochemical differences. The data indicated that the group performing the difficult mental tasks had elevated levels of glutamate, an amino acid, compared to the group performing the easier tasks.

Based on the texts, how would Wiehler and team (Text 2) most likely respond to the "conventional wisdom" discussed in Text 1?

- (A) By suggesting that their own research indicates that glucose levels increase when performing difficult mental tasks

- (B) By arguing that it fails to recognize that elevated levels of glutamate must be solely responsible for mental fatigue

- (C) By explaining that their work indicates that the role of glutamate in mental fatigue should be a topic for further research

- (D) By asserting that it is based on an inaccurate comparison between physical and mental work

Text 1

The solar constant is a theoretical measure of the average radiation from the sun. Although the solar constant varies, the variation is quite small, less than 0.2%. NASA has studied the fluctuations in the solar cycle for over 35 years and has concluded that the solar cycle does not have a major effect on climate.

Text 2

Karin Labitzke and Harry van Loon have uncovered a link between the quasi-biennial oscillation (QBO) and the solar cycle. They gathered data from various locations over the past three solar cycles and found no correlation between the solar cycle and their data until they sorted the data into two categories: those gathered during the QBO's west phase and those gathered during its east phase. A remarkable correlation appeared: temperatures and pressures coincident with the QBO's west phase rose and fell in accordance with the solar cycle.

Based on the texts, how would Labitzke and van Loon (Text 2) most likely respond to NASA's conclusion (Text 1)?

Ⓐ It may be completely dismissed based on Libitzke and van Loon's data correlating the QBO's west phase and the solar cycle.

Ⓑ It is not compelling as a theory regardless of the correlation between the QBO's west phase and the solar cycle in Libitzke and van Loon's data.

Ⓒ It is supported by the correlation between the QBO's west phase and the solar cycle in Libitzke and van Loon's data.

Ⓓ It is plausible but needs further examination based on Libitzke and van Loon's data correlating the QBO's west phase and the solar cycle.

HOW MUCH HAVE YOU LEARNED?

Directions

For testlike practice, give yourself 7 minutes to complete this question set. When you're finished, be sure to study the explanations, even for questions you answered correctly. Full explanations can be found at the end of this chapter.

Reading & Writing

23

Snake venomics, the study of snake venom, includes protemics, the analysis of protein groups, and has yielded some promising results. Because the stability of the blood systems in the snakes' victims is disrupted by snake venom, scientists are hopeful that once the proteins are isolated, some of them may be _____ in treating blood conditions in humans.

Which choice completes the text with the most logical and precise word or phrase?

- (A) innocuous
- (B) deleterious
- (C) exacerbating
- (D) efficacious

24

The following text is from Emilia Pardo-Bazan's 1898 short story "First Love."

But one day—I remember as well as if it were today—in the corner of the top drawer, and lying on some collars of old lace, I saw something gold glittering—I put in my hand, unwittingly crumpled the lace, and drew out a portrait, an ivory miniature, about three inches long, in a frame of gold. I was struck at first sight. A sunbeam streamed through the window and fell upon the alluring form, which seemed to wish to step out of its dark background and come towards me. It was the most lovely creature, such as I had never seen except in the dreams of my adolescence.

As used in the text, what does the word "struck" most nearly mean?

- (A) hit
- (B) sounded
- (C) fascinated
- (D) hurt

25

The following text is adapted from Kate Chopin's 1894 short story, "A Respectable Woman." Gouvernail is a friend of Mrs. Baroda's husband and is visiting the couple.

Gouvernail's personality puzzled Mrs. Baroda, but she liked him. Indeed, he was a lovable, inoffensive fellow. <u>After a few days, when she could understand him no better than at first, she gave over being puzzled and remained piqued.</u> In this mood she left her husband and her guest, for the most part, alone together. Then finding that Gouvernail took no manner of exception to her action, she imposed her society upon him, accompanying him in his idle strolls to the mill and walks along the river. She persistently sought to penetrate the reserve in which he had unconsciously enveloped himself.

Which choice best states the function of the underlined sentence in the text as a whole?

(A) It establishes a contrast with the description of the character presented in the previous sentence.

(B) It elaborates on the character description presented in the previous sentence.

(C) It introduces characteristics of the setting described more fully in the following sentences.

(D) It presents an explanation for the behavior described in the following sentences.

26

In her book *The Creative Life of Animals*, Carol Gigliotti argues that many species of animals display creative behaviors if the definition of creativity is considered from their point of view. Gigliotti considers animal behavior to be creative "if animals in their own cultures can solve problems or create products of value to them." <u>She cites beaver dams; each of which is uniquely designed to accommodate the specific characteristics of the lake or river where it is constructed.</u> Her research also mentions the events of "Julie's earring," when many members of a band of chimpanzees started to wear a piece of grass behind one ear after Julie, a member of the band, began doing so. Gigliotti suggests that, since humans are only one of millions of species, we expand our thinking to consider animals' behaviors and reactions within the contexts of their own lives, and not just from our own.

Which choice best states the function of the underlined sentence in the text as a whole?

(A) It describes an exception to the definition of creativity provided earlier in the text.

(B) It offers an example of a behavior discussed earlier in the text.

(C) It establishes a claim about animal creativity that the following text defends.

(D) It suggests a point of view that should be considered when evaluating animal behavior.

Text 1

Although the dingo dogs of Australia and the wild horses and burros of North America were introduced to these environments by humans, they have become beloved symbols in the regions they occupy. Local residents work with government officials to ensure the populations of these species remain healthy.

Text 2

Dov Sax and colleagues propose that the impact of non-native species can be more objectively evaluated using an analytical framework that includes three measures: the benefits the species may provide humans, the benefits the species may provide the environment, and the relational benefits the species may provide humans. The emotional response people enjoy when they see a beautiful, free-roaming wild animal is an example of this relational benefit.

Based on the texts, how would Sax and colleagues (Text 2) most likely characterize the conclusion presented in Text 1?

(A) As helpful, because it provides an example of a relational benefit of introduced species

(B) As contradictory, because it challenges the idea that habitats should be limited to native species

(C) As puzzling, because introduced species are usually harmful to the environment they enter

(D) As supportive, because it proves their analytical framework to be correct

28

Text 1

Some cells of the human body produce proteins that can break down invading bacteria, thus improving the body's immune response. John MacMicking has identified a protein, APOL3, which breaks down foreign bacteria in a manner similar to that of a detergent acting on grease: part of the protein is attracted to water and another part is attracted to fat. APOL3 perfectly targets the fats of the invading bacteria, never those of the human body. This amazing protein may be the key to the development of a completely new class of antibiotics.

Text 2

Although MacMicking's discovery of the anti-bacterial properties of the naturally occurring protein APOL3 is promising, the current research has only demonstrated effectiveness against the bacteria *Salmonella*. It is likely that other pathologic bacteria will have other defenses against APOL3.

Based on the texts, what would the author of Text 2 most likely say about Text 1's characterization of the discovery involving APOL3?

- (A) It is overly optimistic given additional information about the research of MacMicking and his team.

- (B) It is reasonable given that MacMicking has identified the way APOL3 attacks bacteria.

- (C) It is unexpected given that MacMicking and his team's findings were generally met with enthusiasm.

- (D) It is unfairly dismissive given the progress that MacMicking and his team have reported.

REFLECT

Directions: Take a few minutes to recall what you've learned and what you've been practicing in this chapter. Consider the following questions, jot down your best answer for each one, and then compare your reflections to the expert responses that follow. Use your level of confidence to determine what to do next.

What clues can you use to help you predict the meaning of a word on a Words in Context question?

_____

_____

_____

What questions can you ask yourself to help you answer a Purpose question?

_____

_____

_____

Why is it important to consider viewpoints when answering a Connections question?

_____

_____

_____

How can predicting help you correctly answer Craft and Structure questions? What types of answer choices can you eliminate on Craft and Structure questions?

_____

_____

_____

What are the main differences you see between SAT Craft and Structure questions and those you're used to from tests in school?

_____

_____

_____

How will you approach SAT Reading and Writing questions more strategically as you continue to practice and improve on your performance? Are there any specific habits you will practice to make your approach to SAT Reading and Writing more effective and efficient?

_____

_____

_____

Expert Responses

What clues can you use to help you predict the meaning of a word on a Words in Context question?

Clues from the passage can help you predict the meaning of a word. Clues might include specific words, such as synonyms or antonyms, from the passage that indicate the meaning of the needed word, the immediate and broader context of the passage, and keywords and punctuation in the passage that indicate transitions.

What questions can you ask yourself to help you answer a Purpose question?

When answering a Purpose question about the entire passage, you can ask, "Why did the author write this?" or, "How did the author organize the ideas?" When answering a Purpose question about a portion of the passage, you can ask, "Why did the author decide to include this portion?" and "What would the passage be lacking if the portion were missing?" When answering a Purpose question about the structure of the passage, you can ask, "How are the ideas in the passage organized?"

Why is it important to consider viewpoints when answering a Connections question?

Connections questions often ask about the viewpoints in two different passages, either those of the author or of someone mentioned in the text, and how they are related to one another. To correctly answer a Connections question, you should identify the two relevant viewpoints and, when possible, predict the connection between the viewpoints.

How can predicting help you correctly answer Craft and Structure questions? What types of answer choices can you eliminate on Craft and Structure questions?

When you are able to do so, predicting the correct answer can increase your accuracy and speed by helping you focus in on the one correct answer and avoid spending time comparing the answer choices to one another. Words in Context and Purpose questions often lend themselves to predicting. When eliminating answer choices, toss out any that distort the following: the intended meaning of a word used by the author (Words in Context questions), the author's purpose for writing something (Purpose questions), or viewpoints from the passage (Connections questions).

What are the main differences you see between SAT Craft and Structure questions and those you're used to from tests in school?

Depending on the kinds of classes and teachers you've had in high school, the skills rewarded on SAT Craft and Structure questions may be more or less familiar. In general, Craft and Structure questions do not ask you to simply recall facts, but they instead require you to analyze why or how authors wrote passages, including their choices about words and passage structure, their reasons for writing, and their viewpoints.

How will you approach SAT Reading and Writing questions more strategically as you continue to practice and improve your performance? Are there any specific habits you will practice to make your approach to SAT Reading and Writing more effective and efficient?

There is no one-size-fits-all answer here. Reflect on your own habits in answering SAT Reading and Writing questions and give yourself an honest assessment of your strengths and weaknesses. Consider the strategies you've seen experts use in this chapter, and put them to work in your own practice to increase your accuracy, speed, and confidence.

Next Steps

If you answered most questions correctly in the "How Much Have You Learned?" section, and if your responses to the Reflect questions were similar to those of the SAT expert, then consider Craft and Structure questions an area of strength and move on to the next chapter. Come back to this topic periodically to prevent yourself from getting rusty.

If you don't yet feel confident, review the lessons in this chapter that you have not yet mastered. Then, try the questions you missed again. As always, be sure to review the explanations closely.

Check Your Work – Chapter 19

1.   B
Difficulty: Easy
Category: Craft and Structure
Getting to the Answer: For this Words in Context question, use the context of the passage to determine the meaning of "clipped." Consider the context of the word: clients were clipped for millions of dollars, and then many received refunds. Predict that the company had *scammed* or *overcharged*; this matches choice **(B)** and is correct.

Choices (A) and (C) are both incorrect because neither "cut" nor "busted" makes sense in this context. Eliminate (D); "curtail" means *to make less*, which is the opposite of what occurred.

2.   C
Difficulty: Medium
Category: Craft and Structure
Getting to the Answer: In this passage, Ferguson's "constitution" is "sound," despite its "fatigue," and "he felt at ease." The broad context of this passage includes mention of his stomach, limbs, and ability to sleep at "any hour." Predict that his "constitution" most nearly means his *body* or *health*. Choice **(C)** matches and is correct.

Choices (A), (B), and (D) all have similar meanings: variances of *law* or *decree*.

3.   D
Difficulty: Medium
Category: Craft and Structure
Getting to the Answer: For this Words in Context question, predict a word to replace "branches" that retains the original meaning of the sentence. That sentence says, "The . . . branches . . . form the basis of the . . . system of classification," so *categories* would be a good prediction. This matches **(D)**, the correct answer.

(A), (B), and (C) are alternative definitions of "branches" that do not make sense in the context of the passage. The text is not discussing branches of trees (boughs), branches of a business (offices), or branches of a club (chapters). Using the correct strategy will help when confronted with unfamiliar words. Having a strong prediction before you review the answer choices will aid in avoiding tempting choices or selecting the unfamiliar.

4.   B
Difficulty: Hard
Category: Craft and Structure
Getting to the Answer: For this Words in Context question, use the context of the passage to determine the best strategy for this question. There are limited context clues: Jingmai O'Connor studies prehistoric birds, including their extinction, and the evolution of birds. Eliminate (A) because "discover the link" indicates that there will be a *connection* between dinosaurs and birds. **(B)** most logically completes the passage, as "transition" means *a change from one state to another*, and is correct. Select this choice and move on to the next question.

(C) is incorrect; "imitation" suggests that there exists a *mimicry* or *false resemblance* in the link between dinosaurs and birds, which is not supported by the passage. (D) is far too broad of a term for the context given. The words "development," "evolution," and "link" all point to some sort of transition point or connection event between dinosaurs and birds that O'Connor hopes to find—not the full histories between these animals.

5.   A
Difficulty: Easy
Category: Craft and Structure
Getting to the Answer: The sentence that contains the blank refers to the oversight resulting in "poor outcomes," so predict that the adjective for the oversight was also *limited* or *ineffective*. Choice **(A)** matches that prediction; "insufficient" oversight would mean that the oversight was *not enough* to ensure the intended goals of the facility.

Choice (B), "valuable," is the opposite of what the passage implies; the oversight was not *of great use or worth*. Choice (C), "stringent," means *strict* or *severe*, which would not logically complete the sentence because the reforms are "now" rigorous and involved. (D) is also incorrect because the outcomes were not good, implying that the oversight was *ineffective*.

6. A

Difficulty: Medium

Category: Craft and Structure

Getting to the Answer: The immediate context of the missing word reveals that the correct choice will reflect how people feel (their "mood") when they look at her smile. The first sentence of the passage states that "Everyone brightened at the sight" of the young woman and that "dull dispirited young ones who looked at her…felt they were becoming…full of life and health." Predict that the correct answer will reflect the mood that the young lady was spreading to others: *cheerful* or *happy*. Choice **(A)** is correct. "Amiable" means *agreeable* or *friendly*, which is closely aligned with the prediction.

Choice (B), which means a *state of unhappiness*, is the opposite of the young lady's mood. Choices (C) and (D), which respectively mean *unable to be tolerated* and *causing discomfort*, would illogically complete the sentence: no matter what mood they were in before seeing her smile, everyone "brightened" after seeing it.

7. A

Difficulty: Hard

Category: Craft and Structure

Getting to the Answer: In this passage, the "stained glass windows" that "filter" light onto the floor of the Mosque must be *transparent* or *translucent*, both of which mean that light can pass through, to filter the passing sunlight into different "vibrant" colors. Choice **(A)** matches the prediction and is correct. Darkened glass would obscure or obstruct the sunlight and the "vibrant colors," so (B) is incorrect. Choices (C) and (D) are incorrect because glass that was "murky" or "opaque," which means *light-blocking*, would not filter vibrantly colored light onto the floor.

8. C

Difficulty: Hard

Category: Craft and Structure

Getting to the Answer: Identify the surrounding text for context clues about what "recess" could mean. The "recess" must be a *section* or *area* of her bedroom that holds her bed and is constructed in such a way that it creates shade ("shady"). Eliminate (A) because a break, meaning either a *gap* or an *interruption*, would not logically complete the sentence. Eliminate (B) because a *space made by splitting* or an *indent* would also make the sentence illogical. Choice **(C)** is correct because an

alcove is a *nook*, or *a small recessed section of a room* which most nearly means "recess." On test day, select that choice and move on; (D) is incorrect because an *intermission* is a pause or a break and would not logically complete the sentence.

9. B

Difficulty: Easy

Category: Craft and Structure

Getting to the Answer: When determining the purpose of a text, consider its structure. This passage consists of Charlotte giving an opinion about Jane's chances of finding happiness in marriage and then elaborating on Charlotte's reasoning for that opinion. Thus, the text is structured to tell us about Charlotte's philosophy. Since she believes that happiness in marriage is ultimately up to random chance, find the answer choice that best fits Charlotte's philosophy, which would be **(B)**.

Although Charlotte believes Jane has the same odds of finding happiness in marriage whether or not she rushes into things, (A) is incorrect because it misstates Charlotte's philosophy, which is that happiness is random and cannot be influenced. Choices (C) and (D) are not supported by the passage, as Charlotte is talking about marriage in the abstract rather than her own beliefs and marriage specifically.

10. D

Difficulty: Easy

Category: Craft and Structure

Getting to the Answer: When identifying the author's reason for including a portion of the passage, consider the structure of the entire passage. Here, the text starts with a discussion of how alien life was once considered "impossible or improbable." In the underlined portion, the narrator mentions how "curious" some of the ideas in "those departed days" were. However, nothing specific is listed until the next sentence, which discusses how humans might have "fancied" the existence of Martians and how they were "inferior" to humans. With that in mind, predict what function the underlined portion might serve: *it establishes that people used to have funny ideas about the Martians, without giving details*. This best fits **(D)**.

Choice (A) is incorrect because the focus is on humans and what they once believed. (B) is incorrect because no contrast exists; in fact, the underlined sentence builds upon the ideas of the previous sentence. Choice

(C) is incorrect as the text does not offer specific examples until the subsequent sentence.

11. C
Difficulty: Medium
Category: Craft and Structure
Getting to the Answer: If asked about the purpose of the entire passage, identify its main idea. This passage is focused on "Mr. Toda," describing him as a former samurai who now works as a doorman, and the final sentence describes him as "brave" and "unconquered." With that in mind, make a prediction in your own words about the main idea. It is likely something along the lines of: *Mr. Toda does not mind his new job.* Choice **(C)** best matches that prediction.

Although the passage presents a former samurai working as a doorman, it also notes that it is "well for the world to advance" rather than condemning the world for changing; (A) is incorrect. While the passage mentions how the Japanese have shifted from their traditional clothing to European dress, it nowhere mentions any ban on traditional clothing; (B) is incorrect. The passage shows the old man working as a doorman, but it does not explain how he came to work at that particular building; (D) is incorrect.

12. D
Difficulty: Medium
Category: Craft and Structure
Getting to the Answer: When faced with a difficult question, an elimination strategy can be a useful fallback. Eliminate any answer choices that mention ideas from the passage but misrepresent the author's purpose for mentioning them. Choice (A) can be eliminated because it is factually contradicted by the passage; the man and the dog already know one another. (B) is also contradicted by the passage; the dog is described as wagging its tail at the sight of its owner and trying but failing to stand to meet him. Although the passage does describe Ulysses tearing up at the sight of the dog and hiding that tear from his companion, (C) is incorrect because no reason is given for why Ulysses wishes to hide his emotions. By elimination, **(D)** is correct. Choice **(D)** could also be predicted by the passage's explanation of the history of both Ulysses and the dog Argos, in that neither has seen one another for some time.

13. B
Difficulty: Hard
Category: Craft and Structure
Getting to the Answer: If asked about the function of a portion of the passage, analyze the structure of the passage. Prior to the underlined portion, Eisenhower describes how America has changed and why it needs an armaments industry. After the underlined portion, Eisenhower explains how this new arms industry has "grave implications" for America but does *not* call for its destruction. With that in mind, predict the author's *reason* for including the underlined portion. It might be phrased something like: *an explanation for why the military-industrial complex should be allowed to exist despite its dangers.* With that prediction in mind, choice **(B)** best fits.

Choice (A) is incorrect because Eisenhower does not call for the breakup of the armaments industry, only that it be guarded against. (C) is incorrect because it is the opposite of what the passage states; Eisenhower openly states that he recognizes why the armaments industry has to exist, meaning there is a reason behind it. (D) is incorrect because the passage states the opposite; Eisenhower argues that Americans can "no longer risk emergency improvisation."

14. A
Difficulty: Easy
Category: Craft and Structure
Getting to the Answer: The author's purpose can be summarized roughly as: "This is what the *parfleche* meant to the people who made them." That summary best matches **(A)**. Choice (B) is incorrect because, while the passage discusses the *parfleche,* it does not go over their origin. Choice (C) is likewise incorrect because we do not learn why the French called the *parfleche* what they did. Choice (D) is incorrect because it is the opposite of what the passage states.

15. A
Difficulty: Medium
Category: Craft and Structure
Getting to the Answer: Since the question asks about the structure of the passage, try to determine how the ideas in the passage are organized as you read. The first stanza contains spoken words that the second stanza attributes to a merchant, who asks the Master to build a "vessel" for the "waves": a ship. The second stanza

identifies the Master as "delighted" to build the ship. The last stanza describes how the Master "first" builds a "little model" to make him more "swift and sure" at the "greater labor"; in other words, he builds a model of the ship so it will be easier to build the full-sized ship. Choice **(A)** is correct because it reflects this flow of ideas.

You can eliminate any answer choice that misrepresents any part of the passage. Choice (B) is incorrect because the speech, which contains the phrase "O worthy Master," is made by the merchant, not the Master. Choice (C) is incorrect because the Master is "Delighted" when asked to build the ship. Choice (D) is incorrect because the poem mentions only the Master's first step in shipbuilding, not the "entire process"; further, no alternative methods are mentioned.

16. A

Difficulty: Medium
Category: Craft and Structure
Getting to the Answer: Recall the common forms of incorrect answer choices, which are illustrated here. Choices (B) and (C) are incorrect because they inaccurately reflect the structure of the passage, referring to events that take place outside the underlined portion. Choice (B) is incorrect because the people on stage are established as having "the time of their lives" in the preceding sentence. With (C), the specific details about how the fruit is being thrown back at the audience are shared in the subsequent sentence. Choice (D) is incorrect because it uses a verb ("disputes") that misrepresent the author's reason for writing the passage or underlined portion. The narrator is not disputing the excitement of the people on stage but, instead, elaborating on their reason for being excited. Choice **(A)** is correct by process of elimination. It could also be selected by noting how the wording in the underlined portion matches the idea in **(A)**; the fruit-throwing "couldn't go on for ever" and the people on stage "were making the most of their chances."

17. D

Difficulty: Easy
Category: Craft and Structure
Getting to the Answer: The paleontologists in Text 1 argue that dinosaurs survived a mass extinction event because they tolerated warmer temperatures than their competitors. The team in Text 2 proposes that dinosaurs survived a mass extinction event because they

tolerated colder temperatures than their competitors. Predict that *Olsen's and Jingeng's team would disagree with paleontologists because the Earth's surface was colder, not warmer* and evaluate the choices.

Eliminate (A); this is the paleontologists' view, not the view of Olsen's and Jingeng's team. Eliminate (B) as out of scope; neither text mentions food sources as a factor in dinosaurs' dominance. Eliminate (C); Olsen's and Jingeng's team agree that volcanic activity was involved, so they likely would not challenge that aspect of the paleontologists' argument. Choice **(D)** must be, and is, correct. This choice correctly summarizes the conclusion of Olsen's and Jingeng's team's argument.

18. C

Difficulty: Easy
Category: Craft and Structure
Getting to the Answer: The belief of the retirement savers in Text 1 is that real estate is a better investment for retirement than investing in the stock market. The economists of Text 2 believe that the London Business School study determined that investments in the stock market yielded a much greater return than investments in real estate. Predict that *the economists, using the results of the study, would disagree with the retirement savers.* Eliminate (A) and (B) as out of scope. Although these choices support the economists' belief, Text 2 never mentions selling (A) or taxing (B) either investment. Choice **(C)** paraphrases the results of the London Business School and is correct. Incorrect choice (D) is out of scope; neither text discusses the real estate knowledge needed or the ease of making either investment.

19. B

Difficulty: Medium
Category: Craft and Structure
Getting to the Answer: The "conventional wisdom" in Text 1 is that photosynthesis can't be improved, so crop scientists who use genetic modification focus on improving other characteristics of food crops. Long and colleagues in Text 2 genetically modified plants using a gene that impacts photosynthesis and dramatically improved the yield of soybeans. Predict that *Long would argue that, at least in soybeans, his results indicate the rate of photosynthesis may be improved with genetic modifications.* Keeping the prediction in mind, evaluate the choices.

Eliminate (A); Long and colleagues obtained greater soybean yields using a gene that impacts photosynthesis, not disease resistance. Choice **(B)** matches the prediction and is correct. Eliminate (C) and (D) as out of scope. Neither text discusses the costs of genetic modification (C) or expanding research to different types of soybeans (D).

20. C
Difficulty: Medium
Category: Craft and Structure
Getting to the Answer: The first text claims that video games are generally harmful, offering only "improvement in manual dexterity and computer literacy." The second text outlines a number of areas in which fast-paced video games improved cognitive skills. You need the opinion of the researchers in Text 2, so predict something like, *They'd disagree* or *They'd recommend more research* and evaluate the choices.

Eliminate (A). Although this choice could be an area of disagreement, neither text mentions the amount of time the subjects played video games. Similarly, eliminate (B); neither text discusses comparing the effects of playing video games with those of any other activity. Choice **(C)** identifies the major difference between the two groups of studies and is the correct answer. Since the National Academy of Sciences researchers investigated fast-paced games and found many positive effects, they would encourage the other scientists to reexamine the effects of video games on learning and cognition. Choice (D) is out of scope. Neither text mentions comparing the effects of video games on different age groups.

21. C
Difficulty: Medium
Category: Craft and Structure
Getting to the Answer: The "conventional wisdom" is that mental fatigue is caused by the brain running out of glucose. Wiehler's data indicate that higher levels of glutamate are present in the brains of people who experience mental fatigue. Since the texts present different causes for mental fatigue, predict that *Wiehler and team would recommend that the conventional wisdom be reexamined* and evaluate the choices.

Eliminate (A); this choice misstates Wiehler's results. Wiehler and team found increased glutamate, not glucose, levels in the brains of subjects with mental

fatigue. Eliminate (B); this choice is extreme. Weihler's data provided a possible alternative explanation, but the team never claims glutamate is "solely" responsible for mental fatigue. Choice **(C)** is correct; it is likely that the team believes that the "conventional wisdom" should include some mention of glutamate. Eliminate (D); this choice is out of scope since Text 2 never discusses the comparison of physical and mental work.

22. D
Difficulty: Hard
Category: Craft and Structure
Getting to the Answer: The main idea of Text 1 is that NASA does not have any evidence of the solar cycle affecting climate. The main idea of Text 2 is that the west phase QBO data collected by Labitzke and van Loon were highly correlated with the solar cycle, while the east phase QBO data were not. Predict the correct answer will be something like, *some of their data challenges NASA's conclusion*. Choice **(D)**, the correct answer, matches this prediction. Incorrect choices (A) and (B) go too far. Some of the data of Labitzke and van Loon did not show a correlation, and thus, would support NASA's conclusion. Since the emphasis keywords "remarkable correlation" in Text 2 suggest that some of the data of Labitzke and van Loon contradicts NASA's conclusion, eliminate (C).

23. D
Difficulty: Hard
Category: Craft and Structure
Getting to the Answer: For this Words in Context question, read enough of the text until you've identified the author's view on "snake venom" and "treating blood conditions in humans." The first sentence tells you that the study of snake venom proteins have had "promising results," and the second sentence says the scientists are "hopeful." Predict a positive word like "useful" or "helpful" for the blank. This matches **(D)**, "efficacious," which means *effective* or *able to produce a result*.

Choice (A) "innocuous" means *harmless*. Although a treatment should not harm a human, the scientists are hoping for more than that, they want a positive effect. Choices (B) and (C) are opposite. "Deleterious" means *harmful*, and "exacerbating" means *making worse*. All these choices are incorrect.

24. C
Difficulty: Easy
Category: Craft and Structure
Getting to the Answer: In the passage, "struck" is used to describe the narrator's response to the portrait; later described as "alluring" and "most lovely," the portrait had a quality the narrator "had never seen." A good prediction would be that the narrator was "intrigued" or "very interested" in the portrait, which matches **(C)**, the correct answer.

The incorrect choices are alternative definitions of "struck" that do not fit the context. The narrator was not physically "hit" (A) by the portrait. A clock or alarm may have "sounded" (B) when "struck," but not the narrator. Choice (D), "hurt," is the opposite of the narrator's reaction.

25. D
Difficulty: Medium
Category: Craft and Structure
Getting to the Answer: When identifying the author's reason for including a portion of the passage, consider the structure of the entire passage. Here, the text starts with a description of the favorable relationship between Gouvernail and Mrs. Baroda. Gouvernail is described as "a lovable, inoffensive fellow" and "Mrs. Baroda … liked him," although his "personality puzzled" her. The underlined sentence mentions the result of Mrs. Baroda's confusion; after a few days, she "gave over" or gives up, trying to understand Gouvernail and "remained piqued," or irritated. If you didn't know what "piqued" means, note that you can get a good understanding from the next sentence. If a hostess leaves "her husband and her guest, for the most part, alone together," you can infer that she is unhappy with at least one of them. The next sentence describes Gouvernail's response (or lack of it); he "took no manner of exception to her action," so Mrs. Baroda "impose[s] her society upon him" and tries "to penetrate [his] reserve" or tries to get him to talk with her. The underlined sentence introduced Mrs. Baroda's feelings toward Gouvernail that motivated her actions in the remainder of the text. Using this, or a similar summary, matches **(D)**, the correct answer.

Choices (A) and (B) are incorrect because the previous sentence describes Gouvernail while the underlined sentence describes Mrs. Baroda. So, a description of Mrs. Baroda cannot contrast (A) or elaborate on

(B) a description of Gouvernail. Choice (C) is incorrect because the underlined sentence describes Mrs. Baroda, a character, not a setting.

26. B
Difficulty: Medium
Category: Craft and Structure
Getting to the Answer: When identifying the author's reason for including a portion of the passage, consider the structure of the entire passage. Here, the first two sentences of the text provide Gigliotti's claim: animals can be viewed as creative when they "solve problems or create products of value to them." The underlined sentence follows with an example of a species that does so. Beavers must build a dam customized "to accommodate the specific characteristics of the lake or river where it is constructed." The next sentence provides an example of another species, chimpanzees, that engaged in the creative behavior described in the episode of "Julie's earring." The closing sentence sums up Gigliotti's argument: humans should think about animals "within the contexts of their own lives, and not just from our own." With that in mind, predict what function the underlined portion might serve: *it provides an example of Gigliotti's definition of animal creativity*. This best fits **(B)**.

Incorrect choice (A) is opposite; the underlined sentence is an example of, not an exception to, the definition of animal creativity provided in the previous sentence. Choice (C) is incorrect because the underlined sentence is an example, not a claim. The last sentence, not the underlined one, suggests the point of view to use when viewing animal behavior, making (D) also incorrect.

27. A
Difficulty: Medium
Category: Craft and Structure
Getting to the Answer: The main idea of Text 1 is that three introduced species have become symbols of the areas where they were introduced. The main idea of Text 2 is that Sax and colleagues have a three-part analytical framework for evaluating the impact of non-native species, and that one of these parts is an assessment of the relational benefit the introduced species may provide humans. Predict that Sax and colleagues would consider the introduced species in Text 1 as examples of their idea of a relational benefit. This prediction matches **(A)**, the correct answer.

Choices (B) and (C) are incorrect because they introduce ideas not mentioned in the texts. Sax and colleagues never state that habitats should be limited to native species (B) or that introduced species are usually harmful to their new environments (C). Choice (D) goes too far. Although the species mentioned in Text 1 are examples that fit the framework of Sax and colleagues, these examples alone cannot prove that framework is always valid.

28. A

Difficulty: Medium

Category: Craft and Structure

Getting to the Answer: The main idea of Text 1 is that the APOL3 protein may lead to a new type of antibiotic. The main idea of Text 2 is that APOL3 may not be as effective against other bacteria as it against *Salmonella*. Predict that the author of Text 2 would say that *more testing would be needed to justify the excitement* expressed in Text 1. This prediction matches **(A)**, the correct answer.

Choice (B) is incorrect because, although the author of Text 2 concedes the potential of APOL3, the main idea of Text 2 is that APOL3 may not work against other bacteria. The author of Text 2 would not yet call APOL3 an "amazing protein" that is "key to the development of a completely new class of antibiotics." Choice (C) is incorrect because the author of Text 2 does not base criticism of APOL3 on the reception the discovery generated. Choice (D) is incorrect because Text 1 is not dismissive, but enthusiastic, about the potential of APOL3.

HOW MUCH HAVE YOU LEARNED: READING SKILLS

Directions

This "How Much Have You Learned" section will allow you to measure your growth and confidence in "Reading Skills."

For testlike practice, give yourself 12 minutes for this question set. Be sure to use the Method for SAT Reading and Writing Questions. When you're done, check your answers and read through the explanations, even for the questions you answered correctly. Don't forget to celebrate your progress!

1

The following text is from Hilaire Belloc's 1926 comic novel *The Emerald of Catherine the Great*.

The next year William Bones let his house in Boston and abruptly transported himself and his family to the metropolis. His neighbors were interested to discover that before abandoning them he had purchased not a little property in the town and had even appointed a substantial agent to deal with his rentals. He was clearly an advancing man and their respect for him grew profound when they learned what figure he now cut in a world above their own. In London he was found entertaining largely and standing upon an equal footing with merchants of repute, though not perhaps as yet of the first fortune. Meanwhile he had preferred the name of Bone, in the singular, to that of his earlier life, conceiving it to be more consonant with his present position and his residence in Cornhill and his interests in the banking world.

As used in the text, what does the word "fortune" most nearly mean?

- (A) Luck
- (B) Class
- (C) Treasure
- (D) Destiny

2

The following text is from John Galsworthy's 1922 novel *The Forsyte Saga*.

On June 15, eighteen eighty-six, about four of the afternoon … was the occasion of an "at home" to celebrate the engagement of Miss June Forsyte, old Jolyon's granddaughter, to Mr. Philip Bosinney. In the bravery of light gloves, buff waistcoats, feathers and frocks, the family were present, even Aunt Ann, who now but seldom left the corner of her brother Timothy's green drawing-room, where, under the aegis of a plume of dyed pampas grass in a light blue vase, she sat all day reading and knitting, surrounded by the effigies of three generations of Forsytes. Even Aunt Ann was there; her inflexible back, and the dignity of her calm old face personifying the rigid possessiveness of the family idea.

When a Forsyte was engaged, married, or born, the Forsytes were present.

Which choice best states the function of the underlined sentence in the text as a whole?

- (A) It provides a contrast to the description of the character made earlier in the passage.

- (B) It sets up the character description in the following sentence.

- (C) It establishes a contrast with the description of the setting made earlier in the passage.

- (D) It continues an emphasis of a previous description of the setting that is repeated again later in the text.

3

The development of quantum computing promises computers fast enough to efficiently tackle computations that overwhelm computers today. But if quantum computing is used to solve problems that are impossible to solve with classical computing, is there a way to "check" the results? As a graduate student, Urmila Mahadev devoted over a decade to developing an interactive protocol that can be used as a verification process for quantum computing. Given current limitations, Mahadev's protocol remains purely theoretical, but rapid progress in quantum computing combined with further refinement of the protocol will likely result in real-world implementation within the next decade or two.

According to the text, what is one challenge facing the implementation of quantum computing?

- (A) There is no way to determine that the calculations of a quantum computer are correct if a classical computer cannot solve the same problem.

- (B) Mahadev's protocol has proven to be too expensive and time-consuming to be useful in checking quantum computing calculations.

- (C) Although promising when first presented, Mahadev's protocol has been shown to be incorrect.

- (D) Quantum computers can only be used on large computation problems that are impossible for classical computers.

Reading & Writing

4

Hydroponics is a method of growing fruits and vegetables in water-based nutrient solutions rather than in soil. Because they don't require soil, most hydroponic plants are grown indoors under controlled conditions and are not susceptible to damage from drought, floods, unusual temperatures, or other environmental hazards. However, indoor hydroponic systems must have a reliable electricity supply to maintain consistent lighting and to run the pumps that circulate the nutrient solutions. This suggests that most hydroponic plants _____

Which choice most logically completes the text?

(A) may suffer in areas with dense populations and heavy vehicle traffic.

(B) can be successfully raised without the use of any insecticides.

(C) might not thrive in areas with frequent interruptions in electrical power.

(D) may be completely destroyed if pests enter the enclosure.

5

Doctors have been perplexed when malnourished children, after receiving food supplements from aid agencies and gaining weight, lose weight when they return to their traditional diets, even though these diets provide sufficient calories. Dr. Jeffrey Gordon and Dr. Tahmeed Ahmed believe bacteria found in the human gut, called the microbiome, are responsible. They divided malnourished children into two groups. The first group received an experimental food supplement that was designed to introduce new types of bacteria into the children's guts. The second group received the usual food supplement currently provided by aid agencies. Although the experimental supplement provided fewer calories, the children in the experimental group not only gained weight, but, unlike the children in the second group, continued to improve after the study ended and they returned to their usual diets.

Which choice best describes the function of the second sentence in the overall structure of the text?

(A) It describes the hypothesis that the doctors' research later indicated was incorrect.

(B) It presents the central finding of the doctors' study.

(C) It states the hypothesis confirmed by the doctors' research.

(D) It illustrates a flaw in the doctors' method that is addressed and corrected.

6

Text 1

Japanese light-truck manufacturers are working to standardize the battery and the battery attachments in their electric vehicles so that drained batteries can be quickly exchanged for charged ones at drive-through kiosks. Since the drained batteries could be recharged during times when there is less demand on the electric grid, this system affords greater overall environmental benefits.

Text 2

American car manufacturers use electric vehicle batteries that are built into the design of each type of vehicle and are not easily removed. The costs of standardizing batteries across manufacturers would add substantial costs to the purchase price of electric vehicles. In addition, their electric vehicles could use timers to delay the vehicle's connection to the electric grid until a time of lower demand.

Based on the texts, how would the American car manufacturers (Text 2) most likely respond to the view of the Japanese light-truck manufacturers presented in Text 1?

(A) They would agree that electric vehicles will be the preferred type of vehicle in the immediate future.

(B) They would challenge the idea that it is beneficial to recharge electric vehicle batteries during times of lower demand on the electric grid.

(C) They would argue that the use of a timer offers the same savings, without costly changes to vehicle design.

(D) They would claim that customers are indifferent to how their car batteries are recharged.

7

The following text is from A. E. Housman's 1919 poem, "A Shropshire Lad."

Oh, when I was in love with you,
Then I was clean and brave,
And miles around the wonder grew
How well did I behave.
And now the fancy passes by,
And nothing will remain,
And miles around they'll say that I
Am quite myself again.

What is the main idea of the text?

(A) The narrator was concerned with the reactions of the neighbors.

(B) The narrator did not want to reform the narrator's behavior after falling in love.

(C) The narrator disregarded the comments of the neighbors.

(D) When the narrator was in love, the narrator seemed like a different person.

8

The Oort cloud is a cloud of debris leftover from the formation of the solar system and is the source of comets that are detectable from Earth. Two types of comets enter Earth's atmosphere and are visible as fireballs as they burn up. Icy comets have visible tails of water vapor and dust, while rocky comets do not. Icy comets burn up about 75 kilometers from the Earth's surface, while rocky comets burn up much closer to the Earth's surface. Dr. Denis Vida argues that the Oort cloud is composed of approximately 6% rocky material.

Which finding, if true, would most directly support Dr. Vida's claim?

(A) Icy comets are composed of 94% water and 6% rock.

(B) The tails of icy comets make them 94% more likely to be detected from Earth, compared to rocky comets.

(C) The number of sightings of fireballs at about 45 kilometers from the Earth's surface compared to the number of sightings at about 75 kilometers from the Earth's surface is about 6%.

(D) The number of sightings of fireballs at about 75 kilometers from the Earth's surface compared to the number of sightings at about 45 kilometers from the Earth's surface is about 6%.

9

Although the stereotype of stodgy halls of research _____, today's libraries are vibrant sources for a wide variety of community-based events. As many communities trim social services, libraries become welcome avenues for employment information, children's activities, and leisure time activities.

Which choice completes the text with the most logical and precise word or phrase?

(A) may prevail

(B) holds true

(C) is critical

(D) was lost

10

		U.S. Exports to—	U.S. Imports from—
Germany	1914	$344,794,276	$189,919,136
	1915	$28,863,354	$91,372,710
Britain	1914	$594,271,863	$293,661,304
	1915	$911,794,954	$256,351,675

Prior to 1917, the United States was officially a neutral party in World War I, which started in late 1914. The U.S. claimed a right to freely trade with participants on both sides of the conflict. The German navy had little ability to stop American goods from reaching ports. The British navy, however, severely limited U.S. exports to Germany, even blocking goods such as cloth on the grounds that it could be used for German military uniforms. German public opinion was inflamed by the perception that America was acting dishonestly, proclaiming its neutrality while strengthening the British war effort against them. The origin of this charge can be seen most clearly by comparing U.S. _____.

Which choice most effectively uses data from the table to complete the statement?

Ⓐ exports to Germany in 1914 with U.S. exports to Germany in 1915.

Ⓑ imports from Britain in 1914 with U.S. imports from Britain in 1915.

Ⓒ imports from Germany in 1915 with U.S. imports from Britain in 1915.

Ⓓ exports to Britain from 1914 to 1915 with U.S. exports to Germany from 1914 to 1915.

Check Your Work – How Much Have You Learned: Reading Skills

1. B
Difficulty: Hard
Category: Craft and Structure
Getting to the Answer: The opening of the text describes William Bones as "clearly an advancing man" who now lives "in a world above their own," so Bones is prospering as compared to his former neighbors. The next sentence, which begins "In London," is the one of interest, where the word "fortune" appears. In this sentence Bones is compared to "other merchants of repute" with the contrast keyword "though," so he is of lesser "fortune" than the other merchants. A good prediction could be anything like *wealth* or *finances*, but the only choice with the same connotation, (C) "Treasure," does not fit the context. Eliminate (C). On more challenging questions, your first prediction may need to be refined. Since Bones is being compared to the other merchants, but doesn't quite measure up, another good prediction in context is that he is not of the same *level*. This matches **(B)** "Class," the correct answer.

The remaining incorrect choices, (A) and (D), are alternative definitions of "fortune" that do not fit the context. The comparison is drawn on Bones's position within the community as compared to the other merchants, not on the circumstances that brought him there.

2. D
Difficulty: Hard
Category: Craft and Structure
Getting to the Answer: The question asks for "the function of the underlined sentence," so this is a Purpose question. Read the entire text, because the correct answer to a Purpose question will hinge on the author's reason for writing the text. Often, that reason is revealed towards the end of the passage. Here, the first sentence describes an engagement party where "the family were present, even Aunt Ann." Then, a lengthy description of why Aunt Ann's presence is unusual follows—she seldom leaves home. The beginning of the underlined sentence echoes the emphasis keyword "even"; this repetition highlights how unusual it is for Aunt Ann to be in attendance. The final sentence explains why, "When a Forsyte was engaged, married, or born, the Forsytes were present." A good prediction is something like, *the author used the underlined sentence to describe a feature of the gathering.* This prediction matches **(D)**, the correct answer.

Choices (A) and (B) are incorrect because these focus on Aunt Ann, the character, but the author's intention is to use the description of Aunt Ann to explain why the gathering is important. Choice (C) is incorrect because the underlined sentence continues, not contrasts with, the description of Aunt Ann in the previous sentence.

3. A
Difficulty: Medium
Category: Information and Ideas
Getting to the Answer: Get every clue from the question before starting to read the text. The question requires "one challenge facing the implementation of quantum computing," so read actively, looking for that challenge. The first sentence introduces quantum computing. The second sentence starts with the contrast keyword "but," so expect that some issue with quantum computing is coming up. Indeed, the next phrase outlines the problem: how can quantum computing results be checked if classical computers can't make the same calculations? Reviewing the choices against this information shows **(A)** is the correct answer.

On test day, there's no reason to read any further—there is always only one correct answer. For the record, the rest of the text outlines the research of Urmila Mahadev and says that research holds promise for eventual use to verify quantum computing results. Incorrect choice (B) is not mentioned in the text; there is no discussion of the cost of Mahadev's protocol. Choice (C) contradicts the last sentence of the passage, where Mahadev's protocol is mentioned as part of the "real-world implementation within the next decade or two." Choice (D) goes too far. The text says that quantum computing promises computers fast enough to "efficiently tackle computations that overwhelm computers today," but neither identifies this as an obstacle nor states that this is the "only" use of quantum computers.

4. C

Difficulty: Easy

Category: Information and Ideas

Getting to the Answer: The correct answer to a "logically completes the text" Inference question will refer to ideas mentioned in the text and will not introduce a new concept. Inventory the ideas in the text, then work through the choices by elimination. Here, the first sentence provides the definition of hydroponics, the second describes why hydroponic plants are safe from environmental hazards, and the third mentions why a reliable source of electricity is needed. Eliminate (A) because "dense populations and heavy vehicle traffic" are not mentioned in the text. Although (B) may seem to be true, eliminate this choice since "insecticides" are never discussed. The correct answer is **(C)**. If "most hydroponic plants are grown indoors" and "indoor hydroponic systems must have a reliable electricity supply," then it is likely that "most hydroponic plants might not thrive in areas with frequent interruptions in electrical power." On test day, mark **(C)** confidently and move to the next question. For the record, (D) is incorrect because the danger of "pests" is never mentioned in the text.

5. C

Difficulty: Medium

Category: Craft and Structure

Getting to the Answer: The question asks for "the function of the second sentence," so it is a Purpose question. As you read, describe the *type* of information presented and evaluate how that information is contributing to the author's main idea. The first sentence raises a question: Why do malnourished children who responded well to food supplements later lose weight, even though their diets have enough calories? The keyword "believe" in the second sentence indicates that this sentence presents the doctors' hypothesis. The second sentence is the subject of the question, so eliminate (B) and (D) because these choices do not describe a hypothesis. The third, fourth, and fifth sentences describe the doctors' experiment. Read these quickly because the outcome of the experiment is the key difference between the two remaining choices. The comparison in the final sentence indicates that the experimental group, who received the food supplement that "was designed to introduce new types of bacteria into the children's guts,"

outperformed the group who received the usual supplement. So the hypothesis that "bacteria found in the human gut, called the microbiome, are responsible" was confirmed. Eliminate (A), as the hypothesis was correct. Choice **(C)** is the correct answer.

6. C

Difficulty: Medium

Category: Craft and Structure

Getting to the Answer: Since the question focuses on the view of the American car manufacturers in Text 2, read Text 1 quickly, and focus on the concepts mentioned in Text 2. Text 1 provides an advantage of battery-exchange programs: the batteries can be recharged during times of low electricity demand. Text 2 does not argue against this idea, but points out that American car manufacturers can get the same result in a different way and at a lower cost. This matches **(C)**, the correct answer.

For the incorrect choices, (A) and (D) are not mentioned in the text; there is no discussion of customer preferences for vehicles (A) or charging methods (D). Choice (B) contradicts the text; since the American manufacturers offer an option to recharge batteries during times of lower demand, their view supports, not challenges, this idea.

7. D

Difficulty: Medium

Category: Information and Ideas

Getting to the Answer: The first two lines of the poem say that after falling in love, the narrator was "clean and brave." The next two lines state that because this behavior was unusual, "the wonder grew" at the narrator's behavior. In the next two lines "the fancy passes," meaning the narrator is no longer in love, and "nothing will remain" of the former good behavior. Those who know the narrator for "miles around" will say the narrator's behavior has returned to normal since the narrator is "quite myself again." This summary matches **(D)**, the correct answer.

For the incorrect choices, the narrator describes the neighbor's reactions but never comments on them. Eliminate (A) and (C). The first two lines contradict (B); the narrator's behavior changed because the narrator was in love.

8.   C

Difficulty: Medium

Category: Information and Ideas

Getting to the Answer: Since the question requires "support" of "Dr. Vida's claim," start by quickly scanning the text to identify that claim. The opinion keyword "argues" identifies the last sentence as Dr. Vida's claim: the Oort cloud contains about 6% rocky material. Now, start reading the text from the beginning, summarizing the ideas in your own words. The first sentence says that all comets seen from Earth come from the Oort cloud. The second and third sentences contain characteristics of the two types of comets. It may be helpful to jot down these ideas. Icy comets have tails and burn up about 75 kilometers from the Earth's surface; rocky comets do not have tails and burn up about 45 kilometers from the Earth's surface. Use this summary to evaluate the choices; the correct answer will be based on only these ideas. Eliminate (A); the text never connects the composition of icy comets to the composition of the Oort cloud. Eliminate (B); the text does not connect the detection rate of comets to the composition of the Oort cloud. **(C)** is correct; "fireballs at about 45 kilometers from the Earth's surface" are rocky comets burning up. The fireballs "at about 75 kilometers" are icy comets burning up. If all comets come from the Oort cloud, then the 6% of comets seen from Earth that are "rocky" make it more likely that the Oort cloud is composed of rock at about the same percentage. On test day, mark **(C)** and move to the next question, but for the record, incorrect choice (D) is backward, stating that the *icy* comets are 6% of the comets observed from Earth.

9.   A

Difficulty: Easy

Category: Craft and Structure

Getting to the Answer: Since it starts with the contrast keyword "Although," the phrase ending in the blank is establishing a contrast with libraries that "are vibrant sources for a wide variety of community-based events." A good prediction is any word or phrase that means *used to be true* or *was believed*. Although not a precise match to the prediction, **(A)** coveys the same idea and is the correct answer.

The incorrect choices all change the meaning of the text. (B) contradicts the rest of the passage; "vibrant sources" are not "stodgy halls." Choice (C) says the stereotype *is important*, but the text does not discuss

that concept. Choice (D) says the stereotype "was lost," but again, there is no mention of that loss in the passage.

10.   D

Difficulty: Hard

Category: Information and Ideas

Getting to the Answer: The final sentence states that the "origin of this charge" is made clear by "comparing" something about U.S. exports or imports, as recorded in the table. Yet, what does "this charge" refer to? In the next to last sentence, Germans are described as seeing the U.S. as "acting dishonestly" by claiming "neutrality while strengthening the British war effort." Neutrality is defined at the start of the passage as the "right to freely trade with participants on both sides of the conflict." Thus, it can be deduced that "this charge" involves some sort of trade imbalance that benefits Britain. Reviewing the data table, predict that *the roughly 300-million-dollar increase in U.S. exports to Britain between 1914 and 1915 would, in conjunction with the more than 300 million decrease in US exports to Germany over the same time, support the German claim.* This best fits **(D)**, which is correct.

Choice (A) is incorrect because it does not support the claim that the U.S. was *strengthening* the British war effort; a reduction in U.S. imports to Germany between 1914 and 1915 merely weakens Germany rather than strengthening Britain. (B) is incorrect because U.S. imports from Britain only modestly declined between 1914 and 1915, which does not support the claim. (C) likewise does not support the claim, because it does not show how imports from Europe to the United States strengthen Britain.

HOW MUCH DO YOU KNOW: WRITING SKILLS

Directions

Try the questions that follow, using the Method for SAT Reading and Writing Questions. When you're done, check your answers and read through the explanations in the "Check Your Work" section.

There will be an opportunity for timed practice at the end of the Writing Skills unit.

Reading & Writing

1

Because French collaborators assisted in the development of American Sign Language (ASL), French Sign Language shares almost 60% of its signs with ASL. However, British Sign Language and American Sign Language, though based on a shared spoken language, _____ not mutually intelligible.

Which choice completes the text so that it conforms to the conventions of Standard English?

- (A) is
- (B) are
- (C) was
- (D) were

2

The *Chicago Manual of Style* is a guide for writing that is used by many U.S. publishers and within several academic _____ its first publication by the University of Chicago Press in 1906, the manual has undergone 17 editions and added nearly 1,000 pages to its length, as it continues to specify its style and citation guidelines and to accommodate for changes in English usage over time.

Which choice completes the text so that it conforms to the conventions of Standard English?

- (A) fields, since
- (B) fields since
- (C) fields. Since
- (D) fields and since

3

Ruby-throated hummingbirds have several unique adaptations that make it possible for them to migrate over 1,500 miles between the northeastern United States and Mexico. _____ the hummingbirds use their small size to their advantage by riding along on tail-winds to conserve energy. The hummingbirds also migrate individually, making the already tiny birds even less likely to be spotted by predators.

Which choice completes the text with the most logical transition?

- (A) Next,
- (B) For example,
- (C) Furthermore,
- (D) Hence,

4

While researching a topic, a student has taken the following notes:

- Historian Robert Darnton studies historical texts by analyzing the meanings the text likely held for its writers within their historical context.

- He analyzed and compared a variety of traditional French, German, Italian, and English fairy tales.

- He argues that in the French version of "The Basket of Figs" tale, the hero succeeds because he devises several cunning schemes and outwits those who oppose him.

- He argues that in the German version of "The Basket of Figs" tale, the hero succeeds because he is aided by a variety of magical creatures and objects.

- He suggests that "The Basket of Figs" tales reflect generalizations about their corresponding cultures' worldviews on how to be successful.

The student wants to emphasize a similarity in Darnton's analysis of the two tales. Which choice most effectively uses relevant information from the notes to accomplish this goal?

(A) Darnton argues that the hero in the French version of "The Basket of Figs" succeeds through clever schemes and by using his wits; he argues, however, that the hero in the German version succeeds when assisted by magical creatures and objects.

(B) Darnton studies fairy tales from countries throughout Europe to analyze their meanings, particularly their generalizations about worldviews on success.

(C) Though he analyzes fairy tales from France, Germany, Italy, and England, Darnton specifically studied the French and German versions of "The Basket of Figs."

(D) Darnton suggests that the French and the German versions of "The Basket of Figs" both reflect generalizations about worldviews on success: the French hero succeeds through cleverness, and the German hero succeeds through magical assistance.

5

The first Boston Marathon, held in 1897, was a distance of 24.8 miles, rather than the 26.2 miles that is now the standard marathon length. Most participants in the Boston Marathon today must earn _____ spots in the race by recording a qualifying completion time in another approved marathon.

Which choice completes the text so that it conforms to the conventions of Standard English?

(A) their

(B) they're

(C) its

(D) it's

6

To ensure survival, most human labor in pre-agrarian societies had to be devoted to food acquisition. Over time, the development of large-scale agriculture and irrigation systems during the Neolithic Revolution created food and labor surpluses. _____ this era saw a marked increase in labor specialization, and individuals began to work in areas such as education, skilled crafts, and government.

Which choice completes the text with the most logical transition?

(A) For example,

(B) In other words,

(C) Still,

(D) Consequently,

7

In an effort to understand the characteristics of historical architecture, fine arts _____ use period-appropriate tools to actually build such structures today; these techniques are used in the growing field of experimental archaeology. For instance, the professors recently led their students in a reconstruction of a ceiling truss that had been damaged in the 2019 fire at the medieval Notre Dame Cathedral.

Which choice completes the text so that it conforms to the conventions of Standard English?

(A) professors Rick and Laura Brown

(B) professors, Rick and Laura Brown

(C) professors Rick and Laura Brown,

(D) professors, Rick and Laura Brown,

8

While researching a topic, a student has taken the following notes:

- Scientists did not understand how bacteria are able to coil single proteins into propellers that enable the bacteria to move.
- Researchers from the University of Virginia School of Medicine used a technique called cryo-electron microscopy (cryo-EM) to magnify bacteria propellers more than was possible with microscopes.
- Using cryo-EM allowed the researchers to view the atoms of the propellers.
- The researchers discovered that the atoms of the propeller protein can take on various different structures.
- The researchers discovered that a certain combination of propeller protein structures enables the protein to coil.

The student wants to emphasize the aim of the research study. Which choice most effectively uses relevant information from the notes to accomplish this goal?

- (A) Researchers used cryo-EM to highly magnify the different structures of protein propeller atoms in bacteria.

- (B) Researchers wanted to view bacteria propellers at an atomic level to determine how the propellers are able to coil.

- (C) Researchers used cryo-EM to determine that bacteria propellers have certain combinations of protein structures that allow them to coil.

- (D) Researchers wanted to demonstrate that cryo-EM is a more effective magnifying tool than microscopes by viewing bacteria propellers.

9

Nanoengineers Joseph Wang and Liang-fang Zhang developed microrobots that can deliver antibiotics directly to the lungs of pneumonia-infected mice. In their study, all of the mice treated through the microrobots were cured of their pneumonia after one small dose. _____ intravenous (IV) injections required an antibiotic dose that was thousands of times larger than that of the microrobot dose in order to be effective in curing mice in the study.

Which choice completes the text with the most logical transition?

- (A) Likewise,

- (B) On the other hand,

- (C) Hence,

- (D) Regardless,

10

Foreshadowing the ongoing tension between human work and technology since its theatrical release in 1957, _____ feels professionally threatened by the introduction of a prototype computer into her library workspace.

Which choice completes the text so that it conforms to the conventions of Standard English?

(A) the character Ms. Watson, a research librarian featured in the movie *Desk Set*,

(B) there was a research librarian, Ms. Watson, a character featured in the movie *Desk Set*, who

(C) the research librarian character who is featured in the movie *Desk Set*, Ms. Watson,

(D) the movie *Desk Set* features the character Ms. Watson, a research librarian who

Reading & Writing

Check Your Work – How Much Do You Know: Writing Skills

1.   B

Difficulty: Medium

Category: Standard English Conventions

Getting to the Answer: A quick glance at the choices tells you this question is testing verb agreement, so identify the subject of the verb and the surrounding tense. Starting with the tense may be easier, since the present tense verb "shares" appears in the previous sentence. Eliminate the past tense verbs in (C) and (D). Although the blank follows "language," the commas marking off "though based . . . language" indicate that this is a modifying phrase, which cannot be the subject of a verb. (A) is incorrect. The word "and" makes a plural subject; "British Sign Language and American Sign Language . . . are not mutually intelligible." Answer choice **(B)** is correct.

2.   C

Difficulty: Medium

Category: Standard English Conventions

Getting to the Answer: The answer choices indicate that this question is testing how to combine (or separate) sentence portions, so determine whether the ideas before and after the blank are complete thoughts. The portion before the blank ("The *Chicago Manual of Style* is a guide . . .") is an independent clause that could stand on its own as a sentence. The portion "since . . . in 1906" is a dependent clause that cannot stand on its own, but it is already connected to the independent clause that follows ("the manual has undergone . . . ."). Thus, choice **(C)** is correct because it appropriately creates two sentences by using a period. Choices (A) and (B) are incorrect because they are not appropriate ways to combine independent clauses ("The *Chicago Manual of Style* is a guide . . ." and "the manual has undergone . . . ."), so they result in run-on sentences. Choice (D) is incorrect because a comma would be required to use a FANBOYS conjunction to join the independent clauses.

3.   B

Difficulty: Medium

Category: Expression of Ideas

Getting to the Answer: The question stem indicates that this question is testing transitions. As you read the passage, identify the two ideas that are being connected by the missing transition so you can determine the

relationship between them. The first idea is that ruby-throated hummingbirds have adaptations that enable their long migrations. The second idea concerns one of these adaptations: their small size allows them to ride tailwinds. Since the second idea is *an example* of the first, choice **(B)** is correct. Choice (A) is incorrect because the passage does not present a sequence of events. Choice (C) is incorrect because the continuation transition "Furthermore" would indicate that the hummingbirds' small size is an idea that is *in addition* to their having unique adaptations rather than *an example* of those unique adaptations. Choice (D) is incorrect because it is a cause-and-effect transition; the birds don't ride tailwinds *because* they have unique adaptations.

4.   D

Difficulty: Medium

Category: Expression of Ideas

Getting to the Answer: The question stem asks you to emphasize a similarity between the two fairy tales in terms of Darnton's analysis of the tales, so look for similarities as you read the bullet points. The first two bullet points introduce the topic by stating that Darnton analyzes meanings in historical texts, including fairy tales from several countries. The next two points describe his arguments about the two specific tales. Look for what they have in common: both are versions of "The Basket of Figs" and both concern success. The last point provides something that Darnton thinks is true of *both* tales: they reflect worldviews about success. Use this similarity as your prediction, as it entails a similarity in how Darnton analyzes the tales; **(D)** is correct. Choice (A) is incorrect because it concerns a difference in Darnton's analysis of the two tales. Choice (B) is incorrect because it does not emphasize the two specific tales. Although (C) mentions the two tales, it is incorrect because it does not identify a similarity in Darnton's analysis; it just states that he studied the two tales.

5.   A

Difficulty: Easy

Category: Standard English Conventions

Getting to the Answer: The answer choices indicate that this question tests correct pronoun usage. The pronoun in the blank must be possessive since the "spots" belong to the pronoun's antecedent. Eliminate the contractions ("they are" and "it is") in (B) and (D). Determine the pronoun's antecedent; the "spots" are those of the plural "participants," so **(A)** is correct. Choice (C) is incorrect because although it is a possessive pronoun, it is singular.

6.   D

Difficulty: Medium
Category: Expression of Ideas
Getting to the Answer: The question stem indicates that this question is testing transitions. As you read the passage, identify the two ideas that are being connected by the missing transition so you can determine the relationship between them. The first idea is that the Neolithic Revolution "created food and labor surpluses." The second idea is that labor specialization, or the variety of jobs that were done, increased. The connection between the ideas is that the surpluses *led to* labor specialization, in contrast to labor being mostly for food acquisition in pre-agrarian societies. Look for a cause-and-effect transition in the answer choices; **(D)** is correct. Choice (A) is incorrect because an increase in labor specialization is not *an example* of food and labor surpluses. Choice (B) is incorrect because an increase in labor "specialization" is not another way of stating that there were food and labor "shortages." Choice (C) is incorrect because it is a contrast transition rather than a cause-and-effect transition.

7.   A

Difficulty: Medium
Category: Standard English Conventions
Getting to the Answer: The answer choices indicate that this question is testing comma usage around the phrase "Rick and Laura Brown." In the passage, they are identified as "fine arts professors." Their names are essential, since without this information you would not otherwise know which fine arts professors are being described in the passage. Choice **(A)** is correct, as essential information should not be set off from the rest of the sentence by any punctuation. Choice (B) is incorrect because a comma should not be used to separate the modifier "fine arts professors" from "Rick and Laura Brown." Choice (C) incorrectly separates the subject "Rick and Laura Brown" from its verb (use). Choice (D) is incorrect because it sets off "Rick and Laura Brown" as though it were parenthetical information.

8.   B

Difficulty: Medium
Category: Expression of Ideas
Getting to the Answer: The question stem indicates that you need to identify the aim of the research study, so as you read the bullet points, look for the reason *why* the researchers conducted the study. The first point states that there was something scientists did not understand: how bacteria can coil single proteins. It is likely that gaining insight into this unknown was the goal of the study. The following bullet points describe the study and its results: the researchers used cryo-EM to better magnify propellers and found that a certain combination of structures allows for coiling. Predict that the study's aim was *to determine how the propellers coil*, which matches **(B)**. Choice (A) is incorrect because it describes the procedure of the study rather than its aim. Choice (C) is incorrect because it identifies the result of the study rather than its aim. Choice (D) is incorrect because the goal of the study concerned investigating bacteria propellers, not comparing magnification tools.

9.   B

Difficulty: Medium
Category: Expression of Ideas
Getting to the Answer: The question stem indicates that this question is testing transitions. As you read the passage, identify the two ideas that are being connected by the missing transition so you can determine the relationship between them. The first idea is that the mice in the study were cured by microrobots with one small dose. The second idea is that IV injections also cured the mice, but required a much larger dose. Predict that these ideas about a small dose and a large dose *contrast*: choice **(B)** is correct. Choice (A) is incorrect because the large IV injection is not *similar to* the small microrobot dose. Choice (C) is incorrect because the large IV dose is not *a result of* the small microrobot dose. Choice (D) is incorrect because the focus of the passage is the success of the microrobots doses, so the reader should not *disregard* ("Regardless") the microrobots.

10. D

Difficulty: Medium

Category: Standard English Conventions

Getting to the Answer: The answer choices contain various combinations of modifying phrases, so analyze the sentence in the passage to determine who or what should be modified. The introductory phrase "Foreshadowing the tension . . . since its theatrical release in 1957" should describe "the movie." Choice **(D)** is correct because it is the only answer choice that positions the movie directly after the phrase that modifies it; further, this choice correctly places "a research librarian" next to the noun it modifies: "Ms. Watson." Choices (A) and (C) are incorrect because they result in "since its release in 1957" modifying the character. In choice (B), the phrase incorrectly modifies the vague "there."

CHAPTER 20

EXPRESSION OF IDEAS

LEARNING OBJECTIVES

After completing this chapter, you will be able to:

- Combine statements to create a logical summary that meets a given goal
- Determine the appropriate transition word or phrase to establish logical relationships within the text

HOW MUCH DO YOU KNOW?

Directions

Try the questions that follow. When you're done, check your answers and reasoning against ours in the "Check Your Work" section. If they closely match, you may be able to move quickly through the chapter. If they do not, spend some extra time with the chapter to grow your SAT Reading and Writing skills.

1

While researching a topic, a student has taken the following notes:

- Charlotte Perkins Gilman was an American writer and advocate for women's rights during the late 1800s.
- Her works explored how society, families, and individuals benefited when women were able to act with autonomy.
- In her 1892 short story "The Yellow Wallpaper," the female character suffers when she is confined to a room for a health treatment rather than allowed to move and act freely.
- In her 1898 book *Women and Economics*, Gilman argues that women having the opportunity to enter the workforce would contribute to better families and societies.

The student wants to emphasize a difference between the two works. Which choice most effectively uses relevant information from the notes to accomplish this goal?

(A) Gilman's "The Yellow Wallpaper" addresses a woman's suffering when she is unable to act freely, while *Women and Economics* claims that benefits will come from women being able to work.

(B) Gilman's short story "The Yellow Wallpaper" and her book *Women and Economics* were both published in the late 1800s; the short story was published in 1892, and the book was published in 1898.

(C) Charlotte Perkins Gilman is known not only for her writings as an American author but also for her work as an advocate for women's rights, particularly her view that women's autonomy would lead to positive outcomes.

(D) The themes of Gilman's "The Yellow Wallpaper" and *Women and Economics* explore the idea that women are individuals with rights, addressing concepts such as women as actors in the workforce.

While researching a topic, a student has taken the following notes:

- Researchers from Ohio State University studied the impact of a tomato-heavy diet on the gut microbiome of pigs.

- Half of the pigs in the study were fed a regular diet, and the other half of the pigs were fed a modified diet that was 10% tomato powder.

- The researchers sequenced the microbial DNA in the pigs' waste.

- The sequencing showed a higher ratio of bacteria from the Bacteroidota phylum to bacteria from the Bacillota phylum in the pigs fed the tomato-heavy diet.

- A high ratio of Bacteroidota to Bacillota bacteria in the gut has been linked to health benefits.

The student wants to summarize the study. Which choice most effectively uses relevant information from the notes to accomplish this goal?

(A) Researchers from Ohio State University wanted to know how a diet heavy in tomatoes would impact the gut microbiome of pigs, so they conducted a scientific study.

(B) An Ohio State University study that used microbial DNA sequencing showed that the gut microbiome of pigs fed a tomato-heavy diet had a particular ratio of bacteria that has been associated with health benefits.

(C) Researchers from Ohio State University sequenced the microbial DNA from the waste of pigs that had been fed a tomato-heavy diet and compared it to the microbial DNA from the waste of pigs that had been fed a regular diet.

(D) Knowing that an animal's diet can impact the composition of its gut microbiome, researchers from Ohio State University studied how a special diet impacted the gut microbiome of two groups of pigs.

Reading & Writing

While researching a topic, a student has taken the following notes:

- The U.S. National Park System includes numerous National Historical Parks in its registry.
- National Historical Parks serve to preserve locations that are significant in the history of the United States.
- The battle sites at Lexington and Concord in the state of Massachusetts have together been designated as the Minute Man National Historical Park.
- British troops and American militias engaged in armed conflicts in 1775 in the towns of Lexington and Concord after the British General Gage sent troops to seize possible stockpiles of weapons.
- The 1775 battles at Lexington and Concord began the American Revolutionary War.

The student wants to emphasize why the battle sites at Lexington and Concord were designated as a National Historical Park. Which choice most effectively uses relevant information from the notes to accomplish this goal?

(A) The Minute Man National Historical Park in Massachusetts contains the battle sites of Lexington and Concord, where armed conflicts occurred between British troops and American militias in 1775.

(B) National Historical Parks are part of the U.S. National Park System and have the particular function of preserving locations that are important in the history of the United States.

(C) National Historical Parks preserve locations that are significant in U.S. history, so the battle sites at Lexington and Concord, the locations of the first battles of the Revolutionary War, were designated as the Minute Man National Historical Park.

(D) Lexington and Concord were the sites of the first battles between British troops and American militias in the Revolutionary War; the battles occurred when the Americans resisted the British General Gage's attempt to seize weapons in 1775.

4

The earliest studies of the mysterious prehistoric "sorcerer" painting in the Trois Frères cave in France were based on a sketch of the painting made by archaeologist Henri Breuil. Initial analysis of Breuil's drawing led archaeologists to speculate that the painting depicts a religious shaman. Based on new photographs of the painting, _____ some archaeologists now argue that Breuil's sketch misrepresents the painting by interpreting some cracks in the cave wall as part of the image.

Which choice completes the text with the most logical transition?

(A) meanwhile,

(B) however,

(C) similarly,

(D) for instance,

5

The state of North Carolina adopted the phrase "First in Flight" on its license plates in 1982, referencing the fact that the first powered airplane flight occurred at the beach at Kitty Hawk, North Carolina in 1903. However, the inventors of the airplane, Orville and Wilbur Wright, had developed their airplane design and resided in Dayton, Ohio. _____ the state of Ohio began inscribing "Birthplace of Aviation" on their license plates in 1998.

Which choice completes the text with the most logical transition?

(A) Consequently,

(B) Specifically,

(C) Regardless,

(D) Likewise,

6

Using GPS tracking devices to monitor individual mountain lion's movements, scientists have concluded that California mountain lions are engaging in increasingly risky behaviors as their habitats are threatened. _____ mountain lions near Los Angeles have increased their crossings of major highways by 67% in recent years, likely in response to wildfires that have impacted their previous hunting grounds.

Which choice completes the text with the most logical transition?

(A) Similarly,

(B) Nevertheless,

(C) For instance,

(D) As a result,

Check Your Work

1.   A
Difficulty: Medium
Category: Expression of Ideas
Getting to the Answer: Since the question asks for a difference between the works, look for how the writings differ as you read the bullet points. The last two points address the individual works. The third bullet point describes "The Yellow Wallpaper," stating that the female character suffers when she can't act freely. The last bullet point describes *Women and Economics*, stating that Gilman argues that women should be able to work. The works thus differ in their content, which is accurately summarized in **(A)**; this choice is correct.

Choice (B) is incorrect because it emphasizes a similarity—the publication dates—between the works rather than a difference; note the similarity keyword "both" in the answer choice. Choice (C) is incorrect because it is about Gilman's overall achievements, not about the two specific works. Choice (D) is incorrect because it discusses how the works are similar.

2.   B
Difficulty: Hard
Category: Expression of Ideas
Getting to the Answer: A summary of a study should address all its major components, such as who conducted it, what it studied, its methods, and its conclusions. Look for the major components of the study as you read the bullet points. The first bullet point identifies who conducted the study (Ohio State University researchers) and its aim (determining the impact of a tomato-heavy diet on pigs' gut microbiomes). The next two points describe the study's method (sequencing microbial DNA from the pigs' waste), and the last points provide the results (a bacteria ratio linked with health benefits). Eliminate answer choices that fail to summarize all the important components of the study.

Choice (A) is incorrect because it fails to mention the study's method or results. Choice **(B)** is correct because it provides a complete summary, addressing who conducted the study, what it studied, its method, and its conclusion. Choices (C) and (D) are incorrect because they do not include the study's findings; further, (D) does not specify that the study concerned a tomato-heavy diet.

3.   C
Difficulty: Hard
Category: Expression of Ideas
Getting to the Answer: Based on the question stem, the correct answer will focus on why the Lexington and Concord battle sites were made a National Historical Park. Look for this particular detail as you read the bullet points. The first three points include the ideas that National Historical Parks are historically significant and that the Minute Man National Historical Park contains Lexington and Concord. Thus, if Lexington and Concord were made a National Historical Park, it must be the case that they are historically significant. Indeed, the remaining points concern the events and significance of Lexington and Concord: the last point specifies that they were the locations of the first battles of the American Revolutionary War. Choice **(C)** summarizes the reason why Lexington and Concord were made a National Historical Park and is correct.

Choice (A) is incorrect because it does not explain why the battles were historically significant enough to warrant a designation as a National Historical Park. Choice (B) is incorrect because it does not mention Lexington and Concord. Choice (D) explains why Lexington and Concord are significant, but it is incorrect because it does not address the sites being a National Historical Park.

4.   B
Difficulty: Easy
Category: Expression of Ideas
Getting to the Answer: When asked to find the most logical transition, identify the two ideas that are connected by the transition as you read the passage. The idea before the transition is that the "Initial analysis" of a cave painting was based on a sketch by Breuil and determined the subject is a shaman. The idea after the transition is that archaeologists "now" think the sketch on which the analysis was based is inaccurate. Since the second idea identifies an objection to the initial sketch and its analysis, predict that the ideas contrast; choice **(B)** is correct.

Choice (A) is incorrect because the transition "meanwhile" would illogically indicate that the initial analysis and the "new" analysis happened at the same time.

Choice (C) is incorrect because the ideas are not *similar*. Choice (D) is incorrect because the new criticism of the sketch is not *an example of* (for instance) the initial analysis of the sketch.

5.   A
Difficulty: Hard
Category: Expression of Ideas
Getting to the Answer: When asked to find the most logical transition, identify the two ideas that are connected by the transition as you read the passage. The passage begins by explaining why North Carolina placed a phrase about aviation on their license plates. The idea immediately before the transition is that the inventors of the airplane lived in Ohio; the idea after the transition is that Ohio also used a phrase about aviation on their license plates. Predict that Ohio adopted the phrase *because* the Wright brothers were from Ohio; **(A)** is correct.

Choice (B) is incorrect because Ohio adopting the phrase is not a *specific instance* of the Wrights living in Ohio. Choice (C) is incorrect because Ohio did not adopt the phrase *regardless of* the Wright brothers living in Ohio, but *because* they were from Ohio. Choice (D) is incorrect because the continuation transition "Likewise" would indicate that the Wrights living in Ohio and the state adopting the phrase are *similar* ideas, rather than one idea being the cause of the other.

6.   C
Difficulty: Medium
Category: Expression of Ideas
Getting to the Answer: When asked to find the most logical transition, identify the two ideas that are connected by the transition as you read the passage. The idea before the transition is that mountain lions are showing more risky behaviors due to threats to their habitats. The idea after the transition is that some mountain lions are crossing highways more often due to the impact of wildfires. The second idea is *an example of* a risky behavior, so **(C)** is correct.

Choice (A) is incorrect because the ideas are not just *similar to* each other; the second is a *specific example* of the first. Choice (B) is incorrect because the ideas do not contrast. Choice (D) is incorrect because the mountain lions are not crossing roads more frequently *as a result* of their engaging in more risky behaviors; rather, the road crossings are *an example of* a risky behavior.

SYNTHESIS QUESTIONS

> **LEARNING OBJECTIVE**
>
> After this lesson, you will be able to:
>
> • Combine statements to create a logical summary that meets a given goal

To answer a question like this:

While researching a topic, a student has taken the following notes:

- Julie Mehretu is an Ethiopian-American artist who creates paintings, drawings, and prints.
- Her works have been described as abstract landscapes, as many are based on her interpretations of documents associated with urban environments, including blueprints, city maps, and photos of buildings.
- The media Mehretu uses to create her art include acrylic paint, spray paint, and markers.
- Her work *Stadia I* (2004) features an architectural rendering of a stadium and stylized versions of world flags.
- Her work *Berliner Plätze* (2009) features a hazy depiction of photos of buildings that were destroyed in Berlin in World War II.

The student wants to emphasize a similarity between the two works. Which choice most effectively uses relevant information from the notes to accomplish this goal?

A) Like many of Mehretu's works, both *Stadia I* and *Berliner Plätze* reflect urban documents: *Stadia I* includes an architectural rendering of a stadium, and *Berliner Plätze* includes depictions of old buildings from photos.

B) Mehretu's works, which often include her interpretations of urban documents, consist of paintings, drawings, and prints, and they are usually created using acrylic paint, spray paint, and markers.

C) Mehretu completed *Stadia I* in 2004 and *Berliner Plätze* in 2009.

D) *Stadia I* (2004) includes an architectural rendering of a stadium and stylized world flags; *Berliner Plätze* (2009), however, includes depictions of old buildings from photos.

You need to know this:

How to Identify Synthesis Questions

Synthesis questions will ask you to identify which answer choice accomplishes a specific rhetorical aim. For instance, you might be asked to emphasize a similarity or a difference between ideas. The question stem will identify the rhetorical aim and then ask you which answer choice accomplishes this goal. See the question above for an example of the possible format of a Synthesis question. Also, as shown above, the passage of a Synthesis question will likely consist of a list of bullet point notes about a topic.

How to Synthesize Ideas

To *synthesize* means to bring different ideas together in a logical way that creates one new idea. Fortunately, synthesis question stems will always specify *how* you need to synthesize the ideas. For example, you may need to create a new idea that describes a similarity or a new idea that describes a difference.

The passage on a Synthesis question will likely contain more information than you need to meet the goal specified in the question stem. You do not need to consider all the ideas in the passage equally; as always, read the question

stem first to help you identify what is being asked. Once you identify the specific rhetorical goal (such as finding a similarity), read the passage with that goal in mind. Focus on the ideas that are relevant, and, if possible, see if you can paraphrase how to achieve the goal in your own words. Mentally set aside details that are irrelevant to the goal.

Imagine, for instance, you are asked to synthesize the ideas in the following notes by emphasizing a similarity between two dogs.

- A dog owner manages a dog daycare service and owns two dogs of her own, Astro and Bingo.
- Astro is an 8-year-old golden retriever who enjoys playing fetch with tennis balls.
- Bingo is a 4-year-old Labrador retriever who enjoys playing Frisbee.

Was there any information that was irrelevant to the goal? Did you focus on identifying a similarity as you read? Some information was entirely unrelated to the goal of identifying a similarity between the two dogs, such as the details about the dog owner. Some information was about *differences* between the dogs, such as their specific breeds and ages. What were the similarities? You may have noticed that they are both types of retrievers who enjoy playing. If this were a test question, you'd look for an answer choice that states one or both of these similarities.

Incorrect answers to a Synthesis question may be:

- **Opposite**—Incorrect answers to Synthesis questions may provide the *opposite* of the goal in the question stem, for instance, a difference rather than a similarity.
- **Misused Details**—Incorrect answers to Synthesis questions may include details from the passage that are irrelevant to the goal in the question stem.

The **correct answer** to a Synthesis question will:

- Specifically address the goal identified in the question stem using only relevant information from the passage

You need to do this:

THE METHOD FOR SAT READING AND WRITING

STEP 1 What is the question asking?

STEP 2 What do I need to look for in the passage?.

STEP 3 What answer strategy is best?

- Predict and Match
- Eliminate

Step 1. What is the question asking?

If the question stem identifies a rhetorical aim and asks you which choice "accomplish[es] this goal," it is a Synthesis question.

Step 2. What do I need to look for in the passage?

Restate the goal from the question stem in your own words—perhaps you need to find a similarity between two books or a difference between two artistic styles—and read the passage with this specific aim in mind. As you read each detail, ask yourself whether it is relevant to the goal. If it's not, mentally set it aside. If it is relevant, pay careful attention to that detail. When finished, try to paraphrase a statement in your own words that achieves the goal.

Step 3. What answer strategy is best?

If you paraphrased a way to achieve the goal, use it as your prediction as you look for the one correct match among the answer choices. If needed, eliminate answer choices that do the opposite of the stated goal, as well as those that use details from the passage that are irrelevant to the stated goal.

Whether you predict and match or eliminate (or both), pay careful attention to the keywords in the answer choices. Questions that ask about similarities or differences may contain contrast or continuation words that provide strong hints: if your goal is to find a similarity, for instance, an answer choice that contains contrast words such as "however" or "but" is likely incorrect. On the other hand, the correct answer will likely contain continuation words such as "both" and "and."

Explanation:

The question asks for a specific rhetorical aim and asks which answer choice "accomplish[es] this goal," so this is a Synthesis question. Before you read the passage, restate the goal in your own words: *you need a similarity between two works*. The first bullet point is likely irrelevant to this goal, as it describes just the artist. The second and third bullet points are about Mehretu's work overall; it's possible that the similarity between the two specific works could be related to these bullet points, but don't focus on their details just yet. The last two bullet points finally identify the two works and describe the *content* of each. The second bullet point also described the *content* of Mehretu's works: she bases her work on urban documents. Consider the specific works in light of this use of urban documents; indeed, *Stadia I* has an architectural drawing, and *Berliner Plätze* uses photos of buildings. Predict that *both works are based on urban documents;* this matches **(A)**. Note that this choice includes words that suggest similarity, such as "both" and "and."

Choice (B) is incorrect because it uses details from the passage that are about her works in general, but they are not specific to a similarity between the two identified works. Choice (C) is incorrect because it merely states facts about the works rather than identifying a similarity between them. Be careful: note that the use of "and," in this case, does not signal a similarity. Choice (D) is incorrect because it identifies a difference, as indicated by the contrast word "however."

Try on Your Own

Directions

Take as much time as you need on these questions. Work carefully and methodically. There will be an opportunity for timed practice later in the book.

1

While researching a topic, a student has taken the following notes:

- Some spiders create webs that store mechanical energy.

- A force stretching a spring causes the spring to store mechanical energy that becomes motion when the force is released and the spring bounces back.

- Black widow spiders weave massive webs called cobwebs, and connect the bottoms of the webs to the ground using gumfoot silk.

- The gumfoot silk is stretched tightly between the cobweb and the ground.

- When prey touches gumfoot silk and breaks the attachment to the ground, the silk flies up into the web, trapping the prey.

The student wants to emphasize a similarity between spider webs and springs. Which choice most effectively uses relevant information from the notes to accomplish this goal?

(A) Black widow spiders are a type of spider that build webs capable of storing mechanical energy.

(B) Cobwebs, the massive webs of black widow spiders, are connected to the ground with gumfoot silk.

(C) Springs store energy when a force is applied to stretch the spring; when the force is released, the spring bounces back and converts the stored energy into motion.

(D) Black widow spiders use gumfoot silk to keep tension on their webs, so the silk can act as a spring, propelling the prey into the web when contact with the ground is broken.

While researching a topic, a student has taken the following notes:

- The deepest part of the ocean is called the Challenger Deep, which is 35,814 feet below sea level where pressure levels exceed 16,000 pounds per square inch.

- A bathyscaphe is a self-propelled submersible that is built specifically to withstand the high pressure levels in the deep sea.

- In 1960, using a U.S. Naval bathyscaphe named *Trieste*, Lt. Don Walsh and explorer Jacques Piccard were two of only three people to ever dive to the bottom of the Challenger Deep.

- At 30,000 feet below sea level, Walsh and Piccard made the risky decision to finish the dive after a crack appeared in one of *Trieste*'s plexiglass windows.

- Filmmaker James Cameron was the third person ever to dive to the bottom of the Challenger Deep in 2012.

The student wants to emphasize the significance of the *Trieste*. Which choice most effectively uses relevant information from the notes to accomplish this goal?

Ⓐ Even though *Trieste* was built to withstand pressures of more than 16,000 pounds per square inch, it nevertheless developed a crack in its trip to the Challenger Deep.

Ⓑ *Trieste* was a bathyscaphe built for deep sea diving, able to withstand pressures of more than 16,000 pounds per square inch.

Ⓒ The bottom of the Challenger Deep has been reached by three people: Lt. Don Walsh, Jacques Piccard, and James Cameron.

Ⓓ *Trieste* was the first manned submersible to reach the Challenger Deep, which is the deepest point of the ocean.

3

While researching a topic, a student has taken the following notes:

- Author Jesmyn Ward is the first woman and first Black American to be awarded two National Book Awards for Fiction.

- She was recognized for her novel *Salvage the Bones* in 2011 and her novel *Sing, Unburied, Sing* in 2017.

- The story of *Sing, Unburied, Sing* is primarily narrated by Jojo, who is the 13-year-old son of a white man, Michael, and a Black woman, Leonie, who is a secondary narrator.

- A third narrator, Richie, is the spirit of a murdered teenager who occasionally converses with Jojo as he struggles to accept the circumstances of his death.

The student wants to introduce the novel *Sing, Unburied, Sing* to an audience already familiar with Jesmyn Ward. Which choice most effectively uses relevant information from the notes to accomplish this goal?

(A) Jesmyn Ward uses three principal narrators in her National Book Award-winning novel: a teenage boy, his mother, and the spirit of a murdered teenager.

(B) Black American author Jesmyn Ward followed up her 2011 National Book Award-winning novel *Salvage the Bones* with another award-winning novel, *Sing, Unburied, Sing,* which was published in 2017.

(C) Jesmyn Ward's 2017 novel *Sing, Unburied, Sing* is written from the viewpoints of 13-year-old Jojo, who is biracial; his Black mother, Leonie; and murdered teenager Richie.

(D) *Sing, Unburied, Sing* was not the only National Book Award-winning novel written by Black American author Jesmyn Ward.

4

While researching a topic, a student has taken the following notes:

- Extending over 2,180 miles from Mount Oglethorpe in Georgia to Mount Katahdin in Maine, the Appalachian Trail is a wilderness footpath that traverses the Appalachian Mountains.

- The Trail not only allows people to hike through spectacular natural scenery but also was instrumental in preserving extensive swathes of wilderness.

- Interest in developing the Trail eventually led to the 1964 Wilderness Act, which has protected 109.5 million acres of wilderness across 44 states.

- First championed by Benton MacKaye in 1921, his vision included three different kinds of communities: shelter for hikers, food and farm camps, and private homes.

- Every year, more than three million people visit the Trail, and about three thousand attempt to walk its full length.

The student wants to emphasize a difference between the original plan for the Appalachian Trail and the Trail today. Which choice most effectively uses relevant information from the notes to accomplish this goal?

(A) The Appalachian Trail was established through the efforts of Benton MacKaye, who started in 1921.

(B) Even though the Appalachian Trail extends over 2,180 miles, about three thousand people attempt to walk its full length every year.

(C) The Appalachian Trail is a wilderness hiking path, but Benton MacKay, who first envisioned the Trail, hoped it would include a variety of support communities.

(D) While the Appalachian Trail makes it possible for hikers to enjoy the wilderness, it also spurred the preservation of millions of acres of wilderness in 44 different states.

5

While researching a topic, a student has taken the following notes:

- The Alpha Suffrage Club of Chicago was established in 1913.

- The club engaged Black women in the fight for women's suffrage through voter education, community outreach, and advocacy efforts.

- Investigative journalist and anti-lynching crusader Ida B. Wells helped to co-found the organization.

- Her fame helped to raise the profile of the new organization, especially among Black women in Chicago.

- Attorney and activist Belle Squire helped to co-found the organization.

- Her legal expertise likely contributed to the strategic planning and execution of the Alpha Suffrage Club's mission.

The student wants to emphasize the time of inception and the purpose of Wells and Squire's collaborative work. Which choice most effectively uses relevant information from the notes to accomplish this goal?

(A) Founded in 1913 by Ida B. Wells and Belle Squire, the Alpha Suffrage Club of Chicago was dedicated to engaging Black women in the women's suffrage movement.

(B) Ida B. Wells and Belle Squire co-founded the Alpha Suffrage Club, which aimed to involve Black women in the struggle for women's suffrage by focusing on voter education, community outreach, and advocacy initiatives.

(C) Alpha Suffrage Club co-founders Ida B. Wells and Belle Squire each brought their unique skills and influence to help the new organization succeed.

(D) The year of 1913 marked a turning point in the history of women's suffrage, with activists like Ida B. Wells and Belle Squire becoming involved.

6

Reading & Writing

While researching a topic, a student has taken the following notes:

- Conventional wisdom has maintained that animals must engage in prolonged, consolidated periods of sleep in order to function at peak health.

- In 2023, researchers Paul-Antoine Libourel and Won Young Lee studied the sleep patterns of wild chinstrap penguins using a combination of implants and observation.

- The team found that penguins caring for eggs or chicks slept in thousands of four-second "microsleep" periods, which sum up to 11 hours of total sleep per day.

- The study indicates that fragmented sleep may not be as harmful to animals as previously thought.

The student wants to summarize the study. Which choice most effectively uses relevant information from the notes to accomplish this goal?

Ⓐ For a 2023 study, researchers collected data using both implants and observation on wild chinstrap penguins' sleep patterns while they were caring for eggs or chicks.

Ⓑ Libourel and Lee wanted to know how wild chinstrap penguins obtained sleep while nesting, so they conducted a study.

Ⓒ Knowing that animals need prolonged periods of sleep to be healthy, Libourel and Lee studied penguin sleep patterns in 2023, which had some surprising results.

Ⓓ Libourel and Lee's 2023 study of nesting penguin sleep patterns revealed that the penguins slept in thousands of "microsleep" intervals totaling 11 hours per day.

TRANSITIONS QUESTIONS

LEARNING OBJECTIVE

After this lesson, you will be able to:

* Determine the appropriate transition word or phrase to establish logical relationships within the text

To answer a question like this:

Palov is a traditional rice-based dish in Central Asian countries such as Uzbekistan. Consisting of rice simmered with savory meats and vegetables, palov may seem like a cozy comfort food prepared only in private homes. _____ the dish has a strong community aspect as well. On special occasions such as weddings, skilled chefs sometimes cook a cauldron of palov that can serve hundreds.

Which choice completes the text with the most logical transition?

A) Therefore,

B) Similarly,

C) As a result,

D) However,

You need to know this:

How to Identify Transitions Questions

Transitions questions can be identified by the keywords "logical transition" and typically have the question stem, *Which choice completes the text with the most logical transition?*

How to Identify Transition Relationships

The key to answering Transitions questions is to determine what type of connection exists between the ideas in a passage. To do this, identify the two ideas that are connected by the missing transition word and paraphrase in your own words the relationship between the two ideas. The most common types of transition relationships tested on the SAT include:

* **Continuation**—a continuation of the same point
  * *Cockapoo dogs are great pets. They are highly intelligent;* ***further***, *they have sociable personalities.*
  * The keyword "further" indicates a continuation of the reasons cockapoos are great pets.
* **Contrast**—a change in direction or a point of difference
  * *Cockapoo dogs are great pets;* ***however***, *they can develop painful knots in their fur without consistent grooming.*
  * The keyword "however" indicates a contrast between a positive feature of cockapoos (they are great pets) and a negative feature of cockapoos (they can get knots).
* **Cause-and-effect**—one idea causes another idea or leads to a conclusion
  * *Cockapoo dogs are great pets;* ***therefore***, *they were voted the most popular dog breed in New York City.*
  * The keyword "therefore" indicates a cause-and-effect relationship: because cockapoos are great pets, they were voted most popular.

In the previous examples, note how the transition keywords (*further*, *however*, *therefore*) serve as clues that indicate the type of transition relationship between ideas. A different transition word can entirely change the meaning of a sentence. Consider how different transition words change the meaning of the following sentence:

- Calculus is Kiyana's strongest subject, **and** she prepared thoroughly for the exam.
- Calculus is Kiyana's strongest subject, **yet** she prepared thoroughly for the exam.
- Calculus is Kiyana's strongest subject, **so** she prepared thoroughly for the exam.

The **continuation** transition word (*and*) indicates that Kiyana's thorough preparation for the exam is a continuation of the idea that calculus is her strongest subject. The **contrast** transition word (*yet*) indicates that even though calculus is Kiyana's strongest subject, she still prepared thoroughly for the exam. Finally, the **cause-and-effect** transition word (*so*) indicates that the reason Kiyana prepared thoroughly for the exam was because calculus is her strongest subject.

The table that follows contains examples of common transition words used on the SAT. Becoming familiar with these words will help you understand the connections between ideas in *every* Reading and Writing passage you encounter. In addition, these transition words are often answer choices on Transition questions.

TYPES OF SAT TRANSITION KEYWORDS		
Keyword Type	**What the Keywords Indicate**	**Examples**
Continuation	a continuation of the same point	*moreover, in addition, also, further, and*
Contrast	a change in direction or a point of difference	*but, yet, despite, on the other hand, however*
Cause-and-effect	one idea causes another idea or leads to a conclusion	*thus, therefore, because, since, so*

Transition words are extremely helpful, but be aware that passages often include more subtle clues about the relationships between ideas. Relationships might be indicated by the content of the ideas themselves, or even by punctuation marks, so be thorough in your search for clues about the connections between ideas.

Incorrect answers to a Transitions question may be:

- **Opposite**—Incorrect answers to Transitions questions may give the opposite of the logical relationship between ideas.
- **Distortions**—Incorrect answers to Transitions questions may misrepresent the connection between ideas, such as indicating a cause-and-effect relationship where one does not logically exist.

The **correct answer** to a Transitions question will:

- Precisely reflect the logical relationship between the ideas in the passage

You need to do this:

> ### THE METHOD FOR SAT READING AND WRITING
>
> **STEP 1** What is the question asking?
>
> **STEP 2** What do I need to look for in the passage?.
>
> **STEP 3** What answer strategy is best?
>
> - Predict and Match
> - Eliminate

Step 1. What is the question asking?

If the question stem asks you to fill in the blank with a "logical transition," it is a Transitions question.

Step 2. What do I need to look for in the passage?

To identify the logical transition, you'll need to identify the two ideas that are connected by the blank. Then, determine the relationship between those two ideas; use transition keywords as well as additional clues, such as information in the ideas themselves and punctuation marks, to help you find the relationship.

Step 3. What answer strategy is best?

Transitions questions tend to lend themselves to the strategy of predicting the type of transition needed before looking at the answer choices. Predict a word or phrase that conveys the same type of relationship you found between the ideas: continuation, contrast, cause-and-effect, or another type of connection. Look for the answer choice that matches the meaning of your predicted transition word or phrase, and read your selection back into the passage to make sure it makes sense in context. If needed, eliminate answer choices that are opposite or distortions of the logical relationship between the ideas in the passage.

Explanation:

The keywords "logical transition" signal that this is a Transitions question, so as you read the passage, look for the two ideas that are connected by the blank. The idea before the blank is that palov seems like a food for private homes; the idea after the blank is that palov has a community aspect. The passage doesn't contain obvious transition keywords, so look for other clues about the relationship between these ideas. The words "may seem" suggest that there is a contrast between what is expected about palov (that it's a food for private homes) and the idea about palov that follows (that it's also a community food). The ideas themselves, which concern the private and the communal, also indicate contrast. Predict that the correct answer will be *a contrast transition such as "Nevertheless" or "However"*; **(D)** is correct and logically makes sense when read into the blank.

Choices (A) and (C) are incorrect because they distort the relationship between the ideas by indicating cause-and-effect relationships. Choice (B) is incorrect because it indicates continuation rather than the contrast relationship intended in the passage.

Try on Your Own

Directions

Take as much time as you need on these questions. Work carefully and methodically. There will be an opportunity for timed practice later in the book.

7

Marek participates in an online Renaissance music discussion group that has a library of original articles that are the product of a master's thesis. The author gained no monetary reward for the information (which she made available for free) and receives little praise for it outside the community that shares her interest. She posts because she is passionate about her subject; _____ her enthusiasm for this music inspires her to share what she knows with anyone who would like to learn.

Which choice completes the text with the most logical transition?

Ⓐ nonetheless,

Ⓑ lastly,

Ⓒ however,

Ⓓ indeed,

8

Temperature affects the speed of chemical reactions in two ways. First, temperature increases accelerate the motion of the molecules. _____ the probability that the molecules will collide increases, speeding the rate of the reaction. Second, the amount of energy in the reactants also increases as the temperature rises.

Which choice completes the text with the most logical transition?

Ⓐ For instance,

Ⓑ Finally,

Ⓒ Consequently,

Ⓓ Alternatively,

9

Most plants distribute their seeds using water, winds, or animals to spread them out before the seeds are sown into the ground to sprout the next generation. _____ the only plant currently known to self-sow after fertilization without intervention is the *Arachis hypogaeae*, a legume that is commonly called a "peanut." After the peanut plant's flower has been pollinated, it begins to wither and produce a stake-like peg that slowly descends into the soil. Deep underground, a peanut will form from the tip of that peg.

Which choice completes the text with the most logical transition?

Ⓐ However,

Ⓑ Further,

Ⓒ Additionally,

Ⓓ Since,

10

Whereas many clothing manufacturers have long focused on gaining an advantage over their competitors by producing clothing as inexpensively as possible, sales data in recent years reveals an alternative trend. _____ clothing companies are boosting their sales by marketing fair trade fabrics: materials that are produced by workers who are paid higher, living wages.

Which choice completes the text with the most logical transition?

- Ⓐ Furthermore,
- Ⓑ For this reason,
- Ⓒ Similarly,
- Ⓓ Increasingly,

11

Mosquitoes have a reputation for being irritating, inescapable bloodsuckers. _____ female mosquitoes only require the proteins, iron, and amino acids that are obtained through a blood meal when they are seeking to complete their reproductive process. Indeed, blood is not mosquitoes' primary food source; the majority of mosquitoes, both male and female, feed on nectar and help pollinate the plants from which they feed.

Which choice completes the text with the most logical transition?

- Ⓐ Therefore,
- Ⓑ In fact,
- Ⓒ Because of this,
- Ⓓ However,

12

Georgia, a state located in the southern United States, has long held a reputation for cultivating delicious peaches. In fact, it was one of the first few colonies to plant and harvest peaches. Now, Georgia is officially known as "the Peach State." _____ it only ranks as the fourth largest U.S. producer of this fruit.

Which choice completes the text with the most logical transition?

- Ⓐ Moreover,
- Ⓑ Likewise,
- Ⓒ Nevertheless,
- Ⓓ As a result,

13

Vintage uranium glass is making a resurgence in popularity for many reasons. One reason is that the glass, which is produced by mixing in uranium oxide prior to its melting and forming, is a stunning neon green at its densest and is almost transparent in other areas. _____ the uranium's radioactivity causes the glass to glow when exposed to ultraviolet black light, making it a fascinating statement piece to any place setting.

Which choice completes the text with the most logical transition?

- (A) Subsequently,
- (B) Though,
- (C) Additionally,
- (D) On the other hand,

14

Though many infants do not produce discernible words until around age one, they begin gaining proficiency in their native languages long before that. _____ many linguists agree that a newborn baby's brain is preprogrammed for language acquisition, meaning that it is as natural for a baby to talk as it is for a badger to dig.

Which choice completes the text with the most logical transition?

- (A) In fact,
- (B) Besides,
- (C) However,
- (D) In contrast,

HOW MUCH HAVE YOU LEARNED?

Directions

For testlike practice, give yourself 7 minutes to complete this question set. When you're finished, be sure to study the explanations, even for questions you answered correctly. Full explanations can be found at the end of this chapter.

15

While researching a topic, a student has taken the following notes:

- Charlotte Perkins Gilman was an American writer and advocate for women's rights during the late 1800s.

- Her works explored how society, families, and individuals benefited when women were able to act with autonomy.

- In her 1892 short story "The Yellow Wallpaper," the female character suffers when she is confined to a room for a health treatment rather than allowed to move and act freely.

- In her 1898 book *Women and Economics*, Gilman argues that women having the opportunity to enter the workforce would contribute to better families and societies.

The student wants to emphasize a similarity between the two works. Which choice most effectively uses relevant information from the notes to accomplish this goal?

(A) The American author Gilman wrote both short stories, such as "The Yellow Wallpaper," and books, such as *Women and Economics*.

(B) Gilman's short story "The Yellow Wallpaper" and her book *Women and Economics* both address the importance of women's autonomy.

(C) "The Yellow Wallpaper" is about a woman who cannot act autonomously, while *Women and Economics* advocates for women's economic autonomy.

(D) Since Gilman was an advocate for women's rights, she often wrote about the issue of women acting autonomously.

While researching a topic, a student has taken the following notes:

- Researchers from Ohio State University studied the impact of a tomato-heavy diet on the gut microbiome of pigs.

- Half of the pigs in the study were fed a regular diet, and the other half of the pigs were fed a modified diet that was 10% tomato powder.

- The researchers sequenced the microbial DNA in the pigs' waste.

- The sequencing showed a higher ratio of bacteria from the Bacteroidota phylum to bacteria from the Bacillota phylum in the pigs fed the tomato-heavy diet.

- A high ratio of Bacteroidota to Bacillota bacteria in the gut has been linked to health benefits.

The student wants to present the study and its methodology. Which choice most effectively uses relevant information from the notes to accomplish this goal?

(A) An Ohio State University study revealed that the gut microbiome of pigs fed a tomato-heavy diet had a higher ratio of Bacteroidota bacteria to Bacillota bacteria, which has been associated with various health benefits.

(B) Researchers from Ohio State University studied how different diets can impact the composition of the gut microbiome of different groups of pigs.

(C) Researchers from Ohio State University demonstrated that a high ratio of Bacteroidota bacteria to Bacillota bacteria in the gut microbiome of pigs is linked to health benefits.

(D) Seeking to understand how a tomato-heavy diet impacts the gut microbiome of pigs, researchers from Ohio State University sequenced the microbial DNA in the waste of pigs fed regular or tomato-heavy diets.

While researching a topic, a student has taken the following notes:

- The U.S. National Park System includes numerous National Historical Parks in its registry.
- National Historical Parks serve to preserve locations that are significant in the history of the United States.
- The battle sites at Lexington and Concord in the state of Massachusetts have together been designated as the Minute Man National Historical Park.
- British troops and American militias engaged in armed conflicts in 1775 in the towns of Lexington and Concord after the British General Gage sent troops to seize possible stockpiles of weapons.
- The 1775 battles at Lexington and Concord began the American Revolutionary War.

The student wants to introduce the Minute Man National Historical Park to an audience already familiar with the cause and significance of the battles of Lexington and Concord. Which choice most effectively uses relevant information from the notes to accomplish this goal?

Ⓐ Lexington and Concord were the sites of the first battles between British troops and American militias in the Revolutionary War; the battles occurred when the Americans resisted the British General Gage's attempt to seize weapons in 1775.

Ⓑ Since National Historical Parks preserve locations that are significant in the history of the United States, the Minute Man National Historical Park in Massachusetts contains the battle sites at Lexington and Concord.

Ⓒ The battle sites at Lexington and Concord were together designated as the Minute Man National Historical Park in Massachusetts because in 1775 they were the locations of the first battles of the American Revolutionary War.

Ⓓ National Historical Parks are part of the National Park System and have the particular function of preserving locations that are important in the history of the United States.

18

In her 1912 short story collection *Mrs. Spring Fragrance*, Sui Sin Far writes of the challenges faced by Chinese immigrants in the United States. Her most poignant stories address the anguish of family separations. In the story "In the Land of the Free," immigrant parents fight for ten months to have their infant child restored to them after he is removed by customs officials due to a paperwork issue. _____ a couple in "Children of Peace" lament that their children are growing up in San Francisco's Chinatown rather than among their own families in China.

Which choice completes the text with the most logical transition?

Ⓐ Besides,

Ⓑ By contrast,

Ⓒ In fact,

Ⓓ Similarly,

19

Scientists have identified a number of instances in which human activity has contributed to decreases in the genetic diversity of plant and animal populations. _____ in the case of Atlantic eelgrass, which supports coastal ecosystems throughout the ocean, marine biologists attribute the plant's low genetic diversity to prehistoric natural events. The eelgrass in the Atlantic had only recently migrated from its origin in the Pacific Ocean when the Pleistocene Ice Age began, which limited the eelgrass's development in its new ocean.

Which choice completes the text with the most logical transition?

Ⓐ By contrast,

Ⓑ Second,

Ⓒ Likewise,

Ⓓ Therefore,

20

Synesthesia is a phenomenon in which multiple senses are triggered together, such as perceiving letters as particular colors. Synesthesia may seem incomprehensible to those who don't experience it, yet synesthetes often grow up assuming that their experience of the world is universal. _____ many individuals with synesthesia report that they did not realize their perception was unique until they had reached adulthood.

Which choice completes the text with the most logical transition?

Ⓐ Nevertheless,

Ⓑ Next,

Ⓒ To conclude,

Ⓓ In fact,

REFLECT

Directions: Take a few minutes to recall what you've learned and what you've been practicing in this chapter. Consider the following questions, jot down your best answer for each one, and then compare your reflections to the expert responses that follow. Use your level of confidence to determine what to do next.

What do Synthesis questions ask you to do, and how should you approach them strategically?

_____

_____

_____

What three most common types of transition words are common on the SAT? What are some examples of each type of transition word?

_____

_____

_____

How can predicting help you correctly answer Expression of Ideas questions? What types of answer choices can you eliminate on Expression of Ideas questions?

_____

_____

_____

What are the main differences you see between SAT Expression of Ideas questions and those you're used to from tests in school?

_____

_____

_____

How will you approach SAT Reading and Writing questions more strategically as you continue to practice and improve your performance? Are there any specific habits you will practice to make your approach to SAT Reading and Writing more effective and efficient?

_____

_____

_____

Expert Responses

What do Synthesis questions ask you to do, and how should you approach them strategically?

Synthesis questions ask you to bring ideas from the passage together to achieve a specific rhetorical goal (such as finding a similarity or a difference) that is identified in the question stem. You should restate this goal in your own words, and then read the passage with this specific goal in mind. Focus only on the details that are relevant to the goal, and, when finished reading, make a prediction statement that would achieve the goal. Eliminate answer choices that fail to address the specific goal.

What three most common types of transition words are common on the SAT? What are some examples of each type of transition word?

The three most common types of transitions words on the SAT include: continuation words (such as "moreover" and "further") that indicate a continuation of the same point, contrast words (such as "but" and "however") that indicate a change in direction or a point of difference, and cause-and-effect words (such as "therefore" and "because") that indicate that one idea causes another idea or leads to a conclusion.

How can predicting help you correctly answer Expression of Ideas questions? What types of answer choices can you eliminate on Expression of Ideas questions?

When you are able to do so, predicting the correct answer can increase your accuracy and speed by helping you focus in on the one correct answer and avoid spending time comparing the answer choices to one another. Synthesis and Transitions questions often lend themselves to predicting. When eliminating answer choices, toss out any that fail to address the specific goal (Synthesis questions) and any that distort the connection between the ideas in the passage (Transitions questions).

What are the main differences you see between SAT Expression of Ideas questions and those you're used to from tests in school?

Depending on the kinds of classes and teachers you've had in high school, the skills rewarded on SAT Expression of Ideas questions may be more or less familiar. In general, Expression of Ideas questions do not ask you to simply recall facts, but they instead require you to determine relationships between ideas.

How will you approach SAT Reading and Writing questions more strategically as you continue to practice and improve your performance? Are there any specific habits you will practice to make your approach to SAT Reading and Writing more effective and efficient?

There is no one-size-fits-all answer here. Reflect on your own habits in answering SAT Reading and Writing questions and give yourself an honest assessment of your strengths and weaknesses. Consider the strategies you've seen experts use in this chapter, and put them to work in your own practice to increase your accuracy, speed, and confidence.

Next Steps

If you answered most questions correctly in the "How Much Have You Learned?" section, and if your responses to the Reflect questions were similar to those of the SAT expert, then consider Expression of Ideas questions an area of strength and move on to the next chapter. Come back to this topic periodically to prevent yourself from getting rusty.

If you don't yet feel confident, review the lessons in this chapter that you have not yet mastered. Then, try the questions you missed again. As always, be sure to review the explanations closely.

Check Your Work – Chapter 20

1. D

Difficulty: Easy

Category: Expression of Ideas

Getting to the Answer: Always read the question first, and check the choices as soon as you can predict the answer. Here, the question asks for a similarity between spider webs and springs, so keep this idea in mind as you read the points. The first point provides a fact about spiders: they can make webs that store mechanical energy. The second point provides a fact about springs: when they are stretched, they store mechanical energy. That similarity is enough to identify **(D)** as the correct answer. The remaining points provide additional information, but predicting as you read can save valuable time on test day.

None of the incorrect choices draw a comparison. (A) only discusses spiders, (B) only mentions spider webs, and (C) only discusses springs.

2. D

Difficulty: Easy

Category: Expression of Ideas

Getting to the Answer: The question stem indicates that the correct answer will focus on what makes the *Trieste* important. The first two bullet points detail background information about the Challenger Deep and bathyscaphes; it is not until the third bullet point that Trieste is mentioned as the vehicle in which Walsh and Piccard descended into the Challenger Deep in 1960, which is a strong clue as to why it might be important. The fourth bullet point mentions a complication that happened during the mission, but that detail does not contribute to why the *Trieste* was important. The last bullet does not directly relate to the *Trieste*; it just references another explorer, but importantly, that explorer did not complete his trip until 2012. Predict that the *Trieste* is significant because *it descended to the bottom of the Challenger Deep for the first time.* Choice **(D)** matches that prediction.

Choice (A) should be eliminated because it focuses on a detail about the trip, but not on why the *Trieste* was important. Choice (B) focuses on what the *Trieste* was, but not why it was important; it is incorrect. Choice (C) is incorrect because it does not mention the *Trieste* at all.

3. C

Difficulty: Medium

Category: Expression of Ideas

Getting to the Answer: Since the question stem asks for you to "introduce" the novel, read for information about the novel that would help people understand it as a story. Notice that the stem says that you can assume the reader is familiar with the author, so the correct choice does not have to include background information aimed at introducing Ward. The first two bullet points largely describe Ward; it isn't until the last two bullet points that *Sing, Unburied, Sing* is described as having three narrators. Use this information in your prediction and eliminate both (B) and (D) since neither includes mention of the narrators; both are incorrect. Choice (A) may be tempting, but notice that the choice does not mention the title by name; such information would have to be included in an effective introduction to a book. Eliminate it. Choice **(C)** is the only choice that includes the book title and mention of the three narrators, so it is correct.

4. C

Difficulty: Medium

Category: Expression of Ideas

Getting to the Answer: The question asks for a contrast between the original plan for the Appalachian Trail and the Trail today. Focus on these two ideas as you read the points. Note the details about the Trail mentioned in the first point: its length, starting and ending points, and general description, "a wilderness footpath that traverses the Appalachian Mountains." The second point describes a benefit of the Trail for hikers, and the third point describes how the Trail benefited wilderness preservation. The original plan for the Trail has not yet been mentioned, so expect to find that information coming up in one of the final points. The fourth point (finally!) mentions the original plan. MacKaye wanted to include communities along the way. Read the final point quickly; it only describes the usage of the Trail today. A good prediction would be something like, *MacKaye wanted the Trail to include support communities, but now it is a wilderness path.* This prediction matches **(C)**, the correct answer.

None of the incorrect choices include "the original plan" for the Trail. (A) mentions MacKaye, but not his vision for the Trail. Choices (B) and (D) do present contrasting views of the Trail, but again, lack any mention of "the original plan."

Reading & Writing

5. A
Difficulty: Hard
Category: Expression of Ideas
Getting to the Answer: Notice that the question stem establishes two goals; the correct answer must specify *both* "the time of inception," which means the starting time, *and* the purpose of the two people's collaborative work. Read for this information. The first two bullet points discuss the establishment and purpose of the Alpha Suffrage Club. The next four bullet points discuss the contributions of co-founders Wells and Squire to the Alpha Suffrage Club. This club is the "collaborative work" that the stem alludes to, so return to the first two bullet points to formulate a prediction: *Wells and Squire co-founded the Alpha Suffrage Club in 1913 for the purpose of engaging Black women in the fight for women's suffrage*. Match to choice **(A)**, the correct answer.

Incorrect choices (B) and (D) are missing one of the goals; (B) describes the purpose of the Alpha Suffrage Club, but it does not include the year 1913, and (D) contains the year, but not the purpose of the club. Choice (C) contains neither the purpose nor the year, so it is incorrect as well.

6. D
Difficulty: Hard
Category: Expression of Ideas
Getting to the Answer: The question stem specifies that the correct answer will summarize the study, so read for facts about who conducted the study, when the study was conducted, and what the results were. The first bullet point contains background information about the issue being studied. The second bullet point contains the names of the researchers (Paul-Antoine Libourel and Won Young Lee), the date of the study (2023), and the aim of the study. The last two bullet points contain the results and implications of the study. Make a prediction that includes the researchers, the date of the study, and the results: *Libourel and Lee's 2023 study found that penguins sleep in "microsleep" intervals*. Match this prediction to **(D)**, the correct choice.

All the other choices are incorrect because they do not include a description of the results; furthermore, (A) also leaves out the names of the researchers and (B) leaves out the date.

7. D
Difficulty: Easy
Category: Expression of Ideas
Getting to the Answer: The phrase "logical transition" indicates that this is a Transitions question. To determine the correct transition word to use in context, first determine the relationship between the ideas it must connect. The first part of this sentence describes a person as "passionate," and the second part says that "her enthusiasm . . . inspires her." The second part elaborates on how her passion motivates her, so a continuation transition is needed to connect the two clauses. The correct choice is **(D)**.

Incorrect choices (A) and (C) signal contrast. (B) is incorrect because "lastly" is only a logical transition word at the end of a process or list, wherein the previous items have been laid out.

8. C
Difficulty: Medium
Category: Expression of Ideas
Getting to the Answer: As indicated by the phrase "logical transition," this is a Transitions question. Identify the context clues closest to the blank. The sentence describes part of the process of the first way that temperature affects chemical reactions. The "probability that the molecules will collide" must increase *as a result of* the acceleration of the molecules. This is a cause-and-effect relationship and requires a cause-and-effect transition word. Eliminate (A); "For instance" would indicate that the probability is *an example of* the increased acceleration. Choice (B) is a sequence transition word that illogically interrupts the use of "First" and "Second" in the passage, so eliminate (B). The correct choice is **(C)**; it logically expresses the cause-and-effect relationship indicated in the passage. Incorrect choice (D) is a contrast transition word.

9. A
Difficulty: Medium
Category: Expression of Ideas
Getting to the Answer: The sentence that contains the missing transition word provides little context: the peanut is the "only plant. . .known to self-sow. . .without intervention." Yet, when paired with the passage's first sentence, which states that most plants' seeds are sown with intervention ("using water, winds, or animals"), it becomes clear that a contrast transition word is needed. Choice **(A)** is the only contrast word and is correct.

Incorrect choice (B) signals continuation and choices (C) and (D) are cause-and-effect transition words.

10. D
Difficulty: Hard
Category: Expression of Ideas
Getting to the Answer: Carefully analyze the relationship between the ideas before and after the blank. The sentence before the blank refers to "an alternative trend" that differs from the practice of clothing manufacturers making clothing "as inexpensively as possible." The next sentence explains that clothing companies are selling more fabrics made by workers who are paid better wages. The second sentence thus *describes* the "alternative trend." Look for a transition word in the answer choices that reflects this relationship.

Choice (A) can be eliminated because it is a continuation transition. The increase in sales of free trade fabrics is not *in addition to* the new trend; it *describes* the new trend. Choice (B) is incorrect because there is not a cause-and-effect relationship between the ideas. Choice (C) is a continuation transition and can be eliminated for the same reason as (A). Correct choice **(D)** logically connects the mention of "an alternative trend" to a description of what the new trend entails: increased sales of free trade clothing.

11. D
Difficulty: Medium
Category: Expression of Ideas
Getting to the Answer: The passage opens with the reputation of mosquitoes and then talks about the only time when female mosquitoes require blood. It then further continues that idea with the use of the continuation transition word "indeed," that mosquitoes primarily feed on nectar, not blood. Predict a contrast word such as "but" or "however" to show the comparison between the reality and the reputation about the mosquitoes' diet. Choice **(D)** matches this contrast and is correct.

Choices (A) and (C) are both cause-and-effect transitions, but the mosquitoes' reputation does not change their dietary habitat. Choice (B) is a continuation transition that does not compare the two ideas.

12. C
Difficulty: Easy
Category: Expression of Ideas
Getting to the Answer: Begin by identifying the two ideas that are connected by the blank. The idea before the missing word is that Georgia is known as "the Peach State;" the idea after the blank is that Georgia is only "the fourth largest" producer of peaches. The author is making a contrast between Georgia's claim to fame and its actual rank as a producer of the fruit. Therefore, the correct choice will indicate that this is a contrasting connection. Choice **(C)** is correct.

Incorrect choices (A) and (B) are continuation transition words. Choice (D) signals a cause-and-effect relationship.

13. C
Difficulty: Medium
Category: Expression of Ideas
Getting to the Answer: The correct transition word to use in context will connect the two listed reasons that uranium glass has become popular again. The first reason is found in the second sentence and the second reason is in the last sentence. Therefore, the correct transition word will signal a continuation of the list. Eliminate (A) "subsequently," because even though it is a continuation word, it refers to things that happen at a later time. This passage refers to reasons that are coinciding during this resurgence. Eliminate (B); it creates an illogical contrast. Choice **(C)** is correct; it signals continuation and that the events are concurring. Incorrect choice (D) signals contrast.

14. A
Difficulty: Medium
Category: Expression of Ideas
Getting to the Answer: The sentence that contains the missing transition word provides little context: "linguists agree that a . . . baby's brain is . . . preprogrammed" and it is "natural for a baby to talk." In the preceding sentence, the author claims that infants "begin gaining proficiency in . . . languages long before" they start making "discernible words." These claims are related; the second sentence elaborates on the same general concept that is introduced in the first. Choice **(A)** is the only continuation transition word and is correct.

Incorrect choice (B) signals that the second sentence provides an idea that is additional but separate from the idea in the first sentence; however, both are concerned with infant language acquisition. Choices (C) and (D) are incorrect because they are contrast transition words.

15. B
Difficulty: Medium
Category: Expression of Ideas
Getting to the Answer: Since the question asks for a similarity between the works, look for what the works have in common as you read the bullet points. The third bullet point describes "The Yellow Wallpaper," stating that the female character suffers when she can't act freely. The last bullet point describes *Women and Economics*, stating that Gilman argues that women should be able to work. The content of both addresses women's autonomy, which the second bullet point identified as a general theme of Gilman's writings; choice **(B)** is correct. Note the similarity keyword "both" in this answer choice.

Choices (A) and (D) are incorrect because they address Gilman's work in general rather than a similarity between the two specific works. Choice (C) is incorrect because it highlights a difference, rather than a similarity, between the works; note the contrast keyword "while."

16. D
Difficulty: Hard
Category: Expression of Ideas
Getting to the Answer: The correct answer will "present the study" and its methodology. As you read the bullet points, think about how you would summarize the purpose of the study (present the study), and focus especially on the researchers' method, or the process they used to conduct the study. The first bullet point identifies the purpose of the study: determining the impact of a tomato-heavy diet on pigs' gut microbiomes. The next two points describe the study's methodology: the researchers sequenced the microbial DNA from the waste of pigs fed the regular and the tomato-heavy diets. Eliminate answer choices that fail to summarize the purpose of the study or its methodology.

Choice (A) can be eliminated because it focuses on the findings of the study; it fails to describe the method the researchers used. Choice (B) addresses the purpose of the study, but it is incorrect because it also omits the study's methodology. Choice (C) is incorrect for multiple reasons: it does not include the

study's methodology, and it misrepresents the purpose and conclusion of the study. The study considered a tomato-heavy diet, which is not mentioned in choice (C), and this particular study only identified the presence of the bacteria ratio; it did not demonstrate that the bacteria ratio is linked to health benefits. Choice **(D)** is correct because it accurately summarizes the purpose and the methodology of the study.

17. B
Difficulty: Hard
Category: Expression of Ideas
Getting to the Answer: Based on the question stem, the correct answer must introduce the audience to the Minute Man National Historical Park. The audience knows about the cause and significance of the Lexington and Concord battles but does not know about the Minute Man park. As you read the bullet points, think about what a reader with this background would need to know about the Minute Man park. The first three points include the ideas that National Historical Parks are historically significant and that the Minute Man National Historical Park contains the battle sites at Lexington and Concord. The last two points concern the events and significance of Lexington and Concord—since the question specifies that the audience is already familiar with this information, predict that the correct answer will address the first three points. Choice **(B)** is correct because it introduces the Minute Man National Historical Park in a way that assumes the audience already knows why Lexington and Concord are historically significant.

Choice (C) is incorrect because it unnecessarily specifies why Lexington and Concord are historically significant, while the question stem states that the audience already knows this information. Choices (A) and (D) are incorrect because they fail to mention the Minute Man park; further, all the information in (A) is already known by the audience, according to the question stem.

18. D
Difficulty: Easy
Category: Expression of Ideas
Getting to the Answer: When asked to find the most logical transition, identify the two ideas that are connected by the transition as you read the passage. The passage begins by making the claim that Sui Sin Far wrote about Chinese immigrants experiencing family separations. The sentence before the transition

gives an example of a family's separation from the story "In the Land of the Free." The idea after the transition addresses another example of a family separation in the story "Children of Peace." Since the second story is another similar example of a family separation story, **(D)** is correct.

Choice (A) would incorrectly emphasize how the stories are distinct, rather than highlighting that both stories are about immigrant family separations. Choice (B) is incorrect because the story examples do not contrast. Choice (C) is incorrect because "In fact" would indicate the second story elaborates on the first story, rather than them both being similar examples of immigrant stories.

19. A
Difficulty: Medium
Category: Expression of Ideas
Getting to the Answer: When asked to find the most logical transition, identify the two ideas that are connected by the transition as you read the passage. The first idea is that human activity has led to lower genetic diversity. The second idea is that the low genetic diversity of Atlantic eelgrass is due to "prehistoric natural"—not human—events. These ideas contrast, so **(A)** is correct.

Choice (B) is incorrect because the ideas are not presented in sequence. Choice (C) is incorrect because although both ideas involve decreases in genetic diversity, the passage emphasizes their *different* causes, not their *similarities* (Likewise). Choice (D) is incorrect because the Atlantic eelgrass's low genetic diversity is not a *result of* (Therefore) human activity decreasing genetic diversity in other populations.

20. D
Difficulty: Medium
Category: Expression of Ideas
Getting to the Answer: When asked to find the most logical transition, identify the two ideas that are connected by the transition as you read the passage. The idea before the transition is that many synesthetes often think that everyone perceives the world as they do. The idea after the transition is that many synesthetes don't realize they perceive things differently until they are adults. The second idea elaborates on the first idea, providing a more specific detail about the assumption of many synesthetes, so **(D)** is correct.

Choice (A) is incorrect because the ideas do not contrast (Nevertheless), but rather the second idea builds upon the first. Although the ideas mention "grow[ing] up" and "adulthood," choice (B) is incorrect because the ideas about how synesthetes see themselves are not presented in sequential order in the passage. Choice (C) is incorrect because synesthetes not realizing their perception was unique until adulthood is not the conclusion of the passage; the passage is a summary of synesthesia.

[CHAPTER 21]

STANDARD ENGLISH CONVENTIONS

LEARNING OBJECTIVES

After completing this chapter, you will be able to:

- Determine the correct punctuation and/or conjunctions to form a complete sentence
- Identify and correct inappropriate uses of commas, dashes, semicolons, and colons
- Use punctuation to set off simple parenthetical elements
- Identify and correct subject-verb agreement issues
- Identify and correct verb tense issues
- Identify and correct parallelism issues
- Identify and correct pronoun agreement issues
- Identify and correct modifier agreement issues
- Identify and correct inappropriate uses of apostrophes

HOW MUCH DO YOU KNOW?

Directions

Try the questions that follow. When you're done, check your answers and reasoning against ours in the "Check Your Work" section. If they closely match, you may be able to move quickly through the chapter. If they do not, spend some extra time with the chapter to grow your SAT Reading and Writing skills.

1

The Battle of Myeongnyang took place on October 26, 1597. It saw a Korean fleet of a mere twelve ships under the command of Admiral Yi Sun-sin defeat a Japanese fleet of approximately 130 warships. Japan lost more than thirty warships and roughly half of their sailors in the battle, while _____ amounted to only two sailors. What made Admiral Yi's underdog victory all the more remarkable was that he had no naval training, being a career army officer whose main experience was fighting nomadic horsemen.

Which choice completes the text so that it conforms to the conventions of Standard English?

Ⓐ   Koreas losses

Ⓑ   Koreas' losses'

Ⓒ   Korea's losses

Ⓓ   Korea's losses'

2

Lactic acid does not form during normal daily activities because our muscles have a small store of ATP available, which is easily replenished as it is used. More intense activity, however, quickly uses up that _____ the store is used up, and if the level of oxygen needed for the activity is greater than the amount reaching the muscles, lactic acid starts to build up. The buildup of lactic acid occurs most quickly while engaging in so-called power sports, such as sprinting.

Which choice completes the text so that it conforms to the conventions of Standard English?

Ⓐ   store and once

Ⓑ   store once,

Ⓒ   store; once

Ⓓ   store once

3

The goldfish is the oldest ornamental fish in the world. It has been selectively bred for thousands of years, starting in Ancient China but spreading throughout the world from there. Goldfish are a diminutive breed of carp, typically four inches long. Historians studying this type of fish _____ that they were originally farmed as a food source. Over time, goldfish were selectively bred for variations of color and shape.

Which choice completes the text so that it conforms to the conventions of Standard English?

(A) believes

(B) have believed

(C) believe

(D) will believe

4

Phosphophyllite's name derives in part from its chemical composition (hydrated zinc _____ and from the Greek word *phyllon,* literally "leaf," in a reference to the gem's softness. It rates a mere 3.5 out of 10 on the Mohs scale of hardness, meaning a copper penny's edge would be enough to scratch the gem's surface.

Which choice completes the text so that it conforms to the conventions of Standard English?

(A) phosphate—

(B) phosphate)

(C) phosphate),

(D) phosphate

5

In 1807, President Thomas Jefferson attempted to end British and French attacks on American sea vessels by passing the Embargo Act, which enacted a prohibition on trade with foreign nations that the early twentieth-century _____ "was disastrous" and "ruined … American shipping."

Which choice completes the text so that it conforms to the conventions of Standard English?

(A) historian Albert J. Beveridge claimed

(B) historian Albert J. Beveridge, claimed,

(C) historian, Albert J. Beveridge, claimed,

(D) historian, Albert J. Beveridge, claimed

Reading & Writing

6

The Himalayan blackberry, *Rubus armeniacus*, _____ a thorny shrub native to Eurasia. However, while not native to the state of Washington, it spreads aggressively and forms impenetrable thickets that negatively impact the local ecosystem. Thus, it is considered invasive.

Which choice completes the text so that it conforms to the conventions of Standard English?

(A) was

(B) were

(C) are

(D) is

Check Your Work

1.   C
Difficulty: Easy
Category: Standard English Conventions
Getting to the Answer: An apostrophe is used to indicate the possessive form of a noun. In the blank, the "losses" belong to "Korea," so "Korea" needs an apostrophe to indicate ownership. This makes (A) incorrect. When using a singular noun, the format is an apostrophe followed by an "s." Because there is only one Korea being discussed in the passage, the plural possessive would not be used here; (B) is incorrect. While there is more than one loss being discussed ("losses"), plural nouns are formed without an apostrophe; (D) is incorrect. **(C)** is correct because it uses the singular possessive form of "Korea" and the plural noun "losses."

2.   C
Difficulty: Hard
Category: Standard English Conventions
Getting to the Answer: This passage demonstrates the difficulty posed by complex sentence construction. The part of the sentence immediately after the blank looks like an independent clause ("the store is used up"). However, adding the word "Once" will turn it into a dependent clause. Also, there is a comma plus a conjunction ("and") that appears within that same sentence, creating a sentence structure that can potentially be confusing. In cases like this, it can be helpful to break down the sentence being tested. Focus on finding the independent clause(s). Here, there are two: "More intense activity . . . quickly uses up that store" and "lactic acid starts to build up." These are the two independent clauses that must be correctly connected. Choice **(C)** is correct because it places a semicolon between the two complete thoughts. Incorrect choices (A), (B), and (D) create run-ons.

3.   C
Difficulty: Medium
Category: Standard English Conventions
Getting to the Answer: A verb must agree with its subject in person and number. The plural noun "Historians" thus needs a plural verb, and, from the context of the text, the verb should be present tense. Thus, **(C)** is correct. (A) is incorrect because it is a singular present tense verb, which would not match the plural "Historians." (B) and (D) are inconsistent with the present tense across the verbs throughout the passage; "have believed" is a plural past tense verb, while "will believe" is in future tense.

4.   B
Difficulty: Medium
Category: Standard English Conventions
Getting to the Answer: Parenthetical information is set apart from the sentence's main body. Dashes, parentheses, and commas can all be used for that task. However, the usage of parenthetical elements must be consistent within a given sentence. Parentheses must always come in pairs. Thus, we can eliminate (A) and (D) because they would leave the parentheses unpaired. (C) completes the parentheses, but it adds an unneeded comma. Choice **(B)** is correct.

5.   A
Difficulty: Medium
Category: Standard English Conventions
Getting to the Answer: Every punctuation mark on a Standard English Conventions question must serve a purpose. In this sentence, the name "Albert J. Beveridge" is not parenthetical. Otherwise, the reader would not know which "early twentieth-century historian" made the statement about the Embargo Act. Eliminate (C) and (D), which use sets of commas to set off the name as though it were parenthetical. Neither should a comma separate the noun "Albert J. Beveridge" from its verb, "claimed"; eliminate (B). Nor is any punctuation needed before the integrated quotations that follow the word "claimed." No punctuation is necessary, so **(A)** is correct.

6.   D
Difficulty: Medium
Category: Standard English Conventions
Getting to the Answer: The first sentence is asking for the appropriate verb tense. If the Himalayan blackberry still exists, it should be referred to in present tense. If it is extinct, it should be referred to in the past tense. From the passage's context, we can conclude the Himalayan blackberry still exists, eliminating (A) and (B). The first sentence discusses a singular species of blackberry, the Himalayan blackberry. Thus, we can eliminate (C) because "are" refers to a plural subject while "is" refers to a singular subject. **(D)** is correct.

THE KAPLAN METHOD WITH STANDARD ENGLISH CONVENTIONS QUESTIONS

LEARNING OBJECTIVE

After this lesson, you will be able to:

• Apply the Method to SAT Reading and Writing questions

How to Approach Standard English Conventions Questions

In the previous chapters, you've practiced applying the Method for SAT Reading and Writing to questions that ask about Information and Ideas, Craft and Structure, and Expression of Ideas. You'll use the same method when tackling Standard English Conventions questions but with one important extra task on Step 1. Review the method:

THE METHOD FOR SAT READING AND WRITING

STEP 1 What is the question asking?

• Standard English Conventions questions **ONLY**: Look at the answer choices for clues

STEP 2 What do I need to look for in the passage?

STEP 3 What answer strategy is best?

• Predict and Match
• Eliminate

Note that on Step 1, if you identify the question as a Standard English Conventions question (typically indicated by the stem: *Which choice completes the text so that it conforms to the conventions of Standard English?*), take a moment to glance at the answer choices before looking at the passage. Think about what Standard English conventions you notice in the answer choices. Do they contain variations on punctuation? Different verb tenses? A variety of modifying phrases or pronouns? If you identify a pattern in the answer choices, you'll have a better idea of what type of issue you'll need to correct as you read the passage.

Take a look at the question that follows and think about how you would approach it on test day. Then compare your approach to the explanation that follows.

The Op Art paintings of British artist Bridget Riley are characterized by their effect of creating optical illusions for the _____ waves of lines that appear to move, black and white compositions that seem to contain colors, and geometric patterns that give the impression of pulsations.

Which choice completes the text so that it conforms to the conventions of Standard English?

A) viewer. Including

B) viewer, including

C) viewer, among these were

D) viewer; including

Now consider how an SAT expert might apply the Method for Reading and Writing to this Standard English Conventions question.

Step 1. What is the question asking?

This question asks you to choose the answer choice that "conforms to the conventions of Standard English." Since this question concerns Standard English conventions, be sure to glance at the answer choices for clues about the issue tested *before looking at the passage*. This question contains a variety of punctuation marks after the word "viewer." Since these include different ways of combining the parts of a sentence—including commas, a period, and a semicolon—anticipate that this question will test sentence structure.

Step 2. What do I need to look for in the passage?

Since the answer choices indicate that this question tests sentence structure, be on the lookout for potential sentence fragments or run-ons as you read the passage. Consider whether the parts of the sentence before and after the punctuation are complete thoughts. The first part of the sentence ("The Op Art paintings . . . are characterized by their effect . . .") is a complete idea, or an independent clause. Most of the answer choices have the word "including" after the punctuation; the portion of the sentence beginning "including waves of lines . . . " is a list and is *not* a complete thought on its own.

Step 3. What answer strategy is best?

After evaluating the passage for the issue you identified in Step 1, consider which answer strategy—Predict and Match or Eliminate—works best for you on the question. Here, an expert test taker might realize that a comma should be used to connect a complete thought to a phrase that is not a complete thought. Choice **(B)** appears to be correct; confirm the choice by reading the answer choice back into the sentence. Choice **(B)** correctly uses a comma to connect a complete idea to a phrase.

Alternatively, an expert test taker might evaluate the answer choices and eliminate those that result in sentence fragments or run-ons. Choice (A) can be eliminated because it turns the second part of the sentence into a fragment, since the part beginning "Including" is not a complete thought. Choice (C) is incorrect because the words "among these were" turn the second part of the sentence into a complete thought, and two complete thoughts cannot be joined by only a comma. Finally, choice (D) is incorrect because a semicolon can be used to connect two complete thoughts, not a complete thought and a phrase.

If you were unsure about recognizing sentence fragments and run-ons on this question, don't worry. The rest of the lessons in this chapter will review the specific areas tested on Standard English Conventions questions: basic sentence structure, punctuation, verbs, pronouns, and modifiers. As you work through each lesson, practice applying the Method for Reading and Writing to every Standard English Conventions question. Use the answer choices to identify what issue is being tested, and tailor your approach to reading the passage appropriately. Then, predict or eliminate based on the best approach for you.

SENTENCE STRUCTURE: THE BASICS

LEARNING OBJECTIVE

After this lesson, you will be able to:

- Determine the correct punctuation and/or conjunctions to form a complete sentence

To answer a question like this:

In the late spring of 1953, the New Zealander Sir Edmund Hillary and the Nepali Tenzing Norgay became the first people to walk on the top of the world. After Hillary and Norgay underwent a grueling expedition that spanned several _____ finally reached the summit of Mount Everest.

Which choice completes the text so that it conforms to the conventions of Standard English?

A) months. They

B) months, and they

C) months; they

D) months, they

You need to know this:

Fragments and Run-Ons

A complete sentence must have both a subject and a verb and express a complete thought. If any one of these elements is missing, the sentence is a **fragment**. You can recognize a fragment because the sentence will not make sense as written. There are some examples in the table that follows.

MISSING ELEMENT	EXAMPLE	CORRECTED SENTENCE
Subject	*Ran a marathon.*	*Lola ran a marathon.*
Verb	*Lola a marathon.*	
Complete thought	*While Lola ran a marathon.*	*While Lola ran a marathon, her friends cheered for her.*

The fragment *While Lola ran a marathon* is an example of a dependent clause: it has a subject (Lola) and a verb (ran), but it does not express a complete thought because it starts with a subordinating conjunction (while). Notice what the word *while* does to the meaning: While Lola ran a marathon, what happened? To fix this type of fragment, eliminate the subordinating conjunction or join the dependent clause to an independent clause using a comma. Subordinating conjunctions are words and phrases such as *since, because, unless, although,* and *due to*.

Unlike a dependent clause, an independent clause can stand on its own as a complete sentence. If a sentence has more than one independent clause, those clauses must be properly joined. If they are not, the sentence is a **run-on**: *Morgan enjoys hiking, he climbs a new mountain every summer.* There are several ways to correct a run-on, as shown in the following table.

TO CORRECT A RUN-ON	EXAMPLE
Use a period	*Morgan enjoys hiking. He climbs a new mountain every summer.*
Use a semicolon	*Morgan enjoys hiking; he climbs a new mountain every summer.*
Use a colon	*Morgan enjoys hiking: he climbs a new mountain every summer.*
Use a dash	*Morgan enjoys hiking—he climbs a new mountain every summer.*
Make one clause dependent	*Since Morgan enjoys hiking, he climbs a new mountain every summer.*
Add a FANBOYS conjunction: For, And, Nor, But, Or, Yet, So	*Morgan enjoys hiking, so he climbs a new mountain every summer.*

You need to do this:

To recognize and correct errors involving fragments, run-ons, and semicolons, familiarize yourself with the ways in which they are tested:

- Fragments
  - If a sentence is missing a subject, a verb, or a complete thought, it is a fragment.
  - Correct the fragment by adding the missing element.
- Run-ons
  - If a sentence includes two independent clauses, they must be properly joined.
  - Employ one of the following options to properly punctuate independent clauses:
    - Use a period.
    - Use a semicolon.
    - Use a comma and a FANBOYS (*for*, *and*, *nor*, *but*, *or*, *yet*, *so*) conjunction.
    - Use a colon.
    - Use a dash.
    - Make one clause dependent by using a subordinating conjunction (*since*, *because*, *therefore*, *unless*, *although*, *due to*, etc.).

Explanation:

The portion ending with "months" is a dependent clause because it does not express a complete thought. Eliminate (A); it results in a fragment, as a dependent clause cannot stand alone. Eliminate (B) because using both "after" and "and" creates an error—a comma and a FANBOYS conjunction are used to join two independent clauses. Eliminate (C) because it results in the same error as (A). A semicolon, like a period, is used between two independent clauses. Choice **(D)** is correct because it uses a comma to join the dependent clause with the independent clause that follows.

If sentence formation or semicolons give you trouble, study the preceding information and try these Drill questions before completing the "Try on Your Own" questions that follow. Drill answers can be found in the Check Your Work section at the end of the chapter.

Drill

a. <u>Correct the fragment by adding a subject</u>: Brought snacks to the weekend study session.

b. <u>Correct the fragment by completing the thought</u>: After getting to the stadium.

c. <u>Correct the run-on sentence with a punctuation mark</u>: The new arts center just opened it has a crafts room for children under 13.

d. <u>Correct the run-on sentence with a punctuation mark</u>: Herodotus is known as one of the first historians he is even called "The Father of History."

e. <u>Make one clause dependent to correct the run-on sentence</u>: Herodotus is sometimes accused of making up stories for his histories, he claimed he simply recorded what he had been told.

Try on Your Own

Directions

Take as much time as you need on these questions. Work carefully and methodically. There will be an opportunity for timed practice later in the book.

1

In the early days of railway _____ passenger comfort was not a high priority. Passenger railroad cars were noisy, dirty from the soot of the coal-fired engine, and typically equipped with rows of hard wooden benches and few amenities.

Which choice completes the text so that it conforms to the conventions of Standard English?

Ⓐ travel

Ⓑ travel,

Ⓒ travel;

Ⓓ travel, and

2

Studies have shown that the charged particles released by solar flares, associated with sunspots, can react with the Earth's magnetic _____ the radiation can disrupt satellite communications, radio broadcasts, and even cell phone calls.

Which choice completes the text so that it conforms to the conventions of Standard English?

Ⓐ field,

Ⓑ field;

Ⓒ field, however

Ⓓ field so the

3

Early jazz music, like much of Western music up to that time, generally used chord tones to create melodies. Bebop jazz, in contrast, relied heavily on chromatic ornamentation and borrowed notes from altered _____ new harmonic opportunities for musicians.

Which choice completes the text so that it conforms to the conventions of Standard English?

(A) scales. Opening up

(B) scales; opening up

(C) scales, opening up

(D) scales, and opening up

4

When the 804-foot *Hindenburg* was launched in 1936, it was the largest airship in the world. However, the highly flammable hydrogen gas used to fill the blimp was always a safety concern. On May 6, 1937, in Lakehurst, New Jersey, as the *Hindenburg* _____ suddenly burst into flames, killing 36 of the 97 passengers and crew on board. This horrific disaster marked the end of the use of airships for passenger transportation.

Which choice completes the text so that it conforms to the conventions of Standard English?

(A) landed, it

(B) landed. It

(C) landed; it

(D) landed—it

5

Mauritius, a small island in the Indian Ocean, has a complicated history influenced by several international _____ was first colonized by the Portuguese in 1511, followed by the Dutch, the French, and the British. In 1947, the citizens of the island nation began working toward independence, and formally adopted their constitution in May of 1968.

Which choice completes the text so that it conforms to the conventions of Standard English?

(A) powers, it

(B) powers and it

(C) powers; and it

(D) powers: it

6

In 2021, the UCCA Center for Contemporary Art in Beijing featured a retrospective of the work of Cao Fei, one of China's most prominent multimedia artists. Several major international galleries had previously shown her _____ this was the first exhibition that examined Cao's entire career.

Which choice completes the text so that it conforms to the conventions of Standard English?

Ⓐ work but

Ⓑ work but,

Ⓒ work, but

Ⓓ work, but,

7

The Stroop test is a well-documented tool used to measure cognitive performance. In the test, subjects are shown the name of a color that is printed in colored _____ printed color may match the word, for example, the word "red" printed in red ink, or the printed color may be different from the word, such as the word "red" printed in green ink. The subject's task is to identify the name of the color of the ink, not the word presented, as quickly as possible.

Which choice completes the text so that it conforms to the conventions of Standard English?

Ⓐ ink the

Ⓑ ink the,

Ⓒ ink, the

Ⓓ ink. The

8

Bicycles are, by far, the most popular type of mechanical transportation. Almost 50% of households across the globe have a _____ more than those with cars. In a given year, China's production of bicycles outstrips the entire world's production of automobiles.

Which choice completes the text so that it conforms to the conventions of Standard English?

Ⓐ bicycle, far

Ⓑ bicycle; far

Ⓒ bicycle. Far

Ⓓ bicycle, this is

SENTENCE STRUCTURE: PUNCTUATION

LEARNING OBJECTIVES

After this lesson, you will be able to:

- Identify and correct inappropriate uses of commas, dashes, semicolons, and colons
- Use punctuation to set off simple parenthetical elements

To answer a question like this:

Ascending Mount Everest requires facing extreme dangers, including sudden weather changes, avalanches, and potential altitude sickness. Climbing Everest, however, may be easier than answering non-climbers when they ask why anyone would attempt to scale the mountain. Perhaps George Mallory said it best in 1923 before his ill-fated _____ "Because it is there."

Which choice completes the text so that it conforms to the conventions of Standard English?

A) climb;

B) climb:

C) climb, and

D) climb

You need to know this:

Answer choices often move punctuation marks around, replace them with other punctuation marks, or remove them altogether. When the answer choices include commas, dashes, semicolons, or colons, check to make sure the punctuation is used correctly in context.

Commas

There are two situations in which only commas are used: a series of items and introductory words or phrases.

USE COMMAS TO ...	COMMA(S)
Set off three or more items in a series	*Jeremiah packed a sleeping bag, a raincoat, and a lantern for his upcoming camping trip.*
Separate an introductory word or phrase from the rest of the sentence	*For example, carrots are an excellent source of several vitamins and minerals.*

Commas and Dashes

In many cases, either a comma or a dash may be used to punctuate a sentence. Note that only a comma can be used to set off a leading dependent clause from an independent clause.

USE COMMAS OR DASHES TO …	COMMA(S)	DASH(ES)
Separate independent clauses connected by a FANBOYS conjunction (For, And, Nor, But, Or, Yet, So)	*Jess finished her homework earlier than expected, so she started an assignment that was due the following week.*	*Jess finished her homework earlier than expected—so she started an assignment that was due the following week.*
Separate a dependent clause from an independent clause when the dependent clause is first	*Because Tyson wanted to organize his locker before class, he arrived at school a few minutes early.*	*N/A*
Separate parenthetical elements from the rest of the sentence (use either two commas or two dashes, not one of each; more information on parentheticals follows)	*Professor Mann, who is the head of the English department, is known for assigning extensive projects.*	*Professor Mann—who is the head of the English department—is known for assigning extensive projects.*

Colons and Dashes

A colon or a stand-alone dash can be used to introduce new ideas, often breaking the flow of the sentence. Note that the clause before the colon or dash must be able to stand on its own as a complete sentence.

USE COLONS AND DASHES TO …	COLON	DASH
Introduce and/or emphasize a short phrase, quotation, explanation, example, or list	*Sanjay had two important tasks to complete: a science experiment and an expository essay.*	*Sanjay had two important tasks to complete—a science experiment and an expository essay.*
Separate two independent clauses when the second clause explains, illustrates, or expands on the first sentence	*Highway 1 in Australia is one of the longest national highways in the world: it circles the entirety of the continent and connects every mainland state capital.*	*Highway 1 in Australia is one of the longest national highways in the world—it circles the entirety of the continent and connects every mainland state capital.*

Semicolons

Semicolons can be used in two specific ways. First, as you learned in the previous lesson, a semicolon can be used between two independent clauses, just as a period can. Second, semicolons are used to separate items in complex lists, which are lists in which one or more of the list items contains a comma.

USE SEMICOLONS TO …	SEMICOLON(S)
Join two independent clauses	*Lalia may not be able to come to the study group this weekend; she has to work Saturday afternoon.*
Separate items in a list if those items already include commas	*The salad bar includes hot soup; fruit, including pineapple and watermelon; and a selection of bread.*

Parenthetical Elements

A phrase such as *the capital of France* is considered parenthetical if the rest of the sentence is still grammatically correct when it is removed. Parenthetical elements may appear at the beginning, in the middle, or at the end of a sentence. The SAT frequently tests parentheticals in the middle of a sentence. When a parenthetical phrase appears in the middle of a sentence, do not mix and match; a parenthetical element must begin and end with the same type of punctuation.

PARENTHETICAL ELEMENT PLACEMENT	PARENTHESES	COMMA(S)	DASH(ES)
Beginning	N/A	The capital of France, Paris is a popular tourist destination.	N/A
Middle	Paris (the capital of France) is a popular tourist destination.	Paris, the capital of France, is a popular tourist destination.	Paris—the capital of France—is a popular tourist destination.
End	A popular tourist destination is Paris (the capital of France).	A popular tourist destination is Paris, the capital of France.	A popular tourist destination is Paris—the capital of France.

Unnecessary Punctuation

Knowing when punctuation should not be used is equally important. The SAT frequently has Standard English Conventions questions on which the correct answer is the choice with *no* punctuation, so if the answer choices include punctuation, take time to consider if it should be included at all.

DO NOT USE PUNCTUATION TO ...	INCORRECT	CORRECT
Separate a subject from its verb	The diligent student council, meets every week.	The diligent student council meets every week.
Separate a verb from its object or a preposition from its object	The diligent student council meets, every week.	The diligent student council meets every week.
Set off elements that are essential to a sentence's meaning	The, diligent student, council meets every week.	The diligent student council meets every week.
Separate adjectives that work together to modify a noun	The diligent, student council meets every week.	The diligent student council meets every week.

You need to do this:

If the answer choices include punctuation, ask yourself:

- Is the punctuation used correctly?

  The punctuation needs to be the correct type (comma, dash, semicolon, or colon) and in the correct location.

- Is the punctuation necessary?

  If you cannot identify a reason why the punctuation is included, the punctuation should be removed.

Explanation:

The answer choices contain different ways to use punctuation to introduce Mallory's quote. Since the blank here is intended to emphasize a short quotation, a colon or dash would be appropriate. **(B)** is correct. The semicolon in (A) is used incorrectly because it neither joins two independent clauses nor separates items containing commas in a series or list. Choice (C) is incorrect because a comma with a FANBOYS conjunction is used to join two independent clauses. Choice (D) is incorrect because it omits any punctuation to introduce the quote.

If commas, dashes, and colons give you trouble, study the information above and try these Drill questions before completing the following "Try on Your Own" questions. Edit each sentence to correct the punctuation issue. Drill answers can be found in the Check Your Work section at the end of the chapter.

Drill

a. For my birthday, I asked for my favorite dessert chocolate pecan pie.

b. The story of Emperor Nero playing the fiddle while Rome burned has been debunked by historians but the saying based on the tale remains popular.

c. The fact that koala fingerprints are nearly indistinguishable from human fingerprints, has occasionally led to mistakes at crime scenes.

d. Invented by Sir John Harrington in 1596 the flush toilet actually precedes modern indoor plumbing.

e. Toni Morrison born Chloe Wofford is one of America's most celebrated writers.

Try on Your Own

Directions

Take as much time as you need on these questions. Work carefully and methodically. There will be an opportunity for timed practice later in the book.

9

Although most of the products we buy today are made abroad in places well known to Americans, such as Mexico and China, a quick check of many clothing labels will reveal the name of a country that might not be _____

Which choice completes the text so that it conforms to the conventions of Standard English?

(A) expected Vietnam.

(B) expected; Vietnam.

(C) expected: Vietnam.

(D) expected. Vietnam.

10

What is it in a best-selling novel that causes the modern reader to continue turning the pages? The answer can be a bit slippery. Is it the psychological realism of the characters? Is it the drama of the events they encounter? Is it the modern author's consciousness of the position as author and the _____ with her readers?

Which choice completes the text so that it conforms to the conventions of Standard English?

(A) relationship—distant or intimate, serious or playful—that develops

(B) relationship—distant or intimate, serious or playful, that develops

(C) relationship: distant or intimate, serious or playful—that develops

(D) relationship: distant or intimate, serious or playful, that develops

11

Graphic designers wield a powerful influence over the modern consumer by crafting how we perceive products, services, and ideas. Business _____ on billboards, websites, and streaming platforms; layouts in print and online media; and product designs from T-shirts to the decorated cardboard of cereal boxes are just a few of the many ways the work of graphic designers impacts our daily lives.

Which choice completes the text so that it conforms to the conventions of Standard English?

(A) logos advertisements

(B) logos, advertisements

(C) logos; advertisements

(D) logos: advertisements

12

When people consider different types of communication, they often think of only verbal or written forms. Few, perhaps, think of art as a mode of _____ from early cave paintings and the intricate craftwork of ancient civilizations to contemporary, esoteric, abstract works that challenge traditional notions of aesthetic representation, art has played an essential role in visual communication.

Which choice completes the text so that it conforms to the conventions of Standard English?

(A) communication, however,

(B) communication, however

(C) communication; however

(D) communication; however,

13

Eleanor Catton is a Canadian-born New Zealand author who stunned the literary world with her debut novel, *The Rehearsal*, when she was only twenty-two years old. In 2013, her novel _____ made her, at twenty-eight, the youngest winner of the prestigious Booker Prize.

Which choice completes the text so that it conforms to the conventions of Standard English?

- (A) *The Luminaries*
- (B) *The Luminaries,*
- (C) *The Luminaries—*
- (D) *The Luminaries:*

14

Today's solar panels convert between fifteen and twenty percent of the sun's energy to usable electricity. Scientists researching higher efficiencies experimented with using the oxide _____ in solar panels. Although perovskite has the potential to almost double solar panel efficiencies, it degrades rapidly and is not yet a viable alternative.

Which choice completes the text so that it conforms to the conventions of Standard English?

- (A) mineral perovskite
- (B) mineral, perovskite
- (C) mineral perovskite,
- (D) mineral, perovskite,

15

Although the oldest airships, or "blimps," made passenger air travel commercially possible, they were plagued with problems. Worst of all was the safety concern: hydrogen gas is extremely flammable. Any spark or flame that came near the gas could cause a horrific _____ exactly what happened.

Which choice completes the text so that it conforms to the conventions of Standard English?

- (A) explosion; which is
- (B) explosion: which is
- (C) explosion, which is
- (D) explosion which—is

16

Physical therapists treat health issues with physical methods such as massage and exercise. These professionals work with a broad range of patients in a variety of settings—hospitals, long-term care facilities, private clinics, and patients' _____ are in increasing demand as patients seek to avoid drug and surgical treatments.

Which choice completes the text so that it conforms to the conventions of Standard English?

(A) homes and

(B) homes, and

(C) homes: and

(D) homes—and

AGREEMENT: VERBS

LEARNING OBJECTIVES

After this lesson, you will be able to:

- Identify and correct subject-verb agreement issues
- Identify and correct verb tense issues
- Identify and correct parallelism issues

To answer a question like this:

The new textbook about natural disasters was nearly ready for publication, having undergone review by both a copy editor and a proofreader. However, the editors faced a dilemma when the part of the book devoted to avalanches and landslides _____ found to be inaccurate.

Which choice completes the text so that it conforms to the conventions of Standard English?

A) were

B) was

C) are

D) is

You need to know this:

Verb Tense

Verb tense indicates when an action or state of being took place: in the past, present, or future. The tense of the verb must fit the context of the passage. Each tense can express three different types of action.

TYPE OF ACTION	PAST	PRESENT	FUTURE
Single action occurring only once	Connor **planted** vegetables in the community garden.	Connor **plants** vegetables in the community garden.	Connor **will plant** vegetables in the community garden.
Action that is ongoing at some point in time	Connor **was planting** vegetables in the community garden this morning before noon.	Connor **is planting** vegetables in the community garden this morning before noon.	Connor **will be planting** vegetables in the community garden this morning before noon.
Action that is completed before some other action	Connor **had planted** vegetables in the community garden every year until he gave his job to Jasmine.	Connor **has planted** vegetables in the community garden since it started five years ago.	Connor **will have planted** vegetables in the community garden by the time the growing season starts.

Besides matching the tense of its context, a verb must also result in a complete sentence. For example, if a baseball game is happening in the present, it would not be correct to say *The batter **running** to first base*. Instead, you could say *The batter **is running** to first base* or *The batter **runs** to first base*.

Subject-Verb Agreement

A verb must agree with its subject in person and number:

- Person (first, second, or third)
  - First: *I **ask** a question.*
  - Second: *You **ask** a question.*
  - Third: *She **asks** a question.*
- Number (singular or plural)
  - Singular: *The apple **tastes** delicious.*
  - Plural: *Apples **taste** delicious.*

The noun closest to the verb is not always the subject: *The chair with the clawed feet is an antique.* The singular verb in this sentence, *is*, is closest to the plural noun *feet*. However, the verb's actual subject is the singular noun *chair*, so the sentence is correct as written.

When a sentence includes two nouns, only the conjunction *and* forms a compound subject requiring a plural verb form: *Saliyah and Taylor **are** in the running club.*

Collective nouns are nouns that name entities with more than one member, such as *group*, *team*, and *family*. Even though these nouns represent more than one person, they are grammatically singular and require singular verb forms:

- *The collection of paintings **is** one of the most popular art exhibits in recent years.*
- *The team **looks** promising this year.*

Parallelism

Verbs in a list, a compound, or a comparison must be parallel in form.

FEATURE	EXAMPLE	PARALLEL FORM
A list	*Chloe **formulated** a question, **conducted** background research, and **constructed** a hypothesis before starting the experiment.*	3 simple past verb phrases
A compound	*Nineteenth-century midwestern Native American tribes such as the Omaha taught their children **to hunt** and **to fish**, essential survival skills in the plains.*	2 *to* verb forms
A comparison	*Garrett enjoys **sculpting** as much as **painting**.*	2 *-ing* verb forms

Note that parallelism may be tested using other parts of speech besides verbs. In general, any items in a list, compound, or comparison must be in parallel form. For example, if a list starts with a noun, the other items in the list must also be nouns; if it starts with an adjective, the other items must be adjectives, etc.

INCORRECT	CORRECT
Naomi likes *pumpkin pie and to drink coffee* on chilly weekend afternoons.	Naomi likes *pumpkin pie and coffee* on chilly weekend afternoons. *or* Naomi likes *to eat pumpkin pie and drink coffee* on chilly weekend afternoons.
Which of the dogs is the *most docile and better behaved?*	Which of the dogs is the *most docile and best behaved?* *or* Which of the dogs is the *more docile and better behaved?*
Many of the ingredients in croissants, such as salt, milk, and flour, are similar to **pancakes**.	Many of the ingredients in croissants, such as salt, milk, and flour, are similar to **those in pancakes**.

You need to do this:

If the answer choices include a verb, check that the verb:

- Reflects the correct tense: does it fit the context?
- Agrees with the subject in person and number
- Is parallel in form with other verbs if it appears in a list, compound, or comparison
- Results in a complete sentence

Explanation:

The subject of the verb "_____ found" is the noun "part," which is singular. (Note that the test makers sometimes put prepositional phrases or other descriptive phrases, such as the phrases "of the book" and "devoted to avalanches and landslides," between the subject and verb to make the subject-verb agreement error trickier to spot.)

Since a singular verb is needed, eliminate the plural verbs in (A) and (C). To decide between (B) and (D), look at the context defined by the other verb tense in the sentence. The editors "*faced* a dilemma," so the sentence describes past events. Choice **(B)** is also in the past tense and is consistent with this context. It is the correct answer.

If verbs give you trouble, study the information above and try these Drill questions before completing the following "Try on Your Own" questions. Edit each sentence to correct the verb or parallelism issue. Drill answers can be found in the Check Your Work section at the end of the chapter.

Drill

a. Angel audition for the school play next week.

b. The song, with its upbeat rhythm and catchy lyrics, were wildly popular.

c. The aquatic science club's activities include attending a marine biology lecture, performing a pond ecosystem experiment, and a behind-the-scenes tour at the aquarium.

d. By the time the last runner completed the marathon, the winner has crossed the finish line hours ago.

e. Few people knowing that Stephen Hawking both revolutionized physics and co-wrote children's books with his daughter.

Try on Your Own

Directions

Take as much time as you need on these questions. Work carefully and methodically. There will be an opportunity for timed practice later in the book.

17

Kombucha is a beverage that is traditionally made by fermenting a mixture of tea, sugar, bacteria, and yeast. After two to four weeks, the bacteria and yeast _____ a symbiotic colony on the top layer of the fermenting liquid. This thick, jelly-like, cellulose disc is commonly referred to as "the mother culture" or "scoby," which is an acronym for "symbiotic colony of bacteria and yeast."

Which choice completes the text so that it conforms to the conventions of Standard English?

- (A) form
- (B) are forming
- (C) formed
- (D) forming

18

At 69 Condotti Street in Rome sits what is believed by many to be the smallest country in the world, a country that few have ever heard of. The Sovereign Military and Hospitaller Order of St. John of Jerusalem, of Rhodes, and of Malta, or SMOM, _____ an ancient order of knights well known for its humanitarian activities. The order's headquarters in Rome—a mere 6,000 square meters, or about one acre— is considered an independent state by at least 75 nations.

Which choice completes the text so that it conforms to the conventions of Standard English?

- (A) were
- (B) was
- (C) are
- (D) is

19

The Mount Rushmore National Memorial in South Dakota is on land considered sacred by many sovereign nations, including the Sioux Nation, which had been promised the territory in perpetuity by the 1868 Fort Laramie Treaty. Less than a decade after the treaty had been signed, the discovery of gold brought settlers and prospectors who _____ to force the indigenous people from their land. This led to the 1876 Black Hills War, during which the Lakota Sioux and their allies defended their land rights against the U.S. government. Despite the victory at the Battle of Little Bighorn, the allied nations lost the war and the treaty was broken.

Which choice completes the text so that it conforms to the conventions of Standard English?

(A) have attempted

(B) had attempted

(C) attempt

(D) attempted

20

Urban agriculture has been proposed as a potential solution to the food insecurities that occur in densely populated communities with high economic disparity. Specifically, rooftop gardens can help improve access to fresh fruits and vegetables, _____ the residents in a collective purpose, and beautify the skyline. However, the space is very limited, and rooftop gardeners would benefit from consistent crop rotation and strategic plant selection.

Which choice completes the text so that it conforms to the conventions of Standard English?

(A) engaging

(B) engage

(C) engages

(D) engaged

21

In natural conditions, *Magicicada septendecim*, *M. cassini*, and *M. septendecula* are the three species of North American periodical cicadas with the longest synchronized development time. These cicadas spend the majority of their lives as subterranean plant parasites called nymphs. After 17 years as nymphal cicadas, the brood emerges from the ground, molts into adulthood, and seeks out mates. The typical adult female cicada will die after four to six weeks and _____ up to 600 eggs during that time.

Which choice completes the text so that it conforms to the conventions of Standard English?

(A) will lay

(B) is laying

(C) has laid

(D) laying

22

Over 100 years ago, a San Diego Zoological Society was formed in Southern California in the United States. It was founded as a municipal zoo that would better display the few wild creatures that were housed in Balboa Park. Today, the San Diego Zoo Wildlife Alliance _____ on educating their visitors and integrating transdisciplinary solutions into their sustainable conservation efforts.

Which choice completes the text so that it conforms to the conventions of Standard English?

Ⓐ are concentrating

Ⓑ was concentrating

Ⓒ concentrates

Ⓓ will concentrate

23

The Babylonian king Hammurabi, who reigned between 1792 and 1750 B.C.E., recorded one of the first systems of laws. The 282 edicts of the code of Hammurabi all follow an "If … then …" structure that _____ the conditions required before a punishment can be imposed. Interestingly, many modern legal systems employ this identical structure.

Which choice completes the text so that it conforms to the conventions of Standard English?

Ⓐ establish

Ⓑ establishes

Ⓒ established

Ⓓ are establishing

24

Wallace Chan, a renowned Chinese jewelry artist, is famous not only for his delicate, beautiful creations but also for his many inventive techniques. Among these is the "Wallace cut," a unique method of sculpting a precious gem from within. The front of the finished gem has a smooth facet, but under the surface, a three-dimensional image of the subject _____ both in portrait and in profile.

Which choice completes the text so that it conforms to the conventions of Standard English?

Ⓐ appear

Ⓑ appears

Ⓒ appeared

Ⓓ appearing

AGREEMENT: PRONOUNS

LEARNING OBJECTIVE

After this lesson, you will be able to:

- Identify and correct pronoun agreement issues

To answer a question like this:

The forerunner of the earliest abolition society in the United States, the Pennsylvania Abolition Society, had its first meeting in 1775. The abolitionist movement eventually split in the late 1830s due to disagreement about women's role in activism. Angelina and Sarah Grimké, for instance, advocated for equality even as opposition to _____ public speeches increased.

Which choice completes the text so that it conforms to the conventions of Standard English?

A) her

B) its

C) their

D) them

You need to know this:

Pronoun Forms

A pronoun is a word that takes the place of a noun. Pronouns can take three different forms, each of which is used based on the grammatical role it plays in the sentence.

FORM	PRONOUNS	EXAMPLE
Subjective: The pronoun is used as a subject.	I, you, she, he, it, we, they, who	*Rivka is the student* **who** *will lead the presentation.*
Objective: The pronoun is used as the object of a verb or a preposition.	me, you, her, him, it, us, them, whom	With **whom** will Rivka present the scientific findings?
Possessive: The pronoun expresses ownership.	my, mine, your, yours, her, hers, his, its, our, ours, their, theirs, whose	Rivka will likely choose a partner **whose** work is excellent.

Note that a pronoun in subjective form can, logically, be the subject in a complete sentence. Pronouns that are in objective form cannot.

When a pronoun appears in a compound structure, dropping the other noun or pronoun will show you which form to use—for example: *Leo and me walked into town.* If you were talking about yourself only, you would say, "I walked into town," not "Me walked into town." Therefore, the correct form is subjective, and the original sentence should read: *Leo and I walked into town.*

Pronoun-Antecedent Agreement

A pronoun's antecedent is the noun it logically represents in a sentence. If the noun is singular, the pronoun must be singular; if the noun is plural, the pronoun must be plural.

ANTECEDENT	INCORRECT	CORRECT
selection	*The selection of books was placed in **their** designated location.*	The selection of books was placed in ***its*** designated location.
apples	If apples are unripe, ***it*** should not be purchased.	If apples are unripe, ***they*** should not be purchased.
woman	A woman visiting the zoo fed the giraffes all of the lettuce ***they*** had purchased.	A woman visiting the zoo fed the giraffes all of the lettuce ***she*** had purchased.
sapling	The sapling, along with dozens of flowers, was relocated to where ***they*** would thrive.	The sapling, along with dozens of flowers, was relocated to where ***it*** would thrive.

Ambiguous Pronouns

A pronoun is ambiguous if its antecedent is either missing or unclear. If a question involves a pronoun, make sure you can clearly identify the noun to which the pronoun refers. If the pronoun is ambiguous, replace it with the appropriate noun (or a rephrasing of the appropriate noun). Note that the logical antecedent may not be the noun that appears closest to the pronoun.

AMBIGUOUS PRONOUN USE	CORRECTED SENTENCE
Anthony walked with Cody to the ice cream shop, and ***he*** bought a banana split.	Anthony walked with Cody to the ice cream shop, and ***Anthony*** bought a banana split.

You need to do this:

If a question involves a pronoun, *identify the logical antecedent.* Then, check that the pronoun:

- Has a clear antecedent
  - If there is no clear antecedent, the pronoun is ambiguous. Replace the pronoun with the appropriate noun (or a rephrasing of the appropriate noun).
- Uses the correct form
  - If the pronoun is the subject of a phrase or sentence, use a subjective pronoun such as *I, you, she, he, it, we, they,* or *who.*
  - If the pronoun is the object of a verb or preposition, use an objective pronoun such as *me, you, her, him, it, us, they,* or *whom.*
  - If the pronoun indicates possession, use a possessive pronoun such as *my, mine, your, yours, her, hers, his, its, our, ours, their, theirs,* or *whose.*
- Agrees with its antecedent
  - A singular antecedent requires a singular pronoun; a plural antecedent requires a plural pronoun.

Explanation:

The answer choices indicate that this question tests pronouns, so first identify the logical antecedent. The clear antecedent of the pronoun in the blank is "Angelina and Sarah Grimké," so a possessive form is correct; eliminate (D). Because *two* women "advocated," eliminate the singular pronouns in (A) and (B). The plural possessive in **(C)** is correct.

If pronouns give you trouble, study the information above and try these Drill questions before completing the following "Try on Your Own" questions. Edit each sentence to correct the pronoun issue. Drill answers can be found in the Check Your Work section at the end of the chapter.

Drill

a. Although the teacher gave the student detention after school, she was not angry.

b. My uncle likes to go bowling with my sister and I.

c. My brother moved the box of nails from their usual place in the shed.

d. My favorite singer, who I have wanted to see in person for years, will give a concert a week after my birthday.

e. The cathedral of Notre Dame, with vast vaulted ceilings and intricate carvings, never fails to amaze their visitors.

Try on Your Own

Directions

Take as much time as you need on these questions. Work carefully and methodically. There will be an opportunity for timed practice later in the book.

25

What do mosquitoes, mussels, giraffes, sharks, plant burrs, and dog hair all have in common? In addition to being a part of the natural world that surrounds us, _____ have inspired significant advancements in modern technology through a practice called biomimicry.

Which choice completes the text so that it conforms to the conventions of Standard English?

- Ⓐ we need to
- Ⓑ it continues to
- Ⓒ these biological entities
- Ⓓ the natural world

26

Akira Kurosawa, a Japanese film director, is considered by movie critic Leonard Maltin to be "one of the undisputed giants of cinema." Over his career, Kurosawa's unique blend of Western themes and Eastern settings made _____ arguably the most important Japanese filmmaker in history.

Which choice completes the text so that it conforms to the conventions of Standard English?

(A) them

(B) he

(C) him

(D) his

27

It is perhaps impossible to overestimate the impact of the Sun on our planet Earth. Even though the Sun is situated roughly 100 million miles away from the Earth, _____ provides essentially all of Earth's heat. Functioning like a great thermonuclear reactor, the Sun has a core temperature of nearly 30 million degrees Fahrenheit.

Which choice completes the text so that it conforms to the conventions of Standard English?

(A) it

(B) they

(C) the Sun

(D) the Earth

28

Since the discovery of penicillin, medical specialists have prescribed it to effectively combat bacterial infections, but problems concerning the usage of this antibiotic have begun to emerge. Some people are allergic to penicillin, though the number of _____ truly allergic has low statistical significance. Side effects of the antibiotic are more frequent and include common reactions such as nausea, rash, and vomiting; uncommon reactions such as fever, wheezing, and irregular breathing; and rare, life-threatening reactions such as anaphylaxis and seizures.

Which choice completes the text so that it conforms to the conventions of Standard English?

(A) they whom are

(B) those who are

(C) them

(D) antibiotics that are

29

While the International Coffee Organization reports that the global consumption of coffee beans currently exceeds 22 billion pounds annually, most researchers analyze our consumption in terms of "cups." With so many ways for _____ to enjoy coffee, it stands to reason that a more precise method of quantification needs to be identified to accurately measure how much coffee we consume. How does drinking a pint of cold brew compare to eating a pint of coffee gelato when measuring coffee consumption?

Which choice completes the text so that it conforms to the conventions of Standard English?

Ⓐ us

Ⓑ me

Ⓒ you

Ⓓ them

30

Parkour, the practice of moving from one space to another in the fastest and most efficient way possible without the use of assistive equipment, began in the late 1990s when David Belle and his friends began to use the built environment of cities on the outskirts of Paris to engage in the art of movement. Parkour captured the whole world's attention through viral videos that featured amazing feats that highlighted people's agility and ingenuity. Part of _____ appeal was how accessible the sport was—there were no direct costs associated with participating.

Which choice completes the text so that it conforms to the conventions of Standard English?

Ⓐ their

Ⓑ your

Ⓒ it's

Ⓓ its

31

Hummingbirds are so remarkable as to be almost beyond belief. Weighing about one-tenth of an ounce, much smaller than most other birds, _____ flap their wings over 50 times every second, and their hearts beat around 1,000 times every minute. In addition, most hummingbird species migrate hundreds or even thousands of miles twice each year.

Which choice completes the text so that it conforms to the conventions of Standard English?

Ⓐ they

Ⓑ their

Ⓒ these birds

Ⓓ hummingbirds

32

Sean Sherman is a member of the Oglala Lakota Sioux and an award-winning chef. Realizing that indigenous American foods were completely missing from his professional training, Chef Sherman established North American Traditional Indigenous Food Systems (NATIFS) to not only reclaim traditional ingredients and food preparation methods but also to empower Native Americans to improve _____ lives through food-related businesses.

Which choice completes the text so that it conforms to the conventions of Standard English?

(A) their

(B) there

(C) they're

(D) these

AGREEMENT: MODIFIERS

LEARNING OBJECTIVES

After this lesson, you will be able to:

- Identify and correct modifier agreement issues
- Identify and correct inappropriate uses of apostrophes

To answer a question like this:

The ruins of Puʻukoholā Heiau on the Big Island of Hawaii mark the only remaining major ancient Hawaiian temple. Constructed in 1791 with stones transported miles across the island, _____ first unified the Hawaiian islands.

Which choice completes the text so that it conforms to the conventions of Standard English?

A) Kamehameha I, whose leadership skills are reflected by his building of this impressive temple,

B) the builder, Kamehameha I, whose leadership skills are reflected by this impressive temple,

C) the leadership skills of its builder, Kamehameha I, are reflected in this impressive temple, and he

D) this impressive temple reflects the leadership skills of its builder, Kamehameha I, who

You need to know this:

A **modifier** is a word or phrase that describes, clarifies, or provides additional information about another part of the sentence. Modifier questions require you to identify the part of a sentence being modified and to use the appropriate modifier in the proper place.

In order to be grammatically correct, the modifier must be placed as close to the word it describes as possible. Use context clues in the passage to identify what word or phrase is logically being described by the modifier.

Note that a common way the SAT tests modifiers is with modifying phrases at the beginning of a sentence. Just like any other modifier, the modifying phrase grammatically modifies whatever is right next to it in the sentence. For example, consider the sentence: *While walking to the bus stop, the rain drenched Bob.* The initial phrase, *While walking to the bus stop*, grammatically modifies *the rain*, creating a nonsense sentence. After all, the rain can't walk to a bus stop! Logically, it must be that Bob walked to the bus stop, so the sentence should read: *While walking to the bus stop, Bob was drenched by the rain.*

MODIFIER/MODIFYING PHRASE	INCORRECT	CORRECT
nearly	Andre **nearly** watched the play for four hours.	Andre watched the play for **nearly** four hours.
in individual containers	The art teacher handed out paints to students **in individual containers**.	The art teacher handed out paints **in individual containers** to students.
A scholar athlete	**A scholar athlete**, maintaining high grades in addition to playing soccer were expected of Maya.	**A scholar athlete**, Maya was expected to maintain high grades in addition to playing soccer.

Adjectives and Adverbs

Use adjectives only to modify nouns and pronouns. Use adverbs to modify everything else.

- **Adjectives** are single-word modifiers that describe nouns and pronouns: *Ian conducted an **efficient** lab experiment.*

- **Adverbs** are single-word modifiers that describe verbs, adjectives, or other adverbs: *Ian **efficiently** conducted a lab experiment.*

Note that nouns can sometimes be used as adjectives. For example, in the phrase *the fashion company's autumn collection*, the word *fashion* functions as an adjective modifying *company*, and the word *autumn* functions as an adjective modifying *collection*.

Comparative/Superlative

When comparing similar things, use adjectives that match the number of items being compared. When comparing two items or people, use the **comparative** form of the adjective. When comparing three or more items or people, use the **superlative** form.

COMPARATIVE (TWO ITEMS)	SUPERLATIVE (THREE OR MORE ITEMS)
better, more, newer, older, shorter, taller, worse, younger	best, most, newest, oldest, shortest, tallest, worst, youngest

Apostrophes

USE AN APOSTROPHE TO . . .	EXAMPLE
Indicate the possessive form of a single noun	*My oldest **sister's** soccer game is on Saturday.*
Indicate the possessive form of a plural noun	*My two older **sisters'** soccer games are on Saturday.*
Indicate a contraction (e.g., *don't, can't*)	***They've** won every soccer match this season.*

Note that plural nouns are formed without an apostrophe.

INCORRECT	CORRECT
*Sting **ray's** are cartilaginous fish related to **shark's**.*	*Sting **rays** are cartilaginous fish related to **sharks**.*
*There are many **carnival's** in this area every summer.*	*There are many **carnivals** in this area every summer.*

Possessive Nouns and Pronouns

Possessive nouns and pronouns indicate that something belongs to someone or something. In general, possessive nouns are written with an apostrophe, while possessive pronouns are not.

TO SPOT ERRORS IN POSSESSIVE NOUN OR PRONOUN CONSTRUCTION, LOOK FOR ...	INCORRECT	CORRECT
Two nouns in a row	The **professors lectures** were both informative and entertaining.	The **professor's lectures** were both informative and entertaining.
Pronouns with apostrophes	The book is **her's**.	The book is **hers**.
Words that sound alike	The three friends decided to ride **there** bicycles to the park over **they're** where **their** going to enjoy a picnic lunch.	The three friends decided to ride **their** bicycles to the park over **there** where **they're** going to enjoy a picnic lunch.

To check whether *it's* is appropriate, replace it in the sentence with *it is* or *it has*. If the sentence no longer makes sense, *it's* is incorrect. The following sentence is correct:

The tree frog blends perfectly into its surroundings. When it holds still, it's nearly invisible.

Note that *its'* and *its's* are never correct.

You need to do this:

If a modifying phrase appears next to the blank or in the answer choices:

- Determine which word or words the phrase should be modifying.
- Make sure the modifying phrase is as *near as possible* to what it logically modifies.

If the answer choices include a modifier:

- Determine which word or words the modifier should be modifying.
- Make sure the modifier *agrees with* what it logically modifies.
  - Does the sentence require an adjective or an adverb?
  - Does the noun or pronoun show proper possession?

If the answer choices include an apostrophe, make sure it correctly indicates either possession or a contraction.

Explanation:

The introductory modifying phrase "Constructed in 1791 with stones ..." must refer to the temple. Only **(D)** correctly places the temple so that it is adjacent to the modifying phrase. Choices (A) and (B) are incorrect because they result in Kamehameha I being modified by the introductory phrase "Constructed in 1791 ... ." Likewise, (C) incorrectly results in "the leadership skills" being modified by the phrase.

If modifiers give you trouble, study the information above and try these Drill questions before completing the following "Try on Your Own" questions. Edit each sentence to correct the modifier or apostrophe issue. Drill answers can be found in the Check Your Work section at the end of the chapter.

Drill

a.   Since their invention, the efficiency of computers has grown exponentially.

b.   Estella chose to take the route with the most attractively scenery to her destination.

c.   The leaf-tailed gecko's amazing natural camouflage enables it to blend perfectly into it's surroundings.

d.   Between basketball and baseball, basketball is the most popular sport in the United States.

e.   From Edgar Allan Poe to Monty Python, the infamous Spanish Inquisition has provided material for many artists.

Try on Your Own

Directions

Take as much time as you need on these questions. Work carefully and methodically. There will be an opportunity for timed practice later in the book.

33

Considered the father of the montage, a popular cinematic technique that involves a rapid succession of shots, often superimposed, _____ work contains a clarity and sharpness of composition that make the depth of his plots and the powerful complexity of his juxtaposed images easily accessible to most viewers.

Which choice completes the text so that it conforms to the conventions of Standard English?

Ⓐ   the modern movie has as one of its principal architects Russian director Sergei Eisenstein, whose

Ⓑ   the modern movie has Russian director Sergei Eisenstein to thank as one of its principal architects, because his

Ⓒ   the Russian director Sergei Eisenstein was one of the principal architects of the modern movie. His

Ⓓ   critics name the Russian director Sergei Eisenstein as one of the principal architects of the modern movie, because his

34

Graphic designers have long played an important role in popular culture, crafting the formats, styles, images, and symbols that shape how consumers perceive products and services. However, with the drastic reduction in newspaper and magazine publishing in the last decade, the number of job openings in commercial design has shrunk. Trying to expand their possibilities, _____ continues to be a growing field for tech-minded artists.

Which choice completes the text so that it conforms to the conventions of Standard English?

(A) much graphic design knowledge also now applies to website and web application design, which

(B) many graphic designers' knowledge also now applies to website and web application design, which

(C) website and web application design allows many graphic designers to apply their knowledge, which

(D) many graphic designers are also now applying their knowledge to website and web application design, which

35

The inventions of Nicola Tesla are not just a part of our daily lives; they also continue to be expanded upon to create new advances in science and technology. Tesla's approach to energy transmission, as well as his contributions to radio technology, underlies modern wireless communications, such as radio broadcasting and mobile phones. Unfortunately, despite developing a veritable wealth of innovations, _____

Which choice completes the text so that it conforms to the conventions of Standard English?

(A) they were inventions that brought him only fame, and not fortune, during his lifetime.

(B) he received only fame for them and never saw the fortune his brilliance deserved.

(C) Tesla's fame came without the fortune one would expect his inventions to warrant.

(D) the fortunes that eluded Tesla's grasp were amassed by other inventors.

36

Bebop jazz music flourished briefly in the early 1940s, but quickly encountered heavy resistance. Employing irregular rhythms and discordant sounds, bebop was initially opposed by older jazz musicians, but also, later and more lastingly, by the general public alienated by _____ complexity and sophistication.

Which choice completes the text so that it conforms to the conventions of Standard English?

(A) its

(B) it's

(C) its'

(D) its's

37

Children's zoos often provide hands-on opportunities for children to learn about the most common domesticated animals. In contrast to the guests at zoos and parks that focus on exotic animals, a children's _____ rarely feel intimidated because they are surrounded by many animals with which they are already familiar.

Which choice completes the text so that it conforms to the conventions of Standard English?

(A) zoos visitors

(B) zoos visitors'

(C) zoo's visitors

(D) zoo's visitors'

38

When planning a family, _____ a report from the United States Department of Agriculture estimates that the average cost of raising a child born in 2015 until age seventeen is over $230,000.

Which choice completes the text so that it conforms to the conventions of Standard English?

(A) financial considerations should be kept in mind by future parents, since

(B) financial considerations should be at the forefront of parents' thinking, since

(C) future parents should keep financial considerations in mind, since

(D) financial issues are of paramount importance and should be considered as parents prepare, since

Reading & Writing

39

The studio's films were critically acclaimed successes at the box office, but because advertisers had paid heavily to have their products frequently and prominently placed in them, these productions were frequently criticized _____ lack of artistic integrity.

Which choice completes the text so that it conforms to the conventions of Standard English?

(A) for they're

(B) therefore

(C) for their

(D) for there

40

The Williams sisters, Serena and Venus, revolutionized women's tennis with their powerful, athletic style of play. When compared to her sister, _____ she has won nearly 50% more single titles than Vanessa did throughout the course of their respective careers.

Which choice completes the text so that it conforms to the conventions of Standard English?

(A) Serena is considered the more successful:

(B) Serena's success is notably higher:

(C) the scoreboards reflect Serena's success:

(D) success has been more plentiful for Serena:

HOW MUCH HAVE YOU LEARNED?

Directions

For testlike practice, give yourself 7 minutes to complete this question set. When you're finished, be sure to study the explanations, even for questions you got correct. Full explanations can be found at the end of this chapter.

41

Competition in the job market for graphic designers is _____ the field offers a variety of professional options. Some work in design studios; others work "in-house" for businesses that staff their own graphic designers. Those with more entrepreneurial inclinations can work as freelance graphic designers.

Which choice completes the text so that it conforms to the conventions of Standard English?

- (A) rigorous yet
- (B) rigorous,
- (C) rigorous; even though
- (D) rigorous, but

42

The small, colorless, and blind Ozark cavefish lives most of its life in total darkness and is endangered. In their search for this elusive species, researchers were encouraged by the stability of the caves' groundwater as well as _____ length and the presence of bats.

Which choice completes the text so that it conforms to the conventions of Standard English?

- (A) its
- (B) it's
- (C) their
- (D) they're

43

Of the many forms poetry can _____ triolet, ballad, ode, and epigram, to name a few—none is quite as briefly beautiful as the Japanese haiku. With a complex history and a challenging structure, the haiku is as popular as it is difficult to master.

Which choice completes the text so that it conforms to the conventions of Standard English?

- (A) take
- (B) take—
- (C) take,
- (D) take:

44

Adenosine triphosphate (ATP) is a molecule formed when cells break down glucose. First, the muscle cells break the six-carbon glucose into two three-carbon molecules of pyruvic acid. This makes two ATP molecules available for the muscle cells to use. When enough oxygen is available, the cells _____ to break the pyruvic acid down in a series of steps, each of which produces more ATP. The full cycle releases another 34 ATP molecules, as well as carbon dioxide and water, from one molecule of glucose.

Which choice completes the text so that it conforms to the conventions of Standard English?

- (A) then continues
- (B) did continue
- (C) continue
- (D) continued

45

Although they are best known today for their peculiar niche as floating commercials over sports _____ more commonly called "blimps" today, were widely used for passenger transportation in the early twentieth century. The most infamous was the *Hindenburg*. When the 804-foot *Hindenburg* was launched in 1936, it was the largest airship in the world.

Which choice completes the text so that it conforms to the conventions of Standard English?

- (A) arenas, airships
- (B) arenas; airships,
- (C) arenas, airships,
- (D) arenas: airships,

46

The films of Japanese director Akira Kurosawa enjoy a lofty reputation in the West, but many critics and moviegoers in his home country view his films as neither original nor particularly Japanese. His use of Western ideals and themes—even reinterpreting Western authors such as William Shakespeare and Fyodor Dostoyevsky—leads Japanese cinema lovers, many of _____ see Kurosawa's use of Japanese culture as mere "window dressing" applied to essentially foreign stories, to regard his work with suspicion.

Which choice completes the text so that it conforms to the conventions of Standard English?

- (A) who
- (B) whose
- (C) which
- (D) whom

REFLECT

Directions: Take a few minutes to recall what you've learned and what you've been practicing in this chapter. Consider the following questions, jot down your best answer for each one, and then compare your reflections to the expert responses that follow. Use your level of confidence to determine what to do next.

What additional task should you do when using the Kaplan Method for Reading and Writing on a Standard English Conventions question?

_____

_____

_____

Name at least three ways to correct a run-on sentence.

_____

_____

_____

How should parenthetical elements be punctuated?

_____

_____

_____

If the answer choices indicate that the question tests verbs, what four factors should you check about the verb?

_____

_____

_____

If the answer choices indicate that the question tests pronouns, what three factors should you check about the pronoun?

_____

_____

_____

Where should a modifying phrase be placed?

_____

_____

_____

How will you approach SAT Reading and Writing questions more strategically as you continue to practice and improve your performance? Are there any specific habits you will practice to make your approach to SAT Reading and Writing more effective and efficient?

_____

_____

_____

Expert Responses

What additional task should you do when using the Kaplan Method for Reading and Writing on a Standard English Conventions question?

During Step 1, once you determine that it is a Standard English Conventions question, you should look at the answer choices for clues about what specific issue (such as verb agreement) is being tested. Doing so will help you focus your reading of the passage in Step 2.

Name at least three ways to correct a run-on sentence.

There are a number of ways to fix a run-on sentence on the SAT. The six ways that you are likely to see are: 1) use a period to create two separate sentences, 2) use a semicolon between the two independent clauses, 3) use a colon between the two independent clauses, 4) make one clause dependent, 5) add a FANBOYS conjunction after the comma, or 6) use a dash between the two independent clauses.

How should parenthetical elements be punctuated?

Parenthetical elements should be set off from the rest of the sentence by commas, parentheses, or dashes. If the parenthetical element is in the middle of the sentence, use a matching set of punctuation (for example, two dashes rather than one dash and one comma).

If the answer choices indicate that the question tests verbs, what three factors should you check about the verb?

Make sure that the verb: 1) reflects the correct verb tense based on the context of the passage, 2) agrees with its subject in person and number, 3) is parallel in form with other verbs if it appears in a list, compound, or comparison, and 4) results in a complete sentence.

If the answer choices indicate that the question tests pronouns, what three factors should you check about the pronoun?

Make sure that the pronoun: 1) has a clear and unambiguous antecedent, 2) agrees in number with its antecedent, and 3) uses the correct pronoun form (subjective, objective, or possessive).

Where should a modifying phrase be placed?

Modifying phrases should be placed as near as possible to what they logically modify.

How will you approach SAT Reading and Writing questions more strategically as you continue to practice and improve your performance? Are there any specific habits you will practice to make your approach to SAT Reading and Writing more effective and efficient?

There is no one-size-fits-all answer here. Reflect on your own habits in answering SAT Reading and Writing questions and give yourself an honest assessment of your strengths and weaknesses. Consider the strategies you've seen experts use in this chapter, and put them to work in your own practice to increase your accuracy, speed, and confidence.

Next Steps

If you answered most questions correctly in the "How Much Have You Learned?" section, and if your responses to the Reflect questions were similar to those of the SAT expert, then consider Standard English Conventions an area of strength. Come back to this topic periodically to prevent yourself from getting rusty.

If you don't yet feel confident, review the lessons in this chapter that you have not yet mastered. Then, try the questions you missed again. As always, be sure to review the explanations closely.

Check Your Work – Chapter 21

Drill Answers for Sentence Structure: The Basics

Note: These are not the only ways to correct the sentences; your answers may differ.

a. **My friend** brought snacks to the weekend study session.

b. After getting to the stadium, **we went looking for our seats.**

c. The new arts center just opened**.** It has a crafts room for children under 13.

d. Herodotus is known as one of the first historians**;** he is even called "The Father of History."

e. **Although** Herodotus is sometimes accused of making up stories for his histories, he claimed he simply recorded what he had been told.

Try on Your Own Answers

1. B
Difficulty: Easy
Category: Standard English Conventions
Getting to the Answer: The first part of the sentence is a dependent clause that describes when the actions in the following independent clause occurred. The appropriate punctuation mark to separate a dependent from an independent clause is a comma, so **(B)** is correct. Choice (A) incorrectly eliminates the comma after the dependent clause. The semicolon in (C) must follow an independent, not a dependent, clause. Choice (D) adds an unnecessary conjunction and produces a sentence fragment.

2. B
Difficulty: Medium
Category: Standard English Conventions
Getting to the Answer: The portions of the text before and after the blank are each independent clauses, so you need to combine them according to correct grammar. There are several ways to combine two independent clauses, but only one answer choice offers an acceptable method: **(B)** correctly uses a semicolon to join the two independent clauses. Choice (A) uses a comma and creates a run-on. Choice (C) does not use a FANBOYS conjunction and (D) erroneously omits the comma.

3. C
Difficulty: Hard
Category: Standard English Conventions
Getting to the Answer: Consider the relationship between the portions of the sentence before and after the blank in order to determine how best to combine them. The second clause contributes useful information regarding the results of using the "chromatic ornamentation" and "altered scales." Making this a dependent clause that modifies the independent clause at the start of the sentence will clearly and smoothly show the relationship between the ideas. Choice **(C)** does so with the proper punctuation and is correct. Choice (A) incorrectly uses a period to separate the dependent clause. Choice (B) incorrectly uses a semicolon preceding the dependent clause. Similarly, the comma and FANBOYS conjunction "and" must introduce an independent clause, making (D) incorrect.

4. A
Difficulty: Hard
Category: Standard English Conventions
Getting to the Answer: As you read the sentence containing the blank, be on the lookout for a complete idea, the key feature of an independent clause. Here, the prepositions "on," "in," and "as" all mark the start of modifying phrases, so the correct answer will create a properly punctuated independent clause. Choice **(A)** ends the final modifying phrase with a comma, separating it from the independent clause that follows, and is correct. Choice (B) incorrectly ends the string of modifying phrases with a period, but the multiple phrases do not include a verb. Choices (C) and (D) are incorrect for the same reason. Semicolons (C) and dashes (D) can both be used to separate two independent clauses, not dependent and independent clauses.

5. D
Difficulty: Hard
Category: Standard English Conventions
Getting to the Answer: As you read, mentally reduce the sentence with the blank into its main components. "Mauritius ... has a complicated history" is an independent clause. "It was first colonized ..." is another independent clause. Look for the choice that correctly connects these two complete ideas. Choice **(D)** is correct because a colon can be used to join two

independent clauses when the second clause further explains or clarifies the first. The incorrect choices are improperly punctuated. Choice (A) creates a run-on with its comma usage. Choice (B) uses the FANBOYS conjunction "and" without a comma, and (C) incorrectly uses a semicolon.

6. C
Difficulty: Easy
Category: Standard English Conventions
Getting to the Answer: A quick glance at the choices tells you that every choice contains the FANBOYS conjunction "but," so this question is testing the punctuation between two independent clauses. The correct punctuation is a comma followed by the FANBOYS conjunction, so **(C)** is correct. For the incorrect choices, (A) omits all punctuation, and (B) and (D) incorrectly follow the FANBOYS conjunction with a comma.

7. D
Difficulty: Medium
Category: Standard English Conventions
Getting to the Answer: A quick glance at the choices tells you that this question is testing the punctuation connecting the two parts of the sentence. Replace the blank with "ink the" as you read the sentence containing the blank, and ask yourself, Have I just read a complete idea? Here, "... subjects are shown the name of a color that is printed in colored ink" is a complete idea, and only **(D)** properly connects that clause to "The printed color may match the word ... ," another independent clause. Incorrect choice (A) omits all necessary punctuation, (B) incorrectly inserts a comma after "the," and (C) creates a run-on by connecting two independent clauses with only a comma.

8. A
Difficulty: Medium
Category: Standard English Conventions
Getting to the Answer: A quick glance at the choices tells you that the first word to fill the blank is "bicycle," so reread the sentence including that word to determine if the first clause is independent. "Almost 50% of households ... have a bicycle" is an independent clause. The next clause, "far more ..." is a modifying phrase, so it should be preceded by a comma. Keep this in mind as you evaluate the choices. **(A)** is correct. Choice (B) incorrectly uses a semicolon prior to a modifying phrase, (C) punctuates the modifying phrase as if

it were a complete sentence, and (D) creates a run-on by connecting two complete ideas with only a comma.

Drill Answers for Sentence Structure: Punctuation

Note: These are not the only ways to correct the sentences; your answers may differ.

a. For my birthday, I asked for my favorite dessert**:** chocolate pecan pie.

b. The story of Emperor Nero playing the fiddle while Rome burned has been debunked by historians**,** but the saying based on the tale remains popular.

c. The fact that koala fingerprints are nearly indistinguishable from human fingerprints has occasionally led to mistakes at crime scenes. (Comma deleted)

d. Invented by Sir John Harrington in 1596**,** the flush toilet actually precedes modern indoor plumbing.

e. Toni Morrison**,** born Chloe Wofford**,** is one of America's most celebrated writers. OR Toni Morrison—born Chloe Wofford—is one of America's most celebrated writers.

Try on Your Own Answers

9. C
Difficulty: Medium
Category: Standard English Conventions
Getting to the Answer: "Vietnam" is not a complete sentence, as there is no verb. Look for a choice that will either make "Vietnam" a complete sentence or combine it with the first sentence. Choice **(C)** correctly uses a colon to introduce important information. Choice (A) is missing a comma after "expected," and the semicolon in (B) and the period in (D) must separate two independent clauses, not an independent clause and a single word.

10. A
Difficulty: Medium
Category: Standard English Conventions
Getting to the Answer: A quick glance at the choices indicates that the punctuation surrounding the phrase "distant or intimate, serious or playful" is the issue this question is testing. The phrase is a parenthetical element because it describes the different possible relationships an author may establish with readers and could be eliminated without changing the meaning of the sentence. Expect that the correct answer will

mark off this phrase with a pair of commas or dashes. Choice **(A)** does so and is the correct answer. Choice (B) starts with a dash, but then incorrectly ends the parenthetical element with a comma. Choices (C) and (D) are incorrect because they introduce the parenthetical with a colon.

11. C
Difficulty: Hard
Category: Standard English Conventions
Getting to the Answer: A quick glance at the choices indicates this question is testing the correct punctuation, if any, needed between the words "logos" and "advertisements." Carefully check the information before and after the blank for clues to the structure of the sentence. Here, the best clues are the semicolons following the blank that signal a complex list. The list item "advertisements on billboards, websites, and streaming platforms" contains commas, so the items in the list must be separated by semicolons. Choice **(C)** is correct.

12. D
Difficulty: Hard
Category: Standard English Conventions
Getting to the Answer: A quick glance at the choices indicates that this question is testing the required punctuation between the same two words. Read the sentence containing the blank and look for the complete idea(s). "Few . . . think of art . . ." and ". . . art has played an essential role" are both independent clauses. To join them, use a semicolon, a comma and coordinating (i.e., FANBOYS) conjunction, or a dash. Eliminate (A) and (B), which create run-ons. While "however" does help in connecting the ideas of the first and second clauses, the word is not necessary, and should therefore be set off by a comma. Choice **(D)** is correct.

13. A
Difficulty: Medium
Category: Standard English Conventions
Getting to the Answer: A quick glance at the choices indicates this question is testing the correct punctuation, if any, needed after the title of the book "*The Luminaries*." Read the sentence containing the blank carefully and determine the role the book's title plays in the sentence. Here, "her novel *The Luminaries*" is the subject of the sentence and is followed by the verb

"made." No punctuation should separate a subject from its verb, so **(A)** is correct.

14. A
Difficulty: Hard
Category: Standard English Conventions
Getting to the Answer: A quick glance at the choices indicates this question is testing the correct punctuation, if any, needed around the word "perovskite." Read the sentence containing the blank carefully and determine whether "perovskite" is an essential or parenthetical element. If "perovskite" were removed from the sentence, the reader would not know which mineral the scientists were testing. Therefore, "perovskite" is essential information, part of the noun phrase "oxide mineral perovskite," and no punctuation is needed. Choice **(A)** is correct.

15. C
Difficulty: Medium
Category: Standard English Conventions
Getting to the Answer: Commas set off nonessential information from the main part of the sentence just as parentheses or dashes do. The sentence's concluding phrase "which is exactly what happened" is not necessary for understanding the sentence's main clause, which explains how a spark or flame could ignite the hydrogen and cause an explosion. The use of a semicolon or a colon is not appropriate for setting off nonessential information. Eliminate (A) and (B). A dash can replace a comma as a way to emphasize the parenthetical phrase, which would be appropriate here, but (D) misplaces the dash. Choice **(C)** is correct because it uses the necessary punctuation, a comma, in the proper location.

16. D
Difficulty: Medium
Category: Standard English Conventions
Getting to the Answer: A quick glance at the choices indicates this question is testing the correct punctuation, if any, needed between the words "home" and "and." Carefully check the information before and after the blank for clues to the structure of the sentence. Here, the best clue is the dash before "hospitals" in the clause preceding the blank. This dash introduces the parenthetical element "hospitals, long-term care facilities, private clinics, and patients' homes," so a matching dash must end the element. Choice **(D)** is correct.

Drill Answers for Agreement: Verbs

Note: These are not the only ways to correct the sentences; your answers may differ.

a. Angel **will** audition for the school play next week.

b. The song, with its upbeat rhythm and catchy lyrics, **was** wildly popular.

c. The aquatic science club's activities include attending a marine biology lecture, performing a pond ecosystem experiment, and **participating in** a behind-the-scenes tour at the aquarium.

d. By the time the last runner completed the marathon, the winner **had** crossed the finish line hours ago.

e. Few people **know** that Stephen Hawking both revolutionized physics and co-wrote children's books with his daughter.

Try on Your Own Answers

17. A
Difficulty: Medium
Category: Standard English Conventions
Getting to the Answer: Identify the missing verb's subject to ensure that there is proper subject-verb agreement. The subject in this sentence is the compound "bacteria and yeast," which requires a plural verb. All the answer choices contain plural verbs, so next determine the tense of the missing verb. The text uses the present tense verb "is" to describe the process of making kombucha, so eliminate the past tense verb in (C). The tense in (B) does not match the simple present tense used in the rest of the text; eliminate. Choice (D) does not result in a complete sentence, so eliminate this choice as well. The simple present tense verb in **(A)** is correct.

18. D
Difficulty: Easy
Category: Standard English Conventions
Getting to the Answer: Start by determining whether the subject is singular or plural. Here, the SMOM is a group of knights and a collective noun, so it functions as a singular subject. The use of the singular possessive pronoun "its" at the end of the sentence confirms that the Order is singular. Eliminate (A) and (C). Next, consider the tense. The entire paragraph is in the present tense, so maintain the same tense in this sentence.

Choice **(D)** is correct because "is" is a singular verb in the present tense.

19. D
Difficulty: Medium
Category: Standard English Conventions
Getting to the Answer: Start by identifying the context clues in the sentence. The events in the sentence occur after the treaty of 1868 and before 1876, so the verb will be in the past tense. Eliminate choices (A) and (C). Because this attempt was the final activity, occurring after the discovery, it would neither be considered ongoing nor be completed before some other action. Eliminate (B). Choice **(D)** is correct.

20. B
Difficulty: Easy
Category: Standard English Conventions
Getting to the Answer: The sentence is a list that includes present tense, single-action words: "improve" and "beautify." This is a verb parallelism question. Select the answer choice that is a present tense, single-action verb. Choice **(B)** is correct because it is the only option that meets all those conditions.

21. A
Difficulty: Medium
Category: Standard English Conventions
Getting to the Answer: In this sentence, the singular cicada's future action of egg-laying occurs before its death. The compound verb "will lay" is singular and in the future tense for an action that will be completed before a different action. Choice **(A)** is correct because it is the only option that meets all those conditions.

22. C
Difficulty: Medium
Category: Standard English Conventions
Getting to the Answer: The first word of the second sentence is "today," which signals a shift from the past tense of the previous sentence to the present tense, ongoing action. (B) uses the past tense, and (D) uses the future tense: eliminate them. The subject of the verb is the Alliance, a single collective entity, so (A) can be eliminated because it is a plural verb. Therefore, choice **(C)** is correct because it uses the present tense, singular verb "concentrates."

23. B
Difficulty: Hard
Category: Standard English Conventions
Getting to the Answer: When evaluating a verb, ask yourself, Who/what is performing the action? Here, that question becomes, What is doing the establishing? The answer, "the structure," requires a singular verb. The surrounding verbs, "follow" and "can be," are all in the present tense, so choice **(B)**, the present tense, singular "establishes" is correct. Choices (A) and (D) are incorrect because "establish" and "are" are plural verbs, and a singular verb is required. Choice (C) is incorrect because the other verbs in the sentence are in the present tense; there is no reason to change the tense to the past.

24. B
Difficulty: Medium
Category: Standard English Conventions
Getting to the Answer: A quick glance at the choices indicates that this question is testing the correct form of the verb "appear." To identify the subject, ask yourself, What is appearing? The answer is "image," so eliminate (A), a plural verb. The other verb in the sentence, "has," is in the present tense, so **(B)** is correct. Incorrect choice (C) unnecessarily changes the tense to past, and (D) makes "… image … appearing" a dependent clause. Since the clause starts with a comma and the FANBOYS conjunction "but," the final clause of the sentence must be independent.

Drill Answers for Agreement: Pronouns

Note: These are not the only ways to correct the sentences; your answers may differ.

a. Although the teacher gave the student detention after school, **the student** was not angry. OR Although the teacher gave the student detention after school, **the teacher** was not angry.

b. My uncle likes to go bowling with my sister and **me**.

c. My brother moved the box of nails from **its** usual place in the shed.

d. My favorite singer, **whom** I have wanted to see in person for years, will give a concert a week after my birthday.

e. The cathedral of Notre Dame, with vast vaulted ceilings and intricate carvings, never fails to amaze **its** visitors.

Try on Your Own Answers

25. C
Difficulty: Easy
Category: Standard English Conventions
Getting to the Answer: When a pronoun is in the blank, identify its antecedent. The sentence with the blank pronoun has many nouns near it; however, the most logical antecedent is "all" (of the listed items). Neither "natural world" nor "us" are logical antecedents because they are part of a modifying phrase that describes the listed items. Eliminate (A), (B), and (D) because they do not refer to "all" (of the listed items). Therefore, the correct choice will be a rephrase of the antecedent, so as to avoid ambiguity. Choice **(C)** is correct.

26. C
Difficulty: Easy
Category: Standard English Conventions
Getting to the Answer: The blank should refer to "the most important Japanese filmmaker" as stated later in the sentence. In addition to being singular, the pronoun needs to be in the objective form because the "themes" and "settings" are acting on the filmmaker, the object. The third-person, singular objective pronoun is "him." Choice **(C)** is correct.

27. C
Difficulty: Easy
Category: Standard English Conventions
Getting to the Answer: If a pronoun lacks a clear referent, it needs to be replaced with a rephrasing of the antecedent. The missing verb can only logically refer to the Sun, which provides the Earth's heat. Eliminate (B) and (D). However, the closest noun is Earth; therefore, the blank must be a repeat of the noun, "the Sun." Choice **(C)** is correct. (A) is incorrect because using "it" would create ambiguity.

28. B
Difficulty: Medium
Category: Standard English Conventions
Getting to the Answer: Start with ensuring that you have identified the correct antecedent. The missing pronoun refers to the people who are truly allergic, so eliminate (D). "The people who are allergic" is the subject of the sentence, so eliminate both (A) and (C)

because "whom" and "them" are in the objective form. Choice **(B)** is correct.

29. A

Difficulty: Medium

Category: Standard English Conventions

Getting to the Answer: Since the answer choices are all pronouns, identify the correct antecedent. The end of the previous sentence states that the "researchers analyze our consumption," and the blank refers to those who "enjoy" coffee. Therefore, the correct pronoun must be consistent with the plural pronoun "our" and, since it follows the preposition "for," be an objective pronoun. Choice **(A)** is correct. Although the other answer choices are all objective pronouns, none of them are consistent with the other pronouns in the passage: "our" and "we."

30. D

Difficulty: Medium

Category: Standard English Conventions

Getting to the Answer: The antecedent of the missing pronoun is "parkour" and the "appeal" belongs to the sport, a single entity. Predict that the correct pronoun will be the singular possessive form for a thing. Choice **(D)** is correct. Choice (A) is incorrect because "their" is plural. Choice (B) is the possessive for a person, not a thing. Choice (C) is a contraction for "it is"; there is no apostrophe used for the possessive form of "it."

31. D

Difficulty: Medium

Category: Standard English Conventions

Getting to the Answer: A quick glance at the choices tells you this question is testing pronoun usage. Ask yourself, What flap[s] their wings over 50 times every second? The answer is "hummingbirds." Now, examine the noun closest to the blank. That noun is "birds," but its modifier "other" means the birds are not hummingbirds. Eliminate (A), (B), and (C) because these choices connect the blank to the "other birds." The correct answer, **(D)**, makes it clear that the hummingbirds have these unusual characteristics.

32. A

Difficulty: Easy

Category: Standard English Conventions

Getting to the Answer: The "lives" belong to the "Native Americans," so the blank requires a plural

possessive pronoun, making **(A)** correct. Incorrect choices (B) and (C) sound the same, but (B) indicates a location and (C) is the contraction for "they are." Choice (D) does not reflect possession and is also incorrect.

Drill Answers for Agreement: Modifiers

Note: These are not the only ways to correct the sentences; your answers may differ.

a. Since their invention, **computers have grown exponentially more efficient.**

b. Estella chose to take the route with the most **attractive** scenery to her destination.

c. The leaf-tailed gecko's amazing natural camouflage enables it to blend perfectly into **its** surroundings.

d. Between basketball and baseball, basketball is the **more** popular sport in the United States.

e. The infamous Spanish Inquisition has provided material for many artists, **from Edgar Allan Poe to Monty Python.**

Try on Your Own Answers

33. C

Difficulty: Hard

Category: Standard English Conventions

Getting to the Answer: The sentence begins with a modifier, "Considered the father of montage," which means that the subject of the sentence must be the father of montage. Typically, the subject will immediately follow the opening modifying phrase, but in this sentence the next phrase, "a popular cinematic technique ... superimposed," is an additional description of montage, not the main clause. The main clause begins with the blank, and the first words need to be the subject, the father of montage, Sergei Eisenstein. **(C)** is the only choice that makes Sergei Eisenstein the subject and is correct. Choices (A) and (B) make "the modern movie" the subject, while choice (D) makes "critics" the subject.

34. D

Difficulty: Medium

Category: Standard English Conventions

Getting to the Answer: When a sentence begins with a modifying phrase, whatever follows must be the thing that is modified and is the subject of the sentence. Logically, the modifying phrase "Trying to expand their possibilities" can refer only to the graphic designers. The pronoun "their" is plural and so is "graphic designers." **(D)** is the only choice to place graphic designers after the modifying phrase and is correct.

35. B
Difficulty: Hard
Category: Standard English Conventions
Getting to the Answer: The correct answer will align the modifier with its subject without disrupting the syntax of the remainder of the sentence. The sentence begins with the phrase "developing . . . innovations," which must be followed by a subject that can logically do the action of developing: Tesla. Choice **(B)** is correct. The other choices illogically suggest that the innovations were developed by "they" (the inventions) (A), "Tesla's fame" (C), and "the fortunes" (D).

36. A
Difficulty: Medium
Category: Standard English Conventions
Getting to the Answer: A quick glance at the choices indicates this question is testing the correct form of the pronoun "it." The phrase "complexity and sophistication" are characteristics possessed by "bebop," so the possessive form is required. Choice **(A)** is the correct answer. Choice (B) means "it is" or "it has" and does not make sense within the sentence. The spellings in choices (C) and (D) are always incorrect.

37. C
Difficulty: Medium
Category: Standard English Conventions
Getting to the Answer: A quick glance at the choices indicates this question is testing the correct punctuation and modification of "visitors." Who or what has "visitors"? The "zoo." Any answer choices that do not include the apostrophe to make "zoo's" possessive are incorrect: eliminate (A) and (B). The "visitors," however, are not in possession of anything in this sentence, so you do not need a possessive form. Thus, eliminate (D) and choose **(C)** as the correct answer.

38. C
Difficulty: Medium
Category: Standard English Conventions
Getting to the Answer: This question features a blank immediately following an introductory phrase—a

signal to check for a modification error. Determine what that first phrase is describing. Indeed, in this sentence, it is future parents who would be planning a family, so the phrase "future parents" should be placed right next to the introductory modifying phrase. That makes **(C)** the correct answer, as it is the only choice that does so.

39. C
Difficulty: Easy
Category: Standard English Conventions
Getting to the Answer: To identify the word being modified, ask yourself, What lacks artistic integrity? The answer, "productions," requires a plural pronoun, making **(C)** correct.

40. A
Difficulty: Medium
Category: Standard English Conventions
Getting to the Answer: The sentence containing the blank compares someone to "her sister," and the independent clause after the blank reveals that the "someone" is Serena who is being compared to (more . . . than) Vanessa. The correct answer choice will place the logically compared subject closest to the modifying phrase. The only logical choice is **(A)**, "Serena," and it is correct. Because it is illogical to compare "success," as in (B) and (D), and "scoreboards" (C) with a person (her sister), all other choices are incorrect.

41. D
Difficulty: Medium
Category: Standard English Conventions
Getting to the Answer: The sentence as constructed has two independent clauses. Look for a way to correctly join independent clauses, such as a semicolon or a comma with a FANBOYS (coordinating) conjunction. When considering your options, an elimination strategy can be efficient. Eliminate (A) because there is no comma between "rigorous" and "yet." Choice (B) omits the FANBOYS conjunction and creates a run-on; eliminate (B). Choice (C) makes the second clause dependent and incorrectly connects it to the first clause with a semicolon. Only **(D)** uses a comma and a FANBOYS conjunction, so it is correct.

42. C
Difficulty: Hard
Category: Standard English Conventions
Getting to the Answer: The word "length" logically refers to the caves, not the groundwater. You need the possessive form of the pronoun, but because the word "caves" is plural, you need the plural "their." Choice **(C)** is correct and (A) is incorrect. Choices (B) and (D) are incorrect because they are contractions, not pronouns.

43. B
Difficulty: Easy
Category: Standard English Conventions
Getting to the Answer: A glance at the choices indicates this question is testing what punctuation type should be used. Specifically, the list of poetic types is not essential to the meaning of the sentence, so it needs to be set off from the sentence's main structure. Choice (A) does not do this, so eliminate it. When considering (B), note the dash after "to name a few." Its placement suggests it will be paired with another dash. Thus, **(B)** is correct. Choices (C) and (D) are incorrect because they incorrectly pair the dash with a comma or a colon.

44. C
Difficulty: Medium
Category: Standard English Conventions
Getting to the Answer: This question deals with verbs. First, determine whether the verb refers to a singular or plural noun. The noun "cells" in this clause is plural, so the verb will need to be in plural form as well. Second, determine what verb tense is used elsewhere in the sentence. A quick glance will confirm that the rest of the sentence is written in present tense. Thus, the correct answer will be a plural present tense form of the verb, which fits **(C)**. Choices (A), (B), and (D) are incorrect because they violate that agreement in number and/or tense.

45. C
Difficulty: Hard
Category: Standard English Conventions
Getting to the Answer: The sentence with the blank is long and grammatically complex. Begin by identifying its overall structure. The first sentence begins with the word "Although," which means that its first clause is dependent. The following clause, therefore, must be able to stand alone as an independent clause. **(C)** is correct because it uses commas properly. The comma after "arena" properly connects the dependent clause in the first part of the sentence to the independent clause "airships … were widely used … " in the second part of the sentence. The parenthetical phrase "more … today" is correctly set off by commas.

Choice (A) is incorrect because it lacks a comma after "airships." This choice would set off the phrase "airships more commonly called 'blimps' today," meaning "were widely used" would lack a subject. Thus, (A) does not result in an independent clause. (B) is incorrect because both halves of a sentence divided by a semicolon must be able to stand alone as complete sentences. Likewise, (D) is incorrect because a colon cannot come at the end of an introductory dependent clause.

46. D
Difficulty: Hard
Category: Standard English Conventions
Getting to the Answer: In the text, the word "of" means that the pronoun that follows should be in the objective form. "Who" is in the subjective form; therefore, eliminate (A). Choice (B) is incorrect because "whose" is a possessive pronoun, but an objective pronoun is needed. Choice (C) is incorrect because "many" refers to people, and "which" is used to refer to inanimate objects. Only **(D)** has the right pronoun in objective form and is correct.

HOW MUCH HAVE YOU LEARNED: WRITING SKILLS

Directions

This "How Much Have You Learned" section will allow you to measure your growth and confidence in Writing Skills.

For testlike practice, give yourself 12 minutes for this question set. Be sure to use the Method for SAT Reading and Writing Questions. When you're done, check your answers and read through the explanations, even for the questions you answered correctly. Don't forget to celebrate your progress!

1

In *The Hidden Treasures of Black ASL*, author Carolyn McCaskill documents the differing signs, facial expressions, and grammar that _____ Black American Sign Language a separate, authentic dialect of American Sign Language for the thousands of Black Americans who use it today.

Which choice completes the text so that it conforms to the conventions of Standard English?

- (A) made
- (B) make
- (C) makes
- (D) making

2

In 1967 Katherine Switzer became the first woman to officially complete the Boston Marathon. Switzer ran with an official registration bib after signing "K.V. Switzer" on her entry _____ she was physically accosted during her run by a race official who insisted that women were not permitted to participate. A women's Boston Marathon race was finally established in 1972.

Which choice completes the text so that it conforms to the conventions of Standard English?

- (A) papers; however,
- (B) papers, however,
- (C) papers, however;
- (D) papers, however

3

Butser Ancient Farm in Berkshire, United Kingdom, serves as a kind of living history laboratory. _____ researchers at Butser have used historical methods and materials to replicate a Stone Age–era farm in order to study prehistoric living conditions.

Which choice completes the text with the most logical transition?

(A) Finally,

(B) Specifically,

(C) Similarly,

(D) However,

4

While researching a topic, a student has taken the following notes:

- Historian Robert Darnton studies historical texts by analyzing the meanings the text likely held for its writers within their historical context.

- He analyzed and compared a variety of traditional French, German, Italian, and English fairy tales.

- He argues that in the French version of "The Basket of Figs" tale, the hero succeeds because he devises several cunning schemes and outwits those who oppose him.

- He argues that in the German version of "The Basket of Figs" tale, the hero succeeds because he is aided by a variety of magical creatures and objects.

- He suggests that "The Basket of Figs" tales reflect generalizations about their corresponding cultures' worldviews on how to be successful.

The student wants to emphasize a difference in the origins of the two fairy tales. Which choice most effectively uses relevant information from the notes to accomplish this goal?

(A) The hero in the French tale uses cleverness in order to succeed, while the hero in the German tale uses magical assistance in order to succeed.

(B) The version of "The Basket of Figs" in which the hero makes cunning schemes is of French origin, while the version in which the hero is aided by magic is of German origin.

(C) Robert Darnton has analyzed the meanings of fairy tales that originated from a number of countries throughout Europe.

(D) Robert Darnton suggests that the German hero's success, which was due to his receiving help from magical creatures and objects, reflects a historic German worldview about success.

5

Amazed by the long distance of the bird's seasonal migrations, researchers have investigated the unique migratory characteristics of the ruby-throated hummingbird, including the animal's rapid heart rate, which can exceed 1,200 beats a minute during the journey, and _____ solitary undertaking of the migration.

Which choice completes the text so that it conforms to the conventions of Standard English?

(A) they're

(B) their

(C) it's

(D) its

6

The Green Revolution, which began in the 1950s, has been praised for its successful application of agricultural technologies, such as high-yield seeds and chemical fertilizers, and the resultant increases in staple crop production. _____ the long-term overreliance of some countries on nutritionally sparse cereal crops, such as rice, that were made more plentiful by Green Revolution techniques has led to a more cautious evaluation of the revolution over time.

Which choice completes the text with the most logical transition?

(A) In other words,

(B) Therefore,

(C) Nevertheless,

(D) Finally,

7

The *Chicago Manual of Style* provides writers with two alternative citation style _____ in author-date style, writers include parentheses with the source's author and year following each text that requires citation, while in notes and bibliography style, writers instead include citation numbers that lead the reader to a corresponding footnote or endnote source entry.

Which choice completes the text so that it conforms to the conventions of Standard English?

(A) formats,

(B) formats:

(C) formats and

(D) formats

8

While researching a topic, a student has taken the following notes:

- Scientists did not understand how bacteria are able to coil single proteins into propellers that enable the bacteria to move.
- Researchers from the University of Virginia School of Medicine used a technique called cryo-electron microscopy (cryo-EM) to magnify bacteria propellers more than was possible with microscopes.
- Using cryo-EM allowed the researchers to view the atoms of the propellers.
- The researchers discovered that the atoms of the propeller protein can take on various different structures.
- The researchers discovered that a certain combination of propeller protein structures enables the protein to coil.

The student wants to present the researchers' study and its conclusions. Which choice most effectively uses relevant information from the notes to accomplish this goal?

(A) Researchers wanted to demonstrate that cryo-EM is a more effective magnifying tool than microscopes by viewing bacteria propellers.

(B) Researchers used cryo-EM to highly magnify the different structures of protein propeller atoms in bacteria.

(C) Researchers wanted to view bacteria propellers at an atomic level to determine how the propellers are able to coil.

(D) Researchers used cryo-EM to determine that bacteria propellers have certain combinations of protein structures that allow them to coil.

9

A study published in the *European Journal of Preventative Cardiology* reported that moderate daily coffee drinking, in contrast to coffee avoidance, is correlated with positive health outcomes. For example, researchers identified that subjects who drank coffee showed up to a 20% lower likelihood of incidents of cardiovascular disease over the course of the study. _____ subjects who drank coffee showed up to a 27% lower likelihood of death from any cause during the study.

Which choice completes the text with the most logical transition?

(A) Furthermore,

(B) Nevertheless,

(C) For instance,

(D) Instead,

10

Life Among the Piutes: Their Wrongs and Claims is an 1887 narrative that provides insights into the lives of members of the Piute tribe in the late 1800s. The first published autobiography by a Native American woman, _____ advocated for her people in Washington, D.C., and spoke out against the injustices of the reservation system.

Which choice completes the text so that it conforms to the conventions of Standard English?

- (A) there was a Piute chief's daughter, Sarah Winnemucca Hopkins, who relates her experiences in *Life Among the Piutes* and

- (B) Sarah Winnemucca Hopkins, the daughter of a Piute chief who relates her experiences in *Life Among the Piutes*,

- (C) *Life Among the Piutes* relates the experiences of Sarah Winnemucca Hopkins, a Piute chief's daughter who

- (D) the daughter of a Piute chief, Sarah Winnemucca Hopkins, whose experiences are related in *Life Among the Piutes*,

Check Your Work – How Much Have You Learned: Writing Skills

1. B
Difficulty: Medium
Category: Standard English Conventions
Getting to the Answer: Be on the lookout for the word "and"; it makes a list a plural subject, which requires a plural verb. The other verbs in the sentence, "documents" and "use," as well as the adverb "today," establish the present tense, so predict the correct answer is a plural present tense verb. **(B)** matches the prediction and is correct. For the incorrect choices, (A) unnecessarily changes the tense to past, (C) is a singular verb, and (D) destroys the logic of the sentence.

2. A
Difficulty: Medium
Category: Standard English Conventions
Getting to the Answer: The answer choices indicate that this question is testing how to join portions of sentences. The portion before "however" is an independent clause, with the subject-verb "Switzer ran." The portion after "however" is also an independent clause, with subject-verb "she was … accosted." Without a FANBOYS conjunction, a comma cannot join independent clauses, so eliminate (B) and (D). The remaining choices use semicolons, which can be used to join independent clauses; the choices differ in whether the contrast transition "however" is placed with the first or second clause. Since her official running of the marathon contrasts with her being confronted about it, the intended contrast is between the two clauses themselves. Thus, "however" should be grouped with the second clause; **(A)** is correct. Choice (C) would indicate a contrast between the first clause and the preceding sentence.

3. B
Difficulty: Medium
Category: Expression of Ideas
Getting to the Answer: The question stem indicates that this question is testing transitions. As you read the passage, identify the two ideas that are being connected by the missing transition so that you can determine the relationship between them. The first idea is that Butser Farm is a "living history laboratory." The second idea is that researchers made a replica Stone Age farm to study. The second idea is an *example of*, or *clarifies what is meant by* the first idea: the replica Stone Age farm shows how Butser Farm is a "living history laboratory." Choice **(B)** provides the appropriate type of transition, indicating that the Stone Age farm is a specific way in which Butser is a "living history laboratory," and is correct. Choice (A) is incorrect because the passage does not indicate a chronological relationship between the ideas. Choice (C) is incorrect because the Stone Age farm is not *similar to* being a "living history laboratory," but rather it is *a specific example of* being a "living history laboratory." Choice (D) is incorrect because the ideas do not contrast.

4. B
Difficulty: Medium
Category: Expression of Ideas
Getting to the Answer: The question stem asks you to emphasize a "difference" in the "origins" of the fairy tales; the correct answer will specifically concern a difference in *where the tales came from*, and not another difference between the tales. The third and fourth bullet points describe the two fairy tales, identifying one being of French origin and one being of German origin, so look for this specific difference in the answer choices. Although (A) mentions the "French" and "German" tales, it is incorrect because it emphasizes the content of the stories rather than their origins. Choice **(B)** emphasizes the story's origins. Before selecting this answer, be sure to check its descriptions of the tales against the bullet points; **(B)** describes the tales accurately and is correct. Choice (C) is incorrect because it does not focus on the origins of the two specific tales. Choice (D) is incorrect because it is only about one of the tales.

5. D
Difficulty: Easy
Category: Standard English Conventions
Getting to the Answer: The answer choices indicate that this question is testing pronoun usage. The missing pronoun must be possessive, since the "solitary undertaking" belongs to the pronoun's antecedent. Eliminate the contractions ("they are" and "it is") in (A) and (C). Determine the pronoun's antecedent;

the singular "ruby-throated hummingbird" makes the "solitary undertaking," so **(D)** is correct. Choice (B) is incorrect because although it is a possessive pronoun, it is plural.

6. C
Difficulty: Medium
Category: Expression of Ideas
Getting to the Answer: The question stem indicates that this question is testing transitions. As you read the passage, identify the two ideas that are being connected by the missing transition so you can determine the relationship between them. The first idea is about reasons the Green Revolution is praised. The second idea is that the Green Revolution has been more "cautious[ly]" evaluated over time, in particular, due to overreliance on "nutritionally sparse" crops. These ideas move from praise to reservations, so look for a contrast transition; **(C)** is correct. Choice (A) is incorrect because the second idea is not a restatement of the first idea. Choice (B) is incorrect because the "more cautious evaluation" is not the *result of* its initial praise. Choice (D) is incorrect because the passage is not relaying a sequence of multiple events.

7. B
Difficulty: Medium
Category: Standard English Conventions
Getting to the Answer: The answer choices indicate that this question is testing what punctuation, if any, should be used to join two portions of a sentence. The portion ending in "formats" is an independent clause ("The *Chicago Manual of Style* provides . . ."). The portion after "formats" has a prepositional phrase ("in author-date style") connected to an independent clause ("writers include . . ."). Since two independent clauses are connected, using a comma or no punctuation would result in a run-on, so eliminate (A) and (D). Choice **(B)** is correct because a colon can be used after an independent clause to introduce information that clarifies or explains: here, the portion after the colon specifies the "two alternative citation style formats." Choice (C) is incorrect because a comma must be used with a FANBOYS conjunction when joining independent clauses.

8. D
Difficulty: Medium
Category: Expression of Ideas
Getting to the Answer: The question stem indicates that you need to summarize (or present) and identify the conclusions of the research study, so look for these elements as you read the bullet points. The first point states that there was something scientists did not understand: how bacteria can coil single proteins. The following bullet points describe the study and its results: the researchers used cryo-EM to better magnify propellers and found that a combination of structures allows for coiling. Use this summary of the study and its results as your prediction, which matches **(D)**. Choice **(D)** is correct because it "presents" the study by summarizing its method (use of cryo-EM), and it provides its results (the finding about how the propellers coil). Choices (A) and (C) are incorrect because they concern the aim of the study; further, (A) misrepresents the aim as comparing magnification tools rather than investigating bacteria propellers. Although choice (B) describes the procedure of the study, it is incorrect because it does not mention its conclusions.

9. A
Difficulty: Medium
Category: Expression of Ideas
Getting to the Answer: The question stem indicates that this question is testing transitions. As you read the passage, identify the two ideas that are being connected by the missing transition so you can determine the relationship between them. The first idea is that the study showed that coffee-drinkers had a lower likelihood of cardiovascular disease. The second idea is that the study showed that coffee-drinkers were less likely to die from any cause during the study. The second idea is an *additional* example of the "positive health outcomes" mentioned in the first sentence, so the *continuation* transition in **(A)** is correct. Choices (B) and (D) are incorrect because the two examples of positive health outcomes do not *contrast*. Choice (C) is incorrect because the lower likelihood of death is not *an example of* the lower likelihood of cardiovascular disease.

10. C
Difficulty: Medium
Category: Standard English Conventions
Getting to the Answer: The answer choices indicate that this question is testing modifying phrases. The second sentence's introductory phrase "The first published autobiography by a Native American woman" should modify the book it is describing, *Life Among the Piutes*. Choice **(C)** is correct because it places the book title immediately after the modifying phrase; further, it correctly positions "Sarah Winnemucca Hopkins" next to the phrase that describes her ("a Piute chief's daughter …"). The other choices incorrectly result in "The first published autobiography by a Native American woman" modifying "there" in (A), "Sarah Winnemucca Hopkins" in (B), and "the daughter" in (D).

SAT READING AND WRITING: TIMING AND SECTION MANAGEMENT STRATEGIES

LEARNING OBJECTIVE

After completing this chapter, you will be able to:

- Make quick decisions about which questions to do right away and which to save for later

---

SAT READING AND WRITING: TIMING AND SECTION MANAGEMENT

Timing

The Reading and Writing section is made up of two 32-minute modules, for a total of 64 minutes for the section. Each of the two modules has 27 questions, for a total of 54 Reading and Writing questions. This gives you a little over one minute for each question.

Section Management

To help you navigate the Reading and Writing section accurately and efficiently, recall the test-taking strategies discussed in the Inside the SAT chapter. Review chapter 1 for more details about the strategies.

1. **Triaging the Test**—Start with the questions you find easiest and flag more difficult or time-consuming questions to do later. Use the module review screen to help you navigate through each module.

2. **Elimination**—Strategically eliminate answer choices that you know are incorrect by crossing them out with the on-screen elimination tool. Be on the lookout for incorrect answer types that are common on SAT Reading and Writing, such as Misused Details. (See chapter 17 to review the incorrect answer types.)

3. **Strategic Guessing**—Be sure to answer every question, since there is no wrong-answer penalty. If you're not sure how to do a question or you're nearly out of time, strategically eliminate answer choices, and then use a Letter of the Day to guess an answer.

4. **Living in the Question**—Focus all your energy on the current question.

Keep reading for specifics on how to apply these strategies to the Reading and Writing section.

Pacing

Each question on the SAT Reading and Writing section is accompanied by a short passage, but you definitely do not need to spend the same amount of time on each question. Passages vary both in difficulty and in length—from about 25 to 150 words—so the time you'll spend on each passage will vary. Further, some question types will require more time than others. Consider the following questions, which you practiced in the Reading and Writing lessons of this book, and think about how you might approach a Reading and Writing module that contains these questions on test day.

1. **Text 1**

   Many teenagers have heard that playing video games can negatively affect their learning and socialization. Studies performed in the 1990s supported this claim. Scientists evaluated the content of popular video games and the amount of time teenagers were allowed to spend playing them, connecting video game use to anger issues, obesity, and addiction. The scientists found that the only positive effect of playing video games was an improvement in manual dexterity and computer literacy.

   Text 2

   Researchers from the National Academy of Sciences found in a 2013 study that playing fast-paced video games can improve performance in many areas, such as attention span, spatial navigation, cognition, reasoning, and memory. Researchers tested small pools of gamers and found that those who played action-packed video games were better at tasks involving pattern discrimination and conceptualizing 3-D objects.

   Based on the texts, how would the researchers from the National Academy of Sciences (Text 2) most likely respond to the scientists' findings presented in Text 1?

   A) They would argue that the time spent playing video games per day increased dramatically in the years between the studies.

   B) They would recommend that the scientists compare the effects of playing video games to those of playing contact sports.

   C) They would encourage the scientists to evaluate the effects of video games on a wide variety of learning and performance skills.

   D) They would claim that video games have different effects on people in different age groups.

2. Because French collaborators assisted in the development of American Sign Language (ASL), French Sign Language shares almost 60% of its signs with ASL. However, British Sign Language and American Sign Language, though based on a shared spoken language, _____ not mutually intelligible.

   Which choice completes the text so that it conforms to the conventions of Standard English?

   A) is

   B) are

   C) was

   D) were

On test day, a Connections question like question 1, would appear before a Standard English Conventions question like question 2. Think about everything the Connections question requires you to do. You need to read *two* passages. Based on the question stem, you then have to identify the view of the researchers in Text 2, identify the scientists' findings in Text 1, and, finally, carefully evaluate the statements in the answer choices to determine which accurately reflects the relationship between the passages. On the other hand, the Standard English Conventions question has a brief accompanying passage and just asks you to identify which verb agrees with the subject and tense in the passage. No matter which question you may personally find *easier*, the first question here will likely take you substantially longer to read, analyze, and answer correctly. Adopt the mindset that every question is equally important to your best score. You might decide to flag question 1 and move on to questions like the second one, returning to question 1 from the review screen later as you have time. (See the Connections Questions lesson in chapter 19 and the How Much Do You Know: Writing Skills section for the answers and explanations to these questions.)

Because this is a timed exam, be sure to complete the questions you find easiest to answer first. If a particular question is challenging or is taking you an especially long time, eliminate any answer choices you can, mark a guess, and flag the question to come back to it if you have time. Once you submit your answers for a module, you will not be able to return to it. So before you exit a module, make sure you have an **answer selected for every question**, since there is no penalty for guessing.

Questions of the same type will be grouped together in each Reading and Writing module; for instance, all the Words in Context questions within a module will appear together. Within these question groups, the questions will be in approximate order of difficulty, from easiest to most difficult. Use this structure to help you navigate each module: expect that some groups of questions may take you longer than others, and be ready to flag the more difficult questions, if needed, at the end of each question group to review if you have time at the end of the module.

Using the Digital SAT Test Application Tools

The digital test application includes a **countdown timer** that can help you keep track of your remaining time and manage your pace. Every time you complete a practice test, make sure you time yourself so you can practice your pacing.

The digital testing application will also provide you with **annotation tools** that allow you to make notes or highlight text in the passages and question stems. These tools may help you focus your attention on the keywords and information that are most relevant to answering the question. The digital testing application also gives you the ability to **cross out answer choices** as you eliminate them. *Practice with the tools ahead of time so you can determine if you want to use them, and, if so, figure out how you will use them to your advantage on test day.*

Practicing the SAT Reading and Writing Section

Mastering your section management strategy for SAT Reading and Writing will require practice. **Every time you complete a practice test, apply the strategies from this chapter:** flag questions you find too time-consuming and return to them if you have time while keeping an eye on the clock. Eliminate incorrect answer choices, strategically guess if you need to, and keep your focus on the current question. Make sure you answer every question before you finish each module. And when taking online practice tests, practice navigating the section and using the available tools so you'll be comfortable with the format on test day.

Now that you've learned about section management for the SAT Reading and Writing section, your next step is to **take a practice test**. Be sure to apply the section management strategies you've learned and, as always, carefully **review the practice test answers and explanations** to reflect on your performance.

PART 4

COUNTDOWN TO TEST DAY

CHAPTER 23

COUNTDOWN TO TEST DAY

Two Months before the Test

- Make sure you have an approved laptop or tablet on which to take the digital SAT. Visit the test maker's website, www.collegeboard.org, to ensure you have an acceptable device.

- If you do not have access to a device that meets the technical specifications for the exam application, you can request to borrow one from College Board. Note that you must submit your request at least 30 days before your test day. Check the College Board's website for the most up-to-date details.

- If you haven't done so already, set up a schedule to regularly use your Kaplan study resources (such as this book).

The Week before the Test

- Focus your additional practice on the question types and/or subject areas in which you usually score highest. Now is the time to sharpen your best skills, not cram new information.

- Make sure you are registered for the test. Remember, Kaplan cannot register you. If you missed the registration deadlines, check if you can request Waitlist Status on the test maker's website, www.collegeboard.org.

- If you have not already done so, go to www.collegeboard.org and download the testing application onto the laptop or tablet that you will use to take the test. If you are using a school device and are unable to download the testing application yourself, request help from your school's tech support.

- Open the testing application and complete the exam setup. Once complete, print or email to yourself the admission ticket that you'll use on test day.

- Confirm the location of your test site. Never been there before? Make a practice run to make sure you know exactly how long it will take to get from your home to your test site. Build in extra time in case you hit traffic or construction on the morning of the test.

- Get a great night's sleep the two days before the test.

The Day before the Test

- Review the methods and strategies you learned in this book.

- Put new batteries in your calculator, if using your own.

- If bringing your own laptop or tablet, charge your device overnight to make sure it is fully charged for the exam.

- Pack your backpack or bag for test day with the following items:

  - Laptop or tablet case (or another way to help you remember to pack your device and power cord for the exam)

  - Photo ID

- Admission ticket or printout
- Directions to your test site location
- Several pens or sharpened pencils with erasers (no mechanical pencils or pens that make a clicking noise)
- Approved calculator and extra batteries, if planning to use your own rather than the built-in graphing calculator
- Non-prohibited timepiece, if desired
- Tissues
- Prepackaged snacks, like granola bars
- Bottled water, juice, or sports drink
- Sweatshirt, sweater, or jacket

The Night before the Test

- No studying!
- Do something relaxing that will take your mind off the test, such as watching a movie or playing video games with friends.
- Set your alarm to wake up early enough so that you won't feel rushed.
- Go to bed early, but not too much earlier than you usually do. You want to fall asleep quickly, not spend hours tossing and turning.

The Morning of the Test

- Dress comfortably and in layers. You need to be prepared for any temperature.
- Eat a filling breakfast, but don't stray too far from your usual routine. If you normally aren't a breakfast eater, don't eat a huge meal, but make sure you have something substantial.
- Read something over breakfast. You need to warm up your brain so you don't go into the test cold. Read a few pages of a newspaper, magazine, or favorite novel.
- If bringing your own, make sure to pack your fully charged laptop or tablet and your power cord.
- Get to your test site early. There is likely to be some confusion about where to go and how to sign in, so allow yourself plenty of time, even if you are taking the test at your own school.
- Leave your cell phone at home or in the car. Many test sites do not allow them in the building.
- While you're waiting to sign in or be seated, read more of what you read over breakfast to stay in reading mode.

During the Test

- Be calm and confident. You're ready for this!
- Remember that while the SAT is a more than two-hour marathon, it is also a series of shorter sections. Focus on the section you're working on at that moment; don't think about previous or upcoming sections.
- Use the methods and strategies you have learned in this book as often as you can. Allow yourself to fall into the good habits you built during your practice.
- Don't linger too long on any one question. Mark it and come back to it later.
- Can't figure out an answer? Try to eliminate some choices and take a strategic guess. Remember, there is no penalty for an incorrect answer, so even if you can't eliminate any choices, you should take a guess.

- There will be plenty of questions you *can* answer, so spend your time on those first.
- Maintain good posture throughout the test. It will help you stay alert.
- If you find yourself losing concentration, getting frustrated, or stressing about the time, stop for 30 seconds. Close your eyes, take a few deep breaths, and relax your shoulders. You'll be much more productive after taking a few moments to relax.
- Use your break effectively. During the break, go to the restroom, eat your snacks, and get your energy up for the next section.

After the Test

- Congratulate yourself! Then, reward yourself by doing something fun. You've earned it!
- If you got sick during the test or if something else happened that might have negatively affected your score, you can cancel your scores. Request information from your test proctor or visit the test maker's website for more information.
- Your scores should be available online within a week after your test. The College Board sends scores to colleges 10 days after they are available to you.

PART 5

PRACTICE TEST 1

ABOUT YOUR PRACTICE TEST

The SAT is an *adaptive test*. This means that, for both the Reading and Writing section and the Math section, your performance on the first module of the test section will determine the relative difficulty of the questions you see in the second module. (See chapter 1, Inside the SAT, for more information about the SAT's structure.) Also note that on test day, the SAT will include *pre-test questions* that will not be scored, but as there is no indication of which questions they are, this paper test will grade all of the questions. *While a paper test cannot simulate a digital adaptive test perfectly, the test can still give you an estimate of your current abilities and how you might perform on the digital version of the test.*

To best simulate the digital SAT test day experience, follow these steps as you complete your practice test:

1. Using a timer, give yourself **32 minutes** to complete the *Routing Module of the Reading and Writing section*.

2. Use the answer key at the end of the Reading and Writing Routing Module to calculate your score. If you scored:

    - **19 or more questions correct:** Move on to *Reading and Writing Module B*.
    - **18 or fewer questions correct:** Move on to *Reading and Writing Module A*.

3. Give yourself **32 minutes** to complete *Module A or B* (see step 2) of the Reading and Writing section.

4. Take a **10 minute break**.

5. Give yourself **35 minutes** to complete the *Routing Module of the Math section*.

6. Use the answer key at the end of the Math Routing Module to calculate your score. If you scored:

    - **14 or more questions correct:** Move on to *Math Module B*.
    - **13 or fewer questions correct:** Move on to *Math Module A*.

7. Give yourself **35 minutes** to complete *Module A or B* (see step 6) of the Math section.

To score your practice test:

- Use the answer key to score the Reading and Writing modules and the Math modules.
- Write down your total raw score—the total number of questions you got correct—for all of the Reading and Writing modules and all of the Math modules.
- Convert your raw scores to scaled scores as directed. The score in the right column indicates your estimated scaled score if this were an actual SAT. Enter your scaled scores in the boxes that follow the table.
- Calculate your estimated composite, or overall, score. Simply add together your scaled scores for each section.

Besides the provided in-book practice, be sure to familiarize yourself with the layout and tools of the College Board's testing application to make sure you feel confident navigating the digital SAT on test day.

READING AND WRITING: ROUTING MODULE

Mark your answers either on the pages that follow or on a separate sheet of paper. You will be scoring this Routing Module before going on to the final Reading and Writing Module.

DIRECTIONS

The questions in this section address a number of important reading and writing skills. Each question includes one or more passages, which may include a table or graph. Read each passage and question carefully, and then choose the best answer to the question based on the passage(s).

All questions in this section are multiple-choice with four answer choices. Each question has a single best answer.

1

The following text is from Franz Kafka's 1915 novel *Metamorphosis*.

Gregor then turned to look out the window at the dull weather. Drops of rain could be heard hitting the pane, which made him feel quite sad. "How about if I sleep a little bit longer and forget all this nonsense," he thought.

As used in the text, what does the word "dull" most nearly mean?

- Ⓐ Boring
- Ⓑ Smooth
- Ⓒ Pale
- Ⓓ Drab

2

Art is never _____, nor is it meant to be. A poem written today looks and sounds vastly different from a poem by Shakespeare, and a modern symphony no longer resembles one by Beethoven.

Which choice completes the text with the most logical and precise word or phrase?

- Ⓐ dynamic
- Ⓑ sluggish
- Ⓒ static
- Ⓓ progressive

CONTINUED ➡

Practice Tests

Chemist Carolyn Bertozzi developed biorthogonal chemistry, which entails producing chemical reactions inside living organisms through a relatively _____ procedure; the practice facilitates cutting-edge research because it allows scientists to study the impacts of modified molecules without interfering with the normal biological functioning of an organism's cells.

Which choice completes the text with the most logical and precise word or phrase?

Ⓐ reactive

Ⓑ benign

Ⓒ coherent

Ⓓ injurious

Astronomers typically have difficulty detecting newly-forming planets <u>because the young planets are obscured by large amounts of dust and debris</u>. Astronomer Feng Long, however, has recently discovered a new potential method for identifying young planets. Using extensive data from computer models, Long reports that precisely positioned clusters of material buildup—120 degrees apart—may signal the presence of a new planet.

Which choice best states the function of the underlined portion in the text as a whole?

Ⓐ It provides the cause of a problem for which a possible solution is presented in the sentences that follow.

Ⓑ It establishes a contrast with the problem that is mentioned earlier in the sentence.

Ⓒ It suggests an alternative solution for a problem that differs from the potential solution that is presented in the sentences that follow.

Ⓓ It elaborates on a potential solution for a problem that is mentioned earlier in the sentence.

CONTINUED

5

Meditation has been around for thousands of years, starting as a religious practice. Hindu scripture from around 1500 B.C.E. describes meditating on the divine, and art from this time period shows people sitting cross-legged and solitary in a garden. In China and India around the fifth century B.C.E., other forms of meditation developed. Several religions, including Taoism, Buddhism, Islam, and Christianity, have meditative rites. In 20th-century Europe and America, secular forms of meditation arrived from India. Rather than focusing on spiritual growth, secular meditation emphasizes stress reduction, relaxation, and self-improvement.

Which choice best states the main purpose of the text?

(A) It discusses the history of meditation as a religious practice to illustrate how it can impact spiritual growth.

(B) It argues that religious and secular meditation improve well-being, including the regulation of the impacts of stress.

(C) It presents meditation as a practice that has been historically connected to various world religions.

(D) It describes the history of meditation, from its religious origins to its developing non-religious forms over time.

6

Text 1

First used to replace sugar during the shortages caused by World War I, artificial sweeteners have since grown tremendously in popularity. Many nutritionists believe that artificial sweeteners can be used to replace sugar in the diet of a person suffering from diabetes, a chronic condition that prevents the body from properly regulating blood sugar levels.

Text 2

Jotham Suez and a research team conducted a study of about 400 people and found that the subjects who consumed artificial sweeteners had higher blood sugar levels and impaired abilities to tolerate glucose. They also found that the subjects who consumed artificial sweeteners had different populations of bacteria in their guts compared to the subjects who did not, and they posit that artificial sweetener use was responsible for these differences.

Based on the texts, how would Suez and the research team (Text 2) most likely describe the view of the nutritionists presented in Text 1?

(A) It is seriously compromised by the research team's findings.

(B) It probably holds true only under conditions like those in the research team's study.

(C) It is not compelling as a theory regardless of the data collected by the research team.

(D) It is largely correct but requires a minor refinement in light of the research team's results.

CONTINUED

Practice Tests

7

Text 1

Most geologists believe the continents formed as material bubbled up from the Earth's core. In the presence of water, buoyant granite formed on the underside of the bubbles and become the base upon which a continent would grow. This theory remains unproven, however, because the motion of the continents and the interactions along their edges destroy the geological record, thus making it impossible to study.

Text 2

Tim Johnson and colleagues argue that the original continents were seeded by meteorites. The collision of the meteorites with the hot surface of the Earth caused fragments of the crust to cool and become buoyant patches to which additional material would adhere, forming continents. To support their view, they cite the composition of crystals taken from the oldest known segment of the Earth's crust, which shows that the crystals formed close to the surface of the Earth.

Based on the texts, how would Johnson and colleagues (Text 2) most likely describe the view of the geologists presented in Text 1?

(A) It is largely correct but requires a minor refinement in light of the results obtained by Johnson and colleagues.

(B) It is not compelling as a theory regardless of the data collected by Johnson and colleagues.

(C) It is more likely to be accepted in conjunction with the data provided by Johnson and colleagues.

(D) It may seem plausible but is not supported by the findings of Johnson and colleagues.

8

The programs of the New Deal constituted a collection of measures intended to curb the economic hardships U.S. citizens faced as a result of the Great Depression. For instance, the Public Works Administration provided jobs in an effort to combat high unemployment. Likewise, the Agricultural Adjustment Act sought to raise incomes for impoverished farmers by inflating prices on agricultural commodities.

Which choice best states the main idea of the text?

(A) The goal of the New Deal programs was to address economic difficulties.

(B) The Public Works Administration significantly increased employment.

(C) The Agricultural Adjustment Act was a controversial part of the New Deal.

(D) The Great Depression led to the New Deal.

CONTINUED

9

A now-famous occurrence at the roulette wheel at a casino in Monte Carlo in 1913 has become emblematic of the so-called gambler's fallacy. A roulette wheel has an equal number of red and black spaces, and players can bet on the color on which a ball will land when the wheel is spun. On the night of the incident, the wheel landed on black a surprising 26 times in a row. Bettors lost huge sums of money, based on their mistaken assumption that the wheel was much more likely to break the streak and land on red next. This flawed conception of probability, which fails to consider each independent spin as a discrete event, is the heart of the gambler's fallacy.

Which choice best states the main idea of the text?

(A) In some situations, the probability of any individual event is not influenced by the probability of the events that preceded it.

(B) A roulette wheel landing on black 26 times is just as likely as it landing on red 26 times, assuming the wheel has an equal number of red and black spaces.

(C) The gambler's fallacy is difficult to avoid since it is human nature to assume that a random event that has occurred many times is less likely to occur the next time.

(D) An event at a Monte Carlo casino is a well-known example of the mistaken understanding of probability called the gambler's fallacy.

CONTINUED

10

The following text is from Sir Arthur Conan Doyle's 1887 novel *A Study in Scarlet*.

As the weeks went by, my interest in him and my curiosity as to his aims in life gradually deepened and increased. His very person and appearance were such as to strike the attention of the most casual observer. In height he was rather over six feet, and so excessively lean that he seemed to be considerably taller. His eyes were sharp and piercing, save during those intervals of torpor to which I have alluded; and his thin, hawk-like nose gave his whole expression an air of alertness and decision. His chin, too, had the prominence and square-ness which mark the man of determination. His hands were invariably blotted with ink and stained with chemicals, yet he was possessed of extraordinary delicacy of touch, as I frequently had occasion to observe when I watched him manipulating his fragile philosophical instruments.

According to the passage, as time passes, what does the narrator think about the man he describes?

(A) The man is frequently irritating.

(B) The man is somewhat snobby.

(C) The man is increasingly intriguing.

(D) The man is occasionally generous.

CONTINUED

Practice Tests

"A March in the Ranks Hard-Pressed, and the Road Unknown" is an 1865 poem by Walt Whitman. In the poem, the speaker describes the determination of soldiers to continue despite their heavy losses: _____

Which quotation from "A March in the Ranks Hard-Pressed, and the Road Unknown" most effectively illustrates the claim?

- (A) "A march in the ranks hard-pressed, and the road unknown, / A route through a heavy wood with muffled steps in the darkness, / Our army foil'd with loss severe, and the sullen remnant retreating, / Till after midnight glimmer upon us the lights of a dim-lighted building,"

- (B) "We come to an open space in the woods, and halt by the dim-lighted building, / 'Tis a large old church at the crossing roads, now an impromptu hospital, / Entering but for a minute I see a sight beyond all the pictures and poems ever made, / Shadows of deepest, deepest black, just lit by moving candles and lamps."

- (C) "But first I bend to the dying lad, his eyes open, a half-smile gives he me, / Then the eyes close, calmly close, and I speed forth to the darkness, / Resuming, marching, ever in darkness marching, on in the ranks, / The unknown road still marching."

- (D) "Then before I depart I sweep my eyes o'er the scene fain to absorb it all, / Faces, varieties, postures beyond description, most in obscurity, some of them dead, / Surgeons operating, attendants holding lights, the smell of ether, the odor of blood, / The crowd, O the crowd of the bloody forms, the yard outside also fill'd,"

CONTINUED

12

Germany's International Trade in 1913

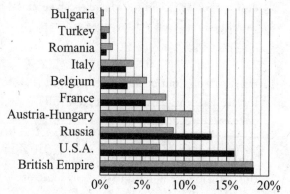

Bulgaria
Turkey
Romania
Italy
Belgium
France
Austria-Hungary
Russia
U.S.A.
British Empire

0%   5%   10%   15%   20%

■ Destination of Germany's Exports   ■ Origin of Germany's Imports

World War I ran from 1914 to 1918. It saw the Central Powers, led by Germany, battle the Allies, principally the British Empire, France, Russia, and, starting in 1917, the United States. In 1909, however, British economist Normal Angell published *The Great Illusion*, which became a best-seller published in over 11 languages. Angell argued that, in the modern world, the 'great illusion' was that international peace was guaranteed through strong militaries. Angell asserted that international trade and economic interconnectedness meant modern war was unlikely due to it potentially costing nations so much money. This idea was welcomed at a time when tensions were rising between Germany and the British Empire over a naval arms race, as _____

Which choice most effectively uses data from the graph to illustrate Angell's claim?

Ⓐ Germany imported more goods from the British Empire than it did from everywhere else combined.

Ⓑ only the United States of America exceeded the British Empire as a destination for German exports.

Ⓒ over 70% of German imports came from the British Empire, France, and Russia, which were the main military rivals of Germany.

Ⓓ around 18% of German exports and imports involved the British Empire, more than those of any other state.

Practice Tests

CONTINUED ➡

13

Economic models have been harshly criticized for not accurately predicting major economic crises such as the Great Depression and the 2008 recession. However, these models are only able to incorporate known, historical trends. Both the Great Depression and the 2008 economic recession were triggered by bank failures: sudden, unusual, and traumatic events impossible to predict. Once the failures occurred, and thus became known, they were incorporated into the economic models of the time that then accurately predicted the future direction of the economy. Since the models can be updated, this implies that economic models _____

Which choice most logically completes the text?

(A) deserve the criticism they have received and should be replaced with a more accurate methodology.

(B) remain useful but cannot be expected to foresee every potentially disruptive influence on the economy.

(C) could have been updated more quickly and thus possibly been used to prevent some of the damage of these events.

(D) have proven their reliability and should be able to predict future crises, since two crisis events are now included.

14

In his most famous project, French philosopher René Descartes sought certainty by mentally stripping away every layer of knowledge that was remotely possible to doubt. Ultimately, Descartes arrived at his memorable conclusion, "I think, therefore I _____ could only be certain of the fact that he was thinking. Building from there, he could work toward rational certainty in other areas of knowledge.

Which choice completes the text so that it conforms to the conventions of Standard English?

(A) am" he

(B) am." He

(C) am," he

(D) am"; He

CONTINUED ➡

15

In early 1878, Constantin Fahlberg began working as a research chemist in a laboratory at Johns Hopkins University, making chemical compounds derived from coal tar. Coal tar was a by-product of steel manufacturing, and compounds derived from _____ had been used as medicines and in dye formulations. Fahlberg was studying ways to add different chemicals to molecules found in coal tar to see if the new compounds formed had other useful properties, and in one of the more famous accidents of modern chemistry, created saccharine, the first artificial sweetener.

Which choice completes the text so that it conforms to the conventions of Standard English?

- (A) these
- (B) them
- (C) him
- (D) it

16

Earth has been struck by asteroids in the past, so scientists have launched a probe that will crash into a small asteroid in an effort to measure the effect the impact has on the path of the asteroid. Although the asteroid is small, it is much larger than the one that struck Siberia in _____ leveled 2,000 square kilometers of forest), so scientists hope to learn enough to be able to protect Earth from future asteroid impacts.

Which choice completes the text so that it conforms to the conventions of Standard English?

- (A) 1908 which
- (B) 1908, which
- (C) 1908 (which
- (D) 1908: which

17

Although some consumers consider home delivery more efficient than driving to several stores to obtain needed supplies, the cardboard needed to produce shipping packages _____ to the household garbage that communities must process.

Which choice completes the text so that it conforms to the conventions of Standard English?

- (A) contributes
- (B) contribute
- (C) are contributing
- (D) have contributed

CONTINUED

Practice Tests

18

Spring has traditionally been the time to plant trees; however, in areas with hot summers and mild winters, fall is the best season to plant. Planting in the _____ new trees the longest possible time to establish good growth and build strength before the stresses of the hot and dry summer months begin.

Which choice completes the text so that it conforms to the conventions of Standard English?

Ⓐ fall gives

Ⓑ fall, for example, gives

Ⓒ fall, in other words, gives

Ⓓ fall, the season before winter, gives

19

Weight-bearing exercise has been shown to benefit participants of all ages and abilities. Although the most obvious example is that of athletes who build the muscle mass and strength that help them excel in their sports, weight-bearing exercise is _____ to enable them to continue with the activities of daily life.

Which choice completes the text so that it conforms to the conventions of Standard English?

Ⓐ important for, the injured and the elderly

Ⓑ important for the injured, and the elderly

Ⓒ important for the injured and the elderly

Ⓓ important, for the injured and the elderly,

20

The Tripitaka Koreana is a collection of over 80,000 woodblocks. Created in the 13th century, it is the oldest and most comprehensive version of the Buddhist canon, with no known errors or typos in its volumes. Each woodblock was made through an elaborate _____ was soaked in sea water for three years, then boiled in salt water, then exposed to wind for three years, then covered in a poisonous lacquer to keep insects from damaging the wood, and finally framed with metal to prevent the wood from warping. This elaborate process created woodblocks that are in pristine condition despite being over 750 years old.

Which choice completes the text so that it conforms to the conventions of Standard English?

Ⓐ process: birch wood

Ⓑ process. Birch wood,

Ⓒ process—birch wood:

Ⓓ process birch wood

CONTINUED

21

The Hohokam people of the Phoenix Basin in the desert of today's southern Arizona constructed villages that encompassed several hundred acres with the largest and most extensive irrigation canals in North America. Remarkably permanent in an area known for settlements that relocated after only a few decades, _____ during which the Hohokam successfully grew crops in the same locations and prospered.

Which choice completes the text so that it conforms to the conventions of Standard English?

- (A) Hohokam villages were home to their people for 1500 years or more,
- (B) there was a period of 1500 years
- (C) 1500 years was the time
- (D) the Hohokam people lived in these villages for 1500 years or more,

---

22

Mary Anning was an English fossil collector in the early 19th century. Despite her many achievements, Anning existed on the outskirts of paleontology. Women were not allowed to join the Geological Society of London. Class politics further stifled Anning, who came from a working-class background. She supported herself by collecting fossils along the shoreline of Lyme Regis, as each winter caused landslides that exposed previously buried fossils. This work was dangerous; _____ Anning herself had one near-miss with a landslide that took the life of her dog.

Which choice completes the text with the most logical transition?

- (A) but,
- (B) though,
- (C) on the other hand,
- (D) indeed,

23

SONAR (Sound Navigation And Ranging) is a system that uses sound waves to measure the depth of water under a boat. SONAR technology was developed during World War I; _____ in 1490, Leonardo da Vinci experimented with the principle by listening to a tube inserted into water in order to detect marine vessels.

Which choice completes the text with the most logical transition?

- (A) since,
- (B) despite,
- (C) however,
- (D) for example,

CONTINUED ➡

K   713

24

A recent survey found that the share of teens between the ages of 13 and 17 who claim to be "almost constantly" on social media has nearly doubled from 24% in 2015 to 46% today. _____ most of the survey responders believe they spend an appropriate amount of time online; only 36% reported that they believe they spend too much time on the internet.

Which choice completes the text with the most logical transition?

Ⓐ Despite this increase,

Ⓑ Illustrating this point,

Ⓒ Subsequently,

Ⓓ Indeed, because of this increase,

25

While researching a topic, a student has taken the following notes:

- Parshvanatha, one of the 23 propagators of the Jain religion, lived in the 9th century B.C.E. and is considered the first documented person to prohibit consuming meat as part of a religious practice.

- Around the 5th century B.C.E., Siddhartha Gautama (the founder of Buddhism) and Pythagoras (the Greek philosopher and mathematician) refrained from eating meat.

- Seitan, a wheat-based meat substitute, was invented in China in the 6th century C.E., and almond milk was first manufactured in 13th century C.E. Europe.

- In the 18th century C.E., Benjamin Franklin sent soybeans to the United States after encountering tofu, a soy-based meat substitute, in London.

- Today, companies manufacturing plant-based meat substitutes make even more options available for consumers who are reducing their consumption of meat.

The student wants to emphasize a difference between past humans who did not eat meat and those who are reducing their meat consumption today. Which choice most effectively uses relevant information from the notes to accomplish this goal?

Ⓐ The practice of refusing to eat meat is not new; this custom has a long and varied history, starting for religious reasons in the 9th century B.C.E. and continuing until the present day.

Ⓑ Unlike people who removed meat from their diets in the past, those who do so today have a wider variety of meat substitutes available.

Ⓒ Soybeans came to the United States through Benjamin Franklin, who came upon tofu, a soy-based meat substitute, while in London.

Ⓓ Those who choose to reduce or eliminate meat from their diets today may choose among seitan, tofu, almond milk, and plant-based manufactured meat when planning their diets.

CONTINUED ➡

26

While researching a topic, a student has taken the following notes:

- Umi Kai crafts traditional *na mea Hawaii* (things of Hawai'i), everyday objects used by his people for generations.

- Committed to preserving his culture, he exclusively uses the same native materials such as shark's teeth, *ohia lehua*, and other native woods as were used by his forebears.

- Using power tools, he crafts items more quickly than his ancestors could, but even with modern methods, his hand-crafted items are time-consuming to produce.

- Looking for quick, inexpensive souvenirs, many tourists purchase items that look as if they are authentically Hawaiian but are actually mass-produced overseas.

- Umi Kai and other traditional Hawaiian artisans continue to seek customers who recognize the value of craftmanship and want to participate in the continuity of traditional Hawaiian culture.

The student wants to emphasize a similarity between Umi Kai and his ancestral craftsmen. Which choice most effectively uses relevant information from the notes to accomplish this goal?

- (A) Umi Kai uses power tools to craft *na mea Hawaii*, or things of Hawai'i, in less time than would have been possible for his ancestors.

- (B) Umi Kai uses local materials, such as shark's teeth and native woods, to handcraft *na mea Hawaii*, or things of Hawai'i, the tools needed for daily life, as did his forebears.

- (C) Although Umi Kai painstakingly handcrafts traditional Hawaiian items, consumers frequently prefer purchasing less expensive imported souvenirs.

- (D) Despite the careful process of collecting natural materials and crafting *na mea Hawaii*, or things of Hawai'i, by hand, Umi Kai must seek out customers who value preserving traditional Hawaiian culture.

CONTINUED

K   715

Practice Tests

While researching a topic, a student has taken the following notes:

- The ancient Bedouin, a nomadic people of the Arabian desert, preserved their cultural history in oral poetry from at least the 3rd century B.C.E.

- Their dominant poetic form was the *Qasida*, epic odes with three parts—the prelude, the desert journey, and the goal of the ode—that were transmitted orally by storytellers who memorized *Qasida* hundreds of lines long and performed public recitations.

- Portions of *Qasida* were found inscribed on rock tablets, and experts identified consistent elements of style, such as repeated word patterns and specific themes.

- By the 6th century B.C.E., the *Qasida* form was adopted in Arabic courts, and the poet Imru' al-Qais, ruler of the Kindah tribal kingdom, became known as the "father of Arabic poetry" for his *Qasida*.

- Some of Imru' al-Qais's *Qasida* were preserved in writing and include themes common to those of the earliest Arabic poetry.

The student wants to emphasize a similarity between the *Qasida* composed in the 3rd century B.C.E. and the *Qasida* composed in the 6th century B.C.E. Which choice most effectively uses relevant information from the notes to accomplish this goal?

- (A) Traditional *Qasida* are poetic odes with three parts: the prelude, the desert journey, and the goal of the ode.

- (B) Although *Qasida* were known among the Bedouin of the 3rd century B.C.E., they were primarily an oral tradition and not recorded in writing until the 6th century B.C.E.

- (C) The *Qasida* of the poet Imru' al-Qais, called the "father of Arabic poetry," include traditional themes of Arabic poetry as used in the earliest *Qasida*.

- (D) The poet Imru' al-Qais was the ruler of the Kindah tribal kingdom but is famous as the "father of Arabic poetry" for his *Qasida*.

This page is intentionally blank.

ANSWER KEY

Reading and Writing: Routing Module

1.	**D**	8.	**A**	15.	**D**	22.	**D**
2.	**C**	9.	**D**	16.	**C**	23.	**C**
3.	**B**	10.	**C**	17.	**A**	24.	**A**
4.	**A**	11.	**C**	18.	**A**	25.	**B**
5.	**D**	12.	**D**	19.	**C**	26.	**B**
6.	**A**	13.	**B**	20.	**A**	27.	**C**
7.	**D**	14.	**B**	21.	**A**		

Instructions

Compare your answers to the answer key and enter the number of correct answers for this stage here. _____ This is your raw score.

If you scored less than 19 correct, turn to the Reading and Writing Module A and continue your test.

If you had 19 or more correct in this routing module, turn to the Reading and Writing Module B and continue your test.

Explanations will be at the end of the practice test.

READING AND WRITING: MODULE A

Mark your answers either on the pages that follow or on a separate sheet of paper. You will be scoring this Module before moving on to the Math section.

DIRECTIONS

The questions in this section address a number of important reading and writing skills. Each question includes one or more passages, which may include a table or graph. Read each passage and question carefully, and then choose the best answer to the question based on the passage(s).

All questions in this section are multiple-choice with four answer choices. Each question has a single best answer.

1

Damage from tropical storms is more often caused by flood water than by high winds. The storms push a wall of water, called a storm surge, ahead of them that washes over coastal land. Flooding can be _____ when the storm surge arrives at high tide, when water levels on the coasts are already at their highest for that day.

Which choice completes the text with the most logical and precise word or phrase?

Ⓐ aggravated

Ⓑ irritated

Ⓒ improved

Ⓓ assisted

2

Poems written in iambic pentameter consist of lines of 10 syllables, each following a strict unstressed-stressed syllable pattern. Despite the _____ of such a structure, poet Alice Oswald chose to employ iambic pentameter in her free-flowing lyrical expression "A Short Story of Falling," a poem that explores the process of rain and its impacts on nature.

Which choice completes the text with the most logical and precise word or phrase?

Ⓐ autonomy

Ⓑ liberty

Ⓒ authority

Ⓓ restrictions

CONTINUED

3

Jim Metzner is a sound engineer who has collected sounds of nature from all over the world and shared them with his audiences for over 40 years. He hesitates to describe his work as "capturing" sound because he perceives every recording as a gift, _____ the creatures on the planet.

Which choice completes the text with the most logical and precise word or phrase?

(A) taken by him from

(B) sought by him from

(C) ascribed to him by

(D) bestowed upon him by

4

Scientists have known for over 50 years that bacteria propel themselves by coiling and uncoiling filaments attached to the cell wall, called flagella, that push the bacteria along like tiny propellers. <u>But flagella are composed of identical protein segments, and strands of identical proteins should simply form a straight structure that can't create motion</u>. Edward Egelman and an international team have determined that the protein in the flagella has 11 different states and that the precise arrangement of these states is what causes the flagella to coil.

Which choice best states the function of the underlined portion in the text as a whole?

(A) It states the hypothesis Egelman and team investigated.

(B) It presents the paradox Egelman and team researched and resolved.

(C) It offers an alternative explanation for the findings of Egelman and team.

(D) It provides additional context to explain how bacteria move.

CONTINUED

5

The following text is from Louisa May Alcott's 1887 novel *Eight Cousins*.

Rose sat all alone in the big best parlor, with her little handkerchief laid ready to catch the first tear, for she was thinking of her troubles, and a shower was expected. She had retired to this room as a good place in which to be miserable; <u>for it was dark and still</u>, full of ancient furniture, somber curtains, and hung all round with portraits of solemn old gentlemen in wigs, severe-nosed ladies in top-heavy caps, and staring children in little bob-tailed coats or short-waisted frocks. It was an excellent place for woe; and the fitful spring rain that pattered on the window-pane seemed to sob, "Cry away: I'm with you."

Which choice best states the function of the underlined portion in the text as a whole?

(A) It establishes a contrast with the description of the setting mentioned earlier in the sentence.

(B) It provides an example that supports the description of the setting mentioned earlier in the sentence.

(C) It sets up the character description presented in the rest of the sentence.

(D) It introduces a character trait that contrasts with the description in the previous sentence.

6

Text 1

Cancers start with a mutation in a single cell, so larger animals with many more cells should have more cancers than smaller ones. Richard Peto noticed that this is not the case. Whales have 1,000 times more cells than humans do but have much lower rates of cancer. Marc Tollis determined that whales have at least 13 different tumor-suppressing genes, suggesting that, as whales evolved to become so large, they also evolved genes to combat cancer.

Text 2

Elephants have 100 times more cells than humans do but have cancer rates that are less than half of human cancer rates. Joshua Schiffman found that elephants have 40 copies of a gene that suppresses cancer, while humans have two copies of this gene.

Which choice best states the relationship between the two texts?

(A) Text 2 takes issue with the main point of Text 1.

(B) Text 2 provides a supporting point to the main idea of Text 1.

(C) Text 2 implies a future modification to the main point of Text 1.

(D) Text 2 illustrates a practical difficulty with the main point of Text 1.

CONTINUED

7

Text 1

Kudzu, an invasive vine, can grow a foot a day, and masses of these plants cover structures, forests, and landscapes in the southern United States. Kudzu grows so thickly that it completely cuts off sunlight to the plants beneath it, killing them and destroying native ecosystems. Fortunately, a new weapon has emerged in the battle against kudzu: goats. Goats not only quickly consume vast amounts of the plants, but their digestive systems also destroy the seeds, so the plants are not transplanted through the goat's manure.

Text 2

Using goats to control invasive plants is an important innovation in curbing many problematic species, but it is not a panacea. After the goats eat the tender foliage, the roots and woody portions of invasive plants must still be removed. In addition, the land needs to be monitored for erosion because the goats' hooves may disrupt structures that stabilize the soil.

Which choice best state the relationship between the two texts?

(A) Text 2 provides a supporting example for the main point of Text 1.

(B) Text 2 illustrates practical difficulties with the main idea of Text 1.

(C) Text 2 takes a dismissive stance regarding the main point of Text 1.

(D) Text 2 uses concrete examples to illustrate the concepts presented in Text 1.

8

The eminence of the U.S. public university network stretches beyond the United States. Students travel from across the globe to study at top programs. Cutting-edge schools like the University of Virginia (UVA) and the University of California at Los Angeles (UCLA) receive continual international attention for their accomplishments in scholarship and research. Programs, faculty, and students from these schools participate in the global conversation in significant ways, working toward a better future for the planet.

Which choice best states the main idea of the text?

(A) Universities such as UVA and UCLA produce world-class scholars.

(B) Faculty from foreign universities participate in global conversations.

(C) U.S. public universities are respected throughout the world.

(D) Most international students consider UCLA their top school choice.

CONTINUED

9

A new theory may shed light on several phenomena of the planet Saturn that astronomers could not previously explain. Scientists now theorize that an additional moon called Chrysalis orbited Saturn until approximately 160 million years ago, when its orbit destabilized and the moon scraped the planet. The remnants of the crashed moon could be the source of Saturn's rings, icy debris that orbits the planet. The rings are thought to have formed about 100 million years ago, long after the formation of Saturn itself but after Chrysalis's theoretical destruction. Further, Chrysalis's gravitational pull on Saturn before the collision and the lack of that pull after the collision—in conjunction with the gravitational influence of Saturn's large planetary neighbor, Neptune—may help explain Saturn's pronounced tilt on its axis.

Which choice best states the main idea of the text?

(A) A new astronomical theory exists that concerns the existence of a former moon of Saturn named Chrysalis that crashed into the planet.

(B) The exact date of Saturn's formation is undetermined, but astronomers estimate that the debris in its rings collected 100 million years ago.

(C) Scientists have a possible understanding of Saturn's rings and its tilt based on a new theory about one of its moons.

(D) Saturn's former moon Chrysalis is believed to have had an influence on Saturn's particular tilt on its axis.

10

One theory about the cause of honeybee colony collapse disorder points to the use of pesticides. Pesticides, which are chemicals used to prevent pest infestation of crops on a large scale around the world, are often picked up by honeybees during their foraging and pollination flights. Scientists have found that more than one pesticide can be found in the honey of one hive. While the presence of one pesticide in a hive would certainly limit the life spans of bees and impair their navigational skills, some researchers theorize that the interaction of two or more pesticides could cause an entire colony to collapse. There are many ingredients in pesticides that are not regulated by world governments, and this leaves a lot of ground for bee scientists to cover when doing their research.

According to the passage, how do some researchers theorize pesticides impact colony collapse disorder?

(A) A single pesticide in a hive could damage bees' navigation skills and lead to colony collapse disorder.

(B) Unregulated pesticides destroy bees' honey and cause colonies to collapse.

(C) The impact of the ingredients in multiple pesticides in a hive could cause colony collapse disorder.

(D) Two specific types of pesticides adhere to bees as they pollinate plants.

Practice Tests

CONTINUED

11

The following text is from Kahlil Gibran's 1923 collection of poetry fables *The Prophet*.

Work is love made visible.

And if you cannot work with love but only with distaste, it is better that you should leave your work and sit at the gate of the temple and take alms of those who work with joy.

For if you bake bread with indifference, you bake a bitter bread that feeds but half man's hunger.

And if you grudge the crushing of the grapes, your grudge distills a poison in the wine. And if you sing though as angels, and love not the singing, you muffle man's ears to the voices of the day and the voices of the night.

The speaker indicates that which of the following is the result if the reader works with a lack of concern when baking bread?

- (A) The product of the labor will be unsatisfying.

- (B) The loaves will be indifferent about who consumes them.

- (C) Only half of those who eat the bread will become full.

- (D) Those who eat the bread will be inspired to sing with love.

CONTINUED

12

Professional line standers are paid to wait in a queue in someone else's place. Some situations that draw line standers are relatively frivolous, such as camping out days in advance for the release of the latest cell phone or video game system. Line-standing also occurs in the U.S. capitol, where political lobbyists have engaged in paying others to queue for them to gain entry to political processes such as Supreme Court hearings; one notorious example saw people waiting for four days outside the hearings on the Affordable Care Act in 2012. Based on a recent series of interviews with several politicians in Washington, D.C., a journalist claims that lobbyist line-standing draws criticism due to concerns that it undermines the fairness of political processes.

Which quotation from the interviews best illustrates the journalist's claim?

Ⓐ "Line-standing strikes some as inherently unfair, but it is just a paid service like anything else. Most of us pay for services to help free up our own time, such as paying a cook to prepare a meal for us. Lobbyist line-standing is essentially based on the same principle."

Ⓑ "Lobbyists should be made to wait in line themselves like everyone else. Otherwise, lobbying in support for political issues will become increasingly elitist, as those with more money can essentially pay their way into hearings while they continue lobbying for their cause elsewhere."

Ⓒ "Line-standing really isn't a matter of concern to serious politicians. If the payoffs merely entail securing early ownership of cutting-edge electronics, the larger societal impact of such a practice is likely insignificant."

Ⓓ "Whether or not lobbyist line-standing is fair is ultimately less important than the fact that the practice creates more paid work in our city. As either someone's primary occupation or as a side job, the more service positions that are available, the better off everyone will be financially."

Practice Tests

The concept of embodied cognition states that our physical interactions with an object are an essential component of how our brains understand the meaning of the word for that object. For example, our brains do not fully comprehend the meaning of the word "pencil" apart from our familiarity with the physical actions of holding and writing with a pencil. Thus, a team at Osaka Metropolitan University hypothesized that the brain's processing of the words for physical objects would be impacted if subjects' body movements were limited. To evaluate this hypothesis, the researchers showed subjects pairs of words on a computer screen. When words for physical objects, such as "cup" and "broom" were displayed, researchers asked the subjects to compare the objects' relative sizes. Some subjects' hands were restrained, while others could move their hands freely.

Which finding from the experiment, if true, would most strongly support the research team's hypothesis?

(A) Subjects whose hands were restrained showed low levels of brain activity in brain scans when shown the words "because" and "although."

(B) Subjects whose hands were restrained showed high levels of brain activity in brain scans when shown the words "because" and "although."

(C) When shown the words "fork" and "chair," subjects whose hands were restrained showed significantly less brain activity in brain scans than did subjects whose hands were not restrained.

(D) When shown the words "fork" and "chair," subjects whose hands were restrained showed the same level of brain activity in brain scans as did subjects whose hands were not restrained.

CONTINUED

14

	Venus	Earth	The Moon	Mars
Gravity (kg/m^3)	8.9	9.8	1.6	3.7
Average Temperature (F°)	867	59	−4	−85
Surface Pressure (bars)	92	1	0	0.01

Some scientists have argued that humanity must become a multi-planet species to minimize our risk of extinction. However, establishing off-world colonies poses severe technological and, indeed, biological challenges. Orthopedist Gaurav Sahota of Grand Lakes University conducted a study of astronauts who had spent several months in zero-gravity conditions, noting a decline in their bone density. Sahota theorized that children born in off-world colonies may suffer from musculoskeletal developmental issues due to being born and raised in conditions with gravity lower than that found on Earth. Sahota argues that this issue would eliminate most of our closest celestial neighbors as viable candidates for settlement. For example, although Mars is often the subject of interest when it comes to colonization, the _____

Which choice most effectively uses data from the table to complete the example?

(A) gravity on Venus is comparatively higher at 8.9 kg/m^3.

(B) gravity on Mars is a mere 3.7 kg/m^3.

(C) gravity on the Moon is slightly higher at 4 kg/m^3.

(D) gravity on Mars is a negligible 0.01 kg/m^3.

15

Researchers are racing to find ways for people to maintain brain health while aging. A recent study examined the effects of non-action video-game training on small sample sizes of aging adults experiencing cognitive decline. Test subjects who completed as few as twenty training sessions with these video games showed an increase in attention span, alertness, and visual memory. They also showed a decrease in distraction. Since these results suggest that there may be ways to stave off mental decline and thus help the elderly maintain functions needed for safe driving and other activities of daily living, the researchers therefore imply that _____

Which choice most logically completes the text?

(A) elderly people who are able to reduce or reverse cognitive decline may be able to live longer independently.

(B) regular playing of video games could completely cure age-related cognitive problems.

(C) playing board games for extended periods of time could have the same effect on cognition as playing video games.

(D) too much time spent playing video games would likely have a negative effect on cognition in aging populations.

16

Françoise Gilot often appeared as the subject of the renowned Pablo Picasso's paintings. However, Annie Maïllis, Gilot's biographer, claims that Gilot created her own abstract _____ it was important to her to have a voice in the projection of her own self-image.

Which choice completes the text so that it conforms to the conventions of Standard English?

(A) self-portraits because

(B) self-portraits; because

(C) self-portraits. Because

(D) self-portraits, and because

17

Among the earliest internet hoaxes was the case of John Titor, a self-proclaimed time traveler. Over the course of 2000 and 2001, Titor posted on a variety of message boards, sharing information about the future during a 'layover' on his mission to retrieve a particular model of computer from the 1970s. Titor revealed an obscure secret feature of that computer model, one its manufacturer had successfully hidden for decades, _____

Which choice completes the text so that it conforms to the conventions of Standard English?

(A) which served as proof of his apparent claims.

(B) which served as apparent proof of his claims.

(C) which served as apparent proof of his claims?

(D) which served as proof of his apparent claims?

CONTINUED

Practice Tests

18

Iranian mathematician Maryam Mirzakhani, born in 1977, was renowned for her contributions to the field of theoretical mathematics, such as in Ergodic theory, hyperbolic geometry, moduli spaces, and symplectic _____ won the prestigious Fields Medal, the first woman to do so.

Which choice completes the text so that it conforms to the conventions of Standard English?

(A) geometry she

(B) geometry, she

(C) geometry. She

(D) geometry and she

19

The cherimoya is a fruit native to South America with a custard-like texture, a taste often compared to ice cream, and, says nutritionist Johan Liebert of Heinrich Heine University Düsseldorf, a host of important vitamins and minerals; for example, adults eating just a single cherimoya will find it contains 60% of _____ daily recommended amount of Vitamin C.

Which choice completes the text so that it conforms to the conventions of Standard English?

(A) it's

(B) its

(C) your

(D) their

20

Ibn Khaldun, writing in his book *The Muqaddimah*, describes *asabiyyah*, a feeling of social cohesion binding people together in a civilization, as possessing a life cycle that, like the life cycle of birds and beasts, _____ an end.

Which choice completes the text so that it conforms to the conventions of Standard English?

(A) having

(B) have

(C) has

(D) had

21

In recent decades, popular novels and their film adaptations have driven the novel market in a new direction. Novels are considered just another entertainment medium, one that ought to enthrall passive readers and relieve them of their daily stresses. The difficulties, challenges, and triumphs of real life are becoming less common as the subjects of popular _____ instead, escapist tales of fantastical lands and escapades prevail.

Which choice completes the text so that it conforms to the conventions of Standard English?

(A) novels;

(B) novels

(C) novels,

(D) novels and

22

Although little-remembered today, the Jubalaires, a Christian gospel group active in the 1940s and 1950s, were among several formative influences on the creation of hip-hop and rap music. This four-man group, by incorporating rhythmic rhyming verses into their _____ together to create a new type of music that would eventually become rap.

Which choice completes the text so that it conforms to the conventions of Standard English?

(A) music harmonized

(B) music harmonized,

(C) music, harmonized,

(D) music, harmonized

23

In the first days of space exploration, one concern was the possibility that astronauts or spacecraft might be hit by meteoroids. Scientists calculated that this possibility was extremely small because meteoroids are rare. Astronauts and spacecraft, _____ would almost certainly collide with micrometeorites, which are about the size of grains of dust and much more common.

Which choice completes the text with the most logical transition?

(A) therefore,

(B) on the other hand,

(C) moreover,

(D) in fact,

CONTINUED

24

Researchers in the RIPE (Realizing Increased Photosynthetic Efficiency) project have developed a bioengineering technique that allows plants to conduct photosynthesis more efficiently. The technique, which reduces the time plants spend in a non-productive state while switching between the photosynthetic processes they use when exposed to sun versus shade, has increased yields in both tobacco and soybean plants in field studies. _____ these results, the researchers hope that further applications of their research will help mitigate world hunger in the future.

Which choice completes the text with the most logical transition?

- (A) Despite
- (B) In addition to
- (C) Exemplifying
- (D) In light of

25

Commissioned by emperors of the early Ming Dynasty, Admiral Zheng He led naval expeditions from China to locations as far away as the Arabian Peninsula and the East African coast in the early 1400s. Eventually, after increased threats from the Yuan Mongols, the Ming government diverted funds to terrestrial defensive measures instead, including an expansion of the Great Wall of China. _____ major state-sponsored sea voyages did not continue after the 1430s.

Which choice completes the text with the most logical transition?

- (A) Therefore,
- (B) Nevertheless,
- (C) Similarly,
- (D) Initially,

CONTINUED

26

While researching a topic, a student has taken the following notes:

- Romero Britto is a Brazilian-born painter and printmaker who lives in Miami, Florida.

- His art style encompasses principles of pop art and cubism, including the use of strong geometric lines.

- His art incorporates bright colors and cheerful subject matter; it reflects the "Happy Art Movement," which he founded to promote art with an optimistic message.

- His work *Mona Cat* (2010), a stylized reworking of da Vinci's classic *Mona Lisa*, features a smirking, cartoonish blue cat wearing a Renaissance gown of many colors.

- His 2009 poster for the 2010 soccer World Cup in South Africa features a soccer ball, covered in rainbow-colored country outlines, hurtling as a comet through a sky of colorful stars with a background of blue streamers.

The student wants to emphasize a difference between Britto's two works. Which choice most effectively uses relevant information from the notes to accomplish this goal?

- (A) Both *Mona Cat* and Britto's World Cup poster make use of bright colors: *Mona Cat* shows a blue cat in a colorful gown, and the World Cup poster displays a background of multicolored stars and blue streamers.

- (B) Britto considers his work, which reflects both pop art and cubism, as part of the optimistic "Happy Art Movement."

- (C) Although Britto was born in Brazil, he currently paints his optimistic art in Miami, Florida.

- (D) Britto's art reflects positivity through diverse subject matter; while *Mona Cat* portrays a cartoon cat dressed in a gown, his World Cup poster depicts a soccer ball as a comet.

CONTINUED

27

While researching a topic, a student has taken the following notes:

- Archaeologists have discovered ancient Egyptian personal letters, which are written on papyrus.

- Letters in ancient Egypt were typically written by elites, such as government officials and landowners, as the common populace was illiterate.

- Several discovered letters contain the written instructions of elites who were traveling and attempting to manage their households while away.

- Two letters written by General Nehesu address an issue about sacks of grain that he had sent to his household but had gone missing, possibly due to in-fighting within the household.

- In several letters, the priest Heqanakht responds to his household's complaints about their low food rations during a season of inadequate river flooding and admonishes his son Merisu to carefully manage his property.

The student wants to emphasize a similarity between the two groups of letters. Which choice most effectively uses relevant information from the notes to accomplish this goal?

- (A) The Nehesu letters were written by a general, while the Heqanakht letters were written by a priest.

- (B) Ancient Egyptian personal letters, which were written on papyrus, were composed by the few in society who were literate, such as government officials and landowners.

- (C) The content of both the Nehesu letters and the Heqanakht letters address household concerns: the Nehesu letters discusses missing grain, and the Heqanakht letters discuss low food rations.

- (D) The Nehesu letters address concerns such as missing grain sacks and household in-fighting; the Heqanakht letters, however, address concerns such as low food rations and property management.

Practice Tests

IF YOU FINISH BEFORE TIME IS CALLED, YOU MAY CHECK YOUR WORK ON THIS MODULE ONLY. ON TEST DAY, YOU WON'T BE ABLE TO MOVE ON TO THE NEXT MODULE UNTIL TIME EXPIRES.   **STOP**

K   733

ANSWER KEY

Reading and Writing: Module A

1. **A**	8. **C**	15. **A**	22. **D**
2. **D**	9. **C**	16. **A**	23. **B**
3. **D**	10. **C**	17. **B**	24. **D**
4. **B**	11. **A**	18. **C**	25. **A**
5. **B**	12. **B**	19. **D**	26. **D**
6. **B**	13. **C**	20. **C**	27. **C**
7. **B**	14. **B**	21. **A**	

Instructions

Compare your answers to the answer key and enter the number of correct answers for this stage here. _____ This is your raw score.

Take a 10-minute break and turn to the Math Routing Module to continue your test.

Explanations will be at the end of the practice test.

READING AND WRITING: MODULE B

Mark your answers either on the pages that follow or on a separate sheet of paper. You will be scoring this Module before moving on to the Math section.

DIRECTIONS

The questions in this section address a number of important reading and writing skills. Each question includes one or more passages, which may include a table or graph. Read each passage and question carefully, and then choose the best answer to the question based on the passage(s).

All questions in this section are multiple-choice with four answer choices. Each question has a single best answer.

1

The following text is from Lucy Maud Montgomery's 1908 novel *Anne of Green Gables*.

"The trouble with you, Anne, is that you're thinking too much about yourself. You should just think of Mrs. Allan and what would be nicest and most agreeable to her," said Marilla, hitting for once in her life on a very sound and pithy piece of advice. Anne instantly realized this.

"You are right, Marilla. I'll try not to think about myself at all."

As used in the text, what does the word "sound" most nearly mean?

- (A) Reasonable
- (B) Clamorous
- (C) Severe
- (D) Secure

Practice Tests

CONTINUED ➡

K 735

2

Marine biologists suspected that rising temperatures were significantly impacting coral reefs off the coast of Australia, but a dearth of _____ data that compares Australia's reefs with that of other reefs throughout the world meant they could not confirm their hypothesis. In response, Rick Stuart-Smith and Graham Edgar of the Reef Life Survey not only collected detailed data about Australia's reefs but also incorporated data from two other major reef studies, which together have helped demonstrate the impacts of rising temperatures on Australian coral reefs, such as decreases in localized reef fish species diversity.

Which choice completes the text with the most logical and precise word or phrase?

Ⓐ accurate

Ⓑ comprehensive

Ⓒ permanent

Ⓓ quantifiable

3

Despite its original reception, the influence of Charles Baudelaire's 1857 poetry volume *Les Fleurs du mal* (*The Flowers of Evil*) over time is _____. Six poems from the volume, which explored themes of decadence and death, were banned by the French government at its initial publication, and Baudelaire was prosecuted and fined. Still, *Les Fleurs du mal* lived on to inspire many top-tier French poets, especially those of the symbolist movement, as well as numerous orchestral and popular music compositions throughout the world, and even an acclaimed 2009 manga series titled *Aku no Hana* (*Flowers of Evil* in Japanese).

Which choice completes the text with the most logical and precise word or phrase?

Ⓐ substantial

Ⓑ paltry

Ⓒ controversial

Ⓓ superior

Practice Tests

CONTINUED

4

The following text is adapted from Sir Arthur Conan Doyle's 1887 short story "A Study in Scarlet."

Yet his zeal for certain studies was remarkable, and within eccentric limits his knowledge was so extraordinarily ample and minute that his observations have fairly astounded me. . . . <u>His ignorance was as remarkable as his knowledge.</u> Of contemporary literature, philosophy and politics he appeared to know next to nothing. . . . My surprise reached a climax, however, when I found incidentally that he was ignorant of the Copernican Theory and of the composition of the solar system.

Which choice best states the function of the underlined sentence in the text as a whole?

- (A) It elaborates on the character trait mentioned in the previous sentence.

- (B) It provides a specific example of the behavior of a character described in the previous sentence.

- (C) It introduces a new setting for the events described in the sentences that follow.

- (D) It establishes a contrast with the character description in the previous sentence.

5

The following text is adapted from Philip Gibbs' 1920 nonfiction book *Now It Can Be Told*.

[British World War I veterans] were told bluntly that they had "wasted" three or four years in the army and could not be of the same value as boys just out of school. The officer class was hardest hit in that way. They had gone straight from the public schools and universities to the army. They had been lieutenants, captains, and majors in the air force, or infantry battalions, or tanks, or trench-mortars. . . . What knowledge had they of use in civil life? None. They scanned advertisements, answered likely invitations, were turned down by elderly men who said: "I've had two hundred applications. And none of you young gentlemen from the army are fit to be my office-boy." They were the same elderly men who had said: "We'll fight to the last ditch. If I had six sons I would sacrifice them all in the cause of liberty and justice."

Which choice best states the main purpose of the text?

- (A) It presents the situation faced by World War I veterans trying to find jobs as a way to critique their decision to fight in the war as younger men.

- (B) It shows that employers were uninterested in hiring World War I veterans because they mistrusted them for their actions during the war.

- (C) It discusses the difficulty that veterans faced trying to find jobs after World War I as their wartime experience offered little attractiveness to employers.

- (D) It illustrates the hypocrisy of an elderly British man who lost six sons in World War I only to insult soldiers who survived the war.

CONTINUED

Text 1

Historians consider primary sources—original documents, records, and accounts created at the time of interest—to be the best materials to use when researching past events. Secondary sources are created after some time passes and include analyses, interpretations, and retellings.

Text 2

In 1981, anthropologist David Pocock advertised for voluntary correspondents from any occupation who were willing to provide their views on a topic that would be sent to them quarterly. Other than asking his respondents to observe carefully and include as much detail as they wished, Pocock provided no direction, only a general topic. Since then Pocock and his colleagues have archived thousands of responses that include maps, diagrams, and letters of varying lengths.

Based on the texts, how would Pocock and colleagues (Text 2) most likely respond to the view of the historians presented in Text 1?

(A) They would argue that significant primary sources are difficult to identify before a historic event occurs.

(B) They would claim to be collecting a substantial archive of primary source documents.

(C) They would criticize the prioritization of primary sources over secondary sources.

(D) They would describe their archive as a collection of secondary sources.

CONTINUED ➡

7

Text 1

Historian J.R. McNeill claims that mosquitoes were historical actors in the Caribbean region in the period 1620 to 1914 since their spreading of the diseases of yellow fever and malaria impacted geopolitical developments in the region. Since various populations had differing levels of immunity or resistance to the diseases, McNeill argues, groups with relatively high protection were more likely to prevail militarily against groups with relatively low protection.

Text 2

When searching for historical causes, scholars must be cautious to avoid strict environmental determinism, which frames the ecological environment as the primary causal factor in historical developments. While aspects of the physical environment, such as climate, soil quality, and the types of wildlife present, undoubtedly influence societies and events, historians must be careful to prioritize human actors as the most critical catalysts of history.

Based on the texts, how would the author of Text 2 most likely describe McNeill's argument (Text 1)?

- (A) The author would dismiss McNeill's claims about the impact of disease-carrying mosquitoes in the historical Caribbean since environmental determinism rejects humans as historical actors.

- (B) The author would tentatively accept McNeill's claims about the impact of disease-carrying mosquitoes in the historical Caribbean but would recommend he conduct similar studies in other historical eras to confirm his findings.

- (C) The author would acknowledge that disease-carrying mosquitoes were a factor in historical events in the Caribbean but would encourage McNeill to give a high causal role to human factors.

- (D) The author would accept that military engagements were a factor in historical events in the Caribbean but would encourage McNeill to also consider environmental factors, such as climate, as well.

8

"Hope is the Thing with Feathers" is a late 1800s poem written by Emily Dickinson.

"Hope" is the thing with feathers—
That perches in the soul—
And sings the tune without the words—
And never stops—at all—

And sweetest—in the Gale—
is heard And sore must be the storm—
That could abash the little Bird
That kept so many warm—

I've heard it in the chillest land—
And on the strangest Sea—
Yet, never, in Extremity,
It asked a crumb—of Me.

What is the main idea of the text?

Ⓐ   The speaker was injured in a storm at sea.

Ⓑ   The speaker is distressed by the storms of life.

Ⓒ   The speaker experiences hope in every circumstance.

Ⓓ   The speaker hopes to hear the sounds of bird songs.

Practice Tests

CONTINUED

9

Scientists have known that women's brains undergo structural changes as a result of pregnancy. They have also found a positive correlation between the decrease in brain volume during pregnancy and feelings of attachment to the new infant. These observations support the hypothesis that the brain changes are an evolutionary adaptation to improve parenting behaviors. In what may be another interesting example of similar evolutionary goals being met by different physiological mechanisms, research by Magdalena Martínez-García indicates similar, but smaller, changes in the brains of new fathers that are also positively correlated with affectionate feelings towards infants.

What is the main idea of the text?

Ⓐ Women lose brain volume during pregnancy, and this loss improves their feelings of attachment to their baby, but men do not, since they do not experience the physical and hormonal effects of pregnancy.

Ⓑ Men lose less brain volume than women do after the birth of their children, yet experience similar feelings of attachment to their children, likely due to similar physiological changes after the birth of their child.

Ⓒ Men and women have similar changes in brain volume after the birth of their children that seem to bestow parenting benefits, but these develop through different physiological processes.

Ⓓ Research by Magdalena Martínez-García has challenged the hypothesis that the brain volume changes seen in men and women after the birth of their children offer improved parenting behaviors.

CONTINUED

10

The following text is from Louisa May Alcott's 1887 novel *Eight Cousins*.

Rose scrambled into the china-closet as rapidly as possible, and there refreshed herself by making faces at Debby, while she settled her plumage and screwed up her courage. Then she crept softly down the hall and peeped into the parlor. No one appeared, and all was so still she felt sure the company was upstairs. So she skipped boldly through the half-open folding-doors, to behold on the other side a sight that nearly took her breath away.

Seven boys stood in a row,—all ages, all sizes, all yellow-haired and blue-eyed, all in full Scotch costume, and all smiling, nodding, and saying as with one voice, "How are you, cousin?"

Rose gave a little gasp and looked wildly about her as if ready to fly, for fear magnified the seven and the room seemed full of boys.

The passage indicates that Rose had which of the following reactions after she enters the parlor?

- (A) She is friendly and greets her cousin by asking how he's doing.

- (B) She is startled and perceives the room as crowded.

- (C) She is nervous but motivates herself to be brave.

- (D) She attempts to be humorous by making some silly faces.

11

The following text is from Mark Twain's and Charles Dudley Warner's 1874 satirical novel, *The Gilded Age*.

"Squire" Hawkins got his title from being postmaster of Obedstown—not that the title properly belonged to the office, but because in those regions the chief citizens always must have titles of some sort, and so the usual courtesy had been extended to Hawkins. The mail was monthly, and sometimes amounted to as much as three or four letters at a single delivery. Even a rush like this did not fill up the postmaster's whole month, though, and therefore he "kept store" in the intervals.

Based on the text, what is true about the postmaster of Obedstown?

- (A) He received the title "Squire" because it was traditionally part of the job of postmaster.

- (B) He has another job because there isn't enough mail to stay busy.

- (C) His only responsibility is to manage the post office.

- (D) He is the chief citizen in charge of Obedstown.

CONTINUED ➡

12

Psychologist Stephen Worchel hypothesized if a commodity is perceived to be scarce, that commodity will be considered more valuable than a commodity that is perceived to be abundant. To evaluate this hypothesis, Worchel and a team of researchers designed a study in which participants in two different groups were asked to rate the value of cookies. One group was presented with only a few cookies in each trial; the other group was presented with a large number of cookies in each trial.

Which finding from the study, if true, would most strongly support Worchel's hypothesis?

(A) In surveys, participants who were presented with a few cookies reported that they perceived the cookies to be in abundant supply.

(B) In surveys, participants who were presented with many cookies reported that they perceived the cookies to be in abundant supply.

(C) Participants who were presented with many cookies consistently rated the cookies as more valuable than did participants who were presented with a few cookies.

(D) Participants who were presented with a few cookies consistently rated the cookies as more valuable than did participants who were presented with many cookies.

CONTINUED

Practice Tests

13

The Prophet is a collection of poetry fables written by Kahlil Gibran and first published in 1923. The poems describe the arrival and teachings of a fictional prophet named Almustafa. In the poems, the speaker, Almustafa, admonishes his listeners that material goods are relatively unimportant: _____

Which quotation from *The Prophet* most effectively illustrates the claim?

(A) "And as he walked he saw from afar men and women leaving their fields and their vineyards and hastening towards the city gates. / And he heard their voices calling his name . . . "

(B) "And with a great voice he said: / When love beckons to you, follow him, / Though his ways are hard and steep."

(C) "Your children are not your children. . . . / You may give them your love but not your thoughts, / For they have their own thoughts. / You may house their bodies but not their souls . . . "

(D) "You give but little when you give of your possessions. / It is when you give of yourself that you truly give. / For what are your possessions but things you keep and guard for fear you may need them tomorrow?"

CONTINUED ➡

14

	Electric Resistivity (ρ)	Thermal Conductivity (σ)	Average Price per Ounce in 2018
Silver	1.59×10^{-8}	6.30×10^7	$15.71
Copper	1.68×10^{-8}	5.96×10^7	$2.93
Gold	2.44×10^{-8}	4.11×10^7	$1,268.93

Electricity generally flows better through metals than through other materials. However, not all metals have the same properties, with their resistivity and conductivity varying. Resistivity is a measure of how strongly a material resists electrical current; maximizing electrical flow requires low resistivity. By contrast, a higher conductivity is better, as such a material will better conduct electrical current. Silver, gold, and copper are metals commonly used to conduct electricity. Silver and gold are restricted to high-end electronic components due to their rarity creating a high price. Copper is used in such components, too, but it also sees widespread use in power lines and home wiring. Researchers at NASA have hypothesized that asteroid mining would massively increase the global supply of precious metals, like silver and gold, allowing for a more energy-efficient infrastructure to be created.

Which choice best describes the data from the table that supports the researchers' hypothesis?

Ⓐ The resistivity of gold is lower than that of copper, but the use of gold is restricted due to its price per ounce.

Ⓑ Gold and silver have higher conductivity than that of copper, but copper is more widely used due to its comparative affordability.

Ⓒ The resistivity of silver is higher than that of gold, which is a better material for electricity, but its use is constrained by its high price per ounce.

Ⓓ The conductivity of silver is higher than that of copper and gold, but copper has a far lower price per ounce than silver.

CONTINUED

15

When colony collapse disorder—the mysterious disappearance of entire colonies of honeybees—was first recognized, beekeepers and scientists assumed that a pathogen was to blame. Indeed, there are several known viruses and pests that can kill off entire hives of honeybees quickly and are extremely hard to prevent. Mites, fungus, and bacterial infections are all common killers. Because of how often they're seen in hives, farmers assumed that these common plights were responsible for colony collapse disorder. However, as time passed and the disorder was studied, researchers noticed something odd. In many cases, there were simply no dead bees to discover, only empty hives. These findings therefore imply that _____

Which choice most logically completes the text?

- (A) understanding the role of pathogens in colony collapse disorder is vital to reducing its occurrence.

- (B) more types of viruses are responsible for the death of honeybees than are currently known by scientists.

- (C) a cause other than known pathogens must be the primary reason for colony collapse disorder.

- (D) farmers' initial assumptions about the cause of colony collapse disorder are confirmed.

16

NASCAR has its roots in the Prohibition Era, when drivers would illegally transport alcohol. These bootleggers would sometimes find themselves pursued by the police. To escape the police, especially on narrow backcountry roads at night, these bootleggers would customize their cars to emphasize two _____ handling and speed. Many of these bootleggers became popular stock car racers in the 1930s and 1940s.

Which choice completes the text so that it conforms to the conventions of Standard English?

- (A) factors

- (B) factors:

- (C) factors;

- (D) factors (

CONTINUED ➡

Practice Tests

17

Between 1934 and 1968, most films released in the United States were subject to censorship by the Hays Code. The code severely restricted what could and could not be shown in films. There were, however, ways to circumvent it. Director Alfred Hitchcock depicted a couple kissing for nearly two and a half minutes despite there being a strict three-second rule for onscreen kisses. He did this by having the actors break off the kiss every three seconds, meaning _____ kissing technically did not violate the Hays Code's time limit.

Which choice completes the text so that it conforms to the conventions of Standard English?

- (A) their
- (B) they're
- (C) there
- (D) its

18

Yoga pants have become an increasingly commonplace fashion in recent years, yet yoga pants are often worn by people who have never practiced yoga themselves. What explains this trend? It is simply the continuing, longtime influence of sports on fashion. Clothing that we now consider _____ only by athletes. Like yoga pants, those items also became popular among the general public.

Which choice completes the text so that it conforms to the conventions of Standard English?

- (A) ordinary—sweatshirts, polo shirts, and tennis shoes, were once worn
- (B) ordinary—sweatshirts, polo shirts, and tennis shoes—were once worn
- (C) ordinary (sweatshirts, polo shirts, and tennis shoes—were once worn
- (D) ordinary: sweatshirts, polo shirts, and tennis shoes, were once worn

Practice Tests

19

Published in the 14th century, *Romance of the Three Kingdoms* is one of the "Four Great Classical Novels" of Chinese literature alongside *Water Margin*, *Journey to the West*, and *Dream of the Red Chamber*. Following a sprawling cast battling over which faction will reunite China during the Three Kingdoms period (220 to 280 C.E.), _____ cultural influence can be seen throughout East Asia.

Which choice completes the text so that it conforms to the conventions of Standard English?

- (A) their
- (B) whose
- (C) it's
- (D) its

20

Xenophon of Athens, among the most famous Greek military leaders, _____ best remembered today for the March of the Ten Thousand, which saw him assume command of a leaderless army, one trapped in hostile territory with enemies on all sides, then lead it to safety.

Which choice completes the text so that it conforms to the conventions of Standard English?

- (A) have been
- (B) was
- (C) were
- (D) is

21

Two English political thinkers, Thomas Hobbes and John Locke, lived through the horrors of the English Civil War. Despite this shared experience, each man came to strikingly different conclusions about human nature. Locke believed that people possess inherent natural rights: to life, liberty, and _____ by contrast, argued that natural rights did not exist. Only through a strong ruler and the willing submission of the people to the laws of that ruler could rights exist.

Which choice completes the text so that it conforms to the conventions of Standard English?

- (A) property, Hobbes,
- (B) property. Hobbes,
- (C) property; Hobbes—
- (D) property. Hobbes

CONTINUED ➡

Practice Tests

22

Though prominently displayed on the Great Seal of the United States, the bald eagle was once considered a threat to small livestock (despite the fact that its diet consists primarily of _____ and was widely hunted in the 19th century. The 1940 Bald Eagle Protection Act sought to preserve the birds' dwindling numbers by not only outlawing the hunting of bald eagles but also prohibiting interference with their nests.

Which choice completes the text so that it conforms to the conventions of Standard English?

(A) fish),

(B) fish)—

(C) fish)

(D) fish);

23

A spontaneous semi-dominant gene mutation in the leopard gecko produces "lemon frost" geckos, which are prized for their unique coloration patterns of white and bright yellow. This gene mutation of the iridophores also causes extensive skin tumors, or iriophoroma, in the majority of the lemon frost geckos. A team of geneticists, led by Longhua Guo at the University of California, Los Angeles, has isolated the location of the specific gene: SPINT1, a tumor suppressor gene that is also related to human skin cutaneous melanoma (SKCM). _____ some scientists have asserted that the potential of this new animal model in the study of melanoma may unlock answers in the quest for a cure, others have cited the need for additional research on the metastatic progression of the lemon frost geckos' iriophoroma before supplanting their current animal models.

Which choice completes the text with the most logical transition?

(A) While

(B) Additionally

(C) Since

(D) Furthermore

CONTINUED ➤

24

The first photographed image of a black hole was captured by using eight separate radio telescopes that were located throughout the world, two of which reside in Mauna Kea on the Big Island of Hawaii. The black hole was _____ given the sobriquet "Pōwehi" by Hawaiian Language and Culture Professor Larry Kimura. Considered to be a fitting reflection of the current understanding of black holes, the name means "embellished dark source of unending creation."

Which choice completes the text with the most logical transition?

- (A) finally
- (B) nonetheless
- (C) subsequently
- (D) however

25

After years of social and academic struggles experienced in formal school settings during his adolescence, Ansel Adams found solace in mastering the piano and hiking through the wilderness. _____ those passions are evident in his award-winning photography, which wielded the rich tonality of black and white to illuminate the nuanced aesthetic he had found in nature.

Which choice completes the text with the most logical transition?

- (A) Conversely,
- (B) Eventually,
- (C) Specifically,
- (D) Consequently,

CONTINUED →

26

While researching a topic, a student has taken the following notes:

- In 2022, about 500 million messages—or tweets—were sent per day on the Twitter messaging platform.

- Data on the number of Twitter messages can be easily known from Twitter's records.

- Sociologists Michael Macy and Scott Golder were interested in investigating the content of Twitter messages, particularly their depiction of emotions over the course of the day.

- The sociologists used computer analysis to detect the presence of words associated with positive and negative emotions in tweets.

- On average, Twitter users across the world made tweets with more positive words in the morning and early evening.

- On average, Twitter users across the world made tweets with more negative words in the afternoon.

The student wants to emphasize the aim of the sociologists' study. Which choice most effectively uses relevant information from the notes to accomplish this goal?

(A) The sociologists wanted to know about the content related to emotions in Twitter messages throughout the day.

(B) We now know that more negative emotion words are used in tweets in the afternoon hours than during the morning hours.

(C) The sociologists determined the number of Twitter messages sent each day and used computers to analyze the messages.

(D) After studying millions of tweets, the sociologists determined that morning and early evening were the times when users make tweets with more positive words.

Practice Tests

CONTINUED

27

While researching a topic, a student has taken the following notes:

- One of the most famous paintings of William Shakespeare is the so-called Flower Portrait, named for the Flower family that owned the portrait.
- The portrait is signed with the date 1609.
- The portrait is similar to the 1623 Droeshout engraving of Shakespeare.
- In 2005, art historians x-rayed the portrait and performed mass spectrometry on paint samples from the portrait.
- The paint sample analysis indicated the presence of a chrome yellow pigment that dates to the early 1800s.
- The historians concluded that the portrait was painted in the 1800s and was based on the Droeshout engraving.

The student wants to make a generalization about the kind of study conducted by the art historians. Which choice most effectively uses relevant information from the notes to accomplish this goal?

Ⓐ Based on mass spectrometry analysis, the art historians claim that the Flower Portrait was painted about 200 years after its signed date.

Ⓑ Art historians have used techniques including x-rays and mass spectroscopy on paint samples to help determine the likely creation date of paintings.

Ⓒ The chrome yellow pigment in the Flowers Portrait is from the 1800s, so the painting could not have been created in 1609.

Ⓓ It is more likely that the Flower Portrait was based upon the Droeshout engraving than that the Droeshout engraving was based upon the Flower Portrait.

This page is intentionally blank.

ANSWER KEY

Reading and Writing: Module B

1. **A**	8. **C**	15. **C**	22. **C**
2. **B**	9. **C**	16. **B**	23. **A**
3. **A**	10. **B**	17. **A**	24. **C**
4. **D**	11. **B**	18. **B**	25. **D**
5. **C**	12. **D**	19. **D**	26. **A**
6. **B**	13. **D**	20. **D**	27. **A**
7. **C**	14. **D**	21. **B**	

Instructions

Compare your answers to the answer key and enter the number of correct answers for this stage here. _____ This is your raw score.

Take a 10-minute break and turn to the Math Routing Module to continue your test.

Explanations will be at the end of the practice test.

MATH: ROUTING MODULE

Mark your answers either on the pages that follow or on a separate sheet of paper. You will be scoring this Routing Module before going on to the final Math Module.

DIRECTIONS

- The questions in this section address a number of important math skills.
- Use of a calculator is permitted for all questions. A reference sheet, calculator, and these directions can be accessed throughout the test.
- Unless otherwise indicated:
  - All variables and expressions represent real numbers.
  - Figures provided are drawn to scale.
  - All figures lie in a plane.
  - The domain of a given function f is the set of all real numbers x for which $f(x)$ is a real number.

For **multiple-choice questions**, solve each question and choose the correct answer from the choices provided. Each multiple-choice question has a single correct answer.

For **student-produced response questions**, solve each question and enter your answer as follows:

- If you find **more than one correct answer**, enter only one answer.
- You can enter up to five characters for a **positive** answer and up to six characters (including the negative sign) for a **negative** answer.
- If your answer is a **fraction** that doesn't fit in the provided space, enter the decimal equivalent.
- If your answer is a **decimal** that doesn't fit in the provided space, enter it by truncating or rounding at the fourth digit.
- If your answer is a **mixed number** (such as $3\frac{1}{2}$), enter it as an improper fraction (**7/2**) or its decimal equivalent (**3.5**).
- Don't enter **symbols** such as a percent sign, comma, or dollar sign.

Examples

ANSWER	ACCEPTABLE WAY TO ANSWER	UNACCEPTABLE: WILL NOT RECEIVE CREDIT
3.5	3.5 3.50 7/2	31/2 3 1/2
$\frac{2}{3}$	2/3 .6666 .6667 0.666 0.667	0.66 .66 0.67 .67
$-\frac{1}{3}$	−1/3 −.3333 −0.333	−.33 −0.33

Reference:

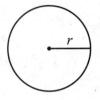

$A = \pi r^2$
$C = 2\pi r$

$A = lw$

$A = \frac{1}{2}bh$

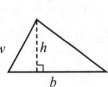

$c^2 = a^2 + b^2$

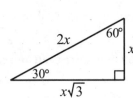

Special Right Triangles

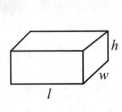

$V = lwh$

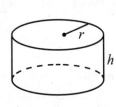

$V = \pi r^2 h$

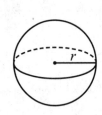

$V = \frac{4}{3}\pi r^3$

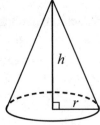

$V = \frac{1}{3}\pi r^2 h$

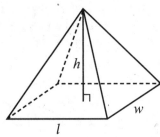

$V = \frac{1}{3}lwh$

The number of degrees of arc in a circle is 360.

The number of radians of arc in a circle is 2π.

The sum of the measures in degrees of the angles of a triangle is 180.

CONTINUED

1

$$\frac{1}{4}(x - 7) = 3$$

What value of x satisfies the equation?

- (A) 3
- (B) 7
- (C) 19
- (D) 28

2

If $f(x) = 5x - 2$, what is $f(x + 3)$?

- (A) $5x + 1$
- (B) $5x + 13$
- (C) $5x + 15$
- (D) $5x + 17$

3

If $4b - 3 > 7$, what is the greatest possible integer value of $-2b + 4$?

- (A) -2
- (B) -1
- (C) 0
- (D) 1

4

Which of the following is equivalent to $\frac{x^2 + 6x + 9}{x^2 + 7x + 12}$?

- (A) $\frac{6x + 9}{7x + 12}$
- (B) $\frac{x + 4}{x + 3}$
- (C) $\frac{x + 3}{x + 4}$
- (D) $x + 3$

5

$$\frac{x^4 y^3}{(x^2)^2 y^m} = 1$$

What is the value of m?

6

A certain type of floor tile covers an area of 7.75 square feet for every three tiles. How many tiles of this type are needed to cover an area of 186 square feet?

- (A) 24
- (B) 72
- (C) 186
- (D) 558

Practice Tests

7

A square has a diagonal length of $12\sqrt{2}$ inches. What is the area of the square in square inches?

- Ⓐ 12
- Ⓑ 24
- Ⓒ 72
- Ⓓ 144

8

$$\frac{2y - (2y + 1)}{3y + 5} = \frac{4y + (3 - 4y)}{y}$$

What is the value of y?

9

$$2y + x = 9$$
$$27 - 3x = 6y$$

The system of equations shown has how many solutions?

- Ⓐ 0
- Ⓑ 1
- Ⓒ 2
- Ⓓ Infinitely many

10

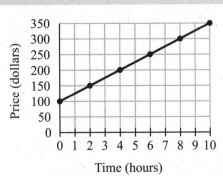

An electrician charges a service call fee, plus an additional fee for every hour on the job. The graph shows the relationship between the hours worked and the total price of the job. Based on the graph, how much would the electrician charge for a job that takes 20 hours?

- Ⓐ $600
- Ⓑ $700
- Ⓒ $1,200
- Ⓓ $1,500

CONTINUED ➡

11

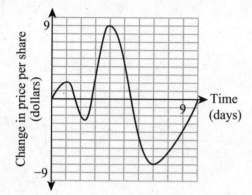

The graph represents the change in price per share (in dollars) of a certain stock during two business weeks. If the coordinates of the maximum are (a, b) and the coordinates of the minimum are (c, d), what is the value of $\frac{d-b}{c-a}$?

(A) -17

(B) $-\dfrac{19}{3}$

(C) $-\dfrac{17}{3}$

(D) 3

12

Kush currently scores 400 on the SAT math section. He sets a goal to improve this score by 1% each day. At this rate, approximately how many days will it take him to score an 800?

(A) 40

(B) 50

(C) 60

(D) 70

13

x	$f(x)$
-1	-1
0	1
1	0

x	$g(x)$
-1	0
0	-1
1	1

For what value of x is the function $h(x) = \dfrac{f(x)}{g(x)}$ undefined?

CONTINUED

14

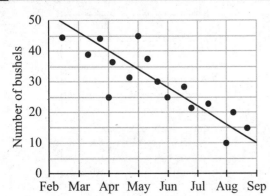

The scatterplot relates the time when a farmer planted a crop to the yield of that crop. Which of the following is the approximate difference, in bushels, between the yield predicted by the line of best fit and the actual yield of the greatest outlier from the predicted value?

(A) 10

(B) 15

(C) 20

(D) 25

15

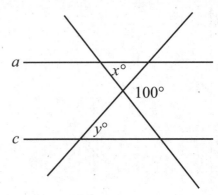

Line a is parallel to line c. Which of the following statements is true?

(A) $x° + y° = 80°$

(B) $x° + y° = 100°$

(C) $x° = y°$

(D) $x° + y° = 180°$

16

$$8x \leq 24y + 40$$
$$3x \leq 6y + 12$$

What is the greatest possible value of x in the system of inequalities?

(A) 2

(B) 1

(C) 0

(D) −1

CONTINUED ➡

17

At a certain store, 4 knives, 5 spoons, and 6 forks cost $7.90. To purchase 2 knives, 2 spoons, and 5 forks would cost $5.80. How much do 2 knives, 3 spoons, and 1 fork cost?

(A) $2.10

(B) $3.30

(C) $4.70

(D) $5.80

18

If $x \neq 3$, $y \neq -5$, and $xy = 15$, which of the following is equivalent to $\dfrac{1}{\dfrac{1}{x-3}+\dfrac{1}{y+5}}$?

(A) $\dfrac{5x-3y}{x+y+2}$

(B) $\dfrac{x+y+2}{(x-3)(y+5)}$

(C) $\dfrac{(x+3)(y-5)}{x+y+2}$

(D) $\dfrac{5-3}{2}$

19

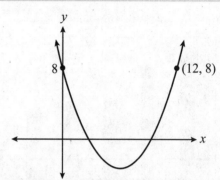

The range of the parabola shown in the graph is $y \geq -4$. If the equation $y = ax^2 + bx + c$ is used to represent the graph, what is the value of a?

(A) $\dfrac{1}{3}$

(B) $\dfrac{2}{3}$

(C) $\dfrac{3}{2}$

(D) 3

20

A thrift store prices a piece of used furniture at $100. The price is marked down an additional p percent every month until it is sold. If the piece of furniture is sold for $64 after two months, what is p?

CONTINUED

Practice Tests

21

Table Wait Time Survey Results

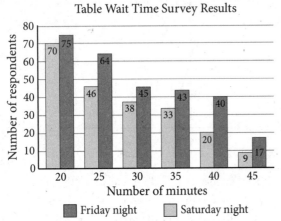

Friday night   Saturday night

A restaurant randomly surveyed customers to determine how long customers are willing to wait for a table on a Friday night versus a Saturday night. On average, approximately how many minutes longer are customers willing to wait for a table on a Saturday night than on a Friday night?

(A) 1.3

(B) 11.3

(C) 34

(D) 68

22

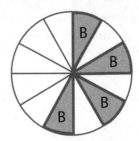

The figure shows a rodeo arena divided into 12 equal sections, 4 of which contain bulls. If $64 + \frac{16\pi}{3}$ yards are needed to reinforce all the edges of the 4 bull sections, what is the radius, in yards, of the arena?

IF YOU FINISH BEFORE TIME IS CALLED, YOU MAY CHECK YOUR WORK ON THIS MODULE ONLY. ON TEST DAY, YOU WON'T BE ABLE TO MOVE ON TO THE NEXT MODULE UNTIL TIME EXPIRES.   **STOP**

762 K

Practice Tests

This page is intentionally blank.

ANSWER KEY

Math: Routing Module

1.	**C**	7.	**D**	13.	**−1**	19.	**A**
2.	**B**	8.	**−15/10, −3/2, or −1.5**	14.	**B**	20.	**20**
3.	**A**	9.	**D**	15.	**B**	21.	**A**
4.	**C**	10.	**A**	16.	**A**	22.	**8**
5.	**3**	11.	**C**	17.	**A**		
6.	**B**	12.	**D**	18.	**A**		

Instructions

Compare your answers to the answer key and enter the number of correct answers for this stage here. _____ This is your raw score.

If you scored less than 14 correct, turn to Math Module A and continue your test.

If you had 14 or more correct in this routing module, turn to Math Module B and continue your test.

Explanations will be at the end of the practice test.

MATH: MODULE A

Mark your answers either on the pages that follow or on a separate sheet of paper. You will be scoring this module and using the results to find your final Math score.

DIRECTIONS

- The questions in this section address a number of important math skills.
- Use of a calculator is permitted for all questions. A reference sheet, calculator, and these directions can be accessed throughout the test.
- Unless otherwise indicated:
  - All variables and expressions represent real numbers.
  - Figures provided are drawn to scale.
  - All figures lie in a plane.
  - The domain of a given function f is the set of all real numbers x for which $f(x)$ is a real number.
- For **multiple-choice questions**, solve each question and choose the correct answer from the choices provided. Each multiple-choice question has a single correct answer.
- For **student-produced response questions**, solve each question and enter your answer as follows:
  - If you find **more than one correct answer**, enter only one answer.
  - You can enter up to five characters for a **positive** answer and up to six characters (including the negative sign) for a **negative** answer.
  - If your answer is a **fraction** that doesn't fit in the provided space, enter the decimal equivalent.
  - If your answer is a **decimal** that doesn't fit in the provided space, enter it by truncating or rounding at the fourth digit.
  - If your answer is a **mixed number** (such as $3\frac{1}{2}$), enter it as an improper fraction (**7/2**) or its decimal equivalent (**3.5**).
  - Don't enter **symbols** such as a percent sign, comma, or dollar sign.

Examples

ANSWER	ACCEPTABLE WAY TO ANSWER	UNACCEPTABLE: WILL NOT RECEIVE CREDIT
3.5	3.5 3.50 7/2	31/2 3 1/2
$\frac{2}{3}$	2/3 .6666 .6667 0.666 0.667	0.66 .66 0.67 .67
$-\frac{1}{3}$	−1/3 −.3333 −0.333	−.33 −0.33

Reference:

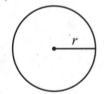

$A = \pi r^2$
$C = 2\pi r$

$A = lw$

$A = \frac{1}{2}bh$

$c^2 = a^2 + b^2$

Special Right Triangles

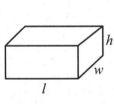

$V = lwh$

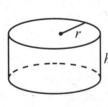

$V = \pi r^2 h$

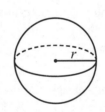

$V = \frac{4}{3}\pi r^3$

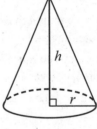

$V = \frac{1}{3}\pi r^2 h$

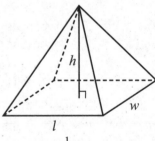

$V = \frac{1}{3}lwh$

The number of degrees of arc in a circle is 360.

The number of radians of arc in a circle is 2π.

The sum of the measures in degrees of the angles of a triangle is 180.

CONTINUED ➡

1

A "pick your own" strawberry farm charges each customer a $10 entry fee, plus $3 per pound of strawberries picked. Which of the following functions describes a customer's total cost in dollars, c, as a function of the number of pounds of strawberries picked, p?

Ⓐ $c(p) = 3p$

Ⓑ $c(p) = 3p + 10$

Ⓒ $c(p) = 10p + 3$

Ⓓ $c(p) = 10p$

2

If $11x - 22 = 4(x - 2)$, what is the value of $2x$?

Ⓐ 2

Ⓑ $\dfrac{20}{7}$

Ⓒ 4

Ⓓ $\dfrac{40}{7}$

3

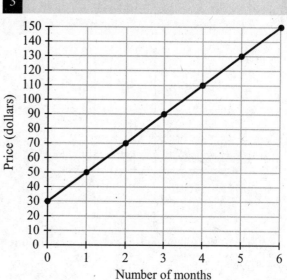

An Internet service charges an initial membership fee plus a fixed monthly cost, as shown in the graph. What is the fixed cost per month, in dollars?

Ⓐ 10

Ⓑ 20

Ⓒ 30

Ⓓ 50

CONTINUED

4

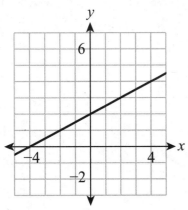

Which of the following is the equation of the line shown?

(A) $y = x + 2$

(B) $y = \frac{1}{2}x$

(C) $y = \frac{1}{2}x + 2$

(D) $y = 2x + 2$

5

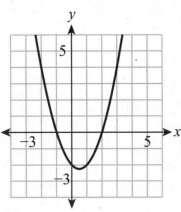

The graph of the function $y = x^2 - x - 2$ is shown. What is the sum of the roots of this function?

6

If $x - y = 6$, what is the value of $x^2 - 2xy + y^2$?

(A) 0

(B) 6

(C) 24

(D) 36

7

If $\sqrt[3]{x} = 8$, what is the value of x?

(A) 2

(B) $\frac{8}{3}$

(C) 24

(D) 512

8

A delivery van travels at an average speed of 30 miles per hour. If the van travels for 8 hours each day, how many miles will it travel in 6 days?

CONTINUED ➡

9

A puppy's weight increases 35 percent each month. If the puppy's initial weight is 10 pounds, approximately how many pounds will the puppy weigh after 4 months?

- Ⓐ 13.5
- Ⓑ 24
- Ⓒ 33
- Ⓓ 150

10

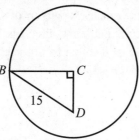

In the figure, point C is the center of the circle, and the measure of angle B is $37°$. Which of the following expresses the length of the radius?

- Ⓐ $15 \sin 37°$
- Ⓑ $15 \tan 37°$
- Ⓒ $15 \cos 37°$
- Ⓓ $15 \tan 53°$

11

A rectangle has a width of $2a$. If the length of the rectangle is 3.5 times its width, what is the perimeter of the rectangle, in terms of a?

- Ⓐ $5.5a$
- Ⓑ $9a$
- Ⓒ $11a$
- Ⓓ $18a$

12

If $\sqrt{xy} = 3$, $y = z^2$, and $z = 6$, what is the value of x?

- Ⓐ $\dfrac{1}{4}$
- Ⓑ $\dfrac{1}{2}$
- Ⓒ 2
- Ⓓ 4

13

If $-4x + 46 \leq x - 4$, what is the minimum value of x?

CONTINUED

14

Suppose the larva of a certain insect species has an initial mass of 10 grams and grows linearly from $t = 0$ to $t = 48$ hours. If the mass of the larva is 14 grams after 48 hours, what was its mass, in grams, at $t = 6$ hours?

- Ⓐ 10.5

- Ⓑ 12.5

- Ⓒ 13

- Ⓓ 14

15

$$|3x - 6| = 2x$$

What is the product of the solutions to the equation shown?

- Ⓐ 6

- Ⓑ $\dfrac{36}{5}$

- Ⓒ $\dfrac{42}{5}$

- Ⓓ 36

16

$$2x^2 + 16x + 2 = 0$$

What is the value of x?

- Ⓐ $\pm 5\sqrt{3} - 15$

- Ⓑ $\sqrt{15} - 8$

- Ⓒ $3\sqrt{5} - 8$

- Ⓓ $\pm\sqrt{15} - 4$

17

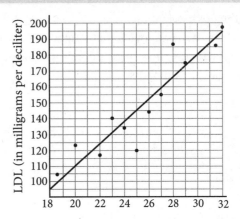

Body mass index (BMI)

The scatterplot shows the relationship between the body mass index and the low-density lipoprotein (LDL) for 12 people, along with the line of best fit for the data. How many of the 12 people have an actual LDL that differs by 10 or more milligrams per deciliter from the LDL predicted by the line of best fit?

- Ⓐ 1

- Ⓑ 2

- Ⓒ 3

- Ⓓ 4

CONTINUED

18

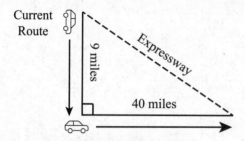

Note: Figure not drawn to scale.

The figure shows the route that Max currently takes to work and back home every day. The city is planning to build an expressway that would cross through the city. Assuming an average gas consumption of 20 miles per gallon, how many gallons of gas will Max save each day by taking the expressway to and from work?

19

Which of the following is equivalent to $\dfrac{3x^2 + 5x - 7}{x + 1}$?

- Ⓐ $3x + 5$
- Ⓑ $3x + 7$
- Ⓒ $3x + 1 + \dfrac{2}{x + 1}$
- Ⓓ $3x + 2 - \dfrac{9}{x + 1}$

20

$$2x^2 - x - 15 = 0$$

Which of the following is a possible value of x?

- Ⓐ 3
- Ⓑ $\dfrac{5}{2}$
- Ⓒ $-\dfrac{2}{5}$
- Ⓓ -3

21

x	$f(x)$
0	−1
1	1
2	7
3	17

Which of the following functions correctly models the data in the table?

- Ⓐ $f(x) = 2x^2 - 1$
- Ⓑ $f(x) = 2x^3 - 1$
- Ⓒ $f(x) = 2^{2x - 1}$
- Ⓓ $f(x) = 2^{x - 1}$

Practice Tests

CONTINUED

22

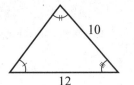 

The ratio of the perimeters of the two triangles in the figure is 7:4. What is the perimeter of the smaller triangle?

This page is intentionally blank.

ANSWER KEY

Math: Module A

1.	**B**	7.	**D**	13.	**10**	19.	**D**
2.	**C**	8.	**1440**	14.	**A**	20.	**A**
3.	**B**	9.	**C**	15.	**B**	21.	**A**
4.	**C**	10.	**C**	16.	**D**	22.	**20**
5.	**1**	11.	**D**	17.	**C**		
6.	**D**	12.	**A**	18.	**16/20, 4/5, 0.8, or .8**		

Instructions

Compare your answers to the answer key and enter the number of correct answers for this stage here. _____ This is your raw score.

Go to the "How to Score Your Practice Test" section to determine your score.

Explanations will be at the end of the practice test.

MATH: MODULE B

Mark your answers either on the pages that follow or on a separate sheet of paper. You will be scoring this module and using the results to find your final Math score.

Examples

ANSWER	ACCEPTABLE WAY TO ANSWER	UNACCEPTABLE: WILL NOT RECEIVE CREDIT
3.5	3.5 3.50 7/2	31/2 3 1/2
$\frac{2}{3}$	2/3 .6666 .6667 0.666 0.667	0.66 .66 0.67 .67
$-\frac{1}{3}$	−1/3 −.3333 −0.333	−.33 −0.33

Reference:

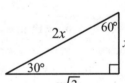
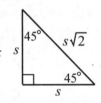

$A = \pi r^2$
$C = 2\pi r$

$A = lw$

$A = \frac{1}{2}bh$

$c^2 = a^2 + b^2$

Special Right Triangles

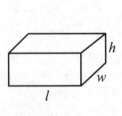
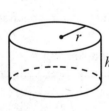

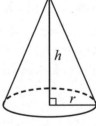
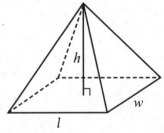

$V = lwh$

$V = \pi r^2 h$

$V = \frac{4}{3}\pi r^3$

$V = \frac{1}{3}\pi r^2 h$

$V = \frac{1}{3}lwh$

The number of degrees of arc in a circle is 360.

The number of radians of arc in a circle is 2π.

The sum of the measures in degrees of the angles of a triangle is 180.

CONTINUED ➡

1

The function $f(x)$ is defined as $f(x) = 2g(x)$, where $g(x) = x + 5$. What is the value of $f(3)$?

2

$$\frac{24x^4 + 36x^3 - 12x^2}{12x^2}$$

Which of the following expressions is equivalent to the expression shown?

Ⓐ $2x^2 + 3x$

Ⓑ $24x^4 + 36x^3$

Ⓒ $2x^2 + 3x - 1$

Ⓓ $24x^4 + 36x^3 - 1$

3

A group of 150 first-year students was randomly selected for a survey that asked whether they were excited to continue their foreign language studies in the next school year. Of this group, 93 said yes, 37 said no, and 20 were not sure. If 1,195 first-year students are currently enrolled in foreign language studies, which of the following is most likely a valid conclusion?

Ⓐ About 740 first-year students are excited to continue foreign language studies next year.

Ⓑ About 440 first-year students are not excited to continue foreign language studies next year.

Ⓒ About 240 first-year students are not excited to continue foreign language studies next year.

Ⓓ About 130 first-year students do not know yet whether they are excited to continue foreign language studies next year.

Practice Tests

CONTINUED ➡

K 777

4

A trucking firm needs to hire at least 8 employees. These employees will be made up of drivers, each paid \$1,120 per week, and mechanics, each paid \$900 per week. The budget for paying these employees is no more than \$8,300 per week. Which of the following inequalities represents this situation, where x is the number of drivers and y is the number of mechanics?

Ⓐ $2,020(x + y) \leq 8,300$
$x + y \geq 8$

Ⓑ $1,120x + 900y \geq 8,300$
$x + y \geq 8$

Ⓒ $1,120x + 900y \leq 8,300$
$x + y \leq 8$

Ⓓ $1,120x + 900y \leq 8,300$
$x + y \geq 8$

5

$$y = 3x^2 + 7x - 4$$
$$y - x = -7$$

How many solutions are there to the system of equations shown?

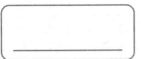

6

A land conservation trust has an initial area of 720 acres. The growth plan will add 84 acres of land to the trust each year. If a function is written in the form $f(x) = ax + b$, where $f(x)$ represents the number of acres of land in the trust and x represents the number of months that have passed, what is the value of x when $f(x) = 1,126$?

Ⓐ 4.83

Ⓑ 13.4

Ⓒ 58

Ⓓ 406

7

$$g(x) = 3x^2 + 12x + 3$$

What is the minimum value of $g(x) + 3$?

Ⓐ -9

Ⓑ -6

Ⓒ -2

Ⓓ 6

8

Which of the following are the roots of the equation $2x^2 + 4x - 3 = 0$?

Ⓐ $\dfrac{-2 \pm \sqrt{10}}{2}$

Ⓑ $-2 \pm \sqrt{5}$

Ⓒ $-1 \pm \sqrt{10}$

Ⓓ $-1 \pm 2\sqrt{10}$

CONTINUED

9

The number of algae cells in a test tube increases at a rate of 50 percent per day. After 3 days, the number of algae cells is 6,750. What was the initial number of algae cells in the test tube?

(A) 2,000

(B) 3,000

(C) 4,500

(D) 6,600

10

Over 5 quizzes, a student's average score is 80. If the lowest score is removed, the average score of the remaining quizzes rises to 83. What is the lowest score of the 5 quizzes?

(A) 28

(B) 35

(C) 68

(D) 77

11

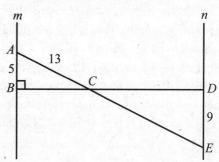

In the figure shown, lines *m* and *n* are parallel. If *AB* is 5, *AC* is 13, and *DE* is 9, what is the length of *BD*?

(A) 12

(B) 21.6

(C) 23.4

(D) 33.6

12

A wholesale food vendor charges $33 for each gallon of maple syrup and $14 for each gallon of pancake syrup. If a restaurant buys 8 gallons of syrup, of which *x* gallons are pancake syrup and the rest are maple syrup, which of the following equations represents the total cost in dollars, *c*?

(A) $c = -19x + 264$

(B) $c = -14x + 33$

(C) $c = 14x$

(D) $c = 19x + 112$

CONTINUED

Practice Tests

13

A landscaping company mows x properties per month for m months. For each property, landscape maintenance starts at c dollars. If the company charges y dollars per square yard and the average lawn area per property is z square yards, which of the following expressions represents the monthly revenue of the landscaping company?

Ⓐ $xyz + c$

Ⓑ $(yz + c)x$

Ⓒ $(yz + c)mx$

Ⓓ $(xyz + c)m$

14

$$2x + 8y = 9$$
$$3x + 5y = 10$$

If (x, y) is a solution to the system of equations shown, what is the value of $\frac{x}{y}$?

[_____]

15

$$\left|\frac{4 + 2x}{x + 2}\right| = x$$

What is the solution set for the equation shown?

Ⓐ No solution

Ⓑ $\{-2\}$

Ⓒ $\{2\}$

Ⓓ $\{-2, 2\}$

16

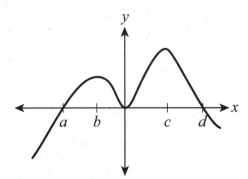

Which of the following equations could be for the graph of the polynomial shown?

Ⓐ $f(x) = -x^2(x + a)(x - d)$

Ⓑ $f(x) = -x^2(x - a)(x - d)$

Ⓒ $f(x) = -x^2(x - b)(x - c)$

Ⓓ $f(x) = -x^2(x + b)(x + c)$

17

$$y = ax^2 - \frac{b^2}{4}$$

Which of the following is equivalent to the equation shown?

Ⓐ $y = \left(\sqrt{ax} + \frac{b}{2}\right)\left(\sqrt{ax} - \frac{b}{2}\right)$

Ⓑ $y = \left(\sqrt{a}\,x + \frac{b}{2}\right)\left(\sqrt{a}\,x - \frac{b}{2}\right)$

Ⓒ $y = \left(\sqrt{ax} - \frac{b}{2}\right)^2$

Ⓓ $y = \left(\sqrt{a}\,x - \frac{b}{2}\right)^2$

CONTINUED ▶

Practice Tests

18

$$y - 2x^2 = 4x + 5$$
$$y - 8 = 5x$$

In the xy-plane, the equations shown intersect at the points $\left(\frac{3}{2}, 15.5\right)$ and (c, d). What is the value of d?

Ⓐ -1

Ⓑ 1

Ⓒ $\frac{3}{2}$

Ⓓ 3

19

Disks		
Metal	Small	Large
Zinc		
Copper		
Total	100	170

A machine shop has a box of metal disks as shown in the table. There are 3 small zinc disks for every 5 large zinc disks and 4 small copper disks for every 7 large copper disks. If a small disk is chosen at random, what is the probability that it will be copper?

20

$$x^2 + y^2 + 12x + 14y = -4$$

What is the radius of the circle given by the equation?

Ⓐ -4

Ⓑ -1

Ⓒ 9

Ⓓ 16

21

Cylinder A and cylinder B are right cylinders. Cylinder A's volume is $\frac{5}{4}$ of cylinder B's volume, and cylinder B's diameter is $\frac{4}{5}$ of cylinder A's diameter. What is the ratio of cylinder B's height to cylinder A's height?

Ⓐ 4:5

Ⓑ 1:1

Ⓒ 5:4

Ⓓ 25:16

22

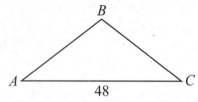

In triangle *ABC*, angle *A* and angle *C* are equal, and *AC* is 48 inches long. If tan $\angle A$ is 0.75, what is the area of the triangle, in square inches?

Practice Tests

This page is intentionally blank.

ANSWER KEY

Math: Module B

1.	**16**	7.	**B**	13.	**B**	19.	**4/10, 2/5, 0.4, or .4**
2.	**C**	8.	**A**	14.	**5**	20.	**C**
3.	**A**	9.	**A**	15.	**C**	21.	**C**
4.	**D**	10.	**C**	16.	**B**	22.	**432**
5.	**1**	11.	**D**	17.	**B**		
6.	**C**	12.	**A**	18.	**D**		

Instructions

Compare your answers to the answer key and enter the number of correct answers for this stage here. _____ This is your raw score.

Go to the "How to Score Your Practice Test" section to determine your score.

Explanations will be at the end of the practice test.

HOW TO SCORE YOUR PRACTICE TEST

Because this is a digital and adaptive exam, scores can vary widely based on the number of correct answers. The following tables give an estimated score range based on the most common scoring logic. Please visit your online resources for the most up-to-date scoring information.

If you were directed to Reading and Writing Module A:

Add the raw score from your Reading and Writing: Routing Module to your raw score from Reading and Writing: Module A.

_____ (Routing) + _____ (Module A) = _____ (Your Total Raw Reading and Writing Score)

Use this table to convert your raw score into your scaled score:

Reading and Writing		Reading and Writing		Reading and Writing	
TOTAL Raw Score	Scaled Score	TOTAL Raw Score	Scaled Score	TOTAL Raw Score	Scaled Score
0	200	21	430	42	610
1	200	22	440	43	630
2	200	23	450	44	640
3	200	24	460	45	640
4	200	25	470	46	N/A
5	200	26	480	47	N/A
6	200	27	490	48	N/A
7	210	28	490	49	N/A
8	220	29	500	50	N/A
9	230	30	510	51	N/A
10	250	31	520	52	N/A
11	280	32	530	53	N/A
12	290	33	540	54	N/A
13	300	34	550		
14	330	35	560		
15	350	36	570		
16	380	37	570		
17	390	38	580		
18	400	39	590		
19	420	40	600		
20	430	41	610		

Your scaled Reading and Writing score from the table is: _____

If you were directed to Reading and Writing Module B:

Add the raw score from your Reading and Writing: Routing Module to your raw score from Reading and Writing: Module B.

_____ (Routing) + _____ (Module B) = _____ (Your Total Raw Reading and Writing Score)

Use this table to convert your raw score into your scaled score:

Reading and Writing		Reading and Writing		Reading and Writing	
TOTAL Raw Score	Scaled Score	TOTAL Raw Score	Scaled Score	TOTAL Raw Score	Scaled Score
0	N/A	21	450	42	630
1	N/A	22	460	43	650
2	N/A	23	470	44	660
3	N/A	24	480	45	660
4	N/A	25	490	46	680
5	N/A	26	500	47	690
6	N/A	27	510	48	700
7	N/A	28	510	49	710
8	N/A	29	520	50	720
9	N/A	30	530	51	730
10	N/A	31	540	52	760
11	N/A	32	550	53	780
12	N/A	33	560	54	800
13	N/A	34	570		
14	N/A	35	580		
15	N/A	36	590		
16	N/A	37	590		
17	N/A	38	600		
18	N/A	39	610		
19	440	40	620		
20	450	41	630		

Your scaled Reading and Writing score from the table is: _____

Practice Tests

If you were directed to Math Module A:

Add the raw score from your Math: Routing Module to your raw score from Math: Module A.

_____ (Routing) + _____ (Module A) = _____ (Your Total Raw Math Score)

Use this table to convert your raw score into your scaled score:

Math		Math	
TOTAL Raw Score	Scaled Score	TOTAL Raw Score	Scaled Score
0	200	25	490
1	200	26	500
2	200	27	510
3	200	28	530
4	200	29	540
5	200	30	560
6	200	31	570
7	220	32	590
8	250	33	610
9	270	34	620
10	290	35	630
11	330	36	N/A
12	350	37	N/A
13	360	38	N/A
14	370	39	N/A
15	380	40	N/A
16	390	41	N/A
17	410	42	N/A
18	410	43	N/A
19	430	44	N/A
20	440		
21	450		
22	460		
23	470		
24	480		

Your scaled Math score from the table is: _____

If you were directed to Math Module B:

Add the raw score from your Math: Routing Module to your raw score from Math: Module B.

_____ (Routing) + _____ (Module B) = _____ (Your Total Raw Math Score)

Use this table to convert your raw score into your scaled score:

Math		Math		Math	
TOTAL Raw Score	Scaled Score	TOTAL Raw Score	Scaled Score	TOTAL Raw Score	Scaled Score
0	N/A	15	380	30	590
1	N/A	16	390	31	600
2	N/A	17	410	32	620
3	N/A	18	430	33	640
4	N/A	19	440	34	650
5	N/A	20	450	35	660
6	N/A	21	460	36	670
7	N/A	22	480	37	690
8	N/A	23	490	38	710
9	N/A	24	500	39	730
10	N/A	25	520	40	750
11	N/A	26	540	41	780
12	N/A	27	550	42	790
13	N/A	28	560	43	800
14	370	29	570	44	800

Your scaled Math score from the table is: _____

To find your composite score, add your Reading and Writing score to your Math score.

_____ (Reading and Writing) + _____ (Math) = _____ (Your Composite Score)

READING AND WRITING: ROUTING MODULE ANSWERS AND EXPLANATIONS

1.   D
Difficulty: Easy
Category: Craft and Structure
Getting to the Answer: Consider how the word "dull" is used in context. The author uses the word to describe the weather, which is rainy. The author also notes that the rain makes Gregor feel "sad" and want to sleep. Predict that "dull" in context means *rainy and depressing*. "Drab" means *cheerless*, so this prediction matches **(D)**, which is correct. The other choices are meanings of "dull" that do not match the context. Sad, rainy weather would not be described as "boring," "smooth," or "pale."

2.   C
Difficulty: Medium
Category: Craft and Structure
Getting to the Answer: Read the passage for clues about the intended meaning of the word for the blank. The sentence with the blank states that art is never *something*. The next sentence gives examples of art changing over time. Predict, then, that art is never *unchanging*. This prediction matches **(C)**, "static," which means *fixed in place*. Choices (A) and (D) are incorrect because their meanings are related to change, the opposite of the intended meaning. Choice (B) is incorrect because "sluggish" means *relatively slow*; the passage does not imply the rate at which art changes.

3.   B
Difficulty: Hard
Category: Craft and Structure
Getting to the Answer: Analyze the passage for clues about the logical meaning of the word in the blank. The missing word describes a type of procedure. The passage describes the procedure as "producing chemical reactions inside living organisms" and as not "interfering with the normal biological function of an organism's cells." Paraphrase this description: the procedure creates chemical reactions inside living cells but doesn't interfere with how they function. Predict that the procedure is *harmless* or *non-interfering*. This matches **(B)**, "benign," which means *not causing harm*. Choice (A) is incorrect because, although the procedure involves a chemical reaction, the procedure itself isn't acting in response to a stimulus. Choice (C), "coherent," means *consistent or understandable*; the procedure may indeed have these qualities, but the passage

describes it as non-interfering. Choice (D) is the opposite of the required meaning.

4.   A
Difficulty: Easy
Category: Craft and Structure
Getting to the Answer: To determine the function of a specific portion of the passage, consider the structure of the passage as a whole. Ask yourself, *Why did the author include this?* The first sentence introduces a "difficulty" facing astronomers (it's hard to detect new planets), and the keyword "because" in the underlined portion signals that it provides a reason for the difficulty (it's hard to see them). The keyword "however" in the next sentence signals that it provides a contrast with the difficulty—a new potential method for detection—which is described in the remainder of the passage. Predict that the underlined portion *gives a reason for a difficulty* or *shows the cause of the problem*. Choice **(A)** is correct. The other choices are incorrect because the underlined portion does not provide a contrast or a solution, but rather an explanation for a problem.

5.   D
Difficulty: Medium
Category: Craft and Structure
Getting to the Answer: Since the correct answer to a question that asks about the purpose of a passage identifies the author's reason for writing, consider the passage's main idea and the author's viewpoint about the main idea. This passage begins by identifying meditation as originally being a religious practice. The following sentences describe meditation's connection to several religions over time. The last sentences discuss the more recent history of meditation, not as a religious practice but as a secular one. The author does not give an opinion about meditation but rather presents an objective description of its history. Therefore, predict that the purpose is to *describe meditation's religious and secular history*. This matches **(D)**. Choices (A) and (C) are incorrect because they omit the passage's discussion of meditation as a secular practice. Further, (A) misrepresents the author's purpose, as the passage never makes the case that meditation impacts spiritual growth. Choice (B) is incorrect because the author makes no arguments about meditation.

6.   A
Difficulty: Medium
Category: Craft and Structure
Getting to the Answer: As you read Text 1, identify the nutritionists' view. The last sentence states that "artificial sweeteners can be used to replace sugar in the diet of a person suffering from diabetes." However, the research results in Text 2 found that people who used artificial sweeteners "had higher blood sugar levels and impaired abilities to tolerate glucose." Since diabetes is a "condition that prevents the body from properly regulating blood sugar levels," predict that *Suez and the researchers would disagree with the nutritionists in Text 1,* making **(A)** the correct answer.

Choices (B) and (D) are incorrect because Suez and the research team's study disagreed, not agreed, with the nutritionists' view. (C) is incorrect because the data collected by the research team is absolutely relevant and directly challenges the nutritionists' view.

7.   D
Difficulty: Hard
Category: Craft and Structure
Getting to the Answer: Focus on identifying the view of the geologists as you read Text 1. The first sentence provides the gist: "the continents formed as material bubbled up from the Earth's core." The first sentence of Text 2 provides the view of Johnson and colleagues: "the original continents were seeded by meteorites." Predict that the correct answer will say that *Johnson and colleagues will disagree with the geologists* and evaluate the choices. Only take the time to go back and understand the rest of the texts if needed. Eliminate (A) and (C) because these choices indicate agreement. Because this is a challenging question, evaluate the reasoning presented in the rest of the text to choose between (B) and (D). The last sentence of Text 1 indicates the view of the geologists hasn't been proven, and the last sentence of Text 2 states that Johnson and colleagues have physical evidence to support their view. Eliminate (B) because the evidence of Johnson and colleagues is relevant to challenging the geologists. **(D)** is correct.

8.   A
Difficulty: Easy
Category: Information and Ideas
Getting to the Answer: The main idea of a passage can often be found in its first sentence; this passage begins by describing the programs of the New Deal as "intended to curb the economic hardships" from the

Great Depression. The words "For instance" signal that the next sentence is an example of such a New Deal program: the Public Works Administration made "an effort to combat high unemployment." The continuation word "Likewise" signals another example: the Agricultural Adjustment Act "sought to raise incomes for impoverished farmers." These are both examples of *New Deal programs trying to reduce economic hardships*, as stated in the first sentence; use this summary as your prediction. Choice **(A)** matches this prediction and is correct.

Choices (B) and (C) are incorrect because they each refer to a single example detail from the passage; further, both choices make claims that go beyond what is discussed in the passage. Choice (D) is incorrect because it reflects one detail from the topic sentence rather than the main idea about the New Deal reducing economic hardships.

9.   D
Difficulty: Medium
Category: Information and Ideas
Getting to the Answer: When determining the main idea of a passage, pay close attention to its first and last sentences. Here, the first sentence states that an occurrence at a casino is now "emblematic," or *representative of*, the gambler's fallacy. The following sentences describe the event, and the last sentence relates the event back to the gambler's fallacy and defines the fallacy. Predict the main idea: *the casino event is an example of the gambler's fallacy.* Choice **(D)** contains this main idea. Further, its definition of the gambler's fallacy matches the definition in the last sentence of the passage, so **(D)** is the correct answer.

Choice (A) summarizes the aspect of probability that is misunderstood in the gambler's fallacy, but it does not address the main idea of the passage about the casino event representing the gambler's fallacy. Choice (B) is incorrect because it focuses only on probability in roulette, not the gambler's fallacy or the Monte Carlo example. Although the passage may suggest that the gambler's fallacy is difficult to avoid, the passage never makes this claim and thus it cannot be the main idea of the passage, so (C) is incorrect.

10. C
Difficulty: Easy
Category: Information and Ideas
Getting to the Answer: The entire text is a description by the narrator, so use the crucial clue in the question,

"as time passes," to identify the correct detail. The detail that answers the question will be marked by keywords to indicate that the narrator's view of the man happens at some *later* point in their relationship. In the first sentence, the keywords "As the weeks went by" identify the next phrase, "my interest in him and my curiosity as to his aims in life gradually deepened and increased" as the correct detail, matching **(C)**.

Because there is no evidence in the passage to support any of the other choices, these are all incorrect.

11. C

Difficulty: Medium

Category: Information and Ideas

Getting to the Answer: Keep the two ideas needed for the correct answer in mind as you read the choices. The correct answer will describe both heavy losses and the soldiers' determination to continue despite these losses. Heavy losses, "loss severe," are described in (A), but "sullen remnant retreating" is not determination to continue. Eliminate (A). Choice (B) simply describes the night setting; eliminate (B). Choice **(C)** is correct. The poignant death of a young man is described, followed by the narrator rushing to join the army as it determinedly "still" marches out into the "darkness" and "unknown." Choice (D) describes the horrific hospital scene but does not address the soldiers' determination; eliminate this choice.

12. D

Difficulty: Medium

Category: Information and Ideas

Getting to the Answer: When analyzing a graph for a Quantitative Command of Evidence question, be sure to carefully examine any titles or labels. In the graph provided, several countries are listed. Each country has two bars: German exports and German imports. Along the bottom of the graph, the percentage is listed. Thus, each bar for each country illustrates what percent of German exports go to that country, as well as what percent of German imports come from that country.

The passage describes how economist Norman Angell claimed that international trade decreases the likelihood of war between nations. It then goes on to add that Angell's idea was welcomed as "tensions were rising between Germany and the British Empire." The question asks for data from the graph to support this claim by Angell.

With a complex Command of Evidence question such as this one, an elimination strategy can often be the most efficient way to determine the correct answer. Choice (A) is factually incorrect; according to the table, Germany imported roughly 18% of its goods from the British Empire, while combining imports from the United States (16%) and Russia (13%) alone constituted 29% percent of German imports. Choice (B) is incorrect because it does not match the data that is depicted on the graph; the British Empire was the largest destination for German exports. Choice (C) is factually incorrect; the British Empire (18%), France (5%), and Russia (13%) amounted to roughly 36% of German imports, far below the 70% claimed in (C). By process of elimination, that leaves **(D)** as the correct answer. However, **(D)** could also be determined as correct through the data table. The claim involves relief at Angell's idea due to rising tensions between the British Empire and Germany; if Britain were Germany's single biggest trading partner, that would make war unlikely according to Angell.

13. B

Difficulty: Hard

Category: Information and Ideas

Getting to the Answer: Note that the question requires a conclusion to the discussion on "economic models" based on the fact that "the models can be updated" so keep these points in mind as you read the text, summarizing the information in your own words. The first sentence states the models are criticized because they failed to predict two major economic crises. The contrast keyword "However" starting the next sentence signals the author's disagreement: the models can only include known information, and the causes of the two economic disruptions were "impossible to predict." The author emphasizes that *once those causes were known and the models updated, the models became accurate*. Matching this summary to the choices yields **(B)** as the correct answer. If the updated models "accurately predicted the future direction of the economy," they remain useful. But since they "are only able to incorporate known, historical trends" and missed two disruptive events, models cannot be expected to foresee every potentially disruptive influence on the economy.

Incorrect choice (A) is the opposite of the author's view; the author defends the models, despite their shortcomings. The speed of updating the models and the prevention of damage mentioned in incorrect choice

Practice Tests

(C) are not discussed in the passage. A correct SAT inference will always be directly supported by the given text. Incorrect choice (D) is extreme; the models missed two major economic crises, so they didn't prove to be *always* reliable. In addition, although the models became more accurate after the crisis events were included, the author describes those events as "impossible to predict." Nothing in the text indicates that the models are now able to predict future crisis events.

14. B
Difficulty: Easy
Category: Standard English Conventions
Getting to the Answer: A quick glance at the choices indicates that this question is testing the punctuation between two phrases. Two other clues are in the choices. First, the words to be added are "am" and "he." Second, the quotation marks close after "am," so usage of the quotation marks is not being tested. As you read, identify whether the portion with the blank consists of two independent clauses or an independent and a dependent clause. This will provide guidance for punctuating it. The sentence consists of two independent clauses ("Ultimately, Descartes arrived . . ." and "he could only be . . . "). Separating the independent clauses into two sentences is the best way to punctuate them. Choice **(B)** is the correct answer.

For the incorrect choices, (A) omits all punctuation between the clauses, (C) creates a run-on by using a comma, and (D) incorrectly capitalizes "He" after a semicolon.

15. D
Difficulty: Easy
Category: Standard English Conventions
Getting to the Answer: A quick glance at the choices identifies this question as testing the correct pronoun. The pronoun should agree with the noun to which it refers, so identify this noun to determine the correct pronoun. The antecedent of the pronoun here is "coal tar," a singular, impersonal noun. Choice **(D)**, "it," is therefore the correct answer.

Incorrect choices (A) and (B) could be used to replace "compounds," but this doesn't make sense in context. The compounds cannot be derived from themselves. Similarly, "him" in (C) would refer to Fahlberg, but the compounds cannot be derived from him.

16. C
Difficulty: Medium
Category: Standard English Conventions
Getting to the Answer: Be sure to read enough of the text before choosing a response. Here, the most important clue is *after* the blank: the closing parenthesis after "forest." The same punctuation is needed at the start of the parenthetical information, so **(C)** is correct.

None of the other choices supply an opening parenthesis, so these choices are all incorrect.

17. A
Difficulty: Medium
Category: Standard English Conventions
Getting to the Answer: A quick glance at the choices indicates that this question is testing verb usage. As you read the text, look for the two clues that will lead to the correct answer: the subject and the tense. The tense is set in the opening phrase; "consumers consider," which is present tense. The subject is "cardboard," a singular noun. Predict that the correct answer will be a singular, present tense verb, and **(A)** matches this prediction.

The incorrect choices are all plural verbs. If you were tempted by some of the incorrect answer choices, notice that "packages" is part of the phrase "needed to produce shipping packages" that modifies "cardboard" and is not the subject.

18. A
Difficulty: Medium
Category: Standard English Conventions
Getting to the Answer: A glance at the choices indicates this question is testing the need for a parenthetical expression since every choice contains "fall . . . gives." On the SAT, if choices are grammatically and logically correct, the shorter the choice, the better. Evaluate the shortest choice first, and only check the longer choices to see if they include essential information. Here, **(A)**, the shortest choice, is correct.

The parenthetical comments in the remaining choices do not add any essential information. Also, the illustration keywords in choice (B) misstate the author's intention: the statement following the blank is an explanation, not an example. Since the meaning of the sentence is clearly conveyed without these comments, these choices are all incorrect.

19. C
Difficulty: Hard
Category: Standard English Conventions
Getting to the Answer: A quick glance at the choices shows the commas in different locations, so this question is testing comma usage. Eliminate (A) for inserting a comma between the preposition "for" and its object "the injured and . . . ." Eliminate (B) because a comma with a FANBOYS conjunction ("and") should be used before an independent clause, and "the elderly to enable them . . ." is not a complete idea. No commas are needed, so **(C)** is correct. To be sure, quickly check (D). The commas in (D) make "for the injured or the elderly" parenthetical, but without this phrase, the pronoun "them" has no logical antecedent. Eliminate (D).

20. A
Difficulty: Hard
Category: Standard English Conventions
Getting to the Answer: The first issue to consider is the punctuation needed, if any, after the word "process." Eliminate (D) because some form of punctuation is needed to avoid a run-on sentence, as the second clause begins with "birch wood." A colon, period, and dash are all viable options in this context. The second issue is to consider the punctuation needed, if any, after the word "wood." Eliminate (B) because it places a comma between the subject "birch wood" and its verb "was." Eliminate (C) because it violates the rules for colons. Namely, the clause before the colon must be able to stand on its own as a complete sentence. "Each woodblock was made through an elaborate process—birch wood" is nonsensical, as birch wood is itself not "an elaborate process." **(A)** is the only grammatically correct choice.

21. A
Difficulty: Hard
Category: Standard English Conventions
Getting to the Answer: The blank follows an introductory modifying phrase that ends with a comma, so the first noun of the blank must be what was "Remarkably permanent" compared to "settlements that relocated." Only the correct answer **(A)** starts with "Hohokam villages," the permanent settlements in an area known for temporary ones.

The remaining choices are all incorrect because the time period in (B) and (C) and "the Hohokam people" in (D), were not "Remarkably permanent" compared to other settlements.

22. D
Difficulty: Easy
Category: Expression of Ideas
Getting to the Answer: Prior to the blank, the text establishes that Anning's work was "dangerous." Immediately following the blank, the death of Anning's dog in a landslide that nearly killed her too is described. Since the information after the blank elaborates on the statement before it, this transition is a *continuation* of ideas. Choice **(D)** is correct as it is the only transition that serves as a continuation. Choices (A), (B), and (C) are all incorrect because they contrast ideas, which is not what the chain of thought calls for here.

23. C
Difficulty: Medium
Category: Expression of Ideas
Getting to the Answer: Since the question asks for a transition, summarize the ideas before and after the blank in your own words, and predict the type of transition needed. The first part of the sentence describes the construction of SONAR during the time of World War I, and the second part notes that Leonardo da Vinci used the same principles about 400 years earlier. Predict that *a contrast keyword, such as "although," is needed*, making **(C)** correct.

Choice (A) is a cause-and-effect transition. Da Vinci's work was a precursor to SONAR, but not a cause of it. Choice (D), an illustration transition, does not express the correct relationship. Eliminate these choices. Choice (B) is a contrast transition, but not the appropriate one for this context. The later development of SONAR was not made *despite* Leonardo da Vinci's experiments.

24. A
Difficulty: Hard
Category: Expression of Ideas
Getting to the Answer: This question is testing a logical transition between the two sentences. Summarize the main idea of each sentence in your own words, then predict the type of transition that would logically connect them. The first sentence states that twice as many surveyed teens say they are "almost constantly"

on social media compared to those who said that in 2015. The second sentence states that the majority believe that they spend an appropriate amount of time online. The author may simply be reporting another fact from the survey, or the author may be drawing a comparison between the large increase in time spent on social media and the teens' perceptions of that increase as an acceptable amount of screen time. Choice **(A)** uses an appropriate contrast keyword phrase and is correct.

Choice (B) is incorrect because "Illustrating this point" is a keyword phrase for an example. The second sentence introduces a new idea; it does not provide an example to support the first sentence. Choice (C) is incorrect because "Subsequently" is a keyword that indicates the order of events, and the text isn't presenting a sequence of events. Choice (D) is incorrect since "Indeed, because" is a keyword phrase emphasizing a cause-and-effect relationship, but the increase in social media time is not the cause of the teens' beliefs.

25. B
Difficulty: Easy
Category: Expression of Ideas
Getting to the Answer: Read the question carefully and make a mental or physical note on the characteristics of the correct answer. Here, a contrast between the earliest people to refrain from eating meat and the later ones will be correct. Eliminate (A); it mentions the earliest people who refrained from meat but shows how their practice is consistent with, not different from, the practice of those who do so today. Choice **(B)** is correct, noting that those who first avoided meat did not have the wide variety of meat substitutes available today. At this point, on test day, move on to the next question, but for the record: eliminate (C) and (D) for not making comparisons. (C) simply states a fact, and (D) only discusses those who do not eat meat today.

26. B
Difficulty: Medium
Category: Expression of Ideas
Getting to the Answer: Read the question carefully and make a mental or physical note on the characteristics of the correct answer. Here, you need a similarity between the artisan Umi Kai and his ancestors. Keep this in mind as you read the choices. Eliminate (A), which contrasts the time needed to craft the items by the two generations of artisans. **(B)** is correct; this choice states Umi Kai is using the same materials to make "things of Hawai'i" as did his ancestors. At this point, on test day, choose **(B)** and move on, but for practice: (C) and (D) draw comparisons between Umi Kai and customers, rather than a similarity between Umi Kai and his ancestors. Eliminate these choices.

27. C
Difficulty: Hard
Category: Expression of Ideas
Getting to the Answer: The question asks for a similarity between third-century and sixth-century B.C.E. Arabic poetry. Keep this in mind, or make a note, as you evaluate the choices. Choice (A) only discusses the construction of *Qasida*; eliminate this choice. Choice (B) cites a difference, not a similarity, between the *Qasida* of the two time periods. Eliminate it. Choice **(C)** mentions the *Qasida* of Imru' al-Qais, so consult the points to establish whether these are relevant to the question. The fourth point confirms these *Qasida* were written in the sixth century B.C.E., and the fifth point states these have themes used since the earliest *Qasida*. Now, verify the time period for the earliest *Qasida*. The first point sets that time period in the third century B.C.E., making **(C)** the correct answer. On test day, choose **(C)** and move to the next question, but for practice: Choice (D) draws a comparison about the fame of Imru' al-Qais but does not mention third-century *Qasida*.

READING AND WRITING: MODULE A ANSWERS AND EXPLANATIONS

1.   A
Difficulty: Easy
Category: Craft and Structure
Getting to the Answer: As you read the text, be on the lookout for clues that will define the meaning of the blank. The first sentence notes that flooding is more dangerous than high winds during tropical storms. The second sentence explains why: the storm pushes a wall of water toward the land. The phrase before the blank indicates the blank is describing "Flooding." The segment after the blank says the wall of water can arrive when the water is already at its highest, so predict that the filled blank will give a meaning like: *the flooding will get worse.* This prediction matches **(A)**, the correct answer. In this context, "aggravated" means *made worse.*

Choice (B), "irritated," means *to annoy,* and is a synonym for "aggravated," but cannot describe flooding. Choice (C) means *to get better* and (D) means *to help,* so these choices give the sentence the opposite meaning. These choices are all incorrect.

2.   D
Difficulty: Medium
Category: Craft and Structure
Getting to the Answer: Since the question stem asks for the most logical and precise word, look for clues about the word's meaning as you read the passage. The first sentence identifies poems with iambic pentameter as having a "strict" pattern. The second sentence states that Oswald used this structure in her "free-flowing" poem "Despite" its *something.* Since "Despite" is a contrast transition, predict that the blank reflects the "strict" structure of iambic pentameter, in contrast to the poem's "free" flow. Choice **(D)** matches "strict" and is correct. Choices (A) and (C) are incorrect because the passage does not imply that iambic pentameter structure entails "autonomy" (*independence*) or "authority" (*power*). Choice (B) is the opposite of the intended meaning.

3.   D
Difficulty: Hard
Category: Craft and Structure
Getting to the Answer: As you read the text, be looking for the clues that will define the blank. The first sentence describes Jim Metzner and his work. The second sentence presents how Metzner does *not* see his work, "He hesitates to describe his work", so he wouldn't describe his work as "capturing" sound. The phrase immediately before the blank explains why: the sounds he records are "gift[s]." Predict a word or phrase associated with a gift; *given to him* (or anything like that) is a good prediction. **(D)** matches the prediction and is correct.

Choices (A) and (B) are opposite; "taken by" and "sought by" are similar to the more active "capturing" of sound that Metzner states is *not* the way he perceives his work. Choice (C) "ascribed to" means *to say something is caused by,* but Metzner believes nature sounds are given to him, not caused by him.

4.   B
Difficulty: Easy
Category: Craft and Structure
Getting to the Answer: The question asks for the purpose of a statement, so, as you read, describe the role of each statement in your own words. Here, the first sentence describes how the flagella move to propel bacteria. Then, the underlined sentence states that flagella should *not* be able to move. The final sentence describes research that explains how the flagella move. Take this summary to the choices. Eliminate (A); the underlined sentence is a statement describing the composition of flagella, not a hypothesis. **(B)** is correct; flagella should not be able to move, yet they do, and Egelman and team explained how this occurs. On test day, choose **(B)** and move on, but for practice: Eliminate (C) as no alternative explanation is mentioned in the test, only Egelman's. Eliminate (D); the underlined sentence presents why flagella shouldn't be able to move bacteria, not context to explain how they do.

5.   B
Difficulty: Medium
Category: Craft and Structure
Getting to the Answer: To determine the function of a specific part of the passage, consider the structure of the passage as a whole. Ask yourself, *Why did the author include this?* The first sentence introduces Rose and describes her as feeling sad and about to cry. The underlined portion refers to the "room" in which Rose is sitting, which is described as "a good place in which

to be miserable." The underlined portion begins a list of features of the room that confirm that it is a good place to be sad, so predict that its function is to *describe the setting*. Choice **(B)** is correct; the detail that the room is "dark and still" supports the idea that the room is "a good place in which to be miserable." Choice (A) is incorrect because the underlined portion supports rather than contrasts the description of the "miserable" room. Choices (C) and (D) are incorrect because the underlined portion does not refer to a character.

6.   B
Difficulty: Easy
Category: Craft and Structure
Getting to the Answer: Text 1 describes a paradox: compared to humans, whales have many more cells that could mutate into cancer, but a much lower incidence of cancer. Text 2 describes this same paradox with the example of elephants. A good prediction for the relationship between the texts would be, *They use different examples to illustrate the same point*. This prediction matches **(B)**, the correct answer.

Incorrect choice (A) states the opposite relationship. The texts support, not contradict, each other. Incorrect choices (C) and (D) misstate the main idea of Text 2. Text 2 does not modify Text 1 (C) or show a difficulty with it (D).

7.   B
Difficulty: Easy
Category: Craft and Structure
Getting to the Answer: Text 1 describes how goats can be used to control kudzu, an invasive plant. Text 2 considers this "an important innovation," but goes on to detail two additional considerations. If you were unsure of the meaning of "panacea," or *cure-all*, use the keyword "but" to understand that the rest of the text is a contrast to the first sentence. Predict that the two passages largely agree, but the second identifies some problems. This prediction matches **(B)**, the correct answer.

Text 2 does not provide any examples of goats controlling invasive plants, so eliminate (A) and (D). (C) is incorrect because Text 2 calls using goats "an important innovation," so the author of Text 2 is not "dismissive" of this idea.

8.   C
Difficulty: Easy
Category: Information and Ideas
Getting to the Answer: Check the first sentence of the passage when looking for its main idea. The first sentence states that the "eminence" of U.S. public universities goes beyond the United States. If unsure of the meaning of "eminence," which means *prominence*, check the rest of the passage for clues. The rest of the passage lists evidence that U.S. universities are respected internationally: foreign students attend U.S. schools, UVA and UCLA have international attention, and U.S. schools contribute to the global conversation. Predict that the first sentence reflects the main idea; **(C)** is correct.

You could also eliminate the other answer choices because they misuse or distort details from the passage. Choice (A) is a detail about two U.S. universities, not the main idea of the passage, which is about U.S universities in general. Choice (B) can be eliminated because the passage is about U.S., not foreign, universities. Choice (D) is incorrect because it is too extreme; the passage states that some foreign students go to U.S. schools, but it never indicates that UCLA is most foreign students' top choice.

9.   C
Difficulty: Medium
Category: Information and Ideas
Getting to the Answer: The first sentence of a passage often contains its main idea; the other sentences in the passage should support the main idea. The first sentence here states that a new theory might explain some things about Saturn. This main idea is broad, so look for details in the passage to fill out the main idea. What is the new theory? What things does the theory explain? The theory is identified in the next sentence: Saturn used to have a moon named Chrysalis. The remaining sentences identify what this new theory about a moon might explain: Saturn's rings and Saturn's "pronounced tilt on its axis." Predict that the main idea is that *a theory about a moon helps explain Saturn's rings and tilt*. This matches **(C)**, which is correct. Choice (A) mentions the moon theory, but it is incorrect because it is incomplete; it fails to include the idea that the theory helps explain phenomena about Saturn. Choice (B) can be eliminated because it does not mention the theory about the moon. Choice (D) is incorrect because it only addresses one of the two phenomena that Chrysalis is thought to have influenced.

10. C
Difficulty: Easy
Category: Information and Ideas
Getting to the Answer: Look for the researchers' theory about pesticides and colony collapse disorder as you read the passage. The next-to-last sentence identifies the theory: two or more pesticides interacting together could cause colony collapse. Use this theory as your prediction; choice **(C)** is correct.

Choice (A) is incorrect because the passage specifies that *one* pesticide would impact bees' life spans and navigation, but the theory is that the interaction of *more than one* pesticide could cause the disorder. Choice (B) is incorrect because although the passage mentions pesticides in honey, it never states that the honey is destroyed. Choice (D) distorts details. Pesticides may stick to bees as they pollinate, but the passage does not specify two particular types of pesticides.

11. A
Difficulty: Hard
Category: Information and Ideas
Getting to the Answer: Identify the detail you should look for as you read the passage: the question asks for the result of baking bread with a lack of concern. Bread is mentioned in the middle of the passage. The speaker states that if you bake with "indifference"—"a lack of concern"—the bread is "bitter" and "feeds but half man's hunger." In other words, the bread would taste bad and not satisfy hunger. The statement about bread is abstract though, so you may want to read the rest of the passage for context. The passage begins by equating work with love and condemns working with "distaste." The rest of the passage gives examples of the negative results of working without love, including bitter bread, poison wine, and unpleasant singing. In each case, the result of the work fails to fulfill its intended purpose, so predict that *baking bread without concern would result in unsatisfying bread;* this matches **(A)**, which is the correct answer.

Choice (B) is incorrect because it is a distortion of a detail; the passage discusses a baker acting with indifference, not the bread itself being indifferent. The other choices also distort details. For (C), the speaker indicates that a person's hunger would only be half satisfied when eating the bread, not that only half of those who eat it will feel full. For (D), singing is mentioned as another example of work that can be done without love, not a result of eating bread.

12. B
Difficulty: Easy
Category: Information and Ideas
Getting to the Answer: Begin by paraphrasing the journalist's claim: line-standing by lobbyists is criticized because it makes political processes unfair. Evaluate the quotes, looking for the one that specifically reflects this criticism. Although it may seem to begin with a criticism, (A) is incorrect because it concludes that line-standing is just "a paid service like anything else." Choice **(B)** is correct. It clearly criticizes the practice of lobbyist line-standing ("Lobbyists should be made to wait in line themselves"), and it provides a reason for the criticism that is related to undermining political fairness (it makes lobbying for political issues more "elitist"). Choice (C) is incorrect because it doesn't address lobbyist line-standing. Choice (D) is an "opposite" type of incorrect answer, as it gives a reason in favor of lobbyist line-standing.

13. C
Difficulty: Medium
Category: Information and Ideas
Getting to the Answer: To determine which statement would support the hypothesis, locate the hypothesis as you read the passage. Paraphrase the hypothesis, located in the third sentence, in your own words: *restricting people's movement impacts how their brains process words for physical objects.* You can predict that this hypothesis would be supported by brain processing results that are different for subjects with and without hand restraints. Choices (A) and (B) can be eliminated because the hypothesis deals with words for *physical objects*; these choices describe results related to viewing *abstract words*, like "because." Further, these results don't compare the brain activity levels to the levels of a group without hand restraints, so they can't be used to indicate the "impact" of hand restraints. Choice **(C)** is correct because it deals with object words and describes different brain activity for subjects with and without hand restraints. Choice (D) is incorrect because it does not indicate a difference in results.

14. B
Difficulty: Medium
Category: Information and Ideas
Getting to the Answer: When analyzing a graph or table for a Quantitative Command of Evidence question, be sure to carefully examine any titles or labels.

Practice Tests

The columns here deal with specific celestial bodies (Venus, Earth, the Moon, and Mars). The rows deal with specific aspects of those bodies. Given that the passage focuses on the problems associated with living in zero gravity or low gravity, the table row dealing with gravity should be kept in mind when answering the question.

Gaurav Sahota claims that children born in less-than-Earth gravity risk developing health problems. Sahota then goes on to state this means "most of our closest celestial neighbors" cannot be settled by humans. Keep Sahota's claim in mind when evaluating choices that go in the blank. The sentence with the blank states that "Mars is often the subject of interest" when it comes to settlement, but sets up a contrast with the word "although." Predict that whatever goes in the blank *should support Sahota and eliminate Mars from consideration for hosting a colony*. Choice **(B)** correctly lists the low gravity of Mars, 3.7 kg/m^3, compared to the 9.8 kg/m^3 listed for Earth.

Although (A) is factually accurate based on the table, as the gravity of Venus is 8.9 kg/m^3, it does not offer a reason to support Sahota and eliminate Mars from contention the way (B) does. (C) is factually wrong; the gravity on the Moon is 1.6 kg/m^3, lower than on Mars. (D) is also factually wrong; the surface pressure on Mars is 0.01 bars; its gravity is 3.7 kg/m^3.

15. A
Difficulty: Easy
Category: Information and Ideas
Getting to the Answer: The correct answer will be a logical conclusion that can be drawn based on what the study results suggest: that it may be possible to decrease mental decline and to allow the elderly to perform daily functions like driving. Evaluate the answer choices with these ideas in mind. Choice **(A)** is correct because preventing mental decline to "maintain functions needed for safe driving and other activities of daily living" could potentially allow the elderly to "live longer independently." Choice (B) can be eliminated because it is too extreme; the passage discusses a possible "stav[ing] off" of mental decline, but it does not suggest video games can "completely cure" age-related cognitive problems. Choice (C) is incorrect because playing board games is out of the passage's scope. Choice (D) is incorrect because it is the opposite of what the study results suggest.

16. A
Difficulty: Easy
Category: Standard English Conventions
Getting to the Answer: The answer choices indicate that you need to determine how the two portions of the sentence should be joined. The clause before the word "because" is an independent clause, with subject "Annie Maïllis" and verb "claims." The portion beginning with "because" is a dependent clause, since it cannot stand on its own as a complete thought. A dependent clause beginning with "because" can appear after an independent clause without any punctuation, so **(A)** is correct. Choices (B) and (D) are incorrect because a semicolon or a comma with a FANBOYS conjunction would join two independent clauses. Choice (C) is incorrect because it turns the portion beginning with "Because" into a sentence fragment.

17. B
Difficulty: Easy
Category: Standard English Conventions
Getting to the Answer: Recall that nouns can sometimes be used as adjectives, which serve to modify nouns and pronouns. The placement of "apparent" varies in the answer choices, modifying either "proof" or "claims." In the context of the passage, Titor offers the secret features of the 1970s computer as evidence that supports his claim to be a time traveler. Predict that this better matches "apparent proof" and eliminate (A) and (D). As (B) and (C) use the same phrasing, determine whether a question mark makes sense in this context. Because it does not, eliminate (C), which leaves **(B)** as the correct answer.

18. C
Difficulty: Easy
Category: Standard English Conventions
Getting to the Answer: The portions of the text before and after the blank are each independent clauses. When nonessential information is removed, the first sentence would be: "Iranian mathematician Maryam Mirzakhani . . . was renowned for her contributions to the field of theoretical mathematics." Likewise, the second sentence would be: "She won the prestigious Fields Medal." This question is testing how to combine (or separate) these clauses according to correct grammar. (A) is incorrect because it creates a run-on. (B) and (D) are incorrect because a comma and a conjunction are both needed to join two independent clauses. Only **(C)** properly arranges these clauses according to correct grammar.

19. D
Difficulty: Easy
Category: Standard English Conventions
Getting to the Answer: The answer choices indicate that this question tests pronouns, so first identify the logical antecedent. The sentence with the blank could be reduced to "adults . . . will find it contains 60% of _____ daily recommend amount of Vitamin C." This makes it clearer that the antecedent of the blank pronoun is "adults." Predict that the correct pronoun will be plural possessive. Choice **(D)** is correct. (A) is incorrect because "it's" is a contraction, not a pronoun. (B) is incorrect because the pronoun "its" is not used in reference to people. (C) is incorrect because "your" is a second-person possessive pronoun, and it would only be appropriate if the antecedent was *you*.

20. C
Difficulty: Medium
Category: Standard English Conventions
Getting to the Answer: The answer choices indicate this question is testing verb tenses. Prepositional phrases and other descriptive phrases can make the subject-verb agreement error trickier to spot. It can help to streamline the sentence: "Ibn Khaldun . . . describes *asabiyyah* . . . as possessing a life cycle that _____ an end." Now it is clearer that the subject being tested is "a life cycle," and that the sentence is in the present tense. **(C)** is correct because it is a third-person singular present tense verb.

Choice (A) is incorrect because "having" is the present participle form of *have*. A present participle is a word that ends in "-ing," is formed from a verb, and is used as an adjective (*The laughing clown*) or to form a verb tense (*I have been laughing*). (B) is incorrect because "have" cannot be used in the third person singular (*he, she, it*), only the third person plural (*they*). (C) is incorrect because "had" is in the past tense.

21. A
Difficulty: Medium
Category: Standard English Conventions
Getting to the Answer: Since the question asks about English conventions, look at the answer choices before reading the passage: the varying punctuation indicates that this question tests how to join clauses. The first portion of the sentence with the blank is an independent clause, with a list as the subject ("difficulties, challenges, and triumphs") and "are becoming" as the

verb. The second part of the sentence begins with the parenthetical "instead," correctly set off by a comma; the rest of the sentence is an independent clause with a compound subject ("escapist tales . . . and escapades") and the verb "prevail." Look in the answer choices for a way to connect two independent clauses; **(A)** is correct.

Choices (B) and (C) result in run-on sentences. A comma with a FANBOYS conjunction could join two independent clauses, but (D) is incorrect because it omits the comma.

22. D
Difficulty: Hard
Category: Standard English Conventions
Getting to the Answer: In this passage, commas set off nonessential information from the main part of the sentence, just as parentheses or dashes might be used to do. The second sentence's middle section "by incorporating rhythmic rhyming verses into their music" is not necessary for understanding that sentence's main clause, which explains that a four-man group harmonized together to create an early form of rap music. Eliminate (A) and (B) because they do not use a comma after "music" to close off the nonessential information from the main part of the sentence. Eliminate (C) because it does not make grammatical sense; "harmonized" could not stand alone in this context. Choice **(D)** is correct because it uses the necessary punctuation, a comma, in the proper location.

23. B
Difficulty: Easy
Category: Expression of Ideas
Getting to the Answer: Since the question stem asks for the logical transition, determine what two ideas are being connected in the passage. The sentences before the needed transition state that the risk of astronauts and spacecraft colliding with meteoroids is low because meteoroids are rare. The sentence with the needed transition states that astronauts and spacecraft would "almost certainly" collide with micrometeorites because micrometeorites are common. These ideas contrast, so look for a contrast transition in the answer choices; **(B)** is correct.

Choice (A) results in an illogical cause-and-effect relationship: the micrometeorites are not encountered because of the small chance of hitting rare meteoroids. Choices (C) and (D) incorrectly use continuation transitions.

24. D
Difficulty: Medium
Category: Expression of Ideas
Getting to the Answer: When identifying the correct transition, determine which two ideas are being connected. After the transition, the words "these results" indicate that the transition will tie the results to the researchers' hope to reduce hunger. Before the transition, the "results" are identified as plants having increased yields. Increased plant yield would be a promising result for reducing hunger, so **(D)** is correct. Choice (A) is incorrect because it is a contrast transition. Choice (B) is incorrect because the researchers' hopes are not *in addition* to these results, but are *based on* these results. Choice (C) is incorrect because the researchers are not examples of the results.

25. A
Difficulty: Hard
Category: Expression of Ideas
Getting to the Answer: Paraphrase the ideas that are connected by the blank so you can determine the appropriate transition between them. The passage begins by describing Zheng He's naval expeditions. The second sentence states that the government "diverted funds to terrestrial defensive measures instead," and the sentence with the blank concludes that "major state-sponsored sea voyages did not continue." In other words, the government switched from paying for sea voyages to paying for land defenses. Predict that *as a result* of this change, sea voyages ended. Choice **(A)** is also a cause-and-effect transition and is correct. Choice (B) is incorrect because ending funding for sea voyages and such voyages stopping are not contrasting ideas. Choice (C) is incorrect because the end of state-sponsored sea voyages is not similar to any idea in the previous sentence. Choice (D) is incorrect because the major sea voyages did not just initially end; rather, they ended altogether after the 1430s.

26. D
Difficulty: Easy
Category: Expression of Ideas
Getting to the Answer: Look for a difference between the two works as you read through the passage.

The last two bullet points address Britto's two specific works; both are described as colorful, but the difference seems to entail their differing subject matter. Evaluate the answer choices, looking for one that correctly identifies the differing subjects and, most likely, uses contrast keywords. Eliminate (A) because it discusses a similarity, the works' use of bright colors, using the continuation transition words "Both" and "and." Eliminate (B) because it addresses features that all of Britto's works have in common; further, it does not mention the two specific works. Even though (C) mentions a difference ("Although"), it is about where Britto has lived, not the two artworks. Choice **(D)** is correct; the choice identifies the art as having "diverse"—or different—subject matter and uses the contrast word "while" to describe the different subjects of the two specific paintings.

27. C
Difficulty: Medium
Category: Expression of Ideas
Getting to the Answer: The question asks you to identify a similarity between the two groups of letters, so look for similarities as you read the passage. The first three bullet points describe overall features that ancient Egyptian personal letters have in common. They are written on papyrus by elites and sometimes give instructions about managing households. Look for these commonalities as you read the last two bullet points, which address the specific letters. Both are written by elites (a general and a priest), and both discuss household management. Choice **(C)** is correct because it reflects the similarity of household concerns in the letters; further, it accurately describes the specific household concerns identified for each group of letters in the passage. Choice (A) is incorrect because it identifies a difference ("while") rather than a similarity. Choice (B) gives an overall description of ancient Egyptian personal letters, but it is incorrect because it does not address the two specific letter groups. Choice (D) describes the two specific letter groups, but it is incorrect because it identifies a difference ("however") rather than a similarity.

READING AND WRITING: MODULE B ANSWERS AND EXPLANATIONS

1.   A
Difficulty: Medium
Category: Craft and Structure
Getting to the Answer: Look for clues about how the word "sound" is used in context. The end of the first paragraph states that Anne realized Marilla had given "very sound and pithy" advice. Anne's statement in the next sentence ("'You are right, Marilla'") shows that Anne agrees with the advice, so predict that the "sound" advice must be *correct* or *good*. Choice **(A)** is correct; Anne must find the advice "reasonable" if she agrees with it. If you were familiar with the word "pithy," which means *concise and meaningful*, this could also serve as a hint; if not, the context of the passage is sufficient to figure out the meaning of "sound." The other answer choices are meanings of "sound"—related to something being *noisy, intense, or stable*—that do not reflect the idea of agreeing with advice.

2.   B
Difficulty: Hard
Category: Craft and Structure
Getting to the Answer: To determine the logical meaning of the word that belongs in the blank, carefully read the passage for clues. The first sentence states that marine biologists had a theory about Australia's reefs, but a "dearth," or *lack*, of some kind of data that compares Australia's reefs with other reefs prevented them from confirming their hypothesis. The answer choices are all words that could describe the type of data needed, so look to the passage for more clues. The next sentence explains that researchers "not only" collected data about Australian reefs "but also" added other data, and "together" this data demonstrated an impact. Predict that the correct answer will reflect the idea that the researchers *combined and used a lot of data*. This matches **(B)**, "comprehensive," which means *all-inclusive* or *broad*.

For (A) and (D), nothing in the passage suggests that existing data was inaccurate or non-quantifiable; rather, the clues point to the breadth of the data. Choice (C) is incorrect because nothing in the passage suggests needing "permanent" data; in fact, data would need to be continually updated to reflect changes over time.

3.   A
Difficulty: Hard
Category: Craft and Structure
Getting to the Answer: When determining the most logical word that fits in a passage, search for the clues provided about its meaning. This passage contains a lot of details, but its ideas are anchored by transition words. "Despite" in the first sentence signals that there is a contrast between the "original reception" of a poetry volume and its influence over time. The next sentence describes the original reception as negative: It faced censorship and its author was prosecuted. "Still" in the next sentence indicates a shift to the positive. The poetry inspired many other significant ("top-tier," "throughout the world," "acclaimed") artworks. Predict that the long-term influence must be either *positive* and/or *significant*. This matches **(A)**, which is correct.

Choice (B) is incorrect because it is the opposite of the intended meaning; "paltry" would mean a *small influence*. For (C), although the poetry was "controversial" *at first*, the blank refers to its influence *over time*; the sentence describing its long-term influence does not indicate controversy, and the poetry's lasting influence must *contrast* with its immediate (negative) reception. Choice (D) is incorrect because the passage does not suggest that the poetry's influence was "superior" to the influence of anything else.

4.   D
Difficulty: Medium
Category: Craft and Structure
Getting to the Answer: To determine the function of a specific sentence, consider the structure of the passage as a whole. Ask yourself, *Why did the author include this?* The passage begins by describing a character as having "extraordinarily ample" knowledge. The underlined sentence, however, states that the character also has great ignorance. The remaining sentences give examples of the character's ignorance. Predict that the underlined sentence either *contrasts with the idea in the previous sentence* or *sets up the examples that follow*. Choice **(D)** is correct.

Choice (A) is incorrect because the underlined sentence creates a contrast, not an elaboration, of the trait in the previous sentence. Choices (B) and (C) are incorrect because the sentence does not concern a behavior or a setting.

5. C
Difficulty: Hard
Category: Craft and Structure
Getting to the Answer: The text describes the experiences of British World War I veterans; specifically, it relates how they had trouble finding jobs after the war, finding no support among the "elderly men" who had supported continuing the war. With that summary in mind, review the answer choices and choose the one that best matches it. That would be **(C)**, which is the correct answer. (A) can be eliminated because it misrepresents the text; the "elderly men" are the ones who make the critique, not the author. Furthermore, the "elderly men" are presented as hypocrites given their earlier insistence that Britain keep fighting in the war. Eliminate (B) because there is nothing in the text to indicate that the lack of interest in hiring veterans was due to mistrust. Instead, the war was seen as offering no practical experience: "What knowledge had they of use in civil life?" Eliminate (D) because, while an elderly man insults British veterans, the death of the elderly man's six sons is offered as a hypothetical. He is described as saying "if" he had six sons, he would be glad for them to die for the sake of victory.

6. B
Difficulty: Easy
Category: Craft and Structure
Getting to the Answer: Summarize the main ideas of the texts as you read. Text 1 defines primary and secondary source documents and describes the historians' preference for primary source documents. Text 2 describes Pocock's archive of impressions received from his voluntary correspondents. Evaluate the choices using these summaries. Eliminate (A). Text 2 does not include any arguments; it simply presents Pocock's work. Choice **(B)** is correct. Since Pocock's project is archiving documents created during specific times, these documents could be considered primary sources by historians investigating those times. At this point on test day, choose **(B)** and move on. But, for the record, eliminate (C) because Text 2 does not offer any criticism. Although Pocock's correspondents may be offering analyses or interpretations, the authors are responding to events as they occur. Since time has not elapsed, these documents are primary, not secondary sources. Eliminate (D).

7. C
Difficulty: Hard
Category: Craft and Structure
Getting to the Answer: To answer the question, make sure you can paraphrase the view of the author of Text 2 and McNeill's argument from Text 1. The crux of McNeill's argument is that mosquitoes were historical actors in the Caribbean. The author of Text 2 claims that historians should avoid "strict environmental determinism," which makes ecological factors the most important causes in history. In the next sentence, the author includes "wildlife" as one of these factors, so the author would likely say that mosquitoes (Text 1) should not be considered the most important historical cause. But author 2 argues only against *strict* environmental determinism and acknowledges that the environment "undoubtedly influence[s]"; thus, the author would likely accept that mosquitoes are *one* historical cause. Text 2 concludes by arguing for the prioritization of human actors as causes. With these subtleties of Text 2 in mind, **(C)** is correct. Author 2 would think mosquitoes played a causal role in the Caribbean but would argue that humans played a bigger role.

Choice (A) is incorrect because the author of Text 2 would not "dismiss" McNeill's claims; rather, Text 2 acknowledges that ecological factors like mosquitoes are influential. Further, (A) misrepresents environmental determinism; Text 2 never claims that environmental determinism entirely rules out human actors. Choice (B) can be eliminated because the author of Text 2 emphasizes environmental versus human causal factors, not a concern about replicating studies in other eras. Choice (D) is incorrect because McNeill already focuses on an environmental factor.

8. C
Difficulty: Medium
Category: Information and Ideas
Getting to the Answer: The poem compares the emotion of hope to a bird. Hope "perches in the soul," and never stops singing, even during storms—the hard times of life. Predict that the correct answer will be something like *to describe hope as persistent*. This matches **(C)**, the correct answer.

Choice (A) is incorrect because "sore must be the storm" refers to a difficult, stormy time of life, not a time when the speaker was injured. Choice (B) is the opposite. Hope is "sweetest—in the Gale—," so the speaker gets the most consolation from hope when life is difficult, like a stormy gale at sea. Choice (D) is incorrect because the first line says the speaker is talking about hope, not actual birds.

9.   C
Difficulty: Hard
Category: Information and Ideas
Getting to the Answer: Since this is a Main Idea question, as you read, be on the lookout for keywords that indicate the author's point of view. The first sentence presents a fact that scientists know: women's brains change during pregnancy. The continuation keyword "also" indicates the next sentence describes another fact: the larger the decrease in brain volume, the more feelings of attachment the women express towards their children. ("They have also found a positive correlation . . .") The next sentence presents the hypothesis that these brain changes are "an evolutionary adaptation to improve parenting behaviors." So far, the author has been neutral, simply presenting several facts. In the following sentence, however, the author speculates that these brain changes may be an "interesting example" of something. At this point, note that anything the author finds "interesting" is likely to be the main idea. The author introduces a coming "example of similar evolutionary goals being met by different physiological mechanisms." Use this statement as your prediction to test the choices, since what follows will simply be the details of the example. Only **(C)**, the correct answer, mentions a single evolutionary goal, "parenting benefits" and "different physiological processes." For the record, the example summarizes Magdalena Martínez-García's research that men have similar (but smaller) reductions in brain volume and similar positive correlations with affectionate behaviors toward their children.

The incorrect choices all contradict the passage. Men do have reductions in brain volume (A), due to different, not similar, physiological changes (B), and Magdalena Martínez-García's work (D) supports, not challenges, the hypothesis.

10.   B
Difficulty: Medium
Category: Information and Ideas
Getting to the Answer: Use the question to focus your reading on finding the relevant detail: Rose's reaction after entering the parlor. She enters the parlor at the end of the first paragraph, and her reactions are described as losing her breath, gasping, looking

around "wildly," being ready to "fly" (run away), and feeling "fear" that makes the room seem like it is full of boys. These reactions reflect surprise and panic; **(B)** is correct. Rose is startled and feels there are even more boys in the room than there are (" fear magnified the seven and the room seemed full of boys").

Choice (A) is incorrect because the passage describes the actions of the seven boys. Choices (C) and (D) are incorrect because they describe Rose before she enters the parlor.

11.   B
Difficulty: Hard
Category: Information and Ideas
Getting to the Answer: The entire text involves the postmaster of Obedstown and his job, so make a mental or physical note of each point as you read, and check it against the choices. The first phrase says "Squire Hawkins got his title from being postmaster of Obedstown"; however, the next phrase states the title does not belong to the job. Eliminate (A). The remainder of the first sentence explains that "Squire" is an honorary title, given as a courtesy to "chief citizens," but does not state Hawkins is "the chief citizen in charge of Obedstown." Eliminate (D). The next sentence describes the monthly mail delivery, and the satiric "as much as three or four letters" indicates the delivery is small. The satire continues in the next sentence that states that "a rush like this" did not fill his time, and that when he wasn't busy with the mail, he "kept store." Eliminate (C), leaving **(B)**, the correct answer.

12.   D
Difficulty: Easy
Category: Information and Ideas
Getting to the Answer: In order to determine which statement would support Worchel's hypothesis, locate the hypothesis as you read the passage. Paraphrase the hypothesis, located in the first sentence, in your own words: *scarce commodities will be considered more valuable*. You can predict that the group that got a few cookies would rate them as more valuable than would the group that got a lot of cookies. This matches **(D)**, which is correct.

Choices (A) and (B) are incorrect because they do not address how valuable the participants considered the cookies, while the hypothesis concerns value ratings. Choice (C) is incorrect because it would weaken the hypothesis.

13. D
Difficulty: Medium
Category: Information and Ideas
Getting to the Answer: You need to choose the quote that illustrates the claim, which is located at the end of the passage: the speaker teaches that material goods are not important. Evaluate the answer choices with this claim in mind. Choice (A) mentions people leaving fields and vineyards, which are material things, but this quote does not encourage the people to leave their fields and vineyards; eliminate (A). Eliminate (B) because it is about love, not material goods. Likewise, eliminate (C), which is about children having their own thoughts and souls. Choice **(D)** is correct because it reflects a down-playing of possessions. The speaker claims that the giving of your possessions amounts to "little," as they are just "things you keep and guard" out of fear.

14. D
Difficulty: Hard
Category: Information and Ideas
Getting to the Answer: When analyzing a graph or table for a Quantitative Command of Evidence question, be sure to carefully examine any titles or labels. The rows in the table list specific metals: silver, copper, and gold. The columns list aspects of those metals: resistivity, conductivity, and average price per ounce in 2018.

NASA researchers claim that asteroid mining will massively increase the global supply of precious metals like silver and gold, allowing for a more energy-efficient infrastructure to be created. It was mentioned in the passage that the use of silver and gold was "restricted to high-end electronic components due to their rarity creating a high price." Thus, it can be inferred that a massive increase in the supply of silver and gold would allow for their use in things other than high-end electronic components. Keep that inference in mind when evaluating the answer choice options, as the correct answer will likely make some reference to price.

Choice (A) is incorrect because, although the use of gold is restricted due to its high price, the table indicates that the resistivity of gold is higher than that of copper. (B) is incorrect for a similar reason; gold has a lower conductivity compared to that of copper. (C) is incorrect because silver has a lower resistivity than gold. **(D)** is correct because silver has higher conductivity than copper and gold, and high conductivity is in line with efficient electricity conduction; copper has a lower price per ounce than silver. Silver's high

price is explained as being due to its "rarity," so asteroid mining would increase the supply of silver. Thus, the price of silver would decrease as silver would no longer be so rare. This would allow silver to take the place of copper in "power lines and home wiring."

15. C
Difficulty: Hard
Category: Information and Ideas
Getting to the Answer: Since you need to identify a logical inference based on the findings, begin by summarizing the researchers' findings about colony collapse disorder: they made the "odd" discovery that the disorder left behind empty hives, but no actual dead bees. Consider why this finding would be "odd." The passage states that beekeepers, scientists, and farmers all assumed a pathogen was killing bees; this theory is significantly weakened, however, since no dead bees were actually found. Choices (A) and (D) are incorrect because the findings imply that pathogens are *not* responsible for colony collapse disorder, as farmers originally assumed. For (B), the second sentence identifies viruses as a type of pathogen that kills bees, but the passage does not suggest unknown viruses kill bees. Choice **(C)** is correct, as the lack of dead bees suggests that known pathogens do not cause colony collapse disorder.

16. B
Difficulty: Easy
Category: Standard English Conventions
Getting to the Answer: Since the blank here is intended to emphasize a brief statement of fact, a colon or dash would be appropriate. Choice **(B)** is correct. (A) is incorrect because it omits any punctuation to introduce the short list. (C) incorrectly uses a semicolon; it neither joins two independent clauses nor separates items containing commas in a series or list. (D) incorrectly uses a parenthesis; while parentheses can be used to set aside parenthetical information, the parentheses must come in a pair to bracket off that information.

17. A
Difficulty: Easy
Category: Standard English Conventions
Getting to the Answer: The choices contain frequently confused versions of possessive pronouns and contractions, so carefully assess the context of the sentence to determine which is correct. Choice **(A)** is correct because *their* is attached to a noun to show ownership;

it establishes whose kissing "did not violate" the "time limit." Choices (B) and (C) are incorrect because they are sound-alikes for *their*. (B) is a contraction for *they are*. (C) refers to a location. Choice (D) is a possessive form not used in reference to humans, so it is inappropriate in this context.

18. B
Difficulty: Medium
Category: Standard English Conventions
Getting to the Answer: Judging by the answer choices, this question deals with the punctuation surrounding the list "sweatshirts, polo shirts, and tennis shoes." The phrase is a parenthetical element because it describes now-common clothes that were once only worn by athletes. A pair of parentheses, commas, or dashes should set it apart from the rest of the sentence. Only **(B)** does so and is correct. Choice (A) starts with a dash but then incorrectly ends the parenthetical with a comma. (C) starts with a parenthesis but then incorrectly ends with a dash. (D) is incorrect because it introduces the parenthetical with a colon.

19. D
Difficulty: Medium
Category: Standard English Conventions
Getting to the Answer: The answer choices indicate that this question tests pronouns, so first identify the logical antecedent. The sentence with the blank pronoun has many nouns near it. However, of the answer choices, the most logical pronoun is "its" because the passage is introduced as an overview of *Romance of the Three Kingdoms*. "Published," "alongside," and "following" are all introducing modifying phrases. Thus, **(D)** is correct. Eliminate (A) and (B) because the antecedent is not a person or people. Eliminate (C) because it is a contraction for "it is," which is commonly mistaken for the pronoun "its."

20. D
Difficulty: Hard
Category: Standard English Conventions
Getting to the Answer: Identify the missing verb's subject to ensure that there is proper subject-verb agreement. The subject in this sentence is not the closest noun; it is "Xenophon," which is singular and requires a singular verb. When dealing with a complex sentence, it can be helpful to reduce the sentence down to its core. In this case: *Xenophon of Athens (blank) best remembered today for the March of the Ten Thousand*.

The "of Athens" is a title for Xenophon, so "Xenophon" is the subject in the sentence. As Xenophon is said to be "best remembered *today*" for the March of the Ten Thousand, the verb is present tense. Only **(D)** fits all that information and is correct.

(A) is incorrect because "have been" requires the subject of the sentence to be *I, you, we*, or a third person plural. (B) and (C) are both incorrect for being in past tense, and (C) is also a plural verb.

21. B
Difficulty: Hard
Category: Standard English Conventions
Getting to the Answer: The first issue to consider is the punctuation needed after the word "property." Eliminate (A) because the use of a comma in this context would create a run-on sentence. The second issue to consider is the punctuation needed, if any, after the word "Hobbes." Eliminate (C) because, while a dash can be used to set aside parenthetical information like "by contrast" from "Hobbes," in this context, a second dash after "contrast" would be needed. A dash and a comma cannot be used together to bracket a parenthetical, and there is already a comma after "contrast." Eliminate (D) because a comma is needed to set off the parenthetical element "by contrast," from "Hobbes." **(B)** is the only grammatical choice and is correct.

22. C
Difficulty: Hard
Category: Standard English Conventions
Getting to the Answer: The answer choices indicate that this question tests the correct punctuation after the end parenthesis. Evaluate the sentence with the blank to determine the sentence's structure. The main subject of the sentence is "the bald eagle," which has a compound verb ("was once considered . . . and was widely hunted.") The parenthetical information is correctly set off by parentheses, but no punctuation is needed between the parts of the compound verb; **(C)** is correct. The other answer choices incorrectly insert punctuation within the compound verb. The semicolon in (D) would be used to join two independent clauses.

23. A
Difficulty: Medium
Category: Expression of Ideas
Getting to the Answer: The sentence that contains the missing transition word has two ideas. The first is the opinion of "some scientists" and the second is the

assertion of "others." These are two separate ideas that need a contrast transition word to logically connect them; they neither continue a shared thought nor have a causational relationship. Choice **(A)** is correct; it logically signals that in spite of the fact that a new model may help provide new answers, others need additional research on this new animal model.

Incorrect choices (B) and (D) signal continuation, and choice (C) conveys a cause-and-effect relationship between the ideas.

24. C

Difficulty: Hard
Category: Expression of Ideas
Getting to the Answer: The sentence that contains the missing transition word states that the black hole was given a nickname by Professor Kimura. This information comes after the claim that the first image was made using two telescopes on a Hawaiian island and before the explanation of what the *nickname*, or "sobriquet," means in the Hawaiian language. Each sentence in the passage builds on the preceding sentence; the correct transition word will signal continuation. Choice (A) is a continuation transition word that conveys that the action took place at the end of a long period, which is not supported by the passage. Eliminate (A). Choices (B) and (D) are contrast transition words; eliminate them. Choice **(C)**, which most nearly means *after*, logically completes the sentence: the "sobriquet" was given after the image was captured using local telescopes.

25. D

Difficulty: Hard
Category: Expression of Ideas
Getting to the Answer: Begin by identifying the two ideas that are connected by the missing word. The idea before the blank is that Ansel Adams mitigated his adolescent struggles by playing the piano and hiking. The idea after the blank is that his photography's visual imagery was a result of his early passions. Therefore, the correct choice will signal this is a cause-and-effect relationship. Choice **(D)** is correct.

Choice (A) is incorrect because it indicates contrast. Choices (B) and (C) signal a continuation of an idea, which does not logically fit this passage. "Eventually" conveys a time and "specifically" is used to refer to an exact purpose or use.

26. A

Difficulty: Medium
Category: Expression of Ideas
Getting to the Answer: Based on the question stem, the correct answer will identify the aim of the study. As you read the bullet points, pay careful attention to identifying *why* the sociologists conducted the study. The study is introduced in the third bullet point, which states that the sociologists wanted to know about the "content" (rather than the quantity, as described in the previous points) of tweets, especially relating to emotions throughout the day. The remaining points do not address the aim, but rather the procedure and findings of the study. So use the information in the third bullet point to predict that the aim was *to study the content about emotions in tweets throughout the day*. Choice **(A)** matches the prediction and is correct.

Choices (B) and (D) are incorrect because they concern the results, rather than the aim, of the study. Choice (C) concerns the procedure, not the aim, of the study and mentions the number, rather than the content, of tweets.

27. A

Difficulty: Hard
Category: Expression of Ideas
Getting to the Answer: Identify the goal that the correct answer will satisfy: a generalization about the kind of study conducted. Since the generalization is about the "kind of study," the correct answer will likely provide details about the methods or nature of the study itself, not just the study's conclusions. Look for both kinds of details as you read the bullet points. The first three points describe the Flower Portrait, which was dated 1609. The next three points summarize the study, including the techniques used (X-ray and mass spectrometry), its finding about a yellow pigment from the 1800s, and its conclusion that the painting was made in the 1800s. Predict that the correct answer will address the study's techniques and conclusions; **(A)** is correct. This choice correctly identifies the technique that dated the painting 200 years later (the early 1800s rather than 1609), as mass spectrometry was used to analyze the paint samples that were found to contain the yellow pigment from the 1800s.

Choice (B) is incorrect because it concerns art historians' techniques in general rather than the study of the Flower Portrait. Choices (C) and (D) are incorrect because they concern the findings and conclusions of the study rather than a generalization about the kind of study it was.

MATH: ROUTING MODULE ANSWERS AND EXPLANATIONS

1. C
Difficulty: Easy
Category: Algebra
Getting to the Answer: Although you could distribute the $\frac{1}{4}$, this would create some unpleasant fractions. An easier approach is to multiply both sides of the equation by 4 to get rid of the fraction and then solve from there:

$$\frac{1}{4}(x - 7) = 3$$
$$x - 7 = 12$$
$$x = 19$$

Choice **(C)** is correct. You could also backsolve by plugging the answer choices into the equation. Start with (B):

$$\frac{1}{4}(x - 7) = 3$$
$$\frac{1}{4}(7 - 7) = 3$$
$$\frac{1}{4}(0) = 3$$
$$0 = 3$$

Since the left side of the equation is smaller than the right, this value of x is too small. Move on to (C):

$$\frac{1}{4}(x - 7) = 3$$
$$\frac{1}{4}(19 - 7) = 3$$
$$\frac{1}{4}(12) = 3$$
$$3 = 3$$

This results in a true statement, so **(C)** is correct.

2. B
Difficulty: Easy
Category: Algebra
Getting to the Answer: Replace x with $x + 3$ in the function and simplify:

$$f(x + 3) = 5(x + 3) - 2$$
$$= 5x + 15 - 2$$
$$= 5x + 13$$

Choice **(B)** is correct.

3. A
Difficulty: Easy
Category: Algebra
Getting to the Answer: Instead of solving for b, see if you can solve for $-2b + 4$ directly. Start by adding 3 to both sides of the inequality to obtain $4b > 10$. Next, divide both sides by -2. Remember that when you divide by a negative, you must flip the inequality sign. You get $-2b < -5$. Now simply add 4 to both sides to obtain the desired expression: $-2b + 4 < -1$. The greatest possible integer value less than -1 is -2, so **(A)** is correct.

4. C
Difficulty: Easy
Category: Advanced Math
Getting to the Answer: To divide these two quadratic expressions, begin by factoring the numerator and denominator. Then cancel terms that appear on both the top and bottom:

$$\frac{x^2 + 6x + 9}{x^2 + 7x + 12} = \frac{(x + 3)(x + 3)}{(x + 4)(x + 3)}$$
$$= \frac{x + 3}{x + 4}$$

Choice **(C)** is correct.

5. 3
Difficulty: Easy
Category: Advanced Math
Getting to the Answer: Apply exponent rules to simplify the expression. Recall that $(x^a)^b = x^{ab}$.

$$\frac{x^4 y^3}{(x^2)^2 y^m} = \frac{x^4 y^3}{x^4 y^m}$$
$$= \frac{y^3}{y^m}$$

Since the expression is equal to 1, m must equal 3. Enter **3**.

6. B
Difficulty: Easy
Category: Problem-Solving and Data Analysis
Getting to the Answer: You can use a straightforward proportion to solve this question.

$$\frac{3 \text{ tiles}}{7.75 \text{ square feet}} = \frac{n \text{ tiles}}{186 \text{ square feet}}$$
$$558 = 7.75n$$
$$72 = n$$

Therefore, **(B)** is correct.

7. D
Difficulty: Easy
Category: Geometry and Trigonometry
Getting to the Answer: By definition, all sides of a square are equal. The diagonal of the square splits it into two 45-45-90 triangles.

Recall that 45-45-90 triangles have a side ratio of $x : x : x\sqrt{2}$. Since the diagonal of the square functions as the hypotenuse of the triangle, $x\sqrt{2} = 12\sqrt{2}$. This means that the side length x is 12. Therefore, the area of the square is $12(12) = 144$. Choice **(D)** is correct.

8. $-15/10$, $-3/2$, or -1.5
Difficulty: Medium
Category: Algebra
Getting to the Answer: Begin by simplifying the numerators of each fraction:

$$\frac{2y - (2y + 1)}{3y + 5} = \frac{4y + (3 - 4y)}{y}$$
$$\frac{2y - 2y - 1}{3y + 5} = \frac{4y + 3 - 4y}{y}$$
$$\frac{-1}{3y + 5} = \frac{3}{y}$$

Then cross-multiply to solve for y:

$$\frac{-1}{3y + 5} = \frac{3}{y}$$
$$-y = 3(3y + 5)$$
$$-y = 9y + 15$$
$$-10y = 15$$
$$y = -\frac{15}{10}$$
$$y = -\frac{3}{2}$$

You may enter **$-15/10$, $-3/2$,** or **-1.5,** the decimal equivalent.

9. D
Difficulty: Medium
Category: Algebra
Getting to the Answer: Recall that the number of solutions to a system of equations is how many times the two lines intersect. If a system has one solution, the lines will intersect at one point and therefore have different slopes and different y-intercepts. If a system has no solutions, the lines will be parallel (same slope but different y-intercepts). If a system has infinitely many solutions, the lines will be on top of each other (same slope and same y-intercept). One way to answer this question is to get both equations into $y = mx + b$ form to make it easy to compare slopes and y-intercepts:

$$2y + x = 9 \qquad 27 - 3x = 6y$$
$$2y = -x + 9 \qquad \frac{27}{6} - \frac{3x}{6} = y$$
$$y = -\frac{x}{2} + \frac{9}{2} \qquad \frac{9}{2} - \frac{x}{2} = y$$
$$y = -\frac{x}{2} + \frac{9}{2}$$

The two lines have the same slope and y-intercept, so **(D)** is correct.

10. A
Difficulty: Medium
Category: Algebra
Getting to the Answer: Whenever you see a line, think of the slope-intercept form $y = mx + b$. According to the graph, the y-intercept is 100. The line rises $50 in every 2-hour increment, so its slope is $\frac{50}{2} = 25$. Therefore, the equation of the line is $y = 25x + 100$. The question asks for the price of a 20-hour job, so plug in $x = 20$ and simplify: $y = \$25(20) + \$100 = \$500 + \$100 = \$600$. Choice **(A)** is correct.

11. C
Difficulty: Medium
Category: Advanced Math
Getting to the Answer: The maximum is the point that has the largest y-value. According to the graph, this is (4, 9). The minimum is the point that has the smallest y-value. This is (7, −8). Therefore, $(a, b) = (4, 9)$ and $(c, d) = (7, -8)$. The question asks for $\frac{d-b}{c-a}$, so plug in these values and simplify:

$$\frac{d-b}{c-a} = \frac{-8-9}{7-4}$$
$$= -\frac{17}{3}$$

Choice **(C)** is correct.

12. D
Difficulty: Medium
Category: Advanced Math
Getting to the Answer: If Kush improves by 1%, then his new score will be 100% + 1% = 101% of his old score. Since $101\% = \frac{101}{100} = 1.01$, his new score after one day will be 400(1.01). Using similar logic, his score two days later will be 400(1.01)(1.01), and his score three days later will be 400(1.01)(1.01)(1.01). You can generalize this idea to $400\,(1.01)^x$, where x is the number of days. Backsolve by plugging in each answer choice for x to see which one yields approximately 800:

(A) $400(1.01)^{40} = 595.55$

(B) $400(1.01)^{50} = 657.85$

(C) $400(1.01)^{60} = 726.68$

(D) $400(1.01)^{70} = 802.71$

Choice **(D)** is correct.

13. −1
Difficulty: Medium
Category: Advanced Math
Getting to the Answer: Recall that division by 0 is undefined. Therefore, a value of x that makes the denominator $g(x)$ equal to 0 would make the function $h(x)$ undefined. According to the table, $g(x) = 0$ when $x = -1$. Enter **−1**.

14. B
Difficulty: Medium
Category: Problem-Solving and Data Analysis
Getting to the Answer: The greatest outlier is located below the line of best fit at approximately April. The predicted yield from the line of best fit is about 40 bushels. The outlier point itself is about 25 bushels. Therefore, the difference is about 40 − 25 = 15 bushels. Choice **(B)** is correct.

15. B
Difficulty: Medium
Category: Geometry and Trigonometry
Getting to the Answer: There are 180° in a straight line, so the angle adjacent to 100° is 180° − 100° = 80°. Use the transversal that forms angle x to identify a corresponding angle:

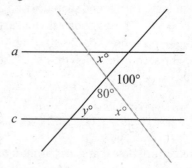

The angles of a triangle add up to 180°, so $x° + y° + 80° = 180°$ and $x° + y° = 180° − 80° = 100°$. Choice **(B)** is correct.

16. A
Difficulty: Hard
Category: Algebra
Getting to the Answer: Clean up the inequalities: divide the top inequality by 8 and the bottom inequality by 3:

$$x \le 3y + 5$$
$$x \le 2y + 4$$

Since both inequalities now have an isolated x, use substitution to set the other sides equal to each other and solve:

$$2y + 4 = 3y + 5$$
$$4 = y + 5$$
$$-1 = y$$

Is this the final answer? No! The question asks for the maximum value of x, not y. Plug -1 in for y in either inequality to determine the maximum value of x:

$$x \le 2y + 4$$
$$x \le 2(-1) + 4$$
$$x \le -2 + 4$$
$$x \le 2$$

The answer is **(A)**.

17. A
Difficulty: Hard
Category: Algebra
Getting to the Answer: Translate each statement into math. Let k represent the price of knives, s represent the price of spoons, and f represent the price of forks. The first sentence is equivalent to $4k + 5s + 6f = 7.90$. Using similar logic, the second sentence translates into $2k + 2s + 5f = 5.80$. The question asks for $2k + 3s + f$. You can obtain this expression directly simply by subtracting the second equation from the first.

$$\begin{array}{r} 4k + 5s + 6f = 7.90 \\ -(2k + 2s + 5f = 5.80) \\ \hline 2k + 3s + f = 2.10 \end{array}$$

Choice **(A)** is correct. Note that since the question gives you three unknowns but only two equations, it is impossible to determine the individual prices of knives, spoons, and forks.

18. A
Difficulty: Hard
Category: Advanced Math
Getting to the Answer: Focus first on the denominator of the fraction. To add these two fractions, you need a common denominator. Here, the common denominator is $(x - 3)(y + 5)$. Multiply the first fraction by $\dfrac{y + 5}{y + 5}$ and the second fraction by $\dfrac{x - 3}{x - 3}$. Then add the numerators and multiply the denominator.

$$\cfrac{1}{\dfrac{1}{x - 3} + \dfrac{1}{y + 5}} = \cfrac{1}{\dfrac{y + 5}{(x - 3)(y + 5)} + \dfrac{x - 3}{(x - 3)(y + 5)}}$$

$$= \cfrac{1}{\dfrac{x + y + 2}{(x - 3)(y + 5)}}$$

$$= \cfrac{1}{\dfrac{x + y + 2}{xy + 5x - 3y - 15}}$$

You are given that $xy = 15$, so plug this in and simplify.

$$\cfrac{1}{\dfrac{x + y + 2}{xy + 5x - 3y - 15}} = \cfrac{1}{\dfrac{x + y + 2}{15 + 5x - 3y - 15}}$$

$$= \cfrac{1}{\dfrac{x + y + 2}{5x - 3y}}$$

Recall that $\dfrac{1}{\frac{a}{b}} = \dfrac{b}{a}$. In other words, you can simplify this expression by taking the reciprocal of the fraction in the denominator:

$$\cfrac{1}{\dfrac{x + y + 2}{5x - 3y}} = \dfrac{5x - 3y}{x + y + 2}$$

Choice **(A)** is correct.

19. A
Difficulty: Hard
Category: Advanced Math
Getting to the Answer: To write the equation of a parabola, you need two things—the vertex and one other point. In this question, you already have a point, but you'll need to think creatively to find the vertex. The vertex of the parabola shown must lie on its axis of symmetry, which is halfway between the pair of symmetric points $(0, 8)$ and $(12, 8)$. This means that the x-coordinate of the vertex is halfway between 0 and 12, which is 6. To find the y-coordinate of the vertex, look at the range, $y \ge -4$. This means that the minimum value of the graph, and hence the y-coordinate of the vertex, is -4. Now, use the vertex $(6, -4)$ to set up a quadratic equation in vertex form: $y = a(x - h)^2 + k$. The result is $y = a(x - 6)^2 - 4$. Plug in either of the given points for x and y to find the value of a. Using $(0, 8)$, the result is:

$$y = a(x - 6)^2 - 4$$
$$8 = a(0 - 6)^2 - 4$$
$$8 = 36a - 4$$
$$12 = 36a$$
$$a = \frac{12}{36} = \frac{1}{3}$$

This matches **(A)**.

20. 20

Difficulty: Hard

Category: Problem-Solving and Data Analysis

Getting to the Answer: Let x represent the price of the furniture after the first month, and use the percent change formula to set up a system of equations.

Percent increase or decrease
$$= \frac{\text{amount of increase or decrease}}{\text{original amount}} \times 100\%$$

Note that the question indicates a percent decrease, so the percent change after the first month is:

$$-p = \frac{x - 100}{100} \times 100\%$$

The percent change after the second month is:

$$-p = \frac{64 - x}{x} \times 100\%$$

Set the two equations equal to each other and solve for x.

$$\frac{x - 100}{100} \times 100\% = \frac{64 - x}{x} \times 100\%$$
$$\frac{x - 100}{100} = \frac{64 - x}{x}$$
$$x(x - 100) = 100(64 - x)$$
$$x^2 - 100x = 6,400 - 100x$$
$$x^2 = 6,400$$
$$x = \sqrt{6,400}$$
$$x = 80$$

Then plug $x = 80$ into one of the equations to determine p.

$$-p = \frac{80 - 100}{100} \times 100\%$$
$$-p = -20\%$$
$$p = 20\%$$

Enter **20**.

You could also answer this question by setting up the exponential decay equation as $100(1 - p)^2 = 64$ to find that $p = .2$ or 20%. Either way, you would enter **20**.

21. A

Difficulty: Hard

Category: Problem-Solving and Data Analysis

Getting to the Answer: The question asks *on average* how much *longer* customers are willing to wait. So, you will need to find a weighted average for each day. Start with Friday. Multiply each wait time by the height of the bar (the number of people willing to wait for that amount of time on that night) to calculate the sum of

minutes waited, and then divide by the total number of people who took the Friday survey:

$$\frac{20(70) + 25(46) + 30(38) + 35(33) + 40(20) + 45(9)}{70 + 46 + 38 + 33 + 20 + 9}$$
$$\frac{1,400 + 1,150 + 1,140 + 1,155 + 800 + 405}{216}$$
$$\frac{6,050}{216} \approx 28$$

Now, do the same thing for Saturday:

$$\frac{20(75) + 25(64) + 30(45) + 35(43) + 40(40) + 45(17)}{75 + 64 + 45 + 43 + 40 + 17}$$
$$\frac{1,500 + 1,600 + 1,350 + 1,505 + 1,600 + 765}{284}$$
$$\frac{8,320}{284} \approx 29.3$$

Therefore, people are willing to wait approximately $29.3 - 28.0 = 1.3$ minutes longer on Saturday than Friday. **(A)** is correct.

22. 8

Difficulty: Hard

Category: Geometry and Trigonometry

Getting to the Answer: Notice that two radii and an arc form each section, so the amount of steel needed for one section is the length of the radius times 2, plus the length of the outer arc.

The arena is divided into 12 equal sections through the center, so divide 360 by 12 to find that the central angle measure for each section is 30 degrees. Now, use the arc length formula:

$$\frac{n°}{360°} \times 2\pi r = \frac{30°}{360°} \times 2\pi r$$
$$= \frac{\pi}{6} r$$

So, the amount of steel needed to enforce 1 bull section is $2r + \frac{\pi}{6}r$ yards, and the amount of steel needed for 4 bull sections is $4\left(2r + \frac{\pi}{6}r\right)$. Set this equal to the total yards given in the question, $64 + \frac{16\pi}{3}$, and solve for r:

$$64 + \frac{16\pi}{3} = 4\left(2r + \frac{\pi}{6}r\right)$$
$$64 + \frac{16\pi}{3} = 8r + \frac{2\pi}{3}r$$

Comparing 64 to $8r$ and $\frac{16\pi}{3}$ to $\frac{2\pi}{3}r$ gives $r = 8$. Enter **8**.

MATH: MODULE A ANSWERS AND EXPLANATIONS

1. B
Difficulty: Easy
Category: Algebra
Getting to the Answer: Since the question specifies that each pound of strawberries, p, costs $3, the correct function must multiply p times 3, or $3p$. That's enough to eliminate (C) and (D). You're also told that each customer pays an up-front entry fee of $10, so that means the function has to add 10 to $3p$. Choice **(B)** is the match.

2. C
Difficulty: Easy
Category: Algebra
Getting to the Answer: Use the standard steps of algebra to solve for x, starting by distributing the 4 into the parentheses on the right side of the equation:

$$11x - 22 = 4x - 8$$
$$11x = 4x + 14$$
$$7x = 14$$
$$x = 2$$

The question asks for the value of $2x$, and that's 4, so **(C)** is correct.

3. B
Difficulty: Easy
Category: Algebra
Getting to the Answer: The graph indicates the number of months on the x-axis and the price in dollars on the y-axis. A quick examination shows a $30 charge before any time has passed—at 0 months—so this represents the initial membership fee. To determine the fixed cost for each month, you can either eyeball the change in cost per month or use the slope formula, $\frac{y_2 - y_1}{x_2 - x_1}$. If you choose to use the slope formula, identify two points along the line, for example, (1, 50) and (2, 70), and then plug the values in to solve for cost per month: $\frac{70 - 50}{2 - 1} = \frac{20}{1}$, or $20 per month. Alternatively, you can look at the change in rise in cost from one month to the next; that's $20.

Choice **(B)** is correct.

4. C
Difficulty: Easy
Category: Algebra
Getting to the Answer: Lines can be represented in the slope-intercept form, $y = mx + b$, in which m represents the slope of the line and b represents the y-intercept (where the line crosses the y-axis).

Examine the graph; you can see that the line crosses the y-axis at 2, so eliminate (B). Next, determine the slope of the line. Slope is $\frac{\text{rise}}{\text{run}}$. You might eyeball the slope and notice that it rises one grid line for every two it runs to the right; that's a slope of $\frac{1}{2}$. Alternatively, you can calculate the slope by picking two points, for example, (0, 2) and (2, 3), and then plug them into the slope formula:

$$m = \frac{y_2 - y_1}{x_2 - x_1}$$
$$m = \frac{3 - 2}{2 - 0}$$
$$m = \frac{1}{2}$$

(C) is correct.

5. 1
Difficulty: Easy
Category: Algebra
Getting to the Answer: The simplest way to find the answer here is to examine the graph of the given quadratic equation. The graph of a quadratic equation takes the form of a parabola, and the roots of the equation are the points where the parabola intersects the x-axis. In this case, those points are at -1 and 2. Thus, the sum is $-1 + 2 = 1$. Enter **1**.

6. D
Difficulty: Easy
Category: Algebra
Getting to the Answer: The key to answering this question efficiently is to recognize that the quadratic expression given, $x^2 - 2xy + y^2$, is a "classic quadratic" equivalent to $(x - y)^2$. Since the question states that $x - y = 6$ and $x^2 - 2xy + y^2 = (x - y)^2$, then $x^2 - 2xy + y^2 = 6^2 = 36$.

Alternatively, if you didn't recognize the classic quadratic, you could solve this question by picking numbers. For example, if you say $x = 8$ and $y = 2$, then the quadratic expression becomes $8^2 - 2(8)(2) + 2^2 = 64 - 32 + 4 = 36$.

Choice **(D)** is correct.

7. D
Difficulty: Easy
Category: Algebra
Getting to the Answer: A root is canceled by raising the root to the same power as the root's index value. For example, a cube (3rd) root is canceled by cubing it (raising it to the 3rd power). In this case, that looks like this:

$$\sqrt[3]{x} = 8$$
$$(\sqrt[3]{x})^3 = 8^3$$
$$x = 8 \times 8 \times 8$$
$$x = 512$$

Choice **(D)** is correct.

8. 1440
Difficulty: Easy
Category: Problem-Solving and Data Analysis
Getting to the Answer: This rates question involves unit conversion from hours to days. You could use either straight multiplication or conversion ratios to solve:

$$6 \text{ days} \times \frac{8 \text{ hours}}{1 \text{ day}} \times \frac{30 \text{ miles}}{1 \text{ hour}} = 1{,}440 \text{ miles}$$

Enter **1440**.

9. C
Difficulty: Easy
Category: Problem-Solving and Data Analysis
Getting to the Answer: When calculating a series of successive percent adjustments, it's important to remember that each successive percent adjustment is based on an adjusted value. Calculating each month's change in weight looks like this:

$$10 + 0.35(10) = 13.5$$
$$13.5 + 0.35(13.5) = 18.225$$
$$18.225 + 0.35(18.225) \approx 24.604$$
$$24.604 + 0.35(24.604) \approx 33.215$$

So after 4 months, the puppy weighs about 33 pounds. However, there's a more efficient way of calculating this: the exponential change formula, $y = a(1 + r)^t$, where y is the final value, a is the starting value, r is

the rate of change, and t is the time. Filling in the given values looks like this:

$$\text{final weight} = 10(1.35)^4 \approx 33.215$$

Therefore, **(C)** is correct.

10. C
Difficulty: Easy
Category: Geometry and Trigonometry
Getting to the Answer: The radius is line BC. Since this is what the question asks you to find, call it r. The radius is adjacent to angle B, which is $37°$. Finally, the hypotenuse is given as 15. Recall that $\cos \theta = \frac{\text{adjacent}}{\text{hypotenuse}}$. Fill in what you know: $\cos 37° = \frac{r}{15}$. Therefore, $r = 15 \cos 37°$, which matches **(C)**.

11. D
Difficulty: Easy
Category: Geometry and Trigonometry
Getting to the Answer: The perimeter of a rectangle is $2(\text{length}) + 2(\text{width})$. In this case, the rectangle's width is $2a$. The question states that the length is 3.5 times the width, so that's $3.5 \times 2a = 7a$.

Plugging these values into the perimeter formula yields $2(7a) + 2(2a) = 14a + 4a = 18a$.

Choice **(D)** is correct.

12. A
Difficulty: Medium
Category: Algebra
Getting to the Answer: Since the question specifies that $y = z^2$ and $z = 6$, plug 6 in for z to find y: $y = 6^2 = 36$.

To isolate x, first cancel the root by squaring both sides of the equation:

$$\sqrt{xy} = 3$$
$$(\sqrt{xy})^2 = 3^2$$
$$xy = 9$$

Now plug 36 in for y and solve for x:

$$xy = 9$$
$$x(36) = 9$$
$$x = \frac{9}{36}$$
$$x = \frac{1}{4}$$

Choice **(A)** is correct.

13. 10
Difficulty: Medium
Category: Algebra
Getting to the Answer: To find the value range of x, systematically isolate x using the rules of algebra:

$$-4x + 46 \leq x - 4$$
$$46 \leq 5x - 4$$
$$50 \leq 5x$$
$$10 \leq x$$

Thus, 10 is the minimum value of x. Enter **10**.

14. A
Difficulty: Medium
Category: Algebra
Getting to the Answer: The equation $y = mx + b$ is used to model linear growth. Since the mass depends on the time elapsed, time is the x-variable and mass is the y-variable. The initial mass is 10 grams, so write this as the point $(0, 10)$. The mass is 14 grams after 48 hours, so write this as $(48, 14)$. First, find the slope: $\frac{y_2 - y_1}{x_2 - x_1} = \frac{14 - 10}{48 - 0} = \frac{4}{48} = \frac{1}{12}$. The point $(0, 10)$ indicates that 10 is the y-intercept. Therefore, the equation is $y = \frac{1}{12}x + 10$. You are asked to find the mass when $t = 6$, so plug in this value for x and simplify:

$$y = \frac{1}{12}x + 10$$
$$= \frac{1}{12}(6) + 10$$
$$= \frac{6}{12} + 10$$
$$= \frac{1}{2} + 10$$
$$= 10.5$$

Choice **(A)** is correct.

15. B
Difficulty: Medium
Category: Advanced Math
Getting to the Answer: Since absolute value gives a non-negative value, the expression inside the absolute value may be equal to $2x$ or $-2x$. In other words, an absolute value equation will "split" into a positive and a negative case. Solving each case gives the two solutions to the equation:

$$3x - 6 = 2x \qquad 3x - 6 = -2x$$
$$-6 = -x \qquad -6 = -5x$$
$$6 = x \qquad \frac{6}{5} = x$$

The question asks for the product of the solutions, which is $6\left(\frac{6}{5}\right) = \frac{36}{5}$. Choice **(B)** is correct.

16. D
Difficulty: Medium
Category: Advanced Math
Getting to the Answer: Before you do anything, notice that you can divide every term by 2. While division by 0 is undefined, dividing 0 by a real number like 2 will always result in 0.

$$x^2 + 8x + 1 = 0$$

You usually solve quadratics by factoring. Unfortunately, this will not work here because you cannot find two real numbers whose product is 1 and sum is 8. Since the coefficient in front of the x^2 term is 1, use completing the square instead. Begin by moving the constant term to the other side.

$$x^2 + 8x = -1$$

Then add $\left(\frac{8}{2}\right)^2 = 16$ to both sides of the equation. This will create a perfect square trinomial that is easy to factor. Solve the resulting equation for x:

$$x^2 + 8x + 16 = -1 + 16$$
$$x^2 + 8x + 16 = 15$$
$$(x + 4)(x + 4) = 15$$
$$(x + 4)^2 = 15$$
$$x + 4 = \pm\sqrt{15}$$
$$x = \pm\sqrt{15} - 4$$

Choice **(D)** is correct.

17. C
Difficulty: Medium
Category: Problem-Solving and Data Analysis
Getting to the Answer: Each grid line along the vertical axis represents 5 units, so look for points that are at least two grid lines away from the line of best fit. The people who have BMIs of 20, 25, and 28 have LDLs that are 10 or more milligrams per deciliter greater than the LDLs predicted by the line of best fit. This represents 3 people. **(C)** is correct.

18. 16/20, 4/5, 0.8, or .8
Difficulty: Medium
Category: Geometry and Trigonometry
Getting to the Answer: Max's current route is $9 + 40 = 49$ miles. Since he must drive to and from work each day, he drives a total of $49(2) = 98$ miles.

Now determine his expressway route. You can find this using the Pythagorean theorem.

$$9^2 + 40^2 = c^2$$
$$81 + 1600 = c^2$$
$$1681 = c^2$$
$$41 = c$$

Since he goes to and from work each day, he drives a total of $41(2) = 82$ miles. Therefore, he will save $98 - 82 = 16$ miles per day by taking the expressway.

Don't stop yet! The question asks how many *gallons* per day he will save. To find this, apply the conversion factor of 20 miles per gallon:

$$16 \text{ miles} \times \left(\frac{1 \text{ gallon}}{20 \text{ miles}}\right) = \frac{16}{20} \text{ gallons} = 0.8 \text{ gallons}$$

Enter **16/20, 4/5, 0.8,** or **.8** into the box.

19. D
Difficulty: Medium
Category: Advanced Math
Getting to the Answer: Simplify the expression using polynomial long division:

$$\begin{array}{r} 3x + 2 \\ x+1\overline{)3x^2 + 5x - 7} \\ -(3x^2 + 3x) \\ \hline 2x - 7 \\ -(2x+2) \\ \hline -9 \end{array}$$

The quotient is therefore $3x + 2 - \dfrac{9}{x+1}$. Choice **(D)** is correct.

20. A
Difficulty: Hard
Category: Algebra
Getting to the Answer: There are a number of ways to answer this question. Backsolving each answer choice into the equation to see which choice makes the equation valid is one way. Choice **(A)** is correct: $2(3)^2 - 3 - 15 = 18 - 3 - 15 = 0$.

Another possible way is to factor the quadratic equation into binomials using reverse-FOIL. Since the leading coefficient is 2, the first term in the two parentheses must be $2x$ and x: $(2x \pm ?)(x \pm ?) = 0$.

The last term in the quadratic is -15, so the last terms of the two binomials have to be factors of -15. There are only four possible pairs: 1 and -15, -1 and 15, -3

and 5, or 3 and -5. It also indicates that there will be one $+$ sign and one $-$ sign in the parentheses.

It may take some trial-and-error to identify the correct factors of -15. Since the coefficient of the middle term in the quadratic is -1, you can eliminate 1 and -15 and -1 and 15, since neither will produce a middle coefficient of -1.

Now test -3 and 5: if the factors are $(2x - 3)(x + 5)$, FOIL-ing yields $2x^2 + 10x - 3x - 15$, which simplifies to $2x^2 + 7x - 15$. That's not a match for the original equation, so reverse the second terms in the parentheses and test them: $(2x + 5)(x - 3) = 2x^2 - 6x + 5x - 15 = 2x^2 - x - 15$. That's a match.

Now set the two values in the parentheses equal to 0 to calculate the possible value of x:

$$2x + 5 = 0$$
$$2x = -5$$
$$x = \frac{-5}{2}$$

This value is not among the answer choices, so try the other parenthesis:

$$x - 3 = 0$$
$$x = 3$$

Choice **(A)** is correct.

21. A
Difficulty: Hard
Category: Advanced Math
Getting to the Answer: Examining the answer choices, you notice that none of them are linear functions. In situations like these, the best strategy is to plug in points from the table and eliminate answer choices that do not match. Start with $(0, -1)$. Plug in 0 for x and see which answer choices yield -1:

(A) $2(0)^2 - 1 = 0 - 1$
            $= -1$

(B) $2(0)^3 - 1 = 0 - 1$
            $= -1$

(C) $2^{2(0)} - 1 = 1 - 1$
            $= 0$

(D) $2^0 - 1 = 1 - 1$
            $= 0$

Eliminate (C) and (D). Now look at the second row of the table. Unfortunately, both (A) and (B) give 1 when you plug in $x = 1$. This does not let you distinguish between them. To decide between (A) and (B), move to the third row. Plug $x = 2$ into the remaining answer choices and see which one yields 7:

$$\text{(A)} \quad 2(2)^2 - 1 = 8 - 1$$
$$= 7$$
$$\text{(B)} \quad 2(2)^3 - 1 = 16 - 1$$
$$= 15$$

Choice **(A)** is correct.

22. 20
Difficulty: Hard
Category: Geometry and Trigonometry
Getting to the Answer: The two triangles have equal angles, so they are similar. Similar triangles have proportional corresponding sides. The perimeter of a triangle is simply the sum of all its sides. Since the ratio of the perimeters is given as 7:4, this is also the ratio of the sides. Use this to find the missing side of the larger triangle.

$$\frac{7}{4} = \frac{x}{\frac{52}{7}}$$
$$7\left(\frac{52}{7}\right) = 4x$$
$$52 = 4x$$
$$13 = x$$

The perimeter of the larger triangle is therefore $10 + 12 + 13 = 35$. Set up another proportion to find the perimeter of the smaller triangle.

$$\frac{4}{7} = \frac{x}{35}$$
$$7x = 140$$
$$x = 20$$

Enter **20**.

MATH: MODULE B ANSWERS AND EXPLANATIONS

1. 16
Difficulty: Easy
Category: Algebra
Getting to the Answer: When you see an expression such as $f(x)$, it means to substitute the given value for x in the function's equation. When there is more than one function involved, pay careful attention to which function should be evaluated first. You are looking for the value of $f(x)$ at $x = 3$. Because $f(x)$ is defined in terms of $g(x)$, evaluate $g(3)$ first by substituting 3 for x in the expression $x + 5$:

$$g(3) = 3 + 5 = 8$$
$$f(3) = 2g(3) = 2(8) = 16$$

The correct answer is **16**.

2. C
Difficulty: Easy
Category: Advanced Math
Getting to the Answer: Don't be tempted—you can't simply cancel one term when a polynomial is divided by a monomial. Instead, find the greatest common factor of *both* the numerator and the denominator. Factor out the greatest common factor from the numerator and from the denominator, and then you can cancel it. The greatest common factor is $12x^2$. Here is the math:

$$\frac{24x^4 + 36x^3 - 12x^2}{12x^2}$$
$$= \frac{\cancel{12x^2}(2x^2 + 3x - 1)}{\cancel{12x^2}}$$
$$= 2x^2 + 3x - 1$$

This matches **(C)**.

3. A
Difficulty: Easy
Category: Problem-Solving and Data Analysis
Getting to the Answer: Find what you need about the group from the follow-up survey. Then, extrapolate to see which answer choice matches your calculations. First, determine the number of first-year students who fall into each of the three groups of the follow-up survey:

Percent excited to continue: $\frac{93}{150} \times 100\% = 62\%$

Percent not excited to continue: $\frac{37}{150} \times 100\% \approx 24.67\%$

Percent who do not know yet whether they are excited to continue: $\frac{20}{150} \times 100\% \approx 13.33\%$

There are 1,195 first-year students currently enrolled in foreign language studies, making the number excited to continue $0.62 \times 1,195 = 740.9 \approx 741$; the number not excited to continue $0.2467 \times 1,195 \approx 294.8 \approx 295$; and the number who do not know yet whether they are excited to continue $0.1333 \times 1,195 \approx 159.3 \approx 159$. Choice (A) states that about 740 first-year students are excited to continue their foreign language studies, which matches these findings. Choice **(A)** is therefore correct.

4. D
Difficulty: Medium
Category: Algebra
Getting to the Answer: Read the question for key phrases to determine the proper inequality signs. The question states that the firm must hire "at least" 8 employees, and x and y represent the numbers of drivers and mechanics, respectively. That means x plus y is greater than or equal to 8. That's "$x + y \geq 8$." You can eliminate (C).

The question also states that drivers earn \$1,120 each and mechanics earn \$900 each and that the firm will pay a total of "no more than \$8,300 per week." That means *1,120 times the number of drivers plus 900 times the number of mechanics is less than or equal to 8,300.* That's "$1,120x + 900y \leq 8,300$." Eliminate (A) and (B). **(D)** is correct.

5. 1
Difficulty: Medium
Category: Algebra
Getting to the Answer: You can graph these two equations to look for the number of intersection points, or you can solve the system algebraically. If doing the latter, start by setting the second equation equal to y by adding x to both sides: $y = x - 7$. Since both equations are equal to y, you can now set them equal to each other: $3x^2 + 7x - 4 = x - 7$. Next, subtract the terms from the right side to yield a quadratic equation set equal to 0: $3x^2 + 6x + 3 = 0$. There are two ways to determine the number of solutions from this equation: by finding the value of the discriminant ($b^2 - 4ac$) or by factoring.

Using the discriminant, you get $36 - 4(3)(3) = 0$. When the discriminant of a quadratic is equal to 0, there is one solution.

Factoring yields $(3x + 3)(x + 1) = 0$. Solving for the value of x in each set of parentheses results in $x = -1$ in both cases. That's one solution.

Enter **1**.

6.   C
Difficulty: Medium
Category: Algebra
Getting to the Answer: Start by filling in the known values. The function described is linear (because the growth is a constant value each year) so b in the function is the starting value, which is 720.

Next, you need to determine the slope, m. The trust will grow by 84 acres per year, but the value of the function represents *months*. Therefore, you have to divide the yearly value, 84, by 12 to find the monthly growth rate (the slope). Thus, $m = 84 \div 12 = 7$. You're looking for the value of x when $f(x) = 1,126$. Plugging these values in yields $1,126 = 7x + 720$. Now use algebra to solve for x:

$$
\begin{aligned}
1{,}126 &= 7x + 720 \\
406 &= 7x \\
58 &= x
\end{aligned}
$$

That's **(C)**.

7.   B
Difficulty: Medium
Category: Advanced Math
Getting to the Answer: The given function $g(x)$ is quadratic, which means it graphs as a parabola. Because the a-coefficient is positive, the parabola opens upward. That means the minimum value of $g(x)$ is the y-value of the vertex (called k).

To solve for the value of k, first solve for the x-coordinate of the vertex, h. Use the equation $h = \dfrac{-b}{2a}$:

$$
\begin{aligned}
h &= \frac{-12}{6} \\
h &= -2
\end{aligned}
$$

Now plug this value into the original equation to solve for k:

$$
\begin{aligned}
k &= 3(-2)^2 + 12(-2) + 3 \\
k &= 12 - 24 + 3 \\
k &= -9
\end{aligned}
$$

That's the minimum value of $g(x)$, but the question asks for the minimum value of $g(x) + 3$, so that's $-9 + 3 = -6$. Choice **(B)** is correct.

You can also solve this by using a graphing calculator, but be careful with this as well. Graphing the equation $y = 3x^2 + 12x + 3$ and visually inspecting the graph will not get you to the correct answer. Since the question asks for $g(x) + 3$, you will either need to add 3 to the results you see, $-9 + 3 = -6$, or graph
$y = 3x^2 + 12x + 3 + 3$
(or $y = 3x^2 + 12x + 6$) to lead you to choice **(B)**.

8.   A
Difficulty: Medium
Category: Advanced Math
Getting to the Answer: The roots of an equation are the same as its solutions. The choices contain radicals, which tells you that the equation can't be factored. Instead, either complete the square or solve the equation using the quadratic formula, whichever you are most comfortable using. The equation is already written in the form $y = ax^2 + bx + c$ and the coefficients are fairly small, so using the quadratic formula is probably the quickest method. Jot down the values that you'll need: $a = 2$, $b = 4$, and $c = -3$. Then, substitute these values into the quadratic formula and simplify:

$$
\begin{aligned}
x &= \frac{-b \pm \sqrt{b^2 - 4ac}}{2a} \\
&= \frac{-(4) \pm \sqrt{(4)^2 - 4(2)(-3)}}{2(2)} \\
&= \frac{-4 \pm \sqrt{16 + 24}}{4} \\
&= \frac{-4 \pm \sqrt{40}}{4}
\end{aligned}
$$

This is not one of the answer choices, so simplify the radical. To do this, look for a perfect square that divides into 40 and take its square root:

$$
\begin{aligned}
x &= \frac{-4 \pm \sqrt{4 \times 10}}{4} \\
&= \frac{-4 \pm 2\sqrt{10}}{4} \\
&= \frac{-2 \pm \sqrt{10}}{2}
\end{aligned}
$$

Be careful—you can't simplify the answer any further because you cannot divide the square root of 10 by 2, so **(A)** is correct.

9.   A
Difficulty: Medium
Category: Advanced Math
Getting to the Answer: The description in the question "increases at a rate of 50 percent per day" indicates exponential growth. The exponential growth formula is $f(x) = f(0) \times (1 + r)^x$, where $f(0)$ is the starting value, r is the rate of increase, and x is the number of time periods. Plug in the known values from the question to solve for $f(0)$:

$$6{,}750 = f(0) \times (1.5)^3$$
$$6{,}750 = f(0) \times 3.375$$
$$\frac{6{,}750}{3.375} = f(0)$$
$$2{,}000 = f(0)$$

Alternatively, you could backsolve to find the answer. Starting with (B), 3,000, you can increase the value by 50% a day for three days:

$$3{,}000 \times 1.5 = 4{,}500$$
$$4{,}500 \times 1.5 = 6{,}750$$
$$6{,}750 \times 1.5 = 10{,}125$$

Since this process reaches the target value, 6,750, after only two days, 3,000 is too large for a starting value. Answer (A) is the only smaller value.

Thus, **(A)** is correct.

10.   C
Difficulty: Medium
Category: Problem-Solving and Data Analysis
Getting to the Answer: First, use the average formula to calculate the sum of the 5 original quizzes:

$$\text{Average} = \frac{\text{sum of terms}}{\text{number of terms}}$$
$$80 = \frac{\text{sum of terms}}{5}$$
$$400 = \text{sum of terms}$$

Next, calculate the sum of the 4 remaining quizzes after the lowest score has been removed:

$$83 = \frac{\text{sum of terms}}{4}$$
$$332 = \text{sum of terms}$$

Now subtract the second sum from the first to determine the difference, which represents the score that was removed: $400 - 332 = 68$. **(C)** is correct.

11.   D
Difficulty: Medium
Category: Geometry and Trigonometry
Getting to the Answer: Lines m and n are parallel, so that means the alternate interior angles formed by AE are the same and the alternate interior angles formed by BD are the same. Since the intersection at point C forms vertical angles, these vertical angles are the same as well. That means triangles ABC and EDC are similar.

Triangle ABC is a right triangle with a side length of 5 and a hypotenuse of 13; while you could use the Pythagorean theorem to solve for the missing side, it's more efficient to recognize that this is a common Pythagorean triple: the 5-12-13. That means the length of BC is 12.

Side AB with a length of 5 corresponds to side DE with a length of 9, so the ratio of side lengths between triangle EDC and triangle ABC is $\frac{9}{5}$. To determine the length of CD, which corresponds to side BC, set up a proportion:

$$\frac{9}{5} = \frac{CD}{BC}$$
$$\frac{9}{5} = \frac{CD}{12}$$
$$108 = 5 \times CD$$
$$21.6 = CD$$

The question asks for the length of BD, and that's $12 + 21.6 = 33.6$. Choice **(D)** is correct.

12.   A
Difficulty: Hard
Category: Algebra
Getting to the Answer: The key to answering this question is to define the number of gallons of each type of syrup. There are 8 gallons in total and x gallons of pancake syrup, so the remaining gallons, $8 - x$, must be maple syrup.

Each gallon of pancake syrup costs \$14 and each gallon of maple syrup costs \$33, so you can set up an equation to represent this cost: $c = 14x + 33(8 - x)$. This equation does not appear among the answer choices, so simplify the equation:

$$c = 14x + 33(8 - x)$$
$$c = 14x + 264 - 33x$$
$$c = -19x + 264$$

Choice **(A)** is correct.

13. B
Difficulty: Hard
Category: Algebra
Getting to the Answer: The average monthly revenue for one property will be the landscape maintenance fee (c) plus the rate per square yards (y) times the average lawn area (z). Thus, the monthly revenue for x properties would be $(c + yz)x$. **(B)** is correct. Note that further multiplying $(c + yz)x$ by m would give the total revenue after m months.

14. 5
Difficulty: Hard
Category: Algebra
Getting to the Answer: When solving a system of linear equations, always check to see if you can cancel out one of the variables by multiplying one or both of the equations by a fairly small number and then adding the two equations. Before you enter an answer, check that you answered the right question (here, the value of $\frac{x}{y}$).

Multiply the top equation by 3 and the bottom equation by -2. Then combine the equations to eliminate the terms that have x's in them:

$$3[2x + 8y = 9] \rightarrow 6x + 24y = 27$$
$$-2[3x + 5y = 10] \rightarrow -6x - 10y = -20$$
$$\overline{14y = 7}$$
$$y = \frac{7}{14}$$
$$y = \frac{1}{2}$$

The question asks for the value of $\frac{x}{y}$, so you need to find the value of x too. Substitute $y = \frac{1}{2}$ into the top equation and solve for x:

$$2x + 8\left(\frac{1}{2}\right) = 9$$
$$2x + 4 = 9$$
$$2x = 5$$
$$x = \frac{5}{2}$$

The value of $\frac{x}{y}$ is $\dfrac{\frac{5}{2}}{\frac{1}{2}} = \frac{5}{2} \times \frac{2}{1} = 5$. Enter **5**.

15. C
Difficulty: Hard
Category: Advanced Math
Getting to the Answer: Since absolute value gives a non-negative value, the expression inside the absolute value may be equal to x or $-x$. Solving for each case gives the solutions to the equation.

$$\frac{4 + 2x}{x + 2} = x \qquad\qquad \frac{4 + 2x}{x + 2} = -x$$
$$4 + 2x = x(x + 2) \qquad 4 + 2x = -x(x + 2)$$
$$4 + 2x = x^2 + 2x \qquad 4 + 2x = -x^2 - 2x$$
$$4 = x^2 \qquad\qquad x^2 + 4x + 4 = 0$$
$$\sqrt{4} = x \qquad\qquad (x + 2)(x + 2) = 0$$
$$\pm 2 = x \qquad\qquad x = -2$$

Note that when $x = -2$, $\frac{4 + 2x}{x + 2}$ is undefined and the absolute value of the expression equals a negative value, which cannot be true. Thus, the only solution is $x = 2$. **(C)** is correct.

16. B
Difficulty: Hard
Category: Advanced Math
Getting to the Answer: The solutions, or x-intercepts, of a polynomial are the factors of that polynomial. This polynomial has x-intercepts of a, 0, and d. The factors that generate those solutions are $(x - a)$, x, and $(x - d)$. **(B)** is correct. Note that the graph *touches* but does not cross the x-axis at $x = 0$, so the factor is raised to an even exponent.

Note that (A) is not correct because the graph shows $x = a$, not $x = -a$. For example, if $a = -3$, the factor would be $x - a$ or $x - (-3)$ and $x = a = -3$, not $x = -a = -(-3) = 3$.

17. B
Difficulty: Hard
Category: Advanced Math
Getting to the Answer: The given equation $y = ax^2 - \frac{b^2}{4}$ follows the classic quadratic pattern $x^2 - y^2 = (x + y)(x - y)$.

Take the square root of each term in $ax^2 - \frac{b^2}{4}$ to find the factors:

$$\sqrt{ax^2} = \sqrt{a}\,\sqrt{x^2} = \sqrt{a}\,x$$
and
$$\sqrt{\frac{b^2}{4}} = \frac{\sqrt{b^2}}{\sqrt{4}} = \frac{b}{2}$$

Thus, $ax^2 - \frac{b^2}{4} = \left(\sqrt{a}x + \frac{b}{2}\right)\left(\sqrt{a}x - \frac{b}{2}\right)$. **(B)** is correct.

18. D
Difficulty: Hard
Category: Advanced Math
Getting to the Answer: Start by rearranging each equation to set each equal to y:

$$y = 2x^2 + 4x + 5$$
$$y = 5x + 8$$

With a graphing calculator, you could graph the two equations to find the point of intersection. Otherwise, since both equations are equal to y, they are also equal to each other. Set them equal, rearrange the two equations into one quadratic that's set equal to 0, and then factor to solve for the values of x:

$$2x^2 + 4x + 5 = 5x + 8$$
$$2x^2 - x - 3 = 0$$
$$(2x - 3)(x + 1) = 0$$
$$x = \frac{3}{2}, x = -1$$

You're given that (c, d) is a point of intersection, and asked to find d, the y-value at that point. You've already been given that $y = 15.5$, where $x = \frac{3}{2}$, so that means $c = -1$. Plug -1 in for x in the equation $y = 5x + 8$ to solve for d:

$$y = 5x + 8$$
$$y = 5(-1) + 8$$
$$y = 3$$

Thus, $d = 3$. The correct answer is **(D)**.

19. 4/10, 2/5, 0.4, or .4
Difficulty: Hard
Category: Problem-Solving and Data Analysis
Getting to the Answer: Although the cells for the numbers of each type and size of disk are empty, you can set up algebraic expressions in each cell based on the information given in the question. Since there are 3 small zinc disks for every 5 large zinc disks, you can denote these as $3z$ and $5z$. There are 4 small copper disks for every 7 large copper disks, so you can denote those $4c$ and $7c$.

Disks		
Metal	Small	Large
Zinc	$3z$	$5z$
Copper	$4c$	$7c$
Total	100	170

You can now set up a system of equations to determine the number of each type of disk:

Small disks: $3z + 4c = 100$
Large disks: $5z + 7c = 170$

Since you're interested in the number of small copper disks, solve the system of equations for c. Because all of the coefficients are different, combination (elimination) is a better approach to solving the system. You'll need to multiply both equations to establish a common coefficient for the z terms in order to cancel them out:

$$5(3z + 4c = 100)$$
$$3(5z + 7c = 170)$$

This multiplication yields the following equations:

$$15z + 20c = 500$$
$$15z + 21c = 510$$

Subtracting the first equation from the second yields $c = 10$. Therefore, the number of small copper disks is $4c = 4 \times 10 = 40$. Since the total number of small disks is 100, the probability that a small disk will be copper is $\frac{40}{100} = 0.4$. Enter **4/10, 2/5, 0.4, or .4**.

20. C
Difficulty: Hard
Category: Geometry and Trigonometry
Getting to the Answer: The question asks for the radius. When the equation of a circle is in the form $(x - h)^2 + (y - k)^2 = r^2$, the r represents the radius. The question gives the equation in general form, so you need to complete the square to put the equation into standard form.

You already have an x^2 and a y^2 in the given equation and the coefficients of x and y are even, so completing the square is fairly straightforward. Start by grouping the x's and y's together. Then, take the coefficient of the x term and divide it by 2, square it, and add it to the two terms with x variables.

Do the same with the *y* term. Remember to add these amounts to the other side of the equation as well. Then factor the perfect squares and simplify:

$$x^2 + y^2 + 12x + 14y = -4$$
$$x^2 + 12x + y^2 + 14y = -4$$
$$(x^2 + 12x + 36) + (y^2 + 14y + 49) = -4 + 36 + 49$$
$$(x + 6)^2 + (y + 7)^2 = 81$$

The equation tells you that r^2 is 81, which means that the radius is $\sqrt{81} = 9$. That's **(C).**

21. C
Difficulty: Hard
Category: Geometry and Trigonometry
Getting to the Answer: Use the volume of a cylinder formula, Volume $= \pi r^2 \times$ height, to set up an equation based on the information in the question. Although you don't have actual values for the radii of the two cylinders, picking numbers will work well here. Since the ratio of diameters between cylinder B and cylinder A is $\frac{4}{5}$, the same ratio applies to their radii. Therefore, you can say cylinder A's radius is 5 and cylinder B's radius is 4, and then plug those values into an equation:

$$\text{volume}_A = \frac{5}{4}\text{volume}_B$$
$$\pi \times 5^2 \times h_A = \frac{5}{4}\pi \times 4^2 \times h_B$$
$$\cancel{\pi} \times 25 \times h_A = \frac{5}{4}\cancel{\pi} \times 16 \times h_B$$
$$25 \times h_A = 20 \times h_B$$
$$\frac{25}{20} \times h_A = h_B$$
$$\frac{25}{20} = \frac{h_B}{h_A}$$

Simplifying the ratio yields $\frac{5}{4}$, or 5:4. Answer choice **(C)** is correct.

22. 432
Difficulty: Hard
Category: Geometry and Trigonometry
Getting to the Answer: The base of the triangle is provided, so finding the area will require determining the height. Since angles A and C are equal, the triangle is isosceles. That means drawing an altitude down will split the triangle into two similar right triangles, each with a leg length of 24.

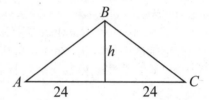

Tangent is $\dfrac{\text{opposite}}{\text{adjacent}}$. In relation to angle *A*, the height, *h*, is the opposite side length and 24 is the adjacent side length. Use this information to determine the length of *h*:

$$\tan\angle A = 0.75$$
$$\frac{\text{opposite}}{\text{adjacent}} = 0.75$$
$$\frac{h}{24} = 0.75$$
$$h = 0.75 \times 24$$
$$h = 18$$

The area of a triangle is $\frac{1}{2} \times$ base $\times$ height. In this case, that's $\frac{1}{2} \times 48 \times 18 = 432$.

Enter **432**.

PART 6

PRACTICE TEST 2

ABOUT YOUR PRACTICE TEST

The SAT is an *adaptive test*. This means that, for both the Reading and Writing section and the Math section, your performance on the first module of the test section will determine the relative difficulty of the questions you see in the second module. (See chapter 1, Inside the SAT, for more information about the SAT's structure.) Also note that on test day, the SAT will include *pre-test questions* that will not be scored, but as there is no indication of which questions they are, this paper test will grade all of the questions. *While a paper test cannot simulate a digital adaptive test perfectly, the test can still give you an estimate of your current abilities and how you might perform on the digital version of the test.*

To best simulate the digital SAT test day experience, follow these steps as you complete your practice test:

1. Using a timer, give yourself **32 minutes** to complete the *Routing Module of the Reading and Writing section*.

2. Use the answer key at the end of the Reading and Writing Routing Module to calculate your score. If you scored:

   - **19 or more questions correct:** Move on to *Reading and Writing Module B*.
   - **18 or fewer questions correct:** Move on to *Reading and Writing Module A*

3. Give yourself **32 minutes** to complete *Module A or B* (see step 2) of the Reading and Writing section.

4. Take a **10 minute break**.

5. Give yourself **35 minutes** to complete the *Routing Module of the Math section*.

6. Use the answer key at the end of the Math Routing Module to calculate your score. If you scored:

   - **14 or more questions correct:** Move on to *Math Module B*.
   - **13 or fewer questions correct:** Move on to *Math Module A*.

7. Give yourself **35 minutes** to complete *Module A or B* (see step 6) of the Math section.

To score your practice test:

- Use the answer key to score the Reading and Writing Modules and Math Modules.
- Write down your total raw score—the total number of questions you got correct—for all of the Reading and Writing modules and all of the Math modules.
- Convert your raw scores to scaled scores as directed. The score in the right column indicates your estimated scaled score if this were an actual SAT. Enter your scaled scores in the boxes that follow the table.
- Calculate your estimated composite, or overall, score. Simply add together your scaled scores for each section.

Besides the provided in-book practice, be sure to complete additional **practice tests online** (www.kaptest.com/moreonline). By taking tests online, you can familiarize yourself with the testing application's layout and tools to make sure you feel confident navigating the digital SAT on test day.

READING AND WRITING: ROUTING MODULE

Mark your answers either on the pages that follow or on a separate sheet of paper. You will be scoring this Routing Module before going on to the final Reading and Writing Module.

DIRECTIONS

The questions in this section address a number of important reading and writing skills. Each question includes one or more passages, which may include a table or graph. Read each passage and question carefully, and then choose the best answer to the question based on the passage(s).

All questions in this section are multiple-choice with four answer choices. Each question has a single best answer.

1

The _____ of soccer as a spectator sport is growing in the United States. This change may be driven by the increasing number of viewers who played the sport as children.

Which choice completes the text with the most logical and precise word or phrase?

Ⓐ popularity

Ⓑ influence

Ⓒ expense

Ⓓ availability

2

Medical research indicates that when sufferers feel the symptoms of a cold or flu starting, it is important to act with _____. The duration and intensity of many common illnesses can be reduced by starting treatment immediately.

Which choice completes the text with the most logical and precise word or phrase?

Ⓐ caution

Ⓑ alacrity

Ⓒ impunity

Ⓓ reluctance

CONTINUED ➡

3

The solar constant is a measurement of the sun's total radiance at a specific point in time. Since the sun's radiance is affected by sunspots, which wax and wane in an eleven-year cycle, the solar constant not only fluctuates, but is also cyclical. Karen Labitzke, Harry van Loon, and Brian Tinsley are working to determine if the fluctuations in the solar constant _____ Earth's weather. Labitzke and van Loon have correlated changes in the solar constant with some temperatures and pressures occurring on Earth, and Tinsley has correlated variations in the solar constant with the position of storms in the North Atlantic.

Which choice completes the text with the most logical and precise word or phrase?

Ⓐ manifest in

Ⓑ disguise as

Ⓒ improve upon

Ⓓ exacerbate

4

The following text is adapted from John Evelyn's 1662 book *Sylva: Or a Discourse of Forest Trees & the Propagation of Timber.*

But to pursue this to some further advantage, as to what concerns the <u>election</u> of your seed, it is to be considered that there is vast difference...in trees even of the same growth and bed, which I judge to proceed from the variety and quality of the seed. This, for instance, is evidently seen in the heart, prosperity, and stature of timber. And therefore choose not your seeds always from the most fruitful trees, which are commonly the most aged and decayed, but from such as are found most solid and fair. Nor, for this reason, covet the largest acorns, but (as husbandmen do their wheat) the most weighty, clean, and bright.

As used in the text, what does the word "election" most nearly mean?

Ⓐ Selection

Ⓑ Vote

Ⓒ Nomination

Ⓓ Liberty

CONTINUED

5

In her 1917 "Address to the United States Congress," Carrie Chapman Catts, president of the National American Woman Suffrage Association, urged Congress to _____ women's grievances by immediately putting forward legislation granting women the right to vote. Citing a history of delays, political tricks, and dishonesty, Catts warned legislators that once women could vote, they would remember those who opposed them with suspicion. She argued that this issue was so important that, despite having to defend themselves in World War I, some of America's allies in that war had already passed legislation expanding the right to vote to women.

Which choice completes the text with the most logical and precise word or phrase?

- (A) complement
- (B) petition
- (C) forewarn
- (D) redress

6

The following text is from A. A. Milne's 1922 novel *The Red House Mystery*.

It was understood—and this, anyhow, on Mark's own authority—that his father had been a country clergyman. It was said that, as a boy, Mark had attracted the notice, and patronage, of some rich old spinster of the neighborhood, who had paid for his education, both at school and university. At about the time when he was coming down from Cambridge, his father had died; leaving behind him a few debts, as a warning to his family, and a reputation for short sermons, as an example to his successor. Neither warning nor example seems to have been effective. Mark went to London, with an allowance from his patron, and (it is generally agreed) made acquaintance with the money-lenders. He was supposed, by his patron and any others who inquired, to be "writing"; but what he wrote, other than letters asking for more time to pay, has never been discovered.

Which choice best states the function of the underlined sentence in the text as a whole?

- (A) It restates the reason the main character left home.
- (B) It introduces the setting described in the following sentences.
- (C) It establishes an important personality trait of the main character.
- (D) It explains the source of the conflict addressed in the previous sentences.

CONTINUED ➡

Practice Tests

7

The following text is from the 1876 poem "Later Life" by Christina Rossetti.

We lack, yet cannot fix upon the lack:
this, not that; yet somewhat, certainly.
We see the things we do not yearn to see
Around us: and what see we glancing back?
Lost hopes that leave our hearts upon the rack,
Hopes that were never ours yet seemed to be,
For which we steered on life's salt stormy sea
Braving the sunstroke and the frozen pack.
If thus to look behind is all in vain,
And all in vain to look to left or right,
Why face we not our future once again,
Launching with hardier hearts across the main,
Straining dim eyes to catch the invisible sight,
And strong to bear ourselves in patient pain?

Which choice best states the main purpose of the text?

(A) To encourage perseverance and hope in the face of life's disillusionments

(B) To demonstrate how disappointments in life can gradually accumulate over a lifetime

(C) To refute the idea that achievement of goals is necessary for a fulfilled life

(D) To question whether memories of the past are more useful guides for behavior than experiences of the present

8

The Pechanga Band of Luiseño Indians views their ancestral lands as their source of life. Wi'áaşal, The Great Oak, is the largest naturally grown oak tree in the western United States and is central to Pechanga people's identity. After the tribe's forced relocation in the late nineteenth century, Wi'áaşal was located just outside of the boundaries of their lands. Concerned with restoring this vital part of their culture to the Pechanga tribe's oversight, the band purchased the ranch that held Wi'áaşal along with the thousand acres surrounding it. Wi'áaşal is now protected and preserved as part of the Pechanga reservation.

According to the text, why was the Pechanga band concerned about Wi'áaşal?

(A) It was growing on land not owned by the Pechanga.

(B) It was endangered by local development.

(C) It could be damaged by too many visitors.

(D) It is so old, it may be near the end of its natural life.

Practice Tests

CONTINUED

K 829

9

Cement is needed to make concrete, one of the most important building materials used throughout the world, but the carbon dioxide released by its manufacture generates about 8% of the world's carbon dioxide emissions. To make concrete by a process that consumes carbon dioxide, rather than produces it, a Colorado company uses cyanobacteria, a bacteria capable of photosynthesis. The bacteria are raised in water, under lights, with the carbon dioxide needed for photosynthesis pumped in. The bacteria generate tiny crystals of calcium carbonate, the main component of limestone, which is then blended with sand or another aggregate to make "bioconcrete." The results have been promising. Bioconcrete cures faster and, in early tests, is as strong as conventional concrete.

Which choice best states the main idea of the text?

Ⓐ Concrete requires cement, and the manufacture of cement generates large amounts of carbon dioxide.

Ⓑ Cyanobacteria may be useful in reducing the carbon dioxide emissions associated with concrete production.

Ⓒ Some bacteria, called cyanobacteria, are capable of photosynthesis, a process that consumes carbon dioxide.

Ⓓ A Colorado company has invented the only known way to reduce the emissions of carbon dioxide in the production of cement.

CONTINUED ➡

The Jungle is a 1906 novel by Upton Sinclair. In the novel, Sinclair portrays Jurgis and Ona, Lithuanian immigrants to Chicago, as persevering with integrity and diligence despite difficult conditions: _____

Which quotation from *The Jungle* most effectively illustrates the claim?

(A) "Jurgis talked lightly about work, because he was young. They told him stories about the breaking down of men, there in the stockyards of Chicago, and of what had happened to them afterward—stories to make your flesh creep, but Jurgis would only laugh. He had only been there four months, and he was young, and a giant besides."

(B) "Jurgis was like a boy, a boy from the country. He was the sort of man the bosses like to get hold of, the sort they make it a grievance they cannot get hold of. When he was told to go to a certain place, he would go there on the run. When he had nothing to do for the moment, he would stand round fidgeting, dancing, with the overflow of energy that was in him."

(C) "There was always the boss prowling about, and if there was a second's delay he would fall to cursing; Lithuanians and Slovaks and such, who could not understand what was said to them, the bosses were wont to kick about the place like so many dogs."

(D) "We will pay them all somehow. I will work harder." That was always what Jurgis said. Ona had grown used to it as the solution of all difficulties—"I will work harder!" He had said that in Lithuania...He had said it again in New York...Now he said it a third time..."

11

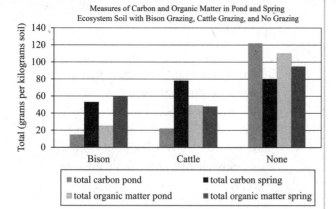

Measures of Carbon and Organic Matter in Pond and Spring Ecosystem Soil with Bison Grazing, Cattle Grazing, and No Grazing

- total carbon pond
- total organic matter pond
- total carbon spring
- total organic matter spring

Allowing access to national forests for grazing has been controversial since the late nineteenth century when a presidential order established these reserves. Conservationists argue that these areas should be pristine and protected from most intrusion, while ranchers demand use of the land to fuel the economic growth and prosperity of local communities. To determine the effects of grazing on the soil of two types of ecosystems found in a national forest, pond and spring, scientists measured an array of soil attributes. Two of these, total carbon and organic matter are summarized in the graph. Based on these results, the scientists found that although any grazing in either ecosystem reduced total carbon and organic matter in the soil, _____

Which choice most effectively uses data from the graph to complete the statement?

(A) bison grazing in the pond ecosystem had very little effect on total carbon levels.

(B) bison grazing in the spring ecosystem had very little effect on total organic matter levels.

(C) cattle grazing in the spring ecosystem had very little effect on total carbon levels.

(D) cattle grazing in the pond ecosystem had very little effect on total organic matter levels.

12

A common insect found worldwide, caddisflies are primarily terrestrial during their adulthood and solely aquatic during their adolescence. Caddisfly larvae use the debris and substrate found in the water to form individual cocoons in which to pupate. It is this natural creative process using found, organic materials that inspired French artist Hubert Duprat's 2014 work "Caddis." Duprat constructed an artificial habitat for caddisfly larvae using clean water with only flakes and rods of gold and tiny pieces of precious and semi-precious stones for their cocoons. Referring to himself as an "architect," Duprat's intention was to _____

Which choice most logically completes the text?

- (A) collaborate with the caddisfly larvae by providing them with building materials that would best showcase the larva's abilities to create organic art.

- (B) profit off of the larvae's labor by selling the cocoons that were built using the supplied materials of gold and precious and semi-precious metals.

- (C) prove that caddisfly larvae would be unable to construct cocoons using materials that were not naturally found in their habitat.

- (D) create an art installation that brought awareness to the ecological impact of the caddisflies' life cycles, with a special emphasis on the pupal stage.

13

Published in 1968, the second edition of the American Psychiatric Association's Diagnostic and Statistical Manual of Mental Disorders, or *DSM-II*, introduced a newly conceptualized disorder listed as the Hyperkinetic Reaction of Childhood, which focused on a child's excessive motor activity. The *DSM-III*, published in 1980, renamed the disorder to Attention Deficit Disorder (ADD) and expanded the symptoms list to include difficulties with attention and impulsivity. A revision of the *DSM-III* brought with it the addition of another disorder Attention Deficit/Hyperactivity Disorder (ADHD), which was listed separate from ADD. However, ADD _____

Which choice most logically completes the text?

(A) was eliminated from the *DSM-5* in 2013, leaving only ADHD and its specific subtypes, or "presentations," as the current iteration of a disorder that was introduced decades ago.

(B) is a very uncommon disorder and it is highly unlikely that future publications of the *DSM* will continue to have modifications to the criteria for a formal diagnosis.

(C) remains one of the most prevalent childhood psychiatric diagnoses for children between the ages of 6–12 years old, and is often comorbid with depression and anxiety.

(D) diagnoses require significant documentation of excessive motor activity, inattention, and hyperactivity, as observed and reported by a board-certified psychologist.

14

Portal fantasies, beginning with Mark Twain's 1889 novel *A Connecticut Yankee in King Arthur's Court*, typically feature a person from Earth transported to a fantastical _____ one strikingly different from that of their everyday ordinary life. In the last decade, portal fantasies have become especially popular in Japan, where they are known as *isekai*, which translates as "different world."

Which choice completes the text so that it conforms to the conventions of Standard English?

(A) setting

(B) setting)

(C) setting;

(D) setting,

CONTINUED

15

Hedy Lamarr is best remembered as a Hollywood _____ her greatest legacy is as an inventor. Working alongside composer George Antheil, she co-developed a system for radio-guided torpedoes during World War II. The frequency-hopping technique these torpedoes used provides a foundation for many technologies central to modern life, including GPS, Bluetooth, and Wi-Fi.

Which choice completes the text so that it conforms to the conventions of Standard English?

- (A) actress,
- (B) actress but
- (C) actress, but
- (D) actress, but,

16

The defeat of a navy by horse-mounted cavalry is a laughable idea, and yet it once happened. In 1795, fourteen Dutch warships in an iced-over port, lacking an escape route, _____ to a French light cavalry regiment after tense negotiations rather than face certain defeat by boarding parties. It was a humiliating loss.

Which choice completes the text so that it conforms to the conventions of Standard English?

- (A) surrender
- (B) surrendered
- (C) surrenders
- (D) will surrender

17

The Xiaozhai Tiankeng sinkhole in China is the largest sinkhole in the world, deep enough that you could stack the Eiffel Tower inside it twice over with room to spare. Its remote location and sheer walls make it cumbersome for humans to _____ those same qualities make it a rich ecological reserve for endangered species like the clouded leopard.

Which choice completes the text so that it conforms to the conventions of Standard English?

- (A) explore, however
- (B) explore, however,
- (C) explore; however,
- (D) explore; however

CONTINUED

Practice Tests

18

The James Webb Space Telescope (JWST) is a space telescope launched in 2021. Unlike any of its predecessors, its primary mission is to conduct infrared astronomy. Designed to capture otherwise invisible infrared light, _____ is better suited to wavelengths of light visible to the human eye.

Which choice completes the text so that it conforms to the conventions of Standard English?

(A) the Hubble Space Telescope is able to perceive astronomical objects that are dimmer, cooler, and farther away than the objects perceivable by its more famous counterpart, the JWST, which

(B) astronomical objects that are dimmer, cooler, and farther away than the objects perceivable by its more famous counterpart, the Hubble Space Telescope, mean the JWST

(C) the JWST is able to perceive astronomical objects that are dimmer, cooler, and farther away than the objects perceivable by its more famous counterpart, the Hubble Space Telescope, which

(D) the objects perceivable by its more famous counterpart, the Hubble Space Telescope, are dimmer, cooler, and farther away, which the JWST

19

Pellagra is a potentially fatal disease resulting from niacin deficiency (vitamin B_3), with its symptoms including the stiffening and peeling of skin exposed to sunlight. This niacin deficiency often results from a diet centered on corn, which needs to undergo nixtamalization via the _____ or a comparable chemical solution. This process is sometimes not practiced in impoverished areas, but it improves the nutritional benefit of corn and cuts the rate of pellagra.

Which choice completes the text so that it conforms to the conventions of Standard English?

(A) alkaline, solution limewater

(B) alkaline solution limewater

(C) alkaline solution, limewater

(D) alkaline solution, limewater,

CONTINUED

20

The earliest known named poet is Enhed-uanna, the daughter of Sargon of Akkad, founder of the Akkadian Empire. She lived in the 23rd century B.C.E. in the Sumerian city-state of Ur. However, there is scholarly debate as to whether or not Enheduanna actually wrote her poems. Only several centuries after her _____ Babylonian scholars attribute several poems to her. This, it seems, was possibly an effort on their part to magnify the legend of Sargon of Akkad, a renowned figure important to Babylonian history.

Which choice completes the text so that it conforms to the conventions of Standard English?

(A) death, did

(B) death, did,

(C) death did

(D) death did,

21

In 1120 C.E., several dozen high-ranking English nobles, including the crown prince, held a party aboard a vessel dubbed *White Ship*. The nobles urged the captain to race across the English Channel to beat the king's ship to port. _____ due to everyone's drunken state, *White Ship* soon struck a rock and capsized. Only one passenger, a French butcher, survived. The death of the crown prince soon led to a brutal period of civil war known as The Anarchy.

Which choice completes the text with the most logical transition?

(A) Thus,

(B) Indeed,

(C) Likewise,

(D) However,

22

The gutter—a term referring to the blank space between two panels—is a critical tool in drawing comics, especially as it relates to storytelling. _____ it invites the reader to use their imagination to fill in the gutter, painting in the events that happen between the two panels, each of which represents a specific point in time.

Which choice completes the text with the most logical transition?

(A) Nevertheless,

(B) Because,

(C) Since,

(D) Specifically,

CONTINUED

23

While researching a topic, a student has taken the following notes:

- *Beowulf* is an old English epic poem.
- Its author is unknown, and it may have originated in oral traditions.
- It consists of almost 3,200 lines.
- The *Iliad* is an ancient Greek epic poem.
- The poem was traditionally attributed to Homer but likely originated in oral traditions.
- It is over 15,000 lines long.

The student wants to compare the lengths of the two poems. Which choice most effectively uses relevant information from the notes to accomplish this goal?

(A) Some historical epic poems, including one originally attributed to Homer, are longer than 3,000 lines.

(B) *Beowulf* is almost 3,200 lines long, while the significantly longer *Iliad* is over 15,000 lines long.

(C) *Beowulf*, which is almost 3,200 lines long, is an Old English epic poem of uncertain authorship.

(D) Both *Beowulf*, which was written in Old English, and the *Iliad*, which was written in ancient Greek, are examples of epic poems.

CONTINUED

24

While researching a topic, a student has taken the following notes:

- Sparta was an ancient Greek city-state known for its military strength.

- Sparta was unusual among ancient governments in that it had a dual kingship, with two hereditary kings from different families ruling at the same time and having equal power.

- One non-military responsibility of the kings was to serve as priests of the god Zeus.

- Another non-military responsibility of the kings was to serve on the *gerousia*, the council of elders.

- The kings were the only members of the *gerousia* that did not have to be older than age 60 to be eligible to serve on the council.

The student wants to emphasize a similarity between the two non-military responsibilities of the kings of ancient Sparta. Which choice most effectively uses relevant information from the notes to accomplish this goal?

- (A) Both of the non-military responsibilities of the kings of ancient Sparta were carried out by a pair of kings who ruled together.

- (B) The dual kings of ancient Sparta had equal power in their role of serving on the *gerousia* council of elders.

- (C) Of the non-military responsibilities of the kings of ancient Sparta, one permitted them to serve on the *gerousia* although they might not yet be 60 years old.

- (D) In addition to serving as priests of the god Zeus, the kings of ancient Sparta served on the *gerousia* council of elders and oversaw the battle readiness of the army to be certain that Sparta continued to be known for its strength.

While researching a topic, a student has taken the following notes:

- Scientists use techniques such as GPS tracking of individual sample animals to approximate regional animal population numbers.

- The Canadian lynx is one of many animals whose population numbers are closely linked to those of another animal species.

- The population of Canadian lynx is at its highest when the numbers of its primary prey, the snowshoe hare, surge approximately every 10 years.

- The population of Canadian lynx significantly declines about 1–2 years after the population of snowshoe hares reaches its lowest.

The student wants to make and support a generalization about the relationships between animal populations. Which choice most effectively uses relevant information from the notes to accomplish these goals?

(A) The numbers of some animal populations are closely related to those of other animals: the population of the Canadian lynx rises and falls in conjunction with the population of its primary prey, the snowshoe hare.

(B) The population numbers of the Canadian lynx vary in relation to the population numbers of its primary prey, the snowshoe hare.

(C) Scientists use techniques such as GPS tracking to approximate regional animal populations; animal population numbers may be closely linked to the population numbers of another animal species.

(D) One example of an animal population is the Canadian lynx, whose population number is at its highest when the number of snowshoe hares surges and significantly declines when the number of snowshoe hares is at its lowest.

Practice Tests

CONTINUED

26

While researching a topic, a student has taken the following notes:

- The main location of the National Air and Space Museum is on the National Mall in Washington, D.C., within short walking distance of other national museums.

- The museum's exhibits include artifacts from the beginning of aviation, such as the Wright brothers' 1903 flyer; a detailed display about the planets; and a collection of artifacts related to space travel, including astronaut Neil Armstrong's spacesuit.

- The Steven F. Udvar-Hazy Center is another location of the National Air and Space Museum, located outside of Washington, D.C., in Virginia.

- The center's exhibits are housed in two massive hangars and include Cold War-era satellites and planes, commercial aircraft such as the first supersonic airliner, and the Space Shuttle *Discovery*.

The student wants to explain an advantage of the organization of the National Air and Space Museum. Which choice most effectively uses relevant information from the notes to accomplish this goal?

(A) The main location of the National Air and Space Museum is accessible to those visiting other museums on the National Mall, and its second location, the Steven F. Udvar-Hazy Center, has the room to display full-sized aircraft.

(B) The Steven F. Udvar-Hazy Center in Virginia has numerous exhibits on display that include actual aircraft and spacecraft, such as planes from the Cold War era, the first supersonic commercial airliner, and the Space Shuttle *Discovery*.

(C) The National Air and Space Museum consists of two locations: the main museum located in Washington, D.C., and the Steven F. Udvar-Hazy Center located in Virginia.

(D) The locations of the National Air and Space Museum display artifacts related to aviation, such as the Wright brothers' 1903 flyer and the first supersonic commercial airliner, as well as artifacts related to space travel, such as astronaut Neil Armstrong's spacesuit and the Space Shuttle *Discovery*.

27

While researching a topic, a student has taken the following notes:

- The earliest evidence of humans using fire to cook was previously dated to 170,000 years ago.
- In a 2022 study, researchers analyzed teeth from fish remains found throughout an archeological site in Israel.
- The researchers were trying to determine whether the fish had been cooked by ancient humans.
- The researchers evaluated the size of the crystal structures found in the fish teeth enamel to determine that they had been exposed to cooking fire temperatures.
- The researchers concluded that the fish had been cooked by fires made by humans approximately 700,000 years ago.

The student wants to present the study and its findings. Which choice most effectively uses relevant information from the notes to accomplish this goal?

(A) Before a 2022 study of the enamel of fish teeth remains, the earliest dated evidence of humans cooking food using fire was from 170,000 years ago.

(B) In 2022, researchers studied the crystal structures in the teeth of fish remains because they wanted to determine whether the fish had been cooked by humans more than 170,000 years ago, the oldest date indicated by previous evidence.

(C) In a 2022 study, researchers determined that the crystal structures in fish teeth remnants from an archeological site in Israel indicated the fish had been cooked by humans earlier than suggested by previous evidence.

(D) In a 2022 study, researchers used techniques to evaluate the size of crystal structures found in the enamel of fish teeth from an archeological site in Israel.

Practice Tests

IF YOU FINISH BEFORE TIME IS CALLED, YOU MAY CHECK YOUR WORK ON THIS MODULE ONLY. ON TEST DAY, YOU WON'T BE ABLE TO MOVE ON TO THE NEXT MODULE UNTIL TIME EXPIRES. **STOP**

842 K

This page is intentionally blank.

ANSWER KEY

Reading and Writing: Routing Module

1.	**A**	8.	**A**	15.	**C**	22.	**D**
2.	**B**	9.	**B**	16.	**B**	23.	**B**
3.	**A**	10.	**D**	17.	**C**	24.	**A**
4.	**A**	11.	**C**	18.	**C**	25.	**A**
5.	**D**	12.	**A**	19.	**B**	26.	**A**
6.	**C**	13.	**A**	20.	**C**	27.	**C**
7.	**A**	14.	**D**	21.	**D**		

Instructions

Compare your answers to the answer key and enter the number of correct answers for this stage here. _____ This is your raw score.

If you scored less than 19 correct, turn to the Reading and Writing Module A and continue your test.

If you had 19 or more correct in this routing module, turn to the Reading and Writing Module B and continue your test.

Explanations will be at the end of the practice test.

READING AND WRITING: MODULE A

Mark your answers either on the pages that follow or on a separate sheet of paper. You will be scoring this Module before moving on to the Math section.

DIRECTIONS

The questions in this section address a number of important reading and writing skills. Each question includes one or more passages, which may include a table or graph. Read each passage and question carefully, and then choose the best answer to the question based on the passage(s).

All questions in this section are multiple-choice with four answer choices. Each question has a single best answer.

1

In vegan cooking, a popular and cost-effective substitute for eggs is aquafaba, a viscous water that is a by-product of boiling legumes such as chickpeas. The starches and proteins _____ the beans during the boiling process aid in the resulting liquid's ability to bind and foam in a manner comparable to that of egg whites.

Which choice completes the text with the most logical and precise word or phrase?

- (A) linked with
- (B) extracted from
- (C) created in
- (D) enriched by

2

The following text is from Jules Verne's 1874 novel *The Mysterious Island*. The voyagers are traveling by hot air balloon.

It was impossible to prevent the escape of gas, which rushed through a large rent in the silk. By lightening the car of all the articles which it contained, the passengers had been able to prolong their suspension in the air for a few hours. But the inevitable catastrophe could only be retarded, and if land did not appear before night, voyagers, car, and balloon must to a certainty vanish beneath the waves.

As used in the text, what does the word "rent" most nearly mean?

- (A) lease
- (B) schism
- (C) rip
- (D) wrest

CONTINUED

Practice Tests

3

Considered to be the longest continually _____ route across the Americas, the Pan-American Highway begins in Ushuaia, Argentina, and stretches nearly 19,000 kilometers to Prudhoe Bay, Alaska. While the majority of the journey may be completed by car, there are two sections that must be navigated on foot.

Which choice completes the text with the most logical and precise word or phrase?

- Ⓐ walkable
- Ⓑ dangerous
- Ⓒ unlivable
- Ⓓ coastal

4

The impact of parasites on ecosystems may be more significant than previously recognized and is worthy of further research. Environmental biologists Connor Meyer and Kira Cassidy studied grey wolf populations and determined that wolves infected with the protozoan parasite *Toxoplasma gondii* displayed bolder behavior than those not infected. The researchers were astonished to discover that these more _____ individuals were eleven times more likely to establish new packs and forty-six times more likely to be a pack leader than non-infected wolves.

Which choice completes the text with the most logical and precise word or phrase?

- Ⓐ innocuous
- Ⓑ venturous
- Ⓒ apprehensive
- Ⓓ tortuous

CONTINUED ➡

5

The Sponsian aureus is a gold coin discovered in large numbers in 1713 in modern-day Hungary, formerly a part of the ancient Roman empire, and has long been considered _____ : unlike authentic examples of ancient Roman coins, the Sponsian aureus was cast, not struck, and composed of gold alloy, instead of pure gold. However, Paul Pearson and four colleagues have recently performed extensive testing and determined from wear marks that the coin was actually in circulation. In addition, since the name "Sponsian" was not known to historians until 1720, Pearson argues that it is more likely the coin was made by a local ancient Roman ruler to commemorate his reign.

Which choice completes the text with the most logical and precise word or phrase?

(A) an exemplar

(B) a depiction

(C) an attribute

(D) a forgery

6

David Sabel, a British media producer, prepared for his career with advanced degrees in both acting and business. Despite the traditional _____ in education between business and the arts, he argues that the ability to combine creativity with effective fund-raising, management, and investor reporting is crucial to keep pace with the rapid changes in the entertainment industry due to technology.

Which choice completes the text with the most logical and precise word or phrase?

(A) amalgamation

(B) conflation

(C) explication

(D) bifurcation

Practice Tests

CONTINUED

7

Pharmaceutical companies dream of a time when their research and development process shifts from looking for illnesses whose symptoms can be ameliorated by a specific drug to choosing a disease and creating a drug to eradicate it. Quantum computing may be the key to that goal. The powerful modeling potential unlocked by quantum computing may also someday be employed by autonomous vehicles to create a world free of traffic jams. With plausible applications in so many fields, it is worthwhile to learn a bit about how quantum computing works.

Which choice best describes the function of the second sentence in the overall structure of the text?

- (A) It restates the goal of pharmaceutical companies.

- (B) It explains why quantum computing will allow for creating specifically-tailored medication on demand.

- (C) It establishes multiple possible applications of quantum computing.

- (D) It introduces the mechanism by which the goal introduced in the first sentence may be made real.

8

Text 1

Marine bycatch are species caught by commercial fishers that are not the target species. For example, a ship fishing for cod may also catch sharks, rays, seals, dolphins, or other species. Bycatch are thrown back into the ocean, but not before some animals are injured, sometimes fatally. Paul Wade and team describe bycatch as the largest human contributor to marine species decline and insist that the commercial fishing industry work to reduce bycatch.

Text 2

Philip Doherty and colleagues are testing a device that is attached just above a fishhook and sends an electrical pulse into the hook. The researchers placed the device on half of the hooks deployed by a commercial fishing ship and compared the bycatch found on these hooks to those without. The hooks with the device caught substantially fewer of the local bycatch species.

Based on the texts, how would Doherty and colleagues (Text 2) most likely respond to the issue described by Wade in Text 1?

- (A) They would offer their experimental results as proof that the issue of marine bycatch can be solved.

- (B) They would present their findings as a potential step toward addressing the amount of marine bycatch.

- (C) They would explain that, while interesting, their data is not relevant to the reduction of marine bycatch.

- (D) They would express regret that their findings indicate the issue of marine bycatch to be more difficult than anticipated.

CONTINUED

Practice Tests

9

The following text is adapted from L.M. Montgomery's 1926 novel *The Blue Castle*. Throughout the story, Mrs. Frederick, refers to her adult daughter Valancy by the nickname Doss.

[Valancy] marched to the tool-room in the barn for her garden knife and she went at the rosebush viciously. A few minutes later horrified Mrs. Frederick came out to the verandah and beheld her daughter slashing insanely among the rosebush boughs. Half of them were already strewn on the walk. The bush looked sadly dismantled.

"Doss, what on earth are you doing? Have you gone crazy?"

"No," said Valancy. She meant to say it defiantly, but habit was too strong for her. She said it deprecatingly. "I—I just made up my mind to cut this bush down. It is no good. It never blooms—never will bloom."

"That is no reason for destroying it," said Mrs. Frederick sternly. "It was a beautiful bush and quite ornamental. You have made a sorry-looking thing of it.... Really, I'm surprised at you. And to do it without consulting *me*!"

Based on the text, which of the following best describes Valancy's usual way of interacting with her mother?

Ⓐ Rebelliously

Ⓑ Amicably

Ⓒ Argumentatively

Ⓓ Submissively

Practice Tests

CONTINUED ▶

10

An artificial intelligence (AI) computer program has established its dominance over most human players in one of the most complex online games. Computers have previously bested masters of backgammon, chess, and go, but unlike these games, more complex online games require verbal and relationship skills: players bargain, cooperate, form alliances, and may break them. It is this added dimension of communication, negotiation, and subterfuge that makes large online games so complex and unpredictable. Yet an AI computer program was ranked in the top ten percent of players in an online gaming tournament, and none of the human competitors realized they were playing against a computer program.

Which choice best states the main idea of the text?

(A) Online games can be extremely complex, so it was unexpected that an AI computer program proved to be unbeatable.

(B) An AI computer program scored well in an online gaming competition, even though the game requires human relationship skills.

(C) Although none of its competitors recognized it as a computer program, an AI computer program lacked the sophistication needed to succeed in a complex online game.

(D) The interpersonal skills of communication, bargaining, and negotiation make some online games difficult and unpredictable.

11

"Books" is an essay by Ralph Waldo Emerson. In the essay, Emerson explores the value of books, arguing that the best books to read are those that have withstood scrutiny over many years: _____

Which quotation from "Books" most effectively illustrates the claim?

(A) "We owe to books those general benefits which come from high intellectual action...They impart sympathetic activity to the moral power."

(B) "Be sure, then, to read no mean books. Shun the spawn of the press on the gossip of the hour. Do not read what you shall learn, without asking, in the street and the train...the scholar knows that the famed books contain, first and last, the best thoughts and facts."

(C) "It is easy to accuse books, and bad ones are easily found; and the best are but records, and not the things recorded; and certainly there is dilettantism enough, and books that are merely neutral and do nothing for us."

(D) "The annals of bibliography afford many examples of the delirious extent to which book-fancying can go, when the legitimate delight in a book is transferred to a rare edition or to a manuscript. This mania reached its height about the beginning of the present century."

A meteorite that struck a small English town in 2021 has provided scientists with crucial information about the origins of Earth. The meteorite was observed entering Earth's atmosphere and its pieces were immediately collected. Although the meteorite was tracked back to its origins in the meteorite belt inside the orbit of Jupiter, the water in the meteorite fragments was found to be composed of the identical isotopes as water on Earth. This finding supports the theory that Earth's water was added to its surface, after the planet's formation, by material from space.

Which finding, if true, would most directly strengthen the author's claim?

(A) Images of the path of the meteorite in the Earth's atmosphere were captured on many official and private cameras.

(B) The pieces of the meteorite that reached the Earth were found several inches below the surface, where they had buried upon impact.

(C) The samples of the meteorite were collected and stored using methods that isolated the fragments from further contact with terrestrial elements.

(D) The evidence obtained from meteorites is not as compelling as geological evidence collected from Earth when evaluating the origins of the planet.

CONTINUED

13

Selected Results of Dating Analyses of Hominid Fossils

Hominid fossil	Year of study	Dating technique	Date assigned (approximate)
"Lucy" *Australopithecus afarensis* skeleton	Initial analysis	Stratigraphic (analysis of surrounding pig skeletons)	3.5–2.9 million years ago
	1992	Radiometric (geochemical dating of nearby volcanic ash)	3.18 million years ago
"Omo I" *Homo sapien* skeleton	Initial analysis	Stratigraphic (analysis of surrounding mollusk shells)	130,000 years ago
	2004	Stratigraphic (analysis of surrounding fossils)	195,000 years ago
	2021	Radiometric (geochemical dating of nearby volcanic ash)	233,000 years ago

One difficulty facing palaeoarchaeologists, researchers who study ancient human remains, is determining accurate dates for the hominid fossils they analyze. Scientific dating methods fall into two broad categories: relative and absolute. Relative dating approximates date ranges based on where a fossil is located in relation to other fossils. For instance, stratigraphy, a type of relative dating, relies on the principle that lower sedimentary layers are older than higher ones. Absolute dating uses techniques such as radiometric dating, which measures the decay of radioactive materials in a fossil. Palaeoarchaeologists today rely on a combination of these methods and claim that subsequent analyses over time can sometimes determine that hominid fossils are older than was previously thought.

Which choice best describes data from the table that support the palaeoarchaeologists' claim?

Ⓐ Based on both stratigraphic and radiometric dating methods, researchers estimate that the "Lucy" skeleton is likely more than 2 million years old.

Ⓑ Researchers utilized stratigraphic analysis in studies of both the "Lucy" skeleton and the "Omo I" skeleton; these studies estimated the former's age at 3.5–2.9 million years and the latter's at 130,000 years.

Ⓒ A 1992 study of the "Lucy" skeleton used radiometric dating of volcanic ash to conclude that the fossil was 3.18 million years old, significantly older than previous estimates of its age.

Ⓓ Repeated analysis of the "Omo I" skeleton eventually determined that it was approximately 100,000 years older than had been indicated when it was initially analyzed.

Practice Tests

CONTINUED

14

One diagnostic tool that is frequently used to test for cardiac muscle injury, or damage to the heart's tissue, is to measure the concentration levels of troponin in a patient's blood because some troponin subunits have shown to be either exclusive to, or significantly higher in, damaged cardiac tissue. In the hospital, when a patient presents with symptoms that could indicate a myocardial infarction, or heart attack, the responding medical team will assess the patient's troponin levels. If the patient's troponin levels are elevated, they will immediately begin treating the patient for a heart attack.

Which finding, if true, would most directly weaken the medical team's reason for relying on this diagnostic tool?

- (A) Researchers have identified a positive correlation between the severity of cardiac muscle injury and higher concentration levels of troponin.

- (B) Recent surveys reported that patients that present with elevated troponin levels typically have shorter wait times in the emergency departments.

- (C) Myocardial infarctions occur when the body's demand for oxygen is unable to be met due to a blockage in the coronary vessels.

- (D) A recent study demonstrated that nearly half of all patients who have experienced any type of acute trauma to the chest will present with elevated troponin levels.

CONTINUED

Average Lobster Body Length, in mm

	2006	2008	2010	2012
Fished area—males	248	252	254	249
Fished area—females	252	243	253	248
Protected area—males	240	268	281	285
Protected area—females	240	260	270	276

Tonje Sordalen hypothesized that Norwegian fishing regulations are contributing to the production of smaller-sized lobsters. Norwegian lobster fishers may only retain lobsters with body lengths longer than 250 mm. Sordalen theorized that the removal of larger individuals from the breeding population was forcing a gradual reduction in lobster body length because a female lobster will usually only mate with a male that is her size or larger. To test this hypothesis, Sordalen and her team collected and measured over 2,000 lobsters across a six-year period, starting in 2006, when several areas protected from lobster fishing were established.

Which choice best describes data from the table that support Sordalen's hypothesis?

Ⓐ The males in the protected area had longer average body lengths than males in the fished areas, even though the rate of change of average body length for protected males was less than that of protected females.

Ⓑ Not only was the rate of change of average body length of males in the protected area greater than that of protected females, but the protected males achieved overall longer body lengths than the fished males.

Ⓒ Females in both fished and protected areas always had rates of change of average body length less that those of the males in the corresponding areas.

Ⓓ Neither the males nor the females in the fished areas showed a significant decrease in average body length during the study period.

Practice Tests

CONTINUED

K 855

16

Ann Kussmaul, an economic historian, tracked the movement of the Industrial Revolution through England by using marriage records. Prior to the Industrial Revolution, villages in farming districts recorded most marriages in the winter, after crops were harvested. In hilly districts, where sheep were raised, most marriages were recorded in the summer, after the busy lambing season in the spring. As the Industrial Revolution and the factory-based labor it demanded moved into the villages, marriages became more evenly distributed throughout the year, indicating that _____

Which choice most logically completes the text?

(A) factory work was not considered to be a better type of employment than agriculture.

(B) the total number of marriages occurring in a village during the year increased as well.

(C) the benefits of the Industrial Revolution were seen more quickly in the cities than in the rural villages.

(D) people's activities were no longer tied as closely to the seasons of the year as they had been in the past.

17

Peacock spiders, a type of jumping spider that is native to Australia, are tiny predators whose excellent eyesight _____ them to easily hunt and capture prey. Their keen vision may be one of the reasons the female peacock spiders are so swiftly wooed by the elaborate mating dances that the males perform.

Which choice completes the text so that it conforms to the conventions of Standard English?

(A) will allow

(B) allow

(C) allows

(D) has allowed

CONTINUED

18

When crafting new work, Sudanese-American poet Safia Elhillo frequently draws on her own experiences as a child of immigrant parents and the complicated emotions of being held between two worlds with her language, culture, and history. Elhillo's newest collection of poetry, *Girls That Never Die* (2022), is a national bestseller, which is unsurprising because her writings _____ lauded before. Her debut collection of poetry, *The January Children* (2017), won both the Sillerman First Book Prize for African Poets and the Arab American Book Award.

Which choice completes the text so that it conforms to the conventions of Standard English?

Ⓐ have been

Ⓑ is

Ⓒ has been

Ⓓ are

19

Trumpeter Miles Davis reached the artistic high point of his career relatively quickly when he was a newcomer in the 1950s. While studying at the Juilliard School of Music in New York by day, Davis haunted the _____ by night, receiving another education entirely. Bebop, the hot, frantic new sound in jazz, was being played by such musical revolutionaries as Charlie Parker, Dizzy Gillespie, and Thelonious Monk, and Davis was sometimes invited up on the bandstand to play with them.

Which choice completes the text so that it conforms to the conventions of Standard English?

Ⓐ city's jazz clubs

Ⓑ city's jazz club's

Ⓒ cities' jazz clubs

Ⓓ cities' jazz club's

20

The first home video game system that connected to a television was only capable of displaying a white line and three white dots on a black _____ by plastic color overlays that players could place directly on the TV screen, the system included instructions on how to modify the appearance of each otherwise identical-looking game.

Which choice completes the text so that it conforms to the conventions of Standard English?

- (A) background and accompanied
- (B) background. Accompanied
- (C) background, accompanied
- (D) background accompanied

21

British scientists Antony Hewish and Sir Martin Ryle won the Nobel Prize in Physics in 1974 for their research in radio astrophysics, which led to the discovery of pulsars. However, it is inaccurate to say that only Hewish and Ryle discovered the recurring bursts of radio waves emitted by a celestial object. _____ findings were based on observations made and documented by Dame Jocelyn Bell Burnell, a graduate student under Hewish at the University of Cambridge.

Which choice completes the text so that it conforms to the conventions of Standard English?

- (A) His
- (B) Their
- (C) Its
- (D) They're

22

Discovered in 1914, the tunnels of the deep subterranean Trois Frères cave in France _____ hundreds of Paleolithic paintings and engravings. Its most famous painting is referred to as "the sorcerer." This mysterious human-like figure that combines parts of various animals seems to stare directly at the viewer, fascinating both archaeologists and the general public alike.

Which choice completes the text so that it conforms to the conventions of Standard English?

- (A) contained
- (B) containing
- (C) contain
- (D) contains

CONTINUED

Practice Tests

23

Suburban zoning laws have forced the ongoing separation of living and commercial spaces. As such, the city dweller's fond experiences of walking down the block to the neighborhood park or café _____ entirely alien to a suburbanite. Should suburban dwellers, on a Saturday morning, desire a change of scenery or a cup of coffee, they must get in their cars and drive some distance.

Which choice completes the text so that it conforms to the conventions of Standard English?

(A) is

(B) were

(C) was

(D) are

24

Political philosophers of the past often argued that the best system of government is one in which everyone in a given society would vote on each and every law. In the past, such a system could only have been feasible in small communities, as it would have been impossible to execute efficiently on a large scale. _____ the existence of modern technology now renders this objection irrelevant. If our society so desires it, all of us may one day digitally cast votes on individual laws from the comfort of our homes.

Which choice completes the text with the most logical transition?

(A) Indeed,

(B) Likewise,

(C) However,

(D) For example,

25

In transportation planning and civil engineering, an important inclusion is road verges, which are strips of grass, bushes, or trees that separate roads from the sidewalk. Road verges play a vital part in pedestrian and driver safety; _____ trees lining a roadway decrease the number of pedestrian fatalities in an area because they act as a buffer.

Which choice completes the text with the most logical transition?

(A) for instance,

(B) therefore,

(C) first,

(D) despite this,

CONTINUED

26

The human eye contains no photoreceptor cells—which facilitate our vision by converting light into electrical signals—in the spot where the optic nerves connect from the eye to the brain, resulting in a "blind spot" in our field of vision. The brain's visual cortex, _____ is able to "fill in" the missing visual information, so that we do not typically experience any lapse in our sight due to the blind spot.

Which choice completes the text with the most logical transition?

(A) similarly,

(B) nevertheless,

(C) indeed,

(D) in other words,

CONTINUED

27

While researching a topic, a student has taken the following notes:

- Niko Luoma is an important artist of the Helsinki School of photography.
- *For Each Minute, Sixty-Five Seconds* is a collection of his photographic interpretations of historic artworks.
- Luoma published the book in 2021.
- It includes abstract interpretations of paintings such as Pablo Picasso's *Weeping Woman*.
- Luoma used some of the same photographic techniques in *For Each Minute, Sixty-Five Seconds* as in his 2012 book *And Time is No Longer an Obstacle*.

The student wants to introduce Niko Luoma and his book *For Each Minute, Sixty-Five Seconds* to a new audience. Which choice most effectively uses relevant information from the notes to accomplish this goal?

(A) Niko Luoma published *And Time is No Longer an Obstacle* before he created *For Each Minute, Sixty-Five Seconds*.

(B) *For Each Minute, Sixty-Five Seconds*, a photography collection published in 2021, consists of abstract photographic interpretations of historic artworks by an artist of the Helsinki School of photography.

(C) In 2021, Niko Luoma of the Helsinki School of photography published *For Each Minute, Sixty-Five Seconds*, which is a collection of his abstract interpretations of historic artworks, including Pablo Picasso's *Weeping Woman*.

(D) *And Time is No Longer an Obstacle* and *For Each Minute, Sixty-Five Seconds*, both published by Niko Lumoa, use similar photographic techniques.

Practice Tests

ANSWER KEY

Reading and Writing: Module A

1.	**B**	8.	**B**	15.	**B**	22.	**C**
2.	**C**	9.	**D**	16.	**D**	23.	**D**
3.	**A**	10.	**B**	17.	**C**	24.	**C**
4.	**B**	11.	**B**	18.	**A**	25.	**A**
5.	**D**	12.	**C**	19.	**A**	26.	**B**
6.	**D**	13.	**D**	20.	**B**	27.	**C**
7.	**D**	14.	**D**	21.	**B**		

Instructions

Compare your answers to the answer key and enter the number of correct answers for this stage here. _____ This is your raw score.

Take a 10-minute break and turn to the Math Routing Module to continue your test.

Explanations will be at the end of the practice test.

READING AND WRITING: MODULE B

Mark your answers either on the pages that follow or on a separate sheet of paper. You will be scoring this Module before moving on to the Math section.

DIRECTIONS

The questions in this section address a number of important reading and writing skills. Each question includes one or more passages, which may include a table or graph. Read each passage and question carefully, and then choose the best answer to the question based on the passage(s).

All questions in this section are multiple-choice with four answer choices. Each question has a single best answer.

1

The following text is adapted from L.M. Montgomery's 1926 novel *The Blue Castle*.

For a moment she was afraid she was going to cry. It was all so—ridiculous. Then she heard Dr. Trent's housekeeper coming down the stairs. Valancy rose and went to the office door.

"The doctor forgot all about me," she said with a twisted smile.

"Well, that's too bad," said Mrs. Patterson sympathetically. "But it wasn't much wonder, poor man. That was a telegram they 'phoned over from the Port. His son has been terribly injured in an auto accident in Montreal.... You'll have to come again, Miss Stirling. I hope it's nothing serious."

"Oh, no, nothing serious," agreed Valancy. She felt a little less humiliated. It was no wonder poor Dr. Trent had forgotten her at such a moment. Nevertheless, she felt very flat and discouraged as she went down the street.

As used in the text, what does the word "flat" most nearly mean?

- (A) Settled
- (B) Subdued
- (C) Bored
- (D) Even

Practice Tests

CONTINUED ➜ **K** 863

2

Robert Liston was a British surgeon notable for several professional achievements; yet, he is largely remembered for _____ event. During the speedy amputation of a patient's leg, Liston accidentally amputated the fingers of his surgical assistant. Both the patient and assistant subsequently died of gangrene. A spectator at the surgery fainted, dying from shock. Thus, Liston is known for conducting the only surgery in history with a 300% mortality rate.

Which choice completes the text with the most logical and precise word or phrase?

- (A) a wily
- (B) a trite
- (C) an infamous
- (D) a glorious

3

Ludonarrative dissonance is a term used in the study and design of video games. It refers to an _____ the narrative of a game's *story*, told through cut-scenes or dialogue, and the narrative created by the *gameplay*. For example, the story might ostensibly be about a thief struggling with the morality of stealing to provide for her family. However, if the fun of gameplay is centered on stealth, sneaking past guards to rob a safe or steal famous artwork, then a clash is created between what the story and gameplay are saying about theft.

Which choice completes the text with the most logical and precise word or phrase?

- (A) ambivalence toward
- (B) expunging of
- (C) incompatibility between
- (D) objectification of

4

A parasocial relationship is where the consumer of a media product perceives a close personal relationship with the performer in that product. While their one-way relationship with the media figure is _____, the consumer can nevertheless experience intense emotions, ranging from romantic love to stinging betrayal. Interest in the study of parasocial relationships first arose in the 1950s, as they were widely noted following the rise of radio and television.

Which choice completes the text with the most logical and precise word or phrase?

- (A) anomalous
- (B) deceptive
- (C) illusory
- (D) scandalous

CONTINUED

Practice Tests

5

The following text is adapted from Sui Sin Far's 1912 short story "Children of Peace." The characters immigrated from China to the United States as young adults and married in San Francisco.

It was seven years since Liu Venti and Pau Tsu had begun their work in San Francisco's Chinatown; seven years of struggle and hardship, working and waiting, living, learning, fighting, failing, loving—and conquering. The victory, to an onlooker, might have seemed small: just a modest school for adult pupils of their own race, a few white night pupils, and a free school for children. But the latter was in itself evidence that Liu Venti and Pau Tsu had not only sailed safely through the waters of poverty, but had reached a haven from which they could enjoy the blessedness of stretching out helping hands to others.

Which choice best describes the function of the underlined portion in the text as a whole?

(A) It provides a summary to show that the characters faced both difficulties and successes over the years.

(B) It emphasizes the length of time in which the characters have lived in a new city in the United States.

(C) It highlights the ever-present instability of the characters' financial situation.

(D) It introduces the theme that education played an important role in achieving success in Chinatown.

6

"Calligraffiti" is art that combines calligraphy, or artistic handwriting, with graffiti, or drawing on a public surface. Artist eL Seed is noted for his monumental installations that use traditional Arabic calligraphy to inscribe inspirational quotations on the sides of buildings. One of his most ambitious and complex projects, "Perceptions," extends over the walls of fifty homes in Cairo, Egypt. The complete inscription, "Anyone who wants to see the sunlight clearly must first wipe his eyes," is only fully visible from one vantage point. For this project, eL Seed used photographs of the neighborhood overlaid with his digitized calligraphy to ensure that the images on every wall of his massive project would align properly.

Which choice best describes the function of the fourth sentence in the overall structure of the text?

(A) It explains the importance of the quotations mentioned earlier in the text.

(B) It sets up the detailed description of the artist's method made earlier in the text.

(C) It describes the reasons behind the author's motivation discussed earlier in the text.

(D) It provides a detail about the complexity of the project that supports a claim made earlier in the text.

CONTINUED

Practice Tests

7

The following text is adapted from Niccolò Machiavelli's 1513 political treatise *The Prince*. Throughout the text, Machiavelli is offering advice to the rulers of kingdoms.

It ought to be remembered that there is nothing more difficult to take in hand, more perilous to conduct, or more uncertain in its success, than to take the lead in the introduction of a new order of things, because the innovator has for enemies all those who have done well under the old conditions, and lukewarm defenders in those who may do well under the new. This coolness arises partly from fear of the opponents, who have the laws on their side, and partly from the incredulity of men, who do not readily believe in new things until they have had a long experience of them.

Which choice best states the main purpose of the text?

(A) It explains why any ruler will encounter difficulty when trying to achieve reform within the kingdom.

(B) It discusses the idea that people who will benefit from reform will nevertheless be skeptical about it ahead of time.

(C) It argues that one should not go against the law when considering what reforms to make as a ruler.

(D) It presents the case for why a ruler cannot risk undertaking any reform however necessary it might be.

CONTINUED

Text 1

Some literary critics argue that Gustave Flaubert's 1856 novel *Madame Bovary* has a strange and subversive theme that undermines its own medium: in short, they say that Flaubert's masterpiece of fiction is a cautionary tale about the dangers of reading novels. As evidence, they point to its unsympathetic protagonist, Emma Bovary, who lives in her books and romanticizes the simplest aspects of daily life as well as her relationships, ultimately becoming entirely dissatisfied with real life.

Text 2

Flaubert's *Madame Bovary* was not meant to be a criticism of fiction itself, but a warning against allowing suggestible people like Emma to have access to novels. It is the other characters' unwillingness to check Emma's literary passions (and even their ignorance of the existence of such a problem) that leads to the disintegration of the Bovary household.

Based on the texts, how would the author of Text 2 most likely respond to the claims of the literary critics in Text 1?

Ⓐ By insisting that *Madame Bovary*'s message is that novels are dangerous for only some readers

Ⓑ By emphasizing that the other characters in *Madame Bovary* also read novels without any adverse effects

Ⓒ By admitting that *Madame Bovary*'s depiction of Emma Bovary demonstrates that the reading of novels is always dangerous

Ⓓ By arguing that the romanticization of daily life can lead to high expectations and dissatisfaction

Practice Tests

CONTINUED ➡

9

The following text is adapted from Thucydides' 5th century B.C.E. work *History of the Peloponnesian War*. During the war, Athens and Sparta each lead an alliance of city-states. Thucydides describes the war's impact on Corcyra, a neutral city-state.

In peace there would have been neither the pretext nor the wish to make such an invitation; but in war, with an alliance always at the command of either political faction for the hurt of their adversaries and their own corresponding advantage, opportunities for bringing in the foreigner were never wanting to the revolutionary parties.... Words had to change their ordinary meaning and to take that which was now given them. Reckless audacity came to be considered the courage of a loyal ally; prudent hesitation, specious cowardice; moderation was held to be a cloak for unmanliness; ability to see all sides of a question, inaptness to act on any.

According to the text, how did the Peloponnesian War undermine the domestic politics of Corcyra?

(A) Public debate became confused as the war led to a change in the definition of many commonplace words, undermining public debate.

(B) The benefits of joining the war were great, but the two political factions could not agree on what to ask of Athens for an alliance.

(C) Each political faction felt itself to be in danger, as their opponent might ally with a foreign power.

(D) Both political factions feared that their city would be invaded and totally destroyed by a foreign power.

K

CONTINUED

10

The following text is adapted from Victor Hugo's 1862 novel *Les Misérables*.

In former times, those severe places where the discipline of the prison delivers the convict into his own hands, were composed of four stone walls, a stone ceiling, a flagged pavement, a camp bed, a grated window, and a door lined with iron. They were called *dungeons*; but the dungeon was judged to be too terrible. Nowadays they are composed of an iron door, a grated window, a camp bed, a flagged pavement, four stone walls, and a stone ceiling, and are called *chambers of punishment*. A little light penetrates towards midday. The inconvenient point about these chambers which, as the reader sees, are not dungeons, is that they allow the persons who should be at work to think.

Which choice best states the main idea of the text?

Ⓐ Dungeons were replaced after the French legislature judged them to be too terrible.

Ⓑ A prisoner who has time to think will often be deeply unhappy.

Ⓒ Little has been done to actually reform prisons.

Ⓓ The midday light that enters the chambers of punishment is harmful to the eyes of prisoners.

11

"The Storm" is a poem by Emily Dickinson first published in 1890. In the poem, Dickinson suggests that, despite violent interludes, life continues undisturbed, writing, _____

Which quotation from "The Storm" most effectively illustrates the claim?

Ⓐ "We barred the windows and the doors / As from an emerald ghost; / The doom's electric moccasin / That very instant passed."

Ⓑ "On a strange mob of panting trees, / And fences fled away, / And rivers where the houses ran / The living looked that day."

Ⓒ "How much can come / And much can go, / And yet abide the world!"

Ⓓ "The bell within the steeple wild / The flying tidings whirled."

12

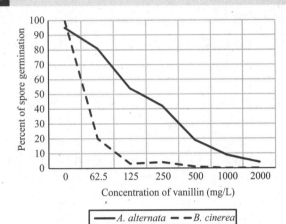

A. alternata ─ ─ B. cinerea

Cherry tomatoes are a highly-valued crop, but after harvest, the fruits are susceptible to gray mold caused by the fungal parasite *Botrytis cinerea* and black rot caused by *Alternaria alternata*. Vanillin is a popular and safe food additive that has also shown antimicrobial and antioxidant effects. Jing Yang and colleagues hypothesized that applying vanillin to cherry tomatoes could extend their shelf life by delaying the onset of gray mold and black rot. The researchers tested the effectiveness of varying concentrations of vanillin on the spore germination of the causative organisms. Although high concentrations of vanillin proved to be effective, Yang and colleagues reported a substantial difference in the preventative abilities of vanillin at lower concentrations, citing _____

Which choice most effectively uses data from the graph to complete the example?

(A) the similarity of the level of the rate of spore reduction of both organisms at concentrations of vanillin over 1000 mg/L.

(B) the higher concentration of vanillin needed before the spore germination rate of the fungus causing gray mold equaled that of the fungus causing black rot.

(C) the observation that, at low concentrations of vanillin, the spore germination rate of the black rot fungus dropped quickly whereas that of the gray mold fungus did not.

(D) a sharp decrease in the rate of gray mold spore germination at a low concentration of vanillin, while a similar decrease in the rate of spore germination of black rot required a much higher concentration.

CONTINUED

13

Some psychologists have argued that even subtle cues that suggest one is being watched can cause a person to act more generously. Psychologists Melissa Bateson, Daniel Nettle, and Gilbert Roberts claim to have found evidence for this effect in a 2006 study, in which the researchers set up an "honesty box" in a university coffee room. Posted signage indicated the prices of various drinks, and students could anonymously take drinks and place their payments into the box. The researchers also displayed a banner above the drink station that showed either a pair of directly staring eyes or a control image of flowers.

Which finding from the researchers' study, if true, would most strongly support their claim?

(A) On average, participants paid approximately the same price for their drinks regardless of whether the image of eyes or the control image was displayed.

(B) In a post-experiment survey, participants who had viewed the image of eyes self-reported increased feelings of anxiety compared with participants who had viewed the control image.

(C) On average, participants paid approximately three times as much for their drinks when the image of eyes rather than the control image was displayed.

(D) In a post-experiment survey, the majority of participants reported that they had not noticed any image displayed on the banner, whether it was the image of eyes or the control image.

Practice Tests

Selected Results of Dating Analyses of Hominid Fossils

Hominid fossil	Year of study	Dating technique	Date assigned (approximate)
"Lucy" *Australopithecus afarensis* skeleton	Initial analysis	Stratigraphic (analysis of surrounding pig skeletons)	3.5–2.9 million years ago
	1992	Radiometric (geochemical dating of nearby volcanic ash)	3.18 million years ago
"Omo I" *Homo sapiens* keleton	Initial analysis	Stratigraphic (analysis of surrounding mollusk shells)	130,000 years ago
	2004	Stratigraphic (analysis of surrounding fossils)	195,000 years ago
	2021	Radiometric (geochemical dating of nearby volcanic ash)	233,000 years ago

Practice Tests

One difficulty facing palaeoarchaeologists, researchers who study ancient human remains, is determining accurate dates for the hominid fossils they analyze. Scientific dating methods fall into two broad categories: relative and absolute. Relative dating approximates date ranges based on where a fossil is located in relation to other fossils. For instance, stratigraphy, a type of relative dating, relies on the principle that lower sedimentary layers are older than higher ones. Absolute dating uses techniques such as radiometric dating, which measures the decay of radioactive materials in a fossil. Palaeoarchaeologists today rely on a combination of these methods and suggest that applying absolute dating techniques to fossils previously analyzed by relative dating may enable researchers to fine-tune broad approximations of dates into more precise estimates.

Which choice best describes data from the table that support the palaeoarchaeologists' suggestion?

Ⓐ The radiometric dating of the "Lucy" skeleton indicated a more specific date within the date range that had been determined by the stratigraphic analysis of the skeleton.

Ⓑ The stratigraphic dating of the "Lucy" skeleton indicated an approximate age of 3.18 million years, which conflicted with the date determined by the radiometric dating of the skeleton.

Ⓒ The initial stratigraphic analysis of the "Omo I" skeleton indicated an approximate age of 130,000 years, while the 2004 stratigraphic analysis of the skeleton indicated an approximate age of 195,000 years.

Ⓓ The radiometric dating of the "Lucy" skeleton approximated its age at 3.18 million years, while the radiometric dating of the "Omo I" skeleton approximated its age as significantly younger, at 233,000 years.

CONTINUED

15

Political scientists argue that the field is a true science, capable of quantifying past evidence and using it to predict future events. They cite the ability of models, such as the one developed by Alan Abramowitz in 1988, to use measurable data to forecast election results. Abramowitz's model uses only three variables: the incumbent president's net approval rating at the end of June of the election year, the change in real Gross Domestic Product in the second quarter of the election year, and a variable indicating whether a president is running for re-election. This model has predicted the winner of each presidential election since 1988, overstating the margin of victory by an average of only 4.5%. In 2012, Abramowitz added a fourth variable to account for the polarization between the two major political parties, which reduced the error in the winning margin of victory by half.

Which finding, if true, would most directly weaken the political scientists' claim?

(A) Of the three variables used in Abramowitz's original model, the change in real Gross Domestic Product in the second quarter of the election year is given the most weight.

(B) Abramowitz's model was less accurate in the period from 1988 through 1996 than in the period from 1996 to 2020.

(C) Political scientists have yet to agree on a clear methodology for measuring partisanship, so Abramowitz's 2012 modification was based on his own analysis.

(D) Several other election prediction models have similar rates of accuracy as that of Abramowitz's model.

16

A decades-old experimental situation called "the marshmallow test" was developed at Stanford University to measure delayed gratification skills in young children. The creators of the study later compared the children's initial results to their later-in-life outcomes and determined that those who demonstrated self-control had higher rates of academic and professional successes. A team of researchers, led by behavioral ecologist Alexandra Schnell, modified this assessment method and used it to determine that cuttlefish with the ability to exert self-control performed better in cognitive performance tests. These findings would suggest that _____

Which choice most logically completes the text?

(A) children and cuttlefish both delay gratification to improve their learning outcomes.

(B) delaying gratification is positively associated with superior learning performance.

(C) the cuttlefishes' self-control may be attributed to their ability to camouflage themselves.

(D) the marshmallow test is the most effective tool for measuring self-control.

CONTINUED

K 873

17

Some psychologists claim that humans have developed a unique nervous system that is capable of recognizing different emotional expressions out of necessity, due to the weight of such recognition in human communication. To test this theory, researchers showed photographs of people displaying emotions of joy, anger, and surprise to a group of trained pigeons. The birds were not only able to distinguish between expressions but were also able to correctly match each image to photographs of other human faces displaying the same expressions. While the experiment's results do not conclusively prove that the pigeons can comprehend the meaning of the tested expressions, _____

Which choice most logically completes the text?

(A) the results do cast doubt upon the theory proposed by the psychologists.

(B) psychologists will likely reject the attempt to draw conclusions about humans based on a study about birds.

(C) the results do suggest that the nervous systems of humans and birds are essentially identical.

(D) the results prove that emotions are important in human communication.

18

The suburb should be the ambiguous halfway point between city and country, away from the noise, congestion, and pollution but not so far away that there's no access to city culture and to all the exciting benefits of urban life. In reality, though, few suburbs have actually approached this ideal. Moreover, the structure of the modern suburb—while offering a respite from city _____ has created health and environmental risks of its own.

Which choice completes the text so that it conforms to the conventions of Standard English?

(A) pollution:

(B) pollution

(C) pollution—

(D) pollution,

CONTINUED

19

In the aftermath of the French Revolution, political and social currents in Europe brought with them significant developments in the world of music. Patronage of the arts no longer exclusively belonged to the _____ increasingly prosperous middle class flocked to public concerts and music festivals, contributing to the development of Romanticism.

Which choice completes the text so that it conforms to the conventions of Standard English?

Ⓐ aristocracy and the

Ⓑ aristocracy the

Ⓒ aristocracy; the

Ⓓ aristocracy, the

20

Lying on the bank of the Yamuna River in northern India is one of the world's most famous and beautiful buildings—the Taj Mahal. Built by the Mughal emperor Shah Jahan as a burial home for his favorite consort, Arjumand Banu Bagam (known as Mumtaz Mahal, "the Elect of the Palace"), _____ soon after her death in 1631. The mausoleum was completed by 1643, and the surrounding complex of buildings and gardens was completed about ten years later.

Which choice completes the text so that it conforms to the conventions of Standard English?

Ⓐ construction of this ornate tomb started

Ⓑ this ornate tomb began being constructed

Ⓒ plans for this ornate tomb's construction started

Ⓓ this ornate tomb's construction started

21

In recent decades, numerous international cities have vied for the distinction of possessing the world's tallest Ferris wheel. The 853-foot Ain Dubai in the United Arab Emirates secured the title in 2021. Other past Ferris wheel record holders include the 394-foot London _____ the 550-foot High Roller in Las Vegas; the 541-foot Singapore Flyer; and the 525-foot Star of Nanchang.

Which choice completes the text so that it conforms to the conventions of Standard English?

Ⓐ Eye, which kick-started the giant Ferris wheel trend when it was completed in 2000;

Ⓑ Eye, which kick-started the giant Ferris wheel trend when it was completed in 2000,

Ⓒ Eye; which kick-started the giant Ferris wheel trend when it was completed in 2000,

Ⓓ Eye which kick-started the giant Ferris wheel trend when it was completed in 2000,

CONTINUED

22

In prehistoric times, humans lived in social groupings of tribes or clans, interacting with no more than a few hundred individuals. Since each tribe had to compete for food, land, and other resources, skirmishes between neighboring groups were inevitable and frequent. Just as adherence to common languages and belief systems _____ shared cultural identity today, mutual tribal systems preserved ancient group integrity, helping people to unite against external forces. Conformity thus became an adaptation for survival; no individual wished to be cut off from the group and left all alone to deal with the many dangers of the outside world.

Which choice completes the text so that it conforms to the conventions of Standard English?

Ⓐ   facilitated

Ⓑ   facilitating

Ⓒ   facilitate

Ⓓ   facilitates

23

Olympus Mons is an enormous shield-type volcano on the surface of the planet Mars. The Mars Orbiter Laser Altimeter, an instrument on the *Mars Global Surveyor* spacecraft, used infrared laser pulses to measure the height of the _____ of the Tharsis Montes volcanic region, this massive geographic feature towers more than 13 miles above the Martian surface and is the tallest known mountain on any planet in the solar system.

Which choice completes the text so that it conforms to the conventions of Standard English?

Ⓐ   volcano. Part

Ⓑ   volcano part

Ⓒ   volcano, part

Ⓓ   volcano and part

CONTINUED

24

The first home video game system, released in 1972, was not a great commercial success, but it introduced features that still character-ize modern home video game systems today. _____ one significant innovation was its use of interchangeable game cartridges.

Which choice completes the text with the most logical transition?

- Ⓐ As a result,
- Ⓑ Likewise,
- Ⓒ In contrast,
- Ⓓ For instance,

25

Given that some of the Founding Fathers of the United States opposed the concept of politi-cal parties, modern citizens may reasonably wonder how the party system arose in the first place. After all, while there may seem to be no essential connection between two issues such as taxation and foreign policy, most of the nation's voters huddle under one of the two all-encompassing ideological umbrellas held out by our two dominant political parties. _____, the origins and endurance of the two-party system might initially seem puzzling to the budding student of political science, but to those who have a background in anthropol-ogy or social psychology, it should come as no surprise.

Which choice completes the text with the most logical transition?

- Ⓐ For instance,
- Ⓑ Indeed,
- Ⓒ However,
- Ⓓ Finally,

CONTINUED ➜

26

While researching a topic, a student has taken the following notes:

- Niko Luoma is an important artist of the Helsinki School of photography.

- The Helsinki School encourages the use of abstract photography to facilitate deep thinking.

- Luoma's 2021 book *For Each Minute, Sixty-Five Seconds* features a collection of his photographic interpretations of historic artworks.

- *For Each Minute, Sixty-Five Seconds* includes abstract interpretations of paintings by artists, including Vincent van Gogh.

The student wants to introduce Niko Luoma's book to an audience already familiar with the Helsinki School of photography. Which choice most effectively uses relevant information from the notes to accomplish this goal?

(A) The Helsinki School, whose artists include *For Each Minute, Sixty-Five Seconds*'s Niko Luoma, uses photography to promote deep thinking.

(B) *For Each Minute, Sixty-Five Seconds* is the work of an artist of the Helsinki School, which emphasizes abstract photography's ability to promote deep thinking.

(C) One artist interpreted by Niko Luoma, who is an important figure in the Helsinki School of photography, is the painter Vincent van Gogh.

(D) The Helsinki School artist Niko Luoma's *For Each Minute, Sixty-Five Seconds* is a photo collection of his abstract interpretations of historic artworks.

CONTINUED ➡

27

While researching a topic, a student has taken the following notes:

- The Volcanic Explosivity Index (VEI) measures the intensity of a volcanic eruption in relation to other volcanic eruptions.

- The VEI of an eruption is determined based on factors, including the quantity of the erupted material.

- The VEI is reported on a scale from 0–8; each increase of 1 denotes a tenfold increase in the intensity of the eruption.

- The eruption of Mount Pelée in 1902 is classified as a 4 on the VEI index, which is described as a "catastrophic" eruption that ejects between 0.1 km^3 and 1 km^3 of material.

- The eruption of Vesuvius in 79 C.E. is classified as a 5 on the VEI index, which is described as a "cataclysmic" level of eruption that ejects between 1 km^3 and 10 km^3 of material.

- The eruption of Krakatoa in 1883 C.E. is classified as a 6 on the VEI index, which is described as a "colossal" level of eruption that ejects between 10 km^3 and 100 km^3 of material.

The student wants to emphasize how intense the eruption of Vesuvius was relative to the eruptions of Mount Pelée and Krakatoa. Which choice most effectively uses relevant information from the notes to accomplish this goal?

(A) The eruption of Vesuvius in 79 C.E. was a 5 on the VEI index, the eruption of Mount Pelée in 1902 C.E. was a 4 on the VEI index, and the eruption of Krakatoa in 1883 C.E. was a 6 on the VEI index.

(B) A classification of 5 on the VEI index, as has been assigned to the eruption of Vesuvius, indicates an eruption that is considered "cataclysmic" and that ejects up to 10 km^3 of material.

(C) While the eruption of Mount Pelée was a 4 on the VEI index and the eruption of Krakatoa was a 6 on the VEI index, the eruption of Vesuvius was classified as a 5 since it ejected more than 1 km^3 of material.

(D) At a 5 on the VEI index, the eruption of Vesuvius ejected more than 1 km^3 of material and was ten times more powerful than the eruption of Mount Pelée but ten times less powerful than the eruption of Krakatoa.

IF YOU FINISH BEFORE TIME IS CALLED, YOU MAY CHECK YOUR WORK ON THIS MODULE ONLY.
ON TEST DAY, YOU WON'T BE ABLE TO MOVE ON TO THE NEXT MODULE UNTIL TIME EXPIRES.

STOP

K   879

ANSWER KEY

Reading and Writing: Module B

1.	**B**	8.	**A**	15.	**C**	22.	**D**
2.	**C**	9.	**C**	16.	**B**	23.	**A**
3.	**C**	10.	**C**	17.	**A**	24.	**D**
4.	**C**	11.	**C**	18.	**C**	25.	**B**
5.	**A**	12.	**D**	19.	**C**	26.	**D**
6.	**D**	13.	**C**	20.	**B**	27.	**D**
7.	**A**	14.	**A**	21.	**A**		

Instructions

Compare your answers to the answer key and enter the number of correct answers for this stage here. _____ This is your raw score.

Take a 10-minute break and turn to the Math Routing Module to continue your test.

Explanations will be at the end of the practice test.

MATH: ROUTING MODULE

Mark your answers either on the pages that follow or on a separate sheet of paper. You will be scoring this Routing Module before going on to the final Math Module.

DIRECTIONS

- The questions in this section address a number of important math skills.

- Use of a calculator is permitted for all questions. A reference sheet, calculator, and these directions can be accessed throughout the test.

- Unless otherwise indicated:

  - All variables and expressions represent real numbers.

  - Figures provided are drawn to scale.

  - All figures lie in a plane.

  - The domain of a given function f is the set of all real numbers x for which $f(x)$ is a real number.

For **multiple-choice questions**, solve each problem and choose the correct answer from the choices provided. Each multiple-choice question has a single correct answer.

For **student-produced response questions**, solve each problem and enter your answer as described below:

- If you find **more than one correct answer**, enter only one answer.

- You can enter up to 5 characters for a **positive** answer and up to 6 characters (including the negative sign) for a **negative** answer.

- If your answer is a **fraction** that doesn't fit in the provided space, enter the decimal equivalent.

- If your answer is a **decimal** that doesn't fit in the provided space, enter it by truncating or rounding at the fourth digit.

- If your answer is a **mixed number** (such as $3\frac{1}{2}$), enter it as an improper fraction (**7/2**) or its decimal equivalent (**3.5**).

- Don't enter **symbols** such as a percent sign, comma, or dollar sign.

Examples

ANSWER	ACCEPTABLE WAY TO ANSWER	UNACCEPTABLE: WILL NOT RECEIVE CREDIT
3.5	3.5 3.50 7/2	31/2 3 1/2
$\frac{2}{3}$	2/3 .6666 .6667 0.666 0.667	0.66 .66 0.67 .67
$-\frac{1}{3}$	−1/3 −.3333 −0.333	−.33 −0.33

Reference:

$A = \pi r^2$
$C = 2\pi r$

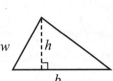

$A = lw$

$A = \frac{1}{2}bh$

$c^2 = a^2 + b^2$

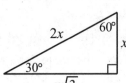

Special Right Triangles

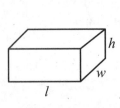

$V = lwh$

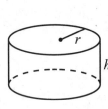

$V = \pi r^2 h$

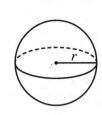

$V = \frac{4}{3}\pi r^3$

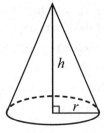

$V = \frac{1}{3}\pi r^2 h$

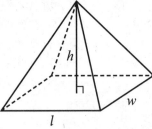

$V = \frac{1}{3}lwh$

The number of degrees of arc in a circle is 360.

The number of radians of arc in a circle is 2π.

The sum of the measures in degrees of the angles of a triangle is 180.

CONTINUED ➡

1

$$S = 10.625\,E + 13.750$$

The equation shown is used to predict a person's salary, S, in thousands of dollars, based on the number of years of work experience, E, the person has. What does 10.625 represent in terms of the model?

Ⓐ The estimated salary, in thousands of dollars, for a person with 13.750 years of work experience.

Ⓑ The estimated increase in a person's salary, in thousands of dollars, every 13.750 years.

Ⓒ The estimated increase in a person's salary, in thousands of dollars, for each one-year increase in work experience.

Ⓓ The estimated increase in a person's work experience, in years, for each thousand of dollars increase in a person's salary.

2

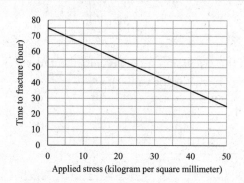

The graph shows the linear relationship between the time to fracture of a concrete blend, y, and applied stress, x. Which of the following equations represents this relationship?

Ⓐ $y + x = -75$

Ⓑ $y - x = -75$

Ⓒ $x + y = 75$

Ⓓ $x - y = 75$

3

A runner ran 4000 meters at a rate of 800 meters per minute. For how many minutes did the runner run?

4

$$\frac{3\left(\sqrt[4]{a^{16}}\right)}{\sqrt{2a^6}}$$

If the expression shown is equivalent to xa^y and $x > 1$, what is the value of y?

(A) 1

(B) $\dfrac{3}{\sqrt{2}}$

(C) 7

(D) 10

5

If $x^2 - 5x = -6$, what are the two possible values of x?

(A) $-1, 6$

(B) $1, -6$

(C) $-2, -3$

(D) $2, 3$

6

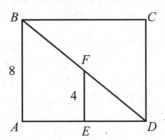

The area of rectangle $ABCD$ is 80. Line segment EF is parallel to AB. What is the area of triangle FED?

(A) 5

(B) 10

(C) 20

(D) 40

7

$$a + \frac{2}{3}b = 12$$

What is b in terms of a?

(A) $12 - \dfrac{3}{2}a$

(B) $12 - \dfrac{2}{3}a$

(C) $18 - \dfrac{3}{2}a$

(D) $18 - \dfrac{2}{3}a$

CONTINUED ➡

8

x	$f(x)$
0	−1
1	1
2	1
3	−1

Which of the following functions best models the data in the table?

(A) $f(x) = -x^2 + 3x - 1$

(B) $f(x) = -2^x + 3x - 1$

(C) $f(x) = -2x + 3$

(D) $f(x) = x^2 - 3x - 1$

9

$$y = 3x - 2$$
$$y + 15 = x^2 - 9x$$

If $x > 0$, what is the value of x?

(A) −1

(B) 4

(C) 12

(D) 13

10

Hamza currently has \$1,000 in his checking account. He makes \$1,200 each week and deposits $\frac{2}{3}$ of that amount into his checking account. Hamza has no other sources of income. How many weeks will it take him to save \$5,000?

(A) 3

(B) 4

(C) 5

(D) 6

11

Anastasia sells a total of 15 pounds of vegetables. Tomatoes are sold for \$2 per pound, and peppers are sold for \$7 per pound. If she makes a total of \$45, how many pounds of peppers does she sell?

(A) 3

(B) 9

(C) 12

(D) 15

12

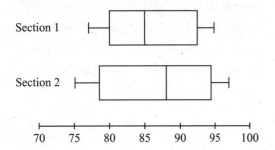

Section 1

Section 2

70   75   80   85   90   95   100

The box plots summarize the final exam grades from two sections of Mr. Horton's physics class. Based on the box plots, which of the following statements must be true?

Ⓐ The range of Section 1 is greater than the range of Section 2.

Ⓑ The mean of Section 1 is less than the mean of Section 2.

Ⓒ The mean of Section 1 is greater than the mean of Section 2.

Ⓓ The median of Section 1 is less than the median of Section 2.

13

x	$f(x)$
-1	1.75
0	1
4	-2

The table shows some values of the linear function f. What is the value of $f(6)$?

Ⓐ -4

Ⓑ -3.5

Ⓒ 3

Ⓓ 4.5

14

If (a, b) is a point in the xy-coordinate plane that lies on the graphs of both $y = x^2 + 3x - 4$ and $y = -x^2 - 3x + 4$, and $a < $ b, what is the value of $a + b$?

Practice Tests

15

The side length of an equilateral triangle is $2\sqrt{10}$ units. What is the area of the triangle, in square units?

- (A) $5\sqrt{3}$
- (B) $10\sqrt{3}$
- (C) 20
- (D) $20\sqrt{3}$

16

Each week, Eugene loses 0.25% of his body weight. Approximately how many weeks will it take him to lose 5% of his original body weight?

- (A) 10
- (B) 20
- (C) 30
- (D) 40

17

$$6y + 15 = -2ax$$
$$2x + 4y = -6$$

If the system of equations has no solutions and a is a constant, what is the value of a?

18

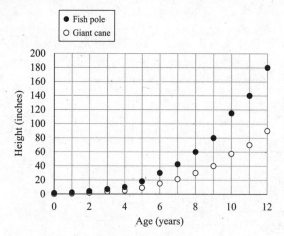

The scatterplot shows the height of two bamboo plant species, fish pole and giant cane, over time. Which of the following statements correctly describes the growth rates of the two bamboo species?

- (A) The average growth rate of the fish pole is the same as that of the great cane from 4 to 8 years and less than that of the great cane from 8 to 12 years.

- (B) The average growth rate of the fish pole is greater than that of the great cane from 4 to 8 years and greater than that of the great cane from 8 to 12 years.

- (C) The average growth rate of the fish pole is greater than that of the great cane from 0 to 6 years and less than that of the great cane from 6 to 12 years.

- (D) The average growth rate of the great cane is greater than that of the fish pole from 0 to 6 years and less than that of the fish pole from 6 to 12 years.

CONTINUED

19

$$x^2 + 6x + y^2 - 10y = k$$

Circle C is defined by the equation, where k is a constant. If the point $(-6, 9)$ lies on the circumference of the circle, what is the value of k?

Ⓐ −29

Ⓑ −9

Ⓒ 5

Ⓓ 25

20

A professor creates a test with 30 questions. He awards 1 point for each correct answer and deducts $\frac{1}{4}$ point for each incorrect answer. If Charles earns a score of 20, what was his ratio of correct to incorrect answers expressed as a fraction?

21

$$2\sqrt{a} + 1 = \frac{b^2}{c}$$

For the given equation, which of the following correctly expresses a in terms of b and c?

Ⓐ $a = \frac{1}{2}\left(\frac{b^2}{c}\right)^2 - 1$

Ⓑ $a = \left[\frac{1}{2}\left(\frac{b^2}{c}\right)\right]^2 - 1$

Ⓒ $a = \frac{1}{2}\left[\left(\frac{b^2}{c} - 1\right)^2\right]$

Ⓓ $a = \left[\frac{1}{2}\left(\frac{b^2}{c} - 1\right)\right]^2$

22

Alena determines that her pet cat has a 60% chance of a successful hunt with a margin of error of 7%. If the cat hunts 300 times in the next year, which of the following could plausibly be the number of successful hunts?

Ⓐ 150

Ⓑ 195

Ⓒ 210

Ⓓ 225

Practice Tests

This page is intentionally blank.

ANSWER KEY

Math: Routing Module

1. **C**	7. **C**	13. **B**	19. **B**
2. **C**	8. **A**	14. **−4**	20. **22/8 or 11/4**
3. **5**	9. **D**	15. **B**	21. **D**
4. **A**	10. **C**	16. **B**	22. **B**
5. **D**	11. **A**	17. **3/2 or 1.5**	
6. **B**	12. **D**	18. **B**	

Instructions

Compare your answers to the answer key and enter the number of correct answers for this stage here. _____ This is your raw score.

If you scored less than 14 correct, turn to Math Module A and continue your test.

If you had 14 or more correct in this routing module, turn to Math Module B and continue your test.

Explanations will be at the end of the practice test.

MATH: MODULE A

Mark your answers either on the pages that follow or on a separate sheet of paper. You will be scoring this module and using the results to find your final Math score.

DIRECTIONS

- The questions in this section address a number of important math skills.
- Use of a calculator is permitted for all questions. A reference sheet, calculator, and these directions can be accessed throughout the test.
- Unless otherwise indicated:
  - All variables and expressions represent real numbers.
  - Figures provided are drawn to scale.
  - All figures lie in a plane.
  - The domain of a given function f is the set of all real numbers x for which $f(x)$ is a real number.

For **multiple-choice questions**, solve each problem and choose the correct answer from the choices provided. Each multiple-choice question has a single correct answer.

For **student-produced response questions**, solve each problem and enter your answer as described below:

- If you find **more than one correct answer**, enter only one answer.
- You can enter up to 5 characters for a **positive** answer and up to 6 characters (including the negative sign) for a **negative** answer.
- If your answer is a **fraction** that doesn't fit in the provided space, enter the decimal equivalent.
- If your answer is a **decimal** that doesn't fit in the provided space, enter it by truncating or rounding at the fourth digit.
- If your answer is a **mixed number** (such as $3\frac{1}{2}$), enter it as an improper fraction (**7/2**) or its decimal equivalent (**3.5**).
- Don't enter **symbols** such as a percent sign, comma, or dollar sign.

Examples

ANSWER	ACCEPTABLE WAY TO ANSWER	UNACCEPTABLE: WILL NOT RECEIVE CREDIT
3.5	3.5 3.50 7/2	31/2 3 1/2
$\frac{2}{3}$	2/3 .6666 .6667 0.666 0.667	0.66 .66 0.67 .67
$-\frac{1}{3}$	−1/3 −.3333 −0.333	−.33 −0.33

Reference:

$A = \pi r^2$
$C = 2\pi r$

$A = lw$

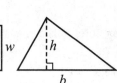
$A = \frac{1}{2}bh$

$c^2 = a^2 + b^2$

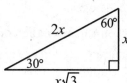
Special Right Triangles

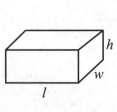
$V = lwh$

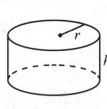
$V = \pi r^2 h$

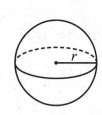
$V = \frac{4}{3}\pi r^3$

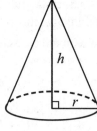
$V = \frac{1}{3}\pi r^2 h$

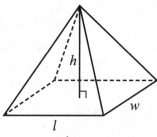
$V = \frac{1}{3}lwh$

The number of degrees of arc in a circle is 360.

The number of radians of arc in a circle is 2π.

The sum of the measures in degrees of the angles of a triangle is 180.

CONTINUED

Practice Tests

1

If 1,220 books were returned to the library and 20% of the returned books were past due, how many of the books were past due?

- (A) 61
- (B) 244
- (C) 976
- (D) 1,464

2

$$y = 6x + 1$$

For the given equation, what is the value of y when $x = -6$?

- (A) -35
- (B) -11
- (C) 13
- (D) 37

3

The function f is defined by the equation $f(x) = \frac{3}{4}x - 8$. What is the value of x when $f(x) = 16$?

- (A) 4
- (B) $\frac{32}{3}$
- (C) 18
- (D) 32

4

$$|2x + 5| = -x + 3$$

What are the possible values of x?

- (A) $x = -8, x = 8$
- (B) $x = -8, x = -\frac{2}{3}$
- (C) $x = -\frac{2}{3}, x = \frac{2}{3}$
- (D) $x = -\frac{2}{3}, x = 8$

5

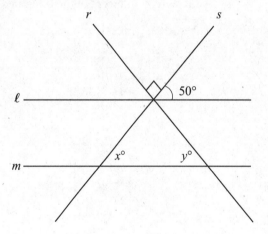

In the figure, lines l and m are parallel. What is the value of $x - y$?

- (A) 10
- (B) 40
- (C) 50
- (D) 90

Practice Tests

CONTINUED

6

$$|9 - 9x| = 81$$

For the equation given, what is the positive value of $1 - x$?

7

The equation $2x - 3y = 18$ is graphed in an xy-plane and translated up 3 units. What is the y-coordinate of the y-intercept of the translated graph?

Ⓐ -15

Ⓑ -6

Ⓒ -3

Ⓓ 21

8

If $3x - 24 = 3$, what is the value of x?

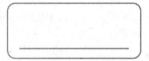

9

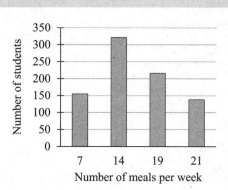

A college offers meal plan options for 7, 14, 19, or 21 meals a week. The bar graph shows the number of students living in McCormick Hall who purchased each type of meal plan for an academic year. How many students purchased the 19 meals a week plan?

Ⓐ 138

Ⓑ 155

Ⓒ 216

Ⓓ 321

10

A seamstress wishes to add a lace trim around a square-shaped pillow, which has a diagonal length of $5\sqrt{2}$ inches. What is the length of lace trim, in inches, that the seamstress needs for all sides of the square-shaped pillow?

Ⓐ 5

Ⓑ 20

Ⓒ 25

Ⓓ 40

CONTINUED ➡

Practice Tests

11

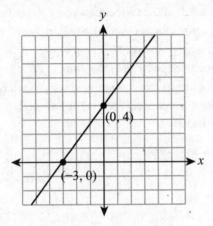

The graph of the linear function $f(x)$ is shown. The linear function $g(x)$ (not shown) is perpendicular to $f(x)$ and has a y-intercept of 3. What is the value of $g(4)$?

(A) -3

(B) $-\dfrac{3}{4}$

(C) 0

(D) 3

12

A garden consists of six rectangular plots and 4 square-shaped plots. Each rectangular plot has a length of 18 feet and a width that is one-third its length. The side length of each square-shaped plot is half the length of a rectangular plot. What is the total area, in square feet, of the garden?

13

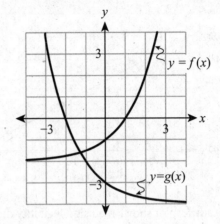

The graph of functions f and g in the xy-plane are shown. If a is the x-coordinate of the x-intercept of f and b is the y-coordinate of the y-intercept of g, what is the value of $a + b$?

(A) -3

(B) -2

(C) -1

(D) 1

Practice Tests

CONTINUED

14

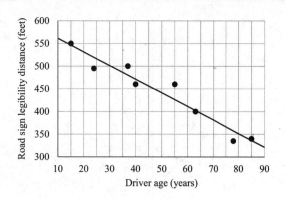

The scatterplot shows road sign legibility distance *d*, in feet, and driver age *a*, in years. Which of the following equations is the most appropriate model for the data shown?

Ⓐ $d = -3a - 590$

Ⓑ $d = -3a + 590$

Ⓒ $d = 3a - 590$

Ⓓ $d = 3a + 590$

15

Siri needs at least 6 medium posts and at least 4 large posts for her garden. Medium posts cost $5, and large posts cost $6. Let *m* represent the number of medium posts and *l* the number of large posts. If she wants to spend no more than $70, which of the following system of inequalities correctly models this situation?

Ⓐ $5m + 6l \leq 70$
$m \geq 6$
$l \geq 4$

Ⓑ $6m + 5l \leq 70$
$m \geq 6$
$l \geq 4$

Ⓒ $5m + 6l \geq 70$
$m \leq 6$
$l \geq 4$

Ⓓ $6m + 5l \geq 70$
$m \geq 6$
$l \leq 4$

16

$$\frac{2x}{x - 5} + \frac{15}{x} = 2$$

What is the value of *x*?

CONTINUED

17

Genre	Number
Action	20
Drama	x
Documentary	4
Romantic comedy	10
Science fiction	11

The table represents the number of movies of distinct genres in Julian's queue on a particular streaming service. Julian chooses one of them at random to watch. If the probability that he picks a drama is $\frac{1}{4}$, how many dramas are in his queue?

- (A) 11
- (B) 15
- (C) 30
- (D) 45

18

x	y
-1	-4
0	-2
1	0
2	2

The table shows certain points on the graph of linear function f. If g represents f translated down 3 units in the xy-coordinate plane, which of the following equations defines g?

- (A) $2x + y = -5$
- (B) $2x - y = -1$
- (C) $2x - y = 2$
- (D) $2x - y = 5$

19

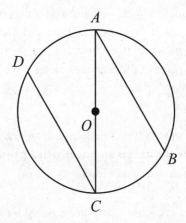

The circle shown has center O and diameter AC. DC is parallel to AB. The length of minor arc AB is twice the length of minor arc BC. What is the measure of the inscribed angle ACD?

- (A) 15°
- (B) 30°
- (C) 45°
- (D) 60°

Practice Tests

CONTINUED

K 897

20

The function $f(x) = 101(0.88)^x$ models the atmospheric pressure, in kilopascals, for every 1,000-meter increase from sea level, where x is the altitude in thousands of meters. Which of the following best interprets "$f(4)$ approximately equals 61"?

Ⓐ The atmospheric pressure at 4,000 meters above sea level is approximately 61 times greater than at sea level.

Ⓑ The atmospheric pressure at 4,000 meters above sea level is approximately 61 kilopascals.

Ⓒ The atmospheric pressure at 61,000 meters above sea level is approximately 4 times greater than that at sea level.

Ⓓ The atmospheric pressure at 61,000 meters above sea level is approximately 4 kilopascals.

21

$$-1 < \frac{x}{4} + 5 < 6$$

What is the minimum possible integer value of $3x - 2$?

Ⓐ -74

Ⓑ -73

Ⓒ -24

Ⓓ -23

22

$$x^{a^2} = x^{b^2}(x^6)^6$$

For the equation given, if $x > 1$ and $a - b = 4$, what is the value of $a + b$?

Ⓐ 3

Ⓑ 6

Ⓒ 8

Ⓓ 9

IF YOU FINISH BEFORE TIME IS CALLED, YOU MAY CHECK YOUR WORK ON THIS MODULE ONLY. ON TEST DAY, YOU WON'T BE ABLE TO MOVE ON TO THE NEXT MODULE UNTIL TIME EXPIRES. STOP

This page is intentionally blank.

ANSWER KEY

Math: Module A

1. **B**	7. **C**	13. **B**	19. **B**
2. **A**	8. **9**	14. **B**	20. **B**
3. **D**	9. **C**	15. **A**	21. **B**
4. **B**	10. **B**	16. **3**	22. **D**
5. **A**	11. **C**	17. **B**	
6. **9**	12. **972**	18. **D**	

Instructions

Compare your answers to the answer key and enter the number of correct answers for this module here. _____ This is your raw score.

Go to the "How to Score Your Practice Test" section to determine your score.

Explanations will be at the end of the practice test.

MATH: MODULE B

Mark your answers either on the pages that follow or on a separate sheet of paper. You will be scoring this module and using the results to find your final Math score.

DIRECTIONS

- The questions in this section address a number of important math skills.

- Use of a calculator is permitted for all questions. A reference sheet, calculator, and these directions can be accessed throughout the test.

- Unless otherwise indicated:

  - All variables and expressions represent real numbers.

  - Figures provided are drawn to scale.

  - All figures lie in a plane.

  - The domain of a given function f is the set of all real numbers x for which $f(x)$ is a real number.

For **multiple-choice questions**, solve each problem and choose the correct answer from the choices provided. Each multiple-choice question has a single correct answer.

For **student-produced response questions**, solve each problem and enter your answer as described below:

- If you find **more than one correct answer**, enter only one answer.

- You can enter up to 5 characters for a **positive** answer and up to 6 characters (including the negative sign) for a **negative** answer.

- If your answer is a **fraction** that doesn't fit in the provided space, enter the decimal equivalent.

- If your answer is a **decimal** that doesn't fit in the provided space, enter it by truncating or rounding at the fourth digit.

- If your answer is a **mixed number** (such as $3\frac{1}{2}$), enter it as an improper fraction (**7/2**) or its decimal equivalent (**3.5**).

- Don't enter **symbols** such as a percent sign, comma, or dollar sign.

Examples

ANSWER	ACCEPTABLE WAY TO ANSWER	UNACCEPTABLE: WILL NOT RECEIVE CREDIT
3.5	3.5 3.50 7/2	31/2 3 1/2
$\frac{2}{3}$	2/3 .6666 .6667 0.666 0.667	0.66 .66 0.67 .67
$-\frac{1}{3}$	−1/3 −.3333 −0.333	−.33 −0.33

Reference:

$A = \pi r^2$
$C = 2\pi r$

$A = lw$

$A = \frac{1}{2}bh$

$c^2 = a^2 + b^2$

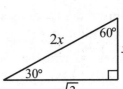

Special Right Triangles

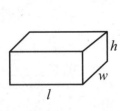

$V = lwh$

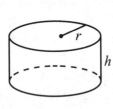

$V = \pi r^2 h$

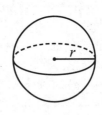

$V = \frac{4}{3}\pi r^3$

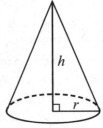

$V = \frac{1}{3}\pi r^2 h$

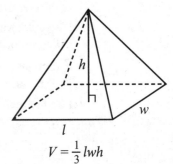

$V = \frac{1}{3}lwh$

The number of degrees of arc in a circle is 360.

The number of radians of arc in a circle is 2π.

The sum of the measures in degrees of the angles of a triangle is 180.

CONTINUED ➤

1

The number x is 130% greater than 75. What is the value of x?

Ⓐ 22.5

Ⓑ 97.5

Ⓒ 172.5

Ⓓ 250

2

Which of the following expressions is equivalent to $\dfrac{x^{\frac{5}{2}}}{\sqrt{x}}$, if $x > 0$?

Ⓐ x^2

Ⓑ x^4

Ⓒ x^5

Ⓓ x^{10}

3

$$t = 3 - \frac{1}{2}d$$

The equation gives the time, t, in hours, a student spends studying for an exam, d days before the day of the exam. What is the time, in hours, the student spends studying 3 days before the day of the exam?

4

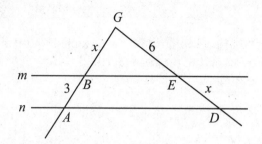

In the figure shown, lines m and n are parallel. What is the value of x?

Ⓐ 3

Ⓑ $3\sqrt{2}$

Ⓒ 9

Ⓓ $9\sqrt{3}$

5

Which of the following expressions is equivalent to $2x^{-2}(4x^5y^2) - 24xy^2$, if $x > 0$?

Ⓐ $-16x^{-9}$

Ⓑ $8xy^2(x^{-11} - 3)$

Ⓒ $8x(x^2 - 3)$

Ⓓ $8xy^2(x^2 - 3)$

CONTINUED

6

$$f(x) = -x^2 + dx$$

What is x-coordinate of the maximum value, in terms of d, of the given function?

Ⓐ $-d$

Ⓑ $-\dfrac{d}{2}$

Ⓒ $\dfrac{d}{2}$

Ⓓ d

7

The linear function f is defined by $f(2) = 9$ and $f(5) = 0$. Which of the following gives the equation for f?

Ⓐ $f(x) = -3x + 5$

Ⓑ $f(x) = -3x + 15$

Ⓒ $f(x) = -\dfrac{1}{3}x + \dfrac{5}{3}$

Ⓓ $f(x) = -\dfrac{1}{3}x + 5$

8

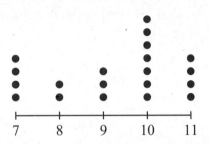

The dot plot represents the distribution of 20 values in data set A. The median of data set B is less than the median of data set A, and the range of data set B is equal to the range of data set A. Which of the following correctly shows the dot plot representing data set B?

Ⓐ
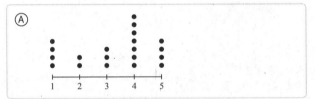

Ⓑ
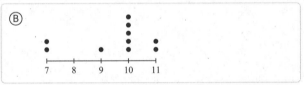

Ⓒ
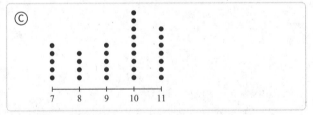

Ⓓ
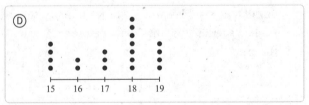

CONTINUED ➡

9

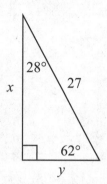

For the given triangle, which of the following is equivalent to $\frac{x}{y}$?

- (A) $\dfrac{\sin(62°)}{\sin(28°)}$

- (B) $\dfrac{\sin(28°)}{\tan(62°)}$

- (C) $\dfrac{\cos(62°)}{\cos(28°)}$

- (D) $\dfrac{\tan(28°)}{\cos(62°)}$

10

The value of y is at least 3 less than twice the value of x. Which inequality gives the possible values of x?

- (A) $x \le \dfrac{1}{2}y + \dfrac{3}{2}$

- (B) $x \ge \dfrac{1}{2}y + \dfrac{3}{2}$

- (C) $x \le -\dfrac{1}{2}y + \dfrac{3}{2}$

- (D) $x \ge -\dfrac{1}{2}y + \dfrac{3}{2}$

11

$$\frac{7x^2 + 30x - 25}{7x + 35}$$

Which of the following expressions is equivalent to the given expression if $x > -5$?

- (A) $\dfrac{7x - 5}{7}$

- (B) $\dfrac{x + 5}{7}$

- (C) $\dfrac{x(7x - 5) - 5(7x - 5)}{7x + 35}$

- (D) $\dfrac{x(7x + 5) + 5(7x + 5)}{7x + 35}$

12

In 1998, the concentration of methyl chloroform in surface waters was 70 parts per million. For each year after 1998, the concentration of methyl chloroform decreased by a factor of 2. If x represents the number of years after 1998 and y represents the concentration of methyl chloroform in parts per million, which equation defines this relationship?

- (A) $y = \dfrac{1}{2}(x)^{70}$

- (B) $y = \dfrac{1}{2}(70)^x$

- (C) $y = 70(x)^{\frac{1}{2}}$

- (D) $y = 70\left(\dfrac{1}{2}\right)^x$

CONTINUED

Practice Tests

13

$$3x < -6$$
$$-6x - y < 15$$

The graph of the solution to the system of inequalities given contains the point $(a, 21)$. If a is an integer, what could be the value of a?

14

Coffee is packaged into 50-pound and 150-pound bags that are loaded into a cargo container. The total cargo weight cannot exceed 37,000 pounds. At least 200 150-pound bags are loaded into the cargo container. If x represents the number of 50-pound bags and y represents the number of 150-pound bags, which inequality represents the number of 50-pound bags loaded into the cargo container?

Ⓐ $x \leq 42$

Ⓑ $x \geq 42$

Ⓒ $x \leq 140$

Ⓓ $x \geq 140$

15

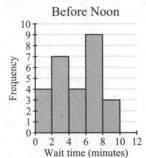
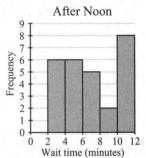

The histograms summarize the time, in minutes, customers waited in line at a license bureau before noon and after noon. What is the positive difference between the approximate means of the two data sets?

Ⓐ 0

Ⓑ 2

Ⓒ 4

Ⓓ 12

16

$$|2x + 4| + 1 = 3x$$

If a is a solution to the given equation, which of the following gives all the possible values of a?

Ⓐ $-\dfrac{3}{5}$

Ⓑ 5

Ⓒ $-\dfrac{3}{5}$ or 5

Ⓓ -1 or 5

CONTINUED

17

$$f(x) = a^x - b$$
$$g(x) = f(x) + 2$$

The graph of $g(x)$ has a y-intercept of $\left(0, \frac{97}{3}\right)$. If a and b are constants and $\frac{a}{b} = \frac{3}{22}$, what is the value of a?

18

$$y = 4x - 16$$
$$y = 52kx$$

For what value of k does the given system of equations have no solution if k is a constant?

19

A cone with a diameter of 10 centimeters and a height of 15 centimeters sits inside a cylinder with the same diameter and height. What is the volume, in cubic centimeters, of the space in the cylinder NOT taken up by the cone?

Ⓐ 100π

Ⓑ 125π

Ⓒ 250π

Ⓓ $1,000\pi$

20

Let $f(x) = ax + b$, where a and b are constants. Which of the following best describes the graph of $f(x - c)$, where c is a constant?

Ⓐ The new line will have a slope of $a - c$ and a y-intercept of b.

Ⓑ The new line will have a slope of a and a y-intercept of $b - ac$.

Ⓒ The new line will be shifted to the left by c units.

Ⓓ The new line will be shifted down by c units.

21

The equation $2x^2 + 4x - 10 = 0$ has solutions of the form $m \pm n\sqrt{6}$. What is the value of $m + n$?

Ⓐ -1

Ⓑ 0

Ⓒ 1

Ⓓ 2

Practice Tests

22

A rectangular prism has a square base that has a side length of s. The height of the prism is 3 times the length of the square's side. Which of the following functions defines the surface area of the square prism, in square inches?

Ⓐ $f(s) = 3s^3$

Ⓑ $f(s) = 6s^2$

Ⓒ $f(s) = 14s^2$

Ⓓ $f(s) = 18s^2$

IF YOU FINISH BEFORE TIME IS CALLED, YOU MAY CHECK YOUR WORK ON THIS MODULE ONLY. ON TEST DAY, YOU WON'T BE ABLE TO MOVE ON TO THE NEXT MODULE UNTIL TIME EXPIRES. STOP

908

Practice Tests

This page is intentionally blank.

ANSWER KEY

Math: Module B

1. **C**	7. **B**	13. **−3, −4, or −5**	18. **1/13, .0769, 0.076,**
2. **A**	8. **A**	14. **C**	**or 0.077**
3. **1.5 or 3/2**	9. **A**	15. **B**	19. **C**
4. **B**	10. **A**	16. **B**	20. **B**
5. **D**	11. **A**	17. **−4**	21. **B**
6. **C**	12. **D**		22. **C**

Instructions

Compare your answers to the answer key and enter the number of correct answers for this module here. _____ This is your raw score.

Go to the "How to Score Your Practice Test" section to determine your score.

Explanations will be at the end of the practice test.

HOW TO SCORE YOUR PRACTICE TEST

Because this is a digital and adaptive exam, scores can vary widely based on the number of correct answers. The following tables give an estimated score range based on the most common scoring logic. Please visit your online resources for additional practice exams and the most up-to-date scoring information.

If you were directed to Reading and Writing Module A:

Add the raw score from your Reading and Writing: Routing Module to your raw score from Reading and Writing: Module A.

_____ (Routing) + _____ (Module A) = _____ (Your Total Raw Reading and Writing Score)

Use this table to convert your raw score into your scaled score:

Reading and Writing	
TOTAL Raw Score	Scaled Score
0	200
1	200
2	200
3	200
4	200
5	200
6	200
7	210
8	220
9	230
10	250
11	280
12	290
13	300
14	330
15	350
16	380
17	390
18	400
19	420
20	430

Reading and Writing	
TOTAL Raw Score	Scaled Score
21	430
22	440
23	450
24	460
25	470
26	480
27	490
28	490
29	500
30	510
31	520
32	530
33	540
34	550
35	560
36	570
37	570
38	580
39	590
40	600
41	610

Reading and Writing	
TOTAL Raw Score	Scaled Score
42	610
43	630
44	640
45	640
46	N/A
47	N/A
48	N/A
49	N/A
50	N/A
51	N/A
52	N/A
53	N/A
54	N/A

Your scaled Reading and Writing score from the table is: _____

If you were directed to Reading and Writing Module B:

Add the raw score from your Reading and Writing: Routing Module to your raw score from Reading and Writing: Module B.

_____ (Routing) + _____ (Module B) = _____ (Your Total Raw Reading and Writing Score)

Use this table to convert your raw score into your scaled score:

Reading and Writing	
TOTAL Raw Score	Scaled Score
0	N/A
1	N/A
2	N/A
3	N/A
4	N/A
5	N/A
6	N/A
7	N/A
8	N/A
9	N/A
10	N/A
11	N/A
12	N/A
13	N/A
14	N/A
15	N/A
16	N/A
17	N/A
18	N/A
19	440
20	450

Reading and Writing	
TOTAL Raw Score	Scaled Score
21	450
22	460
23	470
24	480
25	490
26	500
27	510
28	510
29	520
30	530
31	540
32	550
33	560
34	570
35	580
36	590
37	590
38	600
39	610
40	620
41	630

Reading and Writing	
TOTAL Raw Score	Scaled Score
42	630
43	650
44	660
45	660
46	680
47	690
48	700
49	710
50	720
51	730
52	760
53	780
54	800

Your scaled Reading and Writing score from the table is: _____

If you were directed to Math Module A:

Add the raw score from your Math: Routing Module to your raw score from Math: Module A.

_____ (Routing) + _____ (Module A) = _____ (Your Total Raw Math Score)

Use this table to convert your raw score into your scaled score:

Math	
TOTAL Raw Score	Scaled Score
0	200
1	200
2	200
3	200
4	200
5	200
6	200
7	220
8	250
9	270
10	290
11	330
12	350
13	360
14	370
15	380
16	390
17	410
18	410
19	430
20	440
21	450
22	460
23	470
24	480

Math	
TOTAL Raw Score	Scaled Score
25	490
26	500
27	510
28	530
29	540
30	560
31	570
32	590
33	610
34	620
35	630
36	N/A
37	N/A
38	N/A
39	N/A
40	N/A
41	N/A
42	N/A
43	N/A
44	N/A

Your scaled Math score from the table is: _____

If you were directed to Math Module B:

Add the raw score from your Math: Routing Module to your raw score from Math: Module B.

_____ (Routing) + _____ (Module B) = _____ (Your Total Raw Math Score)

Use this table to convert your raw score into your scaled score:

Math	
TOTAL Raw Score	Scaled Score
0	N/A
1	N/A
2	N/A
3	N/A
4	N/A
5	N/A
6	N/A
7	N/A
8	N/A
9	N/A
10	N/A
11	N/A
12	N/A
13	N/A
14	370

Math	
TOTAL Raw Score	Scaled Score
15	380
16	390
17	410
18	430
19	440
20	450
21	460
22	480
23	490
24	500
25	520
26	540
27	550
28	560
29	570

Math	
TOTAL Raw Score	Scaled Score
30	590
31	600
32	620
33	640
34	650
35	660
36	670
37	690
38	710
39	730
40	750
41	780
42	790
43	800
44	800

Your scaled Math score from the table is: _____

To find your composite score, add your Reading and Writing score to your Math score.

_____ (Reading and Writing) + _____ (Math) = _____ (Your Composite Score)

READING AND WRITING: ROUTING MODULE ANSWERS AND EXPLANATIONS

1.　A
Difficulty: Easy
Category: Craft and Structure
Getting to the Answer: The blank is an adjective describing a characteristic of "soccer as a spectator sport." The next sentence identifies the cause of "this change" as "the increasing number of viewers." Predict a word or phrase that means more people are watching soccer, such as *prevalence*. This prediction matches **(A)**, the correct answer. None of the other choices, by definition, mean an *increasing number*, so these are all incorrect.

2.　B
Difficulty: Easy
Category: Craft and Structure
Getting to the Answer: The blank is an adjective describing a manner of acting when cold or flu symptoms begin. The second sentence of the text defines the blank as meaning *starting treatment immediately*, so a word or phrase meaning *quickly* is a good prediction. Choice **(B)**, "alacrity," means *responding promptly* and is correct. Choices (A), "caution," and (D), "reluctance," are opposite; both mean to delay acting. Choice (C), "impunity," means without punishment or loss and does not fit the context of the passage.

3.　A
Difficulty: Medium
Category: Craft and Structure
Getting to the Answer: The scientists mentioned in the text have discovered connections between the changes in the solar constant and "temperatures and pressures occurring on Earth" and "storms in the North Atlantic." Temperatures, pressures, and storms are aspects of Earth's weather, so the scientists in the passage are studying whether the changes in the solar constant *are seen in* or *have an effect on* Earth's weather. Any word or phrase that matches one of these meanings is a good prediction. This prediction matches **(A)**, the correct answer. None of the incorrect choices fit the context of the passage. There is no indication that the solar cycle *deceives* or *hides its identity* (B), *makes the weather better* (C), or *worse* (D).

4.　A
Difficulty: Medium
Category: Craft and Structure
Getting to the Answer: Use the context of the passage to help determine how the word "election" is being used. The book title indicates that it is about trees and their "propagation," or *reproduction*. In the first sentence, the author refers to "election of your seed" and claims that there is a "vast difference" even among similar trees due to the "quality of the seed." He then gives advice about how to "choose" seeds and acorns; predict that "election of your seed" refers to the reader's *choice* of seeds. Choice **(A)** is correct.

Choices (B) and (C) are incorrect because they are related to "election" in the context of voting. Choice (D) is incorrect because, while "liberty" may entail freedom of choice, the phrase "liberty of your seed" suggests that the seed, rather than the reader, has the ability to choose.

5.　D
Difficulty: Hard
Category: Craft and Structure
Getting to the Answer: Catts cites women's grievances, or complaints, "a history of delays, political tricks, and dishonesty." Predict that Catts wants Congress *to correct*, or *relieve*, these grievances. Any word or phrase with the same meaning is a good prediction. This prediction matches **(D)**, the correct answer. "Redress" means *to set right* or *remedy* the ills committed against women. Incorrect choice (A) is an opposite; "complement" means *to add to* or *to fill up*. Incorrect choices (B) and (C) do not fit the context. "Petition" means *to ask* or *to request*; "forewarn" means *to give an advance warning*.

6.　C
Difficulty: Medium
Category: Craft and Structure
Getting to the Answer: The start of the text is an extended description of Mark, the main character. His father was a clergyman, a wealthy lady paid for his education, and his father died as Mark finished university. Then, there's a description of the father, leading up to the underlined sentence. The father left a few debts "as a warning to his family," so the father intended to warn Mark away from borrowing money. The underlined sentence states that the warning was ineffective, introducing Mark's habit of

borrowing money. The remainder of the passage confirms this trait. Mark "made acquaintance with the money-lenders" and wrote "letters asking for more time to pay." Choice **(C)** is correct.

None of the incorrect choices are mentioned in the text. Neither the reason Mark left home (A), the setting in London (B), nor any description of a conflict (D) are discussed in the passage.

7.   A
Difficulty: Hard
Category: Craft and Structure
Getting to the Answer: The poem opens by describing feelings of "lack" and "the things we do not yearn to see" all around us. The poet then suggests we look back to the past, but there "hopes that were never ours" are found. Then, the poet suggests, since "to look behind is all in vain" and "in vain to look to left or right" in the present, "why face we not our future once again." In the last lines, the poet recognizes the difficulties of moving forward; we'll need "hardier hearts" and "Straining dim eyes to catch the invisible sight." A good summary of the purpose of the poem is to urge the reader to move forward past life's difficulties. This matches **(A)**, the correct answer.

Although the poem does discuss the accumulation of disappointments in life, (B) is incorrect because it ignores the encouragement the poem offers. Choice (C) is incorrect because the poem does not discuss the need for achieving goals. Similarly, the poem does not make any comparisons of memories, so (D) is also incorrect.

8.   A
Difficulty: Easy
Category: Information and Ideas
Getting to the Answer: The keyword phrase "According to the text" indicates that the answer to this question will be clearly stated in the text. The reason "the Pechanga band [was] concerned" is found in the fourth sentence: they wanted to *restore* "this vital part of their culture to the Pechanga tribe's oversight," so they purchased the land containing Wi'áaşal. This prediction matches **(A)**, the correct answer.

All of the incorrect choices introduce issues not raised in the text. There is no mention of "local development" (B), "too many visitors" (C), or the tree's "natural life" (D).

9.   B
Difficulty: Hard
Category: Information and Ideas
Getting to the Answer: The text opens with a description of a problem, the need for concrete despite the carbon dioxide emissions it creates, followed by a possible solution, the bioconcrete process described. This summary best matches **(B)**, the correct answer.

Incorrect choices (A) and (C) are details from the text, but not the main idea: (A) ignores the potential solution provided, and (C) doesn't explain why this photosynthetic bacteria may be helpful. Incorrect choice (D) goes too far. The author identifies the Colorado process as a potential, but not the only, solution.

10.   D
Difficulty: Medium
Category: Information and Ideas
Getting to the Answer: Summarize the claim in the question in your own words before reading the choices. Here, the correct answer will show the immigrants *facing a difficult situation and responding with honesty and effort*. This prediction matches **(D)**, the correct answer because "We will pay them all somehow" indicates Jurgis and Ona must owe a debt, and Jurgis plans to pay it by "work[ing] harder."

None of the incorrect choices support both aspects of the claim. Choice (A) hints at the difficulties Jurgis will face, but he is not yet aware of them. Choice (B) describes Jurgis, but does not mention any problems. Choice (C) gives an example of the difficulty Jurgis faced, but not how he responds to it.

11.   C
Difficulty: Medium
Category: Information and Ideas
Getting to the Answer: First, summarize the information in the text and graph and then, if possible, predict the characteristic of the correct answer. If a prediction doesn't immediately come to mind, compare the choices to the graph and eliminate those that misstate the information presented. The text explains that grazing has an effect on the soil and that the soil in two ecosystems in a national forest, a pond and a spring, were analyzed. The graph indicates the total carbon and total organic matter in areas where bison and cattle were grazed and an area where there was no grazing activity. The phrase before the blank includes the contrast keyword "although," and the contrast

that is made is with "*any* grazing in either ecosystem *reduced* total carbon and organic matter in the soil." Predict that the correct answer will mention a data point that *did not reduce one of the measures very much*. Checking the graph, total carbon levels with cattle grazing in the spring ecosystem were very close to those of the area with no grazing. This prediction matches **(C)**, the correct answer.

All the incorrect choices misread the graph. Both total carbon and total organic matter were higher in both ecosystems with no grazing, indicating that all grazing activities had some effect on these soil measures.

12. A
Difficulty: Easy
Category: Information and Ideas
Getting to the Answer: The answer to an Inference question should be logically supported by the passage, so pay special attention to the author's logical flow of ideas. In this passage, the author introduces that caddisfly larvae use found material to create their cocoons. Next, the artist Duprat was "inspired" by this "natural creative process" that occurs with debris and substrate. He then creates an artificial habitat with specific materials of "only" gold and stones. Finally, the author quotes that Duprat referred to himself as an "architect," who is a person that designs and guides, but doesn't build. Predict an answer that best fits this inference, such as *Duprat intended to work with the natural, creative skills of the insects to create art*. **(A)** best fits this prediction.

Choice (B) is out of scope; while the building materials are mentioned in the passage, making money from the art is never mentioned. (C) is a distortion; the artist was "inspired" by the process and viewed himself as a creative partner (architect), not a researcher seeking to disrupt the process. (D) is a distortion, while the life-cycle is mentioned, it is the larvae's cocoon construction process that inspired Duprat.

13. A
Difficulty: Hard
Category: Information and Ideas
Getting to the Answer: When tackling an Inference question, it can be useful to consider the chain of thought in a passage. This one begins with *DSM-II* "introduc[ing] a new...disorder" for childhood hyperactivity. Next, it is stated that in the subsequent *DSM* edition the disorder was renamed "ADD" and given an

expanded description. Finally, a revision of the third edition resulted in the addition of a similar disorder (ADHD). Predict that the correct choice will *continue outlining changes* to attention and hyperactivity disorders in the *DSM* and will contrast ("However") with the addition of a disorder. Choice **(A)** correctly continues this passage's chain of thought, as the 2013 edition of the *DSM* eliminated one disorder and expanded upon the details of another.

The other answer choices all incorrectly break that chain of thought. (B) is incorrect because the passage identifies multiple changes to this category of disorders throughout the *DSM's* publication and therefore it is not "highly unlikely" that future changes will be made. Nothing in the passage hints at the frequency or age of children being diagnosed; (C) is incorrect because it is out of scope. (D) distorts details from the passage; while some symptoms are listed, the requirements for diagnoses are not included in the passage.

14. D
Difficulty: Easy
Category: Standard English Conventions
Getting to the Answer: The choices indicate that this question is testing the required punctuation, if any. Read the sentence containing the blank and look for the complete idea(s). By removing the nonessential information in the portion before the blank, an independent clause can be identified: "Portal fantasies...typically feature a person from Earth transported to a fantastical setting." The portion after the blank cannot stand alone, so it is a dependent clause. **(D)** is correct, because a comma is the proper way to separate a dependent clause from an independent clause.

Choice (A) is incorrect because punctuation is needed to separate the two clauses; otherwise a run-on is created. Parentheses must come in pairs, so (B) is incorrect. (C) is incorrect because the two clauses joined by a semicolon must be independent. In other words, each half of the sentence must be able to stand alone. This is not the case here, as the portion after the blank is dependent.

15. C
Difficulty: Easy
Category: Standard English Conventions
Getting to the Answer: If a sentence has more than one independent clause, those clauses must be properly joined. If they are not, the sentence is a run-on. A comma

and a conjunction is one way to weld together the two independent clauses; **(C)** is correct. A comma alone does nothing to avoid a run-on, as the second clause is still independent; (A) is incorrect. A comma without a coordinating conjunction between two independent clauses creates a run-on. Coordinating conjunctions can be remembered with the acronym FANBOYS (For, And, Nor, But, Or, Yet, So). (B) is incorrect, as it is contains a FANBOYS conjunction but is missing the required comma. A comma is not needed *after* the coordinating conjunction when joining two independent clauses; (D) is incorrect.

16. B
Difficulty: Medium
Category: Standard English Conventions
Getting to the Answer: The subject of the verb in the blank is the noun "fourteen Dutch warships," which is plural. Note that the test makers sometimes put prepositional phrases or other descriptive phrases, such as "in an iced-over port," between the subject and verb to make the subject-verb agreement issue more challenging to spot, as the singular noun "port" would require a singular verb. Another technique used to make verb questions more difficult is a shifting time frame. Here, the passage is introduced with the idea that cavalry capturing a navy "is a laughable idea," which can lead the reader into assuming the whole passage is in present tense. However, note the final sentence, which uses the past tense "was." Predict that the correct answer will be a past tense plural; **(B)** fits, and it is correct.

Choice (A) is incorrect because it is in plural present tense. (C) is incorrect because it is singular present tense. (D) is incorrect because it is future tense.

17. C
Difficulty: Medium
Category: Standard English Conventions
Getting to the Answer: The first issue to consider is the punctuation needed after the word "however." Eliminate (A) and (D) because "however" needs a comma after it, as "however" is functioning as an introductory clause to "those same qualities make it a rich ecological reserve for endangered species like the clouded leopard." Now consider the punctuation needed after the word "explore." Eliminate (B) because the portions before and after the blank are independent clauses; they must be properly joined. This leaves **(C)**, which is correct because it uses a semicolon to join the two independent clauses as well as a comma after "however."

18. C
Difficulty: Hard
Category: Standard English Conventions
Getting to the Answer: When a sentence begins with a single modifying phrase, whatever follows must be the thing that is modified. Logically, the modifying phrase "Designed to capture otherwise invisible infrared light," can refer only to the James Webb Space Telescope (JWST), which is described in the first sentence as conducting "infrared astronomy." Choice **(C)** is correct. Choices (A), (B), and (D) do not feature a subject that would logically be modified by the modifying phrase.

19. B
Difficulty: Hard
Category: Standard English Conventions
Getting to the Answer: If answer choices include punctuation, take time to consider if it should be included at all. In this passage, "the alkaline solution" is modifying the word "limewater." Predict that there should be no punctuation between any of the words; **(B)** best fits that prediction and is correct. Choices (A), (C), and (D) all incorrectly use a comma or commas to separate adjectives that work together to modify a noun.

20. C
Difficulty: Hard
Category: Standard English Conventions
Getting to the Answer: Commas are used in three situations. First, to set off three or more items in a series. Second, to separate an introductory word or phrase from the rest of the sentence. Third, to separate a dependent clause from an independent clause. None of those situations apply in this context. **(C)** is correct because commas are not needed here. (A) and (B) are incorrect because they set off elements that are essential to a sentence's meaning: "Only several centuries after her death" provides vital information. (D) is incorrect because it separates a verb (did) from the rest of the sentence.

21. D
Difficulty: Easy
Category: Expression of Ideas
Getting to the Answer: The sentence that contains the missing transition word provides little context: "due to everyone's drunken state, *White Ship* soon struck a rock and capsized." Yet, when paired with the passage's previous sentence, which states that after "The nobles urged the captain...to beat the king's ship to port," it

becomes clear that a contrast transition word is needed. A race was urged, *but* the ship quickly sank. Choice **(D)** is the only contrast word and is correct. (A) is incorrect because it is a cause-and-effect transition. (B) and (C) are incorrect because they are continuation transitions.

22. D
Difficulty: Medium
Category: Expression of Ideas
Getting to the Answer: When determining which type of transition to use, consider the logical flow of a passage. The first sentence states: "The gutter...is a critical tool in drawing comics, especially as it relates to storytelling." The second sentence, which contains the missing transition, states: "it invites the reader to use their imagination to fill in the gutter...." In other words, the first sentence introduces the concept of the gutter, and the second sentence describes what the gutter is used for in terms of storytelling. Thus, a continuation transition is needed, which is why **(D)** is correct. (A) is incorrect because it is a contrast transition. (B) and (C) are cause-and-effect transitions. While they may both be tempting answers, they create a dependent clause at the beginning of the sentence that doesn't not logically modify what comes after it: painting in the events. Creating a new error means an incorrect answer choice.

23. B
Difficulty: Easy
Category: Expression of Ideas
Getting to the Answer: Based on the question stem, focus on the details about the lengths of the poems as you read the bullet points. The third point specifies that *Beowulf* is almost 3,200 lines, and the last point specifies that the *Iliad* is over 15,000 lines. Choice **(B)** is correct because it reflects this data and accurately compares the lengths, identifying that the *Iliad* is much longer than *Beowulf*.

Choice (A) is incorrect because it makes a generalization that is true about the length of both poems rather than compares the lengths; further, it does not identify the two specific poems. Choice (C) is incorrect because it focuses only on *Beowulf*. Choice (D) is incorrect because it does not address the poems' lengths.

24. A
Difficulty: Medium
Category: Expression of Ideas
Getting to the Answer: Based on the question stem, look for a way in which the Spartan kings' non-military

responsibilities were similar as you read the bullet points. The first bullet point introduces Sparta, and the second point notes something "unusual" about Sparta's government: it had a dual kingship. The remaining bullet points describe the kings' non-military responsibilities, including serving as priests and on the *gerousia*.

Evaluate the answer choices with these details in mind, eliminating any that do not provide a similarity between the responsibilities of being priests and council members. Choice **(A)** is correct because it identifies something the responsibilities had in common: both were carried out by the dual kings. Choices (B) and (C) are incorrect because they each describe only one of the two responsibilities that were identified in the bullet points. Choice (D) is incorrect because although it identifies the non-military responsibilities, it also includes an extraneous military one, which is beyond the scope of the goal.

25. A
Difficulty: Medium
Category: Expression of Ideas
Getting to the Answer: According to the question stem, the correct answer will "make and support" a general statement about the relationships between animal populations. As you read the bullet points, look for an overall statement that can be made about animal population relationships and an example that supports the generalization. The first bullet point mentions animal populations, but not a *relationship* between populations. The second point introduces a generalization: many population numbers are "closely linked" to another population. The second point also introduces the example of this generalization—the Canadian lynx population—whose relationship with the snowshoe hare population is described in the last two bullet points.

Evaluate the answer choices and eliminate any that do not mention both the generalization *and* the support. Choice **(A)** includes both and is correct. Choice (B) is incorrect because it addresses only the support, not the generalization. On the other hand, choice (C) is incorrect because it addresses the generalization but omits the support. Choice (D) is incorrect because it does not specify the generalization about the relationship between animal populations.

26. A
Difficulty: Hard
Category: Expression of Ideas
Getting to the Answer: Based on the question stem, look for an advantage of the organization of the National Air and Space Museum as you read the bullet points. The first bullet point states that the museum's main location is in Washington, D.C. The second point describes the main location's artifacts. The last two points describe another location of the museum, a center outside of Washington, D.C., and its exhibits. The National Air and Space Museum is organized into two separate locations; think about why this might be advantageous. The description of the main location points out that it is close to other museums; the description of the center specifies that its exhibits are in "two massive hangars" and include planes and a space shuttle. The main location thus has the benefit of being close to other museums, while the center has the benefit of having enough space to exhibit full-sized aircraft. Choice **(A)** summarizes this advantage and is correct.

Choice (B) is incorrect because it only provides a description of the exhibits at the center; it does not explain an advantage of the overall organization of the National Air and Space Museum. Choice (C) identifies the organization, but it is incorrect because it does not address a benefit of this organization. Choice (D) is incorrect because it is a description of the artifacts of the National Air and Space Museum rather than an explanation of why its organization is advantageous.

27. C
Difficulty: Hard
Category: Expression of Ideas
Getting to the Answer: Since the question stem asks you to "present the study and its findings," summarize the important details about the study and specify its findings as you read the bullet points. The second bullet point identifies the focus of the study (fish teeth from an archaeological site). The third point states the aim of the study (determining if humans had cooked the fish). The next point describes the method (evaluating the size of crystal structures in the teeth), and the final point provides the finding (the fish had been cooked 700,000 years ago, longer ago than identified in the first bullet point). Evaluate the choices and eliminate any that omit important details—particularly the findings—of the study.

Choice (A) is incorrect because it emphasizes the previous evidence about humans cooking; further, it fails to describe the method of the study and its specific findings. Choice (B) is incorrect because it focuses only on the aim of the study and omits its findings. Choice **(C)** is correct because it summarizes the study and its findings about the age of the cooked fish. Choice (D) is incorrect because it discusses the method of the study but not its aim or its findings.

READING AND WRITING: MODULE A ANSWERS AND EXPLANATIONS

1. B
Difficulty: Easy
Category: Craft and Structure
Getting to the Answer: The immediate context of the missing word reveals that the correct choice will reflect the connection between the "boiling" beans and the "starches and proteins" in the "resulting liquid." The first sentence of the passage states that aquafaba is "a by-product" of cooking legumes. Predict that the correct answer will reflect the process of the starches and proteins *coming from* or *being produced by* the beans during cooking. Choice **(B)** is correct; "extracted" means *pulled out* or *removed*, which is closely aligned with the prediction.

Choice (A), which means *connected*, does not logically complete the sentence because the starches and proteins are *disconnected from* the beans. Choice (C) is incorrect because the starches and proteins are already present in the beans, not *brought into existence* by the boiling process. Choice (D) would illogically complete the sentence: the starches and proteins are not *improved by* the beans, they are *removed from* the beans.

2. C
Difficulty: Easy
Category: Craft and Structure
Getting to the Answer: Identify the surrounding text for context clues about what "rent" could mean. Because the "gas" is able to "escape...through" the silk, predict that the correct choice will be either a *gap* or *tear*. Choice **(C)** matches the prediction and is correct. Incorrect choice (A), "lease," means *borrow* and does not fit the context of the passage. Neither (B) or (D) logically complete the sentence. "Schism" means *division*, but it's a division within a group caused by differing opinions. "Wrest" means *to forcibly remove*.

3. A
Difficulty: Easy
Category: Craft and Structure
Getting to the Answer: The blank is an adjective describing the continuous route from South America to North America. The second sentence of the text adds that parts of the "journey" may be completed with a car, but "two sections...must be" completed by "foot," so a word or phrase meaning *able to be hiked* or *passable* are good predictions. Choice **(A)** matches the

prediction and is correct. None of the other choices, by definition, mean "walkable," and would not complete the text logically.

4. B
Difficulty: Medium
Category: Craft and Structure
Getting to the Answer: The blank is an adjective describing "these individuals," which the previous sentence identifies as wolves that "displayed bolder behavior" than others. Using *bold*, or another word or phrase with the same meaning, as a prediction matches **(B)**, the correct answer. Note that if you were unfamiliar with the word "venturous," it shares the same root as *adventure*. Using words that you do know can help you make strategic guesses.

None of the incorrect choices mean *bold*. "Innocuous" means *harmless*, "apprehensive" means *timid*, and "tortuous" means *twisted* or *convoluted*.

5. D
Difficulty: Medium
Category: Craft and Structure
Getting to the Answer: The blank is a noun describing the "Sponsian aureus." Note that the colon following the blank indicates that the explanation of the blank is coming up; the "Sponsian aureus" is "unlike authentic examples of ancient Roman coins," so a good prediction is *something that is not authentic*, or *fake*. This prediction matches the correct answer **(D)** because a forgery is *an imitation that is presented as genuine*. For this question, the rest of the text was not needed, but, for the record, supports the correct answer. The contrast keyword "however," introduces the details of Pearson's research that provides the evidence that "the coin was made by a local ancient Roman ruler to commemorate his reign."

Incorrect choice (A) is opposite; an "exemplar" is a *perfect example,* but the Sponsian aureus was thought to be "unlike authentic" coins. The remaining choices do not fit the context. A "depiction" (B) is an *illustration* or *image*, and an "attribute" (C) is a *characteristic*.

6.   D
Difficulty: Hard
Category: Craft and Structure
Getting to the Answer: The blank is a noun describing the "traditional" relationship in education between "business and the arts." Since there is not yet enough information from the text to support a prediction, keep reading. The contrast keyword "Despite" indicates that the part of the sentence after the blank will describe the *opposite* meaning of the blank. Sabel argues that "creativity," associated with the arts, and "fund-raising, management, and…reporting," activities associated with business, must be "combine[d]." A good prediction is any word or phrase that means the opposite of something that is "combine[d]," such as *separated*. This prediction matches **(D)**, "bifurcated," which means *divided into two parts*. Note that the prefix bi- (binary, bifocal, bicycle) means *two*. If you didn't know the precise meaning of "bifurcate," using the prefix could help you make a good strategic guess.

Incorrect choices (A) and (B) are opposites. "Amalgamation" (A) means *combination*, and "conflation" (B) means *an improper combination of two ideas*. "Explication" means *explanation* and doesn't fit the context, making (C) also incorrect.

7.   D
Difficulty: Easy
Category: Craft and Structure
Getting to the Answer: The use of an appropriate verb is important when correctly identifying the author's reason for including a portion of the passage. Choice **(D)** is correct because the underlined portion "introduces" the mechanism, quantum computing, by which the goal of pharmaceutical companies may one day be met. By contrast, (A) incorrectly uses the verb "restates," when the underlined portion does not actually restate anything from the previous section of the passage. (B) is incorrect because the underlined portion does not "explain" why quantum computing will be able to make such medication. (C) is incorrect because the underlined portion does not "establish" *multiple* possible applications of quantum computing.

8.   B
Difficulty: Easy
Category: Craft and Structure
Getting to the Answer: The main idea of Text 1 is that marine bycatch is responsible for extensive damage to some marine species and should be addressed. The main idea of Text 2 is that an experiment showed it is possible to catch "substantially fewer" of bycatch species. Predict that Doherty and his colleagues of Text 2 *would agree that bycatch is a problem and that their data may indicate a path to a solution*. This matches **(B)**, the correct answer.

Incorrect choice (A) goes too far; Doherty's single experiment reduced the bycatch of two species, and that is not enough to prove that the device always will reduce the bycatch of every species in every location. Incorrect choices (C) and (D) misinterpret Text 2. Since the experiment resulted in "substantially fewer" of two species caught, Doherty's results are "relevant" (C) and not a cause for "regret" (D).

9.   D
Difficulty: Medium
Category: Information and Ideas
Getting to the Answer: As you read the passage, look for clues about Valancy's and Mrs. Frederick's interactions. The third paragraph indicates that Valancy wants to speak "defiantly, but habit was too strong for her." Instead, she speaks "deprecatingly." In other words, Valancy is *not* in the habit of speaking to her mother defiantly, so instead she speaks "deprecatingly," or *negatively*, about herself as she explains why she cut the rosebush. Further, Mrs. Frederick refers to Valancy as having "gone crazy," rejects Valancy's reasoning, and is surprised that Valancy acted without asking her first; these details all suggest that Mrs. Frederick typically has a domineering attitude with her daughter. If Valancy does not act "defiantly," predict that she typically acts *obediently* or *compliantly*; choice **(D)** is correct.

Choices (A) and (C) are incorrect because they are the opposite of Valancy's habit of acting non-defiantly. Choice (B), "amicably," means *friendly*. The passage never indicates that Valancy acts with friendliness toward her mother; rather, she does not typically defy her.

10.   B
Difficulty: Easy
Category: Information and Ideas
Getting to the Answer: The text opens and closes with its main idea: an AI computer program defeated most of its human competitors in an online tournament of a complex game. This prediction matches **(B)**, the correct answer. The remainder of the passage is devoted to the

details of the reason why this was unusual: complex online games require human verbal and relationship skills.

Incorrect choice (A) exaggerates the AI program's success; it scored in the top ten percent, but was not undefeated. Choice (C) misstates the AI program's performance; the program was usually successful. Choice (D) is a detail from the passage, but since it never mentions the success of the AI program, it does not summarize the main idea of the text.

11. B
Difficulty: Easy
Category: Information and Ideas
Getting to the Answer: The key to correctly answering a Command of Evidence question is to put the claim in the question into your own shorter and simpler words. Here, the claim "that the best books to read are those that have withstood scrutiny over many years" can be summarized as "the best books are classics." Choice **(B)** supports this claim by stating "the famed books contain…the best thoughts and facts."

None of the incorrect choices address "the best books to read," the topic of the claim; (A) and (C) are general descriptions of books and (D) discusses book-collecting.

12. C
Difficulty: Easy
Category: Information and Ideas
Getting to the Answer: Start by paraphrasing the author's claim in your own words. The author believes that *the water in this meteor supports a theory about how Earth's water originated in space*. Keep this idea firmly in mind as you read the choices. Only one, the correct answer, will directly support the claim.

Eliminate (A). The many images of the meteor's path collected by cameras are not relevant to the water in the meteorite. Eliminate (B). If the pieces of the meteor were dug out of the surface of the Earth, perhaps water or chemicals from the Earth mixed with the meteor fragments. This would make it difficult to determine if the water in the sample came from the Earth or the meteor. **(C)** is correct. If the samples were collected in a way that ensured that the meteor fragments minimized contact with the Earth, this would support the author's claim because the water found in the fragments would most likely be from the meteor, not the Earth. On test day, choose **(C)** with confidence and move on, but for

the record, eliminate (D) as out of scope. The comparison between different methods of evaluating the origin of the planet is not discussed in the text.

13. D
Difficulty: Medium
Category: Information and Ideas
Getting to the Answer: First, based on the question stem, determine the "claim" of the palaeoarchaologists, as stated in the last sentence of the passage: doing multiple analyses of a hominid fossil can show that it is older than was previously thought. Look for evidence in the table that shows a later analysis of a fossil indicating an older date. The later 1992 data about "Lucy" does *not* give an older date than the initial study, but rather a date that falls within the previously estimated range. However, each study of the "Omo I" fossil gives an older date, so predict that the correct answer will describe the "Omo I" studies. Choice **(D)** is correct because it accurately reflects the data (the 2021 study found the skeleton to be 233,000 years old, while the initial analysis found it to be just 130,000 years old) and it gives evidence that multiple analyses can provide older dates.

Choices (A) and (B) are incorrect because, although they are true based on the table, they do not provide evidence of a date estimate changing over multiple analyses of a fossil. Choice (C) is incorrect because it misrepresents the data; although the 1992 study found "Lucy" to be 3.18 million years old, this is not "significantly older" than previous estimates of its age. Rather, it falls within the previously estimated range of 3.5–2.9 million years old.

14. D
Difficulty: Medium
Category: Information and Ideas
Getting to the Answer: This Textual Command of Evidence question is asking for you to identify which finding weakens the team's reliance on a diagnostic tool. So begin by identifying how and why the medical team relies on the test. The first sentence of the passage introduces why the tool is used: "some troponin subunits [are] exclusive…or significantly higher" in damaged heart tissue. Read the rest of the passage to put the use of this tool in context: when a patient has symptoms that "could indicate" a heart attack, the team checks the troponin levels and, if elevated, will "begin treating…for a heart attack." So predict that a finding that would

weaken the reliance on this test will likely involve either *a more effective tool or the troponin levels signaling other trauma*. Eliminate (A) because it restates the information presented in the first sentence. (B) is incorrect; emergency room "wait times" are out of scope. Eliminate (C), an explanation of a heart attack does not affect the passage. Correct choice **(D)** effectively weakens the reliance because "any type of acute" chest trauma, not just heart attacks, will result in higher troponin levels.

15. B
Difficulty: Hard
Category: Information and Ideas
Getting to the Answer: Summarize Sordalen's hypothesis, and then evaluate the choices against the chart. Sordalen's hypothesis is that lobsters in the fished areas would be smaller because larger individuals were removed from the breeding pool. Now, check the choices against the hypothesis. Eliminate (A); the protected males did have longer average body lengths than the fished males, but the rate of change of the body lengths of protected males was greater than that of the protected females. **(B)** is correct. In the protected area, both males and females started at the same size, but the average body length of the males at the end of the study period was longer, so their rate of change in body length was greater. In addition, they grew longer than the males in the fished area. On test day, select **(B)** with confidence and move to the next question. For practice, eliminate (C); in the fished area neither males nor females had consistent rates of change in average body length. In addition, if (C) were true, the comparison between females and males in the same areas would not support Sordalen's hypothesis. Eliminate (D); although it is true that the lobsters in the fished area did not significantly decrease in average body length, without a comparison to the lobsters in the protected area, this information is not sufficient to support the hypothesis.

16. D
Difficulty: Easy
Category: Information and Ideas
Getting to the Answer: Paraphrase the information in the text in your own simpler, but accurate, words. A good paraphrase of this text is something like, "A researcher used marriage records to analyze the spread of the Industrial Revolution in England. When people worked in agriculture, they married when there wasn't a lot of farm work. After they went to work in factories, they married any time during the year." Now match your

summary to the choices, immediately eliminating a choice that introduces a new concept (out of scope) or goes beyond what is stated in the text (extreme.)

Eliminate (A); there is no discussion in the text about which type of work was preferable. Eliminate (B); the research involved how the numbers of marriages were distributed throughout the year, not the total number of marriages. Eliminate (C); there is no mention of any benefits of the Industrial Revolution, nor how those benefits were distributed between the cities and the villages. That leaves **(D)** as the correct answer.

On test day, select **(D)** with confidence and move on, but for practice, the text discusses "people's activities," decisions as to when to get married. These "activities" (the marriages) took place throughout the year after the Industrial Revolution, not in the winter for farmers and the summer for shepherds, so the marriages "were no longer tied as closely to the seasons of the year as they had been in the past."

17. C
Difficulty: Easy
Category: Standard English Conventions
Getting to the Answer: Start by determining whether the subject is singular or plural. Here, the spiders' "eyesight" functions as a singular subject of the clause. Eliminate (B). Next, consider the tense. The sentence containing the blank is in the present tense, "is," with no words indicating a change in tense, so select the verb that is in the present tense. Choice **(C)** is correct because "allows" is a singular verb in the present tense. Incorrect choices (A) and (D) are in the future (will) and past (has) tenses, respectively.

18. A
Difficulty: Easy
Category: Standard English Conventions
Getting to the Answer: Identify the missing verb's subject to ensure that there is proper subject-verb agreement. The subject in this sentence is the closest noun, "her writings," which is plural and requires a plural verb. Eliminate choices (B) and (C), which use "is" and "has," verbs that go with a singular subject. The writing that is being referred to was "lauded" in the past (before the most recent work's recognition); therefore, eliminate (D). Choice **(A)** is correct because "have been" is the correct plural form of the verb and is in the correct tense.

19. A
Difficulty: Easy
Category: Standard English Conventions
Getting to the Answer: Since the answer choices contain various apostrophe placements, determine whether any of the nouns should be in the possessive form. The noun "city" refers to the singular New York City and should be possessive since the "jazz clubs" are in the city. Eliminate (C) and (D) because they use the plural possessive of "city." The "jazz clubs" do not possess anything, so the possessive "club's" in (B) can be eliminated. Choice **(A)** is correct.

20. B
Difficulty: Medium
Category: Standard English Conventions
Getting to the Answer: The answer choices indicate that this question is testing how to join or divide parts of the passage, so determine the types of clauses that are connected by the missing portion. An independent clause, with subject-verb "system...was," appears before the blank. Another independent clause, with subject-verb "system included," appears after the blank. Only choice **(B)** contains a way to punctuate independent clauses—a period—and is correct. Choice **(B)** turns the phrase "Accompanied by plastic color overlays..." into an introductory phrase correctly joined by a comma to the independent clause that follows. The other answer choices result in run-on sentences, as they include incorrect ways to join independent clauses.

21. B
Difficulty: Medium
Category: Standard English Conventions
Getting to the Answer: The referenced "findings" belong to "Hewish and Ryle," so the blank requires a plural possessive pronoun, making **(B)** correct. Incorrect choice (D) sounds the same, but is the contraction for "they are." Incorrect choice (A) is a singular possessive noun rather than plural, and choice (C) is the possessive pronoun for a thing, not people.

22. C
Difficulty: Medium
Category: Standard English Conventions
Getting to the Answer: Since the answer choices contain verbs, determine the verb's subject and the appropriate verb tense based on the passage context. The subject of the verb is the plural "tunnels"; the phrase "of the deep subterranean Trois Frères cave in

France" describes the "tunnels." Eliminate the singular verb in (D). The rest of the paragraph uses the present tense ("combines," "seems") to describe the cave's painting, so eliminate the past tense verb in (A). Also eliminate (B), since it results in a sentence fragment. The plural, present tense verb in **(C)** is correct.

23. D
Difficulty: Hard
Category: Standard English Conventions
Getting to the Answer: Determine the subject and appropriate tense of the missing verb. The subject is the plural "experiences"; the phrase "of walking down the block to the neighborhood park or café" is a prepositional phrase that describes the "experiences." Eliminate the singular verbs in (A) and (C). Based on the context of the passage, the verb should be in the present tense. The phrase "have forced the ongoing separation" in the first sentence indicates that the separation caused by suburban zoning laws is happening in the present, and the last sentence indicates that suburban dwellers must presently "get in their cars and drive." The plural, present tense verb in **(D)** is correct.

24. C
Difficulty: Easy
Category: Expression of Ideas
Getting to the Answer: Determine the two ideas that are connected by the missing transition. The first idea is that in the past, the voting system would have been "impossible" to carry out on a large scale. The second idea is that new technology "renders this objection irrelevant." In other words, the past objection is no longer valid. These ideas require a *contrast* transition, so **(C)** is correct.

Choice (A) is incorrect because the objection now being irrelevant is not a *continuation of* (Indeed) the original objection of the voting system not working on a large scale. Choice (B) is incorrect because the objection now being irrelevant is not *similar to* (Likewise) the original objection. Choice (D) is incorrect because the objection now being irrelevant is not *an example of* the original objection.

25. A
Difficulty: Easy
Category: Expression of Ideas
Getting to the Answer: Begin by identifying the two ideas that are connected by the missing word. The idea before the blank is that road verges are "a vital

part" of transportation safety. The idea after the blank is that trees will "decrease the number of pedestrian fatalities." The writer is making a connection between the ideas using the effect of trees *as an example* of how road verges keep pedestrians safe. Choice **(A)** is correct because it signals the author's continuation of the information: the use of trees as a barrier is an *instance* of the role that road verges play in traffic safety.

Incorrect choice (B) signals a cause-and-effect relationship, however the role of roads verges do not cause the trees to prevent fatalities. Choice (C), which indicates the beginning of a list, illogically completes the passage. (D) is incorrect; the ideas that are connected by the blank do not contrast.

26. B
Difficulty: Hard
Category: Expression of Ideas
Getting to the Answer: Determine the relationship between the two ideas that are connected by the missing transition. The first sentence of the passage describes the "blind spot" in the human eye. The sentence with the transition explains that the brain can "fill in" the blind spot. The ideas that humans have a blind spot but the brain can compensate for the blind spot *contrast*, so the contrast transition in **(B)** is correct.

Choices (A) and (C) are incorrect because the brain's ability to "fill in" the blind spot is not *similar to* (similarly) or *a continuation of* (indeed) the idea that the blind spot exists. Choice (D) is incorrect because the second idea is not a *restatement of* (in other words) the first idea; rather, the brain's ability to "fill in" information explains how the brain prevents a "lapse" in vision despite the blind spot in the eyes.

27. C
Difficulty: Medium
Category: Expression of Ideas
Getting to the Answer: Since the question stem asks you to introduce both Luoma and the book *For Each Minute...*, look for details about both as you read the bullet points. The first point provides an introductory detail about Luoma: he's important in the Helsinki School of photography. The next three bullet points describe *For Each Minute...*, including its contents and date of publication. The last bullet point compares *For Each Minute...* to a different book. Since the correct answer should describe Luoma and *For Each Minute...* "to a new audience," look for an answer choice that summarizes the first four bullet points. Choice **(C)** is correct.

Choices (A) and (D) are incorrect because they focus on comparing *For Each Minute...* with another book; further, they fail to provide any introductory details about Luoma or a description of *For Each Minute...* Choice (B) is incorrect because it omits an introduction of Luoma.

READING AND WRITING: MODULE B ANSWERS AND EXPLANATIONS

1. B
Difficulty: Medium
Category: Craft and Structure
Getting to the Answer: Use the context of the passage to help determine how the word "flat" is being used. The beginning of the passage describes Valancy as almost crying when her doctor apparently forgets about her. Mrs. Patterson is sympathetic and explains that the doctor heard that his son had been injured. Valancy then feels "a little less humiliated." By the end of the passage, Valancy is no longer sad or embarrassed but leaves feeling "very flat and discouraged." Thus, predict that "flat" has a similar tone or meaning to *discouraged*. This matches **(B)**, "subdued," which can mean *quiet* and *depressed*.

The other choices are meanings of "flat" that do not work in context. The correct answer must reflect that Valancy feels disheartened, while choices (A) and (D) suggest that she feels *balanced*. She feels strong emotions throughout the passage; there is no suggestion that she is "bored," as in (C).

2. C
Difficulty: Hard
Category: Craft and Structure
Getting to the Answer: For this Words in Context question, use the context of the passage to lead you to the correct answer. Liston was "notable for several professional achievements" but a contrast is set up where he is remembered for some singular event; the event, where three people died during one of his surgical procedures, is described in detail. From this context, we can infer that the word that goes into the blank, which modifies "event," should be a negative one. Choice **(C)** is correct because "infamous" describes someone or something as *being well-known for a bad reason*, which fits the events of the surgery.

Eliminate (A) because "wily" means *skillful* or *smart*, which is the opposite of how a surgeon who accidentally amputates his assistant's fingers would be described. Eliminate (B) because "trite" means *unoriginal and unimportant*; while "trite" is a negative term like "infamous," the event is described as "the only surgery in history with a 300% mortality rate," which, as events go, is neither unoriginal nor unimportant. Eliminate (D) because a "glorious" event would be one *worthy of admiration*, which is the opposite of this event.

3. C
Difficulty: Hard
Category: Craft and Structure
Getting to the Answer: In this passage, "Ludonarrative dissonance" refers to some relationship between the narrative of a video game's *story* and the narrative created through its *gameplay*. An example is provided through a hypothetical game about a thief. In the story, she is "struggling with the morality of stealing," while the gameplay tells the player that theft is "fun." From this, it can be predicted that something dealing with *contrast* should go in the blank. Choice **(C)** best fits this prediction; the two narratives are incompatible with one another.

Choice (A) is incorrect because no one is presented as feeling "ambivalent," or *having mixed feelings*, toward the narrative of the story and of the gameplay. Instead, the story and gameplay are contradicting one another. (B) is incorrect because "expunging" refers to *deleting* or *removing*, while the example describes two narratives existing side by side. (D) is incorrect because "objectification" refers to *treating a person like an object*, which does not apply here.

4. C
Difficulty: Hard
Category: Craft and Structure
Getting to the Answer: To determine the logical meaning of the word that belongs in the blank, carefully read the passage for clues. The first sentence describes a parasocial relationship as one where a consumer "perceives," meaning they *interpret* or *regard*, their connection with a performer as a close personal relationship. Yet, the second sentence describes this as a "one-way relationship," despite the intense emotions it can provoke. Predict that the correct answer will reflect the idea that parasocial relationships are *exaggerated, even unreal,* relationships. This matches **(C)**, "illusory," which means *false impression*. As in, consumers falsely believe that a two-way relationship exists.

Choice (A) is tempting but contradicted by the third sentence, which discusses how parasocial relationships were "widely noted" in the 1950s, meaning they were commonplace. Thus, they would not be "anomalous," which means *abnormal* or *unusual*. (B) is incorrect because "deceptive" means someone is being *intentionally misled by another party*; the first sentence makes

Practice Tests

clear the parasocial relationship is created by the consumer, who "perceives" a close personal connection that does not exist. (D) is incorrect because it does not fit the context of the passage; no judgement is made whether or not parasocial relationships are "scandalous," meaning *morally offensive to the general public*, only that they were widespread by the 1950s.

5. A
Difficulty: Medium
Category: Craft and Structure
Getting to the Answer: Determine the structure of the passage so you can figure out the function of the underlined portion. The first part of the passage introduces Liu Venti and Pau Tsu and their work in San Francisco. The underlined portion uses various nouns and verbs—both negative and positive—to describe their work. The rest of the passage claims that the schools they established were significant victories. Predict that the underlined portion thus gives an overview of their work establishing schools; the various nouns and verbs emphasize that it was *hard but also successful and rewarding*. This matches **(A)**.

Choice (B) is incorrect because although the underlined portion mentions "seven years," the main focus of the portion is the nature of the work, not its length; further, the clause before the underlined portion already establishes the length of time. Choice (C) is incorrect because the passage later states that the characters had "sailed safely through the waters of poverty" and could now help others, so they are not experiencing "ever-present instability" financially. Choice (D) is incorrect because the underlined portion does not directly address education.

6. D
Difficulty: Hard
Category: Craft and Structure
Getting to the Answer: Summarize the main idea of the text, then decide how the underlined sentence contributes to that idea. The text describes calligraffiti artist eL Seed and his largest project, "Perceptions." The emphasis keywords "monumental," "ambitious and complex," and "massive" point to the author's view of this installation, so a good prediction of the main idea would be *to describe eL Seed's impressive work*. With that main idea, the fact that "The complete inscription...is only visible from one vantage point" emphasizes the size and intricacy of the project, making **(D)** the correct answer.

For the incorrect choices, although the underlined sentence describes the quotation used in "Perceptions," it does not address its importance (A) or the artist's motivations (C). Choice (B) is also incorrect because the description of the artist's methodology appears later, not earlier, in the text.

7. A
Difficulty: Hard
Category: Craft and Structure
Getting to the Answer: Since this is a Purpose question, identify the author's main idea, then ask yourself what the author's reason is for writing about that main idea. In a long, complex sentence like the first one of this passage, it can be helpful to narrow the sentence to its core: "It ought to be remembered that there is nothing more difficult to take in hand...than to take the lead in the introduction of a new order of things." In other words, change is difficult. The second sentence can likewise be trimmed: "This coolness arises partly from fear of the opponents...and partly from the incredulity of men." This meaning is unclear at first glance, but focus on the description of "coolness." Scan the preceding text for temperature-related language that might explain this, such as the "lukewarm defenders" of change. Now, the context is clearer. Defenders of reform are "lukewarm" because they fear the opponents of reform and because they are feeling "incredulity," or an unwillingness to believe in the benefits of change. The overall main idea can be paraphrased as: change is difficult because people either oppose it or only weakly support it. Predict that the author's purpose for writing is to *explain this difficulty to rulers*, since the blurb states that the author is writing to give "advice to the rulers of kingdoms." This prediction matches **(A)**.

Although (B) mentions the problems with supporters of change, it is incorrect because it does not discuss the opponents of change; further, it does not mention being a ruler. Choice (C) is incorrect because it exaggerates a detail from the passage; opponents of change "may have the laws on their side," but Machiavelli still describes change (or reform) as possible, merely difficult to achieve. Choice (D) is likewise not supported by the passage; change might be "perilous to conduct," or dangerous, but Machiavelli does not caution against ever attempting change (or reform).

8.   A
Difficulty: Medium
Category: Craft and Structure
Getting to the Answer: Identify the arguments of Text 2 and of the literary critics in Text 1 as you read the passages. The argument of the literary critics is at the end of the first sentence in Text 1: *Madame Bovary* is a "cautionary tale about the dangers of reading novels." In other words, the novel warns that reading novels is dangerous. Text 2 disagrees, stating that the novel "was not meant to be a criticism of fiction itself." Instead, it is a "warning" about allowing people like Emma unchecked access to novels.

Evaluate the answer choices, eliminating any that do not accurately reflect the disagreement between the views. Choice **(A)** is correct because it summarizes how Text 2 qualifies the argument of the literary critics in Text 1: Text 2 claims that *Madame Bovary* doesn't criticize "fiction itself," but it does argue that people like Emma should not have free access to novels. Choice (B) is incorrect because the texts do not mention whether or not the other characters read novels. Choice (C) is incorrect because it is too extreme; if Text 2 argues that *Madame Bovary* is not "a criticism of fiction itself," the author of Text 2 would not admit that the novel shows that reading novels "is *always* dangerous." Choice (D) is incorrect because it better reflects the evidence provided in Text 1, not the disagreement between the texts.

9.   C
Difficulty: Hard
Category: Information and Ideas
Getting to the Answer: The keywords "According to the passage" indicate that this is a Detail question. The question is asking how the Peloponnesian War undermined the "domestic politics" of Corcyra, a neutral city-state. This wording indicates that politics will be a focus, so search the passage for a detail that explains how the "domestic politics" of the city was influenced by the war. The first sentence states that "in peace" there would have been no reason to "make such an invitation," but the war changed things. An alliance with Athens or Sparta was "always at the command of either political faction for the hurt of their adversaries and their own corresponding advantage." Summarize the explanation in your own words: *unlike in peacetime, the war meant one political faction in the city could ally with a foreign power to crush their domestic opponents.* Use this prediction to find a match among the answer choices; **(C)** is correct.

Choice (A) is a distortion. The war did not literally change the definitions of words; instead, the stress it placed on domestic politics meant that moderation and looking at things from another person's perspective were considered dangerous and unwise. Choice (B) is incorrect because it refers to material not in the passage; a debate over the merits of allying with Athens is not mentioned. Choice (D) is a distortion; while both sides likely feared a foreign invasion, in this passage their fear was based on their domestic enemies allying with foreigners and not the destruction of the city.

10.   C
Difficulty: Hard
Category: Information and Ideas
Getting to the Answer: Since this is a Main Idea question, as you read, be on the lookout for keywords that indicate the author's point of view. The first sentence describes a dungeon. The second sentence states that dungeons were eventually judged to be "too terrible." The third sentence describes their replacement, the "chambers of punishment," although the description is nearly identical to that of a dungeon. The fourth sentence describes how sunlight enters them midday. The fifth and final sentence describes the effects of the light, and explicitly comments to "the reader" that chambers of punishment "are not dungeons." That the author makes so pointed a claim is notable. Use this statement as your prediction to test the choices, since the correct answer will simply summarize it. Only **(C)**, the correct answer, concerns the whole passage.

Choice (A) is out of scope; while dungeons were allegedly reformed for being "too terrible," there is no mention of the French legislature in the passage. Choices (B) and (D) are likewise out of scope, claiming more about the effects of the environment on the prisoner than is stated.

11.   C
Difficulty: Easy
Category: Information and Ideas
Getting to the Answer: This Command of Evidence question requires the correct answer to *refer to both the violent times*, such as the storm in the poem's title, *and the permanence of life*. This prediction matches **(C)**, the correct answer. "How much can come" includes the violence of the storm. "And much can go" may refer to the storm leaving, or the loss of property due to the storm. But at the end, "yet abide[s] the world!", the

world remains and life continues. If you were unsure about the meaning of "abide," recall that "yet" is a contrast keyword, so unlike all the other choices, **(C)** is presenting a difference between the storm and the calm that follows. All of the incorrect choices mention violent aspects of the storm, but not the idea that life continues undisturbed.

12. D
Difficulty: Medium
Category: Information and Ideas
Getting to the Answer: The graph shows how the percent of spores germinating for two types of fungus declined as the concentration of vanillin increased. Since the phrase before the blank refers to "a substantial difference…at lower concentrations," examine the left-hand side of the graph. At the lowest concentration, the spore germination rate of *B. cinerea* was much lower than that of *A. alternata*. A quick glance at the choices reveals that these scientific names are not used; refer back to the text and carefully match the common name "gray mold" with *B. cinerea* and "black rot" with *A. alternata*. This prediction matches **(D)**, the correct answer.

Choice (A) is incorrect because the question requires a difference seen at a low concentration of vanillin, not a similarity at higher levels. Choices (B) and (C) are both backward, claiming that the rate of spore germination for gray mold (*B. cinerea*) was greater than that of black rot (*A. alternata*), but, for all concentrations of vanillin, the opposite is true.

13. C
Difficulty: Medium
Category: Information and Ideas
Getting to the Answer: As indicated in the question stem, begin by identifying the study researchers' claim. The second sentence states that the researchers "claim to have found evidence for this effect." The effect referred to is in the first sentence: cues that suggest you're being watched can make you act more generously. In the specific study described, the image of eyes corresponds with being watched, and how much participants paid for their drinks corresponds with their generosity. Predict that a result that entailed *participants paying more when the image of eyes was displayed* would support the researchers' claim. Choice **(C)** matches this prediction and is correct.

Choices (B) and (D) are incorrect because they do not address participants' generosity (how much they paid).

Choice (A) is incorrect because it provides the opposite of the required support, suggesting that the cue of being watched had no impact on generosity.

14. A
Difficulty: Hard
Category: Information and Ideas
Getting to the Answer: First, based on the question stem, determine the "suggestion" of the palaeoarchaeologists: the last sentence states that they think absolute dating may help them "fine-tune broad approximations" of dates supplied by relative dating. Thus, the correct answer will provide data from the table that shows absolute dating giving a more precise date than a "broad approximation" given by relative dating. The table doesn't mention the terms "absolute" or "relative," but according to the passage, stratigraphy is a type of relative dating, and radiometric dating is a type of absolute dating. In the table, the radiometric dating of the "Lucy" skeleton shows a more precise date (3.18 million years) than the broad range given by its stratigraphic dating (3.5–2.9 million years), thus providing evidence of absolute dating "fine-tuning" relative dating. Choice **(A)** reflects this data and is correct.

Choice (B) is incorrect because it misrepresents the data in the table: the radiometric dating, not the stratigraphic dating, found a date of 3.18 million years ago. Further, the 3.18-million-year age of the skeleton does not conflict with the previous estimate of its age. Choice (C) is incorrect because it describes two instances of relative dating methods (stratigraphic analysis), so it cannot provide evidence of absolute dating "fine-tuning" relative dating. Likewise, (D) is incorrect because it only discusses two instances of absolute (radiometric) dating.

15. C
Difficulty: Hard
Category: Information and Ideas
Getting to the Answer: The political scientists' claim is found in the first sentence; political science is a "true science." Pay close attention to the reason the scientists believe this: models use measured data from the past to predict what will likely happen in the future. Since the question asks you to weaken this claim, the correct answer will include information that challenges political science's ability to either quantify data or to predict outcomes. This prediction matches **(C)**, the correct answer. The new variable added in 2012 does not

have a "clear methodology" for measurement, so the modification that made the model more accurate was not "quantif[ied] past evidence" or "measured data."

The remainder of the text after the claim details Alan Abramowitz's model that uses measured information to accurately predict presidential election results. On test day, read the text, but keep the terms of the claim either firmly in mind or noted on your scratch paper.

None of the incorrect choices challenge the political scientists' definition of a "true science." The weight of the different variables in Abramowitz's model (A) and the relative accuracy of the model in different time periods (B) do not affect either the quantification of data or the prediction of events. If (D) were true, and other political scientists had models that gave accurate predictions based on measured data, the claim would be strengthened, not weakened.

16. B
Difficulty: Easy
Category: Information and Ideas
Getting to the Answer: The correct answer to an Inference question is logically supported by the passage. The first sentence introduces the Stanford marshmallow test and the second sentence summarizes that children who "demonstrated self-control had higher rates of academic...success." In the third sentence, researchers determined that "cuttlefish with...self-control performed better in the cognitive performance tests." With that context in mind, predict that the findings would logically suggest that *both tests show that self-control is an indicator of learning ability*. Choice **(B)** best matches that prediction.

Choice (A) is a distortion. There is nothing in the passage to suggest that the test subjects delay their gratification to improve their learning ability. (C) is out of scope; their camouflage is not mentioned in the passage. (D) is too extreme; the passage identifies the marshmallow test as the measure used, not as "the most effective."

17. A
Difficulty: Medium
Category: Information and Ideas
Getting to the Answer: Based on the last sentence, the correct answer will be a logical inference that can be made from the results of the pigeon study, in which the pigeons could distinguish between and match photos of human expressions. Evaluate the choices and eliminate any that do not logically follow from the

details in the passage. For **(A)**, the first sentence states that some psychologists think that the human nervous system, which can recognize expressions, is "unique." That the pigeons also showed the ability to recognize expressions weakens the claim that the human nervous system is unique. Choice **(A)** is correct.

Choice (B) is incorrect because the passage makes no suggestions about whether or not the psychologists approve of studying birds to draw inferences about humans. Choice (C) is too extreme; the study casts doubt on the claim that one ability of the human nervous system is "unique," but it goes too far to suggest that the nervous systems of humans and birds are therefore "essentially identical." Choice (D) is incorrect because the pigeon study has no relevance to how important emotions are in human communication.

18. C
Difficulty: Easy
Category: Standard English Conventions
Getting to the Answer: Determine the structure of the sentence with the blank so that you can select the appropriate punctuation. The main subject-verb of the sentence is "the structure of the modern suburb...has created." The phrase "while offering a respite from city pollution" is parenthetical, so it should be set off from the rest of the sentence with a set of matching punctuation marks. Since the phrase begins with a dash, it should end with a dash; **(C)** is correct.

Choice (A) is incorrect because a colon is used after an independent clause. Choice (B) is incorrect because it omits the end punctuation on the parenthetical phrase, and (D) is incorrect because it does not result in a matching set of punctuation marks around the parenthetical phrase.

19. C
Difficulty: Medium
Category: Standard English Conventions
Getting to the Answer: Determine whether the portions of the sentence are independent clauses so you can choose the correct way to punctuate them. The portion "Patronage of the arts no longer exclusively belonged to the aristocracy" is an independent clause, and the portion "the increasingly prosperous middle class flocked..." is also an independent clause, each with its own subject-verb and expressing a complete thought. Choice **(C)** is correct because a semicolon is an appropriate way to join independent clauses. Choice (A) is incorrect because a

FANBOYS conjunction (and) must be used with a comma to join independent clauses. Choices (B) and (D) result in run-on sentences.

20. B
Difficulty: Medium
Category: Standard English Conventions
Getting to the Answer: The correct answer choice will place the noun that should be described by the modifier "Built by the Mughal emperor..." at the beginning of the phrase, so that it is as close as possible to the phrase that modifies it. It must be the "ornate tomb" itself that was "Built by the Mughal emperor," so **(B)** is correct. The other answer choices are incorrect because they illogically result in either the "construction" or the "plans," rather than the tomb itself, being constructed by the emperor.

21. A
Difficulty: Hard
Category: Standard English Conventions
Getting to the Answer: The answer choices all contain the same wording but different punctuation, so analyze the structure of the sentence that contains the blank. The rest of the sentence contains phrases separated by semicolons, so the London Eye must be one item in a list. Since the other list items are separated by semicolons, the London Eye item must contain a phrase set off by a comma. Choice **(A)** is correct because it sets off the phrase that describes the London Eye, "which kick-started...," with a comma and ends the list item with a semicolon. The other choices are incorrect because (B) and (D) fail to end the list item with a semicolon, and (C) places the semicolon in the incorrect location.

22. D
Difficulty: Hard
Category: Standard English Conventions
Getting to the Answer: Determine the subject and appropriate tense of the missing verb. The subject of the verb is the singular "adherence," since "to common language and belief systems" is a prepositional phrase that describes the "adherence." Eliminate the plural verb in (C). Although most of the passage is written in the past tense (preserved, became, etc.), the missing verb should be in the present tense because it refers to action happening "today." The singular, present tense verb in **(D)** is correct. Choice (A) is incorrect because it is a past tense verb, and (B) is incorrect because it results in a sentence fragment.

23. A
Difficulty: Hard
Category: Standard English Conventions
Getting to the Answer: Analyze the structure of the clauses surrounding the blank so you can determine which punctuation is correct. The portion ending in the blank contains an independent clause, with subject-verb "The Mars Orbiter Laser Altimeter...used." The portion after the blank also contains an independent clause, with the subject and compound verb "this massive geographic feature towers...and is the tallest." Only choice **(A)** contains a way to punctuate independent clauses, so **(A)** is correct; further, this choice correctly turns "Part of the Tharsis Montes volcanic region" into an introductory modifying phrase set off by a comma.

Choices (B) and (C) are incorrect because they result in run-ons. Choice (D) is incorrect because a FANBOYS conjunction must be accompanied by a comma to join independent clauses.

24. D
Difficulty: Easy
Category: Expression of Ideas
Getting to the Answer: Determine the relationship between the two ideas that are connected by the missing transition. The idea before the transition is that the first home video game system introduced features still used in modern systems. The idea after the transition specifies one such "innovation": interchangeable game cartridges. Since the second idea gives an example of the first, choice **(D)** is correct.

Choice (A) is incorrect because the game system's introduction of features is not *the cause of* the innovation of interchangeable cartridges. Choices (B) and (C) are incorrect because the ideas are not *similar* ("Likewise") or *contrasting* ("In contrast").

25. B
Difficulty: Hard
Category: Expression of Ideas
Getting to the Answer: Determine the ideas that are connected by the missing transition. The first sentence introduces the idea that people today may wonder how the two-party system first developed in the United States, and the second sentence continues this thought by discussing the idea that most voters today are still part of one of the two parties, despite their very broad "ideological umbrellas." The idea after the transition

is that the "origins and endurance" of the party system might be "puzzling" at first to political science students. This final idea reinforces the preceding ideas, so the continuation transition in **(B)** is correct.

Choice (A) is incorrect because the party system being puzzling is not *an example of* (For instance) voters belonging to one of the two parties. Choice (C) is incorrect because the passage structure does not create a *contrast* (However) between the ideas, but rather a *connection* between the idea that people stick to the broad parties and the idea that the party system seems "puzzling." Choice (D) is incorrect because the overall passage does not follow a chronological structure.

26. D

Difficulty: Medium

Category: Expression of Ideas

Getting to the Answer: Based on the question stem, focus on details about Luoma's book as you read the bullet points. The last two points discuss the book *For Each Minute, Sixty-Five Seconds*: it is Luoma's collection of abstract interpretations of historic artworks, including van Gogh's paintings. Since the question stem asks for an introduction to Luoma's book for an audience that's familiar with the Helsinki School, look for an answer choice that emphasizes the book rather than the Helsinki School. Choice **(D)** accurately summarizes the book and is correct.

Choices (A) and (B) are incorrect because they primarily focus on describing the Helsinki School and do not provide any information about the book except its title. Choice (C) is incorrect because it focuses on van Gogh; the choice does not mention the book.

27. D

Difficulty: Hard

Category: Expression of Ideas

Getting to the Answer: Based on the question stem, look for how the intensity of the Vesuvius eruption compares with the intensity of the other eruptions as you read the bullet points. The first three bullet points describe the VEI index, which measures the intensity of eruptions using a scale in which an increase of 1 corresponds with a tenfold increase in intensity. The last three bullet points classify each of the three eruptions, so use these details to help you summarize how Vesuvius compares with the Mount Pelée and Krakatoa eruptions. Vesuvius is classified as a 5, higher than Mount Pelée and lower than Krakatoa. Based on these details, look for an answer choice that both makes an accurate comparison and that emphasizes how "intense" Vesuvius was in relation to the other two eruptions.

Choice (A) can be eliminated; although it accurately classifies the eruptions on the VEI, this statement alone does not give the reader any context for how these classifications compare. Does a higher number indicate a more intense eruption? If so, how much more intense? Choice (B) can also be eliminated, as it only describes the Vesuvius eruption and does not compare it to Mount Pelée and Krakatoa. Choice (C) is incorrect for the same reason as (A): it does not give any context for comparing the intensity of the eruptions. Choice **(D)** is correct because it provides a baseline for the intensity of the Vesuvius eruption (ejecting more than 1 km^3 of material) and compares this intensity to the Mount Pelée and Krakatoa eruptions.

MATH: ROUTING MODULE ANSWERS AND EXPLANATIONS

1.   C
Difficulty: Easy
Category: Algebra
Getting to the Answer: The equation shown is in slope-intercept form, $y = mx + b$. Since E is multiplied by 10.625 in the equation, 10.625 is the slope, which is the change in S per change in E. Thus, a person's salary, S, increases by 10.625 thousands of dollars for every one-year increase in work experience, E. **(C)** is correct.

2.   C
Difficulty: Easy
Category: Algebra
Getting to the Answer: Pick a point on the graph such as (0, 75), and plug it into each of the answer choices to determine which equation is correct.

(A): $75 + 0 \neq -75$, eliminate.

(B): $75 - 0 \neq -75$, eliminate.

(C): $0 + 75 = 75$, **(C)** is correct.

(D): $0 - 75 \neq 75$, eliminate.

Alternatively, you could use the graph to determine the slope and y-intercept. According to the graph, the slope is -1 and the y-intercept is 75. Note that the slope can be found by either finding the rise over run or using two points on the line such (0, 75) and (10, 65), which gives $\frac{65 - 75}{10 - 0} = \frac{-10}{10} = -1$. Thus, the equation is $y = -x + 75$. Rearranged, this gives $y + x = 75$, which matches **(C)**.

3.   5
Difficulty: Easy
Category: Problem-Solving and Data Analysis
Getting to the Answer: You can answer this question by either converting units from meters to minutes, via the rate, or by using the distance formula $D = RT$ to solve for the runner's time. Since the runner ran a distance, D, of 4,000 meters at a rate, R, of 800 meters per minutes, $4,000 = 800T$. Dividing both sides by 800 gives $T = 5$ minutes. Enter **5**.

4.   A
Difficulty: Easy
Category: Advanced Math
Getting to the Answer: When converting a radical to a fractional exponent, the root of the radical becomes the denominator of the fraction. When dividing exponents with the same base, subtract the exponents. Rewrite the expression and simplify:

$$\frac{3\sqrt[4]{a^{16}}}{\sqrt{2}\,a^6} = \frac{3a^{\frac{16}{4}}}{\sqrt{2}\,a^{\frac{6}{2}}} = \frac{3a^4}{\sqrt{2}\,a^3} = \frac{3}{\sqrt{2}}a^{(4-3)} = \frac{3}{\sqrt{2}}a$$

Since the expression is equal to $x a^y$, $y = 1$. **(A)** is correct.

5.   D
Difficulty: Easy
Category: Advanced Math
Getting to the Answer: Rearrange the equation so that all the terms are on one side of the equals sign and 0 is on the other: $x^2 - 5x + 6 = 0$. Use reverse-FOIL to factor: -2 and -3 multiply to 6 and add up to -5, so $(x - 2)(x - 3) = 0$, and $x = 2$ or $x = 3$. Choice **(D)** is correct.

6.   B
Difficulty: Easy
Category: Geometry and Trigonometry
Getting to the Answer: Recall that the area of a rectangle is $A = bh$. Since the area is given as 80 and the height is 8, the base AD must be 10.

Since $ABCD$ is a rectangle, angle BAD is a right angle. You are told that EF is parallel to AB, so angle FED must be a right angle as well. Finally, triangles BAD and FED both share angle D. If two triangles have two equal angles, they are similar. This means that they have proportional corresponding sides. Since the height of triangle FED is half of the height of triangle BAD, the base of triangle FED must be half of the base of triangle BAD. Therefore, the base of triangle FED is 5.

The question asks for the area of triangle FED, so use the formula for the area of a triangle, $A = \frac{1}{2}bh$, to obtain $A = \frac{1}{2}(5)(4) = \frac{1}{2}(20) = 10$. Choice **(B)** is correct.

7. C
Difficulty: Easy
Category: Algebra
Getting to the Answer: The words "in terms of a" mean that the variable a will appear in your answer. Your goal is to get b on one side of the equals sign and get everything else on the other side. Begin by multiplying every term by 3 to clear the fraction:

$$3a + 2b = 36$$

Now isolate b:

$$3a + 2b = 36$$
$$2b = 36 - 3a$$
$$b = 18 - \frac{3}{2}a$$

Choice **(C)** is correct.

8. A
Difficulty: Medium
Category: Advanced Math
Getting to the Answer: Examine the table. Notice that x always increases by 1 but that there is no consistent change in the y-values. Therefore, the function is not linear. Eliminate (C). To decide between the remaining answer choices, plug in values from the table and see which ones you can eliminate.

Begin with the point $(0, -1)$. This means that if you plug in $x = 0$, the result should be -1. Eliminate choices that do not give -1.

(A) $f(0) = -0^2 + 3(0) - 1 = -1$ Keep.

(B) $f(0) = -2^0 + 3(0) - 1 = -2$ Eliminate.

(D) $f(0) = 0^2 - 3(0) - 1 = -1$ Keep.

Eliminate (B). To decide between (A) and (D), think about the shape of the graph. Choice (A) is a downward opening parabola, while (D) is an upward opening parabola. The data in the table matches the downward opening curve because as x increases, y increases but then decreases. If the parabola was upward opening, the y-values would decrease and then increase. Thus, **(A)** is correct.

Alternatively, you could simply plug in another point. For convenience, choose $(1, 1)$.

(A) $f(0) = -1^2 + 3(1) - 1 = -1 + 3 - 1 = 1$ Keep.

(D) $f(0) = 1^2 - 3(1) - 1 = 1 - 3 - 1 = -3$ Eliminate.

Eliminate (D). Once again, **(A)** is correct.

9. D
Difficulty: Medium
Category: Advanced Math
Getting to the Answer: The question presents a system of linear and quadratic equations. Begin by plugging $y = 3x - 2$ into the second equation:

$$3x - 2 + 15 = x^2 - 9x$$

This gives a quadratic equation that can be solved by factoring.

$$3x - 2 + 15 = x^2 - 9x$$
$$3x + 13 = x^2 - 9x$$
$$0 = x^2 - 12x - 13$$
$$0 = (x - 13)(x + 1)$$

This yields $x = 13$ and $x = -1$. Since the question tells you that $x > 0$, $x = 13$ is correct. This matches **(D)**.

Alternatively, you could graph both of these functions in your calculator and look for the intersection point with a positive x-coordinate.

10. C
Difficulty: Medium
Category: Algebra
Getting to the Answer: When modeling real-life situations with linear functions, the y-intercept is the starting amount. Here, the y-intercept is 1,000. The slope is the rate of increase or decrease. Hamza deposits $\$1,200\left(\frac{2}{3}\right) = \$800$ per week, so the slope is 800. Put these two pieces together to obtain the function $f(x) = 800x + 1,000$, where x represents the number of weeks.

The question asks how many weeks it will take Hamza to save $5,000. Plug in 5,000 for $f(x)$ and solve for x:

$$5,000 = 800x + 1,000$$
$$4,000 = 800x$$
$$5 = x$$

Choice **(C)** is correct.

11. A
Difficulty: Medium
Category: Algebra
Getting to the Answer: Create a system of equations to model the situation. Let t represent the number of pounds of tomatoes and p represent the number of pounds of peppers. If Anastasia sells a total of 15 pounds of vegetables, then $t + p = 15$.

If tomatoes are sold for \$2 per pound and there are t pounds of tomatoes, then she makes a total of \$2t from tomatoes. Using similar logic, she makes \$7p from peppers. In total she makes \$45, so $2t + 7p = 45$.

The question asks for the number of pounds of peppers, or p. Rewrite the first equation as $t = 15 - p$ and plug this into the second equation:

$$2(15 - p) + 7p = 45$$
$$30 - 2p + 7p = 45$$
$$30 + 5p = 45$$
$$5p = 15$$
$$p = 3$$

Choice **(A)** is correct.

12. D
Difficulty: Medium
Category: Problem-Solving and Data Analysis
Getting to the Answer: Examine each answer choice systematically. In box plots, the range is represented by the difference between the line that is farthest to the right and the line that is farthest to the left. The range of Section 1 is approximately $95 - 77 = 18$. The range of Section 2 is approximately $97 - 75 = 22$, so (A) is incorrect. Choices (B) and (C) can be eliminated immediately because box plots do not contain information about the mean. In box plots, the median is represented by the line drawn through the middle of the box. Choice **(D)** is correct because the median of Section 1 is approximately 86, while the median of Section 2 is approximately 88.

13. B
Difficulty: Medium
Category: Algebra
Getting to the Answer: A linear function can be written in the form $y = mx + b$. The y-intercept occurs when $x = 0$. According to the table, the y-intercept is 1. The function is now $y = mx + 1$. To find the slope, use the formula $m = \dfrac{y_2 - y_1}{x_2 - x_1}$. To avoid messy decimals, work with the last two points, $(0, 1)$ and $(4, -2)$:

$$m = \frac{-2 - 1}{4 - 0}$$
$$= \frac{-3}{4}$$

The function is therefore $y = -\dfrac{3}{4}x + 1$, or $f(x) = -\dfrac{3}{4}x + 1$. To find $f(6)$, plug in $x = 6$ and simplify:

$$f(6) = \left(-\frac{3}{4}\right)(6) + 1$$
$$= -4.5 + 1$$
$$= -3.5$$

Choice **(B)** is correct.

14. −4
Difficulty: Medium
Category: Advanced Math
Getting to the Answer: To find the points of intersection, set the equations equal to each other and solve for x by factoring:

$$x^2 + 3x - 4 = -x^2 - 3x + 4$$
$$2x^2 + 6x - 8 = 0$$
$$x^2 + 3x - 4 = 0$$
$$(x + 4)(x - 1) = 0$$
$$x = -4 \text{ and } x = 1$$

Plug each solution back into one of the equations to determine the value of y. When $x = -4$, $y = (-4)^2 + 3(-4) - 4 = 0$. When $x = 1$, $y = (1)^2 + 3(1) - 4 = 0$. In this question, a is the x-coordinate and b is the y-coordinate of the solution. The question states that $a < b$, which means that $x < y$. Since $y = 0$, x must be -4, and $a + b = -4 + 0 = -4$. Enter **−4**.

Alternatively, graph the equations and identify which point of intersection meets the criteria that $a < b$. Then, calculate $a + b$.

15. B
Difficulty: Medium
Category: Geometry and Trigonometry
Getting to the Answer: The equilateral triangle can be split into two 30-60-90 triangles with side ratios of $x : x\sqrt{3} : 2x$. $2x$ corresponds to the side of the equilateral triangle, $2\sqrt{10}$. Thus, $x = \sqrt{10}$, which is the base of the 30-60-90 triangle and half of the side length of the equilateral triangle. $x\sqrt{3}$ corresponds to the height of the triangle, so the height is $\sqrt{10} \times \sqrt{3} = \sqrt{30}$ units.

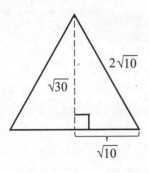

Use the formula for the area of a triangle, $A = \frac{1}{2}bh$, to calculate the area: $A = \frac{1}{2}(2\sqrt{10})(\sqrt{30}) = \sqrt{300} = 10\sqrt{3}$ square units. **(B)** is correct.

16. B
Difficulty: Hard
Category: Advanced Math
Getting to the Answer: If Eugene loses 0.25% of his body weight, then 99.75% of his body weight remains. If his original weight was x, then after one week, he will weigh 99.75% of x, or $0.9975x$. After two weeks, he will weigh 99.75% of this new amount, or $0.9975(0.9975x)$. After three weeks, he will weigh $0.9975(0.9975)(0.9975x)$. You can generalize this pattern as $x(0.9975)^W$, where w is the number of weeks.

If Eugene loses 5% of his original bodyweight x, then his new bodyweight will be $0.95x$. Set up an equation:

$$0.95x = x(0.9975)^W$$
$$0.95 = (0.9975)^W$$

It is possible to use a graphing calculator, or even logarithms, to solve for w, but it is simpler to backsolve by plugging in the answer choices to see which one gives approximately 0.95. Start by trying (B):

$$(0.9975)^{20} \approx 0.951$$

This is the approximate value that you are looking for. Choice **(B)** is correct. If you are concerned that this choice is slightly too big, you can convince yourself by plugging in (C):

$$(0.9975)^{30} \approx 0.928$$

Choice (C) is far too small. Choice **(B)** is verified as correct. There is no need to check any other choices.

17.   3/2 or 1.5
Difficulty: Hard
Category: Algebra
Getting to the Answer: Recall that a system of equations has no solutions if the two lines never touch. This occurs when the two lines are parallel, or when they have the same slope but different y-intercepts.

Begin by rearranging the first equation so that it is in the same format as the second:

$$2ax + 6y = -15$$
$$2x + 4y = -6$$

For the two lines to have the same slope, the coefficients in front of x and y in both equations must match up. Look carefully at the $6y$ in the first equation and the $4y$ in the second equation. To make the $4y$ into a $6y$, you must multiply it by $\frac{3}{2}$. Do this to all of the terms in the second equation:

$$2ax + 6y = -15 \qquad 2ax + 6y = -15$$
$$\frac{3}{2}(2x + 4y = -6) \qquad 3x + 6y = -9$$

Now look at the coefficients of the x terms. You need them to match up as well, so set up an equation and solve for a:

$$2ax = 3x$$
$$2a = 3$$
$$a = \frac{3}{2}$$

Enter **3/2** or **1.5**.

18. B
Difficulty: Hard
Category: Problem-Solving and Data Analysis
Getting to the Answer: The average growth rate for each 4- or 6- year interval can be determined by visualizing a line of best fit for the data points, tracing your fingers on the screen on test day, if needed.

The slope of the line of best fit for each 4-year interval from 4 to 8 years and 8 to 12 years for fish pole is steeper than that for great cane.

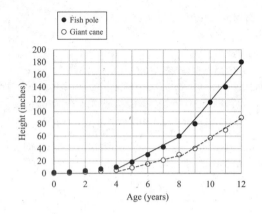

The slope of the line of best fit for each 6-year interval from 0 to 6 years and 6 to 12 years for fish pole is steeper than that for great cane.

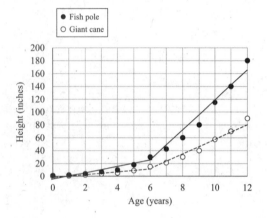

Thus, **(B)** is correct.

19. B
Difficulty: Hard
Category: Geometry and Trigonometry
Getting to the Answer: You're given the equation of a circle, but it's not in standard form, so you'll need to complete the square:

$$x^2 + 6x + 9 - 9 + y^2 - 10y + 25 - 25 = k$$
$$(x + 3)^2 - 9 + (y - 5)^2 - 25 = k$$
$$(x + 3)^2 + (y - 5)^2 - 34 = k$$
$$(x + 3)^2 + (y - 5)^2 = k + 34$$

Thus, the center of the circle is $(-3, 5)$ and $r^2 = k + 34$. Now that you know the coordinates of the circle's center, you can find the radius by calculating the distance between the center and the given point on the circle's circumference, $(-6, 9)$. The formula for the distance between two points is $\sqrt{(y_2 - y_1)^2 + (x_2 - x_1)^2}$, so plug both points into this to find the radius:

$$r = \sqrt{(y_2 - y_1)^2 + (x_2 - x_1)^2}$$
$$r = \sqrt{(9 - 5)^2 + (-6 - (-3))^2}$$
$$r = \sqrt{(4)^2 + (-3)^2}$$
$$r = \sqrt{16 + 9}$$
$$r = \sqrt{25}$$
$$r = 5$$

So, the radius of the circle is 5. According to the standard form of the circle's equation, $r^2 = k + 34$. Plug in 5 for r:

$$5^2 = k + 34$$
$$25 = k + 34$$
$$k = -9$$

Thus, **(B)** is correct.

20. 22/8 or 11/4
Difficulty: Hard
Category: Algebra
Getting to the Answer: Create a system of equations to model the situation. If the test is composed of correct and incorrect answers and there are a total of 30 questions, then $C + I = 30$. Charles received a score of 20. Each correct answer is worth 1 point and each incorrect answer is worth $-\frac{1}{4}$ points, so $C - \frac{1}{4}I = 20$.

Rewrite the second equation as $C = 20 + \frac{1}{4}I$ and plug it into the first equation to solve for I:

$$\frac{1}{4}I + 20 + I = 30$$
$$\frac{5}{4}I + 20 = 30$$
$$\frac{5}{4}I = 10$$
$$5I = 40$$
$$I = 8$$

If $I = 8$, then $C = 30 - 8 = 22$. The question asks for the ratio of correct to incorrect answers, or $\frac{C}{I}$. This is $\frac{22}{8}$. Enter **22/8** or **11/4**.

21. D
Difficulty: Hard
Category: Advanced Math
Getting to the Answer: Use inverse operations to isolate a. First, subtract 1 from both sides and then divide both sides by 2:

$$2\sqrt{a} + 1 = \frac{b^2}{c}$$

$$2\sqrt{a} = \frac{b^2}{c} - 1$$

$$\sqrt{a} = \frac{1}{2}\left(\frac{b^2}{c} - 1\right)$$

Now square both sides:

$$a = \left[\frac{1}{2}\left(\frac{b^2}{c} - 1\right)\right]^2$$

(D) is correct.

22. B
Difficulty: Hard
Category: Problem-Solving and Data Analysis
Getting to the Answer: If the cat has a 60% chance of success with a 7% margin of error, then its chances of success range from $60\% - 7\% = 53\%$ to $60\% + 7\% = 67\%$. A plausible number will be somewhere within this range. Work through each answer choice systematically and see which one fits:

(A) $\frac{150}{300} = 0.50 = 50\%$

(B) $\frac{195}{300} = 0.65 = 65\%$

There is no need to go any further. Choice **(B)** is correct, but for the record:

(C) $\frac{210}{300} = 0.70 = 70\%$

(D) $\frac{225}{300} = 0.75 = 75\%$

MATH: MODULE A ANSWERS AND EXPLANATIONS

1.   B
Difficulty: Easy
Category: Problem-Solving and Data Analysis
Getting to the Answer: The number of past due books is 20% of the number of returned books, 1,220. Rewrite 20% as $\frac{20}{100}$ or 0.2, and translate "of" to multiplication. This gives $0.2 \times 1,220$, which equals 244. **(B)** is correct.

2.   A
Difficulty: Easy
Category: Algebra
Getting to the Answer: Substitute -6 for x in the equation $y = 6x + 1$ and solve for y.

$$y = 6(-6) + 1$$
$$y = -36 + 1$$
$$y = -35$$

(A) is correct.

3.   D
Difficulty: Easy
Category: Algebra
Getting to the Answer: Substitute 16 for $f(x)$ in the equation and then solve for x. First add 8 to both sides and then divide both sides by $\frac{3}{4}$. Note that when dividing by a fraction, multiply by its reciprocal.

$$16 = \frac{3}{4}x - 8$$
$$24 = \frac{3}{4}x$$
$$\frac{4}{3}(24) = x$$
$$32 = x$$

(D) is correct.

4.   B
Difficulty: Easy
Category: Advanced Math
Getting to the Answer: If $|x| = a$, then $x = a$ or $x = -a$. In other words, an absolute value equation will "split" into a positive case and a negative case. Applying this principle here, you obtain:

$$2x + 5 = -x + 3 \qquad 2x + 5 = -(-x + 3)$$

Begin by solving the first equation:

$$2x + 5 = -x + 3$$
$$3x + 5 = 3$$
$$3x = -2$$
$$x = -\frac{2}{3}$$

Now move on to the second equation:

$$2x + 5 = -(-x + 3)$$
$$2x + 5 = x - 3$$
$$x + 5 = -3$$
$$x = -8$$

Thus, $x = -\frac{2}{3}$ or $x = -8$. Quickly check for extraneous solutions: plugging either of these numbers into the right side of the equation will keep the expression $-x + 3$ positive, so neither is an extraneous solution that would create an equation where an absolute value equals a negative number. Choice **(B)** is correct.

5.   A
Difficulty: Easy
Category: Geometry and Trigonometry
Getting to the Answer: You are told that the lines l and m are parallel. This means that they create a set of corresponding angles. Angles that are in the same relative position of each intersection will be equal to each other. In other words, all acute angles are equal and all obtuse angles are equal. Since the 50 degree angle is in the top right corner of the intersection of lines l and s, angle x will also be 50 degrees because it is in the top right corner of the intersection of lines m and s.

The angle next to 50 is given as 90 degrees. This means that the angle directly across from this angle is also 90 degrees.

Now consider the triangle. Two of its angles are 50 and 90. Since there are 180 degrees in a triangle, y must be $180 - 50 - 90 = 40$.

The question asks for the value of $x - y$. You know that $x = 50$ and $y = 40$, so $x - y = 50 - 40 = 10$. Choice **(A)** is correct.

6. 9
Difficulty: Easy
Category: Advanced Math
Getting to the Answer: Since absolute value gives a non-negative value, the expression inside the absolute value may be equal to 81 or −81. Note that the expression inside the absolute value can be rewritten as $9(1 - x)$. Solving for $(1 - x)$ in each case gives:

$$9(1 - x) = 81$$
$$1 - x = 9$$

$$9(1 - x) = -81$$
$$1 - x = -9$$

Enter **9**.

7. C
Difficulty: Easy
Category: Algebra
Getting to the Answer: First rewrite the equation in slope-intercept form, $y = mx + b$:

$$2x - 18 = 3y$$
$$\frac{2}{3}x - 6 = y$$
$$y = \frac{2}{3}x - 6$$

The y-intercept of the original equation is −6. The translated graph is up 3 units, so add 3 to −6: $-6 + 3 = -3$. **(C)** is correct.

8. 9
Difficulty: Easy
Category: Algebra
Getting to the Answer: Add 24 to both sides of the equation to get $3x = 27$. Divide both sides by 3 to get $x = 9$. Enter **9**.

9. C
Difficulty: Easy
Category: Problem-Solving and Data Analysis
Getting to the Answer: The height of the 19 meals per week bar is between 200 and 250. Only choice **(C)** falls between 200 and 250, so **(C)** is correct.

10. B
Difficulty: Easy
Category: Geometry and Trigonometry
Getting to the Answer: The length of lace trim equals the perimeter of the square. The diagonal of the square splits the square into two 45-45-90 triangles with side ratios of $x:x:x\sqrt{2}$. The $x\sqrt{2}$ term corresponds to the diagonal, $5\sqrt{2}$. Thus, $x = 5$, where x corresponds to the side of the square.

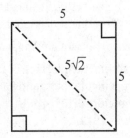

The perimeter of the square is the sum of all four sides, or $4 \times 5 = 20$ centimeters. **(B)** is correct.

11. C
Difficulty: Easy
Category: Algebra
Getting to the Answer: Begin by finding the slope of $f(x)$. Recall that slope $= \frac{y_2 - y_1}{x_2 - x_1}$. Plug the two points shown on the graph into this formula:

$$\text{slope} = \frac{4 - 0}{0 - (-3)}$$
$$= \frac{4}{3}$$

The linear function $g(x)$ is perpendicular to $f(x)$. Perpendicular lines have opposite reciprocal slopes. Therefore, the slope of $g(x)$ is $-\frac{3}{4}$. The question tells you that the y-intercept of $g(x)$ is 3, so the complete function is $g(x) = -\frac{3}{4}x + 3$.

To find $g(4)$, plug in 4 for x and simplify:

$$g(4) = -\frac{3}{4}(4) + 3$$
$$= -3 + 3$$
$$= 0$$

Choice **(C)** is correct.

12. 972
Difficulty: Medium
Category: Geometry and Trigonometry
Getting to the Answer: The formula for the area of a rectangle is $A = l \times w$, where l represents the length and w represents the width. The length of the rectangle is 18 feet, and the width is one-third its length or $\frac{1}{3}(18) = 6$ feet. Thus, the area of one rectangular plot is $18 \times 6 = 108$ square feet. The formula for the area of a square is $A = s^2$, where s is the side length of the square. Since the side length of one square-shaped plot is $\frac{1}{2}(18) = 9$, the area of one square-shaped plot is $9 \times 9 = 81$ square feet. The total area of the garden consisting of six rectangular plots and four square-shaped plots is therefore $6(108) + 4(81) = 648 + 324 = 972$ square feet. Enter **972**.

13. B
Difficulty: Medium
Category: Advanced Math
Getting to the Answer: The x-intercept is where the graph crosses the x-axis. The graph of f crosses the x-axis at $(1, 0)$, so the x-coordinate, or a, is 1. The y-intercept is where the graph crosses the y-axis. The graph of g crosses the y-axis at $(0, -3)$, so the y-coordinate, or b, is -3. Therefore, the value of $a + b$ is $1 + (-3) = -2$. **(B)** is correct.

14. B
Difficulty: Medium
Category: Problem-Solving and Data Analysis
Getting to the Answer: The equation for a linear model in slope intercept form is $y = mx + b$, where m is the slope and b is the y-intercept. The scatterplot shows that the slope is negative (legibility distance decreases as age increases), so eliminate (C) and (D). Note that the x-axis starts at 10, not 0. Extending the x-axis left and extrapolating the line of best fit indicates that the y-intercept is positive, so **(B)** is correct.

Alternatively, you could pick two points on the line such as $(30, 500)$ and $(80, 350)$ to determine the slope: $\frac{y_2 - y_1}{x_2 - x_1} = \frac{350 - 500}{80 - 30} = \frac{-150}{50} = -3$. Then plug one of the points into $y = -3x + b$ to determine the y-intercept: $500 = -3(30) + b$, $b = 590$. **(B)** is correct.

15. A
Difficulty: Medium
Category: Algebra
Getting to the Answer: Start with the easier inequalities first. If Siri needs at least 6 medium posts, then $m \geq 6$. Eliminate (C). Similarly, if she needs at least 4 large posts, then $l \geq 4$. Eliminate (D).

Since medium posts cost \$5, Siri spends a total of $5m$ on medium posts. By the same logic, she spends a total of $6l$ on large posts. Since she wants to spend no more than \$70 total, $5m + 6l \leq 70$. Choice **(A)** is correct.

16. 3
Difficulty: Medium
Category: Advanced Math
Getting to the Answer: To solve a rational equation, begin by clearing the fractions. Do this by multiplying both sides of the equation by the least common of multiple of x and $x - 5$, which is $x(x - 5)$:

$$x(x - 5)\left[\frac{2x}{x - 5} + \frac{15}{x} = 2\right]$$
$$2x^2 + 15(x - 5) = 2x(x - 5)$$

Distribute, collect like terms, and solve for x:

$$2x^2 + 15x - 75 = 2x^2 - 10x$$
$$15x - 75 = -10x$$
$$25x = 75$$
$$x = 3$$

Enter **3**.

17. B
Difficulty: Medium
Category: Problem-Solving and Data Analysis
Getting to the Answer: Probability is equal to $\frac{\text{Number of desired outcomes}}{\text{Number of possible outcomes}}$. The desired outcome is picking a drama movie, of which there are x. Add up the number of movies in each genre to find the total outcomes: $20 + x + 4 + 10 + 11 = x + 45$. So, the probability of picking a drama is $\frac{x}{x + 45}$. The question tells you that this is equal to $\frac{1}{4}$, so set up an equation and cross-multiply to solve for x.

$$\frac{x}{x + 45} = \frac{1}{4}$$
$$4x = x + 45$$
$$3x = 45$$
$$x = 15$$

(B) is correct.

18. D
Difficulty: Medium
Category: Algebra
Getting to the Answer: First, use the information in the table to determine the equation for f. For each increase of x by 1, y increases by 2; this means that f has a slope of 2. Either notice the point $(0, -2)$ in the table or plug this slope and any of the points from the table into the standard equation of a line, $y = mx + b$, to find b, the y-intercept.

$$0 = 2(1) + b$$
$$0 = b + 2$$
$$b = -2$$

So, the equation of f is $y = 2x - 2$, but the question asks for the equation of g. To represent g's translation down 3 units, subtract 3 from f's equation: $y = 2x - 2 - 3 = 2x - 5$. Rearrange this to match the format of the equations in the answer choices: $2x - y = 5$. **(D)** is correct.

19. B
Difficulty: Medium
Category: Geometry and Trigonometry
Getting to the Answer: DC is parallel to AB, so $\angle ACD = \angle CAB$. Use the information about the arc lengths to find the angle measure of CAB. The length of arc AB is twice the length of BC ($AB = 2BC$), so the ratio of the length of BC to the length of AB is $\frac{BC}{BC + AB} = \frac{BC}{BC + 2BC} = \frac{1}{3}$. There are 360° in a circle, and 180° in a semicircle. Thus, the measure of central angle COB is $\frac{1}{3}(180°) = 60°$. The measure of the inscribed angle CAB is half the central angle COB, or $\frac{1}{2}(60°) = 30°$. Since, $\angle ACD = \angle CAB$, $\angle ACD$ also equals 30°. **(B)** is correct.

20. B
Difficulty: Hard
Category: Advanced Math
Getting to the Answer: $f(x)$ represents the estimated atmospheric pressure x thousand meters above sea level. Since $f(4)$ is the value of $f(x)$ when $x = 4$, "$f(4)$ approximately equals 61" means the atmospheric pressure at 4,000 meters above sea level is approximately 61 kilopascals. **(B)** is correct.

21. B
Difficulty: Hard
Category: Algebra
Getting to the Answer: Begin by subtracting 5 from all parts of the inequality:

$$-6 < \frac{x}{4} < 1$$

Then multiply everything by 4 to clear the fraction:

$$-24 < x < 4$$

Be careful! The question asks for the minimum possible integer value of $3x - 2$, not x. Multiply every part of this inequality by 3:

$$-72 < 3x < 12$$

Finally, subtract 2:

$$-74 < 3x - 2 < 10$$

You are looking for the smallest possible integer value of $3x - 2$. This expression cannot actually equal -74, so **(B)** is correct.

22. D
Difficulty: Hard
Category: Advanced Math
Getting to the Answer: Divide both sides by x^{b^2} and then apply exponent rules: $\frac{x^{a^2}}{x^{b^2}} = (x^6)^6$. When dividing exponents with the same base, subtract the exponents, and when raising a power to another power, multiply the exponents: $x^{a^2 - b^2} = x^{36}$. Since all terms have the same base, x, and x does not equal 0 or 1, the exponents are equal: $a^2 - b^2 = 36$. Note that $a^2 - b^2$ is a difference of squares and factors into $(a + b)(a - b)$. Thus, $(a + b)(a - b) = 36$. Substituting 4 for $(a - b)$ and solving for $(a + b)$ gives $(a + b)(4) = 36$, $(a + b) = 9$. **(D)** is correct.

MATH: MODULE B ANSWERS AND EXPLANATIONS

1. C
Difficulty: Easy
Category: Problem-Solving and Data Analysis
Getting to the Answer: Since x is 130% greater than 75, then $x = 75 + \left(\frac{130}{100} \times 75\right) = 75 + 97.5 = 172.5$. **(C)** is correct.

2. A
Difficulty: Easy
Category: Advanced Math
Getting to the Answer: First, convert the radical in the denominator to an exponent: $\frac{x^{\frac{5}{2}}}{\sqrt{x}} = \frac{x^{\frac{5}{2}}}{x^{\frac{1}{2}}}$. Now, use exponent rules to simplify. When a base raised to one exponent is divided by the same base raised to a different exponent, subtract the exponents:
$\frac{x^{\frac{5}{2}}}{x^{\frac{1}{2}}} = x^{\frac{5}{2} - \frac{1}{2}} = x^{\frac{4}{2}} = x^2$. **(A)** is correct.

3. 1.5 or 3/2
Difficulty: Easy
Category: Algebra
Getting to the Answer: To calculate the time spent studying 3 days before the day of the exam, plug 3 for d into $t = 3 - \frac{1}{2}d$ and solve for t: $t = 3 - \frac{1}{2}(3) = 3 - 1.5 = 1.5$. Enter **1.5** or **3/2**.

4. B
Difficulty: Medium
Category: Geometry and Trigonometry
Getting to the Answer: Lines m and n are parallel, so angle A equals its corresponding angle B. Likewise, angle D equals angle E. This allows you to conclude that triangles GBE and GAD are similar. Recall that similar triangles have proportional sides. You can therefore deduce that $\frac{x}{x + 3} = \frac{6}{6 + x}$. Cross-multiply to solve for x:

$$\frac{x}{x + 3} = \frac{6}{6 + x}$$
$$x(6 + x) = 6(x + 3)$$
$$6x + x^2 = 6x + 18$$
$$x^2 = 18$$
$$x = \sqrt{18}$$
$$x = \sqrt{9}\sqrt{2}$$
$$x = 3\sqrt{2}$$

Choice **(B)** is correct.

5. D
Difficulty: Medium
Category: Advanced Math
Getting to the Answer: First, simplify the first term in the expression. When multiplying exponents with the same base, add the exponents.

$$2x^{-2}\left(4x^5 y^2\right) - 24xy^2$$
$$= 8x^{-2 + 5}y^2 - 24xy^2$$
$$= 8x^3 y^2 - 24xy^2$$

Now factor out common terms. Both $8x^3 y^2$ and $24xy^2$ have an $8xy^2$ in common:

$$8xy^2(x^2 - 3)$$

(D) is correct.

6. C
Difficulty: Medium
Category: Advanced Math
Getting to the Answer: The negative sign in front of x^2 indicates the graph of the quadratic opens downward. Thus, the vertex represents the maximum value. The x-coordinate, h, of the vertex can be found using $h = -\frac{b}{2a}$. In the given function, b is d and a is -1. Thus, the x-coordinate of the vertex is $-\frac{d}{2(-1)} = \frac{d}{2}$. **(C)** is correct.

Alternatively, the x-coordinate of the vertex occurs halfway between the x-intercepts. Set the function equal to 0, solve for the x-intercepts, and then find their midpoint:

$$-x^2 + dx = 0$$
$$x(-x + d) = 0$$
$$x = 0 \text{ and } x = d$$

The x-coordinate of the vertex is $\frac{0 + d}{2} = \frac{d}{2}$.

(C) is correct.

7. B
Difficulty: Medium
Category: Algebra
Getting to the Answer: The function notation $f(x) = y$ tells you that when $x = 2$, $y = 9$ and when $x = 5$, $y = 0$. Thus, the points that satisfy the equation for f are $(2, 9)$ and $(5, 0)$. Use the two points to determine the slope of the linear function: $\frac{y_2 - y_1}{x_2 - x_1} = \frac{0 - 9}{5 - 2} = \frac{-9}{3} = -3$.

Eliminate (C) and (D). To find the y-intercept, plug the slope and one of the points into the slope-intercept equation, $y = mx + b$, and solve for b: $0 = -3(5) + b$, $b = 15$. Thus, the equation of f is $f(x) = -3x + 15$. **(B)** is correct.

Alternatively, you could plug the points into each of the answer choices to see which equation satisfies both points.

8. A
Difficulty: Medium
Category: Problem-Solving and Data Analysis
Getting to the Answer: The median is the average of the middle two numbers in a data set with an even number of values that are arranged in ascending or descending order. Since there are 20 values in data set A, the 10th and 11th numbers are in the middle. Both the 10th and 11th numbers have a value of 10, so the median of data set A is 10. The range of a data set is the highest value minus the lowest value. Thus, the range of data set A is $11 - 7 = 4$. Note that the data set range of all four choices is 4 and equal to the range of data set A. (A) has a median of 4, (B) and (C) both have a median of 10, and (D) has a median of 18. Since the median of data set B is less than the median of data set A, **(A)** is correct.

9. A
Difficulty: Medium
Category: Geometry and Trigonometry
Getting to the Answer: Use the acronym SOHCAHTOA to remember the definitions of the three main trig functions: $\sin\theta = \dfrac{opposite}{hypotenuse}$, $\cos\theta = \dfrac{adjacent}{hypotenuse}$, and $\tan\theta = \dfrac{opposite}{adjacent}$. In the given triangle, $\sin 62° = \dfrac{x}{27}$. This means that $x = 27\sin(62°)$. Using similar logic, you can determine that $\sin(28°) = \dfrac{y}{27}$ and that $y = 27\sin(28°)$. The question asks for $\dfrac{x}{y}$. This is $\dfrac{27\sin(62°)}{27\sin(28°)} = \dfrac{\sin(62°)}{\sin(28°)}$. Choice **(A)** is correct.

10. A
Difficulty: Medium
Category: Algebra
Getting to the Answer: Translate English into math: "y is at least" means y is greater than or equal to, "3 less than" means subtract 3, and "twice the value of x"

means 2 times x. Putting it all together gives $y \geq 2x - 3$. Rearranging the inequality to solve for x in terms of y gives:

$$y \geq 2x - 3$$
$$y + 3 \geq 2x$$
$$\frac{y + 3}{2} \geq x$$
$$\frac{1}{2}y + \frac{3}{2} \geq x$$

(A) is correct.

11. A
Difficulty: Medium
Category: Advanced Math
Getting to the Answer: To find the equivalent expression, factor and then simplify. The numerator factors to $(7x - 5)(x + 5)$. In the denominator, factor out a 7 to get $7(x + 5)$. The $x + 5$ terms in the numerator and denominator cancel each other out, leaving $\dfrac{7x - 5}{7}$. **(A)** is correct.

12. D
Difficulty: Hard
Category: Advanced Math
Getting to the Answer: Since the concentration of methyl chloroform decreased by a factor of 2 for each year after 1998, the relationship between x and y is exponential decay. The equation for exponential decay is $y = ab^x$, where a is the value of y when $x = 0$ and $0 < b < 1$. From the question, you know the starting value: when $x = 0$, $y = 70$; thus, $a = 70$. The concentration decreases by a factor of 2, so $b = \dfrac{1}{2}$. The equation is therefore $y = 70\left(\dfrac{1}{2}\right)^x$. **(D)** is correct.

13. −3, −4, or −5
Difficulty: Hard
Category: Algebra
Getting to the Answer: Since the graph of the solution to the system of inequalities contains the point $(a, 21)$, substitute a for x and 21 for y into the second inequality and solve for a:

$$-6a - 21 < 15$$
$$-6a < 15 + 21$$
$$-6a < 36$$
$$a > -6$$

Remember to flip the direction of the inequality when dividing by a negative. Also, substitute a for x in the first inequality and solve for *a* to determine the range of values of *a*:

$$3a < -6$$
$$a < -2$$

Since *a* is an integer that is greater than −6 and less than −2, *a* can be −3, −4, −5. Enter **−3**, **−4**, or **−5**.

14. C

Difficulty: Hard
Category: Algebra
Getting to the Answer: Since *x* represents the number of 50-pound bags and *y* represents the number of 150-pound bags, the total weight is $50x + 150y$. The total cargo weight cannot exceed 37,000 pounds, so $50x + 150y \leq 37,000$. Plug 200 in for *y* and solve for *x*:

$$50x + 150(200) \leq 37,000$$
$$50x + 30,000 \leq 37,000$$
$$50x \leq 7,000$$
$$x \leq 140$$

(C) is correct. At least 200 150-pound bags means a minimum of 200 150-pound bags are loaded into the cargo container. So a maximum of 140 50-pound bags can be loaded into the cargo container.

15. B

Difficulty: Hard
Category: Problem-Solving and Data Analysis
Getting to the Answer: Use the midpoint of each interval to approximate the mean for each data set. The mean wait time before noon is $(4 \times 1) + (7 \times 3) + (4 \times 5) + (9 \times 7) + (3 \times 9) + (0 \times 11)/(4 + 7 + 4 + 9 + 3 + 0) = 135/27 = 5$. The mean wait time after noon is $(0 \times 1) + (6 \times 3) + (6 \times 5) + (5 \times 7) + (2 \times 9) + (8 \times 11)/(0 + 6 + 6 + 5 + 2 + 8) = 189/27 = 7$. Therefore, the positive difference between the means of the two data sets is $|7 - 5| = 2$. **(B)** is correct.

Note that using the left endpoints for both data sets or the right endpoints for both data sets instead of the midpoint to calculate the mean will also give a positive difference of 2. Using the left endpoints gives a before noon mean of 4 and an after noon mean of 6. Using the right endpoints gives a before noon mean of 6 and an after noon mean of 8.

16. B

Difficulty: Hard
Category: Advanced Math
Getting to the Answer: First, subtract 1 from both sides to isolate the absolute value expression on one side: $|2x + 4| = 3x - 1$. Since absolute value gives a non-negative value, the expression inside the absolute value may be equal to $3x - 1$ or $-(3x - 1)$. Solving for *x* in each case gives:

$$|2x + 4| = 3x - 1$$
$$2x + 4 = 3x - 1$$
$$5 = x$$

$$2x + 4 = -(3x - 1)$$
$$2x + 4 = -3x + 1$$
$$5x = -3$$
$$x = -\frac{3}{5}$$

Plug each answer back into the original equation to check for extraneous solutions:

$$|2(5) + 4| + 1 = 3(5)$$
$$|14 + 1| = 15$$
$$15 = 15$$

$$|2x + 4| + 1 = 3x$$
$$\left|2\left(-\frac{3}{5}\right) + 4\right| + 1 = 3\left(-\frac{3}{5}\right)$$
$$\left|-\frac{6}{5} + \frac{20}{5}\right| + \frac{5}{5} = -\frac{9}{5}$$
$$\frac{14}{5} + \frac{5}{5} = -\frac{9}{5}$$
$$\frac{19}{5} \neq -\frac{9}{5}$$

$-\frac{3}{5}$ is an extraneous solution and not correct. The value of *a* is 5. **(B)** is correct.

17. −4
Difficulty: Hard
Category: Advanced Math
Getting to the Answer: Plugging $\left(0, \frac{97}{3}\right)$ into $g(x)$ gives $g(0) = f(0) + 2 = \frac{97}{3}$. Now evaluate $f(0)$: $f(0) = a^0 - b = 1 - b$. Substitute $1 - b$ for $f(0)$ into $g(0)$ and solve for b.

$$g(0) = 1 - b + 2$$
$$\frac{97}{3} = 1 - b + 2$$
$$\frac{97}{3} = 3 - b$$
$$\frac{97}{3} - 3 = -b$$
$$\frac{97}{3} - \frac{9}{3} = -b$$
$$\frac{88}{3} = -b$$
$$-\frac{88}{3} = b$$

Then substitute $-\frac{88}{3}$ for b into $\frac{a}{b} = \frac{3}{22}$ and cross-multiply to find a.

$$\frac{a}{b} = \frac{3}{22}$$
$$\frac{a}{-\frac{88}{3}} = \frac{3}{22}$$
$$22a = 3\left(\frac{-88}{3}\right)$$
$$22a = -88$$
$$a = -4$$

Enter **−4**.

18. 1/13, .0769, 0.076, or 0.077
Difficulty: Hard
Category: Algebra
Getting to the Answer: There is no solution when the coefficient on the x terms are equal, and the lines have the same slope but different y-intercepts, resulting in two lines that will never intersect. Set the x terms equal to each other and solve for k:

$$4x = 52kx$$
$$\frac{4}{52} = k$$
$$\frac{1}{13} = k$$

This can also be solved algebraically. Set the equations equal to each other and solve for x in terms of k to identify when x is undefined. Combine like terms and then factor:

$$4x - 16 = 52kx$$
$$4x - 52kx = 16$$
$$4x(1 - 13k) = 16$$
$$x = \frac{16}{4(1 - 13k)}$$
$$x = \frac{4}{1 - 13k}$$

x is undefined when $1 - 13k = 0$. Solving for k gives $1 = 13k$ and $k = \frac{1}{13}$. Enter **1/13** (**.0769, 0.076,** and **0.077** are also acceptable).

19. C
Difficulty: Hard
Category: Geometry and Trigonometry
Getting to the Answer: The volume of a cylinder is $\pi r^2 h$, and the volume of a cone is $\frac{1}{3}\pi r^2 h$. (Note that these formulas are on the reference sheet of math formulas in the SAT math section.) Thus, the volume of the space in the cylinder not taken up by the cone is $\pi r^2 h - \frac{1}{3}\pi r^2 h = \frac{2}{3}\pi r^2 h$. Since the diameter is 10 centimeters, the radius is $10 \div 2 = 5$ centimeters. Plugging in the radius and height into $\frac{2}{3}\pi r^2 h$ gives $\frac{2}{3}\pi(5)^2 15 = 250\pi$ cubic centimeters. **(C)** is correct.

20. B
Difficulty: Hard
Category: Algebra
Getting to the Answer: Plug $x - c$ into the function and simplify:

$$f(x - c) = a(x - c) + b$$
$$= ax - ac + b$$
$$= ax + b - ac$$

The slope is a, and the y-intercept is $b - ac$. Choice **(B)** is correct.

21. B
Difficulty: Hard
Category: Advanced Math
Getting to the Answer: Begin by dividing all of the terms by 2 to obtain $x^2 + 2x - 5 = 0$. This equation will not factor, so use the quadratic formula to solve for x:

$$x = \frac{-b \pm \sqrt{b^2 - 4ac}}{2a}$$

$$= \frac{-2 \pm \sqrt{2^2 - 4(1)(-5)}}{2(1)}$$

$$= \frac{-2 \pm \sqrt{24}}{2}$$

$$= \frac{-2 \pm \sqrt{4}\sqrt{6}}{2}$$

$$= \frac{-2 \pm 2\sqrt{6}}{2}$$

$$= -1 \pm \sqrt{6}$$

The question tells you that the solutions are of the form $m \pm n\sqrt{6}$, so $m = -1$ and $n = 1$. Therefore, $m + n = -1 + 1 = 0$. Choice **(B)** is correct.

22. C
Difficulty: Hard
Category: Geometry and Trigonometry
Getting to the Answer: The surface area of the rectangular prism with square base is the sum of the areas of all six faces. Two of the faces are squares with side length s, and four of the faces are rectangles with a width of s and height of $3s$. The area of each square is $s \times s$, and the area of each rectangle is $s \times 3s$. Thus, the surface area of the square prism is $2(s^2) + 4(3s^2) = 2s^2 + 12s^2 = 14s^2$. **(C)** is correct.